Microsoft® Office 2007
ILLUSTRATED

SECOND COURSE

Beskeen/Cram/Duffy/Friedrichsen/Wermers

COURSE TECHNOLOGY
CENGAGE Learning™

Australia • Brazil • Japan • Korea • Mexico • Singapore • Spain • United Kingdom • United States

COURSE TECHNOLOGY
CENGAGE Learning

**Microsoft® Office 2007—Illustrated
Second Course**
Beskeen/Cram/Duffy/Friedrichsen/Wermers

Senior Acquisitions Editor: Marjorie Hunt

Senior Product Manager: Christina Kling Garrett

Associate Product Manager: Rebecca Padrick

Editorial Assistant: Michelle Camisa

Senior Marketing Manager: Joy Stark

Marketing Coordinator: Jennifer Hankin

Contributing Author: Jennifer T. Campbell

Developmental Editors: Rachel Biheller Bunin, Barbara Clemens, Pamela Conrad, Lisa Ruffolo

Production Editors: Summer Hughes, Jill Klaffky, Daphne Barbas

Copy Editors: Harold Johnson, Gary Michael Spahl

QA Manuscript Reviewers: Nicole Ashton, John Frietas, Serge Palladino, Jeff Schwartz, Danielle Shaw, Marianne Snow, Teresa Storch, Susan Whalen

Cover Designers: Elizabeth Paquin, Kathleen Fivel

Cover Artist: Mark Hunt

Composition: GEX Publishing Services

© 2008 Course Technology, Cengage Learning

ALL RIGHTS RESERVED. No part of this work covered by the copyright herein may be reproduced, transmitted, stored or used in any form or by any means graphic, electronic, or mechanical, including but not limited to photocopying, recording, scanning, digitizing, taping, Web distribution, information networks, or information storage and retrieval systems, except as permitted under Section 107 or 108 of the 1976 United States Copyright Act, without the prior written permission of the publisher.

> For product information and technology assistance, contact us at
> **Cengage Learning Customer & Sales Support, 1-800-354-9706**
> For permission to use material from this text or product, submit all requests online at **cengage.com/permissions**
> Further permissions questions can be emailed to
> **permissionrequest@cengage.com**

Soft Cover
ISBN-13: 978-1-4239-0513-8
ISBN-10: 1-4239-0513-X

Hard Cover
ISBN-13: 978-1-4239-0515-8
ISBN-10: 1-4239-0515-6

Course Technology
25 Thomson Place
Boston, Massachusetts 02210
USA

Cengage Learning is a leading provider of customized learning solutions with office locations around the globe, including Singapore, the United Kingdom, Australia, Mexico, Brazil, and Japan. Locate your local office at:
international.cengage.com/region

Cengage Learning products are represented in Canada by Nelson Education, Ltd.

For your lifelong learning solutions, visit **course.cengage.com**

Purchase any of our products at your local college store or at our preferred online store **www.ichapters.com**

Trademarks:

Some of the product names and company names used in this book have been used for identification purposes only and may be trademarks or registered trademarks of their respective manufacturers and sellers.

Microsoft and the Office logo are either registered trademarks or trademarks of Microsoft Corporation in the United States and/or other countries. Thomson Course Technology is an independent entity from Microsoft Corporation, and not affiliated with Microsoft in any manner. Microsoft product screen shot(s) reprinted with permission from Microsoft Corporation.

Credit List

PowerPoint Units

Figure	Credit Line
G-13	Courtesy of Karen Beskeen
G-15	Courtesy of Karen Beskeen
H-18	Courtesy of MT Cozzola
H-19	Courtesy of MT Cozzola
H-22	Courtesy of Karen Beskeen

Other photos provided by Barbara Clemens

Printed in the United States of America
3 4 5 6 7 8 9 11 10 09 08

About This Book

Welcome to *Microsoft Office 2007—Illustrated Second Course*! Since the first edition of this book was published in 1995, close to one million students have used various editions of it to master Microsoft Office. We are proud to bring you this latest edition on the most exciting version of Microsoft Office ever to release.

As you probably have heard by now, Microsoft completely redesigned this latest version of Office from the ground up. No more menus! No more toolbars! The software changes Microsoft made were based on years of research during which they studied users' needs and work habits. The result is a phenomenal and powerful new version of the software that will make you and your students more productive and help you get better results faster.

Before we started working on this new edition, we also conducted our own research. We reached out to nearly 100 instructors like you who have used previous editions of this book. Some of you responded to one of our surveys; others of you generously spent time with us on the phone, telling us your thoughts. Seven of you agreed to serve on our Advisory Board and guided our every decision in developing this new edition.

As a result of all the feedback you gave us, we have preserved the features that you love, and made improvements that you suggested and requested. And of course we have covered all the key features of the new software. (For more details on what's new in this edition, please read the Preface.) We are confident that this book and all its available resources will help your students master Microsoft Office 2007.

Advisory Board

We thank our Advisory Board who enthusiastically gave us their opinions and guided our every decision on content and design from beginning to end. They are:

Kristen Callahan, Mercer County Community College
Paulette Comet, Assistant Professor, Community College of Baltimore County
Barbara Comfort, J. Sargeant Reynolds Community College
Margaret Cooksey, Tallahassee Community College
Rachelle Hall, Glendale Community College
Hazel Kates, Miami Dade College
Charles Lupico, Thomas Nelson Community College

Author Acknowledgments

David Beskeen Experience, dedication, hard work, and attention-to-detail with a little humor thrown in are the qualities of a great editor and Rachel Biheller Bunin is truly a great editor—thank you so much! To all of the professionals at Course Technology, led by Christina Kling Garrett, thanks for your hard work. I would also like to especially thank Marjorie Hunt, who fifteen years ago, gave me my first opportunity to use my knowledge of PowerPoint to help others learn. Finally, a special thanks to my wife, Karen, and the "J's", for always being there.

Carol Cram A big thank you to my developmental editor Barbara Clemens for her patience, good humor, and insight! And, as always, everything I do is made possible by Gregg and Julia. They make everything worthwhile.

Jennifer Duffy Many talented people at Course Technology helped to shape this book — thank you all. I am especially indebted to Pam Conrad for her precision editing, sage encouragement, and endless good cheer throughout the many months of writing. On the home front, I am ever grateful to my husband and children for their patience and support.

Lisa Friedrichsen The Access portion is dedicated to my students, and all who are using this book to teach and learn about Access. Thank you. Also, thank you to all of the professionals who helped me create this book.

Lynn Wermers I would like to thank Barbara Clemens for her insightful contributions, great humor, and patience. I would also like to thank Christina Kling Garrett for her encouragement and support in guiding and managing this project.

Preface

Welcome to *Microsoft Office 2007—Illustrated Second Course*. If this is your first experience with the Illustrated series, you'll see that this book has a unique design: each skill is presented on two facing pages, with steps on the left and screens on the right. The layout makes it easy to digest a skill without having to read a lot of text and flip pages to see an illustration.

This book is an ideal learning tool for a wide range of learners—the rookies will find the clean design easy to follow and focused with only essential information presented, and the hotshots will appreciate being able to move quickly through the lessons to find the information they need without reading a lot of text. The design also makes this a great reference after the course is over! See the illustration on the right to learn more about the pedagogical and design elements of a typical lesson.

What's New in This Edition

We've made many changes and enhancements to this edition to make it the best ever. Here are some highlights of what's new:

- **Real Life Independent Challenge**—The new Real Life Independent Challenge exercises offer students the opportunity to create projects that are meaningful to their lives, such as a personal letterhead, a database to track personal expenses, or a budget for buying a house.

- **New Case Study**—A new case study featuring Quest Specialty Travel provides a practical and fun scenario that students can relate to as they learn skills. This fictional company offers a wide variety of tours around the world.

Each two-page spread focuses on a single skill.

Concise text introduces basic principles in the and integrates a real-w case study.

UNIT F — Excel 2007

Saving a Workbook for Distribution

One way to share Excel data is to place, or **publish**, the data on a network or on the Web so that others can access it using their Web browsers. To publish an Excel document to an **intranet** (a company's internal Web site) or the Web, you can save it in an **HTML (Hypertext Markup Language)** format, which is the coding format used for all Web documents. You can also save your Excel file as a **single file Web page** that integrates all of the worksheets and graphical elements from the workbook into a single file. This file format is called MHTML. In addition to distributing files on the Web, you may need to distribute your files to people working with an earlier version of Excel. You can save your files as Excel 97-2003 workbooks. Excel workbooks can be saved in many other formats to support wide distribution and to make them load faster. The most popular formats are listed in Table F-1. Kate asks you to create a workbook version that managers running an earlier version of Excel can open and modify. She also asks you to save the Store Sales workbook in MHT format so she can publish it on the Quest intranet for their sales managers to view.

STEPS

QUICK TIP
You can check your files for unsupported features before saving them by clicking the Office button, pointing to Prepare, then clicking Run Compatibility Checker.

1. **Click the Office button, point to Save As, click Excel 97-2003 Workbook, in the Save As dialog box, navigate to the drive and folder where you store your Data Files, then click Save**
   The Compatibility Checker appears on the screen, alerting you to the features that will be lost by saving in the earlier format. Some Excel 2007 features are not available in earlier versions of Excel.

2. **Click Continue, close the workbook, then reopen the Store Sales.xls workbook**
   [Compatibility Mode] appears in the title bar, as shown in Figure F-16. Compatibility mode prevents you from including Excel features in your workbook that are not supported in Excel 97-2003 workbooks. To exit compatibility mode, you need to save your file in one of the Excel 2007 formats and reopen the file.

3. **Click, point to Save As, click Excel Workbook, if necessary navigate to the drive and folder where you store your Data Files, click Save, then click Yes when you are asked if you want to replace the existing file**
   [Compatibility Mode] remains displayed in the title bar. You decide to close the file and reopen it to exit compatibility mode.

4. **Close the workbook, then reopen the Store Sales.xlsx workbook**
   The title bar no longer displays [Compatibility mode]. You decide to save the file for Web distribution.

QUICK TIP
To ensure that your workbook displays the same way on different computer platforms and screen settings, you can publish it in PDF format. You need to download an Add-in to save files in this format. The PDF format preserves all of the workbook's formatting so that it appears on the Web exactly as it was created.

5. **Click, click Save As, in the Save As dialog box, navigate to the drive and folder where you store your Data Files, change the filename to sales, then click the Save as type list arrow and click Single File Web Page (*.mht, *.mhtml)**
   The Save as type list box indicates that the workbook is to be saved as a Single File Web Page, which is in mhtml or mht format. To avoid problems when publishing your pages to a Web server, it is best to use lowercase characters, omit special characters and spaces, and limit your filename to eight characters with an additional three-character extension.

6. **Click Save, then click Yes**
   The dialog box indicated that some features may not be retained in the Web page file. Excel saves the workbook as an MHT file in the folder location you specified in the Save As dialog box. The MHT file is open on your screen, as shown in Figure F-17. It's a good idea to open an mht file in your browser to see how it will look to viewers.

7. **Close the sales.mht file in Excel, open Windows Explorer, open the sales.mht file, click the Vancouver sheet tab, then close your browser window**

Excel 142   Managing Workbook Data

Hints as well as troubleshooting advice, right where you need it—next to the step itself.

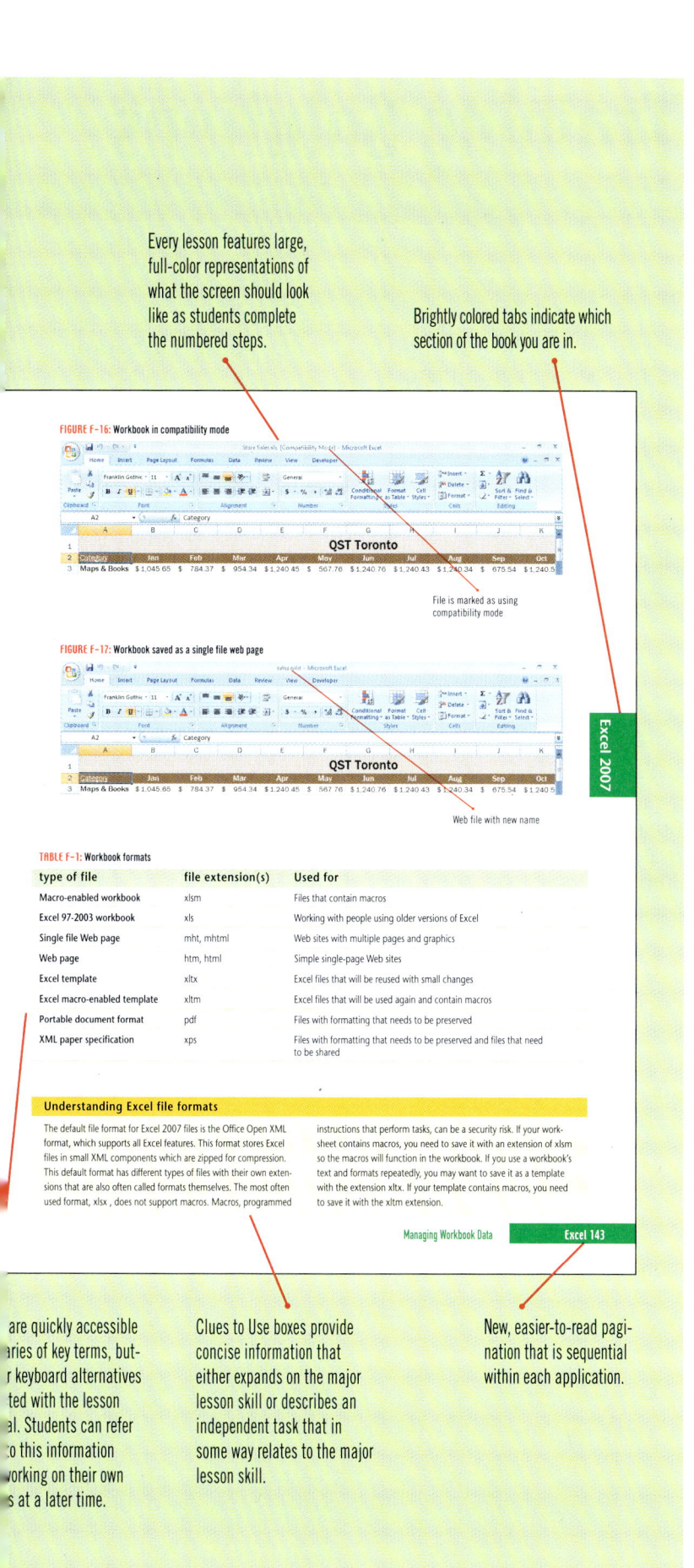

- **Content Improvements**—All of the content in the book has been updated to cover Office 2007 and also to address instructor feedback. See the instructor resource CD for details on specific content changes for each application section.

Assignments

The lessons use Quest Specialty Travel, a fictional adventure travel company, as the case study. The assignments on the light purple pages at the end of each unit increase in difficulty. Data files and case studies provide a variety of interesting and relevant business applications. Assignments include:

- **Concepts Reviews** consist of multiple choice, matching, and screen identification questions.
- **Skills Reviews** provide additional hands-on, step-by-step reinforcement.
- **Independent Challenges** are case projects requiring critical thinking and application of the unit skills. The Independent Challenges increase in difficulty, with the first one in each unit being the easiest. Independent Challenges 2 and 3 become increasingly open-ended, requiring more independent problem solving.
- **Real Life Independent Challenges** are practical exercises in which students create documents to help them with their every day lives.
- **Advanced Challenge Exercises** set within the Independent Challenges provide optional steps for more advanced students.
- **Visual Workshops** are practical, self-graded capstone projects that require independent problem solving.

Every lesson features large, full-color representations of what the screen should look like as students complete the numbered steps.

Brightly colored tabs indicate which section of the book you are in.

FIGURE F-16: Workbook in compatibility mode

File is marked as using compatibility mode

FIGURE F-17: Workbook saved as a single file web page

Web file with new name

TABLE F-1: Workbook formats

type of file	file extension(s)	Used for
Macro-enabled workbook	xlsm	Files that contain macros
Excel 97-2003 workbook	xls	Working with people using older versions of Excel
Single file Web page	mht, mhtml	Web sites with multiple pages and graphics
Web page	htm, html	Simple single-page Web sites
Excel template	xltx	Excel files that will be reused with small changes
Excel macro-enabled template	xltm	Excel files that will be used again and contain macros
Portable document format	pdf	Files with formatting that needs to be preserved
XML paper specification	xps	Files with formatting that needs to be preserved and files that need to be shared

Understanding Excel file formats

The default file format for Excel 2007 files is the Office Open XML format, which supports all Excel features. This format stores Excel files in small XML components which are zipped for compression. This default format has different types of files with their own extensions that are also often called formats themselves. The most often used format, xlsx, does not support macros. Macros, programmed instructions that perform tasks, can be a security risk. If your worksheet contains macros, you need to save it with an extension of xlsm so the macros will function in the workbook. If you use a workbook's text and formats repeatedly, you may want to save it as a template with the extension xltx. If your template contains macros, you need to save it with the xltm extension.

are quickly accessible
ries of key terms, but-
r keyboard alternatives
ted with the lesson
al. Students can refer
o this information
orking on their own
s at a later time.

Clues to Use boxes provide concise information that either expands on the major lesson skill or describes an independent task that in some way relates to the major lesson skill.

New, easier-to-read pagination that is sequential within each application.

Assessment & Training Solutions

SAM 2007

SAM 2007 helps bridge the gap between the classroom and the real world by allowing students to train and test on important computer skills in an active, hands-on environment.

SAM 2007's easy-to-use system includes powerful interactive exams, training, or projects on critical applications such as Word, Excel, Access, PowerPoint, Outlook, Windows, the Internet, and much more. SAM simulates the application environment, allowing students to demonstrate their knowledge and think through the skills by performing real-world tasks.

Designed to be used with the Illustrated series, SAM 2007 includes built-in page references so students can print helpful study guides that match the Illustrated textbooks used in class. Powerful administrative options allow instructors to schedule exams and assignments, secure tests, and run reports with almost limitless flexibility.

Student Edition Labs

Our Web-based interactive labs help students master hundreds of computer concepts, including input and output devices, file management and desktop applications, computer ethics, virus protection, and much more. Featuring up-to-the-minute content, eye-popping graphics, and rich animation, the highly interactive Student Edition Labs offer students an alternative way to learn through dynamic observation, step-by-step practice, and challenging review questions. Also available on CD at an additional cost.

Online Content   Blackboard

Blackboard is the leading distance learning solution provider and class-management platform today. Course Technology has partnered with Blackboard to bring you premium online content. Instructors: Content for use with *Microsoft Office 2007—Illustrated Second Course* is available in a Blackboard Course Cartridge and may include topic reviews, case projects, review questions, test banks, practice tests, custom syllabi, and more.

Course Technology also has solutions for several other learning management systems. Please visit *www.course.com* today to see what's available for this title.

Instructor Resources

The Instructor Resources CD is Course Technology's way of putting the resources and information needed to teach and learn effectively into your hands. With an integrated array of teaching and learning tools that offer you and your students a broad range of technology-based instructional options, we believe this CD represents the highest quality and most cutting edge resources available to instructors today. Many of these resources are available at www.course.com. The resources available with this book are:

- **Instructor's Manual**—Available as an electronic file, the Instructor's Manual includes detailed lecture topics with teaching tips for each unit.
- **Sample Syllabus**—Prepare and customize your course easily using this sample course outline.
- **PowerPoint Presentations**—Each unit has a corresponding PowerPoint presentation that you can use in lecture, distribute to your students, or customize to suit your course.
- **Figure Files**—The figures in the text are provided on the Instructor Resources CD to help you illustrate key topics or concepts. You can create traditional overhead transparencies by printing the figure files. Or you can create electronic slide shows by using the figures in a presentation program such as PowerPoint.
- **Solutions to Exercises**—Solutions to Exercises contains every file students are asked to create or modify in the lessons and end-of-unit material. Also provided in this section, there is a document outlining the solutions for the end-of-unit Concepts Review, Skills Review, and Independent Challenges. An Annotated Solution File and Grading Rubric accompany each file and can be used together for quick and easy grading.

- **Data Files for Students**—To complete most of the units in this book, your students will need Data Files. You can post the Data Files on a file server for students to copy. The Data Files are available on the Instructor Resources CD-ROM, the Review Pack, and can also be downloaded from www.course.com. In this edition, we have included a lesson on downloading the Data Files for this book, see page xxiii.

Instruct students to use the Data Files List included on the Review Pack and the Instructor Resources CD. This list gives instructions on copying and organizing files.

- **ExamView**—ExamView is a powerful testing software package that allows you to create and administer printed, computer (LAN-based), and Internet exams. ExamView includes hundreds of questions that correspond to the topics covered in this text, enabling students to generate detailed study guides that include page references for further review. The computer-based and Internet testing components allow students to take exams at their computers, and also saves you time by grading each exam automatically.

CourseCasts—Learning on the Go. Always available...always relevant.

Want to keep up with the latest technology trends relevant to you? Visit our site to find a library of podcasts, CourseCasts, featuring a "CourseCast of the Week," and download them to your mp3 player at http://coursecasts.course.com.

Our fast-paced world is driven by technology. You know because you're an active participant—always on the go, always keeping up with technological trends, and always learning new ways to embrace technology to power your life.

Ken Baldauf, a faculty member of the Florida State University Computer Science Department, is responsible for teaching technology classes to thousands of FSU students each year. He knows what you know; he knows what you want to learn. He's also an expert in the latest technology and will sort through and aggregate the most pertinent news and information so you can spend your time enjoying technology, rather than trying to figure it out.

Visit us at http://coursecasts.course.com to learn on the go!

COURSECASTS

Brief Contents

	Preface	iv
WORD 2007	Unit E: Creating and Formatting Tables	105
WORD 2007	Unit F: Illustrating Documents with Graphics	129
WORD 2007	Unit G: Working with Themes and Building Blocks	153
WORD 2007	Unit H: Merging Word Documents	177
EXCEL 2007	Unit E: Analyzing Data Using Formulas	105
EXCEL 2007	Unit F: Managing Workbook Data	129
EXCEL 2007	Unit G: Using Tables	153
EXCEL 2007	Unit H: Analyzing Table Data	177
INTEGRATION	Unit D: Integrating Word and Excel	49
ACCESS 2007	Unit E: Modifying the Database Structure	105
ACCESS 2007	Unit F: Creating Multiple Table Queries	137
ACCESS 2007	Unit G: Enhancing Forms	161
ACCESS 2007	Unit H: Analyzing Data with Reports	185
INTEGRATION	Unit E: Integrating Word, Excel, and Access	65

Brief Contents

POWERPOINT 2007	Unit E: Working with Advanced Tools and Masters	97
POWERPOINT 2007	Unit F: Enhancing Charts	121
POWERPOINT 2007	Unit G: Inserting Illustrations, Objects, and Media Clips	145
POWERPOINT 2007	Unit H: Using Advanced Features	169
INTEGRATION	Unit F: Integrating Word, Excel, Access, and PowerPoint	81
PUBLISHER 2007	Unit A: Getting Started with Publisher 2007	1
PUBLISHER 2007	Unit B: Working with Text and Graphics	27
PUBLISHER 2007	Unit C: Creating a Web Publication	53
	Appendix	1
	Glossary	9
	Index	18

Contents

Preface iv

WORD 2007

Unit E: Creating and Formatting Tables — 105

Inserting a Table 106
    Converting text to a table and a table to text
Inserting and Deleting Rows and Columns 108
    Copying and moving rows and columns
Modifying Rows and Columns 110
    Setting advanced table properties
Sorting Table Data 112
    Sorting lists and paragraphs
Splitting and Merging Cells 114
    Changing cell margins
Performing Calculations in Tables 116
    Working with formulas
Applying a Table Style 118
    Using tables to lay out a page
Creating a Custom Format for a Table 120
    Drawing a table
Concepts Review 122
Skills Review 123
Independent Challenges 125
Visual Workshop 128

WORD 2007

Unit F: Illustrating Documents with Graphics — 129

Inserting a Graphic 130
    Adjusting the brightness, contrast, or colors of a picture
Sizing and Scaling a Graphic 132
    Cropping graphics
Positioning a Graphic 134
    Changing the shape of a picture and enhancing it with visual effects
Creating a Text Box 136
    Linking text boxes
Creating WordArt 138
    Enhancing an object with shadows and 3-D effects
Drawing Shapes 140
    Creating an illustration in a drawing canvas

Creating a Chart 142
    Creating SmartArt graphics
Finalizing Page Layout 144
Concepts Review 146
Skills Review 147
Independent Challenges..150
Visual Workshop 152

WORD 2007

Unit G: Working with Themes and Building Blocks — 153

Applying Quick Styles to Text 154
    Saving a document as a Web page
Applying a Theme..156
    Changing the default theme
Customizing a Theme...158
Inserting a Sidebar 160
Inserting Quick Parts 162
Adding a Cover Page..164
Creating Building Blocks 166
    Renaming a building block and editing other properties
Inserting Building Blocks 168
Concepts Review 170
Skills Review 171
Independent Challenges..173
Visual Workshop 176

WORD 2007

Unit H: Merging Word Documents — 177

Understanding Mail Merge..178
Creating a Main Document 180
    Using a mail merge template
Designing a Data Source 182
    Merging with an Outlook data source
Entering and Editing Records..184
Adding Merge Fields 186
    Matching fields
Merging Data 188
Creating Labels 190
    Printing individual envelopes and labels
Sorting and Filtering Records..192
    Inserting individual merge fields
Concepts Review 194
Skills Review 195
Independent Challenges..197
Visual Workshop 200

EXCEL 2007

Unit E: Analyzing Data Using Formulas — 105

Formatting Data Using Text Functions 106
    Using text functions
Summing a Data Range Based on Conditions 108
Consolidating Data Using a Formula 110
    Linking data between workbooks
Checking Formulas for Errors 112
    Correcting circular references
Constructing Formulas Using Named Ranges 114
    Managing workbook names
Building a Logical Formula with the IF Function 116
Building a Logical Formula with the AND Function 118
    Using the OR and NOT logical functions
Calculating Payments with the PMT Function 120
    Calculating future value with the FV function
Concepts Review 122
Skills Review 123
Independent Challenges 125
Visual Workshop 128

EXCEL 2007

Unit F: Managing Workbook Data — 129

Viewing and Arranging Worksheets 130
    Splitting the worksheet into multiple panes
Protecting Worksheets and Workbooks 132
    Freezing rows and columns
Saving Custom Views of a Worksheet 134
    Using Page Break Preview
Adding a Worksheet Background 136
Preparing a Workbook for Distribution 138
    Adding a digital signature to a workbook
    Sharing a workbook
Inserting Hyperlinks 140
    Returning to your document
    Using research tools
Saving a Workbook for Distribution 142
    Understanding Excel file formats
Grouping Worksheets 144
    Creating a workspace
Concepts Review 146
Skills Review 147
Independent Challenges 149
Visual Workshop 152

EXCEL 2007

Unit G: Using Tables — 153

Planning a Table 154
Creating a Table 156
    Coordinating table styles with your document
    Changing table style options
Adding Table Data 158
Finding and Replacing Table Data 160
    Using Find and Select features
Deleting Table Data 162
Sorting Table Data 164
    Sorting a table using conditional formatting
    Specifying a custom sort order
Using Formulas in a Table 166
    Using structured references
Printing a Table 168
    Setting a print area
Concepts Review 170
Skills Review 171
Independent Challenges 172
Visual Workshop 176

EXCEL 2007

Unit H: Analyzing Table Data — 177

Filtering a Table 178
Creating a Custom Filter 180
    Using more than one rule when conditionally formatting data
Filtering a Table with Advanced Filter 182
    Using advanced conditional formatting options
Extracting Table Data 184
    Understanding the criteria range and the copy-to location
Looking Up Values in a Table 186
    Finding records using the DGET function
    Using the HLOOKUP and MATCH functions
Summarizing Table Data 188
Validating Table Data 190
    Restricting cell values and data length
    Adding input messages and error alerts
Creating Subtotals 192
Concepts Review 194
Skills Review 195
Independent Challenges 196
Visual Workshop 200

INTEGRATION

Unit D: Integrating Word and Excel — 49

- Using Paste Special to Modify Formatting 50
- Creating a Hyperlink Between Word and Excel 52
  - Editing and removing a hyperlink
- Creating an Excel Spreadsheet in Word 54
- Embedding an Excel File in Word 56
  - Formatting pasted, embedded, and linked objects
- Changing Link Sources 58
  - Re-establishing links
- Concepts Review 60
- Skills Review 60
- Independent Challenges 63
- Visual Workshop 64

ACCESS 2007

Unit E: Modifying the Database Structure — 105

- Examining Relational Databases 106
  - Using many-to-many relationships
- Designing Related Tables 108
  - Specifying the foreign key field data type
- Creating One-to-Many Relationships 110
  - More on enforcing referential integrity
- Creating Lookup Fields 112
  - Creating multivalued fields
- Modifying Text Fields 114
  - Exploring the Input Mask property
- Modifying Number and Currency Fields 116
- Modifying Date/Time Fields 118
  - Using Smart Tags
- Modifying Validation Properties 120
- Creating Attachment Fields 122
  - Recognizing database formats
- Concepts Review 124
- Skills Review 126
- Independent Challenges 131
- Visual Workshop 136

ACCESS 2007

Unit F: Creating Multiple Table Queries — 137

- Building Select Queries 138
  - Resizing Query Design View
- Using Multiple Sort Orders 140
  - Specifying a sort order different from the field order in the datasheet
- Developing AND Criteria 142
- Developing OR Criteria 144
  - Using wildcard characters in query criteria

Creating Calculated Fields 146
Building Summary Queries..148
Building Crosstab Queries 150
        Using Query Wizards
Building PivotTables and PivotCharts 152
Concepts Review..154
Skills Review 155
Independent Challenges...157
Visual Workshop..160

ACCESS 2007 — Unit G: Enhancing Forms — 161

Creating Subforms 162
Modifying Subforms..164
        Linking the form and subform
Creating Split Forms 166
Adding Tab Controls..168
Adding a Combo Box for Data Entry 170
        Choosing between a combo box and a list box
Adding a Combo Box to Find Records 172
Adding Option Groups...174
        Protecting data
Adding Command Buttons 176
Concepts Review..178
Skills Review 179
Independent Challenges...181
Visual Workshop..184

ACCESS 2007 — Unit H: Analyzing Data with Reports — 185

Creating Summary Reports..186
Creating Parameter Reports 188
Applying Conditional Formatting 190
Adding Lines..192
Using the Format Painter and AutoFormats..194
        Line troubles
Adding Subreports 196
Modifying Section Properties 198
Using Domain Functions 200
Concepts Review..202
Skills Review 203
Independent Challenges...205
Visual Workshop..208

INTEGRATION

Unit E: Integrating Word, Excel, and Access — 65

- Merging from Access to Word 66
- Filtering an Access Data Source 68
- Exporting an Access Table to Word 70
- Exporting an Access Table to Excel 72
- Exporting an Access Report to Word 74
- Concepts Review 76
- Skills Review 76
- Independent Challenges 78
- Visual Workshop 80

POWERPOINT 2007

Unit E: Working with Advanced Tools and Masters — 97

- Drawing and Formatting Connectors 98
  - Drawing a freeform shape
- Using Advanced Formatting Tools 100
  - Creating columns in a text box
- Customizing Animation Effects 102
  - Understanding animation timings
- Creating Custom Slide Layouts 104
  - Restoring the Slide Master layout
- Formatting Master Text 106
  - Exceptions to the Slide Master
- Changing Master Text Indents 108
- Adjusting Text Objects 110
  - More on text spacing
- Customizing Handout and Notes Masters 112
  - Creating handouts in Microsoft Office Word
- Concepts Review 114
- Skills Review 115
- Independent Challenges 117
- Visual Workshop 120

POWERPOINT 2007

Unit F: Enhancing Charts — 121

- Working with Charts in PowerPoint 122
  - Data series and data series mark
- Changing Chart Design and Style 124
  - Save a chart as a template
- Customizing a Chart Layout 126
  - Using the Research task pane
- Formatting Chart Elements 128
  - Saving in PDF and XPS file formats
- Animating a Chart 130
  - Adding voice narrations

Embedding an Excel Chart 132
    Embedding a worksheet
Linking an Excel Worksheet 134
Updating a Linked Excel Worksheet 136
    Using Paste Special
Concepts Review 138
Skills Review 139
Independent Challenges 141
Visual Workshop 144

POWERPOINT 2007

Unit G: Inserting Illustrations, Objects, and Media Clips — 145

Creating Custom Tables 146
    Drawing tables
Designing a SmartArt Graphic 148
    Creating organizational charts
Formatting a SmartArt Graphic 150
    Changing page setup and slide orientation
Inserting an Animation 152
    Inserting movies
Inserting a Sound 154
    Playing music from a CD
Using Macros 156
    Macro security
Adding Action Buttons 158
    The compatibility checker
Inserting a Hyperlink 160
    Changing PowerPoint options
Concepts Review 162
Skills Review 163
Independent Challenges 165
Visual Workshop 168

POWERPOINT 2007

Unit H: Using Advanced Features — 169

Using Templates and Adding Comments 170
    Creating a document workspace
Sending and Reviewing a Presentation 172
    Using PowerPoint's proofing tools
Using Advanced Slide Show Options 174
    Using Presenter view
Creating a Custom Show 176
    Link to a custom slide show
Preparing a Presentation for Distribution 178
    Creating a strong password

	Saving a Presentation for the Web	180
	Publish slides to a Slide Library	
	Packaging a Presentation	182
	Using the Microsoft PowerPoint Viewer	
	Creating a Photo Album	184
	Concepts Review	186
	Skills Review	187
	Independent Challenges	189
	Visual Workshop	192

INTEGRATION

Unit F: Integrating Word, Excel, Access, and PowerPoint — 81

Inserting an Access Table in PowerPoint	82
Inserting Word Objects in PowerPoint	84
Linking an Excel File in PowerPoint	86
Publishing PowerPoint Slides in Word	88
Embedding a PowerPoint Slide in Word	90
Concepts Review	92
Skills Review	92
Independent Challenges	95
Visual Workshop	96

PUBLISHER 2007

Unit A: Getting Started with Publisher 2007 — 1

Defining Desktop Publishing Software	2
Starting Publisher and Viewing the Publisher Window	4
Publisher Tasks	
Creating a Publication Using an Existing Design	6
Customizing Publisher	
Replacing Text in Text Boxes	8
Creating text boxes	
Formatting Text	10
Checking your publication	
Resizing and Moving Objects	12
Aligning objects	
Inserting a Picture	14
Considering image file size	
Saving, Previewing, and Printing a Publication	16
Using the Pack and Go Wizard	
Closing a Publication and Exiting Publisher	18
Using Help	
Concepts Review	20
Skills Review	21
Independent Challenges	22
Visual Workshop	26

PUBLISHER 2007

Unit B: Working with Text and Graphics — 27

Planning a Publication 28
Creating Columns of Text 30
　　Creating columns in existing text boxes
Working with Overflow Text 32
Using Guides 34
　　Using baseline guides
Creating Picture Captions 36
　　Adding your own objects to the Content Library
Creating Headers and Footers 38
　　Creating a drop cap
　　Working with text styles
Wrapping Text Around Objects 40
　　Rotating and flipping objects
Layering and Grouping Objects 42
Merging Information from a Data Source 44
　　Using marketing tools
Concepts Review 46
Skills Review 47
Independent Challenges 49
Visual Workshop 52

PUBLISHER 2007

Unit C: Creating a Web Publication — 53

Understanding and Planning Web Publications 54
　　Publishing a Web site
Creating a New Web Publication 56
Formatting a Web Publication 58
Modifying a Web Form 60
　　Adding multimedia components to a Web publication
Adding Form Controls 62
Previewing a Web Publication 64
Converting a Web Publication to a Web Site 66
　　Formatting Web publications for different audiences
Sending a Publication as an E-mail 68
　　Converting a print publication to a Web site
Concepts Review 70
Skills Review 72
Independent Challenges 75
Visual Workshop 80

Appendix — 1

Glossary — 9

Index — 18

CONTENTS xix

Important Notes for Windows XP Users

The screen shots in this book show Microsoft Office 2007 running on Windows Vista. However, if you are using Microsoft Windows XP, you can still use this book because Office 2007 runs virtually the same on both platforms. There are a few differences that you will encounter if you are using Windows XP. Read this section to understand the differences.

Dialog boxes

If you are a Windows XP user, dialog boxes shown in this book will look slightly different than what you see on your screen. Dialog boxes for Windows XP have a blue title bar, instead of a gray title bar. However, beyond this difference in appearance, the options in the dialog boxes across platforms are the same. For instance, the screen shots below show the Font dialog box running on Windows XP and the Font dialog box running on Windows Vista.

FIGURE 1: Dialog box in Windows XP

FIGURE 2: Dialog box in Windows Vista

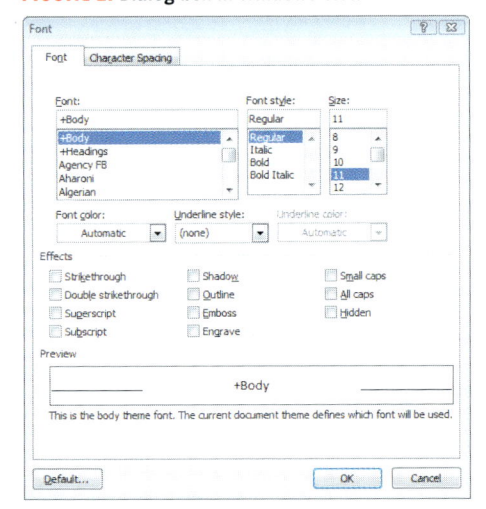

Alternate Steps for Windows XP Users

Nearly all of the steps in this book work exactly the same for Windows XP users. However, there are a few tasks that will require you to complete slightly different steps. This section provides alternate steps for a few specific skills.

Starting a program

1. Click the **Start button** on the taskbar
2. Point to **All Programs**, point to **Microsoft Office**, then click the application you want to use

FIGURE 3: Starting a program

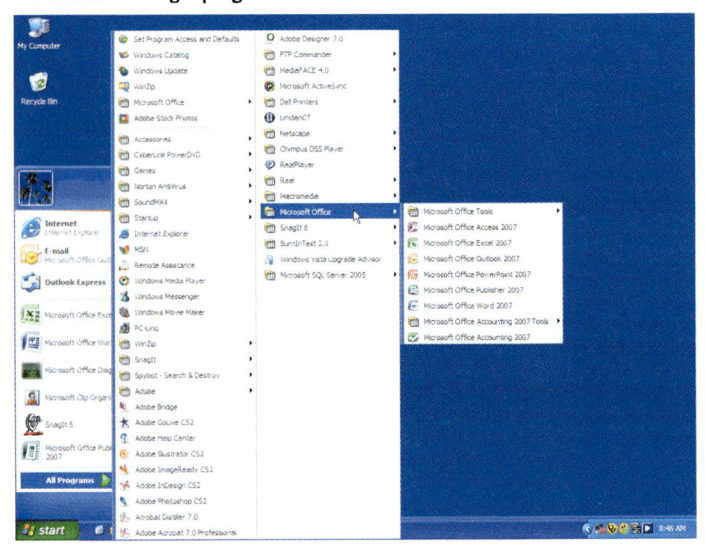

Saving a file for the first time

1. Click the **Office button**, then click **Save As**
2. Type a name for your file in the File name text box
3. Click the **Save in list arrow**, then navigate to the drive and folder where you store your Data Files
4. Click **Save**

FIGURE 4: Save As dialog box

Opening a file

1. Click the **Office button**, then click **Open**
2. Click the **Look in list arrow**, then navigate to the drive and folder where you store your Data Files
3. Click the file you want to open
4. Click **Open**

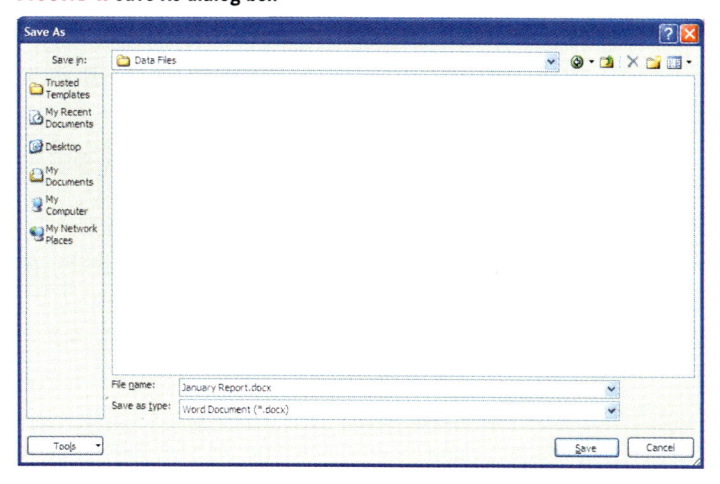

FIGURE 5: Open dialog box

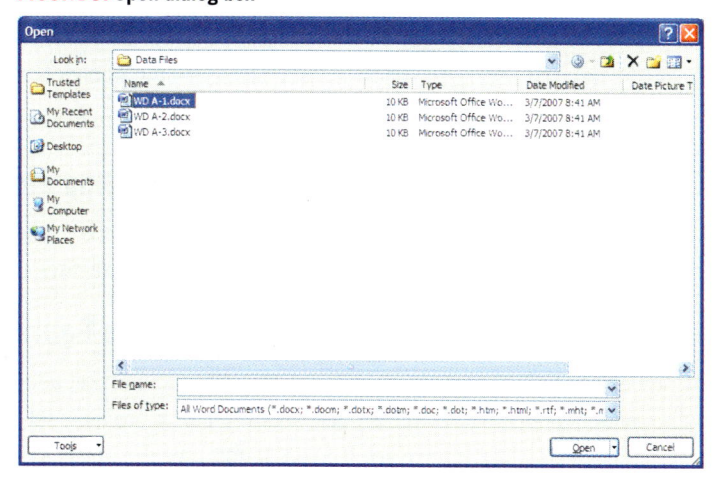

xxi

Read This Before You Begin

Frequently Asked Questions

What are Data Files?

A Data File is a partially completed Word document, Excel workbook, Access database, PowerPoint presentation, or another type of file that you use to complete the steps in the units and exercises to create the final document that you submit to your instructor. Each unit opener page lists the Data Files that you need for that unit.

Where are the Data Files?

Your instructor will provide the Data Files to you or direct you to a location on a network drive from which you can download them. Alternatively, you can follow the instructions on the next page to download the Data Files from this book's Web page.

What software was used to write and test this book?

This book was written and tested using a typical installation of Microsoft Office 2007 on a computer with a typical installation of Microsoft Windows Vista. If you are using this book on Windows XP, please see the next page "Important notes for Windows XP users." If you are using this book on Windows Vista, please see the Appendix at the end of this book.

The browser used for any steps that require a browser is Internet Explorer 7.

Do I need to be connected to the Internet to complete the steps and exercises in this book?

Some of the exercises in this book assume that your computer is connected to the Internet. If you are not connected to the Internet, see your instructor for information on how to complete the exercises.

What do I do if my screen is different from the figures shown in this book?

This book was written and tested on computers with monitors set at a resolution of 1024 × 768. If your screen shows more or less information than the figures in the book, your monitor is probably set at a higher or lower resolution. If you don't see something on your screen, you might have to scroll down or up to see the object identified in the figures.

The Ribbon—the blue area at the top of the screen—in Microsoft Office 2007 adapts to different resolutions. If your monitor is set at a lower resolution than 1024 × 768, you might not see all of the buttons shown in the figures. The groups of buttons will always appear, but the entire group might be condensed into a single button that you need to click to access the buttons described in the instructions.

1024 × 768 Editing Group

Editing Group on the Home Tab of the Ribbon at 1024 × 768

For example, the figures and steps in this book assume that the Editing group on the Home tab in Word looks like the following:

If your resolution is set to 800 × 600, the Ribbon in Word will look like the following figure, and you will need to click the Editing button to access the buttons that are visible in the Editing group.

800 × 600 Editing Group

Editing Group on the Home Tab of the Ribbon at 800 × 600

800 × 600 Editing Group Clicked

Editing Group on the Home Tab of the Ribbon at 800 × 600 is selected to show available buttons

Downloading Data Files for This Book

In order to complete many of the lesson steps and exercises in this book, you are asked to open and save Data Files. A **Data File** is a partially completed Word document, Excel workbook, Access database, PowerPoint presentation, or another type of file that you use as a starting point to complete the steps in the units and exercises. The benefit of using a Data File is that it saves you the time and effort needed to create a file; you can simply open a Data File, save it with a new name (so the original file remains intact), then make changes to it to complete lesson steps or an exercise. Your instructor will provide the Data Files to you or direct you to a location on a network drive from which you can download them. Alternatively, you can follow the instructions in this lesson to download the Data Files from this book's Web page.

1. Start Internet Explorer, type www.course.com in the address bar, then press [Enter]
2. When the Course.com Web site opens, click the Student Downloads link
3. On the Student Downloads page, click in the Search text box, type 9781423905134, then click Go

QUICK TIP
You can also click Student Downloads on the right side of the product page.

4. When the page opens for this textbook, in the left navigation bar, click the Download Student Files link, then, on the Student Downloads page, click the Data Files link
5. If the File Download – Security Warning dialog box opens, click Save. (If no dialog box appears, skip this step and go to Step 6)

TROUBLE
If a dialog box opens telling you that the download is complete, click Close.

6. If the Save As dialog box opens, click the Save in list arrow at the top of the dialog box, select a folder on your USB drive or hard disk to download the file to, then click Save
7. Close Internet Explorer and then open My Computer or Windows Explorer and display the contents of the drive and folder to which you downloaded the file
8. Double-click the file 905134.exe in the drive or folder, then, if the Open File – Security Warning dialog box opens, click Run

QUICK TIP
By default, the files will extract to C:\CourseTechnology\9055134

9. In the WinZip Self-Extractor window, navigate to the drive and folder where you want to unzip the files to, then click Unzip
10. When the WinZip Self-Extractor displays a dialog box listing the number of files that have unzipped successfully, click OK, click Close in the WinZip Self-Extractor dialog box, then close Windows Explorer or My Computer

    You are now ready to open the required files.

UNIT E
Word 2007

Creating and Formatting Tables

Files You Will Need:
WD E-1.docx
WD E-2.docx

Tables are commonly used to display information for quick reference and analysis. In this unit, you learn how to create and modify a table in Word, how to sort table data and perform calculations, and how to format a table with borders and shading. You also learn how to use a table to structure the layout of a page. You are preparing a summary budget for an advertising campaign aimed at the Chicago market. The goal of the ad campaign is to promote winter tours to tropical destinations. You decide to format the budget information as a table so that it is easy to read and analyze.

OBJECTIVES

Insert a table
Insert and delete rows and columns
Modify rows and columns
Sort table data
Split and merge cells
Perform calculations in tables
Apply a table style
Create a custom format for a table

UNIT E
Word 2007

Inserting a Table

A **table** is a grid made up of rows and columns of cells that you can fill with text and graphics. A **cell** is the box formed by the intersection of a column and a row. The lines that divide the columns and rows and help you see the grid-like structure of a table are called **borders**. You can create a table in a document by using the Table command in the Tables group on the Insert tab. Once you have created a table, you can add text and graphics to it. You begin by inserting a blank table and adding text to it.

STEPS

> **QUICK TIP**
> Click the View Ruler button at the top of the vertical scroll bar to display the rulers if they are not already displayed.

1. **Start Word, click the View tab, then click the Page Width button in the Zoom group**

2. **Click the Insert tab, then click the Table button in the Tables group**
   The Table menu opens. It includes a grid for selecting the number of columns and rows you want the table to contain, as well as several commands for inserting a table. Table E-1 describes the function of these commands. As you move the pointer across the grid, a preview of the table with the specified number of columns and rows appears in the document at the location of the insertion point.

3. **Point to the second box in the fourth row to select 2x4 Table, then click**
   A table with two columns and four rows is inserted in the document, as shown in Figure E-1. Black borders surround the table cells. The insertion point is in the first cell in the first row.

> **TROUBLE**
> Don't be concerned if the paragraph spacing under the text in your table is different from that shown in the figures.

4. **Type Location, then press [Tab]**
   Pressing [Tab] moves the insertion point to the next cell in the row.

5. **Type Cost, press [Tab], then type Chicago Tribune**
   Pressing [Tab] at the end of a row moves the insertion point to the first cell in the next row.

6. **Press [Tab], type 27,600, press [Tab], then type the following text in the table, pressing [Tab] to move from cell to cell**

Chicagotribune.com	25,000
Taxi tops	18,000

7. **Press [Tab]**
   Pressing [Tab] at the end of the last cell of a table creates a new row at the bottom of the table, as shown in Figure E-2. The insertion point is located in the first cell in the new row.

> **TROUBLE**
> If you pressed [Tab] after the last row, click the Undo button on the Quick Access toolbar to remove the new blank row.

8. **Type the following, pressing [Tab] to move from cell to cell and to create new rows**

Chicago Defender	18,760
Hellochicago.com	3,250
Bus stops	12,000
Chicago Magazine	12,400

9. **Click the Save button on the Quick Access toolbar, then save the document as Chicago Ad Budget to the drive and folder where you store your Data Files**
   The table is shown in Figure E-3.

TABLE E-1: Table menu commands

command	use to
Insert Table	Create a table with any number of columns and rows and select an AutoFit behavior
Draw Table	Create a complex table by drawing the table columns and rows
Convert Text to Table	Convert selected text that is separated by tabs, commas, or another separator character into a table
Excel Spreadsheet	Insert a blank Excel worksheet into the document as an embedded object
Quick Tables	Insert a table template chosen from a gallery of preformatted tables and replace the placeholder data with your own data

FIGURE E-1: Blank table

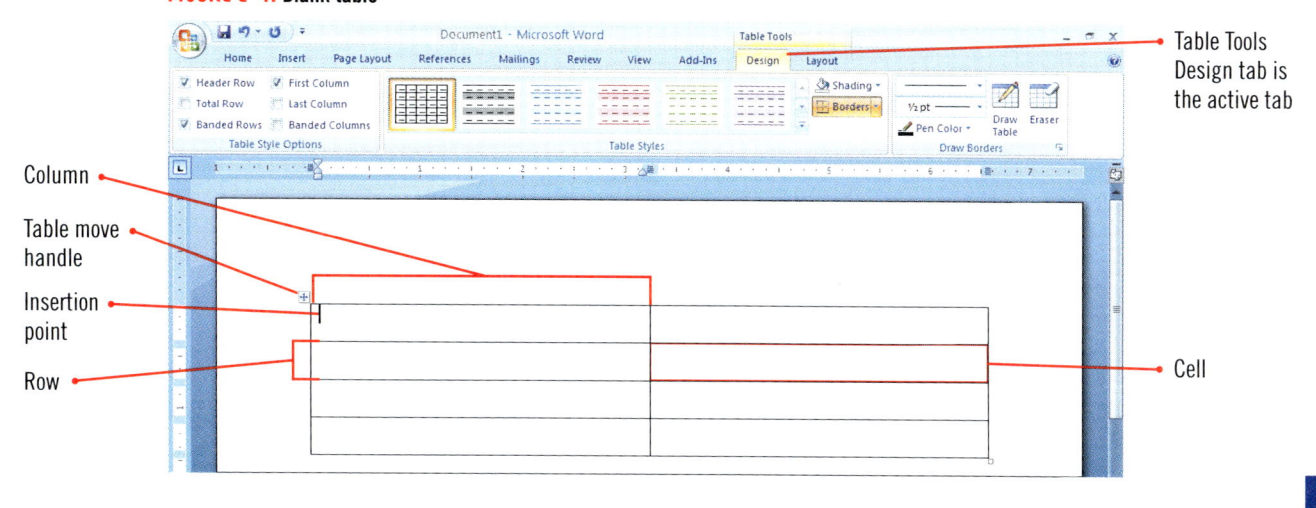

Labels: Column; Table move handle; Insertion point; Row; Cell; Table Tools Design tab is the active tab

FIGURE E-2: New row in table

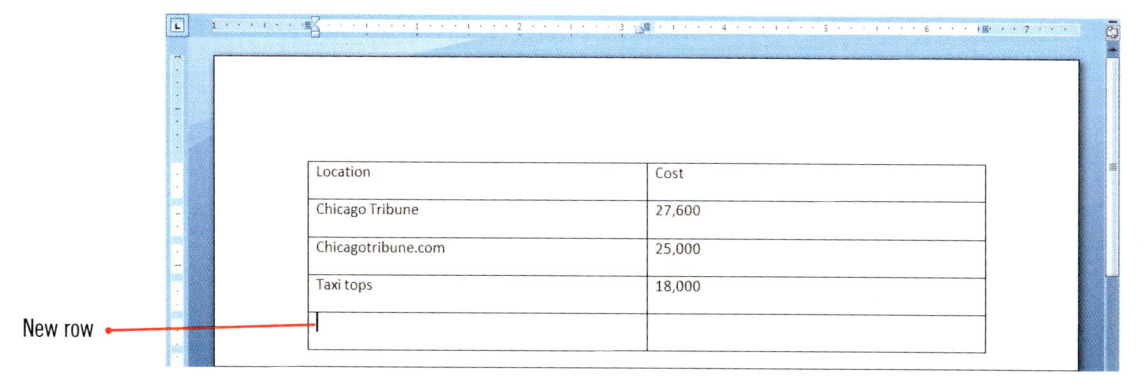

Location	Cost
Chicago Tribune	27,600
Chicagotribune.com	25,000
Taxi tops	18,000

Label: New row

FIGURE E-3: Text in the table

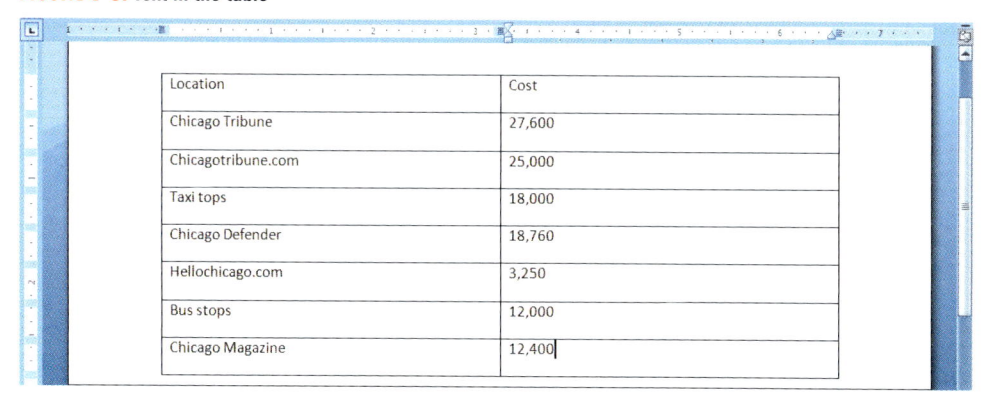

Location	Cost
Chicago Tribune	27,600
Chicagotribune.com	25,000
Taxi tops	18,000
Chicago Defender	18,760
Hellochicago.com	3,250
Bus stops	12,000
Chicago Magazine	12,400

Converting text to a table and a table to text

Another way to create a table is to convert text that is separated by a tab, a comma, or another separator character into a table. For example, to create a two-column table of last and first names, you could type the names as a list with a comma separating the last and first name in each line, and then convert the text to a table. The separator character—a comma in this example—indicates where you want to divide the table into columns, and a paragraph mark indicates where you want to begin a new row. To convert text to a table, select the text, click the Table button in the Tables group on the Insert tab, and then click Convert Text to Table. In the Convert Text to Table dialog box, select from the options for structuring and formatting the table, and then click OK to create the table.

Conversely, you can convert a table to text that is separated by tabs, commas, or some other character by selecting the table, clicking the Table Tools Layout tab, and then clicking the Convert to Text button in the Data group.

Creating and Formatting Tables — Word 107

Inserting and Deleting Rows and Columns

UNIT E — Word 2007

You can easily modify the structure of a table by adding and removing rows and columns. First, you must click or select an existing row or column in the table to indicate where you want to insert or delete a row or a column. You can select any element of a table using the Select command in the Table group on the Table Tools Layout tab, but it is often easier to select rows and columns using the mouse. To insert or delete rows and columns, you use the commands in the Rows & Columns group on the Table Tools Layout tab. You add new rows and columns to the table and delete unnecessary rows.

STEPS

1. **Click the Home tab, then click the Show/Hide ¶ button ¶ in the Paragraph group to display formatting marks**

   An end of cell mark appears at the end of each cell and an end of row mark appears at the end of each row.

2. **Click the Table Tools Layout tab, click the first cell of the Hellochicago.com row, then click the Insert Above button in the Rows & Columns group**

   A new row is inserted directly above the Hellochicago.com row, as shown in Figure E-4. To insert a single row, you simply place the insertion point in the row above or below where you want the new row to be inserted, and then insert the row.

3. **Click the first cell of the new row, type Chicago Sun Times, press [Tab], then type 15,300**

4. **Place the pointer in the margin to the left of the Chicagotribune.com row until the pointer changes to ⇗, click to select the row, press and hold the mouse button, drag down to select the Taxi tops row, then release the mouse button**

   The two rows are selected, including the end of row marks.

   > **QUICK TIP**
   > If the end of row mark is not selected, you have selected only the text in the row, not the row itself.

5. **Click the Insert Below button in the Rows & Columns group**

   Two new rows are added below the selected rows. To insert multiple rows, you select the number of rows you want to insert before inserting the rows.

6. **Click the Chicago Defender row, click the Delete button in the Rows & Columns group, click Delete Rows, select the two blank rows, right-click the selected rows, then click Delete Rows on the shortcut menu**

   The Chicago Defender row and the two blank rows are deleted. If you select a row and press [Delete], you delete only the contents of the row, not the row itself.

   > **QUICK TIP**
   > You can also delete a row or column by pressing [Shift][Delete].

7. **Place the pointer over the top border of the Location column until the pointer changes to ↓, then click**

   The entire column is selected.

8. **Click the Insert Left button in the Rows & Columns group, then type Type**

   A new column is inserted to the left of the Location column, as shown in Figure E-5.

   > **QUICK TIP**
   > To select a cell, place the ▱ pointer over the left border of the cell, then click.

9. **Click in the Location column, click the Insert Right button in the Rows & Columns group, then type Details in the first cell of the new column**

   A new column is added to the right of the Location column.

10. **Press [↓] to move the insertion point to the next cell in the Details column, click the Home tab, click ¶ to turn off the display of formatting marks, enter the text shown in Figure E-6 in each cell in the Details and Type columns, then save your changes**

    You can use the arrow keys to move the insertion point from cell to cell. Notice that text wraps to the next line in the cell as you type. Compare your table to Figure E-6.

Word 108 — Creating and Formatting Tables

FIGURE E-4: Inserted row

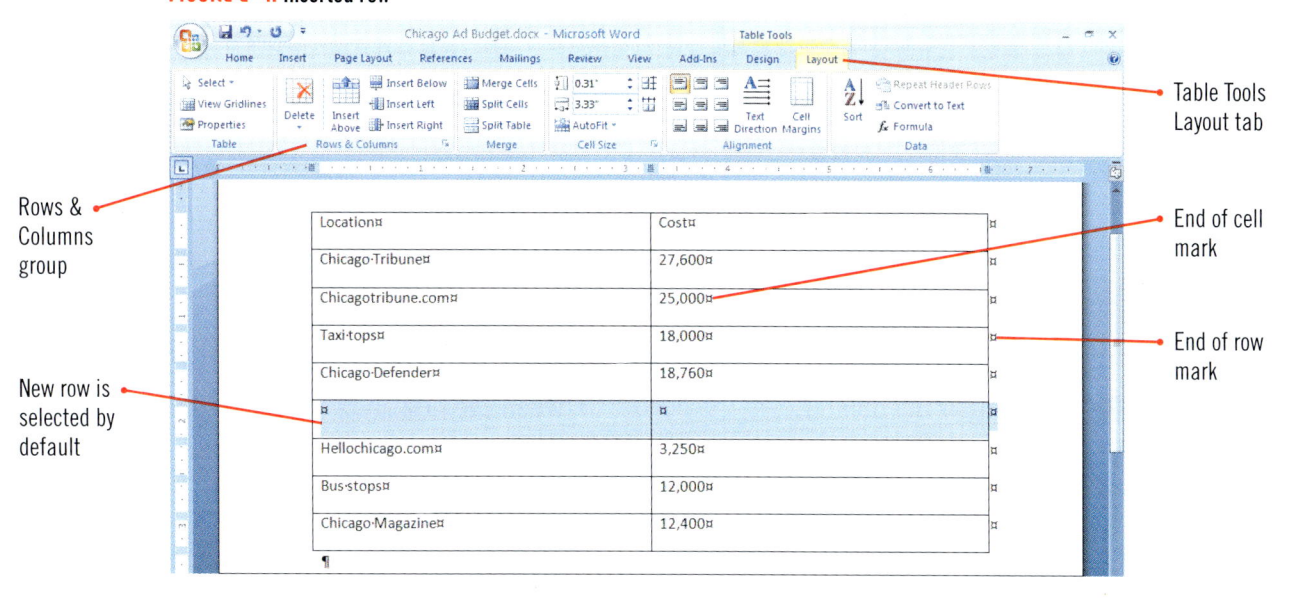

- Rows & Columns group
- New row is selected by default
- Table Tools Layout tab
- End of cell mark
- End of row mark

FIGURE E-5: Inserted column

- New column

FIGURE E-6: Text in Type and Details column

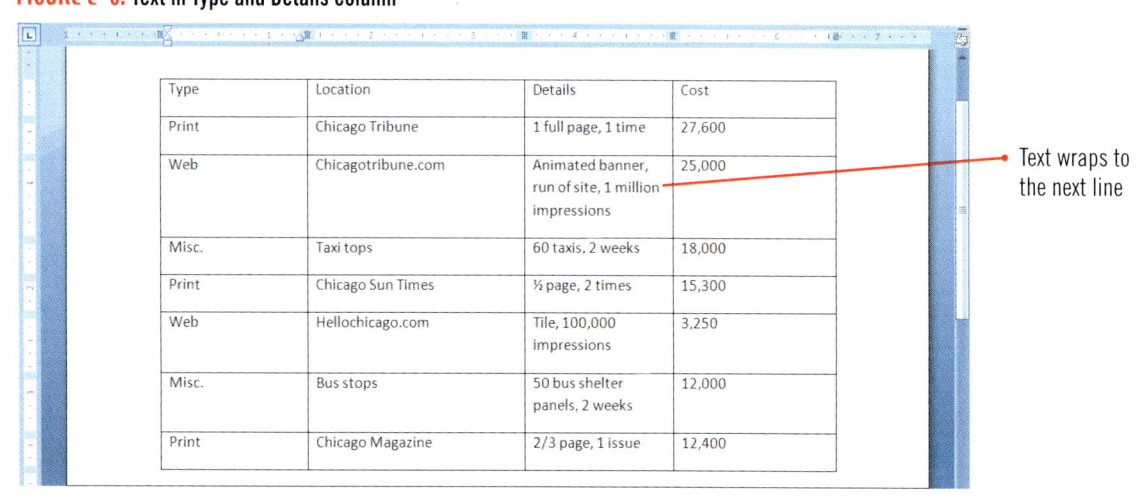

Type	Location	Details	Cost
Print	Chicago Tribune	1 full page, 1 time	27,600
Web	Chicagotribune.com	Animated banner, run of site, 1 million impressions	25,000
Misc.	Taxi tops	60 taxis, 2 weeks	18,000
Print	Chicago Sun Times	½ page, 2 times	15,300
Web	Hellochicago.com	Tile, 100,000 impressions	3,250
Misc.	Bus stops	50 bus shelter panels, 2 weeks	12,000
Print	Chicago Magazine	2/3 page, 1 issue	12,400

- Text wraps to the next line

Copying and moving rows and columns

You can copy and move rows and columns within a table in the same manner you copy and move text. Select the row or column you want to move, then use the Copy or Cut button to place the selection on the Clipboard. Place the insertion point in the location you want to insert the row or column, then click the Paste button to paste the selection. Rows are inserted above the row containing the insertion point; columns are inserted to the left of the column containing the insertion point. You can also copy or move columns and rows by selecting them and using the pointer to drag them to a new location in the table.

Creating and Formatting Tables

UNIT E
Word 2007

Modifying Rows and Columns

Once you create a table, you can easily adjust the size of columns and rows to make the table easier to read. You can change the width of columns and the height of rows by dragging a border, by using the AutoFit command in the Cell Size group on the Table Tools Layout tab, or by setting exact measurements using the Table Row Height and Table Column Width text boxes in the Cell Size group or the Table Properties dialog box. You adjust the size of the columns and rows to make the table more attractive and easier to read. You also center the text vertically in each table cell.

STEPS

QUICK TIP
Press [Alt] as you drag a border to display the column width or row height measurements on the ruler.

1. **Position the pointer over the border between the first and second columns until the pointer changes to ↔, then drag the border to approximately the ½" mark on the horizontal ruler**

   The dotted line that appears as you drag represents the border. Dragging the column border changes the width of the first and second columns: the first column is narrower and the second column is wider. When dragging a border to change the width of an entire column, make sure no cells are selected in the column. You can also drag a row border to change the height of the row above it.

2. **Position the pointer over the right border of the Location column until the pointer changes to ↔, then double-click**

   Double-clicking a column border automatically resizes the column to fit the text.

3. **Double-click the right border of the Details column with the ↔ pointer, then double-click the right border of the Cost column with the ↔ pointer**

   The widths of the Details and Cost columns are adjusted.

4. **Move the pointer over the table, then click the table move handle ⊞ that appears outside the upper-left corner of the table**

   Clicking the table move handle selects the entire table. You can also use the Select button in the Table group on the Table Tools Layout tab to select an entire table.

5. **Click the Home tab, then click the No Spacing button in the Styles group**

   Changing the style to No Spacing removes the paragraph spacing below the text in each table cell.

QUICK TIP
Quickly resize a table by dragging the table resize handle to a new location.

6. **With the table still selected, click the Table Tools Layout tab, click the Distribute Rows button in the Cell Size group, then click in the table to deselect it**

   All the rows in the table become the same height, as shown in Figure E-7. You can also use the Distribute Columns button to make all the columns the same width, or use the AutoFit button to make the width of the columns fit the text, to adjust the width of the columns so the table is justified between the margins, or to set fixed column widths.

7. **Click in the Details column, click the Table Column Width text box in the Cell Size group, type 3.5, then press [Enter]**

   The width of the Details column changes to 3.5".

QUICK TIP
Quickly center a table on a page by selecting the table and clicking the Center button in the Paragraph group on the Home tab.

8. **Click the Select button in the Table group, click Select Table, click the Align Center Left button in the Alignment group, deselect the table, then save your changes**

   The text is centered vertically in each table cell, as shown in Figure E-8. You can use the alignment buttons in the Alignment group to change the vertical and horizontal alignment of the text in selected cells or in the entire table.

Word 110   Creating and Formatting Tables

FIGURE E-7: Resized columns and rows

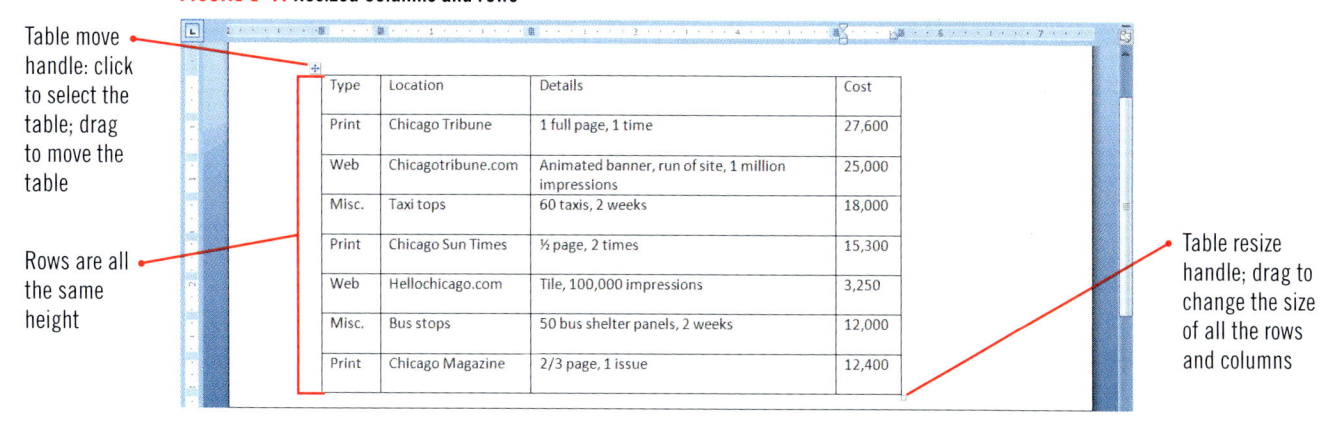

Table move handle: click to select the table; drag to move the table

Rows are all the same height

Type	Location	Details	Cost
Print	Chicago Tribune	1 full page, 1 time	27,600
Web	Chicagotribune.com	Animated banner, run of site, 1 million impressions	25,000
Misc.	Taxi tops	60 taxis, 2 weeks	18,000
Print	Chicago Sun Times	½ page, 2 times	15,300
Web	Hellochicago.com	Tile, 100,000 impressions	3,250
Misc.	Bus stops	50 bus shelter panels, 2 weeks	12,000
Print	Chicago Magazine	2/3 page, 1 issue	12,400

Table resize handle; drag to change the size of all the rows and columns

FIGURE E-8: Text centered vertically in cells

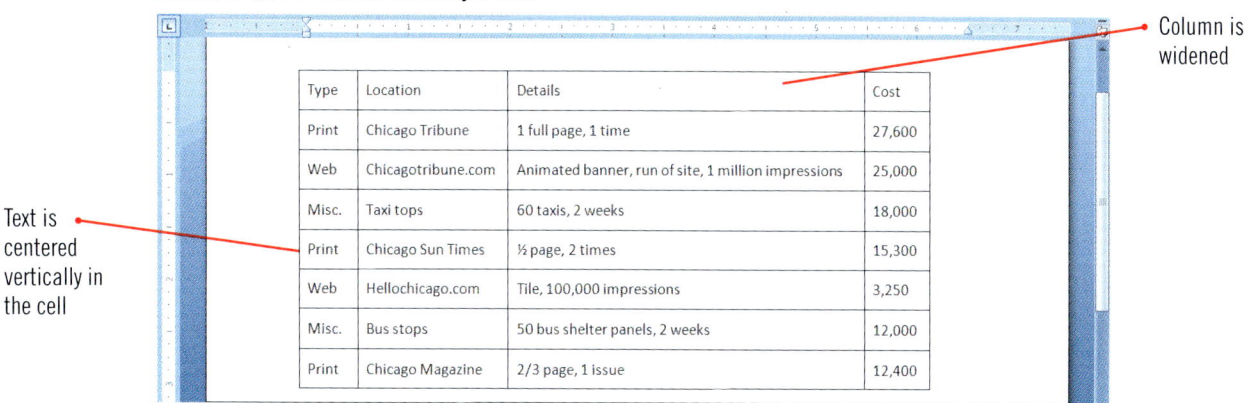

Column is widened

Text is centered vertically in the cell

Type	Location	Details	Cost
Print	Chicago Tribune	1 full page, 1 time	27,600
Web	Chicagotribune.com	Animated banner, run of site, 1 million impressions	25,000
Misc.	Taxi tops	60 taxis, 2 weeks	18,000
Print	Chicago Sun Times	½ page, 2 times	15,300
Web	Hellochicago.com	Tile, 100,000 impressions	3,250
Misc.	Bus stops	50 bus shelter panels, 2 weeks	12,000
Print	Chicago Magazine	2/3 page, 1 issue	12,400

Setting advanced table properties

When you want to wrap text around a table, indent a table, or set other advanced table properties, you click the Properties command in the Table group on the Table Tools Layout tab to open the Table Properties dialog box, shown in Figure E-9. Using the Table tab in this dialog box, you can set a precise width for the table, change the horizontal alignment of the table between the margins, indent the table, and set text wrapping options for the table. You can also click Options on the Table tab to open the Table Options dialog box, which you use to customize the table's default cell margins and the spacing between table cells. Alternatively, click Borders and Shading on the Table tab to open the Borders and Shading dialog box, which you can use to create a custom format for the table. The other tabs in the Table Properties dialog box, the Column, Row, and Cell tabs, allow you to set an exact width for columns, to specify an exact height for rows, and to indicate an exact size for individual cells.

FIGURE E-9: Table Properties dialog box

Creating and Formatting Tables

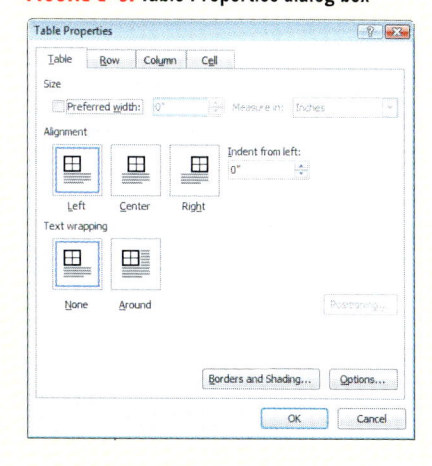

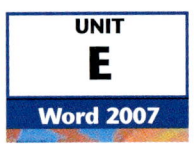

Sorting Table Data

Tables are often easier to interpret and analyze when the data is **sorted**, which means the rows are organized in alphabetical or sequential order based on the data in one or more columns. When you sort a table, Word arranges all the table data according to the criteria you set. You set sort criteria by specifying the column (or columns) by which you want to sort, and indicating the sort order—ascending or descending—you want to use. **Ascending order** lists data alphabetically or sequentially (from A to Z, 0 to 9, or earliest to latest). **Descending order** lists data in reverse alphabetical or sequential order (from Z to A, 9 to 0, or latest to earliest). You can sort using the data in one column or multiple columns. When you sort by multiple columns you must select primary, secondary, and tertiary sort criteria. You use the Sort command in the Data group on the Table Tools Layout tab to sort a table. You sort the table so that all ads of the same type are listed together. You also add secondary sort criteria so that the ads within each type are listed in descending order by cost.

STEPS

1. **Place the insertion point anywhere in the table**
   To sort an entire table, you simply need to place the insertion point anywhere in the table. If you want to sort specific rows only, then you must select the rows you want to sort.

2. **Click the Sort button in the Data group on the Table Tools Layout tab**
   The Sort dialog box opens, as shown in Figure E-10. You use this dialog box to specify the column or columns by which you want to sort, the type of information you are sorting (text, numbers, or dates), and the sort order (ascending or descending). Column 1 is selected by default in the Sort by list box. Since you want to sort your table first by the information in the first column—the type of ad (Print, Web, or Misc.)—you don't change the Sort by criteria.

3. **Click the Descending option button in the Sort by section**
   The ad type information will be sorted in descending—or reverse alphabetical—order, so that the "Web" ads will be listed first, followed by the "Print" ads, and then the "Misc." ads.

4. **In the first Then by section click the Then by list arrow, click Column 4, click the Type list arrow, click Number if it is not already selected, then click the Descending option button**
   Within the Web, Print, and Misc. groups, the rows will be sorted by the cost of the ad—the information contained in the fourth column, which is numbers, not dates or text. The rows will appear in descending order within each group, with the most expensive ad listed first.

5. **Click the Header row option button in the My list has section to select it**
   The table includes a header row that you do not want included in the sort. A **header row** is the first row of a table that contains the column headings.

6. **Click OK, then deselect the table**
   The rows in the table are sorted first by the information in the Type column and second by the information in the Cost column, as shown in Figure E-11. The first row of the table, which is the header row, is not included in the sort.

7. **Save your changes to the document**

> **QUICK TIP**
> To repeat the header row on every page of a table that spans multiple pages, click the Repeat Header Rows button in the Data group on the Table Tools Layout tab.

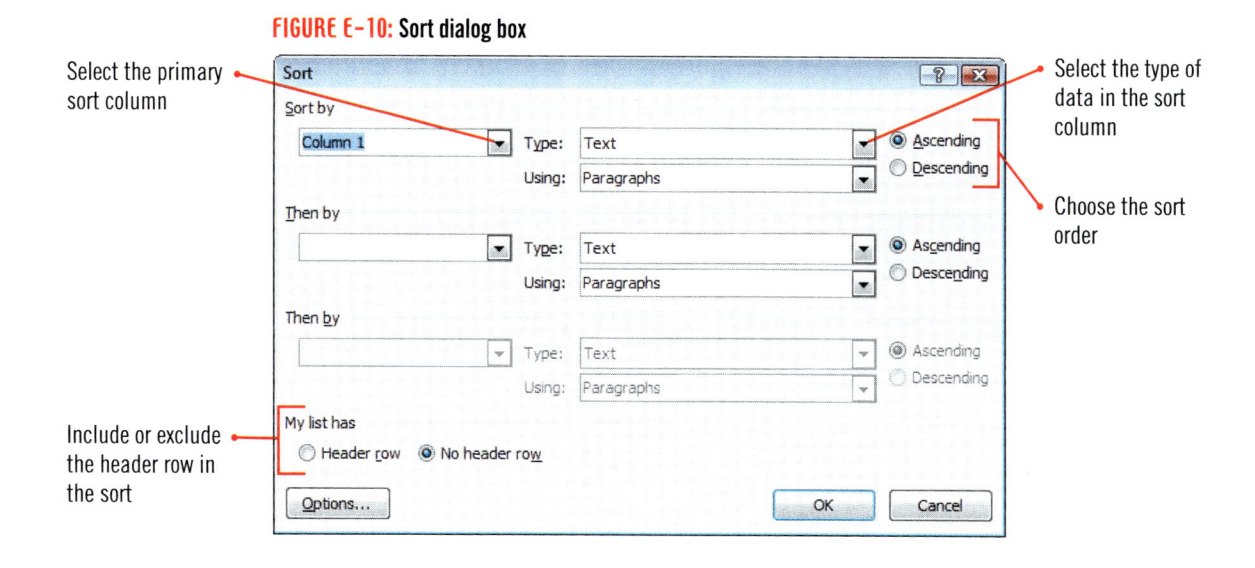

FIGURE E-10: Sort dialog box

- Select the primary sort column
- Include or exclude the header row in the sort
- Select the type of data in the sort column
- Choose the sort order

FIGURE E-11: Sorted table

- Header row is not included in the sort
- First, rows are sorted by type in descending order
- Second, within each type, rows are sorted by cost in descending order

Type	Location	Details	Cost
Web	Chicagotribune.com	Animated banner, run of site, 1 million impressions	25,000
Web	Hellochicago.com	Tile, 100,000 impressions	3,250
Print	Chicago Tribune	1 full page, 1 time	27,600
Print	Chicago Sun Times	½ page, 2 times	15,300
Print	Chicago Magazine	2/3 page, 1 issue	12,400
Misc.	Taxi tops	60 taxis, 2 weeks	18,000
Misc.	Bus stops	50 bus shelter panels, 2 weeks	12,000

Sorting lists and paragraphs

In addition to sorting table data, you can use the Sort command to alphabetize text or sort numerical data. When you want to sort data that is not formatted as a table, such as lists and paragraphs, you use the Sort command in the Paragraph group on the Home tab. To sort lists and paragraphs, select the items you want included in the sort, then click the Sort button. In the Sort Text dialog box, use the Sort by list arrow to select the sort by criteria (paragraphs or fields), use the Type list arrow to select the type of data (text, numbers, or dates), and then click the Ascending or Descending option button to choose a sort order.

When sorting text information in a document, the term "fields" refers to text or numbers that are separated by a character, such as a tab or a comma. For example, you might want to sort a list of names alphabetically. If the names you want to sort are listed in "Last name, First name" order, then last name and first name are each considered a field. You can choose to sort the list in alphabetical order by last name or by first name. Use the Options button in the Sort Text dialog box to specify the character that separates the fields in your lists or paragraphs, along with other sort options.

Creating and Formatting Tables

Splitting and Merging Cells

UNIT E — Word 2007

A convenient way to change the format and structure of a table is to merge and split the table cells. When you **merge** cells, you combine adjacent cells into a single larger cell. When you **split** a cell, you divide an existing cell into multiple cells. You can merge and split cells using the Merge Cells and Split Cells commands in the Merge group on the Table Tools Layout tab. You merge cells in the first column to create a single cell for each ad type—Web, Print, and Misc. You also add a new row to the bottom of the table, and split the cells in the row to create three new rows with a different structure.

STEPS

TROUBLE
If you click below the table to deselect it, the active tab changes to the Home tab. If necessary, click in the table, then click the Table Tools Layout tab to continue with the steps in this lesson.

1. **Select the two Web cells in the first column of the table, click the Merge Cells button in the Merge group on the Table Tools Layout tab, then deselect the text**
   The two Web cells merge to become a single cell. When you merge cells, Word converts the text in each cell into a separate paragraph in the merged cell.

2. **Select the first Web in the cell, then press [Delete]**

3. **Select the three Print cells in the first column, click the Merge Cells button, type Print, select the two Misc. cells, click the Merge Cells button, then type Misc.**
   The three Print cells merge to become one cell and the two Misc. cells merge to become one cell.

4. **Click the Bus stops cell, then click the Insert Below button in the Rows & Columns group**
   A row is added to the bottom of the table.

5. **Select the first three cells in the new last row of the table, click the Merge Cells button, then deselect the cell**
   The three cells in the row merge to become a single cell.

QUICK TIP
To split a table in two, click the row you want to be the first row in the second table, then click the Split Table button in the Merge group.

6. **Click the first cell in the last row, then click the Split Cells button in the Merge group**
   The Split Cells dialog box opens, as shown in Figure E-12. You use this dialog box to split the selected cell or cells into a specific number of columns and rows.

7. **Type 1 in the Number of columns text box, press [Tab], type 3 in the Number of rows text box, click OK, then deselect the cells**
   The single cell is divided into three rows of equal height. When you split a cell into multiple rows, the width of the original column does not change. When you split a cell into multiple columns, the height of the original row does not change. If the cell you split contains text, all the text appears in the upper-left cell.

8. **Click the last cell in the Cost column, click the Split Cells button, repeat Step 7, then save your changes**
   The cell is split into three rows, as shown in Figure E-13. The last three rows of the table now have only two columns.

Creating and Formatting Tables

FIGURE E-12: Split Cells dialog box

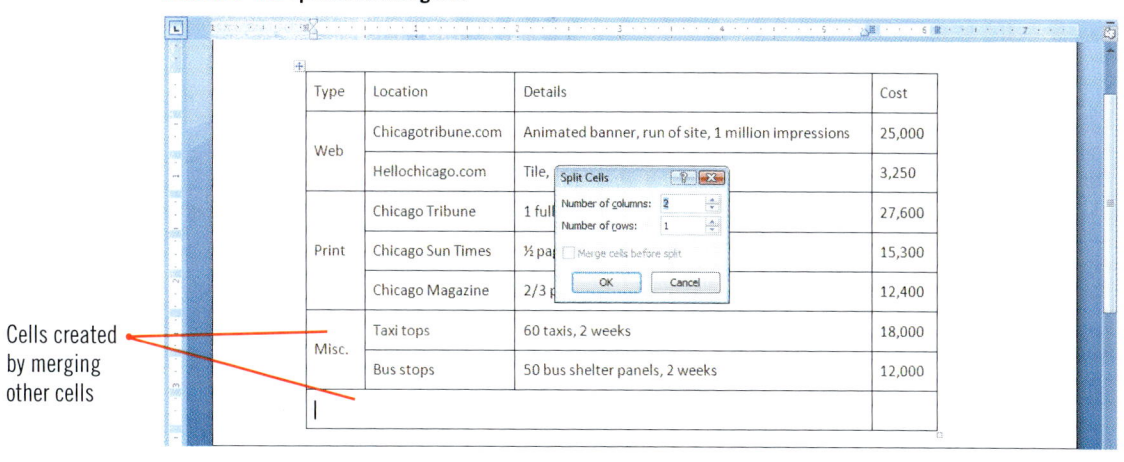

Cells created by merging other cells

FIGURE E-13: Cells split into three rows

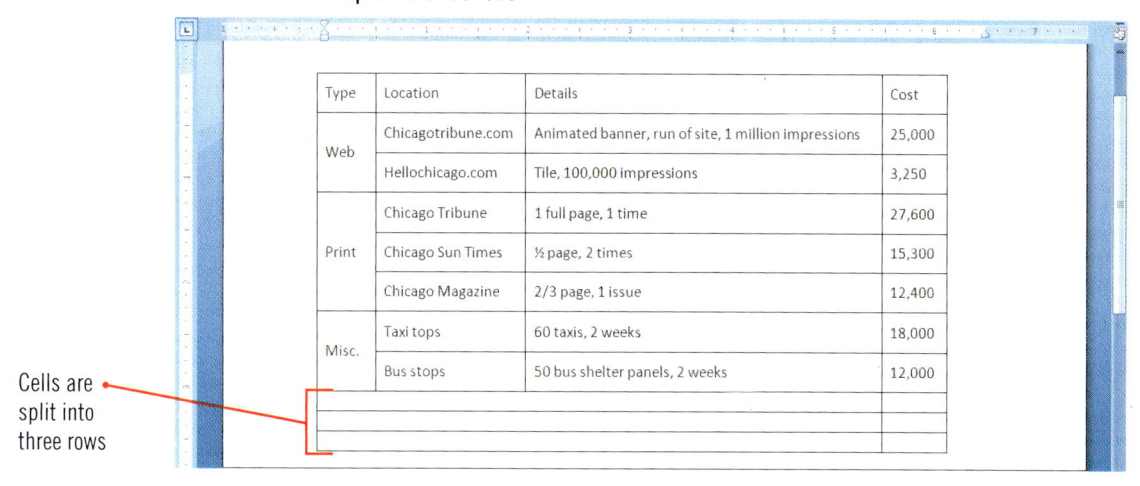

Cells are split into three rows

Changing cell margins

By default, table cells have .08" left and right cell margins with no spacing between the cells, but you can adjust these settings for a table using the Cell Margins button in the Alignment group on the Table Tools Layout tab. First, place the insertion point in the table, and then click the Cell Margins button to open the Table Options dialog box. Enter new settings for the top, bottom, left, and right cell margins in the text boxes in the Default cell margins section of the dialog box, or select the Allow spacing between cells check box and then enter a setting in the Cell spacing section to increase the spacing between table cells. You can also deselect the Automatically resize to fit contents check box in the Options section of the dialog box to turn off the setting that causes table cells to widen to fit the text as you type. Any settings you change in the Table Options dialog box are applied to the entire table.

Creating and Formatting Tables

Performing Calculations in Tables

UNIT E — Word 2007

If your table includes numerical information, you can perform simple calculations in the table. The Formula command allows you to quickly total the numbers in a column or row, and to perform other standard calculations, such as averages. When you calculate data in a table using formulas, you use cell references to refer to the cells in the table. Each cell has a unique **cell reference** composed of a letter and a number; the letter represents its column and the number represents its row. For example, the cell in the third row of the fourth column is cell D3. Figure E-14 shows the cell references in a simple table. You use the Formula command to calculate the total cost of the Chicago ad campaign. You also add information about the budgeted cost and create a formula to calculate the difference between the actual and budgeted costs.

STEPS

> **QUICK TIP**
> If a column or row contains blank cells, you must type a zero in any blank cell before using the SUM function.

1. **Click the first blank cell in column 1, type Total Cost, press [Tab], then click the Formula button in the Data group on the Table Tools Layout tab**
   The Formula dialog box opens, as shown in Figure E-15. The SUM function appears in the Formula text box followed by the reference for the cells to include in the calculation, (ABOVE). The formula =SUM(ABOVE) indicates that Word will sum the numbers in the cells above the active cell.

2. **Click OK**
   Word totals the numbers in the cells above the active cell and inserts the sum as a field. You can use the SUM function to quickly total the numbers in a column or a row. If the cell you select is at the bottom of a column of numbers, Word totals the column. If the cell is at the right end of a row of numbers, Word totals the row.

3. **Select 12,000 in the cell above the total, then type 13,500**
   If you change a number that is part of a calculation, you must recalculate the field result.

> **QUICK TIP**
> To change a field result to regular text, click the field to select it, then press [Ctrl][Shift][F9].

4. **Press [↓], then press [F9]**
   When the insertion point is in a cell that contains a formula, pressing [F9] updates the field result.

5. **Press [Tab], type Budgeted, press [Tab], type 113,780, press [Tab], type Difference, then press [Tab]**
   The insertion point is in the last cell of the table.

6. **Click the Formula button**
   The Formula dialog box opens. Word proposes to sum the numbers above the active cell, but you want to insert a formula that calculates the difference between the actual and budgeted costs. You can type simple custom formulas using a plus sign (+) for addition, a minus sign (–) for subtraction, an asterisk (*) for multiplication, and a slash (/) for division.

> **QUICK TIP**
> Cell references are determined by the number of columns in each row, not by the number of columns in the table. Therefore, rows 9 and 10 have only two columns.

7. **Select =SUM(ABOVE) in the Formula text box, then type =B9-B10**
   You must type an equal sign (=) to indicate that the text following it is a formula. You want to subtract the budgeted cost in the second column of row 10 from the actual cost in the second column of row 9; therefore, you type a formula to subtract the value in cell B10 from the value in cell B9.

8. **Click OK, then save your changes**
   The difference appears in the cell, as shown in Figure E-16.

Creating and Formatting Tables

FIGURE E-14: Cell references in a table

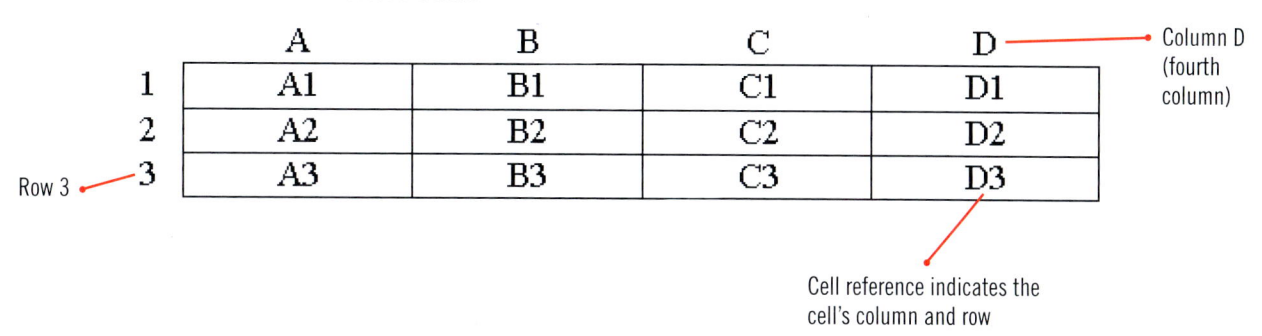

	A	B	C	D
1	A1	B1	C1	D1
2	A2	B2	C2	D2
3	A3	B3	C3	D3

Row 3
Column D (fourth column)
Cell reference indicates the cell's column and row

FIGURE E-15: Formula dialog box

Suggested formula — =SUM(ABOVE)
Suggested range of cells

Formula dialog box fields: Formula, Number format, Paste function, Paste bookmark, OK, Cancel

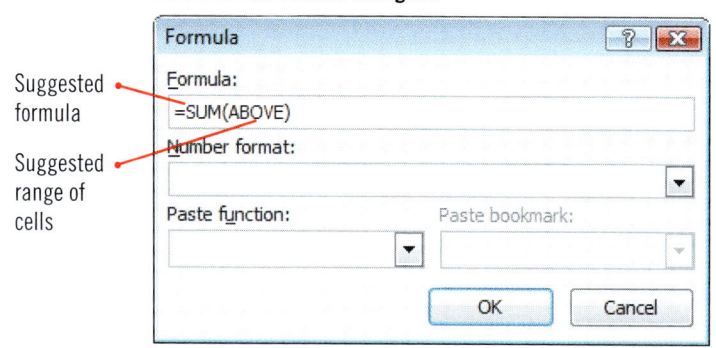

FIGURE E-16: Difference calculated in table

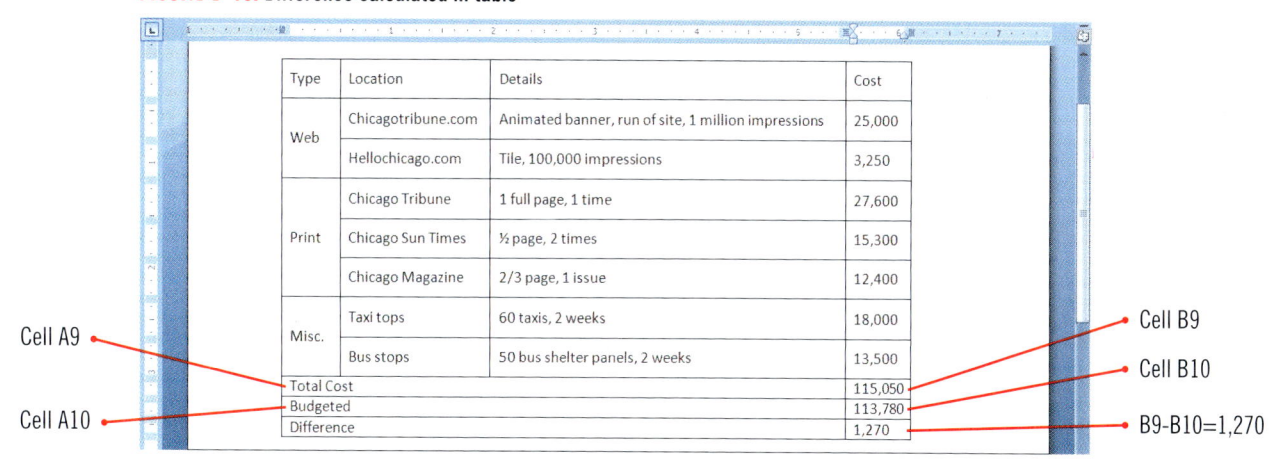

Type	Location	Details	Cost
Web	Chicagotribune.com	Animated banner, run of site, 1 million impressions	25,000
	Hellochicago.com	Tile, 100,000 impressions	3,250
Print	Chicago Tribune	1 full page, 1 time	27,600
	Chicago Sun Times	½ page, 2 times	15,300
	Chicago Magazine	2/3 page, 1 issue	12,400
Misc.	Taxi tops	60 taxis, 2 weeks	18,000
	Bus stops	50 bus shelter panels, 2 weeks	13,500
Total Cost			115,050
Budgeted			113,780
Difference			1,270

Cell A9 — Total Cost row
Cell A10 — Budgeted row
Cell B9 — 115,050
Cell B10 — 113,780
B9−B10=1,270

Working with formulas

In addition to the SUM function, Word includes formulas for averaging, counting, and rounding data, to name a few. To use a Word formula, click the Paste function list arrow in the Formula dialog box, select a function, and then insert the cell references of the cells you want included in the calculation in parentheses after the name of the function. When entering formulas, you must separate cell references by a comma. For example, if you want to average the values in cells A1, B3, and C4, enter the formula =AVERAGE(A1,B3,C4). You must separate cell ranges by a colon. For example, to total the values in cells A1 through A9, enter the formula =SUM(A1:A9). To display the result of a calculation in a particular number format, such as a decimal percentage (0.00%), click the Number format list arrow in the Formula dialog box and select a number format. Word inserts the result of a calculation as a field in the selected cell.

Creating and Formatting Tables

UNIT E
Word 2007

Applying a Table Style

Adding shading and other design elements to a table can help give it a polished appearance and make the data easier to read. Word includes built-in table styles that you can apply to a table to format it quickly. Table styles include borders, shading, fonts, alignment, colors, and other formatting effects. You can apply a table style to a table using the buttons in the Table Styles group on the Table Tools Design tab. You want to enhance the appearance of the table with shading, borders, and other formats, so you apply a table style to the table. After applying a style, you change the theme colors to a more pleasing palette.

STEPS

1. **Click the Table Tools Design tab**
   The Table Tools Design tab includes buttons for applying table styles and for adding, removing, and customizing borders and shading in a table.

   TROUBLE
   If your gallery of table styles does not match the figure, use the ScreenTips to help you locate the correct style.

2. **Click the More button in the Table Styles group**
   The gallery of table styles opens, as shown in Figure E-17. You point to a table style in the gallery to preview the style applied to the table.

3. **Move the pointer over several styles in the gallery, then click the Light Grid – Accent 2 style**
   The Light Grid – Accent 2 style is applied to the table, as shown in Figure E-18. Because of the structure of the table, this style neither enhances the table nor helps make the data more readable.

   QUICK TIP
   Click Clear in the gallery of table styles to remove all borders, shading, and other style elements from the table.

4. **Click the More button in the Table Style group, then click the Light List – Accent 2 style**
   This style works better with the structure of the table, and makes the table data easier to read.

5. **In the Table Style Options group, click the First Column check box to clear it, then click the Banded Columns check box to select it**
   The bold formatting is removed from the first column and column borders are added to the table. When the banded columns or banded rows setting is active, the odd columns or rows are formatted differently from the even columns or rows to make the table data easier to read.

6. **Click the Page Layout tab, click the Theme Colors list arrow in the Themes group, then click Origin in the gallery that opens**
   The color palette for the document changes to the colors used in the Origin theme, and the table color changes to Ice Blue.

   TROUBLE
   When you select the Type column, the first column in the last three rows is also selected.

7. **Click the Table Tools Design tab, click the More button in the Table Styles group, then click the Light List – Accent 1 style**
   The table color changes to Blue-Gray. Notice that the alignment of the text in the table changed back to top left when you applied a table style.

8. **Click the Table Tools Layout tab, click the table move handle to select the table, click the Align Center Left button in the Alignment group, select the Type column, click the Align Center button in the Alignment group, select the Cost column, then click the Align Center Right button in the Alignment group**
   First, the data in the table is left-aligned and centered vertically, then the data in the Type column is centered, and finally the data in the Cost column is right-aligned.

9. **Select the last three rows of the table, click the Bold button B on the Mini toolbar, then click**
   The text in the last three rows is right-aligned and bold is applied.

10. **Select the first row of the table, click the Center button on the Mini toolbar, click the Font Size list arrow on the Mini toolbar, click 14, deselect the row, then save your changes**
    The text in the header row is centered and enlarged, as shown in Figure E-19. You can also use the alignment buttons in the Paragraph group on the Home tab to change the alignment of text in a table.

Word 118   Creating and Formatting Tables

FIGURE E-17: Gallery of table styles

- Options for customizing table style settings
- Modify an existing table style
- Remove a table style from a table
- Create a new table style
- Gallery of table styles (your display may differ)
- Light List – Accent 2 style
- Light Grid – Accent 2 style

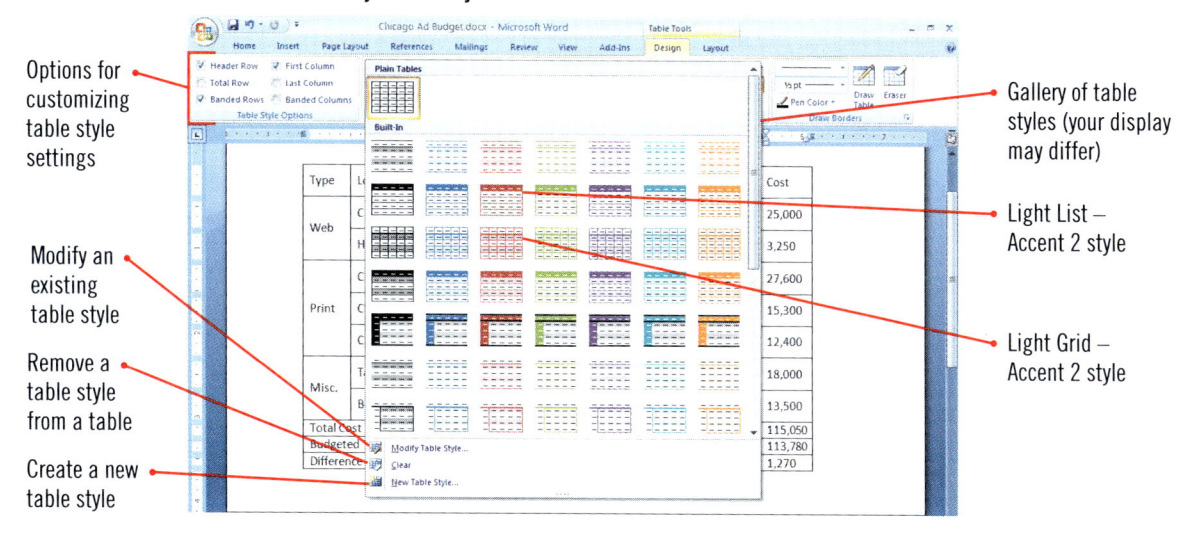

FIGURE E-18: Light Grid – Accent 2 style applied to table

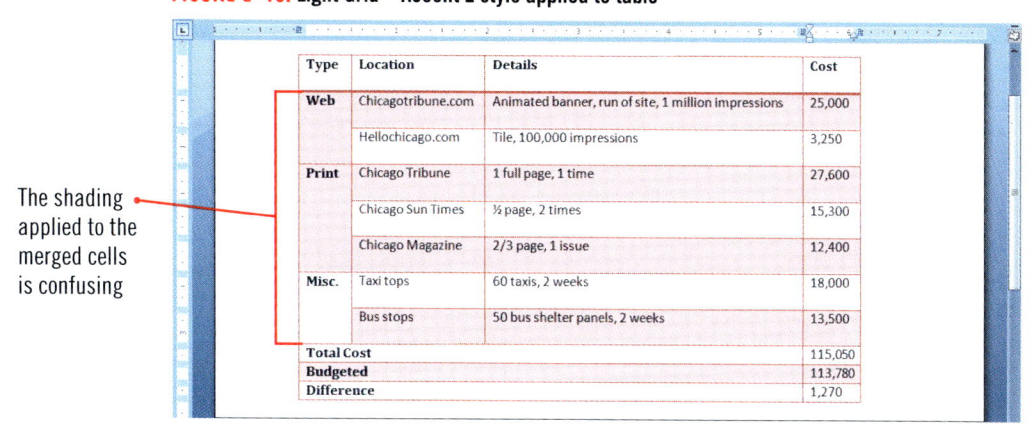

- The shading applied to the merged cells is confusing

FIGURE E-19: Light List – Accent 1 style (Origin theme) applied to table

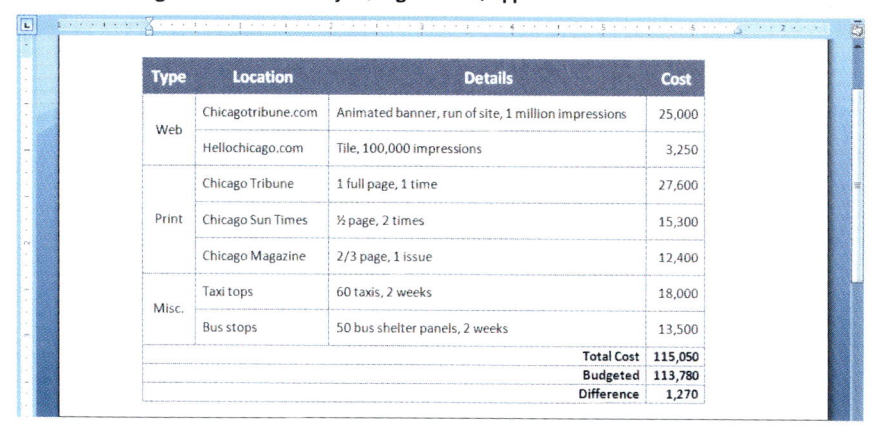

Using tables to lay out a page

Tables are often used to display information for quick reference and analysis, but you can also use tables to structure the layout of a page. You can insert any kind of information in the cell of a table—including graphics, bulleted lists, charts, and other tables (called **nested tables**). For example, you might use a table to lay out a résumé, a newsletter, or a Web page. When you use a table to lay out a page, you generally remove the table borders to hide the table structure from the reader. After you remove borders, it can be helpful to display the table gridlines onscreen while you work. **Gridlines** are blue dotted lines that show the boundaries of cells, but do not print. If your document will be viewed online—for example, if you are planning to e-mail your résumé to potential employers—you should turn off the display of gridlines before you distribute the document so that it looks the same online as it looks when printed. To turn gridlines off or on, click the View Gridlines button in the Table group on the Table Tools Layout tab.

Creating and Formatting Tables

Creating a Custom Format for a Table

You can also use the formatting tools available in Word to create your own table designs. For example, you can add or remove borders and shading, vary the line style, thickness, and color of borders, and change the orientation of text from horizontal to vertical. You adjust the text direction, shading, and borders in the table to make it easier to understand at a glance.

STEPS

1. **Select the Type and Location cells in the first row, click the Merge Cells button in the Merge group on the Table Tools Layout tab, then type Ad Location**
   The two cells are combined into a single cell containing the text "Ad Location."

2. **Select the Web, Print, and Misc. cells in the first column, click the Bold button B on the Mini toolbar, click the Text Direction button in the Alignment group twice, then deselect the cells**
   The text is rotated 270 degrees.

3. **Position the pointer over the right border of the Web cell until the pointer changes to ↔, then drag the border to approximately the ¼" mark on the horizontal ruler**
   The width of the column containing the vertical text narrows.

   > **QUICK TIP**
   > In cells with vertical text, the I-beam pointer is rotated 90 degrees, and the buttons in the Alignment group change to vertical alignment.

4. **Place the insertion point in the Web cell, click the Table Tools Design tab, then click the Shading list arrow in the Table Styles group**
   The gallery of shading colors for the Origin theme opens.

5. **Click Light Yellow, Accent 4 in the gallery as shown in Figure E-20, click the Print cell, click the Shading list arrow, click Lime, Accent 3, click the Misc. cell, click the Shading list arrow, then click Ice Blue, Accent 2**
   Shading is applied to each cell.

6. **Drag to select the six white cells in the Web rows (rows 2 and 3), click the Shading list arrow, then click Light Yellow, Accent 4, Lighter 40%**

7. **Repeat Step 6 to apply Lime, Accent 3, Lighter 40% shading to the Print rows and Ice Blue, Accent 2, Lighter 40% shading to the Misc. rows**
   Shading is applied to all the cells in rows 1-8.

   > **TROUBLE**
   > If gridlines appear, click the Borders list arrow, then click View Gridlines to turn off the display.

8. **Select the last three rows of the table, click the Borders list arrow in the Table Styles group, click No Border on the menu that appears, then click in the table to deselect the rows**
   The top, bottom, left, and right borders are removed from each cell in the selected rows.

   > **QUICK TIP**
   > On the Borders menu, click the button that corresponds to the border you want to add or remove.

9. **Click the Pen Color list arrow in the Draw Borders group, click Blue-Gray, Accent 1, select the Total Cost row, click the Borders list arrow, click Top Border, click the 113,780 cell, click the Borders list arrow, then click the Bottom Border**
   The active pen color for borders changes to Blue-Gray, Accent 1. You use the buttons in the Draw Borders group to change the active pen color, line weight, and line style settings before adding a border to a table. A top border is added to each cell in the Total Cost row, and a bottom border is added below 113,780. The completed table is shown in Figure E-21.

10. **Press [Ctrl][Home], press [Enter], type your name, save your changes, print a copy of the document, close the document, then exit Word**
    Press [Enter] at the beginning of a table to move the table down one line in a document.

FIGURE E-20: Gallery of shading colors from the Origin theme

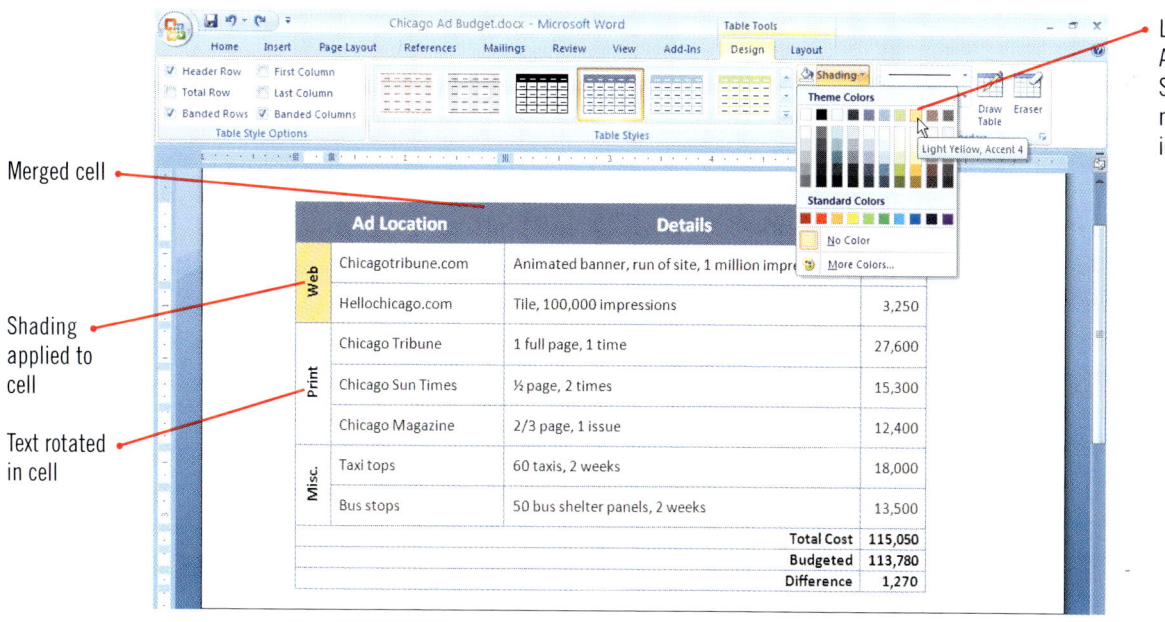

- Merged cell
- Shading applied to cell
- Text rotated in cell
- Light Yellow, Accent 4: use ScreenTips as needed to identify colors

FIGURE E-21: Completed table

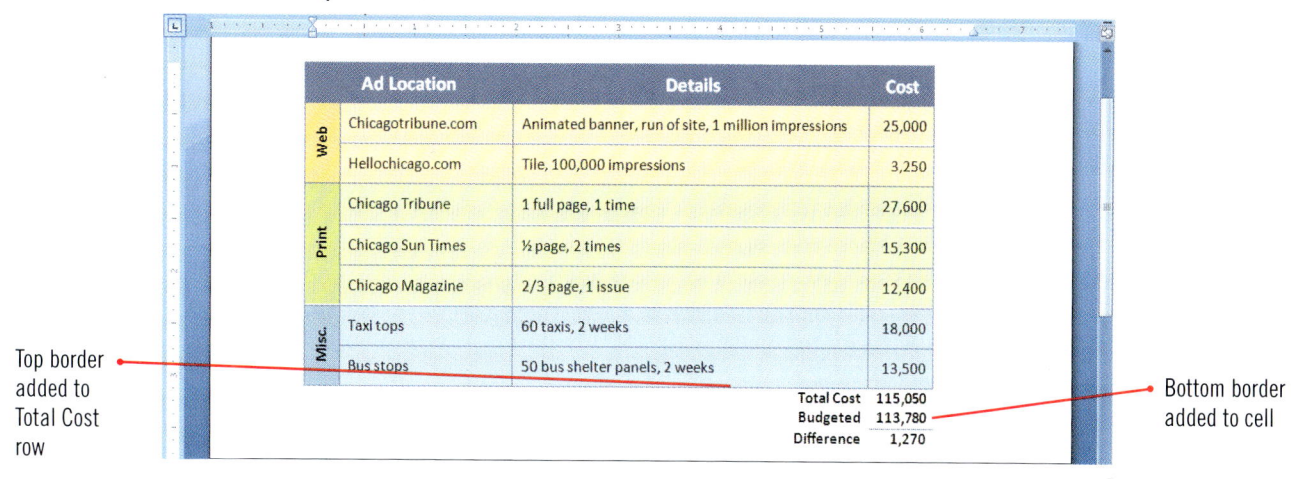

- Top border added to Total Cost row
- Bottom border added to cell

Drawing a table

The Word Draw Table feature allows you to draw table cells exactly where you want them. To draw a table, click the Table button on the Insert tab, and then click Draw Table. If a table is already started, you can click the Draw Table button in the Draw Borders group on the Table Tools Design tab to turn on the Draw pointer, and then click and drag to draw a cell. Using the same method, you can draw borders within the cell to create columns and rows, or draw additional cells attached to the first cell. Click the Draw Table button to turn off the draw feature. The borders you draw are added using the active line style, line weight, and pen color settings.

If you want to remove a border from a table, click the Eraser button in the Draw Borders group to activate the Eraser pointer, and then click the border you want to remove. Click the Eraser button to turn off the erase feature. You can use the Draw pointer and the Eraser pointer to change the structure of any table, not just the tables you draw from scratch.

Creating and Formatting Tables

Practice

▼ CONCEPTS REVIEW

Label each element shown in Figure E-22.

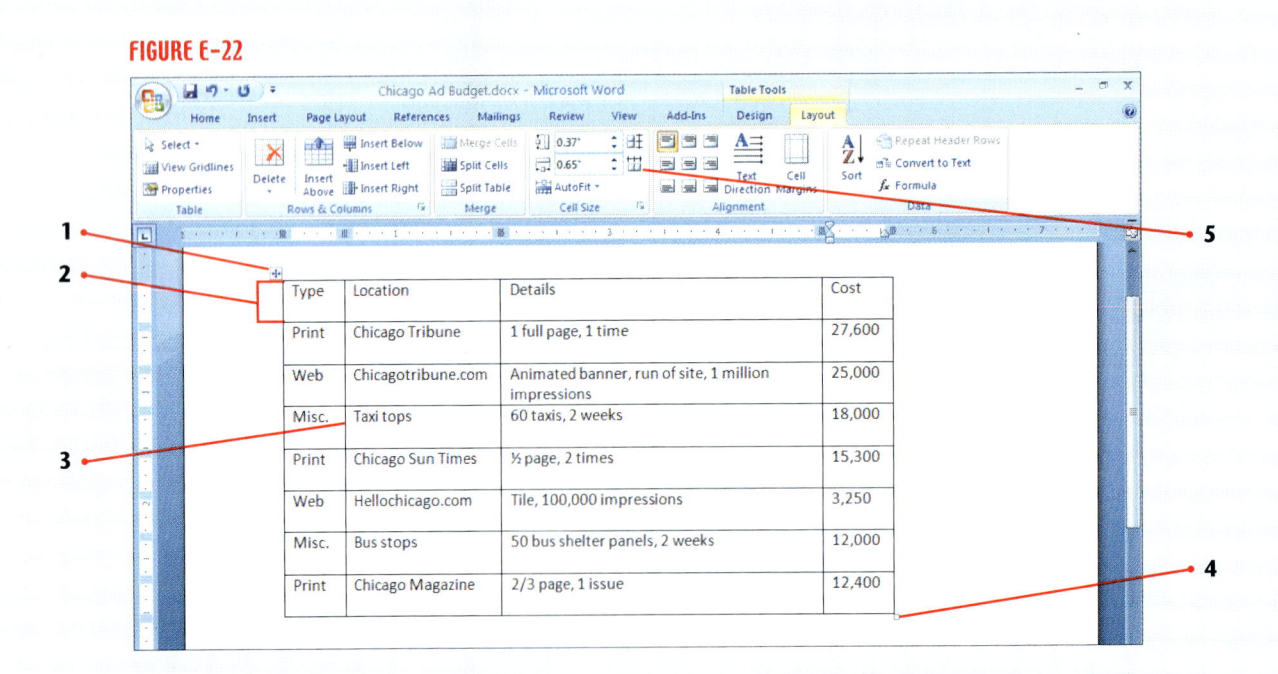

FIGURE E-22

Match each term with the statement that best describes it.

6. Header row
7. Gridlines
8. Split
9. Ascending order
10. Borders
11. Cell
12. Nested table
13. Descending order
14. Merge
15. Cell reference

a. To combine two or more adjacent cells into one larger cell
b. The first row of a table that contains the column headings
c. Lines that separate columns and rows in a table and that print
d. An object inserted in a table cell
e. To divide an existing cell into multiple cells
f. The box formed by the intersection of a column and a row
g. Lines that show columns and rows in a table, but do not print
h. Sort order that organizes text from A to Z
i. Sort order that organizes text from Z to A
j. A cell address composed of a column letter and a row number

Select the best answer from the list of choices.

16. Which of the following is the cell reference for the third cell in the second column?
   a. C2
   b. 2C
   c. 3B
   d. B3

17. Which button do you use to change the alignment of text in a cell?
   a. [A↓Z icon]
   b. [table icon]
   c. [alignment icon]
   d. [A icon]

▼ CONCEPTS REVIEW (CONTINUED)

18. Which of the following is *not* a correct formula for adding the values in cells A1, A2, and A3?
    a. =SUM(A1~A3)
    b. =A1+A2+A3
    c. =SUM(A1:A3)
    d. =SUM(A1,A2,A3)

19. Which of the following is *not* a valid way to add a new row to the bottom of a table?
    a. Right-click the bottom row, point to Insert, then click Insert Rows Below.
    b. Click in the bottom row, then click the Insert Below button in the Rows & Columns group on the Table Tools Layout tab.
    c. Click in the bottom row, open the Properties dialog box, then insert a row using the options on the Row tab.
    d. Place the insertion point in the last cell of the last row, then press [Tab].

20. What happens when you double-click a column border?
    a. The columns in the table are distributed evenly.
    b. The column width is adjusted to fit the text.
    c. A new column is added to the right.
    d. A new column is added to the left.

▼ SKILLS REVIEW

1. **Insert a table.**
   a. Start Word, then save the new blank document as **Mutual Funds** to the drive and folder where you store your Data Files.
   b. Type your name, press [Enter] twice, type **Mutual Funds Performance**, then press [Enter].
   c. Insert a table that contains four columns and four rows.
   d. Type the text shown in Figure E-23, pressing [Tab] to add rows as necessary. (*Note*: Do not format text or the table at this time.)
   e. Save your changes.

2. **Insert and delete rows and columns.**
   a. Insert a row above the Health Care row, then type the following text in the new row:
      Canada   8.24   8.12   8.56
   b. Delete the Europe row.
   c. Insert a column to the right of the 10 Year column, type **Date Purchased** in the header row, then enter a date in each cell in the column using the format MM/DD/YY (for example, 11/27/02).
   d. Move the Date Purchased column to the right of the Fund Name column, then save your changes.

3. **Modify rows and columns.**
   a. Double-click the border between the first and second columns to resize the columns.
   b. Drag the border between the second and third columns to the 2¼" mark on the horizontal ruler.
   c. Double-click the right border of the 1 Year, 5 Year, and 10 Year columns.
   d. Select the 1 Year, 5 Year, and 10 Year columns, then distribute the columns evenly.
   e. Select the table, apply the No Spacing style, select rows 2-7, set the row height to exactly .3", then save your changes.

4. **Sort table data.**
   a. Sort the table data, excluding the header row, in descending order by the information in the 1 Year column.
   b. Sort the table data, excluding the header row, in ascending order by date purchased.
   c. Sort the table data, excluding the header row, by fund name in alphabetical order, then save your changes.

5. **Split and merge cells.**
   a. Insert a row above the header row, then merge the first cell in the new row with the Fund Name cell.
   b. Merge the second cell in the new row with the Date Purchased cell.
   c. Merge the three remaining blank cells in the first row into a single cell, then type **Average Annual Returns** in the merged cell.
   d. Add a new row to the bottom of the table.
   e. Merge the first two cells in the new row, then type **Average Return** in the merged cell.

FIGURE E-23

Fund Name	1 Year	5 Year	10 Year
Computers	16.47	25.56	27.09
Europe	-6.15	13.89	10.61
Natural Resources	19.47	12.30	15.38
Health Care	32.45	24.26	23.25
Financial Services	22.18	21.07	24.44
500 Index	9.13	15.34	13.69

▼ SKILLS REVIEW (CONTINUED)

  f. Select the first seven cells in the first column (from Fund Name to Natural Resources), open the Split Cells dialog box, clear the Merge cells before split check box, then split the cells into two columns.
  g. Type **Trading Symbol** as the heading for the new column, then enter the following text in the remaining cells in the column: **FINX, CAND, COMP, FINS, HCRX, NARS**.
  h. Double-click the right border of the first column to resize the column, then save your changes.

6. **Perform calculations in tables.**
  a. Place the insertion point in the last cell in the 1 Year column.
  b. Open the Formula dialog box, delete the text in the Formula text box, type **=average(above)**, click the Number Format list arrow, scroll down, click 0.00%, then click OK.
  c. Repeat Step b to insert the average return in the last cell in the 5 Year and 10 Year columns.
  d. Change the value of the 1-year return for the Natural Resources fund to **10.35**.
  e. Use [F9] to recalculate the average return for 1 year, then save your changes.

7. **Apply a table style.**
  a. Click the Table Tools Design tab, preview table styles applied to the table, and then apply an appropriate style. Was the style you chose effective?
  b. Apply the Light Shading style to the table, then remove the style from First Column and Banded Rows.
  c. Apply bold to the 1 Year, 5 Year, and 10 Year column headings, and to the bottom row of the table.
  d. Center the table between the margins, center the table title **Mutual Funds Performance**, increase the font size of the title to 14-points, apply bold, then save your changes.

8. **Create a custom format for a table.**
  a. Select the entire table, then use the Align Center button in the Alignment group on the Table Tools Layout tab to center the text in every cell vertically and horizontally.
  b. Center right-align the dates in column 3 and the numbers in columns 4-6.
  c. Center left-align the fund names and trading symbols in columns 1 and 2, but not the column headings.
  d. Center right-align the text in the bottom row. Make sure the text in the header row is still centered.
  e. Change the theme colors to Apex.
  f. Select all the cells in the header row, including the 1 Year, 5 Year, and 10 Year column headings, change the shading color to Lavender, Accent 5, then change the font color to white.
  g. Apply Lavender, Accent 5, Lighter 60% shading to the cells containing the fund names and trading symbols, and Lavender Accent 5, Lighter 80% shading to the cells containing the purchase dates.
  h. To the cells containing the 1 Year, 5 Year, and 10 Year data, respectively, apply Tan, Accent 1, Lighter 60% shading, Lavender, Accent 6, Lighter 60% shading, and Olive Green, Accent 2, Lighter 60% shading.
  i. Apply Lavender Accent 5, Lighter 80% shading to the last row of the table.
  j. Add a ½-point white bottom border to the Average Annual Returns cell.
  k. Add a 1½-point black border around the outside of the table.
  l. Add a ½-point black top border to the 500 Index row and to the last row of the table. (*Hint*: Do not remove any borders.)
  m. Compare your table to Figure E-24, make any necessary adjustments, save your changes, print a copy, close the file, then exit Word.

FIGURE E-24

Mutual Funds Performance

Fund Name	Trading Symbol	Date Purchased	Average Annual Returns		
			1 Year	5 Year	10 Year
500 Index	FINX	5/9/96	9.13	15.34	13.69
Canada	CAND	11/13/03	8.24	8.12	8.56
Computers	COMP	9/23/01	16.47	25.56	27.09
Financial Services	FINS	2/12/01	22.18	21.07	24.44
Health Care	HCRX	3/24/96	32.45	24.26	23.25
Natural Resources	NARS	6/2/98	10.35	12.30	15.38
		Average Return	**16.47%**	**17.78%**	**18.74%**

▼ INDEPENDENT CHALLENGE 1

You are the director of sales for a publishing company with branch offices in six cities around the globe. In preparation for the upcoming sales meeting, you create a table showing your sales projections for the fiscal year 2010.

a. Start Word, then save the new blank document as **2010 Sales** to the drive and folder where you store your Data Files.
b. Type the table heading **Projected Sales in Millions, Fiscal Year 2010** at the top of the document, then press [Enter] twice.
c. Insert a table with five columns and four rows, then enter the data shown in Figure E-25 into the table, adding rows as necessary. (*Note*: Do not format text or the table at this time.)
d. Resize the columns to fit the text.
e. Sort the table rows in alphabetical order by Office.
f. Add a new row to the bottom of the table, type **Total** in the first cell, then enter a formula in each remaining cell in the new row to calculate the sum of the cells above it.
g. Add a new column at the right end of the table, type **Total** in the first cell, then enter a formula in each remaining cell in the new column to calculate the sum of the cells to the left of it. (*Hint*: Make sure the formula you insert in each cell sums the cells to the left, not the cells above. In the last cell in the last column, you can sum the cells to the left or the cells above; either way the total should be the same.)
h. Apply a table style to the table. Select a style that enhances the information contained in the table, and adjust the Table Style Options to suit the content.
i. Center the text in the header row, left-align the remaining text in the first column, then right-align the numerical data in the table.
j. Enhance the table with fonts, font colors, shading, and borders to make the table attractive and easy to read at a glance.
k. Increase the font size of the table heading to 18 points, then center the table heading and the table on the page.
l. Press [Ctrl][End], press [Enter], type your name, save your changes, print the table, close the file, then exit Word.

FIGURE E-25

Office	Q1	Q2	Q3	Q4
Paris	9500	5800	3900	9800
Tokyo	6700	8900	4500	4900
Berlin	8800	8500	6800	7400
Shanghai	5800	7200	4700	8200
New York	8500	7800	9800	9400
Melbourne	7900	6800	3800	6200

▼ INDEPENDENT CHALLENGE 2

You have been invited to speak to your local board of realtors about the economic benefits of living in your city. To illustrate some of your points, you want to distribute a handout comparing the cost of living and other economic indicators in the U.S. cities that offer features similar to your city. You decide to format the data as a table.

a. Start Word, open the file WD E-1.docx, then save it as **City Data** to the drive and folder where you store your Data Files.
b. Center the table heading, then increase the font size to 18 points.
c. Turn on formatting marks, select the tabbed text in the document, then convert the text to a table.
d. Add a row above the first row in the table, then enter the following column headings in the new header row: **City**, **Cost of Living**, **Median Income**, **Average House Cost**, **Bachelor Degree Rate**.
e. Apply an appropriate Table style to the table. Add or remove the style from various elements of the table using the options in the Table Style Options group, as necessary.
f. Adjust the column widths so that the table is attractive and readable. (*Hint*: Allow the column headings to wrap to two lines.)
g. Make the height of each row at least .25".
h. Center Left align the text in each cell in the first column, including the column head.
i. Center Right align the text in each cell in the remaining columns, including the column heads.
j. Center the entire table on the page.
k. Sort the table by cost of living in descending order.

Creating and Formatting Tables

▼ INDEPENDENT CHALLENGE 2 (CONTINUED)

Advanced Challenge Exercise

- Add a new row to the bottom of the table, then type **Average** in the first cell in the new row.
- In each subsequent cell in the Average row, insert a formula that calculates the averages of the cells above it. (*Hint*: For each cell, replace SUM with AVERAGE in the Formula text box, but do not make other changes.)
- Format the Average row with borders, shading, fonts, and other formats, as necessary to enhance the data.

l. On the blank line below the table, type **Note: The average cost of living in the United States is 100.**, italicize the text, then use a tab stop and indents to align the text with the left side of the table if it is not aligned.

m. Enhance the table with borders, shading, fonts, and other formats, if necessary, to make it attractive and readable.

n. Type your name at the bottom of the document, save your changes, print a copy of the table, close the document, then exit Word.

▼ INDEPENDENT CHALLENGE 3

You work in the advertising department at a magazine. Your boss has asked you to create a fact sheet on the ad dimensions for the magazine. The fact sheet should include the dimensions for each type of ad. As a bonus, you could also add a visual representation of the different ad shapes and sizes, shown in Figure E-26. You'll use tables to lay out the fact sheet, present the dimension information, and, if you are performing the ACE steps, illustrate the ad shapes and sizes.

FIGURE E-26

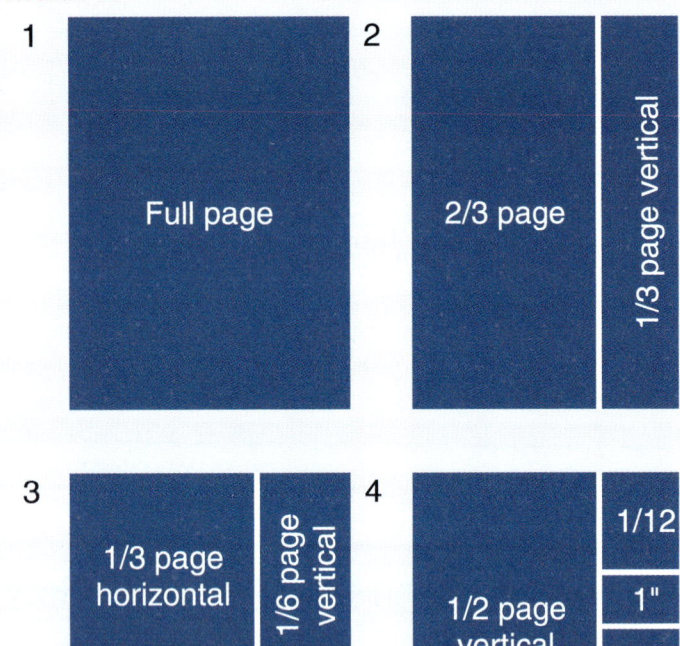

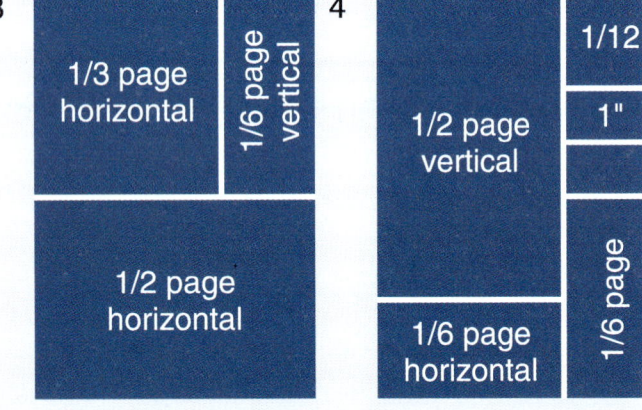

a. Start Word, open the file WD E-2.doc from the drive and folder where you store your Data Files, then save it as **Ad Fact Sheet**. Turn on the display of gridlines, then read the document to get a feel for its contents.

b. Drag the border between the first and second column to approximately the 2¾" mark on the horizontal ruler, resize the second and third columns to fit the text, then make each row in the table .5".

c. Change the alignment of the text in the first column to center left, then change the alignment of the text in the second and third columns to center right.

d. Remove all the borders from the table, then apply a 2¼-point, dark blue, dotted line, inside horizontal border to the entire table. This creates a dark blue dotted line between each row. (*Hint*: Use the Dark Blue, Text 2 color.)

e. In the second blank paragraph under the table heading, insert a new table with three columns and four rows, then merge the cells in the third column of the new blank table.

f. Drag the border between the first and second columns of the new blank table to the 1¼" mark on the horizontal ruler. Drag the border between the second and third columns to the 1½" mark.

g. Select the table that contains text, cut it to the Clipboard, then paste it in the merged cell in the blank table. The table with text is now a nested table in the main table.

h. Split the nested table above the Unit Size (Bleed) row. (*Hint*: Place the insertion point in the Unit Size (Bleed) row, then use the Split Table button.)

▼ INDEPENDENT CHALLENGE 3 (CONTINUED)

i. Scroll up, merge the four cells in the first column of the main table, then merge the four cells in the second column.
j. Split the first column into one column and seven rows.
k. Using the Table Row Height text box in the Cell Size group, change the row height of each cell in the first column so that the rows alternate between exactly 1.8" and .25" in height. Make the height of the first, third, fifth, and seventh rows 1.8". (*Hint*: You can also use the Table Properties dialog box.)
l. Add Dark Blue, Text 2 shading to the first, third, fifth, and seventh cells in the first column, remove all the borders from the main table, then turn off the display of gridlines. The dark blue dotted line borders in the nested table remain.

Advanced Challenge Exercise

- In the first dark blue cell, type **Full Page**, change the font color to white, then center the text vertically in the cell.
- In the Draw Borders group on the Table Tools Design tab, change the Line Style to a single line, change the Line Weight to 2¼ pt, then change the Pen Color to white.
- Be sure the Draw Table pointer is active, then, referring to Figure E-26, draw a vertical border that divides the second dark blue cell into ⅔ and ⅓.
- Label the cells and align the text as shown in the figure. (*Hint*: Change the text direction and alignment before typing text. Take care not to change the size of the cells when you type. If necessary, press [Enter] to start a new line of text in a cell, or reduce the font size of the text.)
- Referring to Figure E-26, divide the third and fourth dark blue cells, then label the cells as shown in the figure.

m. Examine the document for errors, then make any necessary adjustments.
n. Press [Ctrl][End], type your name, save your changes to the document, preview it, print a copy, close the file, then exit Word.

▼ REAL LIFE INDEPENDENT CHALLENGE

This Independent Challenge requires an Internet connection.

A well-written and well-formatted résumé gives you an advantage when it comes to getting a job interview. In a winning résumé, the content and format support your career objective and effectively present your background and qualifications. One simple way to create a résumé is to lay out the page using a table. In this exercise you research guidelines for writing and formatting résumés. You then create your own résumé using a table for its layout.

a. Use your favorite search engine to search the Web for information on writing and formatting résumés. Use the keywords **resume advice**.
b. Print helpful advice on writing and formatting résumés from at least two Web sites.
c. Think about the information you want to include in your résumé. The header should include your name, address, telephone number, and e-mail address. The body should include your career objective and information on your education, work experience, and skills. You may want to add additional information.
d. Sketch a layout for your résumé using a table as the underlying grid. Include the table rows and columns in your sketch.
e. Start Word, open a new blank document, then save it as **My Resumes** to the drive and folder where you store your Data Files.
f. Set appropriate margins, then insert a table to serve as the underlying grid for your résumé. Split and merge cells and adjust the size of the table columns as necessary.
g. Type your résumé in the table cells. Take care to use a professional tone and keep your language to the point.
h. Format your résumé with fonts, bullets, and other formatting features. Adjust the spacing between sections by resizing the table columns and rows.
i. When you are satisfied with the content and format of your résumé, remove the borders from the table, then hide the gridlines if they are visible.
j. Check your résumé for spelling and grammar errors.
k. Save your changes, preview your résumé, print a copy, close the file, then exit Word.

▼ VISUAL WORKSHOP

Create the calendar shown in Figure E-27 using a table to lay out the entire page. (*Hints*: The top and bottom margins are .9", the left and right margins are 1", and the font is Century Gothic. The clip art image is inserted in the table. The clip art image is found using the keyword **coast**. Use a different clip art image or font if the ones shown in the figure are not available.) Type your name in the last table cell, save the calendar with the filename **June 2010** to the drive and folder where you store your Data Files, then print a copy.

FIGURE E-27

June 2010

Sunday	Monday	Tuesday	Wednesday	Thursday	Friday	Saturday
		1	2	3	4	5
6	7	8	9	10	11	12
13	14	15	16	17	18	19
20	21	22	23	24	25	26
27	28	29	30			

UNIT F
Word 2007

Illustrating Documents with Graphics

Files You Will Need:
WD F-1.docx
WD F-2.docx
WD F-3.docx
Fishing Boats.jpg
Stone Barn.jpg

Graphics can help illustrate the ideas in your documents, provide visual interest on a page, and give your documents punch and flair. In addition to clip art, you can add photos or graphics created in other programs to a document, or you can use the graphic features of Word to create your own images. In this unit, you learn how to insert, modify, and position graphics and text boxes, how to draw your own images, and how to illustrate a document with WordArt and charts. You are preparing a flyer advertising QST tours to Mexico. You use the graphic features of Word to illustrate the flyer so that it promotes Mexico as a colorful, warm, lively, and inviting travel destination.

OBJECTIVES

Insert a graphic
Size and scale a graphic
Position a graphic
Create a text box
Create WordArt
Draw shapes
Create a chart
Finalize page layout

Inserting a Graphic

UNIT F
Word 2007

Graphic images you can insert in a document include the clip art images that come with Word, photos taken with a digital camera, scanned art, and graphics created in other graphics programs. To insert a graphic file into a document, you use the Picture command in the Illustrations group on the Insert tab. Once you insert a graphic, you can apply a Picture style to it to enhance its appearance. You have written the text for the Mexico flyer, and now want to illustrate it with digital photographs. You insert a photo file in the document, apply a shadow to the photo, and then wrap text around it to make it a floating graphic.

STEPS

1. **Start Word, open the file WD F-1.docx from the drive and folder where you store your Data Files, save it as Mexico Flyer, click the Show/Hide ¶ button ¶ in the Paragraph group to display formatting marks if necessary, read the flyer to get a feel for its format and contents, then press [Ctrl][Home]**

   The flyer is divided into five sections and includes a hard page break and several inline graphics. The second and fourth sections are formatted in three columns.

2. **Click the Insert tab, then click the Picture button in the Illustrations group**

   The Insert Picture dialog box opens. You use this dialog box to locate and insert graphic files. Most graphic files are **bitmap graphics**, which are often saved with a .bmp, .png, .jpg, .tif, or .gif file extension. To view all the graphic files in a particular location, use the File type list arrow to select All Pictures.

   > **TROUBLE**
   > If you do not see All Pictures, click the File type list arrow, then click All Pictures.

3. **Verify that All Pictures appears in the File type text box, navigate to the location where you store your Data Files, click the file Fishing Boats.jpg, then click Insert**

   The photo is inserted as an inline graphic at the location of the insertion point, as shown in Figure F-1. When a graphic is selected, white circles and squares, called **sizing handles**, appear on the sides and corners of the graphic, a green **rotate handle** appears, and the Picture Tools Format tab appears on the Ribbon. You use this tab to size, crop, position, wrap text around, format, and adjust a graphic.

4. **Click the Picture Effects button in the Picture Styles group, point to Shadow, move the pointer over the shadow styles in the gallery to preview them in the document, then click Offset Diagonal Bottom Right in the Outer section**

   A drop shadow is applied to the photo. You can use the Picture Effects button to apply other visual effects to a graphic, such as a glow, soft edge, reflection, or 3-D rotation.

5. **Click the Picture Effects button, point to Shadow, then click Shadow Options**

   The Format Picture dialog box opens. You use this dialog box to adjust the format settings applied to graphic objects.

6. **Click the Distance up arrow in the Shadow section four times until 7 pt appears, then click Close**

   The distance of the shadow from the picture is increased to 7 points. Notice that as you adjust the settings in the dialog box, the change is immediately applied to the photo.

   > **QUICK TIP**
   > Change a floating graphic to an inline graphic by changing the text wrapping style to In Line with Text.

7. **Click the Text Wrapping button in the Arrange group, then click Tight**

   The text wraps around the sides of the graphic, as shown in Figure F-2, making the graphic a floating object. A floating object is part of the drawing layer in a document and can be moved anywhere on a page, including in front of or behind text and other objects. Notice the anchor that appears in the upper-right corner of the photo next to the Adventure Mexico paragraph. The anchor indicates the floating graphic is **anchored** to the nearest paragraph so that the graphic moves with the paragraph if the paragraph is moved. The anchor symbol appears only when formatting marks are displayed.

   > **QUICK TIP**
   > To position a graphic anywhere on a page, you must apply text-wrapping to it even if there is no text on the page.

8. **Deselect the graphic, then click the Save button on the Quick Access toolbar**

Illustrating Documents with Graphics

FIGURE F-1: Inline graphic

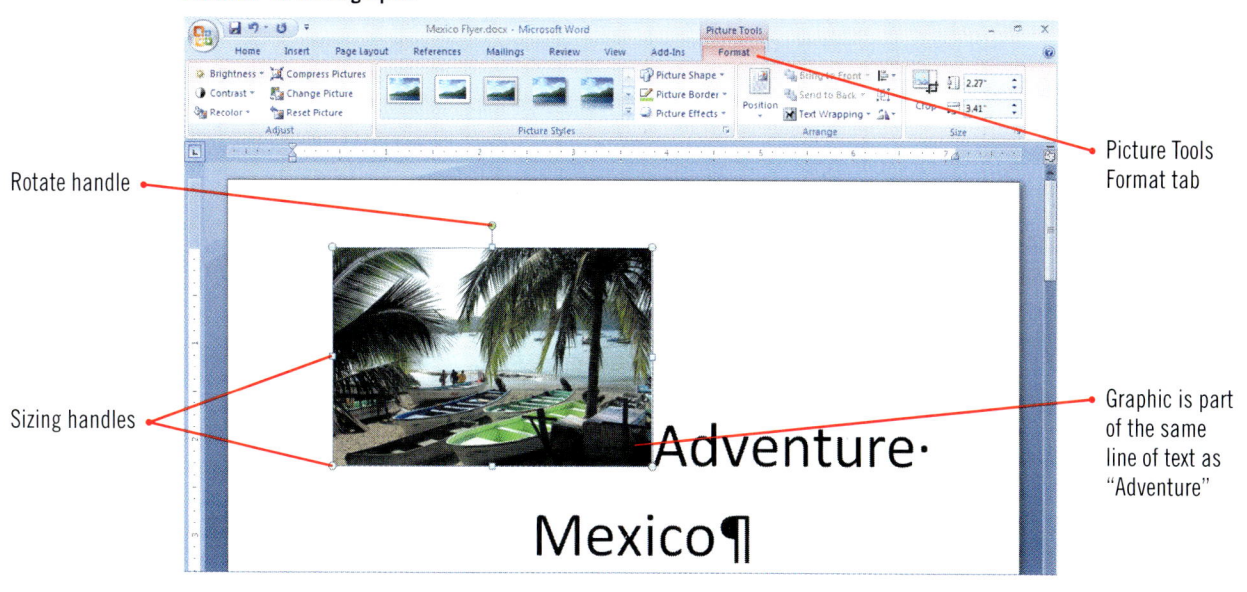

- Picture Tools Format tab
- Rotate handle
- Sizing handles
- Graphic is part of the same line of text as "Adventure"

FIGURE F-2: Floating graphic

- Anchor symbol indicates photo is anchored to the paragraph next to it
- Text wraps around the shape of the graphic

Adjusting the brightness, contrast, or colors of a picture

The Word picture editing features give you the power to enhance the color of photographs and clip art and create interesting visual effects. Using the commands in the Adjust group on the Picture Tools Format tab, you can adjust a picture's relative lightness (**brightness**), alter the difference between its darkest and lightest areas (**contrast**), and recolor a picture to give it a stylized effect, such as sepia tone, grayscale, or duotone.

When you want to alter the brightness or contrast of a picture, you select it, click the Brightness or Contrast button in the Adjust group to open a gallery of percentages that you can preview applied to the picture, and then click the percentage you want to apply. You can also fine tune the brightness or contrast applied to a picture by clicking Picture Corrections Options in the gallery, and then using the sliders in the Picture pane of the Format Picture dialog box to adjust the percentage. See Figure F-3.

If you want to change the colors of a picture, simply select it, click the Recolor button in the Adjust group, and then select one of the color modes or variations in the gallery that opens. After you edit a picture, you can undo any changes that you made to the brightness, contrast, or color by clicking the Reset Picture button in the Adjust group. This command also resets any changes you made to a picture's size, cropping, border, and effects.

FIGURE F-3: Format Picture dialog box

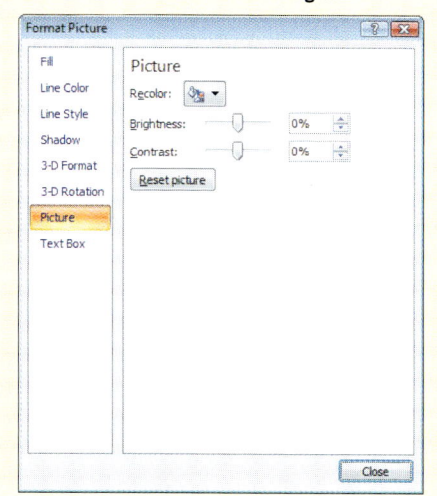

Sizing and Scaling a Graphic

UNIT F · Word 2007

Once you insert a graphic into a document, you can change its shape or size by using the mouse to drag a sizing handle, by using the Shape Width and Shape Height text boxes in the Size group on the Picture Tools Format tab to specify an exact height and width for the graphic, or by changing the scale of the graphic using the Size dialog box. Resizing a graphic with the mouse allows you to see how the image looks as you modify it. Using the text boxes in the Size group or the Size dialog box allows you to set precise measurements. 🎨 You enlarge the photograph.

STEPS

> **TROUBLE**
> Click the View Ruler button 📋 at the top of the vertical scroll bar to display the rulers if they are not already displayed.

1. **Double-click the photo to select it, place the pointer over the middle-right sizing handle, when the pointer changes to ↔, drag to the right until the graphic is about 5" wide**

   As you drag, the transparent image indicates the size and shape of the graphic. You can refer to the ruler to gauge the measurements as you drag. When you release the mouse button, the image is stretched to be wider. Dragging a side, top, or bottom sizing handle changes only the width or height of a graphic.

2. **Click the Undo button 🔄 on the Quick Access toolbar, place the pointer over the lower-right sizing handle, when the pointer changes to ⤡ drag down and to the right until the graphic is about 2 ¾ " tall and 4" wide, then release the mouse button**

   The image is enlarged. Dragging a corner sizing handle resizes the photo proportionally so that its width and height are reduced or enlarged by the same percentage. Table F-1 describes other ways to resize objects using the mouse.

> **QUICK TIP**
> Click a photo once to select it. Double-click a photo to select it and activate the Picture Tools Format tab.

3. **Click the launcher 📋 in the Size group**

   The Size dialog box opens, as shown in Figure F-4. It allows you to enter precise height and width measurements for a graphic or to scale a graphic by entering the percentage by which you want to reduce or enlarge it. When a graphic is sized to scale (or **scaled**), its height to width ratio remains the same.

> **TROUBLE**
> Your height measurement might differ slightly.

4. **Select the measurement in the Height text box in the Scale section, type 130, then click the Width text box in the Scale section**

   The scale of the width changes to 130% and the Height and Width measurements in the Size and rotate section increase proportionally. When the Lock aspect ratio check box is selected, you need to enter only a height or width measurement. Word calculates the other measurement so that the resized graphic is proportional.

5. **Click Close**

   The photo is enlarged to 130% its original size.

> **QUICK TIP**
> Deselect the Lock aspect ratio check box if you want to change a photo's proportions.

6. **Type 4.6 in the Shape Width text box in the Size group, press [Enter], then save your changes**

   The photo is enlarged to be precisely 4.6" wide and approximately 3.07" tall, as shown in Figure F-5. Because the Lock aspect ratio check box is selected in the Size dialog box for this graphic, the photo is sized proportionally when you adjust a setting in either the Shape Height or the Shape Width text box.

Cropping graphics

If you want to use only part of a picture in a document, you can **crop** the graphic to trim the parts you don't want to use. To crop a graphic, select it, then click the Crop button in the Size group on the Picture Tools Format tab. The pointer changes to the cropping pointer ✂, and cropping handles (solid black lines) appear on all four corners and sides of the graphic. To crop one side of a graphic, drag a side cropping handle inward to where you want to trim the graphic. To crop two adjacent sides at once, drag a corner cropping handle inward to the point where you want the corner of the cropped image to be. When you finish adjusting the parameters of the graphic, click the Crop button again to turn off the crop feature. You can also crop a graphic by entering precise crop measurements on the Size tab in the Size dialog box.

FIGURE F-4: Size tab in the Size dialog box

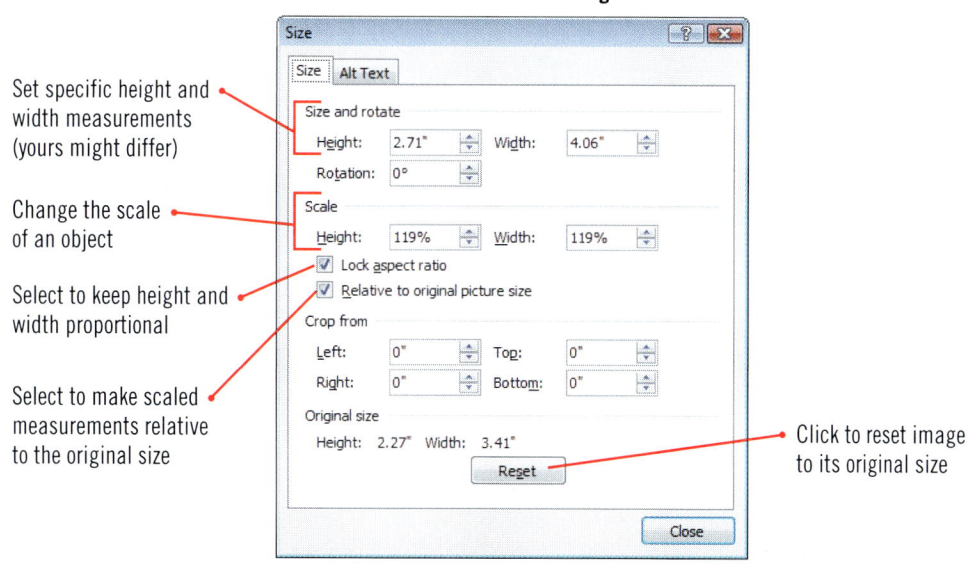

- Set specific height and width measurements (yours might differ)
- Change the scale of an object
- Select to keep height and width proportional
- Select to make scaled measurements relative to the original size
- Click to reset image to its original size

FIGURE F-5: Enlarged photo

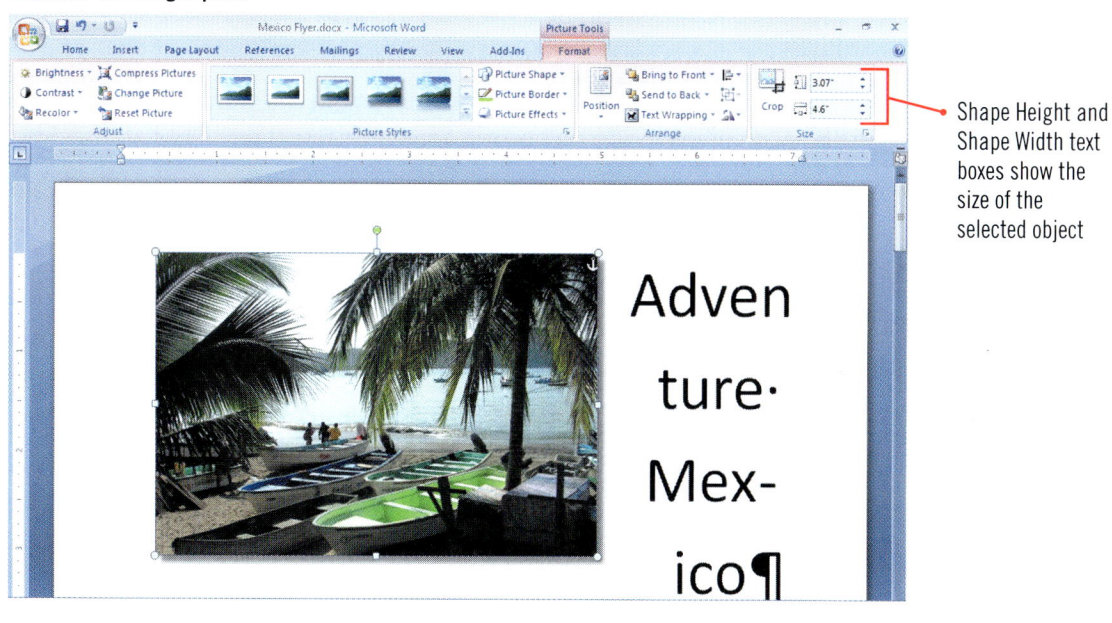

- Shape Height and Shape Width text boxes show the size of the selected object

TABLE F-1: Methods for resizing an object using the mouse

do this	to
Drag a corner sizing handle	Resize a clip art or bitmap graphic and maintain its proportions
Press [Shift] and drag a corner sizing handle	Resize any graphic object and maintain its proportions
Press [Ctrl] and drag a side, top, or bottom sizing handle	Resize any graphic object vertically or horizontally while keeping the center position fixed
Press [Ctrl] and drag a corner sizing handle	Resize any graphic object diagonally while keeping the center position fixed
Press [Shift][Ctrl] and drag a corner sizing handle	Resize any graphic object while keeping the center position fixed and maintaining its proportions

Illustrating Documents with Graphics

UNIT F
Word 2007

Positioning a Graphic

Once you insert a graphic into a document and make it a floating graphic, you can move it by dragging it with the mouse, nudging it with the arrow keys, or setting an exact location for the graphic using the Position command. You experiment with different positions for the photo, and then you move an inline graphic from page 2 to page 1 using Cut and Paste.

STEPS

> **QUICK TIP**
> Press an arrow key to nudge an object in small increments.

1. **Select the photo if it is not already selected, click the Position button in the Arrange group, then click Position in Middle Center with Square Text Wrapping**
   The photo is centered vertically and horizontally on the page and the text wraps around the graphic. Moving an inline graphic using the Position button is a fast way to make it a floating graphic and position it so it is centered or aligned with the margins.

> **QUICK TIP**
> To move an object only horizontally or vertically, press [Shift] as you drag.

2. **Be sure the section break is at the top of your screen, then use the ⁺⁺ pointer to drag the photo up and to the right as shown in Figure F-6**
   As you drag, the transparent image indicates the position of the photo. When you release the mouse button, the photo is moved. Notice that the anchor symbol moved when you moved the graphic.

3. **Click the Position button, click More Layout Options, then click the Picture Position tab in the Advanced Layout dialog box if it is not already selected**
   The Picture Position tab allows you to specify an exact position for a graphic relative to some aspect of the document, such as a margin, column, or paragraph.

> **QUICK TIP**
> You can place a floating graphic anywhere on a page, including outside the margins.

4. **Type 2.44 in the Absolute position text box in the Horizontal section, then type 2.25 in the Absolute position text box in the Vertical section**
   The left side of the photo will be positioned exactly 2.44" from the right margin and the top of the photo will be positioned precisely 2.25" below the top margin.

5. **Click the Text Wrapping tab**
   You use the Text Wrapping tab to change the text wrapping style, to wrap text around only one side of a graphic, and to change the distance between the edge of the graphic and the edge of the wrapped text.

> **QUICK TIP**
> Use the Change Picture button in the Adjust group to replace the current picture with another picture while preserving the formatting and size of the current picture.

6. **Type .1 in the Bottom text box, then click OK**
   The position of the photo is adjusted and the amount of white space under the photo is increased to .1".

7. **Change the Zoom level to 75%, scroll until the section break is at the top of your screen, be sure the photo is still selected, then drag the anchor symbol to the left margin near the top of the first body paragraph if it is not already located there**
   Dragging the anchor symbol to a different paragraph anchors the selected graphic to that paragraph.

8. **Press [Ctrl][End], select the pyramid photo, press [Ctrl][X] to cut the photo, scroll up until the section break at the top of page 1 is at the top of your screen, click the blank paragraph in the first column, then press [Ctrl][V]**
   The inline graphic is pasted above the Quest Specialty Travel Mexico Destinations heading.

9. **Double-click the pyramid photo, click the Position button, click Position in Bottom Left with Square Text Wrapping, then drag the anchor symbol to the margin left of the first body paragraph**
   The pyramid photo becomes a floating graphic aligned in the lower-left corner of the page and anchored to the first body paragraph. Both photos are now anchored to the same paragraph.

10. **Click the Fishing boats photo, click the Home tab, click the Format Painter button ✦ in the Clipboard group, click the pyramid photo with the ⌂I pointer, then click 🖫**
    The shadow format settings are copied from the fishing boats photo to the pyramid photo. Compare your document to Figure F-7.

Illustrating Documents with Graphics

FIGURE F-6: Dragging a graphic to move it

Anchor symbol moves with the graphic

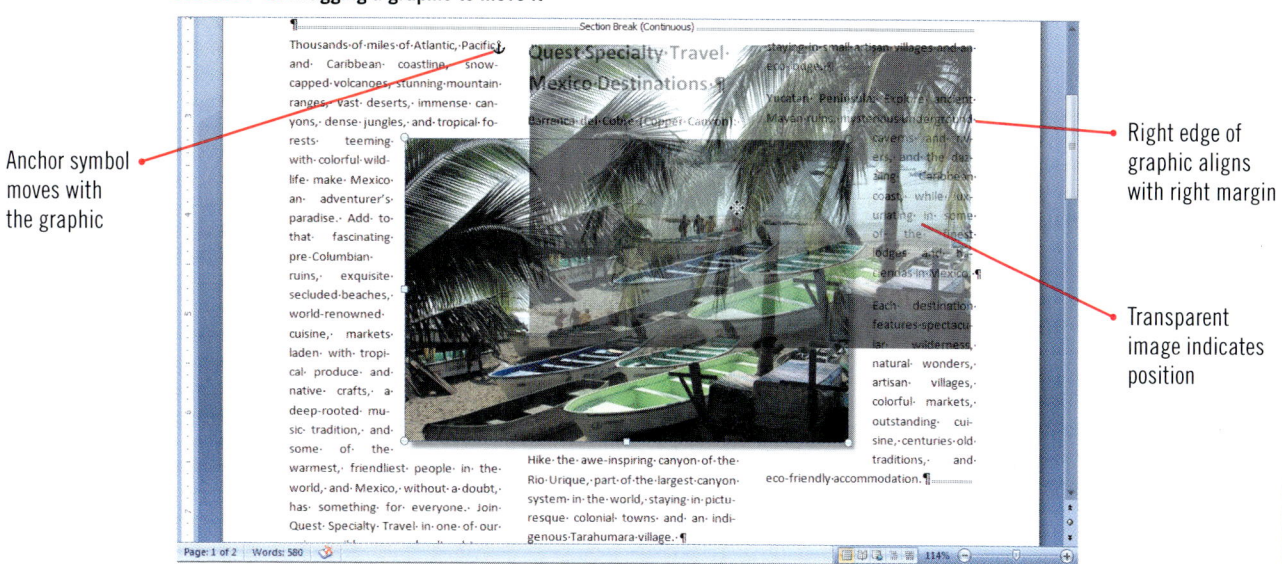

Right edge of graphic aligns with right margin

Transparent image indicates position

FIGURE F-7: Repositioned photos

Selected photo is anchored to this paragraph

Same shadow format applied to both photos

Changing the shape of a picture and enhancing it with visual effects

A fun way to alter the appearance of a picture in a document is to change its shape, either to something sophisticated, such as an oval or a rectangle, or to something playful, such as a star, sun, triangle, or arrow. Another fun way to give a document personality and flair, and help to communicate its message, is to apply a visual effect to a picture, such as a glow, a shadow, a reflection, soft edges, a bevel, or some other effect. When you change the shape of a picture or apply a visual effect, any other formatting you have applied to the picture is preserved. To change the shape of a picture, simply select it, click the Picture Shape button in the Picture Styles group on the Picture Tools Format tab, and then select one of the shapes from the Shape menu that opens. To apply a visual effect, select the picture, click the Picture Effects button in the Picture Styles group, point to a type of effect, and then select from the gallery choices. Figure F-8 shows a photo that is shaped like a cloud and has a bevel effect applied.

FIGURE F-8: Photograph with picture shape and effects applied

Illustrating Documents with Graphics

Creating a Text Box

UNIT F
Word 2007

When you want to illustrate your documents with text, you can create a text box. A **text box** is a container that you can fill with text and graphics. Like other drawing objects, a text box can be resized, formatted with colors, lines, and text-wrapping, and positioned anywhere on a page. You can choose to insert a preformatted text box that you customize with your own text, draw an empty text box and then fill it with text, or select existing text and then draw a text box around it. You use the Text Box button in the Text group or the Shapes button in the Illustrations group on the Insert tab to create a text box. You draw a text box around the QST Mexico Destinations information, resize and position the text box on the page, and then format it using a text box style.

STEPS

1. **Select all the text in columns 2 and 3, including the heading and the last paragraph mark before the section break**
   The text in columns 2 and 3 is selected.

   > **QUICK TIP**
   > To draw an empty text box, click the Text Box button, click Draw Text Box, then click and drag with the ╋ pointer to create the text box.

2. **Click the Insert tab, then click the Text Box button in the Text group**
   A gallery of preformatted text boxes and sidebars opens.

3. **Click Draw Text Box**
   The selected text is formatted as a text box, as shown in Figure F-9. When you draw a text box around existing text or graphics, the text box becomes part of the drawing layer (a floating object).

   > **TROUBLE**
   > Always verify that a text box is sized so that all the text fits.

4. **Click the Text Box Tools Format tab, type 4.1 in the Shape Height text box in the Size group, type 4.65 in the Shape Width text box in the Size group, then press [Enter]**
   The text box is resized to be exactly 4.1" tall and 4.65" wide.

5. **Click the Position button in the Arrange group, then click Position in Bottom Right with Square Text Wrapping**
   The text box is moved to the lower-right corner of the page.

   > **QUICK TIP**
   > To change the vertical alignment or the margins in a text box, click the launcher in the Text Box Styles group, then select from the options on the Text Box tab in the Format Text Box dialog box.

6. **Delete the paragraph mark above the pyramid photo, click the Show/Hide ¶ button ¶ in the Paragraph group on the Home tab, then double-click the text box frame with the pointer**
   Double-clicking the text box frame selects the text box and activates the Text Box Tools Format tab. Clicking inside a text box with the I pointer moves the insertion point inside the text box so the text can be edited.

7. **Click the More button in the Text Box Styles group, move the pointer over the styles in the gallery to preview them applied to the text box, then click Diagonal Gradient – Accent 1**
   A style that includes green gradient shading, a thin green border, and a slight shadow is applied to the text box. You can also create your own designs using the Shape Fill and Shape Outline buttons in the Text Box Styles group.

   > **QUICK TIP**
   > Use the Shadow Effects button to change the style, direction, and color of a shadow.

8. **Click the Shadow On/Off button in the Shadow Effects group**
   The shadow is removed from the text box.

9. **Place the insertion point in the paragraph above the pyramid photo, click the Insert tab, click the Drop Cap button in the Text group, click Drop Cap Options, click Dropped in the Position section, click the Font list arrow, scroll down, click Segoe Script, click the Lines to drop up arrow once, click the Distance from text up arrow once, click OK, deselect the drop cap, then save your changes**
   A drop cap is added to the paragraph. Compare your document to Figure F-10.

FIGURE F-9: Text box

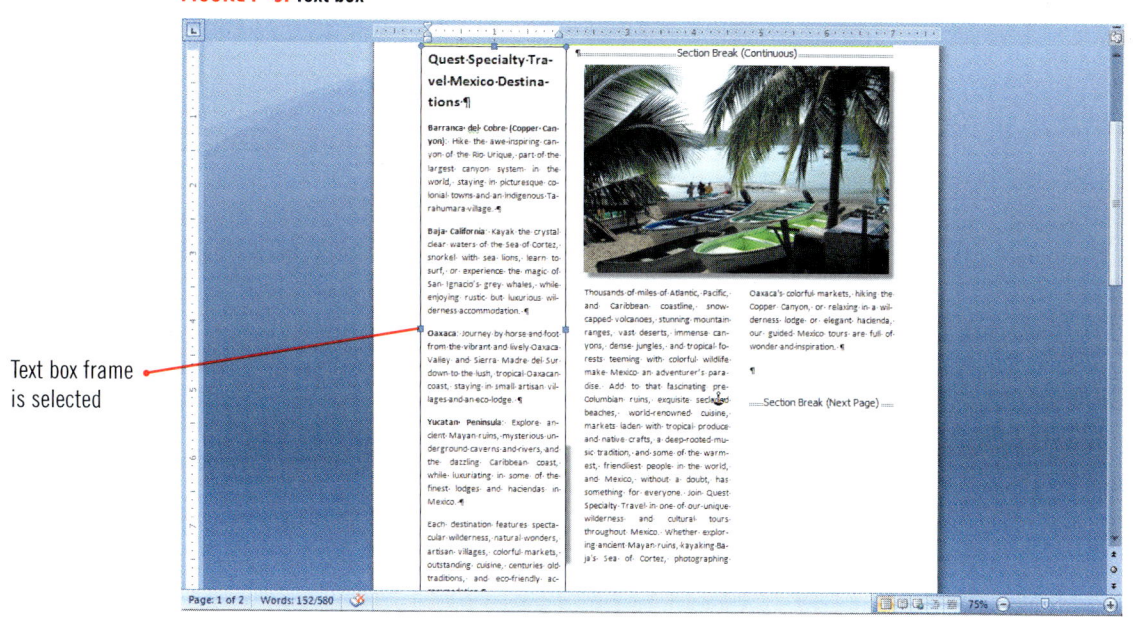

Text box frame is selected

FIGURE F-10: Formatted text box and drop cap

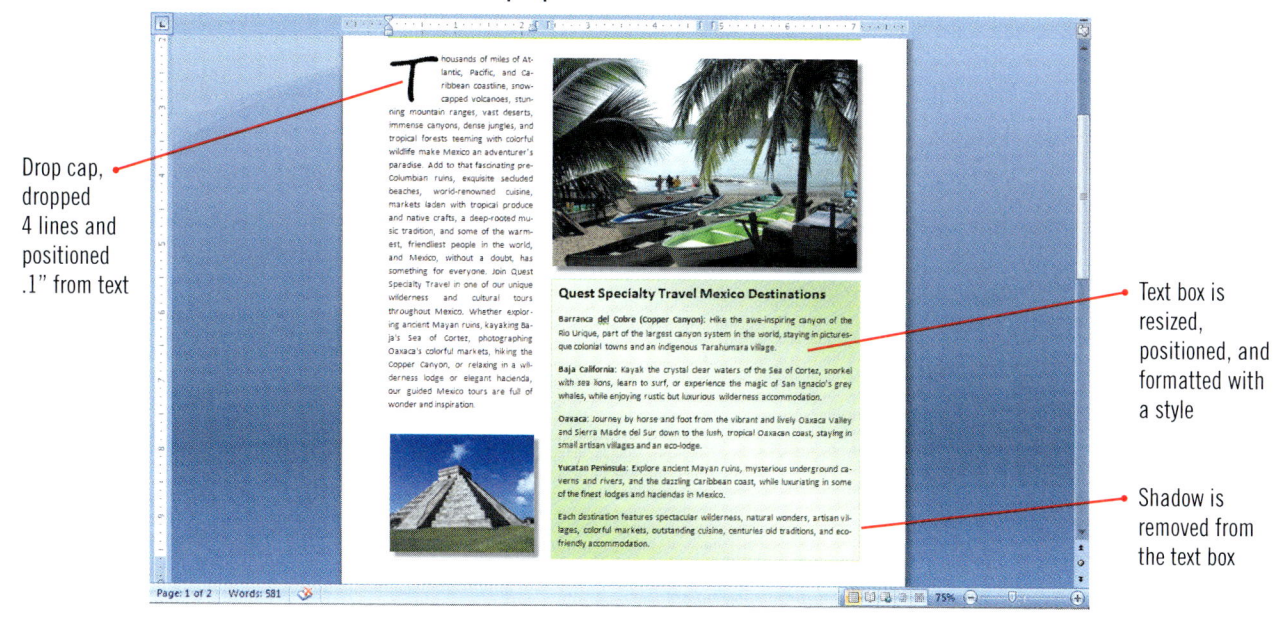

Drop cap, dropped 4 lines and positioned .1" from text

Text box is resized, positioned, and formatted with a style

Shadow is removed from the text box

Linking text boxes

If you are working on a longer document, you might want text to begin in a text box on one page and then continue in a text box on another page. By creating a **link** between two or more text boxes, you can force text to flow automatically from one text box to another, allowing you to size and format the text boxes any way you wish. To link two or more text boxes, you must first create the original text box, fill it with text, and then create a second, empty text box. Then, to create the link, select the first text box, click the Create Link button in the Text group on the Text Box Tools Format tab to activate the pointer, and then click the second text box with the pointer. Any overflow text from the first text box flows seamlessly into the second text box. As you resize the first text box, the flow of text adjusts automatically between the two linked text boxes. If you want to break a link between two linked text boxes so that all the text is contained in the original text box, select the original text box, and then click the Break Link button in the Text group.

Illustrating Documents with Graphics

Word 137

Creating WordArt

UNIT F
Word 2007

Another way to give your documents punch and flair is to use WordArt. **WordArt** is a drawing object that contains text formatted with special shapes, patterns, and orientations. You create WordArt using the WordArt button in the Text group on the Insert tab. Once you have created a WordArt object, you can use the buttons on the WordArt Tools Format tab to change its shape, font, colors, borders, shadows, and other effects to create the impact you desire. You use WordArt to create an impressive heading for the flyer.

STEPS

> **QUICK TIP**
> Triple-clicking a word selects the entire paragraph, including the paragraph mark.

1. **Press [Ctrl][Home], click the View tab, click the Page Width button in the Zoom group, triple-click Adventure Mexico to select it, click the Insert tab, then click the WordArt button in the Text group**
   The WordArt Gallery opens. It includes the styles you can choose for your WordArt.

2. **Click WordArt style 14 (the second style in the third row)**
   The Edit WordArt Text dialog box opens. You enter or edit the text you want to format as WordArt in this dialog box and, if you wish, change the font and font size of the WordArt text.

3. **Click OK**
   The WordArt object appears at the location of the insertion point and the WordArt Tools Format tab becomes the active tab. Like other graphic objects, the WordArt object is an inline graphic until you wrap text around it. Since the object is located where you want it, aligned with the top margin, you decide to leave it as an inline graphic.

4. **Type 7 in the Shape Width text box in the Size group, press [Enter], then click the Shape Height down arrow once**
   The WordArt is enlarged to span the page between the left and right margins.

5. **Click the Spacing button in the Text group, click Tight, click the Even Height button in the Text group, click the Change WordArt Shape button in the WordArt Styles group, then click Double Wave 2**
   The spacing between the characters is decreased, the characters become a uniform height, and the shape of the WordArt text changes, as shown in Figure F-11.

6. **Click the More button in the WordArt Styles group, point to several styles in the gallery to see a preview in the document, then click WordArt style 13 (the first style in the third row)**
   The style of the WordArt object changes.

7. **Click the Shape Fill list arrow in the WordArt Styles group, point to Gradient, then click More Gradients**
   The Fill Effects dialog box opens, as shown in Figure F-12. You use this dialog box to change the fill colors and effects of the WordArt object. Using the Gradient tab, you can select a preset gradient effect or choose colors and shading styles to create your own gradient effect. You can also apply a preset texture using the Texture tab, design a two-color pattern using the Pattern tab, or fill the object with a graphic using the Picture tab.

8. **Make sure the Two colors option button is selected in the Colors section on the Gradient tab, click the Color 1 list arrow, click Light Blue, Accent 5, click the Color 2 list arrow, click Lime, Accent 1, click the Diagonal up option button in the Shading styles section, click the lower-right box in the Variants section, click OK, deselect the object, then save your changes**
   The new fill effects are applied to the WordArt, as shown in Figure F-13.

Illustrating Documents with Graphics

FIGURE F-11: Resized WordArt

- WordArt object is enlarged
- Double Wave 2 shape applied
- Upper- and lower-case characters are the same height

FIGURE F-12: Fill Effects dialog box

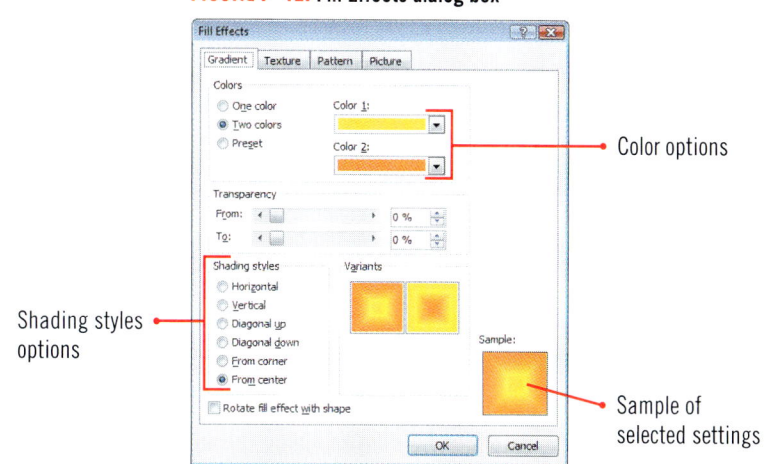

- Color options
- Shading styles options
- Sample of selected settings

FIGURE F-13: Completed WordArt object

- Customized WordArt style

Enhancing an object with shadows and 3-D effects

A fun way to enliven the look of a WordArt or other graphic object is to enhance it with a shadow or three-dimensional effect. The commands in the Shadow Effects group on the active Format tab for that type of object give you the power to apply a variety of shadow styles to an object, change the color of a shadow, and nudge a shadow up, down, right, or left to fine-tune the shadow's placement and depth. The 3-D Effects command on the Format tab is a powerful feature that allows you not only to select from a variety of 3-D styles for an object, but to adjust the tilt, color, direction, and depth of the 3-D effect. In addition, you can alter the direction and intensity of the lighting cast on the object, and change the surface of the 3-D effect to have a matte look, or to resemble plastic, metal, or wire. The best way to learn about shadow and three-dimensional effects is to experiment by applying the effects to an object and seeing what works.

Illustrating Documents with Graphics

UNIT
F
Word 2007

Drawing Shapes

One way you can create your own graphics in Word is to draw shapes. **Shapes** are the rectangles, ovals, lines, callouts, block arrows, stars, banners, hearts, suns, and other drawing objects you can create using the Shapes command in the Illustrations group on the Insert tab. Once you draw a shape, you can add colors, borders, fill effects, shadows, and three-dimensional effects to it to make it come alive in a document. 🎨 You use the Shapes feature to draw a Mayan pyramid in the document.

STEPS

1. **Scroll to the bottom of the document, click the Insert tab, click the Shapes button in the Illustrations group, then click Bevel in the Basic Shapes section of the Shapes menu**
   The Shapes menu contains categories of shapes and lines that you can draw. When you click a shape in the Shapes menu, the pointer changes to +. You draw a shape by clicking and dragging with this pointer.

   > **QUICK TIP**
   > To draw a circle, click the Oval, then press [Shift] while you drag with the pointer.

2. **Position the + pointer in the blank area at the bottom of the page, press [Shift], then drag down and to the right to create a square bevel that is approximately 2" tall and wide**
   Pressing [Shift] as you drag creates a bevel that is perfectly square. When you release the mouse button, sizing handles appear around the bevel to indicate it is selected, as shown in Figure F-14.

   > **TROUBLE**
   > If the shape is not as expected, click the Undo button on the Quick Access toolbar and try again.

3. **Click the Bevel shape in the Insert Shapes group, place the + pointer exactly over the inside upper-left corner of the last bevel you drew, press [Shift], drag down and to the right to create a square bevel that fills the inside of the previous bevel, then repeat this step to create two more bevel shapes inside the stack of bevels**
   When you are finished, the stack of bevels looks like an aerial view of a pyramid.

4. **With the inside bevel still selected, press and hold [Ctrl], click the other three bevel shapes to select them, click the Group button 🔲▾ in the Arrange group, then click Group**
   Grouping converts multiple shapes into a single object that can be sized, positioned, and formatted together.

   > **QUICK TIP**
   > Drag an adjustment handle to modify the shape, but not the size, of a shape.

5. **Click the More button ▾ in the Insert Shapes group, click Sun in the Basic Shapes section, place the + pointer in the upper-left inside corner of the inside bevel, then drag down and to the right to create a sun that fills the top of the pyramid**
   The sun shape includes a yellow diamond-shaped **adjustment handle**.

6. **Position the pointer over the adjustment handle until it changes to ▷, drag the handle to the right about ⅛", click the Shape Fill list arrow 🎨▾ in the Shape Styles group, then click Gold, Accent 3**
   The sun shape becomes narrower and filled with color.

   > **QUICK TIP**
   > To convert a shape to a text box, right-click it, then click Add Text.

7. **Click ▾ in the Insert Shapes group, click Rectangle in the Basic Shapes section, place the + pointer over the topmost horizontal line in the pyramid, draw a rectangle similar to that shown in Figure F-15, click 🎨▾, click Pattern, click the fourth pattern in the second row, click the Foreground Color list arrow, click Blue, Accent 4, then click OK**
   The rectangle is filled with thin blue lines that resemble stairs, as shown in Figure F-15.

8. **With the rectangle selected, press and hold [Ctrl], click the grouped bevel shape and the sun shape to select them, click 🔲▾, click Group, click the Shape Outline list arrow ✏▾ in the Shape Styles group, then click Blue, Accent 4**
   The pyramid shape, sun shape, and rectangle are grouped into a single object, and the lines change to blue.

   > **QUICK TIP**
   > Use the Bring to Front and Send to Back list arrows to shift the order of the layers in a stack of graphic objects.

9. **Click the Rotate button 🔄▾ in the Arrange group, click Rotate Right 90°, then press [F4]**
   The pyramid drawing is rotated 180°. You can also rotate a graphic by dragging the green rotate handle.

10. **Drag the pyramid drawing up to position it temporarily over the third column of text, as shown in Figure F-16, then save your changes**
    The drawing object is automatically formatted as a floating graphic with the In Front of Text wrapping style applied, making it part of the drawing layer. You will finalize the object's position in a later lesson.

Illustrating Documents with Graphics

FIGURE F-14: Bevel shape

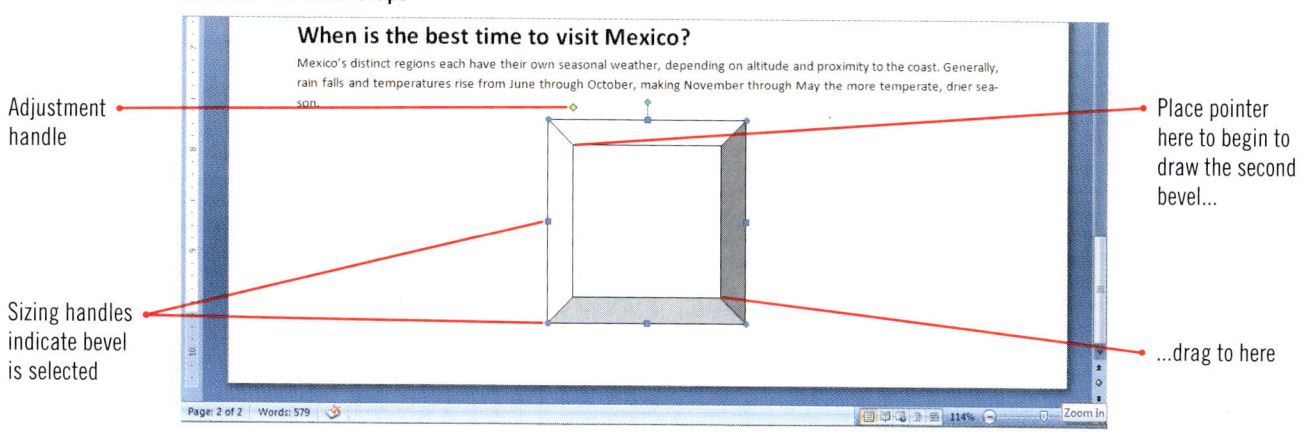

- Adjustment handle
- Sizing handles indicate bevel is selected
- Place pointer here to begin to draw the second bevel...
- ...drag to here

FIGURE F-15: Rectangle added to pyramid

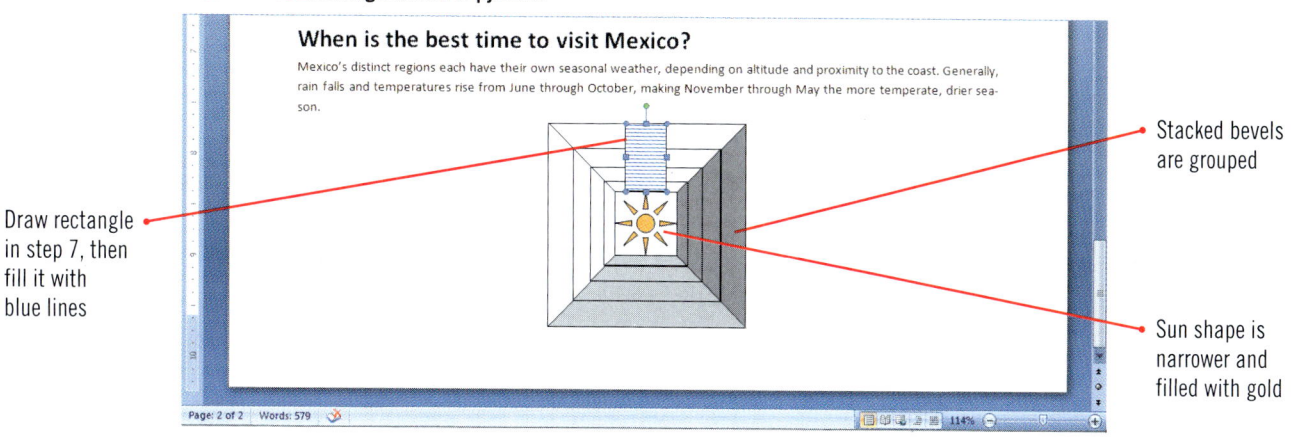

- Draw rectangle in step 7, then fill it with blue lines
- Stacked bevels are grouped
- Sun shape is narrower and filled with gold

FIGURE F-16: Rotated drawing

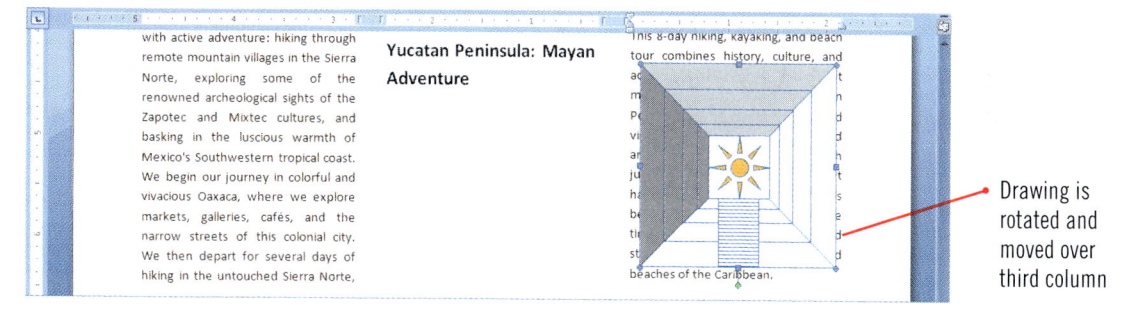

- Drawing is rotated and moved over third column

Creating an illustration in a drawing canvas

A **drawing canvas** is a workspace for creating your own graphics. It provides a frame-like boundary between an illustration and the rest of the document so that the illustration can be sized, formatted, and positioned like a single graphic object. If you are creating an illustration that includes multiple shapes, such as a flow chart, it is helpful to create the illustration in a drawing canvas. To draw shapes or lines in a drawing canvas, click the Shapes button in the Illustrations group, click New Drawing Canvas to open a drawing canvas in the document, and then create and format your illustration in the drawing canvas. When you are finished, right-click the drawing canvas and then click Fit to automatically resize the drawing canvas to fit the illustration. Right-click the drawing canvas again and click Scale Drawing to change the cropping handles on the drawing canvas to sizing handles that you can use to resize the illustration. Once you have resized a drawing canvas, you can wrap text around it and position it by using the Ribbon or dragging the drawing canvas frame. By default, a drawing canvas has no border or background so that it is transparent in a document, but you can add fill and borders to it if you wish.

Illustrating Documents with Graphics

UNIT F
Word 2007

Creating a Chart

Adding a chart can be an attractive way to illustrate a document that includes numerical information. A **chart** is a visual representation of numerical data and usually is used to illustrate trends, patterns, or relationships. The Word chart feature allows you to create many types of charts, including bar, column, pie, area, and line charts. To create a chart, you use the Chart button in the Illustrations group on the Insert tab. You create a chart that shows the average temperature for each season in the four geographic areas where QST Mexico tours are located.

STEPS

1. **Press [Ctrl][End], click the Insert tab, then click the Chart button in the Illustrations group**
   The Insert Chart dialog box opens. You use this dialog box to select the type and style of chart you intend to create. The chart types are listed in the left pane of the dialog box, and the styles for each chart type are listed in the right pane. You want to create a simple column chart.

   > **QUICK TIP**
   > Click the Change Chart Type button in the Type group on the Chart Tools Design tab to change the type of chart.

2. **Click OK**
   A worksheet opens in a Microsoft Excel window and a column chart appears in the Word document. The worksheet and the chart contain placeholder data that you replace with your own data. The chart is based on the data in the worksheet. Any change you make to the data is made automatically to the chart.

3. **Drag the scroll box down to the bottom of the Word document, then click an empty cell in the Excel worksheet**
   The pointer changes to ✥. You use this pointer to select the cells in the worksheet. The blue lines in the worksheet indicate the range of data to include in the chart.

4. **Move the pointer over the lower-right corner of the blue box, when the pointer changes to ⬉ drag the range one column to the right, then release the mouse button**
   The range is enlarged to include five columns and five rows.

   > **TROUBLE**
   > Click the Edit Data button in the Data group on the Chart Tools Design tab to open the worksheet and edit the chart data.

5. **Click the Category 1 cell, type Baja California, click the Category 2 cell, type Oaxaca, press [Enter], type Copper Canyon, replace the remaining placeholder text with the data shown in Figure F-17, click an empty cell, then click the Close button in the Excel window**
   When you click a cell and type, the data in the cell is replaced with the text you type. As you edit the worksheet, the changes you make are reflected in the chart.

6. **Click the chart border to select the object if necessary, click the More button ▼ in the Chart Styles group on the Chart Tools Design tab, then click Style 26**
   A chart style is applied to the chart.

   > **QUICK TIP**
   > Point to any part of a chart to see a ScreenTip that identifies the part.

7. **Click the Layout tab, click the Chart Title button in the Labels group, click Above Chart, type Average Temperature, click the Axis Titles button in the Labels group, point to Primary Vertical Axis Title, click Rotated Title, then type Degrees Celsius**
   A chart title and vertical axis title are added to the chart.

8. **Click the Legend button in the Labels group, then click Show Legend at Top**
   The legend moves above the chart.

   > **QUICK TIP**
   > To change the formatting of any chart element, select it, then click the Format Selection button in the Current Selection group to open the Format Chart Element dialog box.

9. **Right-click Yucatan to select the Horizontal axis, click the Shrink Font button A˅ on the Mini toolbar, right-click the chart title, then click A˅ twice**
   The font sizes of the destination names in the horizontal axis and the chart title are reduced. You can also click a chart element in the chart to select it.

10. **Click the border of the chart object to select the chart area, click the Format tab, click the More button ▼ in the Shape Styles group, click Colored Outline, Dark 1, type 2.5 in the Shape Height text box in the Size group, type 4.1 in the Shape Width text box in the Size group, press [Enter], deselect the chart, then save your changes**
    The completed chart is shown in Figure F-18.

Word 142   Illustrating Documents with Graphics

FIGURE F-17: Chart object in Word and worksheet in Excel

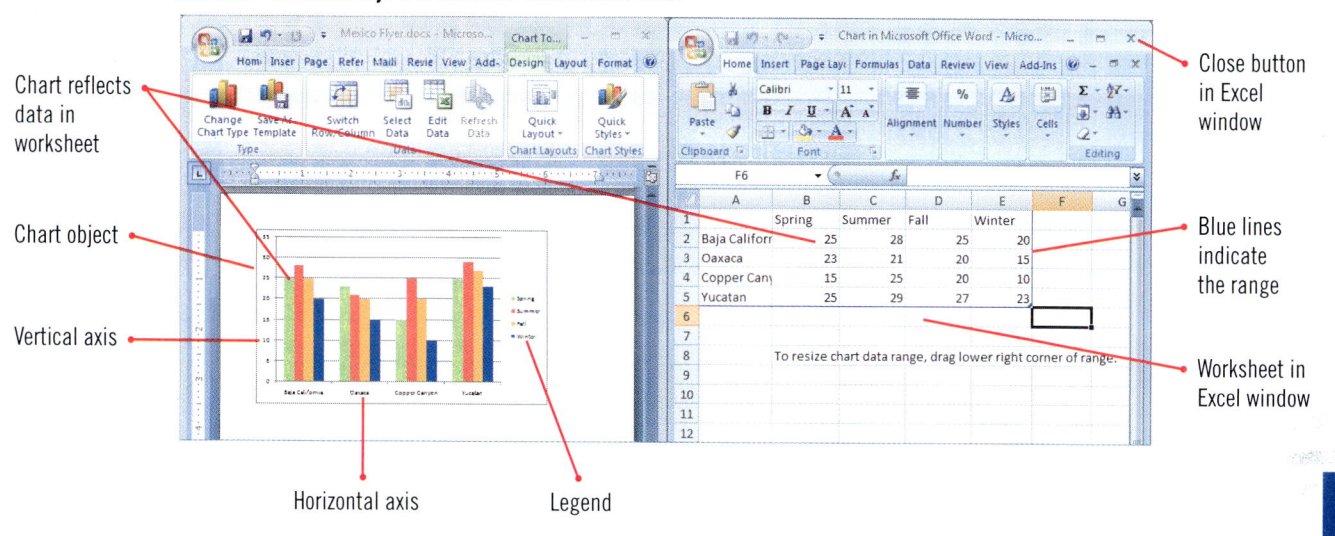

- Chart reflects data in worksheet
- Chart object
- Vertical axis
- Horizontal axis
- Legend
- Close button in Excel window
- Blue lines indicate the range
- Worksheet in Excel window

FIGURE F-18: Completed chart

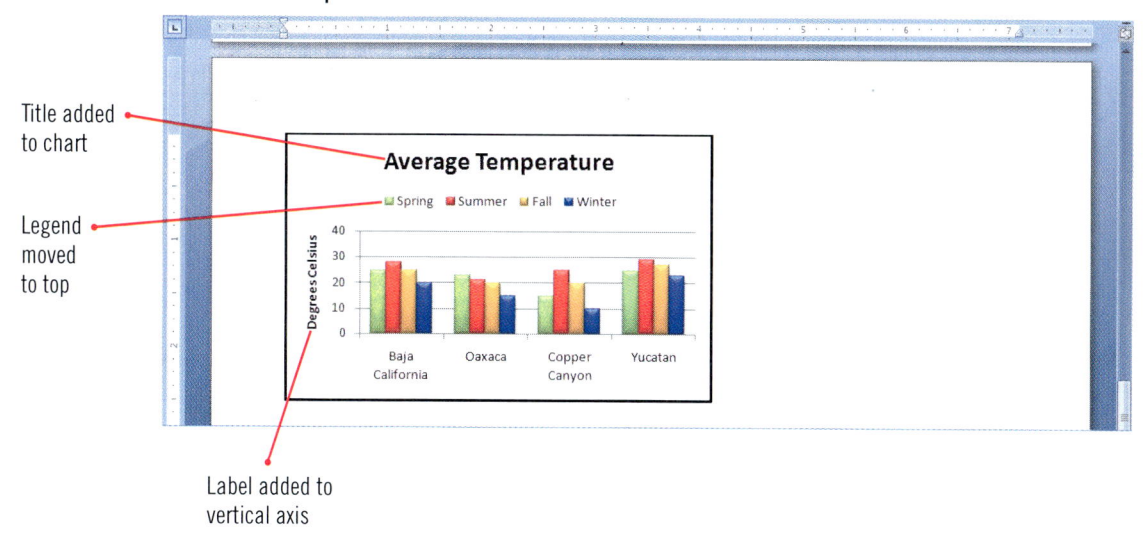

- Title added to chart
- Legend moved to top
- Label added to vertical axis

Creating SmartArt graphics

Diagrams are another way to illustrate concepts in your documents. The powerful Word **SmartArt** feature makes it easy for you to quickly create and format many types of diagrams, including pyramid, target, cycle, and radial diagrams, as well as lists and organization charts. To insert a SmartArt graphic in a document, click the SmartArt button in the Illustrations group on the Insert tab to open the Choose a SmartArt Graphic dialog box. In this dialog box, select a category of diagrams in the left pane, select a specific diagram layout and design in the middle pane, preview the selected diagram layout in the right pane, and then click OK. The SmartArt object appears in the document with placeholder text, and the SmartArt Tools Design and Format tabs are enabled. These tabs contain commands and styles for customizing and formatting the SmartArt graphic and for sizing and positioning the graphic in the document.

Illustrating Documents with Graphics   Word 143

Finalizing Page Layout

UNIT F
Word 2007

When you finish creating the illustrations for a document, it is time to fine-tune the position and formatting of the text and graphics on each page. One way to vary the layout of a page that includes many graphics is to format some of the graphic elements in a text box. You format the Mexico weather information in a text box and adjust the size and position of the other graphic objects so that the text flows smoothly between the columns. Finally, you add a small text box that includes the QST address.

STEPS

1. Move the pointer to the top of page 2, double-click with the pointer, scroll up, move the pointer to the left margin, then drag the pointer to select the heading When is the best time..., the paragraph under it, and the chart object

2. Click the Insert tab, click the Text Box button, click Draw Text Box, click the View tab, click the One Page button in the Zoom group, double-click the top of the page with the pointer, then scroll as needed so the text box is visible on your screen

   The heading, body text, and chart object are moved into a text box.

3. Right-click the chart object, click the Center button on the Mini toolbar, double-click the text box frame, type 4.1 in the Shape Height text box in the Size group, type 4.65 in the Shape Width text box, then press [Enter]

   > **TROUBLE**
   > Don't be concerned if your text box jumps to another location.

   The chart object is centered in the text box and the text box is resized.

4. Scroll to display all of page 2, then with the text box selected, click the Position button in the Arrange group, click Position in Bottom Left..., click the More button in the Text Box Styles group, then click Horizontal Gradient – Accent 5

   The text box is moved to the lower-left corner of page 2, the text wraps around it, and a style is applied.

5. Click the View tab, click the Gridlines check box in the Show/Hide group, click the Page Width button in the Zoom group, then scroll down to view the bottom of the page

   Non-printing **drawing gridlines** appear within the document margins in Print Layout view. You use drawing gridlines to help you size, align, and position objects.

   > **QUICK TIP**
   > You can confirm or modify the size of the selected object by checking the height and width measurements in the Size group on the Drawing Tools Format tab.

6. Double-click the pyramid drawing to select it, drag the object down using the pointer onto a blank area of the drawing grid, press [Shift], then with the pointer, drag the lower-left sizing handle up and to the right until the object is about 1" square

   Use the ruler and the gridlines to help judge the size of the object as you drag.

7. Drag the object to position it as shown in Figure F-19

   You can nudge the drawing with the arrow keys if necessary to position it more precisely on the grid.

   > **QUICK TIP**
   > To align two or more objects to each other, select the objects, click the Align button in the Arrange group, then select an option.

8. Click the Text Box button in the Insert Shapes group, click under the pyramid with the pointer, resize the new text box similar to Figure F-19, click the More button in the Text Box Styles group, then click Horizontal Gradient – Accent 2

   Clicking with the pointer inserts a 1" square text box. After resizing the text box, it should be approximately .9" tall and 2.1" wide and aligned with the column and the bottom margin.

   > **TROUBLE**
   > Reduce the font size of the text in the text box if all the text doesn't fit.

9. Click inside the text box, right-click, then using the Mini toolbar, click the Style list arrow, click No Spacing, click the Center button, click the Bold button, and then type the text shown in Figure F-19 in the text box

   Figure F-19 shows the pyramid drawing reduced and repositioned and the new text box.

10. Click the View tab, click the Gridlines check box, click the Two Pages button, save your changes, print the file, then close the file and exit Word

    The completed document is shown in Figure F-20.

Illustrating Documents with Graphics

FIGURE F-19: Repositioned object and new text box

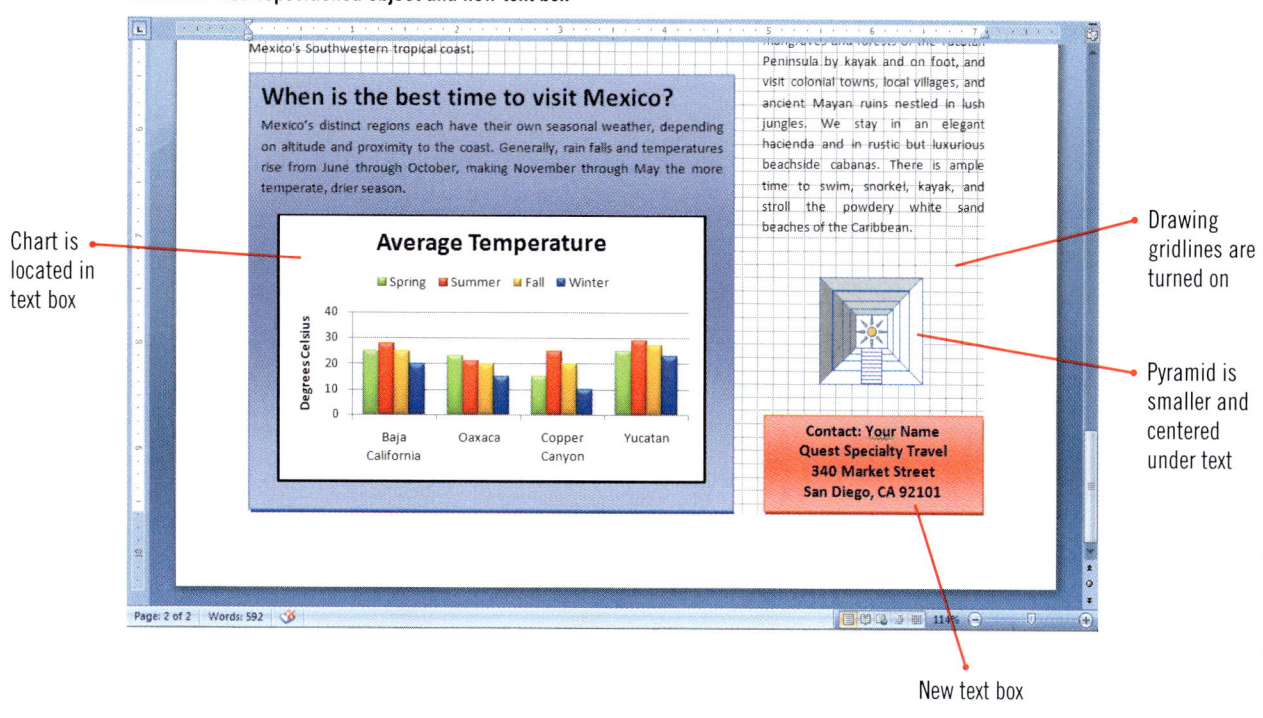

- Chart is located in text box
- Drawing gridlines are turned on
- Pyramid is smaller and centered under text
- New text box

FIGURE F-20: Completed flyer

Illustrating Documents with Graphics

Word 145

Practice

▼ CONCEPTS REVIEW

If you have a SAM user profile, you may have access to hands-on instruction, practice, and assessment of the skills covered in this unit. Log in to your SAM account (http://sam2007.course.com/) to launch any assigned training activities or exams that relate to the skills covered in this unit.

Label the elements shown in Figure F-21.

FIGURE F-21

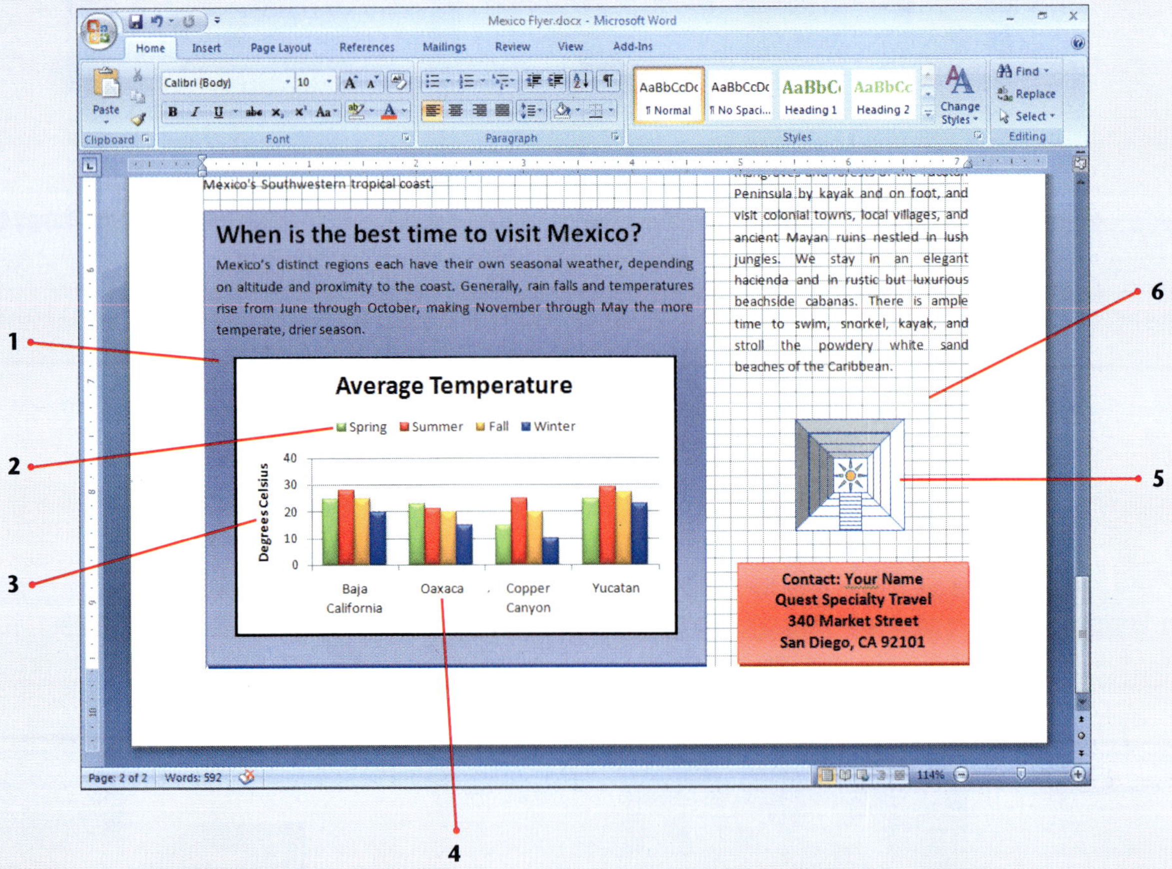

Match each term with the statement that best describes it.

7. Brightness
8. WordArt
9. Drawing gridlines
10. Drawing canvas
11. Floating graphic
12. Text box
13. Chart
14. Contrast

a. Nonprinting lines that are used to align, size, and position objects
b. A graphic to which a text wrapping style has been applied
c. The relative lightness of a picture
d. A graphic object that is a container for text and graphics
e. A workspace for creating graphics
f. A visual representation of numerical data
g. A graphic object composed of specially formatted text
h. The difference between the darkest and lightest areas in a picture

Word 146   Illustrating Documents with Graphics

Select the best answer from the list of choices.

15. Which button is used to change an inline graphic to a floating graphic?
    a. Position
    b. Bring to Front
    c. Send to Back
    d. Change Picture
16. Which button is used to change a photograph to sepia tone?
    a. Brightness
    b. Contrast
    c. Recolor
    d. Picture Effects
17. What do you drag to change a drawing object's shape, but not its size or dimensions?
    a. Rotate handle
    b. Cropping handle
    c. Sizing handle
    d. Adjustment handle
18. Which method do you use to nudge a picture?
    a. Select the picture, then press an arrow key.
    b. Select the picture, then drag a corner sizing handle.
    c. Select the picture, then drag it to a new location.
    d. Select the picture, then drag a top, bottom, or side sizing handle.
19. Which is not an example of a Fill Effect?
    a. Texture
    b. Pattern
    c. Gradient
    d. Glow
20. What style of text wrapping is applied to a shape by default?
    a. Square
    b. In line with text
    c. In front of text
    d. Tight

▼ SKILLS REVIEW

1. **Insert a graphic.**
   a. Start Word, open the file WD F-2.docx from the drive and folder where you store your Data Files, then save it as **Stone Barn CSA Flyer**.
   b. Display formatting marks, scroll down, read the document to get a feel for its contents and formatting, then press [Ctrl][Home].
   c. Select the vegetables photo on page 1, apply square text wrapping, then apply the picture style Simple Frame, Black to the photo.
   d. Use the Format Painter to copy the format settings from the vegetables photo to the photo of the boy, then apply square text wrapping to the photo of the boy.
   e. Scroll down, place the insertion point at the top of page 2, insert the file Stone Barn.jpg from the drive and folder where you store your Data Files, then save your changes.
2. **Size and scale a graphic.**
   a. With the Stone Barn photo still selected, click the Crop button in the Size group.
   b. Drag the bottom-middle cropping handle up approximately 1", drag the top-middle cropping handle down approximately .5", verify that the photo is approximately 2.8" tall, adjust if necessary using the cropping handles, then click the Crop button again.
   c. Deselect the photo, then scroll to page 1.
   d. Resize the vegetable photo proportionally so that it is about 2.7" high and 1.8" wide.
   e. Resize the photo of the boy proportionally so that it is about 1.7" high and 1.1" wide.
   f. Scroll to page 2, then resize the photo of the scale proportionally to be precisely 2.7" high.
   g. Press [Ctrl][Home], then save your changes.
3. **Position a graphic.**
   a. Drag the vegetable photo up so its top is aligned with the first line of body text and its right side is aligned with the right margin.
   b. Change the zoom level to Whole Page, then use the Position command to align the photo of the boy with the middle of the left margin.

Illustrating Documents with Graphics

▼ SKILLS REVIEW (CONTINUED)

    c. Scroll to page 2, use the Position command to align the scale photo with the bottom and right margins, then save your changes.

4. **Create a text box.**
   a. Change the zoom level to Page Width, then scroll to the top of page 1.
   b. Add a drop cap using the default settings for the Dropped option to the first body paragraph, then change the font color of the drop cap to Dark Green, Accent 4.
   c. Select the heading What does Stone Barn Community Farm do?, the paragraph under it, and the two paragraph marks above the page break, then insert a text box.
   d. Delete the paragraph mark after 7 p.m. in the last line of body text on page 1.
   e. Apply the text box style Horizontal Gradient – Accent 4 to the text box, use the Position command to align it with the bottom and right margins, then drag the anchor symbol to the How does it work? paragraph. (*Hint*: The anchor symbol is over the photo of the boy.)
   f. Scroll to page 2, then draw a text box over the bottom of the Stone Barn photo that spans the width of the photo and is approximately .4" high.
   g. Type **Welcome to Stone Barn Community Farm – A USDA Certified Organic Farm** in the text box, center the text, change the font to 12-point Arial Rounded MT Bold, then change the font color to Orange, Accent 1, Lighter 80%.
   h. Remove the fill from the text box, adjust the placement of the text box as necessary so the text is attractively placed over the bottom of the photo, then remove the border from the text box.
   i. Scroll down, select all the green and brown text, then insert a text box.
   j. Resize the text box to be approximately 2.7" tall and 5.4" wide, align it with the lower-left corner of the page, then remove the border from the text box.
   k. Turn off paragraph marks, then save your changes.

5. **Create WordArt.**
   a. Press [Ctrl][Home], triple-click to select Stone Barn Community Farm, insert a WordArt object, select any horizontal WordArt style, then click OK.
   b. Resize the WordArt object to be 7.1" wide and 1.1" tall, then center it between the margins.
   c. Open the WordArt Gallery, then change the style to WordArt style 11.
   d. Change the fill of the object to the texture Green marble.
   e. Change the border color to Dark Green, Accent 4, Lighter 40%.
   f. Change the shadow color to Orange, Accent 1, Darker 25%, then save your changes.

6. **Draw shapes.**
   a. Scroll down to the middle of page 2, select the three-line address, then draw a text box around it.
   b. Move the text box approximately ¾" to the right.
   c. Click the Shapes button, then click the Sun shape.
   d. In a blank area, draw a sun that is approximately .5" tall and wide.
   e. Fill the sun with Orange, Accent 1, apply the gradient style From Center in the Light Variations section, then change the border color to Dark Green, Accent 4.
   f. Move the sun left of the address text box if necessary, then remove the border from the address text box.
   g. Click the Shapes button in the Illustrations group on the Insert tab, then click Rounded rectangle.
   h. Draw a rounded rectangle around the sun and the address, then click the Send to Back button.
   i. Adjust the size of the rectangle to resemble an address label, then save your changes.

7. **Create a chart.**
   a. Scroll up, place the insertion point in the text box on page 1, press [▼] many times as necessary to move the insertion point to the last line in the text box.
   b. Insert a chart, select Bar chart, select Clustered Bar for the style, then click OK.

▼ SKILLS REVIEW (CONTINUED)

c. Type the information shown in Figure F-22, adjust the range to include just the columns and rows that include data, then close Excel.

d. Apply the chart style Style 22 to the chart.

e. Select the chart title text, type Harvest Sales, change the font of the title to 12-point Arial Rounded MT Bold, remove the bold formatting, then change the font color to Orange, Accent 1, Darker 25%.

f. Click the Legend button, then remove the legend from the chart.

g. Click the Axes button, point to Primary Horizontal Axis, then click More Primary Horizontal Axis Options to open the Format Axis dialog box.

h. Click Number in the Left pane, select Percentage in the Category list, change the number of decimal places to 0, then click Close.

i. Resize the chart object to be approximately 2" tall and 3.3" wide, center the chart object in the text box, then save your changes.

8. **Finalize page layout.**

a. Resize the text box that includes the chart to be approximately 3.2" tall and 4.4" wide.

b. Scroll up to page 1, turn on the drawing gridlines in the Show/Hide group on the View tab, then change the zoom level to One Page.

c. Select the vegetable photo, then use the arrow keys to nudge the photo so it extends approximately ¼" outside the right margin.

d. Select the photo of the boy, then use the arrow keys to nudge the photo so it extends approximately ¼" outside the left margin.

e. Select the text box, then use arrow keys to nudge the text box so it extends approximately ¼" outside the right and bottom margins.

f. Using the mouse, carefully enlarge the vegetable photo by dragging the lower-left sizing handle out approximately ¼".

g. Using the mouse, carefully enlarge the photo of the boy by dragging the lower-right sizing handle out approximately ¼".

h. Continue to resize and shift the position of the photographs until all the text fits on page 1 and the layout of page 1 of the flyer looks similar to the completed flyer shown in Figure F-23. Your flyer does not need to match exactly.

i. Type your name in the document footer, save your changes, print the document, close the file, then exit Word.

FIGURE F-22

	A	B	C
1		Series 1	
2	CSA	0.42	
3	U-Pick	0.09	
4	Farm Stand	0.2	
5	Farmers' Market	0.22	
6	Other	0.07	
7			

FIGURE F-23

▼ INDEPENDENT CHALLENGE 1

Your company just completed a major survey of its customer base, and your boss has asked you to prepare a summary of the results for your colleagues. You create a chart for the summary that shows the distribution of customers by age and gender.

a. Start Word, then save a blank document as **Age and Gender Chart** to the location where you store your Data Files.

b. Type **Prepared by** followed by your name at the top of the document, press [Enter] twice, then insert a clustered column chart object into the document.

c. Enter the data shown in Figure F-24 into the worksheet. To begin, delete the data in rows 4 and 5 of the worksheet, and then adjust the range to include 5 columns and 3 rows. When you are finished, minimize the Excel window and maximize the Word window.

d. Use the Switch Row/Column button in the Data group on the Design tab to switch the data so the age groups appear on the horizontal axis.

e. Apply a chart style to the chart, then add the title **Customers by Age and Gender** above the chart.

f. Move the legend to the left side of the chart, then add the horizontal axis title **Age Range**.

g. Click the Axes button, point to Primary Vertical Axis, then click More Primary Vertical Axis Options to open the Format Axis dialog box. Click Number in the Left pane, select Percentage in the Category list, change the number of decimal places to **0**, then click Close.

h. Use the Change Chart Type button in the Type group on the Design tab to change to a different type of column chart, taking care to choose an appropriate type for the data, then format the chart with styles, fills, outlines, and other effects so it is attractive and readable.

i. Save your changes, print the chart, close the file, then exit Word.

FIGURE F-24

	18-34	35-44	45-54	55+
Male	.11	.19	.09	.06
Female	.14	.22	.1	.09

▼ INDEPENDENT CHALLENGE 2

You design ads for bestskivacations.com, a company that specializes in custom ski vacation packages. Your next assignment is to design a full-page ad for a travel magazine. Your ad needs to contain three photographs of ski vacation scenes, such as the photos shown in Figure F-25, the text "Your ski vacation begins here and now," and the Web address "www.bestskivacations.com." If you are performing the ACE steps, your ad will also include a company logo.

a. Start Word, then save a blank document as **Ski Ad** to the drive and folder where your Data Files are located.

b. Change all four page margins to .7".

c. Using keywords such as ski, snowboard, snow, and mountain, find and insert at least three appropriate clip art photographs into the document.

d. Using pencil and paper, sketch the layout for your ad.

e. Change the photos to floating graphics, then format them. You can crop, resize, move, and combine them with other design elements, or enhance them with styles, shapes, borders, and effects.

f. Using text boxes or WordArt, add the text **Your ski vacation begins here and now** and the Web address **www.bestskivacations.com** to the ad.

FIGURE F-25

Advanced Challenge Exercise

- Using shapes and a text box, create a logo that includes a graphic and the company name bestskivacations.com.
- Using the Fill Effects dialog box, fill the shapes with color, gradients, patterns, or textures.
- Group the objects and resize the grouped object to suit your needs, then position the logo in the ad.

g. Adjust the layout, design, and colors in the ad as necessary. When you are satisfied with your ad, type your name in the document header, save your changes, print a copy, close the document, then exit Word.

▼ INDEPENDENT CHALLENGE 3

You are a graphic designer. The public library has hired you to design a bookmark for Literacy Week. Their only request is that the bookmark includes the words Literacy Week. You'll create three different bookmarks for the library.

a. Start Word, then save a blank document as **Literacy Bookmarks** to the location where you store your Data Files.
b. Change all four page margins to .7", change the page orientation to landscape, and change the zoom level to Whole Page.
c. Draw three rectangles. Resize the rectangles to be 6.5" tall x 2.5" wide and move them so they do not overlap. Each rectangle will become a bookmark.
d. In the first rectangle, design a bookmark using shapes.
e. In the second rectangle, design a bookmark using WordArt.
f. In the third rectangle, design a bookmark using clip art.
g. Format the bookmarks with fills, colors, lines, shapes, shadows, and other effects. Be sure to add the words **Literacy Week** to each bookmark.

Advanced Challenge Exercise

- Fill one bookmark with a gradient, one with a texture, and one with a pattern. You might need to revise some aspects of the bookmarks you created in the previous steps.
- To one bookmark, add a photograph and change the shape of the photograph.
- To one bookmark, add curved, scribble, or freeform lines.

h. Type your name in the document header, save your changes, print, close the document, then exit Word.

▼ REAL LIFE INDEPENDENT CHALLENGE

One way to find graphic images to use in your documents is to download them from the Web. Many Web sites feature images that are in the public domain, which means they have no copyright restrictions and permission is not required to use the images. You are free to download these images and use them in your documents, although you must acknowledge the artist or identify the source. Other Web sites include images that are copyrighted and require written permission, and often payment, to use. Before downloading and using graphics from the Web, it's important to research and establish their copyright status and permission requirements. In this exercise you download photographs from the Web and research their copyright restrictions.

a. Start Word, then save a blank document as **Copyright Photos** to the drive and folder where you store your Data Files.
b. Type your name at the top of the page, press [Enter], then create a table with four rows and three columns. Type the following column headings in the header row: **Photo**, **URL**, **Copyright Restrictions**. You will fill this table with the photos you find on the Web and the copyright restrictions for those photos.
c. Use your favorite search engine to search the Web for photographs that you might use for your work or a personal project. Use the keywords **free photo archives** or **free public domain photos**. You can also add a keyword that describes the subject of the photos you want to find.
d. Find at least three Web sites that contain photos you could use in a document. Save a photo from each Web site to your computer, and note the URL and copyright restrictions. To save an image from a Web page, right-click the image, then click the appropriate command on the shortcut menu.
e. Insert the photos you saved from the Web in the Photo column of the table. Resize the photos proportionally so that they are no more than 1.5" tall or 1.5" wide. Wrap text around the photos and center them in the table cells.
f. Enter the URL and the copyright restrictions for the photos in the table. In the Copyright Restrictions column, indicate if the photo is copyrighted or in the public domain, and note the requirements for using that photo in a document.
g. Adjust the formatting of the table so it is easy to read, save your changes, print a copy, close the file, then exit Word.

VISUAL WORKSHOP

Using the file WD F-3.docx (located where you store your Data Files), create the flyer shown in Figure F-26. The photograph is a clip art image found using the keyword "surfer". (*Hints*: To wrap text around the photo, draw a rectangle, layer it behind the photo, remove the border, and then apply Square text wrapping to the rectangle. The photograph uses In Front of Text text wrapping and is formatted with a reflection (Full Reflection, 4 pt offset) and a bevel (Circle).) Type your name in the footer, save the flyer as **Surf Safe**, then print a copy.

FIGURE F-26

Follow the rules
All surfers need to follow basic safety rules before heading into the waves. The key to safe surfing is caution and awareness.

Study the surf
Always study the surf before going in. Select a safe beach with waves under 1 meter, and pick waves that are suitable for your ability.

Use a safe surfboard
A safe surfboard is a surfboard that suits your ability. Beginners need a big, thick surfboard for stability.

Dress appropriately and wear sunscreen
Wear a wet suit that is appropriate for the water temperature or a rash vest to help protect against UV rays. Wear at least SPF 30 broad spectrum sunscreen. Zinc cream also prevents sunburn and guards against UV rays.

NEVER SURF ALONE

Recognize a rip current
A rip current is a volume of water moving out to sea: the bigger the surf, the stronger the rip. Indicators of rips include:
- Brown water from stirred up sand
- Foam on the surface of the water that trails past the break
- Waves breaking on both sides of a rip current
- A rippled appearance between calm water
- Debris floating out to sea

Learn how to escape rips
If you are dragged out by a rip, don't panic! Stay calm and examine the rip conditions before trying to escape the current. Poor swimmers should ride the rip out from the beach and then swim parallel to the shore for 30 or 40 meters. Once you have escaped the rip, swim toward the shore where the waves are breaking or probe with your feet to feel if a sand bar has formed near the edge of the rip. Strong swimmers should swim at a 45 degree angle across the rip.

surf safe

Working with Themes and Building Blocks

UNIT G
Word 2007

Files You Will Need:
WD G-1.docx
WD G-2.docx
WD G-3.docx
WD G-4.docx
WD G-5.docx
WD G-6.docx
WD G-7.docx
WD G-8.docx
WD G-9.docx
WD G-10.docx
QST Logo.jpg

The theme and building block features of Word 2007 streamline the process of designing a professional looking document. Document themes provide coordinated fonts, colors, and effects that you can apply to a document in one easy step, and building blocks offer dozens of preformatted document parts to insert and customize in a document. In this unit you learn how to work with themes, how to add and format sidebars and cover pages, and how to tailor preformatted content quickly and efficiently. You also learn how to create and save your own reusable building blocks for use in other documents. You are preparing a tour summary report for a new QST tour to Kenya. You create a customized theme for the report and simplify the process of designing the layout by using predesigned building blocks. Once the tour report is finished, you save the theme and several reusable pieces of customized content to use in other tour reports.

OBJECTIVES

Apply quick styles to text
Apply a theme
Customize a theme
Insert a sidebar
Insert quick parts
Add a cover page
Create building blocks
Insert building blocks

Applying Quick Styles to Text

Applying a style to text allows you to apply multiple format settings to text in one easy step. A **style** is a set of format settings, such as font, font size, font color, paragraph spacing, and alignment, that are named and stored together. Word includes many **Quick Style sets** — groups of related styles that share common fonts, colors, and formats, and are designed to be used together in a document — that you can use to give your documents a polished and cohesive look. Each Quick Style set includes styles for a title, subtitle, headings, body text, lists, quotes, and other text elements. You apply styles to the tour summary report to help organize the text attractively and make the report easy to read at a glance.

STEPS

1. **Start Word, open the file WD G-1.docx from the drive and folder where you store your Data Files, save it as Mount Kenya Tour, scroll the document to get a feel for its contents, then press [Ctrl][Home]**

   The four-page document includes text, photographs, and a chart.

2. **Select Mount Kenya, Safari, and Beach, click the More button in the Styles group, then move the pointer over the styles in the Quick Styles gallery**

   As you move the pointer over a style in the gallery, a preview of that style is applied to the selected text.

   > **QUICK TIP**
   > To change the active Quick Style set, click the Change Styles button in the Styles group, point to Style Set, then click a new set.

3. **Click Title**

   The Title style is applied to selected text.

4. **Select 15 days/14 nights, Nairobi to Mombasa, click Subtitle in the Styles group, click the Font Color list arrow in the Font group, then click Olive Green, Accent 3, Darker 25%**

   The Subtitle style is applied to the paragraph under the title, and then the font color is changed to olive green. You can modify the format of text to which a style has been applied without changing the style itself.

5. **Select Tour Highlights, click the More button in the Styles group, click Heading 1, then deselect the text**

   The Heading 1 style is applied to the Tour Highlights heading, as shown in Figure G-1.

   > **QUICK TIP**
   > To change the color scheme or fonts used in the active Quick Style set, click the Change Styles button, point to Colors or Fonts, and then select from the options.

6. **Scroll down, then apply the Heading 1 style to each red heading in the document**

   The Heading 1 style is applied to the Tour Highlights, Tour Summary, Planning Your Trip, and What to Bring headings in the report.

7. **Scroll to page 2, select Climate, then click Heading 2 in the Styles group**

   The Heading 2 style is applied to the Climate subheading. The style seems too similar to the Heading 1 style for your purposes.

8. **Select Climate if necessary, click the More button in the Styles group, click Heading 3, click the Font Color list arrow, click Red, Accent 2, then deselect the text**

   The Heading 3 style is applied to the Climate subheading, and the font color is changed to Red, Accent 2, as shown in Figure G-2.

9. **Scroll down, apply the Heading 3 style and the Red, Accent 2 font color to each purple subheading in the document, then save your changes**

   The Heading 3 style and the Red, Accent 2 font color are applied to the Climate, Visa and Vaccination Requirements, Luggage, Clothing and Footwear, and Equipment subheadings in the report.

Working with Themes and Building Blocks

FIGURE G-1: Styles applied to the report

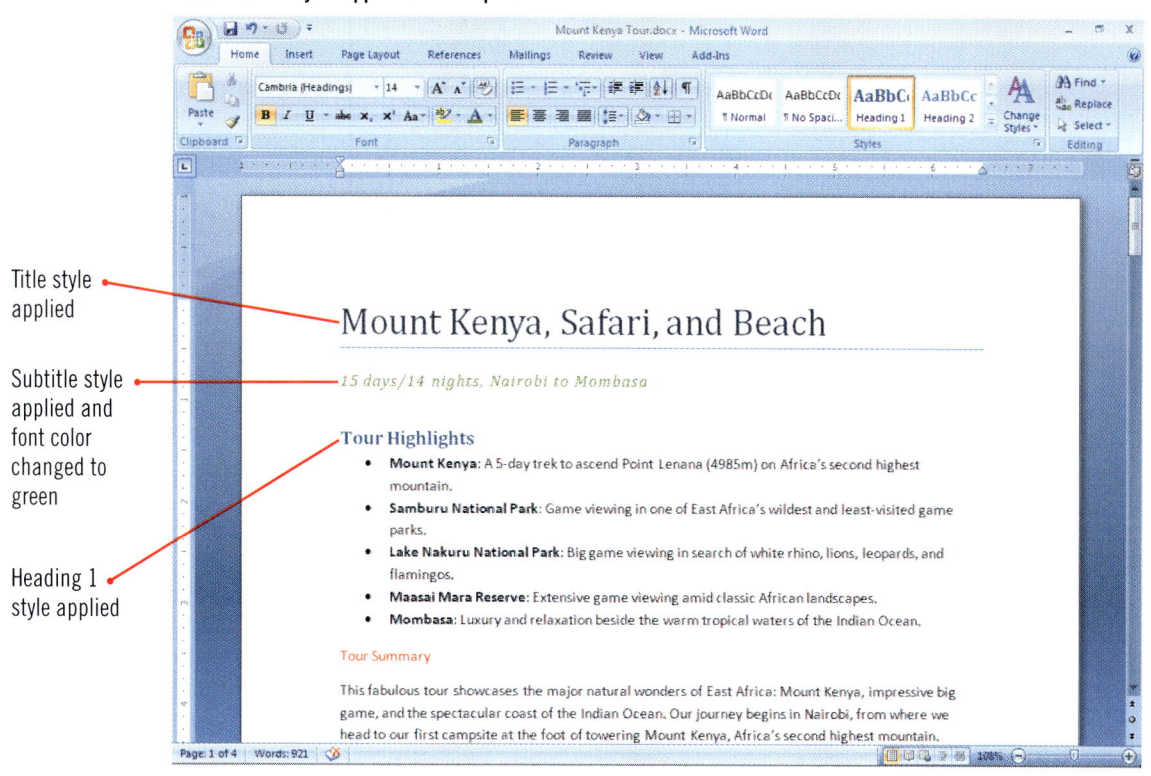

- Title style applied
- Subtitle style applied and font color changed to green
- Heading 1 style applied

FIGURE G-2: Heading 3 style

- Heading 3 style applied and font color changed to red

Saving a document as a Web page

Creating a Web page and posting it on the Internet or an intranet is a powerful way to share information with other people. You can design a Web page from scratch in Word, or you can use the Save As command to save an existing document in HTML format so it can be viewed with a browser. When you save an existing document as a Web page, Word converts the content and formatting of the Word file to HTML and displays the Web page in Web Layout view, which shows the Web page as it will appear in a browser. Any formatting that is not supported by Web browsers is either converted to similar supported formatting or removed from the Web page. For example, if you save a document that contains a floating graphic in HTML format, the graphic will be left- or right-aligned on the Web page. To be able to position text and graphics precisely on a document you plan to save as a Web page, it's best to create a table in the document, and then insert text and graphics in the table cells.

To save a document as a Web page, open the Save As dialog box, and then select a Web page format in the Save as type list box. You have the option of saving the document in Single File Web Page (.mht or .mhtml) format or in Web Page (.htm or .html) format. In a single file Web page, all the elements of the Web page, including the text and graphics, are saved together in a single MIME encapsulated aggregate HTML (MHTML) file, making it simple to publish your Web page or send it via e-mail. By contrast, if you choose to save a Web page as an .htm file, Word automatically creates a supporting folder in the same location as the .htm file. This folder has the same name as the .htm file plus the suffix _files, and it houses the supporting files associated with the Web page, such as graphics.

Working with Themes and Building Blocks

UNIT
G
Word 2007

Applying a Theme

Changing the theme applied to a document is another quick way to set the tone of a document and give it a polished and cohesive appearance, particularly if the text and any tables, charts, shapes, SmartArt objects, or text boxes in the document are formatted with styles. A **theme** is a set of unified design elements, including theme colors, theme fonts for body text and headings, and theme effects for graphics. By default, all documents that you create in Word are formatted with the Office theme, but you can easily apply a different built-in theme to a document. To apply a theme to a document, you use the Themes command in the Themes group on the Page Layout tab. You experiment with different built-in themes and then apply a theme that more closely suits the message you want to convey with the tour summary report.

STEPS

1. **Press [Ctrl][Home], click the Page Layout tab, click the Themes button in the Themes group, then point to Aspect**
   A gallery of built-in Themes opens. When you point to the Aspect theme in the gallery, a preview of the theme is applied to the document, as shown in Figure G-3.

2. **Move the pointer over each theme in the gallery**
   When you point to a theme in the gallery, a preview of the theme is applied to the document. Notice that the font colors and the fonts for the body text and headings to which a style has been applied change when you preview each theme.

3. **Click Opulent, then scroll down to view the theme applied to each page in the document**
   A complete set of new theme colors, fonts, styles, and effects is applied to the document. Notice that while the font of the body text changed, the bold formatting applied to the text under the Tour Highlights heading at the top of page 1 remains. Changing the document theme does not affect the formatting of text to which font formatting has been applied. Only document content that uses theme colors, text that is formatted with a style (including default body text), and table styles and graphic effects change when a new theme is applied.

QUICK TIP
To restore the document to the default theme for the template on which the document is based, click the Themes button, and then click Reset to Theme from Template.

4. **Click the View tab, click the Two Pages button in the Zoom group, then scroll down to see pages 3 and 4**
   The fill effect in the chart at the bottom of the last page is changed to a fill effect from the Opulent theme, as shown in Figure G-4.

5. **Click the Page Layout tab, click the Themes button, then point to each built-in theme in the gallery**
   Notice how each theme affects the formatting of the chart, and, in some cases, the pagination of the document. It's important to choose a theme that not only mirrors the tone, content, and purpose of your document, but also meets your goal for document length.

6. **Click Median**
   The Median theme is applied to the document.

7. **Click the View tab, click the Page Width button in the Zoom group, press [Ctrl][Home], then save your changes**

Working with Themes and Building Blocks

FIGURE G-3: Aspect theme previewed in document

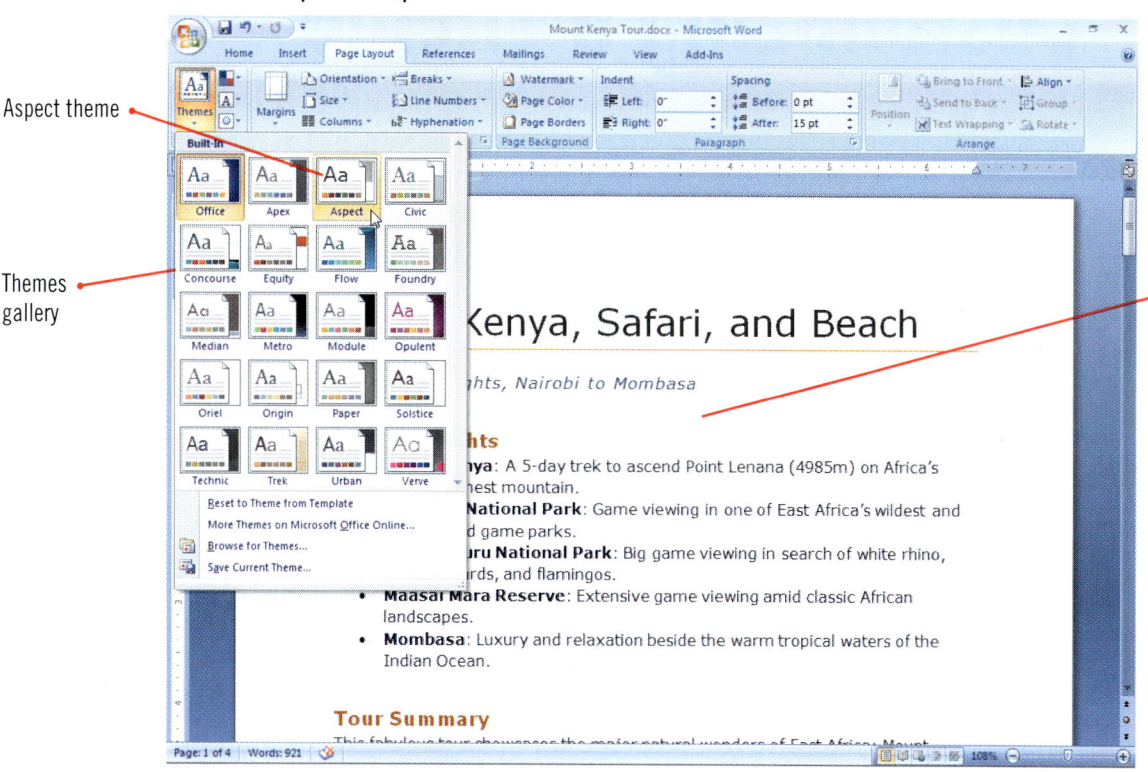

Aspect theme

Themes gallery

Preview of Aspect theme applied to document

FIGURE G-4: Opulent theme applied to document

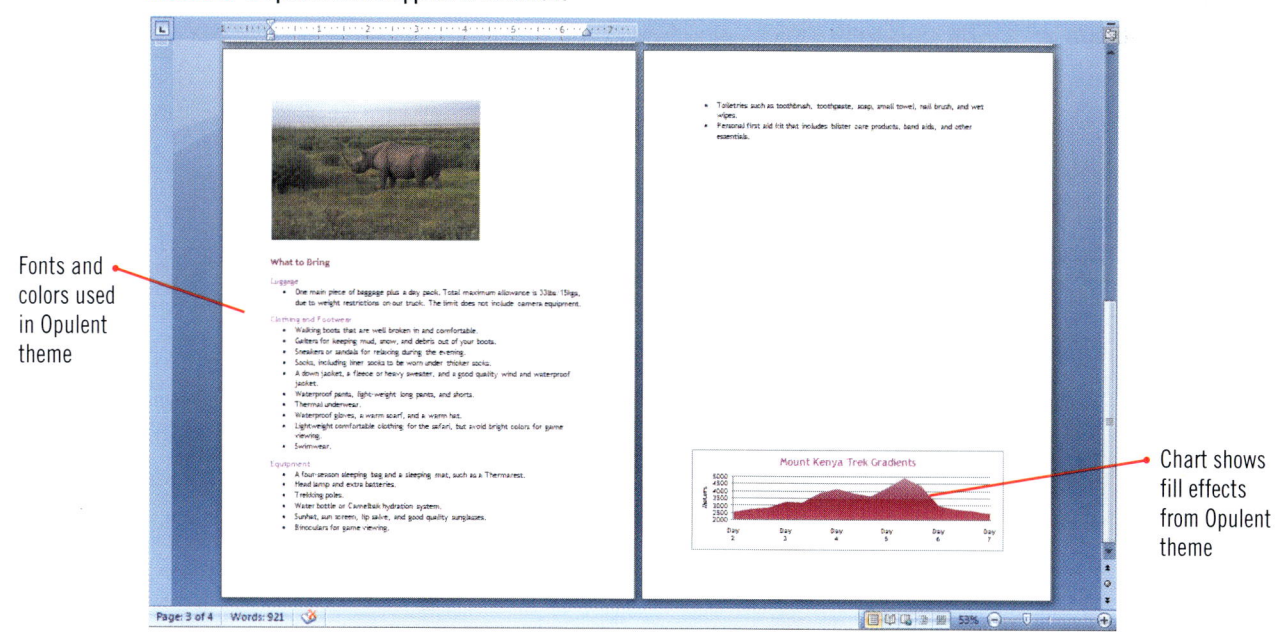

Fonts and colors used in Opulent theme

Chart shows fill effects from Opulent theme

Changing the default theme

By default, all new documents created in Word are formatted with the Office theme, but you can change your settings to use a different theme as the default. To change the default theme to a different built-in or custom theme, press [Ctrl][N] to open a new blank document, click the Themes button in the Themes group on the Page Layout tab, and then click the theme you want to use as the default. If you want to customize the theme before saving it as the new default, use the Theme Colors, Theme Fonts, and Theme Effects buttons in the Themes group to customize the settings for theme colors, fonts, and effects. Alternatively, click the Change Styles button in the Styles group on the Home tab, and then use the Style Set, Colors, and Fonts options to select a new style set, new colors, or new fonts to use in the new default theme. When you are satisfied with the settings for the new default theme, click the Change Styles button again, and then click Set as Default. The Themes gallery will be updated to reflect your changes.

Working with Themes and Building Blocks

Customizing a Theme

UNIT G
Word 2007

When one of the built-in Word themes is not just right for your document, you can customize the theme by changing the theme colors, selecting new theme fonts for headings and body text, and changing the theme effects. You can then save the customized theme as a new theme that you can apply to other documents. You tweak the theme colors, fonts, and effects in the active theme to create a new theme that uses the colors and textures of Kenya and employs fonts that are attractive and easy to read. You then save the settings as a new theme so you can apply the theme to all documents related to Kenya tours.

STEPS

1. **Click the Page Layout tab, then click the Theme Colors button in the Themes group**
   The gallery of theme colors opens. You can select from a palette of built-in theme colors or choose to customize the colors in the active palette. You want a palette that picks up the colors of the Kenyan landscape used in the photographs in the tour report.

2. **Click Oriel, click the Theme Colors button, then click Create New Theme Colors**
   The Oriel colors are applied to the document and the Create New Theme Colors dialog box opens, as shown in Figure G-5. You use this dialog box to change the colors in the active palette and to save the set of colors you create with a new name.

3. **Click the Accent 3 list arrow, click More Colors, click the Custom tab in the Colors dialog box, type 155 in the Red text box, type 187 in the Green text box, type 89 in the Blue text box, then click OK**
   The Accent 3 color changes from dark red to olive green.

> **QUICK TIP**
> To remove a custom theme from the gallery, right-click the theme, then click Delete.

4. **Type Kenya in the Name text box in the dialog box, click Save, then click**
   The new color scheme is saved with the name Kenya, the red subtitle in the document changes to green, and the Kenya color scheme appears in the Custom section in the Theme Colors gallery. The Kenya colors can now be applied to any document.

5. **Click the document to close the Theme Colors gallery if necessary, click the Theme Fonts button in the Themes group, scroll down the gallery of theme fonts, point to several options to preview the fonts applied to the document, then click Equity**
   The heading and body text fonts from the Equity theme are applied to the document.

6. **Click the Theme Fonts button, then click Create New Theme Fonts**
   The Create New Theme Fonts dialog box opens, as shown in Figure G-6. You use this dialog box to select different fonts for headings and body text, and to save the font combination as a new theme font set.

7. **Click the Heading font list arrow, scroll down, click Trebuchet MS, type Tour Reports in the Name text box in the dialog box, then click Save**
   The font of the headings in the report changes to Trebuchet MS, and the Tour Reports theme font set is added to the Custom section of the Theme Fonts gallery.

> **TROUBLE**
> Scroll down if necessary to see the chart.

8. **Press [Ctrl][End], click the Theme Effects button in the Themes group, point to each effect in the gallery to see it previewed in the chart, then click Paper**
   The effects from the Paper theme are applied to the document.

9. **Click the Themes button, click Save Current Theme, type Kenya Tour Report in the File name text box in the Save Current Theme dialog box, then click Save**
   The Kenya theme colors, Tour Reports theme fonts, and theme effects from the Paper theme are saved together as a new theme called Kenya Tour Report in the default location for document themes.

10. **Save your changes, then click the Themes button**
    The new theme appears in the Custom section of the Themes gallery, as shown in Figure G-7.

Working with Themes and Building Blocks

FIGURE G-5: Create New Theme Colors dialog box

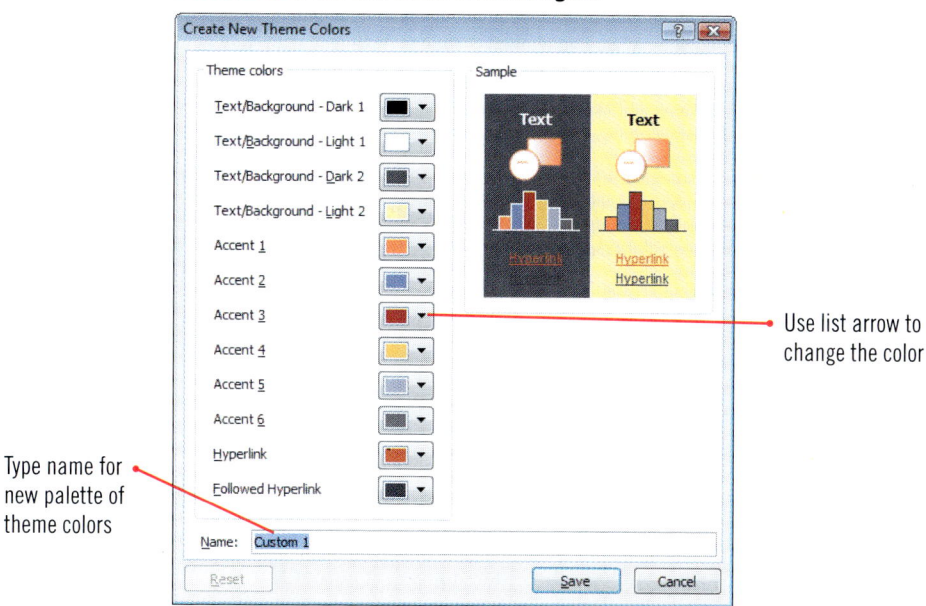

Type name for new palette of theme colors

Use list arrow to change the color

FIGURE G-6: Create New Theme Fonts dialog box

Select font for headings

Select font for body text

Type name for new set of theme fonts

Preview fonts

FIGURE G-7: Custom theme in the Themes gallery

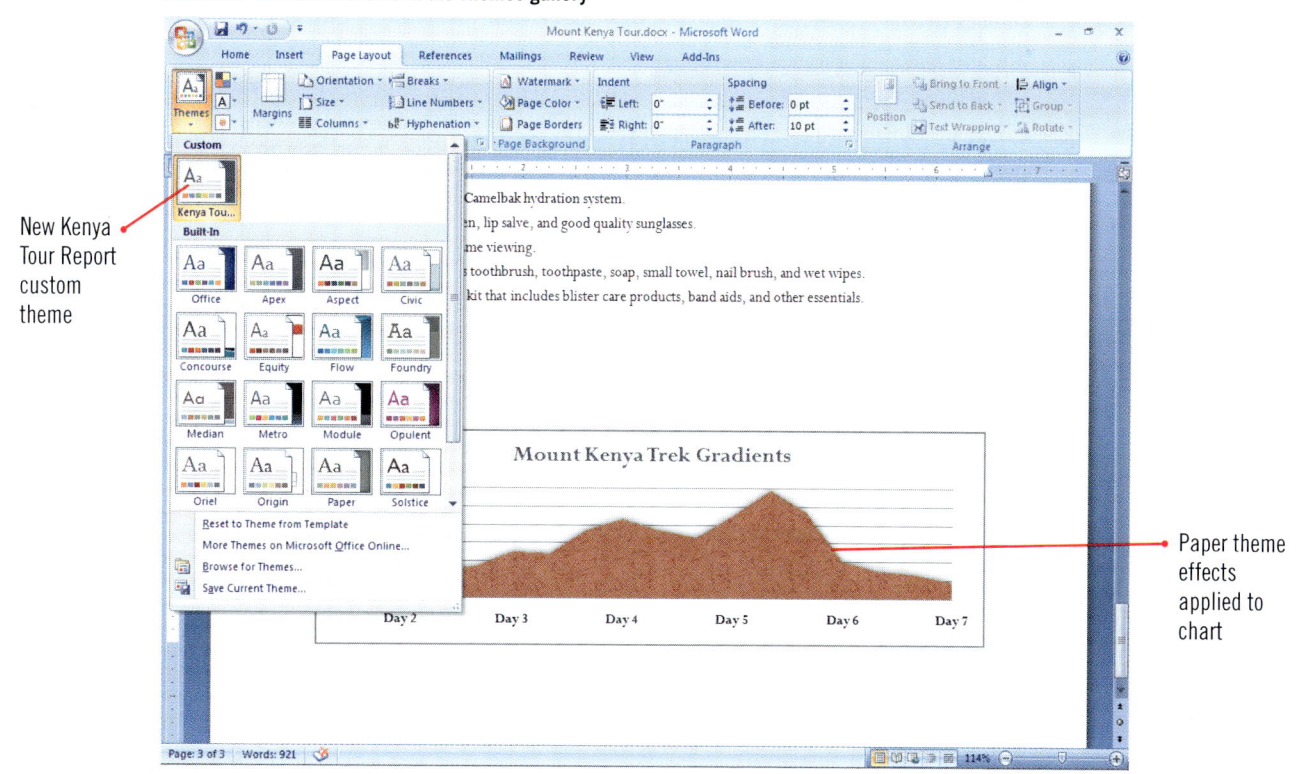

New Kenya Tour Report custom theme

Paper theme effects applied to chart

Working with Themes and Building Blocks

Inserting a Sidebar

UNIT G — **Word 2007**

Another way to design a document quickly and professionally is to use preformatted building blocks. **Building blocks** are the reusable pieces of formatted content or document parts that are stored in galleries, including headers and footers, cover pages, and text boxes. Sidebars and pull quotes are two types of text box building blocks that are frequently used to jazz up the appearance of a text-heavy page and to highlight information. A **sidebar** is a text box that is positioned adjacent to the body of a document and contains auxiliary information. A **pull quote** is a text box that contains a quote or excerpt from an article, formatted in a larger font size and placed on the same page. You use the Text Box command on the Insert tab to insert sidebars and pull quotes. You create a sidebar to display the Tour Highlights information on page 1 and a second sidebar to display information for travelers to Kenya on page 2.

STEPS

1. **Click the document to close the Themes gallery if necessary, press [Ctrl][Home], click the Insert tab, then click the Text Box button in the Text group**
   The Text Box gallery opens. It includes built-in styles for sidebars and pull quotes.

   > **QUICK TIP**
   > The sidebar is anchored to the paragraph where the insertion point is located.

2. **Scroll down the gallery, then click the Tiles Sidebar**
   The Tiles sidebar is inserted at the top of the page. It is composed of a green text box with placeholder text, and a grey shadow. You can type directly in the text box to replace the placeholder text or you can paste text from the document into the text box.

3. **Select Tour Highlights and the bulleted list beneath it, press [Ctrl][X] to cut the text, click the text box, press [Ctrl][V] to paste the text, then press [Backspace]**
   The text is cut from the body of the document and pasted in the sidebar.

4. **Select Tour Highlights, click the Font Color list arrow on the Mini toolbar, click Blue, Accent 2, Darker 25%, select the bulleted list, click the Font Color list arrow, then click White, Background 1**
   The font colors of the text in the sidebar change to blue and white.

   > **QUICK TIP**
   > You can change the format of a sidebar by applying a text box style, adding a shadow, or using the other commands on the Text Box Tools Format tab.

5. **Click the Text Box Tools Format tab, click the Shadow Effects button in the Shadow Effects group, point to Shadow Color, click Blue, Accent 2, Lighter 40%, then deselect the sidebar**
   The shadow color changes to light blue. The completed sidebar is shown in Figure G-8.

   > **QUICK TIP**
   > Sidebars are inserted on the left side of an even-numbered page and on the right side of an odd-numbered page.

6. **Scroll to page 2, place the insertion point in Planning Your Trip, click the View tab, click the One Page button in the Zoom group, click the Insert tab, click the Text Box button, then click Annual Sidebar**
   The Annual Sidebar, an orange text box, is inserted on the left side of the page and anchored to the Planning Your Trip heading paragraph. Rather than type text in the sidebar, you will insert text from a file.

7. **Click the Insert tab, click the Object list arrow in the Text group, then click Text from File**
   The Insert File dialog box opens. You use this dialog box to select the file you want to insert in the sidebar.

8. **Navigate to the drive and folder where you store your Data Files, click the file WD G-2.docx, click Insert, deselect the sidebar, then save your changes**
   The contents of the file WD G-2.docx is inserted in the sidebar, as shown in Figure G-9. When you insert a text file into a text box, it's important to verify that all the text from the file fits in the text box. If not, adjust the size of the text box accordingly.

FIGURE G-8: Tiles sidebar

Blue shadow color

Tiles sidebar

Text pasted in text box and formatted

FIGURE G-9: Annual sidebar

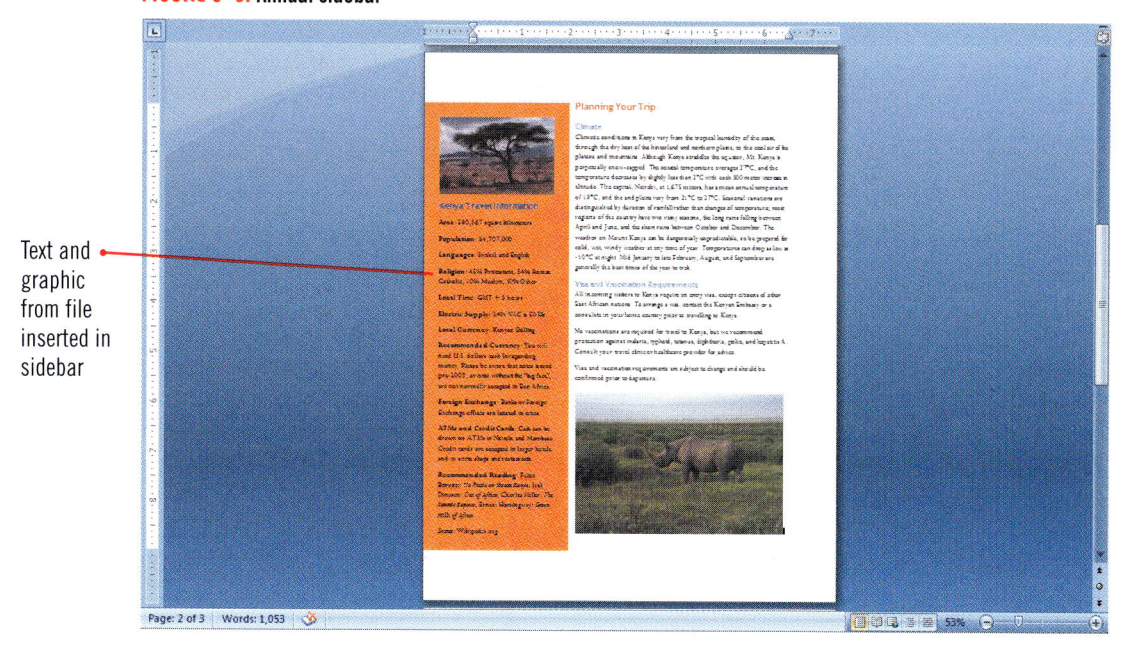

Text and graphic from file inserted in sidebar

Working with Themes and Building Blocks

Word 161

Inserting Quick Parts

UNIT G
Word 2007

The Word Quick Parts feature makes it easy to insert reusable pieces of content into a document. Quick Parts items include fields, such as for the date or a page number, document properties, such as the document title or author, and building blocks. You insert a Quick Part into a document using the Quick Parts command on the Insert tab or on the Header & Footer Tools Design tab. You finalize the design of the three pages by adding a header and a footer building block to the document. You then customize the footer by adding document properties to it using the Quick Parts command.

STEPS

1. **Click the View tab, click the Page Width button in the Zoom group, click the Insert tab, then click the Header button in the Header & Footer group**
   The Header gallery opens and displays the list of predesigned headers.

2. **Scroll down the Header gallery, then click Exposure**
   The Exposure header is added to the document and the Header area opens. The Exposure header includes a property control for the Title document property as well as a content control for the date. A **property control** contains the document property information you entered in the Document Information Panel, or if you did not assign a document property, placeholder text. You can assign or update a document property by typing directly in a property control or by typing in the Document Information Panel.

   > **QUICK TIP**
   > When you update a document property in the Document Information Panel, the property controls of the same type in the document are updated with the information you changed.

3. **Click Type the document title to select the Title property control, type Mount Kenya, Safari, and Beach, click Pick the date, click the Date list arrow, then click Today**
   The title and the current date are added to the header. When you assign or update a document property by typing in a property control, all controls of the same type in the document are updated with the change, as well as the property field in the Document Information Panel.

4. **Click the Header button in the Header & Footer group, then click Annual**
   The header design changes to the Annual design, as shown in Figure G-10.

   > **QUICK TIP**
   > To turn the table gridlines on and off, click the Table Tools Layout tab, then click the View Gridlines button in the Table group.

5. **Click the Footer button in the Header & Footer group, scroll down the Footer gallery, then click Sideline**
   The Sideline footer includes a page number field. Notice that this footer is formatted as a table.

6. **Press [Tab] to move the insertion point to the next table cell, click the Quick Parts button in the Insert group, point to Document Property, click Company, then type Quest Specialty Travel**
   The Company property control is added to the footer and updated to become "Quest Specialty Travel".

7. **Press [→], press [Spacebar], click the Insert tab, click the Symbol list arrow in the Symbols group, click More Symbols, be sure the Font is set to (normal text), type 2022 in the Character code text box, click Insert twice, then click Close**
   Two bullet symbols are added to the footer, as shown in Figure G-11.

8. **Place the insertion point between the two bullet symbols, press [Spacebar], click the Quick Parts button in the Text group, point to Document Property, click Company Phone, type 1-800-555-TOUR, press [→], press [Spacebar], then press [End]**
   The Company Phone property control is added to the footer and updated.

9. **Press [Spacebar], click the Quick Parts button, point to Document Property, click Company Address, type www.questspecialtytravel.com, then press [→]**
   The Company Address property control is added to the footer and updated.

10. **Move the pointer over the footer, click the Table move handle to select the table, click the Bold button B on the Mini toolbar, close the Footer area, then save your changes**
    Bold is applied to the text in the footer. The customized footer is shown in Figure G-12.

Word 162   Working with Themes and Building Blocks

FIGURE G-10: Header formatted using the Annual header style

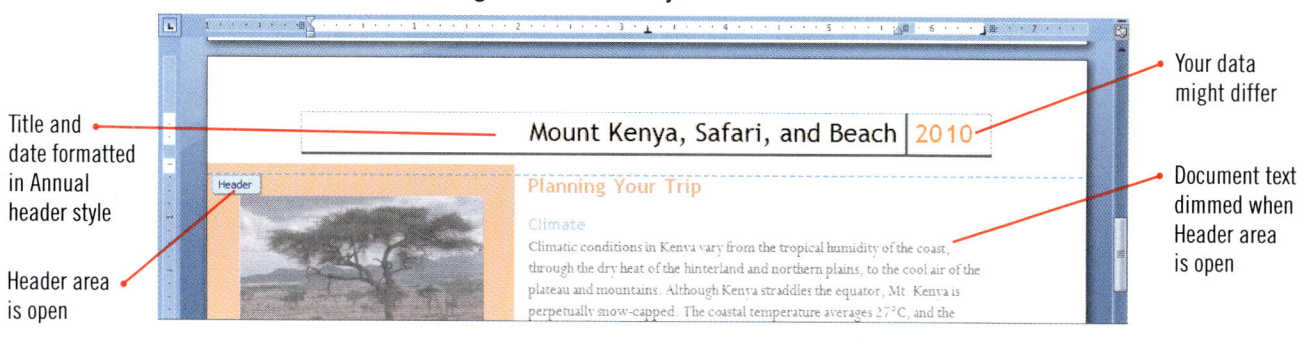

- Title and date formatted in Annual header style
- Header area is open
- Your data might differ
- Document text dimmed when Header area is open

FIGURE G-11: Bullet symbols in Sideline footer

- Table move handle in Footer area
- Company document property
- Bullet symbols

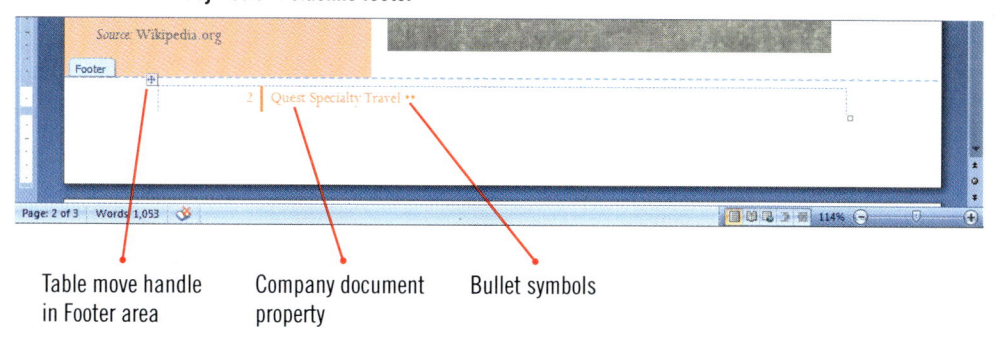

FIGURE G-12: Customized footer

- Company phone document property
- Company address document property

Working with Themes and Building Blocks

Adding a Cover Page

UNIT G
Word 2007

To quickly finalize a report with simplicity or flair, you can insert one of the many predesigned cover pages that come with Word. Cover page designs range from conservative and business-like to colorful and attention-grabbing. Each cover page design includes placeholder text and property controls that you can replace with your own information. You finalize the tour report by inserting an eye-catching cover page that mirrors the design of the report.

STEPS

QUICK TIP
Click the Blank Page button in the Pages group to insert a blank page at the location of the insertion point.

1. **Click the View tab, click the One Page button in the Zoom group, click the Insert tab, then click the Cover Page list arrow in the Pages group**

    The gallery of cover pages opens. Each page design includes placeholder text and property controls.

2. **Scroll down the gallery, then click Motion**

    The Motion cover page is added at the beginning of the document. Notice that the tour name was added automatically to the Title property control and the current year was added automatically to the Date content control.

QUICK TIP
To change the user name and initials, click the Office button, click Word Options, then type a new user name and initials in the User name and Initials text boxes in the Word Options dialog box.

3. **Drag the Zoom slider right to zoom in on the cover page, then scroll down to view the author, company name, and current date controls at the bottom of the page**

    The company name is entered in the Company property control, and today's date is entered in the date control.

4. **Click the Author property control (the first line of text)**

    The text in the Author property control is the default author name for all new documents created on your computer. This information is based on the user name entered in the Word Options dialog box.

5. **Select the text in the Author property control, type your name, click the View tab, then click the One Page button**

    Your name replaces the user name as the Author property for the document.

QUICK TIP
To change to a different cover page design, simply insert a different cover page.

6. **Select the photograph, press [Delete], click the Insert tab, click the Clip Art button in the Illustrations group, type safari in the Search for text box in the Clip Art task pane, click Go, click the lion photograph, then close the Clip Art task pane**

    A photograph of a lion is inserted in the cover page. You can choose a different photograph if the lion photo is not available to you.

7. **Click the Text Wrapping list arrow in the Arrange group on the Picture Tools Format tab, click In Front of Text, then drag the photograph down and to the right to position it under the title and flush with the right edge of the page, as shown in Figure G-13**

QUICK TIP
To remove a cover page from a document, click the Cover Page list arrow in the Pages group, then click Remove Current Cover Page.

8. **Press [Ctrl][Home], click the Insert tab, click the Picture button in the Illustrations group, navigate to the drive and folder where you store your Data Files, click the file QST Logo.jpg, then click Insert**

    The QST logo is added to the cover page.

9. **Click the Position button in the Arrange group, click Position in Bottom Left with Square Text Wrapping, deselect the logo, then save your changes**

    The logo is moved to the bottom left corner of the page.

10. **Print the document**

    The completed tour report is shown in Figure G-14.

Working with Themes and Building Blocks

FIGURE G-13: Cover page

Date, title, and company are automatically entered

Lion photo is flush with edge of page

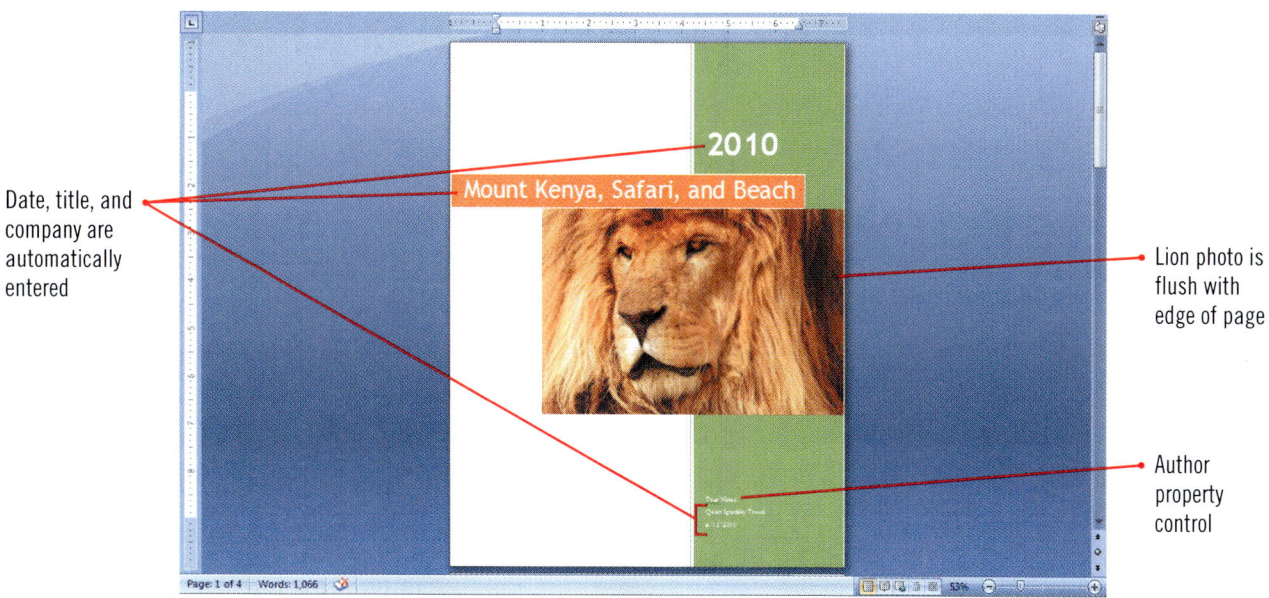

Author property control

FIGURE G-14: Completed tour report

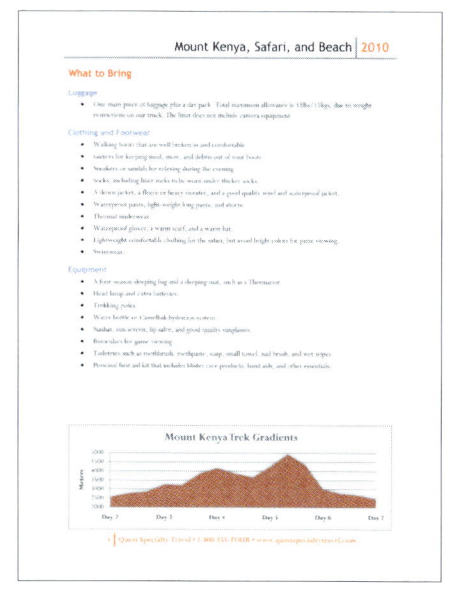

Working with Themes and Building Blocks

Word 165

Creating Building Blocks

UNIT G — Word 2007

When you design a piece of content that you want to use again in other documents, you can save it as a building block in one of the Word galleries. For example, you might want to save your company mission statement or a list of staff names so that you don't have to type and format the information each time you use it in a document. You save an item as a building block using the Quick Parts command. You save the QST logo, the Kenya Travel Information sidebar, the Climate heading and paragraph, and the footer as building blocks so that you can easily include them in other tour reports.

STEPS

1. **Click the logo at the bottom of page 1 to select it, click the Insert tab, click the Quick Parts button in the Text group, then click Save Selection to Quick Part Gallery**

   The Create New Building Block dialog box opens, as shown in Figure G-15. You use this dialog box to enter a unique name and a description for the item and to specify the gallery where you want it to appear. You want the logo to appear in the Quick Parts gallery.

2. **Type QST Logo in the Name text box, click the Description text box, type QST Logo in bottom left corner of tour report cover page, then click OK**

   The logo is added to the Quick Parts gallery.

   > **TROUBLE**
   > Sizing handles appear around the orange text box when the sidebar is selected.

3. **Scroll to page 3, select the orange sidebar, click the Quick Parts button, click Save Selection to Quick Part Gallery, type Kenya Travel Info Sidebar in the Name text box, click the Gallery list arrow, click Text Boxes, click the Category list arrow, click Create New Category, type Kenya, click OK, click the Description text box, type Generic info for travelers to Kenya, click OK, then deselect the text box**

   You add the sidebar to the Text Box gallery and create a new category called Kenya. It's a good idea to assign a descriptive category name to a building block item so that you can sort, organize, and find your building blocks easily.

4. **Click the Text Box button in the Text group, then scroll to the bottom of the Text Box gallery**

   The Kenya Travel Info Sidebar building block is displayed in the Text Box gallery in the Kenya category, as shown in Figure G-16.

   > **QUICK TIP**
   > A text building block can also be saved to the AutoText gallery.

5. **Click the document to close the gallery, select the Climate heading and paragraph on page 3, click the Quick Parts button, click Save Selection to Quick Part Gallery, type Kenya Climate Info in the Name text box, click the Category list arrow, click Create New Category, type Kenya, click OK, then click OK**

   The Climate heading and paragraph are saved in the Quick Parts gallery in the Kenya category.

   > **QUICK TIP**
   > To store paragraph formatting with a building block, make sure to select the final paragraph mark when you select the text.

6. **Click the Quick Parts button to verify that the item was added to the gallery, then point to the QST Logo item in the gallery**

   The gallery includes the QST Logo item in the General category and the Kenya Climate Info item in the Kenya category. When you point to the QST Logo item in the gallery, the name and description appear in a ScreenTip, as shown in Figure G-17.

7. **Click the document, scroll down, double-click the footer, click the Table move handle to select the table in the footer, click the Footer button in the Header & Footer group on the Header & Footer Tools Design tab, then click Save Selection to Footer Gallery**

   The Create New Building Block dialog box opens with Footers automatically selected as the gallery.

8. **Type Tour Report Footer in the Name text box, click OK, then save and close the document**

   The footer is added to the Footers gallery under the General category. In the next lesson you will insert the building blocks you created into a different tour report document.

FIGURE G-15: Create New Building Block dialog box

- Type name for item
- Specify gallery for item
- Select category for item

FIGURE G-16: Kenya Tour Info Sidebar in Text Box gallery

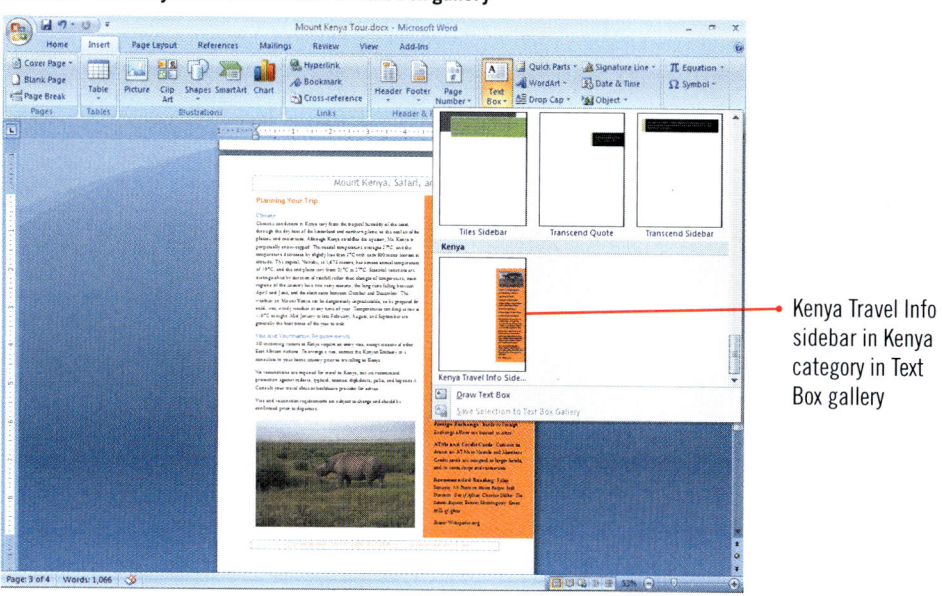

- Kenya Travel Info sidebar in Kenya category in Text Box gallery

FIGURE G-17: Items in Quick Parts gallery

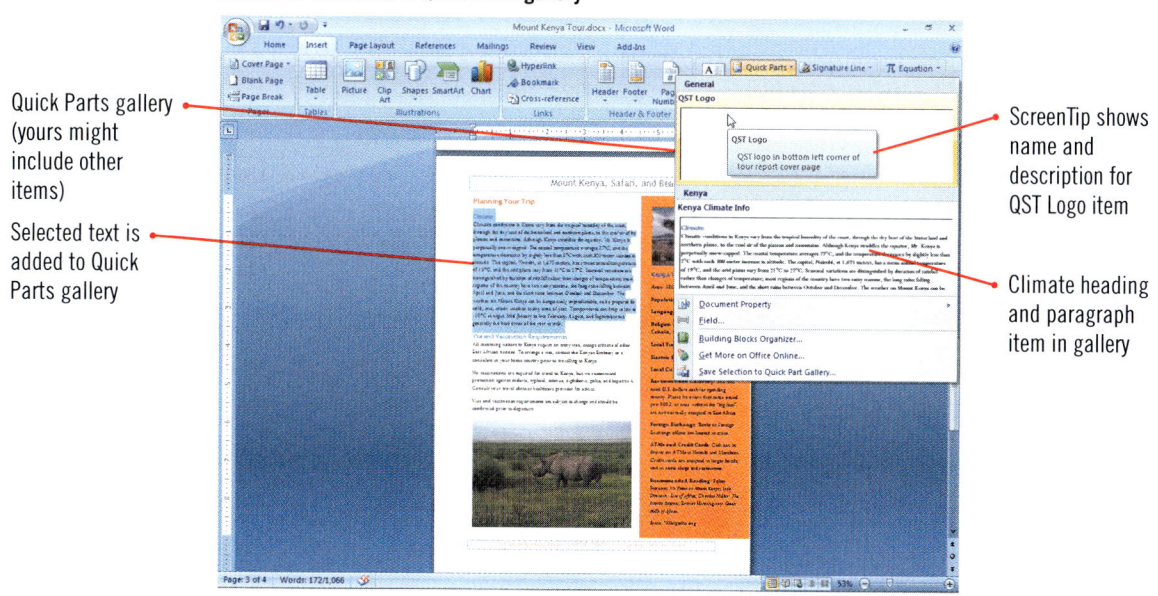

- Quick Parts gallery (yours might include other items)
- Selected text is added to Quick Parts gallery
- ScreenTip shows name and description for QST Logo item
- Climate heading and paragraph item in gallery

Renaming a building block and editing other properties

You can edit the properties of a building block at any time, including changing its name, gallery location, category, and description. To modify building block properties, simply right-click the item in a gallery, and then click Edit Properties. In the Modify Building Block dialog box that opens, edit the item's name or description, or assign it to a new gallery or category. When you are finished, click OK, and then click Yes in the warning box that opens. You can also modify the properties of a building block by selecting the item in the Building Blocks Organizer, and then clicking Edit Properties.

Working with Themes and Building Blocks

Inserting Building Blocks

UNIT G — Word 2007

Once you have created customized building blocks, it is easy to insert them in your documents. You can insert a building block directly from a gallery, or you can use the Building Blocks Organizer to search for, organize, and insert building blocks. You need to create a tour report for a different QST tour to Kenya. You open the tour report file, apply the Kenya theme, and then insert the building blocks you created so that all the Kenya tour reports have common content and a consistent look and feel.

STEPS

1. **Open the file WD G-3.docx** from the drive and folder where you store your Data Files, save it as **Kenya Family Safari**, scroll down, replace **Ron Dawson** with your name at the bottom of page 1, click the **View tab**, then click the **Two Pages button** in the Zoom group

   The Kenya Family Safari tour report includes a cover page, two pages of text formatted with styles, a sidebar, photographs, and a chart.

2. **Click the Page Layout tab**, click the **Themes button** in the Themes group, then click the **Kenya Tour Report theme** in the Custom section of the gallery

   The Kenya Tour Report theme you created is applied to the document.

   > **QUICK TIP**
   > Right-click an item in the Quick Parts gallery to open a menu of locations in which to insert the item.

3. **Press [Ctrl][Home]**, click the **Insert tab**, click the **Quick Parts button** in the Text group, then click the **QST Logo** item in the Quick Parts gallery

   The logo is added to the lower-left corner of the cover page.

   > **TROUBLE**
   > If the insertion point is located on the cover page, the footer will appear on the cover page only.

4. **Click anywhere on page 2**, click the **Footer button** in the Header & Footer group, scroll down the Footer gallery, click **Tour Report Footer** in the General section, zoom as needed to examine the footer in the document, then close headers and footers

   The custom footer you created is added to the Footer area on pages 2 and 3. The property information is automatically entered in the property controls in the footer because the property information was saved previously with the document.

   > **QUICK TIP**
   > To edit the content of a building block, insert the item in a document, edit the item, then save the selection to the same Quick Part gallery using the same name.

5. **Scroll to page 3**, click the **Practical Information heading**, click the **Insert tab**, click the **Quick Parts button** in the Text group, then click **Building Blocks Organizer**

   The Building Blocks Organizer opens as shown in Figure G-18. The Building Blocks Organizer includes a complete list of the built-in and customized building blocks from every gallery. You use the Building Blocks Organizer to sort, preview, insert, delete, and edit the properties of building blocks.

6. **Click the Category column heading** in the list of building blocks

   The building blocks are sorted and grouped by category.

   > **QUICK TIP**
   > To delete a building block, select it in the Building Blocks Organizer, then click Delete.

7. **Scroll down the list to locate the two items in the Kenya category**, click the **Kenya Travel Info Sidebar** item to select it, click **Insert**, click the **Text Box Tools Format tab** if necessary, click the **Shape Fill list arrow** in the Text Box Styles group, then click **Blue, Accent 2**

   The Kenya Travel Information sidebar is inserted on page 3 and the color changes to blue. The sidebar is anchored to the Practical Information heading, where the insertion point is located.

   > **TROUBLE**
   > If you are working on your personal computer, and you want to save the building blocks you created, click Yes to save the Building Blocks.docx file.

8. **Click the blank paragraph** above the chart, click the **Quick Parts button**, click the **Kenya Climate Info** item, then save your changes

   The Climate heading and associated paragraph are inserted above the chart. The completed Kenya Family Safari tour report is shown in Figure G-19.

9. **Print the document, close the file, exit Word**, then click **No** in the warning box to not save the changes to the BuildingBlocks.docx file

   You can choose to save the customized building blocks you created in this session for use in other documents, or you can remove them from the Building Blocks Organizer.

Working with Themes and Building Blocks

FIGURE G-18: Building Blocks Organizer

Click a column heading to sort the building blocks by that criterion

Complete list of building blocks

Preview of selected building block

Word 2007

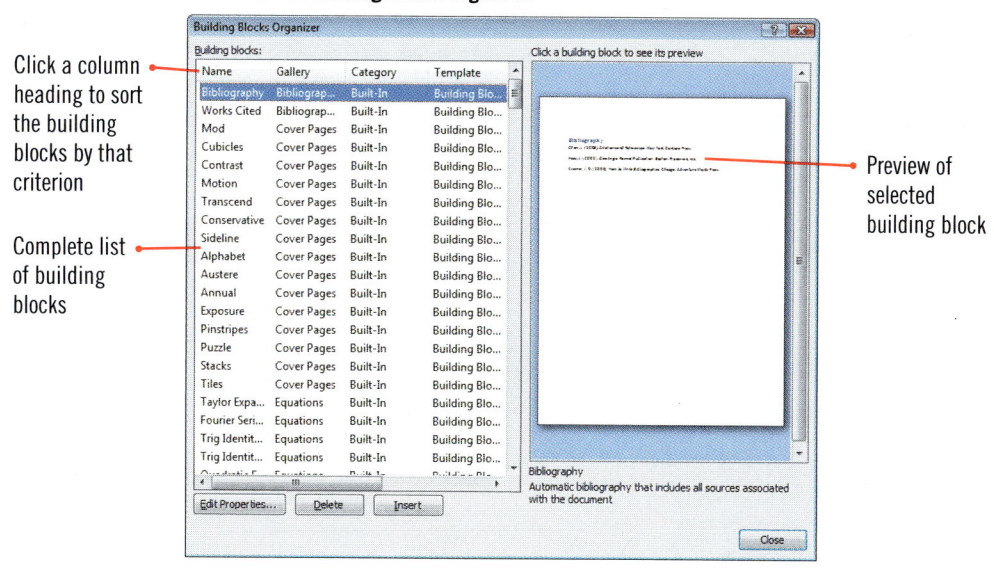

FIGURE G-19: Completed Kenya Family Safari tour report

Logo added

Footer added

Climate information added

Sidebar added

Working with Themes and Building Blocks   Word 169

Practice

▼ CONCEPTS REVIEW

If you have a SAM user profile, you may have access to hands-on instruction, practice, and assessment of the skills covered in this unit. Log in to your SAM account (http://sam2007.course.com/) to launch any assigned training activities or exams that relate to the skills covered in this unit.

Label each element shown in Figure G-20.

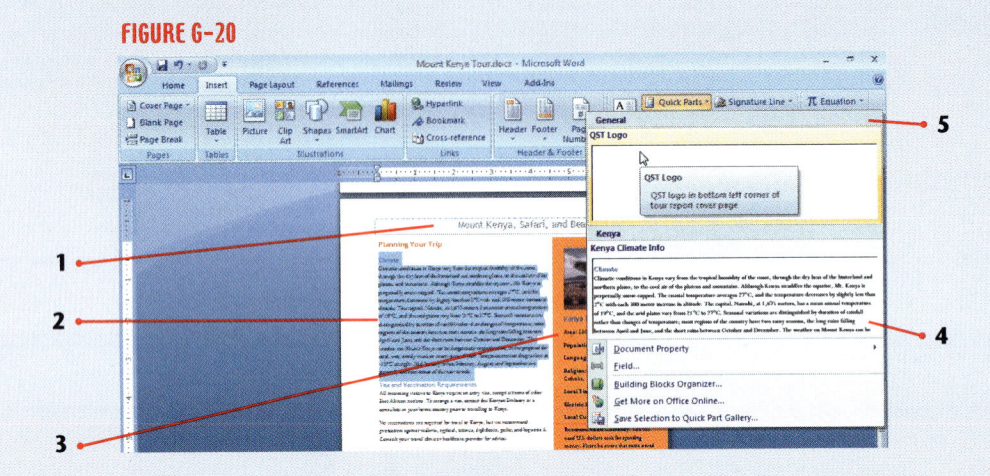

FIGURE G-20

Match each term with the statement that best describes it.

6. Gallery
7. Building block
8. Theme
9. Quick Style set
10. Quick Part
11. Pull quote
12. Style
13. Sidebar

a. A set of unified design elements, including colors, fonts, and effects that are named and stored together
b. A set of format settings, such as font, font color, and paragraph alignment, that are named and stored together
c. A group of related styles that share common fonts, colors, and formats
d. A reusable piece of formatted content or a document part that is stored in a gallery
e. A text box that is positioned adjacent to the body of a document and contains auxiliary information
f. A text box that contains a quote or excerpt from an article, formatted in a larger font size and placed on the same page
g. A field, document property, or other piece of content that can be inserted in a document
h. A location where styles or building blocks are stored

Select the best answer from the list of choices.

14. Which of the following is *not* a design element included in a theme?
    a. Fonts
    b. Picture styles
    c. Colors
    d. Effects

15. Changing which of the following does not change the font used for body text in a document?
    a. Style Set
    b. Theme fonts
    c. Theme
    d. Theme effects

16. Which of the following elements uses theme effects?
    a. SmartArt
    b. ClipArt
    c. Tables
    d. Headers and footers

17. Which of the following is not an example of a building block?
    a. Pull quote
    b. Document property
    c. Footer
    d. Cover page

18. Which of the following statements is false?
    a. Changing a document property in a property control updates the property in the Document Information Panel.
    b. When you change a document theme, the format of text to which font formatting has been applied does not change.
    c. You use the Object command to create a new building block.
    d. When you add a building block to a gallery, it is also added to the Building Block Organizer.

▼ SKILLS REVIEW

1. **Apply quick styles to text.**
    a. Start Word, open the file WD G-4.docx from the drive and folder where you store your Data Files, save it as **Green Home**, read the document, then press [Ctrl][Home].
    b. Apply the Title style to the Greening Your Home heading.
    c. Apply the Subtitle style to the Reducing your personal greenhouse gas emissions heading.
    d. Apply the Heading 1 style to the red headings: Small Steps to Take in Your Home and Yard and Use Green Power.
    e. Apply the Heading 3 style to the purple subheadings, then save your changes. (*Hint*: To make the Heading 3 style available, first apply the Heading 2 style to a subheading, then apply the Heading 3 style to the same subheading.)
2. **Apply a theme.**
    a. Change the view to Two Pages, then open the Themes gallery and preview each theme applied to the document.
    b. Apply the Urban theme, then scroll down to view page 3.
    c. Apply the Concourse theme, apply the Solstice theme, then save your changes.
3. **Customize a theme.**
    a. Change the theme colors to Flow.
    b. Create new theme colors by changing the Accent 1 color to dark green: click the Accent 1 list arrow, click More Colors, click the Custom tab if necessary, type **51** in the Red text box, type **102** in the Green text box, type **0** in the Blue text box, then click OK.
    c. Save the palette of new theme colors with the name **Earth**.
    d. Change the theme fonts to Median, scroll to the bottom of the document, then change the theme effects to Urban.
    e. Save the current theme with the name **Earth**.
    f. Press [Ctrl][Home], change the font color of the title to Dark Green, Accent 1, Darker 25%, then save your changes.
4. **Insert a sidebar.**
    a. Place the insertion point in the title, then insert the Contrast Sidebar.
    b. Select the second paragraph of body text, cut it, paste it in the sidebar, click the Paste Options button, click Match Destination Formatting, then press [Backspace].
    c. Select the sidebar text, use the Shading list arrow to change the Shading Color to Lime, Accent 6, click the Bottom Border list arrow, click Borders and Shading, then change the border color to Lime, Accent 6.
    d. Change the view to One Page, click the subheading Be green in your yard on page 2, then insert the Annual Sidebar.
    e. Insert the text file WD G-5.docx, found in the drive and folder where you store your Data Files, in the sidebar, select all the text in the sidebar, then change the font color to White, Background 1.
    f. Scroll to page 3, click the heading Use Green Power, then insert the Annual Sidebar.
    g. Insert the text file WD G-6.docx, found in the drive and folder where you store your Data Files, in the sidebar, select all the text in the sidebar, change the font color to White, Background 1, then save your changes.
5. **Insert quick parts.**
    a. Change the view to Page Width, insert the Sideline header from the Header gallery, click the Title property control, type **Greening Your Home**, then press [End] to move the insertion point out of the control.
    b. Press [Spacebar], insert a small bullet symbol of your choice, press [Spacebar], insert an Author property control, then add your name to the control as the author.
    c. Insert the Sideline footer from the Footer gallery, close headers and footers, then save your changes.

▼ SKILLS REVIEW (CONTINUED)

6. **Add a cover page.**
   a. Change the view to Two Pages, then press [Ctrl][Home], insert the Pinstripes cover page, zoom in, click the Subtitle control, then type **Reducing your personal greenhouse gas emissions**.
   b. Verify that your name appears in the Author control, then use the Date control to select the current date.
   c. Change the cover page design to the Sideline cover page, right-click the Company control, click Remove Content Control, then verify that the remaining information is accurate.
   d. Save your changes, then print the document. The completed document is shown in Figure G-21.

7. **Create building blocks.**
   a. Change the view to Two Pages, click the upper right corner of the sidebar on page 2 to select it (*Note*: Sizing handles appear around the dark green box when the sidebar is selected.), then use the Quick Parts button to save the selection as a quick part.
   b. Name the building block **Intro Sidebar**, assign it to the Text Boxes gallery, create a category called **Green Reports**, and then click OK.
   c. Scroll down, select the sidebar on page 4, save it as a quick part, name the building block **Measure Your Impact Sidebar**, assign it to the Text Boxes gallery, assign it to the Green Reports category, and then click OK as needed to return to the document.
   d. Zoom in, open the Header area, click the table move handle in the header to select the header, then save the header to the Header Gallery.
   e. Name the building block Green Reports header, create a **Green Reports** category, and then click OK as needed to return to the document.
   f. Close the Header area, save your changes, then close the file without exiting Word.

8. **Insert building blocks.**
   a. Open the file WD G-7.docx from the drive and folder where you store your Data Files, save it as **Green Work**, read the document, then apply the Earth theme.
   b. Scroll to page 2, then insert the Green Reports header from the Green Reports category in the Header gallery.
   c. Replace the information in the Author control with your name if necessary.
   d. Insert the Sideline footer in the document, then close headers and footers.
   e. Click the title on page 2, open the Text Box gallery, then insert the Intro Sidebar from the Green Reports category.
   f. Select the second body paragraph in the document, cut it, select all the text in the sidebar except for the final period, paste the text, click the Paste Options button, click Match Destination Formatting, then press [Backspace] twice to delete the extra line and period.
   g. Scroll to page 3, click On the Road, then open Building Blocks Organizer.
   h. Click the Category heading to sort the items by category, scroll to locate the items in the Green Reports category, click the Measure Your Impact Sidebar, then click Insert.
   i. Save your changes, then print your document. Pages 2 and 3 of the completed document are shown in Figure G-22.
   j. Close the file and exit Word, not saving changes to the Building Blocks.dotx file if prompted.

FIGURE G-21

FIGURE G-22

▼ INDEPENDENT CHALLENGE 1

You volunteer for an organization that promotes literacy in your community. You have written the text for a literacy fact sheet and now want to format it quickly and attractively. You decide to format the fact sheet using styles, themes, and preformatted building blocks. If you are performing the ACE steps, you will also save some of the formatted content so you can use it again in other documents.

a. Start Word, open the file WD G-8.docx from the drive and folder where you store your Data Files, save it as **Literacy Fact Sheet**, then read the document to get a feel for its contents.
b. Apply the Title style to the title Facts on Literacy.
c. Apply the Heading 2 style to the headings Literacy and Poverty, Literacy and Children, and How Can You Help?
d. Press [Ctrl][Home], then add a Cubicles Sidebar to the document.
e. Select the How Can You Help heading and the paragraphs under it, press [Ctrl][X], click the placeholder text in the sidebar, press [Ctrl][V], then use the Paste Options button to match the destination formatting.
f. Apply the Heading 2 style to How Can You Help? in the sidebar, then set the paragraph spacing before the heading to 0 points and after the heading to 12 points.
g. Add a Puzzle (Even Page) footer to the document. Remove the Company property control, type **For more information contact** followed by your name, then replace Confidential with **555-8799**.
h. Preview several themes applied to the document, then select an appropriate theme.
i. If the text flows onto page two or does not all fit in the sidebar, change the theme fonts to a set of fonts that allows the text to fit on one page and in the sidebar. Delete the blank page 2 if necessary.
j. Change the theme colors applied the document elements as necessary to make the document attractive.

Advanced Challenge Exercise

- Select the sidebar, then save it as a building block in the Text Boxes gallery in the General category. Be sure to give the building block a meaningful name and description.
- Open the Footer area, click the Table Move Handle to select the table in the footer, then add the footer to the Footers gallery in the General category. Be sure to give the footer a meaningful name and description.
- Create a new document, type **Teach a Child to Read**, apply the Title style to the text, then save the document as **Literacy ACE** to the drive and folder where you store your Data Files.
- Open the Building Blocks Organizer, locate the sidebar building block you created, then insert it in the document.
- Open the Footer gallery, insert the footer you created, save your changes, print the document, then close the file.

k. Save your changes, print the document, then close the file and exit Word, not saving changes to the Building Blocks.dotx file if prompted.

▼ INDEPENDENT CHALLENGE 2

You work for the Community Relations department at your local hospital. You have written the text for a report on annual giving, and now you need to format the report. You decide to start with a report template and then customize the report with a preformatted text box, a sidebar, a new cover page, and theme elements.

a. Start Word, create a new document using the Oriel Report template, then save it as **Annual Giving Report**.
b. Scroll the document to get a feel for its content and layout, then press [Ctrl][Home].
c. On the cover page, type **Springfield Community Hospital Annual Giving** in the Title property control. (*Note*: Text typed in the Title property control is formatted in small caps.)
d. Type **Invitation to Donors** in the Subtitle property control, remove the Abstract content control, type your name in the Author property control, then select today's date in the Date content control.
e. Scroll to page 2, click the body of the report to select the content control, insert the text file WD G-9.docx, found on the drive and folder where you store your Data Files, then scroll down to view the format and content of the report.
f. Press [Ctrl][Home], then format the following headings in the Heading 1 style: Capital Campaign Exceeds its Goal, Types of Gifts, Planned and Deferred Giving, Named Endowments Leave Lasting Impressions, and Frost Society.
g. Experiment by applying different heading styles to the Annual Fund Gifts subheading: Apply the Heading 2 style to the subheading, apply the Heading 3 style to the subheading, and then apply the Heading 4 style to the subheading.

▼ **INDEPENDENT CHALLENGE 2 (CONTINUED)**

h. Apply the Heading 4 style to the following subheadings: Memorial or Tribute Gifts, Charitable Bequests, Charitable Gift Annuity, Charitable Remainder Trust, Edna and Franklin Frost Society Members.

i. Click the first body paragraph on page 2, insert a text box using the pull quote style of your choice from the Text Box gallery, then reposition the text box so the page is attractive, if necessary.

j. Select the last paragraph of text under the Capital Campaign Exceeds its Goal heading, cut the paragraph and paste it to the pull quote, then use the Paste Options button to match the destination formatting.

k. Scroll to page 4, click the Frost Society heading, insert a sidebar of your choice, then cut the Edna and Franklin Frost Society Members heading and the list that follows it from the body text and paste it in the sidebar. Use the Paste Options button to match the destination formatting, then apply the Heading 4 style to the heading in the sidebar.

l. Using the Cover Page command, insert a different cover page for the report. Update or remove the content and property controls as necessary.

m. Experiment with different themes, theme colors, theme fonts, and theme effects, and then use these tools to customize the look of the report. Adjust the elements of the report as necessary to make sure each page is attractive and the text fits comfortably on 4 pages. Figure G-23 shows a sample finished report.

n. Save your changes to the document, print a copy, close the document, then exit Word.

FIGURE G-23

▼ **INDEPENDENT CHALLENGE 3**

You are in charge of publicity for the Sydney Triathlon 2010 World Cup. One of your responsibilities is to create a two-page flyer that captures the spirit of the event and provides the basic details. You format the flyer using styles, themes, and building blocks, keeping in mind that in the end the content needs to fit on two pages. Figure G-24 shows one possible design, but you will create your own design. If you are completing the ACE steps, you will also create a custom theme that can be used for other documents related to the triathlon.

a. Start Word, open the file WD G-10.docx from the drive and folder where you store your Data Files, then save it as **Triathlon Flyer**, then read the document.

b. Apply the Title style to the title and the Heading 1 style to the following headings: The Triathlon, The Course, Best Views, Public Transport and Road Closures, and The Athletes. Apply other styles to the text as you see fit.

c. Change the Style Set to Modern, apply an appropriate theme, then change the theme colors or theme fonts as necessary to achieve the look you want.

d. Add a continuous section break before The Athletes, then format the second section in two columns using the default column settings.

e. Add a manual page break before the Public Transport and Road Closures heading.

FIGURE G-24

Word 174 Working with Themes and Building Blocks

▼ INDEPENDENT CHALLENGE 3 (CONTINUED)

f. Click The Triathlon heading on page 1, insert a sidebar of your choice on page 1, then cut the Best Views heading and paragraphs from the document, including the photo of the Sydney Opera House, and paste it in the sidebar. (*Hint*: Do not cut the page break.) Keep the source formatting for the selection.

g. Click The Athletes heading on page 2, insert a sidebar of your choice on page 2, then cut the Public Transport and Road Closures heading and paragraphs from the document and paste them in the sidebar. Keep the source formatting for the selection.

h. Adjust the size, color, alignment, text wrapping, and position of the sidebar text boxes and the photographs so that the layout of each page is attractive.

i. Adjust the font and paragraph formatting of the document text so that the text is readable and the overall layout of the flyer is harmonious. All the text should now fit on two pages.

Advanced Challenge Exercise

- Customize one or more of the theme colors you used in the flyer, then save the new palette of theme colors with the name Triathlon.
- Adjust the colors of text and other elements in the document as necessary.
- Save the customized theme with the name Triathlon.

j. Add your name to the header, save your changes, print the document, close the file, then exit Word.

▼ REAL LIFE INDEPENDENT CHALLENGE

In this Independent Challenge, you will design and save at least one building block for your work or personal use. Your building block might be the masthead for a newsletter, a cover page for your academic papers or your business reports, a header or footer that includes your company logo, a SmartArt object, a letterhead, a graphic object, a mission statement or disclaimer, or some other item that you use repeatedly in the documents you create.

a. Determine the building block(s) you want to create. If you frequently create documents that include several standard items, such as a newsletter that includes a masthead, a header, a footer, and a text box with the address of your organization, you will want to create several building blocks.

b. Start Word, then save the blank document as **Building Block 1** to the drive and folder where you store your Data Files.

c. Create your first building block. Whenever possible, insert fields and property controls as appropriate. Format the item using themes, styles, fonts, colors, borders, fill effects, shadows, and other effects, as necessary.

d. When you are satisfied with the content and format of the item, select it, including the final paragraph mark, if appropriate, and then save it as a new building block. Make sure to give the item a meaningful name, description, and category, and to save it to the appropriate gallery so you can find it easily.

e. Repeat steps c and d to create as many building blocks as necessary for your documents.

f. Type your name at the top of the document, then save, print, and close the document.

g. Open a blank document, then save it as **Building Block 2** to the drive and folder where you store your Data Files.

h. Create a document in which to use your building block(s). Insert the building block(s) you created, and then format, adjust, and position the building blocks appropriately.

i. Type your name in the document header (or another appropriate location), save the document, print it, and then close the file and exit Word. If you want to save the building blocks you created for future use, save the Building Blocks.dotx file when prompted.

Working with Themes and Building Blocks

▼ VISUAL WORKSHOP

Create the cover page shown in Figure G-25 using the Exposure cover page design. Replace the photograph with the clip art photograph shown in the figure, replace the placeholder text with the text shown in the figure, increase the font size of the abstract text to 16 points, change the theme colors to Oriel, then delete the second page. Save the document as **Aquarium Cover Page**, then print the document. (*Hints*: Locate the photograph using the keyword **coral**. Choose another photo if the photo shown is not available to you. To delete the second page, delete the page break on the cover page.)

FIGURE G-25

UNIT H
Word 2007

Merging Word Documents

Files You Will Need:
WD H-1.docx
WD H-2.mdb
WD H-3.docx
WD H-4.mdb

A mail merge operation combines a standard document, such as a form letter, with customized data, such as a set of names and addresses, to create a set of personalized documents. You can perform a mail merge to create letters, labels, and other documents used in mass mailings, or to create standard documents that typically include customized information, such as business cards. In this unit, you learn how to use both the Mail Merge task pane and the commands on the Mailings tab to perform a mail merge. You need to send a letter to people who recently booked a QST tour, confirming their reservation and receipt of their nonrefundable deposit. You also need to send a general information packet to all participants in upcoming QST tours. You use mail merge to create a personalized form letter and mailing labels for the information packet.

OBJECTIVES

Understand mail merge
Create a main document
Design a data source
Enter and edit records
Add merge fields
Merge data
Create labels
Sort and filter records

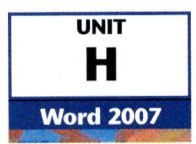

Understanding Mail Merge

When you perform a **mail merge**, you merge a standard Word document with a file that contains customized information for many individuals or items. The standard document is called the **main document**. The file with the unique data for individual people or items is called the **data source**. Merging the main document with a data source results in a merged document that contains customized versions of the main document, as shown in Figure H-1. The Mail Merge task pane steps you through the process of setting up and performing a mail merge. You can also perform a mail merge using the commands on the Mailings tab. You decide to use the Mail Merge task pane to create your form letters and the commands on the Mailings tab to create your mailing labels. Before beginning, you explore the steps involved in performing a mail merge.

DETAILS

- **Create the main document**

  The main document contains the text—often called **boilerplate text**—that appears in every version of the merged document. The main document also includes the merge fields, which indicate where the customized information is inserted when you perform the merge. You insert the merge fields in the main document after you have created or selected the data source. You can create a main document using either the current document, a template, or an existing document.

- **Create a data source or select an existing data source**

  The data source is a file that contains the unique information for each individual or item. It provides the information that varies in every version of the merged document. A data source is composed of data fields and data records. A **data field** is a category of information, such as last name, first name, street address, city, or postal code. A **data record** is a complete set of related information for an individual or an item, such as one person's name and address. It is easiest to think of a data source file as a table: the header row contains the names of the data fields (the **field names**), and each row in the table is an individual data record. You can create a new data source, or you can merge a main document with an existing data source, such as a data source created in Word, an Outlook contact list, an Access database, or an Excel worksheet.

- **Identify the fields to include in the data source and enter the records**

  When you create a new data source, you must first identify the fields to include. It's important to think of and include all the fields before you begin to enter data. For example, if you are creating a data source that includes addresses, you might need to include fields for a person's middle name, title, department name, or country, even though every address in the data source does not include that information. Once you have identified the fields and set up your data source, you are ready to enter the data for each record.

- **Add merge fields to the main document**

  A **merge field** is a placeholder that you insert in the main document to indicate where the data from each record should be inserted when you perform the merge. For example, in the location you want to insert a zip code, you insert a zip code merge field. The merge fields in a main document must correspond with the field names in the associated data source. Merge fields must be inserted, not typed, in the main document. The Mail Merge task pane and the Mailings tab provide access to the dialog boxes you use to insert merge fields.

- **Merge the data from the data source into the main document**

  Once you have established your data source and inserted the merge fields in the main document, you are ready to perform the merge. You can merge to a new file, which contains a customized version of the main document for each record in the data source, or you can merge directly to a printer or e-mail message.

FIGURE H-1: Mail merge process

Data source document — Field name

Tour	Title	First Name	Last Name	Address Line 1	City	State	Zip Code	Country
Old Japan	Ms.	Linda	Barker	62 Cloud St.	Bellevue	WA	83459	US
Egypt	Mr.	Bob	Cruz	23 Plum St.	Boston	MA	02483	US
Old Japan	Ms.	Joan	Yatco	456 Elm St.	Chicago	IL	60603	US
Yucatan	Ms.	Anne	Butler	48 East Ave.	Vancouver	BC	V6F 1AH	CANADA
Alaska	Mr.	Fred	Silver	56 Pearl St.	Cambridge	MA	02139	US

Data record

Main document

Quest Specialty Travel
340 West Market Street • San Diego, CA 92101
Tel: (619) 555-1223 • Fax: (619) 555-0937 • www.questspecialtytravel.com

June 12, 2010

«AddressBlock»

«GreetingLine»

Thank you for your reservation and $250 deposit to secure your participation in QST's exciting «Tour» tour. You will be joining an exclusive group of fellow QST travelers for an inspiring, adventurous, and memorable experience of a lifetime.

Your reservation and nonrefundable deposit guarantee your place on the tour until 30 days prior to departure. At this point, a 50% nonrefundable advance payment is required to confirm your participation. Payment in full is required one week prior to commencement of the tour. We recommend purchasing a travel insurance policy, as no refunds will be given due to weather or personal circumstances.

Thank you for choosing Quest Specialty Travel. We look forward to travelling with you.

Sincerely,

Ron Dawson
Marketing Manager

Merge fields — Boilerplate text

Merged document

Quest Specialty Travel
340 West Market Street • San Diego, CA 92101
Tel: (619) 555-1223 • Fax: (619) 555-0937 • www.questspecialtytravel.com

June 12, 2010

Ms. Linda Barker
62 Cloud St.
Bellevue, WA 83459

Dear Ms. Barker:

Thank you for your reservation and $250 deposit to secure your participation in QST's exciting Old Japan tour. You will be joining an exclusive group of fellow QST travelers for an inspiring, adventurous, and memorable experience of a lifetime.

Your reservation and nonrefundable deposit guarantee your place on the tour until 30 days prior to departure. At this point, a 50% nonrefundable advance payment is required to confirm your participation. Payment in full is required one week prior to commencement of the tour. We recommend purchasing a travel insurance policy, as no refunds will be given due to weather or personal circumstances.

Thank you for choosing Quest Specialty Travel. We look forward to travelling with you.

Sincerely,

Ron Dawson
Marketing Manager

Customized information

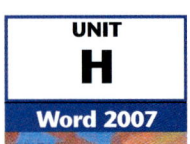

UNIT H
Word 2007
Creating a Main Document

The first step in performing a mail merge is to create the main document—the file that contains the boilerplate text. You can create a main document from scratch, save an existing document as a main document, or use a mail merge template to create a main document. The Mail Merge task pane walks you through the process of selecting the type of main document to create. You use an existing form letter for your main document. You begin by opening the Mail Merge task pane.

STEPS

TROUBLE
A document, blank or otherwise, must be open in the program window for the commands on the Mailings tab to be available.

1. **Start Word, click the Mailings tab, click the Start Mail Merge button in the Start Mail Merge group, then click Step by Step Mail Merge Wizard**
   The Mail Merge task pane opens, as shown in Figure H-2, and displays information for the first step in the mail merge process: selecting the type of merge document to create.

2. **Make sure the Letters option button is selected, then click Next: Starting document to continue with the next step**
   The task pane displays the options for the second step: selecting the starting document (the main document). You can use the current document, start with a mail merge template, or use an existing file.

QUICK TIP
If you choose "Use the current document" and the current document is blank, you can create a main document from scratch. Either type the boilerplate text at this step, or wait until the task pane prompts you to do so.

3. **Select the Start from existing document option button, make sure (More files...) is selected in the Start from existing list box, then click Open**
   The Open dialog box opens.

4. **Navigate to the location where you store your Data Files, select the file WD H-1.docx, then click Open**
   The letter that opens contains the boilerplate text for the main document. Notice the filename in the title bar is Document1. When you create a main document that is based on an existing document, Word gives the main document a default temporary filename.

5. **Click the Save button on the Quick Access toolbar, then save the main document with the filename Client Deposit Letter Main to the drive and folder where you store your Data Files**
   It's a good idea to include "main" in the filename so that you can easily recognize the file as a main document.

6. **Click the Zoom level button on the status bar, click the Text width option button, click OK, select April 19, 2010 in the letter, type today's date, scroll down, select Ron Dawson, type your name, press [Ctrl][Home], then save your changes**
   The edited main document is shown in Figure H-3.

7. **Click Next: Select recipients to continue with the next step**
   You continue with Step 3 of 6 in the next lesson.

Using a mail merge template

If you are creating letters or faxes, you can use a mail merge template to start your main document. Each template includes boilerplate text, which you can customize, and merge fields, which you can match to the field names in your data source. To create a main document that is based on a mail merge template, click the Start from a template option button in the Step 2 of 6 Mail Merge task pane, and then click Select template. In the Select Template dialog box, select a template from the Letters or Faxes tab that includes the word "Merge" in its name, and then click OK to create the document. Once you have created the main document, you can customize it with your own information: edit the boilerplate text, change the document format, or add, remove, or modify the merge fields.

Before performing the merge, make sure to match the names of the merge fields used in the template with the field names used in your data source. To match the field names, click the Match Fields button in the Write & Insert Fields group on the Mailings tab, and then use the list arrows in the Match Fields dialog box to select the field name in your data source that corresponds to each address field component in the main document. You can also create a main document that is based on a template by using a template to create the main document and then adding merge fields to it.

Merging Word Documents

FIGURE H-2: Step 1 of 6 Mail Merge task pane

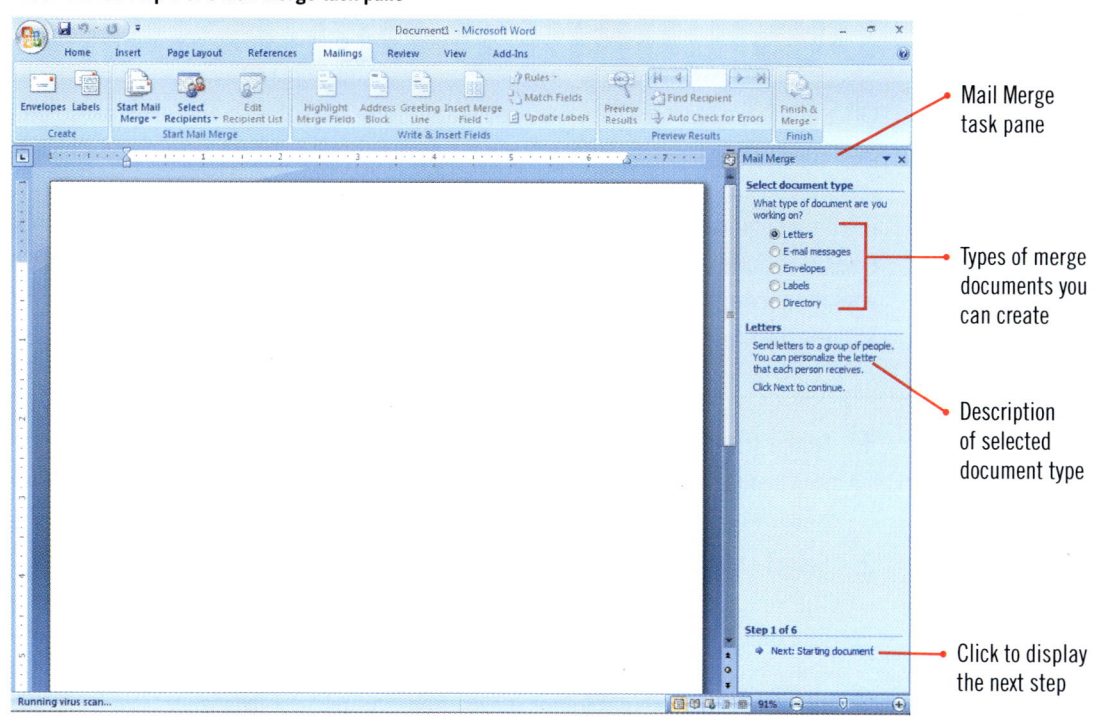

- Mail Merge task pane
- Types of merge documents you can create
- Description of selected document type
- Click to display the next step

FIGURE H-3: Main document with Step 2 of 6 Mail Merge task pane

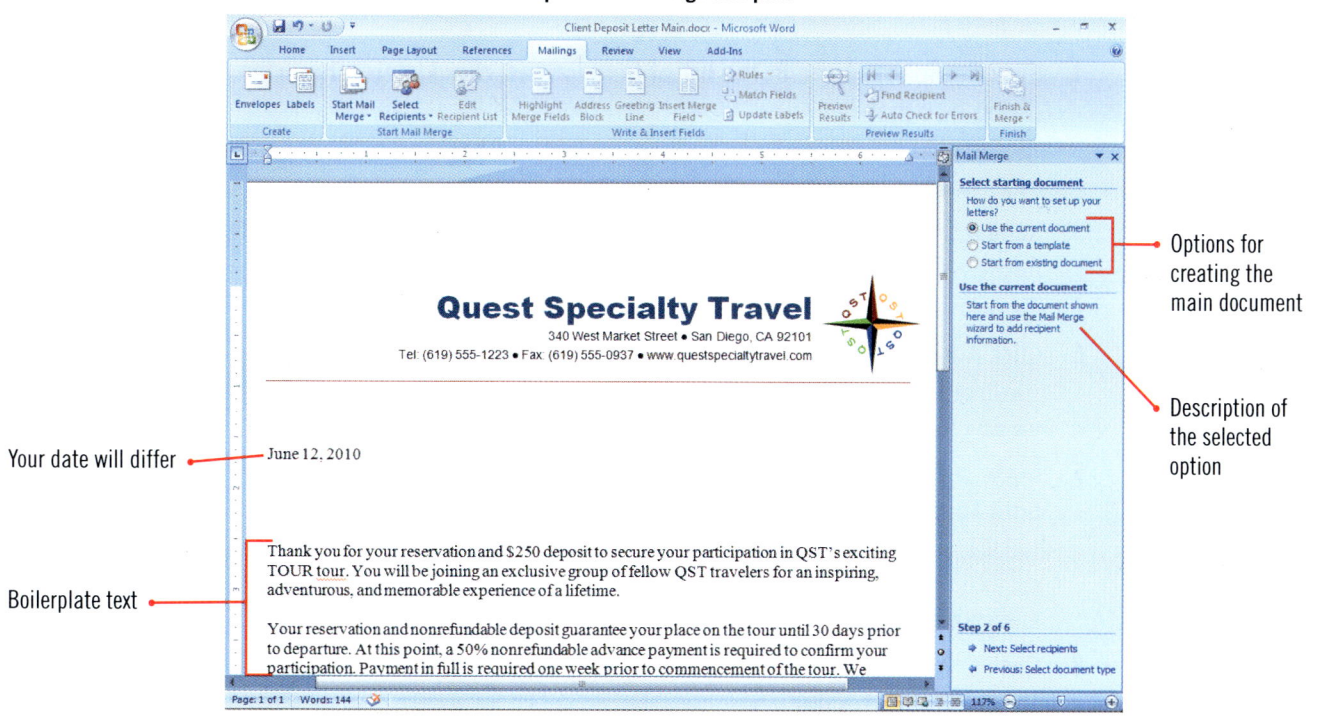

- Your date will differ
- Boilerplate text
- Options for creating the main document
- Description of the selected option

Merging Word Documents

Word 181

Designing a Data Source

UNIT H — Word 2007

Once you have identified the main document, the next step in the mail merge process is to identify the data source, the file that contains the information that is used to customize each version of the merge document. You can use an existing data source that already contains the records you want to include in your merge, or you can create a new data source. When you create a new data source you must determine the fields to include—the categories of information, such as a first name, last name, city, or zip code—and then add the records. You create a new data source that includes fields for the client name, client address, and tour booked by the client.

STEPS

1. **Make sure Step 3 of 6 is displayed at the bottom of the Mail Merge task pane**
   Step 3 of 6 involves selecting a data source to use for the merge. You can use an existing data source, a list of contacts created in Microsoft Outlook, or a new data source.

2. **Select the Type a new list option button, then click Create**
   The New Address List dialog box opens, as shown in Figure H-4. You use this dialog box both to design your data source and to enter records. The column headings in the Type recipient information... section of the dialog box are fields that are commonly used in form letters, but you can customize your data source by adding and removing columns (fields) from this table. A data source can be merged with more than one main document, so it's important to design a data source to be flexible. The more fields you include in a data source, the more flexible it is. For example, if you include separate fields for a person's title, first name, middle name, and last name, you can use the same data source to create an envelope addressed to "Mr. John Montgomery Smith" and a form letter with the greeting "Dear John."

3. **Click Customize Columns**
   The Customize Address List dialog box opens. You use this dialog box to add, delete, rename, and reorder the fields in the data source.

4. **Click Company Name in the list of field names, click Delete, then click Yes in the warning dialog box that opens**
   Company Name is removed from the list of field names. The Company Name field is no longer a part of the data source.

5. **Repeat Step 4 to delete the Address Line 2, Home Phone, Work Phone, and E-mail Address fields**
   The fields are removed from the data source.

6. **Click Add, type Tour in the Add Field dialog box, then click OK**
   A field called "Tour," which you will use to indicate the name of the tour booked by the client, is added to the data source.

7. **Make sure Tour is selected in the list of field names, then click Move Up eight times or until Tour is at the top of the list**
   The field name "Tour" is moved to the top of the list, as shown in Figure H-5. Although the order of field names does not matter in a data source, it's convenient to arrange the field names logically to make it easier to enter and edit records.

8. **Click OK**
   The New Address List dialog box shows the customized list of fields, with the Tour field first in the list. The next step is to enter each record you want to include in the data source. You add records to the data source in the next lesson.

Merging Word Documents

FIGURE H-4: New Address List dialog box

Enter data for the first record

Column headings are the field names

Click to modify the fields included in the data source

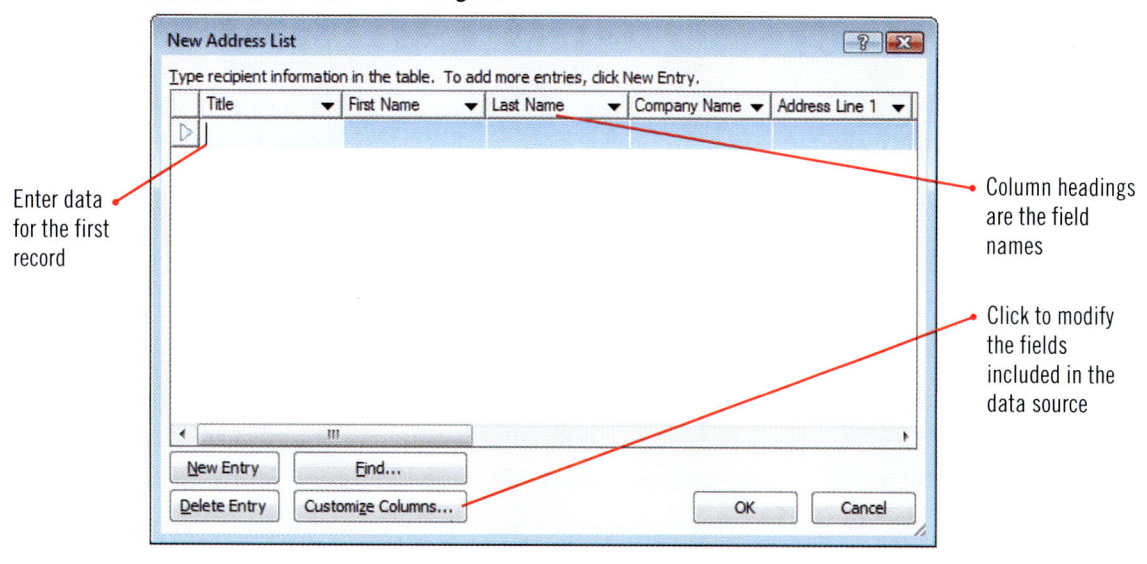

FIGURE H-5: Customize Address List dialog box

Fields in the data source; Tour field is listed first

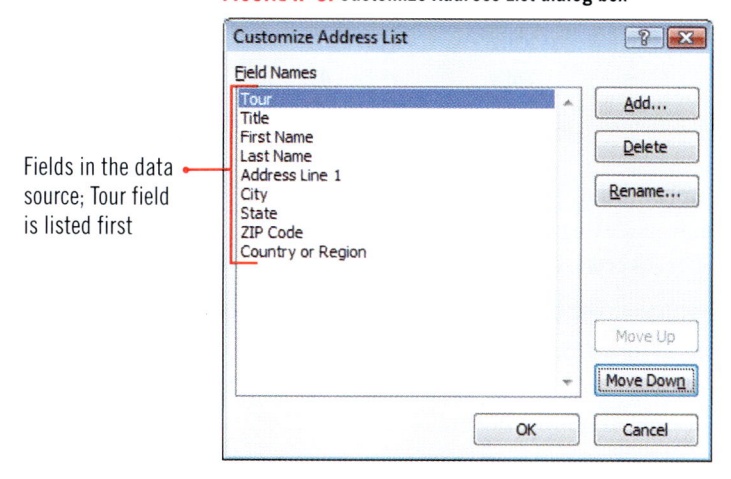

Merging with an Outlook data source

If you maintain lists of contacts in Microsoft Outlook, you can use one of your Outlook contact lists as a data source for a merge. To merge with an Outlook data source, click the Select from Outlook contacts option button in the Step 3 of 6 Mail Merge task pane, then click Choose Contacts Folder to open the Choose Profile dialog box. In this dialog box, use the Profile Name list arrow to select the profile you want to use, then click OK to open the Select Contacts dialog box. In this dialog box, select the contact list you want to use as the data source, and then click OK. All the contacts included in the selected folder appear in the Mail Merge Recipients dialog box. Here you can refine the list of recipients to include in the merge by sorting and filtering the records. When you are satisfied, click OK in the Mail Merge Recipients dialog box.

Merging Word Documents

UNIT H
Word 2007

Entering and Editing Records

Once you have established the structure of a data source, the next step is to enter the records. Each record includes the complete set of information for each individual or item you include in the data source. You create a record for each new QST client.

STEPS

QUICK TIP
Be careful not to add spaces or extra punctuation after an entry in a field, or these will appear when the data is merged.

1. **Verify the insertion point is in the Tour text box in the New Address List dialog box, type Old Japan, then press [Tab]**
   "Old Japan" appears in the Tour field and the insertion point moves to the next column in the table, the Title field.

2. **Type Ms., press [Tab], type Linda, press [Tab], type Barker, press [Tab], type 62 Cloud St., press [Tab], type Bellevue, press [Tab], type WA, press [Tab], type 83459, press [Tab], then type US**
   Data is entered in all the fields for the first record.

QUICK TIP
You can also press [Tab] at the end of the last field to start a new record.

3. **Click New Entry**
   The record for Linda Barker is added to the data source and the dialog box displays empty fields for the next record, as shown in Figure H-6. It's okay to leave a field blank if you do not need it for a record.

4. **Enter the following four records, pressing [Tab] to move from field to field, and clicking New Entry at the end of each record except the last:**

Tour	Title	First Name	Last Name	Address Line 1	City	State	ZIP Code	Country
Egypt	Mr.	Bob	Cruz	23 Plum St.	Boston	MA	02483	US
Old Japan	Ms.	Joan	Yatco	456 Elm St.	Chicago	IL	60603	US
Yucatan	Ms.	Anne	Butler	48 East Ave.	Vancouver	BC	V6F 1AH	CANADA
Alaska	Mr.	Fred	Silver	56 Pearl St.	Cambridge	MA	02139	US

5. **Click OK**
   The Save Address List dialog box opens. Data sources are saved by default in the My Data Sources folder so that you can easily locate them to use in other merge operations. Data sources you create in Word are saved in Microsoft Office Address Lists (*.mdb) format.

TROUBLE
If a check mark appears in the blank record under Fred Silver, click the check mark to eliminate the record from the merge.

6. **Type QST Client Data in the File name text box, navigate to the drive and folder where you store your Data Files, then click Save**
   The data source is saved, and the Mail Merge Recipients dialog box opens, as shown in Figure H-7. The dialog box shows the records in the data source in table format. You can use the dialog box to sort and filter records, and to select the recipients to include in the mail merge. You will learn more about sorting and filtering in a later lesson. The check marks in the second column indicate the records that will be included in the merge.

7. **Click QST Client Data.mdb in the Data Source list box at the bottom of the dialog box, then click Edit**
   The Edit Data Source dialog box opens, as shown in Figure H-8. You use this dialog box to edit a data source, including adding and removing fields, editing field names, adding and removing records, and editing existing records.

8. **Click Ms. in the Title field of the Joan Yatco record to select it, type Dr., click OK, then click Yes**
   The data in the Title field for Joan Yatco changes from "Ms." to "Dr." and the Edit Data Source dialog box closes.

QUICK TIP
If you want to add new records or modify existing records, click Edit recipient list in the task pane.

9. **Click OK in the Mail Merge Recipients dialog box**
   The dialog box closes. The file type and filename of the data source attached to the main document now appear under Use an existing list in the Mail Merge task pane.

Merging Word Documents

FIGURE H-6: Record in New Address List dialog box

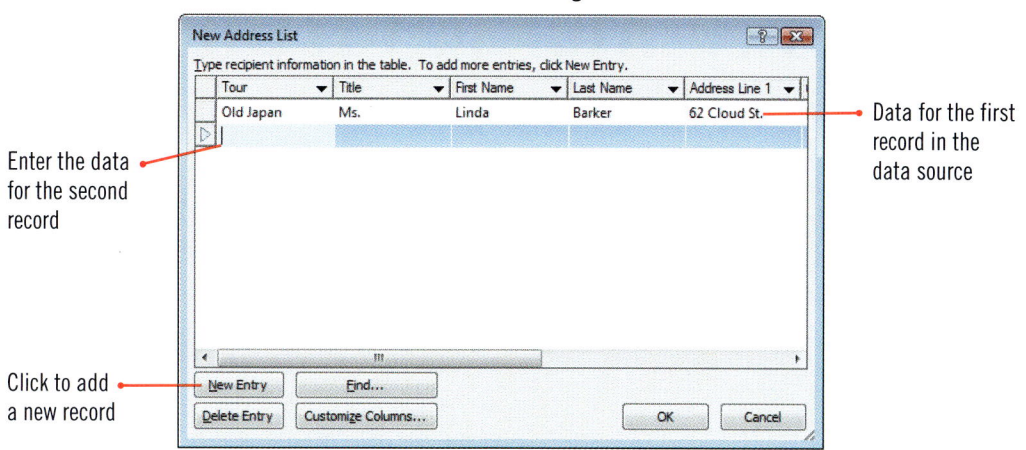

- Data for the first record in the data source
- Enter the data for the second record
- Click to add a new record

FIGURE H-7: Mail Merge Recipients dialog box

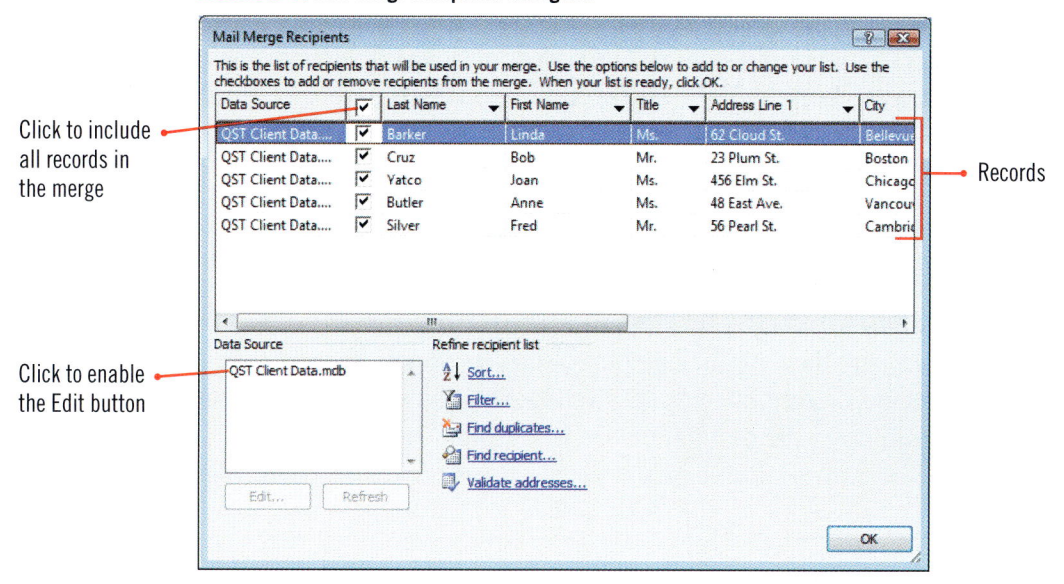

- Click to include all records in the merge
- Records
- Click to enable the Edit button

FIGURE H-8: Edit Data Source dialog box

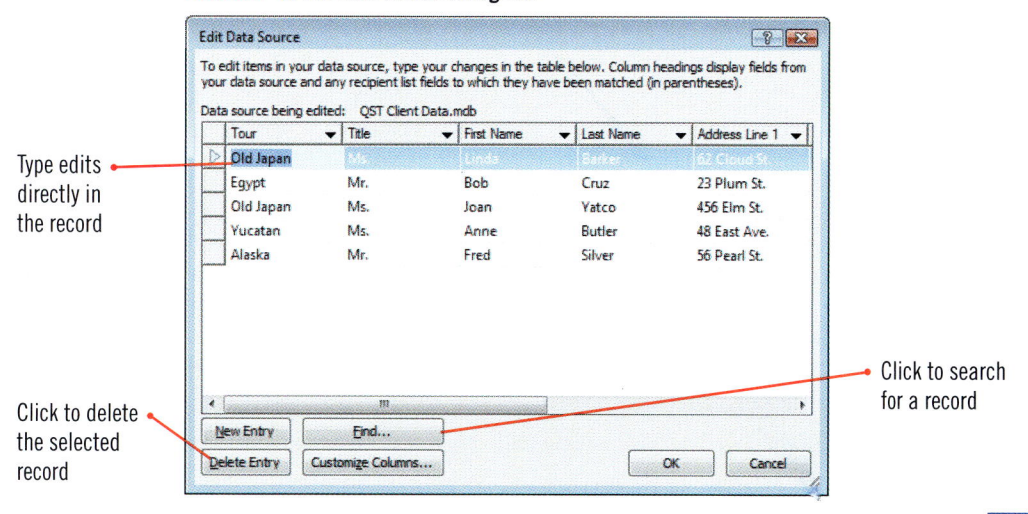

- Type edits directly in the record
- Click to search for a record
- Click to delete the selected record

Merging Word Documents Word 185

UNIT H
Word 2007

Adding Merge Fields

After you have created and identified the data source, the next step is to insert the merge fields in the main document. Merge fields serve as placeholders for text that is inserted when the main document and the data source are merged. The names of merge fields correspond to the field names in the data source. You can insert merge fields using the Mail Merge task pane or the Address Block, Greeting Line, and Insert Merge Field buttons in the Write & Insert Fields group on the Mailings tab. You cannot type merge fields into the main document. You use the Mail Merge task pane to insert merge fields for the inside address and greeting of the letter. You also insert a merge field for the tour destination in the body of the letter.

STEPS

QUICK TIP
Display and hide formatting marks in this lesson as necessary.

1. **Click Next: Write your letter in the Mail Merge task pane**
   The Mail Merge task pane shows the options for Step 4 of 6, writing the letter and inserting the merge fields in the main document. Since your form letter is already written, you are ready to add the merge fields to it.

QUICK TIP
You can also click the Address Block button in the Write & Insert Fields group on the Mailings tab to insert an address block.

2. **Place the insertion point in the blank line above the first body paragraph, then click Address block in the Mail Merge task pane**
   The Insert Address Block dialog box opens, as shown in Figure H-9. You use this dialog box to specify the fields you want to include in an address block. In this merge, the address block is the inside address of the form letter. An address block automatically includes fields for the street, city, state, and postal code, but you can select the format for the recipient's name and indicate whether to include a company name or country in the address.

3. **Scroll the list of formats for a recipient's name to get a feel for the kinds of formats you can use, then click Mr. Joshua Randall Jr. if it is not already selected**
   The selected format uses the recipient's title, first name, and last name.

4. **Make sure the Only include the country/region if different than: option button is selected, select United States in the text box, type US, then deselect the Format address according to the destination country/region check box**
   You only need to include the country in the address block if the country is different than the United States, so you indicate that all entries in the Country field except "US" should be included in the printed address.

QUICK TIP
You cannot simply type chevrons around a field name. You must insert merge fields using the Mail Merge task pane or the buttons in the Write & Insert Fields group on the Mailings tab.

5. **Click OK, then press [Enter] twice**
   The merge field AddressBlock is added to the main document. Chevrons (<< and >>) surround a merge field to distinguish it from the boilerplate text.

6. **Click Greeting line in the Mail Merge task pane**
   The Insert Greeting Line dialog box opens. You want to use the format "Dear Mr. Randall:" (the recipient's title and last name, followed by a colon) for a greeting. The default format uses a comma, so you have to change the comma to a colon.

7. **Click the , list arrow, click :, click OK, then press [Enter]**
   The merge field GreetingLine is added to the main document.

QUICK TIP
You can also click the Insert Merge Field button or list arrow in the Write & Insert Fields group on the Mailings tab to insert a merge field.

8. **In the body of the letter select TOUR, then click More items in the Mail Merge task pane**
   The Insert Merge Field dialog box opens and displays the list of field names included in the data source.

9. **Make sure Tour is selected, click Insert, click Close, press [Spacebar] to add a space between the merge field and "tour" if there is no space, then save your changes**
   The merge field Tour is inserted in the main document, as shown in Figure H-10. You must type spaces and punctuation after a merge field if you want spaces and punctuation to appear in that location in the merged documents. You preview the merged data and perform the merge in the next lesson.

Merging Word Documents

FIGURE H-9: Insert Address Block dialog box

Formats for the recipient's name

Click to match the default address field names to the field names used in your data source

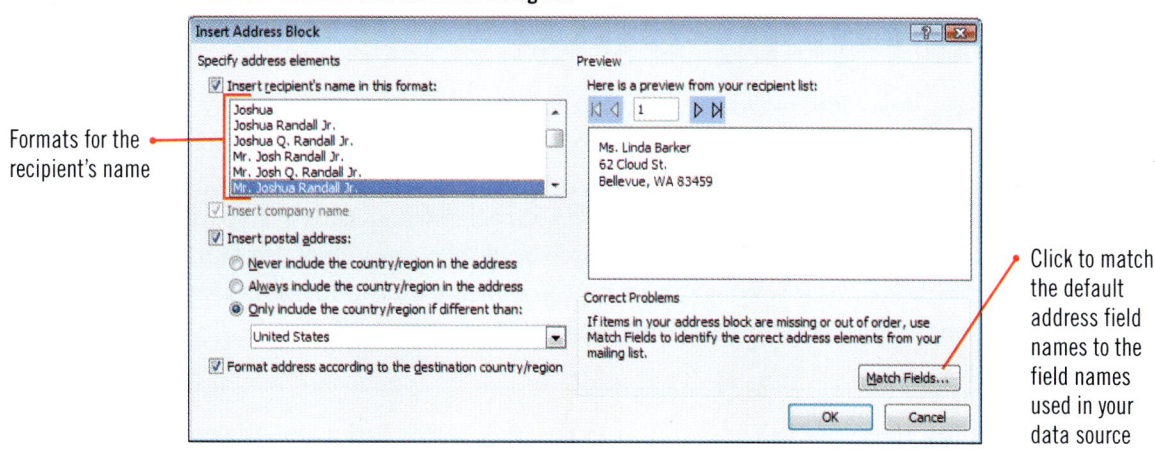

FIGURE H-10: Merge fields in the main document

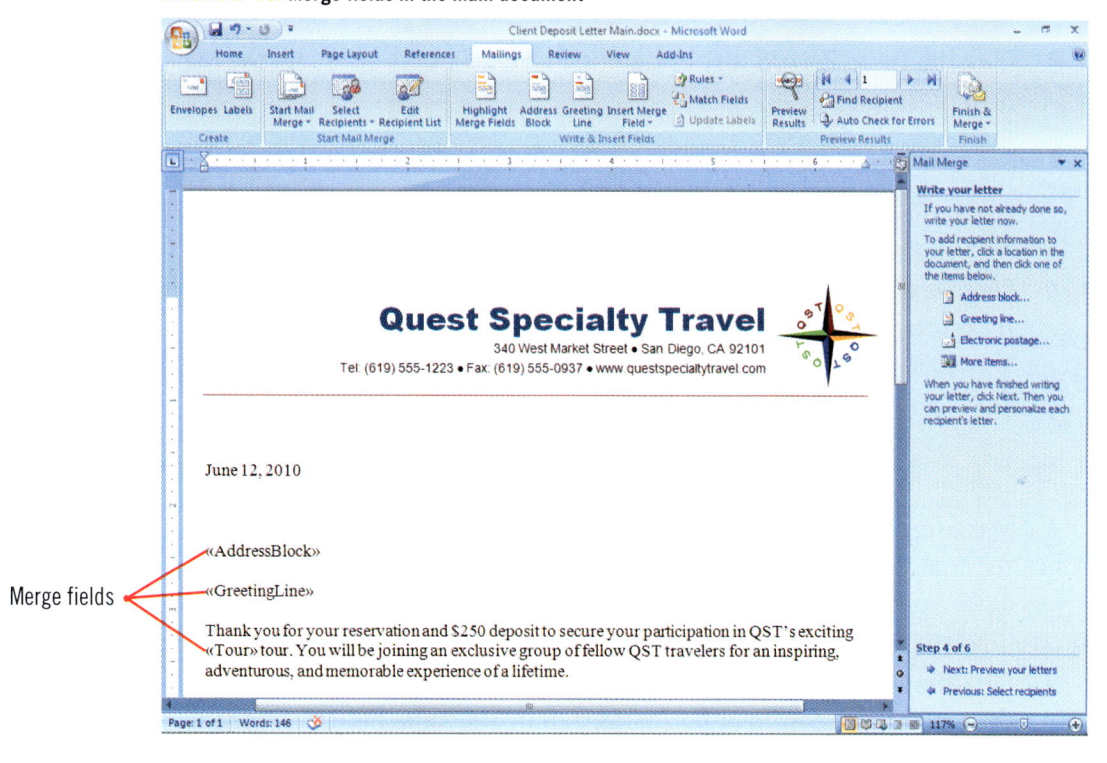

Merge fields

Matching fields

The merge fields you insert in a main document must correspond with the field names in the associated data source. If you are using the Address Block merge field, you must make sure that the default address field names correspond with the field names used in your data source. If the default address field names do not match the field names in your data source, click Match Fields in the Insert Address Block dialog box, then use the list arrows in the Match Fields dialog box to select the field name in the data source that corresponds to each default address field name. You can also click the Match Fields button in the Write & Insert Fields group on the Mailings tab to open the Match Fields dialog box.

Merging Word Documents   Word 187

Merging Data

UNIT H
Word 2007

Once you have added records to your data source and inserted merge fields in the main document, you are ready to perform the merge. Before merging, it's a good idea to preview the merged data to make sure the printed documents will appear as you want them to. You can preview the merge using the task pane or the Preview Results button in the Preview Results group on the Mailings tab. When you merge the main document with the data source, you must choose between merging to a new file or directly to a printer. Before merging the form letter with the data source, you preview the merge to make sure the data appears in the letter as you intended. You then merge the two files to a new document.

STEPS

QUICK TIP
To adjust the main document, click the Preview Results button in the Preview Results group on the Mailings tab, then make any necessary changes. Click the Preview Results button again to preview the merged data.

1. **Click Next: Preview your letters in the Mail Merge task pane, then scroll down as necessary to see the tour name in the document**
   The data from the first record in the data source appears in place of the merge fields in the main document, as shown in Figure H-11. Always preview a document to verify that the merge fields, punctuation, page breaks, and spacing all appear as you intend before you perform the merge.

2. **Click the Next Recipient button >> in the Mail Merge task pane**
   The data from the second record in the data source appears in place of the merge fields.

3. **Click the Go to Record text box in the Preview Results group on the Mailings tab, type 4, then press [Enter]**
   The data for the fourth record appears in the document window. The non-US country name, in this case Canada, is included in the address block, just as you specified. You can also use the First Record, Previous Record, Next Record, and Last Record buttons in the Preview Results group to preview the merged data. Table H-1 describes other commands on the Mailings tab.

QUICK TIP
If your data source contains many records, you can merge directly to a printer to avoid creating a large file.

4. **Click Next: Complete the merge in the Mail Merge task pane**
   The options for Step 6 of 6 appear in the Mail Merge task pane. Merging to a new file creates a document with one letter for each record in the data source. This allows you to edit the individual letters.

5. **Click Edit individual letters to merge the data to a new document**
   The Merge to New Document dialog box opens. You can use this dialog box to specify the records to include in the merge.

6. **Make sure the All option button is selected, then click OK**
   The main document and the data source are merged to a new document called Letters1, which contains a customized form letter for each record in the data source. You can now further personalize the letters without affecting the main document or the data source.

7. **Click the Zoom level button on the status bar, click the Page width option button, click OK, scroll to the fourth letter (addressed to Ms. Anne Butler), place the insertion point before V6F in the address block, then press [Enter]**
   The postal code is now consistent with the proper format for a Canadian address.

8. **Click the Save button on the Quick Access toolbar to open the Save As dialog box, then save the merged document as Client Deposit Letter Merge to the drive and folder where you store your Data Files**
   You may decide not to save a merged file if your data source is large. Once you have created the main document and the data source, you can create the letters by performing the merge again.

9. **Click the Office button, click Print, click the Current page option button in the Page range section of the Print dialog box, click OK, then close all open Word files, saving changes if prompted**
   The letter to Anne Butler prints.

Merging Word Documents

FIGURE H-11: Preview of merged data

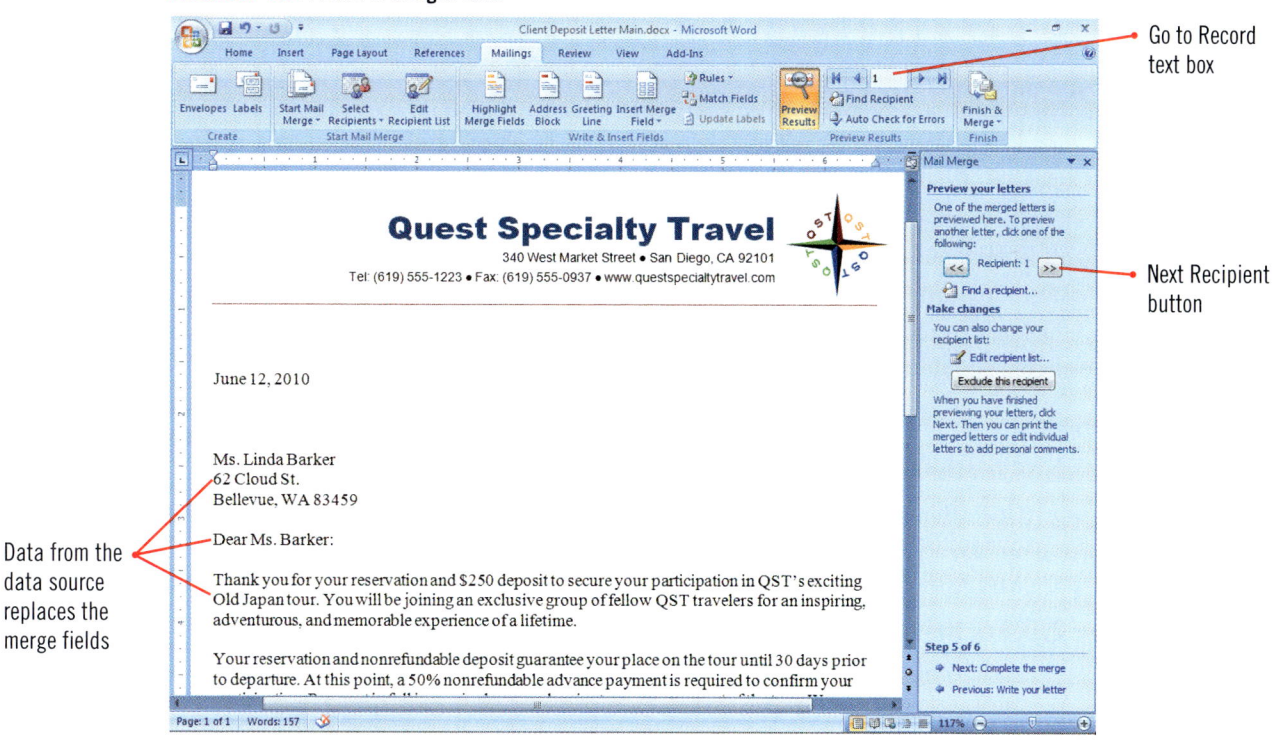

Go to Record text box

Next Recipient button

Data from the data source replaces the merge fields

TABLE H-1: Commands on the Mailings tab

command	use to
Envelopes	Create and print an individual envelope
Labels	Create and print an individual label
Start Mail Merge	Select the type of mail merge document to create and start the mail merge process
Select Recipients	Attach an existing data source to a main document or create a new data source
Edit Recipient List	Edit, sort, and filter the associated data source
Highlight Merge Fields	Highlight the merge fields in the main document
Address Block	Insert an Address Block merge field in the main document
Greeting Line	Insert a Greeting Line merge field in the main document
Insert Merge Field	Insert a merge field from the data source in the main document
Rules	Set rules to control how Word merges the data in the data source with the main document
Match Fields	Match the names of address or greeting fields with the field names used in the data source
Update Labels	Update all the labels in a label main document to match the content and formatting of the first label
Preview Results	Switch between viewing the main document with merge fields or with merged data
Find Recipient	Search for a specific record in the merged document
Auto Check for Errors	Check for and report errors in the merge
Finish & Merge	Specify whether to merge to a new document or directly to a printer or e-mail, and then complete the merge

Merging Word Documents

Creating Labels

UNIT H
Word 2007

You can also use the Mail Merge task pane or the commands on the Mailings tab to create mailing labels or print envelopes for a mailing. When you create labels or envelopes, you must select a standard label or envelope size to use as the main document, select a data source, and then insert the merge fields in the main document before performing the merge. In addition to mailing labels, you can use mail merge to create labels for CDs, videos, and other items, and to create documents that are based on standard or custom label sizes, such as business cards, name tags, and postcards. You decide to use the commands on the Mailings tab to create mailing labels for the information packet you need to send to participants in upcoming QST tours. You create a new label main document and attach an existing data source.

STEPS

1. **Click the Office button, click New, make sure Blank document is selected, click Create, click the Zoom level button on the status bar, click the Page width option button if necessary, click OK, then click the Mailings tab**

   A blank document must be open for the commands on the Mailings tab to be available.

QUICK TIP
To create an envelope mail merge, click Envelopes to open the Envelope Options dialog box, select an envelope size on the Envelope Options tab, click a Feed method on the Printing Options tab, and then click OK.

2. **Click the Start Mail Merge button in the Start Mail Merge group, click Labels, click the Label vendors list arrow, then click Microsoft if necessary**

   The Label Options dialog box opens, as shown in Figure H-12. You use this dialog box to select a label size for your labels and to specify the type of printer you plan to use. The name Microsoft appears in the Label vendors list box. You can use the Label vendors list arrow to select other brand name label vendors, such as Avery or Office Depot. The many standard-size labels for mailings, CD/DVD faces, business cards, postcards, and other types of labels are listed in the Product number list box. The type, height, width, and page size for the selected product are displayed in the Label information section.

TROUBLE
If your labels do not match Figure H-13, click the Undo button on the Quick Access toolbar, then repeat step 3, making sure to click the second instance of 30 Per Page.

3. **Click the second instance of 30 Per Page in the Product number list, click OK, click the Table Tools Layout tab, click View Gridlines in the Table group to turn on the display of gridlines if necessary, then click the Mailings tab**

   A table with gridlines appears in the main document, as shown in Figure H-13. Each table cell is the size of a label for the label product you selected.

4. **Save the label main document with the filename Client Labels Main to the drive and folder where you store your Data Files**

   Next, you need to select a data source for the labels.

5. **Click the Select Recipients button in the Start Mail Merge group, then click Use Existing List**

   The Select Data Source dialog box opens.

QUICK TIP
To create or change the return address for an envelope mail merge, click the Office button, click Word Options, click Advanced in the left pane of the Word Options dialog box, then enter the return address in the Mailing address text box in the General section in the right pane.

6. **Navigate to the drive and folder where you store your Data Files, open the file WD H-2.mdb, then save your changes**

   The data source file is attached to the label main document and <<Next Record>> appears in every cell in the table except the first cell, which is blank. In the next lesson you sort and filter the records before performing the mail merge.

Word 190 Merging Word Documents

FIGURE H-12: Label Options dialog box

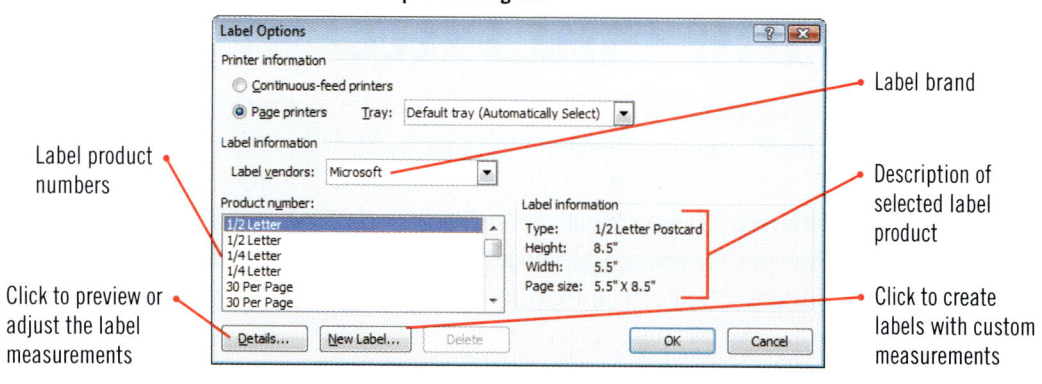

- Label product numbers
- Click to preview or adjust the label measurements
- Label brand
- Description of selected label product
- Click to create labels with custom measurements

FIGURE H-13: Label main document

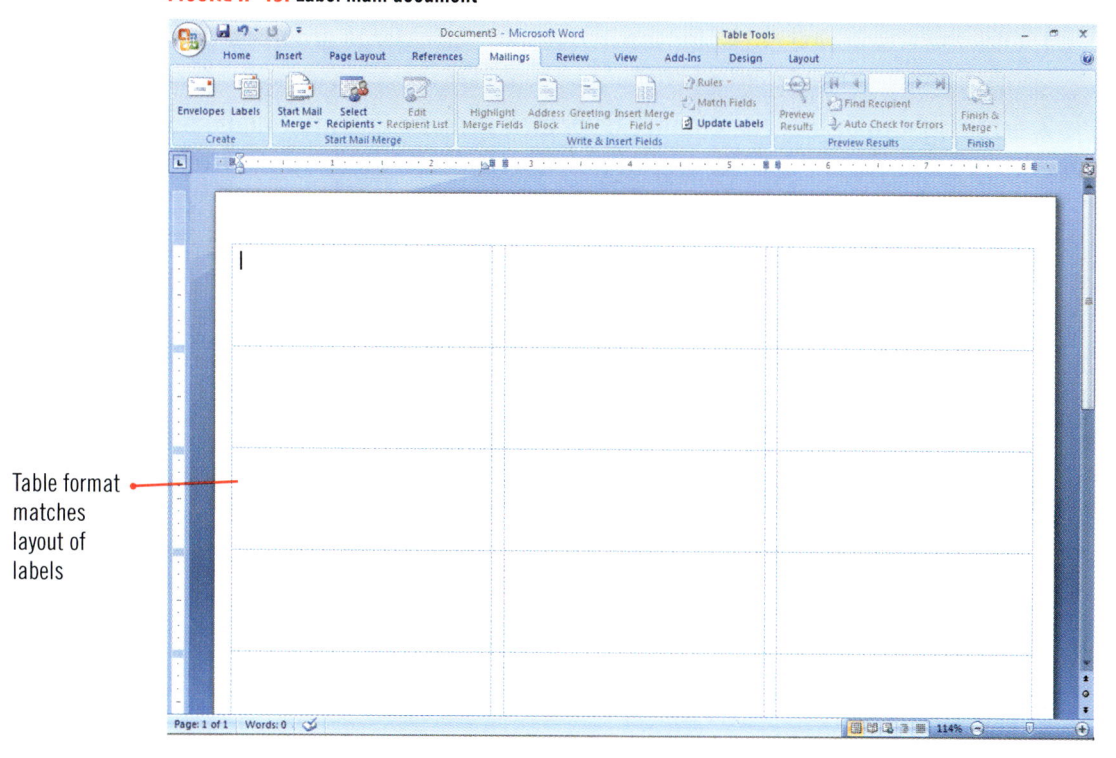

- Table format matches layout of labels

Printing individual envelopes and labels

The Mail Merge feature enables you to easily print envelopes and labels for mass mailings, but you can also quickly format and print individual envelopes and labels using the Envelopes or Labels commands in the Create group on the Mailings tab. Simply click the Envelopes button or Labels button to open the Envelopes and Labels dialog box. On the Envelopes tab, shown in Figure H-14, type the recipient's address in the Delivery address box and the return address in the Return address box. Click Options to open the Envelope Options dialog box, which you can use to select the envelope size, change the font and font size of the delivery and return addresses, and change the printing options. When you are ready to print the envelope, click Print in the Envelopes and Labels dialog box. The procedure for printing an individual label is similar to printing an individual envelope: enter the recipient's address in the Address box on the Labels tab, click Options to select a label product number, click OK, and then click Print.

FIGURE H-14: Envelopes and Labels dialog box

Merging Word Documents

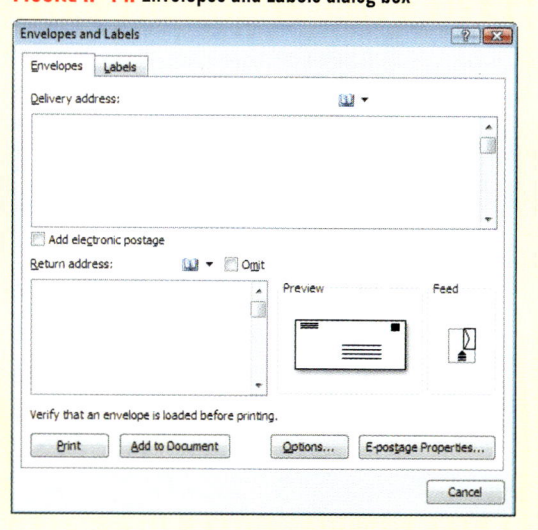

Sorting and Filtering Records

UNIT H
Word 2007

If you are using a large data source, you might want to sort and/or filter the records before performing a merge. **Sorting** the records determines the order in which the records are merged. For example, you might want to sort an address data source so that records are merged alphabetically by last name or in zip code order. **Filtering** the records pulls out the records that meet specific criteria and includes only those records in the merge. For instance, you might want to filter a data source to send a mailing only to people who live in the state of New York. You can use the Mail Merge Recipients dialog box both to sort and to filter a data source. You apply a filter to the data source so that only United States addresses are included in the merge. You then sort those records so that they merge in zip code order.

STEPS

1. **Click the Edit Recipient List button in the Start Mail Merge group**
   The Mail Merge Recipients dialog box opens and displays all the records in the data source.

2. **Scroll right to display the Country field, then click the Country column heading**
   The records are sorted in ascending alphabetical order by country, with Canadian records listed first. If you want to reverse the sort order, you can click the column heading again.

3. **Click the Country column heading list arrow, then click US on the menu that opens**
   A filter is applied to the data source so that only the records with "US" in the Country field will be merged. The grayish-blue arrow in the Country column heading indicates that a filter has been applied to the column. You can filter a data source by as many criteria as you like. To remove a filter, click a column heading list arrow, then click "All."

   > **QUICK TIP**
   > Use the options on the Filter tab to apply more than one filter to the data source.

4. **Click Sort in the Refine recipient list section of the dialog box**
   The Filter and Sort dialog box opens with the Sort Records tab displayed. You can use this dialog box to apply more advanced sort and filter options to the data source.

5. **Click the Sort by list arrow, click ZIP Code, click the first Then by list arrow, click Last Name, then click OK**
   The Mail Merge Recipients dialog box now displays only the records with a US address sorted first in zip code order, and then alphabetically by last name, as shown in Figure H-15.

   > **QUICK TIP**
   > Sorting and filtering a data source does not alter the records in a data source; it simply reorganizes the records for the current merge only.

6. **Click OK**
   The sort and filter criteria you set are saved for the current merge.

7. **Click the Address Block button in the Write & Insert Fields group, then click OK in the Insert Address Block dialog box**
   The Address Block merge field is added to the first label.

8. **Click the Update Labels button in the Write & Insert Fields group**
   The merge field is copied from the first label to every label in the main document.

   > **QUICK TIP**
   > To change the font or paragraph formatting of merged data, format the merge fields before performing a merge, including the chevrons.

9. **Click the Preview Results button in the Preview Results group**
   A preview of the merged label data appears in the main document, as shown in Figure H-16. Only U.S. addresses are included, and the labels are organized in zip code order, with recipients with the same zip code listed in alphabetical order.

10. **Click the Finish & Merge button in the Finish group, click Edit Individual Documents, click OK in the Merge to New Document dialog box, replace Ms. Carmen Landfair with your name in the first label, save the document as Client Labels US Only Zip Code Merge to the drive and folder where you store your Data Files, print the labels, save and close all open files, then exit Word**

Merging Word Documents

FIGURE H-15: US records sorted in zip code order

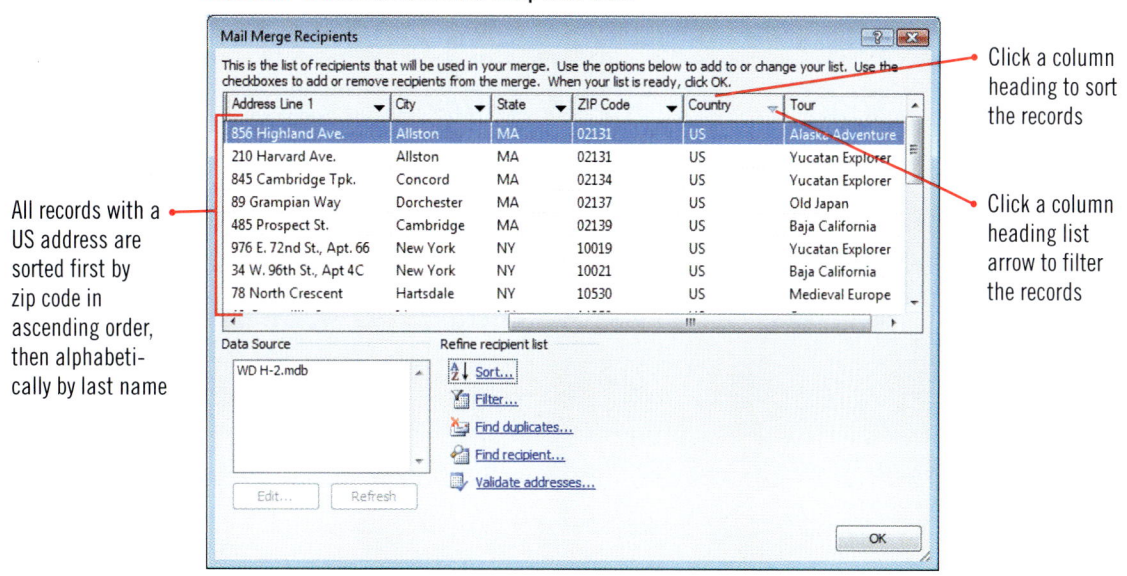

All records with a US address are sorted first by zip code in ascending order, then alphabetically by last name

Click a column heading to sort the records

Click a column heading list arrow to filter the records

FIGURE H-16: Merged labels

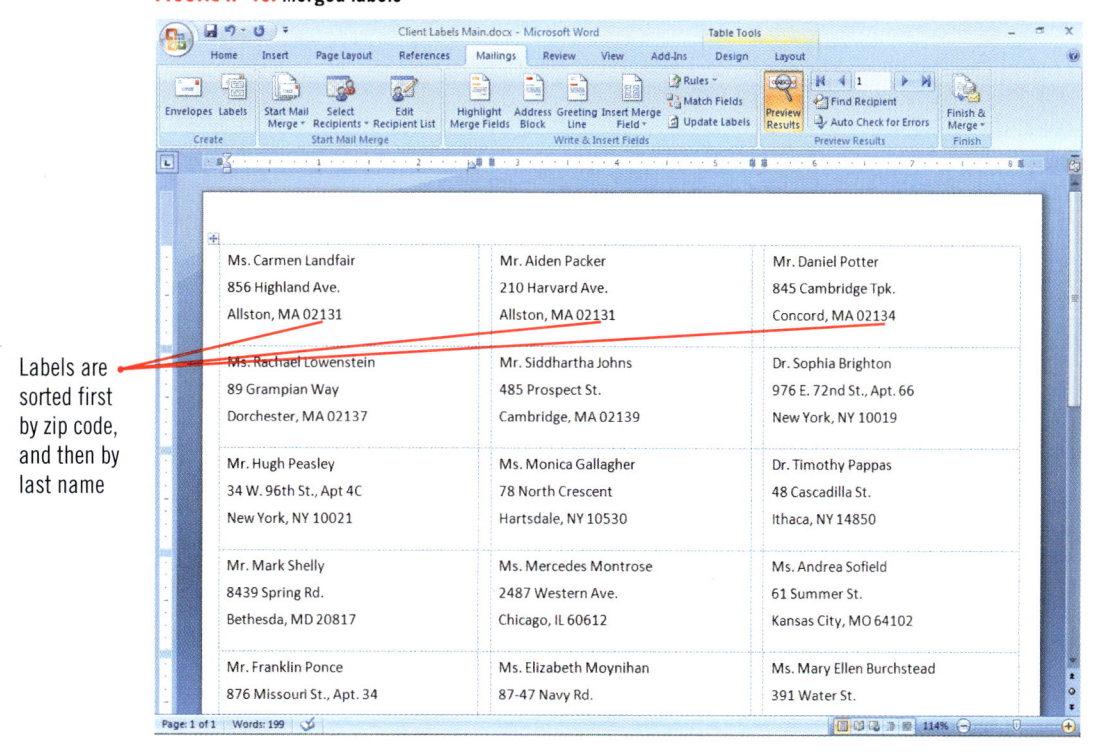

Labels are sorted first by zip code, and then by last name

Inserting individual merge fields

You must include proper punctuation, spacing, and blank lines between the merge fields in a main document if you want punctuation, spaces, and blank lines to appear between the data in the merge documents. For example, to create an address line with a city, state, and zip code, you insert the City merge field, type a comma and a space, insert the State merge field, type a space, and then insert the ZIP Code merge field: <<City>>, <<State>> <<ZIP Code>>.

You can insert an individual merge field by clicking the Insert Merge Field list arrow in the Write & Insert Fields group and then selecting the field name from the menu that opens. Alternatively, you can click the Insert Merge Field button to open the Insert Merge Field dialog box, which you can use to insert several merge fields at once by clicking a field name in the dialog box, clicking Insert, clicking another field name, clicking Insert, and so on. When you have finished inserting the merge fields, click Close to close the dialog box. You can then add spaces, punctuation, and lines between the merge fields you inserted in the main document.

Merging Word Documents

Practice

▼ CONCEPTS REVIEW

If you have a SAM user profile, you may have access to hands-on instruction, practice, and assessment of the skills covered in this unit. Log in to your SAM account (http://sam2007.course.com/) to launch any assigned training activities or exams that relate to the skills covered in this unit.

Describe the function of each button shown in Figure H-17.

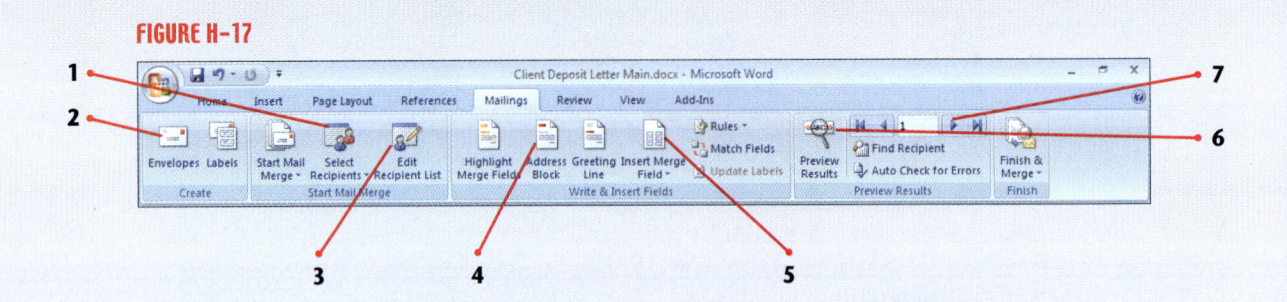

FIGURE H-17

Match each term with the statement that best describes it.

8. Data field
9. Main document
10. Data source
11. Data record
12. Boilerplate text
13. Merge field
14. Sort
15. Filter

a. A file that contains customized information for each item or individual
b. A category of information in a data source
c. A complete set of information for one item or individual
d. A placeholder for merged data in the main document
e. To organize records in a sequence
f. To pull out records that meet certain criteria
g. The standard text that appears in every version of a merged document
h. A file that contains boilerplate text and merge fields

Select the best answer from the list of choices.

16. In a mail merge, which type of file contains the information that varies for each individual or item?
    a. Main document
    b. Data source
    c. Filtered document
    d. Sorted document

17. To change the font of merged data, which element should you format?
    a. Merge field
    b. Data record
    c. Field name
    d. Boilerplate text

18. Which command is used to synchronize the field names in a data source with the merge fields in a document?
    a. Update Labels
    b. Rules
    c. Highlight Merge Fields
    d. Match Fields

19. Which action do you perform on a data source in order to merge only certain records?
    a. Sort records
    b. Edit records
    c. Delete records
    d. Filter records

20. Which action do you perform on a data source to reorganize the order of the records for a merge?
    a. Sort records
    b. Edit records
    c. Delete records
    d. Filter records

Merging Word Documents

▼ SKILLS REVIEW

1. **Create a main document.**
   a. Start Word, change the style of the document to No Spacing, then open the Mail Merge task pane.
   b. Use the Mail Merge task pane to create a letter main document, click Next, then select the current (blank) document.
   c. At the top of the blank document, type **New England Humanities Council**, press [Enter], then type **1375 Harbor Street, Portsmouth, NH 03828; Tel: 603-555-8457; www.nehumanities.org**
   d. Press [Enter] five times, type today's date, press [Enter] five times, then type **We are delighted to receive your generous contribution of AMOUNT to the New England Humanities Council (NEHC).**
   e. Press [Enter] twice, then type **Whether we are helping adult new readers learn to read or bringing humanities programs into our public schools, senior centers, and prisons, NEHC depends upon private contributions to ensure that free public humanities programs continue to flourish in CITY and throughout the REGION region.**
   f. Press [Enter] twice, type **Sincerely,** press [Enter] four times, type your name, press [Enter], then type **Executive Director.**
   g. Center the first two lines of text, change the font of New England Humanities Council to 28 point Bernard MT Condensed, then remove the hyperlink. (*Hint*: Right-click the hyperlink.)
   h. Save the main document as **Donor Thank You Main** to the drive and folder where you store your Data Files.

2. **Design a data source.**
   a. Click Next, select the Type a new list option button in the Step 3 of 6 Mail Merge task pane, then click Create.
   b. Click Customize Columns in the New Address List dialog box, then remove these fields from the data source: Company Name, Address Line 2, Country or Region, Home Phone, Work Phone, and E-mail Address.
   c. Add an **Amount** field and a **Region** field to the data source. Be sure these fields follow the ZIP Code field.
   d. Rename the Address Line 1 field **Street**, then click OK to close the Customize Address List dialog box.

3. **Enter and edit records.**
   a. Add the following records to the data source:

Title	First Name	Last Name	Street	City	State	Zip Code	Amount	Region
Mr.	John	Conlin	34 Mill St.	Exeter	NH	03833	$250	Seacoast
Mr.	Bill	Webster	289 Sugar Hill Rd.	Franconia	NH	03632	$1000	Seacoast
Ms.	Susan	Janak	742 Main St.	Derby	VT	04634	$25	North Country
Mr.	Derek	Gray	987 Ocean Rd.	Portsmouth	NH	03828	$50	Seacoast
Ms.	Rita	Murphy	73 Bay Rd.	Durham	NH	03814	$500	Seacoast
Ms.	Amy	Hunt	67 Apple St.	Northfield	MA	01360	$75	Pioneer Valley
Ms.	Eliza	Pope	287 Mountain Rd.	Dublin	NH	03436	$100	Monadnock

   b. Save the data source as **Donor Data** to the drive and folder where you store your Data Files.
   c. Change the region for record 2 (Bill Webster) from Seacoast to **White Mountain**.
   d. Click OK to close the Mail Merge Recipients dialog box.

4. **Add merge fields.**
   a. Click Next, then in the blank line above the first body paragraph, insert an Address Block merge field.
   b. In the Insert Address Block dialog box, click Match Fields.
   c. Click the list arrow next to Address 1 in the Match Fields dialog box, click Street, then click OK.
   d. In the Insert Address Block dialog box, select the Never include the country/region in the address option button, then click OK.
   e. Press [Enter] twice, insert a Greeting Line merge field using the default greeting line format, then press [Enter].
   f. In the first body paragraph, replace AMOUNT with the Amount merge field.
   g. In the second body paragraph, replace CITY with the City merge field and REGION with the Region merge field. (*Note*: Make sure to insert a space before or after each merge field as needed.) Save your changes to the main document.

▼ SKILLS REVIEW (CONTINUED)

5. Merge data.

a. Click Next to preview the merged data, then scroll through each letter, examining it carefully for errors.

b. Click the Preview Results button on the Mailings tab, make any necessary adjustments to the letter, save your changes, then click the Preview Results button to return to the preview of the document.

c. Click Next, click Edit individual letters, then merge all the records to a new file.

d. Save the merged document as **Donor Thank You Merge** to the drive and folder where you store your Data Files, print a copy of the last letter, shown in Figure H-18, then save and close all open files.

FIGURE H-18

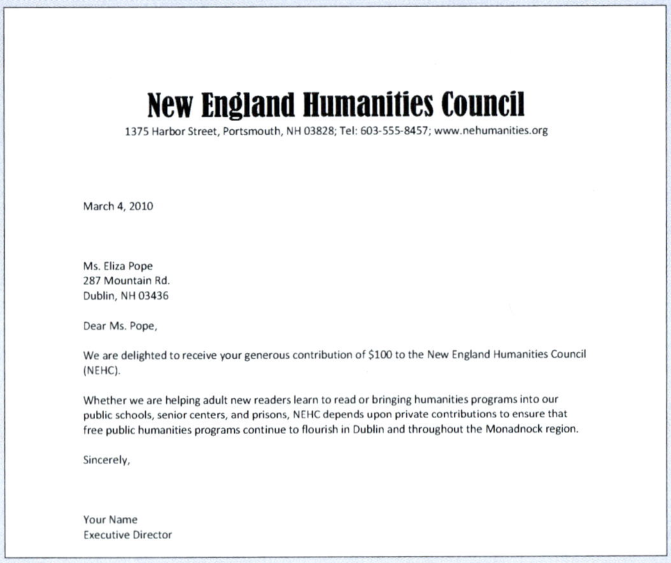

New England Humanities Council
1375 Harbor Street, Portsmouth, NH 03828; Tel: 603-555-8457; www.nehumanities.org

March 4, 2010

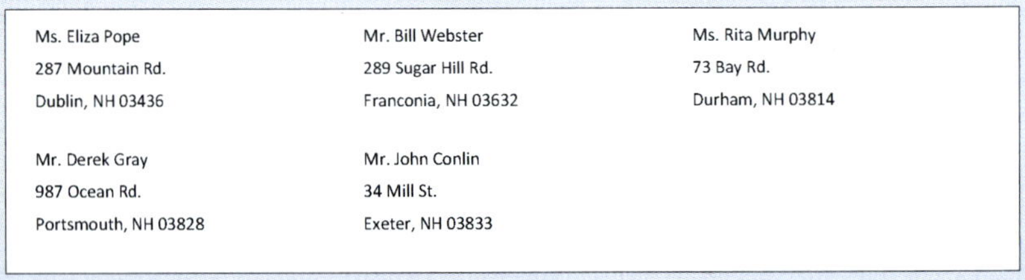

Ms. Eliza Pope
287 Mountain Rd.
Dublin, NH 03436

Dear Ms. Pope,

We are delighted to receive your generous contribution of $100 to the New England Humanities Council (NEHC).

Whether we are helping adult new readers learn to read or bringing humanities programs into our public schools, senior centers, and prisons, NEHC depends upon private contributions to ensure that free public humanities programs continue to flourish in Dublin and throughout the Monadnock region.

Sincerely,

Your Name
Executive Director

6. Create labels.

a. Open a new blank document, click the Start Mail Merge button on the Mailings tab, then create a label main document.

b. In the Label Options dialog box, select Avery US Letter 5160 labels, then click OK.

c. Click the Select Recipients button, then open the Donor Data.mdb file you created.

d. Save the label main document as **Donor Labels Main** to the drive and folder where you store your Data Files.

7. Sort and filter records.

a. Click the Edit Recipient List button, filter the records so that only the records with NH in the State field are included in the merge, sort the records in zip code order, then click OK.

b. Insert an Address Block merge field using the default settings, click the Preview Results button, then notice that the street address is missing and the address block includes the region.

c. Click the Preview Results button, then click the Match Fields button to open the Match Fields dialog box.

d. Click the list arrow next to Address 1, click Street, scroll down, click the list arrow next to Country or Region, click (not matched), then click OK.

e. Click the Preview Results button to preview the merged data, and notice that the address block now includes the street address and the region name is missing.

f. Click the Update Labels button, examine the merged data for errors, then correct any mistakes.

g. Merge all the records to an individual document, shown in Figure H-19, then save the merged file as **Donor Labels NH Only Merge** to the drive and folder where you store your Data Files.

h. In the first label, change Ms. Eliza Pope to your name, print the document, save and close all open Word files, then exit Word.

FIGURE H-19

Ms. Eliza Pope	Mr. Bill Webster	Ms. Rita Murphy
287 Mountain Rd.	289 Sugar Hill Rd.	73 Bay Rd.
Dublin, NH 03436	Franconia, NH 03632	Durham, NH 03814
Mr. Derek Gray	Mr. John Conlin	
987 Ocean Rd.	34 Mill St.	
Portsmouth, NH 03828	Exeter, NH 03833	

▼ INDEPENDENT CHALLENGE 1

You are the director of the Eliot Arts Center (EAC). The EAC is hosting an exhibit of ceramic art in the city of Cambridge, Massachusetts, and you want to send a letter advertising the exhibit to all EAC members with a Cambridge address. You'll use Mail Merge to create the letter. If you are performing the ACE steps and are able to print envelopes on your printer, you will also use Word to print an envelope for one letter.

a. Start Word, then using either the Mailings tab or the Mail Merge task pane, create a letter main document using the file WD H-3.docx, found in the drive and folder where you store your Data Files.
b. Replace Your Name with your name in the signature block, then save the main document as **EAC Member Letter Main**.
c. Use the file WD H-4.mdb, found in the location where you store your Data Files, as the data source.
d. Sort the data source by last name, then filter the data so that only records with Cambridge as the city are included in the merge.
e. Insert an Address Block and a Greeting Line merge field in the main document, then preview the merged letters.
f. Merge all the records to a new document, then save it as **EAC Member Letter Merge**.

Advanced Challenge Exercise

- If you can print envelopes, select the inside address in the first merge letter, then click the Envelopes button in the Create group on the Mailings tab.
- On the Envelopes tab, verify that the Omit check box is not selected, then type your name in the Return address text box along with the address **60 Crandall Street, Concord, MA 01742.**
- Click Options. On the Envelope Options tab, make sure the Envelope size is set to Size 10, then change the font of the Delivery address and the Return address to Times New Roman.
- On the Printing Options tab, select the appropriate Feed method for your printer, then click OK.
- Click Add to Document, click No if a message box opens asking if you want to save the new return address as the default return address, then print the envelope.

g. Print the first merge letter, close all open Word files, saving changes, and then exit Word.

▼ INDEPENDENT CHALLENGE 2

One of your responsibilities at Green Mountain Forestry, a growing forestry services company, is to create business cards for the staff. You use mail merge to create the cards so that you can easily produce standard business cards for future employees.

a. Start Word, then use the Mailings tab or the Mail Merge task pane to create labels using the current blank document.
b. Select Microsoft Business Card 2" high x 3.5" wide labels. (*Hint*: Select the seventh instance of Business Card in the Product number list box.)
c. Create a new data source that includes the fields and records shown below:

Title	First Name	Last Name	Phone	Fax	E-mail	Hire Date
President	Sandra	Bryson	(541) 555-3982	(541) 555-6654	sbryson@gmf.com	1/12/07
Vice President	Philip	Holm	(541) 555-2323	(541) 555-4956	pholm@gmf.com	3/18/09

d. Add six more records to the data source, including one with your name as the Administrative Assistant.
e. Save the data source with the filename **GMF Employee Data** to the drive and folder where you store your Data Files, then sort the data by Title.

▼ INDEPENDENT CHALLENGE 2 (CONTINUED)

f. In the first table cell, create the Green Mountain Forestry business card. Figure H-20 shows a sample business card, but you should create your own design. Include the company name, a street address, and the Web site address www.gmforestry.com. Also include First Name, Last Name, Title, Phone, Fax, and E-mail merge fields. (*Hint*: If your design includes a graphic, insert the graphic before inserting the merge fields. Insert each merge field individually, adjusting the spacing between merge fields as necessary.)

FIGURE H-20

Green Mountain Forestry

Allison Smythe
Marketing Director

476 Mountain Road, Jackson, OR 97535
Tel: (541) 555-9988
Fax: (541) 555-3456
E-mail: asmythe@gmf.com
Web: www.gmforestry.com

g. Format the business card with fonts, colors, and other formatting features. (*Hint*: Make sure to select the entire merge field, including the chevrons, before formatting.)
h. Update all the labels, preview the data, make any necessary adjustments, then merge all the records to a new document.
i. Save the merge document as **GMF Business Cards Merge** to the drive and folder where you store your Data Files, print a copy, then close the file.
j. Save the main document as **GMF Business Cards Main** to the drive and folder where you store your Data Files, close the file, then exit Word.

▼ INDEPENDENT CHALLENGE 3

You need to create a team roster for the children's softball team you coach. You decide to use mail merge to create the team roster. If you are completing the ACE steps, you will also use mail merge to create mailing labels.

a. Start Word, then use the Mailings tab or the Mail Merge task pane to create a directory using the current blank document.
b. Create a new data source that includes the following fields: First Name, Last Name, Age, Position, Parent First Name, Parent Last Name, Address, City, State, Zip Code, and Home Phone.
c. Enter the following records in the data source:

First Name	Last Name	Age	Position	Parent First Name	Parent Last Name	Address	City	State	Zip Code	Home Phone
Sophie	Wright	8	Shortstop	Kerry	Wright	58 Main St.	Camillus	NY	13031	555-2345
Will	Jacob	7	Catcher	Bob	Jacob	32 North Way	Camillus	NY	13031	555-9827
Brett	Eliot	8	First base	Olivia	Eliot	289 Sylvan Way	Marcellus	NY	13032	555-9724
Abby	Herman	7	Pitcher	Sarah	Thomas	438 Lariat St.	Marcellus	NY	13032	555-8347

d. Add five additional records to the data source using the following last names and positions:
O'Keefe, Second base
George, Third base
Goleman, Left field
Siebert, Center field
Choy, Right field
Make up the remaining information for these five records.
e. Save the data source as **Softball Team Data** to the drive and folder where you store your Data Files, then sort the records by last name.
f. Insert a table that includes five columns and one row in the main document.
g. In the first table cell, insert the First Name and Last Name merge fields, separated by a space.
h. In the second cell, insert the Position merge field.

▼ INDEPENDENT CHALLENGE 3 (CONTINUED)

i. In the third cell, insert the Address and City merge fields, separated by a comma and a space.
j. In the fourth cell, insert the Home Phone merge field.
k. In the fifth cell, insert the Parent First Name and Parent Last Name merge fields, separated by a space.
l. Preview the merged data and make any necessary adjustments. (*Hint*: Only one record is displayed at a time when you preview the data.)
m. Merge all the records to a new document, then save the document as **Softball Roster Merge** to the drive and folder where you store your Data Files.
n. Press [Ctrl][Home], press [Enter], type **Wildcats Team Roster 2010** at the top of the document, press [Enter], type **Coach:** followed by your name, press [Enter], then center the two lines.
o. Insert a new row at the top of the table, then type the following column headings in the new row: **Name, Position, Address, Phone, Parent Name.**
p. Format the roster to make it attractive and readable, save your changes, print a copy, then close the file.
q. Close the main document without saving changes.

Advanced Challenge Exercise

- Open a new blank document, then use Mail Merge to create mailing labels using Avery US Letter 5162 address labels.
- Use the Softball Team Data data source you created, and sort the records first in zip code order, and then alphabetically by parent last name.
- In the first table cell, create your own address block using the Parent First Name, Parent Last Name, Address, City, State, and Zip Code merge fields. Be sure to include proper spacing and punctuation.
- Update all the labels, preview the merged data, merge all the records to a new document, then type your name centered in the document header.
- Save the document as **Softball Labels Merge ACE** to the drive and folder where you store your Data Files, print a copy, close the file, then close the main document without saving changes.

r. Exit Word.

▼ REAL LIFE INDEPENDENT CHALLENGE

Mail merge can be used not only for mailings, but to create CD/DVD labels, labels for file folders, phone directories, business cards, and many other types of documents. In this independent challenge, you design and create a data source that you can use at work or in your personal life, and then you merge the data source with a main document that you create. Your data source might include contact information for your friends and associates, inventory for your business, data on one of your collections (such as music or photos), or some other type of information.

a. Determine the content of your data source, list the fields you want to include, and then determine the logical order of the fields. Be sure to select your fields carefully so that your data source is flexible and can be merged with many types of documents. Generally it is better to include more fields, even if you don't enter data in them for each record.
b. Start Word, start a mail merge for the type of document you want to create (such as a directory or a label), then create a new data source.
c. Customize the columns in the data source to include the fields and organization you determined in step a.
d. Add at least 5 records to the data source, then save it as **Your Name Data** to the location where you store your Data Files.
e. Write and format the main document, insert the merge fields, preview the merge, make any necessary adjustments, then merge the files to a document.
f. Adjust the formatting of the merge document as necessary, add your name to the header, print a copy, save the merge document as **Your Name Merge Document**, save the main document as **Your Name Main Document**, both to the drive and folder where you store your Data Files, then close all open files and exit Word.

▼ VISUAL WORKSHOP

Using mail merge, create the postcards shown in Figure H-21. Use Avery US Letter 3263 wide postcard labels for the main document and create a data source that contains at least four records, including your name. Save the data source as **Patient Data**, save the merge document as **Patient Appointment Card Merge**, and save the main document as **Patient Appointment Card Main**, all to the drive and folder where you store your Data Files. (*Hints*: Notice that the postcard label main document is formatted as a table. To layout the postcard, insert a nested table with two columns and one row in the upper-left postcard; add the text, graphic, and merge field to the nested table; and then remove the outside borders on the nested table. The clip art graphic uses the keyword "tooth" and the font is Comic Sans MS.) Print a copy of the postcards.

FIGURE H-21

Sylvia T. Ramirez, D.D.S.
425 East 72nd Street, New York, NY 10021
Telephone: 212-555-0890

Mr. Francisco Cortez
874 East 86th Street
Apt. 3B
New York, NY 10028

Our records indicate it is time for your dental cleaning and exam. Please call our office now to schedule your appointment.

Sylvia T. Ramirez, D.D.S.
425 East 72nd Street, New York, NY 10021
Telephone: 212-555-0890

Mr. Thomas Parker
756 Lexington Avenue
Apt. 6C
New York, NY 10024

Our records indicate it is time for your dental cleaning and exam. Please call our office now to schedule your appointment.

Analyzing Data Using Formulas

UNIT E — Excel 2007

Files You Will Need:
EX E-1.xlsx
EX E-2.xlsx
EX E-3.xlsx
EX E-4.xlsx
EX E-5.xlsx
EX E-6.xlsx
EX E-7.xlsx

As you have learned, formulas and functions help you to analyze worksheet data. As you learn how to use different types of formulas and functions, you will discover more valuable uses for Excel. In this unit, you will gain a deeper understanding of Excel formulas and learn how to use several Excel functions. Kate Morgan, QST's vice president of sales, uses Excel formulas and functions to analyze sales data for the U.S. region and to consolidate sales data from several worksheets. Because management is considering adding a new regional branch, Kate asks you to estimate the loan costs for a new office facility and to compare tour sales in the existing U.S. offices.

OBJECTIVES

Format data using text functions
Sum a data range based on conditions
Consolidate data using a formula
Check formulas for errors
Construct formulas using named ranges
Build a logical formula with the IF function
Build a logical formula with the AND function
Calculate payments with the PMT function

Formatting Data Using Text Functions

UNIT E — Excel 2007

Often, data you import needs restructuring or reformatting to be understandable and attractive, or to match the formatting of other data in your worksheet. Instead of handling these tasks manually in each cell, you can use Excel conversion tools and text functions to perform these tasks automatically for a range of cell data. The Convert Text to Columns feature breaks data fields in one column into separate columns. Your data elements should be separated by a **delimiter**, or separator, such as a space, comma, or semicolon. The text function PROPER capitalizes (converts to a proper noun) the first letter in a string of text as well as any text following a space. For example, if cell A1 contains the text string marketing department, then =PROPER(A1) would display Marketing Department. The CONCATENATE function is used to join two or more strings into one text string. Kate has received the U.S. sales representatives' data from the human resources department. She asks you to use text formulas to format the data into a more useful layout.

STEPS

1. Start Excel, open the file EX E-1.xlsx from the drive and folder where you store your Data Files, then save it as Sales Data

2. On the Sales Reps sheet, select the range A4:A15, click the Data tab, then click the Text to Columns button in the Data Tools group

   The Convert Text to Columns Wizard opens, as shown in Figure E-1. The data fields on your worksheet are separated by commas, which will act as delimiters.

3. If necessary, click the Delimited option button to select it, click Next, in the Delimiters area of the dialog box click the Comma check box to select it if necessary, click any other selected check boxes to deselect them, then click Next

   You instructed Excel to separate your data at the comma delimiter.

4. Click the Text option button in the Column data format area, click the General column to select it in the Data preview area, click the Text option button in the Column data format area, then click Finish

   The data are separated into three columns of text. You want to format the letters to the correct cases.

> **QUICK TIP**
> You can move the Function Arguments dialog box if it overlaps a cell or range that you need to click. You can also click the Collapse Dialog Box button, select the cell or range, then click the Expand Dialog box button to return to the Function Arguments dialog box.

5. Click cell D4, click the Formulas tab, click the Text button in the Function Library group, click PROPER, with the insertion point in the Text text box, click cell A4, then click OK

   The name is copied from cell A4 to cell D4 with the correct uppercase letters for proper names. The remaining names and the cities are still in lowercase letters.

6. Drag the fill handle to copy the formula in cell D4 to cell E4, then copy the formulas in cells D4:E4 into the range D5:E15

   You want to format the years data to be more descriptive.

> **QUICK TIP**
> Excel automatically inserts quotation marks to enclose the space and the Years text.

7. Click cell F4, click the Text button in the Function Library group, click CONCATENATE, with the insertion point in the Text1 text box, click cell C4, press [Tab], with the insertion point in the Text2 text box, press [Spacebar], type Years, then click OK

8. Copy the formula in cell F4 into the range F5:F15, click the Insert tab, click the Header & Footer button in the Text group, click the Go to Footer button in the Navigation group, enter your name in the center text box, click cell A1, then click the Normal button in the status bar

9. Save your file, then print the worksheet and compare your work to Figure E-2

Excel 106 — Analyzing Data Using Formulas

FIGURE E-1: Convert Text to Columns dialog box

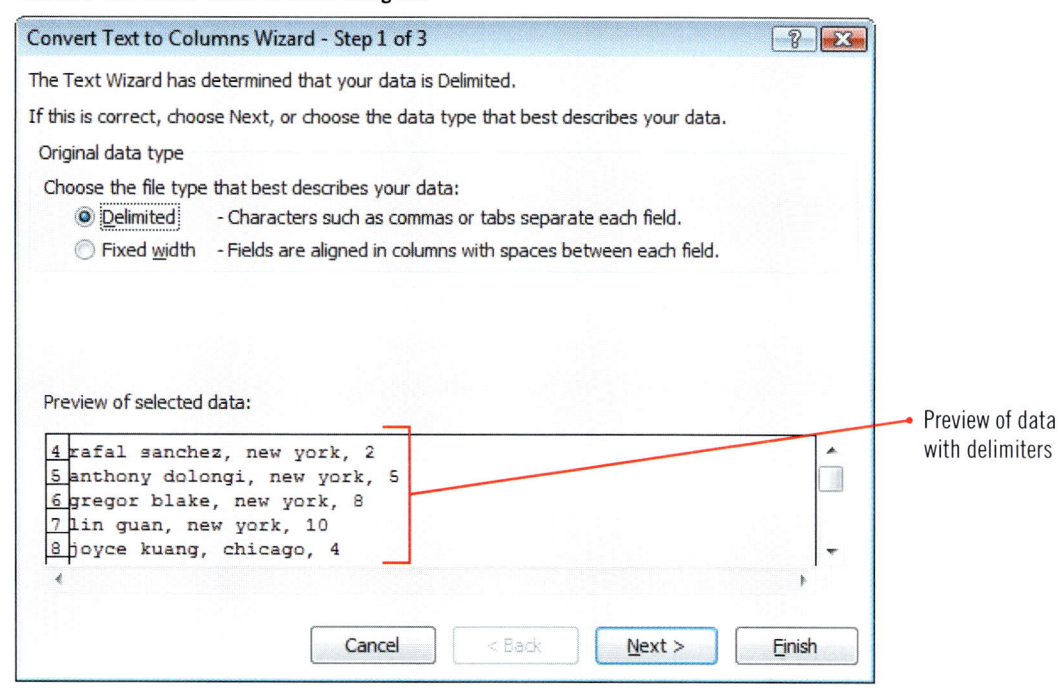

Preview of data with delimiters

FIGURE E-2: Worksheet with data formatted in columns

Using text functions

Other commonly used text functions include UPPER, LOWER, and SUBSTITUTE. The UPPER function converts text to all uppercase letters, the LOWER function converts text to all lowercase letters, and SUBSTITUTE replaces text in a text string. For example, if cell A1 contains the text string Today is Wednesday, then =LOWER(A1) would produce today is wednesday, =UPPER(A1) would produce TODAY IS WEDNESDAY, and =SUBSTITUTE(A1, "Wednesday", "Tuesday") would result in Today is Tuesday.

If you want to copy and paste data formatted using text functions, you need to select Values Only from the Paste Options drop-down list to paste the cell values rather than the text formulas.

Analyzing Data Using Formulas

UNIT E
Excel 2007

Summing a Data Range Based on Conditions

You have learned how to use the SUM, COUNT, and AVERAGE functions for data ranges. You can also use Excel functions to sum, count, and average data in a range based on criteria, or conditions, you set. The SUMIF function conditionally totals cells in a sum range that meet given criteria. For example, you can total the values in a column of sales where a sales rep name equals Joe Smith (the criterion). Similarly, the COUNTIF function counts cells and the AVERAGEIF function averages cells in a range based on a specified condition. The format for the SUMIF function appears in Figure E-3. Kate asks you to analyze the New York branch's January sales data to provide her with information about each tour.

STEPS

1. **Click the NY sheet tab, click cell G7, click the Formulas tab, click the More Functions button in the Function Library group, point to Statistical, then click COUNTIF**

   The Function Arguments dialog box opens, as shown in Figure E-4. You want to count the number of times Pacific Odyssey appears in the Tour column. The formula you use will say, in effect, "Examine the range I specify, then count the number of cells in that range that contain "Pacific Odyssey." You will specify absolute addresses for the range so you can copy the formula.

2. **With the insertion point in the Range text box, select the range A6:A25, press [F4], press [Tab], with the insertion point in the Criteria text box, click cell F7, then click OK**

   The number of Pacific Odyssey tours, 4, appears in cell G7. You want to calculate the total sales revenue for the Pacific Odyssey tours.

   > **QUICK TIP**
   > You can also sum, count, and average ranges with multiple criteria using the functions SUMIFS, COUNTIFS, and AVERAGEIFS

3. **Click cell H7, click the Math & Trig button in the Function Library group, scroll down the list of functions, then click SUMIF**

   The Function Arguments dialog box opens. You want to enter two ranges and a criterion; the first range is the one where you want Excel to search for the criteria entered. The second range contains the corresponding cells that will be totaled when the criterion you want Excel to search for in the first range is met.

4. **With the insertion point in the Range text box, select the range A6:A25, press [F4], press [Tab], with the insertion point in the Criteria text box, click cell F7, press [Tab], with the insertion point in the Sum_range text box, select the range B6:B25, press [F4], then click OK**

   Your formula asks Excel to search the range A6:A25, and where it finds the value shown in cell F7 (that is, when it finds the value Pacific Odyssey), add the corresponding amounts from column B. The revenue for the Pacific Odyssey tours, 12403, appears in cell H7. You want to calculate the average price paid for the Pacific Odyssey tours.

5. **Click cell I7, click the More Functions button in the Function Library group, point to Statistical, then click AVERAGEIF**

6. **With the insertion point in the Range text box, select the range A6:A25, press [F4], press [Tab], with the insertion point in the Criteria text box, click cell F7, press [Tab], with the insertion point in the Average_range text box, select the range B6:B25, press [F4], then click OK**

   The average price paid for the Pacific Odyssey tours, 3101, appears in cell I7.

7. **Select the range G7:I7, then drag the fill handle to fill the range G8:I10**

   Compare your results with those in Figure E-5.

8. **Add your name to the center of the footer, save the workbook, then preview and print the worksheet**

FIGURE E-3: Format of SUMIF function

$$\text{SUMIF}(\underline{\text{range}}, \underline{\text{criteria}}, [\underline{\text{sum\_range}}])$$

- The range the function searches
- The condition that must be satisfied in the range
- The range where the cells that meet the condition will be totaled

FIGURE E-4: COUNTIF function in the Function Arguments dialog box

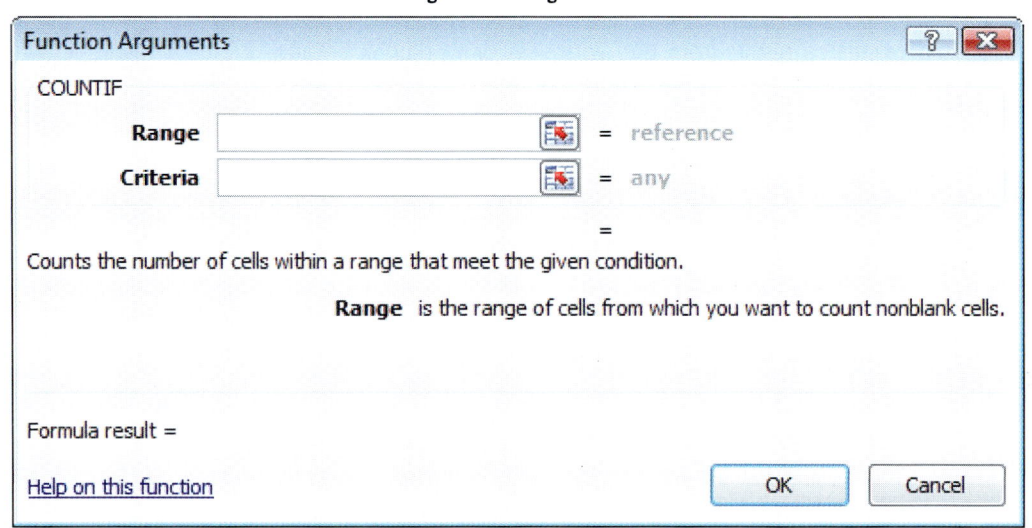

FIGURE E-5: Worksheet with conditional statistics

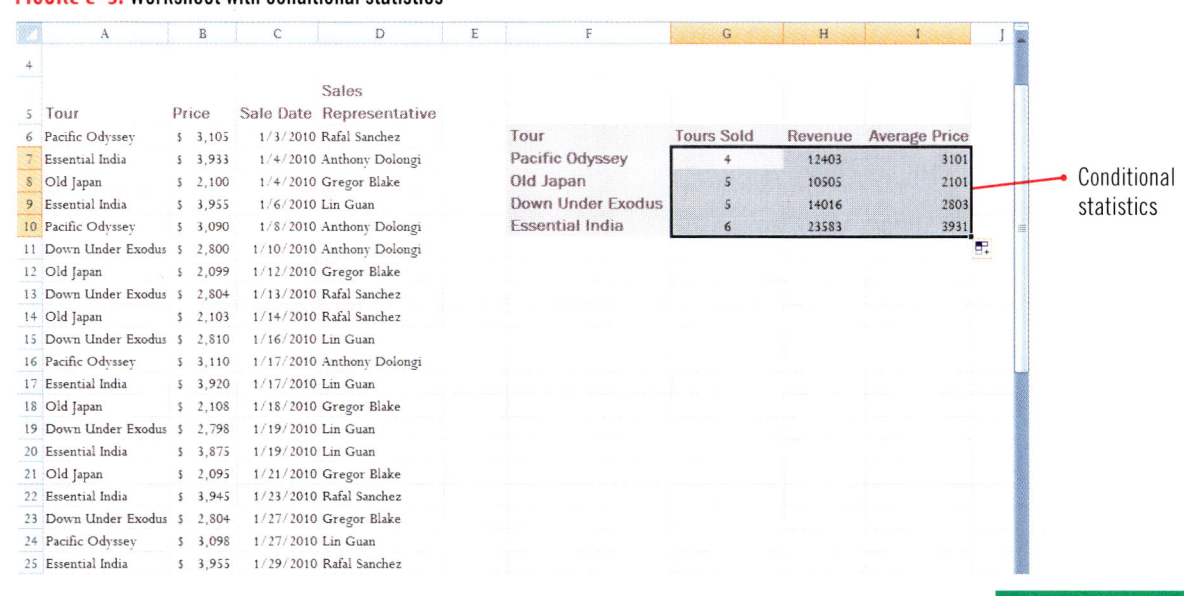

	A	B	C	D	E	F	G	H	I
4									
5	Tour	Price	Sale Date	Sales Representative		Tour	Tours Sold	Revenue	Average Price
6	Pacific Odyssey	$ 3,105	1/3/2010	Rafal Sanchez		Pacific Odyssey	4	12403	3101
7	Essential India	$ 3,933	1/4/2010	Anthony Dolongi		Old Japan	5	10505	2101
8	Old Japan	$ 2,100	1/4/2010	Gregor Blake		Down Under Exodus	5	14016	2803
9	Essential India	$ 3,955	1/6/2010	Lin Guan		Essential India	6	23583	3931
10	Pacific Odyssey	$ 3,090	1/8/2010	Anthony Dolongi					
11	Down Under Exodus	$ 2,800	1/10/2010	Anthony Dolongi					
12	Old Japan	$ 2,099	1/12/2010	Gregor Blake					
13	Down Under Exodus	$ 2,804	1/13/2010	Rafal Sanchez					
14	Old Japan	$ 2,103	1/14/2010	Rafal Sanchez					
15	Down Under Exodus	$ 2,810	1/16/2010	Lin Guan					
16	Pacific Odyssey	$ 3,110	1/17/2010	Anthony Dolongi					
17	Essential India	$ 3,920	1/17/2010	Lin Guan					
18	Old Japan	$ 2,108	1/18/2010	Gregor Blake					
19	Down Under Exodus	$ 2,798	1/19/2010	Lin Guan					
20	Essential India	$ 3,875	1/19/2010	Lin Guan					
21	Old Japan	$ 2,095	1/21/2010	Gregor Blake					
22	Essential India	$ 3,945	1/23/2010	Rafal Sanchez					
23	Down Under Exodus	$ 2,804	1/27/2010	Gregor Blake					
24	Pacific Odyssey	$ 3,098	1/27/2010	Lin Guan					
25	Essential India	$ 3,955	1/29/2010	Rafal Sanchez					

Conditional statistics

Analyzing Data Using Formulas

Consolidating Data Using a Formula

UNIT E — Excel 2007

When you want to summarize similar data that exists in different sheets or workbooks, you can **consolidate**, or combine and display, the data in one sheet. For example, you might have entered departmental sales figures on four different store sheets that you want to consolidate on one summary sheet, showing total departmental sales for all stores. The best way to consolidate data is to use cell references to the various sheets on a consolidation, or summary, sheet. Because they reference other sheets that are usually behind the summary sheet, such references effectively create another dimension in the workbook and are called **3-D references**, as shown in Figure E-6. You can reference, or **link** to, data in other sheets and in other workbooks. Linking to a worksheet or workbook is a better method than retyping calculated results from the worksheet or workbook because the data values on which calculated totals depend might change. If you reference the values, any changes to the original values are automatically reflected in the consolidation sheet. Kate asks you to prepare a January sales summary sheet comparing the total U.S. revenue for the tours sold in the month.

STEPS

> **QUICK TIP**
> You can also consolidate data using named ranges. For example, you might have entered team sales figures using the names team1, team2, and team3 on different sheets that you want to consolidate on one summary sheet. As you enter the summary formula you can click the Formulas tab, click the Use in Formula button in the Defined Names group, and select the range name.

1. **Click the US Summary Jan sheet tab**

   Because the US Summary Jan sheet (which is the consolidation sheet) will contain the reference to the data in the other sheets, the cell pointer must reside there when you initiate the reference.

2. **Click cell B7, click the Formulas tab, click the AutoSum button in the Function Library group, click the NY sheet tab, press and hold [Shift] and click the Miami sheet tab, click cell G7, then click the Enter button ✓ on the formula bar**

   The US Summary Jan sheet becomes active, and the formula bar reads =SUM(NY:Miami!G7), as shown in Figure E-7. NY:Miami references the NY, Chicago, and Miami sheets. The ! (exclamation point) is an **external reference indicator**, meaning that the cells referenced are outside the active sheet; G7 is the actual cell reference you want to total in the external sheets. The result, 12, appears in cell B7 of the US Summary Jan sheet; it is the sum of the number of Pacific Odyssey tours sold and referenced in cell G7 of the NY, Chicago, and Miami sheets. Because the Revenue data is in the column to the right of the Tours Sold column on the NY, Chicago, and Miami sheets, you can copy the tours sold summary formula, with its relative addresses, into the cell that holds the revenue summary information.

3. **Drag the fill handle to copy the formula in cell B7 to cell C7**

   The result, 37405, appears in cell C7 of the US Summary Jan sheet, showing the sum of the Pacific Odyssey tour revenue referenced in cell H7 of the NY, Chicago, and Miami sheets.

> **QUICK TIP**
> You can also use a summary worksheet to consolidate yearly sales figures. Place data for each quarter on a separate sheet. On a summary sheet, use a row for each quarter that references each quarter's sales. Then sum the quarterly information to display total yearly sales.

4. **In the US Summary Jan sheet, with the range B7:C7 selected, drag the fill handle to fill the range B8:C10**

   You can test a consolidation reference by changing one cell value on which the formula is based and seeing if the formula result changes.

5. **Click the Chicago sheet tab, edit cell A6 to read Pacific Odyssey, then click the US Summary Jan sheet tab**

   The number of Pacific Odyssey tours sold is automatically updated to 13 and the revenue is increased to 40280, as shown in Figure E-8.

6. **Click the Insert tab, click the Header & Footer button in the Text group, click the Go to Footer button, enter your name in the center text box, click cell A1, then click the Normal button 🔲 in the status bar**

Analyzing Data Using Formulas

FIGURE E-6: Consolidating data from three worksheets

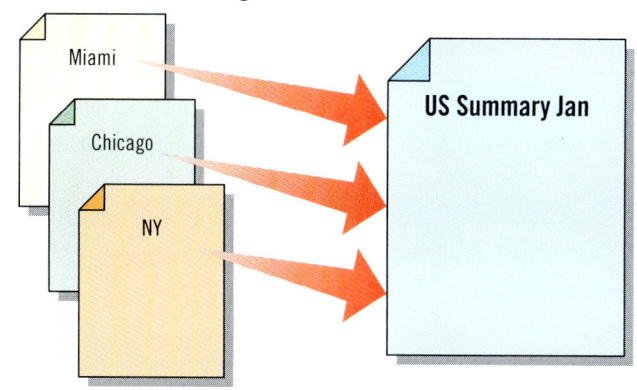

FIGURE E-7: Worksheet showing total Pacific Odyssey tours sold

Formula with 3-D reference

Total Pacific Odyssey tours sold in all three branches

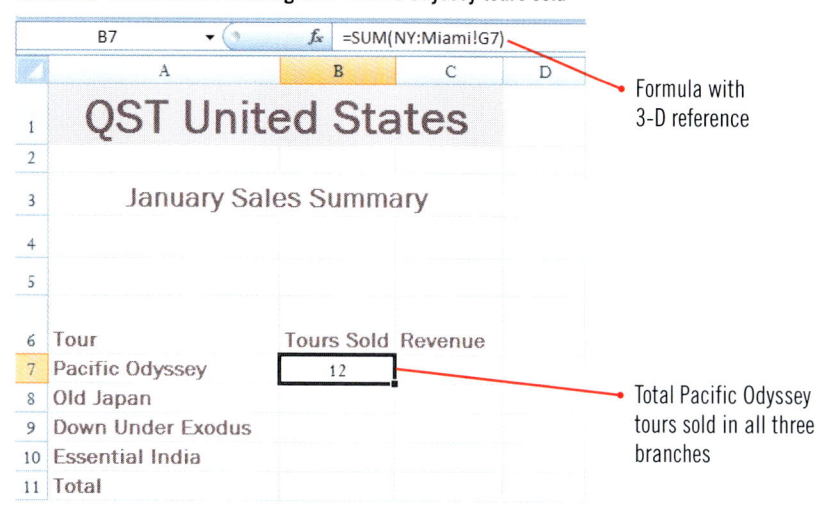

FIGURE E-8: US Summary Jan worksheet with updated totals

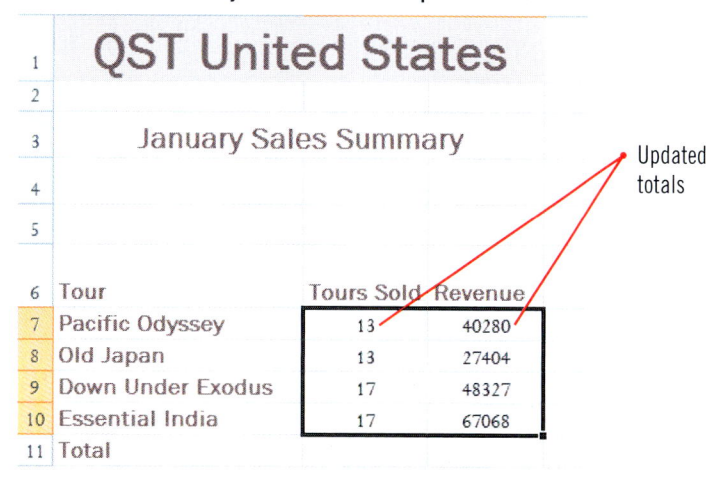

Updated totals

Linking data between workbooks

Just as you can link data between cells in a worksheet and between sheets in a workbook, you can link workbooks so that changes made in referenced cells in one workbook are reflected in the consolidation sheet in the other workbook. To link a single cell between workbooks, open both workbooks, select the cell to receive the linked data, type = (the equal sign), select the cell in the other workbook containing the data to be linked, then press [Enter]. Excel automatically inserts the name of the referenced workbook in the cell reference. For example, if the linked data is contained in cell C7 of worksheet New in the Products workbook, the cell entry reads ='[Product.xlsx]New'!$C$7. To perform calculations, enter formulas on the consolidation sheet using cells in the supporting sheets. If you are linking more than one cell, you can copy the linked data to the Clipboard, select the upper left cell in the workbook to receive the link, click the Home tab, click the Paste list arrow, then click Paste Link.

Analyzing Data Using Formulas

UNIT E
Excel 2007
Checking Formulas for Errors

When formulas result in errors, Excel displays an error value based on the error type. See Table E-1 for a description of the error types and error codes that might appear in worksheets. The IFERROR function simplifies the error-checking process for your worksheets. This function displays a message or value that you specify, rather than the one automatically generated by Excel, if there is an error in a formula. Kate asks you to use formulas to compare the tour revenues for January. You will use the IFERROR function to help catch formula errors.

STEPS

1. **Click cell B11, click the Formulas tab, click the AutoSum button in the Function Library group, then click the Enter button ✓ on the formula bar**
   The number of tours sold, 60, appears in cell B11.

2. **Drag the fill handle to copy the formula in cell B11 into cell C11**
   The tour revenue total of 183079 appears in cell C11. You decide to enter a formula to calculate the percentage of revenue the Pacific Odyssey tour represents by dividing the individual tour revenue figures by the total revenue figure. To help with error checking, you decide to enter the formula using the IFERROR function.

3. **Click cell B14, click the Logical button in the Function Library group, click IFERROR, with the insertion point in the Value text box, click cell C7, type /, click cell C11, press [Tab], in the Value_if_error text box, type ERROR, then click OK**
   The percentage of Pacific Odyssey tour revenue of 22.00% appears in cell B14. You want to be sure that your error message will display properly, so you decide to test it by intentionally creating an error. You copy and paste the formula—which has a relative address in the denominator, where an absolute address should be used.

4. **Drag the fill handle to copy the formula in cell B14 into the range B15:B17**
   The ERROR value appears in cells B15:B17, as shown in Figure E-9. The errors are a result of the relative address for C11 in the denominator of the copied formula. Changing the relative address of C11 in the copied formula to an absolute address of $C$11 will correct the errors.

> **QUICK TIP**
> You can also check formulas for errors using the buttons in the Formula Auditing group on the Formulas tab.

5. **Double-click cell B14, select C11 in the formula, press [F4], then click ✓ on the formula bar**
   The formula now contains an absolute reference to cell C11.

6. **Copy the corrected formula in cell B14 into the range B15:B17**
   The tour revenue percentages now appear in all four cells, without error messages, as shown in Figure E-10.

7. **Save the workbook, print the worksheet, then close the workbook**

Correcting circular references

A cell with a circular reference contains a formula that refers to its own cell location. If you accidentally enter a formula with a circular reference, a warning box opens, alerting you to the problem. Click OK to open a Help window explaining how to find the circular reference. In simple formulas, a circular reference is easy to spot. To correct it, edit the formula to remove any reference to the cell where the formula is located.

Excel 112 Analyzing Data Using Formulas

FIGURE E-9: Worksheet with error codes

B14 =IFERROR(C7/C11,"ERROR")

— Relative reference to cell C11

	A	B	C	D
1	QST United States			
2				
3	January Sales Summary			
4				
5				
6	Tour	Tours Sold	Revenue	
7	Pacific Odyssey	13	40280	
8	Old Japan	13	27404	
9	Down Under Exodus	17	48327	
10	Essential India	17	67068	
11	Total	60	183079	
12				
13	Tour Revenue as a Percentage			
14	Pacific Odyssey	22.00%		
15	Old Japan	ERROR		
16	Down Under Exodus	ERROR		
17	Essential India	ERROR		
18				

— Error values

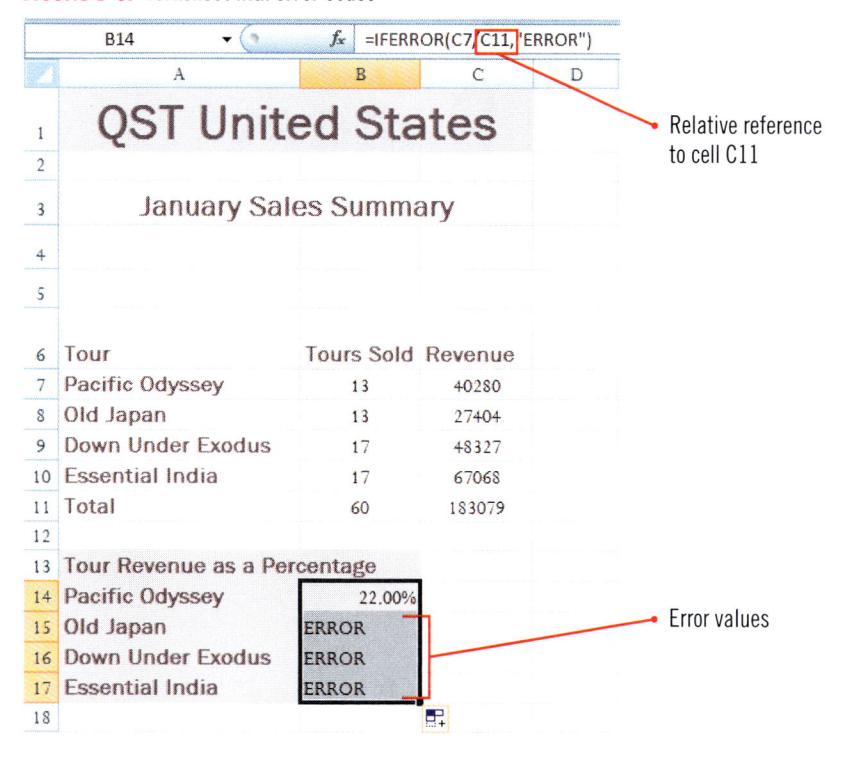

FIGURE E-10: Worksheet with tour percentages

B14 =IFERROR(C7/$C$11,"ERROR")

— Absolute reference to cell C11

	A	B	C	D
1	QST United States			
2				
3	January Sales Summary			
4				
5				
6	Tour	Tours Sold	Revenue	
7	Pacific Odyssey	13	40280	
8	Old Japan	13	27404	
9	Down Under Exodus	17	48327	
10	Essential India	17	67068	
11	Total	60	183079	
12				
13	Tour Revenue as a Percentage			
14	Pacific Odyssey	22.00%		
15	Old Japan	14.97%		
16	Down Under Exodus	26.40%		
17	Essential India	36.63%		
18				

— Tour percentages

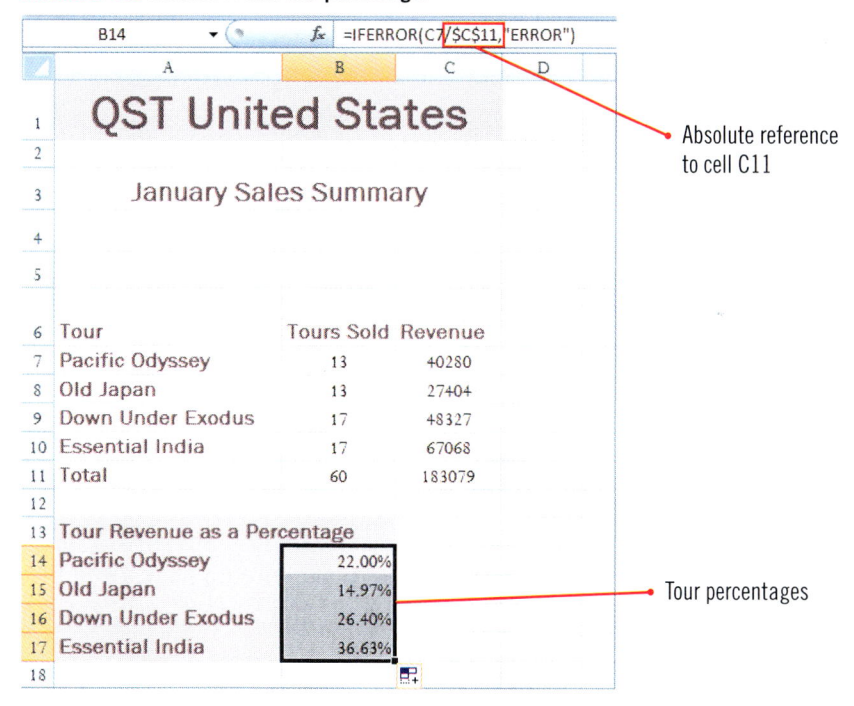

TABLE E-1: Understanding error values

error value	cause of error	error value	cause of error
#DIV/0!	A number is divided by 0	#NAME?	Formula contains text error
#NA	A value in a formula is not available	#NULL!	Invalid intersection of areas
#NUM!	Invalid use of a number in a formula	#REF!	Invalid cell reference
#VALUE!	Wrong type of formula argument or operand	#####	Column is not wide enough to display data

Analyzing Data Using Formulas

Constructing Formulas Using Named Ranges

To make your worksheet easier to follow, you can assign names to cells and ranges. You can also use names in formulas to make them easier to build and to reduce formula errors. For example, a formula named revenue-cost is easier to understand than the formula A5-A8. Names can use uppercase or lowercase letters as well as digits, but cannot have spaces. After you name a cell or range, you can define its **scope**, or the worksheets where it can be used. When defining a name's scope, you can limit its use to a worksheet or make it available to the entire workbook. If you move a named cell or range, its name moves with it, and if you add or remove rows or column to the worksheet the ranges are adjusted to their new position in the worksheet. When used in formulas, names become absolute cell references by default. Kate asks you to calculate the number of days before each tour departs. You will use range names to construct the formula.

STEPS

1. **Open the file EX E-2.xlsx from the drive and folder where you store your Data Files, then save it as Tours**

2. **Click cell B4, click the Formulas tab if necessary, click the Define Name button in the Defined Names group**

   The New Name dialog box opens, as shown in Figure E-11. You can name ranges containing dates to make formulas that perform date calculations easier to build.

   > **QUICK TIP**
   > Because names can not contain spaces, underscores are often used between words to replace spaces, making names with multiple words easier to read.

3. **Type current_date in the Name text box, click the Scope list arrow, click April Tours, then click OK**

   The name assigned to cell B4, current_date, appears in the Name box. Because its scope is the April Tours worksheet, the range name current_date will appear on the name list on that worksheet only. You can also name ranges that contain dates.

4. **Select the range B7:B13, click the Define Name button in the Defined Names group, enter tour_date in the Name text box, click the Scope list arrow, click April Tours, then click OK**

   Now you can use the named range and named cell in a formula. The formula =tour_date–current_date is easier to understand than =B7-$B$4.

   > **QUICK TIP**
   > Named cells and ranges can be used as a navigational tool in a worksheet by selecting the name in the Name box. The named cell or range becomes active.

5. **Click cell C7, type =, click the Use in Formula button in the Defined Names group, click tour_date, type –, click the Use in Formula button, click current_date, then click the Enter button on the formula bar**

   The number of days before the Pacific Odyssey tour departs, 10, appears in cell C7. You can use the same formula to calculate the number of days before the other tours depart.

6. **Drag the fill handle to copy the formula in cell C7 into the range C8:C13, then compare your formula results with those in Figure E-12**

7. **Save the workbook**

FIGURE E-11: New Name dialog box

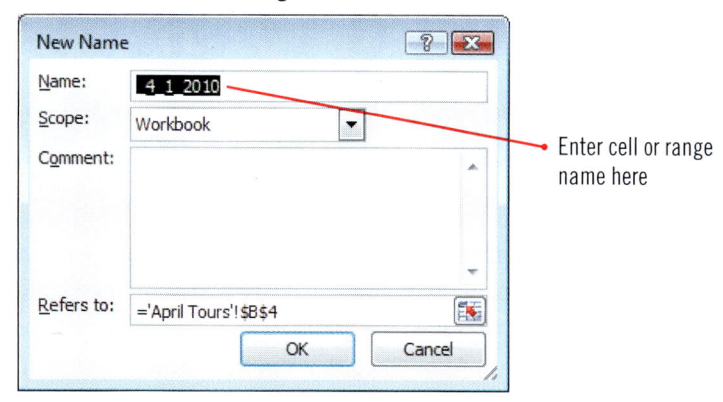

Enter cell or range name here

FIGURE E-12: Worksheet with days before departure

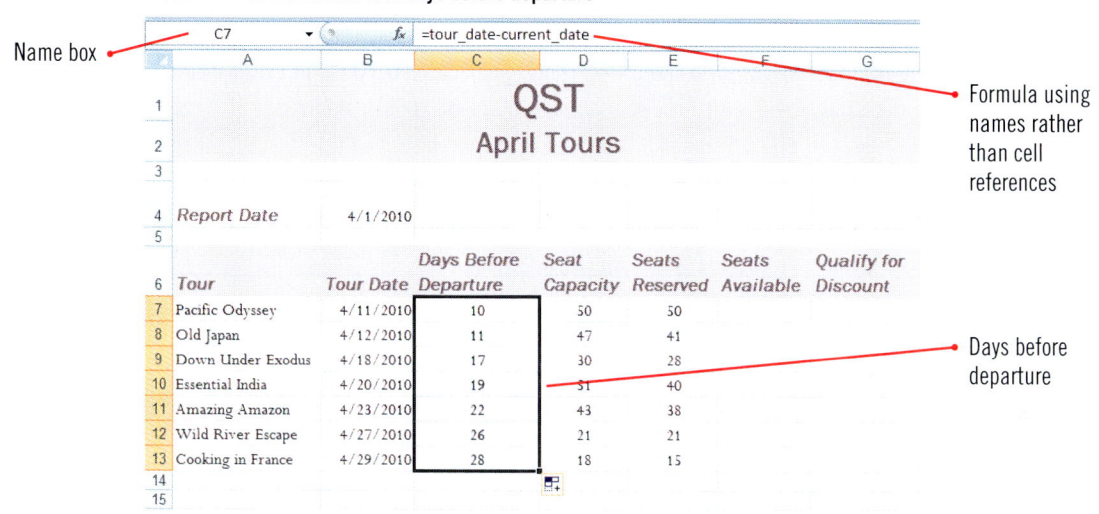

Name box

Formula using names rather than cell references

Days before departure

Managing workbook names

You can use the Name Manager to create, delete, and edit names in a workbook. Click the Name Manager button in the Defined Names group on the Formulas tab to open the Name Manager dialog box, as shown in Figure E-13. Click the New button to create a new named cell or range, click Edit to change a highlighted cell name, and click Delete to remove a highlighted name. Click Filter to see options for displaying specific criteria for displaying names.

FIGURE E-13: Name Manager dialog box

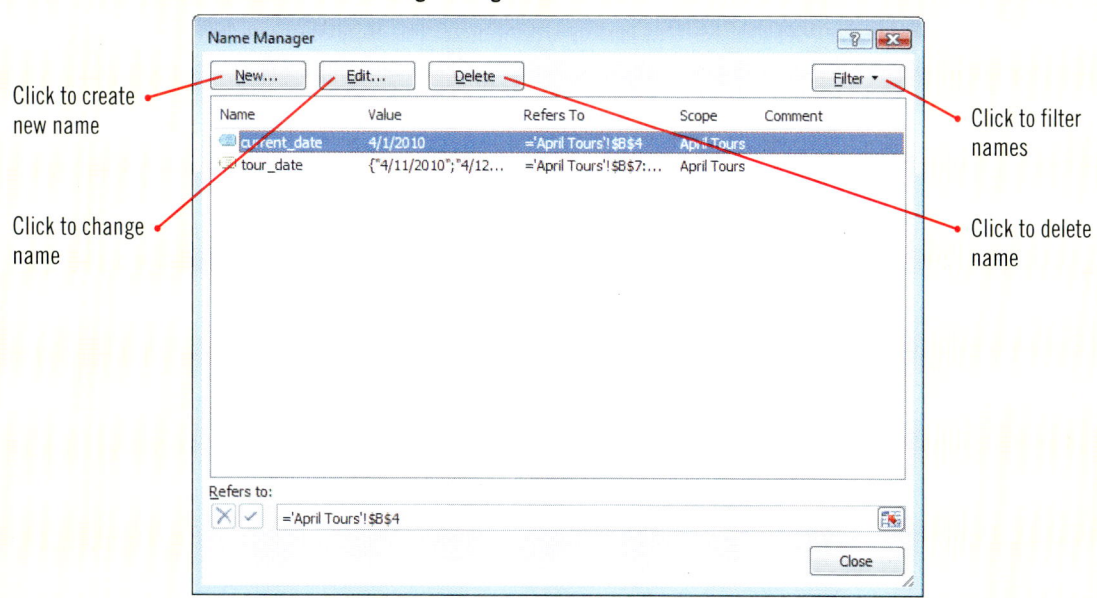

Click to create new name

Click to change name

Click to filter names

Click to delete name

Analyzing Data Using Formulas

Building a Logical Formula with the IF Function

UNIT E — Excel 2007

You can build a logical formula using an IF function. A **logical formula** makes calculations based on criteria that you create, called **stated conditions**. For example, you can build a formula to calculate bonuses based on a person's performance rating. If a person is rated a 5 (the stated condition) on a scale of 1 to 5, with 5 being the highest rating, he or she receives an additional 10% of his or her salary as a bonus; otherwise, there is no bonus. A condition that can be answered with a true or false response is called a **logical test**. The IF function has three parts, separated by commas: a condition or logical test, an action to take if the logical test or condition is true, and an action to take if the logical test or condition is false. Another way of expressing this is: IF(test_cond,do_this,else_this). Translated into an Excel IF function, the formula to calculate bonuses might look like this: IF(Rating=5,Salary*0.10,0). In other words, if the rating equals 5, multiply the salary by 0.10 (the decimal equivalent of 10%), then place the result in the selected cell; if the rating does not equal 5, place a 0 in the cell. When entering the logical test portion of an IF statement, you typically use some combination of the comparison operators listed in Table E-2. Kate asks you to use an IF function to calculate the number of seats available for each tour in April.

STEPS

1. **Click cell F7, on the Formulas tab, click the Logical button in the Function Library group, then click IF**

   The Function Arguments dialog box opens. You want the function to calculate the seats available as follows: If the seat capacity is greater than the number of seats reserved, calculate the number of seats that are available (capacity–number reserved), and place the result in cell F7; otherwise, place the text "None" in the cell.

2. **With the insertion point in the Logical_test text box, click cell D7, type >, click cell E7, then press [Tab]**

   The symbol (>) represents "greater than." So far, the formula reads "If the seating capacity is greater than the number of reserved seats,". The next part of the function tells Excel the action to take if the capacity exceeds the reserved number of seats.

3. **With the insertion point in the Value_if_true text box, click cell D7, type –, click cell E7, then press [Tab]**

   This part of the formula tells the program what you want it to do if the logical test is true. Continuing the translation of the formula, this part means "Subtract the number of reserved seats from the seat capacity." The last part of the formula tells Excel the action to take if the logical test is false (that is, if the seat capacity does not exceed the number of reserved seats).

4. **Enter None in the Value_if_false text box, then click OK**

   The function is complete, and the result, None (the number of available seats), appears in cell F7, as shown in Figure E-14.

5. **Drag the fill handle to copy the formula in cell F7 into the range F8:F13**

   Compare your results with Figure E-15.

6. **Save the workbook**

Analyzing Data Using Formulas

FIGURE E-14: Worksheet with IF function

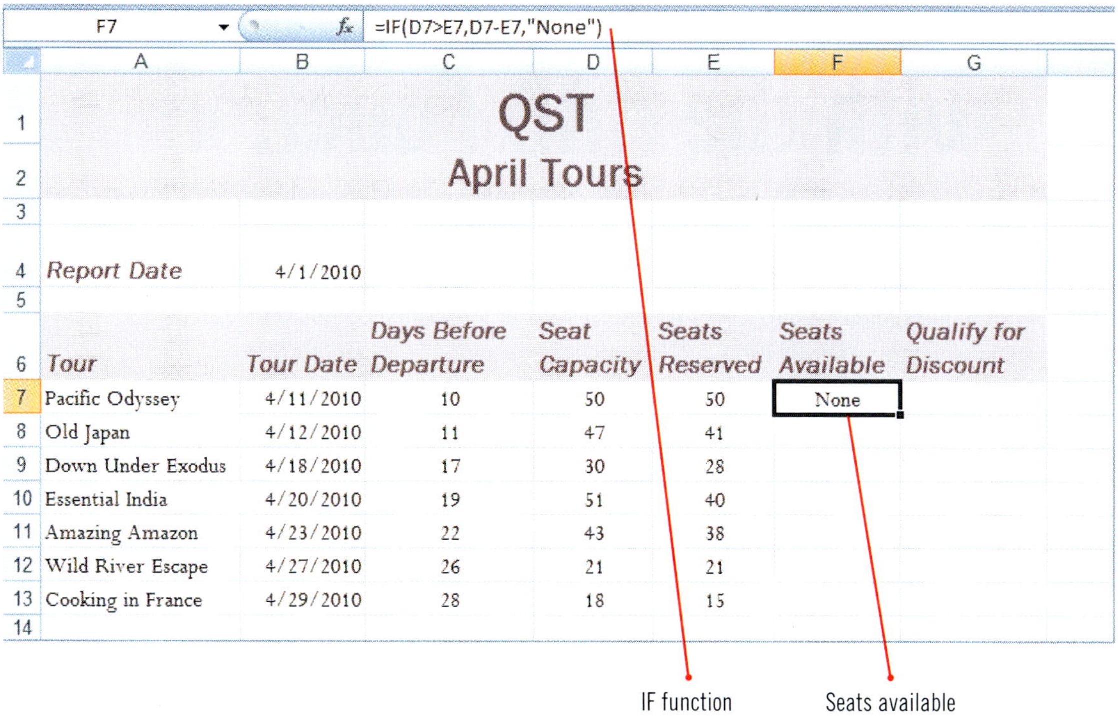

	A	B	C	D	E	F	G
	F7		fx	=IF(D7>E7,D7-E7,"None")			
1				QST			
2				April Tours			
3							
4	Report Date	4/1/2010					
5							
6	Tour	Tour Date	Days Before Departure	Seat Capacity	Seats Reserved	Seats Available	Qualify for Discount
7	Pacific Odyssey	4/11/2010	10	50	50	None	
8	Old Japan	4/12/2010	11	47	41		
9	Down Under Exodus	4/18/2010	17	30	28		
10	Essential India	4/20/2010	19	51	40		
11	Amazing Amazon	4/23/2010	22	43	38		
12	Wild River Escape	4/27/2010	26	21	21		
13	Cooking in France	4/29/2010	28	18	15		
14							

IF function — Seats available

FIGURE E-15: Worksheet showing seats available

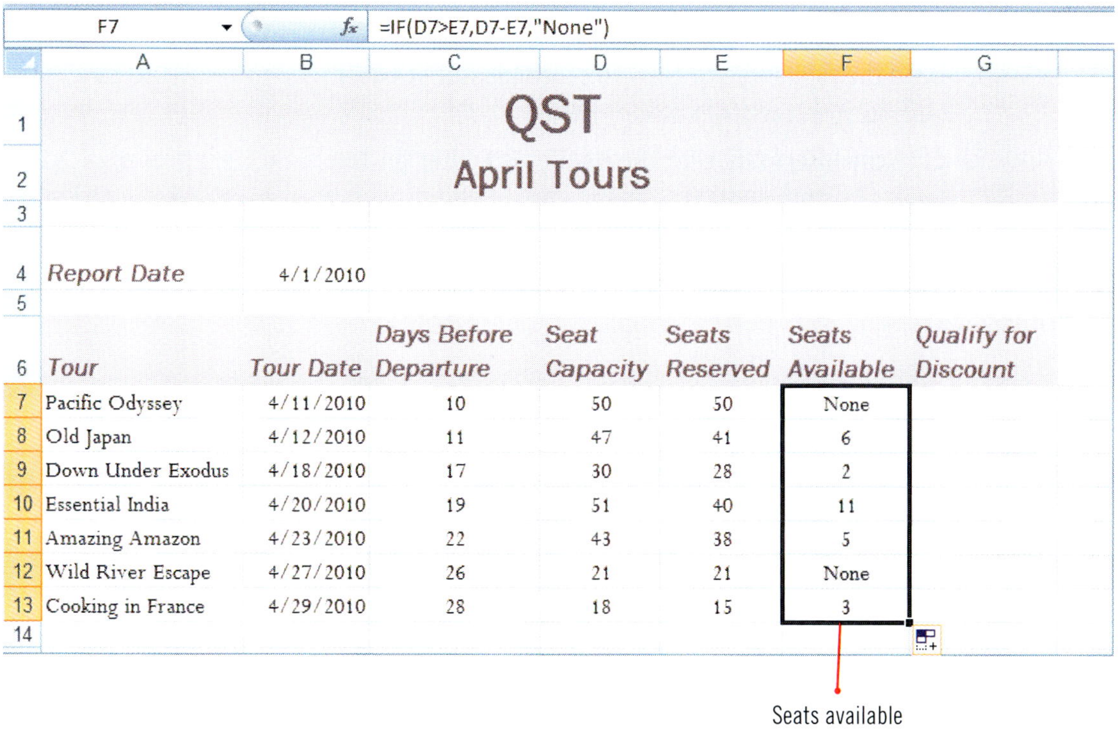

	A	B	C	D	E	F	G
	F7		fx	=IF(D7>E7,D7-E7,"None")			
1				QST			
2				April Tours			
3							
4	Report Date	4/1/2010					
5							
6	Tour	Tour Date	Days Before Departure	Seat Capacity	Seats Reserved	Seats Available	Qualify for Discount
7	Pacific Odyssey	4/11/2010	10	50	50	None	
8	Old Japan	4/12/2010	11	47	41	6	
9	Down Under Exodus	4/18/2010	17	30	28	2	
10	Essential India	4/20/2010	19	51	40	11	
11	Amazing Amazon	4/23/2010	22	43	38	5	
12	Wild River Escape	4/27/2010	26	21	21	None	
13	Cooking in France	4/29/2010	28	18	15	3	
14							

Seats available

TABLE E-2: Comparison operators

operator	meaning	operator	meaning
<	Less than	<=	Less than or equal to
>	Greater than	>=	Greater than or equal to
=	Equal to	<>	Not equal to

Analyzing Data Using Formulas

Building a Logical Formula with the AND Function

UNIT E — **Excel 2007**

You can also build a logical function using the AND function. The AND function evaluates all of its arguments and **returns**, or displays, TRUE if every logical test in the formula is true. The AND function returns a value of FALSE if one or more of its logical tests is false. The AND function arguments can include text, numbers, or cell references. Kate wants you to analyze the tour data to find tours that qualify for discounting. You will use the AND function to check for tours with seats available and that depart within 21 days.

STEPS

1. **Click cell G7, click the Logical button in the Function Library group, then click AND**

   The Function Arguments dialog box opens. You want the function to evaluate the discount qualification as follows: There must be seats available and the tour must depart within 21 days.

2. **With the insertion point in the Logical1 text box, click cell F7, type < >, type "None", then press [Tab]**

   > **TROUBLE**
   > If you get a formula error, check to be sure that you typed the quotation marks around None.

   The symbol (<>) represents "not equal to ." So far, the formula reads "If the number of seats available is not equal to None,"—in other words, if it is an integer. The next logical test checks the number of days before the tour departs.

3. **With the insertion point in the Logical2 text box, click cell C7, type <21, then click OK**

   The function is complete, and the result, FALSE, appears in cell G7, as shown in Figure E-16.

4. **Drag the fill handle to copy the formula in cell G7 into the range G8:G13**

   Compare your results with Figure E-17.

5. **Click the Insert tab, click the Header & Footer button in the Text group, click the Go to Footer button, enter your name in the center text box, click cell A1, then click the Normal button in the status bar**

6. **Save the workbook, then preview and print the worksheet**

Using the OR and NOT logical functions

The OR logical function has the same syntax as the AND function, but rather than returning TRUE if every argument is true, the OR function will return TRUE if any of its arguments are TRUE. It will only return FALSE if all of its arguments are FALSE. The NOT logical function reverses the value of its argument. For example NOT(TRUE) reverses its argument of TRUE and returns FALSE. This can be used in a worksheet to ensure that a cell is not equal to a particular value. See Table E-3 for examples of the AND, OR, and NOT functions.

TABLE E-3: Examples of AND, OR, and NOT functions with cell values A1=10 and B1=20

function	formula	result
AND	=AND(A1>5,B1>25)	FALSE
OR	=OR(A1>5,B1>25)	TRUE
NOT	=NOT(A1=0)	TRUE

Analyzing Data Using Formulas

FIGURE E-16: Worksheet with AND function

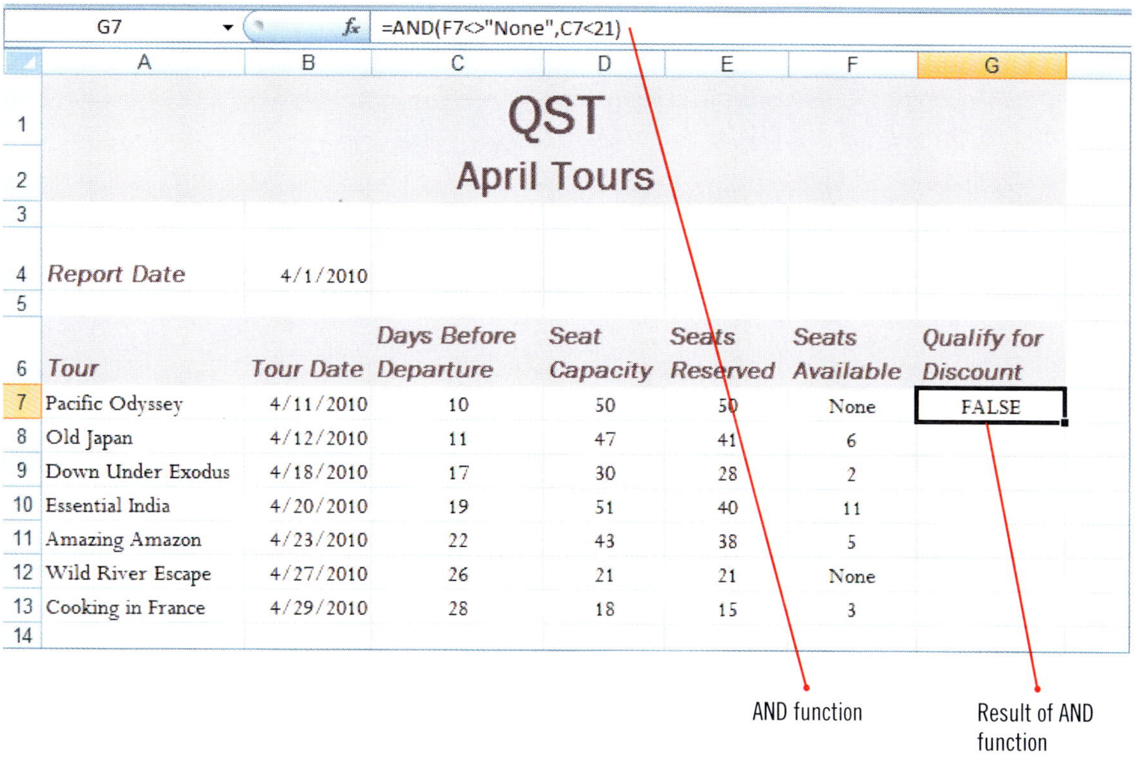

	G7		fx	=AND(F7<>"None",C7<21)			
	A	B	C	D	E	F	G
1			QST				
2			April Tours				
3							
4	Report Date	4/1/2010					
5							
6	Tour	Tour Date	Days Before Departure	Seat Capacity	Seats Reserved	Seats Available	Qualify for Discount
7	Pacific Odyssey	4/11/2010	10	50	50	None	FALSE
8	Old Japan	4/12/2010	11	47	41	6	
9	Down Under Exodus	4/18/2010	17	30	28	2	
10	Essential India	4/20/2010	19	51	40	11	
11	Amazing Amazon	4/23/2010	22	43	38	5	
12	Wild River Escape	4/27/2010	26	21	21	None	
13	Cooking in France	4/29/2010	28	18	15	3	
14							

AND function → Result of AND function

FIGURE E-17: Worksheet with discount status evaluated

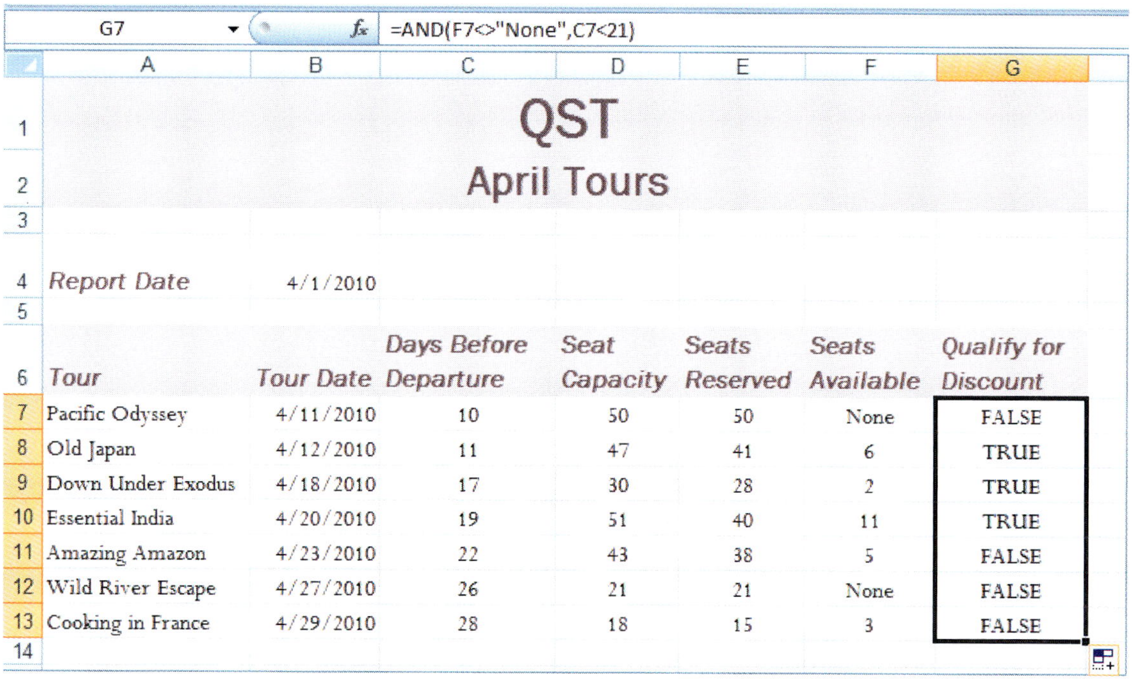

	G7		fx	=AND(F7<>"None",C7<21)			
	A	B	C	D	E	F	G
1			QST				
2			April Tours				
3							
4	Report Date	4/1/2010					
5							
6	Tour	Tour Date	Days Before Departure	Seat Capacity	Seats Reserved	Seats Available	Qualify for Discount
7	Pacific Odyssey	4/11/2010	10	50	50	None	FALSE
8	Old Japan	4/12/2010	11	47	41	6	TRUE
9	Down Under Exodus	4/18/2010	17	30	28	2	TRUE
10	Essential India	4/20/2010	19	51	40	11	TRUE
11	Amazing Amazon	4/23/2010	22	43	38	5	FALSE
12	Wild River Escape	4/27/2010	26	21	21	None	FALSE
13	Cooking in France	4/29/2010	28	18	15	3	FALSE
14							

Calculating Payments with the PMT Function

UNIT E
Excel 2007

PMT is a financial function that calculates the periodic payment amount for money borrowed. For example, if you want to borrow money to buy a car, and you know the principal amount, interest rate, and loan term, the PMT function can calculate your monthly payment. Say you want to borrow $20,000 at 6.5% interest and pay the loan off in five years. The Excel PMT function can tell you that your monthly payment will be $391.32. The main parts of the PMT function are: PMT(rate, nper, pv). See Figure E-18 for an illustration of a PMT function that calculates the monthly payment in the car loan example. For several months, QST's United States region has been discussing opening a new branch in San Francisco. Kate has obtained quotes from three different lenders on borrowing $259,000 to begin the expansion. She obtained loan quotes from a commercial bank, a venture capitalist, and an investment banker. She wants you to summarize the information using the Excel PMT function.

STEPS

1. **Click the Loan sheet tab, click cell F5, click the Formulas tab, click the Financial button in the Function Library group, scroll down the list of functions, then click PMT**

2. **With the insertion point in the Rate text box, click cell D5 on the worksheet, type /12, then press [Tab]**
   You must divide the annual interest by 12 because you are calculating monthly, not annual, payments.

   > **QUICK TIP**
   > Be consistent about the units you use for rate and nper. If you express nper as the number of monthly payments, then express the interest rate as a monthly rate.

3. **With the insertion point in the Nper text box, click cell E5; click the Pv text box, click cell B5, then click OK**
   The payment of (5445.81) in cell F5 appears in red, indicating that it is a negative amount. Excel displays the result of a PMT function as a negative value to reflect the negative cash flow the loan represents to the borrower. To show the monthly payment as a positive number, you can place a minus sign in front of the Pv cell reference in the function. The Fv and Type arguments are optional: The argument Fv is the future value, or the total amount you want to obtain after all payments. If you omit it, Excel assumes the Fv is 0. The Type argument indicates when the payments are made; 0 is the end of the period, and 1 is the beginning of the period. The default is the end of the period.

   > **QUICK TIP**
   > You can use the keyboard shortcut of [Ctrl] + [Enter] rather than clicking the Enter button. This enters the formula and leaves the cell selected.

4. **Double-click cell F5 and edit it so it reads =PMT(D5/12,E5,-B5), then click the Enter button on the formula bar**
   A positive value of $5,445.81 now appears in cell F5, as shown in Figure E-19. You can use the same formula to generate the monthly payments for the other loans.

5. **With cell F5 selected, drag the fill handle to fill the range F6:F7**
   A monthly payment of $8,266.30 for the venture capitalist loan appears in cell F6. A monthly payment of $11,826.41 for the investment banker loan appears in cell F7. The loans with shorter terms have much higher payments. You will not know the entire financial picture until you calculate the total payments and total interest for each lender.

   > **QUICK TIP**
   > You can print the worksheet gridlines and also column and row headings by clicking the Print check boxes under Gridlines and Headings in the Sheet Options group of the Page Layout tab.

6. **Click cell G5, type =, click cell E5, type *, click cell F5, then press [Tab], in cell H5, type =, click cell G5, type –, click cell B5, then click**

7. **Copy the formulas in cells G5:H5 into the range G6:H7, then click cell A1**
   Your worksheet appears as shown in Figure E-20. You can experiment with different interest rates, loan amounts, or terms for any one of the lenders; the PMT function generates a new set of values automatically.

8. **Add your name to the center section of the footer, save the workbook, preview and print the worksheet, then close the workbook and exit Excel**

Analyzing Data Using Formulas

FIGURE E-18: Example of PMT function for car loan

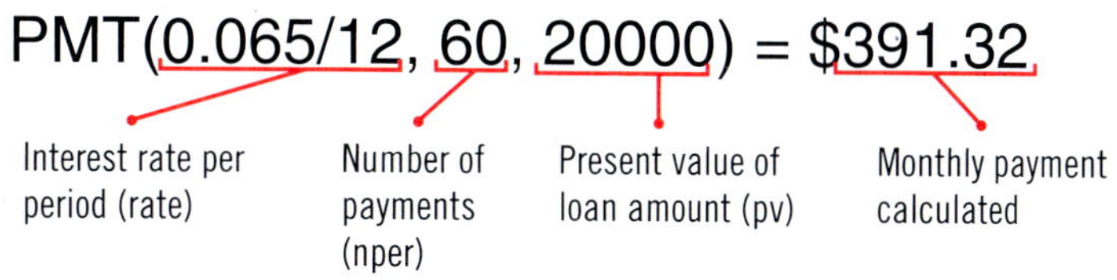

$$\text{PMT}(\underbrace{0.065/12}_{\text{Interest rate per period (rate)}}, \underbrace{60}_{\substack{\text{Number of} \\ \text{payments} \\ \text{(nper)}}}, \underbrace{20000}_{\substack{\text{Present value of} \\ \text{loan amount (pv)}}}) = \underbrace{\$391.32}_{\substack{\text{Monthly payment} \\ \text{calculated}}}$$

FIGURE E-19: PMT function calculating monthly loan payment

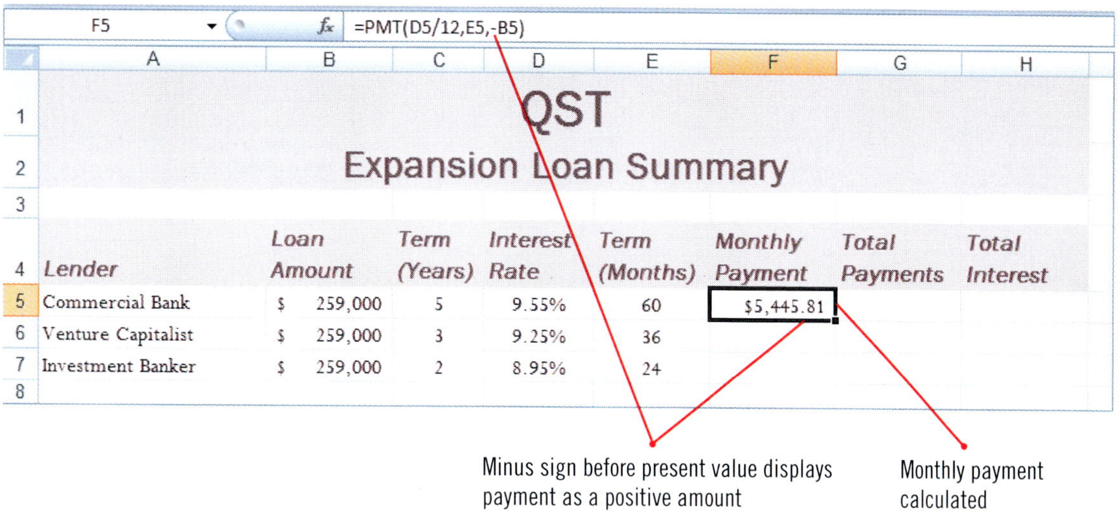

F5 · fx =PMT(D5/12,E5,-B5)

	A	B	C	D	E	F	G	H
1				QST				
2				Expansion Loan Summary				
3								
4	Lender	Loan Amount	Term (Years)	Interest Rate	Term (Months)	Monthly Payment	Total Payments	Total Interest
5	Commercial Bank	$ 259,000	5	9.55%	60	$5,445.81		
6	Venture Capitalist	$ 259,000	3	9.25%	36			
7	Investment Banker	$ 259,000	2	8.95%	24			
8								

Minus sign before present value displays payment as a positive amount

Monthly payment calculated

FIGURE E-20: Completed worksheet

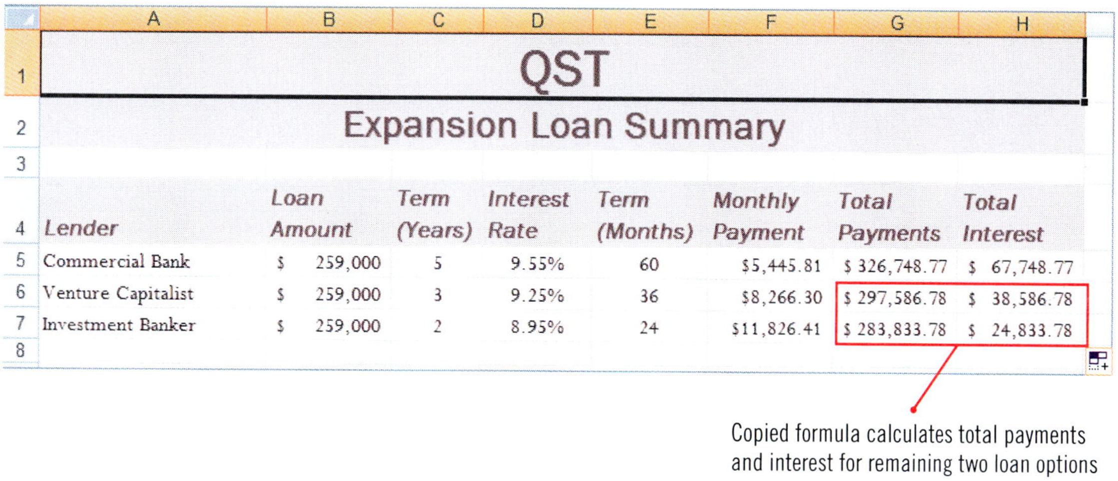

	A	B	C	D	E	F	G	H
1				QST				
2				Expansion Loan Summary				
3								
4	Lender	Loan Amount	Term (Years)	Interest Rate	Term (Months)	Monthly Payment	Total Payments	Total Interest
5	Commercial Bank	$ 259,000	5	9.55%	60	$5,445.81	$ 326,748.77	$ 67,748.77
6	Venture Capitalist	$ 259,000	3	9.25%	36	$8,266.30	$ 297,586.78	$ 38,586.78
7	Investment Banker	$ 259,000	2	8.95%	24	$11,826.41	$ 283,833.78	$ 24,833.78
8								

Copied formula calculates total payments and interest for remaining two loan options

Calculating future value with the FV function

You can use the FV (Future Value) function to determine the amount of money a given monthly investment will amount to, at a given interest rate, after a given number of payment periods. The syntax is similar to that of the PMT function: FV(rate,nper,pmt,pv,type). The rate is the interest paid by the financial institution, the nper is the number of periods, and the pmt is the amount that you deposit. For example, suppose you want to invest $1000 every month for the next 12 months into an account that pays 12% a year, and you want to know how much you will have at the end of 12 months (that is, its future value). You enter the function FV(.01,12,-1000), and Excel returns the value $12,682.50 as the future value of your investment. As with the PMT function, the units for the rate and nper must be consistent. If you made monthly payments on a three-year loan at 6% annual interest, you use the rate .06/12 and 36 periods (12*3). The arguments pv and type are optional; pv is the present value, or the total amount the series of payments is worth now. If you omit it, Excel assumes the pv is 0. The "type" argument indicates when the payments are made; 0 is the end of the period, and 1 is the beginning of the period. The default is the end of the period.

Analyzing Data Using Formulas

Practice

▼ CONCEPTS REVIEW

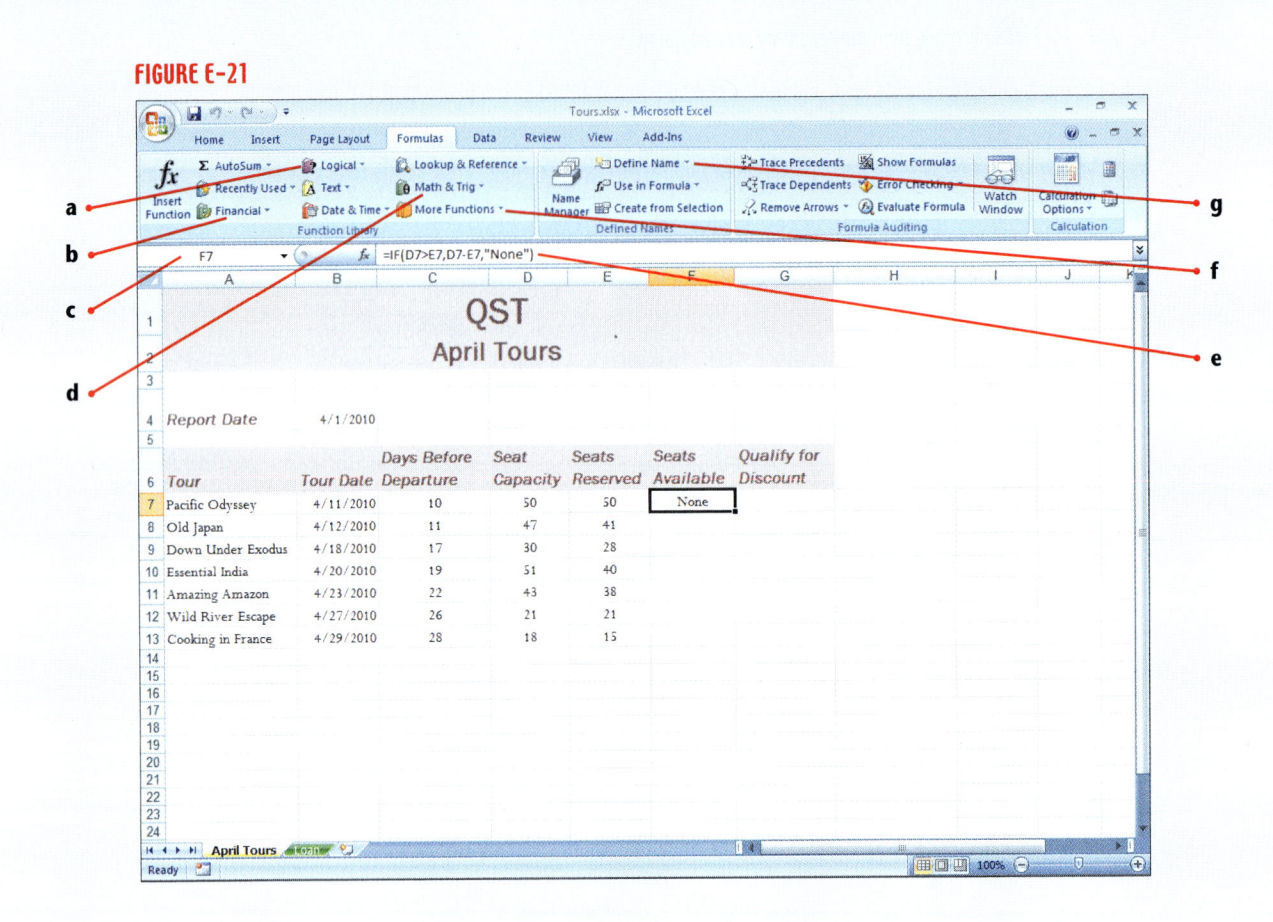

FIGURE E-21

1. Which element points to the area where the name of a selected cell or range is displayed?
2. Which element points to a logical formula?
3. Which element do you click to add a statistical function to a worksheet?
4. Which element do you click to name a cell or range?
5. Which element do you click to insert an IF function into a worksheet?
6. Which element do you click to add a PMT function to a worksheet?
7. Which element do you click to add a SUMIF function to a worksheet?

Match each term with the statement that best describes it.

8. SUMIF
9. PROPER
10. test_cond
11. FV
12. PV

a. Function used to change the first letter of a string to uppercase
b. Function used to determine the future amount of an investment
c. Part of the PMT function that represents the loan amount
d. Part of the IF function in which the conditions are stated
e. Function used to conditionally total cells

Excel 122   Analyzing Data Using Formulas

Select the best answer from the list of choices.

13. **When you enter the rate and nper arguments in a PMT function, you must:**
    a. Use monthly units instead of annual units.
    b. Multiply both units by 12.
    c. Divide both values by 12.
    d. Be consistent in the units used.

14. **To express conditions such as less than or equal to, you can use a(n):**
    a. Statistical function.
    b. PMT function.
    c. Text formula.
    d. Comparison operator.

15. **Which of the following statements is false?**
    a. If you move a named cell or range, its name moves with it.
    b. Named ranges make formulas easier to build.
    c. Names cannot contain spaces.
    d. When used in formulas, names become relative cell references by default.

16. **Which of the following is an external reference indicator in a formula?**
    a. :
    b. &
    c. !
    d. =

▼ SKILLS REVIEW

1. **Format data using text functions.**
   a. Start Excel, open the file EX E-3.xlsx from the drive and folder where you store your Data Files, then save it as **Reviews**.
   b. On the Managers worksheet, select the range A2:A9 and, using the Text to Columns button on the Data tab, separate the names into two text columns. (*Hint*: The delimiter is a space.)
   c. In cell D2, enter the text formula to convert the first letter of the department in cell C2 to uppercase, then copy the formula in cell D2 into the range D3:D9.
   d. In cell E2, enter the text formula to convert all letters of the department in cell C2 to uppercase, then copy the formula in cell E2 into the range E3:E9.
   e. In cell F2, use the text formula to convert all letters of the department in cell C2 to lowercase, then copy the formula in cell F2 into the range F3:F9.
   f. In cell G2, use the text formula to substitute "Human Resources" for "hr" in cell F2. (*Hint*: In the Function Arguments dialog box, Text is F2, Old_text is hr, and New_text is Human Resources.) Copy the formula in cell G2 into the range G3:G9 to change the other cells containing hr to Human Resources. (Note that the marketing and sales entries will not change because the formula searches for the text hr).
   g. Save your work, then enter your name in the worksheet footer. Compare your screen to Figure E-22.
   h. Display the formulas in the worksheet, then print the worksheet.
   i. Redisplay the formula results.

   FIGURE E-22

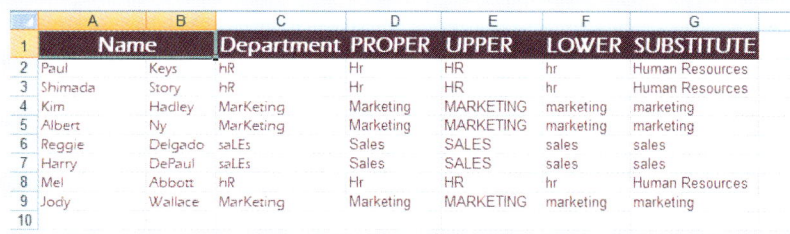

	A	B	C	D	E	F	G
1	Name		Department	PROPER	UPPER	LOWER	SUBSTITUTE
2	Paul	Keys	hR	Hr	HR	hr	Human Resources
3	Shimada	Story	hR	Hr	HR	hr	Human Resources
4	Kim	Hadley	MarKeting	Marketing	MARKETING	marketing	marketing
5	Albert	Ny	MarKeting	Marketing	MARKETING	marketing	marketing
6	Reggie	Delgado	saLEs	Sales	SALES	sales	sales
7	Harry	DePaul	saLEs	Sales	SALES	sales	sales
8	Mel	Abbott	hR	Hr	HR	hr	Human Resources
9	Jody	Wallace	MarKeting	Marketing	MARKETING	marketing	marketing
10							

2. **Sum a range of data conditionally.**
   a. Make the HR sheet active.
   b. In cell B20, use the COUNTIF function to count the number of employees with a rating of 5.
   c. In cell B21, use the AVERAGEIF function to average the salaries of employees with a rating of 5.
   d. In cell B22, enter the SUMIF function that totals the salaries of employees with a rating of 5.
   e. Format cells B21 and B22 with the Number format using commas and no decimals. Save your work.

▼ SKILLS REVIEW (CONTINUED)

3. **Consolidate data using a formula.**
   a. Make the Summary sheet active.
   b. In cell B4, use the AutoSum function to total cell F15 on the HR and Accounting sheets.
   c. Format cell B4 with the Accounting number format.
   d. Enter your name in the worksheet footer, then save your work. Compare your screen to Figure E-23.
   e. Display the formula in the worksheet, then print the worksheet.
   f. Redisplay the formula results in the worksheet.

   FIGURE E-23

	A	B
1	Payroll Summary	
2		
3		Salary
4	TOTAL	$ 565,787.00
5		
6		

4. **Check formulas for errors.**
   a. Make the HR sheet active.
   b. In cell I6, use the IFERROR function to display "ERROR" in the event that the formula F6/F15 results in a formula error. (*Note*: This formula will generate an intentional error, which you will correct in a moment.)
   c. Copy the formula in cell I6 into the range I7:I14.
   d. Correct the formula in cell I6 by making the denominator, F15, an absolute address.
   e. Copy the new formula in cell I6 into the range I7:I14.
   f. Format the range I6:I14 as percentage with two decimal places.
   g. Save your work.

5. **Construct formulas using named ranges.**
   a. On the HR sheet, name the range C6:C14 **review_date** and limit the scope of the name to the HR worksheet.
   b. In cell E6, enter the formula **=review_date+183**, using the Use in Formula button to enter the cell name.
   c. Copy the formula in cell E6 into the range E7:E14.
   d. Use the Name Manager to add a comment of "Date of last review" to the review_date name. (*Hint*: In the Name Manager dialog box, click the review_date name, then click Edit to enter the comment.)
   e. Save your work.

6. **Build a logical formula with the IF function.**
   a. In cell G6, use the Function Arguments dialog box to enter the formula **=IF(D6=5,F6*0.05,0)**
   b. Copy the formula in cell G6 into the range G7:G14.
   c. In cell G15, use AutoSum to total the range G6:G14.
   d. Format the range G6:G15 with the Currency number format, using the $ symbol and no decimal places.
   e. Save your work.

7. **Build a logical formula with the AND function.**
   a. In cell H6, use the Function Arguments dialog box to enter the formula **=AND(G6>0,B6>5)**.
   b. Copy the formula in cell H6 into the range H7:H14.
   c. Enter your name in the worksheet footer, save your work, compare your worksheet to Figure E-24, then print the worksheet.
   d. Make the Accounting sheet active.
   e. In cell H6, indicate if the employee needs more development hours to reach the minimum of 5: Use the Function Arguments dialog box for the NOT function to enter **B6>5** in the Logical text box. Copy the formula in cell H6 into the range H7:H14.
   f. In cell I6, indicate if the employee needs to enroll in a quality class, as indicated by a rating less than 5 and having less than 5 development hours: Use the Function Arguments dialog box for the OR function to enter **D6<>5** in the Logical1 text box and **B6<=5** in the Logical2 text box. Copy the formula in cell I6 into the range I7:I14.

FIGURE E-24

Last Name	Professional Development Hours	Review Date	Rating	Next Review	Salary	Bonus	Pay Bonus	Percentage of Total
Barry	5	2/1/2010	4	8/3/2010	19,840	$0	FALSE	7.21%
Gray	8	3/1/2010	5	8/31/2010	26,700	$1,335	TRUE	9.71%
Greenwood	1	7/1/2010	3	12/31/2010	33,200	$0	FALSE	12.07%
Hemsley	3	4/1/2010	5	10/1/2010	25,500	$1,275	FALSE	9.27%
Kim	9	3/1/2010	3	8/31/2010	37,500	$0	FALSE	13.63%
Manchevski	8	5/1/2010	5	10/31/2010	36,500	$1,825	TRUE	13.27%
Marley	10	6/1/2010	4	12/1/2010	37,500	$0	FALSE	13.63%
Smith	6	1/1/2010	3	7/3/2010	28,600	$0	FALSE	10.40%
Storey	1	9/1/2010	5	3/3/2011	29,700	$1,485	FALSE	10.80%
				Total	$ 275,040	$5,920		

Department Statistics
Rating of 5
Number: 4
Average Salary: 29,600
Total Salary: 118,400

▼ SKILLS REVIEW (CONTINUED)

g. Enter your name in the worksheet footer, save your work, compare your screen to Figure E-25, then print the worksheet.

8. **Calculate payments with the PMT function.**

   a. Make the Loan sheet active.
   b. In cell B9, determine the monthly payment using the loan information shown: Use the Function Arguments dialog box to enter the formula **=PMT(B5/12,B6,-B4)**.
   c. In cell B10, enter the formula **=B9*B6**.
   d. In cell B11, enter the formula **=B10-B4**, then compare your screen to Figure E-26.
   e. Enter your name in the worksheet footer, save the workbook, then print the worksheet.
   f. Close the workbook, then exit Excel.

FIGURE E-25

FIGURE E-26

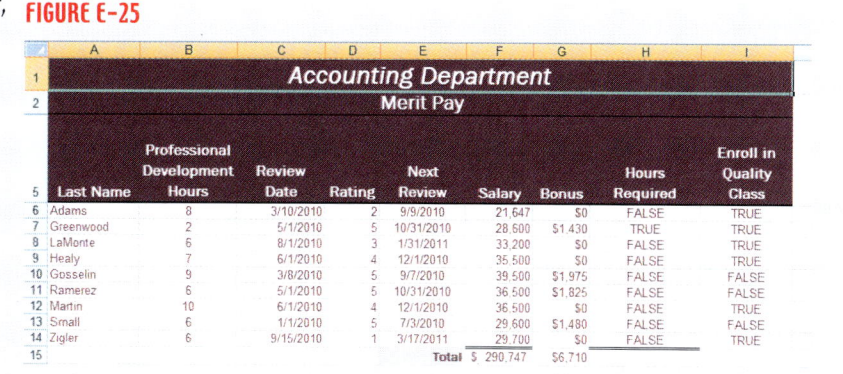

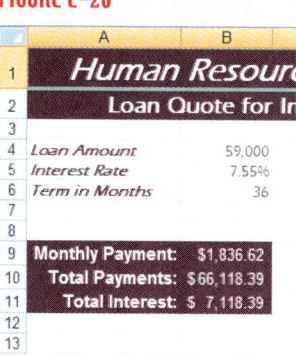

▼ INDEPENDENT CHALLENGE 1

As the accounting manager of Travel Well, a travel insurance company, you are reviewing the accounts payable information for your advertising accounts and prioritizing the overdue invoices for your collections service. You will analyze the invoices and use logical functions to emphasize priority accounts.

a. Start Excel, open the file EX E-4.xlsx from the drive and folder where you store your Data Files, then save it as **Ad Accounts**.
b. Name the range B7:B13 **invoice_date** and give the name a scope of the accounts payable worksheet.
c. Name the cell B4 **current_date** and give the name a scope of the accounts payable worksheet.
d. Enter a formula using the named range invoice_date in cell E7 that calculates the invoice due date by adding 30 to the invoice date.
e. Copy the formula in cell E7 to the range E8:E13.
f. In cell F7, enter a formula using the named range invoice_date and the named cell current_date that calculates the invoice age by subtracting the invoice date from the current date.
g. Copy the formula in cell F7 to the range F8:F13.
h. In cell G7, enter an IF function that calculates the number of days an invoice is overdue, assuming that an invoice must be paid in 30 days. (*Hint*: The Logical_test should check to see if the age of the invoice is greater than 30, the Value_if_true should calculate the current date minus the invoice due date, and the Value_if_false should be 0). Copy the IF function into the range G8:G13.
i. In cell H7, enter an AND function to prioritize the overdue invoices that are more than $1000 for collection services. (*Hint:* The Logical1 condition should check to see if the number of days overdue is more than 0 and the Logical2 condition should check if the amount is more than 1000). Copy the AND function into the range H8:H13.
j. Enter your name in the worksheet footer, then save, preview, and print the worksheet.
k. Close the workbook, then exit Excel.

Advanced Challenge Exercise

- Use the "Refers to:" text box in the Name Manager dialog box to verify that the names in the worksheet refer to the correct ranges.
- Use the filter in the Name Manager dialog box to verify that your names are scoped to the worksheet and not the workbook.
- Use the filter in the Name Manager dialog box to verify that your names are defined, free of errors, and not part of a table.

▼ INDEPENDENT CHALLENGE 2

You are an auditor with a certified public accounting firm. Goals, a manufacturer of ice skating products based in Quebec, has contacted you to audit its first-quarter sales records. The management at Goals is considering opening a branch in Great Britain and needs its sales records audited to prepare the business plan. Specifically, they want to show what percent of annual sales each category represents. You will use a formula on a summary worksheet to summarize the sales for January, February, and March and to calculate the overall first-quarter percentage of the sales categories.

a. Start Excel, open the file EX E-5.xlsx from the drive and folder where you store your Data Files, then save it as **Goals Sales**.

b. In cell B10 of the Jan, Feb, and Mar sheets, enter the formulas to calculate the sales totals for the month.

c. For each month, in cell C5, create a formula calculating the percent of sales for the Sticks sales category. Use a function to display "ERROR" if there is a mistake in the formula. Verify that the percent appears with two decimal places. Copy this formula as necessary to complete the % of Sales data for all sales categories on all sheets. If any cells display "ERROR", fix the formulas in those cells.

d. In column B of the Summary sheet, use formulas to total the sales categories for the Jan, Feb, and Mar worksheets.

e. Locate the first-quarter sales total in cell B10 of the Summary sheet. Calculate the percent of each sales category on the Summary sheet. Use a function to display "ERROR" if there is a mistake in the formula. Copy this formula as necessary. If any cells display "ERROR", fix the formulas in those cells.

f. Enter your name in the Summary worksheet footer, then save, preview, and print the worksheet.

g. On the Products sheet, separate the product list in cell A1 into separate columns of text data. (*Hint*: The products are delimited with commas.) Widen the columns as necessary. Use the second row to display the products with the first letter of each word in uppercase, as shown in Figure E-27.

h. Enter your name in the Products worksheet footer, then save, preview, and print the worksheet.

i. Close the workbook, then exit Excel.

FIGURE E-27

	A	B	C	D	E	F
1	sticks	ice skates	apparel	pads	equipment bags	
2	Sticks	Ice Skates	Apparel	Pads	Equipment Bags	
3						

▼ INDEPENDENT CHALLENGE 3

As the owner of Best Dressed, a clothing boutique with a growing clientele, you are planning to expand your business into a neighboring city. Because you will have to purchase additional inventory and renovate your new rental space, you decide to take out a $20,000 loan to finance your expansion expenses. You check three loan sources: the Small Business Administration (SBA), your local bank, and a consortium of investors. The SBA will lend you the money at 7.5% interest, but you have to pay it off in three years. The local bank offers you the loan at 8.25% interest over four years. The consortium offers you a 7% loan, but they require you to pay it back in two years. To analyze all three loan options, you decide to build a loan summary worksheet. Using the loan terms provided, build a worksheet summarizing your options.

a. Start Excel, open a new workbook, then save it as **Dress Shop Loan**.

b. Using Figure E-28 as a guide, enter labels and worksheet data for the three loan sources. (*Hint*: The Aspect theme is used with Orange Accent 1 as the fill color in the first two rows and Orange, Accent 1, Darker 25% as the text color in the calculation area.)

c. Enter the monthly payment formula for your first loan source (making sure to show the payment as a positive amount), copy the formula as appropriate, then name the range containing the monthly payment formulas **Monthly_Payment** with a scope of the workbook.

FIGURE E-28

	A	B	C	D	E	F	G
1	Best Dressed						
2	Loan Options						
3							
4	Loan Source	Loan Amount	Interest Rate	# Payments	Monthly Payment	Total Payments	Total Interest
5	SBA	20,000	7.50%	36			
6	Bank	20,000	8.25%	48			
7	Investors	20,000	7.00%	24			
8							

Analyzing Data Using Formulas

▼ INDEPENDENT CHALLENGE 3 (CONTINUED)

d. Name the cell range containing the number of payments **Number_Payments** with the scope of the workbook.

e. Enter the formula for total payments for your first loan source using the named ranges Monthly_Payment and Number_Payments, then copy the formula as necessary.

f. Name the cell range containing the formulas for Total payments **Total_Payments**. Name the cell range containing the loan amounts **Loan_Amount**.

g. Enter the formula for total interest for your first loan source using the named ranges Total_Payments and Loan_Amount, then copy the formula as necessary.

h. Format the worksheet using formatting appropriate to the worksheet purpose, then enter your name in the worksheet footer.

i. Save, preview, and print the worksheet in landscape orientation, on a single page.

Advanced Challenge Exercise

- Turn on the print gridlines option for the worksheet.
- Turn on the printing of row and column headings.
- Print the worksheet formulas with the worksheet gridlines and headings on one page.
- Display the worksheet values.

j. Close the workbook then exit Excel.

▼ REAL LIFE INDEPENDENT CHALLENGE

You decide to create a weekly log of your daily aerobic exercise. As part of this log, you record your aerobic activity along with the number of minutes spent working out. If you do more than one activity in a day, for example, if you bike and walk, record each as a separate event. Along with each activity, you record the location where you exercise. For example, you may walk in the gym or outdoors. You will use the log to analyze the amount of time that you spend on each type of exercise.

a. Start Excel, open the file EX E-6.xlsx from the drive and folder where you store your Data Files, then save it as **Workout**.

b. Use the structure of the worksheet to record your aerobic exercise activities. Change the data in columns A, B, C, D, and F to reflect your activities, locations, and times. If you do not have any data to enter, use the provided worksheet data.

c. Use a SUMIF function in the column G cells to calculate the total minutes spent on each activity.

d. Enter an AVERAGEIF function in the column H cells to average the number of minutes spent on each activity.

e. Enter a COUNTIF function in the column I cells to calculate the number of sessions spent on each activity.

Advanced Challenge Exercise

- Enter one of your activities with a specific location, such as Walk Outdoors, in a column F cell, then enter the SUMIFS function in the adjacent column G cell that calculates the total number of minutes spent on that activity in the specific location (such as walking ...outdoors).
- Enter the AVERAGEIFS function in the corresponding column H cell that calculates the average number of minutes spent on the activity in the specified location.
- Enter the COUNTIFS function in the corresponding column I cell that calculates the number of days spent on the activity in the specific location.

f. Enter your name in the worksheet footer, then save, preview, and print the worksheet.

g. Close the workbook, then exit Excel.

▼ VISUAL WORKSHOP

Open the file EX E-7.xlsx from the drive and folder where you store your Data Files, then save it as **Quarterly Sales Summary**. Create the worksheet shown in Figure E-29 using the data in columns B, C, and D. (*Hints*: Use AND formulas to determine if a person is eligible for a bonus, and use IF formulas to enter the bonus amounts. An employee with a performance rating of seven or higher and who meets the sales quota receives a bonus of one percent of the sales. If the rating is less than seven, or if the sales amounts are less than the quota, no bonus is awarded.) Enter your name in the worksheet footer, then preview and print the worksheet.

FIGURE E-29

	A	B	C	D	E	F
1			Bonus Pay Summary			
2						
3	Last Name	Quota	Sales	Performance Rating	Eligible	Bonus Amount
4	Allen	$100,000	$125,400	7	TRUE	$1,254
5	Gray	$80,000	$75,420	3	FALSE	$0
6	Greenwood	$90,000	$83,540	9	FALSE	$0
7	Hanson	$120,000	$132,980	5	FALSE	$0
8	Kerns	$150,000	$147,650	8	FALSE	$0
9	Maloney	$140,000	$149,800	5	FALSE	$0
10	Martin	$135,000	$132,200	7	FALSE	$0
11	Smith	$100,000	$98,650	3	FALSE	$0
12	Storey	$90,000	$96,700	9	TRUE	$967
13						

UNIT F
Excel 2007

Managing Workbook Data

Files You Will Need:

EX F-1.xlsx
EX F-2.xlsx
EX F-3.gif
EX F-4.xlsx
EX F-5.xlsx
EX F-6.xlsx
EX F-7.gif
Classifications.xlsx
Expenses.xlsx
Hardware.xlsx
Logo.gif
Price Information.xlsx
Toronto Sales.xlsx

As you analyze data using Excel, you will find that your worksheets and workbooks become more complex. In this unit, you will learn several Excel features to help you manage workbook data. In addition, you will want to share workbooks with coworkers, but you need to ensure that they can view your data while preventing unwarranted changes. You will learn how to save workbooks in different formats and how to prepare workbooks for distribution. Kate Morgan, the vice president of sales at Quest Specialty Travel, asks for your help in analyzing yearly sales data from the Canadian branches. When the analysis is complete, she will distribute the workbook for branch managers to review.

OBJECTIVES

View and arrange worksheets
Protect worksheets and workbooks
Save custom views of a worksheet
Add a worksheet background
Prepare a workbook for distribution
Insert hyperlinks
Save a workbook for distribution
Group worksheets

Viewing and Arranging Worksheets

UNIT F
Excel 2007

As you work with workbooks made up of multiple worksheets, you may need to compare data in the various sheets. To do this, you can view each worksheet in its own workbook window, called an **instance**, and display the windows in an arrangement that makes it easy to compare data. When you work with worksheets in separate windows, you are working with different views of the same worksheet; the data itself remains in one file. 🎨 Kate asks you to compare the monthly store sales totals for the Toronto and Vancouver branches. Because the sales totals are on different worksheets, you want to arrange the worksheets side by side in separate windows.

STEPS

1. **Start Excel, open the file EX F-1.xlsx from the drive and folder where you store your Data Files, then save it as Store Sales**

2. **With the Toronto sheet active, click the View tab, then click the New Window button in the Window group**

   There are now two instances of the Store Sales workbook on the task bar: Store Sales.xlsx:1 and Store Sales.xlsx:2. The Store Sales.xlsx:2 window is active—you can see its button selected on the taskbar, and the filename in the title bar has :2 after it.

3. **Click the Vancouver sheet tab, click the Switch Windows button in the Window group, then click Store Sales.xlsx:1**

   The Store Sales.xlsx:1 instance is active. The Toronto sheet is active in the Store Sales.xlsx:1 workbook and the Vancouver sheet is active in the Store Sales.xlsx:2 workbook.

   > **QUICK TIP**
   > You can use the View Side by Side button in the Window group to arrange the windows in their previous configuration. The Synchronous Scrolling button below the View Side by Side button is active by default, allowing you to scroll through the arranged worksheets simultaneously.

4. **Click the Arrange All button in the Window group**

   The Arrange Windows dialog box, shown in Figure F-1, provides configurations for displaying the worksheets. You want to view the workbooks vertically.

5. **Click the Vertical option button to select it, then click OK**

   The windows are arranged vertically, as shown in Figure F-2. You can activate a workbook by clicking one of its cells. You can also view only one of the workbooks by hiding the one you do not wish to see.

6. **Scroll horizontally to view the data in the Store Sales.xlsx:1 workbook, click anywhere in the Store Sales.xlsx:2 workbook, scroll horizontally to view the data in the Store Sales.xlsx:2 workbook, then click the Hide button in the Window group**

   When you hide the second instance, only the Store Sales.xlsx:1 workbook is visible.

   > **QUICK TIP**
   > You can also hide a worksheet by right-clicking its sheet tab and clicking Hide from the shortcut menu. To display the hidden sheet, right-click any sheet tab, click Unhide, then in the Unhide dialog box, select the sheet, then click OK.

7. **Click the Unhide button in the Window group; click Store Sales.xlsx:2, if necessary, in the Unhide dialog box; then click OK**

   The Store Sales.xlsx:2 book appears.

8. **Close the Store Sales.xlsx:2 instance, then maximize the Toronto worksheet in the Store Sales.xlsx workbook**

   Closing the Store Sales.xlsx:2 instance leaves only the first instance open, which is now named Store Sales.xlsx in the title bar.

FIGURE F-1: Arrange Windows dialog box

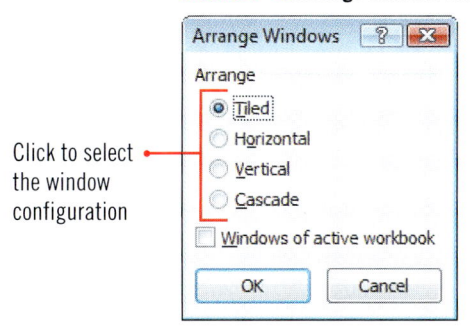

Click to select the window configuration

FIGURE F-2: Windows displayed vertically

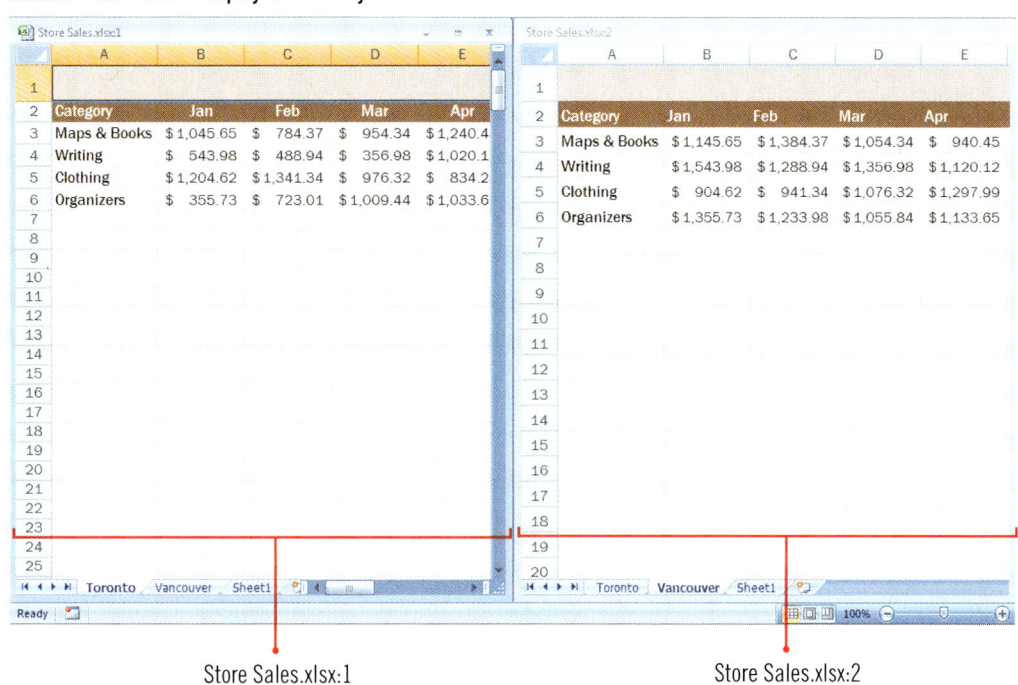

Store Sales.xlsx:1   Store Sales.xlsx:2

Splitting the worksheet into multiple panes

Excel lets you split the worksheet area into vertical and/or horizontal panes, so that you can click inside any one pane and scroll to locate information in that pane while the other panes remain in place, as shown in Figure F-3. To split a worksheet area into multiple panes, drag a split box (the small box at the top of the vertical scroll bar or at the right end of the horizontal scroll bar) in the direction you want the split to appear. To remove the split, move the pointer over the split until the pointer changes to a double-headed arrow, then double-click.

FIGURE F-3: Worksheet split into two horizontal and two vertical panes

Break in row numbers indicates split sheet

Worksheet divided into 4 panes

Break in column letters indicates split sheet

Horizontal split box

Vertical split box

Managing Workbook Data

Protecting Worksheets and Workbooks

To protect sensitive information, Excel allows you to **lock** selected cells so that other people are able to view the data (values, numbers, labels, formulas, etc.) in those cells, but not change it. Excel locks all cells by default, but this protection does not take effect until you activate the Excel protection feature. A common worksheet protection strategy is to unlock cells in which data will be changed, sometimes referred to as the **data entry area**, and to lock cells in which the data should not be changed. Then, when you protect the worksheet, the unlocked areas can still be changed. Because the Toronto sales figures for January through March have been confirmed as final, Kate asks you to protect that area of the worksheet so the figures cannot be altered.

STEPS

1. **On the Toronto sheet, select the range E3:M6, click the Home tab, click the Format button in the Cells group, click Format Cells, then in the Format Cells dialog box click the Protection tab**

   The Locked check box in the Protection tab is already checked, as shown in Figure F-4. This check box is selected by default, meaning that all the cells in a new workbook start out locked. However, cell locking is not applied unless the protection feature is also activated. The protection feature is inactive by default. Because the April through December sales figures have not yet been confirmed as final and may need to be changed, you do not want those cells to be locked when the protection feature is activated.

   QUICK TIP
   To hide any formulas that you don't want to be visible, select the cells that contain formulas that you want to hide, then click the Hidden check box on the Protection tab to select it. The formula will be hidden after the worksheet is protected.

2. **Click the Locked check box to deselect it, then click OK**

   The data remains unlocked until you set the protection in the next step.

3. **Click the Review tab, then click the Protect Sheet button in the Changes group**

   The Protect Sheet dialog box opens, as shown in Figure F-5. In the "Allow users of this worksheet to" list, you can select the actions that you want your worksheet users to be able to perform. The default options protect the worksheet while allowing users to select locked or unlocked cells only. You choose not to use a password.

4. **Verify that Protect worksheet and contents of locked cells is checked and that Select locked cells and Select unlocked cells are checked, then click OK**

   You are ready to test the new worksheet protection.

5. **In cell B3, type 1 to confirm that locked cells cannot be changed, then click OK**

   When you attempt to change a locked cell, a dialog box, shown in Figure F-6, reminds you of the protected cell's read-only status. **Read-only format** means that users can view but not change the data.

6. **Click cell F3, type 1, and notice that Excel allows you to begin the entry, press [Esc] to cancel the entry, then save the workbook**

   Because you unlocked the cells in columns E through M before you protected the worksheet, you can make changes to these cells. You decide to protect the workbook, but you want users to open the workbook without typing a password first.

7. **Click the Protect Workbook button in the Changes group, in the Protect Structure and Windows dialog box make sure the Structure check box is selected, click the Windows check box to select it, then click OK**

   You are ready to test the new workbook protection.

8. **Right-click the Toronto sheet tab**

   The Insert, Delete, Rename, Move or Copy, Tab Color, Hide, and Unhide menu options are not available. You decide to remove the workbook and worksheet protections.

9. **Click the Unprotect Workbook button in the Changes group, then click the Unprotect Sheet button to remove the worksheet protection**

FIGURE F-4: Protection tab in Format Cells dialog box

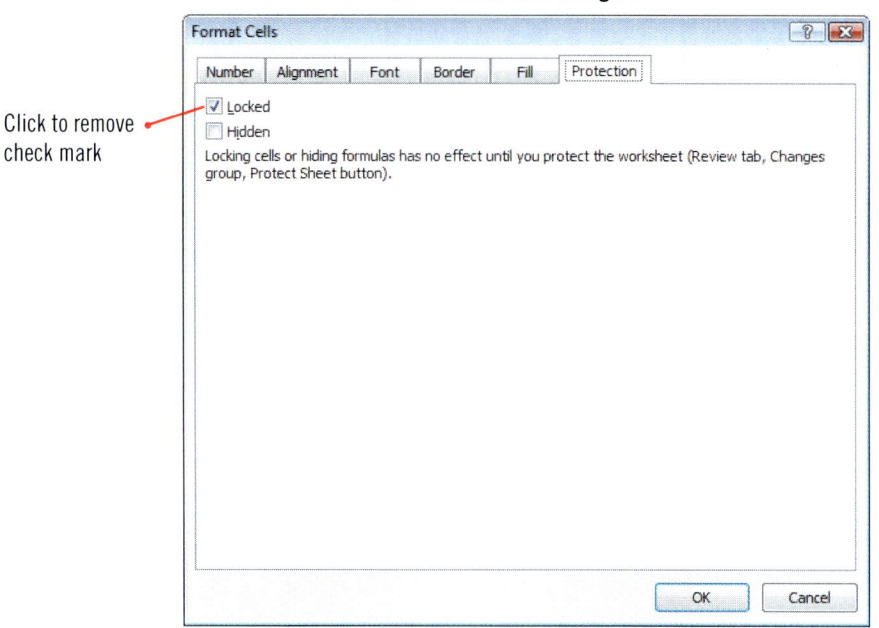

Click to remove check mark

FIGURE F-5: Protect Sheet dialog box

Prevents locked cells from changes

Allows users to select worksheet cells

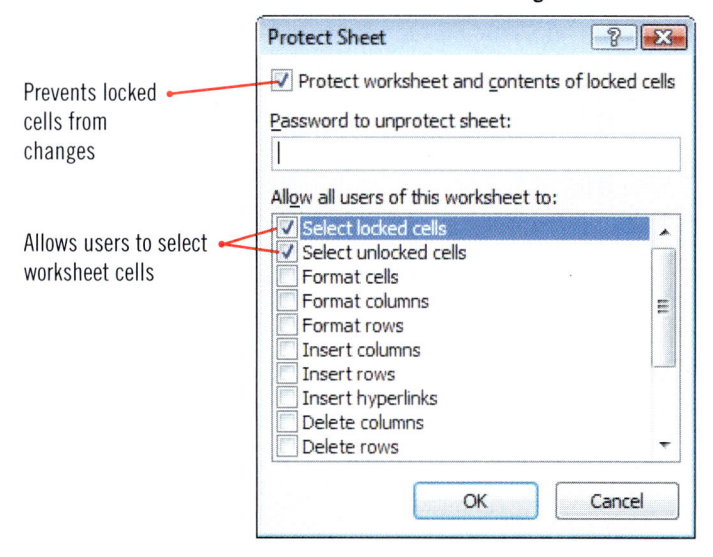

FIGURE F-6: Reminder of protected cell's read-only status

Freezing rows and columns

As the rows and columns of a worksheet fill up with data, you might need to scroll through the worksheet to add, delete, modify, and view information. You can temporarily freeze columns and rows so you can keep labeling information in view as you scroll. **Panes** are the columns and rows that **freeze**, or remain in place, while you scroll through your worksheet. To freeze panes you need to click the View tab, click the Freeze Panes button in the Window group then click Freeze Panes. Excel freezes the columns to the left and the rows above the selected cell. You can also select Freeze Top Row or Freeze First Column to freeze the top row or left worksheet column.

Managing Workbook Data

UNIT F
Excel 2007

Saving Custom Views of a Worksheet

A **view** is a set of display and/or print settings that you can name and save, then access at a later time. By using the Excel Custom Views feature, you can create several different views of a worksheet without having to create separate sheets. For example, if you often hide columns in a worksheet, you can create two views, one that displays all of the columns and another with the columns hidden. You set the worksheet display first, then name the view. Because Kate wants to generate a sales report from the final sales data for January through March, she asks you to save the first-quarter sales data as a custom view. You begin by creating a view showing all of the worksheet data.

STEPS

1. **With the Toronto sheet active, click the View tab, then click the Custom Views button in the Workbook Views group**

   The Custom Views dialog box opens. Any previously defined views for the active worksheet appear in the Views box. No views are defined for the Toronto worksheet. You decide to add a named view that shows all the worksheet columns.

   QUICK TIP
   To delete views from the active worksheet, select the view in the Custom Views dialog box, then click Delete.

2. **Click Add**

   The Add View dialog box opens, as shown in Figure F-7. Here, you enter a name for the view and decide whether to include print settings and hidden rows, columns, and filter settings. You want to include the selected options.

3. **In the Name box, type Year Sales, then click OK**

   You have created a view called Year Sales that shows all the worksheet columns. You want to set up another view that will hide the April through December columns.

4. **Select columns E through M, right-click the selected area, then click Hide on the shortcut menu**

   You are ready to create a custom view of the January through March sales data.

5. **Click cell A1, click the Custom Views button in the Workbook Views group, click Add, in the Name box type First Quarter, then click OK**

   You are ready to test the two custom views.

   TROUBLE
   If you receive the message "Some view settings could not be applied," turn off worksheet protection by clicking the Unprotect Sheet button in the Changes group of the Review tab.

6. **Click the Custom Views button in the Workbook Views group, click Year Sales in the Views list, then click Show**

   The Year Sales custom view displays all of the months' sales data. Now you are ready to test the First Quarter custom view.

7. **Click the Custom Views button in the Workbook Views group, then with First Quarter in the Custom Views dialog box selected, click Show**

   Only the January through March sales figures appear on the screen, as shown in Figure F-8.

8. **Return to the Year Sales view, then save your work**

Managing Workbook Data

FIGURE F-7: Add View dialog box

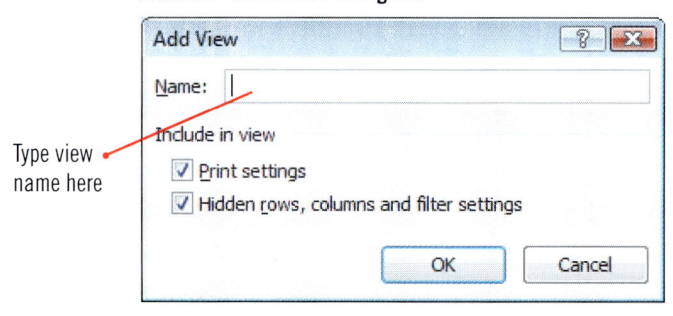

Type view name here →

FIGURE F-8: First Quarter view

January–March sales figures →

→ Break in column letters indicates hidden columns

Using Page Break Preview

The vertical and horizontal dashed lines in the Normal view of worksheets represent page breaks. Excel automatically inserts a page break when your worksheet data doesn't fit on one page. These page breaks are **dynamic**, which means they adjust automatically when you insert or delete rows and columns and when you change column widths or row heights. Everything to the left of the first vertical dashed line and above the first horizontal dashed line is printed on the first page. You can manually add or remove page breaks by clicking the Page Layout tab, clicking the Breaks button in the Page Setup group, then clicking the appropriate command. You can also view and change page breaks manually by clicking the View tab, then clicking the Page Break Preview button in the Workbook Views group, or by clicking the Page Break Preview button on the status bar, then clicking OK. You can drag the blue page break lines to the desired location, as shown in Figure F-9. If you drag a page break to the right to include more data on a page, Excel shrinks the type to fit the data on that page. To exit Page Break Preview, click the Normal button in the Workbook Views group.

FIGURE F-9: Page Break Preview window

Drag blue page break lines to change page breaks

Managing Workbook Data

Adding a Worksheet Background

UNIT F — **Excel 2007**

In addition to using a theme's font colors and fills, you can make your Excel data more attractive to view by adding a picture to the worksheet background. Companies often use their logo as a worksheet background. A worksheet background will display on the screen but will not print with the worksheet. If you want to add a worksheet background that appears on printouts, you can add a **watermark**, a translucent background design that prints behind your data. To add a watermark, you add the image to the worksheet header or footer. Kate asks you to add the Quest logo to the printed background of the Toronto worksheet. You will begin by adding the logo as a worksheet background.

STEPS

1. **With the Toronto sheet active, click the Page Layout tab, then click the Background button in the Page Setup group**

   The Sheet Background dialog box opens.

2. **Navigate to the drive and folder where you store your Data Files, click Logo.gif, then click Insert**

   The Quest logo is tiled behind the worksheet data. It appears twice because the graphic is **tiled**, or repeated, to fill the background.

3. **Preview the Toronto worksheet, then click the Close Print Preview button**

   Because the logo is only for display purposes, it will not print with the worksheet, so is not visible in Print Preview. You want the logo to print with the worksheet, so you decide to remove the background and add the logo to the worksheet header.

4. **Click the Delete Background button in the Page Setup group, click the Insert tab, then click the Header & Footer button in the Text group**

   The Design tab of the Header & Footer Tools appears, as shown in Figure F-10. The Header & Footer group buttons add preformatted headers and footers to a worksheet. The Header & Footer Elements buttons allow you to add page numbers, the date, the time, pictures, and names to the header or footer. The Navigation group buttons move the insertion point from the header to the footer and back. The Options group buttons specify special circumstances for the worksheet's headers and footers. You want to add a picture to the header.

5. **With the insertion point in the center section of the header, click the Picture button in the Header & Footer Elements group, navigate to the drive and folder where you store your Data Files, click Logo.gif, then click Insert**

   A code representing a picture, &[Picture], appears in the center of the header.

6. **Click cell A1, then click the Normal button on the Status Bar**

   You want to scale the worksheet data to print on one page.

7. **Click the Page Layout tab, click the Width list arrow in the Scale to Fit group, click 1 page, click the Height list arrow in the Scale to Fit group, click 1 page, then preview the worksheet**

   Your worksheet should look like Figure F-11.

8. **Click the Close Print Preview button, then save the workbook**

Managing Workbook Data

FIGURE F-10: Design tab of the Header & Footer tools

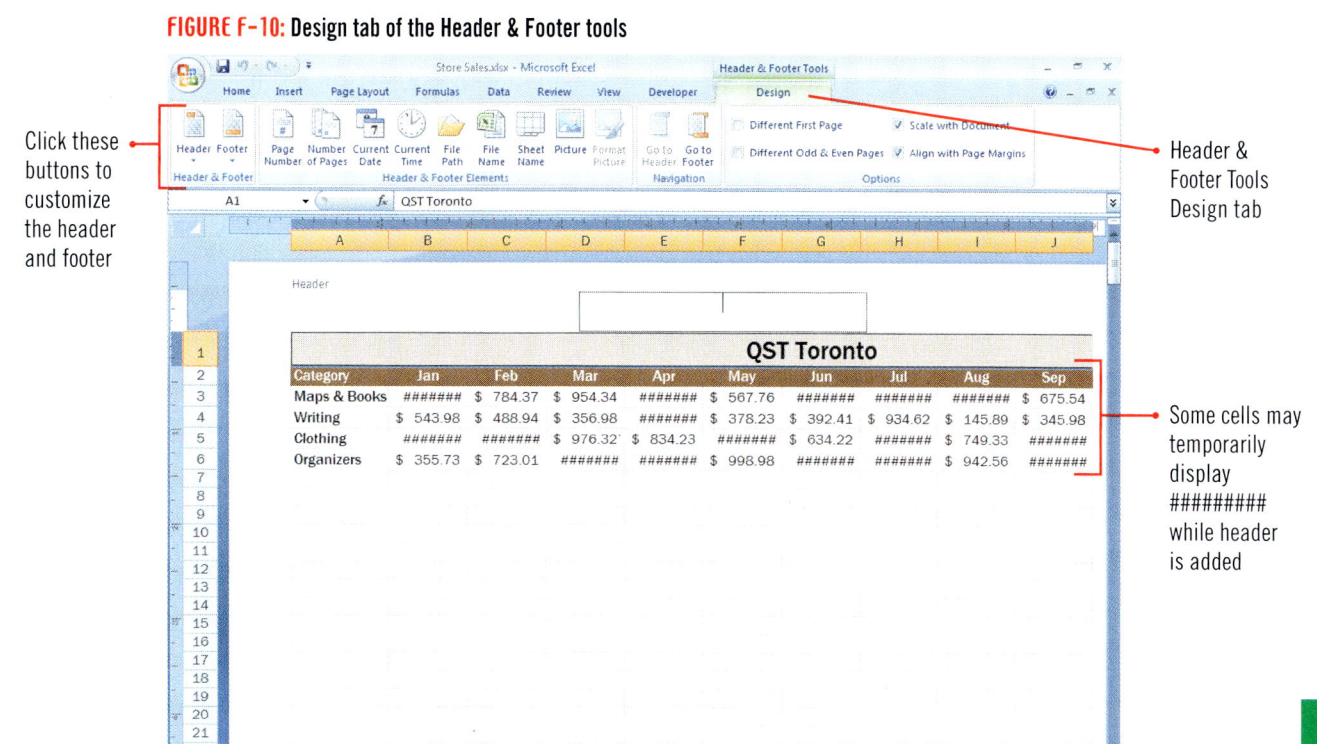

Click these buttons to customize the header and footer

Header & Footer Tools Design tab

Some cells may temporarily display ######### while header is added

FIGURE F-11: Preview of Toronto worksheet with logo in the background

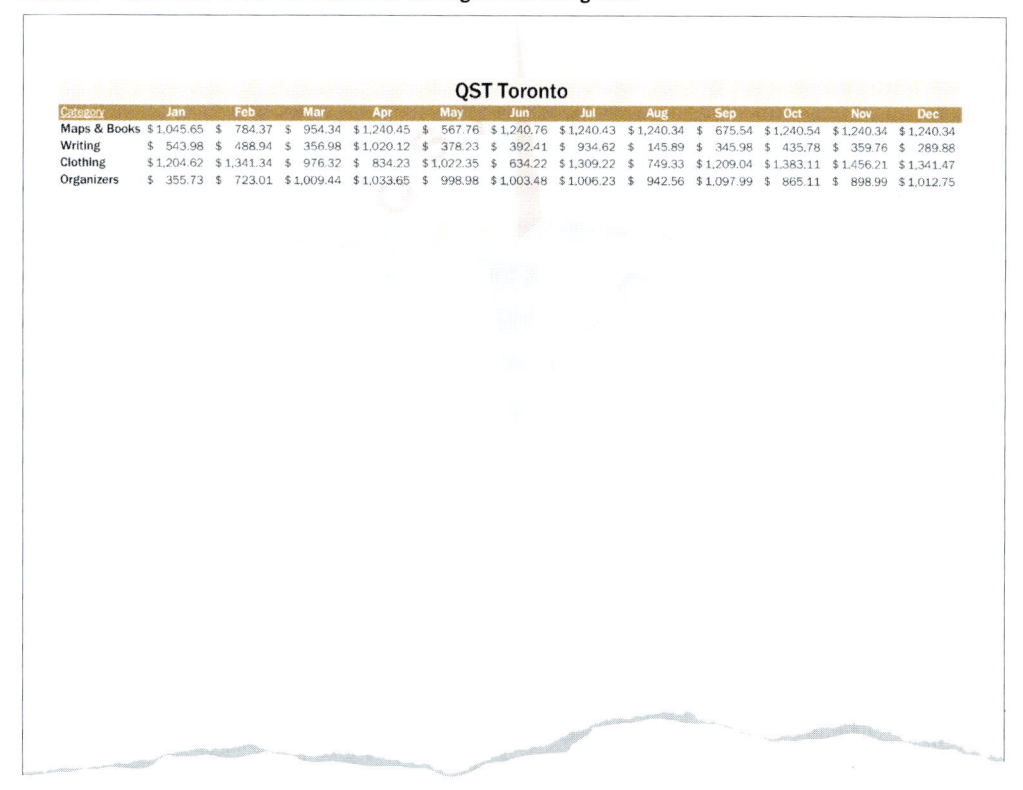

Managing Workbook Data

Preparing a Workbook for Distribution

UNIT F — Excel 2007

If you are collaborating with others and want to share a workbook with them, you might want to remove sensitive information, such as headers, footers, or hidden elements, before distributing the file. You can use the Document Inspector feature to find and remove hidden data and personal information in your workbooks. On the other hand, you might want to add helpful information, called **properties**, to a file to help others identify, understand, and locate it, such as keywords, the author's name, a title, the status, and comments. **Keywords** are terms users can search for that will help them locate your workbook. Properties are a form of **metadata**, information that describe data and are used in Microsoft Windows document searches. You enter properties in the Document Properties Panel. In addition, to insure that others do not make unauthorized changes to your workbook, you can mark a file as final, which changes it to a read-only file, which others can open but not alter. To protect the workbook and prepare it for distribution to the sales managers, Kate asks you to remove sensitive information, add document properties, and mark the workbook as final.

STEPS

1. **Click the Office button, point to Prepare, then click Inspect Document**
   The Document Inspector dialog box opens, as shown in Figure F-12. It lists items that you can have Excel evaluate for personal information. All the components are selected by default.

2. **Click Inspect**
   After inspecting your document, the inspector displays the inspection results. Areas with personal information have a ! in front of them. Headers and footers are also flagged. You want to keep the file's header and footer and remove personal information.

3. **Click Remove All next to Document Properties and Personal Information, then click Close**
   You decide to add keywords to help the sales managers find the worksheet using the search words Toronto or Vancouver.

   > **QUICK TIP**
   > You can view a file's summary information by clicking the Document Properties list arrow in the Document Properties Panel, then clicking Advanced Properties.

4. **Click, point to Prepare, then click Properties**
   The Document Properties Panel appears at the top of the worksheet, as shown in Figure F-13. You decide to add a title, status, keywords, and comments.

5. **In the Title text box type Store Sales, in the Keywords text box type Toronto Vancouver store sales, in the Status text box type DRAFT, then in the Comments text box type The first-quarter figures are final., then click the Close button on the Document Properties Panel**
   You are ready to mark the workbook as final.

   > **QUICK TIP**
   > If you have Windows Rights Management Services (RMS) client software installed, you can use the Information Rights Management (IRM) feature to specify access permissions. Click the Office button, point to Prepare, point to Restrict Permission, then select permission options.

6. **Click, point to Prepare, click Mark as Final, click OK, then click OK again**
   The workbook is saved as a read-only file. [Read-Only] appears in the title bar.

7. **Click cell B3, then type 1 to confirm that the cell cannot be changed**
   Marking a workbook as final prevents accidental changes to the workbook. However, it is not a strong form of workbook protection because a workbook recipient can remove this Final status and edit the document. You decide to remove the read-only status from the workbook so that it is again editable.

8. **Click, point to Prepare, then click Mark as Final**
   The title bar no longer displays [Read-Only] after the workbook title, indicating that you can now edit the workbook.

Managing Workbook Data

FIGURE F-12: Document Inspector dialog box

Items you can inspect for personal information

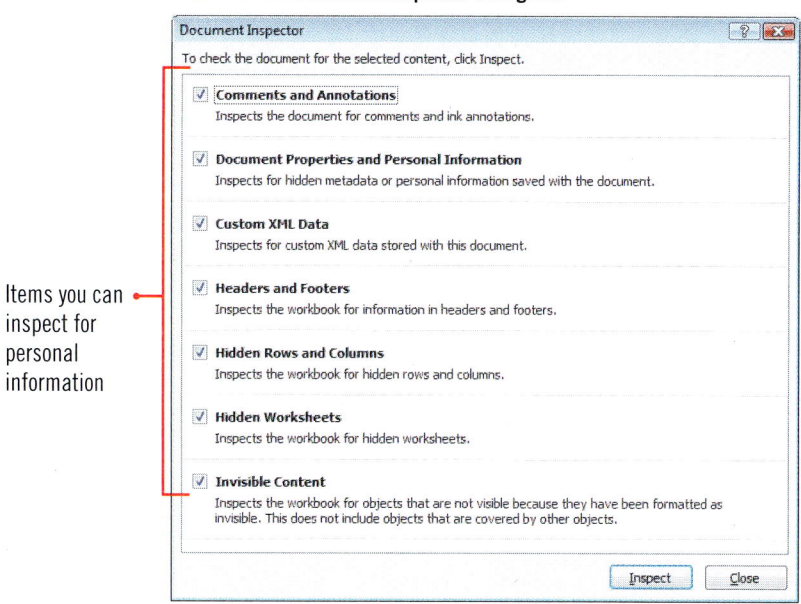

FIGURE F-13: Document Properties Panel

Adding a digital signature to a workbook

You can digitally sign a workbook to establish its validity and prevent it from being changed. You must obtain a valid certificate from a certificate authority to authenticate the workbook. To add a signature line in a workbook, click the Insert tab, click the Signature Line button in the Text group, then click OK. In the Signature Setup dialog box, enter information about the signer of the worksheet and then click OK. To add a signature, double-click the signature line, click OK, if prompted with a Get a Digital ID dialog box, click the Create your own digital ID option button, save your file if prompted, in the Sign dialog box click Select Image next to the sign box, browse to the location where your signature is saved, click Sign, then click OK. To add the certificate authenticating the workbook, click the Office button, point to Prepare, click Add a Digital Signature, then click OK. In the Sign dialog box click Sign, then click OK. The workbook will be saved as read-only and it will not be able to be changed by other users.

Sharing a workbook

You can make an Excel file a **shared workbook** so that several users can open and modify it at the same time. Click the Review tab, click the Share Workbook button in the Changes group, then on the Editing tab of the Share Workbook dialog box click "Allow changes by more than one user at the same time. This also allows workbook merging." If you get an error that the workbook cannot be shared because privacy is enabled, click the Office button, click Excel Options, click the Trust Center category on the left side of the dialog box, click Trust Center Settings, click Privacy Options in the list on the left, click the "Remove personal information from file properties on save" check box to deselect it, then click OK twice. When you share workbooks, it is often helpful to **track** modifications, or identify who made which changes. You can track all changes to a workbook by clicking the Track Changes button in the Changes group, and then clicking Highlight Changes. To resolve the tracked changes in a workbook, click the Track Changes button, then click Accept/Reject Changes. The changes are displayed one by one. You can accept the change or, if you disagree with any of the changes, you can reject them.

Managing Workbook Data

UNIT F
Excel 2007

Inserting Hyperlinks

As you manage the content and appearance of your workbooks, you may want the workbook user to view information in another location. It might be nonessential information or data that is too detailed to place in the workbook itself. In these cases, you can create a hyperlink. A **hyperlink** is an object (a filename, word, phrase, or graphic) in a worksheet that, when you click it, displays, or "jumps to," another location, called the **target**. The target can also be a worksheet, another document, or a site on the World Wide Web. For example, in a worksheet that lists customer invoices, at each customer's name, you might create a hyperlink to an Excel file containing payment terms for each customer. Kate wants managers who view the Store Sales workbook to be able to view the item totals for each sales category in the Toronto sheet. She asks you to create a hyperlink at the Category heading so that users can click the hyperlink to view the items for each category.

STEPS

1. **Click cell A2 on the Toronto worksheet**

2. **Click the Insert tab if necessary, then click the Hyperlink button in the Links group**

   The Insert Hyperlink dialog box opens, as shown in Figure F-14. The icons under "Link to" on the left side of the dialog box let you specify the type of location you want the link to jump to: an existing file or Web page, a place in the same document, a new document, or an e-mail address. Because you want the link to display an already-existing document, the selected first icon, Existing File or Web Page, is correct, so you won't have to change it.

   > **QUICK TIP**
   > To remove a hyperlink or change its target, right-click it, then click Remove Hyperlink or Edit Hyperlink.

3. **Click the Look in list arrow, navigate to the location where you store your Data Files if necessary, then click Toronto Sales.xlsx in the file list**

   The filename you selected and its path appear in the Address text box. This is the document users will see when they click the hyperlink. You can also specify the ScreenTip that users see when they hold the pointer over the hyperlink.

4. **Click ScreenTip, type Items in each category, click OK, then click OK again**

   Cell A2 now contains underlined red text, indicating that it is a hyperlink. The color of a hyperlink depends on the worksheet theme colors. You need to change the text color of the hyperlink text so it is visible on the dark background. After you create a hyperlink, you should check it to make sure that it jumps to the correct destination.

5. **Click the Home tab, click the Font Color list arrow in the Font group, click the White, Background 1 color (first color in the Theme Colors), move the pointer over the Category text, view the ScreenTip, then click once**

   After you click, the Toronto Sales workbook opens, displaying the Sales sheet, as shown in Figure F-15.

   > **QUICK TIP**
   > If you link to a Web page, you must be connected to the Internet to test the link.

6. **Close the Toronto Sales workbook, then save the Store Sales workbook**

Returning to your document

After you click a hyperlink and view the destination document, you will often want to return to your original document that contains the hyperlink. To do this, you can add the Back button to the Quick Access Toolbar. However, the Back button does not appear in the Quick Access toolbar by default; you need to customize the toolbar. (If you are using a computer in a lab, check with your system administrator to see if you have permission to do this.) To customize the Quick Access toolbar, click the Office button, click Excel Options, click Customize in the Excel Options dialog box, click the "Choose Commands from" list arrow, select All Commands, click the Back button, click Add>>, then click OK.

FIGURE F-14: Insert Hyperlink dialog box

Locations a hyperlink can jump to

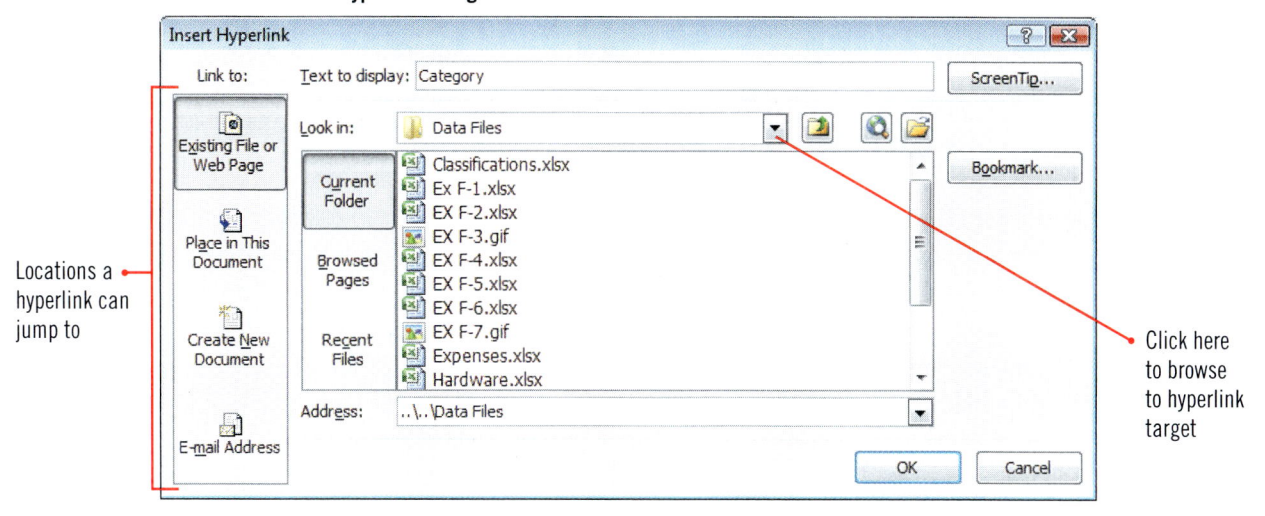

Click here to browse to hyperlink target

FIGURE F-15: Target document

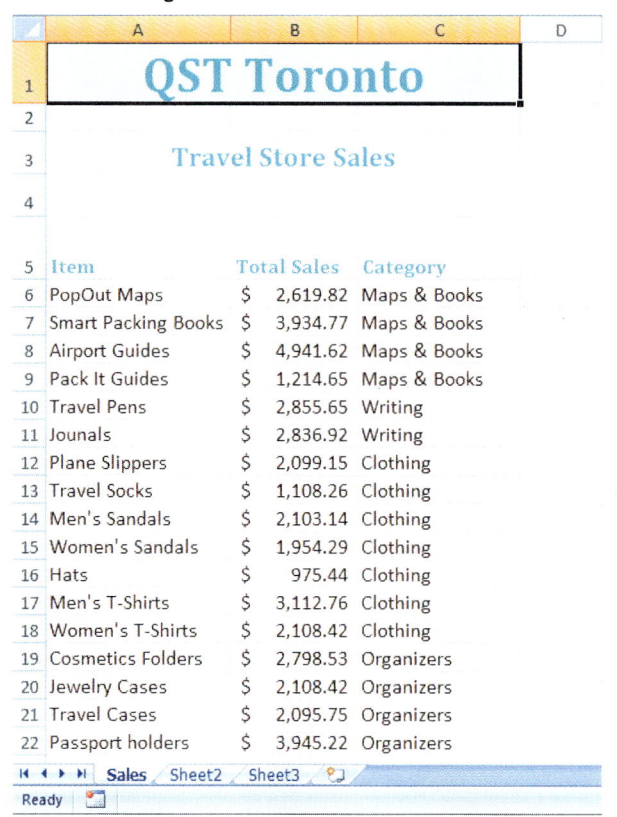

	A	B	C	D
1	QST Toronto			
2				
3	Travel Store Sales			
4				
5	Item	Total Sales	Category	
6	PopOut Maps	$ 2,619.82	Maps & Books	
7	Smart Packing Books	$ 3,934.77	Maps & Books	
8	Airport Guides	$ 4,941.62	Maps & Books	
9	Pack It Guides	$ 1,214.65	Maps & Books	
10	Travel Pens	$ 2,855.65	Writing	
11	Jounals	$ 2,836.92	Writing	
12	Plane Slippers	$ 2,099.15	Clothing	
13	Travel Socks	$ 1,108.26	Clothing	
14	Men's Sandals	$ 2,103.14	Clothing	
15	Women's Sandals	$ 1,954.29	Clothing	
16	Hats	$ 975.44	Clothing	
17	Men's T-Shirts	$ 3,112.76	Clothing	
18	Women's T-Shirts	$ 2,108.42	Clothing	
19	Cosmetics Folders	$ 2,798.53	Organizers	
20	Jewelry Cases	$ 2,108.42	Organizers	
21	Travel Cases	$ 2,095.75	Organizers	
22	Passport holders	$ 3,945.22	Organizers	

Using research tools

You can access resources online and locally on your computer using the Research task pane. To open the Research task pane, click the Review tab, then click the Research button in the Proofing group. You can click the Thesaurus button in the Proofing group for help with synonyms. You can click the Translate button in the Proofing group to translate your text into a selected language. The Search for text box in the Research pane allows you to specify a research topic. The Research pane has a drop-down list of the resources available to search for your topic.

Managing Workbook Data   Excel 141

UNIT F
Excel 2007
Saving a Workbook for Distribution

One way to share Excel data is to place, or **publish**, the data on a network or on the Web so that others can access it using their Web browsers. To publish an Excel document to an **intranet** (a company's internal Web site) or the Web, you can save it in an **HTML (Hypertext Markup Language)** format, which is the coding format used for all Web documents. You can also save your Excel file as a **single file Web page** that integrates all of the worksheets and graphical elements from the workbook into a single file. This file format is called MHTML. In addition to distributing files on the Web, you may need to distribute your files to people working with an earlier version of Excel. You can save your files as Excel 97-2003 workbooks. Excel workbooks can be saved in many other formats to support wide distribution and to make them load faster. The most popular formats are listed in Table F-1. Kate asks you to create a workbook version that managers running an earlier version of Excel can open and modify. She also asks you to save the Store Sales workbook in MHT format so she can publish it on the Quest intranet for their sales managers to view.

STEPS

> **QUICK TIP**
> You can check your files for unsupported features before saving them by clicking the Office button, pointing to Prepare, then clicking Run Compatibility Checker.

1. **Click the Office button, point to Save As, click Excel 97-2003 Workbook, in the Save As dialog box, navigate to the drive and folder where you store your Data Files, then click Save**

   The Compatibility Checker appears on the screen, alerting you to the features that will be lost by saving in the earlier format. Some Excel 2007 features are not available in earlier versions of Excel.

2. **Click Continue, close the workbook, then reopen the Store Sales.xls workbook**

   [Compatibility Mode] appears in the title bar, as shown in Figure F-16. Compatibility mode prevents you from including Excel features in your workbook that are not supported in Excel 97-2003 workbooks. To exit compatibility mode, you need to save your file in one of the Excel 2007 formats and reopen the file.

3. **Click, point to Save As, click Excel Workbook, if necessary navigate to the drive and folder where you store your Data Files, click Save, then click Yes when you are asked if you want to replace the existing file**

   [Compatibility Mode] remains displayed in the title bar. You decide to close the file and reopen it to exit compatibility mode.

4. **Close the workbook, then reopen the Store Sales.xlsx workbook**

   The title bar no longer displays [Compatibility mode]. You decide to save the file for Web distribution.

> **QUICK TIP**
> To ensure that your workbook displays the same way on different computer platforms and screen settings, you can publish it in PDF format. You need to download an Add-in to save files in this format. The PDF format preserves all of the workbook's formatting so that it appears on the Web exactly as it was created.

5. **Click, click Save As, in the Save As dialog box, navigate to the drive and folder where you store your Data Files, change the filename to sales, then click the Save as type list arrow and click Single File Web Page (*.mht, *.mhtml)**

   The Save as type list box indicates that the workbook is to be saved as a Single File Web Page, which is in mhtml or mht format. To avoid problems when publishing your pages to a Web server, it is best to use lowercase characters, omit special characters and spaces, and limit your filename to eight characters with an additional three-character extension.

6. **Click Save, then click Yes**

   The dialog box indicated that some features may not be retained in the Web page file. Excel saves the workbook as an MHT file in the folder location you specified in the Save As dialog box. The MHT file is open on your screen, as shown in Figure F-17. It's a good idea to open an mht file in your browser to see how it will look to viewers.

7. **Close the sales.mht file in Excel, open Windows Explorer, open the sales.mht file, click the Vancouver sheet tab, then close your browser window**

Excel 142   Managing Workbook Data

FIGURE F-16: Workbook in compatibility mode

File is marked as using compatibility mode

FIGURE F-17: Workbook saved as a single file web page

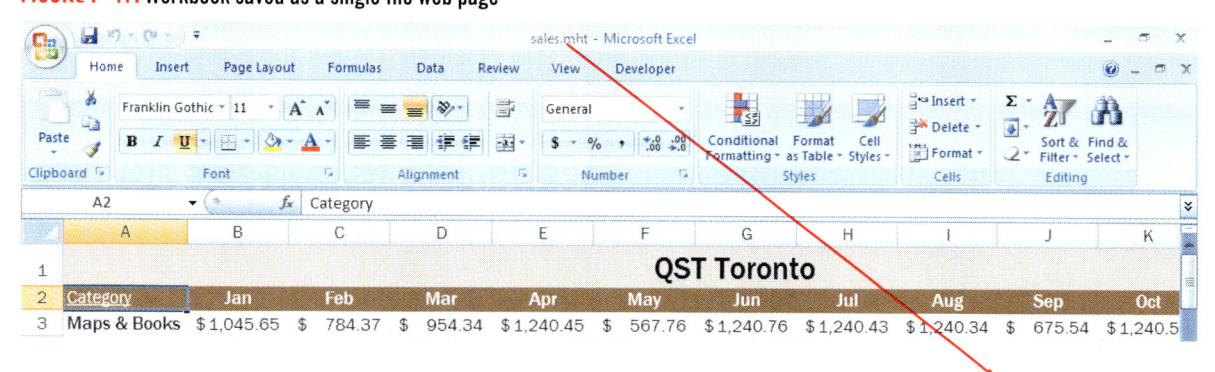

Web file with new name

TABLE F-1: Workbook formats

type of file	file extension(s)	Used for
Macro-enabled workbook	xlsm	Files that contain macros
Excel 97-2003 workbook	xls	Working with people using older versions of Excel
Single file Web page	mht, mhtml	Web sites with multiple pages and graphics
Web page	htm, html	Simple single-page Web sites
Excel template	xltx	Excel files that will be reused with small changes
Excel macro-enabled template	xltm	Excel files that will be used again and contain macros
Portable document format	pdf	Files with formatting that needs to be preserved
XML paper specification	xps	Files with formatting that needs to be preserved and files that need to be shared

Understanding Excel file formats

The default file format for Excel 2007 files is the Office Open XML format, which supports all Excel features. This format stores Excel files in small XML components which are zipped for compression. This default format has different types of files with their own extensions that are also often called formats themselves. The most often used format, xlsx, does not support macros. Macros, programmed instructions that perform tasks, can be a security risk. If your worksheet contains macros, you need to save it with an extension of xlsm so the macros will function in the workbook. If you use a workbook's text and formats repeatedly, you may want to save it as a template with the extension xltx. If your template contains macros, you need to save it with the xltm extension.

Managing Workbook Data

Grouping Worksheets

UNIT F — Excel 2007

You can group worksheets to work on them as a collection so that data entered into one worksheet is automatically entered into all of the selected worksheets. This is useful for data that is common to every sheet of a workbook, such as headers and footers, or for column headings that will apply to all monthly worksheets in a yearly summary. Grouping worksheets can also be used to print multiple worksheets at one time. Kate asks you to add the text Quest to the footer of both the Toronto and Vancouver worksheets. You will also add one-inch margins to the left and right sides of both worksheets.

STEPS

1. Open the Store Sales.xlsx file from the drive and folder where you store your Data Files

2. With the Toronto sheet active, press and hold [Shift], click the Vancouver sheet, then release [Shift]

   Both sheet tabs are selected, and the title bar now contains [Group], indicating that the worksheets are grouped together, so any changes you make to the Toronto sheet will also be made to the Vancouver sheet.

3. Click the Insert tab, then click the Header & Footer button in the Text group

4. On the Header & Footer Tools Design tab, click the Go to Footer button in the Navigation group, type Quest in the center section of the footer, enter your name in the left section of the footer, click cell A1, then click the Normal button on the Status Bar

   You decide to check the footers in Print Preview.

5. With the worksheets still grouped, click the Office button, point to Print, click Print Preview, then click the Next Page button in the Preview group

   Because the worksheets are grouped, both pages contain the footer with Quest and your name. The worksheets would look better with a wider top margin.

6. Click the Close Print Preview button, click the Page Layout tab, click the Margins button in the Page Setup group, click Custom Margins, in the Top text box type 1, then click OK

7. Preview and print the worksheets

   The Toronto worksheet is shown in Figure F-18; the Vancouver worksheet is shown in Figure F-19. You decide to ungroup the worksheets.

8. Right-click the Toronto worksheet sheet tab, then click Ungroup Sheets

9. Save the workbook, then close it and exit Excel

Creating a workspace

If you work with several workbooks at a time, you can group them so that you can open them in one step by creating a **workspace**, a file with an .xlw extension. Then, instead of opening each workbook individually, you can open the workspace. To create a workspace, open the workbooks you wish to group, then position and size them as you would like them to appear. Click the View tab, click the Save Workspace button in the Window group, type a name for the workspace file, navigate to the location where you want to store it, then click Save. Remember, however, that the workspace file does not contain the workbooks themselves, so you still have to save any changes you make to the original workbook files. If you work at another computer, you need to have the workspace file and all of the workbooks that are part of the workspace.

FIGURE F-18: Toronto worksheet

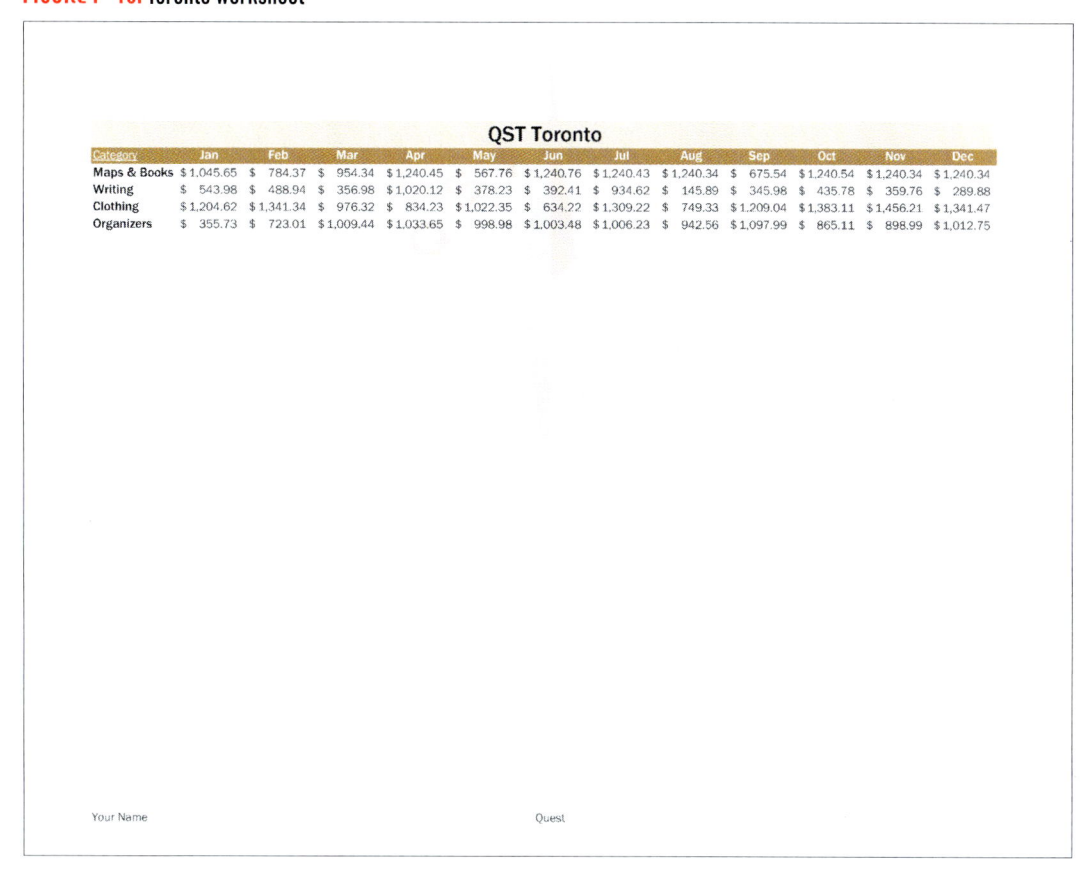

QST Toronto

Category	Jan	Feb	Mar	Apr	May	Jun	Jul	Aug	Sep	Oct	Nov	Dec
Maps & Books	$1,045.65	$ 784.37	$ 954.34	$1,240.45	$ 567.76	$1,240.76	$1,240.43	$1,240.34	$ 675.54	$1,240.54	$1,240.34	$1,240.34
Writing	$ 543.98	$ 488.94	$ 356.98	$1,020.12	$ 378.23	$ 392.41	$ 934.62	$ 145.89	$ 345.98	$ 435.78	$ 359.76	$ 289.88
Clothing	$1,204.62	$1,341.34	$ 976.32	$ 834.23	$1,022.35	$ 634.22	$1,309.22	$ 749.33	$1,209.04	$1,383.11	$1,456.21	$1,341.47
Organizers	$ 355.73	$ 723.01	$1,009.44	$1,033.65	$ 998.98	$1,003.48	$1,006.23	$ 942.56	$1,097.99	$ 865.11	$ 898.99	$1,012.75

Your Name   Quest

FIGURE F-19: Vancouver worksheet

QST Vancouver

Category	Jan	Feb	Mar	Apr	May	Jun	Jul	Aug	Sep	Oct	Nov	Dec
Maps & Books	$1,145.65	$1,384.37	$1,054.34	$ 940.45	$1,567.76	$1,040.76	$ 940.43	$1,140.34	$1,275.54	$ 940.54	$1,040.34	$1,040.34
Writing	$1,543.98	$1,288.94	$1,356.98	$1,120.12	$1,311.22	$1,392.41	$1,134.62	$1,145.89	$1,194.86	$ 835.78	$ 859.76	$ 889.88
Clothing	$ 904.62	$ 941.34	$1,076.32	$1,297.99	$ 922.35	$1,234.22	$1,509.22	$1,049.33	$1,009.04	$1,283.11	$1,126.21	$1,141.47
Organizers	$1,355.73	$1,233.98	$1,055.84	$1,133.65	$1,298.98	$1,303.48	$1,106.23	$ 842.56	$1,197.99	$ 965.11	$ 988.99	$1,112.75

Your Name   Quest

Practice

▼ CONCEPTS REVIEW

FIGURE F-20

[Screenshot of Excel View tab with labels a-g pointing to various ribbon elements and worksheet features]

1. Which element do you click to organize windows in a specific configuration?
2. Which element points to a ScreenTip for a hyperlink?
3. Which element points to a hyperlink?
4. Which element do you click to open the active worksheet in a new window?
5. Which element do you click to name and save a set of display and/or print settings?
6. Which element do you click to group workbooks so that they open together as a unit?
7. Which element do you click to view and change the way worksheet data is distributed on printed pages?

Match each term with the statement that best describes it.

8. Data entry area
9. Hyperlink
10. Watermark
11. HTML
12. Dynamic page breaks

a. Web page format
b. Portion of a worksheet that can be changed
c. Translucent background design on a printed worksheet
d. An object that when clicked displays another worksheet or a Web page
e. Adjusted automatically when rows and columns are inserted or deleted

Select the best answer from the list of choices.

13. You can establish the validity of a workbook by adding a _____.
    a. Keyword
    b. Custom Views
    c. Digital signature
    d. Template

14. You can group several workbooks in a _____ so they can be opened together rather than individually.
    a. Workgroup
    b. Consolidated workbook
    c. Workspace
    d. Work unit

Excel 146   Managing Workbook Data

15. Which of the following formats means that users can view but not change data in a workbook?
    a. Macro
    b. PDF
    c. Read-only
    d. Template

16. You can group noncontiguous worksheets by pressing and holding _____ while clicking the sheet tabs that you want to group.
    a. [Ctrl]
    b. [Spacebar]
    c. [Alt]
    d. [F6]

▼ SKILLS REVIEW

1. **View and arrange worksheets.**
   a. Start Excel, open the file EX F-2.xlsx from the drive and folder where you store your Data Files, then save it as **Chicago Budget**.
   b. Activate the 2010 sheet if necessary, then open the 2011 sheet in a new window.
   c. Activate the 2010 sheet in the Chicago Budget.xlsx:1 workbook. Activate the 2011 sheet in the Chicago Budget.xlsx:2 workbook.
   d. View the Chicago Budget.xlsx:1 and Chicago Budget.xlsx:2 workbooks tiled horizontally. View the workbooks in a vertical arrangement.
   e. Hide the Chicago Budget.xlsx:2 instance, then unhide the instance. Close the Chicago Budget.xlsx:2 instance and maximize the Chicago Budget.xlsx workbook.
   f. Split the 2010 sheet into two horizontal panes. (*Hint*: Drag the Horizontal split box.) Remove the split by double-clicking it, then save your work.

2. **Protect worksheets and workbooks.**
   a. On the 2010 sheet, unlock the expense data in the range C9:F17.
   b. Protect the sheet without using a password.
   c. To make sure the other cells are locked, attempt to make an entry in cell D4. You should see the error message displayed in Figure F-21.
   d. Change the first-quarter mortgage expense to 4500.
   e. Protect the workbook's structure and windows without applying a password. Right-click the 2010 and 2011 worksheets to verify that you cannot insert, delete, rename, move, copy, hide, or unhide the sheets, or change their tab color.
   f. Unprotect the workbook. Unprotect the 2010 worksheet.
   g. Save the workbook.

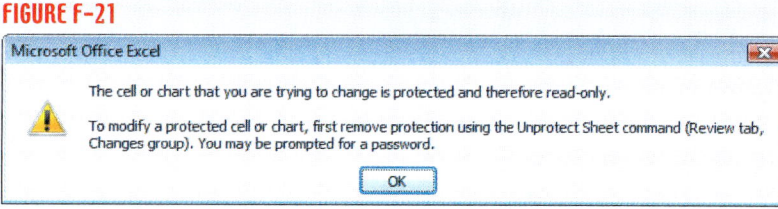

   FIGURE F-21

3. **Save custom views of a worksheet**
   a. Using the 2010 sheet, create a view of the entire worksheet called **Entire 2010 Budget**.
   b. Hide rows 8 through 19, then make a new view called **Income** showing only the income data.
   c. Use the Custom Views dialog box to display all of the data on the 2010 worksheet.
   d. Use the Custom Views dialog box to display only the income data on the 2010 worksheet.
   e. Use the Custom Views dialog box to return to the Entire 2010 Budget view.
   f. Save the workbook.

4. **Add a worksheet background.**
   a. Use EX F-3.gif as a worksheet background for the 2010 sheet.
   b. Delete the background image on the 2010 sheet.
   c. Add EX F-3.gif to the 2010 header.
   d. Preview the 2010 worksheet to verify that the background will print, then exit Print Preview and save the workbook.
   e. Add your name to the center section of the 2010 worksheet footer, then print the worksheet.

▼ SKILLS REVIEW (CONTINUED)

5. **Prepare a workbook for distribution.**
   a. Inspect the workbook and remove any document properties, personal information, and header and footer information.
   b. Use the Document Properties Panel to add a title of Quarterly Budget and the keywords café and Chicago.(*Hint*: Separate the keywords with a space.) If you are using your own computer, add your name in the Author text box.
   c. Mark the workbook as final and verify that [Read-Only] is in the title bar.
   d. Remove the final status of the workbook.
   e. Save the workbook.
6. **Insert hyperlinks.**
   a. On the 2010 worksheet, make cell A8 a hyperlink to the file **Expenses.xlsx** in your Data Files folder.
   b. Test the link, then print Sheet 1 of the Expenses workbook.
   c. Return to the Chicago Budget workbook, edit the hyperlink in cell A8, adding a ScreenTip that reads **Expense Details**, then verify that the ScreenTip appears.
   d. On the 2011 worksheet, enter the text **Based on 2010 budget** in cell A21.
   e. Make the text in cell A21 a hyperlink to cell A1 in the 2010 worksheet. (*Hint*: Use the Place in This Document button and note the cell reference in the Type the cell reference text box.)
   f. Test the hyperlink.
   g. Remove the hyperlink in cell A8 of the 2010 worksheet.
   h. Save the workbook.
7. **Save a workbook for distribution.**
   a. Save the Chicago Budget workbook as a single file Web page with the name chicago.mht. Close the chicago.mht file in Excel, then open the chicago.mht file in your Web browser. Close your browser window and reopen the Chicago Budget.xlsx file.
   b. If you have the PDF Add-in installed on your computer, save the Chicago Budget workbook as a PDF file.
   c. Save the Chicago Budget workbook as an Excel 97-2003 workbook and review the results of the Compatibility Checker.
   d. Close the Chicago Budget.xls file and reopen the Chicago Budget.xlsx file.
   e. Save the file as a macro-enabled template in the drive and folder where you store your Data Files. (*Hint*: Select the type Excel Macro-Enabled template xltm in the Save as type list.)
   f. Close the template file, then reopen the Chicago Budget.xlsx file.
8. **Grouping worksheets.**
   a. Group the 2010 and 2011 worksheets.
   b. Add your name to the center footer section of the worksheets.
   c. Save the workbook, then preview both sheets.
   d. Print both sheets, compare your sheets to Figure F-22, then ungroup the sheets.
   e. Close all open files and exit Excel.

FIGURE F-22

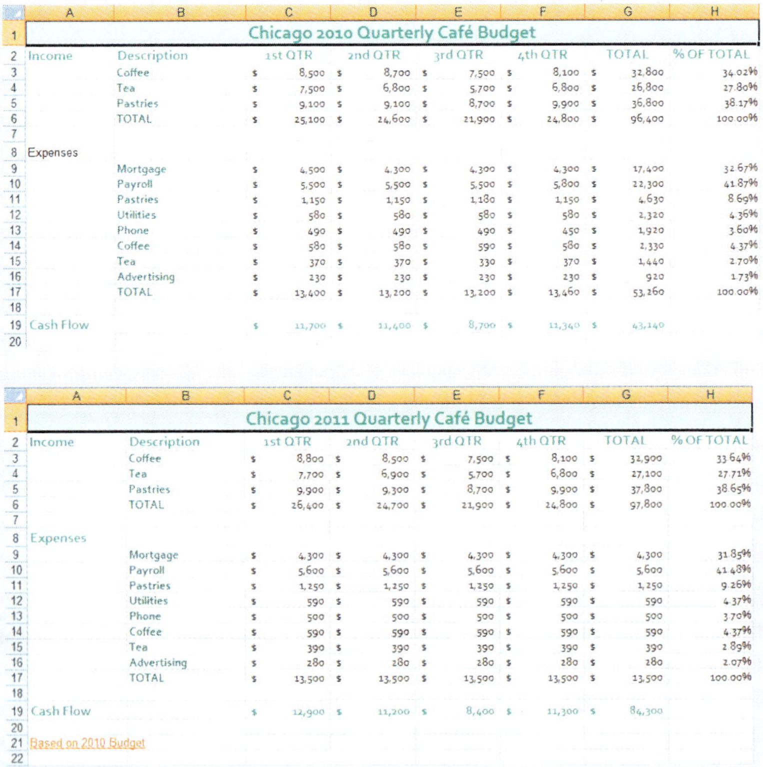

	A	B	C	D	E	F	G	H
1	Chicago 2010 Quarterly Café Budget							
2	Income	Description	1st QTR	2nd QTR	3rd QTR	4th QTR	TOTAL	% OF TOTAL
3		Coffee	$ 8,500	$ 8,700	$ 7,500	$ 8,100	$ 32,800	34.02%
4		Tea	$ 7,500	$ 6,800	$ 5,700	$ 6,800	$ 26,800	27.80%
5		Pastries	$ 9,100	$ 9,100	$ 8,700	$ 9,900	$ 36,800	38.17%
6		TOTAL	$ 25,100	$ 24,600	$ 21,900	$ 24,800	$ 96,400	100.00%
7								
8	Expenses							
9		Mortgage	$ 4,500	$ 4,300	$ 4,300	$ 4,300	$ 17,400	32.67%
10		Payroll	$ 5,500	$ 5,500	$ 5,500	$ 5,800	$ 22,300	41.87%
11		Pastries	$ 1,150	$ 1,150	$ 1,180	$ 1,150	$ 4,630	8.69%
12		Utilities	$ 580	$ 580	$ 580	$ 580	$ 2,320	4.36%
13		Phone	$ 490	$ 490	$ 490	$ 450	$ 1,920	3.60%
14		Coffee	$ 580	$ 580	$ 590	$ 580	$ 2,330	4.37%
15		Tea	$ 370	$ 370	$ 330	$ 370	$ 1,440	2.70%
16		Advertising	$ 230	$ 230	$ 230	$ 230	$ 920	1.73%
17		TOTAL	$ 13,400	$ 13,200	$ 13,200	$ 13,460	$ 53,260	100.00%
18								
19	Cash Flow		$ 11,700	$ 11,400	$ 8,700	$ 11,340	$ 43,140	
20								

	A	B	C	D	E	F	G	H
1	Chicago 2011 Quarterly Café Budget							
2	Income	Description	1st QTR	2nd QTR	3rd QTR	4th QTR	TOTAL	% OF TOTAL
3		Coffee	$ 8,800	$ 8,500	$ 7,500	$ 8,100	$ 32,900	33.64%
4		Tea	$ 7,700	$ 6,900	$ 5,700	$ 6,800	$ 27,100	27.71%
5		Pastries	$ 9,900	$ 9,300	$ 8,700	$ 9,900	$ 37,800	38.65%
6		TOTAL	$ 26,400	$ 24,700	$ 21,900	$ 24,800	$ 97,800	100.00%
7								
8	Expenses							
9		Mortgage	$ 4,300	$ 4,300	$ 4,300	$ 4,300	$ 4,300	31.85%
10		Payroll	$ 5,600	$ 5,600	$ 5,600	$ 5,600	$ 5,600	41.48%
11		Pastries	$ 1,250	$ 1,250	$ 1,250	$ 1,250	$ 1,250	9.26%
12		Utilities	$ 590	$ 590	$ 590	$ 590	$ 590	4.37%
13		Phone	$ 500	$ 500	$ 500	$ 500	$ 500	3.70%
14		Coffee	$ 590	$ 590	$ 590	$ 590	$ 590	4.37%
15		Tea	$ 390	$ 390	$ 390	$ 390	$ 390	2.89%
16		Advertising	$ 280	$ 280	$ 280	$ 280	$ 280	2.07%
17		TOTAL	$ 13,500	$ 13,500	$ 13,500	$ 13,500	$ 13,500	100.00%
18								
19	Cash Flow		$ 12,900	$ 11,200	$ 8,400	$ 11,300	$ 84,300	
20								
21	Based on 2010 Budget							
22								

▼ INDEPENDENT CHALLENGE 1

You manage Old City Photo, a photo supply company located in Montreal, Canada. You are organizing your first-quarter sales in an Excel worksheet. Because the sheet for the month of January includes the same type of information you need for February and March, you decide to enter the headings for all of the first-quarter months at the same time. You use a separate worksheet for each month and create data for three months.

a. Start Excel, create a new workbook, then save it as **Photo Sales.xlsx** in the drive and folder where you store your Data Files.

b. Name the first sheet January, name the second sheet February, and name the third sheet March.

c. Group the worksheets.

d. With the worksheets grouped, use Table F-2 as a guide to enter the row and column labels that need to appear on each of the three sheets. Add the headings in rows one and two. Center the first row across columns A and B. Enter the labels with the data in the range B3:B9 and the Total label in cell A10.

e. Enter the formula to sum the Amount column in cell B10. Ungroup the worksheets and enter your own data for each of the sales categories in the January, February, and March sheets.

f. Display each worksheet in its own window, then arrange the three sheets vertically.

g. Hide the window displaying the March sheet. Unhide the March sheet window.

h. Split the March window into two panes, the upper pane displaying rows one through five and the lower pane displaying rows six through ten. Scroll through the data in each pane, then remove the split.

i. Close the windows displaying Photo Sales.xlsx:2 and Photo Sales.xlsx:3, then maximize the Photo Sales.xlsx workbook.

j. Add the keywords **photo supplies** to your workbook, using the Document Properties Panel.

k. Group the worksheets again.

l. Add headers that include your name in the left section to all three worksheets.

m. With the worksheets still grouped, format the worksheets appropriately.

n. Ungroup the worksheets, then mark the workbook status as final.

o. Save the workbook, preview and print the three worksheets, then exit Excel.

TABLE F-2

Old City Photo	
	Amount in $ (Canada)
Cameras	
Color Processing	
B & W Processing	
Film	
Digital Media	
Frames	
Darkroom Supplies	
TOTAL	

▼ INDEPENDENT CHALLENGE 2

As the payroll manager at Media Communications, an advertising firm, you decide to organize the weekly timecard data using Excel worksheets. You use a separate worksheet for each week and track the hours for employees with different job classifications. A hyperlink in the worksheet provides pay rates for each classification and custom views limit the information that is displayed.

a. Start Excel, open the file EX F-4.xlsx from the drive and folder where you store your Data Files, then save it as **Timesheets**.

b. Compare the data in the workbook by arranging the Week 1, Week 2, and Week 3 sheets horizontally.

c. Maximize the Week 1 window. Unlock the hours data in the Week 1 sheet and protect the worksheet. Verify that the employee names, numbers, and classifications cannot be changed. Verify that the total hours data can be changed, but do not change the data.

d. Unprotect the Week 1 sheet and create a custom view called **Complete Worksheet** that displays all of the worksheet data.

e. Hide column E and create a custom view of the data in the range A1:D22. Give the view a name of **Employee Classifications**. Display each view, then return to the Complete Worksheet view.

▼ INDEPENDENT CHALLENGE 2 (CONTINUED)

f. Add a page break between columns D and E so that the Total Hours data prints on a second page. Preview the worksheet, then remove the page break. (*Hint*: Use the Breaks button on the Page Layout tab.)

g. Add a hyperlink to the Classification heading in cell D1 that links to the file Classifications.xlsx. Add a ScreenTip that reads Pay rates, then test the hyperlink. Compare your screen to Figure F-23.

h. Save the workbook as an Excel 97-2003 workbook, reviewing the Compatibility Checker information. Close the Timesheets.xls file, then reopen the Timesheets.xlsx workbook.

i. Group the three worksheets and add your name to the center section of the footer.

j. Save the workbook, then preview the grouped worksheets.

k. Ungroup the worksheets and add two-inch top and left margins to the Week 1 worksheet.

l. Hide the Week 2 and Week 3 worksheets.

m. Inspect the file and remove all document properties, personal information, headers, footers, and hidden worksheets.

n. Add the keyword hours to the workbook, save the workbook, then mark it as final.

FIGURE F-23

	A	B
1	**Media Communications**	
2	Classifications	Pay Rate
3	Associate	$37
4	Sr. Associate	$45
5	Assistant	$22
6	Sr. Assistant	$30
7		

Advanced Challenge Exercise

- Remove the final status from the workbook.
- If you have Windows Rights Management Services client software installed on your computer, restrict the permissions to the workbook by granting only yourself permission to change the workbook.
- If you have a valid certificate authority, add a digital signature to the workbook.
- Delete the hours data in the worksheet and save the workbook as an Excel Template.

o. Add your name to the center footer section, save the workbook, print the Week 1 worksheet, close the workbook and exit Excel.

▼ INDEPENDENT CHALLENGE 3

One of your responsibilities as the office manager at your technology training company is to order paper supplies for the office. You decide to create a spreadsheet to track these orders, placing each month's orders on its own sheet. You create custom views that will focus on the categories of supplies. A hyperlink will provide the supplier's contact information.

a. Start Excel, open the file EX F-5.xlsx from the drive and folder where you store your Data Files, then save it as **Supplies**.

b. Arrange the sheets for the three months horizontally to compare supply expenses, then close the extra workbook windows and maximize the remaining window.

c. Create a custom view of the entire January worksheet named **All Supplies**. Hide the paper, pens, and miscellaneous supply data and create a custom view displaying only the hardware supplies. Call the view **Hardware**.

d. Display the All Supplies view, group the worksheets, and create totals for the total costs in cell D28 on each month's sheet.

e. With the sheets grouped, add the sheet name to the center section of each sheet's header and your name to the center section of each sheet's footer.

f. Use the compatibility checker to view the unsupported features in earlier Excel formats.

g. Add a hyperlink in cell A1 of the January sheet that opens the file Hardware.xlsx. Add a ScreenTip of **Hardware Supplier**. Test the link, viewing the ScreenTip, then return to the Supplies workbook.

h. Create a workspace that includes the workbooks Supplies.xlsx and Hardware.xlsx in the tiled layout. Name the workspace **Office Supplies**. (*Hint*: Save Workspace is a button on the View tab in the Window group.)

i. Hide the Hardware.xlsx workbook.

j. Unhide the Hardware.xlsx workbook.

▼ INDEPENDENT CHALLENGE 3 (CONTINUED)

k. Close the Hardware.xlsx file and maximize the Supplies.xlsx worksheet.
l. Save the Supplies workbook as a macro-enabled workbook.
m. Print the January worksheet, close the workbook, and exit Excel.

▼ REAL LIFE INDEPENDENT CHALLENGE

Excel can be a useful tool in planning vacations. Whether you are planning a trip soon or in the distant future, you can use Excel to organize your travel budget. Use the table below as a guide in organizing your travel expenses. After your data is entered, you create custom views of the data, add a hyperlink and keywords, and save the file in an earlier version of Excel.

a. Start Excel, create a new workbook, then save it as **Travel Budget** in the drive and folder where you store your Data Files.
b. Enter your travel budget data using the relevant items from the Table F-3.
c. Add a hyperlink to your accommodations label that links to a Web page with information about the hotel, campground, B & B, or inn that you will stay at on your trip.
d. Create a custom view called **Entire Budget** that displays all of the budget information. Create a custom view named **Transportation** that displays only the transportation data. Check each view, then display the entire budget.
e. Add appropriate keywords to the workbook.
f. Add a footer that includes your name on the left side of the printout.
g. Unlock the price information in the worksheet. Protect the worksheet without using a password.
h. Save the workbook, then print the worksheet.
i. Save the workbook in Excel 97-2003 format.
j. Close the Travel Budget.xls file.

Advanced Challenge Exercise

- Open the Travel Budget.xlsx file and unprotect the worksheet.
- Enable the workbook to be changed by multiple people simultaneously.
- Set up the shared workbook so that all future changes will be tracked.
- Change the data for two of your dollar amounts.
- Review the tracked changes and accept the first change and reject the second change
- Save the workbook.

k. Exit Excel.

TABLE F-3

	Amount
Transportation	
Air	
Auto	
Train	
Cab	
Bus	
Accommodations	
Hotel	
Campground fees	
Bed & Breakfast	
Inn	
Meals	
Food	
Beverage	
Miscellaneous	
Admissions fees	
Souvenirs	

▼ VISUAL WORKSHOP

Start Excel, open the file EX F-6.xlsx from the drive and folder where you store your Data Files, then save it as **Summer Rentals**. Create the worksheet shown in Figure F-24. Enter your name in the footer, then print the worksheet. The text in cell A18 is a hyperlink to the Price Information workbook; the worksheet background is the Data File EX F-7.gif, and the picture in the header is the file EX F-7.gif.

FIGURE F-24

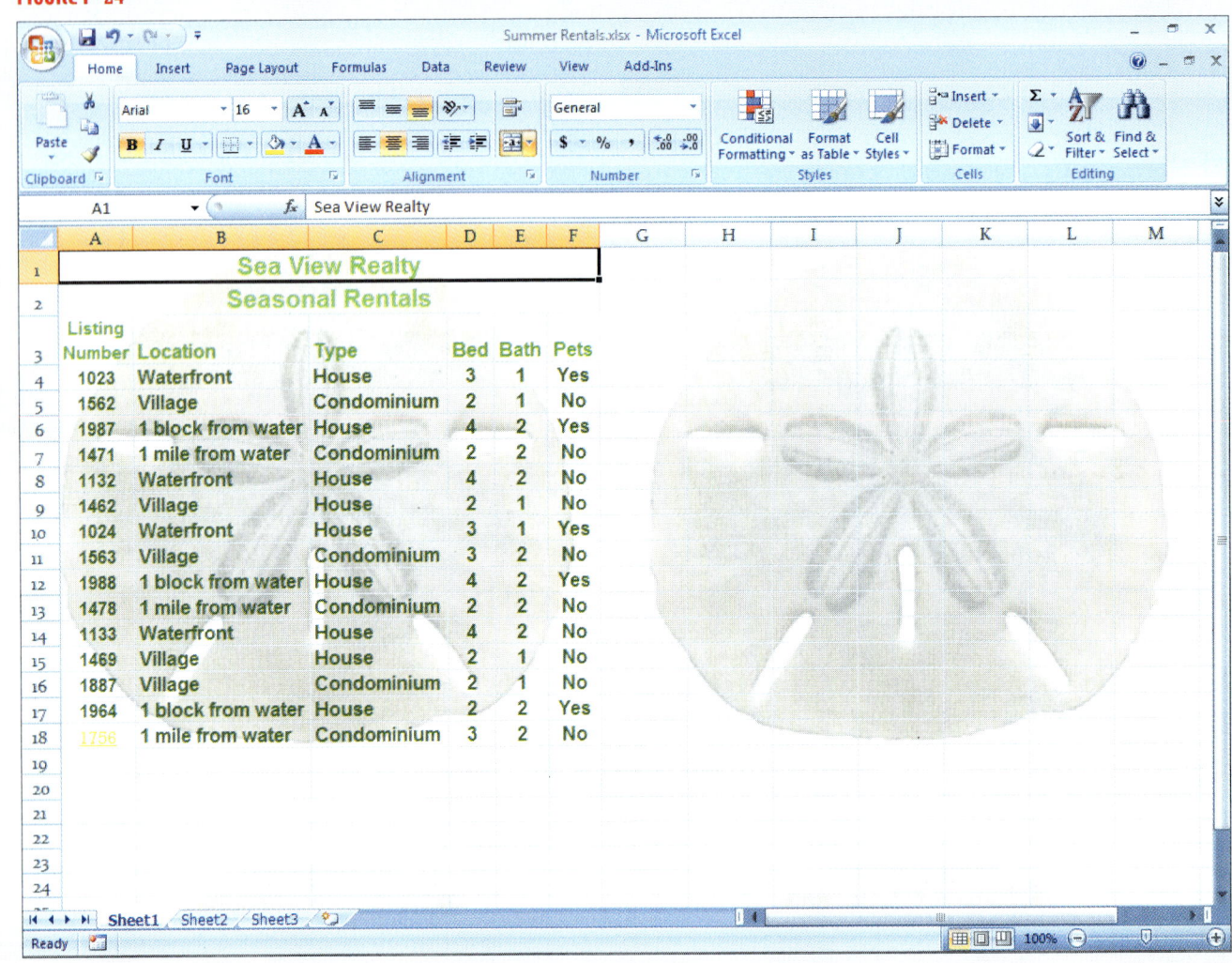

Sea View Realty
Seasonal Rentals

Listing Number	Location	Type	Bed	Bath	Pets
1023	Waterfront	House	3	1	Yes
1562	Village	Condominium	2	1	No
1987	1 block from water	House	4	2	Yes
1471	1 mile from water	Condominium	2	2	No
1132	Waterfront	House	4	2	No
1462	Village	House	2	1	No
1024	Waterfront	House	3	1	Yes
1563	Village	Condominium	3	2	No
1988	1 block from water	House	4	2	Yes
1478	1 mile from water	Condominium	2	2	No
1133	Waterfront	House	4	2	No
1469	Village	House	2	1	No
1887	Village	Condominium	2	1	No
1964	1 block from water	House	2	2	Yes
1756	1 mile from water	Condominium	3	2	No

UNIT G
Excel 2007

Using Tables

Files You Will Need:
EX G-1.xlsx
EX G-2.xlsx
EX G-3.xlsx
EX G-4.xlsx
EX G-5.xlsx

In addition to using Excel spreadsheet features, you can analyze and manipulate data in a table structure. An Excel **table** is an organized collection of rows and columns of similarly structured data in a worksheet. For example, a table might contain customer, sales, or inventory information. When you designate a particular range of worksheet data as a table, its formatting is extended when you add data and all table formulas are updated to include the new data. Without a table, you would have to manually adjust formatting and formulas every time data is added to a range. In this unit, you'll learn how to plan and create a table; add, change, find, and delete information in a table; and then sort, perform table calculations, and print a table. Quest uses tables to analyze tour data. The vice president of sales, Kate Morgan, asks you to help her build and manage a table of 2010 tour information.

OBJECTIVES

Plan a table
Create a table
Add table data
Find and replace table data
Delete table data
Sort table data
Use formulas in a table
Print a table

Planning a Table

UNIT G · Excel 2007

When planning a table, consider what information you want your table to contain and how you want to work with the data, now and in the future. As you plan a table, you should understand its most important components. A table is organized into rows called records. A **record** contains data about an object, person, or other type of table item. Records are composed of fields. **Fields** are columns in the table; each field describes a characteristic of the record, such as a customer's last name or street address. Each field has a **field name**, which is a column label, such as "Address," that describes its contents. Tables usually have a **header row** as the first row that contains the field names. To plan your table, use the steps below. See Table G-1 for additional planning guidelines. Kate asks you to compile a table of the 2010 tours. Before entering the tour data into an Excel worksheet, you plan the table contents.

DETAILS

As you plan your table, use the following guidelines:

- **Identify the purpose of the table**
  Determine the kind of information the table should contain. You want to use the tours table to quickly find all departure dates of a particular tour. You also want to display the tours in order of departure date.

- **Plan the structure of the table**
  Determine the fields that are necessary to achieve the table's purpose. You have worked with the sales department to determine the type of information that they need to obtain about each tour. Figure G-1 shows a layout sketch for the table. Each row will contain one tour record. The columns represent fields that contain pieces of descriptive information you will enter for each tour, such as the name, departure date, and duration.

- **Document the table design**
  In addition to your table sketch, you should make a list of the field names that documents the type of data and any special number formatting required for each field. Field names should be as short as possible while still accurately describing the column info. When naming fields it is important to use text rather than numbers because numbers may be interpreted as parts of formulas. Your field names should be unique and not easily confused with cell addresses, such as the name D2. Your Tours table will contain eight field names, each one corresponding to the major characteristics of the 2010 tours. Table G-2 shows the documentation of the field names in your table.

TABLE G-1: Guidelines for planning a table

worksheet structure guidelines	row and column content guidelines
Tables can be created from any contiguous range of cells on your worksheet	Plan and design your table so that all rows have similar items in the same column
A table should not have any blank rows or columns	Do not insert extra spaces at the beginning of a cell because this can affect sorting and searching
Data in your table can be used independently of data outside of the table on the worksheet	Instead of blank rows or columns between your labels and your data, use formatting to make column labels stand out from the data
Data can be organized on a worksheet using multiple tables to define sets of related data	Use the same format for all cells below the field name in a column

FIGURE G-1: Table layout sketch

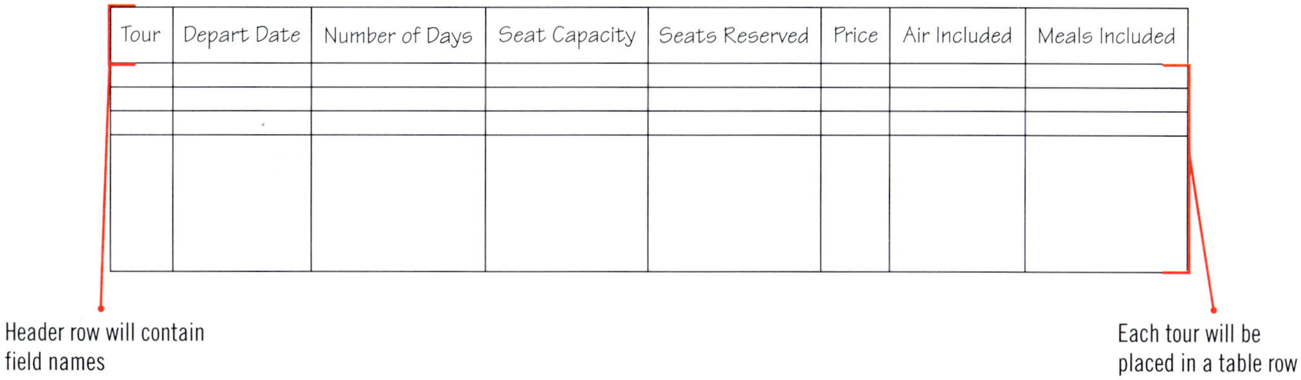

Tour	Depart Date	Number of Days	Seat Capacity	Seats Reserved	Price	Air Included	Meals Included

Header row will contain field names

Each tour will be placed in a table row

TABLE G-2: Table documentation

field name	type of data	description of data
Tour	Text	Name of tour
Depart Date	Date	Date tour departs
Number of Days	Number with 0 decimal places	Duration of the tour
Seat Capacity	Number with 0 decimal places	Maximum number of people the tour can accommodate
Seats Reserved	Number with 0 decimal places	Number of reservations for the tour
Price	Accounting with 0 decimal places and $ symbol	Tour price (This price is not guaranteed until a 30% deposit is received)
Air Included	Text	Yes: Airfare is included in the price No: Airfare is not included in the price
Meals Included	Text	Yes: Breakfast and dinner included in the price No: Meals are not included in the price

Using Tables

UNIT G
Excel 2007

Creating a Table

Once you have planned the table structure, the sequence of fields, and appropriate data types, you are ready to create the table in Excel. After you create a table, a Table Tools Design tab appears, containing a gallery of table styles. **Table styles** allow you to easily add formatting to your table by using preset formatting combinations that define fill color, borders, and type style and color. Kate asks you to build a table with the 2010 tour data. You begin by entering the field names. Then you enter the tour data that corresponds to each field name, create the table, and format the data using a table style.

STEPS

1. **Start Excel, open the file EX G-1.xlsx from the drive and folder where you store your Data Files, then save it as 2010 Tours**

2. **Beginning in cell A1 of the Practice sheet, enter each field name in a separate column, as shown in Figure G-2**
   Field names are usually entered in the first row of the table.

   TROUBLE
   Don't worry if your field names are wider than the cells; you will fix this later.

3. **Enter the information from Figure G-3 in the rows immediately below the field names, leaving no blank rows**
   The data appears in columns organized by field name.

4. **Select the range A1:H4, click the Format button in the Cells group, click AutoFit Column Width, then click cell A1**
   Resizing the column widths this way is faster than double-clicking the column divider lines.

5. **With cell A1 selected, click the Insert tab, then click the Table button in the Tables group, in the Create Table dialog box verify that your table data is in the range $A$1:$H$4 and make sure My table has headers is checked, then click OK**
   Filter list arrows, which let you display portions of your data, appear next to each column header. When you create a table, Excel automatically applies a default table style. The Table Tools Design tab appears and the Table Styles group displays a gallery of table formatting options. You decide to use a different table style from the gallery.

6. **Click the Table Styles More button, scroll to view all of the table styles, then move the mouse pointer over several styles without clicking**
   As you point to each table style, Live Preview shows you what your table will look like with the style applied. However, you only see a preview of each style; you need to click a style to apply it.

7. **Click the Table Style Medium 7 to apply it to your table, then click cell A1**
   Compare your table to Figure G-4.

Coordinating table styles with your document

The Table Styles gallery on the Table Tools Design tab has three style categories: Light, Medium, and Dark. Each category has numerous design types; for example, in some of the designs, the header row and total row are darker and the rows alternate colors. The available table designs use the current workbook theme colors so the table coordinates with your existing workbook content. If you select a different workbook theme and color scheme in the Themes group on the Page Layout tab, the Table Styles gallery uses those colors. You can modify gallery styles further by using the options in the Table Style Options group on the Table Tools Design tab; for example, if you select Header Row, the table styles in the gallery will all display distinctive header rows.

Using Tables

FIGURE G-2: Field names entered in row 1

	A	B	C	D	E	F	G	H	I
1	Tour	Depart Date	Number of Days	Seat Capacity	Seats Reserved	Price	Air Included	Meals Included	
2									

FIGURE G-3: Three records entered in the worksheet

	A	B	C	D	E	F	G	H	I
1	Tour	Depart Date	Number of Days	Seat Capacity	Seats Reserved	Price	Air Included	Meals Included	
2	Pacific Odyssey	1/11/2010	14	50	50	3105	Yes	No	
3	Old Japan	1/12/2010	21	47	41	2100	Yes	No	
4	Down Under Exodus	1/18/2010	10	30	28	2800	Yes	Yes	
5									

FIGURE G-4: Formatted table with three records

Labels: Table Style Medium 7; Filter list arrows; Table Tools Design tab; Table styles More button; Table formatting options in Table Styles gallery

Changing table style options

You can modify a table's appearance by using the check boxes in the Table Styles Options group on the Table Tools Design tab. For example, you can turn on or turn off the following options: **banding**, which creates different formatting for adjacent rows and columns; special formatting for first and last columns; Total Row, which calculates totals for each column; and Header Row, which displays or hides the header row. Use these options to modify a table's appearance either before or after applying a Table Style. For example, if your table has banded rows, you can select the Banded Columns check box to change the table to display with banded columns. Also, you may want to deselect the Header Row check box to hide a table's header row if a table will be included in a presentation. Figure G-5 shows the available table style options.

You can also create your own table style by clicking the Table Styles More button, then at the bottom of the Table Styles Gallery, clicking New Table Style. In the New Table Quick Style dialog box, name the style in the Name text box, click a table element, then format selected table elements by clicking Format. You can also set a custom style as the default style for your tables by checking the Set as default table quick style for this document check box. You can click Clear at the bottom of the Table Styles gallery if you want to clear a table style.

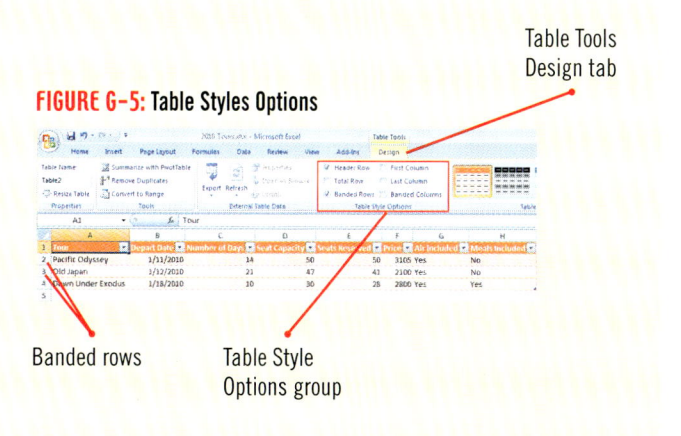

FIGURE G-5: Table Styles Options

Labels: Banded rows; Table Style Options group; Table Tools Design tab

Using Tables

UNIT G
Excel 2007

Adding Table Data

You can add records to a table by typing data directly below the last row of the table. After you press [Enter], the new row is added to the table and the table formatting is extended to the new data. When the active cell is the last cell of a table, you can add a new row by pressing [Tab]. You can add rows in any table location. If you decide you need additional data fields, you can add new columns to a table. Another way to expand a table is to drag the sizing handle in a table's lower-right corner; drag down to add rows and drag to the right to add columns. After entering all of the 2010 tour data, Kate decides to offer two additional tours. She also wants the table to display the number of available seats for each tour and whether visas are required for the destination.

STEPS

1. **Activate the 2010 Tours sheet**
   The sheet contains the 2010 tour data.

2. **Click cell A65 in the table, enter the data for the new Costa Rica Rainforest tour, as shown in Figure G-6, then press [Enter]**
   The new Costa Rica tour is part of the table. You want to enter a record about a new January tour above row 6.

3. **Click the inside left edge of cell A6 to select the table row data, click the Insert list arrow in the Cells group, then click Insert Table Rows Above**
   Clicking the left edge of the first cell in a table row selects the entire table row. A new blank row 6 is available to enter the new record.

   > **QUICK TIP**
   > You can select a table column by clicking the top edge of the field name. Be careful not to click a column letter or row number, however, because this selects the entire worksheet column or row. You can select the table data by clicking the upper-left corner of the first table cell. Clicking a second time will include the table header in the selection.

4. **Click cell A6, then enter the Nepal Trekking record, as shown in Figure G-7**
   The new Nepal tour is part of the table. You want to add a new field that displays the number of available seats for each tour.

5. **Click cell I1, enter the field name Seats Available, then press [Enter]**
   The new field becomes part of the table and the header formatting extends to the new field. The AutoCorrect menu allows you to undo or stop the automatic table expansion, but in this case, you decide to leave this feature on. You want to add another new field to the table to display tours that require visas, but this time you will add the new field by resizing the table.

   > **QUICK TIP**
   > You can also resize a table by clicking the Table Tools Design tab, clicking the Resize Table button in the Properties group, selecting the new data range for the table, then clicking OK.

6. **Scroll down until cell I66 is visible, drag the sizing handle in the table's lower-right corner one column to the right to add column J to the table, as shown in Figure G-8.**
   The table range is now A1:J66 and the new field name is Column1.

7. **Click cell J1, enter Visa Required, then press [Enter]**

8. **Click the Insert tab, click the Header & Footer button in the Text group, enter your name in the center header text box, click cell A1, click the Normal button in the status bar, then save the workbook**

FIGURE G-6: New record in row 65

61	Galapagos Adventure	12/20/2010	14	15	1	$ 3,100	Yes	Yes
62	Pacific Odyssey	12/21/2010	14	50	10	$ 3,105	Yes	No
63	Essential India	12/30/2010	18	51	15	$ 3,933	Yes	Yes
64	Old Japan	12/31/2010	21	47	4	$ 2,100	Yes	No
65	Costa Rica Rainforests	1/30/2010	7	20	0	$ 2,590	Yes	Yes
66								

New record in row 65

FIGURE G-7: New record in row 6

	A	B	C	D	E	F	G	H
1	Tour	Depart Date	Number of Days	Seat Capacity	Seats Reserved	Price	Air Included	Meals Included
2	Pacific Odyssey	1/11/2010	14	50	50	$ 3,105	Yes	No
3	Old Japan	1/12/2010	21	47	41	$ 2,100	Yes	No
4	Down Under Exodus	1/18/2010	10	30	28	$ 2,800	Yes	Yes
5	Essential India	1/20/2010	18	51	40	$ 3,933	Yes	Yes
6	Nepal Trekking	1/31/2010	14	18	0	$ 4,200	Yes	Yes
7	Amazing Amazon	2/23/2010	14	43	38	$ 2,877	No	No
8	Cooking in France	2/28/2010	7	18	15	$ 2,822	Yes	No
9	Pearls of the Orient	3/12/2010	14	50	15	$ 3,400	Yes	No
10	Silk Road Travels	3/18/2010	18	25	19	$ 2,190	Yes	Yes

New record in row 6

Excel 2007

FIGURE G-8: Resizing a table using the resizing handles

60	Panama Adventure	12/18/2010	10	50	21	$ 2,304	Yes	Yes
61	Galapagos Adventure	12/20/2010	14	15	1	$ 3,100	Yes	Yes
62	Galapagos Adventure	12/20/2010	14	15	1	$ 3,100	Yes	Yes
63	Pacific Odyssey	12/21/2010	14	50	10	$ 3,105	Yes	No
64	Essential India	12/30/2010	18	51	15	$ 3,933	Yes	Yes
65	Old Japan	12/31/2010	21	47	4	$ 2,100	Yes	No
66	Costa Rica Rainforests	1/30/2010	7	20	0	$ 2,590	Yes	Yes
67								
68								
69								

Drag sizing handle to add column J

Using Tables

Finding and Replacing Table Data

UNIT G
Excel 2007

From time to time, you need to locate specific records in your table. You can use the Excel Find feature to search your table for a particular record. You can also use the Replace feature to locate and replace existing entries or portions of entries with information you specify. If you don't know the exact spelling of the text you are searching for, you can use wildcards to help locate the records. **Wildcards** are special symbols that substitute for unknown characters. In response to feedback from the sales representatives about customers' lack of familiarity of Istria, Kate wants to replace "Istria" with "Croatia" in all of the tour names. She also wants to know how many Pacific Odyssey tours are scheduled for the year. You begin by searching for records with the text "Pacific Odyssey".

STEPS

1. **Click cell A1 if necessary, click the Home tab, click the Find & Select button in the Editing group, then click Find**

   The Find and Replace dialog box opens, as shown in Figure G-9. In this dialog box, you enter criteria that specify the records you want to find in the Find what text box. You want to search for records whose Tour field contains the label "Pacific Odyssey".

2. **Type Pacific Odyssey in the Find what text box, then click Find Next**

   A2 is the active cell because it is the first instance of Pacific Odyssey in the table.

3. **Click Find Next and examine the record for each found Pacific Odyssey tour until no more matching cells are found in the table and the active cell is A2 again, then click Close**

   There are four Pacific Odyssey tours.

4. **Return to cell A1, click the Find & Select button in the Editing group, then click Replace**

   The Find and Replace dialog box opens with the Replace tab selected and the insertion point in the Replace with text box, as shown in Figure G-10. You will search for entries containing "Istria" and replace them with "Croatia". You are not sure of the spelling of Istria, so you will use the * wildcard to help you locate the records containing the correct tour name.

5. **Delete any text in the Find what text box, type Is* in the Find what text box, click the Replace with text box, then type Croatia**

   The asterisk (*) wildcard stands for one or more characters, meaning that the search text Is* will find words such as "Is", "Isn't", and "Islington". Because you notice that there are other table entries containing the text "is" with a lowercase "i" (in the Visa Required column heading), you need to make sure that only capitalized instances of the letter I are replaced.

6. **Click Options >>, click the Match case check box to select it, click Options <<, then click Find Next**

   Excel moves the cell pointer to the first occurrence of "Istria".

7. **Click Replace All, click OK, then click Close**

   The dialog box closes. Excel made two replacements, in cells A22 and A51. The Visa Required field heading remains unchanged because the "is" in "Visa" is lowercase.

8. **Save the workbook**

> **QUICK TIP**
> You can also use the question mark (?) wildcard to represent any single character. For example, using "to?" as your search text would only find 3-letter words beginning with "to", such as "top" and "tot"; it would not find "tone" or "topography".

FIGURE G-9: Find and Replace dialog box

Type Pacific Odyssey here

FIGURE G-10: The Replace tab in the Find and Replace dialog box

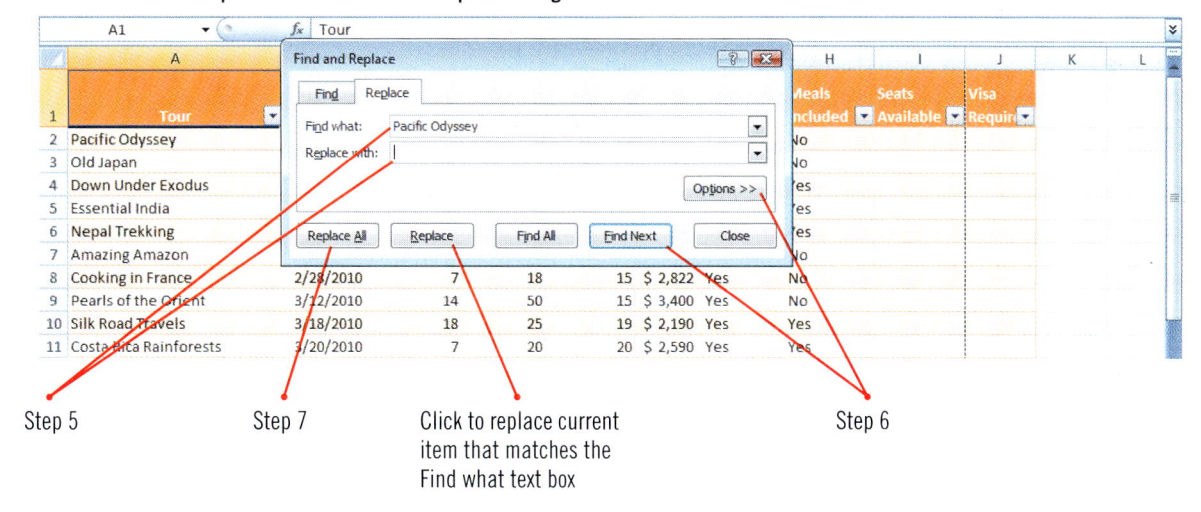

Step 5   Step 7   Click to replace current item that matches the Find what text box   Step 6

Using Find and Select features

You can also use the Find feature to navigate to a specific place in a workbook by clicking the Find & Select button in the Editing group, clicking Go To, typing a cell address, then clicking OK. Clicking the Find & Select button also allows you to find comments and conditional formatting in a worksheet by clicking Go to Special. You can use the Go to Special dialog box to select cells that contain different types of formulas, objects, or data validation. Some Go to Special commands also appear on the Find & Select menu. Using this menu, you can also change the mouse pointer shape to the Select Objects pointer so you can quickly select drawing objects when necessary. To return to the standard Excel pointer, press [Esc].

Using Tables   Excel 161

Deleting Table Data

In order to keep a table up to date, you need to be able to periodically remove records. You may even need to remove fields if the information stored in a field becomes unnecessary. You can delete table data using the Delete button or by dragging the sizing handle at the table's lower right corner. You can also easily delete duplicate records from a table. Kate is canceling the Old Japan tour that departs on 1/12/2010 and asks you to delete the record from the table. You will also remove any duplicate records from the table. Because the visa requirements are difficult to keep up with, Kate asks you to delete the field with visa information.

STEPS

1. **Click the left edge of cell A3 to select the table row data, click the Delete button list arrow in the Cells group, then click Delete Table Rows**

   The Old Japan tour is deleted and the Down Under Exodus tour moves up to row 3, as shown in Figure G-11. You can also delete a table row or a column using the Resize Table button in the Properties group of the Table Tools Design tab, or by right-clicking the row or column, pointing to Delete on the shortcut menu, then clicking Table Columns or Table Rows. You decide to check the table for duplicate records.

2. **Click the Table Tools Design tab, then click the Remove Duplicates button in the Tools group**

   The Remove Duplicates dialog box opens, as shown in Figure G-12. You need to select the columns that the program should use to evaluate duplicates. Because you don't want to delete tours with the same destination but different departure dates, you will look for duplicate data in all of the columns.

   > **QUICK TIP**
   > You can also remove duplicates from worksheet data by clicking the Data tab, then clicking the Remove Duplicates button in the Data Tools group.

3. **Make sure that "My data has headers" is checked and that all the columns headers are checked, then click OK**

   Two duplicate records are found and removed, leaving 63 rows in the table, including the header row. You want to remove the last column, which contains space for visa information.

4. **Click OK, scroll down until cell J63 is visible, drag the sizing handle of the table's lower-right corner one column to the left to remove column J from the table**

   The table range is now A1:I63 and the Visa Required field no longer appears in the table.

5. **Delete the contents of cell J1, return to cell A1, then save the workbook**

FIGURE G-11: Table with row deleted

	A	B	C	D	E	F	G	H	I	J
1	Tour	Depart Date	Number of Days	Seat Capacity	Seats Reserved	Price	Air Included	Meals Included	Seats Available	Visa Required
2	Pacific Odyssey	1/11/2010	14	50	50	$ 3,105	Yes	No		
3	Down Under Exodus	1/18/2010	10	30	28	$ 2,800	Yes	Yes		
4	Essential India	1/20/2010	18	51	40	$ 3,933	Yes	Yes		
5	Nepal Trekking	1/31/2010	14	18	0	$ 4,200	Yes	Yes		
6	Amazing Amazon	2/23/2010	14	43	38	$ 2,877	No	No		
7	Cooking in France	2/28/2010	7	18	15	$ 2,822	Yes	No		
8	Pearls of the Orient	3/12/2010	14	50	15	$ 3,400	Yes	No		
9	Silk Road Travels	3/18/2010	18	25	19	$ 2,190	Yes	Yes		
10	Costa Rica Rainforests	3/20/2010	7	20	20	$ 2,590	Yes	Yes		
11	Green Adventures in Ecuador	3/23/2010	18	25	22	$ 2,450	No	No		
12	African National Parks	4/7/2010	30	12	10	$ 4,870	Yes	Yes		
13	Experience Cambodia	4/10/2010	12	40	21	$ 2,908	Yes	No		
14	Old Japan	4/14/2010	21	47	30	$ 2,100	Yes	No		
15	Down Under Exodus	4/18/2010	10	30	20	$ 2,800	Yes	Yes		
16	Essential India	4/20/2010	18	51	31	$ 3,933	Yes	Yes		
17	Amazing Amazon	4/23/2010	14	43	30	$ 2,877	No	No		
18	Catalonia Adventure	5/9/2010	14	51	30	$ 3,100	Yes	No		
19	Treasures of Ethiopia	5/18/2010	10	41	15	$ 3,200	Yes	Yes		
20	Monasteries of Bulgaria	5/20/2010	7	19	11	$ 2,103	Yes	Yes		
21	Cooking in Croatia	5/23/2010	7	12	10	$ 2,110	No	No		
22	Magnificent Montenegro	5/27/2010	10	48	4	$ 1,890	No	No		
23	Catalonia Adventure	6/9/2010	14	51	15	$ 3,100	Yes	No		
24	Nepal Trekking	6/9/2010	14	18	18	$ 4,200	Yes	Yes		
25	Corfu Sailing Voyage	6/10/2010	21	12	10	$ 3,190	Yes	No		
26	Poland by Bike	6/11/2010	10	15	10	$ 2,600	Yes	No		

Row is deleted and tours move up one row

FIGURE G-12: Remove Duplicates dialog box

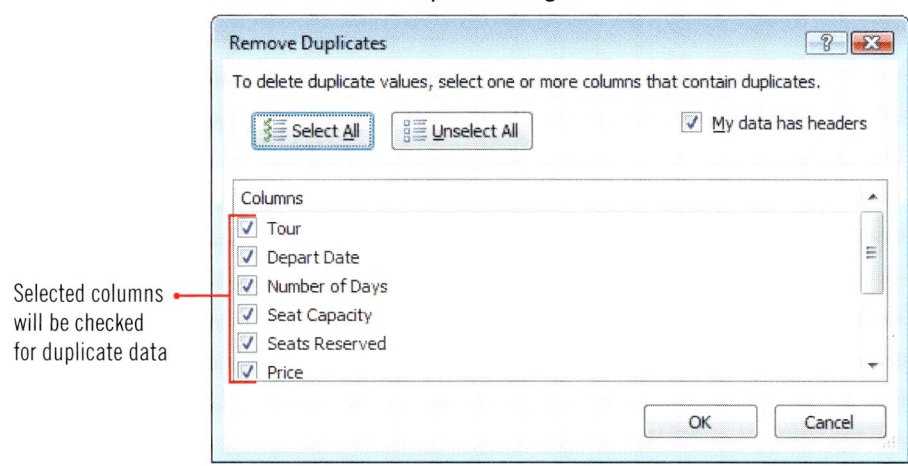

Selected columns will be checked for duplicate data

Using Tables

Sorting Table Data

UNIT G — Excel 2007

Usually, you enter table records in the order in which you receive information, rather than in alphabetical or numerical order. When you add records to a table, you usually enter them at the end of the table. You can change the order of the records any time using the Excel **sort** feature. You can sort a table in ascending or descending order on one field using the filter list arrows next to the field name. In **ascending order**, the lowest value (the beginning of the alphabet or the earliest date) appears at the top of the table. In a field containing labels and numbers, numbers appear first in the sorted list. In **descending order**, the highest value (the end of the alphabet or the latest date) appears at the top of the table. In a field containing labels and numbers, labels appear first. Table G-3 provides examples of ascending and descending sorts. Because the data is structured as a table, Excel changes the order of the records while keeping each record, or row of information, together. Kate wants the tour data sorted by departure date, displaying tours that depart the soonest at the top of the table.

STEPS

QUICK TIP
Before you sort records, consider making a backup copy of your table or create a field that numbers the records so you can return them to their original order, if necessary.

1. **Click the Depart Date filter list arrow, then click Sort Oldest to Newest**
   Excel rearranges the records in ascending order by depart date, as shown in Figure G-13. The Depart Date filter list arrow has an upward pointing arrow indicating the ascending sort in the field. You can also sort the table on one field using the Sort & Filter button.

2. **Click the Home tab, click any cell in the Price column, click the Sort & Filter button in the Editing group, then click Sort Largest to Smallest**
   Excel sorts the table, placing those records with the higher price at the top. The Price filter list arrow now has a downward pointing arrow next to the filter list arrow, indicating the descending sort order. You can also rearrange the table data using a **multilevel sort**. This type of sort rearranges the table data using different levels. If you use two sort levels, the data is sorted by the first field and the second field is sorted within each grouping of the first field. Since you have many groups of tours with different departure dates, you want to use a multilevel sort to arrange the table data by tours and then by departure dates within each tour.

QUICK TIP
You can also add a multilevel sort by clicking the Data tab and then clicking the Sort button in the Sort & Filter group.

3. **Click the Sort & Filter button in the Editing group, then click Custom Sort**
   The Sort dialog box opens, as shown in Figure G-14.

QUICK TIP
You can include capitalization as a sort criterion by clicking Options in the Sort dialog box, then selecting the Case sensitive box. When you choose this option, lowercase entries precede uppercase entries.

4. **Click the Sort by list arrow, click Tour, click the Order list arrow, click A to Z, click Add Level, click the Then by list arrow, click Depart Date, click the second Order list arrow, click Oldest to Newest if necessary, then click OK**
   Figure G-15 shows the table sorted alphabetically in ascending order (A-Z) by Tour and, within each tour, in ascending order by the Depart Date.

5. **Save the workbook**

Sorting a table using conditional formatting

If conditional formats have been applied to a table, you can sort the table using conditional formatting to arrange the rows. For example, if cells are conditionally formatted with color, you can sort a field on Cell Color, using the color with the order of On Top or On Bottom in the Sort dialog box.

TABLE G-3: Sort order options and examples

option	alphabetic	numeric	date	alphanumeric
Ascending	A, B, C	7, 8, 9	1/1, 2/1, 3/1	12A, 99B, DX8, QT7
Descending	C, B, A	9, 8, 7	3/1, 2/1, 1/1	QT7, DX8, 99B, 12A

Using Tables

FIGURE G-13: Table sorted by depature date

Up arrow indicates ascending sort in the field

FIGURE G-14: Sort dialog box

Click to delete sort levels

Click to add additional sort levels

Click to display fields

FIGURE G-15: Table sorted using two levels

Table is sorted alphabetically in ascending order

Table is sorted by departure date within each tour

Specifying a custom sort order

You can identify a custom sort order for the field selected in the Sort by box. Click the Order list arrow in the Sort dialog box, click Custom List, then click the desired custom order. Commonly used custom sort orders are days of the week (Sun, Mon, Tues, Wed, etc.) and months (Jan, Feb, Mar, etc.); alphabetic sorts do not sort these items properly.

Using Tables   Excel 165

UNIT G
Excel 2007

Using Formulas in a Table

Many tables are large, making it difficult to know from viewing them the "story" the table tells. The Excel table calculation features help you summarize table data so you can see important trends. After you enter a single formula into a table cell, the **calculated columns** feature fills in the remaining cells with the formula's results. The column continues to fill with the formula results as you enter rows in the table. This makes it easy to update your formulas because you only need to edit the formula once, and the change will fill in to the other column cells. The **structured reference** feature allows your formulas to refer to table columns by names that are automatically generated when you create the table. These names automatically adjust as you add or delete table fields. An example of a table reference is =[Sales]–[Costs], where Sales and Costs are field names in the table. Tables also have a specific area at the bottom called the **table total row** for calculations using the data in the table columns. The cells in this row contain a dropdown list of functions that can be used for the column calculation. The table total row adapts to any changes in the table size. Kate wants you to use a formula to calculate the number of available seats for each tour. You will also add summary information to the end of the table.

STEPS

1. **Click cell I2, then type =[**
   A list of the table field names is displayed, as shown in Figure G-16. Structured referencing allows you to use the names that Excel created when you defined your table to reference fields in a formula. You can choose a field by clicking it and pressing [TAB] or by double-clicking the field name.

2. **Click [Seat Capacity], press [Tab], then type]**
   Excel begins the formula, placing [Seat Capacity] in the cell in blue and framing the Seat Capacity data in a blue border.

3. **Type -[, double-click [Seats Reserved], then type]**
   Excel places [Seats Reserved] in the cell in green and outlines the Seats Reserved data in a green border.

4. **Press [Enter]**
   The formula result, 2, is displayed in cell I2. The table column also fills with the formula displaying the number of available seats for each tour.

5. **Click the AutoCorrect Options list arrow**
   Because the calculated columns option saves time, you decide to leave the feature on. You want to display the total number of available seats on all of the tours.

6. **Click any cell inside the table, click the Table Tools Design tab, then click the Total Row check box in the Table Style Options group to select it**
   A total row appears at the bottom of the table and the sum of the available seats, 1035, is displayed in cell I64. You can select other formulas in the total row.

7. **Click cell C64, then click the cell list arrow on the right side of the cell**
   The list of available functions appears, as shown in Figure G-17. You want to find the average tour length.

8. **Click Average, then save your workbook**
   The average tour length, 13 days, appears in cell C64.

> **QUICK TIP**
> You can undo the calculated column results by clicking Undo Calculated Column in the AutoCorrect Options list. You can turn off the Calculated Columns feature by clicking Stop Automatically Creating Calculated Columns in the AutoCorrect Options list.

Excel 166 Using Tables

FIGURE G-16: Table field names

	A	B	C	D	E	F	G	H	I
1	Tour	Depart Date	Number of Days	Seat Capacity	Seats Reserved	Price	Air Included	Meals Included	Seats Available
2	African National Parks	4/7/2010	30	12	10	$ 4,870	Yes	Yes	=[
3	African National Parks	10/27/2010	30	12	8	$ 4,870	Yes	Yes	
4	Amazing Amazon	2/23/2010	14	43	38	$ 2,877	No	No	
5	Amazing Amazon	4/23/2010	14	43	30	$ 2,877	No	No	
6	Amazing Amazon	8/23/2010	14	43	18	$ 2,877	No	No	
7	Catalonia Adventure	5/9/2010	14	51	30	$ 3,100	Yes	No	
8	Catalonia Adventure	6/9/2010	14	51	15	$ 3,100	Yes	No	
9	Catalonia Adventure	10/9/2010	14	51	11	$ 3,100	Yes	No	
10	Cooking in Croatia	5/23/2010	7	12	10	$ 2,110	No	No	
11	Cooking in Croatia	9/23/2010	7	12	7	$ 2,110	No	No	
12	Cooking in France	2/28/2010	7	18	15	$ 2,822	Yes	No	

Dropdown list: Tour, Depart Date, Number of Days, Seat Capacity, Seats Reserved, Price, Air Included, Meals Included, Seats Available

Table field names

FIGURE G-17: Functions in the Total Row

	Tour	Depart Date	Number of Days	Seat Capacity	Seats Reserved	Price	Air Included	Meals Included	Seats Available
51	Pacific Odyssey	7/7/2010	14	50	35	$ 3,105	Yes	No	15
52	Pacific Odyssey	9/14/2010	14	50	20	$ 3,105	Yes	No	30
53	Pacific Odyssey	12/21/2010	14	50	10	$ 3,105	Yes	No	40
54	Panama Adventure	6/18/2010	10	50	29	$ 2,304	Yes	Yes	21
55	Panama Adventure	12/18/2010	10	50	21	$ 2,304	Yes	Yes	29
56	Pearls of the Orient	3/12/2010	14	50	15	$ 3,400	Yes	No	35
57	Pearls of the Orient	9/12/2010	14	50	11	$ 3,400	Yes	No	39
58	Silk Road Travels	3/18/2010	18	25	19	$ 2,190	Yes	Yes	6
59	Silk Road Travels	9/18/2010	18	25	9	$ 2,190	Yes	Yes	16
60	Treasures of Ethiopia	5/18/2010	10	41	15	$ 3,200	Yes	Yes	26
61	Treasures of Ethiopia	11/18/2010	10	41	12	$ 3,200	Yes	Yes	29
62	Wild River Escape	6/27/2010	10	21	21	$ 1,944	No	No	0
63	Wild River Escape	8/27/2010	10	21	11	$ 1,944	No	No	10
64	Total								1035

Dropdown list: None, Average, Count, Count Numbers, Max, Min, Sum, StdDev, Var, More Functions...

Functions available in the Total Row

Using structured references

Structured references make it easier to work with formulas that use table data. You can reference all of the table, columns in the table, or specific data. What makes structured references helpful to use in formulas is that they automatically adjust as data ranges change in a table, so you don't need to edit formulas. When you create a table from worksheet data, Excel creates a default table name such as Table1. This references all of the table data but not the header row or any total rows. To refer to a table such as Table1 with its header row, you need to use the reference =Table1[#All]. Excel also names each column of a table which can be referenced in formulas. For example, in Table 1, the formula =Table1[Sales] references the data in the Sales field.

Using Tables

Printing a Table

UNIT G — Excel 2007

You can determine the way a table will print using the Page Layout tab. Because tables often have more rows than can fit on a page, you can define the first row of the table (containing the field names) as the **print title**, which prints at the top of every page. You can also scale the table to print more or fewer rows on each page. Most tables do not have any descriptive information above the field names on the worksheet, so to augment the field name information, you can use headers and footers to add identifying text, such as the table title or the report date. Kate asks you for a printout of the tour information. You begin by previewing the table.

STEPS

1. **Click the Office button, point to Print, then click Print Preview**
   The status bar reads Preview: Page 1 of 3. All of the field names in the table fit across the width of the page.

2. **In the Print Preview window, click the Next Page button in the Preview group to view the second page, then click Next Page again to view the third page**
   The third page contains only one record and the total row, so you will scale the table to print on two pages.

3. **Click the Close Print Preview button, click the Page Layout tab, click the Width list arrow in the Scale to Fit group, click 1 page, click the Height list arrow, then click 2 pages**
   You decide to preview the table again to view the changes in scale.

   > **QUICK TIP**
   > You can hide or print headings and gridlines using the check boxes in the Sheet Options group on the Page Layout tab. You might want to hide a worksheet's headings if it will be displayed in a presentation.

4. **Click the Office button, point to Print, click Print Preview, then click the Next Page button in the Preview group**
   The records are scaled to fit on two pages. The status bar reads Preview: Page 2 of 2. Because the records on page 2 appear without column headings, you want to set up the first row of the table, which contains the field names, as a repeating print title.

5. **Click the Close Print Preview button, click the Print Titles button in the Page Setup group, click inside the Rows to repeat at top text box under Print titles, click any cell in row 1 on the table, then compare your Page Setup dialog box to Figure G-18**
   When you select row 1 as a print title, Excel automatically inserts an absolute reference to the row that will repeat at the top of each page.

6. **Click Print Preview, click the Next Page button to view the second page, then click the Close Print Preview button**
   Setting up a print title to repeat row 1 causes the field names to appear at the top of each printed page. The printout would be more informative with a header to identify the table information.

   > **QUICK TIP**
   > You can also add headers and footers by clicking the Page Layout View in the status bar.

7. **Click the Insert tab, click the Header & Footer button in the Text group, click the left header section text box, then type 2010 Tours**

8. **Select the left header section information, click the Home tab, click the Increase Font Size button A˙ in the Font group twice to change the font size to 14, click the Bold button B in the Font group, click any cell in the table, then click the Normal button in the status bar**

9. **Save the table, preview then print it, close the workbook, then exit Excel**
   Compare your printed table with Figure G-19.

Excel 168 Using Tables

FIGURE G-18: Page Setup dialog box

Print title is set to row 1

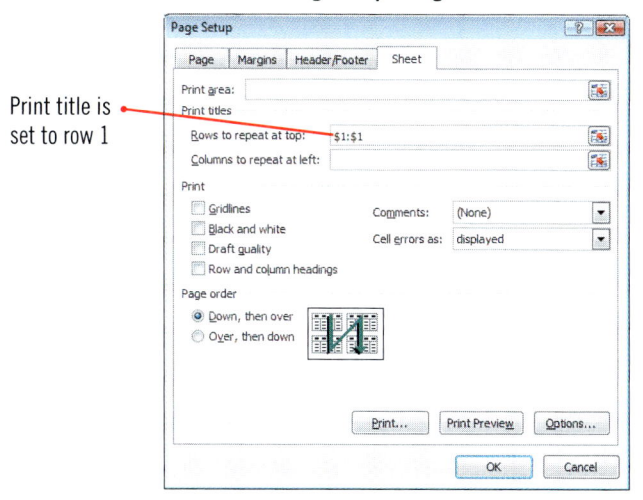

FIGURE G-19: Completed table

2010 Tours — Your Name

Tour	Depart Date	Number of Days	Seat Capacity	Seats Reserved	Price	Air Included	Meals Included	Seats Available
African National Parks	4/7/2010	30	12	10	$ 4,870	Yes	Yes	2
African National Parks	10/27/2010	30	12	8	$ 4,870	Yes	Yes	4
Amazing Amazon	2/23/2010	14	43	38	$ 2,877	No	No	5
Amazing Amazon	4/23/2010	14	43	30	$ 2,877	No	No	13
Amazing Amazon	8/23/2010	14	43	18	$ 2,877	No	No	25
Catalonia Adventure	5/9/2010	14	51	30	$ 3,100	Yes	No	21
Catalonia Adventure	6/9/2010	14	51	15	$ 3,100	Yes	No	36
Catalonia Adventure	10/9/2010	14	51	11	$ 3,100	Yes	No	40
Cooking in Croatia	5/23/2010	7	12	10	$ 2,110	No	No	2
Cooking in Croatia	9/23/2010	7	12	7	$ 2,110	No	No	5
Cooking in France	2/28/2010	7	18	15	$ 2,822	Yes	No	3
Cooking in France	8/29/2010	7	18	5	$ 2,822	Yes	No	13
Corfu Sailing Voyage	6/10/2010	21	12	10	$ 3,190	Yes	No	2
Corfu Sailing Voyage	7/9/2010	21	12	1	$ 3,190	Yes	No	11
Costa Rica Rainforests	1/30/2010	7	20	0	$ 2,590	Yes	Yes	20
Costa Rica Rainforests	3/20/2010	7	20	20	$ 2,590	Yes	Yes	0
Costa Rica Rainforests	6/20/2010	7	20	2	$ 2,590	Yes	Yes	18
Down Under Exodus	1/18/2010	10	30	28	$ 2,800	Yes	Yes	2
Down Under Exodus	4/18/2010	10	30	20	$ 2,800	Yes	Yes	10
Essential India	1/20/2010	18	51	40	$ 3,933	Yes	Yes	11
Essential India	4/20/2010	18	51	31	$ 3,933	Yes	Yes	20
Essential India	8/20/2010	18	51	20	$ 3,933	Yes	Yes	31
Essential India	9/11/2010	18	51	20	$ 3,933	Yes	Yes	31
Essential India	12/30/2010	18	51	15	$ 3,933	Yes	Yes	36
Exotic Morocco	6/12/2010	7	38	25	$ 1,900	Yes	No	13
Exotic Morocco	10/31/2010	7	38	15	$ 1,900	Yes	No	23
Experience Cambodia	4/10/2010	12	40	21	$ 2,908	Yes	No	19
Experience Cambodia	10/31/2010	12	40	2	$ 2,908	Yes	No	38
Galapagos Adventure	7/2/2010	14	15	12	$ 3,100	Yes	Yes	3
Galapagos Adventure	12/20/2010	14	15	1	$ 3,100	Yes	Yes	14
Green Adventures in Ecuador	3/23/2010	18	25	22	$ 2,450	No	No	3
Green Adventures in Ecuador	10/23/2010	18	25	12	$ 2,450	No	No	13
Ireland by Bike	6/11/2010	10	15	10	$ 2,600	Yes	No	5
Wild River Escape	6/27/2010			10				21
Wild River Escape	8/27/2010			10				21
Total				13				1035

Setting a print area

Sometimes you will want to print only part of a worksheet. To do this, select any worksheet range, click the Office button, click Print, in the Print dialog box choose Selection under Print what, then click OK. If you want to print a selected area repeatedly, it's best to define a **print area**, which prints when you use the Quick Print feature. To set a print area, click the Page Layout tab, click the Print Area button in the Page Setup group, then click Set Print Area. You can extend the print area by selecting a range, clicking the Print Area button, then clicking Add to Print Area. If you want to print the table rather than a print area, click the Ignore print areas check box in the Print what section of the Print dialog box. To clear a print area, click the Print Area button, then click Clear Print Area.

Using Tables Excel 169

Practice

▼ CONCEPTS REVIEW

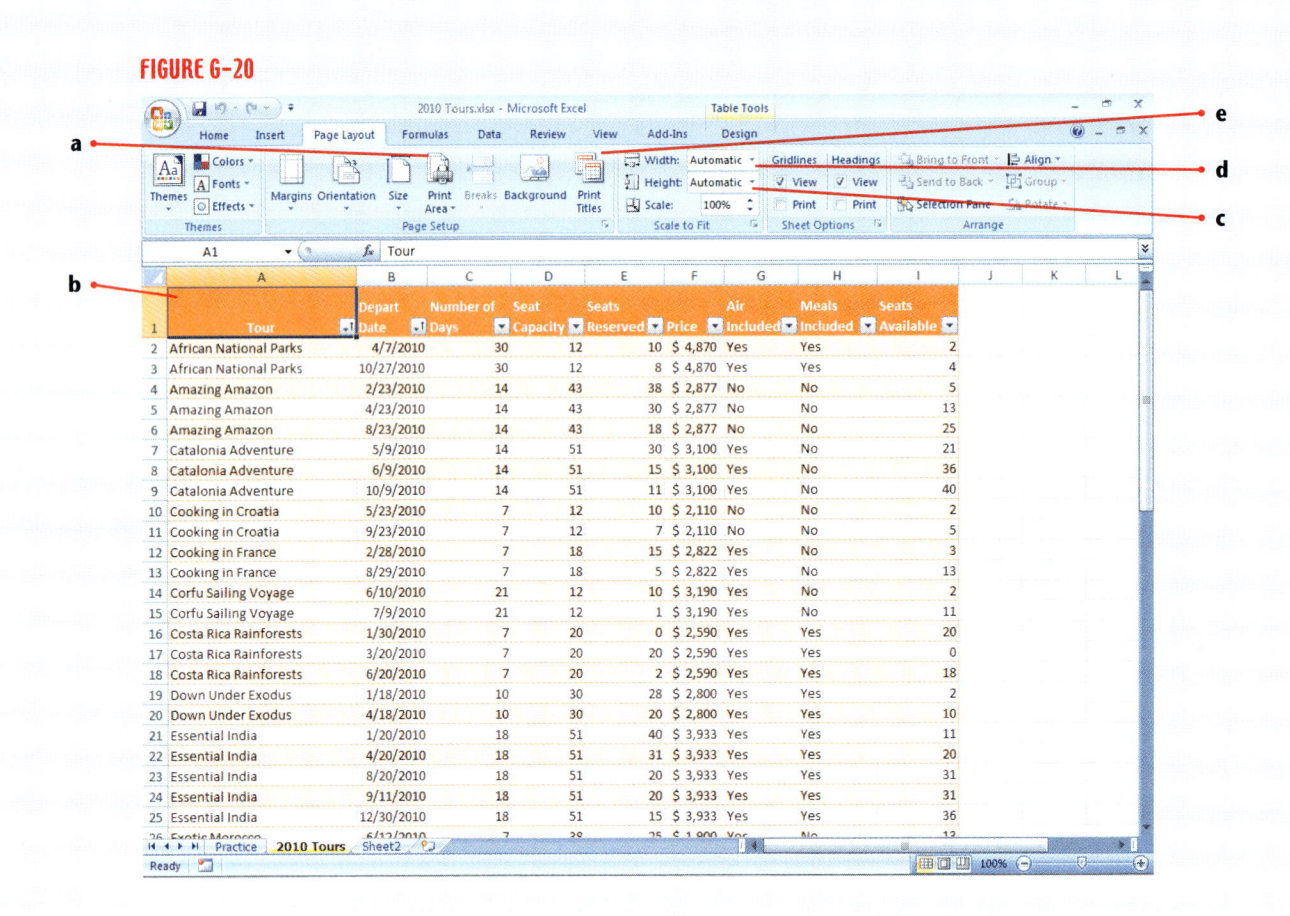

If you have a SAM user profile, you may have access to hands-on instruction, practice, and assessment of the skills covered in this unit. Log in to your SAM account (http://sam2007.course.com/) to launch any assigned training activities or exams that relate to the skills covered in this unit.

FIGURE G-20

1. Which element points to a field that has been sorted in ascending order?
2. Which element do you click to adjust the number of rows printed on a page?
3. Which element do you click to adjust the number of fields printed on a page?
4. Which element do you click to print field names at the top of every page?
5. Which element do you click to set a range in a table that will print using Quick Print?

Match each term with the statement that best describes it.

6. Header row
7. Record
8. Table
9. Field
10. Sort

a. Organized collection of related information in Excel
b. Arrange records in a particular sequence
c. Column in an Excel table
d. First row of a table containing field names
e. Row in an Excel table

Excel 170 Using Tables

Select the best answer from the list of choices.

11. Which of the following Excel sorting options do you use to sort a table of employee names in order from Z to A?
    a. Absolute
    b. Ascending
    c. Alphabetic
    d. Descending

12. Which of the following series appears in descending order?
    a. 4, 5, 6, A, B, C
    b. 8, 6, 4, C, B, A
    c. 8, 7, 6, 5, 6, 7
    d. C, B, A, 6, 5, 4

13. You can easily add formatting to a table by using:
    a. Table styles.
    b. Print titles.
    c. Print areas.
    d. Calculated columns.

14. When printing a table on multiple pages, you can define a print title to:
    a. Include appropriate fields in the printout.
    b. Include the sheet name in table reports.
    c. Include field names at the top of each printed page.
    d. Exclude from the printout all rows under the first row.

▼ SKILLS REVIEW

1. **Create a table.**
   a. Start Excel, open the file EX G-2.xlsx from the drive and folder where you store your data files, then save it as **Employees**.
   b. Using the Practice sheet, enter the field names in the first row and the first two records in rows two and three, as shown in Table G-4. Create a table using the data you entered.

   TABLE G-4

Last Name	First Name	Years Employed	Position	Full/Part Time	Training Completed
Leone	Sally	5	Book Sales	F	Y
Mello	Donato	3	Video Sales	P	N

   c. Create a table with a header row using the data on the Staff sheet. Adjust the column widths, if necessary, to display the field names.
   d. Apply a table style of Light 12 to the table and adjust the columns widths if necessary.
   e. Enter your name in the center section of the worksheet footer, then save the workbook.

2. **Add table data.**
   a. Add a new record in row seven for **Hank Worthen**, a five-year employee in book sales. Hank works full time and has completed training. Adjust the height of the new row to match the other table rows.
   b. Insert a row above Jay Kherian's record and add a new record for **Stacy Atkins**. Stacy works full time, has worked at the company for two years in video sales, and has not completed training.
   c. Insert a new data field in cell G1 with a label **Weeks Vacation**. Adjust the column width and wrap the label in the cell to display the field name with Weeks above Vacation.
   d. Add a new column to the table by dragging the table's sizing handle and give the new field a label of **Employee #**.
   e. Save the file.

3. **Find and replace table data.**
   a. Return to cell A1.
   b. Open the Find and Replace dialog box and if necessary uncheck the Match Case option. Find the first record that contains the text **Book Sales**.
   c. Find the second record that contains the text **Book Sales**.
   d. Replace all Video text in the table with **Movie**.
   e. Save the file.

▼ SKILLS REVIEW (CONTINUED)

4. **Delete table data.**
   a. Go to cell A1.
   b. Delete the record for **Sally Leone**.
   c. Use the Remove Duplicates button to confirm that the table does not have any duplicate records.
   d. Delete the **Employee #** column from the table, then delete its column header.
   e. Save the file.

5. **Sort table data.**
   a. Sort the table by years employed in largest to smallest order.
   b. Sort the table by last name in A to Z order.
   c. Sort the table first by Full/Part Time in A to Z order and then by last name in A to Z order.
   d. Check the table to make sure the records appear in the correct order.
   e. Save the file.

6. **Use formulas in a table.**
   a. In cell G2, enter the formula that calculates an employee's vacation time; base the formula on the company policy that employees working at the company less than three years have two weeks of vacation. At three years of employment and longer, an employee has three weeks of vacation time. Use the table's field names where appropriate. (*Hint:* The formula is: **=IF([Years Employed]<3,2,3)**)
   b. Check the table to make sure the formula filled into the cells in column G and that the correct vacation time is calculated for all cells in the column. **FIGURE G-21**
   c. Add a Total Row and verify the accuracy of the total number of vacation weeks.
   d. Change the function in the Total Row to display the average number of vacation weeks.
   e. Compare your table to Figure G-21, then save the workbook.

	A	B	C	D	E	F	G
1	Last Name	First Name	Years Employed	Position	Full/Part Time	Training Completed	Weeks Vacation
2	Atkins	Stacy	2	Movie Sales	F	N	2
3	Guan	Joyce	1	Book Sales	F	N	2
4	Kherian	Jay	1	Book Sales	F	Y	2
5	Worthen	Hank	5	Book Sales	F	Y	3
6	Mello	Donato	3	Movie Sales	P	N	3
7	Rabin	Mimi	1	Movie Sales	P	Y	2
8	Total						2.333333333
9							

7. **Print a table.**
   a. Add a header that reads **Employees** in the center section, then format the header in bold with a font size of 16.
   b. Add column A as a print title that repeats at the left of each printed page.
   c. Preview your table to check that the last names appear on both pages.
   d. Change the page orientation to landscape, save the workbook, then print the Staff sheet.
   e. Close the workbook, then exit Excel.

▼ INDEPENDENT CHALLENGE 1

You are the marketing director for a national sporting goods store. Your assistants have created an Excel worksheet with customer data including the results of an advertising survey. You will create a table using the customer data and analyze the survey results to help focus the company's advertising expenses in the most successful areas.

   a. Start Excel, open the file EX G-3.xlsx from the drive and folder where you store your Data Files, then save it as **Customers**.
   b. Create a table from the worksheet data and apply Table Style Light 20. Widen the columns as necessary to display the table data.

▼ INDEPENDENT CHALLENGE 1 (CONTINUED)

c. Use the data below to add the two records shown in Table G-5 to the table:

TABLE G-5

Last Name	First Name	Street Address	City	State	Zip	Area Code	Ad Source	Comments
Ross	Cathy	92 Arrow St.	Seattle	WA	98101	206	Yellow Pages	found ad informative
Janis	Steve	402 9th St.	Seattle	WA	98001	206	Newspaper	found in restaurant section

d. Find, then delete the record for Mary Ryder.

e. Click cell A1 and replace all instances of TV with WWIN TV, making sure the case is properly matched. Compare your table to Figure G-22.

f. Remove duplicate records where all fields are identical.

g. Sort the list by Last Name in A to Z order.

h. Sort the list again by Area Code in Smallest to Largest order.

i. Sort the table first by State in A to Z order, then within the state, by Zip in Smallest to Largest order.

FIGURE G-22

	A	B	C	D	E	F	G	H	I
1	Last Name	First Name	Street Address	City	State	Zip	Area Code	Ad Source	Comments
2	Kim	Kathy	19 North St.	San Francisco	CA	94177	415	Newspaper	favorite with friends
3	Jacobs	Martha	Hamilton Park St.	San Francisco	CA	94107	415	Newspaper	no comments
4	Majors	Kathy	1 Spring St.	San Luis	CA	94018	510	Radio	loved ad voice
5	Wong	Sandy	2120 Central St.	San Francisco	CA	93772	415	Newspaper	graphics caught eye
6	Hesh	Gayle	1192 Dome St.	San Diego	CA	93303	619	Newspaper	great ads
7	Chavez	Jane	11 Northern St.	San Diego	CA	92208	619	WWIN TV	interesting ad
8	Chelly	Yvonne	900 Sola St.	San Diego	CA	92106	619	Newspaper	likes description of products
9	Smith	Carolyn	921 Lopez St.	San Diego	CA	92104	619	Newspaper	likes ad prose
10	Owen	Scott	72 Yankee St.	Brookfield	CT	06830	203	Newspaper	no comments
11	Wallace	Salvatore	100 Westside St.	Chicago	IL	60620	312	Newspaper	likes graphics
12	Roberts	Bob	56 Water St.	Chicago	IL	60618	771	Newspaper	likes ad graphic
13	Miller	Hope	111 Stratton St.	Chicago	IL	60614	773	Newspaper	likes ad in local newspaper
14	Duran	Maria	Galvin St.	Chicago	IL	60614	773	Subway	no comments
15	Roberts	Bob	56 Water St.	Chicago	IL	60614	312	Newspaper	liked photo
16	Graham	Shelley	989 26th St.	Chicago	IL	60611	773	Yellow Pages	great store description
17	Kim	Janie	9 First St.	San Francisco	CA	94177	415	Newspaper	great ads
18	Kim	Janie	9 First St.	San Francisco	CA	94177	415	Newspaper	great ads
19	Williams	Tasha	1 Spring St	Reading	MA	03882	413	Newspaper	likes font we use
20	Julio	Manuel	544 Cameo St.	Belmont	MA	02483	617	Newspaper	no comments
21	Masters	Latrice	88 Las Puntas Rd.	Boston	MA	02205	617	Yellow Pages	likes clear store location
22	Kooper	Peter	671 Main St.	Cambridge	MA	02138	617	WWIN TV	no comments
23	Kelly	Shawn	22 Kendall St.	Cambridge	MA	02138	617	Yellow Pages	found under "cafés"
24	Rodriguez	Virginia	123 Main St.	Boston	MA	02007	617	Radio	loves radio personality
25	Frei	Carol	123 Elm St.	Salem	MA	01970	978	Newspaper	no comments
26	Stevens	Crystal	14 Waterford St.	Salem	MA	01970	508	Radio	does not like radio personality
27	Ichikawa	Pam	232 Shore Rd.	Boston	MA	01801	617	Newspaper	told friends
28	Paxton	Gail	100 Main St.	Woburn	MA	01801	508	Newspaper	no comments
29	Spencer	Robin	293 Serenity Dr.	Concord	MA	01742	508	Radio	loved radio personality
30	Lopez	Luis	1212 City St.	Kansas City	MO	64105	816	WWIN TV	liked characters
31	Nelson	Michael	229 Rally Rd.	Kansas City	MO	64105	816	Yellow Pages	found under "Compact Discs"
32	Lee	Ginny	3 Way St.	Kansas City	MO	64102	816	Radio	intrigued by announcer

j. Scale the table width to 1 page and the height to 2 pages.

k. Enter your name in the center section of the worksheet footer.

l. Add a centered header that reads **Customer Survey Data** in bold with a font size of 16.

m. Add print titles to repeat the first row at the top of printed pages.

n. Save the workbook, preview it, then print the table on two pages.

Advanced Challenge Exercise

- Create a print area that prints only the first six columns of the table.
- Print the print area.
- Clear the print area.

o. Save the workbook, close the workbook, then exit Excel.

▼ INDEPENDENT CHALLENGE 2

You own Around the World, a travel bookstore located in New Zealand. The store sells travel-related items such as maps, travel books, journals, and DVDs of travel destinations. Your customers are primarily tour guides who purchase items in quantities of ten or more for their tour customers. You decide to plan and build a table of sales information with eight records using the items sold.

a. Prepare a plan for a table that states your goal, outlines the data you need, and identifies the table elements.

b. Sketch a sample table on a piece of paper, indicating how the table should be built. Create a table documenting the table design including the field names, type of data, and description of the data.

▼ INDEPENDENT CHALLENGE 2 (CONTINUED)

c. Start Excel, create a new workbook, then save it as **Store Items** in the drive and folder where you store your Data Files. Enter the field names from Table G-6 in the designated cells.

d. Enter eight data records using your own data.

e. Create a table using the data in the range A1:E9. Adjust the column widths as necessary.

f. Apply the Table Style Light 4 to the table.

g. Add the following fields to the table: **Subtotal** in cell F1, and **Total** in cell G1.

h. Add the label **Tax** in cell H1 and click the first option in the AutoCorrect Options to undo the table AutoExpansion. Enter **.125** in cell I1 (the 12.5% Goods and Services tax).

i. Enter formulas to calculate the subtotal (Quantity*Cost) in cell F2 and the total (including tax) in cell G2. Check that the formulas were filled down both of the columns. (*Hint*: Remember to use an absolute reference to the tax rate cell.)

j. Format the Cost, Subtotal, and Total columns using the Accounting number format with two decimal places and the symbol $ English (New Zealand). Adjust the column widths as necessary.

k. Add a new record to your table in row 10. Add another record above row 4.

l. Sort the table in ascending order by Item.

m. Enter your name in the worksheet footer, then save the workbook.

n. Preview the worksheet, use the Scale to Fit width option to scale the worksheet to print on one page.

o. Print the worksheet, close the workbook, then exit Excel.

TABLE G-6

Cell	Field name
A1	Customer Last
B1	Customer First
C1	Item
D1	Quantity
E1	Cost

▼ INDEPENDENT CHALLENGE 3

You are the project manager at a local advertising firm. You are managing your accounts using an Excel worksheet and have decided that a table will provide additional features to help you keep track of the accounts. You will use the table sorting features and table formulas to analyze your account data.

a. Start Excel, open the file EX G-4.xlsx from the drive and folder where you store your Data Files, then save it as **Accounts**.

b. Create a table with the worksheet data and apply Table Style Light 3.

c. Sort the table on the Budget field using the Smallest to Largest order. Compare your table to Figure G-23.

d. Sort the table using two fields, by Contact in A to Z order, then by Budget in Smallest to Largest order.

e. Add the new field label **Balance** in cell G1 and adjust the column width as necessary. Format the Budget, Expenses, and Balance columns using the Accounting format with no decimal places.

FIGURE G-23

	A	B	C	D	E	F	G
1	Project	Deadline	Code	Budget	Expenses	Contact	
2	Kelly	2/1/2010	AA1	100000	30000	Connie Blake	
3	Vincent	1/15/2010	C43	100000	150000	Jane Smith	
4	Jaffrey	3/15/2010	A3A	200000	210000	Kate Jeung	
5	Karim	4/30/2010	C43	200000	170000	Connie Blake	
6	Landry	11/15/2010	V53	200000	210000	Jane Smith	
7	Kaplan	9/30/2010	V51	300000	320000	Jane Smith	
8	Graham	7/10/2010	V13	390000	400000	Charlie Katter	
9	Lannou	10/10/2010	C21	450000	400000	Connie Blake	
10	Mason	6/1/2010	AA5	500000	430210	Jane Smith	
11	Melon	12/15/2010	B12	810000	700000	Nelly Atli	
12							

f. Enter a formula in cell G2 that uses structured references to table fields to calculate the balance on an account as the Budget minus the Expenses.

g. Add a new record for a project named **Franklin** with a deadline of **2/15/2010**, a code of **AB2**, a budget of **200000**, expenses of **150000**, and a contact of **Connie Blake**.

h. Verify that the formula accurately calculated the balance for the new record.

i. Replace all of the Jane Smith data with **Jane Jacobson** and adjust the column width as necessary.

j. Enter your name in the center section of the worksheet footer, add a center section header of **Accounts** using formatting of your choice, then save the workbook.

▼ INDEPENDENT CHALLENGE 3 (CONTINUED)

Advanced Challenge Exercise

- Sort the table on the Balance field using the smallest to largest order.
- Use conditional formatting to format the cells of the table containing negative balances with a dark green text on a green fill.
- Sort the table using the order of no cell color on top.
- Format the table to emphasize the Balance column and turn off the banded rows. (*Hint*: Use the Table Style Options on the Table Tools Design tab.)
- Compare your table with Figure G-24.

FIGURE G-24

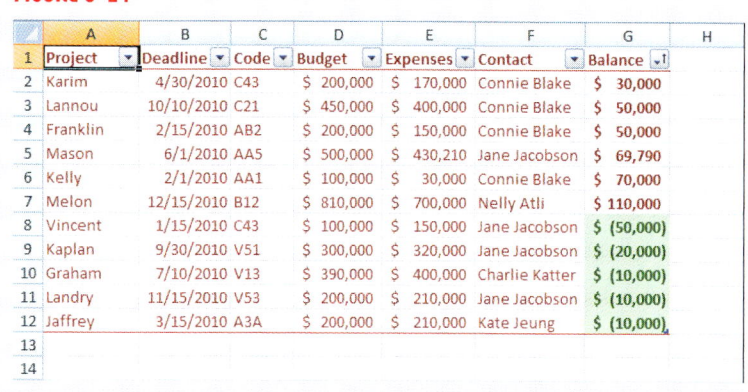

	A	B	C	D	E	F	G
1	Project	Deadline	Code	Budget	Expenses	Contact	Balance
2	Karim	4/30/2010	C43	$ 200,000	$ 170,000	Connie Blake	$ 30,000
3	Lannou	10/10/2010	C21	$ 450,000	$ 400,000	Connie Blake	$ 50,000
4	Franklin	2/15/2010	AB2	$ 200,000	$ 150,000	Connie Blake	$ 50,000
5	Mason	6/1/2010	AA5	$ 500,000	$ 430,210	Jane Jacobson	$ 69,790
6	Kelly	2/1/2010	AA1	$ 100,000	$ 30,000	Connie Blake	$ 70,000
7	Melon	12/15/2010	B12	$ 810,000	$ 700,000	Nelly Atli	$ 110,000
8	Vincent	1/15/2010	C43	$ 100,000	$ 150,000	Jane Jacobson	$ (50,000)
9	Kaplan	9/30/2010	V51	$ 300,000	$ 320,000	Jane Jacobson	$ (20,000)
10	Graham	7/10/2010	V13	$ 390,000	$ 400,000	Charlie Katter	$ (10,000)
11	Landry	11/15/2010	V53	$ 200,000	$ 210,000	Jane Jacobson	$ (10,000)
12	Jaffrey	3/15/2010	A3A	$ 200,000	$ 210,000	Kate Jeung	$ (10,000)

k. Save the workbook, print the table, close the workbook, then exit Excel.

▼ REAL LIFE INDEPENDENT CHALLENGE

You have decided to organize your recording collection using a table in Excel. This will enable you to easily find songs in your music library. You will add records as you purchase new music and delete records if you discard a recording.

a. Use the fields Title, Artist, Genre, and Format and prepare a diagram of your table structure.
b. Document the table design by detailing the type of data that will be in each field and a description of the data. For example, in the Format field you may have mp3, aac, wma, or other formats.
c. Start Excel, create a new workbook, then save it as **Music Titles** in the drive and folder where you store your Data Files.
d. Enter the field names into the worksheet, enter the records for seven of your music recordings, then save the workbook.
e. Create a table that contains your music information. Resize the columns as necessary.
f. Choose a Table Style and apply it to your table.
g. Add a new field with a label of Comments. Enter information in the new table column describing the setting in which you listen to the title, such as driving, exercising, entertaining, or relaxing.
h. Sort the records by the Format field using A to Z order.
i. Add a record to the table for the next recording you will purchase.
j. Add a Total row to your table and verify that the Count function accurately calculated the number of your recordings.
k. Enter your name in the worksheet footer, then save the workbook.
l. Print the table, close the workbook, then exit Excel.

▼ VISUAL WORKSHOP

Start Excel, open the file EX G-5.xlsx from the drive and folder where you store your Data Files, then save it as **Products**. Sort the data as shown in Figure G-25. The table is formatted using Table Style Light 3. Add a header with the file name that is centered and formatted in bold with a size of 18. Enter your name in the worksheet footer. Save the workbook, preview and print the table, close the workbook, then exit Excel.

FIGURE G-25

Products.xlsx

Order Number	Order date	Amount	Shipping	Sales Rep
1134	4/30/2010	$ 200,000	Air	Edward Callegy
1465	11/15/2010	$ 210,000	Air	Edward Callegy
7733	3/15/2010	$ 230,000	Air	Edward Callegy
2889	2/15/2010	$ 300,000	Air	Edward Callegy
1532	10/10/2010	$ 450,000	Air	Edward Callegy
9345	1/15/2010	$ 100,000	Ground	Gary Clarkson
5623	2/1/2010	$ 130,000	Air	Gary Clarkson
1112	9/30/2010	$ 300,000	Ground	Gary Clarkson
2156	6/1/2010	$ 500,000	Ground	Gary Clarkson
2134	7/10/2010	$ 390,000	Ground	Ned Blair
2144	12/15/2010	$ 810,000	Ground	Ned Blair

UNIT H
Excel 2007

Analyzing Table Data

Files You Will Need:
EX H-1.xlsx
EX H-2.xlsx
EX H-3.xlsx
EX H-4.xlsx
EX H-5.xlsx
EX H-6.xlsx

Excel data tables let you manipulate and analyze data in many ways. One way is to filter a table so that it displays only the rows that meet certain criteria. In this unit, you will display selected records using the filter feature, create a custom filter, and filter a table using an Advanced Filter. In addition, you will learn to insert automatic subtotals, use lookup functions to locate table entries, and apply database functions to summarize table data that meet specific criteria. You'll also learn how to restrict entries in a column by using data validation. The vice president of sales, Kate Morgan, asks you to extract information from a table of the 2010 scheduled tours to help the sales representatives with customer inquiries. She also asks you to prepare summaries of the tour sales for a presentation at the international sales meeting.

OBJECTIVES

Filter a table
Create a custom filter
Filter a table with Advanced Filter
Extract table data
Look up values in a table
Summarize table data
Validate table data
Create subtotals

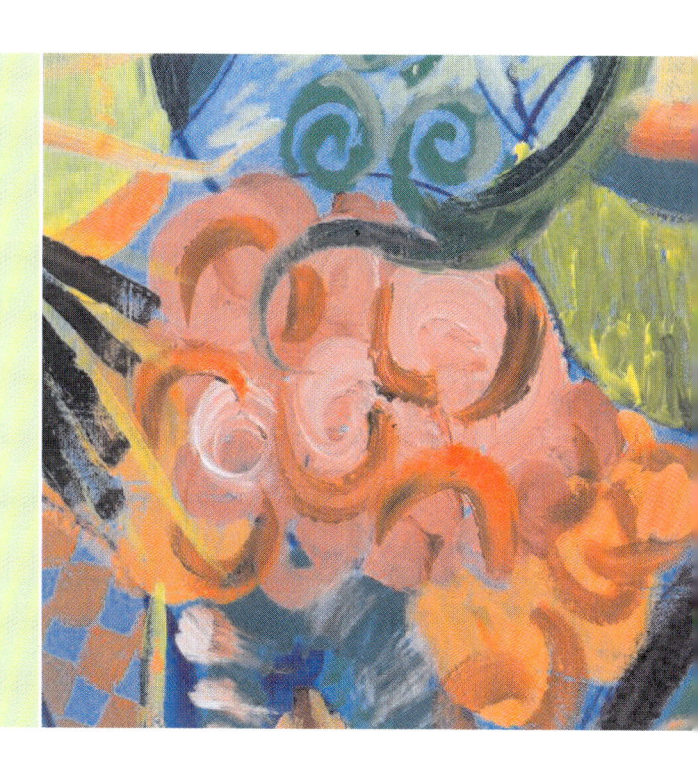

Filtering a Table

UNIT H
Excel 2007

When you create a table, arrows automatically appear next to each column header. These arrows are called **filter list arrows**, or **list arrows**, and you can use them to **filter** a table to display only the records that meet criteria you specify, temporarily hiding records that do not meet those criteria. For example, you can use the filter list arrow next to the Tour field header to display only records that contain Nepal Trekking in the Tour field. Once you filter data, you can copy, chart, and print the displayed records. You can easily clear a filter to redisplay all the records. Kate asks you to display only the records for the Pacific Odyssey tours. She also asks for information about the tours that sell the most seats and the tours that depart in March.

STEPS

1. **Start Excel, open the file EX H-1.xlsx from the drive and folder where you save your Data Files, then save it as Tours**

2. **Click the Tour list arrow**

   Sort options appear at the top of the menu, advanced filtering options appear in the middle, and at the bottom is a list of the tour data from column A, as shown in Figure H-1. Because you want to display data for only the Pacific Odyssey tours, your **search criterion** (the text you are searching for) is Pacific Odyssey. You can select one of the Tour data options in the menu, which acts as your search criterion.

   > **QUICK TIP**
   > You can also filter or sort a table by the color of the cells if conditional formatting has been applied.

3. **In the list of tours for the Tour field, click Select All to clear the checks from the tours, scroll down the list of tours, click the Pacific Odyssey check box, then click OK**

   Only those records containing Pacific Odyssey in the Tour field appear, as shown in Figure H-2. The row numbers for the matching records change to blue, and the list arrow for the filtered field has a filter icon. Both indicate that there is a filter in effect and that some of the records are temporarily hidden.

4. **Move the pointer over the Tour list arrow**

   The ScreenTip (Tour: Equals "Pacific Odyssey") describes the filter for the field, meaning that only the Pacific Odyssey records appear. You decide to remove the filter to redisplay all of the table data.

5. **Click the Tour list arrow, then click Clear Filter From "Tour"**

   You have cleared the Pacific Odyssey filter, and all the records reappear. You want to display the most popular tours, those that are in the top five percent of seats reserved.

6. **Click the Seats Reserved list arrow, point to Number Filters, click Top 10, select 10 in the middle box, type 5, click the Items list arrow, click Percent, then click OK**

   Excel displays the records for the top five percent in the number of Seats Reserved field, as shown in Figure H-3. You decide to clear the filter to redisplay all the records.

   > **TROUBLE**
   > If the Clear command is not available, check to be sure the active cell is inside the table.

7. **Click the Home tab, click the Sort & Filter button in the Editing group, then click Clear**

   You have cleared the filter and all the records reappear. You want to find all of the tours that depart in March.

8. **Click the Depart Date list arrow, point to Date Filters, point to All Dates in the Period, then click March**

   Excel displays the records for the four tours that leave in March. You decide to clear the filter and display all of the records.

   > **QUICK TIP**
   > You can also clear a filter by clicking the Clear button in the Sort & Filter group on the Data tab.

9. **Click Sort & Filter button in the Editing group, click Clear, then save the workbook**

Excel 178   Analyzing Table Data

FIGURE H-1: Worksheet showing filter options

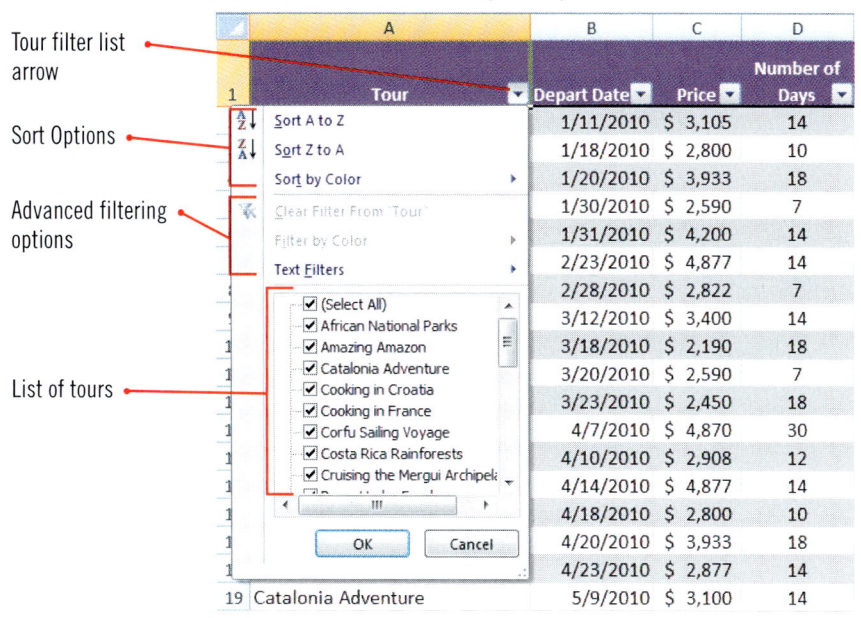

- Tour filter list arrow
- Sort Options
- Advanced filtering options
- List of tours

FIGURE H-2: Table filtered to show Pacific Odyssey tours

	A	B	C	D	E	F	G	H	I
1	Tour	Depart Date	Price	Number of Days	Seat Capacity	Seats Reserved	Seats Available	Air Included	Meals Included
2	Pacific Odyssey	1/11/2010	$ 3,105	14	50	30	20	Yes	No
34	Pacific Odyssey	7/7/2010	$ 3,105	14	50	32	18	Yes	No
48	Pacific Odyssey	9/14/2010	$ 3,105	14	50	26	24	Yes	No
61	Pacific Odyssey	12/21/2010	$ 3,105	14	50	50	0	Yes	No
64									

- Matching row numbers are blue and sequence indicates that not all rows appear
- Filter displays only Pacific Odyssey tours
- Filter icon

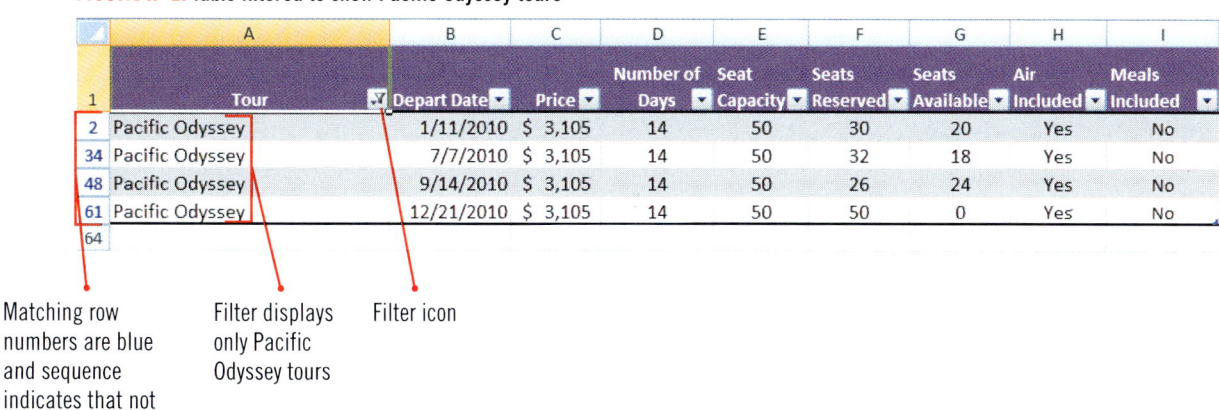

FIGURE H-3: Table filtered with top 5% of Seats Reserved

	A	B	C	D	E	F	G	H	I
1	Tour	Depart Date	Price	Number of Days	Seat Capacity	Seats Reserved	Seats Available	Air Included	Meals Included
18	Amazing Amazon	4/23/2010	$ 2,877	14	50	48	2	No	No
37	Kayak Newfoundland	7/12/2010	$ 1,970	7	50	49	1	Yes	Yes
45	Cooking in France	8/29/2010	$ 2,822	7	50	48	2	Yes	No
61	Pacific Odyssey	12/21/2010	$ 3,105	14	50	50	0	Yes	No
64									

Table filtered with top 5% in this field

Analyzing Table Data

Creating a Custom Filter

UNIT H
Excel 2007

So far, you have filtered rows based on an entry in a single column. You can perform more complex filters by using options in the Custom Filter dialog box. For example, your criteria can contain comparison operators such as "greater than" or "less than" that let you display values above or below a certain amount. You can also use **logical conditions** like And and Or to narrow a search even further. You can have Excel display records that meet a criterion in a field *and* another criterion in that same field. This is often used to find records between two values. For example, by specifying an And logical condition, you can display records for customers with incomes between $40,000 *and* $70,000. You can also have Excel display records that meet either criterion in a field by specifying an Or condition. The Or condition is used to find records that satisfy either of two values. For example, in a table of book data you can use the Or condition to find records that contain either Beginning *or* Introduction in the title name. Kate wants to locate water tours for customers who like boating adventures. She also wants to find tours that depart between February 15, 2010 and April 15, 2010. She asks you to create custom filters to find the tours satisfying these criteria.

STEPS

1. **Click the Tour list arrow, point to Text Filters, then click Contains**
   The Custom AutoFilter dialog box opens. You enter your criteria in the text boxes. The left text box on the first line currently displays "contains." You want to display tours that contain the word sailing in their names.

2. **Type sailing in the right text box on the first line**
   You want to see entries that contain either sailing or cruising.

> **QUICK TIP**
> When specifying criteria in the Custom AutoFilter dialog box, you can use the ? wildcard to represent any single character and the * wildcard to represent any series of characters.

3. **Click the Or option button to select it, click the left text box list arrow on the second line, select contains, then type cruising in the right text box on the second line**
   Your completed Custom AutoFilter dialog box should match Figure H-4.

4. **Click OK**
   The dialog box closes, and only those records having sailing or cruising in the Tour field appear in the worksheet. You want to find all tours that depart between February 15, 2010 and April 15, 2010.

5. **Click the Tour list arrow, click Clear Filter From "Tour", click the Depart Date list arrow, point to Date Filters, then click Custom Filter**
   The Custom AutoFilter dialog box opens. The word "equals" appears in the left text box on the first line. You want to find the departure dates that are between February 15, 2010 and April 15, 2010 (that is, after February 15th *and* before April 15th).

6. **Click the left text box list arrow on the first line, click is after, then type 2/15/2010 in the right text box on the first line**
   The And condition is selected, which is correct.

7. **Click the left text box list arrow on the second line, select is before, type 4/15/2010 in the right text box on the second line, then click OK**
   The records displayed have departing dates between February 15, 2010 and April 15, 2010. Compare your records to those shown in Figure H-5.

8. **Add your name to the center section of the footer, scale the page width to one page, then preview and print the filtered table**
   The worksheet prints using the existing landscape orientation, on one page with your name in the footer.

9. **Click the Depart Date list arrow, then click Clear Filter From "Depart Date"**
   You have cleared the filter, and all the tour records reappear.

FIGURE H-4: Custom AutoFilter dialog box

FIGURE H-5: Results of custom filter

	A	B	C	D	E	F	G	H	I
1	Tour	Depart Date	Price	Number of Days	Seat Capacity	Seats Reserved	Seats Available	Air Included	Meals Included
7	Cruising the Mergui Archipelago	2/23/2010	$ 4,877	14	50	42	8	No	No
8	Cooking in France	2/28/2010	$ 2,822	7	50	18	32	Yes	No
9	Pearls of the Orient	3/12/2010	$ 3,400	14	50	22	28	Yes	No
10	Silk Road Travels	3/18/2010	$ 2,190	18	50	44	6	Yes	Yes
11	Costa Rica Rainforests	3/20/2010	$ 2,590	7	50	32	18	Yes	Yes
12	Green Adventures in Ecuador	3/23/2010	$ 2,450	18	50	45	5	No	No
13	African National Parks	4/7/2010	$ 4,870	30	50	18	32	Yes	Yes
14	Experience Cambodia	4/10/2010	$ 2,908	12	50	29	21	Yes	No
15	Cruising the Mergui Archipelago	4/14/2010	$ 4,877	14	50	20	30	No	No
64									

Depature dates are between 2/15 and 4/15

Using more than one rule when conditionally formatting data

You can apply conditional formatting to table cells in the same way that you can format a range of worksheet data. You can add multiple rules by clicking the Home tab, clicking the Conditional Formatting button in the Styles group, then clicking New Rule for each additional rule that you want to apply. You can also add rules using the Conditional Formatting Rules Manager, which displays all of the rules for a data range. To use the Rules Manager, click the Home tab, click the Conditional Formatting button in the Styles group, click Manage Rules, then click New Rule for each rule that you want to apply to the data range.

Filtering a Table with Advanced Filter

UNIT H
Excel 2007

The Advanced Filter command lets you search for data that matches criteria in more than one column, using And and Or conditions. For example, you can use Advanced Filter to find Tours that leave before a certain date *and* have meals included. To use advanced filtering, you must create a criteria range. A **criteria range** is a cell range containing one row of labels (usually a copy of the column labels) and at least one additional row underneath the row of labels that contains the criteria you want to match. Placing the criteria in the same row indicates that the records you are searching for must match both criteria; that is, it specifies an **And condition**. Placing the criteria in the different rows indicates that the records you are searching for must match only one of the criterion; that is, it specifies an **Or condition**. Kate wants to identify tours that depart after 6/1/2010 and that cost less than $2000. She asks you to use the Advanced Filter to retrieve these records. You begin by defining the criteria range.

STEPS

1. **Select table rows 1 through 6, click the Insert list arrow in the Cells group, click Insert Sheet Rows; click cell A1, type Criteria Range, then click the Enter button ✓ on the Formula bar**

   Six blank rows are added above the table. Excel does not require the label Criteria Range, but it is useful in organizing the worksheet. It is also helpful to see the column labels.

2. **Select the range A7:I7, click the Copy button in the Clipboard group, click cell A2, click the Paste button in the Clipboard group, then press [Esc]**

   Next, you want to list records for only those tours that depart after June 1, 2010 and that cost under $2000.

3. **Click cell B3, type >6/1/2010, click cell C3, type <2000, then click ✓**

   You have entered the criteria in the cells directly beneath the Criteria Range labels, as shown in Figure H-6.

4. **Click any cell in the table, click the Data tab, then click the Advanced button in the Sort & Filter group**

   The Advanced Filter dialog box opens, with the table range already entered. The default setting under Action is to filter the table in its current location ("in-place") rather than copy it to another location.

TROUBLE
If your filtered records don't match Figure H-7, make sure there are no spaces between the > symbol and the 6 in cell B3 and the < symbol and the 2 in cell C3.

5. **Click the Criteria range text box, select range A2:I3 in the worksheet, then click OK**

   You have specified the criteria range and performed the filter. The filtered table contains eight records that match both criteria—the departure date is after 6/1/2010 and the price is less than $2000, as shown in Figure H-7. You'll filter this table even further in the next lesson.

Excel 182   Analyzing Table Data

FIGURE H-6: Criteria in the same row

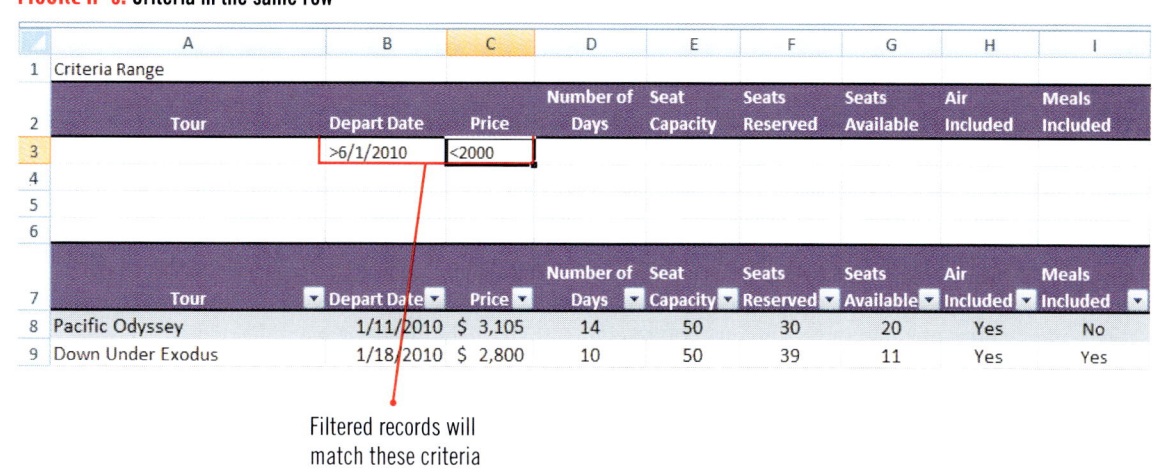

	A	B	C	D	E	F	G	H	I
1	Criteria Range								
2	Tour	Depart Date	Price	Number of Days	Seat Capacity	Seats Reserved	Seats Available	Air Included	Meals Included
3		>6/1/2010	<2000						
4									
5									
6									
7	Tour	Depart Date	Price	Number of Days	Seat Capacity	Seats Reserved	Seats Available	Air Included	Meals Included
8	Pacific Odyssey	1/11/2010	$ 3,105	14	50	30	20	Yes	No
9	Down Under Exodus	1/18/2010	$ 2,800	10	50	39	11	Yes	Yes

Filtered records will match these criteria

FIGURE H-7: Filtered table

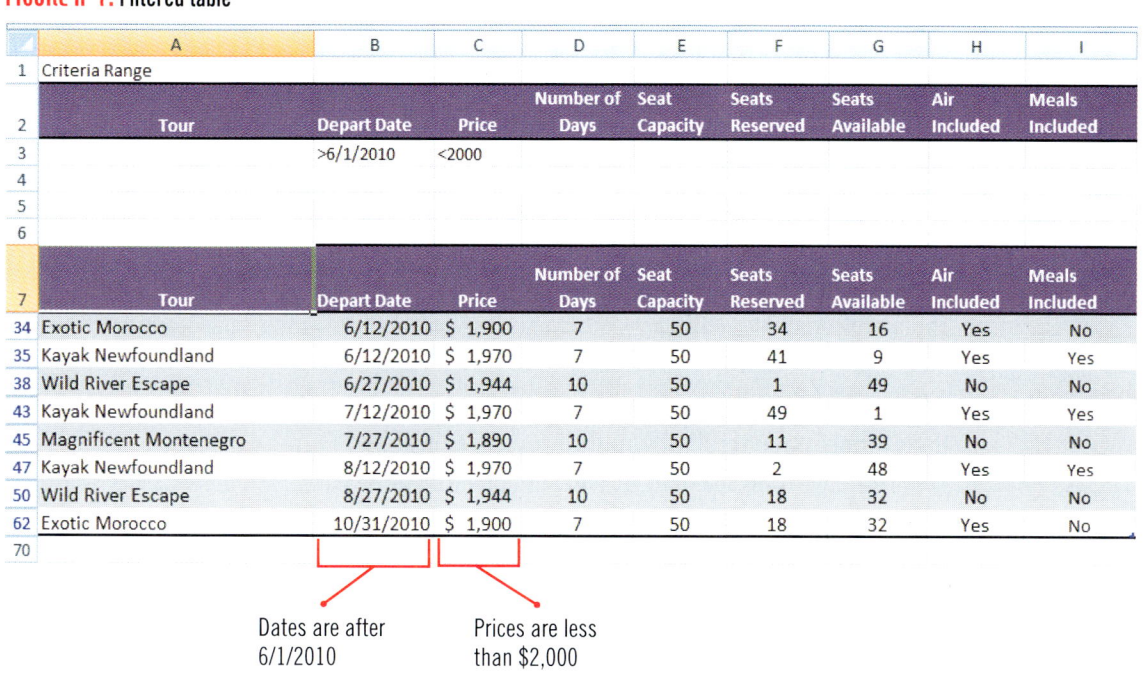

	A	B	C	D	E	F	G	H	I
1	Criteria Range								
2	Tour	Depart Date	Price	Number of Days	Seat Capacity	Seats Reserved	Seats Available	Air Included	Meals Included
3		>6/1/2010	<2000						
4									
5									
6									
7	Tour	Depart Date	Price	Number of Days	Seat Capacity	Seats Reserved	Seats Available	Air Included	Meals Included
34	Exotic Morocco	6/12/2010	$ 1,900	7	50	34	16	Yes	No
35	Kayak Newfoundland	6/12/2010	$ 1,970	7	50	41	9	Yes	Yes
38	Wild River Escape	6/27/2010	$ 1,944	10	50	1	49	No	No
43	Kayak Newfoundland	7/12/2010	$ 1,970	7	50	49	1	Yes	Yes
45	Magnificent Montenegro	7/27/2010	$ 1,890	10	50	11	39	No	No
47	Kayak Newfoundland	8/12/2010	$ 1,970	7	50	2	48	Yes	Yes
50	Wild River Escape	8/27/2010	$ 1,944	10	50	18	32	No	No
62	Exotic Morocco	10/31/2010	$ 1,900	7	50	18	32	Yes	No
70									

Dates are after 6/1/2010

Prices are less than $2,000

Using advanced conditional formatting options

You can emphasize top or bottom ranked values in a field using conditional formatting. To highlight the top or bottom values in a field, select the field data, click the Conditional Formatting button on the Home tab, point to Top/Bottom Rules, select a Top or Bottom rule, if necessary enter the percentage or number of cells in the selected range that you want to format, select the format for the cells that meet the top or bottom criteria, then click OK. You can also format your worksheet or table data using icon sets and color scales based on the cell values. A **color scale** uses a set of two, three, or four fill colors to convey relative values. For example, red could fill cells to indicate they have higher values and green could signify lower values. To add a color scale, select a data range, click the Home tab, click the Conditional Formatting button in the Styles group, then point to Color Scales. On the submenu, you can select preformatted color sets or click More Rules to create your own color sets. **Icon sets** let you visually communicate relative cell values by adding icons to cells based on the values they contain. An upward-pointing green arrow might represent the highest values, and downward-pointing red arrows could represent lower values. To add an icon set to a data range, select a data range, click the Conditional Formatting button in the Styles group, then point to Icon Sets. You can customize the values that are used as thresholds for color scales and icon sets by clicking the Conditional Formatting button in the Styles group, clicking Manage Rules, clicking the rule in the Conditional Formatting Rules Manager dialog box, then clicking Edit Rule.

Analyzing Table Data

UNIT H
Excel 2007

Extracting Table Data

Whenever you take the time to specify a complicated set of search criteria, it's a good idea to extract the matching records, rather than filtering it in-place. When you **extract** data, you place a copy of a filtered table in a range that you specify in the Advanced Filter dialog box. This way, you won't accidentally clear the filter or lose track of the records you spent time compiling. To extract data, you use an advanced filter and enter the criteria beneath the copied field names, as you did in the previous lesson. 🎨 Kate needs to filter the table one step further to reflect only the Exotic Morocco or Kayak Newfoundland tours in the current filtered table. She asks you to complete this filter by specifying an Or condition, which you will do by entering two sets of criteria in two separate rows. You decide to save the filtered records by extracting them to a different location in the worksheet.

STEPS

1. **In cell A3, enter Exotic Morocco, then in cell A4, enter Kayak Newfoundland**
   The new sets of criteria need to appear in two separate rows, so you need to copy the previous filter criteria to the second row.

2. **Copy the criteria in B3:C3 to B4:C4**
   The criteria are shown in Figure H-8. When you perform the advanced filter this time, you indicate that you want to copy the filtered table to a range beginning in cell A75, so that Kate can easily refer to the data, even if you perform more filters later.

3. **Click the Data tab if necessary, then click Advanced in the Sort & Filter group**

4. **Under Action, click the Copy to another location option button to select it, click the Copy to text box, then type A75**
   The last time you filtered the table, the criteria range included only rows 2 and 3, and now you have criteria in row 4.

> **TROUBLE**
> Make sure the criteria range in the Advanced Filter dialog box includes the field names and the number of rows underneath the names that contain criteria. If you leave a blank row in the criteria range, Excel filters nothing and shows all records.

5. **Edit the contents of the Criteria range text box to show the range $A$2:$I$4, click OK, then if necessary scroll down until row 75 is visible**
   The matching records appear in the range beginning in cell A75, as shown in Figure H-9. The original table, starting in cell A7, contains the records filtered in the previous lesson.

6. **Select the range A75:I80, click the Office button 🟠, click Print, under Print what click the Selection option button, click Preview, then click Print**
   The selected area prints.

7. **Press [Ctrl][Home], then click the Clear button in the Sort & Filter group**
   The original table is displayed starting in cell A7, and the extracted table remains in A75:I80.

8. **Save the workbook**

FIGURE H-8: Criteria in separate rows

	A	B	C	D	E	F	G	H	I
1	Criteria Range								
2	Tour	Depart Date	Price	Number of Days	Seat Capacity	Seats Reserved	Seats Available	Air Included	Meals Included
3	Exotic Morocco	>6/1/2010	<2000						
4	Kayak Newfoundland	>6/1/2010	<2000						
5									

Two sets of criteria on separate lines indicates an OR condition

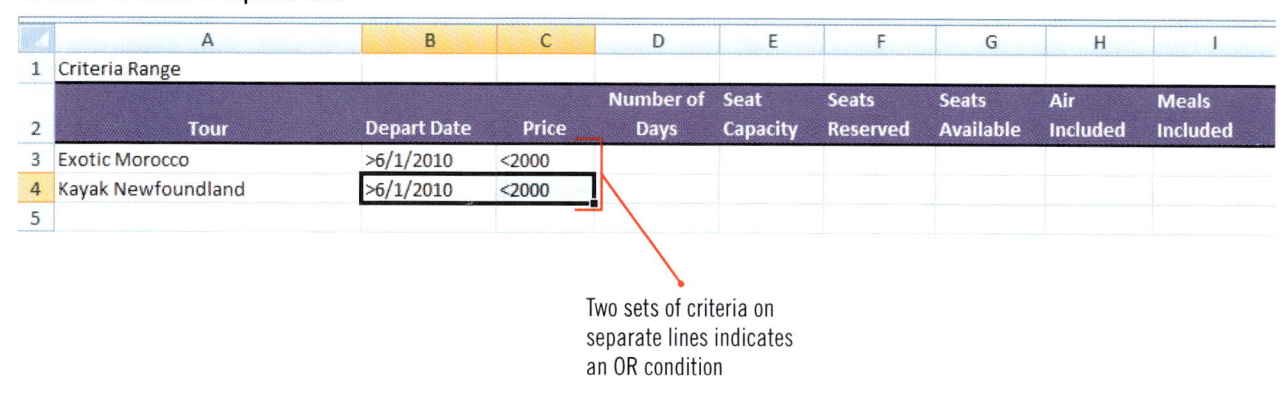

FIGURE H-9: Extracted data records

	Tour	Depart Date	Price	Number of Days	Seat Capacity	Seats Reserved	Seats Available	Air Included	Meals Included
75	Tour	Depart Date	Price	Number of Days	Seat Capacity	Seats Reserved	Seats Available	Air Included	Meals Included
76	Exotic Morocco	6/12/2010	$ 1,900	7	50	34	16	Yes	No
77	Kayak Newfoundland	6/12/2010	$ 1,970	7	50	41	9	Yes	Yes
78	Kayak Newfoundland	7/12/2010	$ 1,970	7	50	49	1	Yes	Yes
79	Kayak Newfoundland	8/12/2010	$ 1,970	7	50	2	48	Yes	Yes
80	Exotic Morocco	10/31/2010	$ 1,900	7	50	18	32	Yes	No

Only Exotic Morocco and Kayak Newfoundland tours appear

Departure date after 6/1/2010

Price is less than $2000

Understanding the criteria range and the copy-to location

When you define the criteria range and the copy-to location in the Advanced Filter dialog box, Excel automatically creates the names Criteria and Extract for these ranges in the worksheet. The criteria range includes the field names and any criteria rows underneath them. The extract range includes just the field names above the extracted table. You can select these ranges by clicking the Name box list arrow, then clicking the range name. If you click the Name Manager button in the Defined Names group on the Formulas tab, you will see these new names and the ranges associated with the names.

Analyzing Table Data

Looking Up Values in a Table

UNIT H — Excel 2007

The Excel VLOOKUP function helps you locate specific values in a table. VLOOKUP searches vertically (V) down the far left column of a table, then reads across the row to find the value in the column you specify, much as you might look up a number in a phone book: You locate a person's name, then read across the row to find the phone number you want. Kate wants to be able to find a tour destination by entering the tour code. You will use the VLOOKUP function to accomplish this task. You begin by viewing the table name so you can refer to it in a Lookup function.

STEPS

> **QUICK TIP**
> You can change table names to better represent their content so they are easier to use in formulas. Click the table in the list of names in the Name Manager text box, click Edit, type the new table name in the Name text box, then click OK.

1. **Click the Lookup sheet tab, click the Formulas tab, then click the Name Manager button in the Defined Names group**

   The named ranges for the workbook appear in the Name Manager dialog box, as shown in Figure H-10. The Criteria and Extract ranges appear at the top of the range name list. At the bottom of the list is information about the three tables in the workbook. Table1 refers to the table on the Tours sheet, Table2 refers to the table on the Lookup sheet, and Table3 refers to the table on the Subtotals worksheet. These table names were automatically generated when the table was created by the Excel structured reference feature.

2. **Click Close**

   You want to find the tour represented by the code 675Y. The VLOOKUP function lets you find the tour name for any trip code. You will enter a trip code in cell L2 and a VLOOKUP function in cell M2.

3. **Click cell L2, enter 675Y, click cell M2, click the Lookup & Reference button in the Function Library group, then click VLOOKUP**

   The Function Arguments dialog box opens, with boxes for each of the VLOOKUP arguments. Because the value you want to find is in cell L2, L2 is the Lookup_value. The table you want to search is the table on the Lookup sheet, so its assigned name, Table2, is the Table_array.

> **QUICK TIP**
> If you want to find only the closest match for a value, enter TRUE in the Range_lookup text box. However, this can give misleading results if you are looking for an exact match. If you use FALSE and Excel can't find the value, you see an error message.

4. **With the insertion point in the Lookup_value text box, click cell L2, click the Table_array text box, then type Table2**

   The column containing the information that you want to find and display in cell M2 is the second column from the left in the table range, so the Col_index_num is 2. Because you want to find an exact match for the value in cell L1, the Range_lookup argument is FALSE.

5. **Click the Col_index_num text box, type 2, click the Range_lookup text box, then enter FALSE**

   Your completed Function Arguments dialog box should match Figure H-11.

6. **Click OK**

   Excel searches down the leftmost column of the table until it finds a value matching the one in cell L2. It finds the tour for that record, Catalonia Adventure, then displays it in cell M2. You use this function to determine the tour for one other trip code.

7. **Click cell L2, type 439U, then click the Enter button on the formula bar**

   The VLOOKUP function returns the value of Cooking in France in cell M2.

8. **Press [Ctrl][Home], then save the workbook**

Finding records using the DGET function

You can also use the DGET function to find a record in a table that matches specified criteria. For example, you could use the criteria of L1:L2 in the DGET function. When using DGET, you need to include [#All] after your table name in the formula to include the column labels that are used for the criteria range.

Excel 186   Analyzing Table Data

FIGURE H-10: Named ranges in the workbook

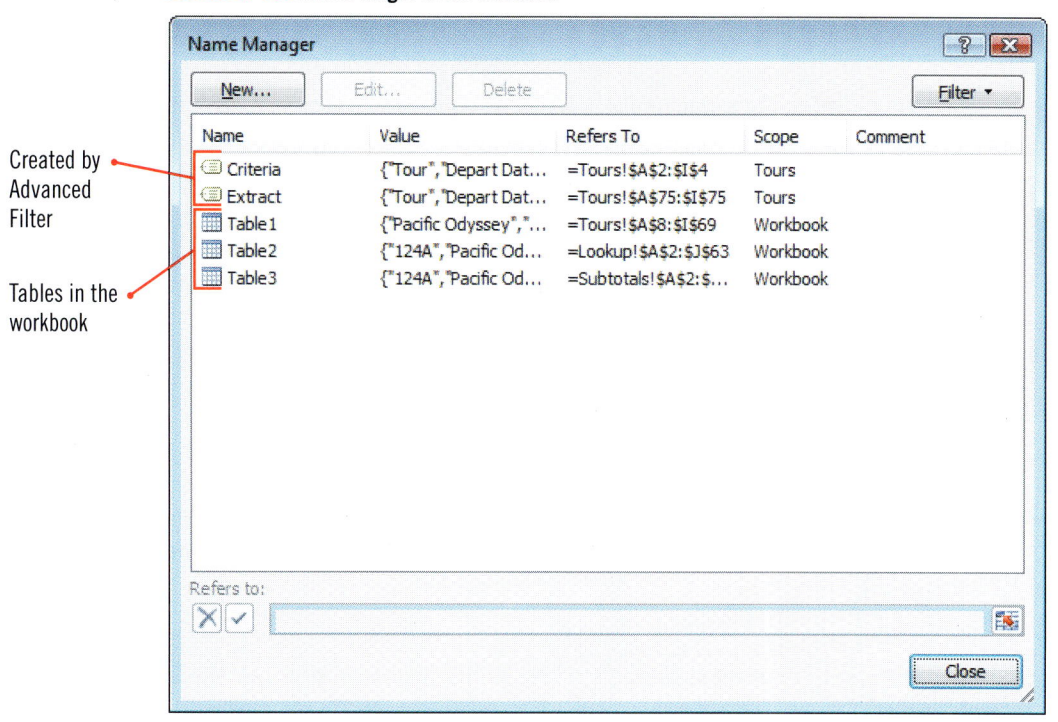

Created by Advanced Filter → Criteria, Extract

Tables in the workbook → Table1, Table2, Table3

FIGURE H-11: Completed Function Arguments dialog box for VLOOKUP

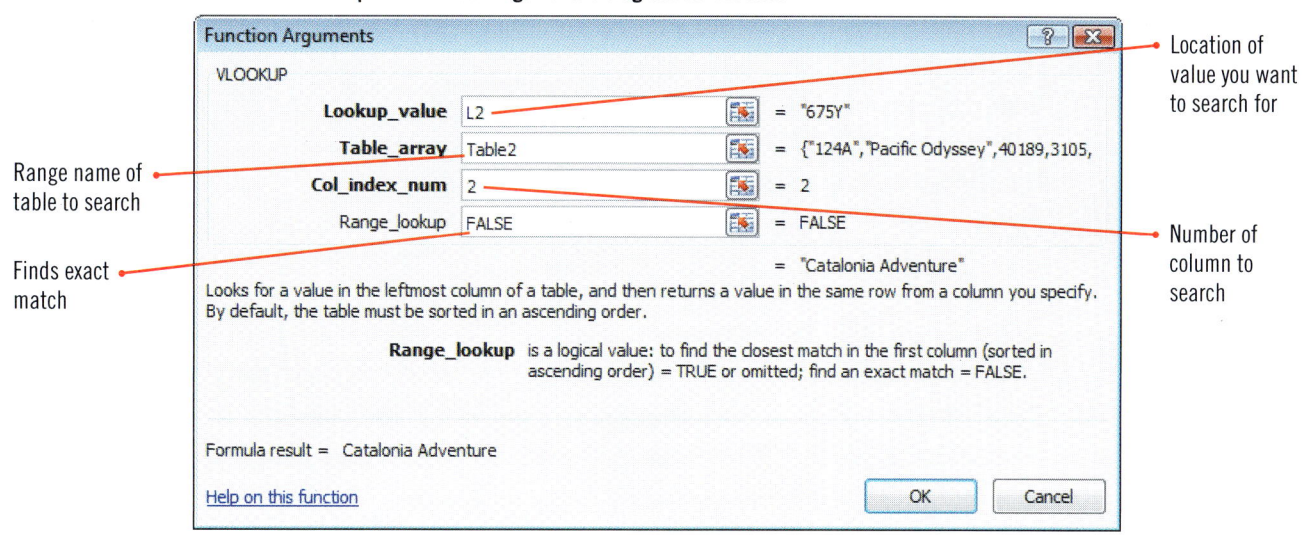

- Location of value you want to search for → Lookup_value: L2
- Range name of table to search → Table_array: Table2
- Number of column to search → Col_index_num: 2
- Finds exact match → Range_lookup: FALSE

Formula result = Catalonia Adventure

Using the HLOOKUP and MATCH functions

The VLOOKUP (Vertical Lookup) function is useful when your data is arranged vertically, in columns. The HLOOKUP (Horizontal Lookup) function is useful when your data is arranged horizontally, in rows. HLOOKUP searches horizontally across the upper row of a table until it finds the matching value, then looks down the number of rows you specify. The arguments for this function are identical to those for the VLOOKUP function, with one exception. Instead of a Col_index_number, HLOOKUP uses a Row_index_number, which indicates the location of the row you want to search. For example, if you want to search the fourth row from the top, the Row_index_number should be 4. You can use the MATCH function when you want the position of an item in a range. The MATCH function uses the syntax: MATCH (lookup_value,lookup_array,match_ type) where lookup_value is the value you want to match in the lookup_array range. The match_type can be 0 for an exact match, 1 for matching the largest value that is less than or equal to lookup_value, or –1 for matching the smallest value that is greater than or equal to lookup_value.

Analyzing Table Data

Summarizing Table Data

UNIT H
Excel 2007

Because a table acts much like a database, database functions allow you to summarize table data in a variety of ways. When working with a sales activity table, for example, you can use Excel to count the number of client contacts by sales representative or to total the amount sold to specific accounts by month. Table H-1 lists database functions commonly used to summarize table data. Kate is considering adding tours for the 2010 schedule. She needs your help in evaluating the number of seats available for scheduled tours.

STEPS

1. **Review the criteria range for the Pacific Odyssey tour in the range L6:L7**
   The criteria range in L6:L7 tells Excel to summarize records with the entry Pacific Odyssey in the Tour column. The functions will be in cells N6 and N7. You use this criteria range in a DSUM function to sum the seats available for only the Pacific Odyssey tours.

2. **Click cell N6, click the Insert Function button in the Function Library group, in the Search for a function text box type database, click Go, click DSUM under Select a function, then click OK**
   The first argument of the DSUM function is the table, or database.

   > **QUICK TIP**
   > Because the DSUM formula uses the column headings to locate and sum the table data, the header row needs to be included in the database range.

3. **In the Function Arguments dialog box, with the insertion point in the Database text box, move the pointer over the upper-left corner of the Trip Code column header until the pointer becomes ↘, click once, then click again**
   The first click selects the table's data range and the second click selects the entire table, including the header row. The second argument of the DSUM function is the label for the column that you want to sum. You want to total the number of available seats. The last argument for the DSUM function is the criteria that will be used to determine which values to total.

   > **TROUBLE**
   > If your Function Arguments dialog box does not match Figure H-12, click Cancel and repeat steps 2 – 4.

4. **Click the Field text box, then click cell H1, Seats Available; click the Criteria text box and select the range L6:L7**
   Your completed Function Arguments dialog box should match Figure H-12.

5. **Click OK**
   The result in cell N6 is 62. Excel totaled the information in the column Seats Available for those records that meet the criterion of Tour equals Pacific Odyssey. The DCOUNT and the DCOUNTA functions can help you determine the number of records meeting specified criteria in a database field. DCOUNTA counts the number of nonblank cells. You will use DCOUNTA to determine the number of tours scheduled

6. **Click cell N7, click 𝑓𝑥 on the formula bar, in the Search for a function text box type database, click Go, select DCOUNTA from the Select a function list, then click OK**

7. **With the insertion point in the Database text box, move the pointer over the upper-left corner of the Trip Code column header until the pointer becomes ↘, click once, click again to, click the Field text box and click cell B1, click the Criteria text box and select the range L6:L7, then click OK**
   The result in cell N7 is 4, meaning that there are four Pacific Odyssey tours scheduled for the year. You also want to display the number of seats available for the Cooking in France tours.

8. **Click cell L7, type Cooking in France, then click the Enter button ✓ on the formula bar**
   Figure H-13 shows that only three seats are available in the Cooking in France tours.

Excel 188   Analyzing Table Data

FIGURE H-12: Completed Function Arguments dialog box for DSUM

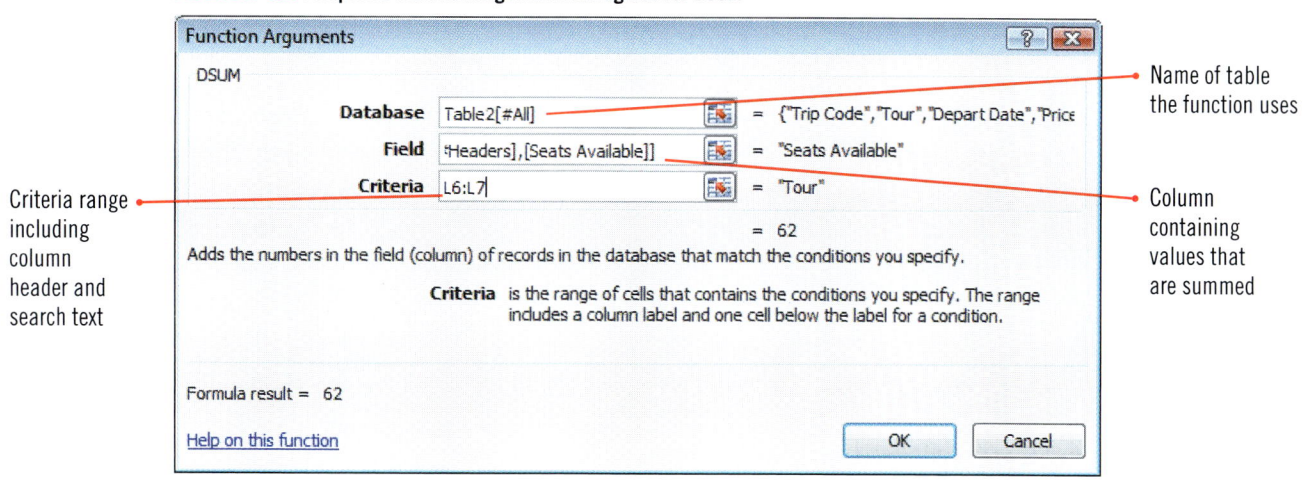

- Criteria range including column header and search text
- Name of table the function uses
- Column containing values that are summed

FIGURE H-13: Result generated by database functions

TABLE H-1: Common database functions

function	result
DGET	Extracts a single record from a table that matches criteria you specify
DSUM	Totals numbers in a given table column that match criteria you specify
DAVERAGE	Averages numbers in a given table column that match criteria you specify
DCOUNT	Counts the cells that contain numbers in a given table column that match criteria you specify
DCOUNTA	Counts the cells that contain nonblank data in a given table column that match criteria you specify

Analyzing Table Data

Excel 189

UNIT H
Excel 2007
Validating Table Data

When setting up data tables, you want to help ensure accuracy when you or others enter data. The Excel data validation feature allows you to do this by specifying what data users can enter in a range of cells. You can restrict data to whole numbers, decimal numbers, or text. You can also specify a list of acceptable entries. Once you've specified what data the program should consider valid for that cell, Excel displays an error message when invalid data is entered and can prevent users from entering any other data that it considers to be invalid. Kate wants to make sure that information in the Air Included column is entered consistently in the future. She asks you to restrict the entries in that column to two options: Yes and No. First, you select the table column you want to restrict.

STEPS

> **QUICK TIP**
> To specify a long list of valid entries, type the list in a column elsewhere in the worksheet, then type the list range in the Source text box.

1. **Click the top edge of the Air Included column header**
   The column data is selected.

2. **Click the Data tab, click the Data Validation button in the Data Tools group, click the Settings tab if necessary, click the Allow list arrow, then click List**
   Selecting the List option lets you type a list of specific options.

3. **Click the Source text box, then type Yes, No**
   You have entered the list of acceptable entries, separated by commas, as shown in Figure H-14. You want the data entry person to be able to select a valid entry from a drop-down list.

> **TROUBLE**
> If you get an invalid data error, make sure that cell I1 is not included in the selection. If I1 is included, open the Data Validation dialog box, click Clear All, click OK, then begin with step 1 again.

4. **Click the In-cell dropdown check box to select it if necessary, then click OK**
   The dialog box closes, and you return to the worksheet.

5. **Click the Home tab, click any cell in the last table row, click the Insert list arrow in the Cells group, click Insert Table Row Below, click cell I64, then click the list arrow to display the list of valid entries**
   The dropdown list is shown in Figure H-15. You could click an item in the list to have it entered in the cell, but you want to test the data restriction by entering an invalid entry.

6. **Click the list arrow to close the list, type Maybe, then press [Enter]**
   A warning dialog box appears to prevent you from entering the invalid data, as shown in Figure H-16.

7. **Click Cancel, click the list arrow, then click Yes**
   The cell accepts the valid entry. The data restriction ensures that records contain only one of the two correct entries in the Air Included column. The table is ready for future data entry.

8. **Delete the last table row, then save the workbook**

9. **Add your name to the center section of the footer, select the range L1:N7, click the Office button, click Print, under Print what, click the Selection option button, click Preview, then click Print**

Restricting cell values and data length

In addition to providing an in-cell drop-down list for data entry, you can use data validation to restrict the values that are entered into cells. For example, if you want to restrict cells to values less than a certain number, date, or time, click the Data tab, click the Data Validation button in the Data Tools group, and on the Settings tab, click the Allow list arrow, select Whole number, Decimal, Date, or Time, click the Data list arrow, select less than, then in the bottom text box, enter the maximum value. You can also limit the length of data entered into cells by choosing Text length in the Allow list, clicking the Data list arrow and selecting less than, then entering the maximum length in the Maximum text box.

Analyzing Table Data

FIGURE H-14: Creating data restrictions

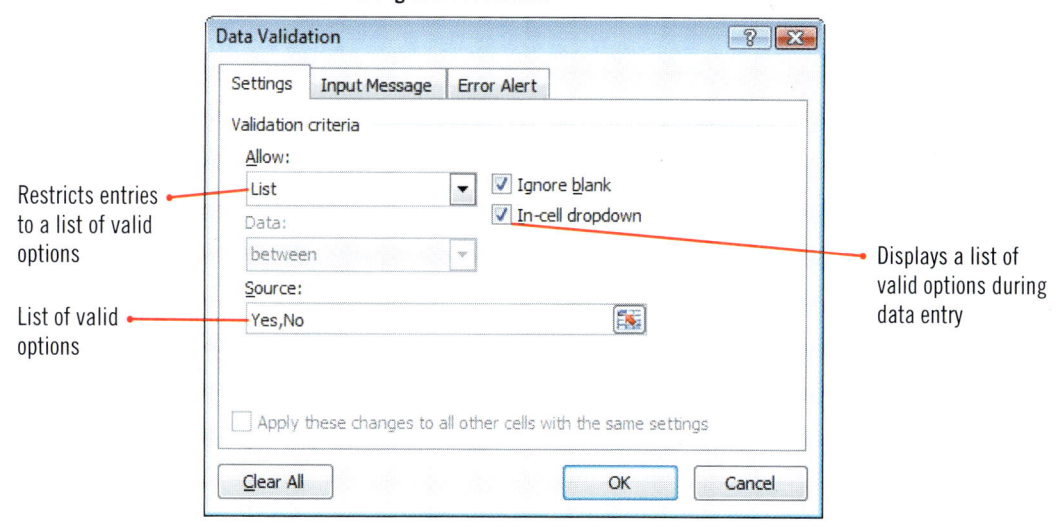

- Restricts entries to a list of valid options
- List of valid options
- Displays a list of valid options during data entry

FIGURE H-15: Entering data in restricted cells

61	307R	Pacific Odyssey	12/21/2010	$ 3,105	14	50	50	0	Yes	No
62	927F	Essential India	12/30/2010	$ 3,933	18	50	31	19	Yes	Yes
63	448G	Old Japan	12/31/2010	$ 2,100	21	50	44	6	Yes	No
64								0		
65										
66										

Dropdown list

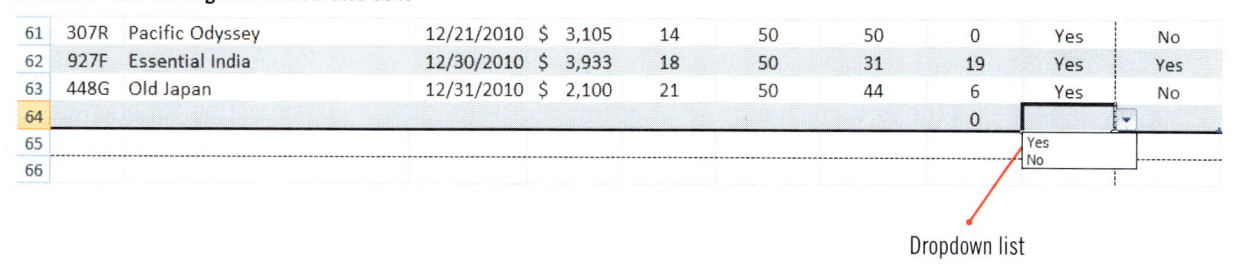

FIGURE H-16: Invalid data warning

Adding input messages and error alerts

You can customize the way data validation works by using the two other tabs in the Data Validation dialog box: Input Message and Error Alert. The Input Message tab lets you set a message that appears when the user selects that cell; for example, the message might contain instructions about what type of data to enter. On the Input Message tab, enter a message title and message, then click OK. The Error Alert tab lets you set one of three alert levels if a user enters invalid data. The Information level displays your message with the information icon but allows the user to proceed with data entry. The Warning level displays your information with the warning icon and gives the user the option to proceed with data entry or not. The Stop level, which you used in this lesson, displays your message and only lets the user retry or cancel data entry for that cell.

Analyzing Table Data

Creating Subtotals

UNIT H
Excel 2007

The Excel Subtotals feature provides a quick, easy way to group and summarize a range of data. Usually, you create subtotals with the SUM function, but you can also summarize data groups with functions such as COUNT, AVERAGE, MAX, and MIN. Subtotals cannot be used in a table structure. Before you can add subtotals to a table, you must first convert the data to a range and sort it. Kate wants you to group data by tours, with subtotals for the number of seats available and the number of seats reserved. You begin by converting the table to a range.

STEPS

1. **Click the Subtotals sheet tab, click any cell inside the table, click the Table Tools Design tab, click the Convert to Range button in the Tools group, then click Yes**

   Before you can add the subtotals, you must first sort the data. You decide to sort it in ascending order, first by tour and then by departure date.

2. **Click the Data tab, click the Sort button in the Sort & Filter group, in the Sort dialog box click the Sort by list arrow, click Tour, then click the Add Level button, click the Then by list arrow, click Depart Date, verify that the order is Oldest to Newest, then click OK**

   You have sorted the range in ascending order, first by tour, then by departure date.

3. **Click any cell in the data range, then click the Subtotal button in the Outline group**

   The Subtotal dialog box opens. Here you specify the items you want subtotaled, the function you want to apply to the values, and the fields you want to summarize.

4. **Click the At each change in list arrow, click Tour, click the Use function list arrow, click Sum; in the Add subtotal to list, click the Seats Reserved and Seats Available check boxes to select them, if necessary, then click the Meals Included check box to deselect it**

5. **If necessary, click the Replace current subtotals and Summary below data check boxes to select them**

   Your completed Subtotal dialog box should match Figure H-17.

> **QUICK TIP**
> You can click the [−] button to hide or the [+] button to show a group of records in the subtotaled structure.

6. **Click OK, then scroll down so row 90 is visible**

   The subtotaled data appears, showing the calculated subtotals and grand total in columns G and H, as shown in Figure H-18. Notice that Excel displays an outline to the left of the worksheet, with outline buttons to control the level of detail that appears. The button number corresponds to the detail level that is displayed. You want to show the second level of detail, the subtotals and the grand total.

7. **Click the outline symbol 2**

   The subtotals and the grand totals appear.

> **QUICK TIP**
> You can remove subtotals in a worksheet by clicking the Subtotal button and clicking Remove All. The subtotals no longer appear, and the Outline feature is turned off automatically.

8. **Add your name to the center section of the footer, scale the worksheet width to print on one page, save, preview the worksheet, then print it**

9. **Close the workbook and exit Excel**

FIGURE H-17: Completed Subtotal dialog box

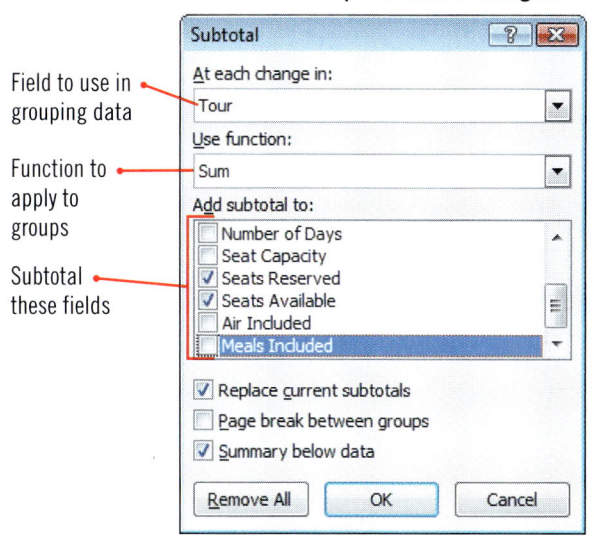

- Field to use in grouping data → At each change in: Tour
- Function to apply to groups → Use function: Sum
- Subtotal these fields → Add subtotal to: Seats Reserved, Seats Available

FIGURE H-18: Portion of subtotaled table

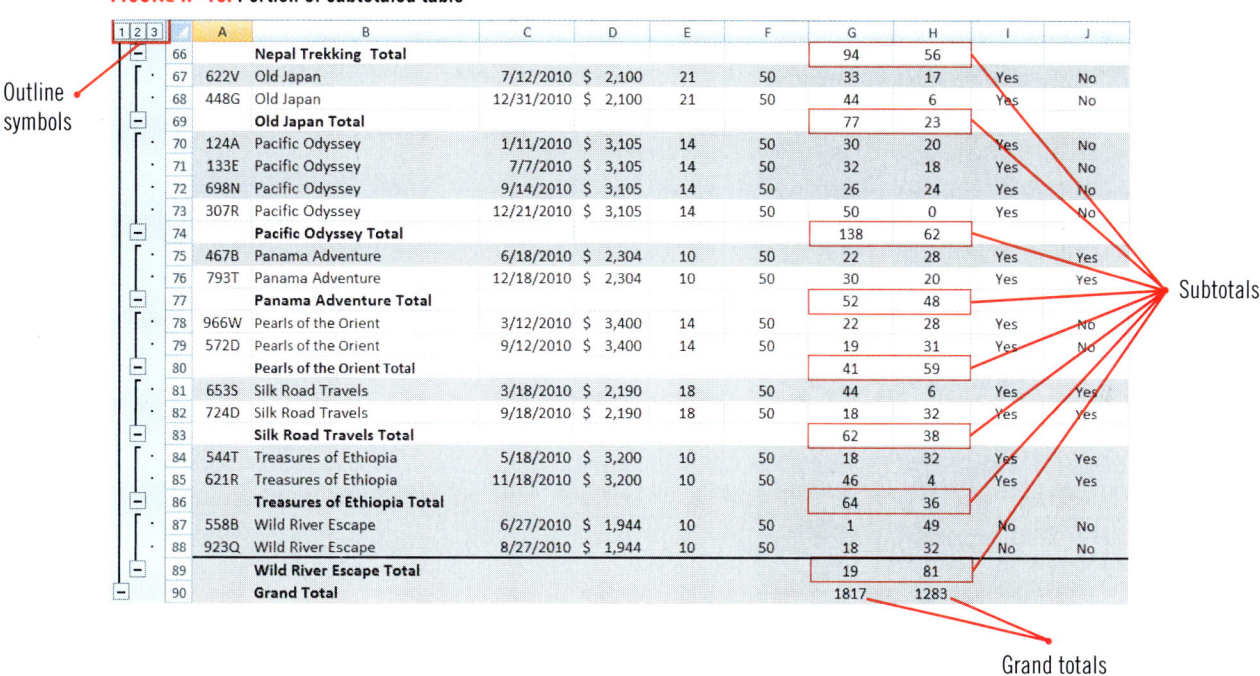

Outline symbols

	A	B	C	D	E	F	G	H	I	J
66		Nepal Trekking Total					94	56		
67	622V	Old Japan	7/12/2010	$ 2,100	21	50	33	17	Yes	No
68	448G	Old Japan	12/31/2010	$ 2,100	21	50	44	6	Yes	No
69		**Old Japan Total**					77	23		
70	124A	Pacific Odyssey	1/11/2010	$ 3,105	14	50	30	20	Yes	No
71	133E	Pacific Odyssey	7/7/2010	$ 3,105	14	50	32	18	Yes	No
72	698N	Pacific Odyssey	9/14/2010	$ 3,105	14	50	26	24	Yes	No
73	307R	Pacific Odyssey	12/21/2010	$ 3,105	14	50	50	0	Yes	No
74		**Pacific Odyssey Total**					138	62		
75	467B	Panama Adventure	6/18/2010	$ 2,304	10	50	22	28	Yes	Yes
76	793T	Panama Adventure	12/18/2010	$ 2,304	10	50	30	20	Yes	Yes
77		**Panama Adventure Total**					52	48		
78	966W	Pearls of the Orient	3/12/2010	$ 3,400	14	50	22	28	Yes	No
79	572D	Pearls of the Orient	9/12/2010	$ 3,400	14	50	19	31	Yes	No
80		**Pearls of the Orient Total**					41	59		
81	653S	Silk Road Travels	3/18/2010	$ 2,190	18	50	44	6	Yes	Yes
82	724D	Silk Road Travels	9/18/2010	$ 2,190	18	50	18	32	Yes	Yes
83		**Silk Road Travels Total**					62	38		
84	544T	Treasures of Ethiopia	5/18/2010	$ 3,200	10	50	18	32	Yes	Yes
85	621R	Treasures of Ethiopia	11/18/2010	$ 3,200	10	50	46	4	Yes	Yes
86		**Treasures of Ethiopia Total**					64	36		
87	558B	Wild River Escape	6/27/2010	$ 1,944	10	50	1	49	No	No
88	923Q	Wild River Escape	8/27/2010	$ 1,944	10	50	18	32	No	No
89		**Wild River Escape Total**					19	81		
90		**Grand Total**					1817	1283		

Subtotals

Grand totals

Practice

SAM — If you have a SAM user profile, you may have access to hands-on instruction, practice, and assessment of the skills covered in this unit. Log in to your SAM account (http://sam2007.course.com/) to launch any assigned training activities or exams that relate to the skills covered in this unit.

▼ CONCEPTS REVIEW

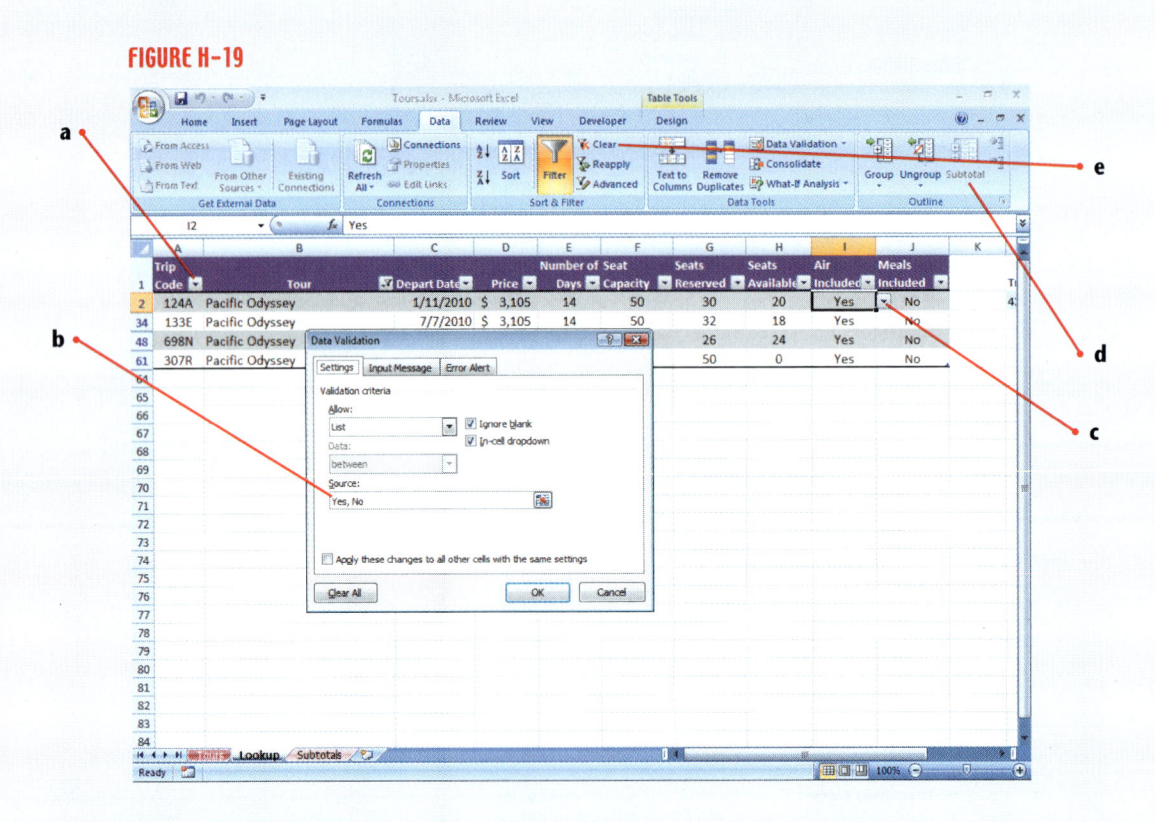

FIGURE H-19

1. Which element do you click to specify acceptable data entries for a table?
2. Which element points to a field's list arrow?
3. Which element do you click to group data and summarize data in a table?
4. Which element would you click to remove a filter?
5. Which element points to an In-cell dropdown list arrow?

Match each term with the statement that best describes it.

6. DSUM
7. Data validation
8. Criteria range
9. Extracted table
10. Table_array

a. Cell range when Advanced Filter results are copied to another location
b. Range in which search conditions are set
c. Restricts table entries to specified options
d. Name of the table searched in a VLOOKUP function
e. Function used to total table values that meet specified criteria

Select the best answer from the list of choices.

11. The _____ logical condition finds records matching both listed criteria.
    a. Or
    b. And
    c. True
    d. False

12. What does it mean when you select the Or option when creating a custom filter?
    a. Both criteria must be true to find a match.
    b. Neither criterion has to be 100% true.
    c. Either criterion can be true to find a match.
    d. A custom filter requires a criteria range.

Excel 194   Analyzing Table Data

13. What must a data range have before subtotals can be inserted?

a. Enough records to show multiple subtotals
b. Grand totals
c. Formatted cells
d. Sorted data

14. Which function finds the position of an item in a table?

a. MATCH
b. VLOOKUP
c. DGET
d. HLOOKUP

▼ SKILLS REVIEW

1. Filter a table.

a. Start Excel, open the file EX H-2.xlsx from the drive and folder where you store your Data Files, then save it as **Salary Summary**.
b. With the Compensation sheet active, filter the table to list only records for employees in the Boston branch.
c. Clear the filter, then add a filter that displays the records for employees in the Boston and Philadelphia branches.
d. Redisplay all employees, then use a filter to show the three employees with the highest annual salary.
e. Redisplay all the records, then save the workbook.

2. Create a custom filter.

a. Create a custom filter showing employees hired before 1/1/2007 or after 12/31/2007.
b. Create a custom filter showing employees hired between 1/1/2007 and 12/31/2007.
c. Enter your name in the worksheet footer, save the workbook, then preview and print the filtered worksheet.
d. Redisplay all records.
e. Save the workbook.

3. Filter and extract a table with Advanced Filter.

a. You want to retrieve a list of employees who were hired before 1/1/2008 and who have an annual salary of more than $80,000 a year. Define a criteria range by inserting six new rows above the table on the worksheet and copying the field names into the first row.
b. In cell D2, enter the criterion **<1/1/2008**, then in cell G2 enter **>80000**.
c. Click any cell in the table.
d. Open the Advanced Filter dialog box.
e. Indicate that you want to copy to another location, enter the criteria range **A1:J2**, verify that the List range is $A$7:$J$17, then indicate that you want to place the extracted list in the range starting at cell **A20**.
f. Confirm that the retrieved list meets the criteria as shown in Figure H-20.
g. Save the workbook, then preview and print the worksheet.

FIGURE H-20

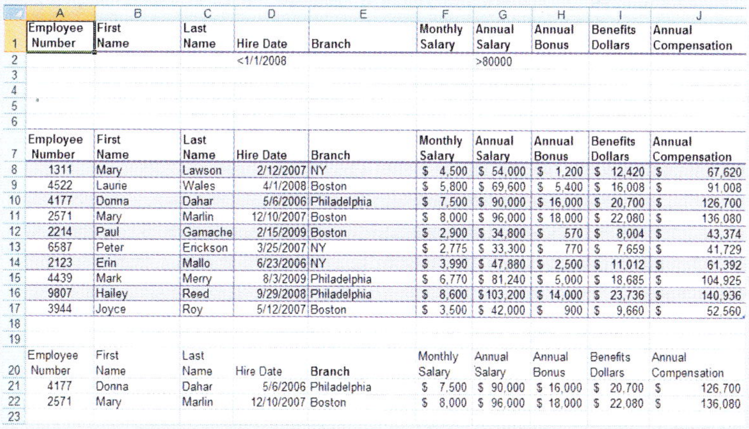

	A	B	C	D	E	F	G	H	I	J
1	Employee Number	First Name	Last Name	Hire Date	Branch	Monthly Salary	Annual Salary	Annual Bonus	Benefits Dollars	Annual Compensation
2				<1/1/2008			>80000			
3										
4										
5										
6										
7	Employee Number	First Name	Last Name	Hire Date	Branch	Monthly Salary	Annual Salary	Annual Bonus	Benefits Dollars	Annual Compensation
8	1311	Mary	Lawson	2/12/2007	NY	$ 4,500	$ 54,000	$ 1,200	$ 12,420	$ 67,620
9	4522	Laurie	Wales	4/1/2008	Boston	$ 5,800	$ 69,600	$ 5,400	$ 16,008	$ 91,008
10	4177	Donna	Dahar	5/6/2006	Philadelphia	$ 7,500	$ 90,000	$ 16,000	$ 20,700	$ 126,700
11	2571	Mary	Marlin	12/10/2007	Boston	$ 8,000	$ 96,000	$ 18,000	$ 22,080	$ 136,080
12	2214	Paul	Gamache	2/15/2009	Boston	$ 2,900	$ 34,800	$ 570	$ 8,004	$ 43,374
13	6587	Peter	Erickson	3/25/2007	NY	$ 2,775	$ 33,300	$ 770	$ 7,659	$ 41,729
14	2123	Erin	Mallo	6/23/2006	NY	$ 3,990	$ 47,880	$ 2,500	$ 11,012	$ 61,392
15	4439	Mark	Merry	8/3/2009	Philadelphia	$ 6,770	$ 81,240	$ 5,000	$ 18,685	$ 104,925
16	9807	Hailey	Reed	9/29/2008	Philadelphia	$ 8,600	$ 103,200	$ 14,000	$ 23,736	$ 140,936
17	3944	Joyce	Roy	5/12/2007	Boston	$ 3,500	$ 42,000	$ 900	$ 9,660	$ 52,560
18										
19										
20	Employee Number	First Name	Last Name	Hire Date	Branch	Monthly Salary	Annual Salary	Annual Bonus	Benefits Dollars	Annual Compensation
21	4177	Donna	Dahar	5/6/2006	Philadelphia	$ 7,500	$ 90,000	$ 16,000	$ 20,700	$ 126,700
22	2571	Mary	Marlin	12/10/2007	Boston	$ 8,000	$ 96,000	$ 18,000	$ 22,080	$ 136,080
23										

4. Look up values in a table.

a. Click the Summary sheet tab. Use the Name Manager to view the table names in the workbook, then close the dialog box.
b. You will use a lookup function to locate an employee's annual compensation; enter the Employee Number **2214** in cell A17.
c. In cell B17, use the VLOOKUP function and enter **A17** as the Lookup_value, **Table2** as the Table_array, **10** as the Col_index_num, and **FALSE** as the Range_lookup; observe the compensation displayed for that employee number, then check it against the table to make sure it is correct.
d. Enter another Employee Number, **4177**, in cell A17 and view the annual compensation for that employee.
e. Format cell B17 with the Accounting format with no decimal places and the $ symbol.
f. Save the workbook.

▼ SKILLS REVIEW (CONTINUED)

5. Summarize table data.

a. You want to enter a database function to average the annual salaries by branch, using the NY branch as the initial criterion. In cell E17, use the DAVERAGE function and click the top left corner of cell A1 twice to select the table and its header row as the Database, select cell G1 for the Field and select the range D16:D17 for the Criteria.

b. Test the function further by entering the text **Philadelphia** in cell D17. When the criterion is entered, cell E17 should display 91480.

c. Format cell E17 in Accounting format with no decimal places and the $ symbol.

d. Save the workbook.

6. Validation table data.

a. Select the data in column E of the table and set a validation criterion specifying that you want to allow a list of valid options.

b. Enter a list of valid options that restricts the entries to **NY**, **Boston**, and **Philadelphia**. Remember to use a comma between each item in the list.

c. Indicate that you want the options to appear in an in-cell dropdown list, then close the dialog box.

d. Add a row to the table. Go to cell E12, then select Boston in the dropdown list.

e. Select column F in the table and indicate that you want to restrict the data entered to only whole numbers. In the Minimum text box, enter **1000**; in the Maximum text box, enter **20000**. Close the dialog box.

f. Click cell F12, enter **25000**, then press [Enter]. You should get an error message.

g. Click Cancel, then enter **17000**.

h. Complete the new record by adding an Employee Number of 1112, a First Name of Caroline, a Last Name of Dow, a Hire Date of 2/1/2010, and an Annual Bonus of $1000. Format the range F12:J12 as Accounting with no decimal places and using the $ symbol. Compare your screen to Figure H-21.

i. Add your name to the center section of the footer, save, preview the worksheet and fit it to one page if necessary, then print it.

FIGURE H-21

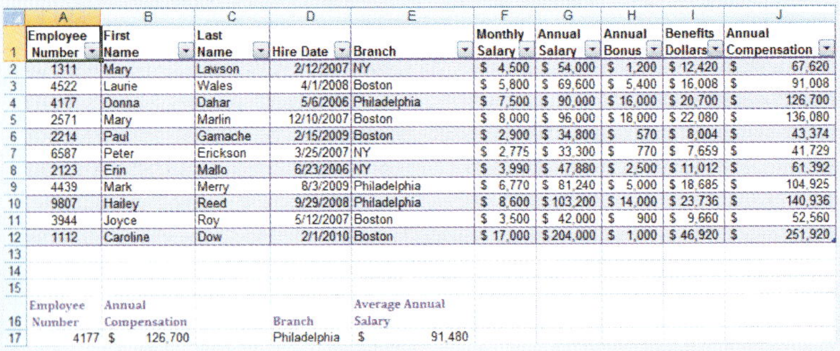

	A	B	C	D	E	F	G	H	I	J
1	Employee Number	First Name	Last Name	Hire Date	Branch	Monthly Salary	Annual Salary	Annual Bonus	Benefits Dollars	Annual Compensation
2	1311	Mary	Lawson	2/12/2007	NY	$ 4,500	$ 54,000	$ 1,200	$ 12,420	$ 67,620
3	4522	Laurie	Wales	4/1/2008	Boston	$ 5,800	$ 69,600	$ 5,400	$ 16,008	$ 91,008
4	4177	Donna	Dahar	5/6/2006	Philadelphia	$ 7,500	$ 90,000	$ 16,000	$ 20,700	$ 126,700
5	2571	Mary	Marlin	12/10/2007	Boston	$ 8,000	$ 96,000	$ 18,000	$ 22,080	$ 136,080
6	2214	Paul	Gamache	2/15/2009	Boston	$ 2,900	$ 34,800	$ 570	$ 8,004	$ 43,374
7	6587	Peter	Erickson	3/25/2007	NY	$ 2,775	$ 33,300	$ 770	$ 7,659	$ 41,729
8	2123	Erin	Mallo	6/23/2006	NY	$ 3,990	$ 47,880	$ 2,500	$ 11,012	$ 61,392
9	4439	Mark	Merry	8/3/2009	Philadelphia	$ 6,770	$ 81,240	$ 5,000	$ 18,685	$ 104,925
10	9807	Hailey	Reed	9/29/2008	Philadelphia	$ 8,600	$ 103,200	$ 14,000	$ 23,736	$ 140,936
11	3944	Joyce	Roy	5/12/2007	Boston	$ 3,500	$ 42,000	$ 900	$ 9,660	$ 52,560
12	1112	Caroline	Dow	2/1/2010	Boston	$ 17,000	$ 204,000	$ 1,000	$ 46,920	$ 251,920
13										
14										
15										
16	Employee Number	Annual Compensation		Branch	Average Annual Salary					
17	4177	$ 126,700		Philadelphia	$ 91,480					

7. Create subtotals using grouping and outlines.

a. Click the Subtotals sheet tab.

b. Use the Department field list arrow to sort the table in ascending order by department.

c. Convert the table to a range.

d. Group and create subtotals by department, using the SUM function, then click the AnnualCompensation checkbox if necessary in the Add Subtotal to list.

e. Click the 2 outline button on the outline to display only the subtotals and the grand total. Compare your screen to Figure H-22.

f. Enter your name in the worksheet footer, save the workbook, preview, then print the subtotals and grand total.

g. Save the workbook, close the workbook, then exit Excel.

FIGURE H-22

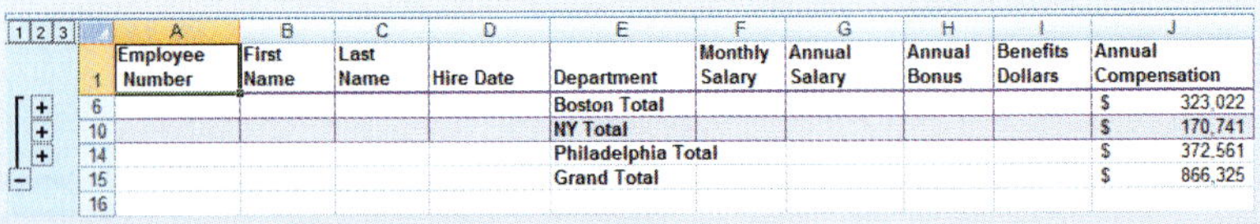

	A	B	C	D	E	F	G	H	I	J
1	Employee Number	First Name	Last Name	Hire Date	Department	Monthly Salary	Annual Salary	Annual Bonus	Benefits Dollars	Annual Compensation
6					Boston Total					$ 323,022
10					NY Total					$ 170,741
14					Philadelphia Total					$ 372,561
15					Grand Total					$ 866,325
16										

▼ INDEPENDENT CHALLENGE 1

As the owner of Preserves, a gourmet food store located in Dublin, Ireland, you spend a lot of time managing your inventory. To help with this task, you have created an Excel table of your jam inventory. You want to filter the table and add subtotals and a grand total to the table. You also need to add data validation and summary information to the table.

▼ INDEPENDENT CHALLENGE 1 (CONTINUED)

a. Start Excel, open the file EX H-3.xlsx from the drive and folder where you store your Data Files, then save it as **Jams**.

b. Using the table data on the Inventory sheet, create a filter to generate a list of rhubarb jams. Enter your name in the worksheet footer, save the workbook, then preview and print the table. Clear the filter.

c. Use a Custom Filter to generate a list of jams with a quantity greater than 20. Preview, then print the table. Clear the filter.

d. Copy the labels in cells A1:F1 into A16:F16. Type **Gooseberry** in cell B17 and type **Small** in cell C17. Use the Advanced Filter with a criteria range of A16:F17 to extract a table of small gooseberry jams to the range of cells beginning in cell A20. Save the workbook, preview, then print the table with the extracted information.

e. Click the Summary sheet tab, select the table data in column B. Open the Data Validation dialog box, then indicate you want to use a validation list with the acceptable entries of **Gooseberry, Blackberry, Rhubarb**. Make sure the In-cell dropdown check box is selected.

f. Test the data validation by trying to change a cell in column B of the table to Strawberry.

g. Using Figure H-23 as a guide, enter a function in cell G18 that calculates the total quantity of blackberry jam in your store. Enter your name in the worksheet footer, save the workbook, then preview and print the worksheet.

h. Use the filter list arrow for the Type of Jam field to sort the table in ascending order by type of jam. Convert the table to a range. Insert subtotals by type of jam using the SUM function, then select Quantity in the Add Subtotal to table box. Use the appropriate button on the outline to display only the subtotals and grand total. (Note that the number of Blackberry Jams calculated in cell G22 is incorrect after subtotals are added because the subtotals are included in the database calculation.) Save the workbook, preview, then print the range containing the subtotals and grand total.

FIGURE H-23

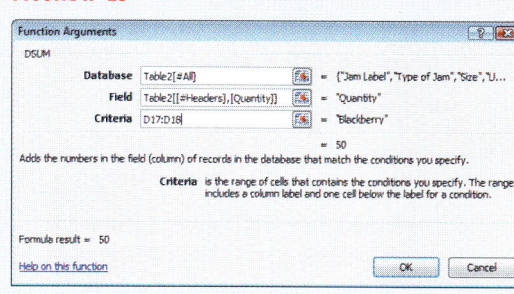

FIGURE H-24

Advanced Challenge Exercise

- Clear the subtotals from the worksheet.
- Use conditional formatting to add icons to the quantity field using the following criteria: quantities greater than or equal to 20 are formatted with a green check mark, quantities greater than or equal to 10 but less than 20 are formatted with a yellow exclamation point, and quantities less than 10 are formatted with a red x. Use Figure H-24 as a guide to adding the formatting rule, then compare your Quantity values to Figure H-25. (*Hint*: You may need to click in the top Value text box for the correct value to display for the red x.)
- Save the workbook, preview then print the worksheet.

i. Close the workbook, then exit Excel.

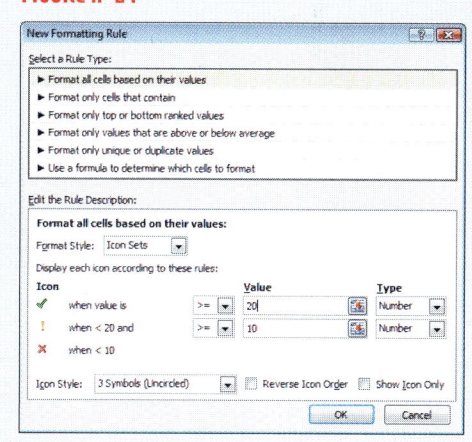

FIGURE H-25

	A	B	C	D	E	F
1	Jam Label	Type of Jam	Size	Unit Price	Quantity	Total
2	Tipperary Ranch	Blackberry	Medium	6.00	! 11	66.00
3	Galway Estate	Blackberry	Small	5.25	! 12	63.00
4	Wexford Hills	Blackberry	Medium	5.75	! 15	86.25
5	Kerry Lane	Blackberry	Small	6.55	! 12	78.60
6	Tipperary Ranch	Gooseberry	Small	5.75	x 6	34.50
7	Cork Estate	Gooseberry	Small	5.75	x 8	46.00
8	Wexford Hills	Gooseberry	Small	5.75	✓ 21	120.75
9	Kerry Lane	Gooseberry	Medium	7.25	! 18	130.50
10	Tipperary Ranch	Rhubarb	Small	6.50	x 5	32.50
11	Galway Estate	Rhubarb	Small	6.25	! 11	68.75
12	Wexford Hills	Rhubarb	Small	5.25	✓ 31	162.75
13	Kerry Lane	Rhubarb	Medium	7.55	✓ 24	181.20
14						

▼ INDEPENDENT CHALLENGE 2

You recently started a personalized pet tag business, called Paw Tags. The business sells engraved cat and dog tags. Customers order tags for their cat or dog and provide you with the name of the pet and whether they want engraving on one or both sides of the tag. You have put together an invoice table to track sales for the month of October. Now that you have this table, you would like to manipulate it in several ways. First, you want to filter the table to retrieve only tags retailing for more than a particular price and ordered during a particular part of the month. You also want to subtotal the unit price and total cost columns by tag and restrict entries in the Order Date column. Finally, you would like to add database and lookup functions to your worksheet to efficiently retrieve data from the table.

▼ INDEPENDENT CHALLENGE 2 (CONTINUED)

a. Start Excel, open the file EX H-4.xlsx from the drive and folder where you store your Data Files, then save it as **Paw Tags**.
b. Use the Advanced Filter to show tags with a price of $12.99 ordered before 10/15/2010, using cells A27:B28 to enter your criteria and filtering the table in place. (*Hint*: You don't need to specify an entire row as the criteria range.) Enter your name in the worksheet footer, save the workbook, then print the filtered table. Clear the filter, then save your work again.
c. Use the Data Validation dialog box to restrict entries to those with order dates on or after 10/1/2010 and before or on 10/31/2010. Test the data restrictions by attempting to enter an invalid date in cell D25.
d. Enter **23721** in cell F28. Enter a VLOOKUP function in cell G28 to retrieve the total based on the invoice number entered in cell F28. Make sure you have an exact match with the invoice number. Test the function with the invoice number 23718.
e. Enter the date **10/1/2010** in cell I28. Use the database function, DCOUNT, in cell J28 to count the number of invoices for the date in cell I28. Save the workbook.
f. Sort the table in ascending order by Tag, then convert the table to a range. Create subtotals showing the number of cat and dog tags in the Invoice Number column. Save your subtotaled data, then preview and print the Invoice worksheet.

Advanced Challenge Exercise

- Clear the subtotals and create a table using the data in the range A1:J25. Change the font color of the column headers to white. If the font headers are not visible, change the font color to one that contrasts with the fill color of your headers.
- Use the filtering feature to display only the Cat tags, then add a total row to display the number of cat tags in cell E26. Change the font color in cells A26 and E26 to white. If the contents of cells A26 and E26 are not visible, change the font color to one that contrasts with the fill color for those cells. Delete the total in cell J26.
- Use conditional formatting to format the cells where the Total is greater than $12.00 with light red fill and dark red text.
- Using the Total Filter arrow, sort the table by color to display the totals exceeding $12.00 on top. Filter the table by color to display only the rows with totals greater than $12.00.

g. Save the workbook, print the Invoice worksheet, close the workbook, then exit Excel.

▼ INDEPENDENT CHALLENGE 3

You are the manager of Green Mountain, a gift shop in Burlington, Vermont. You have created an Excel table that contains your order data, along with the amounts for each item ordered and the date the order was placed. You would like to manipulate this table to display product categories and ordered items meeting specific criteria. You would also like to add subtotals to the table and add database functions to total orders. Finally, you want to restrict entries in the Category column.

a. Start Excel, open the file EX H-5.xlsx from the drive and folder where you store your Data Files, then save it as **Gifts**.
b. Using the table data, create an advanced filter that retrieves, to its current location, records with dates before 9/10/2010 and whose orders were greater than $1000, using cells A37:E38 to enter your criteria for the filter. Clear the filter.
c. Create an advanced filter that extracts records with the following criteria to cell A42: orders greater than $1000 having dates either before 9/10/2010 or after 9/24/2010. (*Hint*: Recall that when you want records to meet one criterion or another, you need to place the criteria on separate lines.) Enter your name in the worksheet footer, then preview and print the worksheet.
d. Use the DSUM function in cell H2 to let worksheet users find the total order amounts for the category entered in cell G2. Format the cell containing the total order using the Accounting format with the $ symbol and no decimals. Test the DSUM function using the Food category name. (The sum for the Food category should be $5,998.) Print the worksheet.
e. Use data validation to create an in-cell drop-down that restricts category entries to Food, Clothing, Book, Personal. Use the Error Alert tab of the Data Validation dialog box to set the alert level to the Warning style with the message "Data is not valid." Test the validation in the table with valid and invalid entries.

▼ INDEPENDENT CHALLENGE 3 (CONTINUED)

f. Sort the table by category in ascending order. Add Subtotals to the order amounts by category. The total order amount in cell H2 will be incorrect after adding subtotals because the subtotals will be included in the database calculation.

g. Use the outline to display only category names with subtotals and the grand total.

Advanced Challenge Exercise

- Clear the subtotals from the worksheet.
- Conditionally format the 1-Month Order data using Top/Bottom Rules to emphasize the cells containing the top 10 percent with yellow fill and dark yellow text.
- Add another rule to format the bottom 10 percent in the 1-Month Order column with a light blue fill.

h. Save the workbook, preview, then print the worksheet.

i. Close the workbook, then exit Excel.

▼ REAL LIFE INDEPENDENT CHALLENGE

You decide to organize your business and personal contacts using the Excel table format. You want to use the table to look up cell, home, and work phone numbers. You also want to include addresses and a field documenting whether the contact relationship is personal or business. You enter your contact information in an Excel worksheet that you will convert to a table so you can easily filter the data. You also use lookup functions to locate phone numbers when you provide a last name in your table. Finally, you restrict the entries in one of the fields to values in drop-down lists to simplify future data entry and reduce errors.

a. Start Excel, open a new workbook, then save it as **Contacts** in the drive and folder where you store your Data Files.

b. Use the structure of Table H-2 to enter at least six of your personal and business contacts into a worksheet. (*Hint*: You will need to format the Zip column using the Zip Code type of the Special category.) In the Relationship field, enter either Business or Personal. If you don't have phone numbers for all the phone fields, leave them blank.

TABLE H-2

Last name	First name	Cell phone	Home phone	Work phone	Street address	City	State	Zip	Relationship

c. Use the worksheet information to create a table. Use the Name Manager dialog box to edit the table name to Contacts.

d. Create a filter that retrieves records of personal contacts. Clear the filter.

e. Create a filter that retrieves records of business contacts. Clear the filter.

f. Restrict the Relationship field entries to Business or Personal. Provide an in-cell drop-down list allowing the selection of these two options. Add an input message of **Select from the dropdown list**. Add an Information level error message of **Choose Business or Personal**. Test the validation by adding a new record to your table.

g. Below your table, create a phone lookup area with the following labels in adjacent cells: **Last name**, **Cell phone**, **Home phone**, **Work phone**.

h. Enter one of the last names from your table under the label Last Name in your phone lookup area.

i. In the phone lookup area, enter lookup functions to locate the cell phone, home phone, and work phone numbers for the contact last name that you entered in the previous step. Make sure you match the last name exactly.

j. Enter your name in the center section of the worksheet footer, save the workbook, preview, then print the worksheet on one page.

k. Close the workbook, then exit Excel.

▼ VISUAL WORKSHOP

Open the file EX H-6.xlsx from the drive and folder where you save your Data Files, then save it as **Schedule**. Complete the worksheet as shown in Figure H-26. Cells B18:E18 contain lookup functions that find the instructor, day, time, and room for the course entered in cell A18. Use HIS101 in cell A18 to test your lookup functions. The range A22:G27 is extracted from the table using the criteria in cells A20:A21. Add your name to the worksheet footer, save the workbook, then preview and print the worksheet.

FIGURE H-26

	A	B	C	D	E	F	G
1	Spring 2011 Schedule of History Classes						
2							
3	Course number	ID #	Time	Day	Room	Credits	Instructor
4	HIS100	1245	8:00 - 9:00	M,W,F	126	3	Walsh
5	HIS101	1356	8:00 - 9:30	T,TH	136	3	Guan
6	HIS102	1567	9:00 - 10:00	M,W,F	150	3	Marshall
7	HIS103	1897	10:00 - 11:30	T,TH	226	3	Benson
8	HIS104	3456	2:00 - 3:30	M,W,F	129	4	Paulson
9	HIS200	4678	12:00 - 1:30	T,TH	156	3	Dash
10	HIS300	7562	3:00 - 4:30	M,W,F	228	4	Christopher
11	HIS400	9823	11:00 - 12:00	M,W,F	103	3	Robbinson
12	HIS500	7123	3:00 - 4:30	T,TH	214	3	Matthews
13							
14							
15							
16							
17	Course Number	Instructor	Day	Time	Room		
18	HIS101	Guan	T,TH	8:00 - 9:30	136		
19							
20	Day						
21	M,W,F						
22	Course number	ID #	Time	Day	Room	Credits	Instructor
23	HIS100	1245	8:00 - 9:00	M,W,F	126	3	Walsh
24	HIS102	1567	9:00 - 10:00	M,W,F	150	3	Marshall
25	HIS104	3456	2:00 - 3:30	M,W,F	129	4	Paulson
26	HIS300	7562	3:00 - 4:30	M,W,F	228	4	Christopher
27	HIS400	9823	11:00 - 12:00	M,W,F	103	3	Robbinson
28							

UNIT D
Integrating Word and Excel

Files You Will Need:
INT D-1.docx
INT D-2.xlsx
INT D-3.xlsx
INT D-4.docx
INT D-5.xlsx
INT D-6.xlsx
INT D-7.docx
INT D-8.xlsx
INT D-9.docx
INT D-10.xlsx
INT D-11.docx
INT D-12.xlsx
INT D-13.docx

As you have learned, you use Word to create documents that contain primarily text and you use Excel to create workbooks that contain primarily values and calculations. Sometimes, the documents you create in Word need to include values that result from calculations you made in an Excel worksheet. You can embed an Excel worksheet in a Word document and use Excel tools to modify it, or you can insert an Excel file directly into a Word document. When you don't want to include Excel data in your Word document, but you still want your readers to access the information, you can create a hyperlink from a Word document to an Excel worksheet. You can also create a hyperlink from an Excel worksheet to a Word document. You are working as an assistant to Bertram Lamont, the manager of the corporate division of QST London, one of the two international branches of Quest Specialty Travel. Bertram is in charge of selling QST tours to corporate clients. He has asked you to link business letters created in Word with invoices created in Excel.

OBJECTIVES

Use Paste Special to modify formatting
Create a hyperlink between Word and Excel
Create an Excel spreadsheet in Word
Embed an Excel file in Word
Change link sources

UNIT D
Integration

Using Paste Special to Modify Formatting

When you paste an object into an Office program using the Paste Special command, you can specify how you want that object to appear. You can choose to retain the original formatting of the pasted object, you can remove all the formatting, or you can even paste the object as a picture that you can enhance with special effects, border styles, fill colors, 3D formatting, shadows, and rotation effects. Figure D-1 shows all the Paste Special options available and how each option formats the pasted value of $8.00. Bertram Lamont, the manager of the corporate division of QST London, accompanies every invoice he sends to corporate clients with a letter. Bertram asks you to modify the letter so that it contains information related to a tour to Scotland taken by the employees of Southwark Consultants.

STEPS

1. Start Word, open the file **INT D-1.docx** from the drive and folder where you store your Data Files, save it as **Southwark Consultants Letter 1**, start Excel, open the file **INT D-2.xlsx** from the drive and folder where you store your Data Files, then save it as **Southwark Consultants Invoices**

2. In Excel, click cell **G17**, enter the formula **=A17*F17**, copy the formula to the range **G18:G21**, click cell **G22**, click the **Sum button Σ** in the Editing group, press **[Enter]**, select the range **F17:G22**, click the **Accounting Number Format button list arrow $** in the Number group, then click **£ English (United Kingdom)** as shown in Figure D-2

QUICK TIP
In the Paste Special dialog box, you can choose to paste a copied object in a variety of formats, most of which are also available when you paste an object as a link.

3. Select the range **A10:A13**, click the **Copy button** in the Clipboard group, switch to Word, select **INSIDE ADDRESS**, click the **Paste button list arrow**, then click **Paste Special**

In the Paste Special dialog box, you can choose to paste a copied object in a variety of formats, most of which are also available when you paste an object as a link.

4. Click the **Paste link option button**, click **Unformatted Text**, click **OK**, then press **[Enter]** once to add a blank line below the text

You can modify the formatting of pasted text just as you would modify any Word text.

5. Select the four lines of pasted text, change the font to **Calibri**, then change the font size to **12 point**

6. Switch to Excel, select the range **B17:B21**, click the **Copy button**, switch to Word, select **ITEMS** below paragraph 2, click the **Paste list arrow**, click **Paste Special**, click the **Paste link option button**, click **Formatted Text (RTF)**, then click **OK**

The four cells are pasted in the form of a long, thin table. When you select the Formatted Text (RTF) option, you can modify the pasted object in the same way you would modify any Word table.

QUICK TIP
Be sure you deselect Banded Columns and not Banded Rows so every other row is shaded.

7. Delete one blank line above the pasted table, move the mouse over the upper-left corner of the table, click the **table select icon**, click the **Table Tools Design tab**, select the **Light Shading - Accent 1** table style (light blue), click the **Banded Columns check box** to deselect it, double-click the right border of the pasted table, then click outside the table

The column width of the pasted table expands so all the information is visible.

8. Switch to Excel, click cell **G22**, click the **Copy button**, switch to Word, select **XX** in paragraph 2, paste the item as a linked Microsoft Office Excel Worksheet Object

9. Click after Dear, type **Ms. Winton:**, save the document, compare the letter to Figure D-3, switch to Excel, then save and close the workbook

FIGURE D-1: Paste Special Options from Excel to Word

Value in Excel pasted in Word

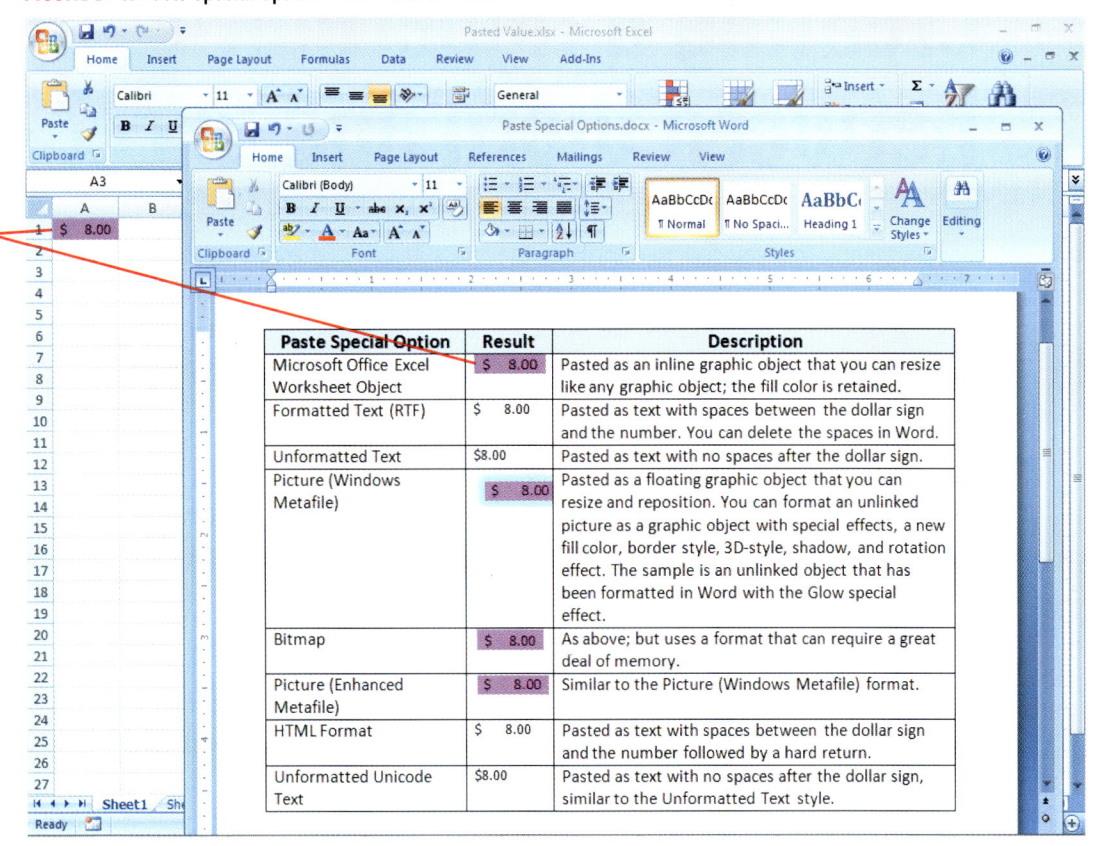

Paste Special Option	Result	Description
Microsoft Office Excel Worksheet Object	$ 8.00	Pasted as an inline graphic object that you can resize like any graphic object; the fill color is retained.
Formatted Text (RTF)	$ 8.00	Pasted as text with spaces between the dollar sign and the number. You can delete the spaces in Word.
Unformatted Text	$8.00	Pasted as text with no spaces after the dollar sign.
Picture (Windows Metafile)	$ 8.00	Pasted as a floating graphic object that you can resize and reposition. You can format an unlinked picture as a graphic object with special effects, a new fill color, border style, 3D-style, shadow, and rotation effect. The sample is an unlinked object that has been formatted in Word with the Glow special effect.
Bitmap	$ 8.00	As above; but uses a format that can require a great deal of memory.
Picture (Enhanced Metafile)	$ 8.00	Similar to the Picture (Windows Metafile) format.
HTML Format	$ 8.00	Pasted as text with spaces between the dollar sign and the number followed by a hard return.
Unformatted Unicode Text	$8.00	Pasted as text with no spaces after the dollar sign, similar to the Unformatted Text style.

FIGURE D-2: Modifying the Currency style

£ English (United Kingdom) currency style selected

FIGURE D-3: Letter containing three linked Excel objects

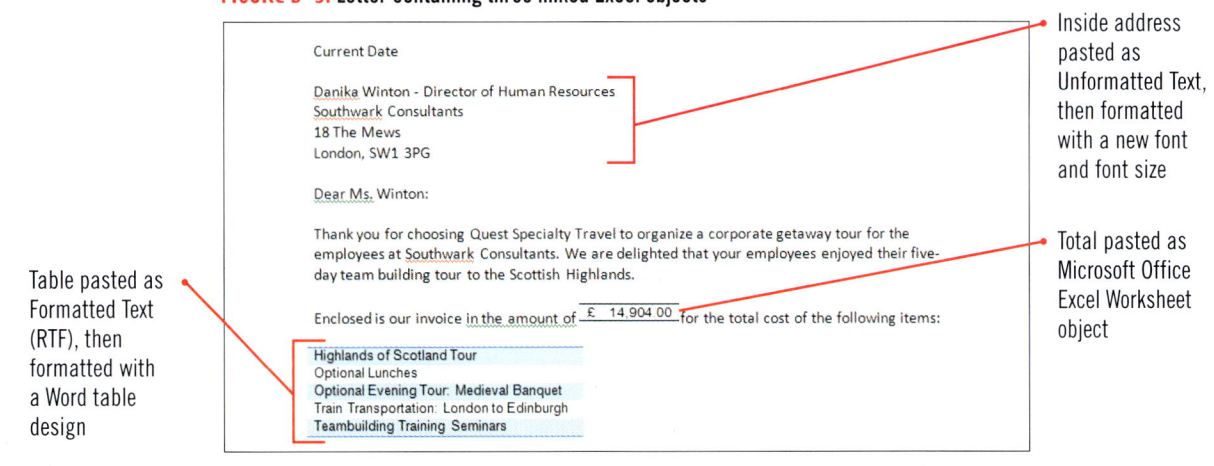

Inside address pasted as Unformatted Text, then formatted with a new font and font size

Total pasted as Microsoft Office Excel Worksheet object

Table pasted as Formatted Text (RTF), then formatted with a Word table design

Integrating Word and Excel

Integration 51

UNIT D Integration

Creating a Hyperlink Between Word and Excel

You can create hyperlinks to access data from other documents and programs. A **hyperlink** is a text element or graphic that you click to display another place in a file, other files created in the same or other programs, or a location on the Internet. When you copy, paste, and link data between programs, you actually bring the data into the destination file. When you click a hyperlink from a source file to a location in a destination file, the destination file opens. You often create hyperlinks between two files that you plan to send electronically. Instead of combining all the information into one file in one program, you can create two documents, such as a letter or other document in Word, and a spreadsheet showing calculations in Excel, and insert hyperlinks in one document that open the other document. The person who receives the two files can use the hyperlinks to jump quickly between them. Bertram plans to send an electronic copy of both the letter and the invoice to Southwark Consultants. He asks you to create a hyperlink between the letter in Word and the invoice in Excel so that the client can view the invoice directly from the letter.

STEPS

1. **In Word, select the word here in the first sentence of the third paragraph**

2. **Click the Insert tab, click the Hyperlink button in the Links group, then verify that Existing File or Web Page is selected**

   In the Insert Hyperlink dialog box, you can create a link to an existing file or to a place in the current document, or you can create a hyperlink that opens a new document or opens an e-mail program so you can send an e-mail.

3. **Click the Browse for File button, navigate to the location where your Solution Files are stored, then double-click the filename Southwark Consultants Invoices.xlsx**

   The Insert Hyperlink dialog box appears as shown in Figure D-4. You can include text in a ScreenTip that appears when users point to the hyperlink. This text can advise users what will happen when they click the hyperlink.

4. **Click ScreenTip in the Insert Hyperlink dialog box, then type This link opens Southwark Consultants Invoices in Excel**

5. **Click OK, then click OK again**

   The word "here" becomes blue and underlined, indicating that it is now a hyperlink that, when clicked, will open another document, which in this case is the Excel invoice.

6. **Move your pointer over here, read the ScreenTip that appears as shown in Figure D-5, press [Ctrl], then click the here**

   The link opens the Southwark Consultants Invoices file.

7. **In Excel, click cell A28, type Thank you for your business!, format it with italics, center it across the range A28:G28, then enter the current date in cell G10 and your name in cell G13**

8. **Click the Office button, point to Print, click Print Preview, then click the Page Setup button in the Print group**

9. **Click the Margins tab if necessary, click the Horizontally check box if it's not already selected, click OK, compare your screen to Figure D-6, click the Print button in the Print group, then click OK in the Print dialog box**

   A copy of Invoice 702 for Southwark Consultants prints, with the invoice data centered between the left and right margins.

FIGURE D-4: Insert Hyperlink dialog box

ScreenTip button

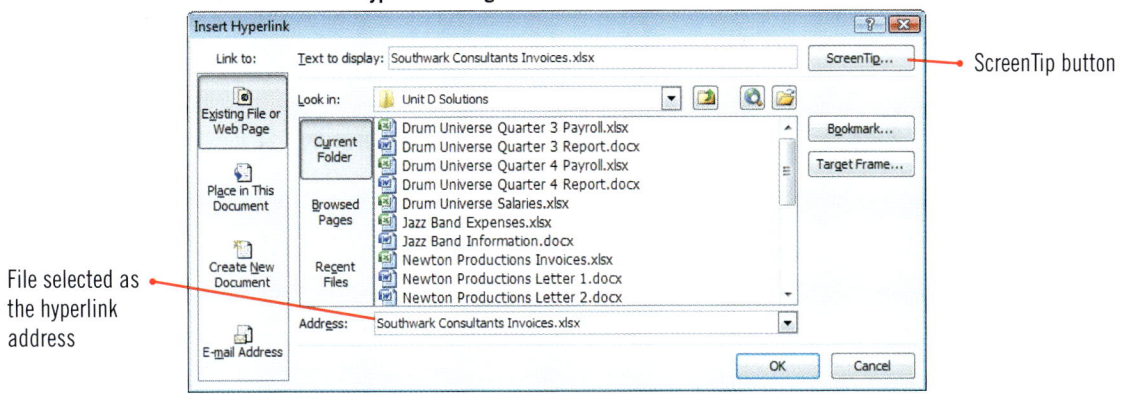

File selected as the hyperlink address

FIGURE D-5: Viewing the ScreenTip

ScreenTip appears when the mouse moves over the hyperlink

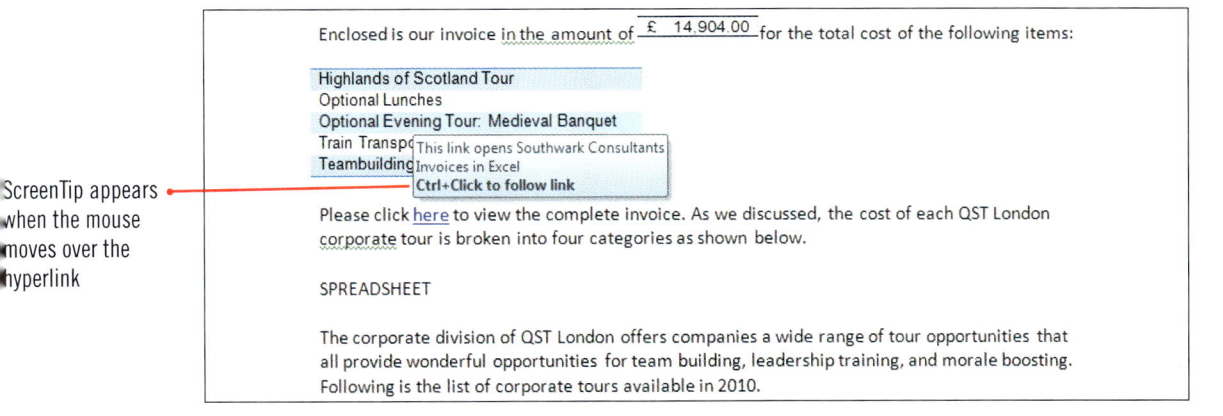

FIGURE D-6: Invoice in Print Preview

Editing and removing a hyperlink

To edit a hyperlink, right-click the underlined text, then click Edit Hyperlink. In the Edit Hyperlink dialog box, you can change the destination of the hyperlink, modify the ScreenTip, and even remove the hyperlink. You can also remove a hyperlink by right-clicking it, then clicking Remove Hyperlink. The underlining that identifies the text as a hyperlink is removed; however, the text itself remains.

Integrating Word and Excel Integration 53

UNIT D
Integration

Creating an Excel Spreadsheet in Word

In cases where you don't need to store spreadsheet data in a separate Excel file, you can use the Table command to create an Excel spreadsheet in Word and then use Excel tools to enter labels and values and make calculations. The Excel spreadsheet object is an embedded object in the Word file. To modify it, you double-click it and then use Excel tools that become available inside of the Word program window. You need the letter to break down the corporate tour price into its component parts. You create the data in an embedded Excel spreadsheet so that you can use Excel tools to make calculations and apply formatting.

STEPS

1. Switch to Word, then select SPREADSHEET below paragraph 3
2. On the Insert tab, click the Table button, then click Excel Spreadsheet
   A blank Excel spreadsheet appears in the Word document, and Excel tools appear in the Ribbon. However, Microsoft Word still appears in the title bar, indicating that you are working in Excel from within the Word program.
3. Enter the spreadsheet labels and values shown in Figure D-7, adjust column widths if necessary, select the range A1:E1, center and bold the labels, change the fill color to Blue, Accent 1, Darker 50% and the font color to White Background 1, then format the range A2:E2 with the £ English (United Kingdom) accounting format
4. Click cell E2, click the Sum button Σ in the Editing group, then press [Enter]
5. Click cell A3, enter the formula =A2/$E$2, copy the formula to the range B3:D3, then with the cells still selected, click the Percent Style button % in the Number group
6. Drag the sizing handles on the spreadsheet object to reduce its size so it displays only the data in the range A1:E3
7. Click outside the spreadsheet object to return to Word, then delete SPREADSHEET
8. Double-click the spreadsheet object, change the cost of Lodging to £490.00, click outside the spreadsheet object, then save the document
   The total updates to reflect the change in Lodging. The completed spreadsheet object appears in Word as shown in Figure D-8.
9. Switch to Excel, then save and close Southwark Consultants Invoices.xlsx

FIGURE D-7: Excel spreadsheet embedded in Word

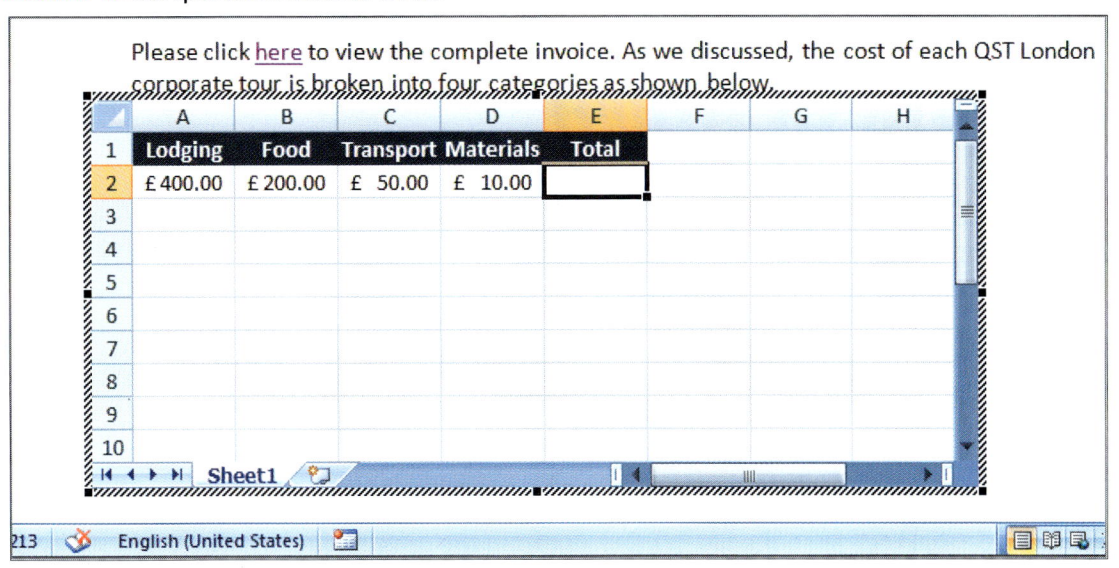

FIGURE D-8: Completed spreadsheet object

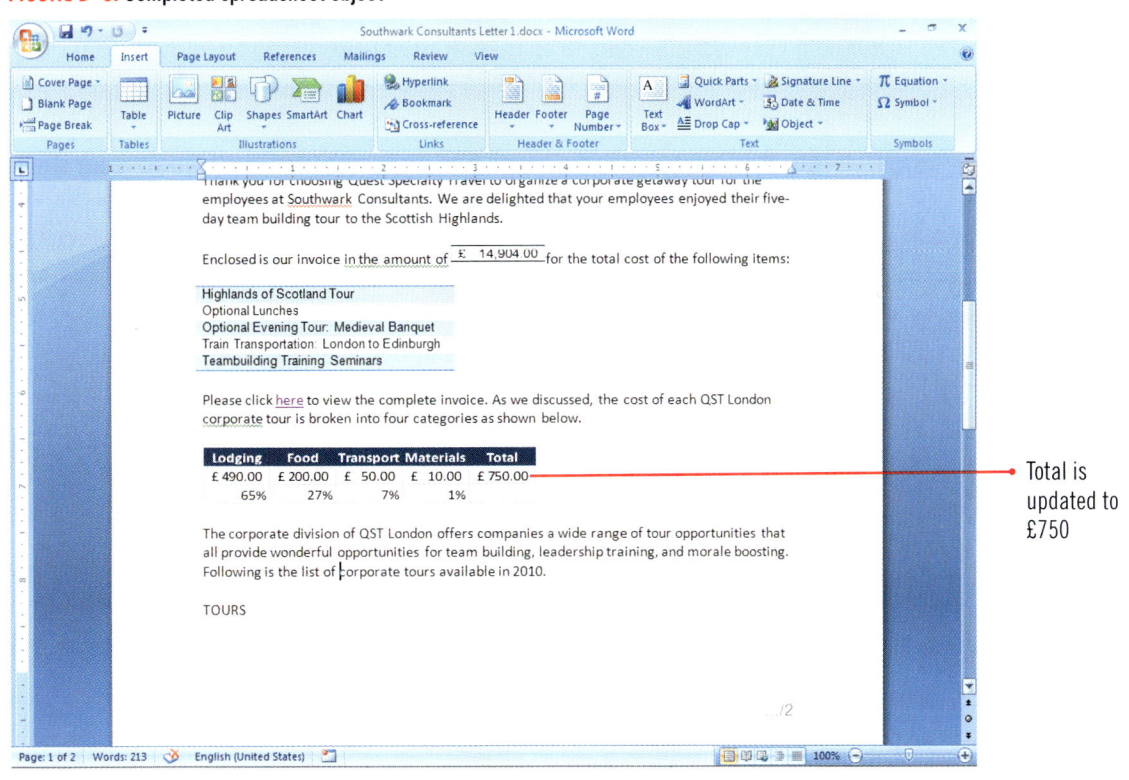

Total is updated to £750

Integrating Word and Excel   Integration 55

UNIT D
Integration

Embedding an Excel File in Word

In Unit A, you learned that when you embed a Word file in an Excel spreadsheet, the original Word formatting is retained. You then edit the embedded file by double-clicking it and using Word tools to make changes to the text and formatting. You use the same procedure to embed an Excel file in Word. In general, when you create a file in one program and embed it into another program, the formatting of the original file is retained. Table D-1 summarizes the integration tasks you performed In this unit. You want the letter to include the list of corporate tours offered by QST London in 2010. This list is already saved in an Excel file, which you decide to embed in your Word letter.

STEPS

1. In Excel, open the file **INT D-3.xlsx** from the drive and folder where you store your Data Files, save it as **QST London Tours**, then close the file

2. In Word, click to place the insertion point to the left of the paragraph that begins, "The corporate division of QST London", then press [Ctrl][Enter] to insert a page break

TROUBLE
If you click the Object button list arrow, you need to select Object from the list of options.

3. Select **TOURS**, then on the Insert tab, click the **Object button** in the Text group

4. Click the **Create from File** tab

5. Click **Browse**, navigate to where you stored QST London Tours.xlsx, double-click **QST London Tours.xlsx**, then click **OK**

   You do not anticipate needing to update the list of tours, so you insert the Excel file into the Word document as an Excel object that is not linked to the source file. Any changes you make to the Excel file in Word are not made to the source file.

6. Delete **TOURS** and the extra blank line, if necessary, then double-click the Excel object

   The object is embedded, so you edit it by double-clicking it and using the source program tools. The Excel Ribbon and tabs replace the Word ones; however, the title bar shows that you are still working in the Word document and using Excel tools only to modify the embedded Excel file. The Verve theme was applied to the inserted Excel file. You want the fill colors in the worksheet to match the colors used to format the letter.

7. Click the **Page Layout tab**, click **Colors** in the Themes group, then click **Office**

   The fill colors change to those of the Office color scheme as shown in Figure D-9.

8. Click outside the embedded worksheet object to return to Word, enter your name where indicated in the closing, then enter the current date where indicated at the top of the document

9. Show the document in Print Preview, view the letter in Two Pages view as shown in Figure D-10, print a copy, close Print Preview, then save the document

---

Formatting pasted, embedded, and linked objects

When you work with Copy and Paste Special options, as you did in the first lesson of this unit, you select options in the Paste Special dialog box to format the copied object. With embedded objects, you double-click them in the destination program to change content or formatting using the source program's tools. For linked objects, such as a chart or a worksheet range, you modify the object in the source program, which will then automatically update in the destination program. The exception occurs when you link an entire file to a document in a destination program. In that case, you can modify the object either by double-clicking it in the destination program or by changing it in the source program.

FIGURE D-9: Modifying fill colors in an embedded Excel file

Word title bar shows that Word is the host program

Excel Ribbon and tabs used to edit the embedded file

Fill colors now match those in the letter

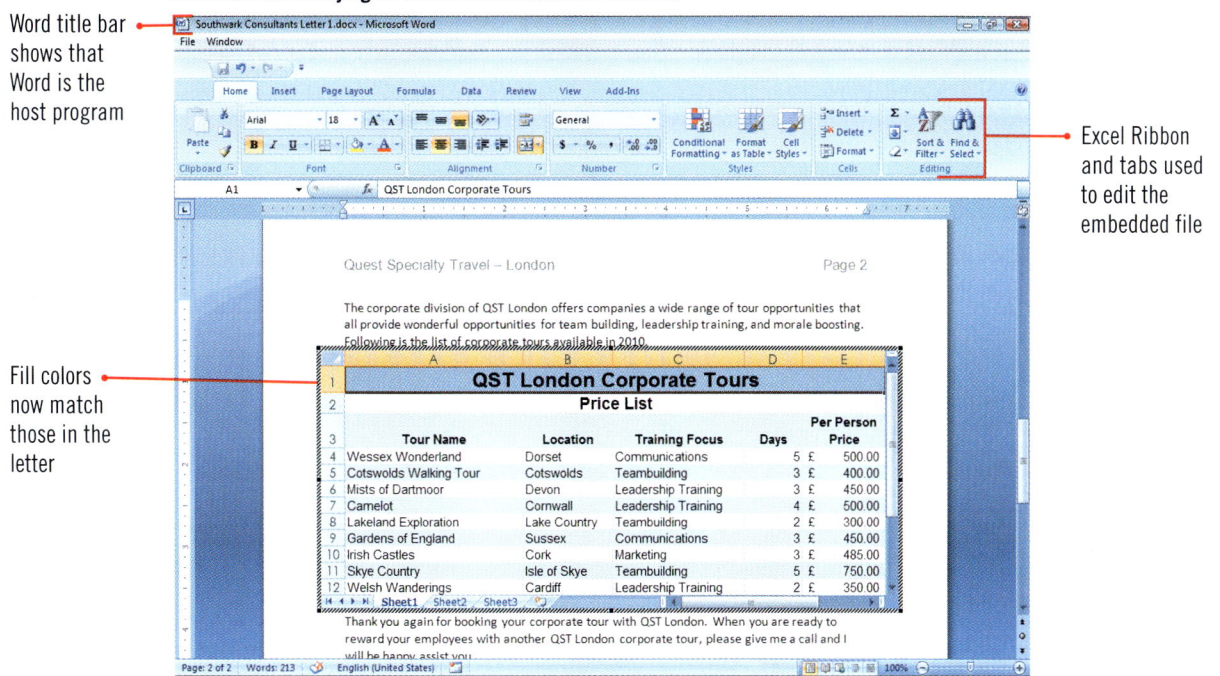

FIGURE D-10: Completed Letter 1 in Two Page view

Current date

Formatted worksheet object

Your name

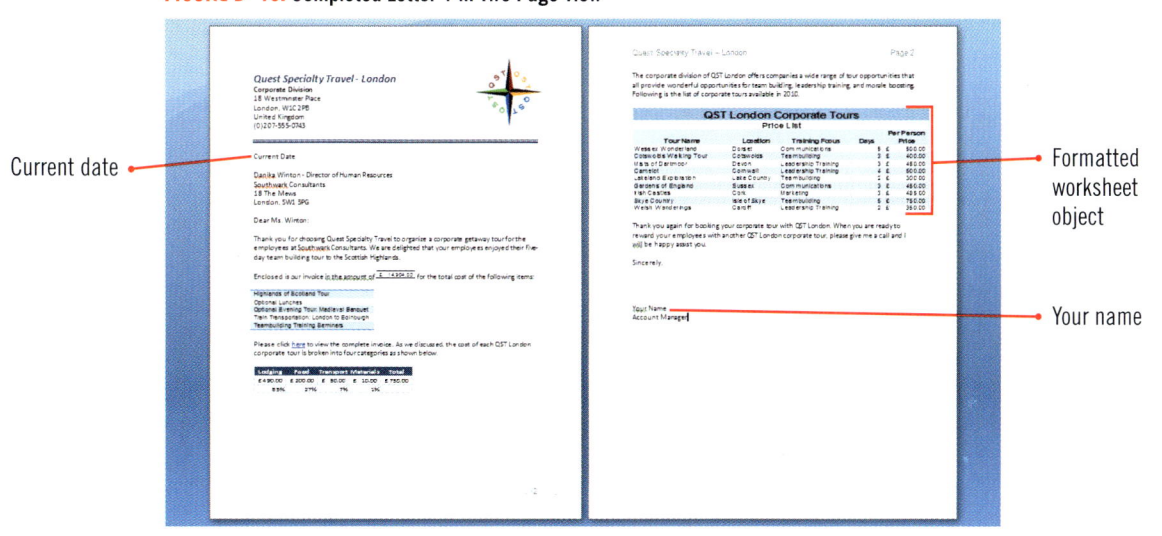

TABLE D-1: Unit D Integration Tasks

object	command	source program(s)	destination program	result	connection type	page no.
Excel range	Copy/Paste Special/Paste Link	Excel	Word	Unformatted text, then formatted in Word	Link	50
Excel file	Insert/Hyperlink/Existing File or Web Page	Excel	Word	Underlined word that users click to view source document	Hyperlink	52
Excel spreadsheet object	Insert/Table/Excel spreadsheet	Excel	Word	Embedded Excel spreadsheet object	Embed	54
Excel spreadsheet file	Insert/Object/Create from File/Browse	Excel	Word	Embedded Excel spreadsheet file	Embed	56

Integrating Word and Excel   Integration 57

UNIT D
Integration

Changing Link Sources

You can change the source of any link that you create between two files, even when the files are created in different source programs. You use the Links dialog box to change link sources and then update links. **QST London has hosted another tour for Southwark Consultants.** To save time, you decide to change the links in the Southwark Consultants Letter 1 file so that they reference a new sheet in the Southwark Consultants Invoices file. All the other information in the letter remains the same.

STEPS

1. **Save the letter as Southwark Consultants Letter 2, locate the third paragraph, which begins "Please", press and hold [Ctrl], then click the hyperlinked text here to open Southwark Consultants Invoices.xlsx**

2. **Click the Select All button** in the upper-left corner of the worksheet window, click the **Copy button** in the Clipboard group, then click the **Insert Worksheet button** as shown in Figure D-11

3. **Click the Paste button, double-click the Sheet1 tab, type 703, press [Enter], modify the data in the new worksheet as shown in Figure D-12, then save the workbook**
   The new total in cell G22 should be £14,664.00.

4. **Switch to Word, click the Office button, point to Prepare, scroll to and click Edit Links to Files, click the second link, then click Change Source**
   The first link references the name and address of the person receiving the letter and invoice. The letter is being sent to the same company, so you do not need to change the link to the name and address. The second link references the total invoice amount.

5. **Click Southwark Consultants Invoices.xlsx in the list of files, click the Item button, change 702 to 703 as shown in Figure D-13, click OK, then click Open**
   The second link will now reference the invoice amount in the worksheet named 703. The third link references the item list.

> **TROUBLE**
> If the list of tours below paragraph 2 collapses, double-click the right edge to restore the column widths.

6. **Click the third link, click Change Source, click Southwark Consultants Invoices.xlsx, click the Item button, change 702 to 703, click OK, click Open, then click OK**
   The third link now references the item list in the worksheet called 703. The total in paragraph 2 is now £14,664 and the item list reflects the revised items (Skye Country and Scottish Banquet).

> **QUICK TIP**
> You cannot modify the hyperlink to an Excel file to go to a specific worksheet.

7. **Locate the third paragraph, which begins "Please", press and hold [Ctrl], then click the hyperlinked text here**
   The Southwark Consultants Invoices file appears with Sheet 703 showing because it is the currently active sheet.

8. **Preview the 703 invoice, then change the setup so that the printed invoice is centered horizontally between the left and right margins**

9. **Print a copy of the invoice, print a copy of Southwark Consultants Letter 2, then save and close both files**

FIGURE D-11: Inserting a new Excel worksheet

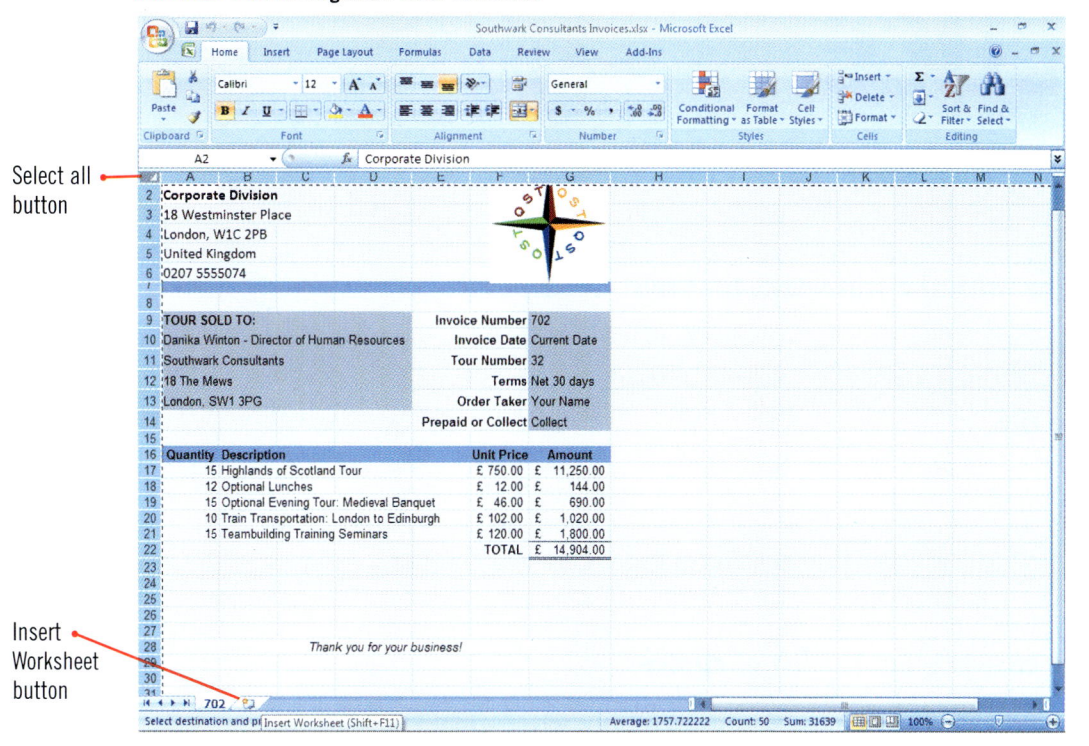

FIGURE D-12: Information updated in Invoice 703

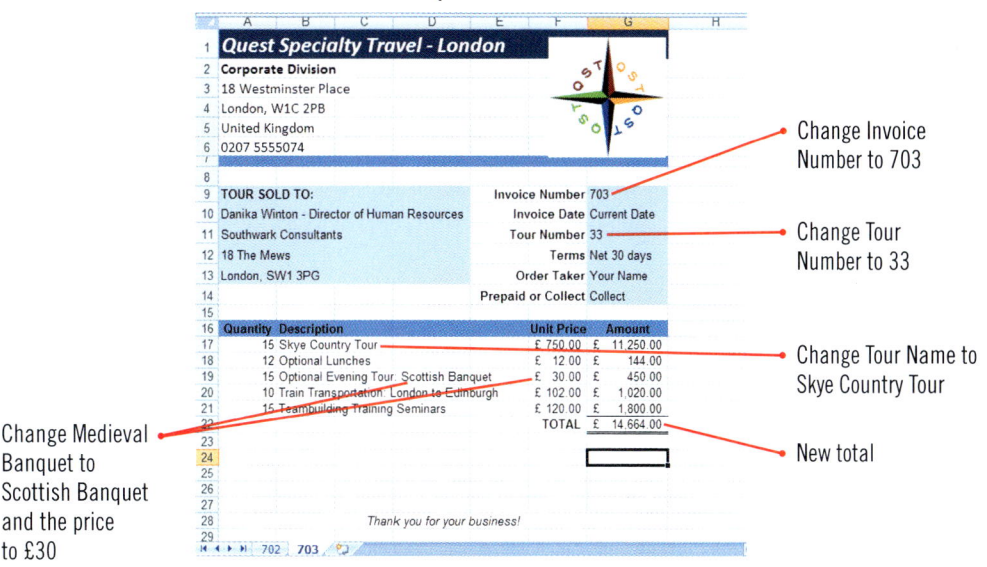

FIGURE D-13: Changing the source location of a link

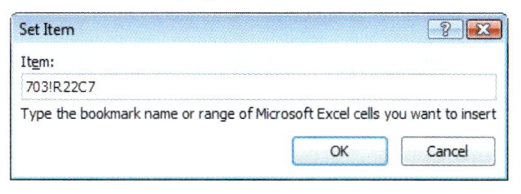

Re-establishing links

When you open a Word file that is linked to an Excel file, you receive the following message: "This document contains links that may refer to other files. Do you want to update this document with the data from the linked files?" You can click "Yes" to re-establish the links between the two files or you can click "No" to open the Word file without linking to the Excel file. If you choose "Yes" to re-establish links, you need to double-click the right edge of any linked worksheet object to restore the column widths.

Practice

▼ **CONCEPTS REVIEW**

If you have a SAM user profile, you may have access to hands-on instruction, practice, and assessment of the skills covered in this unit. Log in to your SAM account (http://sam2007.course.com/) to launch any assigned training activities or exams that relate to the skills covered in this unit.

Match each term with the statement that best describes it.

1. Hyperlink
2. Object
3. Edit Links to File
4. Item
5. Formatted Text (RTF)

a. Select from the Paste Special dialog box to retain the formatting of a pasted object
b. Colored or underlined text or a graphic that, when clicked, opens a different file
c. Command used to paste an Excel object as a table in Word
d. Access from Prepare in the Office menu to update links
e. Select to set the exact location of a link

Select the best answer from the list of choices.

6. Which of the following Paste Special options do you select when you want a value pasted from Excel to retain all formatting?
   a. Formatted Text (RTF)
   b. Microsoft Office Excel Worksheet Object
   c. Word Hyperlink
   d. HTML Format
7. From which tab in Word do you access the Hyperlink command?
   a. Insert
   b. Hyperlink
   c. Review
   d. Add-Ins
8. In Word, which group on the Insert tab contains the command you select to insert an Excel spreadsheet?
   a. Tables
   b. Links
   c. Text
   d. Illustrations
9. In the Links dialog box, which of the following options do you select to edit the source of a link?
   a. Open Source
   b. Edit Source
   c. Change Source
   d. Update Source
10. How do you insert an Excel file in Word?
    a. Office menu, Open command
    b. Insert tab, Object button
    c. Insert tab, File button
    d. Insert tab, Embed button

▼ **SKILLS REVIEW**

1. **Use Paste Special to modify formatting.**
   a. Start Word, open the file INT D-4.docx from the drive and folder where you store your Data Files, save it as **Newton Productions Letter 1**, start Excel, open the file INT D-5.xlsx from the drive and folder where you store your Data Files, then save it as **Newton Productions Invoices**.
   b. In Excel, enter the formula to calculate the total invoice amount for the first item, then copy the formula to the appropriate range.
   c. In cell G21, calculate the subtotal, in cell G22, calculate the tax on the subtotal as 7%, then in cell G23, calculate the total. (*Hint*: To calculate the tax, multiply the value in cell G21 by .07.)
   d. Apply the Euro currency style to all currency amounts, then verify that the total is €9630.00.
   e. Copy the range A10:A14, switch to Word, then paste the copied range as a link in Unformatted Text, replacing INSIDE ADDRESS.

▼ SKILLS REVIEW (CONTINUED)

    f. Change the font size of the pasted text to 12-point, then add a blank line below it.

    g. In Excel, copy the range B17:B20, paste it to replace ITEMS in Word as a link in Formatted Text (RTF), then remove one of the blank lines above the table.

    h. Format the table with the Light Grid - Accent 6 table style. (*Hint*: The style is orange; to expand the selection of table designs, click the More button in the Table Styles group, then read each ScreenTip to find the required style name.)

    i. Deselect Banded Columns, then adjust the table width to show each cell's text on one line.

    j. In Excel, copy cell G23, then paste it as a linked Microsoft Office Excel Worksheet Object, replacing XX in paragraph 2 of the Word document.

    k. Add the name **Brianna Leary:** after Dear, save the document, switch to Excel, then save and close the workbook.

2. **Create a hyperlink between Word and Excel.**

    a. Select the word "here" in the first sentence of the third paragraph.

    b. Open the Insert Hyperlink dialog box, then verify that Existing File or Web Page is selected.

    c. If necessary, navigate to the location where you saved Newton Productions Invoices and select that document.

    d. Create a ScreenTip that uses the text **This link opens Newton Productions Invoices in Excel**, then return to the document.

    e. Test the hyperlink.

    f. In Excel, type **Thank you for your business!** in cell A26, format it with italics, center it across the range A26:G26, then enter the current date and your name where indicated in cells G11 and G13.

    g. View the workbook in Print Preview, set up the workbook to print so it is centered horizontally between the left and right margins on the page, print a copy of the workbook, then save it.

3. **Create an Excel spreadsheet in Word.**

    a. In Word, select SPREADSHEET below paragraph 3, then insert a new Excel worksheet.

    b. Enter labels and values for the worksheet as shown in Table D-2.

    c. For the first item, calculate the Per Pack Price as the product of the Price multiplied by the Discount, subtracted from the price. (*Hint*: The formula is =B2-(B2*C2).) Copy the formula as necessary.

    d. Apply the Accounting Number format using the Euro style to the appropriate cells.

    e. Bold and center the labels in row 1, fill them with Orange, Accent 6, Lighter 40%, then adjust column widths as necessary.

TABLE D-2

Number	Price	Discount	Per Pack Price
50 to 100	5	25%	
101 to 300	5	30%	
301 to 500	5	35%	
Over 500	5	50%	

    f. Reduce the size of the spreadsheet object so only the data appears, click outside the spreadsheet object to return to Word, then delete SPREADSHEET, if necessary.

    g. Edit the spreadsheet object by changing the discount for 301 to 500 snack packs to 40%, then click outside the spreadsheet object and save the document.

    h. Use the hyperlink to display the Newton Productions Invoices file in Excel, then change the price of the Snack Packs to the appropriate discount price ($3.00).

    i. Update the link containing the invoice amount in Word, verify that the new total is €8,346.00, then save the document.

    j. Save and close the Excel workbook.

4. **Embed an Excel file in Word.**

    a. In Excel, open the file INT D-6.xlsx from the drive and folder where you store your Data Files, save it as **Newton Productions Products**, then close the file.

    b. In Word, insert a page break after the second table, before the paragraph that begins "You may also wish…".

    c. Insert the Newton Productions Products file as an object from a file to replace EVENTS.

    d. Open the embedded file in the source program from within Word.

    e. Change the color scheme to Opulent, click outside the embedded file to return to Word, then delete EVENTS.

    f. Enter your name where indicated in the closing, enter the current date where indicated at the top of the document, then save and print the document.

▼ SKILLS REVIEW (CONTINUED)

5. **Change link sources.**
   a. Save the letter as **Newton Productions Letter 2**, follow the here hyperlink to open the Newton Productions Invoices file in Excel, then select the worksheet, copy it, then paste it to a new worksheet.
   b. Name the new worksheet **121**, then save the workbook.
   c. In Word, open the Links dialog box, then change the source of the second link to the new worksheet in the Newton Production Products file.
   d. Change the source of the third link to the new worksheet.
   e. Restore the column widths of the linked worksheet object, if necessary.
   f. Switch to Excel, then on sheet 121 of the Invoices file, change the quantity of breakfast platters to **50** and the quantity of lunch platters to **75**.
   g. In Word, update the invoice amount object in paragraph 2, then verify that the total is now €6,366.50.
   h. Preview the letter, compare it to Figure D-14, then print a copy.
   i. Preview the 121 invoice, change the setup so the invoice is centered horizontally, compare the invoice to Figure D-15, then print a copy.
   j. Save and close both files.

FIGURE D-14

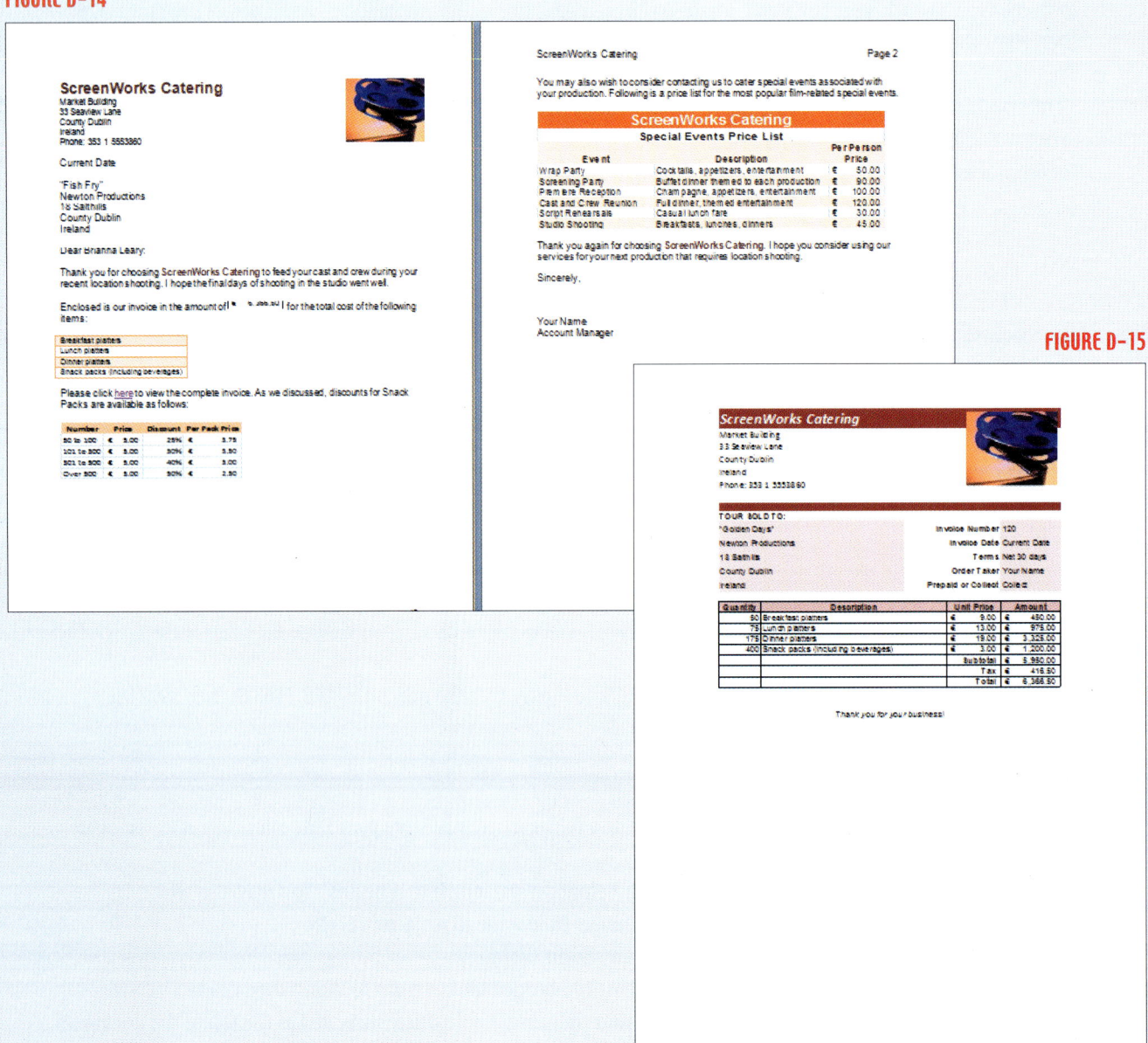

FIGURE D-15

▼ INDEPENDENT CHALLENGE 1

You work for Wessex Books, a small, independent publisher of mysteries and historical romances based in Boston. Several of the authors that Wessex Books handles are about to embark on a tour across Canada and the United States. Your supervisor has asked you to create a fact sheet about the authors that she can refer to as she plans the tour. You open the fact sheet in Word and then add objects from data stored in an Excel worksheet.

a. In Word, open the file INT D-7.docx from the drive and folder where you store your Data Files, then save it as **Wessex Books Fact Sheet**.

b. In Excel, open the file INT D-8.xlsx from where you store your Data Files, then save it as **Wessex Books Information**.

c. In Excel, calculate the total revenue generated by the six authors, calculate the share of the total revenue earned by each author, then calculate the average revenue generated by each author. (*Hint*: To calculate the share of total revenue, enter the formula in C4 that divides the author's revenue by total revenue, being sure to use an absolute reference for Total Revenue in cell B10, then copy the formula to the range C5:C9. To calculate the Average revenue in cell B11, enter the formula =AVERAGE(B4:B9).)

d. Format the values in column C in the Percent style.

e. Select the range containing the author information (A4:C9), then sort the six authors in alphabetical order. Note that the order of the authors shown in the column chart will also change.

f. Copy the cells containing information about the top three authors (cells A4:C6), then paste them as a link in Formatted Text (RTF) over AUTHORS following paragraph 1 in the Word document. Format the copied object with the table design of your choice, deselect Banded Columns, adjust the width of the columns, then remove any extra blank lines around the table.

g. In Excel, copy the values for total and average revenue and paste them as links to the appropriate areas of the Word document using the formatting option you prefer.

h. Create a hyperlink to the Excel file from "here" in the Sales by Author paragraph. Enter **This link opens an Excel workbook containing statistical information about the authors.** as the ScreenTip.

i. Test the hyperlink.

j. In Word, replace COSTS below the Tour Costs paragraph with a new Excel spreadsheet using the data shown in Table D-3. Use formulas to determine the cost of each item and the total cost of all the expenses. Format all dollar amounts with the Accounting Number format, and resize the worksheet object so that only the data appears.

k. Apply the Concourse theme to the spreadsheet object, fill rows 3 and 5 with the same accent color you used to format the table below paragraph 1, then fill row 1 with a darker shade of the same accent color.

l. Click outside the worksheet to return to Word, switch to Excel, change Maria Cellini's name to Maria Anton and her revenue to $2,300,000.

m. In Word, update the three links and restore the width of the table under paragraph 1, if necessary. Enter your name where indicated in the footer, print a copy, save and close the document, then save and close the Excel workbook.

TABLE D-3

Item	Unit	Quantity	Cost	Total
Airfares	Flight	24	$500.00	
Hotels	Night	6	$1,200.00	
Meals	Day	6	$900.00	
Miscellaneous	Day	6	$350.00	
			Total Cost	

▼ VISUAL WORKSHOP

Start Word, open the file INT D-13.docx from where you store your Data Files, then save it as **Jazz Band Information**. As shown in Figure D-16, insert the Excel worksheet object, make the required calculations, then format the object as shown. Search for **jazz band** to find the clip art picture or insert a clip art picture of your choice. Include your name where shown in the Word document, print a copy, then save and close the document.

FIGURE D-16

Jasper Teen Jazz Band
Florida Bound!

In 2010, the Jasper Teen Jazz Band will embark on a five-day, four-concert tour of sunny Florida! The band will perform three solo concerts and then participate in a massed jazz band at a grand finale concert hosted by Epcot Center at Disney World! Each band member should bring both the casual and the concert uniforms. The tour will be fully chaperoned with three assistants in addition to the band leader.

The table shown below breaks down costs for the tour. Please make sure your teen has sufficient funds for the extra meals, attractions, and spending money.

Expense	Unit	Unit Cost	Number	Total
Airfare from Edmonton	Ticket	$ 600.00	1	$ 600.00
Hotel	Night	$ 75.00	5	$ 375.00
Meals (prepaid)	Meal	$ 10.00	12	$ 120.00
Meals (extra)	Meal	$ 15.00	3	$ 45.00
Entrance Fees	Attraction	$ 60.00	3	$ 180.00
			Grand Total	$ 1,320.00

Your Name

UNIT E
Access 2007

Modifying the Database Structure

Files You Will Need:
Quest-E.accdb
Training-E.accdb
Member1.jpg
Sunset.jpg

In this unit, you refine a database by adding a new table to an existing database and linking tables using one-to-many relationships to create a relational database. You work with fields that have different data types, including Text, Number, Currency, Date/Time, and Yes/No, to define the data stored in the database. You create and use Attachment fields to store images. You also modify table and field properties to format and validate data. Working with Mark Rock, the tour developer for U.S. group travel at Quest Travel Services, you are developing an Access database to track the tours, customers, and sales for his division. The database consists of multiple tables that you can link, modify, and enhance to create a relational database.

OBJECTIVES

Examine relational databases
Design related tables
Create one-to-many relationships
Create Lookup fields
Modify Text fields
Modify Number and Currency fields
Modify Date/Time fields
Modify validation properties
Create Attachment fields

Examining Relational Databases

The purpose of a relational database is to organize and store data in a way that minimizes redundancy and maximizes your flexibility when querying and analyzing data. To accomplish these goals, a relational database uses related tables of data rather than a single large table. At one time, the Sales department at Quest Travel Services tracked information about their tour sales using a single Access table called Sales, shown in Figure E-1. You see a data redundancy problem because of the duplicate tour and customer information entered into a single table. You decide to study the principles of relational database design to help Quest Travel Services reorganize these fields into a correctly designed relational database.

DETAILS

To redesign a list into a properly structured relational database, follow these principles:

- **Design each table to contain fields that describe only one subject**

  Currently, the Sales table in Figure E-1 contains three subjects: tours, customers, and sales data. Putting multiple subjects in a single table creates redundant data. For example, the customer's name must be reentered every time that customer purchases a different tour. Redundant data causes extra data-entry work, a higher rate of data-entry inconsistencies and errors, and larger physical storage requirements. Moreover, it limits the user's ability to search for, analyze, and report on the data. These problems are minimized by implementing a properly designed relational database.

- **Identify a primary key field or key field combination for each table**

  A **primary key field** is a field that contains unique information for each record. An employee number field often serves this purpose in a table that stores employee data. A customer number field usually serves this purpose in a table that stores customer data. Although using the employee or customer's last name as the primary key field might work in a small database, it is generally a poor choice because it does not accommodate two employees or customers that have the same last name. A **key field combination** uses more than one field to uniquely identify each record.

- **Build one-to-many relationships between the tables of your database using a field common to each table**

  To tie the information from one table to another, a field must be common to each table. This linking field is the primary key field on the "one" side of the relationship and the **foreign key field** on the "many" side of the relationship. To create a one-to-many relationship between the tables, the primary key field contains a unique entry for each record in the "one" table, but the foreign key field can contain the same value in several records in the "many" table. Table E-1 describes common examples of one-to-many relationships. You are not required to give the linking field the same name in the "one" and "many" tables.

  The new design for the fields of the tour database is shown in Figure E-2. One customer can purchase many tours, so the Customers and Sales tables have a one-to-many relationship based on the linking CustNo field. One tour can have many sales, so the Tours and Sales tables also have a one-to-many relationship based on the common TourID field (named TourNo in the Tours table).

Using many-to-many relationships

As you design your database, you might find that two tables have a **many-to-many relationship**. To join them, you must establish a third table called a **junction table**, which contains two foreign key fields to serve on the "many" side of separate one-to-many relationships with the two original tables. The Customers and Tours tables have a many-to-many relationship because one customer can purchase many tours and one tour can have many customers purchase it. The Sales table serves as the junction table to link the three tables together.

FIGURE E-1: Sales as a single table

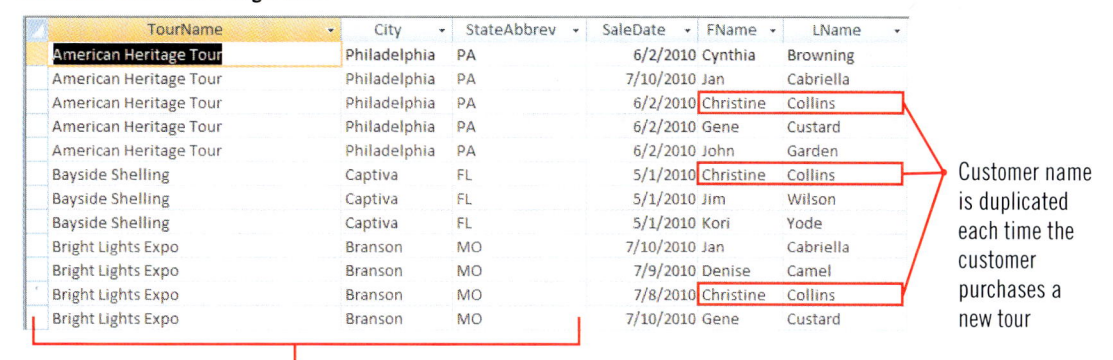

TourName	City	StateAbbrev	SaleDate	FName	LName
American Heritage Tour	Philadelphia	PA	6/2/2010	Cynthia	Browning
American Heritage Tour	Philadelphia	PA	7/10/2010	Jan	Cabriella
American Heritage Tour	Philadelphia	PA	6/2/2010	Christine	Collins
American Heritage Tour	Philadelphia	PA	6/2/2010	Gene	Custard
American Heritage Tour	Philadelphia	PA	6/2/2010	John	Garden
Bayside Shelling	Captiva	FL	5/1/2010	Christine	Collins
Bayside Shelling	Captiva	FL	5/1/2010	Jim	Wilson
Bayside Shelling	Captiva	FL	5/1/2010	Kori	Yode
Bright Lights Expo	Branson	MO	7/10/2010	Jan	Cabriella
Bright Lights Expo	Branson	MO	7/9/2010	Denise	Camel
Bright Lights Expo	Branson	MO	7/8/2010	Christine	Collins
Bright Lights Expo	Branson	MO	7/10/2010	Gene	Custard

Customer name is duplicated each time the customer purchases a new tour

Each tour name, city, state, and tour start date is duplicated each time a new person purchases that tour

FIGURE E-2: Sales data split into three related tables

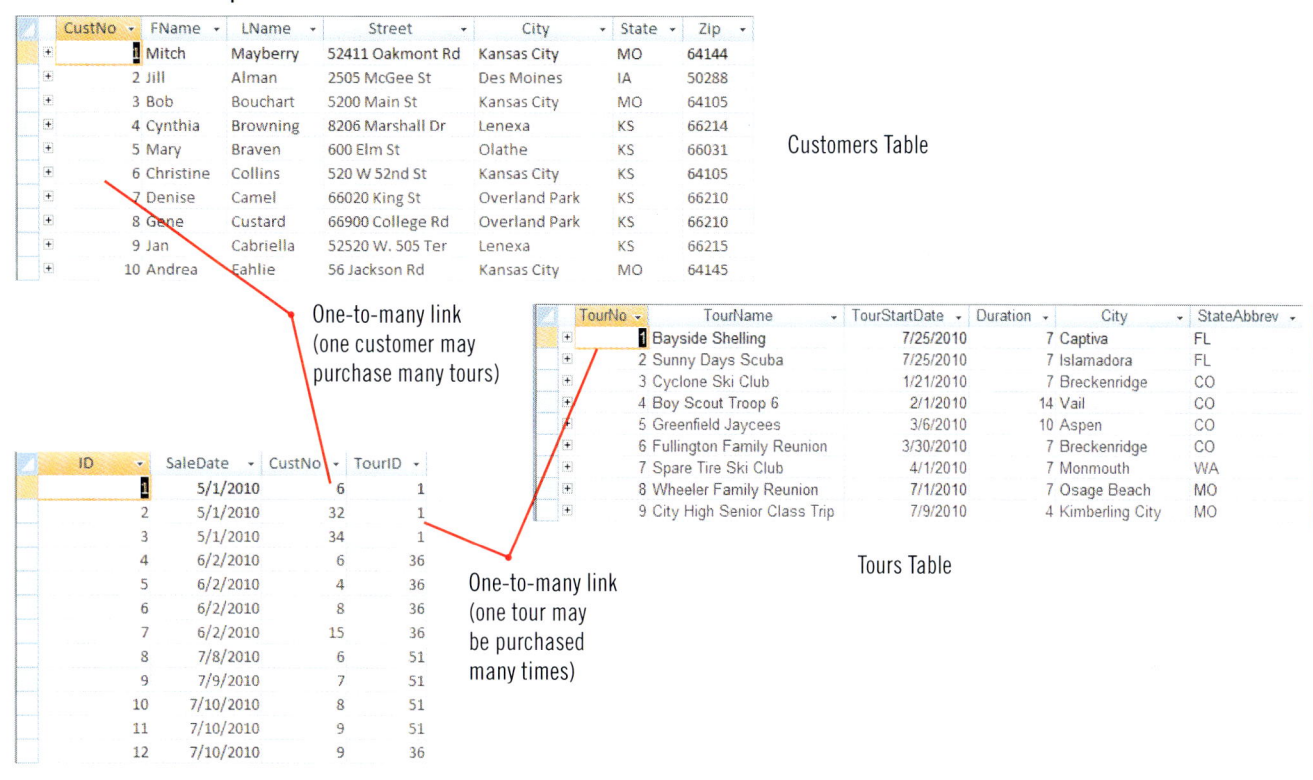

Customers Table

CustNo	FName	LName	Street	City	State	Zip
1	Mitch	Mayberry	52411 Oakmont Rd	Kansas City	MO	64144
2	Jill	Alman	2505 McGee St	Des Moines	IA	50288
3	Bob	Bouchart	5200 Main St	Kansas City	MO	64105
4	Cynthia	Browning	8206 Marshall Dr	Lenexa	KS	66214
5	Mary	Braven	600 Elm St	Olathe	KS	66031
6	Christine	Collins	520 W 52nd St	Kansas City	KS	64105
7	Denise	Camel	66020 King St	Overland Park	KS	66210
8	Gene	Custard	66900 College Rd	Overland Park	KS	66210
9	Jan	Cabriella	52520 W. 505 Ter	Lenexa	KS	66215
10	Andrea	Eahlie	56 Jackson Rd	Kansas City	MO	64145

One-to-many link (one customer may purchase many tours)

Tours Table

TourNo	TourName	TourStartDate	Duration	City	StateAbbrev
1	Bayside Shelling	7/25/2010	7	Captiva	FL
2	Sunny Days Scuba	7/25/2010	7	Islamadora	FL
3	Cyclone Ski Club	1/21/2010	7	Breckenridge	CO
4	Boy Scout Troop 6	2/1/2010	14	Vail	CO
5	Greenfield Jaycees	3/6/2010	10	Aspen	CO
6	Fullington Family Reunion	3/30/2010	7	Breckenridge	CO
7	Spare Tire Ski Club	4/1/2010	7	Monmouth	WA
8	Wheeler Family Reunion	7/1/2010	7	Osage Beach	MO
9	City High Senior Class Trip	7/9/2010	4	Kimberling City	MO

Sales Table

ID	SaleDate	CustNo	TourID
1	5/1/2010	6	1
2	5/1/2010	32	1
3	5/1/2010	34	1
4	6/2/2010	6	36
5	6/2/2010	4	36
6	6/2/2010	8	36
7	6/2/2010	15	36
8	7/8/2010	6	51
9	7/9/2010	7	51
10	7/10/2010	8	51
11	7/10/2010	9	51
12	7/10/2010	9	36

One-to-many link (one tour may be purchased many times)

TABLE E-1: Common one-to-many relationships

table on "one" side	table on "many" side	linking field	description
Products	Sales	ProductID	A ProductID field must have a unique entry in a Products table, but is listed many times in a Sales table as many copies of that item are sold
Students	Enrollments	StudentID	A StudentID field must have a unique entry in a Students table, but is listed many times in an Enrollments table as multiple classes are recorded for the same student
Employees	Promotions	EmployeeID	An EmployeeID field must have a unique entry in an Employees table, but is listed many times in a Promotions table as the employee is promoted over time

Modifying the Database Structure

UNIT E
Access 2007

Designing Related Tables

After you develop a valid relational database design, you are ready to define the tables in Access. Using **Table Design View**, you can specify all characteristics of a table including field names, data types, field descriptions, field properties, lookup properties, and primary key field designations. Using the new database design, you are ready to create the Sales table.

STEPS

1. **Start Access, open the Quest-E.accdb database, then enable content if prompted**
   The Customers, States, TourCategories, and Tours tables already exist in the database. You need to create the Sales table.

2. **Click the Create tab on the Ribbon, then click the Table Design button**
   Table Design View opens, allowing you to enter field names and specify data types and field properties for the new table. Field names should be as short as possible, but long enough to be descriptive. The field name you enter in Table Design View is used as the default name for the field in all later queries, forms, and reports.

   > **QUICK TIP**
   > When specifying field data types, you can type the first letter of the data type to quickly select it.

3. **Type SalesNo, press [Enter], click the Data Type list arrow, click AutoNumber, then press [Enter] twice to move to the next row**
   The AutoNumber data type, which automatically assigns the next available integer in the sequence to each new record, works well for the SalesNo field because each sales number should be unique.

4. **Type the other field names, data types, and descriptions as shown in Figure E-3**
   Field descriptions entered in Table Design View are optional, but are helpful in that they provide further information about the field.

   > **TROUBLE**
   > If you set the wrong field as the primary key field, click the Primary Key field button again to toggle it off.

5. **Click SalesNo in the Field Name column, then click the Primary Key button on the Design tab**
   A **key symbol** appears to the left of SalesNo to indicate that this field is defined as the primary key field for this table.

   > **QUICK TIP**
   > To delete or rename an existing table, right-click it in the Navigation Pane, then click Delete or Rename.

6. **Click the Save button on the Quick Access toolbar, type Sales in the Table Name text box, click OK, then close the table**
   The Sales table is now displayed as a table object in the Quest-E database Navigation Pane, as shown in Figure E-4.

FIGURE E-3: Table Design View for the new Sales table

Primary Key button

Field names | Data types | Descriptions

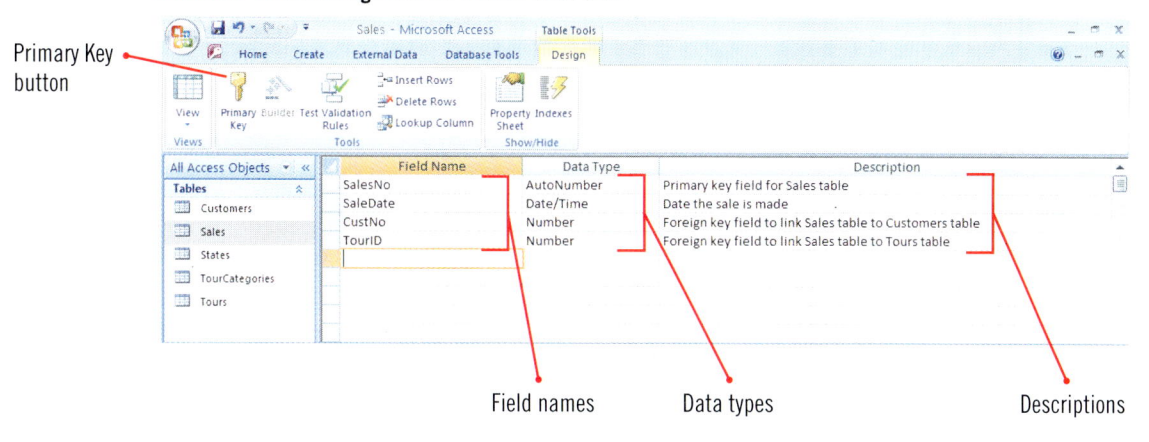

FIGURE E-4: Sales table in the Quest-E database Navigation Pane

Sales table in Navigation Pane

Specifying the foreign key field data type

A foreign key field in the "many" table must have the same data type (Text or Number) as the primary key it is related to in the "one" table. An exception to this rule is when the primary key field in the "one" table has an AutoNumber data type. In this case, the linking foreign key field in the "many" table must have a Number data type. Also note that a Number field used as a foreign key field must have a Long Integer Field Size property to match the Field Size property of the AutoNumber primary key field.

Modifying the Database Structure

Creating One-to-Many Relationships

UNIT E
Access 2007

After creating the tables you need, you link the tables together in appropriate one-to-many relationships before building queries, forms, or reports using fields from multiple tables. Your database design shows that the common CustNo field should link the Customers table to the Sales table, and that the TourID field should link the Tours table to the Sales table. You are ready to define the one-to-many relationships between the tables of the Quest-E database.

STEPS

1. **Click the Database Tools tab on the Ribbon, then click the Relationships button**
   The States, Tours, and TourCategories table field lists appear in the Relationships window. The primary key fields are identified with a small key symbol to the left of the field name. You need to add the Customers and Sales table field lists to this window.

   > **QUICK TIP**
   > Drag the table's title bar to move the field list.

2. **Click the Show Table button on the Design tab, click Sales, click Add, click Customers, click Add, click Close, then maximize the window**
   With all of the field lists in the Relationships window, you're ready to link the Sales and Customers tables to the rest of the relational database.

   > **QUICK TIP**
   > Drag the bottom border of the field list to display all of the fields.

3. **Click TourNo in the Tours table field list, then drag it to the TourID field in the Sales table field list**
   Dragging a field from one table to another in the Relationships window links the two tables by the selected fields and opens the Edit Relationships dialog box, as shown in Figure E-5. Recall that referential integrity helps ensure data accuracy.

4. **Click the Enforce Referential Integrity check box in the Edit Relationships dialog box, then click Create**
   The **one-to-many line** shows the linkage between the TourNo field of the Tours table and the TourID field of the Sales table. The "one" side of the relationship is the unique TourNo value for each record in the Tours table. The "many" side of the relationship is identified by an infinity symbol pointing to the TourID field in the Sales table. The CustNo field should link the Customers table to the Sales table.

   > **QUICK TIP**
   > Right-click a relationship line, then click Delete if you need to delete a relationship and start over.

5. **Click CustNo in the Customers table field list, drag it to CustNo in the Sales table field list, click the Enforce Referential Integrity check box, then click Create**
   The updated Relationships window should look like Figure E-6.

   > **TROUBLE**
   > Click the Landscape button on the Print Preview tab if the report is too wide for portrait orientation.

6. **Click the Relationship Report button on the Design tab, click the Print button, then click OK**
   A printout of the Relationships window, called the Relationship report, shows how your relational database is designed and includes table names, field names, primary key fields, and one-to-many relationship lines. This printout is helpful as you later create queries, forms, and reports that use fields from multiple tables.

   > **QUICK TIP**
   > Add your name as a label to the Report Header section in Report Design View and reprint the report if you want your name on the printout.

7. **Click the Close Print Preview button on the Print Preview tab, close the Report Design View window, then click No when prompted to save the report**

8. **Close the Relationships window, then click Yes if prompted to save changes**

FIGURE E-5: Edit Relationships dialog box

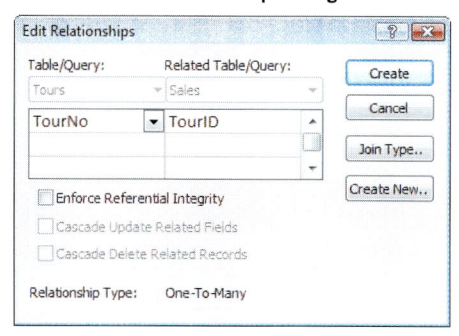

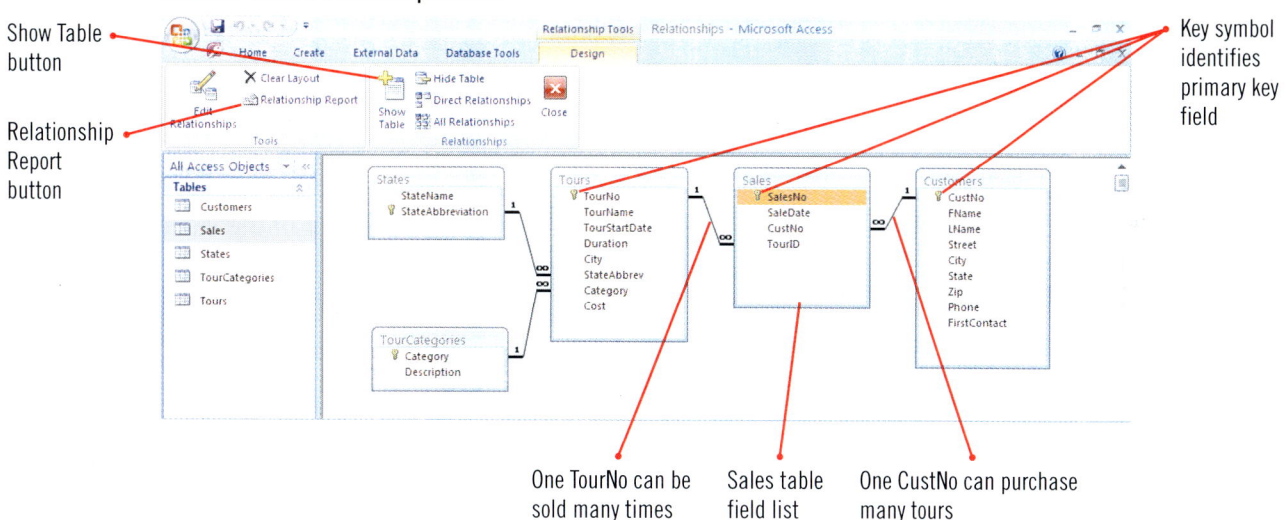

FIGURE E-6: Final Relationships window

Show Table button

Relationship Report button

Key symbol identifies primary key field

One TourNo can be sold many times

Sales table field list

One CustNo can purchase many tours

More on enforcing referential integrity

Recall that referential integrity is a set of rules to help ensure that no orphan records are entered or created in the database. An orphan record is a record in the "many" table that doesn't have a matching entry in the linking field of the "one" table. (For example, an orphan record in the Quest database is a record in the Sales table that contains a TourID entry but has no match in the TourNo field of the Tours table, or a record in the Sales table that contains a CustNo entry but no match in the Customers table.) Referential integrity prevents orphan records in multiple ways. By enforcing referential integrity, you cannot allow a **null entry** (nothing) in a foreign key field nor can you make an entry in the foreign key field that does not match a value in the linking field of the "one" table (such as a Sales record with a TourID not included in the Tours table). Referential integrity also prevents you from deleting a record in the "one" table that has a matching entry in the foreign key field of the "many" table (such as a Customer record with a CustNo associated with a Sales record). You should enforce referential integrity on all one-to-many relationships if possible. Unfortunately, if you are working with a database that already contains orphan records, you cannot enforce this powerful set of rules.

Modifying the Database Structure

UNIT E
Access 2007
Creating Lookup Fields

A **Lookup field** is a field that contains Lookup properties. **Lookup properties** are field properties that allow you to supply a drop-down list of values for a field. The values can be stored in another table or directly stored in the **Row Source** Lookup property of the field. Fields that are good candidates for Lookup properties are those that contain a defined set of appropriate values such as State, Gender, or Department. You can set Lookup properties for a field in Table Design View using the **Lookup Wizard**. The FirstContact field in the Customers table identifies how the customer first made contact with Quest Specialty Travel such as being referred by a friend, finding the company through the Internet, or responding to a direct mail advertisement. You can use the Lookup Wizard to provide a set of defined values as a drop-down list for the FirstContact field.

STEPS

1. **Right-click the Customers table in the Navigation Pane, click Design View, then maximize Table Design View**

   You access the Lookup Wizard from the Data Type list for the field in which you want to apply Lookup properties.

2. **Click the Text data type for the FirstContact field, click the Data Type list arrow, then click Lookup Wizard**

   The Lookup Wizard starts and prompts you for information about where you want the lookup column to get its values.

3. **Click the I will type in the values that I want option button, click Next, click the first cell in the Col1 column, type Friend, press [Tab], then type the rest of the values as shown in Figure E-7**

   These are the values to populate the lookup value list for the FirstContact field.

4. **Click Next, then click Finish to accept the default label and complete the Lookup Wizard**

   Note that the data type for the FirstContact field is still Text. The Lookup Wizard is a process for setting Lookup property values for a field, not a data type itself.

> **QUICK TIP**
> The **Limit to List** Lookup property determines whether you can enter a new value into a field with other lookup properties, or whether the entries are limited to the drop-down list.

5. **Click the Lookup tab to observe the new Lookup properties for the FirstContact field as shown in Figure E-8**

   The Lookup Wizard helped you enter the correct Lookup properties for the FirstContact field, but you can always enter or edit them directly if you know what values you want to use for each property. The Row Source property stores the values that are provided in the drop-down list for a Lookup field.

6. **Click the View button on the Design tab, click Yes when prompted to save the table, press [Tab] eight times to move to the FirstContact field, click the FirstContact list arrow as shown in Figure E-9, then click Friend**

   The FirstContact field now provides a list of values that are valid for this field.

7. **Close the Customers table**

Creating multivalued fields

Multivalued fields allow you to make more than one choice from a drop-down list for a field. As a database designer, multivalued fields allow you to select and store more than one choice without having to create a more advanced database design. To create a multivalued field, use the Lookup Wizard and select the Allow Multiple Values check box for the question that asks "Do you want to store multiple values for this lookup?" This feature is only available for an Access database created or saved in Access 2007 file format.

Access 112 — Modifying the Database Structure

FIGURE E-7: Entering a Lookup list of values

Drop-down list of values

FIGURE E-8: Viewing Lookup properties

Data Type for FirstContact field is still Text

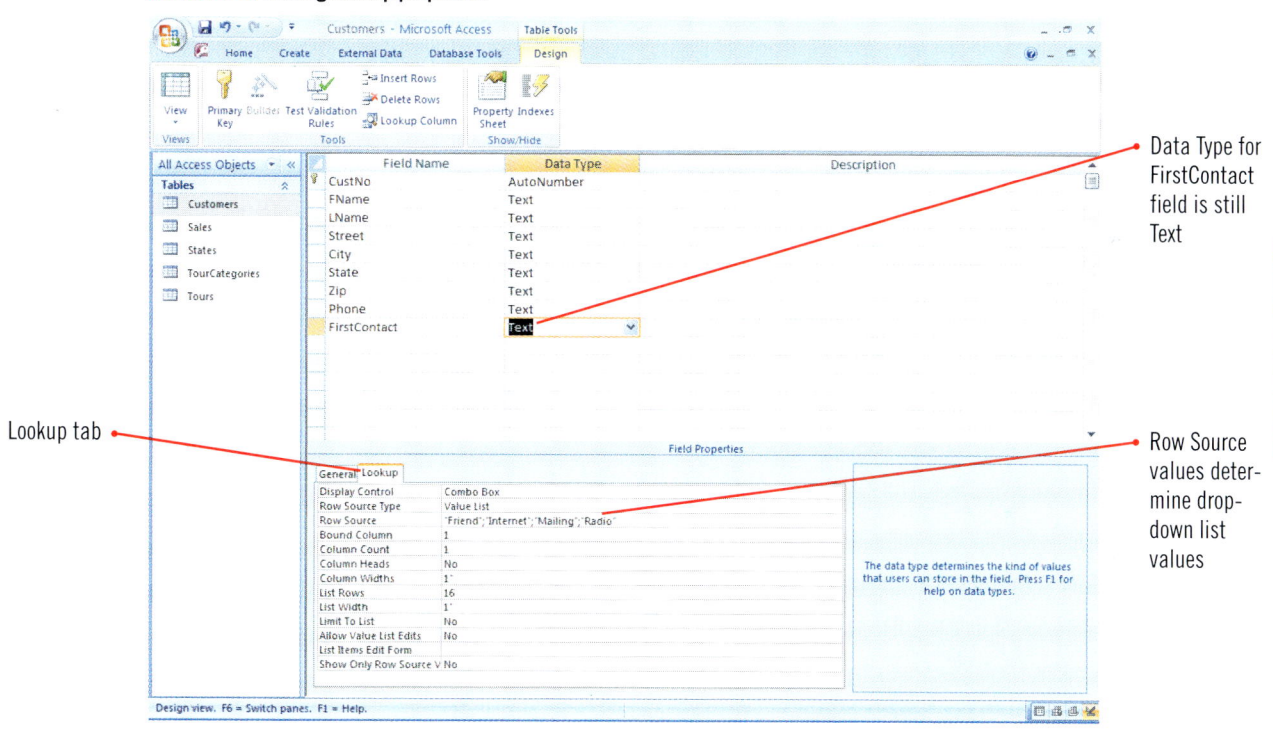

Lookup tab

Row Source values determine drop-down list values

FIGURE E-9: Using a Lookup field in a datasheet

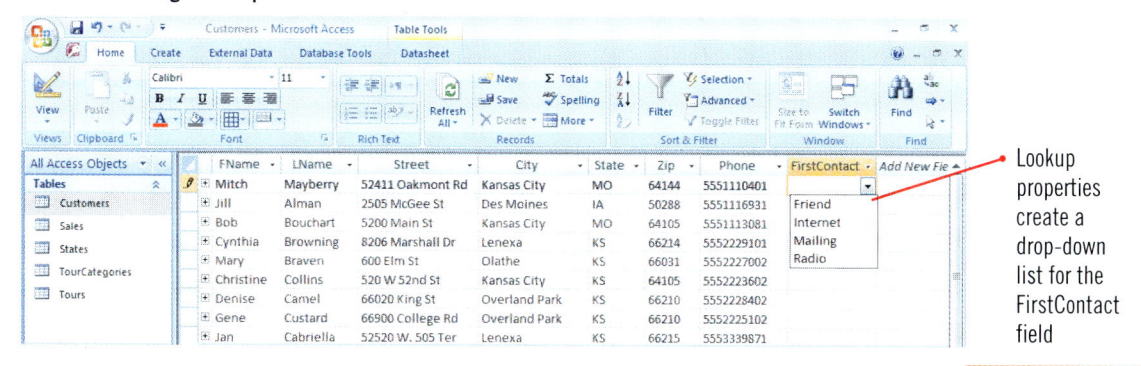

Lookup properties create a drop-down list for the FirstContact field

Modifying the Database Structure

Modifying Text Fields

UNIT E
Access 2007

Field properties are the characteristics that apply to each field in a table, such as Field Size, Default Value, or Caption. These properties help ensure database accuracy and clarity because they restrict the way data is entered, stored, and displayed. You modify field properties in Table Design View. See Table E-2 for more information on Text field properties. After reviewing the Customers table with Mark Rock, you decide to make field property changes to several Text fields in that table.

STEPS

1. **Right-click the Customers table in the Navigation Pane, then click Design View on the shortcut menu**

   The Customers table opens in Design View. The field properties appear on the General tab of the lower half of the Table Design View window and display the properties of the selected field. Field properties change depending on the field's data type. For example, when you select a field with a Text data type, the Field Size property is visible. However, when you select a field with a Date/Time data type, Access controls the Field Size property, so that property is not displayed. Many field properties are optional, but for those that require an entry, Access provides a default value.

2. **Press [↓] to move through each field while viewing the field properties in the lower half of the window**

   The **field selector button** to the left of the field indicates which field is currently selected.

   > **QUICK TIP**
   > Because no entries in the FirstContact field are greater than 20 characters, you do not lose any data by making this property change.

3. **Click the FirstContact field name, double-click 255 in the Field Size property text box, type 20, click the Save button on the Quick Access toolbar, then click Yes**

   The maximum and the default value for the Field Size property for a Text field is 255. In general, however, you want to make the Field Size property for Text fields only as large as needed to accommodate the longest entry. You can increase the size later if necessary. In some cases, shortening the Field Size property helps prevent typographical errors. For example, you should set the Field Size property for a State field that stores two-letter state abbreviations to 2 to prevent errors such as TXX.

4. **Change the Field Size property to 30 for the FName and LName fields, click , then click Yes**

   No existing entries are greater than 30 characters for either of these fields, so no data is lost. The **Input Mask** property provides a visual guide for users as they enter data. It also helps determine what types of values can be entered into a field.

   > **TROUBLE**
   > If the Input Mask Wizard is not installed on your computer, you can complete this step by typing !(999) 000-0000;;_ directly into the Input Mask property for the Phone field.

5. **Click the Phone field name, click the Input Mask property text box, click the Build button click the Phone Number input mask, click Next, click Next, then click Finish**

   Table Design View of the Customers table should look like Figure E-10, which shows the Input Mask property entered for the Phone field.

6. **Click , click the View button on the Design tab, press [Tab] enough times to move to the Phone field for the first record, type 5554441234, then press [Enter]**

   The Phone Input Mask property creates an easy-to-use visual guide to facilitate accurate data entry.

7. **Close the Customers table**

FIGURE E-10: Changing Text field properties

Phone field is selected

Input Mask property

Build button

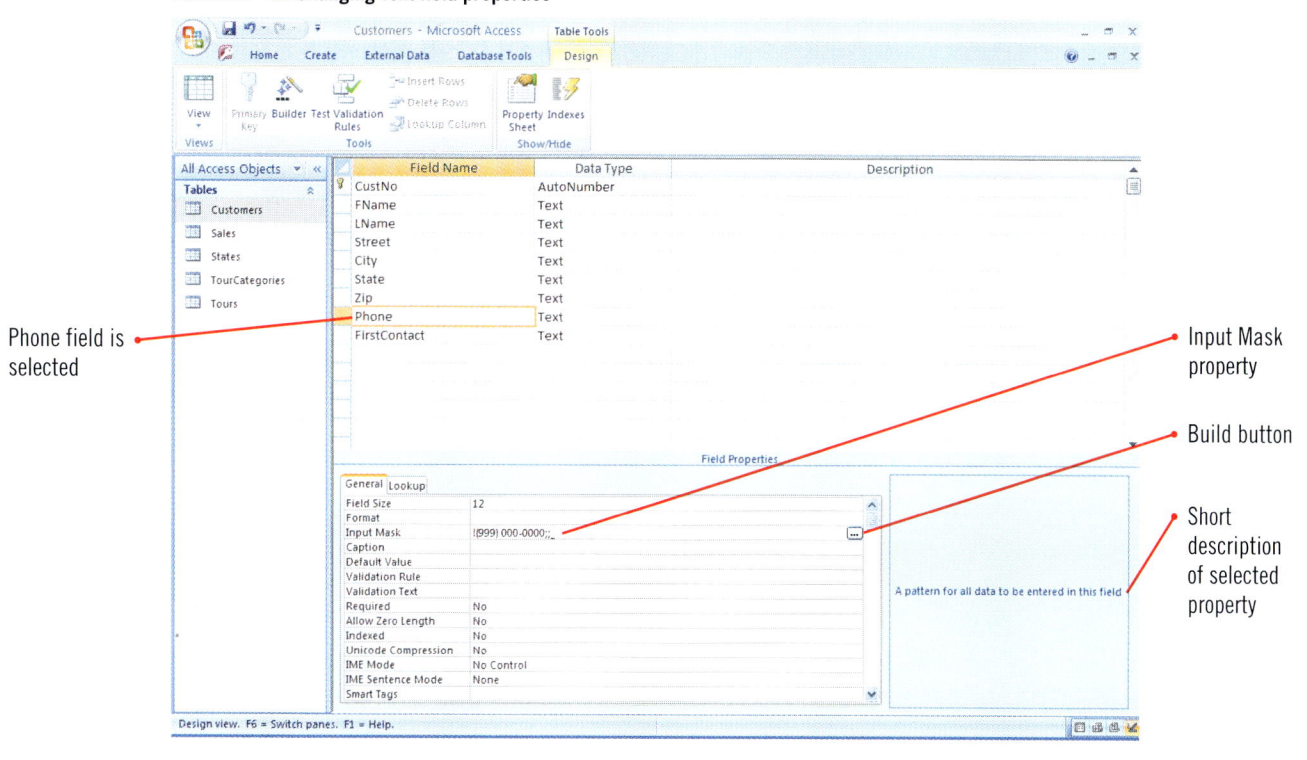

Short description of selected property

TABLE E-2: Common Text field properties

property	description	sample field	sample property entry
Field Size	Controls how many characters can be entered into the field	State	2
Format	Controls how information will be displayed and printed	State	> (displays all characters in uppercase)
Input Mask	Provides a pattern for data to be entered	Phone	!(999) 000-0000;1;_
Caption	Describes the field in the first row of a datasheet, form, or report; if the Caption property is not entered, the field name itself is used to label the field	Emp#	Employee Number
Default Value	Displays a value that is automatically entered in the given field for new records	City	Kansas City
Required	Determines if an entry is required for this field	LastName	Yes

Exploring the Input Mask property

The Input Mask property provides a pattern for data to be entered, using three parts separated by semicolons. The first part provides a pattern for what type of data can be entered. For example, 9 represents an optional number, 0 a required number, ? an optional letter, and L a required letter. The second part determines whether all displayed characters (such as dashes in a phone number) are stored in the field. For the second part of the input mask, a 0 entry stores all characters such as 555-7722, and a 1 entry stores only the entered data, 5557722. The third part of the input mask determines which character Access uses to guide the user through the mask. Common choices are the asterisk (*), underscore (_), or pound sign (#).

Modifying the Database Structure

UNIT E
Access 2007

Modifying Number and Currency Fields

Although some properties for Number and Currency fields are the same as the properties of Text fields, each data type has its own list of valid properties. Numeric and Currency fields have similar properties because they both contain numeric values. Currency fields store values that represent money, and Number fields store values that represent values such as quantities, measurements, and scores. The Tours table contains both a Number field (Duration) and a Currency field (Cost). You want to modify the properties of these two fields.

STEPS

1. **Right-click the Tours table in the Navigation Pane, click Design View on the shortcut menu, click the Duration field name, then maximize Table Design View**

   The default Field Size property for a Number field is Long Integer. See Table E-3 for more information on the options for the Field Size property of a Number field. Access controls the size of Currency fields to control the way numbers are rounded in calculations, so the Field Size property isn't available for Currency fields.

2. **Click Long Integer in the Field Size property text box, click the Field Size list arrow, then click Byte**

   Choosing a Byte value for the Field Size property allows entries from 0 to 255, so it greatly restricts the possible values and the storage requirements for the Duration field.

   > **QUICK TIP**
   > The Property Update Options button allows you to propagate field properties in the queries, forms, and reports that use the Cost field.

3. **Click the Cost field name, click Auto in the Decimal Places property text box, click the Decimal Places list arrow, then click 0**

   Your Table Design View should look like Figure E-11. Because all of Quest's tours are priced at a round dollar value, you do not need to display cents in the Cost field.

4. **Save the table, then view the datasheet**

   Because none of the current entries in the Duration field is greater than 255, which is the maximum value allowed by a Number field with a Byte Field Size, you don't lose any data. You want to test the new property changes.

5. **Press [Tab] three times to move to the Duration field for the first record, type 800, then press [Tab]**

   Because 800 is larger than the Byte Field Size property allows (0-255), an Access error message appears indicating that the value isn't valid for this field.

6. **Press [Esc] twice to remove the inappropriate entry in the Duration field, then press [Tab] four times to move to the Cost field**

   The Cost field is set to display zero digits after the decimal point.

7. **Type 750.25 in the Cost field of the first record, press [↓], then click $750 in the Cost field of the first record**

   Although the Decimal Places property for the Cost field dictates that entries in the field are *formatted* to display zero digits after the decimal point, 750.25 is the actual value stored in the field. Modifying the Decimal Places property does not change the actual data. Rather, the Decimal Places property only changes the way the data is *presented*.

8. **Click the Undo button on the Quick Access toolbar to restore the Cost entry to $750, then close the Tours table**

FIGURE E-11: Changing Currency and Number field properties

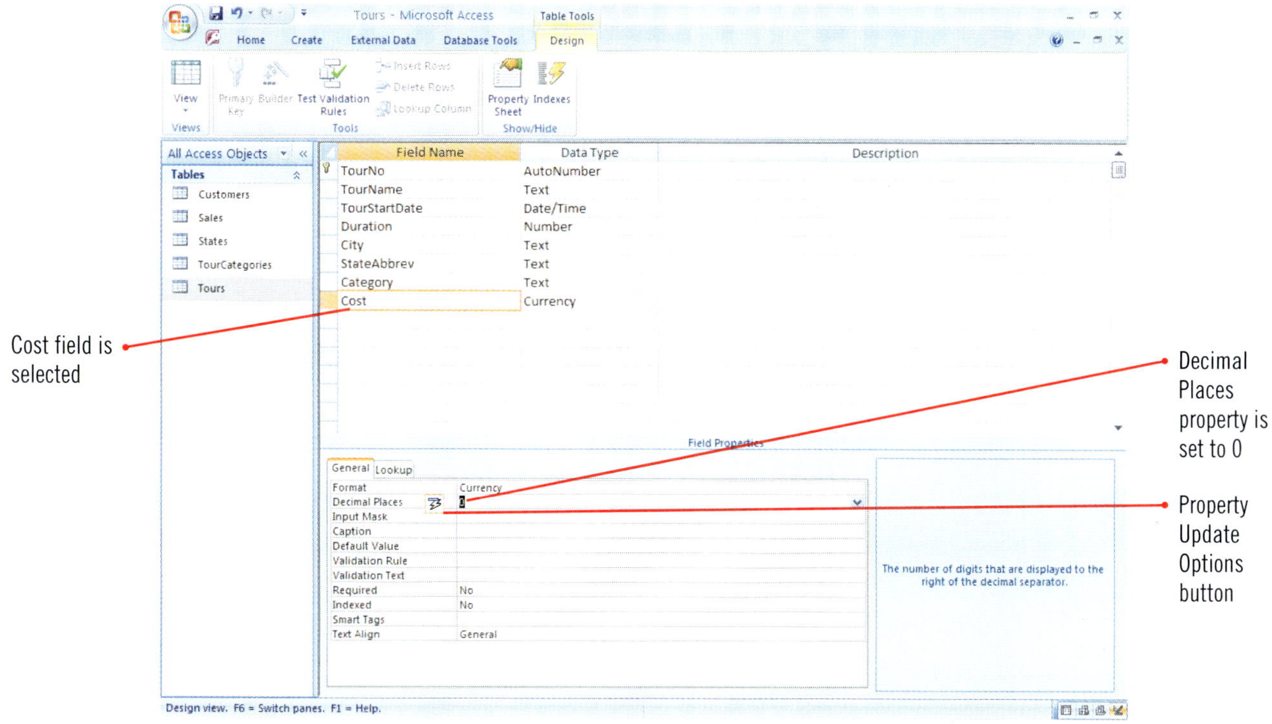

Cost field is selected

Decimal Places property is set to 0

Property Update Options button

TABLE E-3: Common Number field properties

property	description
Field Size	Determines the largest number that can be entered in the field, as well as the type of data (e.g., integer or fraction)
Byte	Stores numbers from 0 to 255 (no fractions)
Integer	Stores numbers from –32,768 to 32,767 (no fractions)
Long Integer	Stores numbers from –2,147,483,648 to 2,147,483,647 (no fractions)
Single	Stores numbers (including fractions with six digits to the right of the decimal point) times 10 to the –38th to +38th power
Double	Stores numbers (including fractions with over 10 digits to the right of the decimal point) in the range of 10 to the –324th to +324th power
Decimal Places	The number of digits displayed to the right of the decimal point

Modifying the Database Structure

UNIT E
Access 2007

Modifying Date/Time Fields

Many properties of the Date/Time field, such as Input Mask, Caption, and Default Value, work the same way as they do in fields with a Text or Number data type. One difference, however, is the **Format** property, which helps you format dates in various ways such as January 25, 2006; 25-Jan-06; or 01/25/2006. You want to change the format of Date/Time fields in the database to display two digits for the month and day values and four digits for the year, as in 05/05/2010.

STEPS

1. **Right-click the Tours table in the Navigation Pane, click Design View on the shortcut menu, click the TourStartDate field name, then maximize Table Design View**

   You want the tour start dates to appear with two digits for the month and day, such as 07/05/2010, instead of the default presentation of dates, 7/5/2010.

   > **QUICK TIP**
   > Click any property box, then press F1 to open the Microsoft Access Help window to the page that describes that property.

2. **Click the Format property box, then click the Format list arrow**

   Although several predefined Date/Time formats are available, none matches the format you want. To define a custom format, enter symbols that represent how you want the date to appear.

3. **Type mm/dd/yyyy then press [Enter]**

   The updated Format property for the TourStartDate field shown in Figure E-12 sets the date to appear with two digits for the month, two digits for the day, and four digits for the year. The parts of the date are separated by forward slashes.

4. **Save the table, display the datasheet, then click the New (blank) record button on the navigation bar**

   To test the new Format property for the TourStartDate field, you can add a new record to the table.

   > **QUICK TIP**
   > Access assumes that years entered with two digits from 30 to 99 refer to the years 1930 through 1999, and 00 to 29 refers to the years 2000 through 2029. To enter a year before 1930 or after 2029, enter all four digits of the year.

5. **Press [Tab] to move to the TourName field, type Missouri Eagles, press [Tab], type 9/1/10, press [Tab], type 7, press [Tab], type Hollister, press [Tab], type MO, press [Tab], type a (for Adventure), press [Tab], then type 700**

   Your screen should look like Figure E-13. The new record is entered into the Tours table. The Format property for the TourStartDate field makes the entry appear as 09/01/2010, as desired.

Access 118   Modifying the Database Structure

FIGURE E-12: Changing Date/Time field properties

TourStartDate field is selected

Custom Format property

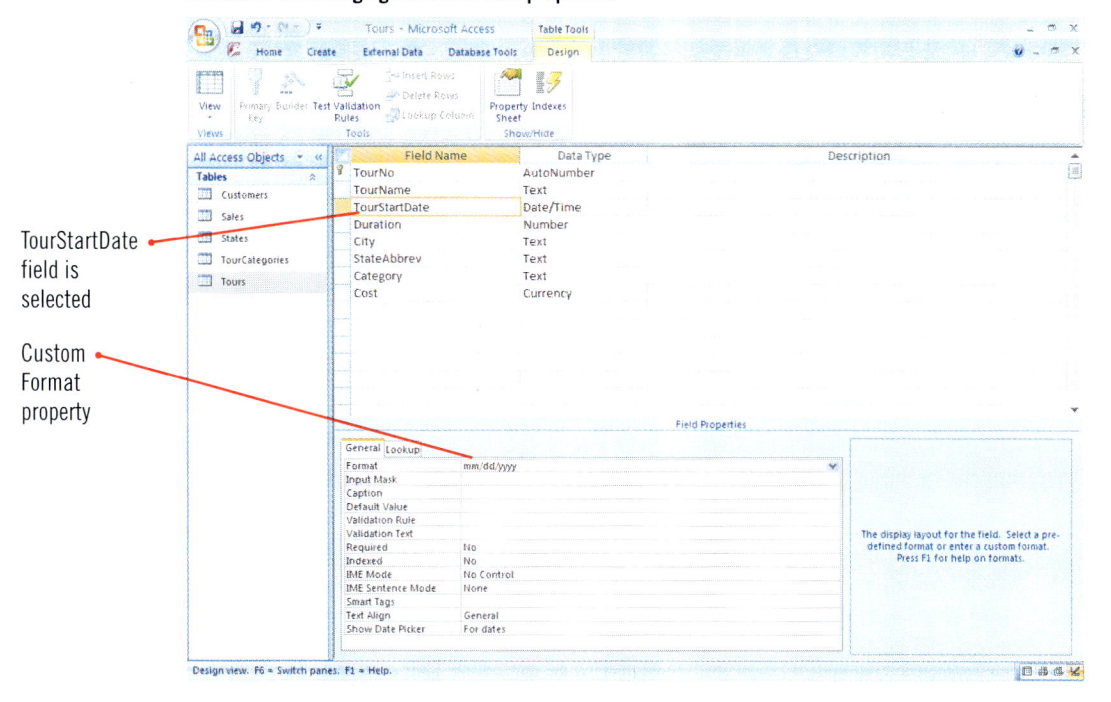

FIGURE E-13: Testing the Format property for the TourStartDate field

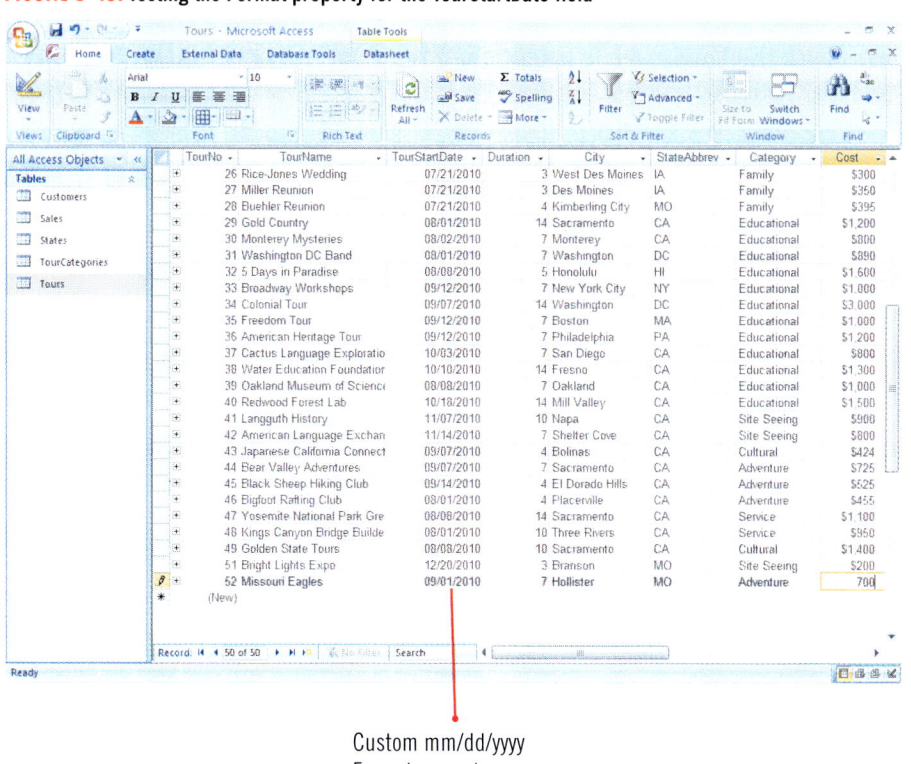

Custom mm/dd/yyyy Format property

Using Smart Tags

The Property Update Options button is an Access Smart Tag. **Smart Tags** are buttons that appear in certain conditions. They provide a small menu of options to help you work with the task at hand. Access provides the Property Update Options Smart Tag to help you quickly apply property changes to other objects of the database that use the field. The **Error Indicator button** Smart Tag helps identify potential design errors. For example, if you are working in Form Design View and add a text box to the form but do not correctly bind it to an underlying field, the Error Indicator button appears by the text box to alert you to the problem.

Modifying the Database Structure

Access 119

Modifying Validation Properties

The **Validation Rule** property determines what entries a field can accept. For example, a Validation Rule for a Date/Time field might require date entries on or after 1/1/2010. A Validation Rule for a Currency field might indicate that valid entries fall between $0 and $1,500. You use the **Validation Text** property to display an explanatory message when a user tries to enter data that doesn't meet the criteria for a valid field entry established by the Validation Rule. Therefore, the Validation Rule and Validation Text field properties help you prevent unreasonable data from being entered into the database. Mark Rock reminds you that Quest tours start no earlier than January 1, 2010. You can use the validation properties to establish this rule for the TourStartDate field.

STEPS

1. **Click the View button on the Home tab to return to Design View, click the TourStartDate field if it isn't already selected, click the Validation Rule property box, then type >=1/1/2010**

   This entry forces all dates in the TourStartDate field to be greater than or equal to 1/1/2010. See Table E-4 for more examples of Validation Rule expressions. The Validation Text property provides a helpful message to the user when the entry in the field breaks the rule entered in the Validation Rule property.

2. **Click the Validation Text box, then type Date must be on or after 1/1/2010**

   The Design View of the Tours table should now look like Figure E-14. Access modifies a property to include additional syntax by changing the entry in the Validation Rule property to >=#1/1/2010#. Pound signs (#) are used to surround date criteria.

3. **Save the table, then click Yes when asked to test the existing data with new data integrity rules**

   Because no dates in the TourStartDate field are earlier than 1/1/2010, Access finds no date errors in the current data and saves the table. You now want to test that the Validation Rule and Validation Text properties work when entering data in the datasheet.

4. **Click the View button on the Design tab to display the datasheet, press [Tab] twice to move to the TourStartDate field, type 1/1/06, then press [Tab]**

   Because you tried to enter a date that was not true for the Validation Rule property for the TourStartDate field, a dialog box opens and displays the Validation Text entry, as shown in Figure E-15.

5. **Click OK to close the validation message**

   You now know that the Validation Rule and Validation Text properties work properly.

6. **Press [Esc] to reject the invalid date entry in the TourStartDate field**

7. **Close the Tours table**

FIGURE E-14: Entering validation properties

[Screenshot of Access table design view with TourStartDate field selected, showing Validation Rule property `>=#1/1/2010#` and Validation Text property "Date must be on or after 1/1/2010"]

TourStartDate field is selected

Validation Rule property

Validation Text property

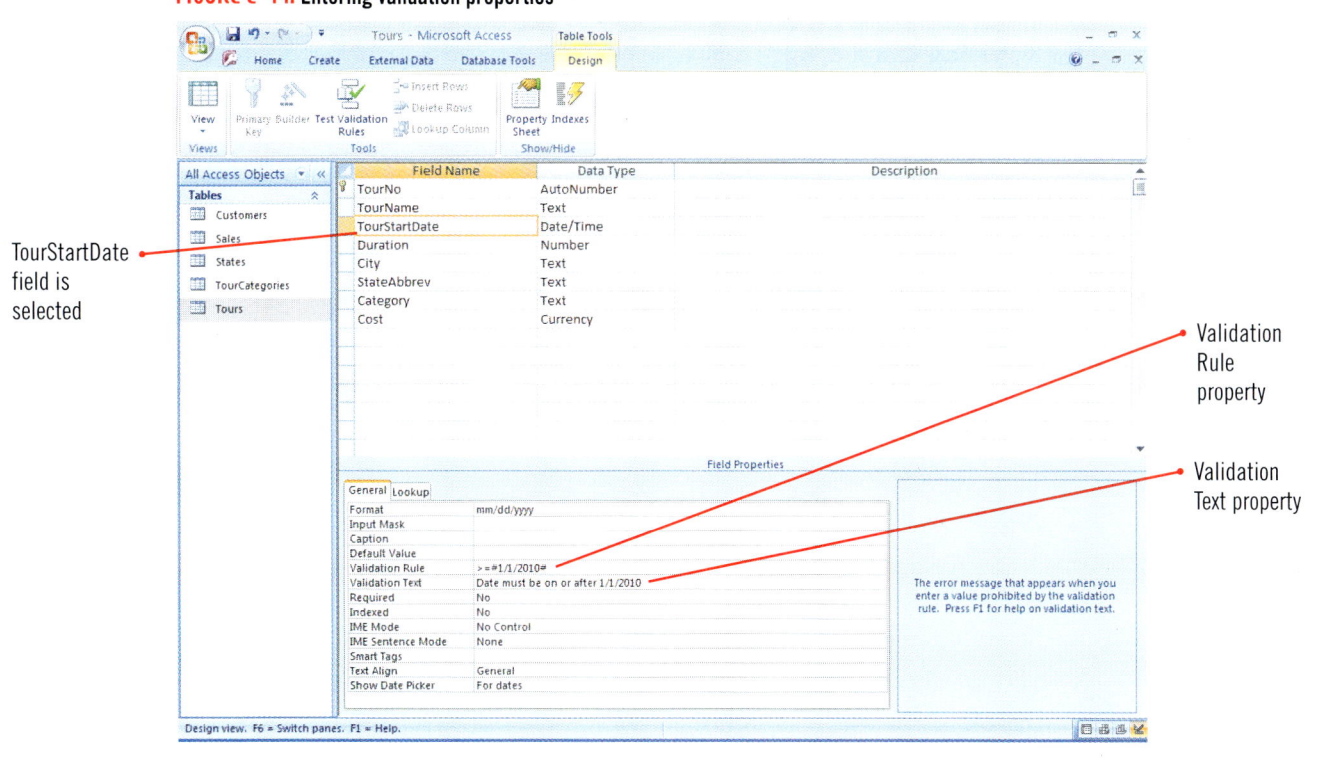

FIGURE E-15: Validation Text message

[Screenshot of Tours datasheet with Microsoft Office Access message box displaying "Date must be on or after 1/1/2010"]

Validation Text property

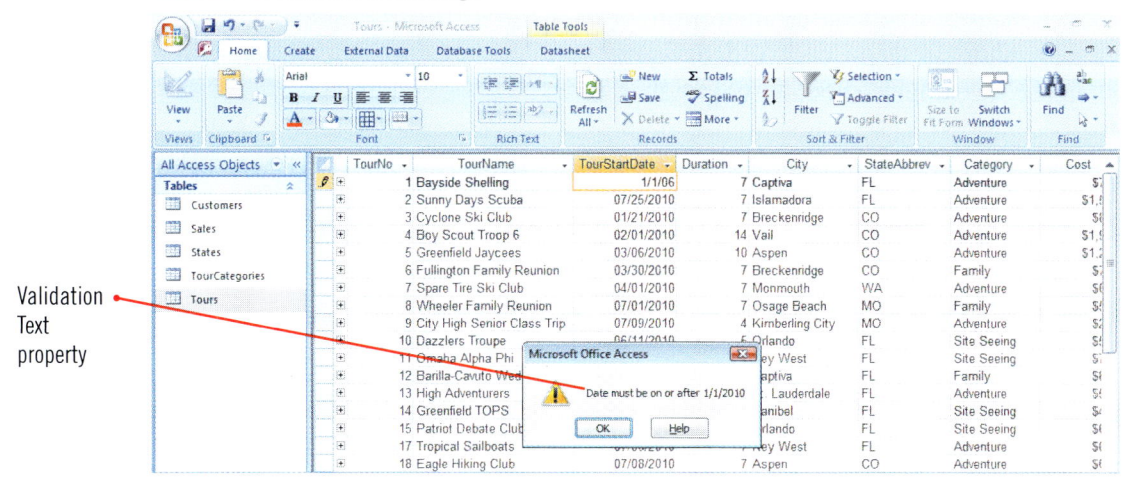

TABLE E-4: Validation Rule expressions

data type	validation rule expression	description
Number or Currency	>0	The number must be positive
Number or Currency	>10 And <100	The number must be between 10 and 100
Number or Currency	10 Or 20 Or 30	The number must be 10, 20, or 30
Text	"IA" Or "NE" Or "MO"	The entry must be IA, NE, or MO
Date/Time	>=#7/1/93#	The date must be on or after 7/1/1993
Date/Time	>#1/1/10# And <#1/1/12#	The date must be between 1/1/2010 and 1/1/2012

Modifying the Database Structure   Access 121

Creating Attachment Fields

UNIT E
Access 2007

An **Attachment field** allows you to attach an external file such as a Word document, PowerPoint presentation, Excel workbook, or image file to a record. Earlier versions of Access allowed you to link or embed external data using the **OLE** (object linking and embedding) data type. The Attachment data type is superior to OLE because it stores data more efficiently; stores more file formats, such as JPEG images; and requires no additional software to view the files from within Access. Mark Rock asks you to incorporate images on forms and reports to help describe and market each tour. You can use an Attachment field to store JPEG images that help illustrate each tour in the Tours table.

STEPS

1. **Right-click the Tours table in the Navigation Pane, click Design View, then maximize Table Design View**

   You can add the new field below the Cost field.

2. **Click the Field Name cell below Cost, type Picture, press [Tab], click the Data Type list arrow, then click Attachment**

   Now that you created the new Attachment field, you're ready to add data to it in Datasheet View.

3. **Click the Save button on the Quick Access toolbar, click the View button on the Design tab to switch to Datasheet View, then press [Tab] enough times to move to the new Attachment field**

   The Attachment field cell displays a small paper clip icon with the number of files attached to the field in parentheses, as shown in Figure E-16. You have not attached any files to this field yet, so each record shows zero (0) file attachments. You can attach files to this field directly from Datasheet View.

4. **Right-click the attachment icon for the first record, click Manage Attachments on the shortcut menu, click Add, navigate to the drive and folder where you store your Data Files, double-click Sunset.jpg, then click OK**

   The Sunset.jpg file is now included with the first record, and the datasheet reflects that one (1) file is attached to the Picture field of the first record. You can add more than one file attachment to the same field, but good database practices encourage you to add only one piece of information per field. Therefore, if you want to also attach a Word document listing the trip itinerary to this record, good database practices encourage you to add a second Attachment field to handle this information. You can view all types of file attachments directly from the datasheet. You can also view images from a form or report that displays this information.

5. **Right-click the attachment icon for the first record, click Manage Attachments on the shortcut menu, then double-click Sunset.jpg to open it**

   The image opens in the program that is associated with the .jpg extension on your computer. Figure E-17 shows the Sunset.jpg image as displayed by Windows Photo Gallery, but a different program on your computer might be associated with the .jpg file extension. **JPEG** is an acronym for Joint Photographic Experts Group, which defines the standards for the compression algorithms that allow image files to be stored in an efficient compressed format. Because the size requirements of JPEG images are minimized, the JPEG file format is ideal for storing large numbers of pictures in a database or for transporting images across a network.

6. **Close the window that displays the Sunset.jpg image, click Cancel in the Attachments dialog box, close the Tours table, close the Quest-E.accdb database, then exit Access**

FIGURE E-16: Attachment field in Datasheet View

— New Attachment field

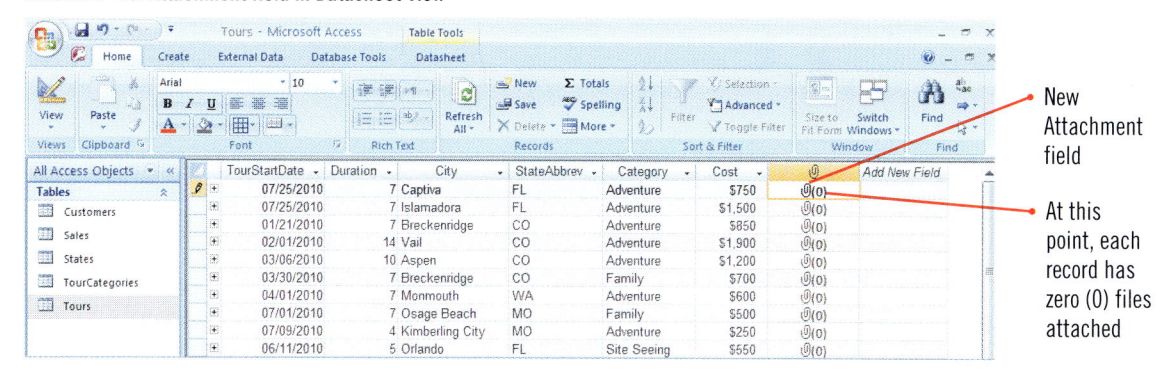

— At this point, each record has zero (0) files attached

FIGURE E-17: Viewing a JPEG image

This image appears in Windows Photo Gallery, but your image might appear in a different program

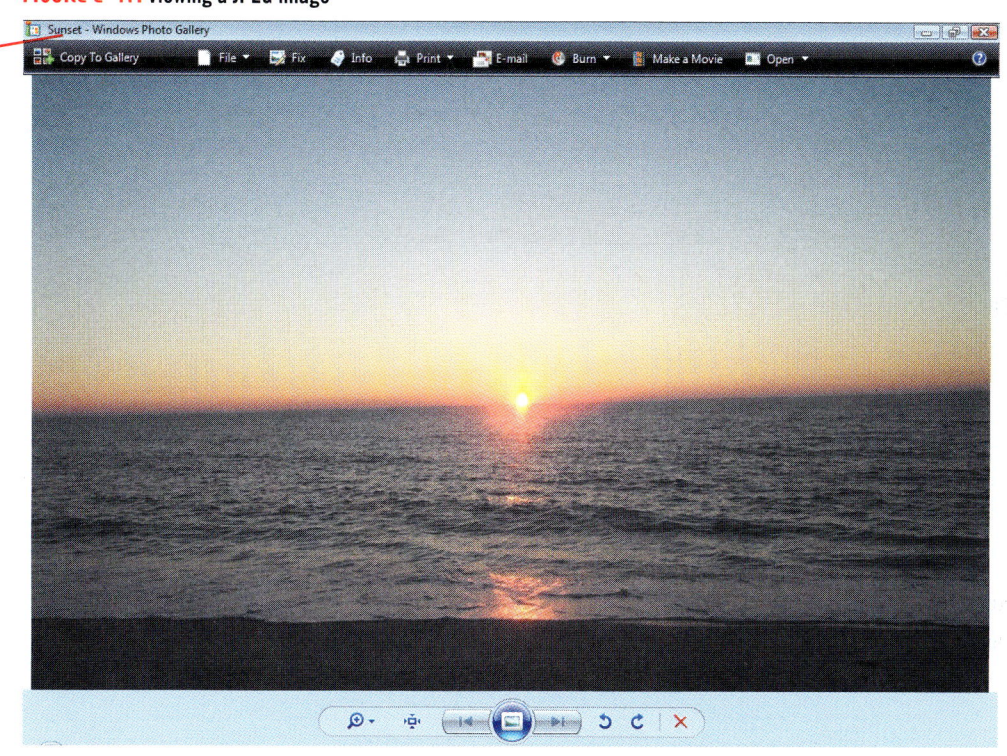

Recognizing database formats

When you create a new, blank database in Microsoft Office Access 2007, Access gives the file the .accdb extension and formats it as an Access 2007 database. Access 2007 displays the version of the current database file in the title bar when you first open the database. The **.accdb** file extension usually means the database is an Access 2007 format database, but note that Access 2007 format databases are *not* readable by earlier versions of Access such as Access 2000, Access 2002 (XP), or Access 2003. Some features such as multivalued fields and Attachment fields are only available when working on an Access 2007 database. In some cases, you might prefer to use Access 2007, but create or convert database files to an earlier Access format such as Access 2000 or Access 2002-2003. This option is helpful if you share the database with users who are still using earlier versions of Access. In Microsoft Office Access 2007, to save an existing database to a different version, use the Save As command on the Office button menu. Using this feature, Access 2000, 2002-2003 databases are given an **.mdb** file extension.

Modifying the Database Structure

Practice

SAM — If you have a SAM user profile, you may have access to hands-on instruction, practice, and assessment of the skills covered in this unit. Log in to your SAM account (http://sam2007.course.com/) to launch any assigned training activities or exams that relate to the skills covered in this unit.

▼ CONCEPTS REVIEW

Identify each element of Table Design View shown in Figure E-18.

FIGURE E-18

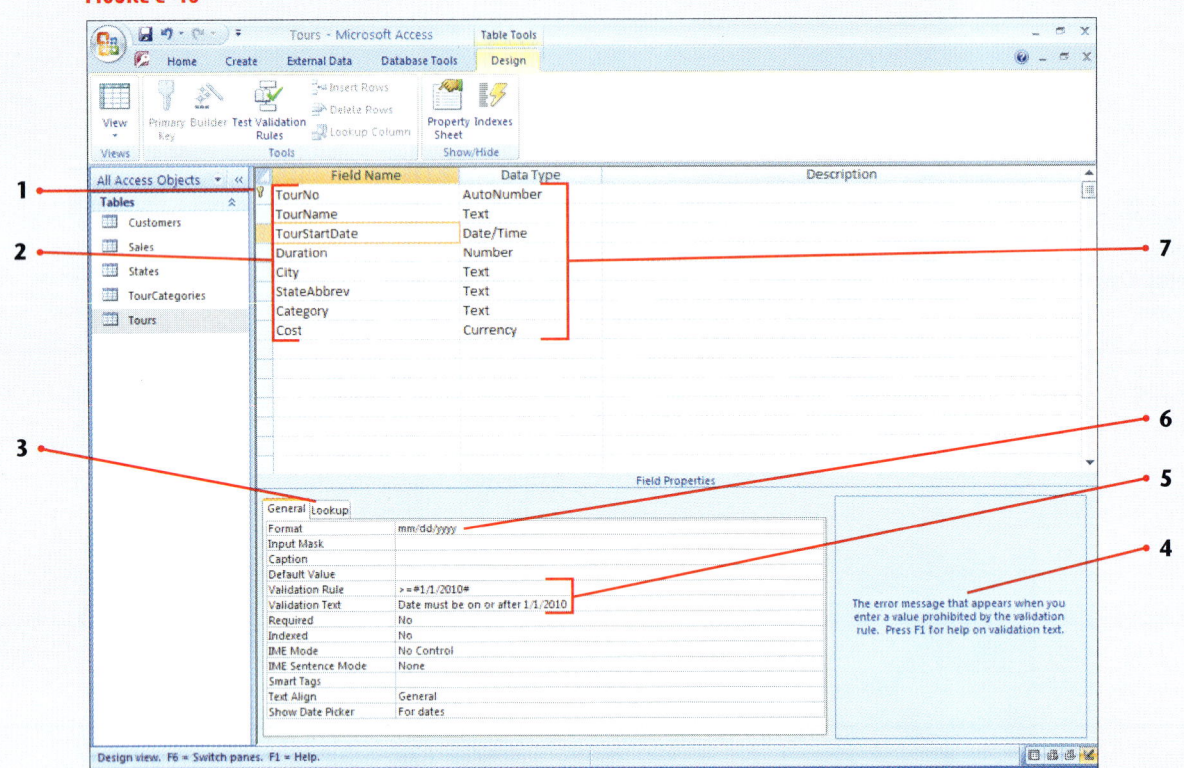

Match each term with the statement that best describes it.

8. Primary key field
9. Validation properties
10. Table Design View
11. Row Source
12. Relational database
13. Input Mask
14. Lookup properties
15. Multivalued field
16. Attachment field

a. Field that allows you to store external files such as a Word document, PowerPoint presentation, Excel workbook, or image files
b. Field that allows you to make more than one choice from a drop-down list for a field
c. Field that holds unique information for each record in the table
d. Several tables linked together in one-to-many relationships
e. Field properties that allow you to supply a drop-down list of values for a field
f. Access window where all characteristics of a table, such as field names and field properties, are defined
g. Field properties that help you prevent unreasonable data entries for a field
h. Field property that provides a visual guide as you enter data
i. Lookup property that determines where the Lookup field gets its list of values

Select the best answer from the list of choices.

17. **Which of the following problems most clearly indicates that you need to redesign your database?**
    a. The Input Mask Wizard has not been used.
    b. Referential integrity is enforced on table relationships.
    c. Not all fields have Validation Rule properties.
    d. There is duplicated data in the field of several records of a table.

18. **Which of the following is *not* defined in Table Design View?**
    a. The primary key field
    b. Field Size properties
    c. Duplicate data
    d. Field data types

19. **What is the purpose of enforcing referential integrity?**
    a. To prevent incorrect entries in the primary key field
    b. To prevent orphan records from being entered
    c. To require an entry for each field of each record
    d. To force the application of meaningful validation rules

20. **To create a many-to-many relationship between two tables, you must create:**
    a. A junction table.
    b. Combination primary key fields in each table.
    c. A one-to-many relationship between the two tables, with referential integrity enforced.
    d. Foreign key fields in each table.

▼ SKILLS REVIEW

1. **Examine relational databases.**
   a. List the fields needed to create an Access relational database to manage membership information for a philanthropic club, community service organization, or international aid group.
   b. Identify fields that would contain duplicate values if all of the fields were stored in a single table.
   c. Group the fields into subject matter tables, then identify the primary key field for each table.
   d. Assume that your database contains two tables: Members and ZipCodes. If you did not identify these two tables earlier, regroup the fields within these two table names, then identify the primary key field for each table, the foreign key field in the Members table, and how the tables would be related using a one-to-many relationship.

2. **Design related tables.**
   a. Start Access 2007, then click the New Blank Database button.
   b. Type **Membership-E** in the File Name box, click the Folder icon to navigate to the drive and folder where you store your Data Files, click OK, then click Create.
   c. Use Table Design View to create a new table with the name **Members** and the field names and data types shown in Figure E-19.

   FIGURE E-19

field name	data type
FirstName	Text
LastName	Text
Street	Text
Zip	Text
Phone	Text
Birthdate	Date/Time
Dues	Currency
MemberNo	Text
MemberType	Text
CharterMember	Yes/No

   d. Specify MemberNo as the primary key field, save the Members table, then close it.
   e. Use Table Design View to create a new table named **ZipCodes** with the field names and data types shown in Figure E-20.

   FIGURE E-20

field name	data type
Zip	Text
City	Text
State	Text

   f. Identify Zip as the primary key field, save the ZipCodes table, then close it.
   g. Use Table Design View to create a third new table called **Activities** with the field names and data types shown in Figure E-21.

   FIGURE E-21

field name	data type
ActivityNo	AutoNumber
MemberNo	Text
ActivityDate	Date/Time
Hours	Number

   h. Identify ActivityNo as the primary key field, save the Activities table, then close it.

▼ SKILLS REVIEW (CONTINUED)

3. **Create one-to-many relationships.**
   a. Open the Relationships window, double-click Activities, double-click Members, then double-click ZipCodes to add all three tables to the Relationships window. Close the Show Table dialog box.
   b. Resize all field lists as necessary so that all fields are visible, then drag the Zip field from the ZipCodes table to the Zip field in the Members table to create a one-to-many relationship between the ZipCodes table and Members table, using the common Zip field.
   c. Enforce referential integrity, and create the one-to-many relationship between ZipCodes and Members.
   d. Drag the MemberNo field from the Members table to the MemberNo field in the Activities table to create a one-to-many relationship between the Members table and the Activities table, using the common MemberNo field.
   e. Enforce referential integrity, and create the one-to-many relationship between Members and Activities. See Figure E-22.
   f. Create a Relationship report for the Membership-E database, add your name as a label to the Report Header section of the report in Report Design View, then print the report.
   g. Close the Relationship report without saving the report, then close the Relationships window. Save the changes to the Relationships window if prompted.

FIGURE E-22

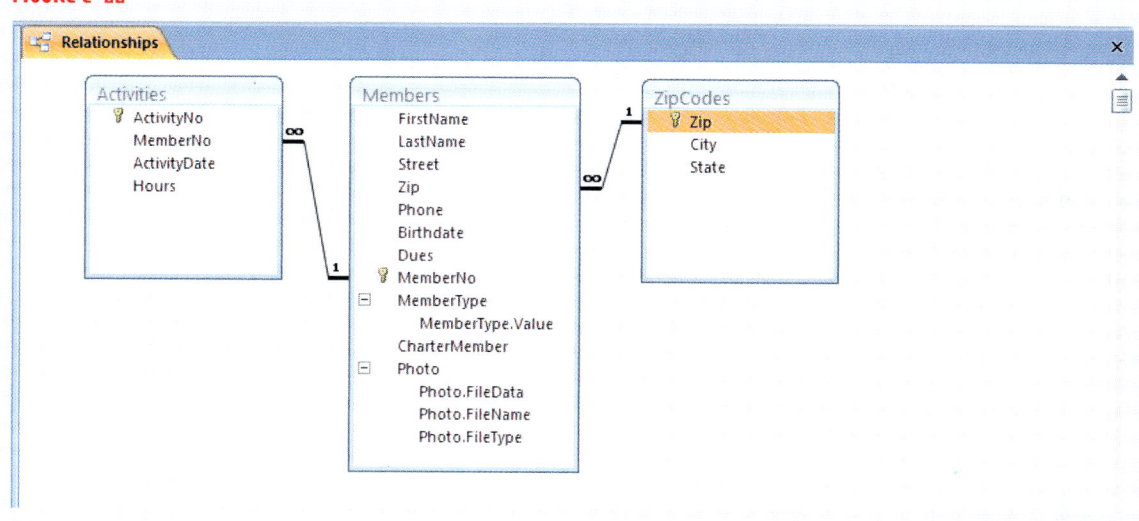

▼ SKILLS REVIEW (CONTINUED)

4. **Create Lookup fields.**
   a. Open the Members table in Design View, then start the Lookup Wizard for the MemberType field.
   b. Select the option that allows you to enter your own values, then enter **Active**, **Inactive**, **Teen**, **Adult**, and **Senior** as the values for the lookup column.
   c. Use the default MemberType label, check the Allow Multiple Values check box, finish the Lookup Wizard, and confirm that you want to allow multiple values.
   d. Save and close the Members table.

5. **Modify Text fields.**
   a. Open the ZipCodes table in Design View.
   b. Change the Field Size property of the State field to **2** then save the ZipCodes table and display it in Datasheet View.
   c. Enter a record with the zip code, city, and state for your school. Try to enter more than two characters in the State field, then close the ZipCodes table.
   d. Open the Members table in Design View. Use the Input Mask Wizard to create an Input Mask property for the Phone field. Choose the Phone Number Input Mask. Accept the other default options provided by the Input Mask Wizard. (*Hint*: If the Input Mask Wizard is not installed on your computer, type **!(999) 000-0000;;_** for the Input Mask property for the Phone field.) See Figure E-23.
   e. Change the Field Size property of the FirstName, LastName, and Street fields to **30**. Save the Members table.
   f. Open the Members table in Datasheet View and enter a new record with your name in the FirstName and LastName fields and your school's Street, Zip, and Phone field values. Note the effect of the Input Mask on the Phone field. Enter **1/1/1985** for the Birthdate field, **200** for Dues, and **1** for MemberNo. Choose both Active and Adult for the MemberType field, and do not check the CharterMember field.

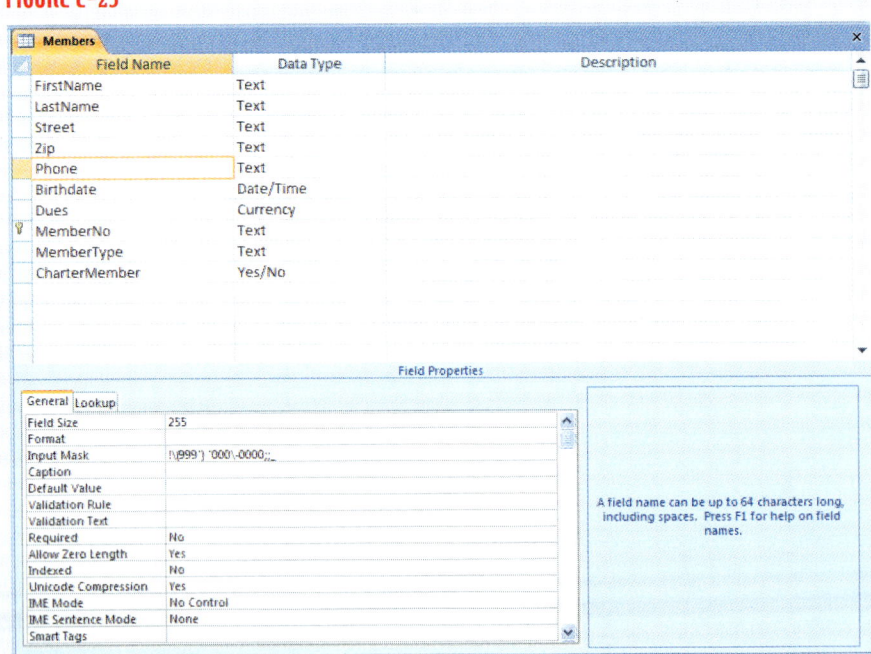

FIGURE E-23

▼ SKILLS REVIEW (CONTINUED)

6. **Modify Number and Currency fields.**
   a. Open the Members table in Design View.
   b. Change the Decimal Places property of the Dues field to **0**. Save and close the Members table.
   c. Open the Activities table in Design View.
   d. Change the Field Size property of the Hours field to **Byte**. Save and close the Activities table.

7. **Modify Date/Time fields.**
   a. Open the Members table in Design View.
   b. Change the Format property of the Birthdate field to **mm/dd/yyyy**
   c. Save and close the Members table.
   d. Open the Activities table in Design View.
   e. Change the Format property of the ActivityDate field to **mm/dd/yyyy**
   f. Save and close the Activities table

8. **Modify field validation properties.**
   a. Open the Members table in Design View.
   b. Click the Birthdate field name, click the Validation Rule text box, then type **<1/1/2000** (Note that Access automatically adds pound signs around date criteria in the Validation Rule property.)
   c. Click the Validation Text box, then type **Birthdate must be before 1/1/2000**
   d. Save and allow the changes, then open the Members table in Datasheet View.
   e. Test the Validation Text and Validation Rule properties by tabbing to the Birthdate field and entering a date after 1/1/2000 such as 1/1/2001. Click OK when prompted with the Validation Text message, press [Esc] to return the Birthdate field value to 01/01/1985, then close the Members table.

▼ SKILLS REVIEW (CONTINUED)

9. **Create Attachment fields.**
   a. Open the Members table in Design View, then add a new field with the field name Photo and an Attachment data type, as shown in Figure E-24. Save the table.
   b. Display the Members table in Datasheet View, then attach the **Member1.jpg** file (provided in the drive and folder where you store your Data Files) to the new Photo field for the first record.
   c. Close the Members table.
   d. Use the Form Wizard to create a form based on all of the fields in the Members table. Use a Columnar layout, a Civic style, and title the form **Members Entry Form**.
   e. Print the first page of the Members Entry Form that shows the picture stored in the Photo field, then close the form.
   f. Close the Membership-E.accdb database, then exit Access.

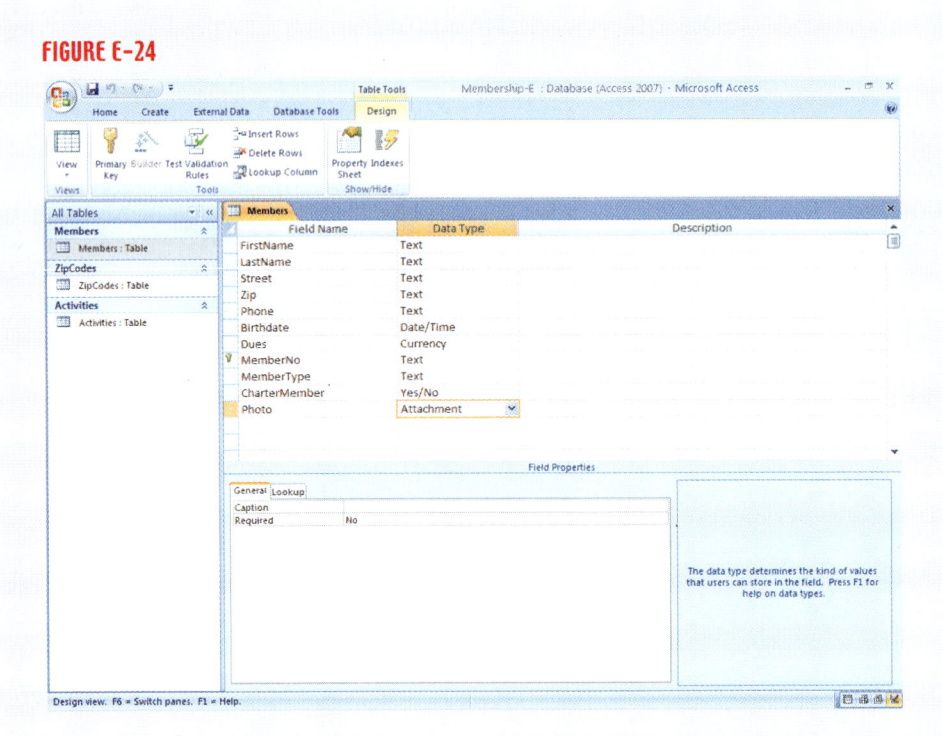

FIGURE E-24

▼ INDEPENDENT CHALLENGE 1

As the manager of a music store's instrument rental program, you decide to create a database to track rentals to schoolchildren. The fields you need to track are organized with four tables: Instruments, Rentals, Customers, and Schools.

   a. Start Access, then create a new blank database called **MusicStore-E.accdb** in the folder where you store your Data Files.
   b. Use Table Design View to create the four tables in the MusicStore-E database using the information shown in Figure E-25. The primary key field for each table is identified with bold text.

FIGURE E-25

table	field name	data type
Customers	FirstName	Text
	LastName	Text
	Street	Text
	City	Text
	State	Text
	Zip	Text
	CustNo	Text
	SchoolNo	Text
Instruments	Description	Text
	SerialNo	Text
	MonthlyFee	Currency
Schools	SchoolName	Text
	SchoolNo	Text
Rentals	**RentalNo**	AutoNumber
	CustNo	Text
	SerialNo	Text
	RentalDate	Date/Time

   c. Enter **>3/1/2010** as the Validation Rule property for the RentalDate field of the Rentals table. This change allows only dates later than 3/1/2010 to be entered into this field.
   d. Enter **Dates must be after March 1, 2010** as the Validation Text property to the RentalDate field of the Rentals table. Note that Access adds pound signs (#) to the date criteria entered in the Validation Rule as soon as you enter the Validation Text property.
   e. Save and close the Rentals table.

▼ INDEPENDENT CHALLENGE 1 (CONTINUED)

f. Open the Relationships window, add all four tables to the window, as shown in Figure E-26, and create one-to-many relationships as shown. Be sure to enforce referential integrity on each relationship.

g. Preview the Relationship report, add your name as a label to the Report Header section, then print the report, making sure that all fields of each table are visible.

h. Close the Relationship report without saving it. Close the Relationships window, then save the layout if prompted.

i. Close the MusicStore-E.accdb database, then exit Access.

FIGURE E-26

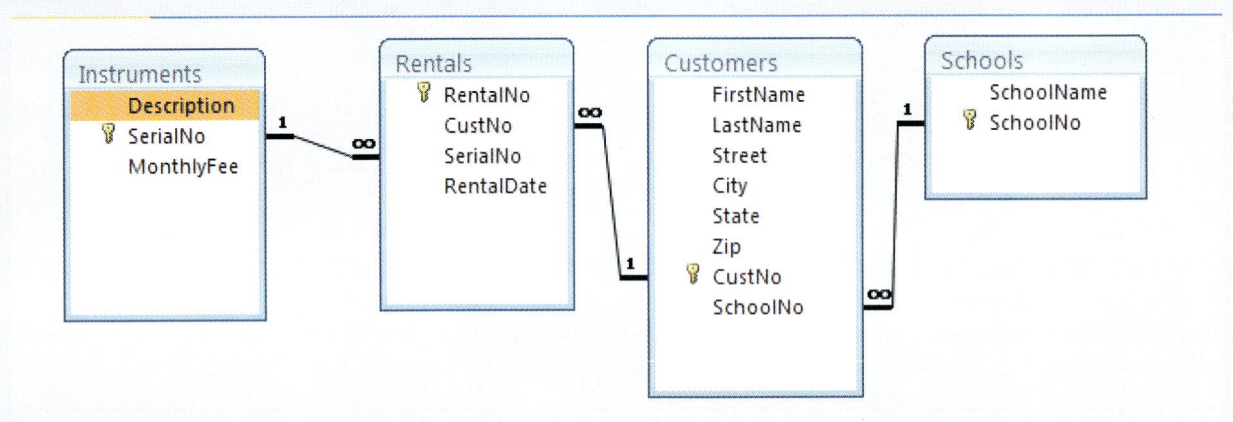

Instruments	Rentals	Customers	Schools
Description	RentalNo	FirstName	SchoolName
SerialNo	CustNo	LastName	SchoolNo
MonthlyFee	SerialNo	Street	
	RentalDate	City	
		State	
		Zip	
		CustNo	
		SchoolNo	

Relationships: Instruments 1—∞ Rentals ∞—1 Customers ∞—1 Schools

▼ INDEPENDENT CHALLENGE 2

You're a member and manager of a recreational baseball team and decide to create an Access database to manage player information, games, and batting statistics.

This Independent Challenge requires an Internet connection.

a. Start Access, then create a new database called **Baseball-E.accdb** in the drive and folder where you store your Data Files.
b. Create a **Players** table with fields and appropriate data types to record the player first name, last name, and uniform number. Make the uniform number field the primary key field.
c. Create a **Games** table with fields and appropriate data types to record an automatic game number, date of the game, opponent's name, home score, and visitor score. Make the game number field the primary key field.
d. Create an **AtBats** table with fields and appropriate data types to record hits, at bats, the game number, and the uniform number of the player. This table does not need a primary key field.
e. In the Relationships window, create a one-to-many relationship with referential integrity between the Games and AtBats table, using the common game number field.
f. In the Relationships window, create a one-to-many relationship with referential integrity between the Players and AtBats table, using the common uniform number field. The final Relationships window is shown in Figure E-27.
g. Use the Relationship Report button to create a report of the Relationships window, then print it. Close the Relationship report without saving it. Close the Relationships window, saving changes if prompted.

FIGURE E-27

h. Using an Internet search tool, find the roster for a baseball team in your area, and enter nine players into the Players table. One of the players should have your name. Print the Players datasheet.
i. Research the games that this team has previously played, and enter one game record into the Games table.
j. Using the GameNo value of **1** and the UniformNo values from the Players table, enter nine records into the AtBats table to represent the batting statistics for the nine players for that game. Your entries do not need to represent a specific game, but they should be realistic. (*Hint*: Most players bat three or four times per game. A player cannot have more hits in a game than at bats.)
k. Print the AtBats datasheet.
l. Close the Baseball-E.accdb database, then exit Access.

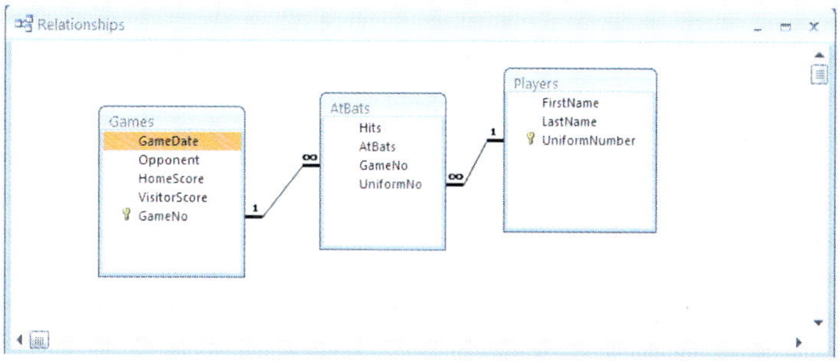

▼ INDEPENDENT CHALLENGE 3

You want to create a database that documents blood bank donations by the employees of your company. Start by designing the database on paper, including the tables, field names, data types, and relationships. You want to track information such as employee name, department, blood type, date of donation, and the hospital that is earmarked to receive the donation. You also want to track basic hospital information, such as the hospital name and address.

a. On paper, create three balanced columns by drawing two vertical lines from the top to the bottom of the paper. Label the columns **Table**, **Field Name**, and **Data Type**, from left to right.

b. In the middle column, list all of the fields that need to be tracked to record the blood donations. When creating your field lists for each table, be sure to separate personal names into at least two fields, FirstName and LastName, so that you can easily sort, filter, and find data based on either part of a person's name.

c. In the first column, identify the table that contains this field. (*Hint*: In this case, you should identify three tables: Employees, Donations, and Hospitals.)

d. Identify the primary key field for each table by circling it. You might have to add a new field to each table if you do not have an existing field that naturally serves as the primary key field. (*Hint*: Each employee is identified with a unique EmployeeID, each hospital with a unique HospitalID, and each donation with a DonationID.)

e. In the third column, identify the appropriate data type for each field.

f. After identifying all field names, table names, and data types for each field, reorder the fields so that the fields for each table are listed together.

g. On a new sheet of paper, sketch the field lists for each table as they would appear in the Access Relationships window. Circle the primary key fields for each table. Include the one-to-many join lines as well as the "one" and "infinity" symbols to identify the "one" and "many" sides of the one-to-many relationship. To help determine how you should create the relationships between the tables, note that one employee can make several blood donations. One hospital can receive many donations. (*Hint*: When building a one-to-many relationship between two tables, one field must be common to both tables. To create a common field, you might need to return to your field lists in Step f and add a foreign key field to the table on the "many" side of the relationship in order to link the tables.)

Advanced Challenge Exercise

- Build the database you designed in Access with the name **BloodDrive-E.accdb**. Don't forget to enforce referential integrity on the two one-to-many relationships in this database.
- Print the Relationship report with your name added as a label to the Report Header section. Close the Relationship report without saving it, then close the Relationships window and save the layout changes.
- Add Lookup properties to the blood type field to provide only valid blood type entries of **A–**, **A+**, **B–**, **B+**, **O–**, **O+**, **AB–**, and **AB+** for this field.
- Close BloodDrive-E.accdb, then exit Access.

▼ REAL LIFE INDEPENDENT CHALLENGE

You want to document the books you've read by creating and storing the information in a relational database. You design the database on paper by identifying the tables, field names, data types, and relationships between the tables.

a. Complete Steps a through g as described in Independent Challenge 3, using the new case information. You like to read multiple books from the same author, so you should separate the author information into a separate table to avoid duplicate author name entries in the Books table. You also want to track information including the book title, category (such as Biography, Mystery, or Science Fiction), rating (a numeric value from 1–10 that indicates how much you liked the book), date you read the book, author's first name, and author's last name. When creating primary key fields, note that each book has an ISBN—International Standard Book Number—that is a unique number assigned to every book. To uniquely identify each author, use an AuthorNo field. Do not use the AuthorLastName field as the primary key field for the Authors table because it does not uniquely identify authors who have the same last names.

Advanced Challenge Exercise

- In Access, build the database you designed. Name the database **Books-E.accdb**, and save it in the drive and folder where you store your Data Files. Don't forget to enforce referential integrity on the one-to-many relationship in this database.
- Print the Relationship report with your name added as a label to the Report Header section. Close the Relationship report without saving it, then close the Relationships window and save the layout changes.
- Add Lookup properties to the field that identifies book categories. Include at least four types of book categories in the list.
- Add at least three records to each table and print them.
- Close Books-E.accdb, then exit Access.

▼ VISUAL WORKSHOP

Open the **Training-E.accdb** database, and create a new table called Vendors using the Table Design View shown in Figure E-28 to determine field names and data types. Make the following property changes: Change the Field Size property of the VState field to **2**, the VZip field to **9**, and VPhone field to **10**. Change the Field Size property of the VendorName, VStreet, and VCity fields to **30**. Apply a Phone Number Input Mask to the VPhone field. Be sure to specify that the VendorID field is the primary key field. Enter one record into the datasheet with your last name in the VendorName field and your school's contact information in the other fields. Print the datasheet in landscape orientation.

FIGURE E-28

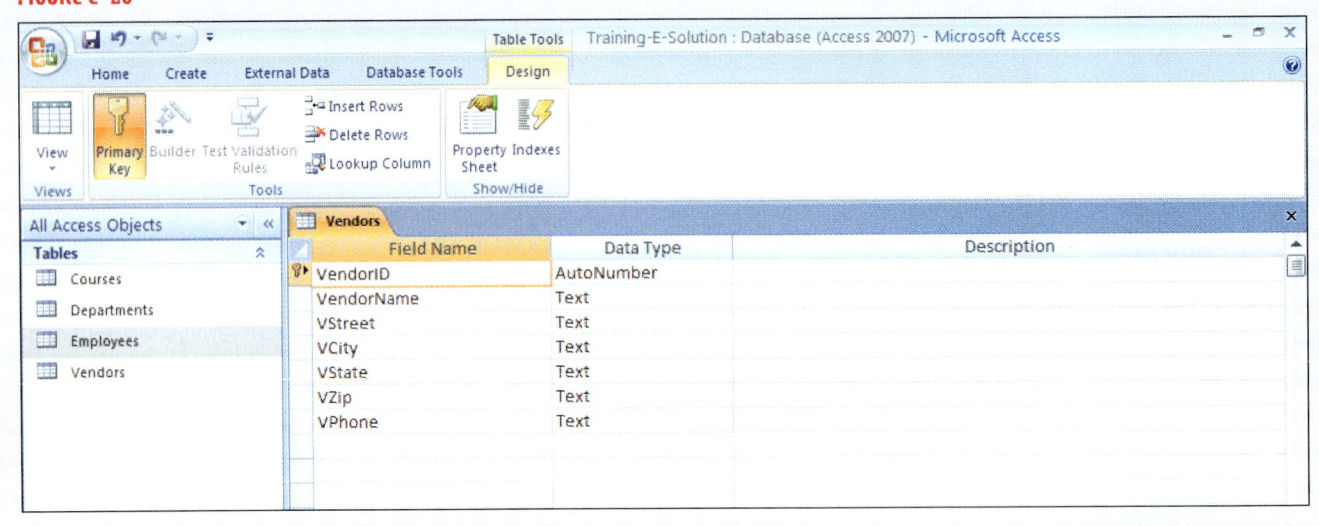

UNIT F
Access 2007

Creating Multiple Table Queries

Files You Will Need:
Quest-F.accdb
Membership-F.accdb
MusicStore-F.accdb
RealEstate-F.accdb
Scholarships-F.accdb
Training-F.accdb

Queries are database objects that organize fields from one or more tables into a single datasheet. A **select query**, the most common type of query, retrieves fields from related tables and displays records in a datasheet. Select queries are used to select only certain records from a database. They can also sort records, calculate new fields of data, or calculate statistics such as the sum or average of a given field. You can also present data selected by a query in Query PivotTable View or Query PivotChart View. These views display information about summarized groups of records in a crosstabular report or graph. The Quest database has been updated to contain more customers, tours, and sales. You help Mark Rock, a Quest tour developer for U.S. travel, create queries to analyze this information.

OBJECTIVES

Build select queries
Use multiple sort orders
Develop AND criteria
Develop OR criteria
Create calculated fields
Build summary queries
Build crosstab queries
Build PivotTables and PivotCharts

UNIT F
Access 2007

Building Select Queries

You can create select queries by using the **Simple Query Wizard** or by building the query in **Query Design View**. Creating a select query with the Simple Query Wizard is fast and easy, but learning how to use Query Design View gives you more flexibility and options when selecting and presenting information. When you open (or **run**) a query, the fields and records that you have selected for the query are presented as a datasheet in **Query Datasheet View**. Query Datasheet View does not present a duplicate copy of the data stored in the tables. Rather, it displays table data in a new arrangement, sometimes called a **logical view** of the data. If you edit data using a query datasheet, the changes are actually made to the underlying table as if you were working directly in a table datasheet. Mark Rock asks you to create a query to answer the question, "Who is purchasing our tours?" You can select fields from the Customers, Sales, and Tours tables using Query Design View to display a single datasheet that answers this question.

STEPS

1. **Start Access, open the Quest-F.accdb database from the drive and folder where you store your Data Files, then enable content if prompted**

2. **Click the Create tab on the Ribbon, then click the Query Design button**
   The Show Table dialog box opens and lists all the tables in the database. You use the Show Table dialog box to add the tables that contain the fields you want to view in the final query datasheet.

   TROUBLE
   If you add a table to Query Design View twice by mistake, click the title bar of the extra field list, then press [Delete].

3. **Double-click Customers, double-click Sales, double-click Tours, click Close, then maximize Query Design View**
   Recall that the upper part of Query Design View displays the fields for each of the three selected tables in **field lists**, with the name of the associated table shown in the field list title bar. Primary key fields are identified with a small key icon to the left of the field. To rearrange the field lists in Query Design View, drag the title bar of a field list to move it, or drag the edge of a field list to resize it. Relationships between tables are displayed with **one-to-many join lines** that connect the linking fields. You add the fields that you want the query to display in the columns in the lower part of Query Design View, known as the **query design grid**.

4. **Drag the FName field in the Customers table field list to the first column of the query design grid**
   The order in which you place the fields in the query design grid is the order they appear in the datasheet. When you drag a field to the query design grid, any existing fields move to the right to accommodate the new field.

   TROUBLE
   Drag the bottom edge of the Tours field list down to view all of the fields in that table.

5. **Double-click the LName field in the Customers field list, double-click the SaleDate field in the Sales field list, double-click the TourName field in the Tours field list, then double-click the Cost field in the Tours field list as shown in Figure F-1**
   If you add the wrong field to the query design grid, you can delete it by clicking the **field selector**, a thin gray bar above each field name, then pressing [Delete]. Deleting a field from the query design grid removes it from the logical view of this query's datasheet, but does not delete the field from the database. A field is defined and the field's contents are stored in a table object only.

6. **Click the View button on the Design tab to run the query and open the query datasheet**
   The resulting datasheet looks like Figure F-2. The datasheet shows the five fields selected in Query Design View: FName and LName from the Customers table, SaleDate from the Sales table, and TourName and Cost from the Tours table. The datasheet displays 40 records that represent 40 sales. The query has selected the name Christine Collins several times—even though this name is recorded only once in the Customers table—because she is related to many sales in the Sales table. The Bayside Shelling tour has been selected for the datasheet several times—though it is physically recorded only once in the Tours table—because it is related to many sales in the Sales table.

Access 138   Creating Multiple Table Queries

FIGURE F-1: Query Design View with five fields in the query design grid

- View button
- One-to-many join lines
- Tours field list has been resized to show all fields
- Field selectors
- Resize bar
- Query design grid

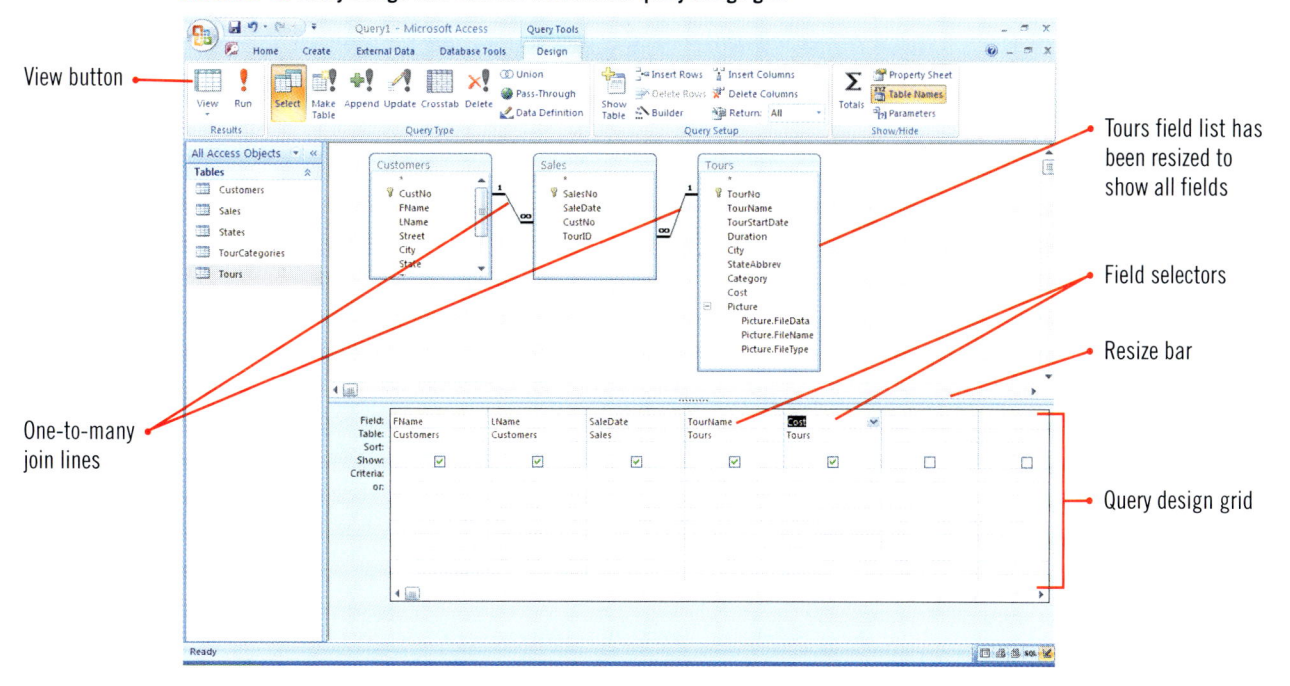

FIGURE F-2: Query datasheet showing related information from three tables

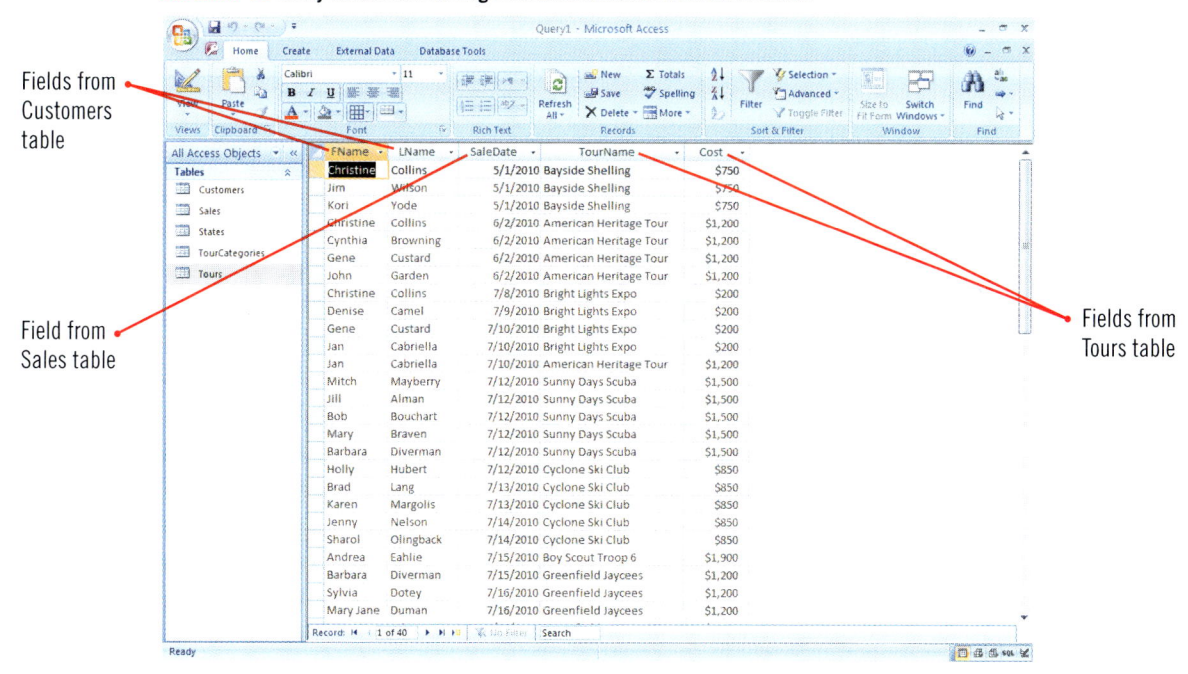

- Fields from Customers table
- Field from Sales table
- Fields from Tours table

Resizing Query Design View

Drag the **resize bar**, a thin gray bar that separates the field lists from the query design grid, up or down to provide more room for the upper (field lists) or lower (query design grid) panes of Query Design View. By dragging the resize bar down, you can create enough room to resize each field list so that you can see all field names for each table.

Creating Multiple Table Queries

UNIT F
Access 2007
Using Multiple Sort Orders

Sorting refers to reordering records in either ascending or descending order based on the values in a field. Queries allow you to specify more than one sort field in Query Design View. Sort orders are evaluated from left to right, meaning that the sort field farthest to the left is the primary sort field. Sort orders defined in Query Design View are saved with the query object. You want to list the records in alphabetical order based on the customer's last name. If the customer has purchased more than one tour, you decide to further sort the records by the sale date.

STEPS

1. **Click the View button on the Home tab to return to Query Design View**

   To sort the records by last name then by sale date, the LName field must be the primary sort field, and the SaleDate field must be the secondary sort field.

2. **Click the LName field Sort cell in the query design grid, click the Sort list arrow, click Ascending, click the SaleDate field Sort cell in the query design grid, click the Sort list arrow, then click Ascending**

   The resulting query design grid should look like Figure F-3.

3. **Click the View button on the Design tab to see the query datasheet**

   The records of the datasheet are now listed in ascending order based on the values in the LName field. When the same value appears in the LName field, the records are further sorted by the date in the SaleDate field. Christine Collins purchased three tours, but she prefers to be called "Chris." You want to fix this error in the query datasheet.

   > **QUICK TIP**
   > You can resize the columns of a datasheet by pointing to the right column border that separates the field names, then dragging ↔ left or right to resize the columns. Double-click ↔ to automatically adjust the column width to fit the widest entry.

4. **Double-click any occurrence of Christine, type Chris, then press [↓]**

   Because this name is physically stored only once in the Customers table (but selected three times for this query), all three records that contained the name "Christine" are automatically updated to "Chris," as shown in Figure F-4. In a properly designed relational database, editing any occurrence of a value in a table, query, or form automatically updates all other occurrences of that data in every other database object. You also need to update the price of the Sunny Days Scuba tour.

5. **Select any occurrence of $1,500 for the Cost field in one of the first three records, type 1400, click Sunny Days Scuba, click the Selection button, then click Equals "Sunny Days Scuba"**

   Because the Sunny Days Scuba tour is physically stored only once in the Tours table (but selected five times for this query), all occurrences of the price for the Sunny Days Scuba tour are now changed from $1,500 to $1,400, regardless of where they are sorted or if they are filtered in the datasheet. When Access saves a query object, it saves **Structured Query Language (SQL)** statements. You can view or work with SQL using Access query objects.

6. **Click the View button arrow on the Home tab, then click SQL View**

   The SQL statements determine what fields are selected, how the tables are joined, and how the resulting records are sorted. Fortunately, you do not have to be able to write or understand SQL to use Access. The easy-to-use Query Design View gives you a way to select and sort data from underlying tables without being an SQL programmer.

7. **Close the SQL window, click Yes when prompted to save the changes, type CustomerSales in the Query Name text box, then click OK**

   The query is now saved and listed as a query object in the Navigation Pane.

Access 140   Creating Multiple Table Queries

FIGURE F-3: Specifying multiple sort orders in Query Design View

Primary sort order

Secondary sort order

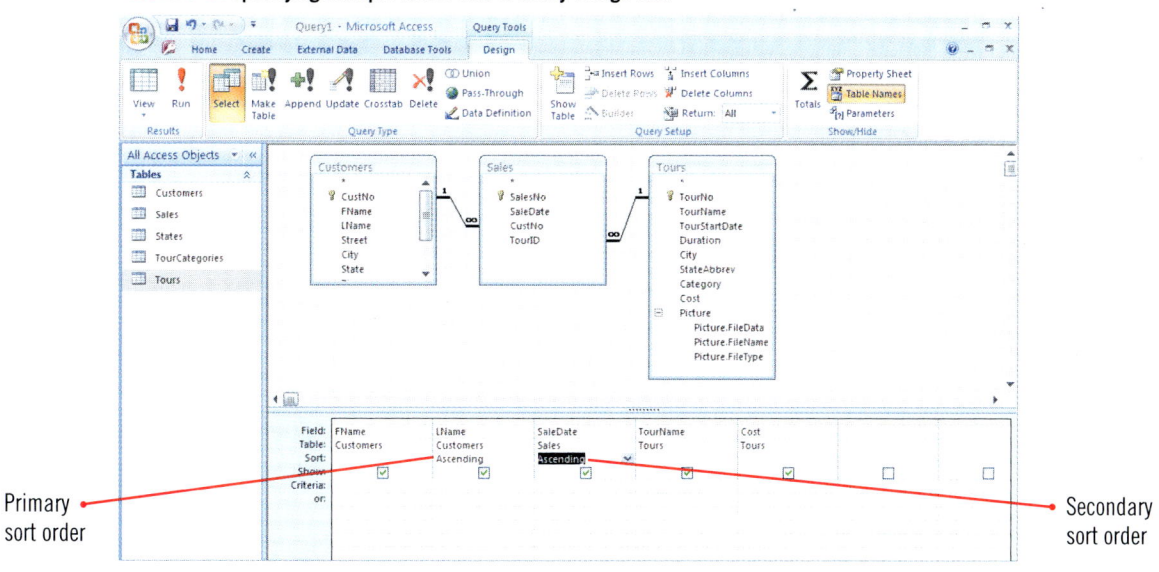

FIGURE F-4: Records sorted by LName, then by SaleDate

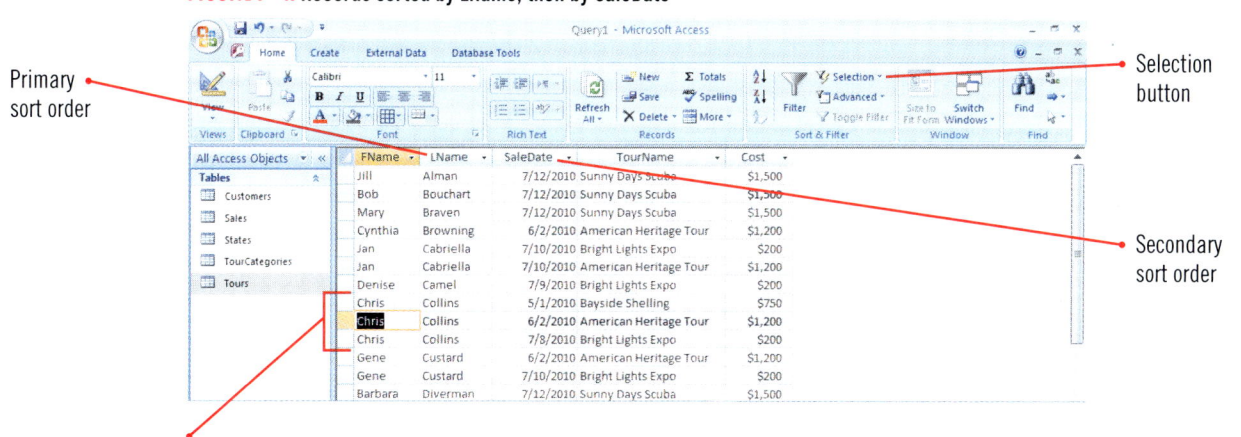

Primary sort order

Selection button

Secondary sort order

All three occurrences of Christine are changed to Chris

Specifying a sort order different from the field order in the datasheet

If your database has several customers with the same last name, you can include a secondary sort on the first name field to distinguish the customers. If you also want to display the fields in a first name, last name order, you can use the solution shown in Figure F-5. You can add a field to the query design grid twice and use the Show check box to sort the fields in one order (LName, FName), yet display the fields in the resulting datasheet in another order (FName, LName).

FIGURE F-5: Sorting on a field that is not displayed

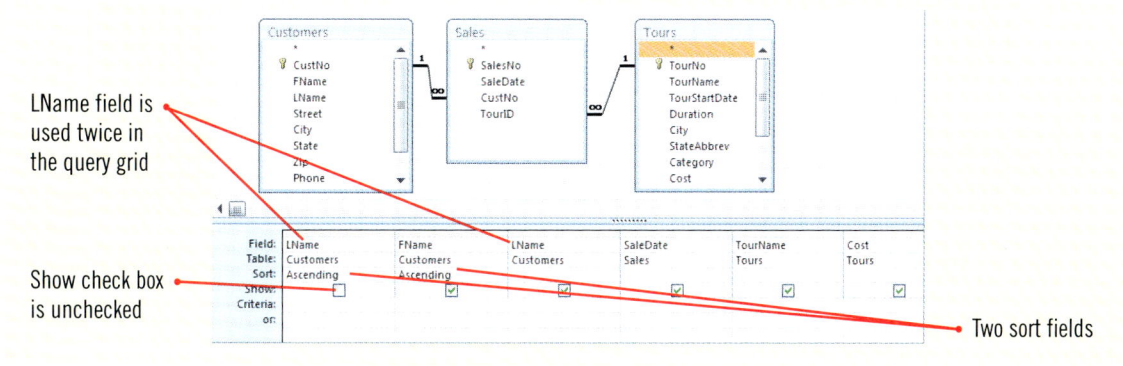

LName field is used twice in the query grid

Show check box is unchecked

Two sort fields

Creating Multiple Table Queries

Access 141

Developing AND Criteria

You can limit the number of records that appear on the resulting datasheet by entering criteria in Query Design View. **Criteria** are tests, or limiting conditions, for which the record must be true to be selected for a datasheet. To create **AND criteria**, which means the query selects a record only if *all* criteria are true, enter two or more criteria on the same Criteria row of the query design grid. To create AND criteria for the *same field*, enter the two criteria in the same Criteria cell separated by the AND operator. Mark Rock predicts strong sales for adventure tours during the month of July. He asks you to create a list of the existing tour sales that meet those criteria.

STEPS

1. **Double-click CustomerSales in the Navigation Pane to open it in Datasheet View, click the View button arrow on the Home tab, click Design View, then maximize Query Design View**

    To query for adventure tours, you need to add the Category field and "Adventure" criterion for this field in the query grid.

2. **Double-click the Category field in the Tours field list to add it to the query grid, click the first Criteria cell for the Category field, then type adventure**

    To find all tours in the month of July for the year 2010, use the asterisk (*) **wildcard character** in the day portion of the SaleDate criterion.

    > **QUICK TIP**
    > Criteria are not case sensitive, so adventure, Adventure, and ADVENTURE are equivalent criteria entries.

3. **Click the first Criteria cell for the SaleDate field, type 7/*/2010, then press [↓]**

    As shown in Figure F-6, Access assists you with **criteria syntax**, rules by which criteria need to be entered. Access automatically adds quotation marks around text criteria in Text fields such as "adventure" in the Category field. The criteria in Number, Currency, and Yes/No fields are not surrounded by any characters. Access also adds the **Like operator** to the SaleDate field criterion because it includes the wildcard asterisk character. (Access uses the Like operator to find values in a field that match the pattern you specify.) See Table F-1 for more information on common Access comparison operators and criteria syntax.

4. **Click the Office button, click Save As, type JulyAdventure, then click OK**

    The query is saved with the new name, JulyAdventure, as a new object in the Quest-F.accdb database.

5. **Click the View button on the Design tab to view the query results**

    The query results are shown in Figure F-7.

6. **Close the JulyAdventure datasheet**

FIGURE F-6: Entering AND criteria on the same row

SaleDate field criterion

Category field criterion

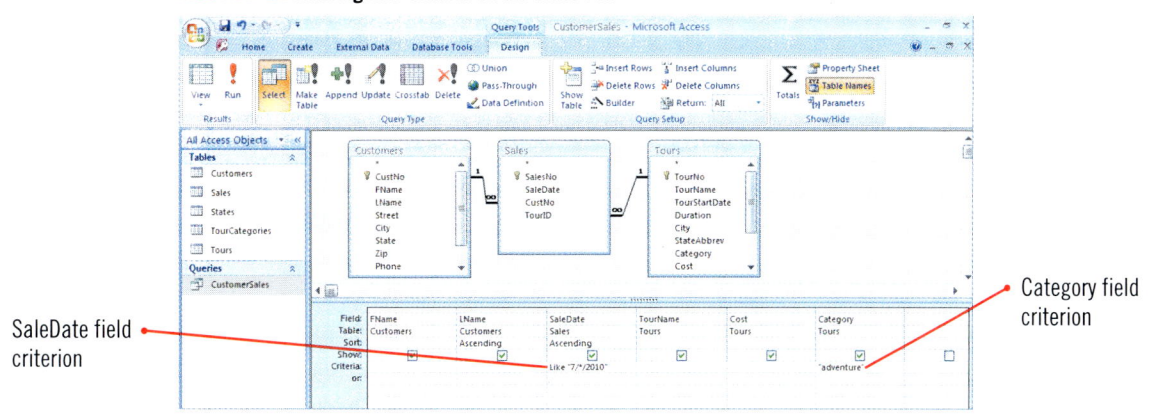

FIGURE F-7: Datasheet for July Adventure records

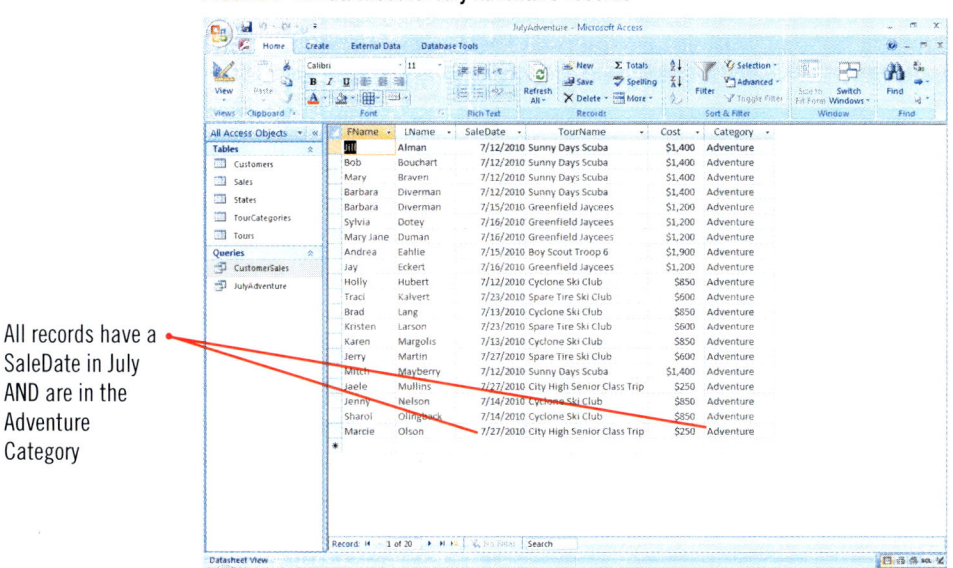

All records have a SaleDate in July AND are in the Adventure Category

TABLE F-1: Common comparison operators

operator	description	example	result
>	Greater than	>50	Value exceeds 50
>=	Greater than or equal to	>=50	Value is 50 or greater
<	Less than	<50	Value is less than 50
<=	Less than or equal to	<=50	Value is 50 or less
<>	Not equal to	<>50	Value is any number other than 50
Between...And	Finds values between two numbers or dates	Between #2/2/2006# And #2/2/2010#	Dates between 2/2/2006 and 2/2/2010, inclusive
In	Finds a value that is one of a list	In ("IA","KS","NE")	Value equals IA or KS or NE
Null	Finds records that have no entry in a particular field	Null	No value has been entered in a field
Is Not Null	Finds records that have any entry in a particular field	Is Not Null	Any value has been entered in a field
Like	Finds records that match the criterion	Like "A*"	Value starts with A
Not	Finds records that do not match the criterion	Not 2	Numbers other than 2

Creating Multiple Table Queries

UNIT F
Access 2007

Developing OR Criteria

In a query, all criteria entries define which records are selected for the resulting datasheet. Whereas AND criteria *narrow* the number of records in the resulting datasheet by requiring that a record be true for multiple criteria, OR criteria *expand* the number of records that appear in the datasheet because a record needs to be true *for only one* of the criteria rows selected. You enter **OR criteria**, which means the query selects records where *any one* criterion is true, in the query design grid on different lines (criteria rows). Because each criteria row of the query design grid is evaluated separately, more OR criteria entries in the query grid produce more records for the resulting datasheet. Based on excellent July sales of adventure tours, Mark Rock inquires about July sales for educational tours. He asks you to modify the JulyAdventure query to expand the number of records to include sales for educational tours, too.

STEPS

1. **Right-click the JulyAdventure query in the Navigation Pane, click Design View on the shortcut menu, then maximize Query Design View**

   To add OR criteria, you have to enter criteria in the next available "or" row of the query design grid. By default, the query grid displays eight rows for additional OR criteria, but you can add even more rows using the Insert Rows button on the Design tab.

2. **In the Category column, click the or Criteria cell below "adventure", type educational, then click the View button on the Design tab**

   The datasheet expands from 20 records to 25 to include five tours in the Educational category. Because no date criterion is used in the SaleDate field, you see all Educational tour records instead of only those with a SaleDate in July. To select only those tours in July, you need to add more criteria to Query Design View.

3. **Click the View button on the Home tab to return to Query Design View, click the next SaleDate Criteria cell, type 7/*/2010, then press [↓] as shown in Figure F-8**

   Each criteria row is evaluated separately, which is why you must put the same date criterion for the SaleDate field in *both* rows of the query design grid if you want to select July records for both tour categories.

4. **Click the View button on the Design tab to return to Datasheet View**

   The resulting datasheet selects 21 records, as shown in Figure F-9. All of the records have a Category entry of Adventure or Educational and a SaleDate in July.

5. **Click the Office button, click Save As, type JulyAdventureOrEducational, then click OK**

   The JulyAdventureOrEducational query is saved as a new query object.

   > **QUICK TIP**
   > To rename an object from the Navigation Pane, right-click it, then choose Rename on the shortcut menu.

6. **Close the JulyAdventureOrEducational query**

   The Quest-F.accdb Navigation Pane displays the three queries you created.

Access 144

Creating Multiple Table Queries

FIGURE F-8: Entering OR criteria on different rows

Insert Rows button

SaleDate field criteria

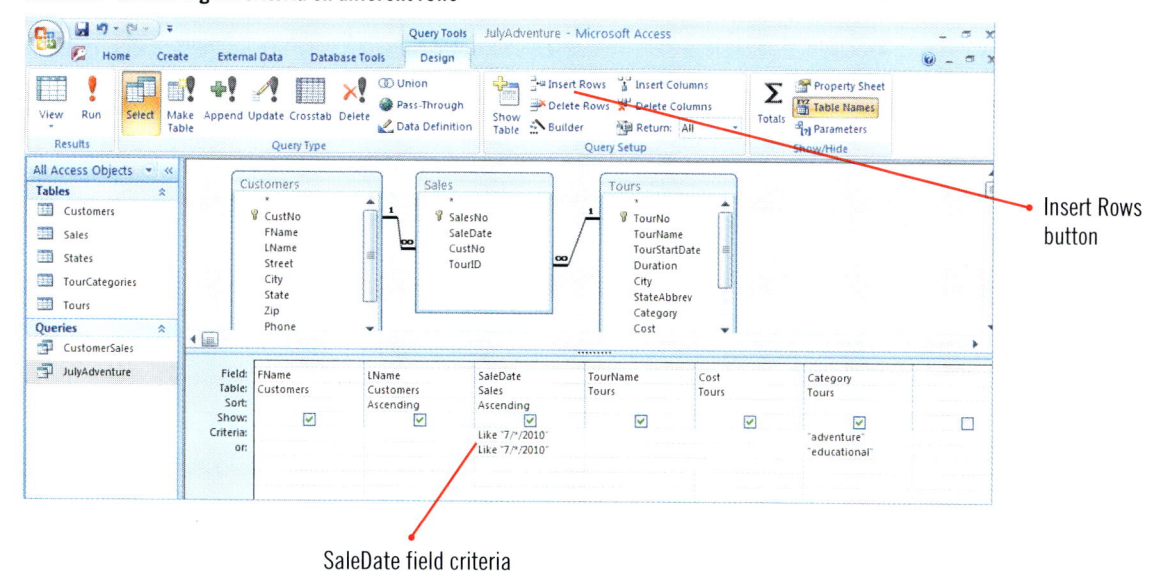

FIGURE F-9: OR criteria add more records to the datasheet

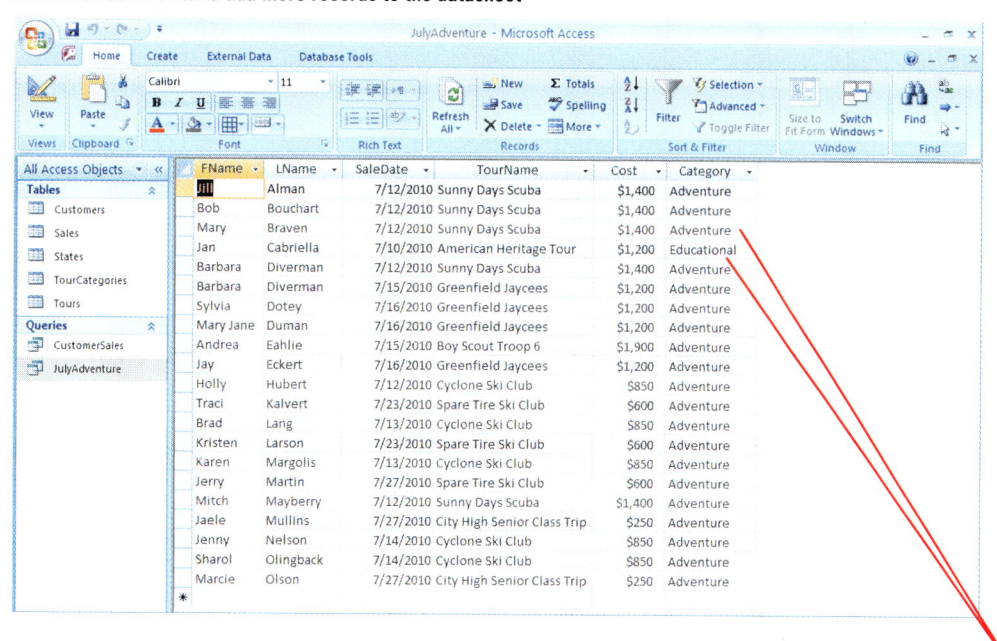

Adventure and Educational tours with a SaleDate in July

Using wildcard characters in query criteria

To search for a pattern, use a wildcard character to represent any character in the criteria entry. Use a ? (question mark) to search for any single character and an * (asterisk) to search for any number of characters. Wildcard characters are often used with the Like operator.

For example, the criterion Like "10/*/2010" finds all dates in October of 2010, and the criterion Like "F*" finds all entries that start with the letter F.

Creating Multiple Table Queries   Access 145

Creating Calculated Fields

UNIT F — Access 2007

A **calculated field** is a field of data that can be created based on the values of other fields. For example, you can calculate the value for a Tax field by multiplying the value of the Sales field by a percentage. To create a calculated field and automatically populate every record with the correct value for that field, define the new calculated field in Query Design View using an expression that describes the calculation. An **expression** is a combination of field names, operators (such as +, –, /, and *), and functions that result in a single value. A **function** is a predefined formula that returns a value such as a subtotal, count, or the current date. See Table F-2 for more information on arithmetic operators and Table F-3 for more information on functions. Mark Rock asks you to find the number of days between a sale and the tour's start date. To determine this information, you can create a calculated field called LeadTime that subtracts the SaleDate from the TourStartDate.

STEPS

1. **Click the Create tab on the Ribbon, click the Query Design button, double-click Tours, double-click Sales, click Close in the Show Table dialog box, then maximize Query Design View**

   First you add the fields to the grid that you want to display in the query.

2. **Double-click the TourName field, double-click the TourStartDate field, double-click the Cost field, then double-click the SaleDate field**

   You create a calculated field in the Field cell of the design grid by entering a new descriptive field name followed by a colon, then an expression. Field names you use in an expression must be surrounded by square brackets.

   > **QUICK TIP**
   > To display a long entry in a field cell, you can also right-click the cell, then click Zoom.

3. **Click the blank Field cell in the fifth column, type LeadTime:[TourStartDate]-[SaleDate], then drag the ✥ pointer on the right edge of the fifth column selector to the right to display the entire entry as shown in Figure F-10**

4. **Click the View button on the Design tab to observe the calculated LeadTime field in the datasheet**

   The LeadTime field calculates correctly, showing the number of days between the TourStartDate and the SaleDate. You can create another calculated field to determine the commission paid on each sale, which is calculated as 10% of the Cost field.

   > **QUICK TIP**
   > You do not need to show the fields used in the expression (in this case, TourStartDate and Cost) in the query, but displaying them helps you determine if the expression is calculating correctly.

5. **Click the View button on the Home tab to return to Query Design View, click the blank Field cell in the sixth column, type Commission:[Cost]*0.1, then click the View button on the Design tab**

   The resulting datasheet, with two calculated fields, is shown in Figure F-11. Any change to a field value that is used in an expression for a calculated field automatically updates the calculation as well.

6. **Press [Tab], type 7/26/2010 in the TourStartDate field for the first record, press [Tab], type 800 in the Cost field for the first record, then press [↓]**

   The LeadTime and Commission calculated fields for the first three records of this query datasheet update automatically because the TourStartDate and Cost fields for the first three records are all based on the same tour, Bayside Shelling, which is physically entered in the database once in the Tours table.

7. **Click the Save button 🖫 on the Quick Access toolbar, type LeadTimesAndCommissions in the Save As dialog box, click OK, then close the datasheet**

   The query is saved as an object in the database.

Creating Multiple Table Queries

FIGURE F-10: Creating a calculated field

- A colon (:) separates the field name from the expression
- Lead time is the new calculated field name
- Drag the column separator to widen the column
- [TourStartDate]-[SaleDate] is the expression

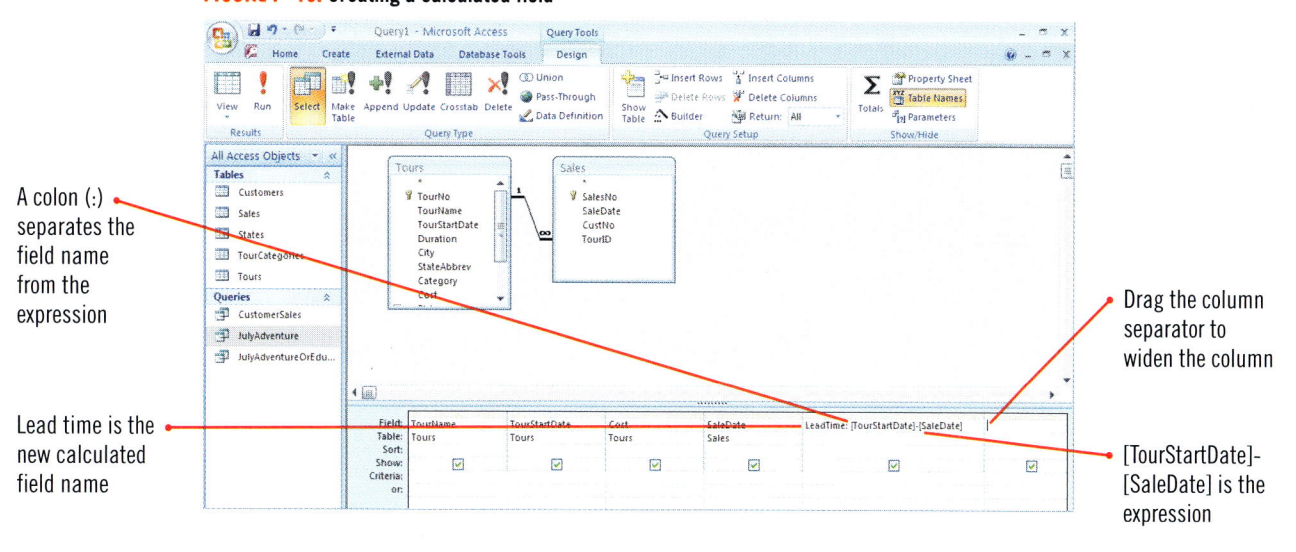

FIGURE F-11: Viewing and testing the calculated fields

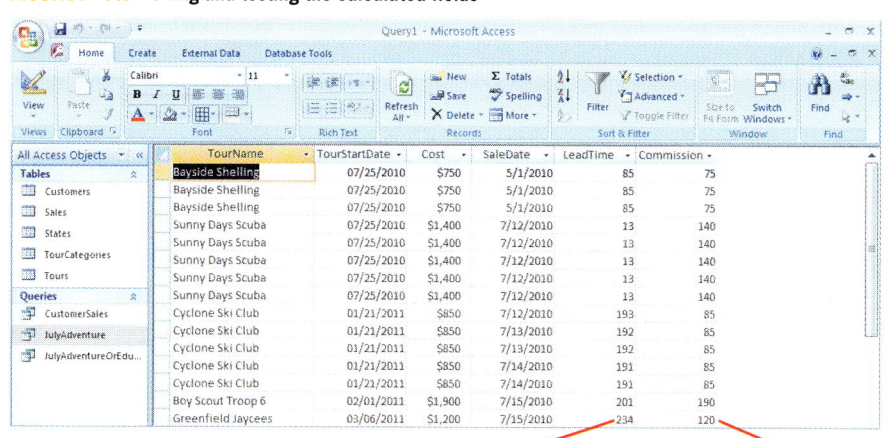

- LeadTime calculated field, which subtracts the SaleDate value from the TourStartDate value
- Commission calculated field, which multiplies the Cost field value by 0.1

TABLE F-2: Arithmetic operators

operator	description
+	Addition
–	Subtraction
*	Multiplication
/	Division
^	Exponentiation

TABLE F-3: Common functions

function	sample expression and description
DATE	DATE()-[BirthDate] Calculates the number of days between today and the date in the BirthDate field
PMT	PMT([Rate],[Term],[Loan]) Calculates the monthly payment on a loan where the Rate field contains the monthly interest rate, the Term field contains the number of monthly payments, and the Loan field contains the total amount financed
LEFT	LEFT([LastName],2) Returns the first two characters of the entry in the LastName field
RIGHT	RIGHT([Partno],3) Returns the last three characters of the entry in the Partno field
LEN	LEN([Description]) Returns the number of characters in the Description field

Access expressions are not case sensitive, so DATE()-[BirthDate] is equivalent to date()-[birthdate] and DATE()-[BIRTHDATE]. Therefore, use capitalization in expressions in any way that makes the expression easier to read.

Creating Multiple Table Queries

Building Summary Queries

UNIT F
Access 2007

A **summary query** calculates statistics about groups of records. To create a summary query, you add the **Total row** to the query design grid to specify how you want to group and calculate the statistics using aggregate functions. In Access 2007, you can also add a Total row to the bottom of any table or query datasheet. **Aggregate functions** calculate a statistic such as a subtotal, count, or average on a given field in a group of records. Some aggregate functions, such as Sum or Avg (Average), can be used only on fields with Number or Currency data types. Other functions, such as Min (Minimum), Max (Maximum), or Count, can also be used on Text fields. Table F-4 provides more information on aggregate functions. A key difference between the statistics displayed by a summary query and those displayed by calculated fields is that summary queries provide calculations that describe a *group of records*, whereas calculated fields provide a new field of information for *each record*. Mark Rock asks you to calculate total sales per tour category. You can use the Total row and build a summary query to provide these statistics.

STEPS

1. **Click the Create tab on the Ribbon, click the Query Design button, double-click Sales, double-click Tours, click Close in the Show Table dialog box, then maximize Query Design View**

   It doesn't matter in what order you add the field lists to Query Design View.

2. **Double-click the SalesNo field, double-click the Category field, double-click the Cost field, then click the View button on the Design tab to view the datasheet**

   Forty records are displayed, representing all 40 records in the Sales table. You can add a Total row to any datasheet.

   TROUBLE
   If the sum total is not completely displayed in the Cost field, widen the column to show the entire value.

3. **Click the Totals button on the Home tab, click the Total cell below the Cost field, click the Total list arrow, then click Sum**

   The Total row is added to the bottom of the datasheet and displays the sum total of the Cost field, $34,350. Other Total row statistics you can select include Average, Count, Maximum, Minimum, Standard Deviation, and Variance. To create subtotals per Category, you need to modify the query in Query Design View.

4. **Click the View button on the Home tab to return to Query Design View, click the Totals button on the Design tab, click Group By in the SalesNo column, click the list arrow, click Count, click Group By in the Cost column, click the list arrow, then click Sum**

   The Total row is added to the query grid below the Table row. To calculate summary statistics for each category, the Category field is the Group By field, as shown in Figure F-12.

5. **Click the View button on the Design tab to display the datasheet, widen each column as necessary to view all field names, click in the Total row for the SumOfCost field, click the list arrow, then click Sum**

   The Adventure category leads all others with a count of 23 sales totaling $22,650. The total revenue for all sales is $34,350, as shown in Figure F-13.

   QUICK TIP
   Because Access inserts the name of the query in the header of the datasheet printout, you can include your name or initials in the query name to uniquely identify a printout.

6. **Click the Save button on the Quick Access toolbar, type CategorySummary, click OK, then close the datasheet**

Creating Multiple Table Queries

FIGURE F-12: Summary Query Design View

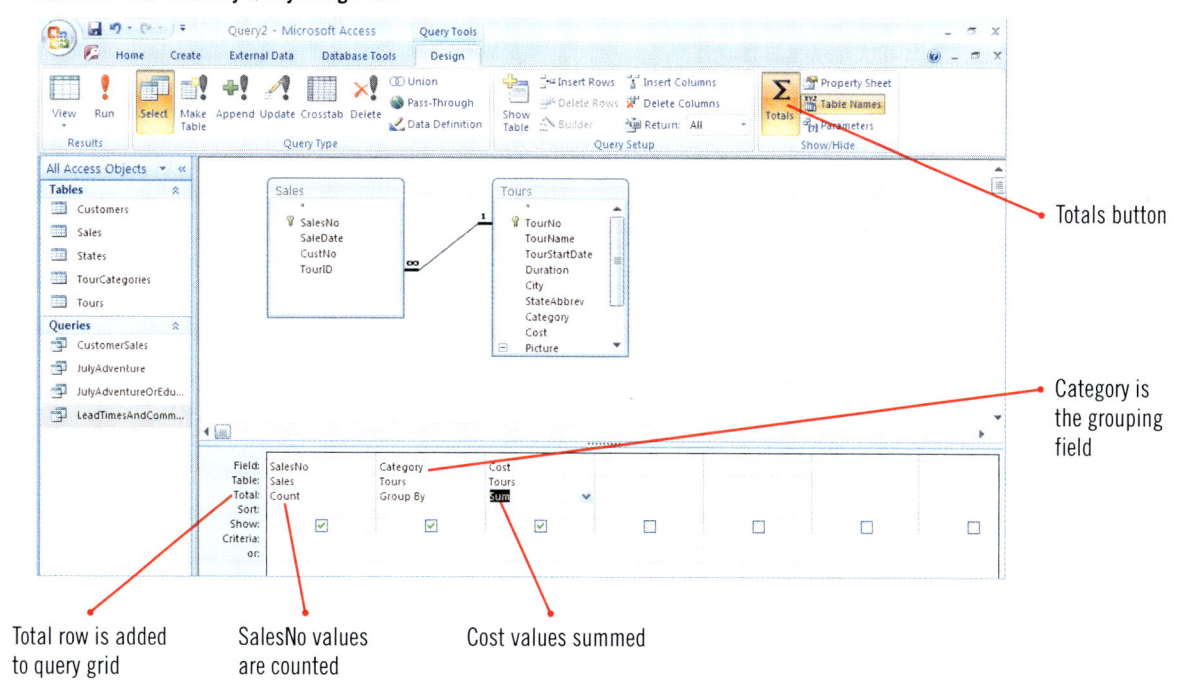

- Totals button
- Category is the grouping field
- Total row is added to query grid
- SalesNo values are counted
- Cost values summed

FIGURE F-13: Summarized and totaled records

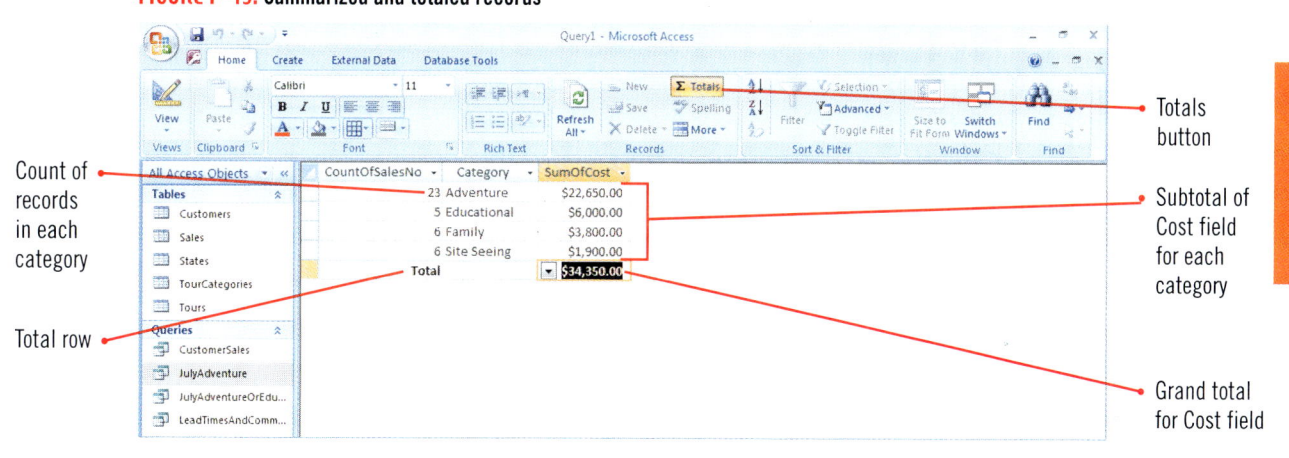

- Count of records in each category
- Total row
- Totals button
- Subtotal of Cost field for each category
- Grand total for Cost field

TABLE F-4: Aggregate functions

aggregate function	used to find the
Sum	Total of values in a field
Avg	Average of values in a field
Min	Minimum value in a field
Max	Maximum value in a field
Count	Number of values in a field (not counting null values)
StDev	Standard deviation of values in a field
Var	Variance of values in a field
First	Field value from the first record in a table or query
Last	Field value from the last record in a table or query

UNIT F
Access 2007

Building Crosstab Queries

A **crosstab query** calculates a statistic, such as a sum or average of a field, by grouping records according to a second field in a column heading position and a third field used in a row heading position. You can use the **Crosstab Query Wizard** to guide you through the steps of creating a crosstab query, or you can build the crosstab query from scratch using Query Design View. Mark Rock asks you to continue your analysis of costs per category by summarizing the cost values for each tour within each category. A crosstab query works well for this request because you want to subtotal the Cost field as summarized by two other fields, TourName and Category.

STEPS

1. **Click the Create tab on the Ribbon, click the Query Design button, double-click Tours, double-click Sales, click Close in the Show Table dialog box, then maximize Query Design View**

   The fields you need for your crosstab query come from the Tours table, but you also need to include the Sales table in this query to display the tour information for all 40 records in the Sales table.

2. **Double-click the TourName field, double-click the Category field, then double-click the Cost field**

   The first step in creating a crosstab query is to create a select query with the three fields you want to use in the crosstabular report.

3. **Click the View button on the Design tab to review the unsummarized datasheet of 40 records, then click the View button on the Home tab to return to Query Design View**

   To summarize these 40 records in a crosstabular report, you need to change the current select query into a crosstab query.

4. **Click the Crosstab button on the Design tab**

   Note that two new rows are added to the query grid—the Total row and the Crosstab row. The Total row helps you determine which fields group or summarize the records, and the **Crosstab row** identifies which of the three positions each field takes in the crosstab report: Row Heading, Column Heading, or Value. The **Value field** is typically a numeric field, such as Cost, that can be summed or averaged.

5. **Click Group By in the Total cell of the Cost field, click the list arrow, click Sum, click the Crosstab cell for the TourName field, click the list arrow, click Row Heading, click the Crosstab cell for the Category field, click the list arrow, click Column Heading, click the Crosstab cell for the Cost field, click the list arrow, then click Value**

   The completed Query Design View should look like Figure F-14. Note the choices made in the Total and Crosstab rows of the query grid.

6. **Click the View button on the Design tab to review the crosstab datasheet**

   The final crosstab datasheet is shown in Figure F-15. The datasheet summarizes all 40 sales records by the Category field used as the column headings and by the TourName field used in the row heading position. Although you can switch the row and column heading fields without changing the numeric information on the crosstab datasheet, you should generally place the field with the most entries (in this case TourName) in the row heading position so that the printout is taller (versus wider).

7. **Click the Save button on the Quick Access toolbar, type TourCrosstab as the query name, click OK, then close the datasheet**

   Crosstab queries appear with a crosstab icon to the left of the query name in the Navigation Pane.

FIGURE F-14: Query Design View of a crosstab query

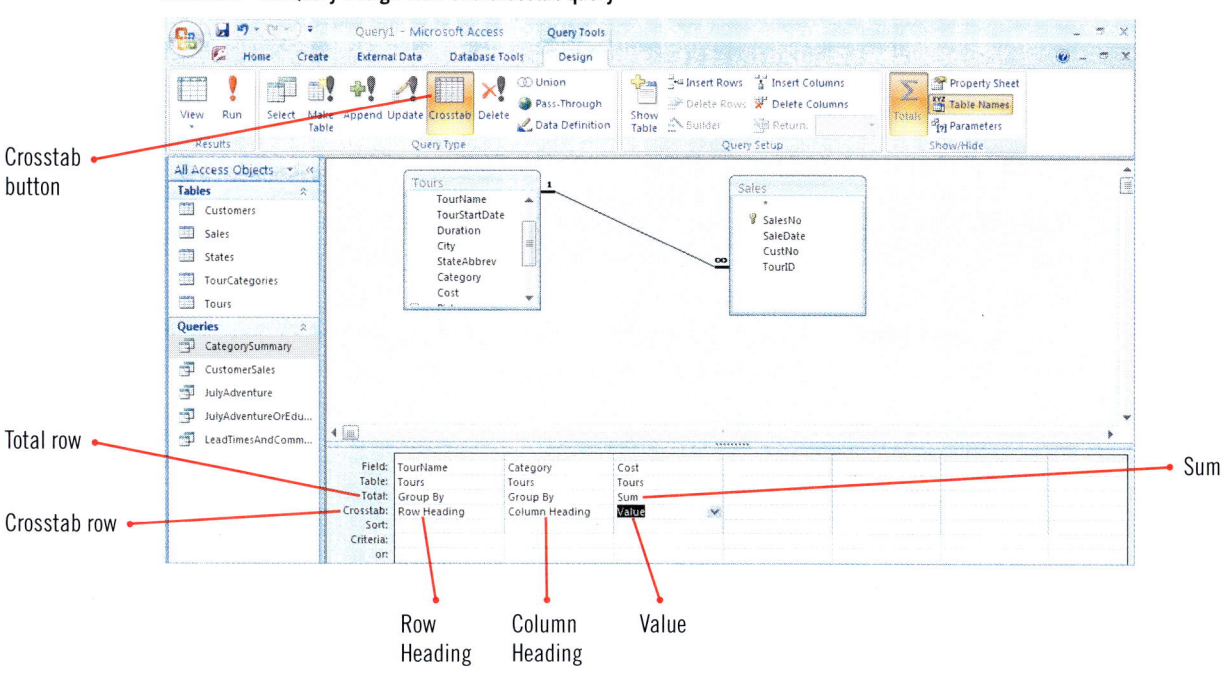

- Crosstab button
- Total row
- Crosstab row
- Sum
- Row Heading
- Column Heading
- Value

FIGURE F-15: Crosstab query datasheet

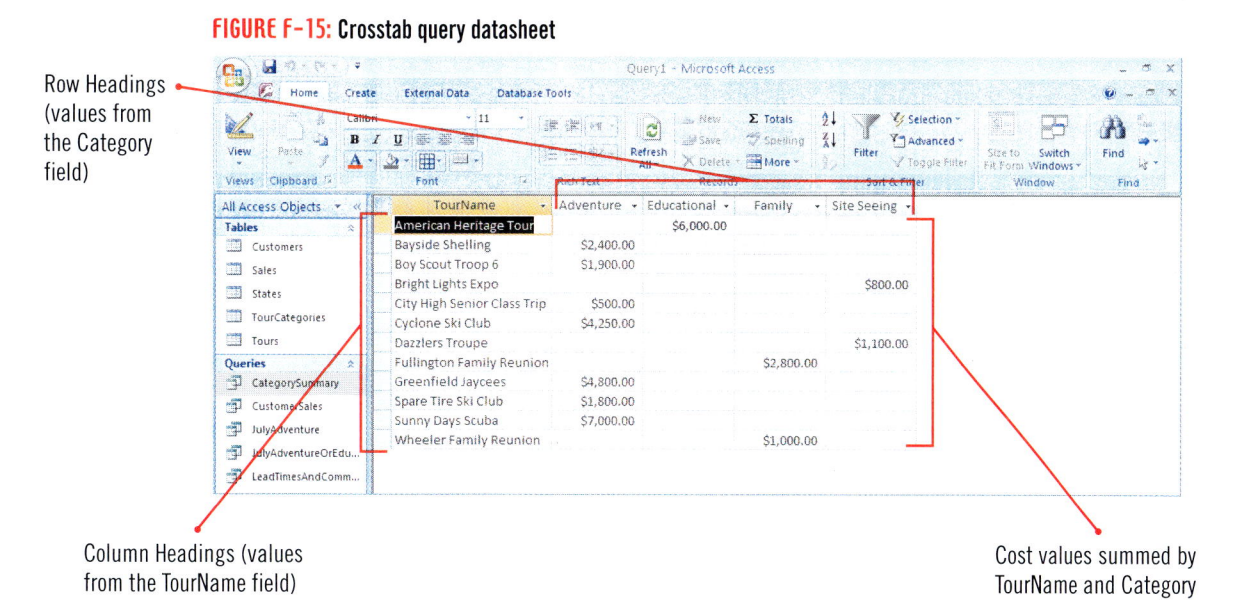

- Row Headings (values from the Category field)
- Column Headings (values from the TourName field)
- Cost values summed by TourName and Category

TourName	Adventure	Educational	Family	Site Seeing
American Heritage Tour		$6,000.00		
Bayside Shelling	$2,400.00			
Boy Scout Troop 6	$1,900.00			
Bright Lights Expo				$800.00
City High Senior Class Trip	$500.00			
Cyclone Ski Club	$4,250.00			
Dazzlers Troupe				$1,100.00
Fullington Family Reunion			$2,800.00	
Greenfield Jaycees	$4,800.00			
Spare Tire Ski Club	$1,800.00			
Sunny Days Scuba	$7,000.00			
Wheeler Family Reunion			$1,000.00	

Using Query Wizards

Four query wizards are available to help you build queries including the Simple (which creates a select query), Crosstab, Find Duplicates, and Find Unmatched Query Wizards. The **Find Duplicates Query Wizard** is used to determine whether a table contains duplicate values in one or more fields. The **Find Unmatched Query Wizard** is used to find records in one table that do not have related records in another table. To use the query wizards, click the Query Wizard button on the Create tab.

Creating Multiple Table Queries

UNIT F
Access 2007

Building PivotTables and PivotCharts

A **PivotTable** calculates a statistic, such as a sum or average, by grouping records like a crosstab query with the additional benefit of allowing you to filter the data. A **PivotChart** is a graphical presentation of the data in the PivotTable. You build a PivotTable using **PivotTable View**. Similarly, you design PivotCharts in **PivotChart View**. The PivotChart and PivotTable Views are bound to one another so that when you make a change in one view, the other view is automatically updated. You use PivotChart View to graphically present summary information about the tours sold within each category.

STEPS

TROUBLE
If this is the first time you are using PivotChart View, a dialog box might open indicating that Access is setting up a new feature.

TROUBLE
To remove a field, drag it out of the PivotChart window.

TROUBLE
You might need to move or resize the Chart Field List title to see the Drop Series Fields Here drop area.

QUICK TIP
The field's list arrow changes from black to blue if you use the field to filter the data.

1. **Double-click the Customers table to open its datasheet, then maximize the datasheet**
   You can view data of any existing table, query, or form in PivotTable and PivotChart views.

2. **Click the View button arrow on the Home tab, then click PivotChart View**
   In PivotChart View, you drag a field from the Chart Field List to a **drop area**, a position on the chart where you want the field to appear. The fields in the **Chart Field List** are the fields in the underlying object, in this case, the Customers table. The relationship between drop areas on a PivotChart, PivotTable, and crosstab query are summarized in Table F-5.

3. **Drag FirstContact from the Chart Field List to the Drop Category Fields Here drop area**
   When you successfully drag a field to a drop area, the drop area displays a blue border. FirstContact field values now appear on the x-axis, also called the **category axis**.

4. **Drag State from the Chart Field List to the Drop Series Fields Here drop area, then drag LName to the Drop Data Fields Here drop area as shown in Figure F-16**
   Because the LName field has a Text data type, when added to the Data Fields drop area, the field values are counted (rather than summed). Therefore, on this chart, the y-axis, also called the **value axis**, counts how many people from each state are added to the database for each FirstContact group displayed on the category axis. The colors of the bars represent state values, but are not identified until you add a legend.

5. **Click the Field List button to toggle it off, then click the Legend button on the Design tab to toggle it on**
   The legend now shows that the blue bars represent the state of Iowa (IA), the dark red bars represent Kansas (KS), and the green bars represent Missouri (MO). To view the information as a PivotTable, you change the view.

6. **Click the View button arrow on the Design tab, then click PivotTable View**
   The PivotTable appears showing the actual values for the data graphed in the PivotChart. PivotTables are very similar in structure to crosstab queries, but also allow you to move and filter the data. For example, if you want to analyze one state at a time, you might move the State field to the Filter Fields position and the City field to the Column Fields position.

7. **Drag the State field from the PivotTable to the Drop the Filter Fields Here position, drag the City field from the PivotTable Field List to the Drop Column Fields Here position, click the State list arrow, click the (All) check box to clear all check marks, click KS, then click OK**
   The filtered PivotTable should look like Figure F-17.

8. **Save and close the Customers table, close the Quest-F.accdb database, and exit Access**

Creating Multiple Table Queries

FIGURE F-16: PivotChart View

- Field List button
- LName in Data area
- Value axis
- FirstContact in Category area
- Legend button
- Chart Field List
- State in Series area
- Category axis

FIGURE F-17: Filtered PivotTable View

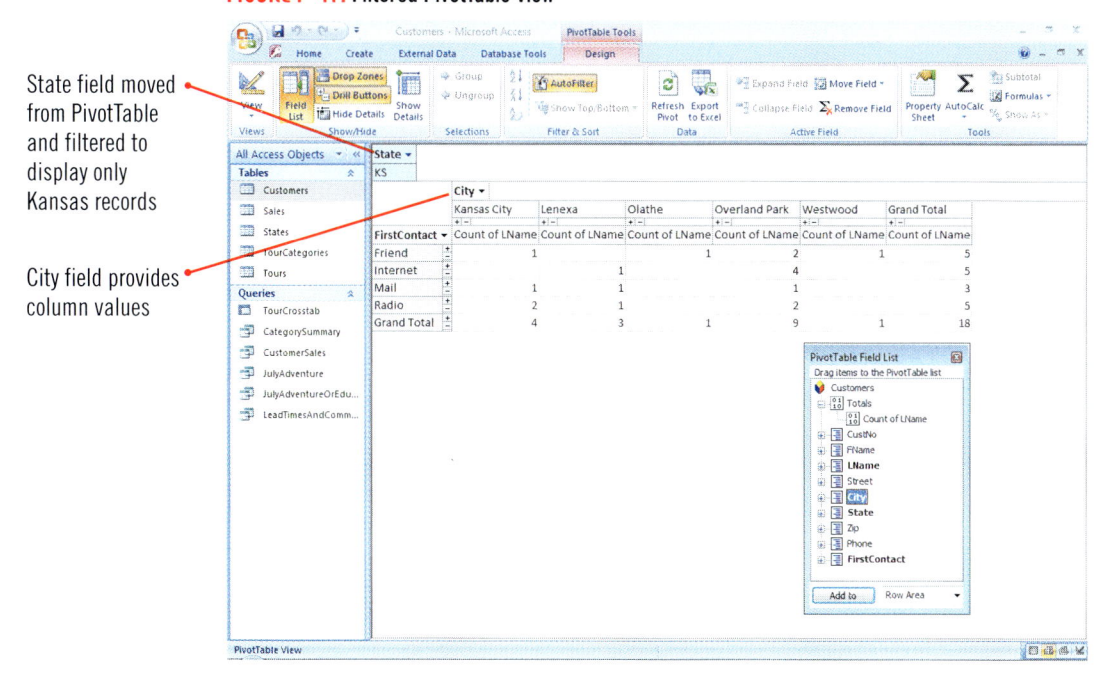

- State field moved from PivotTable and filtered to display only Kansas records
- City field provides column values

TABLE F-5: PivotTable and PivotChart drop areas

drop area on PivotTable	drop area on PivotChart	crosstab query field position
Filter Field	Filter Field	(NA)
Row Field	Category Field	Row Heading
Column Field	Series Field	Column Heading
Totals or Detail Field	Data Field	Value

Creating Multiple Table Queries

Access 153

Practice

▼ CONCEPTS REVIEW

If you have a SAM user profile, you may have access to hands-on instruction, practice, and assessment of the skills covered in this unit. Log in to your SAM account (http://sam2007.course.com/) to launch any assigned training activities or exams that relate to the skills covered in this unit.

Identify each element of the Query Design View shown in Figure F-18.

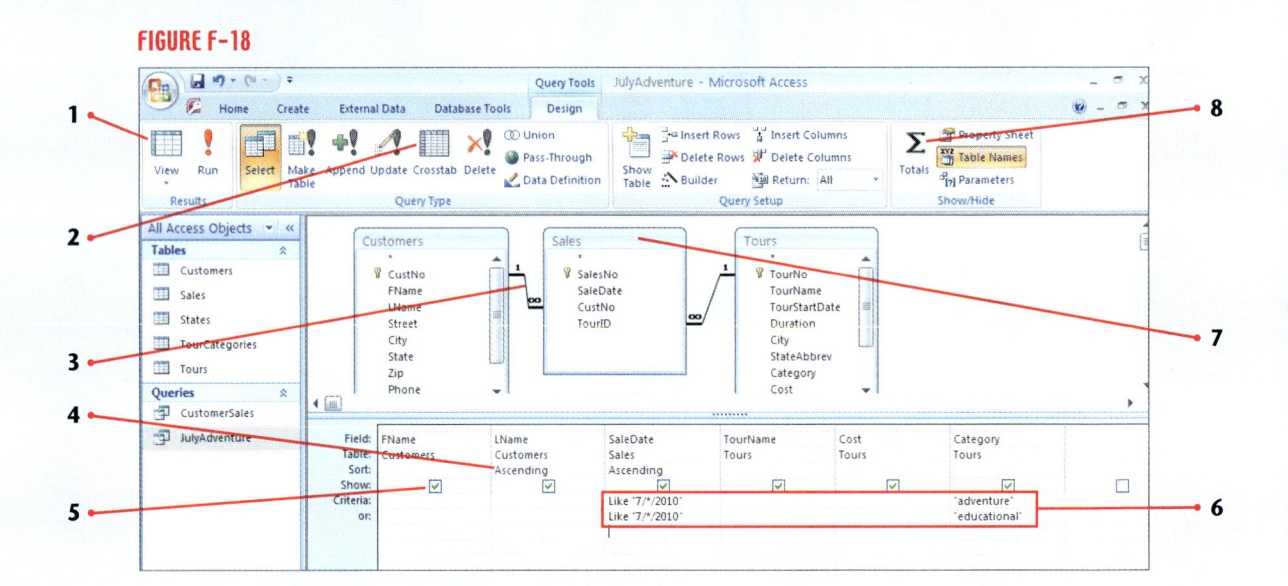

FIGURE F-18

Match each term with the statement that best describes its function.

9. Select query
10. Wildcard character
11. AND criteria
12. Sorting
13. OR criteria

a. Entered on one row of the query design grid
b. Entered on more than one row of the query design grid
c. Asterisk (*) or question mark (?) used in query criteria
d. Retrieves fields from related tables and displays records in a datasheet
e. Placing the records of a datasheet in a certain order

Select the best answer from the list of choices.

14. The query datasheet can best be described as a:
    a. Duplication of the data in the underlying table's datasheet.
    b. Separate file of data.
    c. Logical view of the selected data from an underlying table's datasheet.
    d. Second copy of the data in the underlying tables.

15. Queries may *not* be used to:
    a. Calculate new fields of data.
    b. Set the primary key field for a table.
    c. Enter or update data.
    d. Sort records.

16. When you update data in a table that is also displayed in a query datasheet:
    a. The data is automatically updated in the query.
    b. You must relink the query to the table to refresh the data.
    c. You must also update the data in the query datasheet.
    d. You can choose whether to update the data in the query.

17. **Which of the following is *not* an aggregate function available to a summary query?**
    a. Avg
    b. Subtotal
    c. Count
    d. Max
18. **The order in which records in a query are sorted is determined by:**
    a. The order in which the fields are defined in the underlying table.
    b. The left-to-right position of the fields in the query design grid that contain a sort order choice.
    c. The importance of the information in the field.
    d. The alphabetic order of the field names.
19. **The presentation of data in a crosstab query is most similar to:**
    a. Report Print Preview.
    b. PivotChart View.
    c. Table Datasheet View.
    d. PivotTable View.
20. **A crosstab query is generally constructed with how many fields?**
    a. 1
    b. 3
    c. Between 5 and 10
    d. More than 10
21. **In a crosstab query, which field is the most likely candidate for the Value position?**
    a. FName
    b. Department
    c. Cost
    d. Country

▼ SKILLS REVIEW

1. **Build select queries.**
   a. Start Access and open the **Membership-F.accdb** database from the drive and folder where you store your Data Files, and enable content if prompted.
   b. Create a new select query in Query Design View using the Names and Zips tables.
   c. Add the following fields to the query design grid in this order:
      - First, Last, and Street from the Names table
      - City, State, and Zip from the Zips table
   d. In Datasheet View, replace the Last value in the Quentin Garden record with your last name.
   e. Save the query as **AddressList**, print the datasheet, then close the query.
2. **Use multiple sort orders.**
   a. Open the AddressList query in Query Design View.
   b. Drag the First field from the Names field list to the third column in the query design grid to make the first three fields in the query design grid First, Last, and First.
   c. Add the ascending sort criterion to the second and third fields in the query design grid, and uncheck the Show check box in the third column. The query is now sorted in ascending order by Last, then by First, though the order of the fields in the resulting datasheet still appears as First, Last.
   d. Use Save As to save the query as **SortedAddressList**, view the datasheet, print the datasheet, then close the query.
3. **Develop AND criteria.**
   a. Open the AddressList query in Design View.
   b. Type **M*** (the asterisk is a wildcard) in the Last field Criteria cell to choose all people whose last name starts with M. Access assists you with the syntax for this type of criterion and enters Like "M*" in the cell when you click elsewhere in the query design grid.
   c. Enter **KS** as the AND criterion for the State field. Be sure to enter the criterion on the same line in the query design grid as the Like "M*" criterion.
   d. View the datasheet. It should select only those people from Kansas with a last name that starts with the letter M.
   e. Enter a new value in the City field of the first record to uniquely identify the printout.
   f. Use Save As to save the query as **KansasM**, then print and close the datasheet.

Creating Multiple Table Queries

▼ SKILLS REVIEW (CONTINUED)

4. **Develop OR criteria.**
   a. Open the KansasM query in Query Design View.
   b. Enter **M*** in the second Criteria row (the or row) of the Last field.
   c. Enter **IA** as the criterion in the second Criteria row (the or row) of the State field so that those people from IA with a last name that starts with the letter M are added to this query.
   d. Use Save As to save the query as **KansasIowaM**, view and print the datasheet, then close the query.

5. **Build calculated fields.**
   a. Create a new select query in Query Design View using only the Names table.
   b. Add the following fields to the query design grid in this order: First, Last, Birthday.
   c. Create a calculated field called Age in the fourth column of the query design grid by entering the expression: **Age: (Now()-[Birthday])/365** to determine the age of each person in years based on the information in the Birthday field.
   d. Sort the query in descending order on the calculated Age field, then view the datasheet.
   e. Return to Query Design View, right-click the calculated Age field, click Properties, then change the Format property to Standard and the Decimal Places property to 0. Close the Property Sheet.
   f. Save the query with the name **AgeCalculation**, view the datasheet, print the datasheet, then close the query.

6. **Build summary queries.**
   a. Create a new select query in Query Design View using the Names and Activities tables.
   b. Add the following fields: First and Last from the Names table, Hours from the Activities table.
   c. Add the Total row to the query design grid, then change the aggregate function for the Hours field from Group By to Sum.
   d. Sort in descending order by Hours.
   e. Save the query as **HoursSummary**, view the datasheet, print the datasheet, then close the query.

7. **Build crosstab queries.**
   a. Create a select query with the City and State fields from the Zips table and the Dues field from the Names table. Save the query as **DuesCrosstab**, then view the datasheet.
   b. Return to Query Design View, then click the Crosstab button to add the Total and Crosstab rows to the query design grid.
   c. Specify City as the crosstab row heading, State as the crosstab column heading, and Dues as the summed value field within the crosstab datasheet.
   d. View, print, then save and close the datasheet.

8. **Build PivotTables and PivotCharts.**
   a. Create a select query with the State field from the Zips table and the CharterMember and Dues fields from the Names table. Save it as **DuesPivot**, then run the query.
   b. Switch to PivotChart View, open the Chart Field List if it is not already visible, then drag the State field to the Drop Category Fields Here drop area, the CharterMember field to the Drop Series Fields Here drop area, and the Dues field to the Drop Data Fields Here drop area.
   c. Close the field list, display the legend, then print the PivotChart, which should look similar to the one as shown in Figure F-19.
   d. Switch to PivotTable View, close the field list, filter for only the states of Kansas (KS) and Missouri (MO), then print the PivotTable.
   e. Save and close the DuesPivot query, close the Membership-F.accdb database, then exit Access.

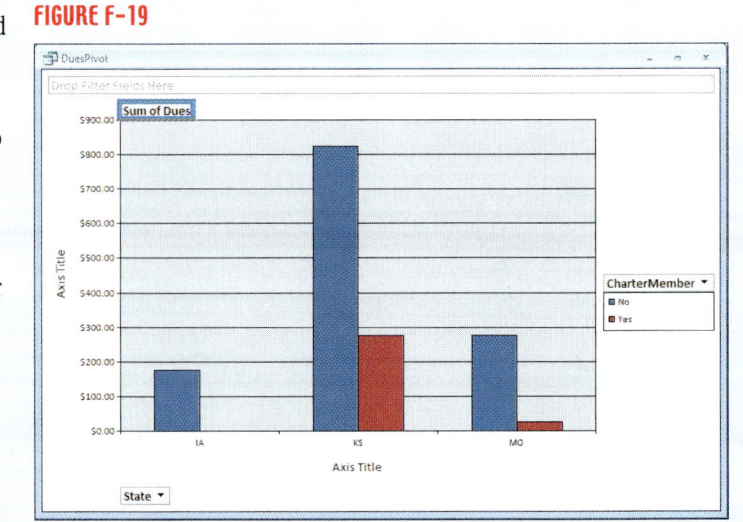

FIGURE F-19

▼ INDEPENDENT CHALLENGE 1

As the manager of a music store's instrument rental program, you have created a database to track rentals to schoolchildren. Now that several rentals have been made, you want to query the database for several different datasheet printouts to analyze school information.

a. Start Access and open the **MusicStore-F.accdb** database from the drive and folder where you store your Data Files, and enable content if prompted.

b. In Query Design View, create a query with the following fields in the following order:
   - SchoolName field from the Schools table
   - Date field from the Rentals table
   - Description field from the Instruments table

   (*Hint*: Although you don't use any fields from the Customers table, you need to add the Customers table to this query to make the connection between the Schools table and the Rentals table.)

c. Sort in ascending order by SchoolName, then in ascending order by Date.

d. Save the query as **SchoolRentals**, view the datasheet, replace Lincoln Elementary with your elementary school name, then print the datasheet.

e. Modify the SchoolRentals query by deleting the Description field. Use the Totals button to group the records by SchoolName and to count the Date field. Print the datasheet and use Save As to save the query as **SchoolCount**. Close the datasheet.

f. Create a crosstab query named **SchoolCrosstab** based on the SchoolRentals query. Remove the sort orders. Use Description as the row heading position and SchoolName in the column heading position. Count the Date field.

g. Save, view, print, and close the SchoolCrosstab query.

h. Modify the SchoolRentals query so that only those schools with the word Elementary in the SchoolName field are displayed. (*Hint*: You have to use wildcard characters in the criteria.)

i. Use Save As to save the query as **ElementaryRentals**, then view, print, and close the datasheet.

j. Close the MusicStore-F.accdb database, then exit Access.

▼ INDEPENDENT CHALLENGE 2

As the manager of a music store's instrument rental program, you have created a database to track rentals to schoolchildren. The database has already been used to answer several basic questions, and now that you've shown how easy it is to get the answers using queries, more questions are being asked. You can use queries to analyze customer and rental information.

a. Start Access and open the **MusicStore-F.accdb** database from the drive and folder where you store your Data Files, and enable content if prompted.

b. In Query Design View, create a query with the following fields in the following order:
   - Description and MonthlyFee fields from the Instruments table
   - LastName, Zip, and City fields from the Customers table

   (*Hint*: Although you don't need any fields from the Rentals table in this query's datasheet, you need to add the Rentals table to this query to make the connection between the Customers table and the Instruments table.)

c. Add the Zip field to the first column of the query grid, and specify an ascending sort order for this field. Uncheck the Show check box for the first Zip field so that it does not appear in the datasheet.

d. Specify an ascending sort order for the Description field.

e. Save the query as **ZipAnalysis**.

f. View the datasheet, replace Johnson with your last name in the LastName field, then print and close the datasheet.

g. Modify the ZipAnalysis query by adding criteria to find the records where the Description is equal to **viola**.

h. Use Save As to save this query as **Violas**.

▼ INDEPENDENT CHALLENGE 2 (CONTINUED)

Advanced Challenge Exercise

- On a piece of paper, write how many records the Violas query contains.
- Modify the Violas query with AND criteria to further specify that the City must be **Ankeny**.
- Save this query as **AnkenyViolas**. On your paper, note how many records the AnkenyViolas query contains. Briefly explain how AND criteria affect this number.
- Modify the AnkenyViolas query with OR criteria that find all violas or violins, regardless of where they are located.
- Use Save As to save this query as **ViolasViolins**. On your paper, note how many records the Violas and Violins query contains. Briefly explain how OR criteria affect this number.
- In Query Design View, create a crosstab query that uses the Description field from the Instruments table for the column headings, the SchoolName field from the Schools table for the row headings, and that Sums the MonthlyFee field.
- Save the crosstab query as **RentalCrosstab**, preview the datasheet, then print the datasheet in landscape orientation so that it fits on one page.

i. Close the MusicStore-F.accdb database, then exit Access.

▼ INDEPENDENT CHALLENGE 3

As a real estate agent, you use an Access database to track residential real estate listings in your area. You can use queries to answer questions about the real estate and to analyze home values.

a. Start Access and open the **RealEstate-F.accdb** database from the drive and folder where you store your Data Files, and enable content if prompted.

b. In Query Design View, create a query with the following fields in the following order:
- AgencyName from the Agencies table
- AgentFirst and AgentLast from the Agents table
- SqFt and Asking from the Listings table

c. Sort the records in descending order by the Asking field.

d. Save the query as **AskingPrices**, view the datasheet, enter your own last name instead of Zacharias for the most expensive listing, then print the datasheet.

e. In Query Design View, modify the AskingPrices query by creating a calculated field that determines price per square foot. The new calculated field's name should be **SquareFootCost** and the expression should be the asking price divided by the square foot field, or **[Asking]/[SqFt]**.

f. Remove any former sort orders, sort the records in descending order based on the SquareFootCost calculated field, and view the datasheet.

g. Return to Query Design View, right-click the SquareFootCost field, click Properties, then change the Format property to **Currency** and the Decimal Places property to **2**.

h. Use Save As to save the query as **SquareFootCostAnalysis**, then view, print, and close the datasheet.

▼ INDEPENDENT CHALLENGE 3 (CONTINUED)

Advanced Challenge Exercise

- Open the SquareFootCostAnalysis query in Design View, then delete the AgentFirst, AgentLast, and SqFt fields.
- View the datasheet, then change the Sun and Ski Realtors agency name to your last name's Agency.
- In Design View, add the Total row, then Sum the Asking field and use the Avg (Average) aggregate function for the SquareFootCost calculated field. In Datasheet View, add the Total row and display the sum of the Asking Field.
- Print the query, save the query as **SummarizedSquareFootCostAnalysis** as shown in Figure F-20, then close it.

FIGURE F-20

AgencyName	SumOfAskin	SquareFootCost
Student Last Name's Agency	1358563	$103.29
Ridgedale Realtors	866899	$92.43
Camden and Camden Realtors	1289500	$66.56
Three Lakes Realtors	951700	$63.35
Total	4466662	

i. Close the RealEstate-F.accdb database, then exit Access.

▼ REAL LIFE INDEPENDENT CHALLENGE

One way to use Access in your real life is in a community service project. People in schools and nonprofit agencies often inherit databases created by others and need help extracting information from them. Suppose you're working with the local high school guidance counselor to help her with an Access database she inherited that is used to record college scholarship opportunities. You can help her keep the database updated and create several queries.

This Independent Challenge requires an Internet connection.

a. Start Access and open the **Scholarships-F.accdb** database from the drive and folder where you store your Data Files.
b. Conduct some research on the Internet to find at least five new scholarships. One of the five should be directed at business students; another should be directed at education majors. Add the five new records to the Scholarships table using the existing fields.
c. Create a query called **Business** that displays all the scholarship information except the ID for all scholarships with the word "business" anywhere in the Description field. (*Hint*: Use an appropriate wildcard character both before and after the word "business.")
d. Add OR criteria to the Business query to also select all scholarships that have the word "education" anywhere in the Description field. Save the query with the name **BusinessOrEducation**.
e. Create a query that selects the ScholarshipName, DueDate, and Amount from the Scholarships table, and sorts the records in ascending order by DueDate, then descending order by Amount. Name the query **ScholarshipMasterList**.

Advanced Challenge Exercise

- View the ScholarshipMasterList query in PivotTable view, then drag the Amount field to the Drop Totals or Detail Fields Here area, the ScholarshipName field to the Drop Row Fields Here area, and the DueDate By Month field to the Drop Filter Fields Here area.
- Filter the PivotTable for only those scholarships in the first quarter of the year 2010 as shown in Figure F-21.
- Save the query with the name **ScholarshipPivot**.

f. Save and close the ScholarshipPivot query, close the Scholarships-F.accdb database, then exit Access.

FIGURE F-21

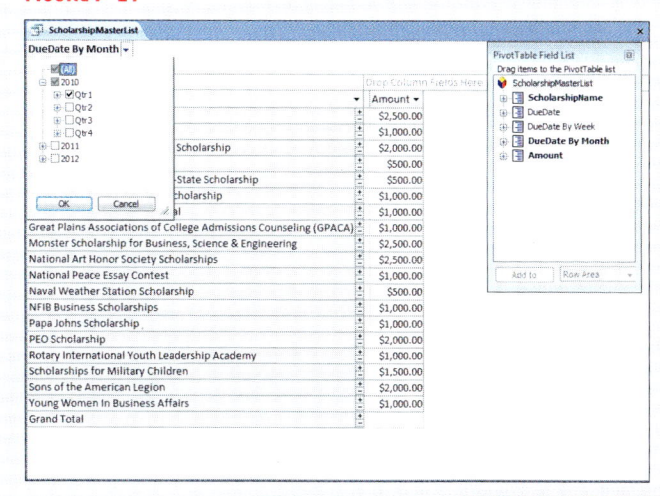

Creating Multiple Table Queries

▼ VISUAL WORKSHOP

Open the **Training-F.accdb** database from the drive and folder where you store your Data Files, and enable content if prompted. In Query Design View, create a new select query with the Location field from the Employees table, the Cost and CourseID fields from the Courses table, and the Passed field from the Attendance table. Display the query in PivotChart View, then modify it as shown in Figure F-22. Note that the Passed field is in the Filter area. Filter the data for CourseIDs Access1 and Access2 and for the Passed value of Yes. Click the Show Legend button on the Design tab to display the legend below the Location field in the Series field area. Right-click the Axis Title for the x-axis, click Properties, click the Format tab, and add your name as the Caption. Save the query with the name **AccessGraduates**, then print it.

FIGURE F-22

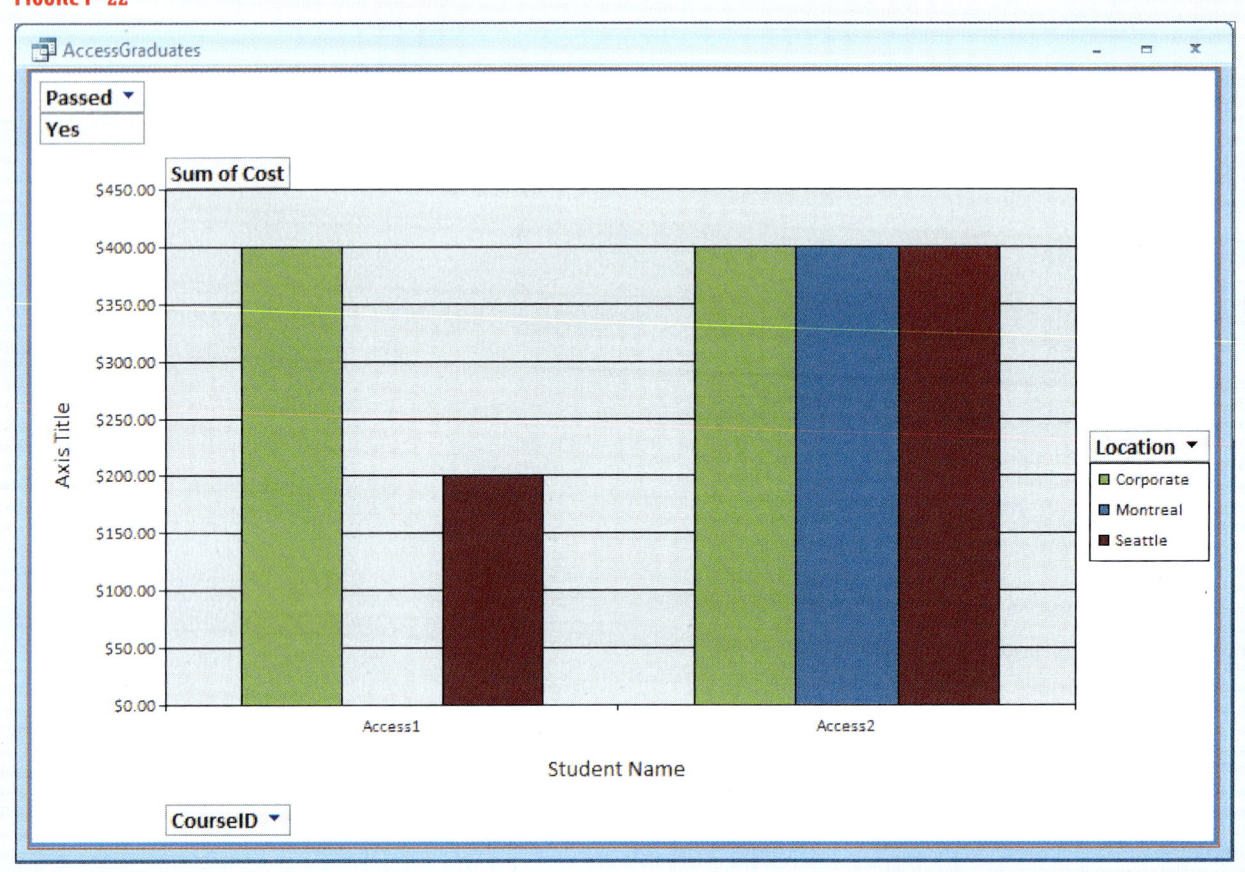

UNIT G
Access 2007

Enhancing Forms

Files You Will Need:
Quest-G.accdb
Membership-G.accdb
MusicRentals-G.accdb
InstrumentRentals-G.accdb
Equipment-G.accdb
Scholarships-G.accdb
RealEstate-G.accdb

A **form** is a database object designed to make data easy to find, enter, and edit. Forms are created by using **controls** such as labels, text boxes, combo boxes, and command buttons, which help you manipulate more quickly and reliably than working in a datasheet. A form that contains a **subform** allows you to work with related records in an easy-to-use screen arrangement. For example, a form/subform combination allows you to display customer data and all of the orders placed by that customer at the same time. Mark Rock wants to improve the usability of the forms in the Quest database. You will build and improve forms by working with subforms, split forms, combo boxes, option groups, and command buttons to enter, find, and filter data.

OBJECTIVES

Create subforms

Modify subforms

Create split forms

Add tab controls

Add a combo box for data entry

Add a combo box to find records

Add option groups

Add command buttons

UNIT G
Access 2007

Creating Subforms

A **subform** is a form within a form. The form that contains the subform is called the **main form**. A main form/subform combination displays the records of two tables that are related in a one-to-many relationship. The forms are linked by a common field, so only those records that are associated with the main form appear in the subform. For example, if a main form contains a customer record, the subform might contain all of the sales related to that customer. When you use the Form Wizard to create a form/subform combination, you create both the main form and the subform in one process. If the main form already exists, you can use the **Subform/Subreport control** to start the Subform Wizard, which guides you through adding the subform to the main form in Form Design View. A form **layout** is the general way that the data and controls are arranged on the form. Columnar is the most popular layout for a main form, and datasheet is the most popular layout for a subform, but you can modify these choices by changing the form's **Default View property** in Form Design View. See Table G-1 for a description of form layouts. You decide to create a form/subform using the Form Wizard. The main form will display fields from the Tours table and the subform will display fields from the Sales and Customers tables to show the many sales for each tour.

STEPS

1. Start Access, then open the Quest-G.accdb database from the drive and folder where you store your Data Files, then enable content if prompted

2. Click the Create tab on the Ribbon, click the More Forms button, then click Form Wizard

   The Form Wizard starts and prompts you to select the fields of the main form/subform combination. You want the main form to display tour information, and the subform to display sales information including customer name. These fields come from three tables: Tours, Sales, and Customers.

3. Click the Tables/Queries list arrow, click Table: Tours, click the Select All Fields button, click the Tables/Queries list arrow, click Table: Sales, click, click the Tables/Queries list arrow, click Table: Customers, double-click FName, double-click LName, then click Next

   Because the Tours and Sales tables are linked in a one-to-many relationship in the Relationships window, the Form Wizard recognizes the opportunity to create a form/subform combination for the selected fields.

4. Click by Tours as shown in Figure G-1 (if it is not already selected), then click Next

5. Click Next to accept the Datasheet layout, click Aspect, click Next, click Finish to accept the default names for the form and subform, then maximize the Tours form

   By default, subforms are created with a Datasheet layout. The Tours form opens and includes the Sales subform in Datasheet layout, as shown in Figure G-2.

6. Click the Next record button on the navigation bar for the main form several times to view the sales for each tour

   The sales for each tour appear in the subform as you move through the records of the main form. Notice that the third tour, Cyclone Ski Club, has 10 sales because it has 10 sales in the subform. The fourth tour, Boy Scout Troop 6, has only two sales in the subform.

7. Close the Tours form

   When you close a main form, any subforms that it contains close as well.

Enhancing Forms

FIGURE G-1: Form Wizard showing main form and subform

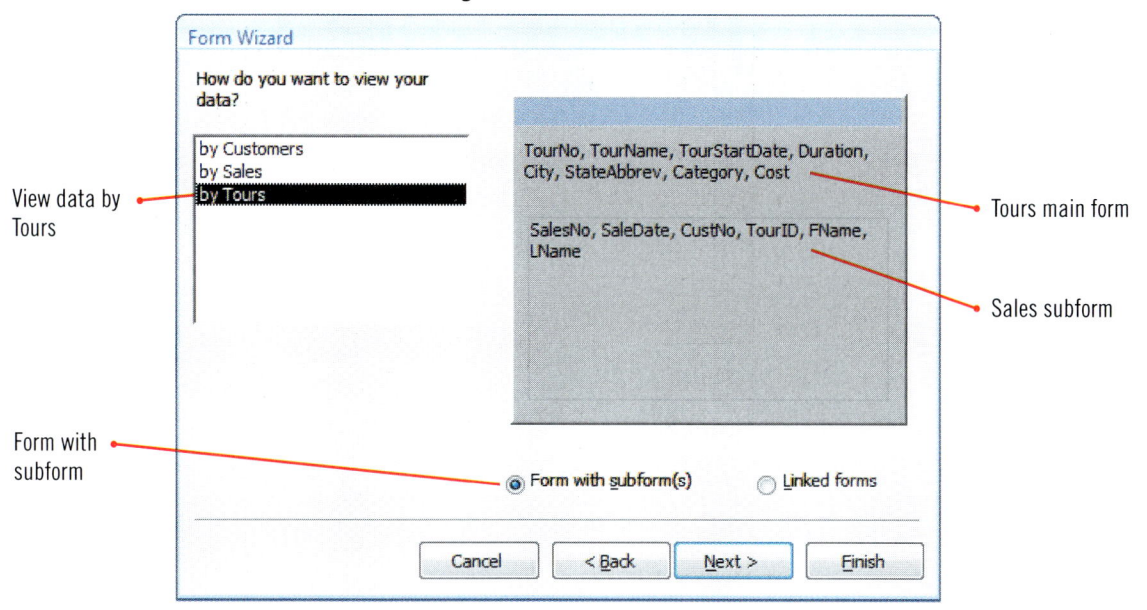

FIGURE G-2: Tours main form with sales subform

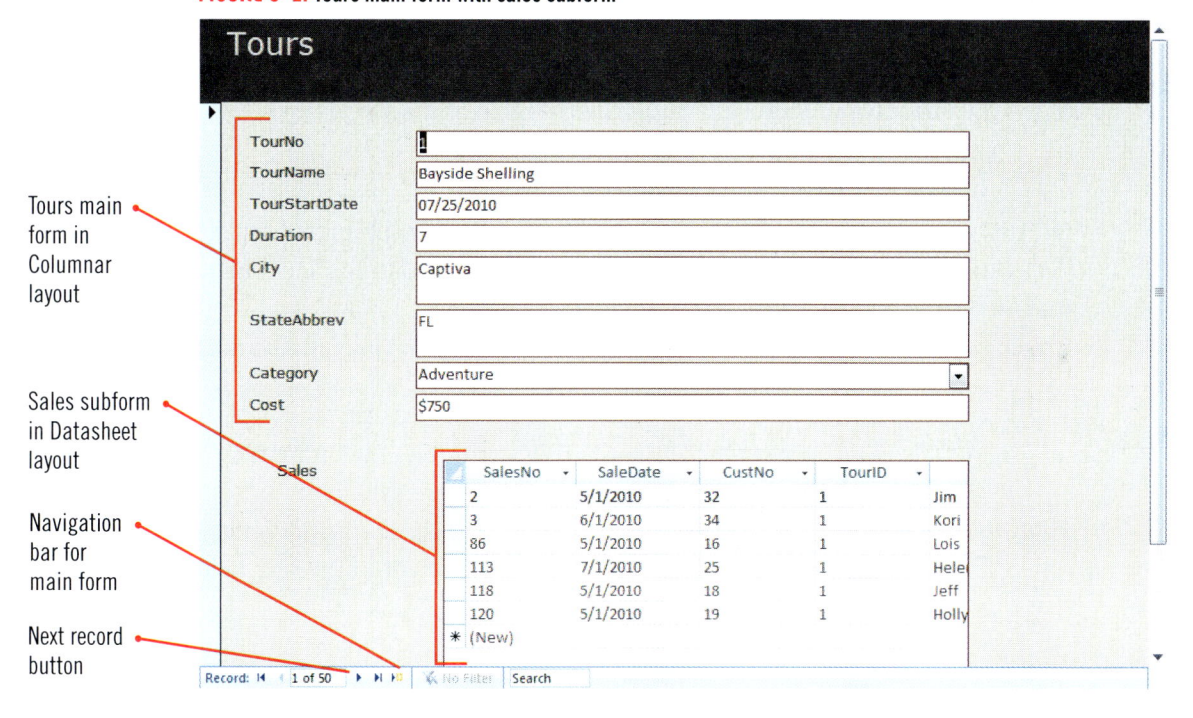

TABLE G-1: Form layouts

layout	description
Columnar	Each field appears on a separate row with a label to its left
Tabular	Each field appears as an individual column and each record is presented as a row
Datasheet	Fields and records are displayed as they appear in a table or query datasheet
PivotTable	Fields are organized in a PivotTable arrangement
PivotChart	Fields are organized in a PivotChart arrangement

Enhancing Forms

UNIT G
Access 2007

Modifying Subforms

You modify a subform, like any other form, in Form Design View. Often, however, it is easiest to work in Form Design View of the main form, as it allows you to modify both the main form and subform in the same view. To modify the fields that either the main form or subform contain, you work with the **Record Source** property of the forms. You want to change some of the fields in the subform and widen it to display all of the fields. Mark Rock also asks you to modify some of the labels in the main form.

STEPS

1. **Click the Navigation list arrow in the Navigation Pane, click Forms (if not already selected), right-click Tours, click Design View on the shortcut menu, then maximize the Design View window**

   The Tours main form opens in Form Design View. First you'll modify the labels in the main form to display them more clearly.

2. **Click the TourNo label in the main form, edit it to read Tour No, then finish editing the labels in the main form as shown in Figure G-3**

   With the labels modified in the main form, you turn your attention to the subform. You decide that you don't really need the SalesNo field in the subform, but in addition to the name of the customer who purchased that tour, you want to see the customer's city in the City field. To modify the fields that a form displays, you work with the Record Source property of the form.

3. **Click the edge of the subform to select it, then double-click the form selector button to open the Property Sheet for the subform**

   The Property Sheet for the subform opens as shown in Figure G-4.

4. **Click the Data tab in the Property Sheet (if not already selected), click the Record Source property Build button to open the Query Builder for the subform, delete the SalesNo field in the query grid, double-click the City field in the Customers field list, click the Close button on the Design tab, then click Yes**

   The Record Source property allows you to modify—add or delete—the fields that may be used on the form. Notice that the SalesNo field now displays an **error indicator**, a small green triangle in the upper-left corner of the SalesNo text box in the subform. You already know the reason for this error—the SalesNo field is no longer selected in the Record Source for this form. If you did not know the cause of the error, however, you could use the Error Checking Options button to get more information.

   > **TROUBLE**
   > You might have to scroll in the main form or subform to see all of the controls.

5. **Click the Property Sheet button on the Design tab to close it, click the SalesNo text box, press [Delete], click the Add Existing Fields button, then drag the City field from the Field List to just under the LName text box on the subform**

   The layout of the subform is datasheet, so the Cost field added to the bottom of the list of fields will appear as a new column on the right edge of the datasheet. You also need to widen the subform to display all of the fields it contains.

6. **Click the edge of the subform to select it, drag the left edge of the subform to the left to widen it, click the Add Existing Fields button to close the Field List, click the Form View button on the Design tab, then resize the columns in the subform so that all of the fields are visible**

   The final form/subform should look like Figure G-5. Continue to make additional enchancements in Form Design View as desired.

7. **Save and close the Tours main form and Sales subform**

Access 164

Enhancing Forms

FIGURE G-3: Modifying the labels in the Tours main form

Modify the labels in the Tours main form

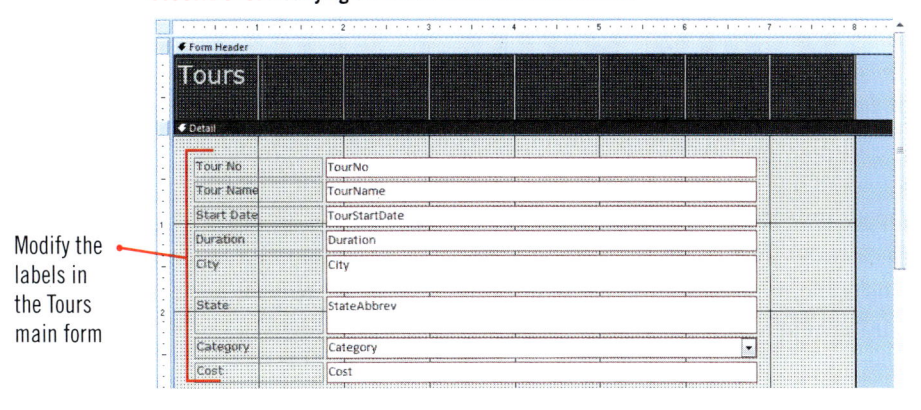

FIGURE G-4: Modifying the Record Source on the Sales subform

Form selector button for subform

Edge of the Sales subform

Property Sheet for the form

Build button

Record Source property

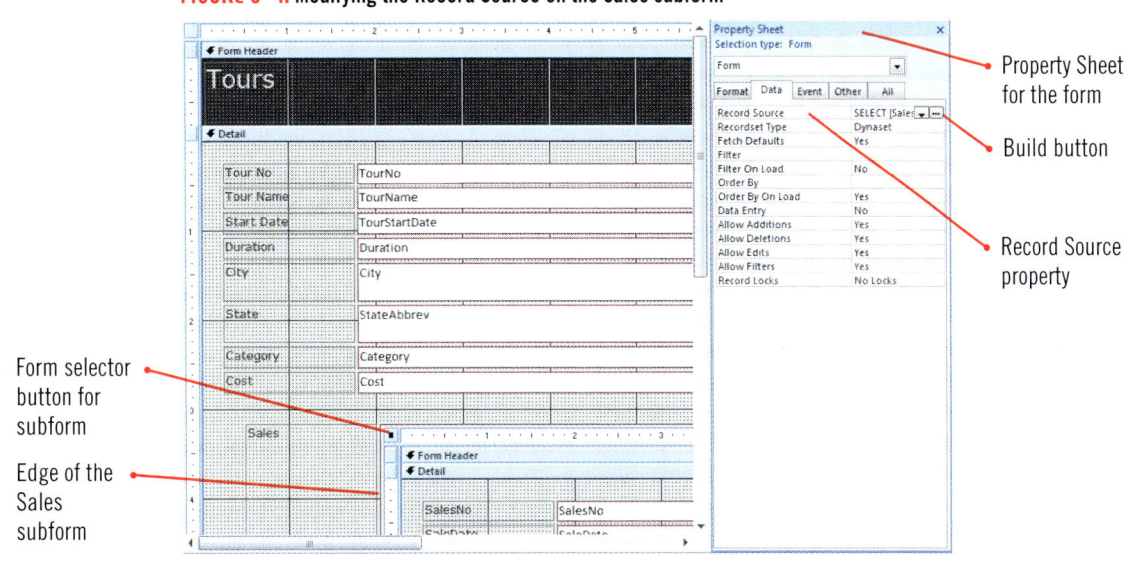

FIGURE G-5: Final form/subform

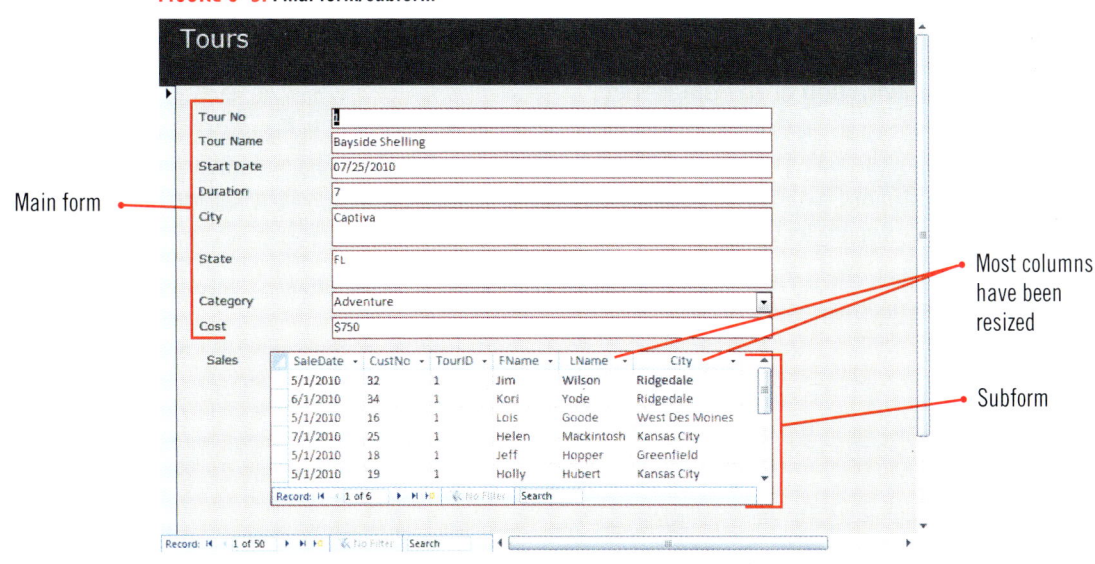

Main form

Most columns have been resized

Subform

Linking the form and subform

If the form and subform do not appear to be correctly linked, examine the subform's property sheet, paying special attention to the **Link Child Fields** and **Link Master Fields** properties on the Data tab. These properties tell you which field serves as the link between the main form and subform.

Enhancing Forms

UNIT G
Access 2007

Creating Split Forms

A **split form** shows you two views of the same data at one time: a traditional form and a datasheet view. A split form is similar to a form/subform in that a split form contains a traditional form view on the top and a datasheet view of data on the bottom of the form. A split form is different, however, because it is only *one* form object instead of two used together as in a form/subform. A split form also shows two views of the *same* data at one time, whereas a form/subform shows two different (but related) sets of data in the main form and subform. You decide to create a split form to be able to productively find, view, and enter customer information.

STEPS

1. **Click the Navigation list arrow in the Navigation Pane, click Tables, click Customers, click the Create tab, click the Split Form button, then maximize the new form**

    The new Customers form appears in Layout View as shown in Figure G-6. Note that the same fields are used in the upper and lower portions of the window, but the layout shows only one record in the top portion, and organizes multiple records as a datasheet in the lower portion. Because the two views of a split form display the *same* data in two different views, the record displayed in the upper portion is also shown in the lower portion of the window. In this case, the record for Mitch Mayberry is displayed both ways. You can switch to Form View to work with the data.

2. **Click the Form View button on the Format tab, then click the Next record button on the navigation bar several times**

    Observe that the record displayed in the upper portion of the split form matches the selected record in the lower datasheet view. You can use a split form, or any form, to sort and filter data.

3. **Click any occurrence of Kansas City in the datasheet portion of the form, click the Selection button on the Home tab, then click Equals "Kansas City"**

    The ten records with Kansas City in the City field of the datasheet are filtered in the lower portion of the split form, and the first record is displayed in the upper portion. To further organize the records, you can sort the filtered list in alphabetical order based on the LName field.

4. **Click any LName field value in the datasheet, click the Ascending button on the Home tab, then press [↓] to watch the record in the upper portion change based on the navigation of the datasheet**

    The Customers split form is both filtered and sorted as shown in Figure G-7. You can use the sort and filter buttons on a form just as you can in a datasheet. When sorting and filtering a split form, however, more than one record is visible in the datasheet portion of the form, which sometimes makes it easier to find the data you're looking for.

5. **Click the Save button on the Quick Access toolbar, click OK, then close the Customers split form**

Enhancing Forms

FIGURE G-6: Customers split form in Layout View

Drag the split bar to resize the views of the form

Next record button

FIGURE G-7: Filtering and sorting the Customers split form in Form View

Selection button

Ascending button

Enhancing Forms

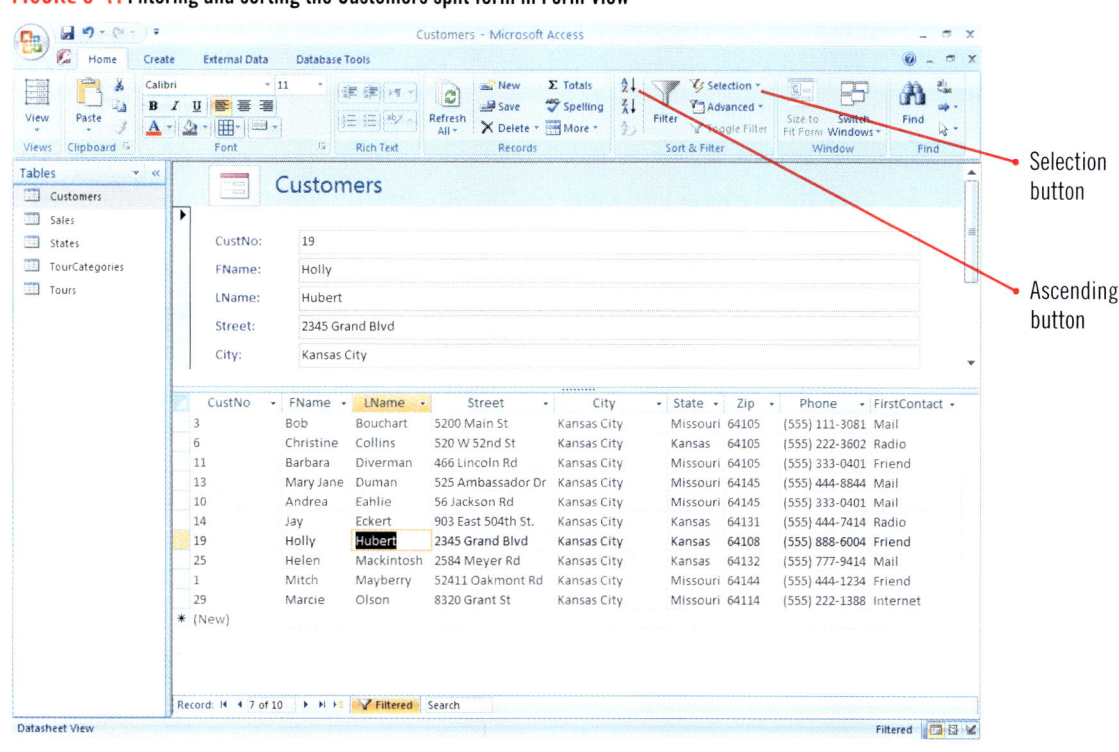

Access 167

Adding Tab Controls

UNIT G
Access 2007

The **tab control** is used to create a three-dimensional aspect to a form so that many controls can be organized and displayed by clicking the tabs. You have already used tab controls because many Access dialog boxes use tabs to organize information. For example, the Property Sheet uses tab controls to organize properties identified by categories: Format, Data, Event, Other, and All. You previously created a form used to update tour data called the Tour Update form. Mark Rock asks you to find a way to organize and present tour information based on three categories: General Info, Dates, and Costs. You decide to use tab controls.

STEPS

1. Click the Navigation list arrow in the Navigation Pane, click Forms, right-click Tour Update, click Design View on the shortcut menu, then maximize the form

    The Tour Update form appears in Design View. Currently, only two fields from the Tours table appear on the form, TourNo and TourName. You can add the tab control next.

2. Click the Tab Control button on the Design tab, then click below the Tour No label on the form

    Your screen should look like Figure G-8. By default, the tab control you added has two pages with the default names of Page20 and Page21. You can change these to more descriptive names, but the default text refers to how many total controls have been added to the form over the life of the form.

   TROUBLE
   If the numbers of your pages are different, continue with the step as you revise these names anyway.

3. Double-click Page20 to open its Property Sheet, click the Other tab (if it is not already selected), double-click Page20 in the Name property text box, type General Info, click the Page21 tab on the form, double-click Page21 in the Name text box of the property sheet, type Dates, then press [Enter]

    The first two pages on the tab control now describe the information they will organize, but you need a third page named Costs before adding the appropriate controls to each page.

4. Right-click the Dates tab, click Insert Page, double-click Page22 in the Name property text box, type Costs, then close the Property Sheet

    With the pages in place on the tab control, you're ready to add controls to each page.

   TROUBLE
   In Form Design View you can undo many actions by clicking the Undo button on the Quick Access toolbar.

5. Click the General Info page on the tab control, click the Add Existing Fields button on the Design tab to display the Field List, click City in the Field List, press and hold [Shift], click StateAbbrev in the Field List, click Category in the Field List, release [Shift], then drag the highlighted fields to the top middle area of the General Info page

    Your screen should look similar to Figure G-9. Three fields are added to the General Info page on the tab control.

   QUICK TIP
   A tab control becomes black when you are successfully adding controls to a page.

6. Click the Dates page on the tab control, click TourStartDate in the Field List, press and hold [Shift], click Duration in the Field List, release [Shift], drag the two highlighted fields to the middle of the Dates page, click the Costs page on the tab control, then drag the Cost field to the middle of the Costs page

    You can add any type of control, even a subform control, to a tab control page.

7. Click the Form View button on the Design tab, click the Dates tab, click the Costs tab, click the General Info tab, then click the Next record button on the navigation bar to observe the tab control in Form View as shown in Figure G-10

8. Save and close the Tour Update form

Enhancing Forms

FIGURE G-8: Adding a tab control

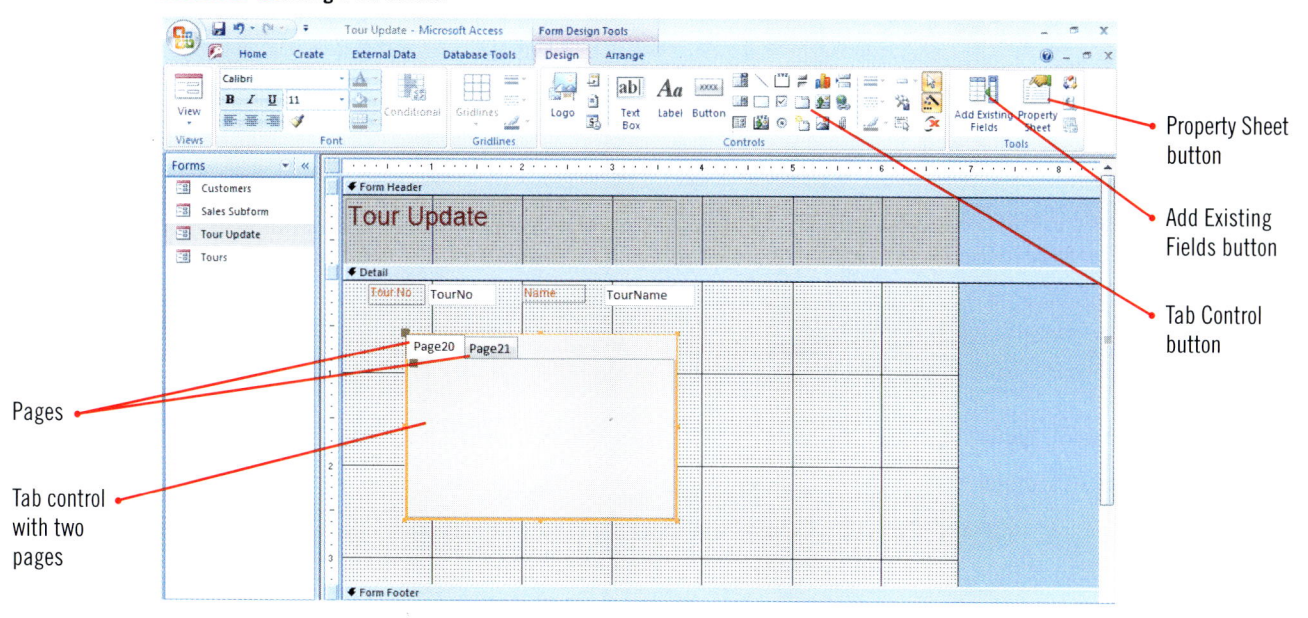

- Property Sheet button
- Add Existing Fields button
- Tab Control button
- Pages
- Tab control with two pages

FIGURE G-9: Adding fields to a tab control in Form Design View

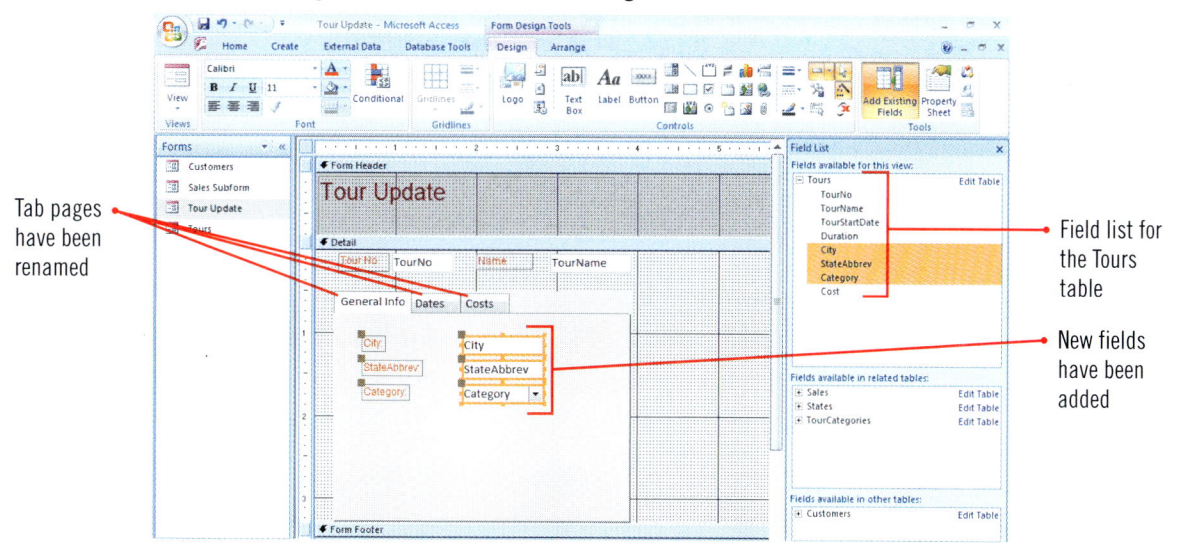

- Tab pages have been renamed
- Field list for the Tours table
- New fields have been added

FIGURE G-10: Working with a tab control in Form View

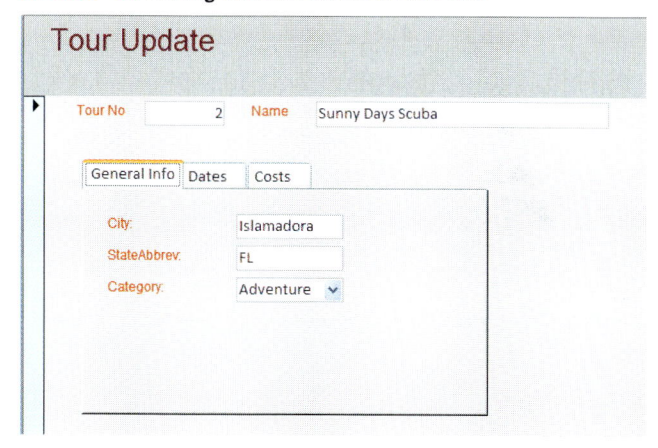

Tour Update

| Tour No | 2 | Name | Sunny Days Scuba |

General Info | Dates | Costs

- City: Islamadora
- StateAbbrev: FL
- Category: Adventure

Enhancing Forms

Access 169

UNIT G
Adding a Combo Box for Data Entry

If a finite set of values can be identified for a field, using a combo box instead of a text box control on a form allows the user to select and enter data faster and more accurately. Both the **list box** and **combo box** controls provide a list of values from which the user can choose an entry. A combo box also allows the user to type an entry from the keyboard; therefore, it is a "combination" of the list box and text box controls. You can create a combo box by using the **Combo Box Wizard**, or you can change an existing text box or list box into a combo box. Fields with Lookup properties are automatically created as combo boxes on new forms. All Quest tours last 3, 4, 5, 7, 10, or 14 days. Because the Duration field contains a limited number of values, you decide to convert the existing Duration text box on the Tour Info form into a combo box.

STEPS

1. Right-click Tour Update in the Navigation Pane, click Design View, click the Dates tab, click the Duration text box to select it, right-click the Duration text box, point to Change To, then click Combo Box

   Now that the control has been changed from a text box to a combo box, you are ready to populate the list with the appropriate duration values.

   > **QUICK TIP**
   > For more information on any property, click the property then press [F1].

2. Click the Property Sheet button on the Design tab, click the Data tab in the Property Sheet, click the Row Source Type property box, click its list arrow, then click Value List

   The **Row Source Type** property determines the source of the control's data—the source of the values in the combo box list. The three possible choices for the Row Source Type property include Table/Query, Value List, and Field List. They work hand-in-hand with the **Row Source** property, which specifies the actual table, values, or field used in the list.

   > **QUICK TIP**
   > The title bar of the property sheet identifies the name of the control that you are currently working with.

3. Click the Row Source property, click the Build button [...], then type the values for the list into the Edit List Items dialog box as shown in Figure G-11

   The Edit List Items dialog box also allows you to specify a default value. Because the most common tour duration is 7 days, you'll set 7 as the default value.

4. Click the Default Value text box, type 7, click OK, click the Property Sheet button to toggle it off, then click the Form View button on the Design tab

   Access automatically created the Category field on the General Info tab as a combo box because it is assigned Lookup properties in the Tours Table Design View. The Duration combo box is on the Dates tab.

5. Click Dates tab, click the Duration list arrow, then click 10 to change the duration for the first tour, Bayside Shelling, from 7 to 10 as shown in Figure G-12

   Also note that you can add items to the combo box list in Form View by clicking the **Edit List Items button**. To inactivate this feature, you change the combo box's **Allow Value List Edits** property to No in the combo box's property sheet. Another combo box property, the **Limit to List** property, controls whether a user can directly type an entry into the combo box that doesn't already appear on the list. To test the default value setting, you start entering a new record.

6. Click the New (blank) record button on the navigation bar to observe 7 as the default value for the Duration combo box

FIGURE G-11: Creating a combo box for the Duration field

List items

Default Value text box

Duration field is selected

Row Source Build button

Row Source Type property

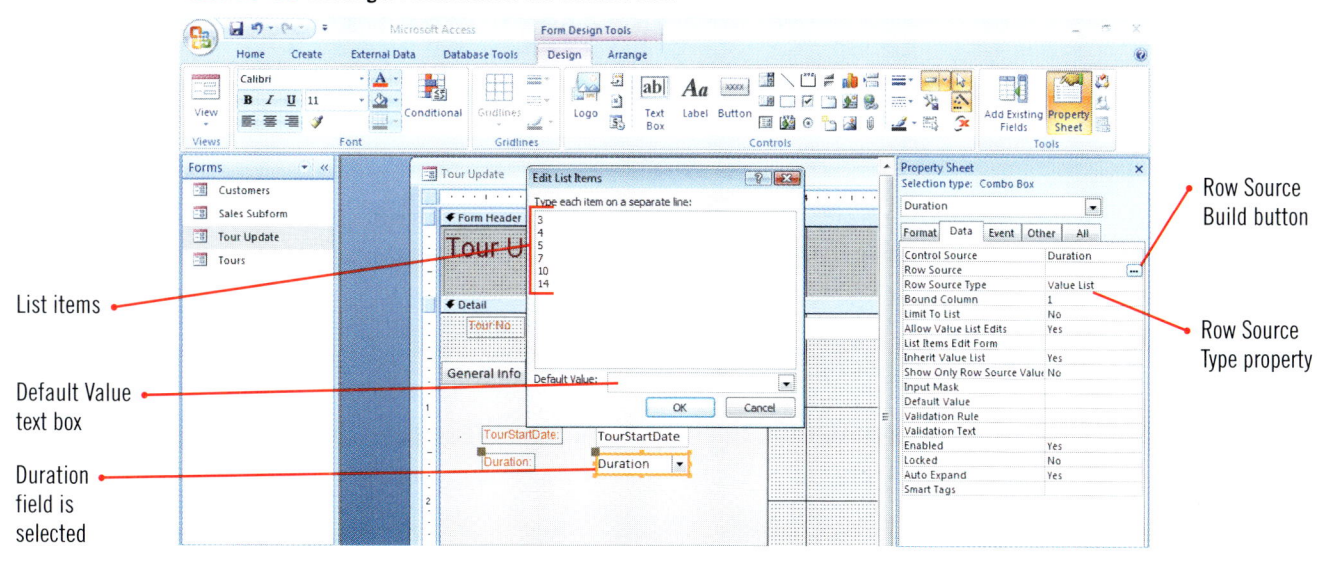

FIGURE G-12: Using the new Duration combo box

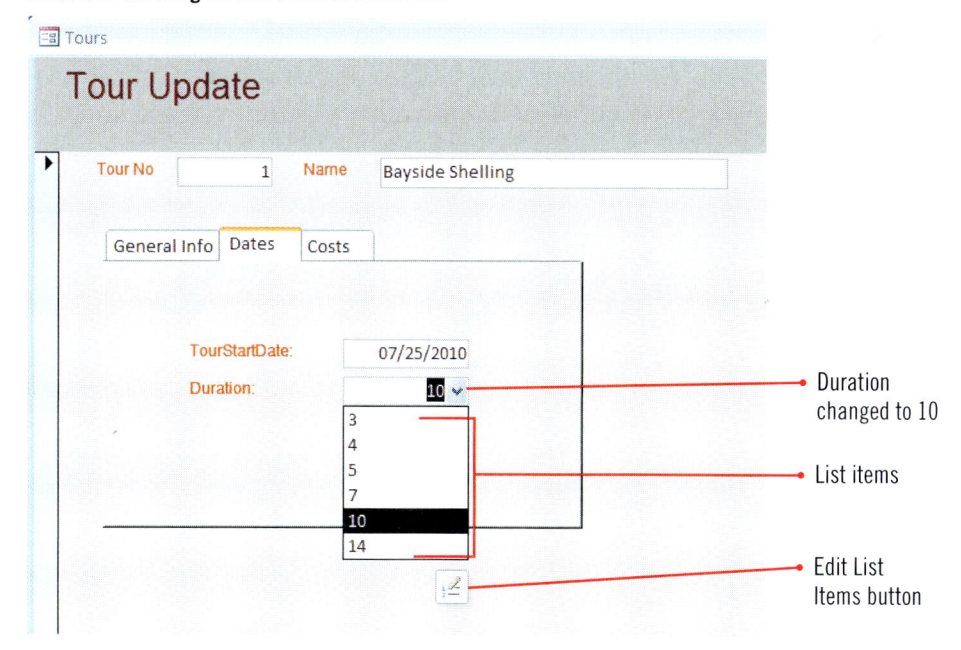

Duration changed to 10

List items

Edit List Items button

Choosing between a combo box and a list box

The list box and combo box controls are very similar, but the combo box is more popular for two reasons. While both provide a list of values from which the user can choose to make an entry in a field, the combo box also allows the user to make a unique entry from the keyboard (unless the Limit To List property is set to Yes). More importantly, however, most users like the drop-down list action of the combo box. A list box also provides a list of values through which the user scrolls and selects a choice, but has no "drop-down" action.

Enhancing Forms Access 171

Adding a Combo Box to Find Records

Most combo boxes are used to enter data; however, you can also use the combo box control to find records. When you use a combo box to find data, you must carefully identify it as a tool for finding and retrieving records so that the user doesn't confuse the combo boxes used to enter data with one used to find a record. You decide to add a combo box to help quickly locate the desired tour on the Tour Update form. You will use the Combo Box Wizard to help guide your actions in building this new combo box.

STEPS

1. **Click the View button arrow on the Home tab, click Design View, click the TourName text box, then press [Delete] to remove it from the form**

   Instead of changing the existing TourName text box into a combo box, you'll add the TourName combo box back to the form using the Combo Box Wizard.

2. **Click the Combo Box button on the Design tab, then click just above the right edge of the tab control**

   > **TROUBLE**
   > If the Combo Box Wizard doesn't start, delete the new combo box control, make sure the Use Control Wizards button is selected, which starts the wizards as needed, then redo Step 2.

   The Combo Box Wizard opens as shown in Figure G-13. The first two options create a combo box used to enter data in a field. The difference between the two options determines the source of the data in the drop-down list. The third option corresponds to what you want to do now—use the combo box to find a record.

3. **Click the Find a record option button, click Next, double-click TourName, click Next, double-click the right edge of the TourName column to view all of the items in the list, click Next, type FIND A TOUR as the label for the combo box, then click Finish**

   You test the combo box in Form View.

4. **Click the Form View button, click the FIND A TOUR list arrow, then click Greenfield Jaycees**

   The Greenfield Jaycees tour (Tour No 5) appears in the form, but you want to sort the combo box list values in ascending order. You must make this change in Form Design View.

5. **Click the View button arrow, click Design View, then double-click the new combo box to open its Property Sheet**

   To sort the values in ascending order, you work with the control's Row Source Property.

6. **Click the Data tab in the Property Sheet, click the Row Source property, then click the Build button**

   > **QUICK TIP**
   > To modify the number of items the combo box displays, use the List Rows property on the Format tab.

   The Query Builder opens, allowing you to modify the fields or sort order of the values in the combo box list.

7. **Click the Sort cell for the TourName field, click the list arrow, click Ascending, click the Close button on the Design tab, then click Yes when prompted to save the changes**

   Test the combo box in Form View.

8. **Click the Property Sheet button to close the Property Sheet, click , click the FIND A TOUR list arrow, then scroll and click Gold Country**

   The form finds and displays Tour No 29 for the Gold Country tour in Sacramento, CA as shown in Figure G-14.

FIGURE G-13: Choices in the Combo Box Wizard

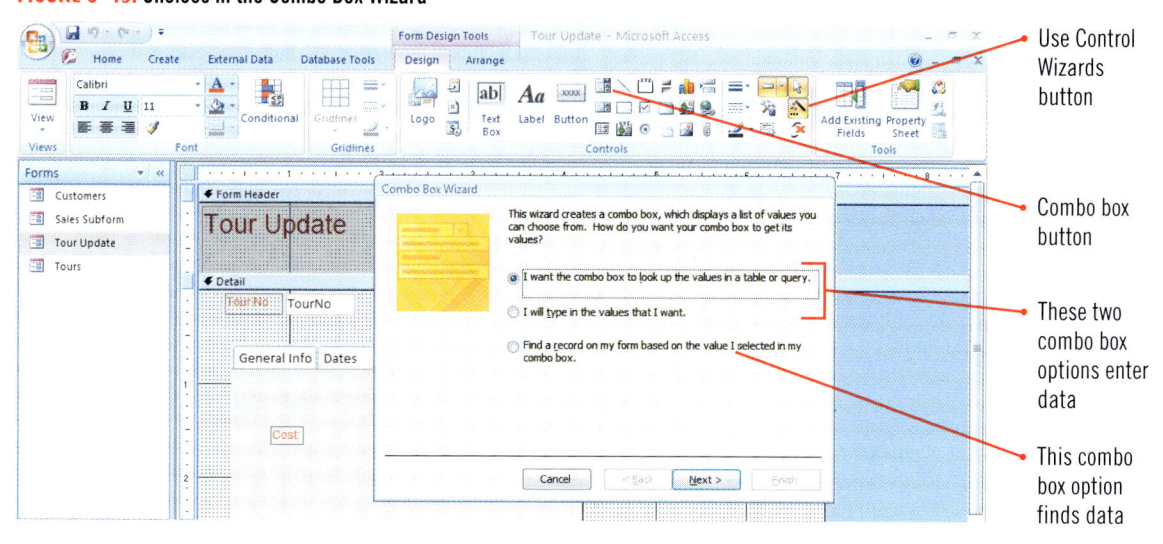

- Use Control Wizards button
- Combo box button
- These two combo box options enter data
- This combo box option finds data

FIGURE G-14: New combo box used to find tour names

- New combo box used to find a record

Enhancing Forms Access 173

Adding Option Groups

UNIT G
Access 2007

An **option group** is a special type of bound control that is often used when only a few values are available for a field. You place **option button** controls within the option group to determine the value that is selected in the field. Each option button represents a different value that can be entered into the field bound to the option group. Option buttons within an option group are mutually exclusive; only one can be chosen at a time. Another way to select the data for the Duration field is to use option buttons within an option group. You can modify the Tour Update form to investigate this alternative.

STEPS

1. Click the View button arrow, click Design View, click the Dates tab, click the Duration combo box, then press [Delete]

   After deleting the Duration combo box and its associated label, you are ready to add the Duration field back to the form as an option group.

2. Click the Option Group button on the Design tab, then click below the TourStartDate text box on the tabbed control

   The **Option Group Wizard** guides you as you develop an option group. The first question asks about label names for the option buttons. You'll enter all of the possible Quest tour durations.

3. Type 3 days, press [Tab], then enter the options as shown in Figure G-15

   The next question prompts you for the actual values associated with each option button.

4. Click Next, click the No, I don't want a default option button, click Next, then enter the option values to correspond with their labels as shown in Figure G-16

   The values are the actual data that are entered into the field and correspond with the **Option Value property** of each option button. The label names are just clarifying labels.

5. Click Next, click the Store the value in this field list arrow, click Duration, click Next, click Next to accept Option buttons in an Etched style, click Next, type Duration as the caption, then click Finish

   View the new option group in Form View.

6. Click the Form View button on the Design tab, use the FIND A TOUR list arrow to find the Colonial Tour, click the Dates tab, then click the 10 days option button

   Your screen should look like Figure G-17. You changed the duration of this tour from 14 to 10 days. To add more option buttons to this option group later, work in Form Design View and use the Option Button button on the Design tab to add the new option button to the option group. Modify the value represented by that option button by opening the option button's property sheet and changing the Option Value property.

7. Save and close the Tour Update form

Protecting data

You may not want to allow all users who view a form to change all the data that appears on that form. You can design forms to limit access to certain fields by changing the Enabled and Locked properties of a control. The **Enabled property** specifies whether a control can have the focus in Form View. The **Locked property** specifies whether you can edit data in a control in Form View.

Enhancing Forms

FIGURE G-15: Option Group Wizard

- Option Group button
- Option Button button
- New option group

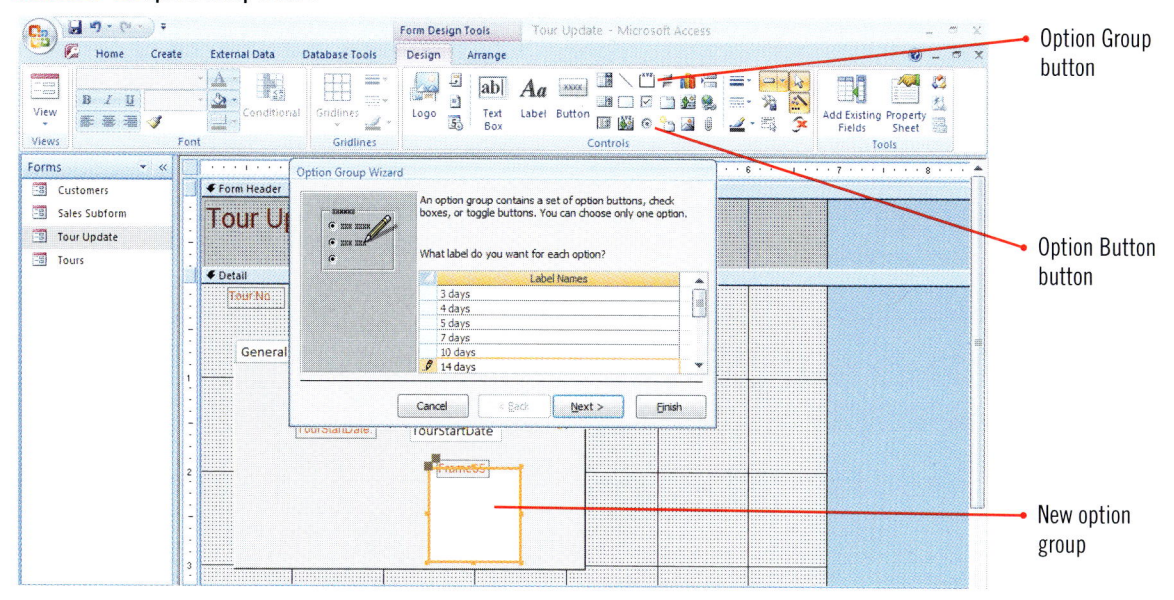

FIGURE G-16: Specifying the option button values

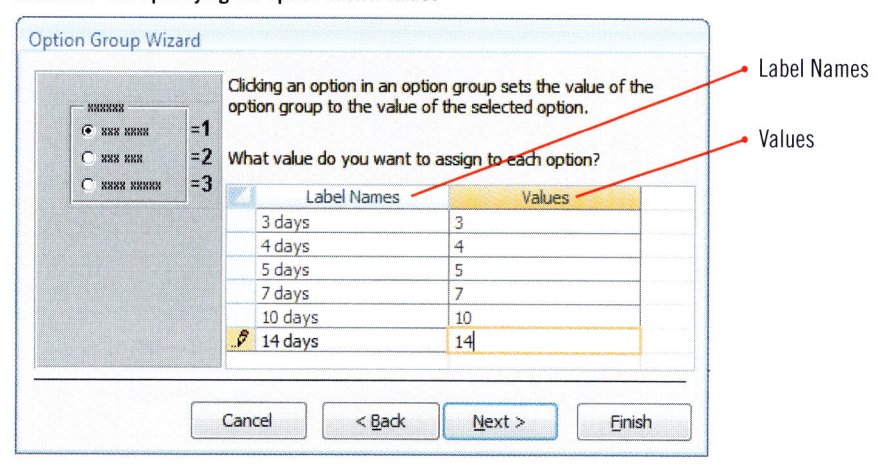

- Label Names
- Values

FIGURE G-17: Using an option group

Selecting an option button enters the value associated with it

New option group bound to the Duration field

Enhancing Forms Access 175

UNIT G
Access 2007
Adding Command Buttons

A **command button** is used to initiate a common action in Form View such as printing the current record, opening another form, or closing the current form. Command buttons are often added to the Form Header or Form Footer sections. **Sections** determine where controls appear on the screen and print on paper. See Table G-2 for more information on form sections. You add a command button to the Form Header section of the Tours form to help other Quest employees print only the current record.

STEPS

1. **Double-click Tours in the Navigation Pane, then maximize the form**
   You plan to add the new command button to the right side of the Form Header section to print the current record.

2. **Click the View button arrow on the Home tab, click Design View, click the Button button on the Design tab, then click the right side of the Form Header section**
   The Command Button Wizard opens, listing over 30 of the most popular actions for the command button, organized within six categories as shown in Figure G-18.

3. **Click Record Operations in the Categories list, click Print Record in the Actions list, click Next, click Next to accept the default picture, type PrintCurrentRecord as the button name, then click Finish**
   Adding this command button to print only the current record helps avoid creating an unintended printout that prints every record. The **Display When property** of the Form Header determines when the controls in that section appear on screen and print.

4. **Double-click the Form Header section bar to open its Property Sheet, click the Format tab, click Always for the Display When property, click the Display When list arrow, click Screen Only, then click the Property Sheet button on the Design tab to toggle off the Property Sheet**
   Now the Print Record button appears on the screen when you are working in the form, but does not appear on printouts. You'll make one more modification to the form—to add your name as a label for identification purposes.

5. **Click the Label button on the Design tab, click to the right of the TourNo text box in the Detail section, type Created by your name, then press [Enter]**
   Save and test the form.

6. **Click the Save button on the Quick Access toolbar, click the Form View button on the Design tab, then click the Print button you added to the Form Header section to confirm that only one record prints and that the Form Header controls do not appear on the printout**
   The final Tours form should look like Figure G-19.

7. **Save and close the Tours form, then close the Quest-G.accdb database**

TABLE G-2: Form sections

section	description
Detail	Appears once for every record
Form Header	Appears at the top of the form and often contains command buttons or a label with the title of the form
Form Footer	Appears at the bottom of the form and often contains command buttons or a label with instructions on how to use the form
Page Header	Appears at the top of a printed form with information such as page numbers or dates
Page Footer	Appears at the bottom of a printed form with information such as page numbers or dates

FIGURE G-18: Command Button Wizard

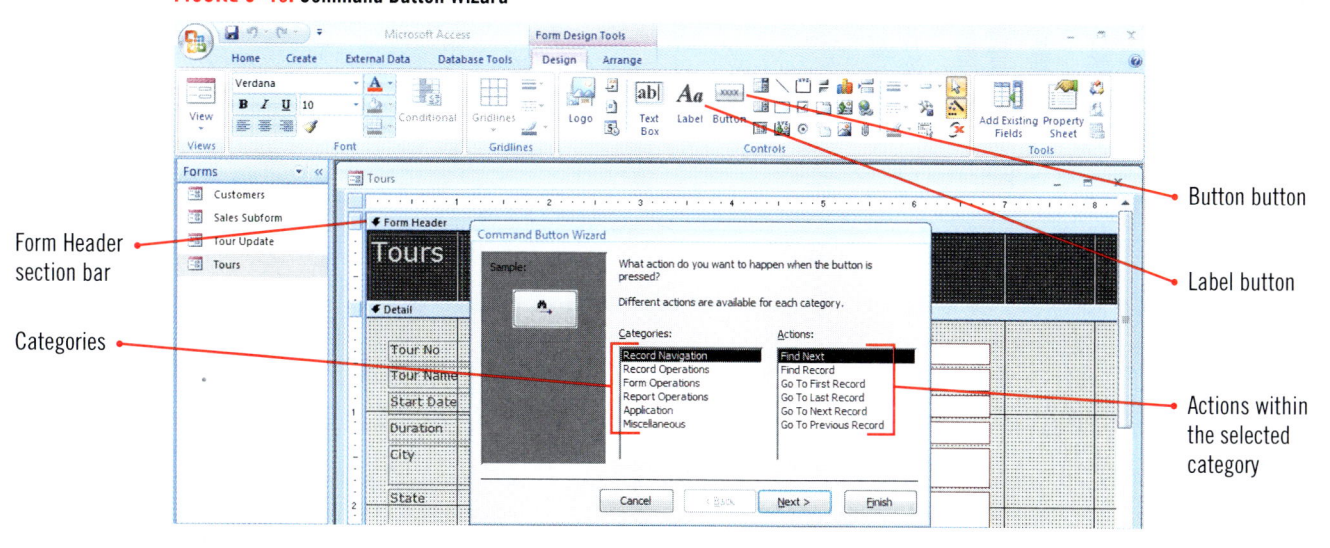

- Form Header section bar
- Categories
- Button button
- Label button
- Actions within the selected category

FIGURE G-19: Final Tours form

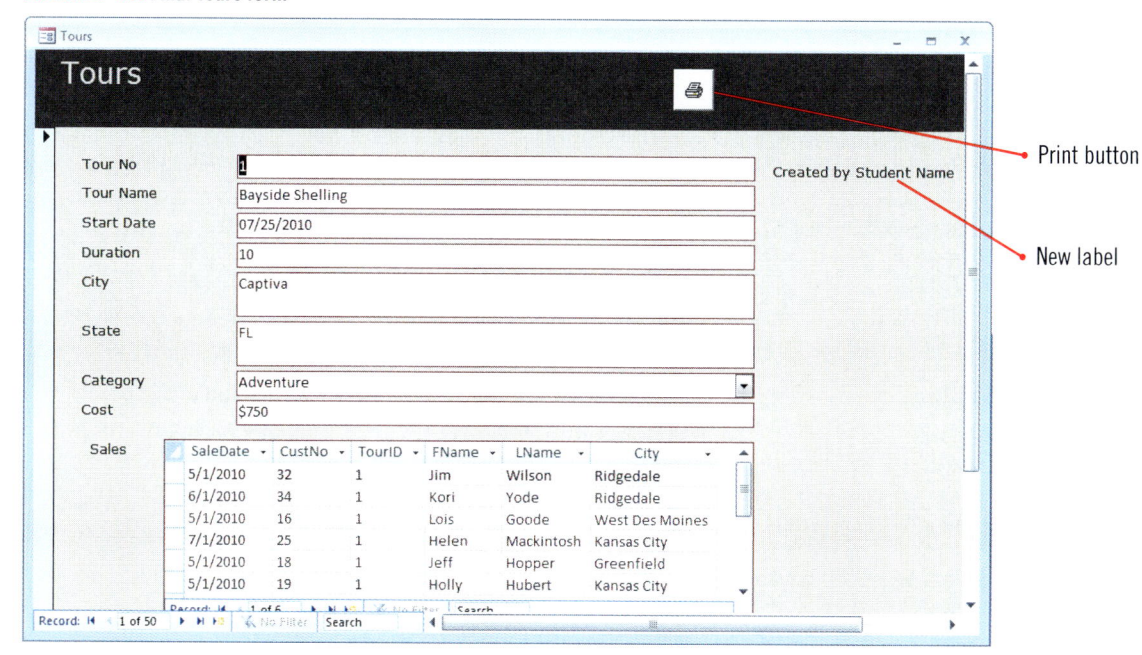

- Print button
- New label

Enhancing Forms

Access 177

Practice

▼ CONCEPTS REVIEW

If you have a SAM user profile, you may have access to hands-on instruction, practice, and assessment of the skills covered in this unit. Log in to your SAM account (http://sam2007.course.com/) to launch any assigned training activities or exams that relate to the skills covered in this unit.

Identify each element of the Form Design View shown in Figure G-20.

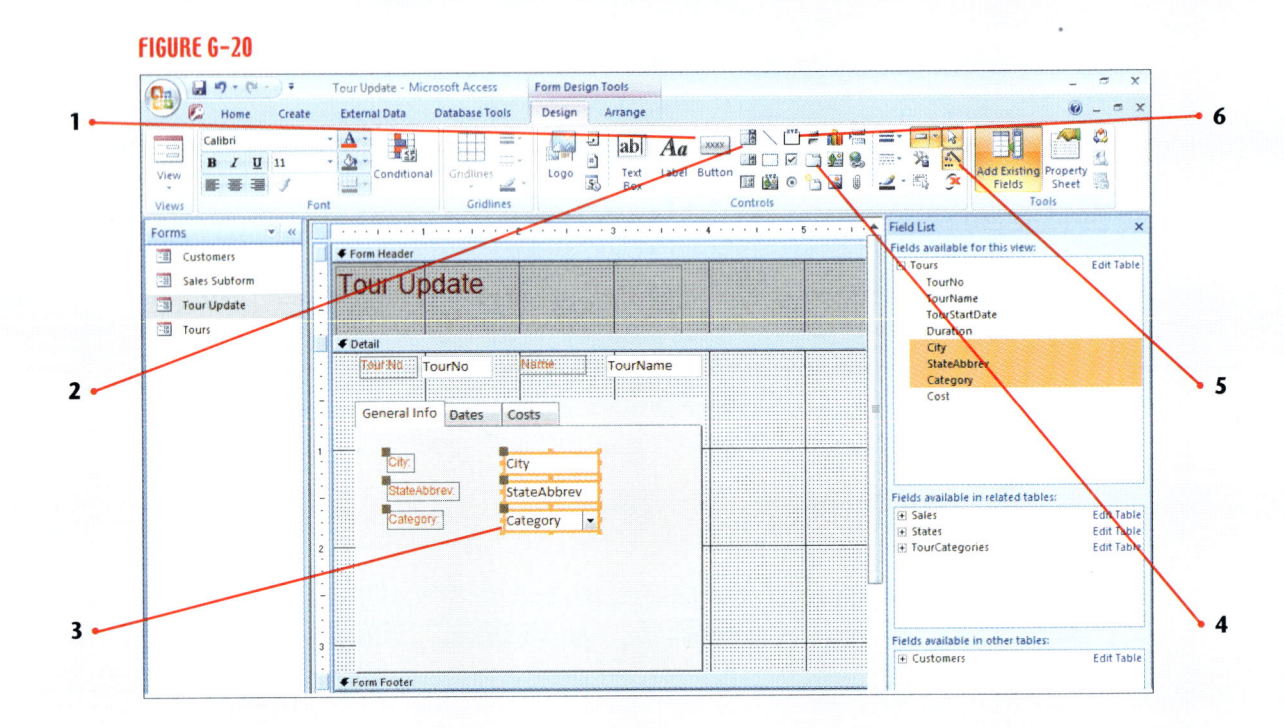

FIGURE G-20

Match each term with the statement that best describes its function.

7. Command button
8. Subform
9. Control
10. Option group
11. Combo box

a. An element you add to a form such as a label, text box, or list box
b. A control that shows records that are related to one record shown in the main form
c. An unbound control that executes an action when it is clicked
d. A bound control that is really both a list box and a text box
e. A bound control that displays a few mutually exclusive entries for a field

Select the best answer from the list of choices.

12. Which control works best to display three choices, 1, 2, or 3, for a Rating field?
    a. Option group
    b. Label
    c. Text box
    d. Command button

13. Which control would you use to initiate a print action?
    a. Option group
    b. Command button
    c. Text box
    d. List box

14. Which control would you use to display a drop-down list of 50 states?
    a. Check box
    b. Field label
    c. Combo box
    d. List box

15. To view many related records within a form, use a:
    a. Link control.
    b. List box.
    c. Design template.
    d. Subform.
16. Which of the following form properties defines the fields and records that appear on a form?
    a. Default View
    b. Record Source
    c. Row Source
    d. List Items Edit Form
17. Which is a popular layout for a main form?
    a. Datasheet
    b. PivotTable
    c. Global
    d. Columnar
18. Which is a popular layout for a subform?
    a. Global
    b. PivotTable
    c. Columnar
    d. Datasheet
19. Which Form Header property determines when the controls in that section appear on screen and print?
    a. Display When
    b. Section Visible
    c. Special Effect
    d. Can Shrink
20. Which control is most commonly used within an option group?
    a. Option Button
    b. Toggle Button
    c. Command Button
    d. Check Box

▼ SKILLS REVIEW

1. **Create subforms.**
   a. Start Access and open the **Membership-G.accdb** database from the drive and folder where you store your Data Files. Enable content if prompted.
   b. Click the Database Tools tab, then click the Relationships button.
   c. Click the Relationship Report button.
   d. The Relationships for Membership-G appears as a report in Print Preview. In Report Design View, insert your name as a label in the Report Header section, then print the report.
   e. Close the Relationships report window without saving the report, and then close the Relationships window.
   f. Use the Form Wizard to create a form/subform combination based on the First, Last, and CharterMember fields in the Names table, and the ActivityDate and Hours fields in the Activities table. Use the printout of the relationships report to answer the Form Wizard question about how you want to view your data. The answer to this question determines which fields go in the main form, and which fields go in the subform. Use a Datasheet layout and an Origin style, and name the form **Names Main Form** and **Activities Subform**.

2. **Modify subforms.**
   a. In Form Design View, make the subform both wider and taller so that more records can be viewed at the same time.
   b. Open the Field List for the main form, and add the Birthday field between the Last text box and CharterMember check box.
   c. Save, then close the Names Main Form.

3. **Create split forms.**
   a. Click the Names table in the Navigation Pane, then use the Split Form button on the Create tab to create a split form based on the Names table.
   b. Maximize the form, filter for all members whose dues are $25, then sort the records in ascending order based on the Last field. Your screen should look like Figure G-21. (*Hint*: If all of the fields are not visible in the upper portion of the split form, drag the split bar that separates the two sections of the form.)
   c. Save the form as **Names Split Form**, then close it.

FIGURE G-21

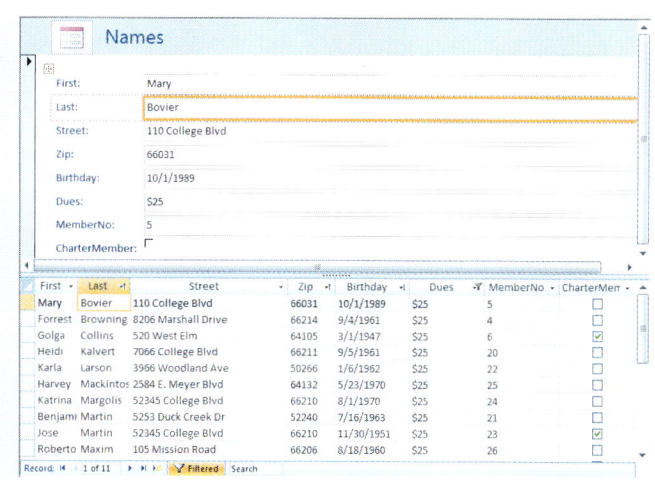

▼ SKILLS REVIEW (CONTINUED)

4. **Add tab controls.**
   a. Open Member Entry Form in Design View.
   b. Add a tab control and rename the two pages to be **Address** and **Activities**.
   c. Resize the tab control to fill the space available on the form under the existing controls.
   d. Open the Field List, then add the **Street** field from the Names table to the top of the Address page.
   e. Add the **Zip** field from the Names table to the bottom of the Address page.
   f. Add the **City** and **State** fields between the existing Street and Zip fields to the Address page from the Zips table in the Field List then close the Field List.
   g. Use your moving and alignment skills to order the fields top to bottom as: Street, City, State, and Zip. Right-align the right edges of these four new text boxes on the Address page and make the vertical spacing between the controls equal.
   h. Click the Activities page to bring it forward, then use the Subform/Subreport button on the Design tab to add the existing Activities Subform to that page. Use the rest of the defaults in the Subform Wizard, which helps you connect the main form and subform using the common MemberNo field.
   i. Resize the Activities Subform to fill the Activities page.
   j. Save and view the Member Entry Form in Form View. Sort the records in ascending order based on the MemberNo and move between the records of the main form observing the fields in both pages of the tab control. MemberNo 1, Micah Zecharius, should have an address in Shawnee, KS, and five activity records. Return to Design View and move or resize any controls that do not completely display the data they contain.

5. **Add a combo box for data entry.**
   a. Open the Member Entry Form in Design View, then right-click the Zip text box and change it to a combo box control.
   b. In the Property Sheet of the new combo box, click the Row Source property, then click the Build button.
   c. Select the Zips table only for the query, and then double-click the Zip field to add it as the only column of the query grid.
   d. Close the Query Builder window, and save the changes.
   e. Close the Property Sheet, then save and view the Member Entry Form in Form View.
   f. In the first record for MemberNo 1, change the Zip to **64153** using the new combo box. Notice that the City and State fields automatically change to Blue Springs, MO to reflect the zip code choice.
   g. Save and close the Member Entry Form.

6. **Add a combo box to find records.**
   a. Open the Names Main Form in Design View.
   b. Use the Combo Box Wizard to add to the right side of the Form Header section a new combo box that finds records in the form.
   c. Select the First and Last fields, make sure that each column is wide enough to view all values, and label the combo box **FIND THIS MEMBER**.
   d. Widen the new combo box to be about 2" wide, change the label text to white, save the Names Main form, then view it in Form View.
   e. Use the FIND THIS MEMBER combo box to find the Benjamin Martin record. Notice that the entries in the combo box are not alphabetized on last name.
   f. Return to Form Design View, and use the Row Source property for the combo box to add an ascending sort order to the Last field. Close the Query Builder, saving changes. View the Names Main Form in Form View, and find the record for Sherry Walker. Note that the entries in the combo box list are now sorted in ascending order by the Last field.
   g. Find the record for Micah Zecharius using the combo box, change the record to your own first and last names, print only that record, then save and close the Names Main Form. (*Hint*: To print only one record, choose the Selected Record(s) option in the Print dialog box.)

7. **Add option groups.**
   a. Open the Member Entry Form in Design View, then delete the Dues text box and label in the main form.
   b. Using the Option Group Wizard, add the Dues field back to the form just below the Birthday text box.
   c. Enter **$25** and **$50** as the label names, then accept $25 as the default choice.
   d. Change the values to **25** and **50** to correspond with the labels.

▼ SKILLS REVIEW (CONTINUED)

e. Store the value in the Dues field, choose Option buttons with an Etched style, type the caption **Annual Dues**, then click Finish.

f. Move and resize the new Dues option group and other controls as needed, save the Member Entry Form, display it in Form View, use the combo box to find the record with your name, then change the Annual Dues to **$25**.

8. **Add command buttons.**
   a. Open the Member Entry Form in Design View.
   b. Use the Command Button Wizard to add a command button to the right side of the Form Header section.
   c. Choose the Print Record action from the Record Operations category.
   d. Display the text **Print Current Record** on the button, then name the button **PrintButton**.
   e. Save the form, display it in Form View, then print the record for yourself. The final form should look similar to Figure G-22.
   f. Navigate to the record with your own name, change the month and day of the Birthday entry to your own, then print the record using the new Print Current Record command button.
   g. Save, then close the Member Entry Form.
   h. Close the Membership-G.accdb database.

FIGURE G-22

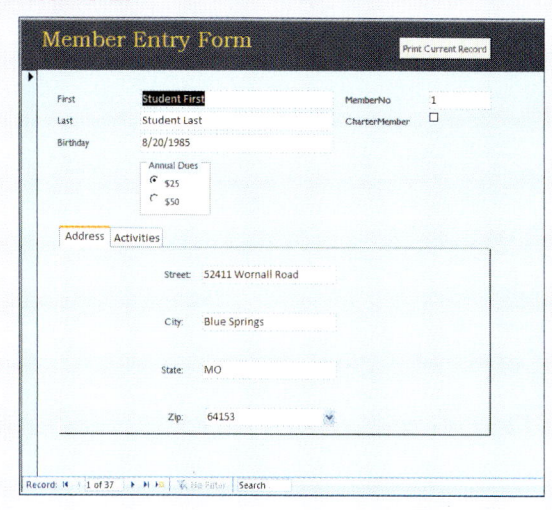

▼ INDEPENDENT CHALLENGE 1

As the manager of a music store's instrument rental program, you have created a database to track instrument rentals to schoolchildren. Now that several rentals have been made, you want to create a form/subform to make it easy for users to enter a new rental record.

a. Start Access, then open the database **MusicRentals-G.accdb** from the drive and folder where you store your Data Files. Enable content if prompted.

b. Using the Form Wizard, create a new form based on all of the fields in the Customers and Rentals tables.

c. View the data by Customers, choose a Datasheet layout for the subform and an Opulent style, then accept the default form titles of Customers for the main form and Rentals Subform for the subform.

d. Add another record to the rental subform for Amanda Smith by typing **888335** as the SerialNo entry and **5/1/10** as the RentalDate entry. (*Hint*: If the RentalDate field isn't visible, press [Tab] to move to it.) Note that no entries are necessary in the RentalNo field because it is an AutoNumber field nor the CustNo field as it is the foreign key field that connects the main form to the subform and is automatically populated when the forms are in this arrangement.

e. Save and close the Customers form.

f. Open the Rentals Subform in Form Design View and change the subform to show only the SerialNo, Date, and the Description for the instrument. You don't need to see the RentalNo or CustNo fields in the subform.

g. Delete the RentalNo and CustNo fields, open the Field List, and drag the Description field from the Field List (*Hint*: Look in the Instruments related table) to just under the Date field. Remember that the subform is in a datasheet layout so precise positioning of the controls in Form Design View is not necessary.

h. Save and close the Rentals Subform, then open the Customers main form in Form View.

i. Resize the columns in the subform so that all fields are visible.

j. In Form Design View, add a combo box to the right side of the Form Header to find records based on the data in the FirstName and LastName fields. Label the combo box FIND CUSTOMER: and change the label text to white so that it is visible on the dark background.

k. Use the Row Source property of the combo box to sort the list in ascending order on LastName, and widen the control.

l. Open the Customers main form in Form View and search for the record Kris Joy. Change that name to your own, and print only this record. (*Hint*: To print only one record, choose the Selected Record(s) option in the Print dialog box.)

m. Save and close the Customers form, close the MusicRentals-G.accdb database, then exit Access.

▼ INDEPENDENT CHALLENGE 2

As the manager of a music store's instrument rental program, you have created a database to track instrument rentals to schoolchildren. You add command buttons to a form to make it easier to use.

a. Start Access, then open the database **InstrumentRentals-G.accdb** from the drive and folder where you store your Data Files. Enable content if prompted.
b. Using the Form Wizard, create a form/subform using all the fields of both the Customers and Schools tables.
c. View the data by Schools, use a Datasheet layout for the subform, then choose a Northwind style.
d. Accept the default names of Schools for the main form and Customers Subform for the subform.
e. Resize the subform columns to view all of the data in Form View. Use Form Design View to delete the SchoolNo field from the subform, and to resize the subform as necessary to display all columns.
f. In Form Design View, add a command button to the middle of the Form Header. The action should print the current record and display the text **Print School Record**. Name the button **PrintButton**.

Advanced Challenge Exercise

- Add a second command button to the right of the Print School Record button using the Command Button Wizard. The action should add a new record and display the text **Add New School**. Name the button **AddButton**.
- Add a third command button to the right side of the Form Header section using the Command Button Wizard. The action should close the form and display the text **Close**. Name the button **CloseButton**.
- Align the top edges of all three buttons.
- Open the Property Sheet for the Form Header and give the Display When property the **Screen Only** value. Close the Property Sheet, then save the Schools form.
- Display the form in Form View, click the Add New School button, add the name of your high school to the SchoolName field, allow the SchoolNo to increment automatically, then add the information of a friend as the first record within the subform. Note that the CustNo and SchoolNo fields in the subform will be entered automatically.

g. Use the Print School Record button to print only this new school record.
h. Close the Schools form, close the InstrumentRentals-G.accdb database, then exit Access.

▼ INDEPENDENT CHALLENGE 3

As the manager of an equipment rental program, you have created a database to track equipment rentals. Now that the users are becoming accustomed to forms, you add a combo box and option group to make the forms easier to use.

a. Start Access, then open the database **Equipment-G.accdb** from the drive and folder where you store your Data Files. Enable content if prompted.
b. Using the Form Wizard, create a form/subform using all the fields of both the Equipment and Rentals tables.
c. View the data by Equipment, use a Datasheet layout for the subform, and choose a Concourse style.
d. Enter the name **Equipment Main Form** for the main form and **Rentals Subform** for the subform. In Form View, resize the columns of the subform so that all data is clearly visible.
e. In Form Design View of the Equipment Main Form, delete the Deposit text box and label.
f. Add the Deposit field as an option group to the right side of the main form using the Option Group Wizard.
g. Enter the Label Names as **$0**, **$50**, and **$100**. Do not specify a default option. The corresponding values for the option buttons should be **0**, **50**, and **100**.
h. Store the value in the Deposit field. Use Option buttons with an Etched style.
i. Caption the option group **Deposit**, save the form, then view it in Form View. Resize and move controls as necessary.
j. Specify a **$50** deposit for each of the first three records (Weed Eater, Weed Whacker, and Mulching Mower). Save and close the Equipment Main Form.

▼ INDEPENDENT CHALLENGE 3 (CONTINUED)

Advanced Challenge Exercise

- In Table Design View of the Equipment table, add a field named **Condition** with a Text data type. This field will record the condition of the instrument as Excellent, Good, Fair, or Poor.
- Start the Lookup Wizard for the Condition field, and choose the "I will type in the values that I want" option button.
- Enter **Excellent**, **Good**, **Fair**, and **Poor** as the four possible values, and accept the name **Condition** as the label for the lookup column. Save and close the Equipment table.
- In Form Design View of the Equipment Main Form, open the Field List and add the Condition field to just below the WeeklyRate text box. Note that the Condition field is automatically added as a combo box control due to the Lookup properties it was given in Table Design View of the Equipment table where it is defined.
- Save the form then display it in Form View. Move through the records, selecting Excellent as the Condition value choice for the first two records and Good for the third record.

k. In Design View, add a command button to the Form Header section that prints the current record. Use the text **Print** on the button and give it the meaningful name of PrintButton. Add your own name as a label under the Equipment Main Form label.

l. Print only the record for the Weed Eater.

m. Save and close the Equipment Main Form, close the Equipment-G.accdb database, and then exit Access.

▼ REAL LIFE INDEPENDENT CHALLENGE

One way to use Access in your real life is in a community service project. People in schools and nonprofit agencies often inherit databases created by others and need help extracting information from them. Suppose you're working with the local high school guidance counselor to help her with an Access database she inherited that is used to record college scholarship opportunities. You can help her keep the database updated by creating some easy to use forms.

a. Start Access and open the **Scholarships-G.accdb** database from the drive and folder where you store your Data Files. Enable content if prompted.

b. Create a split form for the Scholarships table. Save and name the form **Scholarships**.

c. Move and resize controls as necessary to expand the size of the Description field as shown in Figure G-23.

d. Add a combo box to find a scholarship by name to the Form Header section with the label **FIND SCHOLARSHIP:**. Widen the control as necessary and change its List Rows property to **50**.

e. Modify the Row Source property of the combo box so that the scholarships are sorted in ascending order based on the scholarship name.

f. Use the combo box to find the Patrick Charnon Scholarship. Change "Patrick Charnon" to your name in both the ScholarshipName text box as well as the Description field, then print only that record by using the Selected Record(s) option on the Print dialog box.

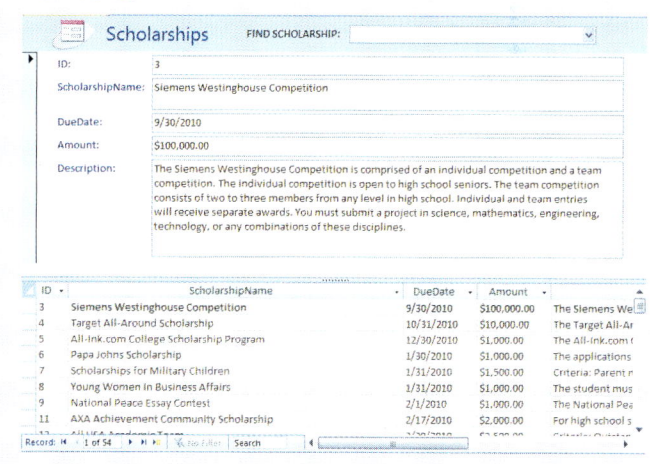

g. Save and close the Scholarship form, close the Scholarships-G.accdb database, then exit Access.

FIGURE G-23

▼ VISUAL WORKSHOP

Open the **RealEstate-G.accdb** database from the drive and folder where you store your Data Files. Enable content if prompted. Use the Form Wizard to create a new form. Select all the fields from the Agencies, Agents, and Listings tables. View the data by Agencies which will create two subforms as one agency has many agents and one agent has many listings. Use a datasheet layout for each subform, and Equity style for the main form, and accept the default names for the forms. Resize the columns in the datasheets to show more fields, and also resize the subforms themselves to better use the width of the form. In Form View, navigate to the Camden and Camden Realtors agency in the main form, navigate to Shari Duncan in the Agents subform as shown in Figure G-24, then change Shari's name to your own. Use the Selected Record(s) option button in the Print dialog box to print that record.

FIGURE G-24

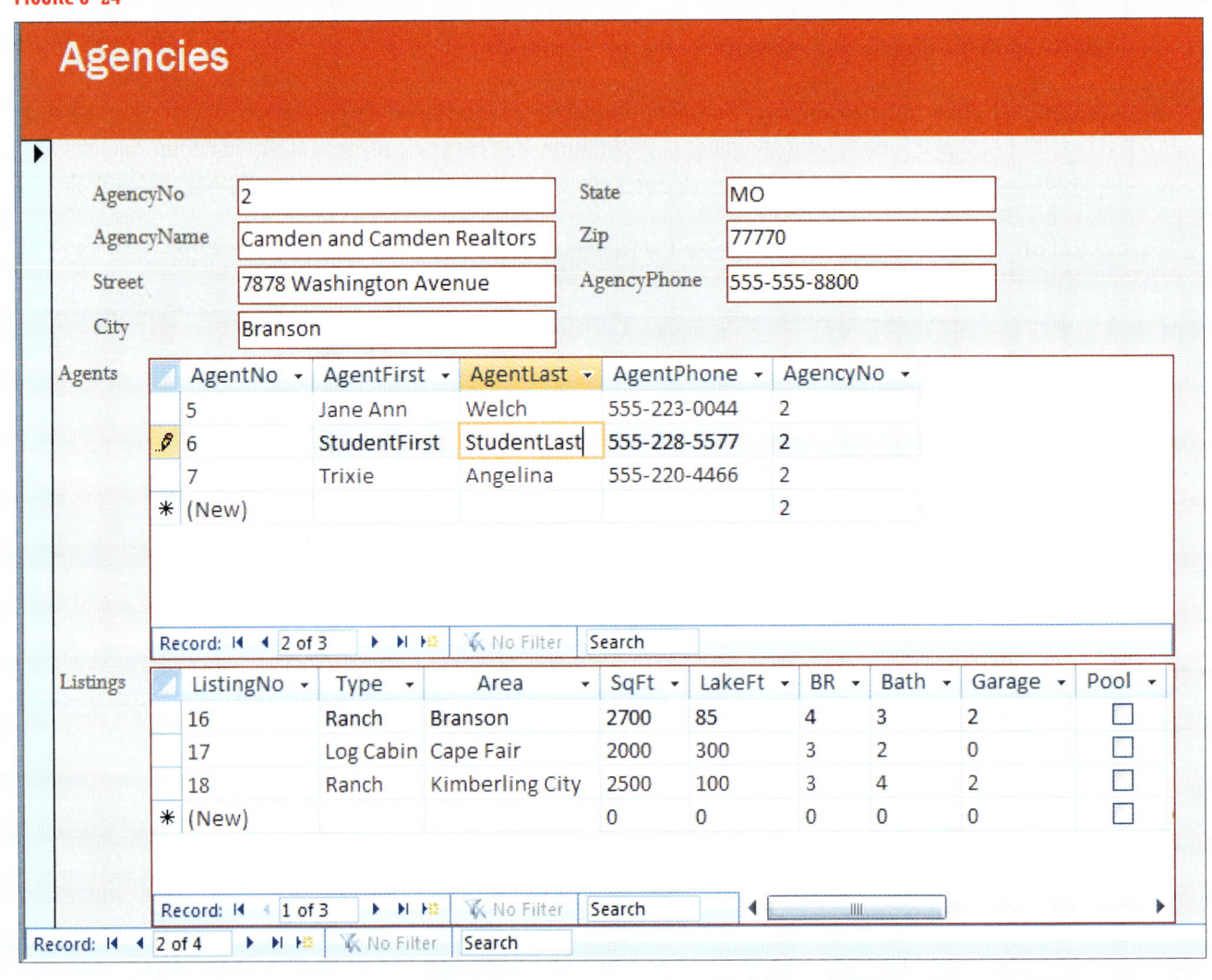

Agencies

AgencyNo	2	State	MO
AgencyName	Camden and Camden Realtors	Zip	77770
Street	7878 Washington Avenue	AgencyPhone	555-555-8800
City	Branson		

Agents

AgentNo	AgentFirst	AgentLast	AgentPhone	AgencyNo
5	Jane Ann	Welch	555-223-0044	2
6	StudentFirst	StudentLast	555-228-5577	2
7	Trixie	Angelina	555-220-4466	2
(New)				2

Record: 2 of 3

Listings

ListingNo	Type	Area	SqFt	LakeFt	BR	Bath	Garage	Pool
16	Ranch	Branson	2700	85	4	3	2	☐
17	Log Cabin	Cape Fair	2000	300	3	2	0	☐
18	Ranch	Kimberling City	2500	100	3	4	2	☐
(New)			0	0	0	0	0	☐

Record: 1 of 3

Record: 2 of 4

Analyzing Data with Reports

UNIT H
Access 2007

Files You Will Need:
Quest-H.accdb
RealEstate-H.accdb
MusicRentals-H.accdb
InstrumentRentals-H.accdb
Equipment-H.accdb
Scholarships-H.accdb
Training-H.accdb

Although you can print data in forms and datasheets, **reports** give you more control over how data is printed and greater flexibility in presenting summary information. To create a report, you use bound controls, such as text boxes, to display data and unbound controls, such as lines, graphics, and labels, to clarify the data. Using additional report design skills, such as building summary reports and parameter reports and applying conditional formatting, you can create reports that not only present but also analyze and clarify the information.

OBJECTIVES

Create summary reports
Create parameter reports
Apply conditional formatting
Add lines
Use the Format Painter and AutoFormats
Add subreports
Modify section properties
Use domain functions

UNIT H
Access 2007

Creating Summary Reports

Summary reports are reports that show statistics on groups of records. As the amount of data in your database grows over time, you probably become more interested in summary statistics that analyze groups of records rather than details about the specific data in each record. You create summary reports by using Access functions such as Sum, Count, or Avg in expressions that calculate the desired statistic. These expressions are entered in text boxes in report group header or footer sections. Therefore, you need to understand report sections and calculated expressions so you can create summary reports effectively. Table H-1 reviews report sections. The Group Footer section is most commonly used to calculate statistics on groups of records. 🎨 Mark Rock asks for a report to summarize the revenue for each tour category. You can create a summary report to satisfy this request.

STEPS

1. **Start Access, open the Quest-H.accdb database from the drive and folder where you store your Data Files, enable content if prompted, click the Create tab, click the Report Design button, then maximize the report window**

   The first step in building a report from scratch in Report Design View is to select the fields you want for the form. You do this by setting the report's Record Source property.

2. **Double-click the report selector button ■ to open the Property Sheet, click the Data tab, click the Record Source Build button ⋯, double-click Tours, double-click Sales, then click Close**

3. **Scroll down and double-click Category in the Tours field list, then double-click Revenue in the Sales field list**

   The Revenue field represents what was actually charged at the time of the sale. Tours are sometimes discounted for various reasons.

4. **Click the Close button on the Query Tools Design tab, click Yes to save changes, click the Property Sheet button on the Design tab to close the Property Sheet, then click the Group & Sort button if the Group, Sort, and Total pane is not open**

   With the fields selected for the report, the next step is to specify the Category field as the grouping field.

5. **Click the Add a group button in the Group, Sort, and Total pane, then click Category**

   The Category Header section appears in Report Design View. To identify each new tour category, you add the Category field to this report section.

6. **Click the Add Existing Fields button on the Design tab, then drag the Category field to the left side of the Category Header section**

   To sum the revenue for each category, you need to add an expression to a text box that subtotals the Revenue for each Category. You use the Access Sum function.

7. **Click the Text Box button abl on the Design tab, click to the right of the Category control in the Category Header section, click Unbound in the new text box, type =Sum([Revenue]), press [Enter], then change, move, resize, and align the controls as shown in Figure H-1**

   A summary report doesn't need a Detail section, so you can close the Detail section.

> **TROUBLE**
> You must scroll down in order to see the bottom edge of the Detail section.

8. **Close the Group, Sort, and Total pane, drag the top edge of the Page Footer section up to completely close the Detail section, click the Home tab, click the View button arrow, then click Print Preview**

   The summarized revenue for each category is shown in the one-page summary report in Figure H-2.

9. **Close Print Preview, save the report with the name Category Revenue Summary, then close it**

Access 186 Analyzing Data with Reports

FIGURE H-1: Design View of summary report

- Group & Sort button
- New expression to subtotal Revenue
- Group on Category field
- Add Existing Fields button
- Text Box button

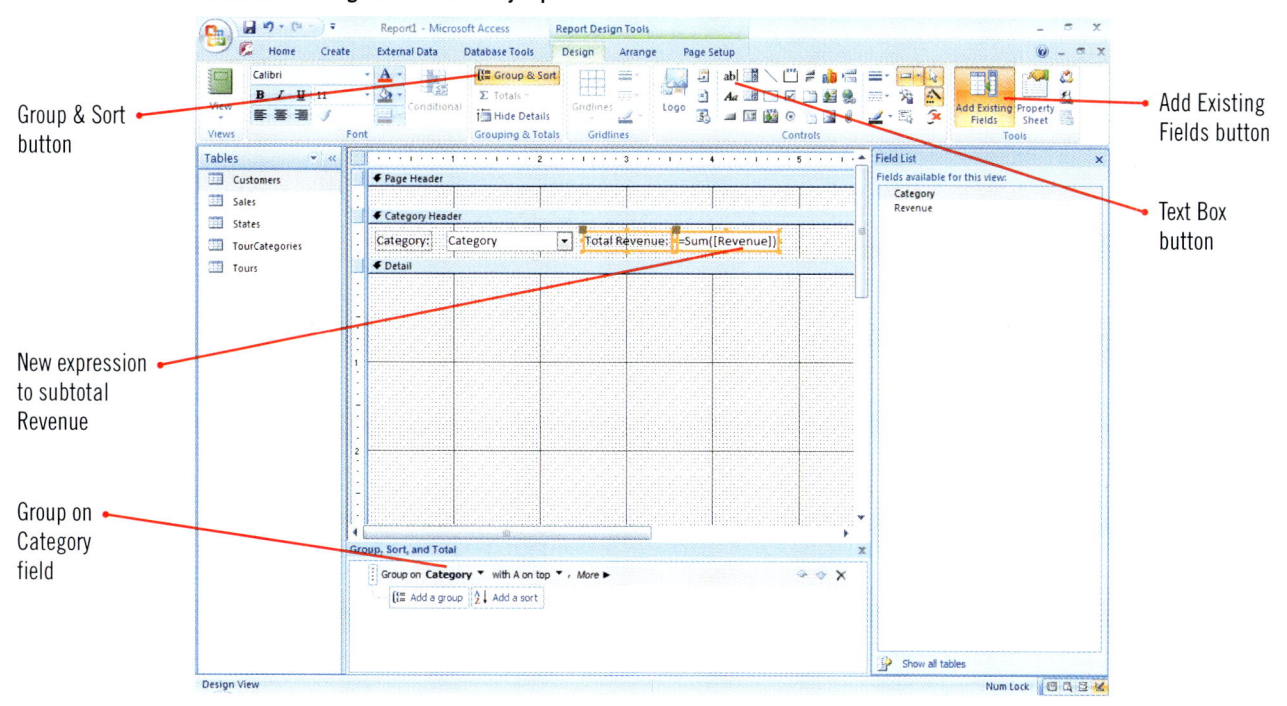

FIGURE H-2: Print Preview of summary report

Category:	Adventure	Total Revenue:	45965
Category:	Cultural	Total Revenue:	3000
Category:	Educational	Total Revenue:	24190
Category:	Family	Total Revenue:	8470
Category:	Service	Total Revenue:	3325
Category:	Site Seeing	Total Revenue:	8180

- Each row represents many records for each category
- Total revenue subtotaled by category

TABLE H-1: Review of report sections

section	where does this section print?	what is this section most commonly used for?
Report Header	At the top of the first page of the report	To print a title or logo
Page Header	At the top of every page (but below the Report Header on page one)	To print titles, dates, or page numbers at the top of every page
Group Header	Before every group of records	To identify the value of the grouping field
Detail	Once for every record	To display data for every record in the report
Group Footer	After every group of records	To calculate summary statistics on groups of records
Page Footer	At the bottom of every page	To print dates or page numbers at the bottom of every page

Analyzing Data with Reports

Creating Parameter Reports

UNIT H
Access 2007

A **parameter report** prompts you for criteria to determine the records to use for the report. To create a parameter report, you base the report on a parameter query by setting the report's Record Source property to the name of the parameter query. Mark Rock requests a report that shows all tour sales for a given period. You use a parameter query to prompt the user for the dates, then build the report on that query.

STEPS

1. Click the Create tab, click the Query Design button, double-click Customers, double-click Sales, double-click Tours, click Close, then maximize the query window

   You want fields from all three records in the report, so you add them to the query that will supply the report's records.

2. Double-click FName, LName, SaleDate, Revenue, and TourName

   To select only those tours sold in a given period, you add parameter prompts to the SaleDate field.

3. Click the Criteria cell for the SaleDate field, type Between [Enter start date] and [Enter end date], then widen the SaleDate column to see the entire entry as shown in Figure H-3

   To test the query, run it and enter dates in the parameter prompts.

> **QUICK TIP**
> You can shorten date criteria by entering only two digits for the year, as in 6/1/10.

4. Click the View button on the Design tab to run the query, type 6/1/2010 in the Enter start date box, click OK, type 6/30/2010 in the Enter end date box, then click OK

   Twenty-five records are displayed in the datasheet, each with a SaleDate value in June 2010. To create a parameter report, you use the Report Wizard to build a report on this query.

5. Click the Save button on the Quick Access toolbar, type SalesParameter as the new query name, click OK, then close the query

   You use the Report button on the Create tab to quickly build a report on the SalesParameter query.

6. Click the SalesParameter query in the Navigation Pane, click the Create tab, click the Report button, type 7/1/2010 in the Enter start date box, click OK, type 7/31/2010 in the Enter end date box, then click OK

   The report is displayed in Layout View with records in July 2010. You decide to preview and save the report.

7. Click the View button arrow on the Format tab, click Print Preview, click the One Page button on the Print Preview tab to view an entire page, then maximize the window as shown in Figure H-4

8. Close Print Preview, save the report with the name SalesParameter, then close it

FIGURE H-3: Creating parameter criteria in a query

Parameter prompt for SaleDate field

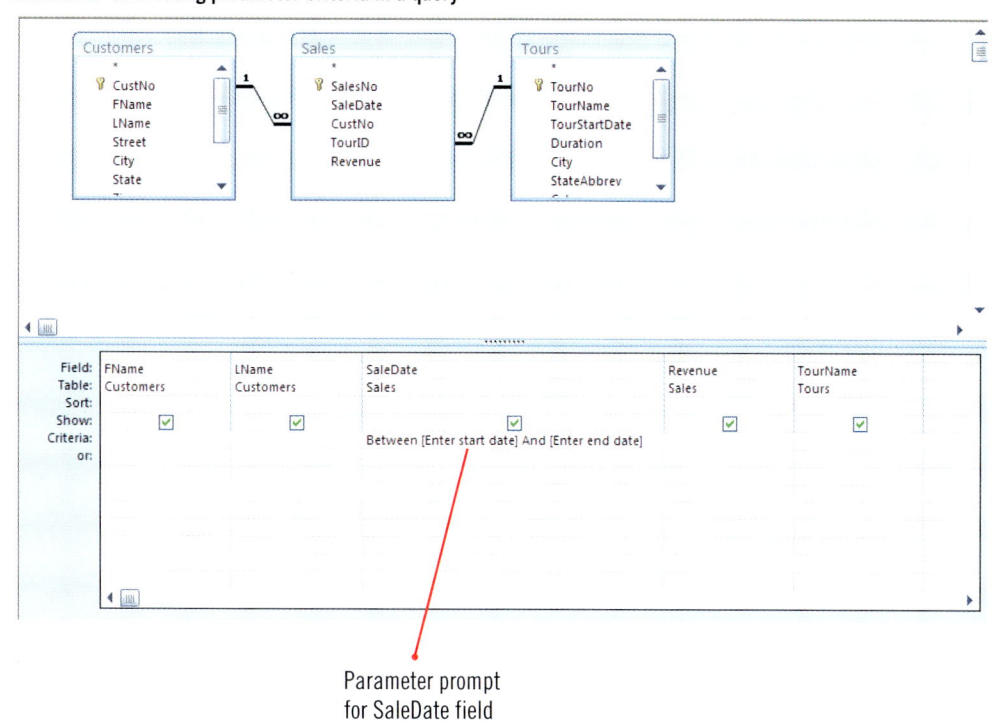

FIGURE H-4: Previewing the parameter report

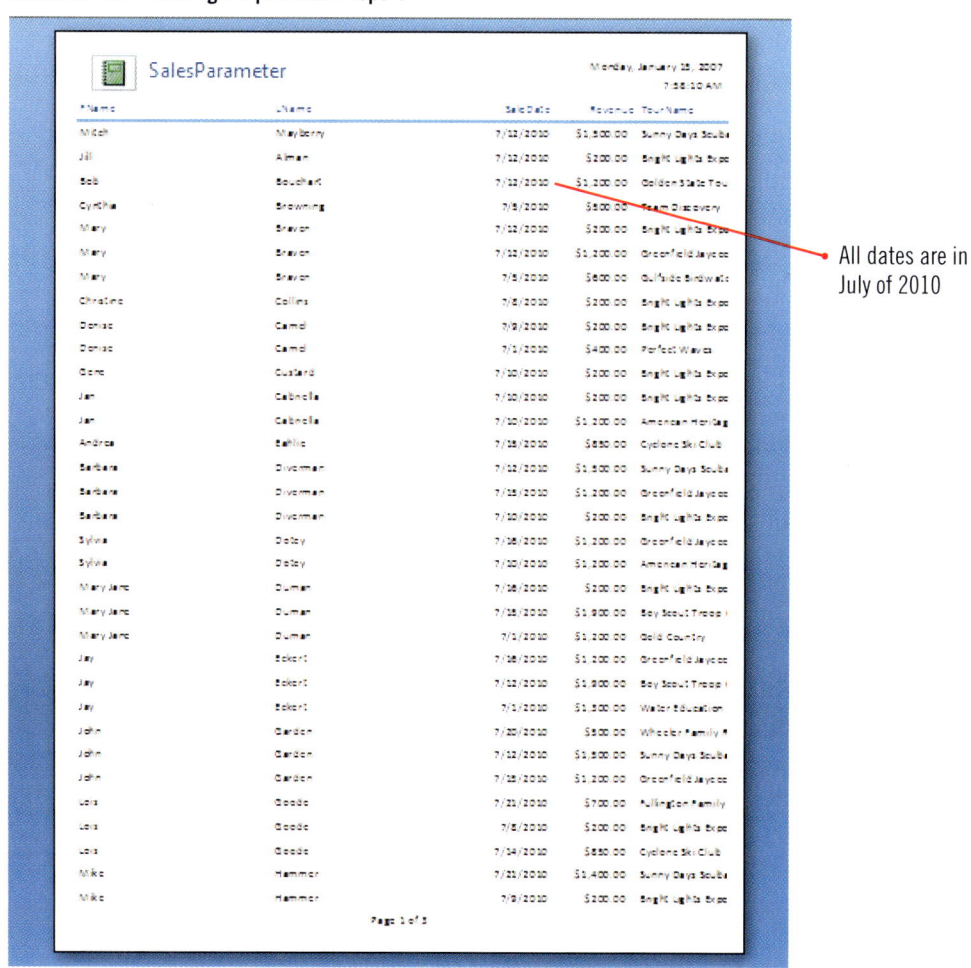

All dates are in July of 2010

Analyzing Data with Reports
Access 189

Applying Conditional Formatting

Conditional formatting allows you to change the appearance of a control on a form or report based on criteria you specify. Conditional formatting helps you highlight important or exceptional data on a form or report. When formatting several controls at the same time, you might find it helpful to group the controls. When you **group controls**, a formatting choice you make for any control in the group is applied to every control in the group. You want to apply conditional formatting to the SalesParameter report to emphasize different revenue levels as well as make other formatting modifications.

STEPS

1. **Right-click the SalesParameter report in the Navigation Pane, click Design View, close the Field List, then maximize the report**

    You notice that you don't need as much room on the report for the FName or LName fields, but that the TourName field needs more space. First, you can resize these controls to better display the data.

2. **Use your resizing skills to resize the text box controls in the Detail section as shown in Figure H-5, making sure that the right edge of the report is aligned with the 8-inch mark on the ruler**

    Notice that when you resize FName or LName, **group selection handles** surround the text box and its associated label in the Page Header section, so resizing any control in the group resizes *every* control in the group. Click the Remove button on the Arrange tab if you want to remove this grouping effect, but in this case, the grouped controls allowed you to resize the controls more productively. Make sure that the right edge of a report is no greater than 8 inches on the vertical ruler so the printout fits on one 8.5 x 11-inch sheet of paper with .25-inch left and right margins.

3. **Click the Revenue text box in the Detail section, then click the Conditional button on the Design tab**

    The Conditional Formatting dialog box opens, asking you to define the conditional formatting rules. You want Revenue values between 500 and 1000 to be formatted in bold text, and values equal to or greater than 1000 to be formatted with both bold text and a light green fill/back color.

> **QUICK TIP**
> You can add up to three conditional formats for any combination of selected controls.

4. **Click the text box to the right of the between arrow, type 500, press [Tab], type 999, click the Bold button B, click the Add button to add Condition 2, click the between list arrow, click greater than or equal to, press [Tab], type 1000, click B for Condition 2, click the Fill/Back Color button arrow for Condition 2, then click a light green box**

    The Conditional Formatting dialog box should look like Figure H-6.

5. **Click OK in the Conditional Formatting dialog box, click the View button arrow on the Design tab, click Print Preview, type 8/1/10 in the Enter start date box, click OK, type 8/31/10 in the Enter end date box, click OK, then click the Zoom pointer as necessary to zoom into the top portion of the report as shown in Figure H-7**

    Conditional formatting made the Revenue value for two tours bold because the values are between 500 and 1000. It made the Revenue for the Broadway workshops appear bold and with a light green fill color because the value is greater than 1000. Default formatting was applied to the Revenue value for the Japanese California Connection tour because it does not meet any of the conditions.

6. **Click the Close Print Preview button on the Print Preview tab, click the Label button Aa on the Design tab, click to the right of the SalesParameter label, then type your name**

7. **Save, print, then close the SalesParameter report**

Analyzing Data with Reports

FIGURE H-5: Design View of SalesParameter report after controls and report are resized

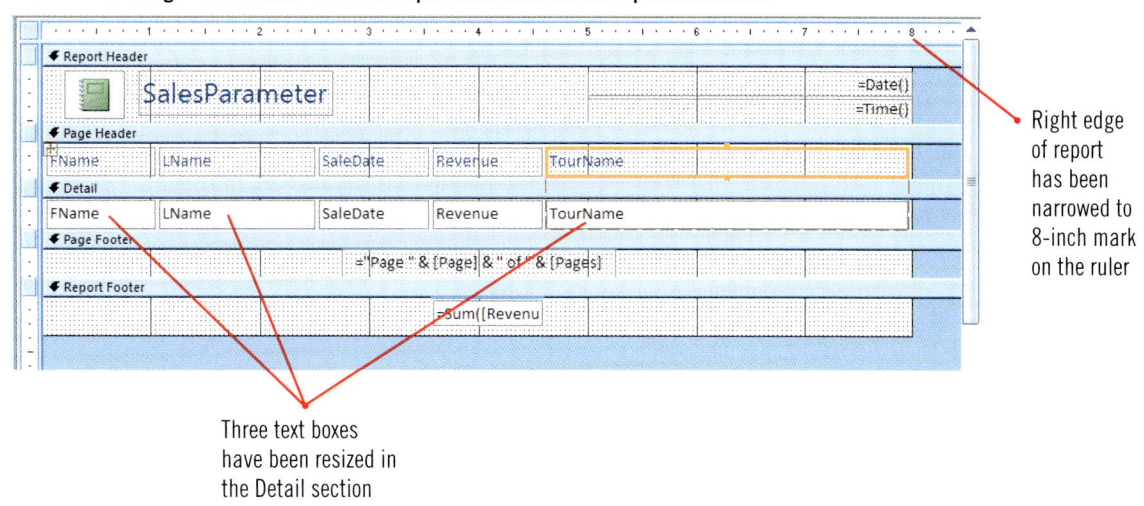

Right edge of report has been narrowed to 8-inch mark on the ruler

Three text boxes have been resized in the Detail section

FIGURE H-6: Conditional Formatting dialog box

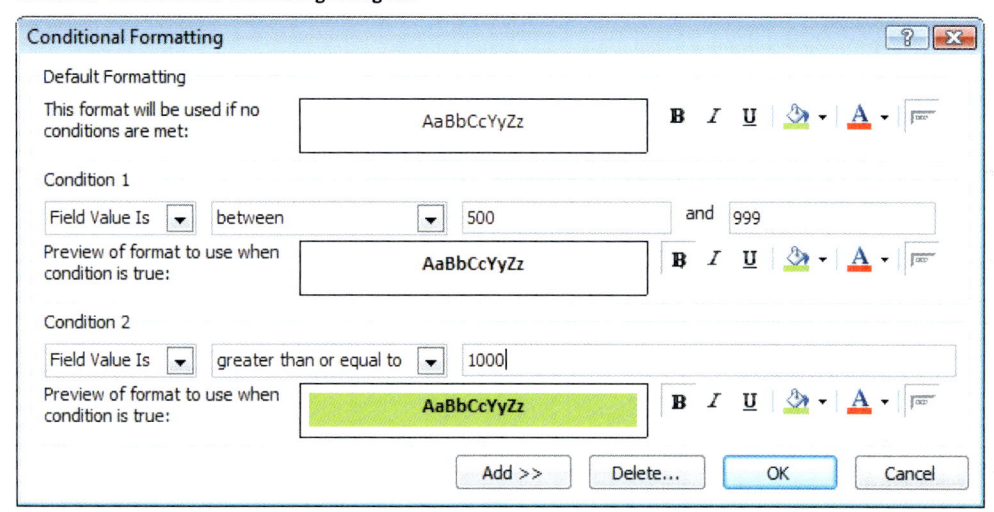

FIGURE H-7: Conditional formatting applied to SalesParameter report

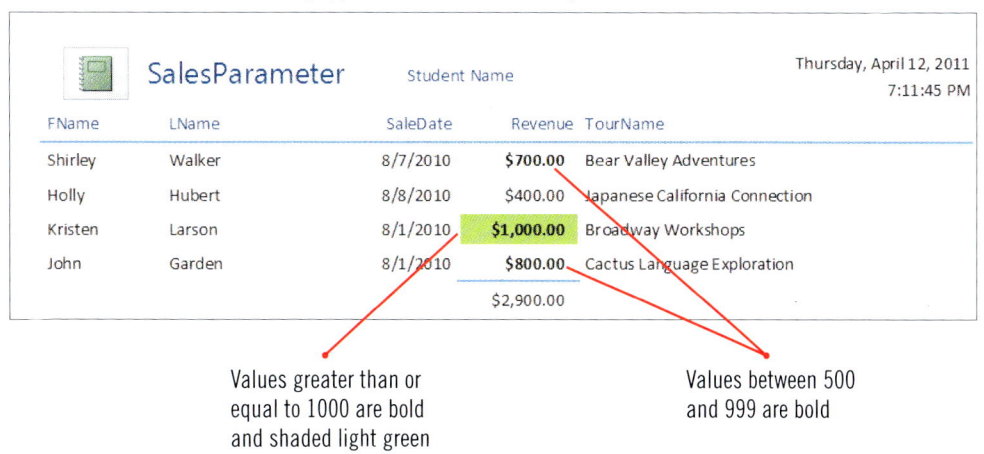

FName	LName	SaleDate	Revenue	TourName
Shirley	Walker	8/7/2010	$700.00	Bear Valley Adventures
Holly	Hubert	8/8/2010	$400.00	Japanese California Connection
Kristen	Larson	8/1/2010	**$1,000.00**	Broadway Workshops
John	Garden	8/1/2010	$800.00	Cactus Language Exploration
			$2,900.00	

Thursday, April 12, 2011
7:11:45 PM

Student Name

Values greater than or equal to 1000 are bold and shaded light green

Values between 500 and 999 are bold

Analyzing Data with Reports

UNIT H
Access 2007

Adding Lines

Unbound controls such as labels, lines, and rectangles can enhance the clarity of a report. When you create a report with the Report Wizard, it often creates line controls at the top or bottom of the report sections to visually separate the sections on the report. You can add, delete, or modify lines to best suit your needs. For example, you might want to separate the report header and page header information from the rest of the report with a line, or use lines to call attention to totals. 🎨 Mark Rock likes the data on the Category Revenue Summary report, but he asks you to enhance the report with labels, formatting, and a grand total. You plan to add lines to separate report sections and to indicate subtotals and grand totals.

STEPS

1. **Right-click the Category Revenue Summary report in the Navigation Pane, click Design View, then maximize the report**

   Your first step is to create a report title. Because you want the title to print at the top of only the first page, you need to open the Report Header section.

2. **Click the Arrange tab, click the Report Header/Footer button in the Show/Hide group, click the Design tab, click the Label button, click the left side of the Report Header section, type Category Revenue Summary Report, then press [Enter]**

   You're ready to add a line to separate the Report Header from the rest of the report.

3. **Drag the top edge of the Page Header section down to about the 0.5-inch mark on the vertical ruler, click the Line button on the Design tab, press and hold [Shift], then drag from the lower-left edge of the Report Header section to the right edge as shown in Figure H-8**

   Pressing [Shift] while drawing a line makes sure that the line stays in a perfectly horizontal position. You also want to add a grand total to the Report Footer section to total all revenue. You can copy and paste the text box with the calculation from the Category Header to the Report Footer section to accomplish this task.

4. **Click the =Sum([Revenue]) text box in the Category Header section, press [Ctrl][C] to copy the control, click the Report Footer section bar, then press [Ctrl][V] to paste the control**

5. **Press [→] enough times to align the new controls in the Report Footer section directly under the corresponding controls in the Category Header section, edit the label in the Report Footer section to read Grand Total:, then drag the bottom edge of the Report Footer section down to about the 0.5-inch mark on the ruler**

   With the Report Footer section resized, it is tall enough to add lines to help identify the grand total figure.

6. **Click the Line button, press and hold [Shift], drag from just above the left edge of the text box with the calculation in the Report Footer section to the right edge of the text box, press [Ctrl][C] to copy the line, press [Ctrl][V] twice to paste the line twice, then move the two copies of the line to just under the text box as shown in Figure H-9**

   The single line above the calculation in the Report Footer section indicates that the numbers in the column above it are being added. Double lines under a calculation indicate a grand total. One other quick formatting change that can improve the report is to apply a Currency format to the calculations.

QUICK TIP
Double-clicking a property label toggles through the choices for that property.

7. **Select the =Sum([Revenue]) text box in the Category Header section and the =Sum([Revenue]) text box in the Report Footer section, click the Property Sheet button on the Design tab, click the Format tab, click the Format property list arrow, click Currency, double-click the Decimal Places property to set it to 0, click the View button arrow on the Design tab, then click Print Preview**

   The final Category Revenue Summary report is shown in Figure H-10.

8. **Close Print Preview, then save and close the Category Revenue Summary report**

FIGURE H-8: New line added to Report Header section

Report Header section has been resized

Line button

New line in the Report Header section

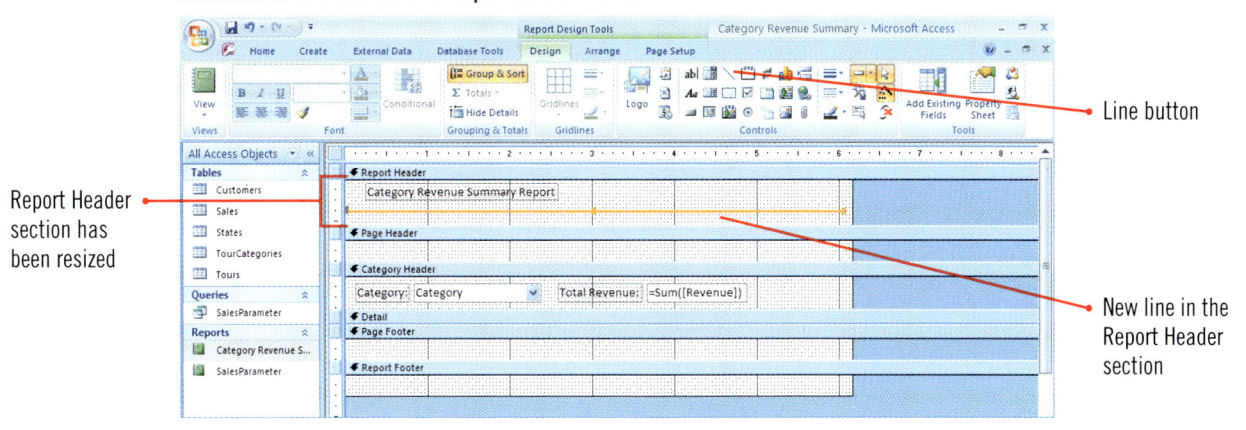

FIGURE H-9: New lines added to Report Footer section

Report Footer section has been resized

Three new lines in the Report Footer section help identify the grand total

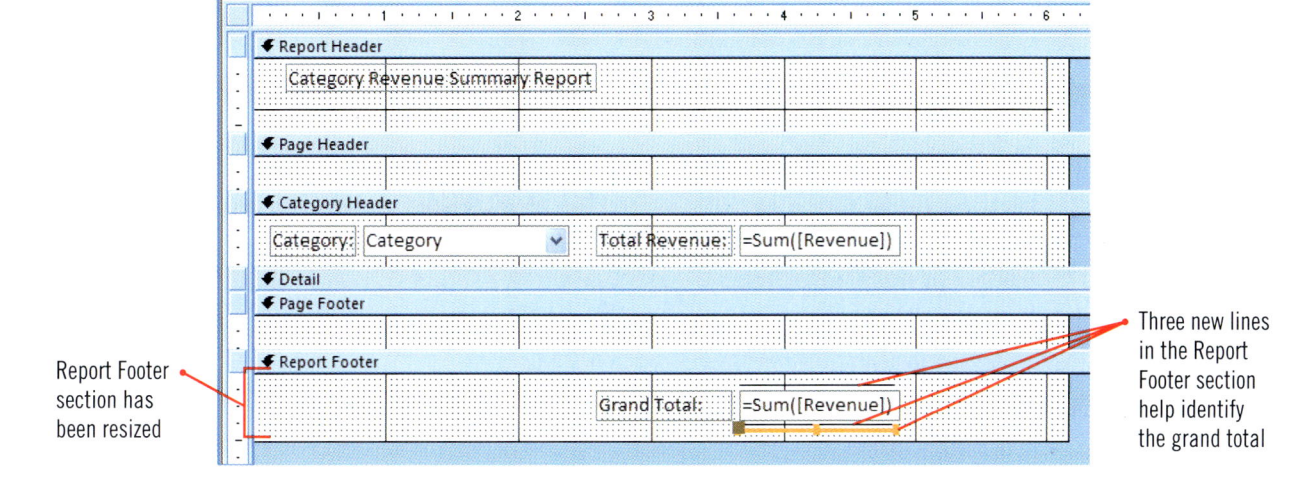

FIGURE H-10: Final Category Revenue Summary Report

New line in the Report Header section

Category Revenue Summary Report			
Category:	Adventure	Total Revenue:	$45,965
Category:	Cultural	Total Revenue:	$3,000
Category:	Educational	Total Revenue:	$24,190
Category:	Family	Total Revenue:	$8,470
Category:	Service	Total Revenue:	$3,325
Category:	Site Seeing	Total Revenue:	$8,180
		Grand Total:	$93,130

Calculations now have a Currency format

Three new lines in the Report Footer section help identify the grand total

Analyzing Data with Reports

Access 2007

Access 193

UNIT H
Access 2007

Using the Format Painter and AutoFormats

The **Format Painter** is a tool used to copy multiple formatting properties from one control to another in Form or Report Design View. **AutoFormats** are predefined formats that you apply to a form or report to set all of the formatting enhancements such as font, color, and alignment. Access provides several AutoFormats that you can use. You think the Category Revenue Summary report can be improved with a few formatting embellishments. You can use the Format Painter to quickly change the characteristics of selected labels in the Category Revenue Summary report, then apply an AutoFormat.

STEPS

1. **Right-click the Category Revenue Summary report in the Navigation Pane, click Design View, close the Property Sheet, then maximize the report**

   Because you don't have any controls in either the Page Header or Page Footer sections, you decide to remove those sections from Report Design View. You also want to change the font size and color of the label in the Report Header section before using the Format Painter and an AutoFormat.

2. **Click the Arrange tab, then click the Page Header/Footer button in the Show/Hide group to toggle those sections off**

   You can make other formatting changes in Layout View.

3. **Click the Home tab, click the View button arrow, click Layout View, click the Category Revenue Summary Report label, click the Font Size list arrow 10, click 18, and move the line in the Report Header section down as needed so that it doesn't touch the edge of the label**

   Next, you can apply an AutoFormat to see how it affects the report.

4. **Click the AutoFormat button arrow, then click the Solstice AutoFormat (fourth row, fifth column)**

   The Solstice AutoFormat gives the Report Header section a tan background. If there were controls in the Detail section of this report, more formatting changes would be applied. You decide to bold and change the color of the values in all of the Revenue text boxes. You also want to make sure the values in these text boxes are right-aligned.

5. **Click the Grand Total: label, click the Bold button B on the Format tab, click $45,965 to select all the Total Revenue values, click B, click the Font Color button arrow A, click the Green box in the top row of the Standard Colors, then click the Align Text Right button**

   The Format Painter will help you quickly copy these three formatting embellishments from one control to another.

TROUBLE
Your fonts and colors may be slightly different than the figures depending on how Access 2007 was installed on your computer.

6. **Click the Format Painter button on the Format tab, then click the Grand Total value**

   Report Layout View should look like Figure H-11. Now view the report in Print Preview.

7. **Click the View button arrow, then click Print Preview**

   The formatted report should look like Figure H-12.

8. **Close Print Preview, then save and close the Category Revenue Summary report**

   You can also press [Esc] to release the Format Painter.

FIGURE H-11: Report Design View of formatted Category Revenue Summary report

- Font Size list arrow
- Bold button
- Format Painter button
- Font Color list arrow
- Calculations are formatted

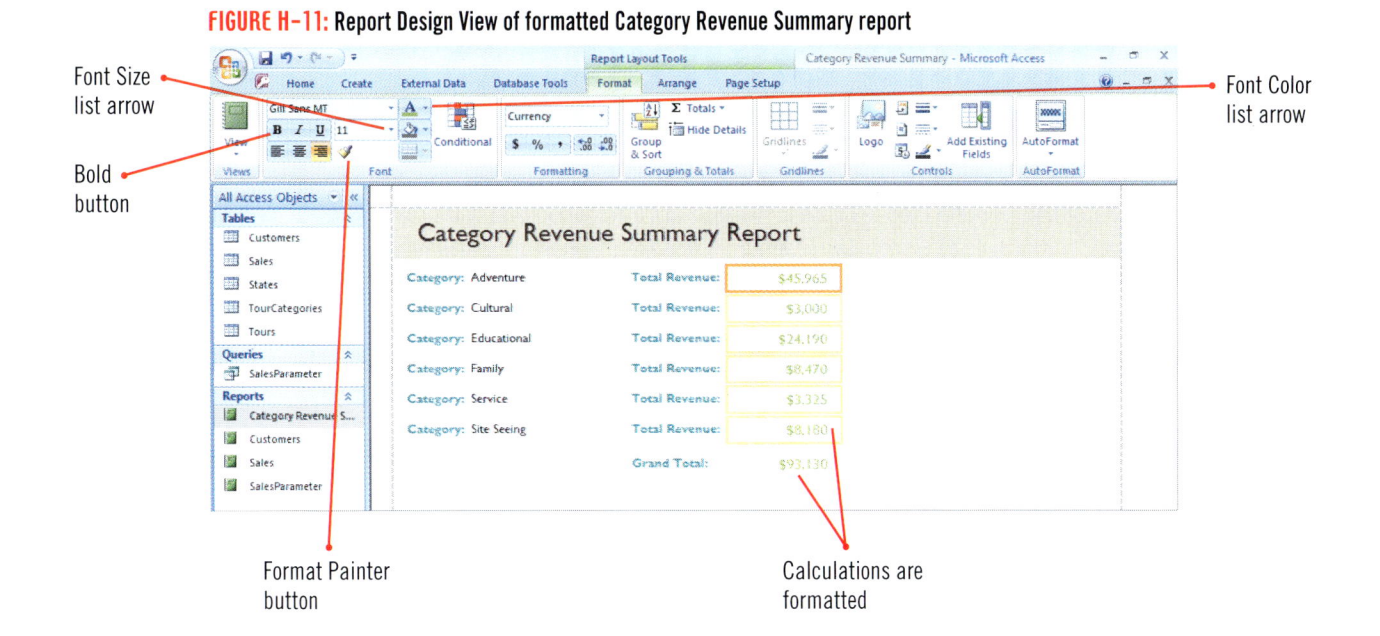

FIGURE H-12: Print Preview of formatted Category Revenue Summary report

Category Revenue Summary Report

Category:	Adventure	Total Revenue:	$45,965
Category:	Cultural	Total Revenue:	$3,000
Category:	Educational	Total Revenue:	$24,190
Category:	Family	Total Revenue:	$8,470
Category:	Service	Total Revenue:	$3,325
Category:	Site Seeing	Total Revenue:	$8,180
		Grand Total:	$93,130

Line troubles

Sometimes lines are difficult to find in Report Design View because they are placed against the edge of a section or the edge of other controls. To find lines that are positioned next to the edge of a section, drag the section bar to expand it to expose the line. Recall that to draw a perfectly horizontal line, you hold [Shift] while creating or resizing it. Also note that it is easy to accidentally widen a line beyond the report margins, thus creating extra unwanted pages in your printout. To fix this problem, narrow any controls that extend beyond the margins of the printout and drag the right edge of the report to the left. Also note that the default left and right margins for an 8.5 x 11-inch sheet of paper are often .25 inches each, so a report in portrait orientation must be no wider than 8 inches and a report in landscape orientation must be no wider than 10.5 inches.

Analyzing Data with Reports
Access 195

UNIT H
Access 2007

Adding Subreports

A **subreport** control displays a report within another report. The report that contains the subreport control is called the **main report**. You use the subreport control when you want to link two reports together to automate printing. You also use a subreport control when you want to change the order in which information automatically prints. For example, if you want report totals (generally found in the Report Footer section, which prints on the last page) to print on the first page, you could use a subreport to present the grand total information, and place it in the main report's Report Header section, which prints first. You want the Category Revenue Summary report to automatically print at the end of a similar report that shows all of the sales revenue detail. You use a subreport to accomplish this.

STEPS

1. **Click the Create tab, click the Report Wizard button, click the Tables/Queries list arrow, click Table: Sales, double-click SaleDate, double-click Revenue, click the Tables/Queries list arrow, click Table: Tours, double-click TourName, double-click Category, then click Next**
   With the fields selected for the detailed report, you continue working through the Report Wizard.

2. **Click by Sales (if not already selected), click Next, double-click Category as a grouping level, click Next, click the first sort list arrow, click SaleDate, click Next, accept a Stepped layout and Portrait orientation by clicking Next, click Solstice for the style, click Next, then click Finish**
   The report opens in Print Preview.

3. **Click the Next Page button ▶ on the navigation bar to observe the detail records grouped by Category, click the Close Print Preview button on the Print Preview tab to switch to Report Design View, then maximize the window**
   You want the Category Summary Revenue report to print as the first page of this report, so you add it as a subreport control to the Report Header.

4. **Click the Sales label in the Report Header section, press [Delete], click the Subform/Subreport button on the Design tab, click the left side of the Report Header section, click the Category Revenue Summary report in the SubReport Wizard, click Next, click None when asked how you want the reports to be linked, click Next, then click Finish to accept the default label**
   Report Design View now looks like Figure H-13. The Report Header section contains the Category Revenue Summary report, which will now print as the first page of the Sales report.

5. **Click the View button arrow on the Design tab, then click Print Preview**
   The report appears in Print Preview, and you notice that the entire value for the first category, "Adventure," isn't completely displayed in the main report. You decide to modify the report to widen the Category text box and to add your name as a label to the Page Footer section.

6. **Click the Close Print Preview button on the Print Preview tab, widen the Category text box in the Category Header section, click the Label button, click in the Page Footer section above the =Now() expression, type your name, then move or resize any controls as needed**

7. **Click the View button arrow on the Design tab, click Print Preview, then click the One Page Zoom button on the Print Preview tab as shown in Figure H-14**

8. **Close Print Preview, then save and close the Sales report**

Access 196

Analyzing Data with Reports

FIGURE H-13: Subreport in Report Design View

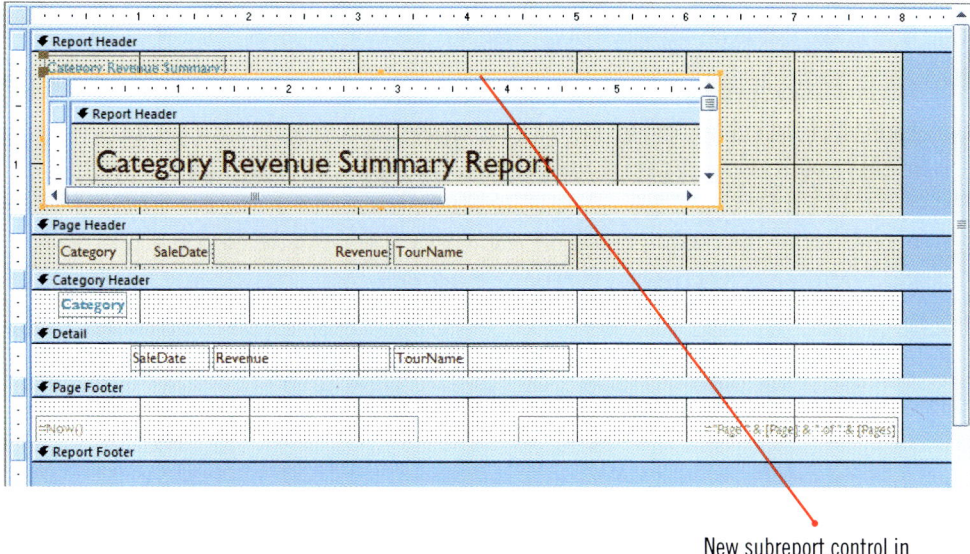

New subreport control in the Report Header section

FIGURE H-14: Subreport in Print Preview

- Subreport
- Category text box is resized
- Your name is added to the Report Footer section

Analyzing Data with Reports

Access 197

UNIT H
Access 2007

Modifying Section Properties

Report **section properties**, the characteristics that define each section, can be modified to improve report printouts. For example, you might want each new Group Header to print at the top of a new page. Or, you might want to modify section properties to format that section with a background color. Mark Rock asks you to modify the Sales report so that each new category prints at the top of a new page. You also decide to make the detail records more readable by alternating the background color of each row. You make these section property changes in Report Design View.

STEPS

1. **Right-click the Sales report, click Design View, then maximize the report**

   To force each new category to print at the top of a new page, you modify the Category Header using its property sheet.

2. **Double-click the Category Header bar, click the Format tab, then double-click the Force New Page property to change the value to Before Section**

   The second change you want to make is to modify the back color of alternating rows in the Detail section. You could make this change in the Detail section's property sheet, or use the Alternate Fill/Back Color button on the Design tab.

3. **Click the Detail section bar to display the properties for this section in the Property Sheet, click the Alternate Fill/Back Color button arrow, then click the Light Gray 2 box (first column, third row of the Standard Colors palette)**

   Design View for the report now looks like Figure H-15. Note that the **Back Color** and **Alternate Back Color** property are specified with a **hexadecimal** number (numbers that consist of numbers 0-9 as well as letters A-H). If you know that number, you can enter it directly in the Property Sheet. Both the Back Color and Alternate Back Color properties provide a Build button to select or mix a color from a palette of choices.

4. **Click the View button arrow on the Design tab, click Print Preview, click the One Page button on the Print Preview tab, then click the Next Page button on the navigation bar several times to observe that all categories after the first (Adventure) start printing at the top of a new page**

   Although alternating gray and white as the background colors for the detail records makes them easier to follow across the page, you want to change the background color of the Report Header and Page Header.

5. **Click the Close Print Preview button on the Print Preview tab to switch to Report Design View, click the Page Header section to display the Page Header properties, select #E7DEC9 in the Back Color property, press [Ctrl][C] to copy the hexadecimal number, click the Detail section to display its properties, select #D8D8D8 in the Alternate Back Color property, press [Ctrl][V] to paste #E7DEC9 into this property**

   With the matching alternate back color, you're ready to preview and print the report.

TROUBLE
If the alternating color of the Detail section doesn't match the Report and Page Header color, make sure that you modified the Detail section's Alternate Back Color property in Report Design View.

6. **Click the View button arrow on the Design tab, click Print Preview, click the One Page button on the Print Preview tab, click the Last Page button on the navigation bar, click the Print button on the Print Preview tab, click the From box, type 8, click the To box, type 8, then click OK**

   The last page of the Sales report is shown in Figure H-16.

7. **Save the report, then close it**

Access 198   Analyzing Data with Reports

FIGURE H-15: Specifying section properties in Report Design View

- Alternate Fill/Back Color button
- Report Selector button
- Report Selector button for subform
- Detail section bar is selected
- Hexadecimal number
- Alternate Back Color property

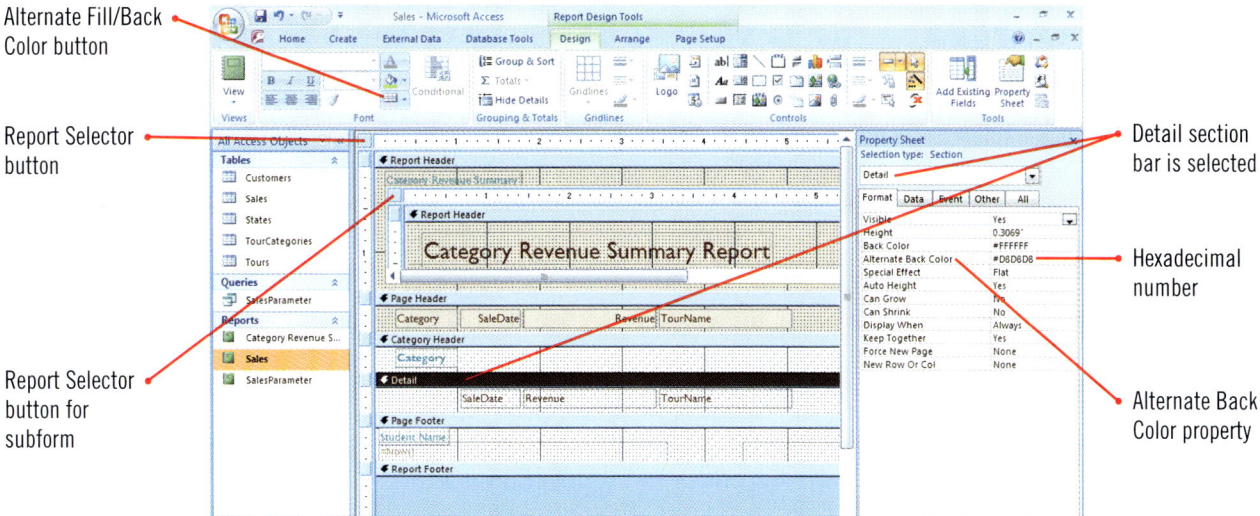

FIGURE H-16: Viewing section properties in Print Preview

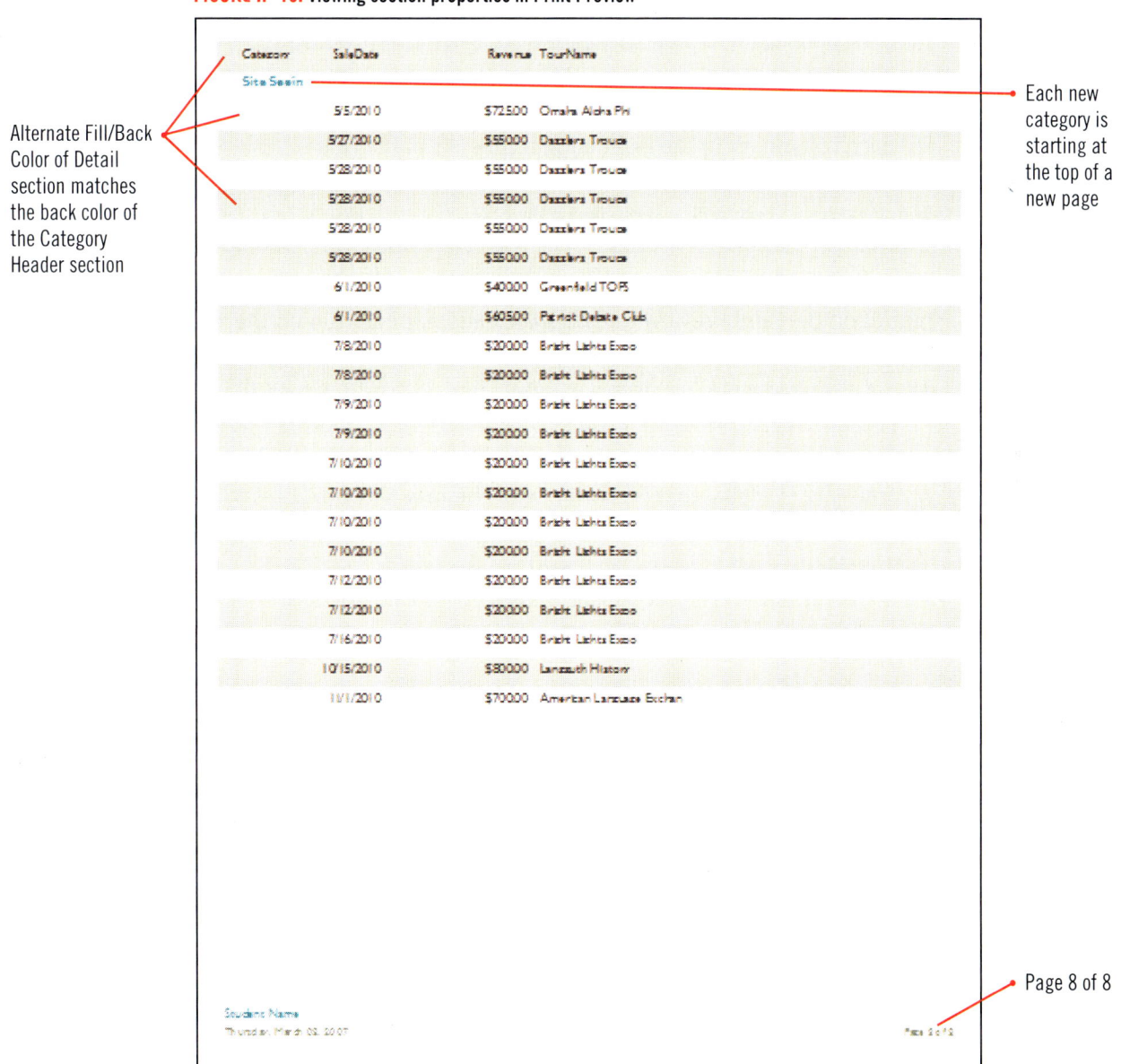

- Alternate Fill/Back Color of Detail section matches the back color of the Category Header section
- Each new category is starting at the top of a new page
- Page 8 of 8

Analyzing Data with Reports

UNIT H
Access 2007

Using Domain Functions

Domain functions, also called domain aggregate functions, are functions that can display a calculation on a form or a report using a field that is not included in the Record Source property for the form or report. Domain functions start with a "D" for "domain" such as DSum, DAvg, DMin, and DMax, and perform the same calculation as their Sum, Avg, Min, Max, and Count counterparts. Regular functions require only one argument, the field that is to be used for the calculation such as =Sum([Price]). Domain functions have two required arguments: the field that is to be used for the calculation and the domain name. The **domain** is the recordset (table or query) that contains the field used in the calculation. A third optional argument allows you to select given records for the calculation based on criteria you specify. Mark Rock asks you to build a report listing all of the customers and including a subtotal of the money they have spent on Quest tours as recorded by the Revenue field in the Sales table. You decide to create a basic report on the Customers table, and then use a domain function to calculate the maximum revenue value.

STEPS

1. **Click the Customers table in the Navigation Pane, click the Create tab, click the Report button, close the Property Sheet, then maximize the report**
   The report opens in Layout View, which allows you to see data while making changes such as resizing controls. Because the report exceeds the width of a regular sheet of paper, you decide to narrow the fields and switch to landscape orientation before adding the domain function.

2. **For each column, drag the right edge to the left to resize the fields to be as narrow as possible yet wide enough to view the data as shown in Figure H-17**
   With the columns narrowed, you can switch the page orientation to landscape to fit all of the columns on a single sheet of paper and provide room for the revenue calculation you plan to add to the report.

3. **Click the View button arrow on the Format tab, click Print Preview, click the One Page button on the Print Preview tab, click the Landscape button on the Print Preview tab, then click OK if a message indicates that the report is too wide for the paper**
   You can make other formatting changes in Report Design View when you add the revenue calculation.

> **QUICK TIP**
> The arguments for domain functions are string expressions, so they must be enclosed in quotation marks.

4. **Close Print Preview, click the View button arrow on the Format tab, click Design View, scroll to the right, click the Text Box button, click to the right of the FirstContact control, click the label that is created with the new text box, press [Delete], click Unbound in the new text box, type =DSum("[Revenue]", "Sales", "[CustNo] ="&[CustNo]), then drag the right edge of the report to narrow it**
   The expression sums the Revenue field found in the Sales domain (Sales table) for every CustNo in the Sales table that is equal to the CustNo in this report. You are now ready to format the new text box, then preview and print the report.

5. **Click the new text box, click the Property Sheet button on the Design tab, click the Format tab, click the Format property list arrow, click Currency, double-click the Decimal Places property to change it to 0, click the Label button, click in the Report Footer section, then type your name**
   With the DSum expression and your name as a label in place and the width of the report narrowed, you're ready to preview and print the report for the last time.

6. **Click the View button arrow on the Design tab, click Print Preview, click the One Page button on the Print Preview tab, then print both pages of the report**
   The first page of the printout should look like Figure H-18.

7. **Save the report with the name Customers, close the Customers report, close the Quest-H.accdb database, and exit Access**

FIGURE H-17: Resizing fields in Report Layout View

Each column has been narrowed

Drag right edge of each column to the left

Customers

Thursday, March 08, 2010
9:15:33 AM

CustNo	FName	LName	Street	City	State	Zip	Phone	FirstContact
1	Mitch	Mayberry	52411 Oakmont Rd	Kansas City	Missouri	64144	(555) 444-1234	Friend
2	Jill	Alman	2505 McGee St	Des Moines	Iowa	50288	(555) 111-6931	Friend
3	Bob	Bouchart	5200 Main St	Kansas City	Missouri	64105	(555) 111-3081	Mail
4	Cynthia	Browning	8206 Marshall Dr	Lenexa	Kansas	66214	(555) 222-9101	Mail
5	Mary	Braven	600 Elm St	Olathe	Kansas	66031	(555) 222-7002	Friend
6	Christine	Collins	520 W 52nd St	Kansas City	Kansas	64105	(555) 222-3602	Radio
7	Denise	Camel	66020 King St	Overland Park	Kansas	66210	(555) 222-8402	Internet
8	Gene	Custard	66900 College Rd	Overland Park	Kansas	66210	(555) 222-5102	Radio
9	Jan	Cabriella	52520 W. 505 Ter	Lenexa	Kansas	66215	(555) 333-9871	Internet
10	Andrea	Eahlie	56 Jackson Rd	Kansas City	Missouri	64145	(555) 333-0401	Mail
11	Barbara	Diverman	466 Lincoln Rd	Kansas City	Missouri	64105	(555) 333-0401	Friend
12	Sylvia	Dotey	96 Lowell St	Overland Park	Kansas	66210	(555) 444-4404	Internet
13	Mary Jane	Duman	525 Ambassador Dr	Kansas City	Missouri	64145	(555) 444-8844	Mail
14	Jay	Eckert	903 East 504th St.	Kansas City	Kansas	64131	(555) 444-7414	Radio
15	John	Garden	305 W. 99th St	Lenexa	Kansas	66215	(555) 566-4344	Radio
16	Lois	Goode	900 Barnes St	West Des Moines	Iowa	50265	(555) 666-1324	Mail

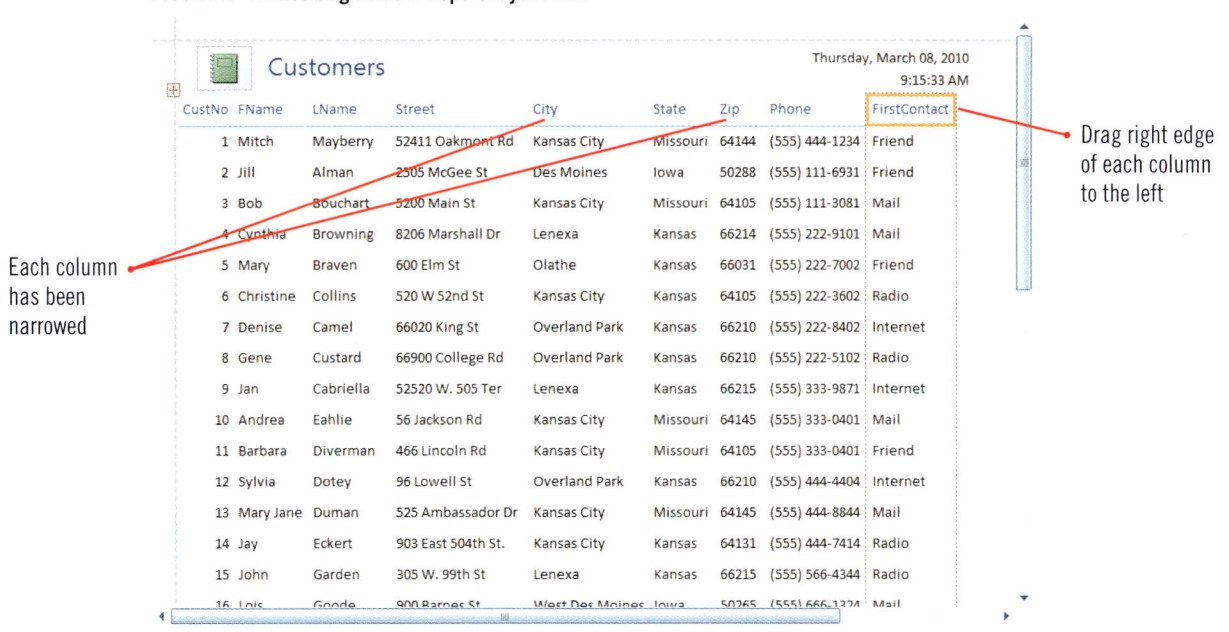

FIGURE H-18: Viewing the DSum function in Print Preview

Customers

Thursday, March 08, 2010
9:20:22 AM

CustNo	FName	LName	Street	City	State	Zip	Phone	FirstContact	
1	Mitch	Mayberry	52411 Oakmont Rd	Kansas City	Missouri	64144	(555) 444-1234	Friend	$2,075
2	Jill	Alman	2505 McGee St	Des Moines	Iowa	50288	(555) 111-6931	Friend	$1,550
3	Bob	Bouchart	5200 Main St	Kansas City	Missouri	64105	(555) 111-3081	Mail	$2,620
4	Cynthia	Browning	8206 Marshall Dr	Lenexa	Kansas	66214	(555) 222-9101	Mail	$2,900
5	Mary	Braven	600 Elm St	Olathe	Kansas	66031	(555) 222-7002	Friend	$2,000
6	Christine	Collins	520 W 52nd St	Kansas City	Kansas	64105	(555) 222-3602	Radio	$3,750
7	Denise	Camel	66020 King St	Overland Park	Kansas	66210	(555) 222-8402	Internet	$600
8	Gene	Custard	66900 College Rd	Overland Park	Kansas	66210	(555) 222-5102	Radio	$2,705
9	Jan	Cabriella	52520 W. 505 Ter	Lenexa	Kansas	66215	(555) 333-9871	Internet	$1,900
10	Andrea	Eahlie	56 Jackson Rd	Kansas City	Missouri	64145	(555) 333-0401	Mail	$1,650
11	Barbara	Diverman	466 Lincoln Rd	Kansas City	Missouri	64105	(555) 333-0401	Friend	$2,900
12	Sylvia	Dotey	96 Lowell St	Overland Park	Kansas	66210	(555) 444-4404	Internet	$4,750
13	Mary Jane	Duman	525 Ambassador Dr	Kansas City	Missouri	64145	(555) 444-8844	Mail	$3,300
14	Jay	Eckert	903 East 504th St.	Kansas City	Kansas	64131	(555) 444-7414	Radio	$4,795
15	John	Garden	305 W. 99th St	Lenexa	Kansas	66215	(555) 566-4344	Radio	$5,750
16	Lois	Goode	900 Barnes St	West Des Moines	Iowa	50265	(555) 666-1324	Mail	$3,900
17	Mike	Hammer	624 Richmond Ter	Clive	Iowa	50266	(555) 666-0865	Mail	$3,800
18	Jeff	Hopper	4435 Main St	Greenfield	Iowa	50849	(555) 777-8774	Internet	$2,650
19	Holly	Hubert	2345 Grand Blvd	Kansas City	Kansas	64108	(555) 888-6004	Friend	$2,200
20	Traci	Kalvert	7066 College Rd	Overland Park	Kansas	66211	(555) 999-7154	Internet	$1,400
21	Brad	Lang	5253 Duck Creek Dr	Iowa City	Iowa	52240	(555) 999-8777	Friend	$2,250
22	Kristen	Larson	3966 Woodland St	West Des Moines	Iowa	50266	(555) 222-8908	Internet	$2,825

Page 1 of 2

Results of expression using the DSum function for each customer

Practice

SAM

If you have a SAM user profile, you may have access to hands-on instruction, practice, and assessment of the skills covered in this unit. Log in to your SAM account (http://sam2007.course.com/) to launch any assigned training activities or exams that relate to the skills covered in this unit.

▼ CONCEPTS REVIEW

Identify each element of the Report Design View shown in Figure H-19.

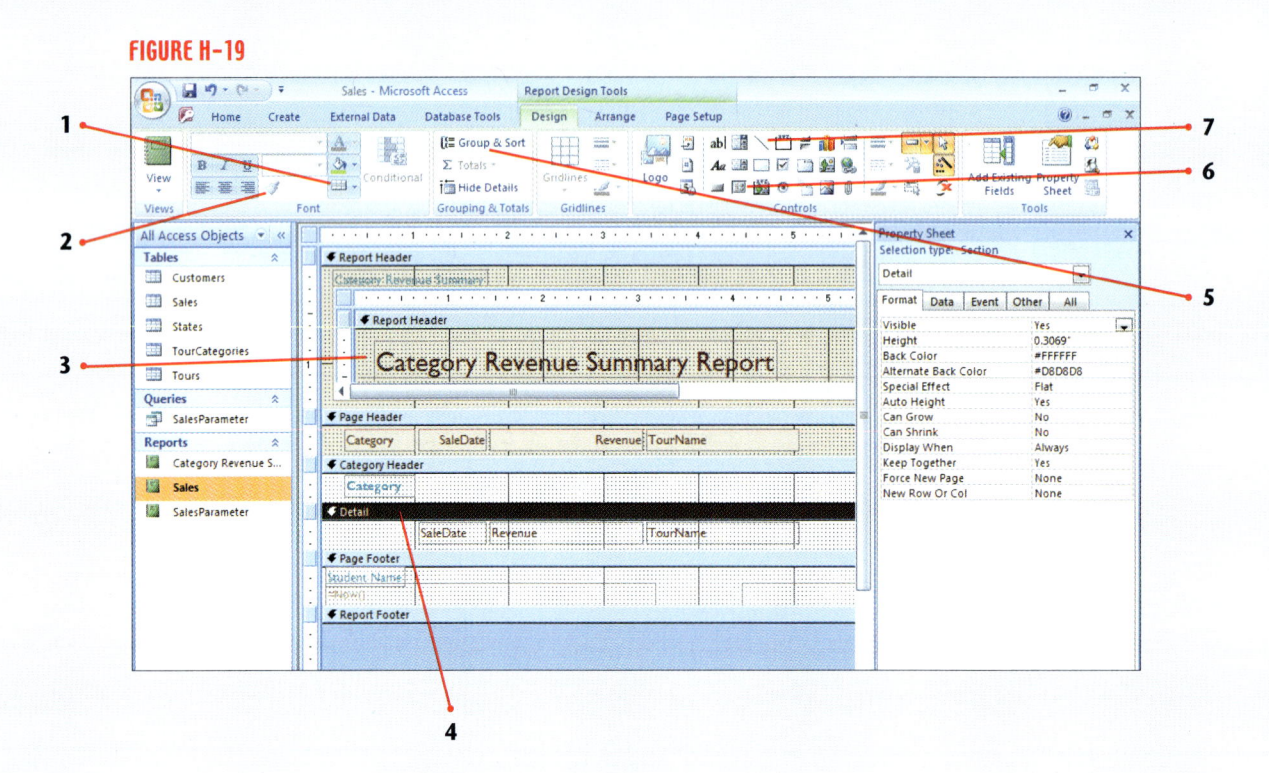

FIGURE H-19

Match each term with the statement that best describes its function.

8. Summary reports
9. Parameter report
10. Conditional formatting
11. Format Painter
12. Domain

a. Prompts the user for the criteria by which the records for the report are selected
b. A way to change the appearance of a control on a form or report based on criteria you specify
c. Used to show statistics on groups of records
d. The recordset (table or query) that contains the field used in the calculation
e. Used to copy multiple formatting properties from one control to another in Report Design View

Select the best answer from the list of choices.

13. Which control would you use to visually separate groups of records on a report?
    a. Option group
    b. Image
    c. Bound Object Frame
    d. Line

14. Which of the following is *not* a Detail section property?
    a. Alternate Back Color
    b. Force New Page
    c. Display When
    d. Calculate

Analyzing Data with Reports

15. **What feature allows you to apply the formatting characteristics of one control to another?**
    a. AutoContent Wizard
    b. AutoFormat
    c. Report Layout Wizard
    d. Format Painter
16. **Which key do you press when creating a line to make it perfectly horizontal?**
    a. [Shift]
    b. [Alt]
    c. [Ctrl]
    d. [Home]
17. **If you want to apply the same formatting characteristics to several controls at once, you might consider _____ them.**
    a. AutoFormatting
    b. AutoPainting
    c. Grouping
    d. Exporting
18. **In a report, an expression used to calculate values is entered in which type of control?**
    a. Text Box
    b. Label
    c. Combo Box
    d. Command Button
19. **The Page Header/Footer and Report Header/Footer buttons are found on which tab of the Ribbon?**
    a. Home
    b. Create
    c. Design
    d. Arrange
20. **What button allows you to change the appearance of a control in every other record on the report?**
    a. Font Color
    b. Alternate Fill/Back Color
    c. Conditional
    d. Group & Sort

▼ SKILLS REVIEW

1. **Create summary reports.**
   a. Open the **RealEstate-H.accdb** database from the drive and folder where you store your Data Files and enable content if prompted.
   b. Create a new report in Report Design View. Include the AgencyName from the Agencies table and the Asking field from the Listings table in the Record Source property. (*Hint*: Include the Agents table in the query builder as well to properly link the Agents table to the Listings table.)
   c. Add AgencyName as a grouping field, then add the AgencyName field to the AgencyName Header section.
   d. Add a text box to the right side of the AgencyName Header section and enter the following expression into the text box: **=Sum([Asking])**
   e. Modify the label to read **Subtotal of Asking Price:**
   f. Move, resize, and align the tops of all controls in the AgencyName Header section so that they are clearly visible.
   g. Apply a Currency format and change the Decimal Places property to **0** for the new text box that contains the expression.
   h. Completely close the Detail section.
   i. Add a label to the Page Header section that reads **Subtotal of Asking Prices by Agency**.
   j. Add a label to the Page Footer section with your name. Preview the report. Continue to modify, resize, and move controls as needed in order to see all data.
   k. Save the report with the name **Asking Price Summary Report**, then close it.

2. **Create parameter reports.**
   a. Create a query in Query Design View, including the AgentFirst, AgentLast, and AgentPhone fields from the Agents table. Include the Type, Area, SqFt, and Asking field from the Listings table.
   b. In the Asking field, include the following parameter criteria: **<[Enter maximum asking price]**
   c. Save the query as **AskingParameter**, then close it.
   d. Click the AskingParameter query in the Navigation Pane, then click Report on the Create tab. Enter **200000** in the Enter maximum asking price box, then click OK.
   e. Work in Layout View to narrow each column to be only as wide as necessary.
   f. In Report Design View add a label with your name to the Report Header section and make sure the report is no wider than 8 inches.
   g. Preview the report again, entering **200000** in the prompt, then print it.
   h. Save the report with the name **AskingParameter**, then close it.

▼ SKILLS REVIEW (CONTINUED)

3. **Apply conditional formatting.**
   a. Open the AskingParameter report in Report Design View, then add a calculated field to the right of the Asking text box with the expression **=[Asking]/[SqFt]**. Delete the label associated with the new text box. Format the new calculation with a Currency format and 0 for the Decimal Places property.
   b. Add a label to the Page Header section above the new calculation with the caption **Cost per Sq Ft**.
   c. Move, resize, and align controls as necessary to keep the report within the 8-inch mark of the ruler.
   d. Conditionally format the new calculated text box so that values less than or equal to 50 are formatted with bold, green text, and values greater than or equal to 100 are formatted with bold, red text.
   e. Test the report in Print Preview, entering a value of **150000** when prompted.

4. **Add lines.**
   a. Open the AskingParameter report in Design View, then use the Group, Sort, and Total pane to add a sort order. Order the fields in descending (largest to smallest) order on the Asking field.
   b. Add a text box to the Report Footer section directly below the Asking text box in the Detail section with the expression **=Sum([Asking])**.
   c. Modify the label to read **Grand Total:**.
   d. Draw one short horizontal line just above the =Sum([Asking]) calculation, then copy and paste it twice and move the second and third copy of the short lines below the =Sum([Asking]) calculation to indicate a grand total.
   e. Modify the Asking text box and the =Sum([Asking]) text box to be formatted with a Currency format and Decimal Places property of 0.
   f. Save the report, then preview the changes using a value of **125000** when prompted. Move, resize, and align any controls as needed to improve the report.

5. **Use the Format Painter and AutoFormats.**
   a. Open the AskingParameter Report in Layout View using a value of 175000 when prompted.
   b. Change the AskingParameter label to **Asking Price Analysis**.
   c. Click the AutoFormat arrow button, then click the Foundry option (first column, third row). If labels overlap in the Report Header section, reduce the font size of the label with your name so that all labels are clearly visible.
   d. Use the Format Painter to copy the format from the Asking text box in the Detail section to the =Sum([Asking]) text box and label in the Report Footer section.
   e. Move, resize, and align the text boxes and label as needed to improve the report.
   f. Save the report, then preview the changes. Return to Design View and change the color of the three lines in the Report Footer section to black using the Line Color button on the Design tab.

6. **Add subreports.**
   a. Expand the vertical size of the Report Header section so it is about 2 inches in vertical height.
   b. Insert the Asking Price Summary Report as a subreport using the SubReport Wizard. Specify None for the link between the main report and subreport, and accept the default name Asking Price Summary Report for the subreport.
   c. Save and preview the report using **225000** when prompted. Return to Report Design View, and resize and move the subreport control as needed to clearly see all of the data.

7. **Modify section properties.**
   a. In Report Design View of the Asking Price Analysis report, modify the Detail section so that alternating rows have a Light Gray 1 shade.
   b. Save and preview the report using **275000** when prompted. The top of the first page of the final report is shown in Figure H-20. Your fonts and colors might be slightly different depending on how Access 2007 was installed on your computer.
   c. Print the Asking Price Analysis report, then close it.

8. **Use domain functions.**
   a. Create a new table named **StandardText** with two new fields: Disclaimer, with a Memo data type, and DisclaimerID, with an AutoNumber data type. The DisclaimerID field should be set as the primary key field.

▼ SKILLS REVIEW (CONTINUED)

b. Add one record to the table with the following entry in the Disclaimer field:
   The realtor makes no warranty or representation with respect to the accuracy of the listing.

c. Close the StandardText table.

d. Create a new report in Report Design view, and specify StandardText in the Record Source property for the report. Open the Report Footer section, then enter the following expression in a new text box in the Report Footer section:
   =DLookup("[Disclaimer]", "StandardText","[DisclaimerID] ="&1)

e. Delete the label associated with the new text box, then resize the text box so it is 6.25 inches wide.

f. Add your name to the Report Header section, close the Detail section, save the report with the name **StandardReport**, then print and close the report. In the future, you could use a domain function in this way to add standard disclaimers to various reports.

g. Close the RealEstate-H.accdb database, and exit Access.

FIGURE H-20

▼ INDEPENDENT CHALLENGE 1

As the manager of a music store's instrument rental program, you created a database to track instrument rentals to schoolchildren. Now that several instruments have been purchased, you need to create a report listing the rental transactions for each instrument.

a. Start Access, open the database **MusicRentals-H.accdb** from the drive and folder where you store your Data Files, and enable content if needed.

b. Use the Report Wizard to create a report based on the FirstName and LastName fields in the Customers table, the RentalDate field from the Rentals table, and the Description and MonthlyFee fields from the Instruments table.

c. View the data by Instruments, do not add any more grouping levels, sort the data in ascending order by RentalDate, use a Block layout and Portrait orientation, use an Urban style, and title the report **Instrument Rental Report**.

d. Open the report in Design View, then change the first grouping level from SerialNo to Description, and open the Description Footer section.

e. Enter the expression **=Count([MonthlyFee])** to a new, unbound control in the text box in the Description Footer section and change the label to **Times Rented:**

f. Add your name as a label to the Report Header section.

g. Save and preview the report as shown in Figure H-21. (Your colors and fonts might look slightly different.)

h. Move, resize, and align controls as needed, then print the report.

i. Save and close the Instrument Rental Report, close the MusicRentals-H.accdb database, then exit Access.

FIGURE H-21

▼ INDEPENDENT CHALLENGE 2

As the manager of a music store's instrument rental program, you have created a database to track instrument rentals to schoolchildren. Now that the rental program is underway, you need to create a summary report that shows how many instruments have been rented by each school.

a. Start Access, open the database **InstrumentRentals-H.accdb** from the drive and folder where you store your Data Files, and enable content if needed.

b. Use Report Design View to create a summary report. Use the Record Source property to add the SchoolName field from the Schools table and the RentalDate field from the Rentals table to the query. (*Hint*: Include the Customers table to build the proper relationships between the Schools and the Rentals table.)

c. Close the Query Builder window and save the changes.

d. Add SchoolName as a grouping field, and add the SchoolName field to the left side of the SchoolName Header section.

e. Add a text box with the following expression to the right side of the SchoolName Header section: **=Count([RentalDate])**.

f. Modify the caption of the new label to read **Number of rentals for this school:**.

g. Move, resize, and align the controls in the SchoolName Header section so that all controls are clearly visible, and completely close the Detail section.

h. Preview the report and continue to modify the controls in the SchoolName Header section as necessary.

i. Add a label to the Page Header section with your name.

j. Save the report with the name **School Summary Report**.

k. Apply a Trek AutoFormat as shown in Figure H-22. (Your colors and fonts might look slightly different.)

l. Print then close the School Summary Report, close the InstrumentRentals-H.accdb database, then exit Access.

FIGURE H-22

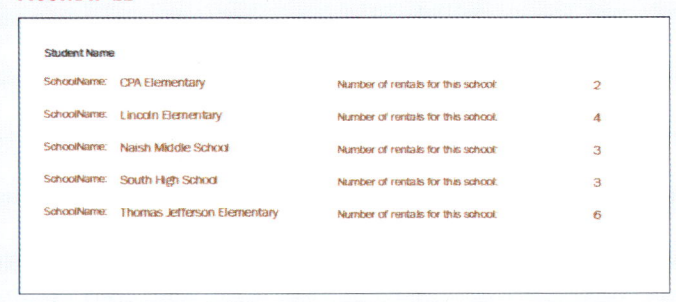

▼ INDEPENDENT CHALLENGE 3

As the manager of an equipment rental program, you have created a database to track rentals. You need to build a parameter report for this database.

a. Start Access, open the database **Equipment-H.accdb** from the drive and folder where you store your Data Files, and enable content if prompted.

b. Create a query with the RentalDate field from the Rentals table; the Description, DailyRate, WeeklyRate, Deposit, and Condition fields from the Equipment table; and the FirstName and LastName fields from the Customers table.

c. Enter the parameter criteria **Between [Enter start date] And [Enter end date]** for the RentalDate field.

d. Save the query with the name **RentalParameter** and close it.

e. Use the Report Wizard to create a report on all fields in the RentalParameter query. View the data by Equipment, do not add any more grouping or sorting levels, and use an Outline layout and a Landscape orientation. Use a Flow style. Title the report **Equipment Rental Report**.

f. To respond to the prompts, enter **3/1/10** for the start date and **3/31/10** for the end date.

g. Change the text color to black for all controls in the Description Header section except for the RentalDate, FirstName, and LastName labels.

h. Add your name as a label to the Report Header section. Format it with a color and size so that it is clearly visible.

▼ INDEPENDENT CHALLENGE 3 (CONTINUED)

Advanced Challenge Exercise

- Add spaces between all words in the labels in the Description Header section so that, for example, DailyRate becomes Daily Rate. Be careful to add spaces to the *label* controls and not the *text box* controls.
- Modify the Record Source property so that the records are sorted in ascending order on the Description field.
- Move and resize controls so they are within an 8-inch width and improve the report's appearance, then change the page orientation to portrait.
- Close up any extra space in the Report Header and Description Header sections.

FIGURE H-23

i. Display the report for RentalDates **3/1/10** through **3/31/10**, then print it. If you completed all of the Advanced Challenge Exercise steps, your printout should look similar to Figure H-23. (Your background colors and fonts might look slightly different.)

j. Save and print the Equipment Rental Report, close the Equipment-H.accdb database, then exit Access.

▼ REAL LIFE INDEPENDENT CHALLENGE

One way to use Access in your real life is in a community service project. People in schools and nonprofit agencies often inherit databases created by others and need help extracting information from them. Suppose you're working with the local high school guidance counselor to help her with an Access database she inherited that is used to record college scholarship opportunities. You can help her analyze scholarships by building a report with conditional formatting.

a. Start Access and open the **Scholarships-H.accdb** database from the drive and folder where you store your Data Files. Enable content if necessary.

b. Use the Report Wizard to create a report based on the Scholarships table. Include all of the fields. Add Amount as the grouping level, then click the Grouping Options button in the Report Wizard. Choose 10000s (ten thousands) as the Grouping interval. Sort the records by DueDate in a descending order. Use a Stepped layout and a Landscape orientation. Use a None style, and title the report **Scholarship Listing**.

c. Preview the report, then add your name as a label next to the report title.

d. In Report Layout View, narrow most of the text boxes in the Detail section so that you can widen the Description field on the right side of the report and give the field as much room as possible.

e. Center the values in the ID and Amount fields.

Advanced Challenge Exercises

- In Report Design View, click the Report Selector button, then use the Record Source property and Query Builder to select all of the fields in the Scholarships table. Enter the following parameter criteria in the DueDate field: **Between [Enter start date] and [Enter end date]**.
- Close and save the Query Builder.
- Apply the Equity AutoFormat to the report.

FIGURE H-24

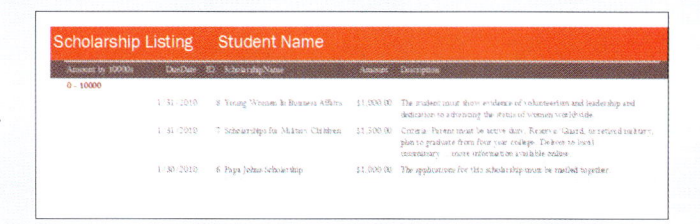

f. Preview the report using **1/1/10** and **1/31/10** dates, then print it. If you completed all of the Advanced Challenge Exercises, the report should look like Figure H-24. (Your background colors and fonts might look slightly different.) Close the report and the Scholarships-H.accdb database.

▼ VISUAL WORKSHOP

Open the **Training-H.accdb** database from the drive and folder where you store your Data Files. Enable content if necessary. Use the Report Wizard to create the report shown in Figure H-25. Select the First, Last, and Location fields from the Employees table and the Description and Hours fields from the Courses table. View the data by Employees, do not add any more grouping levels, sort in ascending order by Description, and use the Summary Options to sum the hours. Use the Stepped, Portrait, and Module style options. Title the report **Employee Education Report**. In Report Design View, enter your name as a label in the Report Header section in a font and color that is easily visible. Use Layout View to widen text boxes to display all values clearly. In Report Design View, delete the long calculated field and the Sum label in the SSN Footer section, and add conditional formatting so that the =Sum([Hours]) field appears in bold with a bright yellow background if the value is greater than or equal to 100. (*Hint*: The =Sum([Hours]) calculation is in a text box on the right side of the SSN Footer and Report Footer sections, but they may not be visible depending on how the text boxes are currently sized. Click the ruler to the left of the SSN Footer section or the left of the Report Footer section to find and select small controls.) Add a black, horizontal subtotal line above the =Sum([Hours]) field in the SSN Footer section, and add two lines to indicate a grand total below the =Sum([Hours]) field in the Report Footer section. Make other changes as necessary so that the first page of your report looks like Figure H-25. (Your background colors and fonts might look slightly different.)

FIGURE H-25

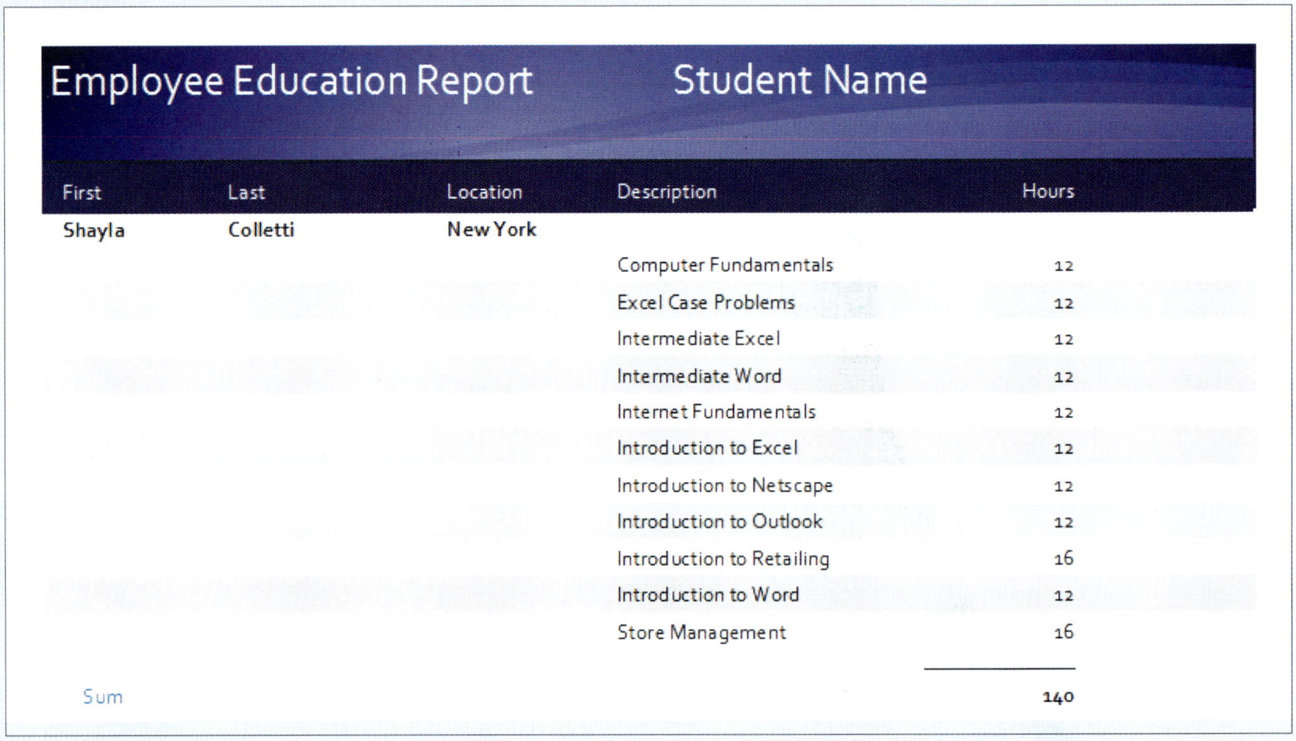

Employee Education Report — Student Name

First	Last	Location	Description	Hours
Shayla	Colletti	New York		
			Computer Fundamentals	12
			Excel Case Problems	12
			Intermediate Excel	12
			Intermediate Word	12
			Internet Fundamentals	12
			Introduction to Excel	12
			Introduction to Netscape	12
			Introduction to Outlook	12
			Introduction to Retailing	16
			Introduction to Word	12
			Store Management	16
Sum				140

UNIT E
Integration

Integrating Word, Excel, and Access

Files You Will Need:
INT E-1.accdb
INT E-2.docx
INT E-3.docx
INT E-4.accdb
INT E-5.docx
INT E-6.docx
INT E-7.accdb
INT E-8.accdb
INT E-9.docx
INT E-10.accdb
INT E-11.docx
INT E-12.accdb

As you have learned, many businesses maintain Access databases that contain the names, addresses, and other useful information about customers, suppliers, employees, and inventory. You can combine information stored in a database with Word to produce form letters, labels, and directories. You can also include in a Word document the charts and spreadsheets that you create from Access data you exported to Excel. Finally, you can export tables and reports that you create in Access into a Word document so you can format them attractively for printing. You work as the assistant to Bertram Lamont, the manager of the corporate division of QST London. Bertram has asked you to merge an Access database with a form letter that confirms the participation of clients in corporate tours. Bertram would also like you to create a report in Word that includes a report you export from Access and a chart created from data you export from Access to Excel.

OBJECTIVES

Merge from Access to Word
Filter an Access data source
Export an Access table to Word
Export an Access table to Excel
Export an Access report to Word

UNIT E
Integration

Merging from Access to Word

You can merge data from an Access database containing the names, addresses, and other information about a company's customers, contacts, and suppliers with a letter you create in Word to produce a series of individually addressed form letters. You can initiate the merge process directly from Access by using the Merge it with Microsoft Office Word feature to merge an active table with a Word document. You want to merge information contained in an Access database with a form letter that welcomes tour participants who have signed up for one of QST London's corporate tours. In Access, you first need to create a query datasheet that contains all the fields required for the form letter.

STEPS

> **QUICK TIP**
> To save the database with a new name, click the Office button, point to Save As, click Access 2007 Database, navigate to the drive and folder where you store your Data Files, type the new filename, then click Save.

1. **Start Access, open the file INT E-1.accdb in the drive and folder where you store your Data Files, then save it as QST London Corporate Tours**
   Each of the three tables in the database is related, so you can create a query datasheet for the form letter that contains fields from all three tables.

2. **Double-click QST London Participants: Table in the list of database objects, click the New (blank) record button to move to a new blank record, press [Tab], type Ms., press [Tab], type Marie, press [Tab], type Scott, press [Tab], click the list arrow, click Markham Consultants, press [Tab], click the list arrow, then click Cornish Quest**

3. **Close the table, double-click QST London Company: Table in the list of database objects, then click the Expand button next to record 1 to view the tour participants who work for Markham Consultants as shown in Figure E-1**
   Marie Scott is one of the tour participants who works for Markham Consultants.

4. **Close the QST London Company table, click the Create tab, click the Query Wizard button in the Other group, then click OK**
   You accept the Simple Query Wizard and move to the dialog box where you select all the fields that you want to include in the table you will merge with a form letter you create in Word.

5. **Click Company Name in the Available Fields list, click the Select Single Field button, click > again to insert Address 1, then click > again to insert Address 2**

6. **Click the Tables/Queries list arrow, click Table: QST London Participants, add the fields Title, First Name, and Last Name, click the Tables/Queries list arrow, click Table: QST London Tours, then add the fields Tour Name, Location, Start Date, and Capacity**
   The Simple Query Wizard dialog box lists fields from all three tables as shown in Figure E-2.

7. **Click Next, click Next, select QST London Company Query, type QST London Letter Query, click Finish, then close the query datasheet**

8. **Click QST London Letter Query in the list of database objects (any of the three versions listed), click the External Data tab, click the More button in the Export group, then click Merge it with Microsoft Office Word as shown in Figure E-3**

9. **Click OK, navigate to the drive and folder where you store your Data Files, double-click INT E-2.docx, click QST London Letter on the taskbar, then save the document as QST London Letter**
   The form letter is linked to the Access database. In the next lesson you insert the merge fields and run the merge.

FIGURE E-1: Viewing related records in the QST London Company table

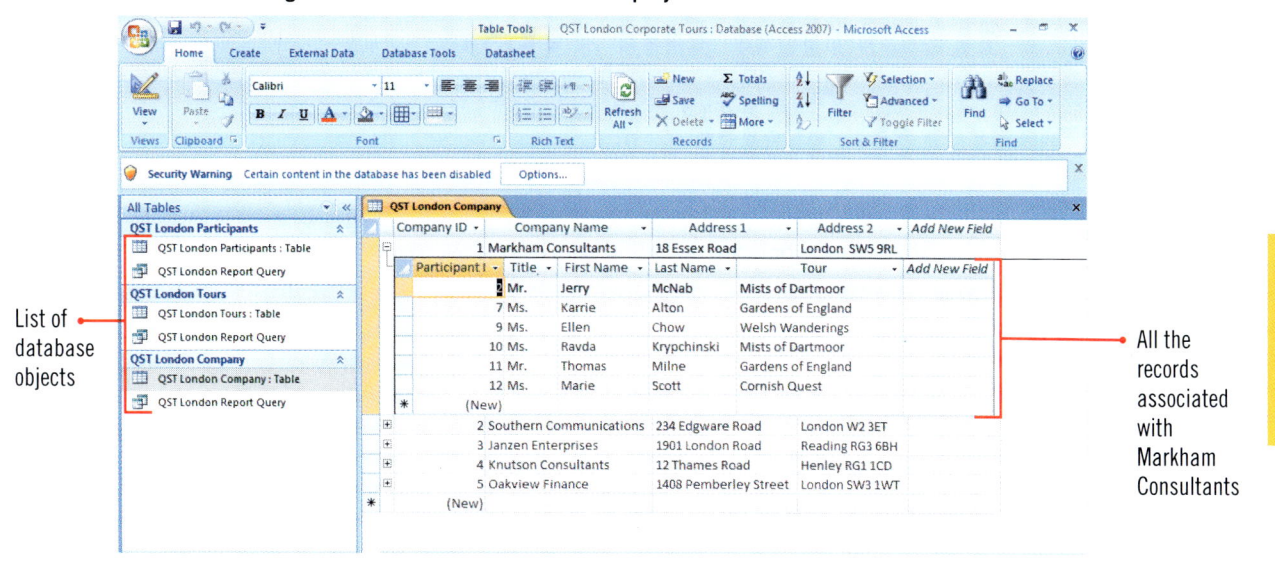

- List of database objects
- All the records associated with Markham Consultants

FIGURE E-2: Fields entered from three tables

- Table/Queries list arrow

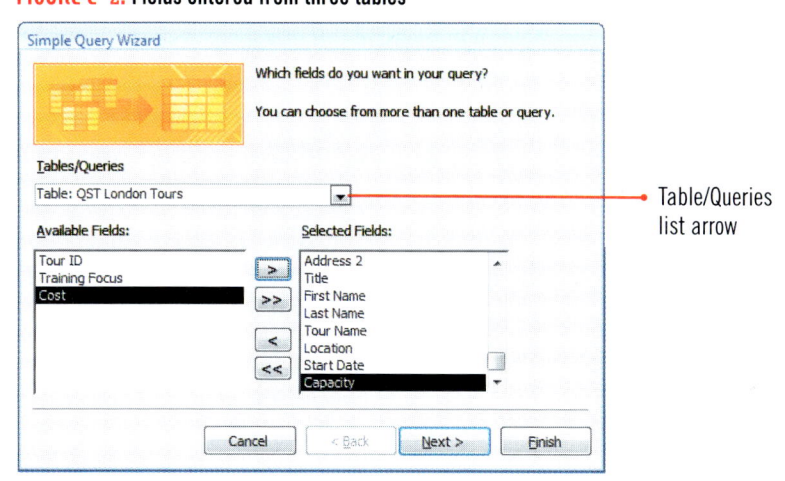

FIGURE E-3: Merging from an Access table to Word

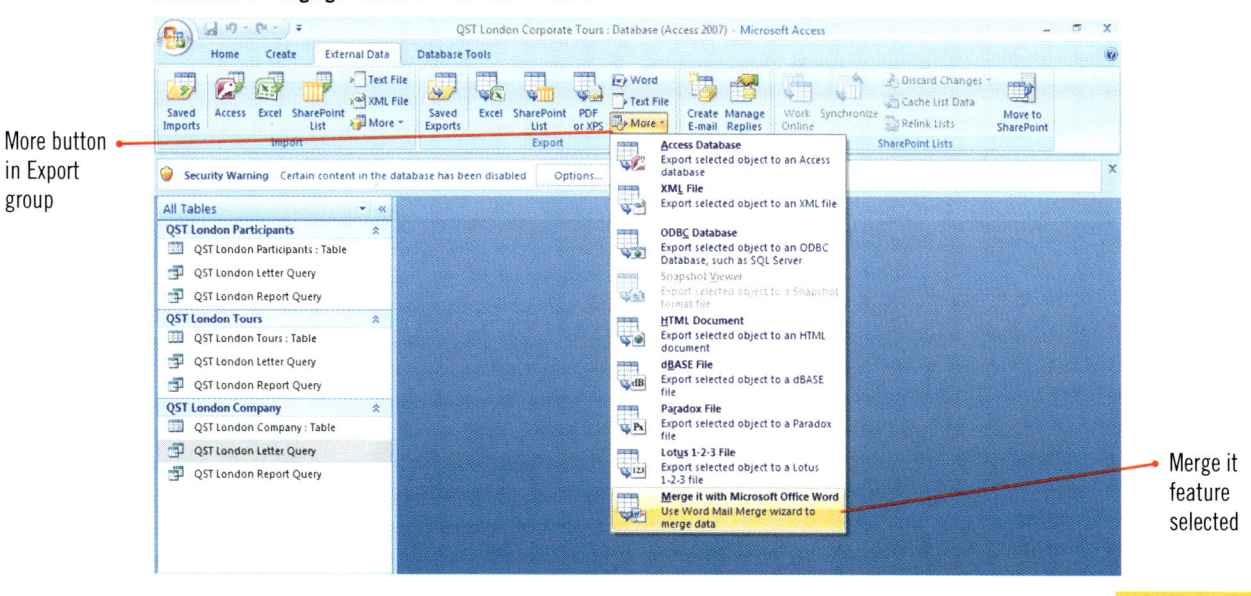

- More button in Export group
- Merge it feature selected

Filtering an Access Data Source

UNIT E Integration

You can choose which records you want to merge from an Access table to a Word document. For example, you may want to merge only the records of people who live in a particular state or only the records of people who are a certain age. You edit the recipients list in Word and use the filtering options to select the records you want to use in the merge. Bertram asks you to print only the records of participants who have purchased the Skye Country tour to Scotland or the Welsh Wanderings tour to Wales. You select the required records, insert the merge fields in the form letter, then run the merge.

STEPS

1. Maximize the Word window, if necessary, close the Mail Merge task pane, type the current date where indicated, then type your name where indicated in the closing

2. In the Start Mail Merge group on the Mailings tab, click the **Edit Recipient List button**
   In the Mail Merge Recipients dialog box, you can select which recipients you want to receive the form letter.

3. Scroll right to view all the fields you will include in the form letter, then click **Filter**
   The Filter and Sort dialog box opens. In this dialog box, you can specify the criteria that each of the records you want to merge should meet. You want to select only those people who will take a corporate tour in Wales or Scotland.

4. Click the **Field list arrow**, scroll to and click **Location**, then in the Compare to text box, type **Wales**

5. Press [Tab], click the **And list arrow**, click **Or**, select the **Location** field again, in the Compare to text box, type **Scotland** as shown in Figure E-4, then click **OK**
   Only the two participants who will take a corporate tour in Wales or Scotland appear.

> **TROUBLE**
> Make sure you click the list arrow on the Insert Merge Field button, not the button itself. If you click the button, click Cancel.

6. Click **OK**, click in the second blank line below the date, in the Write & Insert Fields group, click the **Insert Merge Field button list arrow**, click **Title**, press [Spacebar], click the **Insert Merge Field button list arrow**, click **First_Name**, press [Spacebar], click the **Insert Merge Field button list arrow**, select **Last_Name**, then press [Enter]

7. Insert the **Company_Name** field, press [Enter], insert the **Address_1** field, press [Enter], insert the **Address_2** field, click after Dear, press [Spacebar] once, then insert the **Title** and **Last_Name** fields separated by a space and followed by a colon (:)

> **QUICK TIP**
> Make sure you include a space following each merge field.

8. As shown in Figure E-5, insert the appropriate merge fields for TOUR_NAME, LOCATION, CAPACITY, START_DATE, TITLE, and LAST_NAME to replace the placeholders

9. Click the **Preview Results button** in the Preview Results group, click the **Next Record button** ▶ to view the data for Ellen Chow, compare your letter to Figure E-6, click the **Finish & Merge button** in the Finish group, click **Print Documents**, click **OK**, click **OK**, then save and close the document
   The document is merged with the filtered records, and the two letters are printed. If you open the QST London Letter again, you can choose to print letters to different participants by editing the recipient list. When you open the letter in Word, a message appears, telling you that the letter is linked to the QST Corporate Tours database.

FIGURE E-4: Setting filter criteria

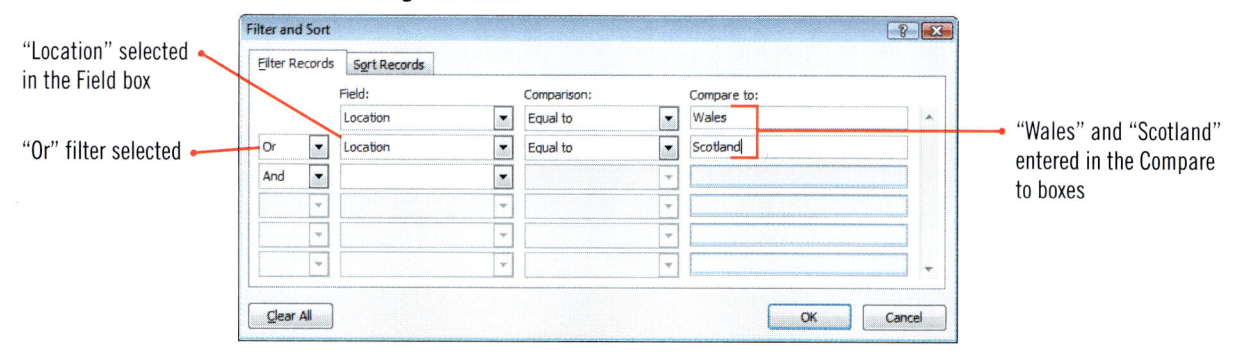

"Location" selected in the Field box

"Or" filter selected

"Wales" and "Scotland" entered in the Compare to boxes

FIGURE E-5: Adding merge fields to a form letter in Word

Insert Merge Field list arrow

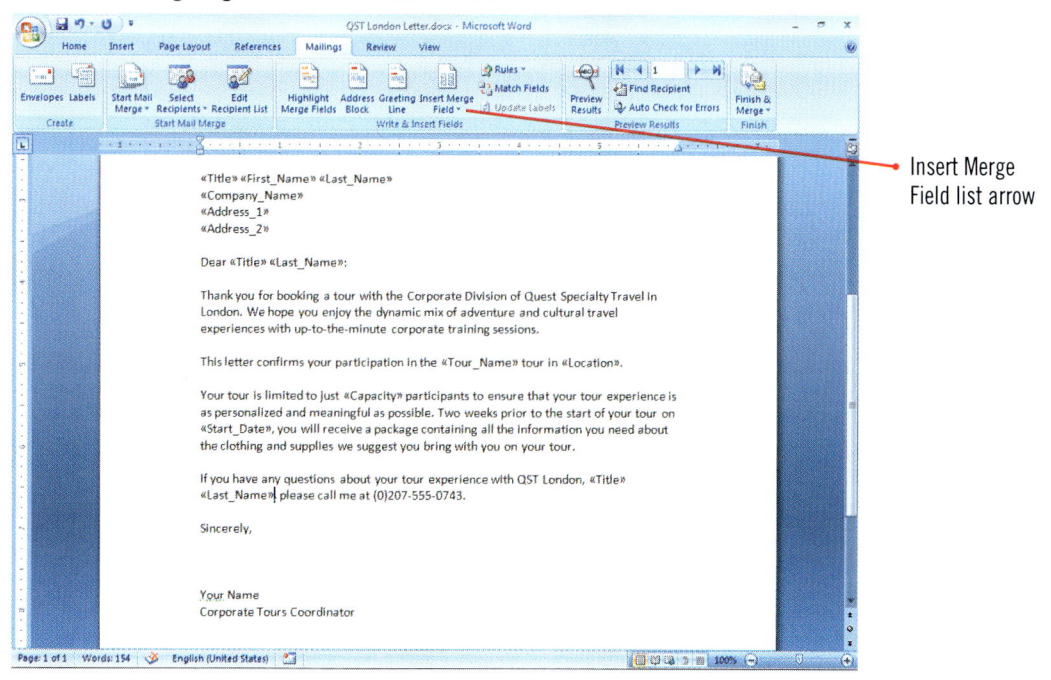

FIGURE E-6: Completed letter for Ellen Chow

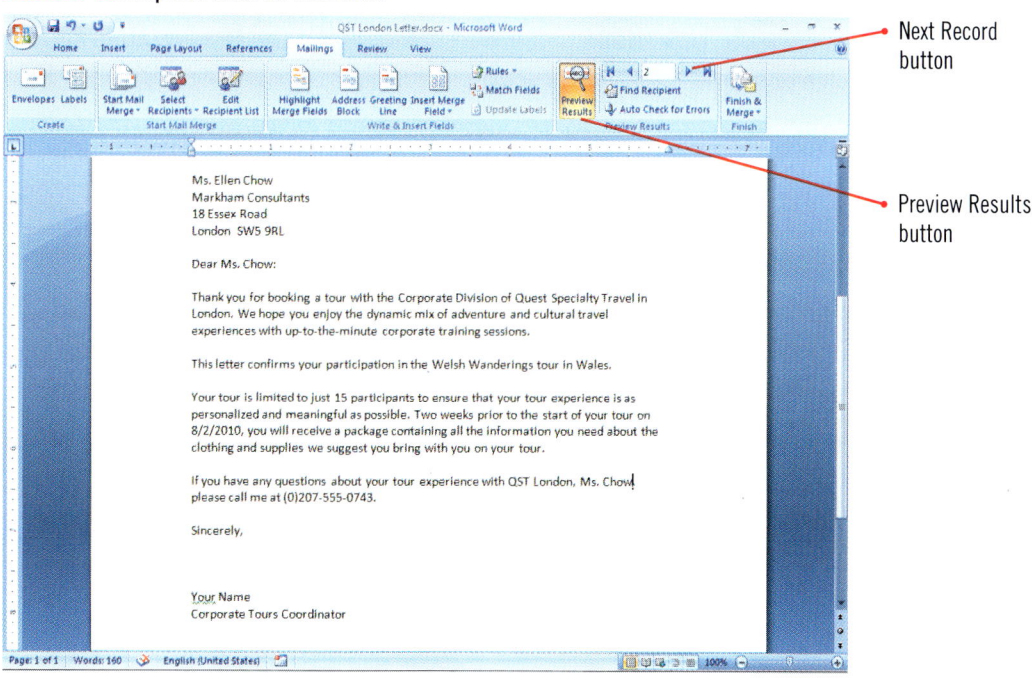

Next Record button

Preview Results button

Integrating Word, Excel, and Access   Integration 69

Exporting an Access Table to Word

UNIT E — Integration

When you want to include an Access table in a Word document, you first export it to a document that is saved in Rich Text Format (.rtf), which is the only format Access supports for exporting to Word. By default, the RTF document is saved in the My Documents folder with the same name as the Access table and an .rtf file extension. However, you can change the location and filename of the table when you export it. Then you can open the RTF document in Word, format the table just as you would any table, and copy the table into an existing Word document. An Access table imported into Word is not linked, so any changes you make to the database in Access will not appear in the table exported to Word. You export an Access table to Word when you will not need to update the exported information when the database information changes. 🎨 Bertram has written a two-page report for the QST London directors about the corporate tours he managed in 2010. He asks you to complete the report with objects copied from Access and Excel. The first object is a table that you export from Access.

STEPS

1. **In Word, open the file INT E-3.docx from the location where you store your Data Files, then save it as QST London Corporate Tours Report**

   First you want to create a query with selected information from the Tours table.

2. **In Access, click the Create tab, click the Query Wizard button in the Other group, click OK, click the Tables/Queries list arrow, click Table: QST London Tours, add the fields Tour Name, Location, Training Focus, and Start Date, click Next, then click Finish**

3. **Close the query datasheet, click QST London Tours Query in the list of database objects, click the External Data tab, then in the Export Group, click the Word button**

   The Export - RTF File dialog box opens.

4. **Click Browse, navigate to the location where you save your files, click Save, then click the Open the destination file after the export operation is complete check box as shown in Figure E-7**

   You select this option to save time.

   > **QUICK TIP**
   > The Access program button will blink because the Export - RTF File dialog box is still open.

5. **Click OK, click the Access program button on the taskbar, then click Close**

   Access exports the file into a new document that is automatically saved as QST London Tours Query.rtf.

6. **In the QST London Tours Query document in Word, move the mouse pointer over the upper-left corner of the table, click the table select icon ⊞, click the Copy button 📋 in the Clipboard group, then switch to the QST London Corporate Tours Report document**

7. **Select TOUR LIST below paragraph 1, then click the Paste button**

8. **Select the table, click the Table Tools Design tab, select the Light Grid - Accent 2 table design (light blue), click the Banded Rows check box to deselect it, click the Home tab, click the Center button ≡ in the Paragraph group, then click away from the table to deselect it**

   The Access table appears in Word as shown in Figure E-8. This table is not linked to the Access database.

9. **Save the report, show the QST London Tours Query document, then close it**

FIGURE E-7: Export - RTF File dialog box

Select this option → ☑ **Open the destination file after the export operation is complete.**

Your filename path will be different

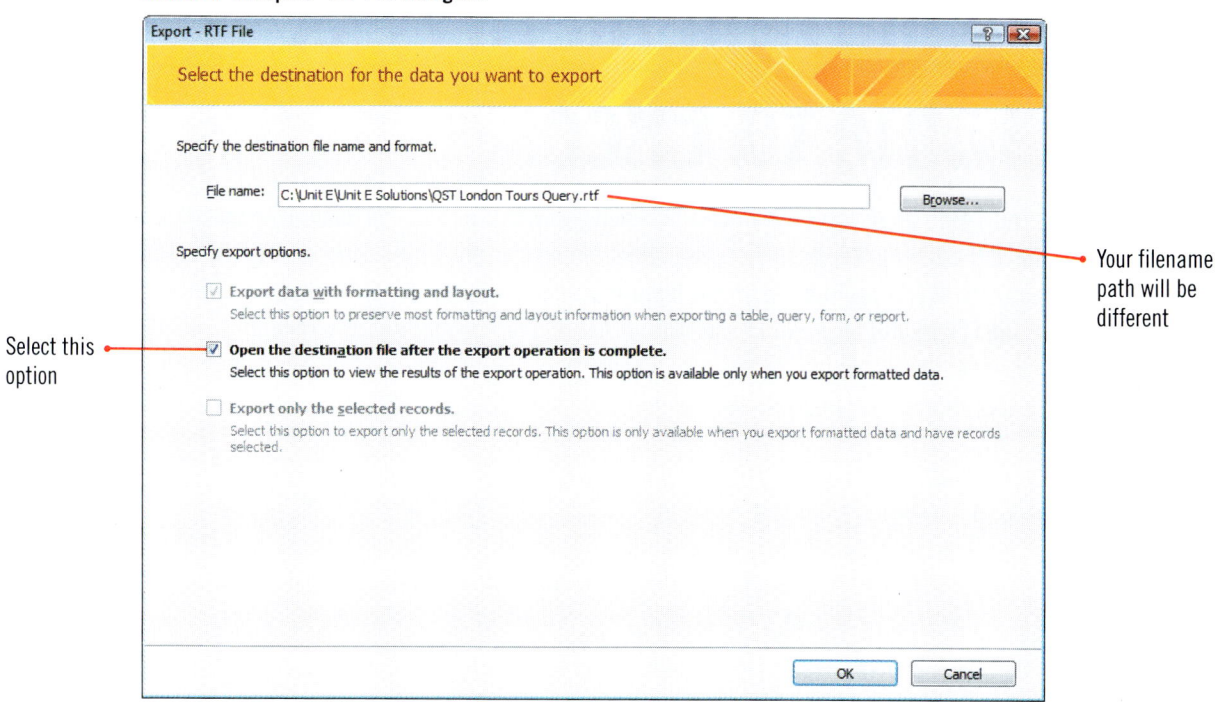

FIGURE E-8: Access table exported to Word and formatted

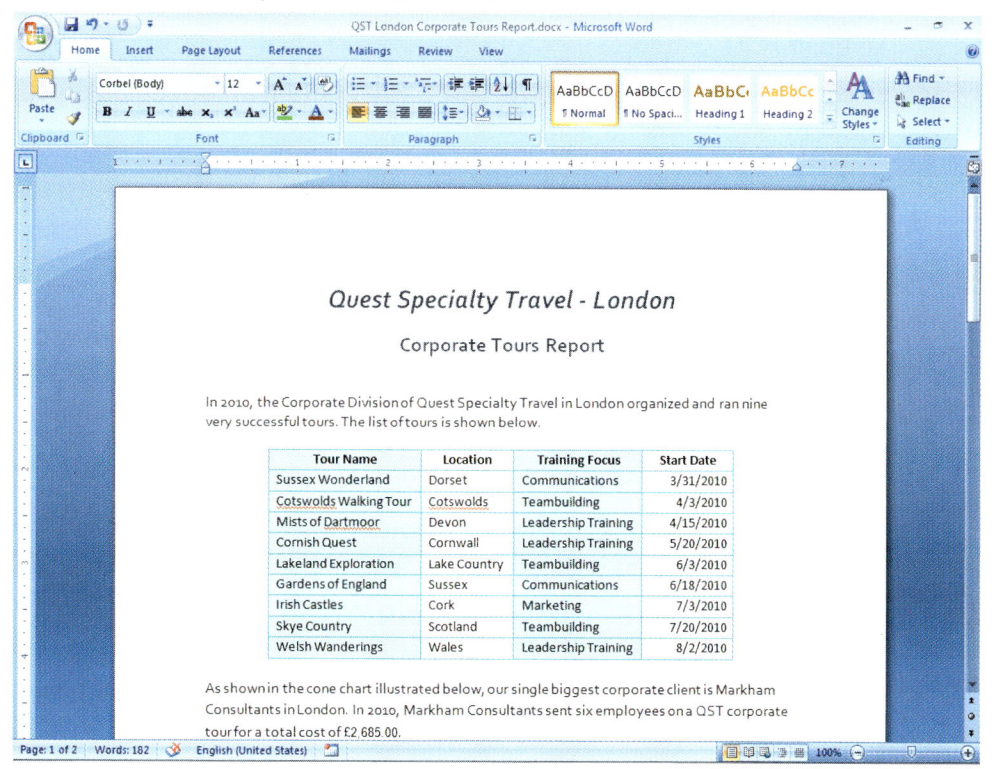

Quest Specialty Travel - London
Corporate Tours Report

In 2010, the Corporate Division of Quest Specialty Travel in London organized and ran nine very successful tours. The list of tours is shown below.

Tour Name	Location	Training Focus	Start Date
Sussex Wonderland	Dorset	Communications	3/31/2010
Cotswolds Walking Tour	Cotswolds	Teambuilding	4/3/2010
Mists of Dartmoor	Devon	Leadership Training	4/15/2010
Cornish Quest	Cornwall	Leadership Training	5/20/2010
Lakeland Exploration	Lake Country	Teambuilding	6/3/2010
Gardens of England	Sussex	Communications	6/18/2010
Irish Castles	Cork	Marketing	7/3/2010
Skye Country	Scotland	Teambuilding	7/20/2010
Welsh Wanderings	Wales	Leadership Training	8/2/2010

As shown in the cone chart illustrated below, our single biggest corporate client is Markham Consultants in London. In 2010, Markham Consultants sent six employees on a QST corporate tour for a total cost of £2,685.00.

Integrating Word, Excel, and Access

UNIT E
Integration

Exporting an Access Table to Excel

You export an Access table into Excel when you want to use Excel features to manipulate, analyze, filter, or edit the table data, but when you don't need to maintain a connection between the Access and Excel objects. When you use the Export feature, you create a new Excel file that is not linked to the Access database. Changes you make to the data in Access are not made to the data in Excel. You create a query in Access containing the data you want to analyze and chart in Excel, export the query datasheet to Excel, then create a cone chart that you copy to the report in Word.

STEPS

1. In Access, create a query that includes the fields from the QST London Company and Tours tables, shown in Figure E-9, click **Finish**, close the query datasheet, click any occurrence of the **QST London Company Query** in the list of database objects, click the **External Data tab**, then in the Export Group, click the **Excel button**

2. Click **Browse**, navigate to where you save your Data Files and click **Save**, click **OK**, then click **Close**

   The QST London Company Query datasheet is exported as an Excel file called QST London Company Query.xlsx.

3. Start Excel, open **QST London Company Query.xlsx**, maximize the window and widen columns as necessary to view all the data, select the range **D2:D13**, click the **Accounting Number Format button list arrow** $ in the Number group, then click **£ English (United Kingdom)**

4. Select the range **A1:D13**, click the **Sort & Filter button** in the Editing group, then click **Sort A to Z**

5. With the cells still selected, click the **Data tab**, then in the Outline group, click the **Subtotal button**

   In the Subtotal dialog box, you can choose to calculate the total tour expenses made by each company.

6. Click the **At each change in list arrow**, click **Company Name**, click the **Cost check box** if necessary to select it, click **OK**, then click **2** in the Grouping pane and widen the Cost column as shown in Figure E-10

   The Subtotal feature calculates the total spent on tours by each company. For example, Markham Consultants spent £2,650.00 on corporate tours in 2010. By selecting 2 in the Grouping pane, you collapse the Subtotal list so it contains only company totals.

7. Click cell **A4**, double-click **Total** in the formula bar, press **[Delete]**, press **[Backspace]**, then delete **Total** and the space before it from each of the remaining four company names

TROUBLE
If you clicked 3 in step 6 to expand the Subtotals list, the chart will show all the list entries.

8. Select the range **A4:A18** (only five cells are selected), press and hold **[Ctrl]**, select the range **D4:D18**, release **[Ctrl]**, click the **Insert tab**, click the **Column** button in the Charts group, select the **Clustered Cone** chart type, click **Series 1** in the chart legend, then press **[Delete]**

9. Click the chart border, copy the chart, switch to Word, select **CONE CHART**, click the **Paste button**, click to the left of the chart to select it, click the **Center button** in the Paragraph group, deselect the chart, then save the document

   The chart is pasted into Word as a link to the Excel spreadsheet, as shown in Figure E-11.

Integrating Word, Excel, and Access

FIGURE E-9: Fields for the QST London Company Query

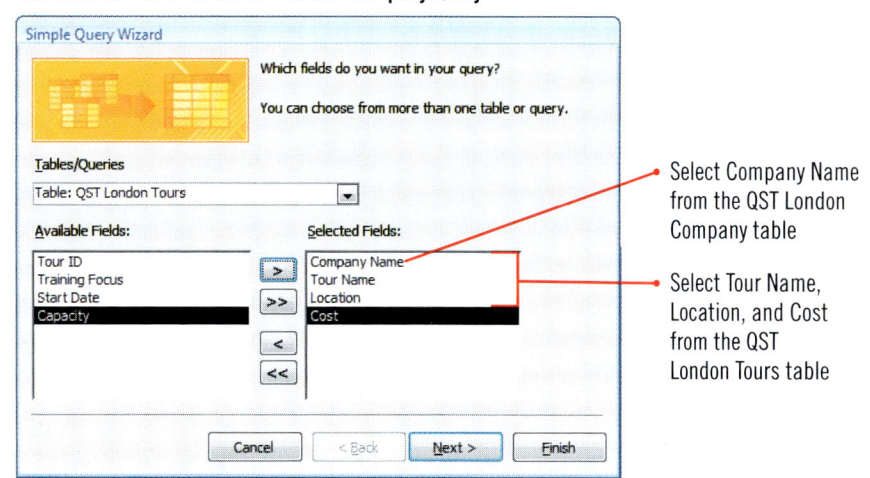

- Select Company Name from the QST London Company table
- Select Tour Name, Location, and Cost from the QST London Tours table

FIGURE E-10: Collapsing the Subtotal list to level 2

- Grouping pane
- Click 2 to collapse the Subtotal list

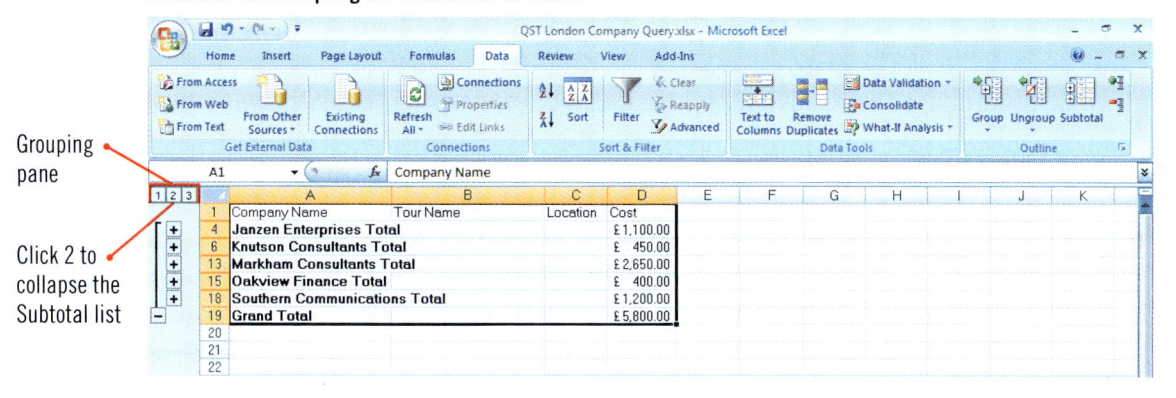

	Company Name	Tour Name	Location	Cost
4	Janzen Enterprises Total			£1,100.00
6	Knutson Consultants Total			£ 450.00
13	Markham Consultants Total			£2,650.00
15	Oakview Finance Total			£ 400.00
18	Southern Communications Total			£1,200.00
19	Grand Total			£5,800.00

FIGURE E-11: Cone chart copied to Word

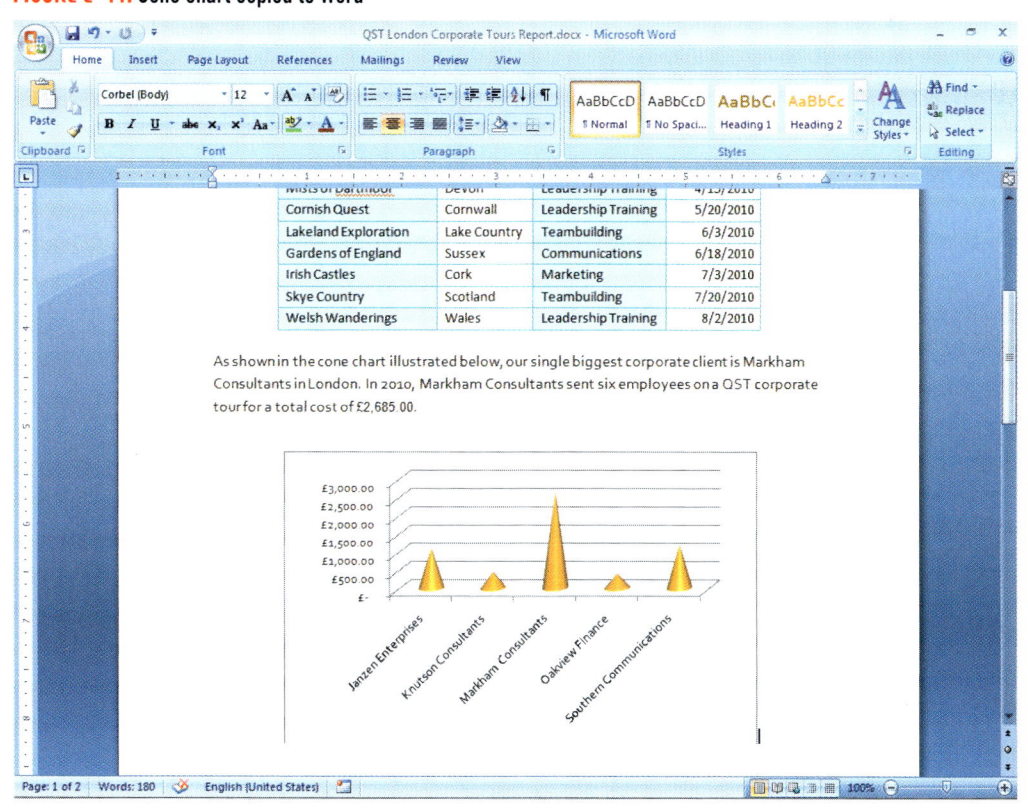

Mists of Dartmoor	Devon	Leadership Training	4/15/2010
Cornish Quest	Cornwall	Leadership Training	5/20/2010
Lakeland Exploration	Lake Country	Teambuilding	6/3/2010
Gardens of England	Sussex	Communications	6/18/2010
Irish Castles	Cork	Marketing	7/3/2010
Skye Country	Scotland	Teambuilding	7/20/2010
Welsh Wanderings	Wales	Leadership Training	8/2/2010

As shown in the cone chart illustrated below, our single biggest corporate client is Markham Consultants in London. In 2010, Markham Consultants sent six employees on a QST corporate tour for a total cost of £2,685.00.

Integrating Word, Excel, and Access

UNIT E
Integration

Exporting an Access Report to Word

If you don't need to modify database information in Excel, you can export an Access report to a Rich Text Format (.rtf) file that you can then open and modify in Word. You can then use Word tools to convert the report into a table that you can format easily. An Access report that you export to an .rtf file is not linked to the Access database. Table E-1 summarizes the integration tasks you performed In this unit. You create the report in Access and then export it to Word so that you can format it as a Word table.

STEPS

1. In Access, click any occurrence of the QST London Report Query in the list of database objects, click the Create tab, then in the Reports group, click the Report Wizard button

2. Click the Select All Fields button >> to add all the fields from the QST London Report Query datasheet, then click Next four times

3. Click the Block option button In the Layout section, click the Landscape option button, click Next, select the None report design if necessary, click Next, name the report QST London Report, click Finish, then click the Close Print Preview button

   When you create a report that you then plan to export to Word, you simplify your formatting tasks when you do not apply one of the Access report designs.

4. Click the View button list arrow in the Views group, click Layout View, close the Field list pane, then use the mouse to adjust the widths of the various fields as shown in Figure E-12

5. Close the report, click Yes to save it, click QST London Report in the list of database objects, click the External Data tab, click the Word button in the Export group, click the Open the destination file after the export operation is complete check box to select it, click OK, click the Access program button on the taskbar, then click Close

   Access exports the file to the location where you store your files and names the document QST London Report.rtf. In Word, the document is formatted with Tab characters that separate the data columns. You need to show the hidden formatting symbols so that you can remove selected Tab characters and then convert the text into a table.

TROUBLE
Do not remove the Tab character to the left of each participant's name.

6. Show the QST London Report.rtf document in Word, click the Show/Hide ¶ button ¶ in the Paragraph group, press [Delete] to remove the Tab character to the left of QST London Report, then remove the Tab character to the left of Company Name and the name of each of the five companies as shown in Figure E-13

7. Select the text from Company Name to Gardens of England, click the Insert tab, click the Table button in the Tables group, click Convert Text to Table, then click OK to accept four columns for the table

8. With the table still selected, double-click any column divider to reduce column widths, click the Home tab, click the Copy button in the Clipboard group, switch to the report in Word, select REPORT on page 2, click the Paste button, select the table, apply the Medium Shading 1 – Accent 2 table design, center the table, then deselect it

9. Type your name where indicated in the document footer, save the document, print a copy, then save and close all open files and programs

FIGURE E-12: Modifying column widths in an Access report

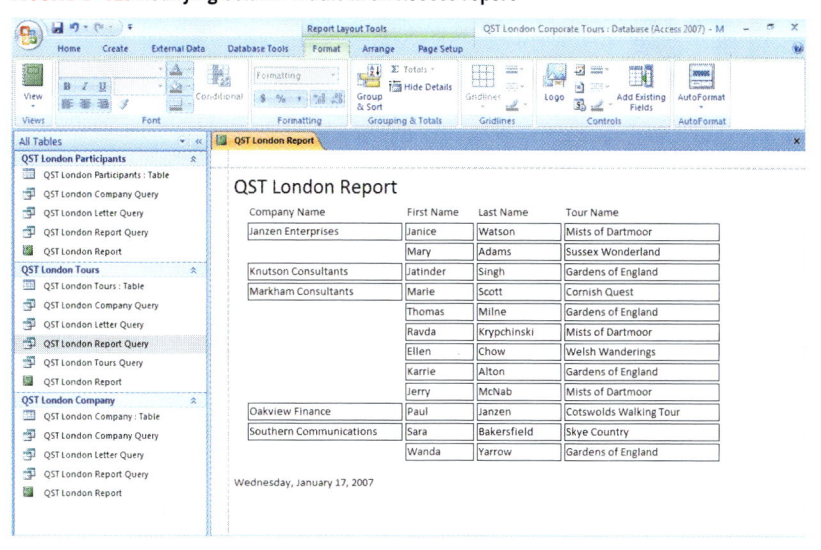

FIGURE E-13: Selected Tab characters removed

Company names now flush left

Tab character

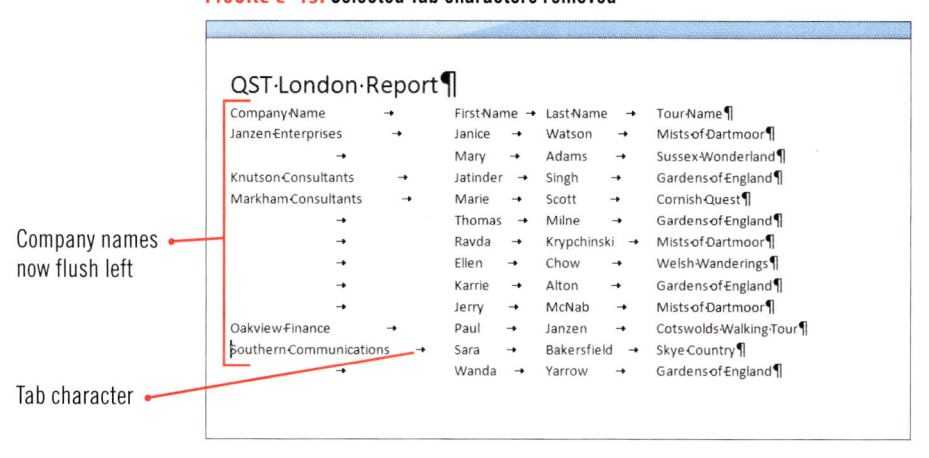

TABLE E-1: Unit E Integration tasks

object	command	source program	destination program	result	connection	page no.
Access query	Merge it with Microsoft Office Word	Access	Word	The fields and records from the Access query datasheet merge into a letter created in Word	Linked	66
Access table	Word button in the External Data tab	Access	Word	The Access table is saved in Rich Text Format with the table structure intact. The .rtf file is opened and formatted in Word	None	70
Access table	Excel button on the External Data tab	Access	Excel	The Access table is exported as an Excel file. In Excel, the table data can be filtered, sorted, and edited	None	72
Access report	Word button on the External Data tab	Access	Word	The Access report is saved in Rich Text Format with the structure defined with tabs. The .rtf file is opened in Word where it can be converted to a table	None	74

Integrating Word, Excel, and Access

Practice

If you have a SAM user profile, you may have access to hands-on instruction, practice, and assessment of the skills covered in this unit. Log in to your SAM account (http://sam2007.course.com/) to launch any assigned training activities or exams that relate to the skills covered in this unit.

▼ CONCEPTS REVIEW

Match each term with the statement that best describes it.

1. Query Wizard
2. Filter
3. Rich Text
4. Export
5. External Data

a. Send an Access table to Word or Excel
b. In Access, click to access functions used to share Access objects with other programs
c. Use to show only selected records in a mail merge
d. Use to create a datasheet containing all the fields you want to include in a mail merge
e. Format of an Access table or report exported to Word

▼ SKILLS REVIEW

1. **Merge from Access to Word.**
   a. Start Access, open the file INT E-4.accdb from where you store your Data Files, then save it as **Techno Conference**.
   b. Open the Techno Delegates table, then add a new record for **Ms. Debra McNair** with the data **Track A** and **Bantock Enterprises**.
   c. Open the Techno Company table, then view the records associated with record 6 for Bantock Enterprises.
   d. Close the Techno Company table, then use the Query Wizard to create a query that includes the Company, Address1, Address2, and Country fields from the Techno Company table, the Title, First Name, and Last Name fields from the Techno Delegates table, and the Workshop1, Time1, Workshop2, and Time2 fields from the Techno Workshops table.
   e. Name the query **Techno Letter Query**.
   f. Use the Merge it with Microsoft Office Word function to merge the Techno Letter query with the data file INT E-5.docx.
   g. Save the Word document as **Techno Conference Registration Letter**.

2. **Filter an Access data source.**
   a. Maximize the Word window, close the Mail Merge task pane, type the current date where indicated, then type your name where indicated in the closing.
   b. Open the Mail Merge Recipients dialog box, view all the fields, then open the Filter and Sort dialog box.
   c. On the Filter tab, select the Country field, enter **Italy** in the Compare to text box, then close the dialog boxes.
   d. In the letter, insert the appropriate merge fields over the placeholders shown in uppercase letters.
   e. Preview the two letters, complete the merge, print a copy of the two letters, then save and close the letter document.
   f. Compare the printed letter for Dena Martelli to Figure E-14.

FIGURE E-14: Completed letter for Dena Martelli

2010 Techno Conference
802 Iris Drive, Dublin 10, Ireland
Phone: 353 1 5557700

Current Date

Ms. Dena Martelli
Martelli Roma
Via del pastini 110
Roma 00186
Italy

Dear Dena:

Welcome to the 2010 Techno Conference, held this year in Dublin, Ireland. The conference starts on September 21 at 0800 hours with a keynote speech by Dame Edna Janzen, author of the best-selling book *The Challenge of 21st Century Technology*.

This letter confirms your participation in the following workshops:

- XML Made Easy at 0900 hours
- Open Source at 1300 hours

Thank you, Dena, for your participation in the 2010 Techno Conference. If you have any questions, please call me at 353 1 5557700.

Sincerely,

Your Name
Conference Organizer

Integration 76 Integrating Word, Excel, and Access

▼ SKILLS REVIEW (CONTINUED)

3. Export an Access table to Word.
   a. In Word, open the file INT E-6.docx from the drive and folder where you store your Data Files, then save it as **Techno Conference Report**.
   b. In Access, create a query called **Techno Workshops Query** that includes the Workshop1, Time1, Workshop2, and Time2 fields from the Techno Workshops table.
   c. Close the query datasheet, then export the Techno Workshops Query to Word as an .rtf file called **Techno Workshops Query.rtf**. Make sure you specify that Access should open the RTF file after the export operation is complete.
   d. Close the Export – RTF dialog box in Access, then in Word, copy the table and paste it over WORKSHOP LIST in the Techno Conference Report document.
   e. Apply the Light Shading – Accent 1 table design (light purple) to the table, then deselect the Banded Rows option and verify that Banded Columns is selected.
   f. Center the table and adjust column widths so the data for each row fits on one row.
   g. Save the document, switch to the Techno Workshop Query document, then close it.

4. Export an Access table to Excel.
   a. In Access, create a query called **Techno Conference Query** that includes the Company field from the Techno Company table and the Track, Workshop1, Workshop2, and Cost fields from the Techno Workshops table.
   b. Export the Techno Conference Query to a new Excel spreadsheet called **Techno Conference Query.xlsx**.
   c. In Excel, open **Techno Conference Query.xlsx**, widen columns as necessary, apply the Euro Currency style to the range E2:E22, then sort the table in alphabetical order by the Company field.
   d. Create a Subtotal list that calculates the total workshop costs incurred by each of the six companies.
   e. Click 2 in the Grouping pane to collapse the Subtotal list, delete "Total" from each company name, then use the [Ctrl] key to select the range A10:A28 and E10:E28.
   f. Create a Column chart using the Clustered Pyramid chart type, then remove the chart legend.
   g. Copy the chart, paste it in the appropriate area of the Word report, center the chart, then save the document.

5. Export an Access report to Word.
   a. In Access, use the Report Wizard to create a report called **Techno Report** from all the fields in the Techno Report Query. Select the Block layout style, the Landscape orientation, and the None report design.
   b. In Layout view, adjust the widths of the various fields so all data is visible.
   c. Close and save the report, then export it to an RTF file called **Techno Report.rtf** that opens in Word.
   d. In Word, show the formatting marks, then delete the Tab character to the left of Techno Report, Company, and the names of each of the six companies.
   e. Select the text from Company to the end of the text (not including the date and page number), then convert the text to a table containing five columns.
   f. Reduce column widths as necessary, copy the table, then paste it over REPORT on page 2 of the Word report.
   g. Apply the Medium List 2 – Accent 1 table design, adjust column widths as necessary, then center the table.
   h. Show the report in Two Pages view, then compare it to Figure E-15.
   i. Type your name where indicated in the document footer, save the document, print a copy, then save and close all open files and programs.

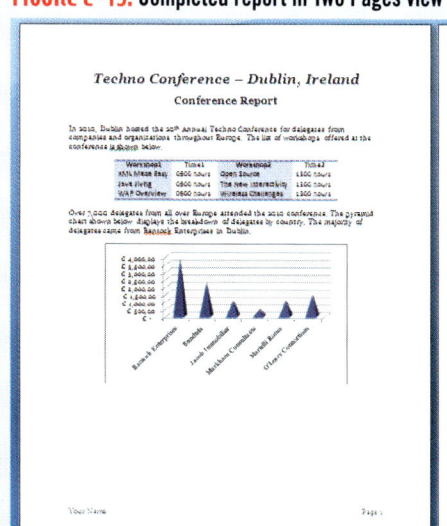

FIGURE E-15: Completed report in Two Pages view

▼ INDEPENDENT CHALLENGE 1

You work in the Human Resources department at Evergreen Marketing in Seattle. Since installing DVD burners on all its office computers, the department has accumulated stacks of DVDs containing data, images, training films, and programs. A co-worker has already organized information about the DVDs in an Access database. Your job is to use the Mail Merge feature to create labels for the DVD cases. You also want to create a chart in Excel to show the total gigabytes of data in your DVDs by category.

a. In Access, open the file INT E-7.accdb from the location where you store your Data Files, then save it as **Evergreen Marketing DVD List**.

b. Create a query called **Evergreen DVD Labels** that contains the Category, Data Description, Date Burned, and Gigabytes fields from the Evergreen DVD List table.

c. Use the Merge it with Microsoft Office Word function to merge the Evergreen DVD Labels Query to a new Word document. (*Hint*: Click the "Create a new document and then link the data to it" option button.)

d. In Word, close the Mail Merge task pane and maximize the window, click the Start Mail Merge button, then click Labels.

e. In the Label Options dialog box, click the Page printers option button to select it if necessary, scroll to and click Media Label in the Product number box, then click OK. The DVD label you selected will produce a 4.62" x 4.62" label.

f. Insert and format merge fields, add additional text, then insert a clip art picture above the company name. (*Hint*: Change the Before spacing above Data Description to 50 point and the font size to 18 pt, change the font size of the Date Burned and Gigabytes lines to 14 point, change the font color of Evergreen Marketing to Olive Green, Accent 3 Darker 50% and the font size to 24 pt, then search for "disk" to find the clip art picture. Center all the data.

g. Preview the labels, complete the merge, select the Print Documents option, then enter 1 in the From text box and 2 in the To text box to print just the first two labels.

h. Save the document as **Evergreen Marketing DVD Labels**, then close the document.

i. In Access, export the Evergreen DVD List table to Excel as a new file called **Evergreen DVD List.xlsx**.

j. Open the new document in Excel, delete column 1 (containing the ID numbers), sort the table in alphabetical order by Category, then use the Subtotal function to calculate the total gigabytes for each category of DVD.

k. Group the Subtotal list to Level 2, remove "Total" from each Category cell, then change the labels so that each one is plural to match images (for example, change "database" to "databases," "document" to "documents," etc.).

l. Select the range containing the Category labels and the range containing the Gigabyte totals, then create a pie chart showing the breakdown of categories by gigabytes.

m. Select Chart Layout 1, change the chart title to **Data Sizes**, apply the chart style of your choice, position the chart below the data, type your name in a cell below the chart, save and print the workbook, then close all files and exit all programs.

▼ INDEPENDENT CHALLENGE 2

You are helping to organize the Pacific Spirit Recreation Conference in San Francisco. Recreation professionals from all over northern California meet at the conference to learn strategies for holding special events related to four recreational areas: skiing, sailing, mountaineering, and cycling. Your first task is to create a form letter that welcomes people to the conference. Then you will create a report in Access that you publish and format in Word.

a. In Access, open the file INT E-8.accdb from the location where you store your Data Files, then save it as **Pacific Spirit Conference**.

b. In Access, add two records to the Pacific Attendees table. You determine the names and addresses, then specify that one person lives in San Francisco and will attend the Skiing workshops at the conference, and the other person lives in Sacramento and will attend the Sailing workshops.

c. View the Pacific Workshops table, then view how many attendees will attend the Skiing workshops.

d. Create a query called **Pacific Spirit Letter Query** that includes all the fields except the ID field from the Pacific Attendees table and all the fields except the Package ID field from the Pacific Workshops table.

e. Merge the query with the Data File called INT E-9.docx, then save the file as **Pacific Spirit Welcome Letter**.

f. In Word, insert the merge fields where required, then filter the Recipient list so that letters are sent only to attendees who live in either Carmel or Reno. Insert your name and today's date in the appropriate locations.

g. Preview the form letters, print the two letters, then save and close the document.

h. In Access, create a query called **Pacific Workshops Query** that includes the Recreation field from the Pacific Workshops table, and the First Name, Last Name, and City fields from the Pacific Attendees table.

i. Use the Report Wizard to create a report called **Pacific Workshops** from all the fields in the Pacific Workshops Query. Select the Block outline style, the Landscape format, and the None report design.

j. In Layout view, adjust the widths of the various fields so all data is visible, close and save the report, then export it to an .rtf file called **Pacific Workshops.rtf**.

k. In Word, delete extra Tab characters, convert selected text to a table consisting of four columns, then adjust column widths.

l. Click to the right of **Pacific Workshops** at the top of the document, press [Enter], clear the formatting, then type the following sentence: **This year, participants attended workshops related to four recreation areas: Cycling, Sailing, Skiing, and Mountaineering. For the second year in a row, the sailors top the list!**

m. Press [Enter] following the sentence, change the page orientation to Portrait and the margins to Normal, format the table attractively using the table design of your choice, then center the table. Note that the document is saved in the .rtf format rather than the .docx format. As a result, some of the table formatting features such as banded columns and banded rows are not available.

n. Type your name in place of the date at the bottom of the document, press [Delete] several times to remove the page number, save the document, print a copy, then save and close all open files and programs.

▼ VISUAL WORKSHOP

You manage the office for Northeast Computers, a small retail outlet that sells computers, software, and accessories in New England. In Access, open the file INT E-12.accdb from where you store your Data Files, then save it as **Northeast Computers**. Export the table to an Excel file called **Northeast Sales.xlsx**, make the required calculations, then use the Sort and Subtotal functions to create the column chart shown in Figure E-16. Select Chart Style 2 if necessary. Save the spreadsheet, print a copy, then close all open files and programs.

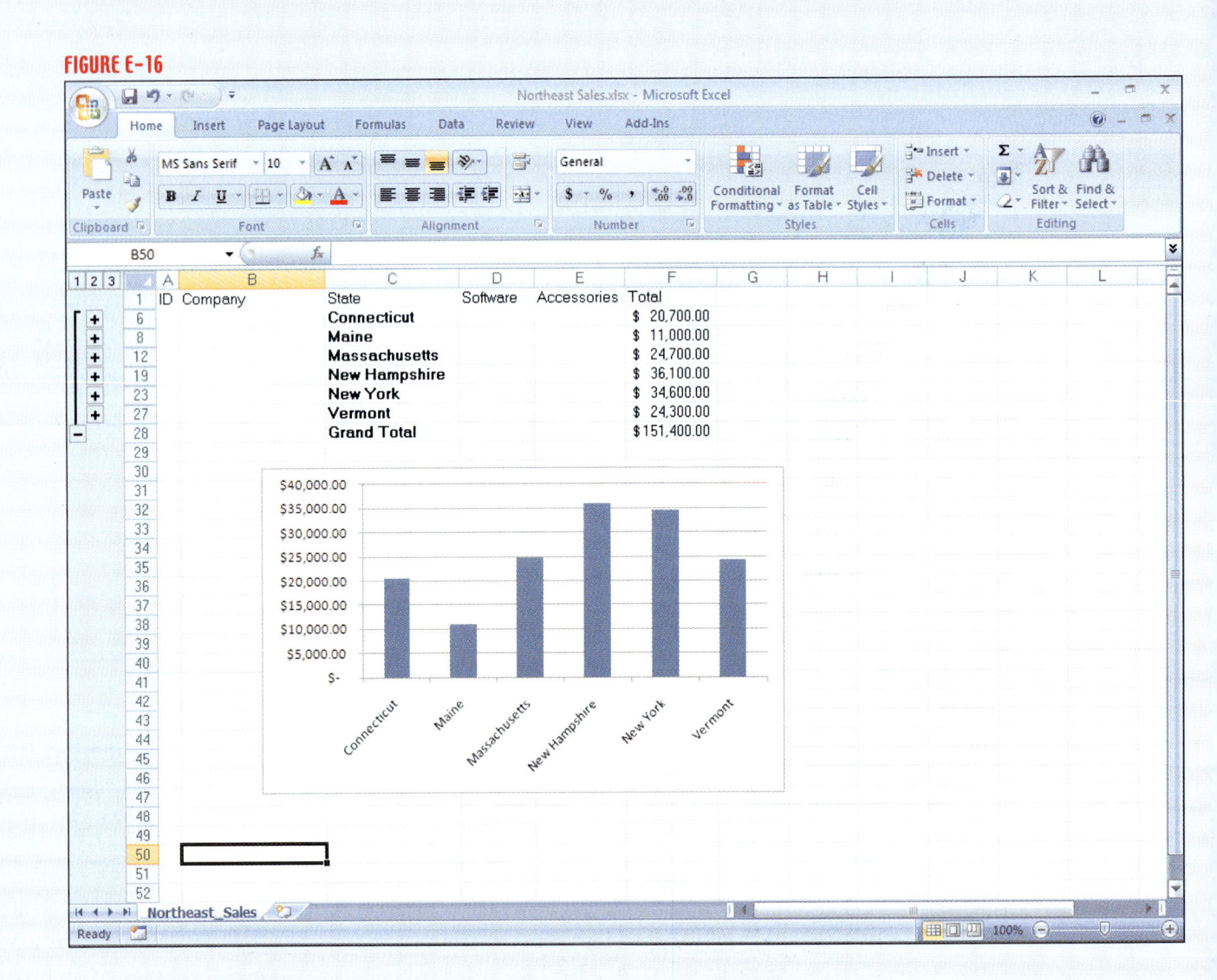

FIGURE E-16

State	Total
Connecticut	$ 20,700.00
Maine	$ 11,000.00
Massachusetts	$ 24,700.00
New Hampshire	$ 36,100.00
New York	$ 34,600.00
Vermont	$ 24,300.00
Grand Total	$151,400.00

Working with Advanced Tools and Masters

UNIT E — PowerPoint 2007

Files You Will Need:
PPT E-1.pptx
PPT E-2.pptx
PPT E-3.pptx
PPT E-4.pptx
PPT E-5.pptx
PPT E-6.pptx

Once you have learned the basics of creating a presentation and running a slide show, you are ready to learn more advanced features of PowerPoint. Learning to use advanced features like Connector shapes, the Format Painter tool, and customized slide layouts helps you create impressive presentations. Knowing how to modify masters allows you the freedom to customize the slides, handouts, and notes of your presentation. As the assistant to Ellen Latsky, the European tour developer for Quest Specialty Travel, you have been working on a tour proposal presentation, which Ellen will give later in the year. After receiving some initial feedback from Ellen, you revise the presentation by enhancing some shapes, customizing animations, and customizing the master views.

OBJECTIVES

Draw and format connectors
Use advanced formatting tools
Customize animation effects
Create custom slide layouts
Format master text
Change master text indents
Adjust text objects
Customize Handout and Notes Masters

Drawing and Formatting Connectors

UNIT E — PowerPoint 2007

PowerPoint has a number of connector tools that enable you to create three different types of connector lines or arrows—straight, elbow (bent), or curved. For example, use the connector tools to connect shapes with a line or arrow. Use the Curve tool to create a freeform curved line. Once you have drawn a line or connector, you can format it using Quick Styles, outline color, and effects. The Curved Arrow connector tool will work well to complete the diagram on Slide 4.

STEPS

1. **Start PowerPoint, open the presentation PPT E-1.pptx from the drive and folder where you store your Data Files, save the presentation as QuestE, click the View tab on the Ribbon, click the Arrange All button in the Window group, then click the Slide 4 thumbnail in the Slides tab**

   Slide 4 of the presentation appears.

2. **Click the Home tab on the Ribbon, click the Shapes button in the Drawing group, in the Lines section click the Curved Arrow Connector button, then position + on the top connection site of Shape 1**

   Notice that Shape 1 has six possible connection sites to anchor a line or arrow. See Figure E-1.

3. **Drag the pointer to the ■ on the bottom of Shape 2**

   Red handles (circles) appear at either end of the arrow connector, indicating that it is attached to the two shapes. The arrow has an adjustment handle (yellow diamond) which allows you to alter the path of the arrow.

   > **TROUBLE**
   > If you accidentally release the mouse before you reach a connection site, an endpoint is created at the end of the connector. Drag the connector endpoint to the correct connection site.

4. **Position the pointer over the arrow head, then drag the arrow to the ■ on the left side of Shape 2**

   The arrow now flows from the top of Shape 1 to the left side of Shape 2.

5. **Click the Shapes button, right-click in the Shapes gallery, then click Lock Drawing Mode**

   Locking the drawing mode allows you to draw the same shape over and over without having to select its button in the Shapes Gallery each time.

6. **Drag from the left ■ on Shape 2 to the bottom ■ on Shape 3, drag from the bottom ■ on Shape 3 to the right ■ on Shape 4, drag from the right ■ on Shape 4 to the top ■ on Shape 1, then press [Esc]**

   You created three more arrows. Pressing [Esc] unlocks the drawing mode.

7. **Right-click the bottom-right arrow, then click Format Shape**

   The Format Shape dialog box opens so you can format the connector arrow.

   > **QUICK TIP**
   > If you rearrange shapes that are joined with connector lines, the connector lines remain attached and move with the shapes.

8. **Type 2 in the Width text box, in the Arrow settings section click the End type list arrow, click the Arrow icon, click the End size list arrow, then click the Arrow R Size 8 icon**

   The style of the arrow changes to a more distinct style.

9. **In the left pane click Shadow, click the Presets list arrow, click the Offset Diagonal Bottom Right icon, click the Distance down arrow once, then in the left pane click Line Color**

   The shadow gives the arrow some depth. You can also change the color of the arrow.

10. **Click the Color list arrow, click Red, Accent 3 in the Theme Colors section, click Close, click in a blank area of the slide, then save the presentation**

    Compare your screen to Figure E-2.

FIGURE E-1: Shape showing connection sites

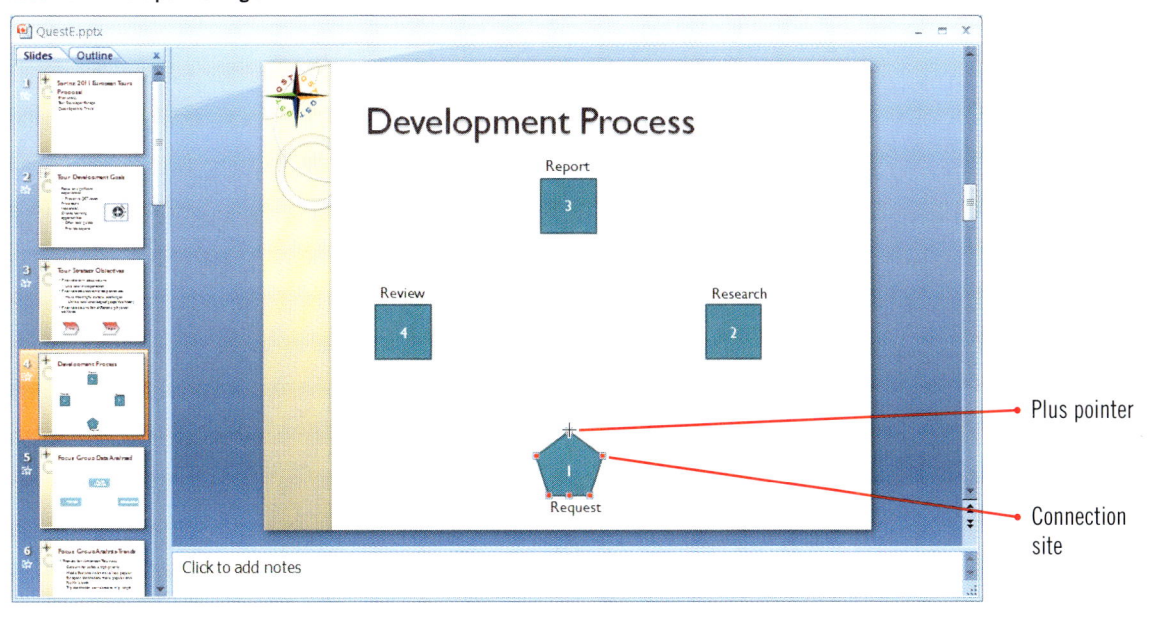

- Plus pointer
- Connection site

FIGURE E-2: Slide showing formatted connector arrow

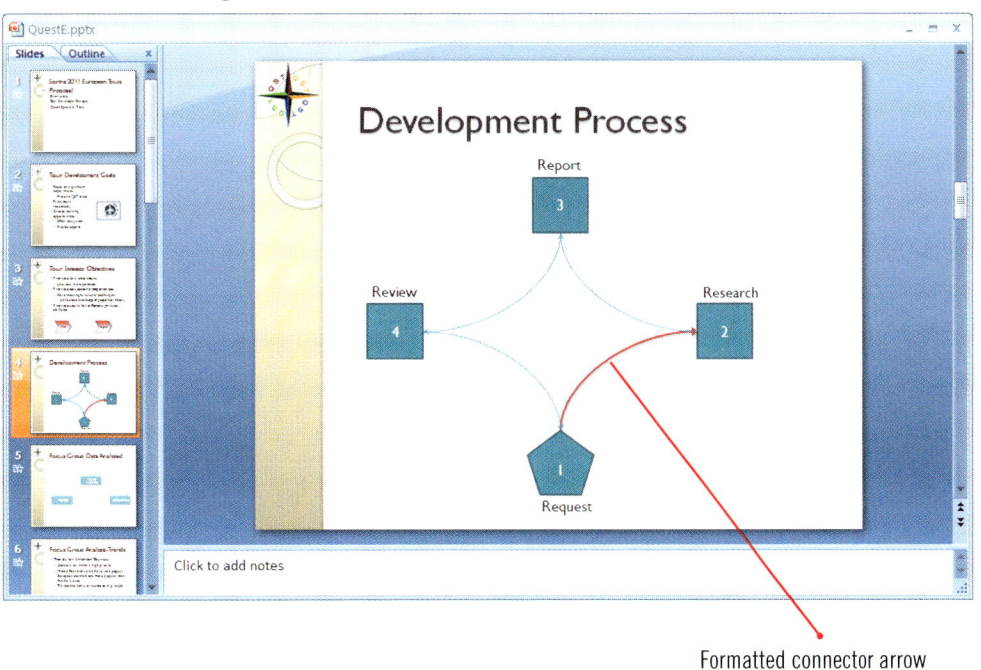

Formatted connector arrow

Drawing a freeform shape

A freeform shape can consist of straight lines, freehand (or curved) lines, or a combination of the two. To draw a freeform shape, click the Shapes button in the Drawing group on the Ribbon, then click the Freeform button in the Lines section. Drag the pointer to draw the desired shape, then double-click when you are done. To draw a straight line with the Freeform tool, click where you want to begin the line, drag the pointer, then double-click to deactivate the Freeform tool. To edit a freeform object, right-click the object, then click Edit Points on the shortcut menu.

Working with Advanced Tools and Masters

Using Advanced Formatting Tools

UNIT E — PowerPoint 2007

With PowerPoint's advanced formatting tools, you can change attributes such as fill texture, 3-D effects, and shadow for text and shapes. If you have multiple objects that you want to format, you can use the Format Painter to pick up the attributes from one object and apply them to another object. You decide to use the advanced formatting tools to enhance the diagram on Slide 4.

STEPS

> **QUICK TIP**
> If you click the Format Painter button once, you can apply formatting attributes to only one object.

1. **Click the red arrow, double-click the Format Painter button in the Clipboard group, then position the Format Painter pointer over one of the blue arrows**
   The Format Painter tool "picks up" the attributes of an object and copies them to the next object you select. Double-clicking the Format Painter button allows you to apply the same formatting to multiple objects on the slide without having to reselect the tool.

2. **Click each of the three blue arrows, then press [Esc]**
   Now all of the arrow connectors are formatted alike as shown in Figure E-3.

3. **Right-click Shape 1, click Format Shape on the shortcut menu to display the Format Shape dialog box, click the Picture or texture fill option button, then click the Texture list arrow**
   The Format Shape dialog box opens and the texture gallery appears.

> **QUICK TIP**
> To add effects to a text box and modify its fill and outline, click the text box, then click the appropriate button in the Shape Styles group on the Drawing Tools Format tab.

4. **Click the Brown marble square, drag the dialog box title bar to move the dialog box off of Shape 1, then click 3-D Format in the left pane**
   The brown marble texture fills the shape. The 3-D Format options appear in the dialog box.

5. **In the Bevel section click the Top list arrow, click the Slope icon, in the Surface section click the Lighting list arrow, then in the Special section click the Two Point icon**
   The lighting effect defines the bevel effect better.

6. **In the Depth section type 20 in the Depth text box, then click 3-D Rotation in the left pane**
   Changing the depth lengthens the effect from the default of 0 points to 20 points.

7. **Click the Presets list arrow, in the Perspective section click the Perspective Left icon in the top row, then click Close**
   The shape changes perspective and you can see the effect and the depth of the effect better. The number in the shape is hard to see, but you can apply formatting to make the characters more visible.

8. **Click the Font list arrow in the Font group, then click Arial Black**
   The text in Shape 1 is now easy to read.

9. **Double-click in the Clipboard group, click each of the three remaining shapes, then click again to turn off the Format Painter**
   Now all the shapes on the slide have the same fill, font, and 3D effects.

10. **Click in a blank area of the slide, then save your changes**
    Compare your screen with Figure E-4.

Working with Advanced Tools and Masters

FIGURE E-3: Slide showing formatted connector arrows

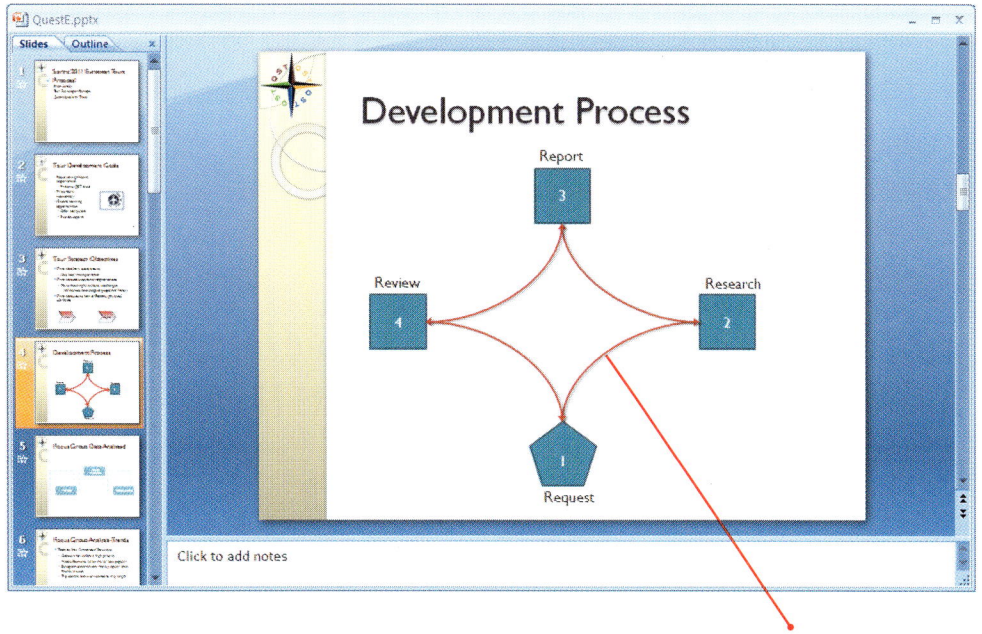

All connector arrows are formatted with the same attributes

FIGURE E-4: Slide showing formatted shapes

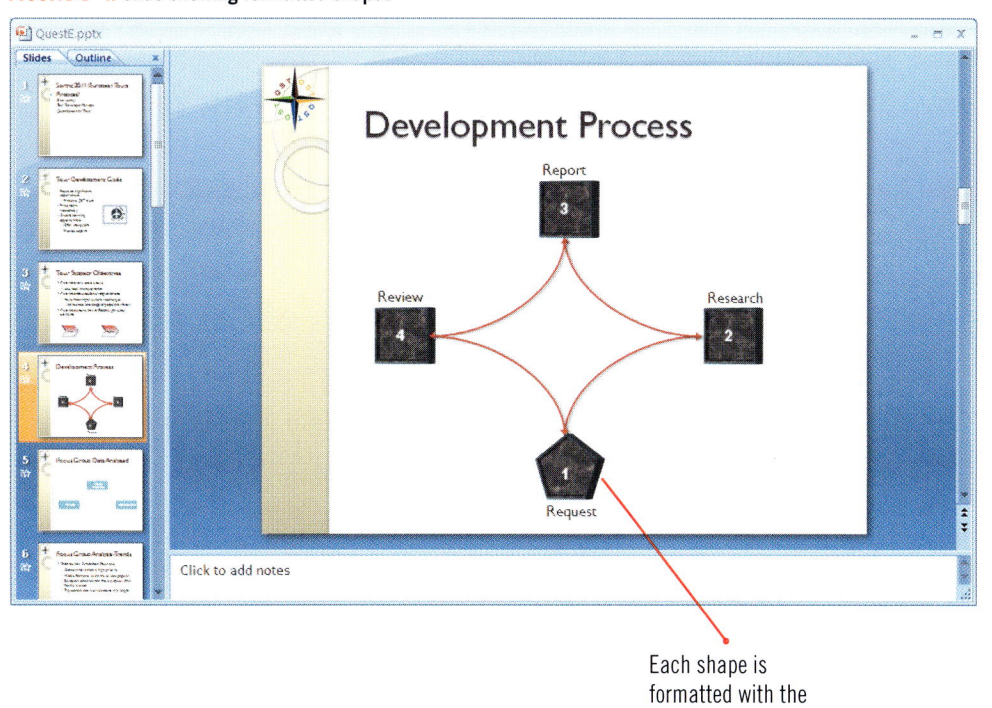

Each shape is formatted with the same attributes

Creating columns in a text box

In PowerPoint 2007, you have the ability to create columns within text objects when the information you are working with fits better in a column format. Select the text object, click the Columns button in the Paragraph group on the Home tab, then click either Two Columns, Three Columns, or More Columns. The More Columns option allows you to set up to 16 columns and customize the spacing between columns. You can display the ruler to set specific widths for the columns and further customize the columns.

Working with Advanced Tools and Masters

Customizing Animation Effects

Animating objects allows you to focus on key information and control how information flows on the slide during a slide show. The simplest way to animate an object is to apply a standard animation effect using the Animate list arrow in the Animations group; however, you can apply and customize other animation effects using the Custom Animation task pane which includes animation effects not found in the Animate list on the Ribbon. You can customize effect options including starting time, direction, and speed. You decide to apply animation effects to the arrows and shapes on Slide 4 and then customize the effects to highlight the shapes.

STEPS

1. **Click Shape 1, click the Animations tab on the Ribbon, then click the Custom Animation button in the Animations group**

   The Custom Animation task pane opens.

2. **Click Add Effect in the Custom Animation task pane, point to Emphasis, click More Effects, in the Subtle section click Flash Bulb, then click OK**

   As soon as you select an animation effect, the effect is previewed on the slide and an animation tag appears next to the shape.

3. **Click the red arrow between Shape 1 and Shape 2, click Add Effect in the Custom Animation task pane, point to Entrance, click More Effects, in the Basic section click Strips, then click OK**

   An animation effect is applied to the connector arrow from Shape 1 to Shape 2. Compare your screen with Figure E-5.

4. **Apply the Emphasis Flash Bulb animation effect to Shape 2, apply the Entrance Strips animation effect to the arrow between Shape 2 and Shape 3, then apply the Flash Bulb and Strips animation effects in alternating order to the rest of the lines and shapes in the diagram**

   When you are finished, each shape has the Flash Bulb animation effect and each arrow has the Strips animation effect. There are a total of eight animation effects on the slide.

   > **TROUBLE**
   > If you want to delete the animation effect, select the effect in the Custom Animation task pane, then click Remove.

5. **Click the Play button at the bottom of the Custom Animation task pane**

   Three of the arrows do not move in the correct direction. The direction of an animation effect is set by default but can be changed.

6. **Click the arrow between Shape 1 and Shape 2, click the Direction list arrow in the Custom Animation task pane, click Right Up, click the arrow between Shape 2 and Shape 3, click the Direction list arrow click Left Up, click the arrow between Shape 4 and Shape 1, click the Direction list arrow, click Right Down, then click Play**

   The animation effects applied to the arrows now play correctly. You can also adjust the speed of the animations.

7. **Press [Ctrl], in the Custom Animation task pane click items 2, 4, 6, and 8 in the animation list, release [Ctrl], click the Speed list arrow, click Fast, then click Play**

   All the animations play the way you want them too. Compare your screen to Figure E-6.

8. **Click the Custom Animation task pane Close button ×, then save your changes**

FIGURE E-5: Slide showing applied animation effects

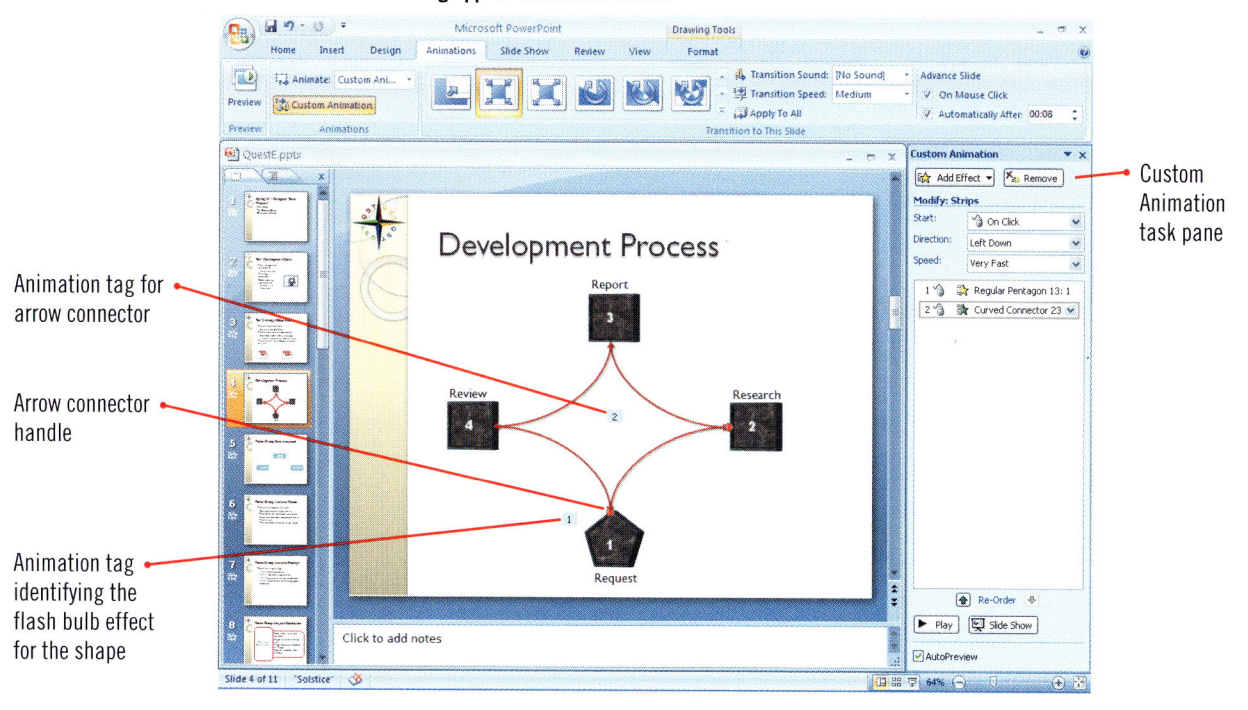

- Animation tag for arrow connector
- Arrow connector handle
- Animation tag identifying the flash bulb effect for the shape
- Custom Animation task pane

FIGURE E-6: Slide showing completed animation effects

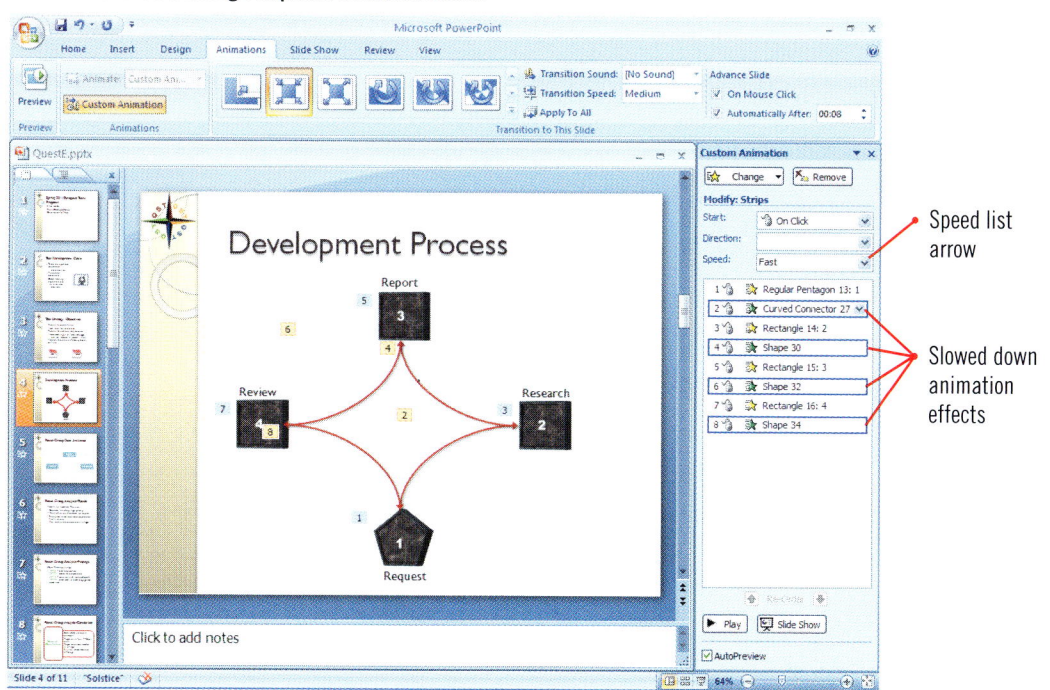

- Speed list arrow
- Slowed down animation effects

Understanding animation timings

Each animated object on a slide has a starting time in relation to the other animated objects. There are three different starting time options: Start On Click, Start With Previous, and Start After Previous. The Start On Click timing option starts the animation effect when you click the mouse. A small mouse icon appears next to the animation effect in the animation list when this timing option is applied. The Start With Previous timing option begins the animation effect at the same time as the previous effect in the animation list, so two or more animation effects play at once. This timing option does not display an icon in the animation list. The Start After Previous timing option, which displays a clock icon in the animation list, begins the animation effect immediately after the previous effect in the animation list finishes playing without clicking the mouse.

Working with Advanced Tools and Masters

Creating Custom Slide Layouts

The standard slide layouts supplied in PowerPoint are adequate to create the majority of slides for your presentation. However, if you are consistently modifying a standard slide layout for presentations, having a custom slide layout that you can reuse would be helpful. To create a custom slide layout, you choose from eight different placeholders to draw on the slide, including text, chart, and media placeholders. You create and save custom slide layouts in Slide Master view, which then become a part of the presentation. You need to create a custom slide layout for the presentation that displays picture thumbnails on the slide that you can use as navigation buttons during a slide show.

STEPS

1. **Click the View tab on the Ribbon, click the Slide Master button in the Presentation Views group, right-click a blank area of the slide, then click Ruler**
   Slide Master view opens and the ruler displays.

2. **Click the last slide layout in the left pane, then click the Insert Layout button in the Edit Master group**
   A new slide layout is added to the presentation and appears in the Slide pane with a title text placeholder and footer placeholders as shown in Figure E-7. The new slide layout contains all of the slide background elements associated with the current theme. The default placeholders are not needed.

3. **In the Master Layout group, click the Title check box, click the Footers check box, then click the Insert Placeholder button arrow**
   The default placeholders are removed from the slide layout. The eight available placeholder options appear in the placeholder gallery.

4. **Click Picture, then position + on the slide so the pointer is lined up at the 2" marks on both the vertical and horizontal rulers**
   As you move the pointer on the slide its position is identified on the rulers by dotted lines.

5. **Drag a box down and to the right until the pointer is lined up with the 0" marks on the rulers**
   A 2" picture placeholder appears on the slide. You can duplicate the placeholder.

6. **Click the Home tab on the Ribbon, click the Paste button arrow in the Clipboard group, click Duplicate, then duplicate the picture placeholder two more times**
   There are four picture placeholders on the slide.

> **QUICK TIP**
> To position placeholders precisely on the slide, use Guides and the Align commands to help you.

7. **Drag each placeholder to a position on the slide as shown in Figure E-8, then click the Slide Master tab on the Ribbon**
   The placeholders are arranged on the slide layout.

8. **Click the Title check box in the Master Layout group, then click the Rename button in the Edit Master group**
   The title text placeholder is added back to the slide layout, and the Rename Layout dialog box opens.

> **QUICK TIP**
> The new Picture slide layout also appears in the Layout gallery.

9. **Type Picture, click Rename, then position the pointer over the slide layout thumbnail**
   The new name of the custom slide layout appears in the ScreenTip.

10. **Right-click a blank area of the slide, click Ruler, click the Normal button on the status bar, then save your changes**

FIGURE E-7: New custom slide layout

Default placeholders

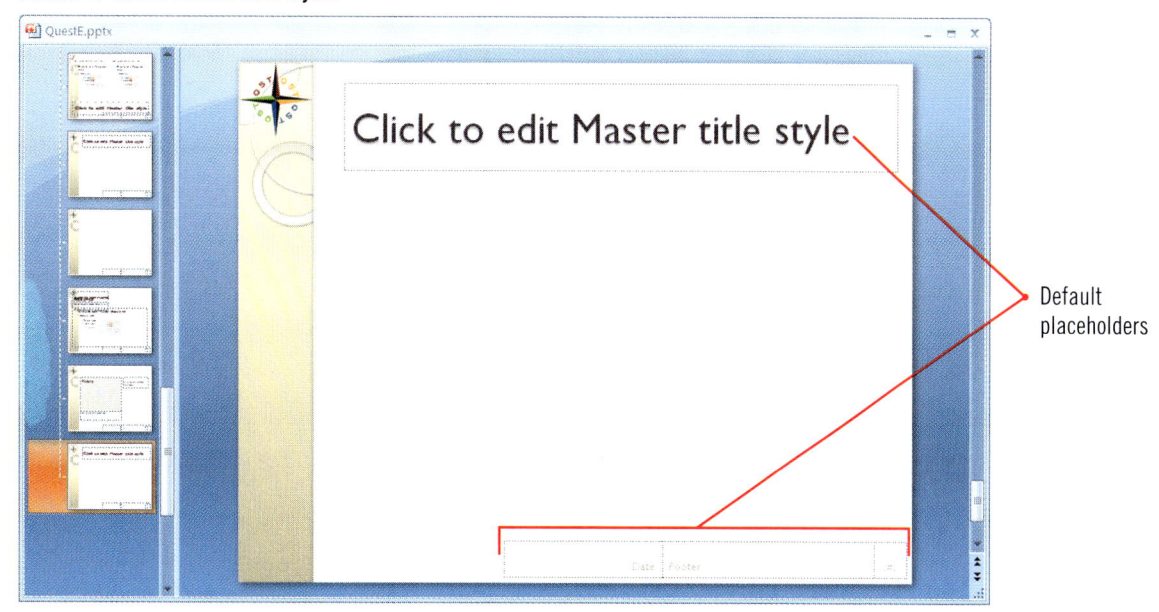

FIGURE E-8: Custom slide layout with new picture placeholders

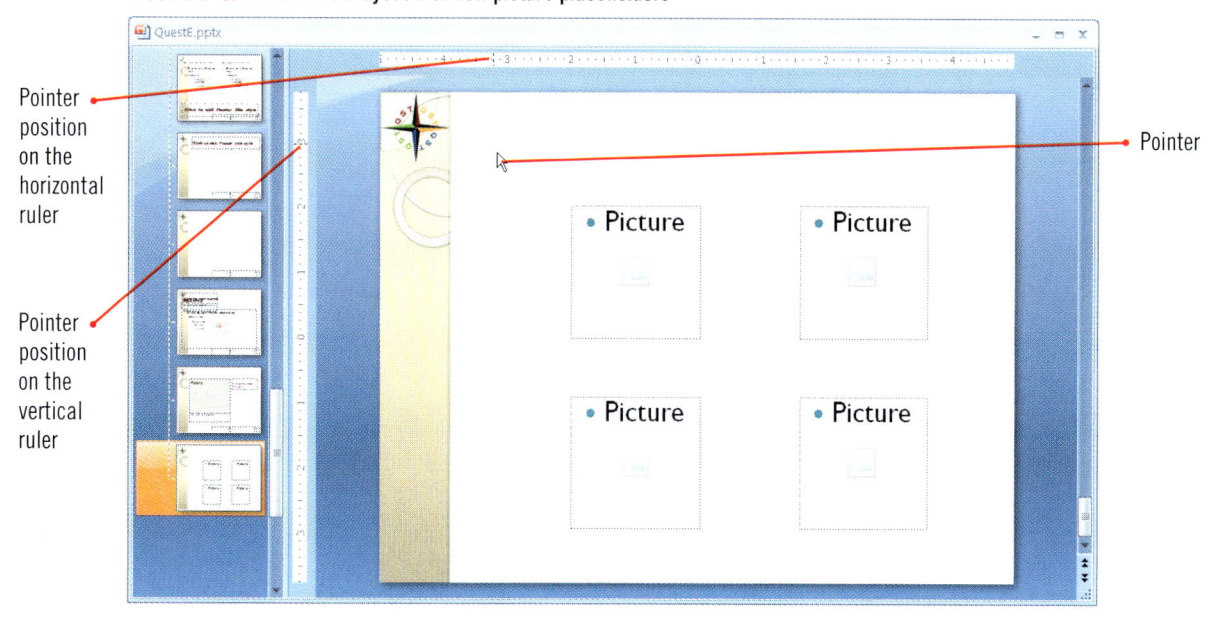

Pointer position on the horizontal ruler

Pointer position on the vertical ruler

Pointer

Restoring the Slide Master layout

If the Slide Master is missing a placeholder, you can click the Master Layout button in the Master Layout group to reapply the placeholder. Clicking the Master Layout button opens the Master Layout dialog box, as shown in Figure E-9. Click the placeholder check box to reapply the placeholder. To restore a slide layout in Slide Master view, click the Insert Placeholder button arrow in the Master Layout group, click the desired type of placeholder, then draw the placeholder on the Slide Master layout.

FIGURE E-9: Master Layout dialog box

Working with Advanced Tools and Masters

Formatting Master Text

To ensure that you use a consistent blend of fonts and font styles throughout the presentation, you should format slide text using standard theme fonts or make changes to the text placeholders in Slide Master view. A font theme defines two fonts—a major font (for headings) and a minor font (for body text). The fonts used in a theme can be the same font or two contrasting fonts. You can also make specific changes to master text, by opening the Slide Master view and changing the text color, style, size, and bullet type. When you change a bullet type, you can use a character symbol from a font, a picture from the Clip Gallery (or other source), or an image that you scan into your computer. You decide to make a few formatting changes to the master text placeholder of your presentation.

STEPS

1. **Click the Design tab on the Ribbon, click the Fonts button in the Themes group, slowly move your pointer over the visible font themes in the gallery, click the down scroll arrow twice, then click Equity**

   The font theme for the whole presentation changes from the Solstice theme to the Equity theme. When you change a theme, whether it's the font theme, color theme, effects theme, or design theme, you actually change the Slide Master. You like the new font theme, but decide to make some minor changes in Slide Master view.

2. **Press [Shift], click the Normal button on the status bar, release [Shift], then click the Solstice Slide Master thumbnail (first thumbnail) in the left pane**

   Slide Master view appears with the Slide Master displayed in the Slide pane.

3. **Right-click Click to edit Master text styles in the master text placeholder, click the Bullets button list arrow on the Mini toolbar, then click Bullets and Numbering**

   The Bullets and Numbering dialog box opens. The Bulleted tab is selected; the Numbered tab is used to create sequentially numbered or lettered bullets.

   > **QUICK TIP**
   > To insert a picture bullet, click Picture in the Bullets and Numbering dialog box, then click the desired bullet.

4. **Click Customize, click the Font list arrow, then click Webdings**

   The available bullet choices change.

5. **Scroll to the top of the dialog box, click the symbol shown in Figure E-10, then click OK**

   The new symbol appears in the Bullets and Numbering dialog box.

6. **Click the Color list arrow, in the Theme Colors section click Indigo, Accent 6, click the Size down arrow until 65 appears, then click OK**

   The color and size of the new bullet in the first level of the master text placeholder is modified.

   > **QUICK TIP**
   > To reset the bullet to the default symbol, click Reset in the Bullets and Numbering dialog box. Clicking Reset does not change the color or size back to their original default settings.

7. **Click the Normal button on the status bar, then click the Slide 2 thumbnail in the Slides pane**

   You see how the changes affect the body text bullets in Normal view. Compare your screen to Figure E-11.

8. **Save your changes**

FIGURE E-10: Symbol dialog box

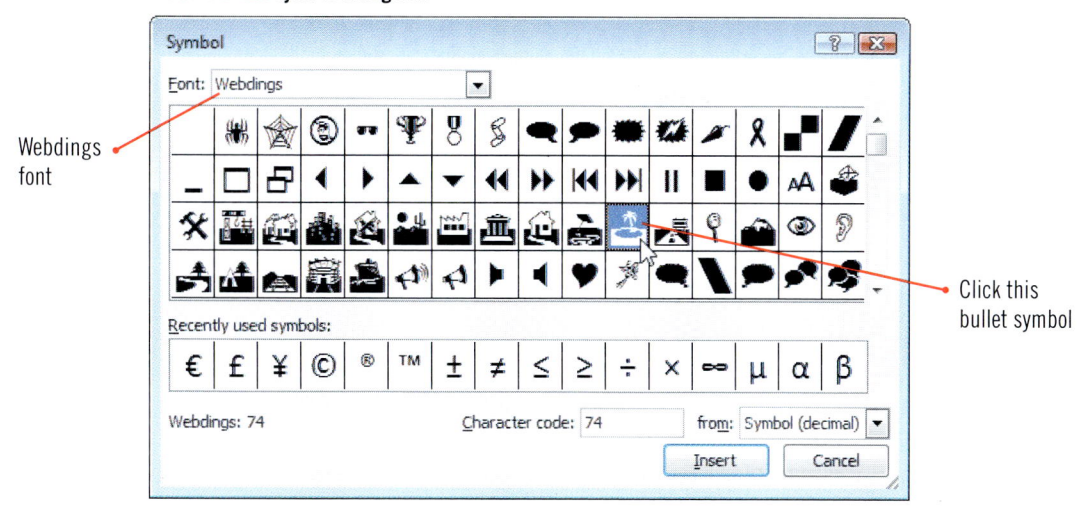

Webdings font • Click this bullet symbol

FIGURE E-11: Slide showing new bullets

New bullet symbol

Exceptions to the Slide Master

If you change the format of text on a slide and then apply a different theme to the presentation, the slide that you formatted retains the text formatting changes you made rather than taking the new theme formats. These format changes that differ from the Slide Master are known as **exceptions**. Exceptions can only be changed on the individual slides where they occur. For example, you might change the font and size of a particular text object on a slide to make it stand out and then decide later to add a different theme to your presentation. The text you formatted before you applied the theme is an exception, and it is unaffected by the new theme. Another way to override the Slide Master is to remove the background graphics on one or more slides. You might want to do this to get a clearer view of your slide text. Click the Design tab, then click the Hide Background Graphics check box in the Background group to select it.

Working with Advanced Tools and Masters

Changing Master Text Indents

Master text and content placeholders have nine levels of text, called **indent levels**. You can modify indent levels using PowerPoint's ruler. For example, you can change the space between a bullet and text of an indent level or change the position of the whole indent level. The position of each indent level on the ruler is represented by two small triangles and a square called **indent markers**. You can modify an indent level by moving these indent markers on the ruler. You can also set tabs on the horizontal ruler, which identifies where a text indent or a column of text begins. By clicking the **tab selector** located at the far left of the horizontal ruler, you are able to choose which of the four tab options you want to use. Table E-1 describes PowerPoint's indent and tab markers. To better emphasize the text in the master text placeholder, you change the first two indent levels.

STEPS

1. **Press [Shift], then click the Normal button on the status bar, release [Shift], then click the Solstice Slide Master thumbnail (first thumbnail) in the left pane**
   Slide Master view opens.

2. **Click anywhere in the first line of text in the master text placeholder, click the View tab on the Ribbon, then click the Ruler check box in the Show/Hide group**
   The horizontal and vertical rulers for the master text placeholder appear. The indent markers, on the horizontal ruler, are set so that the first line of text in each level—in this case, the bullet—begins to the left of subsequent lines of text. This is called a **hanging indent**.

   TROUBLE
   If you accidentally drag an indent marker past the ½" mark, click the Undo button on the Quick Access toolbar.

3. **Position the pointer over the Hanging Indent marker, then drag to the ½" mark on the ruler**
   The space between the first indent level bullet and text increases. Compare your screen to Figure E-12.

4. **Click anywhere in the second line of text in the master text placeholder, then drag the Left indent marker to the ⅞" position shown in Figure E-13**
   The whole indent level moves to the right.

5. **Click the Normal button on the status bar, then click the Slide 7 thumbnail in the Slides pane**
   Slide Master view closes and Slide 7 appears, showing the indent changes in the body text object. A left tab stop on the ruler will allow you to move a word and align it with text above it.

6. **Click to the left of the word combined in the body text object to place the insertion point, then click under the 2 in the horizontal ruler**
   A left-aligned tab appears in the ruler.

7. **Press [Tab]**
   The word "combined" moves to the right and is aligned with the text above it as shown in Figure E-14.

8. **Click the Ruler check box in the Show/Hide group, then save your changes**
   The rulers close and are no longer visible.

Working with Advanced Tools and Masters

FIGURE E-12: First-level text with moved hanging indent marker

— Move the hanging indent to here
— Space between the bullet and text increases

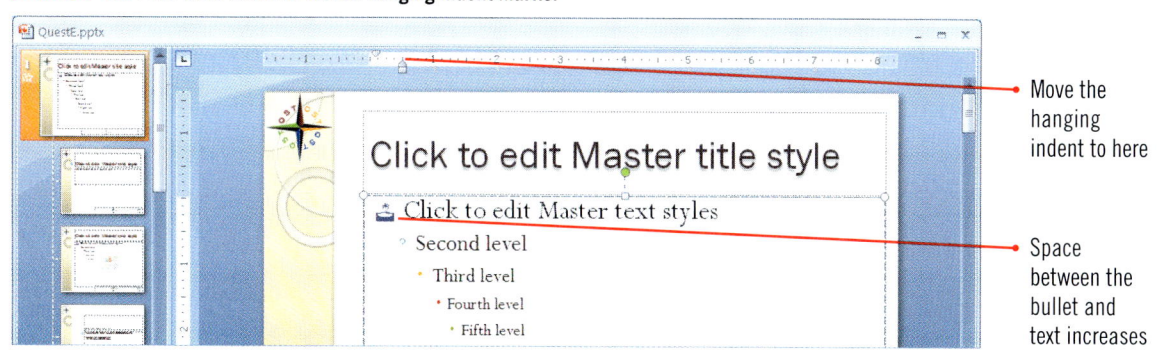

FIGURE E-13: Slide showing moved second-level indent

— Left indent marker
— Indent level moves to the right

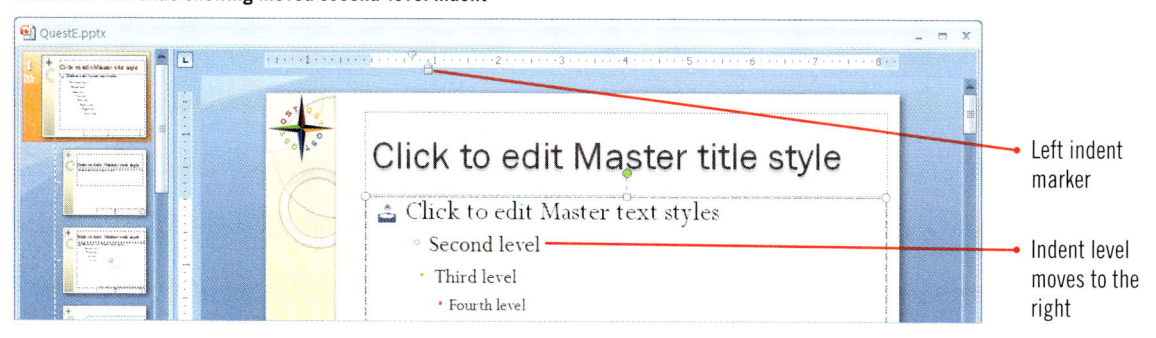

FIGURE E-14: Slide showing left tab stop

— Left tab stop
— Tabbed word

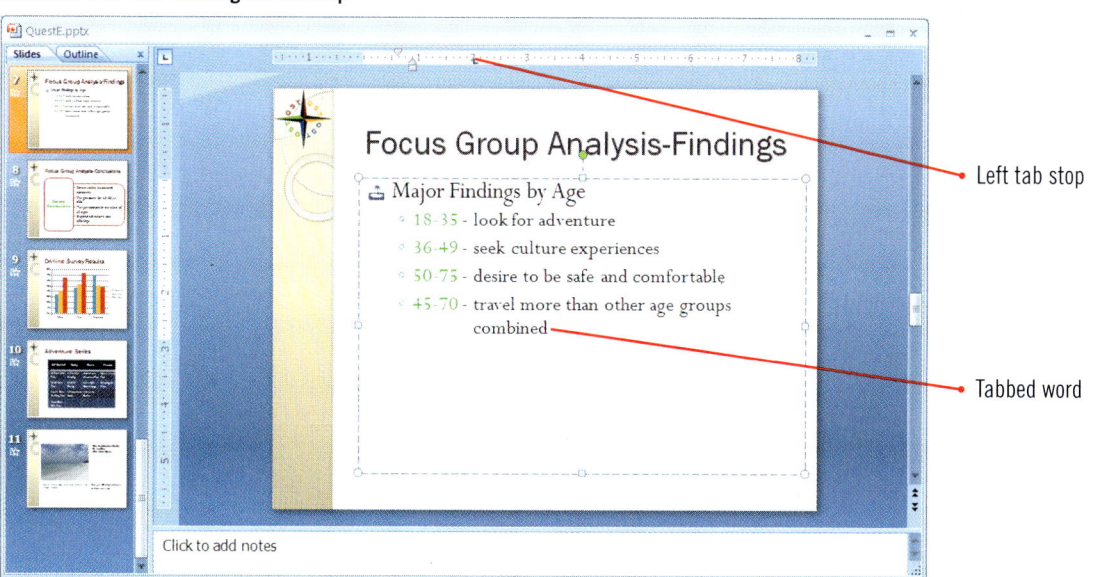

TABLE E-1: Indent and Tab Markers

symbol	name	function
▽	First line indent marker	Controls the position of the first line of text in an indent level
△	Hanging indent marker	Controls the position of the hanging indent
☐	Left indent marker	Controls the position of subsequent lines of text in an indent level
⌊	Left-aligned tab	Aligns tab text on the left
⊥	Center-aligned tab	Aligns tab text in the center
⌋	Right-aligned tab	Aligns tab text on the right
⊥.	Decimal-aligned tab	Aligns tab text on a decimal point

Working with Advanced Tools and Masters

Adjusting Text Objects

You have complete control over the placement of text in PowerPoint, whether the text is in a shape or in a text object. All text in PowerPoint is created within a text box, which has **margins** that determine the distance between the edge of the text and all four edges of the text box. The space between lines of text or bullets can also be modified. There are two types of text spacing in PowerPoint: paragraph spacing and leading (rhymes with "wedding"). **Paragraph spacing** is the space before and after paragraphs (bullet levels). **Leading** refers to the amount of space between lines of text within the same paragraph (bullet level). Using the text alignment feature, you can move text within text boxes or shapes. You decide to move the text margin in the shapes on Slide 3 and then change paragraph spacing of the text object on Slide 7.

STEPS

1. **Click the Home tab on the Ribbon, click the Slide 3 thumbnail in the Slides tab, right-click a blank area of the slide, then click Ruler**

   Slide 3 appears in the slide pane with the rulers showing.

2. **Right-click the text Aim in the left arrow, click Format Shape on the shortcut menu, then drag the Format Shape dialog box to the right so you can see the indent markers on the ruler**

   When you right-click the text in the shape, the individual object is selected within the grouped object and the indent markers for the text appear in the ruler.

   > **QUICK TIP**
   > Easily rotate a shape or text box by dragging its rotate handle.

3. **Click Text Box in the left pane, in the Internal margin section click the Left up arrow until 0.3" appears, then click Close**

   Compare your screen to Figure E-15. The text margin moves to the right in the arrow and the text is centered in the shape.

4. **Right-click the text Higher in the right arrow, click Format Shape on the shortcut menu, then click Text Box in the left pane**

   The Format Shape dialog box opens.

5. **Click the Left up arrow until 0.3" appears, click the Wrap text in shape check box to remove the check mark, then click Close**

   The text margin is changed in the arrow shape. In order for the text not to automatically wrap within the shape, you turned the wrapping feature off.

   > **QUICK TIP**
   > You can also precisely change tab stops in the Paragraph dialog box, by clicking Tabs to open the Tab dialog box.

6. **Click the Slide 7 thumbnail in the Slides tab, select the four second-level bullets in the body text object, click the Line Spacing button in the Paragraph group, then click Line Spacing Options**

   The Paragraph dialog box opens.

7. **In the Spacing section type 24 in the Before text box, type 12 in the After text box, then click OK**

   The spacing before and after each bullet on Slide 7 increases.

8. **Click the Align Text button in the Paragraph group, click More Options, in the Text layout section click the Vertical alignment list arrow, click Middle Centered, then click Close**

   All of the text is aligned to the middle center of the text box. Compare your screen to Figure E-16.

9. **Right-click a blank area of the slide, click Ruler to close the ruler, then save your changes**

FIGURE E-15: Slide showing changed text margin

Changed text margin

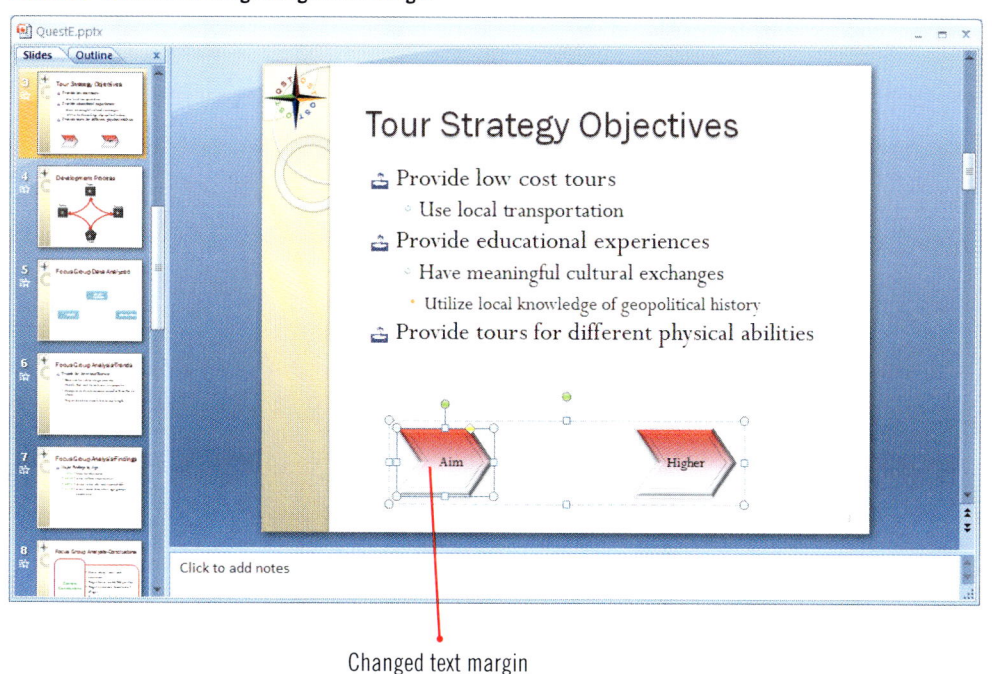

FIGURE E-16: Slide showing changed line spacing

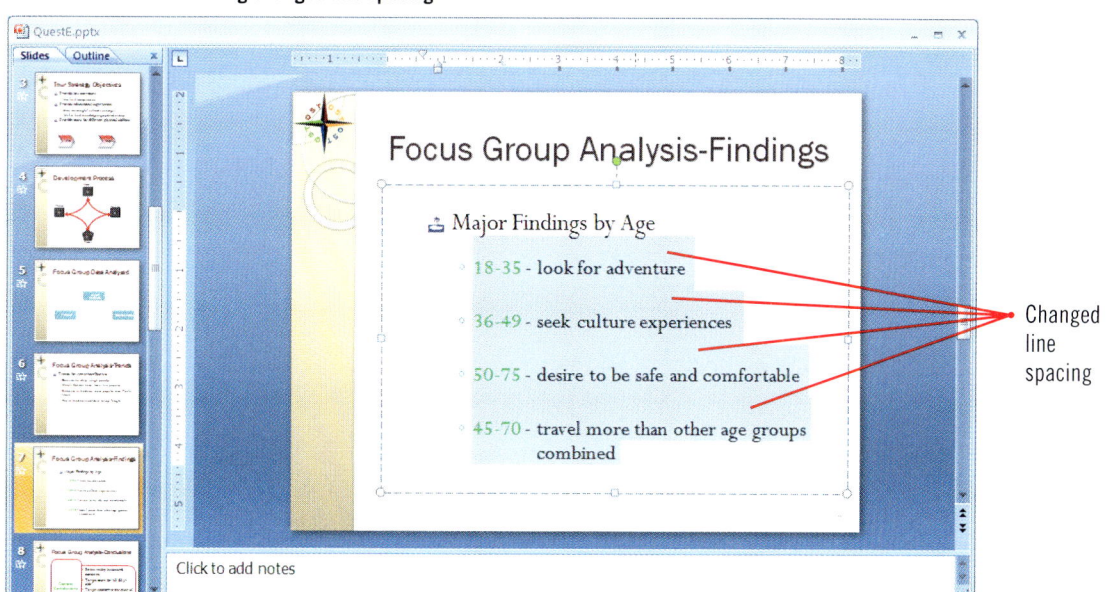

Changed line spacing

More on text spacing

The differences between paragraph spacing and leading can be confusing if you aren't used to working with text layouts, so let's look at the pages in this book for help. This paragraph you are reading has space between the lines of text; that space is called line spacing or leading. Now, look at the numbered steps of this lesson. The space between each numbered step is an example of paragraph spacing. So, when you add a hard return to create a new paragraph, that space is paragraph spacing. Paragraph spacing is often larger than leading, which helps distinguish paragraphs from individual lines of text within a paragraph.

Customizing Handout and Notes Masters

UNIT E
PowerPoint 2007

It is often helpful to provide your audience with supplemental materials to use during a presentation. Creating handouts for your audience provides them a way to follow along and take notes during your presentation and keep for future use. As the presenter, creating notes pages that you can refer to while giving the presentation can be extremely useful, especially when your presentation is complex or detailed. Before you create handouts or notes pages you might want to customize them to fit your specific needs. Ellen Latsky has asked you to prepare some supplemental materials for this presentation. You customize the Handout Master by changing the slides per page and the background style. Then you change the Notes Master by changing the page setup and the notes page orientation. Finally, you print both handouts and notes pages.

STEPS

1. **Click the View tab on the Ribbon, then click the Handout Master button in the Presentation Views group**

   The presentation's Handout Master view appears, showing a page with six large empty placeholders that represent where the slides will appear when you print handouts. There are four small placeholders, one in each corner of the slide, which are the header, footer, date, and number placeholders. Notice that the date placeholder displays today's date.

2. **Click the Background Styles button in the Background group, then click Style 9**

   When you print handouts on a color printer, they will have a gradient fill background.

3. **Click the Slides Per Page button in the Page Setup group, then click 3 Slides**

   Three slide placeholders appear on the left side of the handout as shown in Figure E-17.

   > **QUICK TIP**
   > To change the orientation of the slides on the handout, click the Slide Orientation button in the Page Setup group.

4. **Click the Header placeholder, drag the Zoom Slider to 100%, type European Tour Proposal, press [Pg Dn], click the Footer placeholder, then type Your Name**

   Now your handouts are ready to print.

5. **Click the Fit slide to current window button on the status bar, click the Office button, click Print, in the Print what list box click Handouts, in the Slides per page list box click 3, then click OK**

   Handouts of the presentation print using the options you've set.

6. **Click the Close Master View button in the Close group, click the View tab on the Ribbon, then click the Notes Master button in the Presentation Views group**

   Notes Master view opens showing four corner placeholders—one each for the header, footer, date, and number—a large notes text box placeholder, and a large Slide Master image placeholder.

7. **Click the Notes Page Orientation button in the Page Setup group, then click Landscape**

   The page orientation changes to landscape. Notice that all of the text placeholders are now stretched out. Compare your screen to Figure E-18.

8. **Click the Office button, click Print, in the Print what list box click Notes Pages, then click OK**

   Notes pages of the presentation print in landscape orientation.

9. **Click the Close Master View button in the Close group, save your work, then exit PowerPoint**

FIGURE E-17: Handout Master view

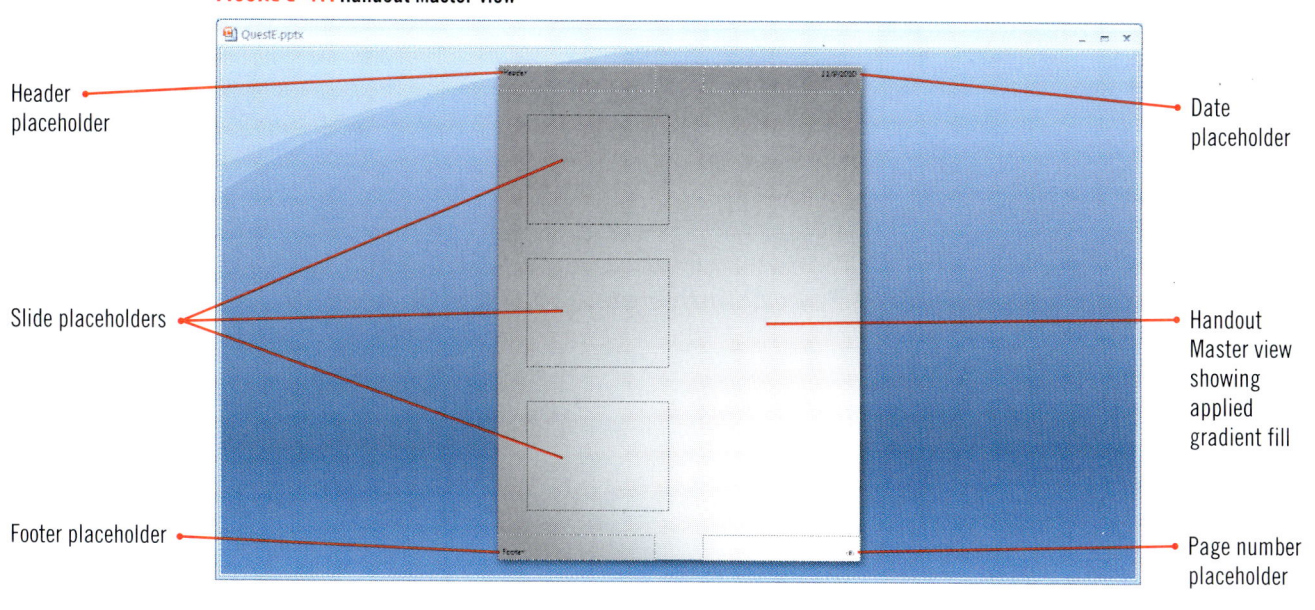

- Header placeholder
- Slide placeholders
- Footer placeholder
- Date placeholder
- Handout Master view showing applied gradient fill
- Page number placeholder

FIGURE E-18: Notes Master view

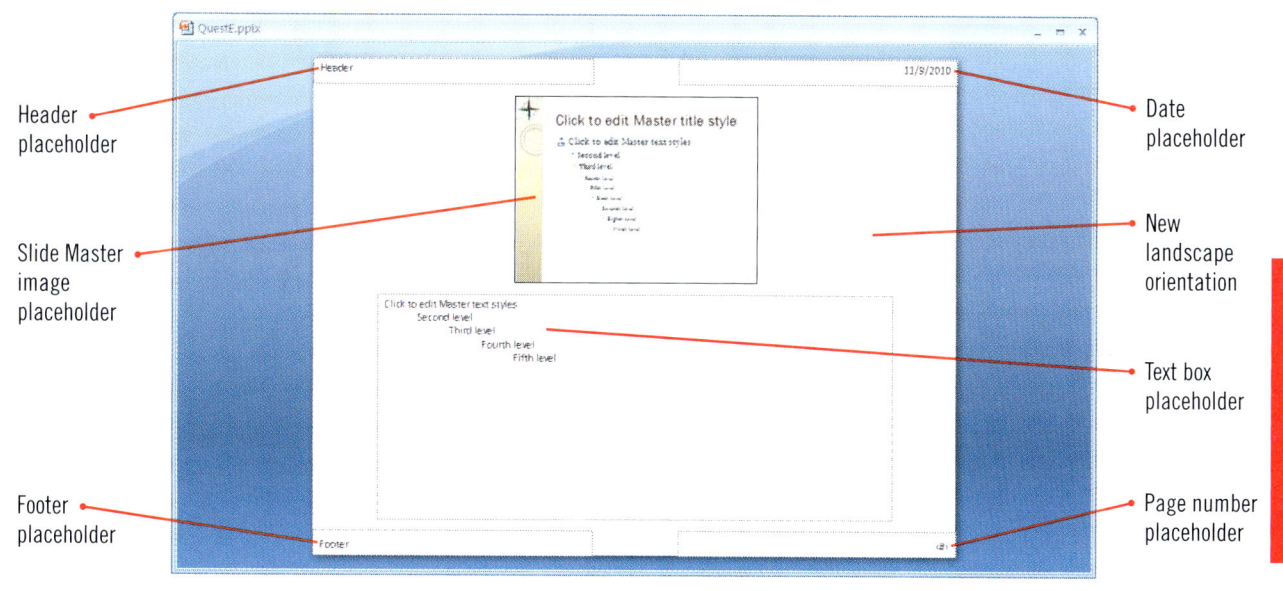

- Header placeholder
- Slide Master image placeholder
- Footer placeholder
- Date placeholder
- New landscape orientation
- Text box placeholder
- Page number placeholder

Creating handouts in Microsoft Office Word

Sometimes it's helpful to use a word processing program like Microsoft Office Word to create detailed handouts or notes pages. You might also want to create a Word document based on the outline of your presentation. To send your presentation to Word, click the Office button, point to Publish, then click Create Handouts in Microsoft Office Word. The Send to Microsoft Office Word dialog box opens and provides you with five document layout options from which to choose. There are two layouts that include notes entered in the Notes pane. Select a layout, then click OK. Word opens and a new document opens with your inserted presentation, using the layout you selected. To send just the text of your presentation to Word, click the Outline only document layout.

Working with Advanced Tools and Masters   PowerPoint 113

Practice

▼ CONCEPTS REVIEW

If you have a SAM user profile, you may have access to hands-on instruction, practice, and assessment of the skills covered in this unit. Log in to your SAM account (http://sam2007.course.com/) to launch any assigned training activities or exams that relate to the skills covered in this unit.

Label each of the elements of the PowerPoint window shown in Figure E-19.

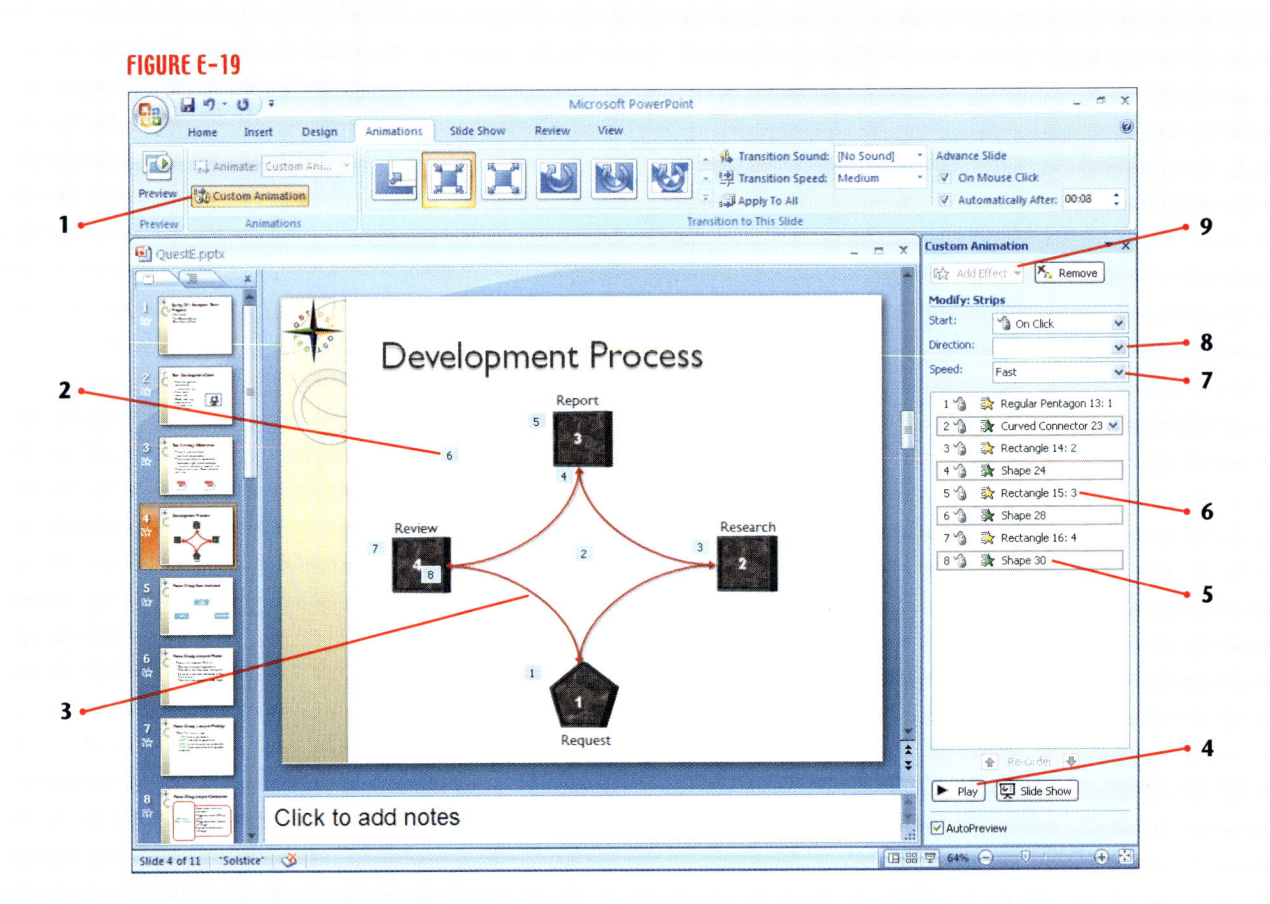

FIGURE E-19

Match each of the terms with the statement that describes its function.

10. Format Painter tool
11. Tab
12. Indent level
13. Hanging indent
14. Leading
15. Paragraph spacing

a. Identifies where the text indent or column of text begins
b. A text level in a text object, usually started with a bullet
c. Picks up attributes from an object and applies them to another object
d. The space between lines of text
e. The space after a hard return
f. The first line of text begins to the left of subsequent lines of text

Working with Advanced Tools and Masters

Select the best answer from the list of choices.

16. What appears at either end of a line or arrow that indicates it's attached to two shapes?
    a. Red handles
    b. Anchor points
    c. Attachment sites
    d. Connection handles
17. What is a connection site?
    a. An attachment point for a placeholder in a custom layout
    b. The anchor point of a text box
    c. The end of a connector arrow
    d. The attachment point on a shape for a connector
18. The small triangles and square that represent the position of each level in a text placeholder are:
    a. Ruler marks.
    b. Indent levels.
    c. Indent markers.
    d. Tabs.
19. Which of the following statements about connectors is not correct?
    a. The line connector has a rotate handle in the middle of it to adjust the line's path.
    b. You can attach a connector to different points on a shape.
    c. You can draw more than one connector at the same time by locking the drawing mode.
    d. Rearranging shapes connected with connectors moves the connectors to better connection sites.
20. In PowerPoint, tabs:
    a. Determine the location of margins.
    b. Determine spacing between lines of text.
    c. Identify where a text indent begins.
    d. Can be only left- or center-aligned.
21. The Format Painter button:
    a. Changes the order of shapes on a slide.
    b. Is the feature you use to paint objects in PowerPoint.
    c. Picks up and applies formatting attributes from one object or slide to another.
    d. Allows you to change the type of shape.

▼ SKILLS REVIEW

1. **Draw and format connectors.**
    a. Start PowerPoint and open the presentation PPT E-2.pptx, then save it as **BookShop** to the drive and folder where you store your Data Files.
    b. Go to Slide 4, click the Shapes button in the Drawing group, right-click Elbow Arrow Connector, then click Lock Drawing Mode.
    c. Position the pointer over the left connection site of the Plant shape, then drag to the top connection site of the Regional Warehouse shape.
    d. Position the pointer over the right connection site of the Plant shape, drag to the top connection site of the Individual Stores shape, then press [Esc].
    e. Click the Shapes button, click Line, position the pointer over the right connection site of the Regional Warehouse shape, then drag to the left connection site of the Individual Stores shape.
    f. Select all three connectors, right-click one of the connectors, click Format Object, make the connectors 2 pt wide and change the line color to Black, click Close, then deselect the objects.
    g. Right-click the connector between Regional Warehouse shape and the Individual Stores shape, click Format Shape, click the Dash Type list arrow, click Dash Dot, then click Close.
    h. Change the Elbow Arrow connectors' arrow heads End type to Diamond Arrow and their End size to Arrow R Size 9.
    i. Save the presentation.
2. **Use advanced formatting tools.**
    a. Go to Slide 1.
    b. Right-click the text object in the lower-right corner of the slide, then click Format Shape.
    c. Click the Gradient fill option button, click the Preset colors list arrow, then click Moss.
    d. Click Line Style in the left pane, then click the Width up arrow until 3 pt appears.

▼ SKILLS REVIEW (CONTINUED)

   e. Click Shadow in the left pane, click the Presets list arrow, click Offset Bottom, click the Distance up arrow until 5 pt appears, then click Close.
   f. Double-click the Format Painter button in the Clipboard group to pick up the format of the selected text box on the title slide, apply it to each of the diamond objects on Slide 4, then press [Esc].
   g. Save your changes.

3. **Customize animation effects.**
   a. Click the Animations tab, click the Plant shape, click the Custom Animation button, then click Add Effect.
   b. Point to Entrance, click More Effects, click Diamond, then click OK.
   c. Select the arrow connectors, add the Strips Entrance effect, then select the right arrow connector.
   d. Click the Direction list arrow, click Right Down, then click Play.
   e. Select the Regional Warehouse and Individual Stores shapes, add the Dissolve In Entrance effect, add the Flash Bulb Emphasis effect, then click Play.
   f. Select the dotted line, add the Ease In Entrance effect, then click Play.
   g. Select the arrow connectors, change the animation speed to Fast, then click Play.
   h. Close the task pane, then save your changes.

4. **Create custom slide layouts.**
   a. Switch to Slide Master view, then click the last slide layout in the left pane.
   b. Display the ruler and the drawing guides, then insert a new layout.
   c. Add a 3" square Media placeholder, move the vertical guide left to 4.49, move the horizontal guide up to 0.98, then move the Media placeholder to the intersection of the guides.
   d. Move the vertical guide right to 0.47 to the left of the zero mark, add a 4" × 3" Table placeholder, then move the placeholder to the intersection of the guides.
   e. Name the custom slide layout Media Table, turn off guides, then save your work.

5. **Format master text.**
   a. Click the Flow Slide Master in the left pane, then make the first-level bulleted item in the master text placeholder bold.
   b. Change the bullet symbol of the first-level bullet to a character bullet. In the Wingdings character set, select character code 38, the sixth bullet from the left in the first row.
   c. Use the Bullets and Numbering dialog box to set the size of the bullet to 75% of the text.
   d. Change the bullet color to the Theme Color Green, Accent 5.
   e. Change the bullet symbol color of the second indent level to the Theme Color Dark Teal, Text 2.
   f. Save your changes.

6. **Change Master text indents.**
   a. Move the hanging indent marker of the first-level bullet to the ½" mark on the ruler and left indent marker of the second-level bullet as shown in Figure E-20.
   b. Hide the rulers, switch to Normal view, then save the presentation.

   FIGURE E-20

7. **Adjust text objects.**
   a. Press [Shift], right-click anywhere in the body text object on Slide 2, then click Format Shape on the shortcut menu.
   b. Click Text Box in the left pane, then change the vertical alignment of the text to Top Centered.
   c. Adjust the internal margin on the left and right sides to 0.5".
   d. Click the Resize shape to fit text option button, then click Close.

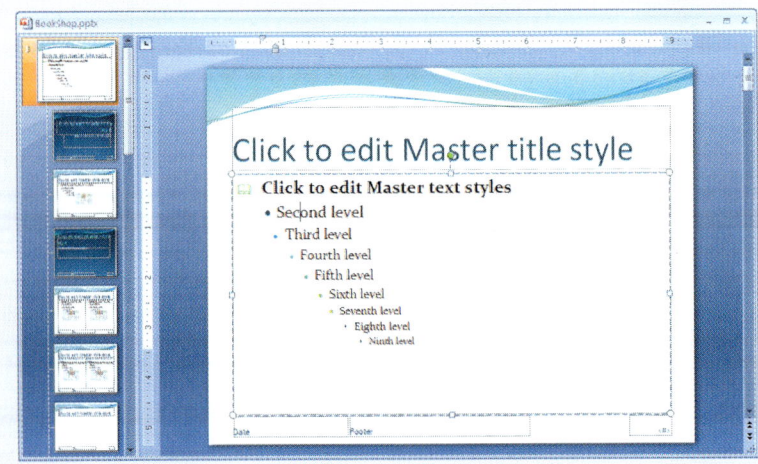

▼ SKILLS REVIEW (CONTINUED)

e. Figure E-21 shows you the completed presentation.

f. Save your changes.

8. Customize Handout and Notes Masters.

a. Switch to Handout Master view.

b. Change the slides per page to 4 slides, then change the handout orientation to Landscape.

c. In the header text placeholder type **BookShop**, then in the footer text placeholder type **Your Name**.

d. Close Handout Master view, then switch to Notes Master view.

e. Change the background style to Style 5, in the header text placeholder type **Product Report**, then in the footer text placeholder type **Your Name**.

f. Close Notes Master view, save your changes, then print the presentation as handouts, 2 slides per page.

g. Close the presentation and exit PowerPoint.

FIGURE E-21

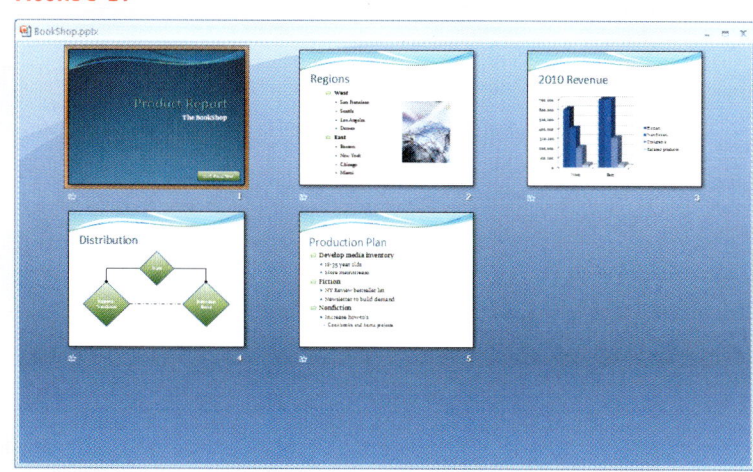

▼ INDEPENDENT CHALLENGE 1

You work in marketing at ZZ101 Records in Los Angeles, California. ZZ101 Records is a record label that specializes in alternative music and hip hop. As a growing record company, your business is looking for investment capital to expand its business markets and increase sales. It is your responsibility to develop a presentation that the owners can present to potential investors. You have been working on the content of the presentation and now you are ready to add custom animations and customize Slide Master text.

a. Open the presentation PPT E-3.pptx from the drive and folder where you store your Data Files, then save it as **ZZ101**.

b. Preview the presentation in Slide Show view.

c. Bold the first-level indent text, then change the bullet style in the first-level indent. See Figure E-22. (*Hint*: The bullet is a Webdings font (Character code 43) and is 85% of text size.)

d. Convert the text on Slide 4 to a SmartArt graphic using the Vertical Box List SmartArt graphic layout, then apply the Moderate Effect SmartArt Style to the graphic.

e. Select Slide 6, create at least two shapes connected by connectors and format all of the objects using advanced formatting techniques you learned in the lesson.

f. Use the Custom Animation task pane to apply animation effects to objects and text on at least three slides, then preview the presentation in Slide Show view.

g. Add your name to the notes and handouts footers, save the presentation, then print the slides of your final presentation as handouts in pure black and white.

h. Close the presentation and exit PowerPoint.

FIGURE E-22

Working with Advanced Tools and Masters

▼ INDEPENDENT CHALLENGE 2

You are the owner of The Reef Catering in Melbourne, New South Wales, Australia. You have built your business on private parties, wedding receptions, and special events over the last five years. To expand, you decide to pursue the business and hotel markets. Use PowerPoint to develop a presentation that you can use to gain corporate catering accounts.

a. Open the presentation PPT E-4.pptx from the drive and folder where you store your Data Files, then save it as **Reef**.
b. View the Oriel Slide Master slide. Change the Font theme to Foundry, then change the bullet in the first-level indent level to an arrow bullet.
c. Search PowerPoint clip art and add a koala bear to the Oriel Slide Master and the Title Slide Layout. Format the clip art as necessary.
d. Connect the shapes on Slide 4 using arrow connectors. Draw an Elbow arrow connector between each shape formatted with a 3 pt dash line and an Arrow R Size 7 end arrow style.
e. Switch to Slide 2 and change the text alignment and line spacing to create the best look.
f. Change the left internal margin of each shape on Slide 4 to 0".
g. Create a new custom slide layout using three different placeholders, then save the new layout as **Custom1**.
h. View the presentation in Slide Show view. Add your name to the handouts footer.
i. Save and print the presentation as handouts, 2 slides per page.

Advanced Challenge Exercise

- Switch to Slide 5, then select the body text object.
- Click the Home tab on the Ribbon, then click the Columns button in the Paragraph group.
- Click Two Columns.
- Save the presentation as **Reef ACE** to the drive and folder where you store your Data Files, then print the presentation as handouts, 2 slides per page.

j. Close the presentation and exit PowerPoint.1

▼ INDEPENDENT CHALLENGE 3

You are a computer game designer for The Zone, an Internet interactive game developer. One of your responsibilities is to develop new interactive game concepts and present the information at a company meeting. Complete the presentation provided, which promotes two new interactive Internet game concepts you've developed. Use the following game ideas in your presentation or create two of your own.

- **US Forces I** is an interactive World War II game where you play an American serviceman. You have the option to play with and against others online to achieve one of six different objectives.
- **TopSecret** is an interactive contemporary action/adventure game where you create a secret government agent who has to battle against evil forces to save nations or the world from destruction.

a. Open the presentation PPT E-5.pptx from the drive and folder where you store your Data Files, then save it as **Zone**. If you develop your own material, open a new presentation, storyboard the ideas for the presentation, then create at least six slides. What do you want your audience to know about the product idea?
b. Apply a theme. Modify the theme as necessary, such as changing background objects, font theme, color theme, or effect theme.
c. Use clip art, photos, shapes, and other objects as necessary to enhance the presentation.
d. Edit any text and add any additional information to create a professional presentation.
e. Format the bullet and text in the Master text and title placeholders on the master slide layout to fit the subject matter.
f. Create a custom slide layout, name it **Concept**, then apply it to at least one slide in the presentation.

▼ INDEPENDENT CHALLENGE 3 (CONTINUED)

g. Change the page orientation of the Notes Master view to Landscape, add your name to the notes and handouts footer, then save the presentation.
h. View the presentation in Slide Show view.
i. Print the notes pages in pure black and white.

Advanced Challenge Exercise

- Click the Office button, point to Publish, then click Create Handouts in Microsoft Office Word.
- Click the Blank lines below slides option button, then click OK.
- Save the document as **Zone Handouts** to the drive and folder where you store your Data Files.
- Print the handouts, close the document, then exit Word.

j. Close the presentation and exit PowerPoint.

▼ REAL LIFE INDEPENDENT CHALLENGE

You work for the operations manager at the Southern State University student union. You have been working on a presentation that you eventually will publish to the college Web site that describes all of the services offered at the student union. Complete work on the presentation by working with masters and animation effects.

a. Open the presentation PPT E-6.pptx from the drive and folder where you store your Data Files, then save it as **SSU Union**.
b. Apply animation effects to all the objects in the presentation. Customize the animation speed and property as necessary.
c. Create a custom slide layout and apply it to a slide.
d. Format the bullet and text in the Master text and title placeholders on the master slide layout to fit the subject matter.
e. Modify master text indents on the master slide layout.
f. Change the page orientation of Handout Master view to Landscape, add your name to the notes and handouts footer, and save the presentation.
g. Adjust the alignment and line spacing of at least one text object.
h. View the presentation in Slide Show view.
i. Print the final presentation as notes pages in pure black and white.
j. Close the presentation and exit PowerPoint.

▼ VISUAL WORKSHOP

Create a slide that looks like the example in Figures E-23. Be sure to use connector lines. Add your name to the handout footer, then save the presentation as **Development**. Print the Slide view of the presentation. In addition, submit the final presentation as a printed handout.

FIGURE E-23

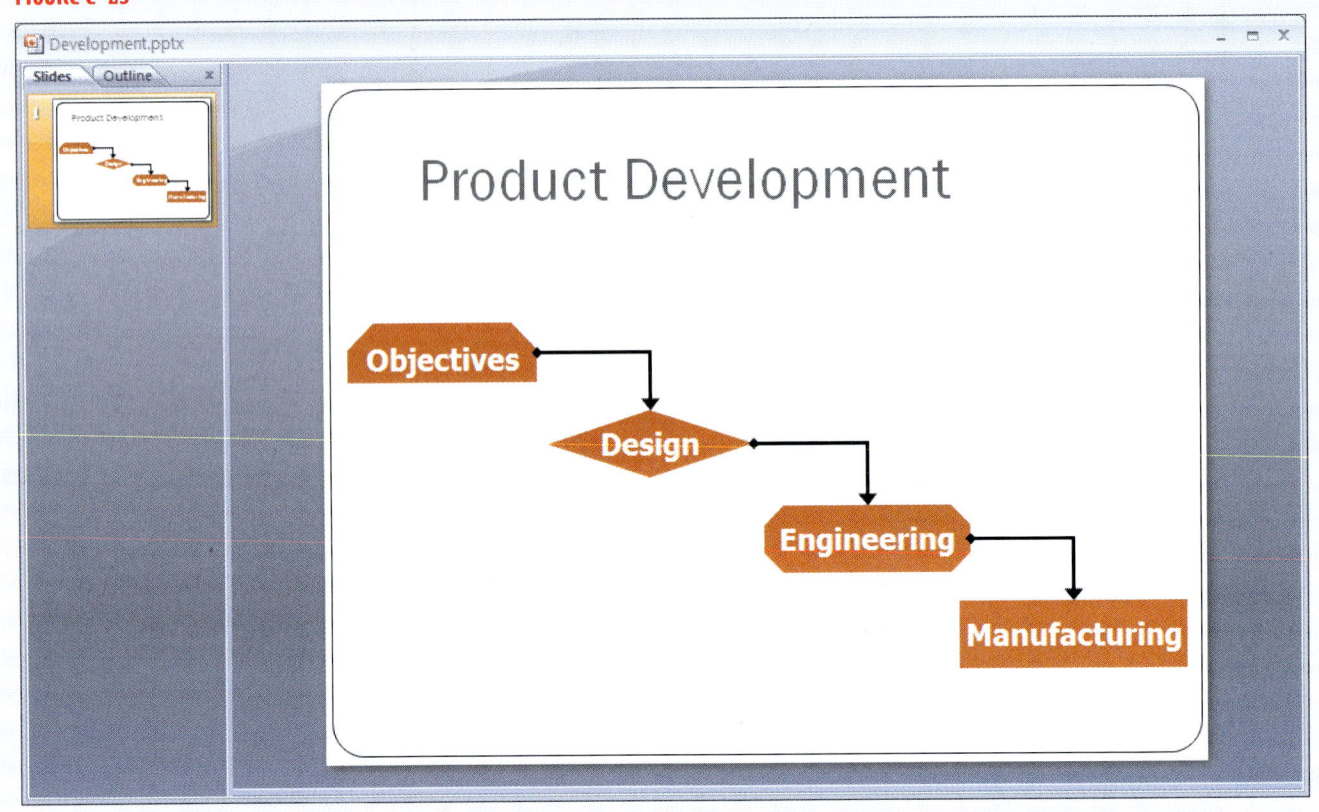

UNIT F
PowerPoint 2007

Enhancing Charts

Files You Will Need:
PPT F-1.pptx
PPT F-2.xlsx
PPT F-3.xlsx
PPT F-4.pptx
PPT F-5.xlsx
PPT F-6.xlsx
PPT F-7.pptx
PPT F-8.pptx
PPT F-9.pptx
PPT F-10.xlsx
PPT F-11.xlsx
PPT F-12.pptx
PPT F-13.xlsx
PPT F-14.xlsx

A PowerPoint presentation is first and foremost a visual communication tool. Slides that deliver information with relevant graphics have a more lasting impact on an audience than slides with plain text. The most effective way to display numerical data is to show the data graphically in a chart. You can show numerical data in many different ways including columns, bars, lines, or pie wedges. Deciding which type of chart best illustrates your data is important to consider when choosing a chart type. For example, a pie chart is designed to display data from one data series in proportion to the sum of all of the data series; whereas, a column chart is designed to display data changes over time or for demonstrating comparisons among data points. In this unit, you continue to work on the Quest Specialty Travel (QST) presentation that includes charts. You customize the chart layout, format chart elements, and animate the chart. Finally, you insert an Excel chart and link an Excel worksheet to the presentation.

OBJECTIVES

Work with charts in PowerPoint
Change chart design and style
Customize a chart layout
Format chart elements
Animate a chart
Embed an Excel chart
Link an Excel worksheet
Update a linked Excel worksheet

Working with Charts in PowerPoint

One of the best ways to enhance a presentation is to insert graphic elements such as a chart. When you have numerical data that you want to compare, a chart helps the audience visualize and understand the information. Because Excel is now fully integrated with PowerPoint, you can easily create fantastic-looking charts on the presentation slides. As you continue to develop the QST presentation, you plan to include charts on several slides.

DETAILS

Overview of charting in PowerPoint:

- **Create charts using Excel from PowerPoint**

  If you have Microsoft Office 2007 installed on your computer, PowerPoint uses Excel, by default, to create charts. If you don't have Excel, Microsoft Graph opens and displays a chart and a datasheet with sample data on your slide. You can enter your own data in the Graph datasheet or import data from another source. When you create a chart directly from a presentation slide using the Chart button, a sample chart is placed on the slide and a separate Excel window opens beside the PowerPoint window displaying the chart's data in a worksheet. Displaying both program windows at the same time provides you with the ability to work directly on the chart in the Excel window and see the changes on the slide in the PowerPoint window. See Figure F-1.

  > **QUICK TIP**
  > If you open a presentation with a chart that was created in Microsoft Graph, PowerPoint will recognize it and allow you to open and edit it using Excel.

- **Embed or link a chart**

  You have some options to choose from when considering how you want to insert an Excel chart (or any other object) to your presentation. There are two ways in which you can add a chart to a slide: you can embed it or link it. An embedded chart is an object created in another program and inserted in a slide. An embedded chart becomes a part of the presentation like a picture or a piece of clip art. The embedded chart's data is stored in an Excel worksheet that is incorporated into the presentation file. You can embed a chart in PowerPoint by creating it using the Chart button or by copying a chart from Excel and pasting it on a slide. A linked chart is different in that the chart that is displayed on the slide is not saved with the presentation. A linked chart is an object that is created in another program and is saved in a separate file. If you want to make changes to a linked Excel chart, you must open the saved Excel file that holds the chart.

- **Modify charts using styles and layouts**

  Because document themes and theme effects are alike for all Office programs, you can apply a specific theme or effect to a chart in Excel and PowerPoint will recognize the formatting. By using themes and effects, you don't have to format individual elements of a chart to match the colors and graphics in your PowerPoint file. You can, however, refine individual elements, such as the chart area, plot area, data series, or the legend of your chart. There are a number of chart layouts that you can apply to quickly change the layout of your chart. The chart layout specifies where chart elements, such as axes titles, data labels, and the legend, are displayed within the chart area. You cannot create your own chart layouts and styles, but you can create a template of a customized chart, which you can use later to apply to another chart.

  > **QUICK TIP**
  > A chart template does not save theme or style information, only chart type information.

- **Add advanced formatting to charts**

  You have a number of formatting options to choose from if you want to modify specific elements of a chart. The predefined styles will not always give you exactly the formatting options you want for a chart. For example, you may want to alter the way data labels look or how axes are displayed. You can specify the axes scales and adjust the interval between the values or categories. You can also add tick marks and specify the intervals between data points. **Tick marks** are small lines of measurement that intersect an axis and identify the categories, values, or series in a chart. Trendlines and error bars added to a chart provide more information about the data. A **trendline** is a graphical representation of an upward or downward trend in a data series, also used to predict future trends. **Error bars** identify potential error amounts relative to each data marker in a data series. Figure F-2 displays some advanced formatting items.

  > **QUICK TIP**
  > If you do not have Excel 2007 installed on your computer, you will not be able to utilize any of the advanced charting capabilities in the 2007 Microsoft Office system.

FIGURE F-1: PowerPoint and Excel windows open

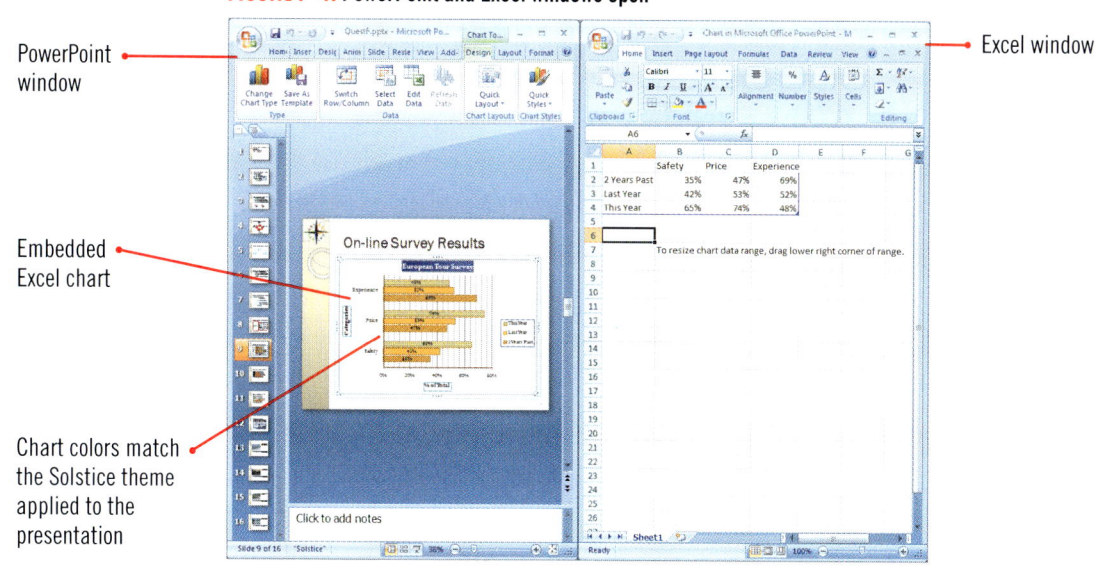

- PowerPoint window
- Embedded Excel chart
- Chart colors match the Solstice theme applied to the presentation
- Excel window

FIGURE F-2: Formatted chart

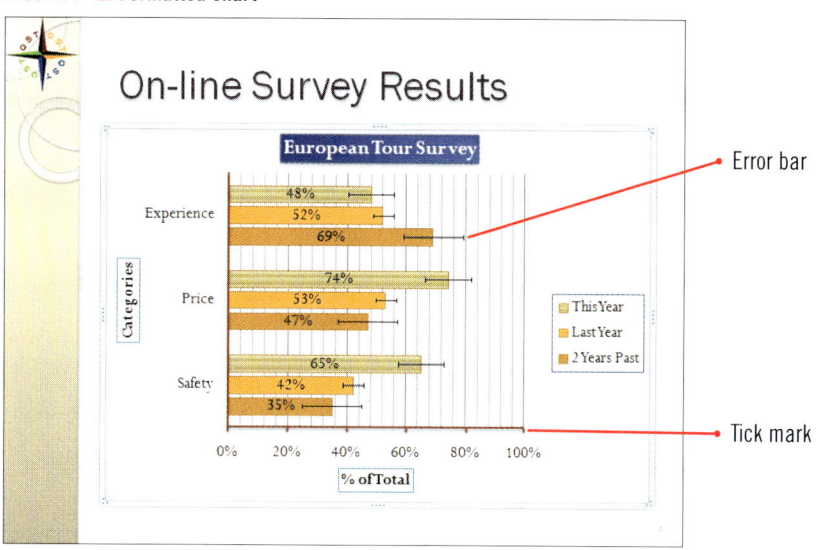

- Error bar
- Tick mark

Data series and data series markers

Each column or row of data in the worksheet is called a data series. Each data series has corresponding data markers in the chart, which are graphical representations such as bars, columns, or pie wedges. Figure F-3 shows how each data series marker in the chart corresponds to the data in the chart. Notice the correlation between the data in the Safety column of the datasheet and the data series markers in the chart.

FIGURE F-3: Chart and worksheet

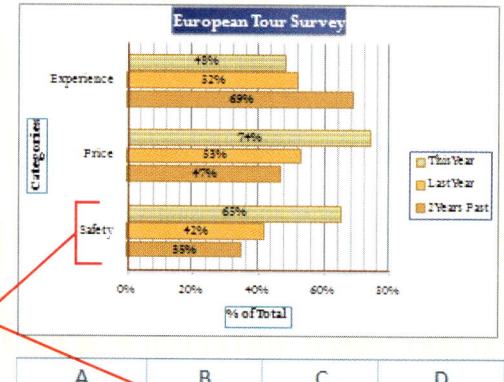

- Safety data series

	A	B	C	D
	Safety	Price	Experience
2 Years Past	35%	47%	69%
Last Year	42%	53%	52%
This Year	65%	74%	48%

Enhancing Charts

Changing Chart Design and Style

Being able to use Excel to create charts in PowerPoint offers you many advantages including the ability to format charts using Excel's Chart tools to customize the design, layout, and formatting. After you create a chart, you can immediately change the way it looks by individually changing different chart elements or by applying a predefined chart layout or style. The chart layout options are in the Quick Layout gallery. For example, you can select a chart layout that adds a chart title and moves the legend to the bottom of the chart. You can also easily change the color and effects of chart elements by applying one of the styles found in the Chart Quick Styles gallery. The chart that includes survey results needs some work. You change the chart layout, style, and type of the chart on Slide 9.

STEPS

1. **Start PowerPoint, open the presentation PPT F-1.pptx from the drive and folder where you store your Data Files, save the presentation as QuestF, click the View tab on the Ribbon, click the Arrange All button in the Window group, then click the Slide 9 thumbnail in the Slides tab**

   Slide 9 appears in the Slide pane.

2. **Click the chart, then click the Chart Tools Design tab on the Ribbon**

   The chart is selected and ready to edit.

3. **Click the More button in the Chart Layouts group, then click Layout 9 in the Quick Layout gallery**

   This particular layout option adds a chart title and value and category axis titles to the chart as shown in Figure F-4.

4. **Click the Chart Title, type European Tour Survey, click the Vertical (Value) Axis Title, type % of Total, click the Horizontal (Category) Axis Title, then type Categories**

   The new chart labels help identify aspects of the chart.

5. **Click the More button in the Chart Styles group, then click Style 36**

   The Style 36 option changes the colors of the data series markers to better match the presentation colors. This new style option also adds a light background color behind the data series markers, for better contrast with the graph.

6. **Click the Change Chart Type button in the Type group**

   The Change Chart Type dialog box opens.

7. **Click Bar in the left pane, make sure that Clustered Bar is selected, then click OK**

   The data series markers change from columns to bars and rotate 90 degrees.

8. **Click a blank area of the slide, then click the Save button on the Quick Access toolbar**

   Compare your screen to Figure F-5.

FIGURE F-4: Chart showing new layout

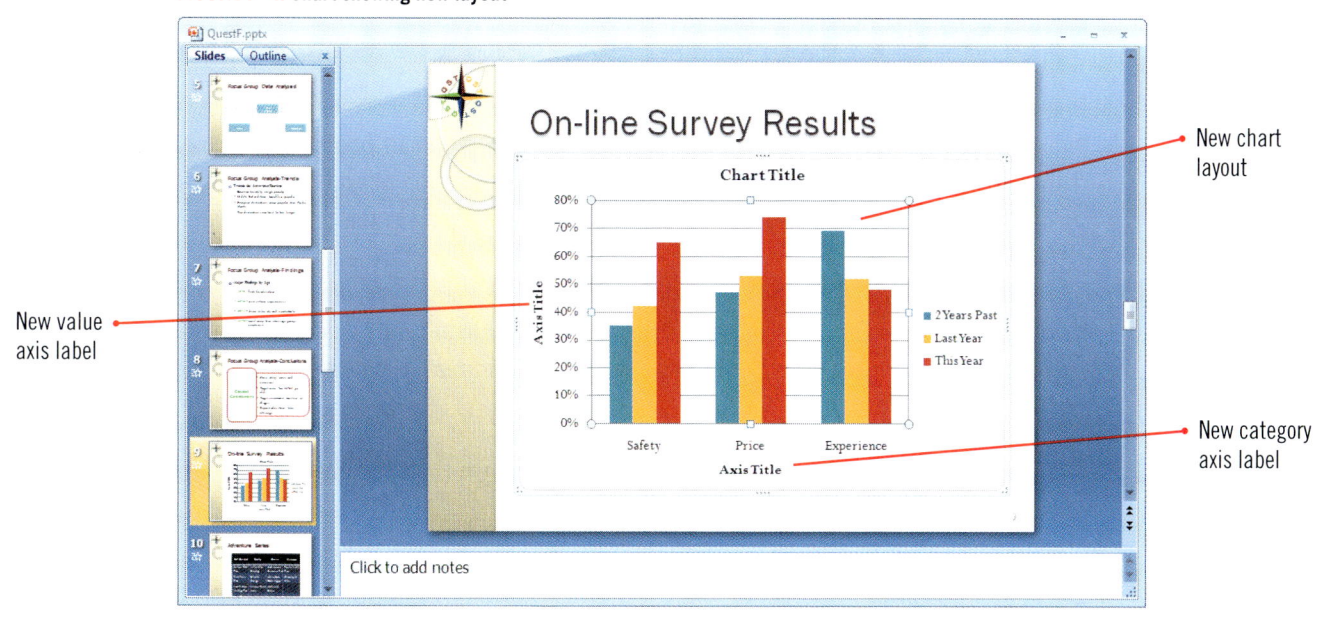

[Screenshot of PowerPoint slide "On-line Survey Results" with a column chart titled "Chart Title" showing Safety, Price, and Experience categories with 2 Years Past, Last Year, and This Year data series. Callouts: "New value axis label", "New chart layout", "New category axis label".]

FIGURE F-5: Chart showing new style and labels

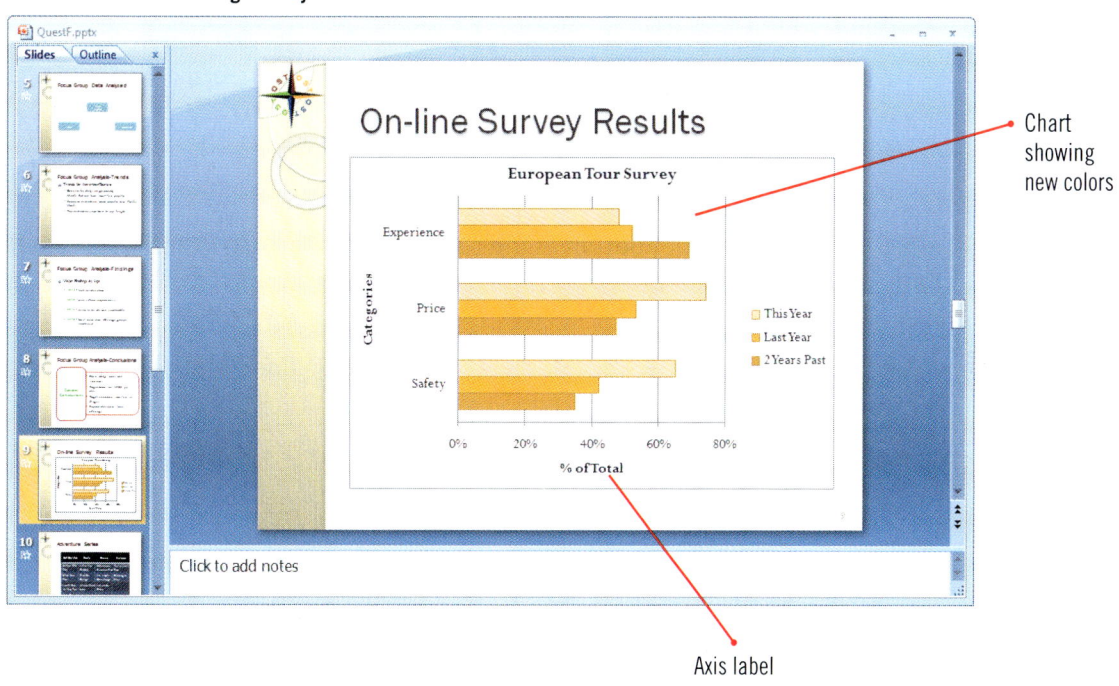

[Screenshot of PowerPoint slide "On-line Survey Results" with a horizontal bar chart titled "European Tour Survey" showing Experience, Price, and Safety categories with This Year, Last Year, and 2 Years Past data series in orange/yellow colors. Callouts: "Chart showing new colors", "Axis label".]

Save a chart as a template

If you create a customized chart that you want to reuse, you can save it as a template (*.crtx) to the Charts Template folder. Then, instead of re-creating the chart type, you can simply apply the chart template to an existing chart or create a new chart based on the template. To save a chart as a template, select the chart you want to save, then click the Save As Template button in the Type group on the Chart Tools Design tab. To apply a chart template to an existing chart, click the Change Chart Type button in the Type group, click Templates, then click the chart template.

Enhancing Charts PowerPoint 125

Customizing a Chart Layout

One of the many advantages of using Excel to create charts in PowerPoint is the ability you have to customize chart elements, such as labels, axes, gridlines, and the chart background. For example, you can change the plot area color so the data markers are distinctly set off or you can add gridlines to a chart to make it easier to read. Gridlines help make the data easier to read in the chart and extend from the horizontal or vertical axes across the plot area. There are two types of gridlines: major gridlines and minor gridlines. **Major gridlines** identify major units on the axis and are usually identified by a tick mark. **Minor gridlines** identify minor units on the axis and can also be identified by a tick mark. You decide to improve the appearance of the Survey Results chart by customizing some elements of the chart.

STEPS

QUICK TIP
You can easily add or remove a legend by clicking the Legend button in the Labels group on the Chart Tools Layout tab.

1. **Click the chart, click the Chart Tools Layout tab on the Ribbon, then click the Gridlines button in the Axes group**
   The Gridlines menu opens. The chart already has major gridlines on the vertical axis.

2. **Point to Primary Vertical Gridlines, then click Major & Minor Gridlines on the gallery**
   This adds minor vertical gridlines to the chart as shown in Figure F-6. Notice that the major gridlines are darker in color than the minor gridlines and are identified by a tick mark on the value axis at each unit of value.

3. **Click the Data Table button in the Labels group, then click Show Data Table with Legend Keys**
   You like seeing the data on the chart because it helps define the data markers, but using the data table takes up too much room on the slide and significantly decreases the size of the chart.

4. **Click the Data Table button in the Labels group, click None, click the Data Labels button in the Labels group, then click Center**
   The data table closes and data labels appear in the center of each data marker.

5. **Click the Axis Titles button in the Labels group, point to Primary Horizontal Axis Title, then click More Primary Horizontal Axis Title Options**
   The Format Axis Title dialog box opens.

6. **Click Border Color in the left pane, click the Solid line option button, click the Color list arrow, click the Brown, Accent 5 color box, then click Close**
   A brown border appears around the value axis title. The category axis title would also look good with a border around it.

QUICK TIP
To format any chart element quickly, right-click the element, then choose a command from the submenu or the Mini toolbar.

7. **Click the Vertical (Category) Axis Title, then press [F4]**
   A brown border appears around the category axis title. Pressing [F4] repeats the last formatting action.

8. **Click a blank area of the slide, then save your presentation**
   Compare your screen to Figure F-7.

Enhancing Charts

FIGURE F-6: Chart showing new minor gridlines

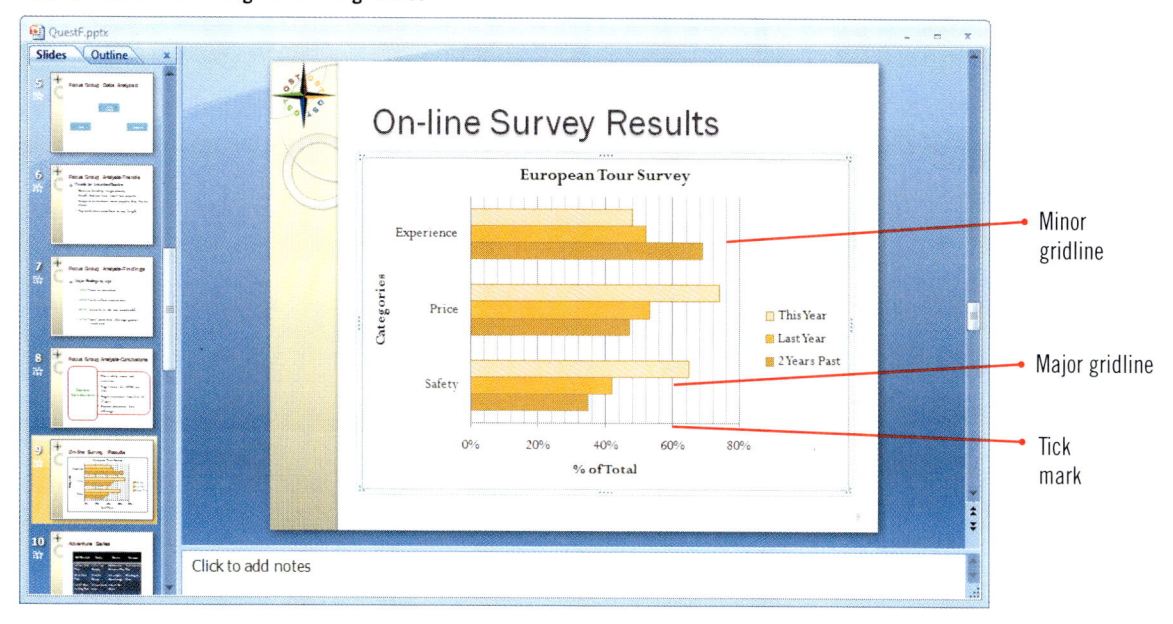

- Minor gridline
- Major gridline
- Tick mark

FIGURE F-7: Chart showing added and formatted elements

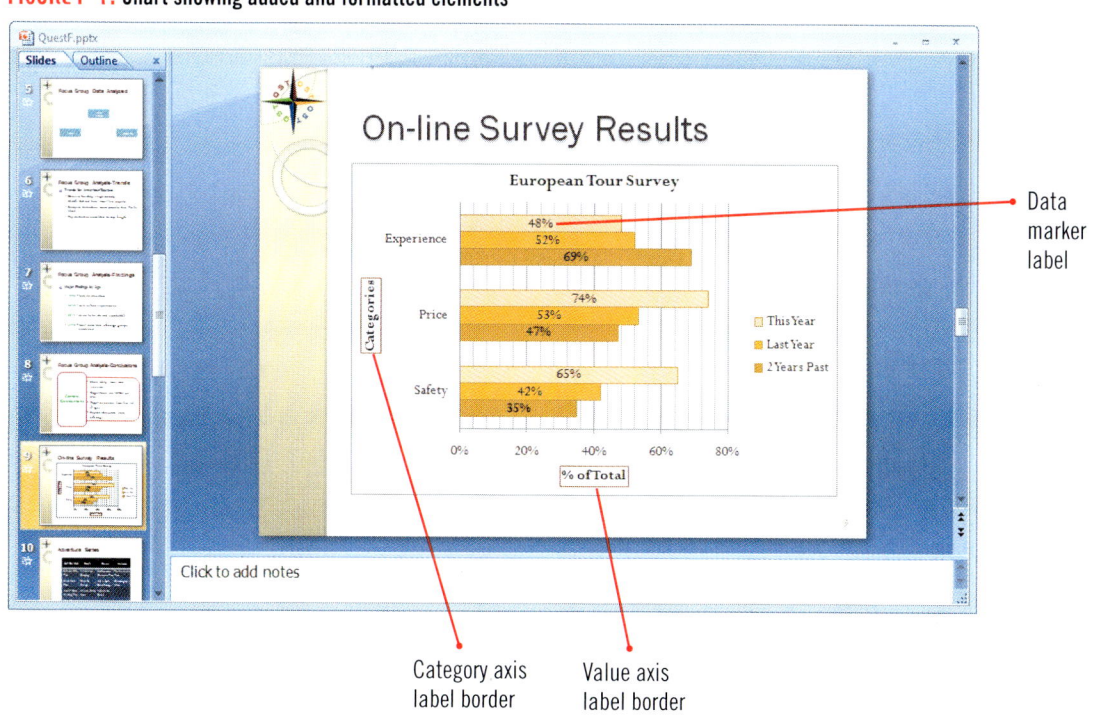

- Data marker label
- Category axis label border
- Value axis label border

Using the Research task pane

Sometimes when you are developing a presentation, you need help formulating your ideas or researching a subject. PowerPoint has an extensive set of online tools found in the Research task pane that gives you immediate access to many different kinds of information. The Research task pane provides the following research tools: an English dictionary, an English, French, and Spanish thesaurus, a word and phrase translator, four research Web sites (including an encyclopedia), and two business research Web sites. To open the Research task pane, click the Research button in the Proofing group on the Review tab. The Research options link at the bottom of the Research task pane provides additional research books and research sites that you can add to the Research task pane.

Enhancing Charts

Formatting Chart Elements

Quick Styles in PowerPoint provide you with a number of choices to modify all the elements in a chart. Even with all the Quick Style choices, you still may want to format individual elements to make the chart easy to look at and comprehend. Overall, you like what you have done to the European Tour survey chart so far, but you decide to format some individual elements of the chart to better fit the QST presentation design.

STEPS

QUICK TIP
You can also click a data marker in the chart to select all of the data series markers.

1. **Click the Chart, click the Chart Area list arrow in the Current Selection group, then click Series "This Year"**
   All of the This Year data markers are selected in the chart.

2. **Click the Chart Tools Format tab on the Ribbon, click the Shape Fill button in the Shape Styles group, point to Gradient, then click More Gradients**
   The Format Data Series dialog box opens.

3. **Drag the dialog box title bar to the left to move the dialog box off the chart, type –25 in the Series Overlap text box, then click Fill in the left pane**
   A small space is applied between the data markers for each data series in the chart. You can enter a value from –100% to 100% in the Series Overlap text box. A negative number adds space between each data marker while a positive number overlaps the data markers.

4. **Click the Gradient fill option button, click the Preset colors list arrow, click Gold (4th row), then click Close**
   The This Year data series markers change to a gold color. Compare your screen to Figure F-8.

5. **Click the chart title, then click the More button in the Shape Styles group**
   The Shapes Style gallery opens.

6. **Click Moderate Effect – Accent 6 (5th row), then click any one of the numbers on the value axis**
   Applying the new style to the chart title makes it stand out. Clicking any of the numbers on the value axis selects the entire axis.

7. **Click the More button in the Shape Styles group, click Moderate Line – Accent 5, click any one of the words on the Vertical (Category) Axis, then click Moderate Line – Accent 5 in the Shape Styles group**
   The new style applies a brown color and shadow to the axis and better defines the plot area.

8. **Right-click the chart legend, click Format Legend in the submenu, click Border Color in the left pane, then click the Solid line option button**
   A solid border line appears around the legend.

9. **Click the Color list arrow, click Indigo, Accent 6 (top row), then click Close**

10. **Click a blank area of the slide, then save the presentation**
    Compare your screen to Figure F-9.

Enhancing Charts

FIGURE F-8: Chart showing modified data markers

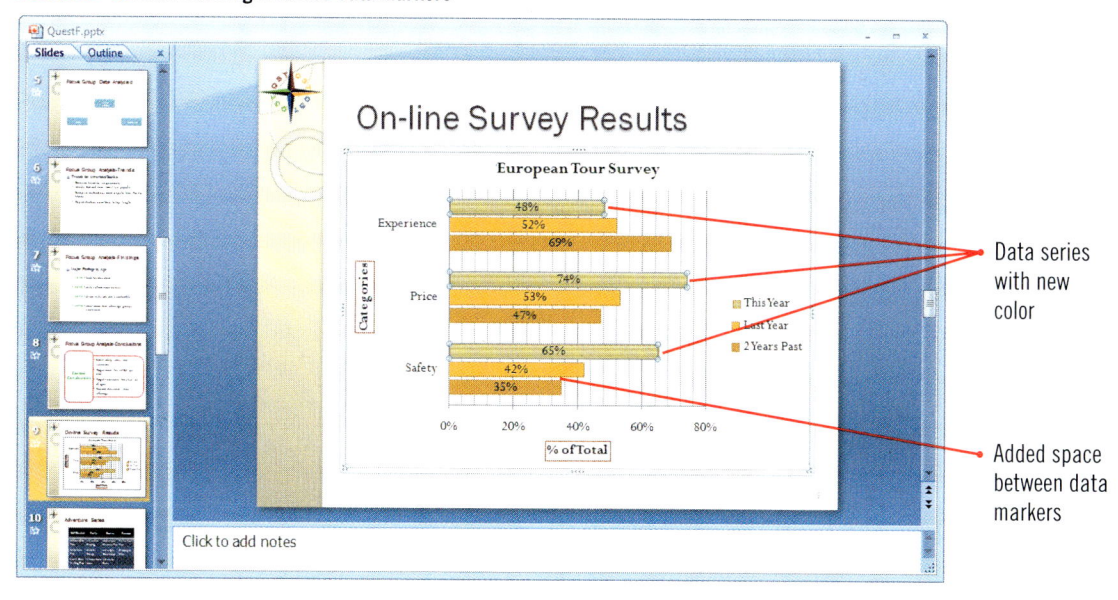

- Data series with new color
- Added space between data markers

FIGURE F-9: Completed chart

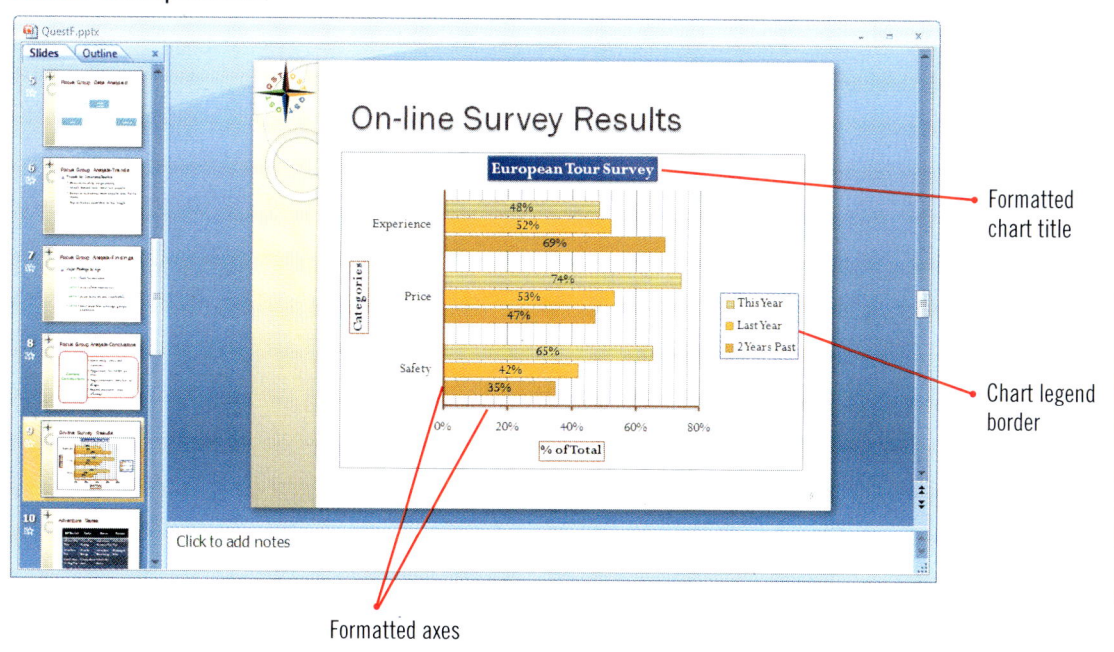

- Formatted chart title
- Chart legend border
- Formatted axes

Saving in PDF and XPS file formats

In certain situations, for example when sharing sensitive or legal materials with others, you may find it necessary to save your presentation file in a fixed layout format. A **fixed layout format** is a specific file format that "locks" the file from future change and allows others only the ability to view or print the presentation. To be able to save or export a presentation in a fixed layout format directly from PowerPoint, you first must download and install the Save as PDF or XPS add-in from the Microsoft Office 2007 Web site. (You may also choose another software solution that enables you to create a fixed layout format file.) Once you have the add-in installed, click the Office button, point to Save As, then click PDF or XPS. The Save As dialog box opens. Select the appropriate file type and other options to save your presentation in a fixed layout format. To view a fixed layout format presentation, you need appropriate viewer software that you can download from the Internet.

Enhancing Charts

Animating a Chart

UNIT F — PowerPoint 2007

You can animate elements of a chart, much in the same way you animate text and graphics. You can animate the entire chart as one object or you can animate the data markers. There are two options for animating data markers individually: by series or by category. Animating data markers individually by series displays data markers of each data series (or the same colored data markers). Animating data markers individually by category displays the data markers of each category in the chart. If you choose to animate the chart's data markers as a series, the entire data series animates as a group; the same is true for animating data markers by category. And, of course, you have complete control over the animation speed and the animation playing order. If you animate the chart background, individual data series markers, and other objects or text on the slide, it may be difficult for your audience to distinguish the key information on the slide. You decide to animate only the data series markers of the chart.

STEPS

1. **Click the Animations tab on the Ribbon, then click the Custom Animation button in the Animations group**
   The Custom Animation task pane opens.

   > **QUICK TIP**
   > Exit animation effects cause an object to leave the slide. To add an exit animation, click the Add Effect button, point to Exit, then select an effect.

2. **Click the chart, click the Add Effect button in the Custom Animation task pane, point to Entrance, then click More Effects**
   The Add Entrance Effect dialog box opens.

3. **In the Basic section, click Fly In, then click OK**
   The Fly In animation effect is added to the chart, and the chart is added to the animations list as Chart 5. Compare your screen to Figure F-10.

4. **Click the Chart 5 list arrow in the animations list in the Custom Animation task pane, then click Effect Options**
   The Fly In dialog box opens.

   > **QUICK TIP**
   > Due to the large number of animation options available with charts and other objects, be careful how many options and objects you animate on one slide.

5. **Click the Chart Animation tab, click the Group chart list arrow, click By Element in Series, click the Start animation by drawing the chart background check box to remove the check mark, then click OK**
   The Fly In dialog box closes. Then, each data series marker, by series, flies in from the bottom of the slide beginning with the 2 Years Past data series. Notice that there are nine animation tags on the chart, one for each data series marker. The chart background, which would have been animated by default, is not animated.

6. **Click the Direction list arrow in the Custom Animation task pane, click From Left, click the Speed list arrow, then click Fast**
   The direction of the animation effect now comes from the left and is slowed down slightly.

7. **Click the Chart 5 list arrow in the animations list, click Effect Options, in the Settings section, click the Smooth start check box, then click the Smooth end check box**
   Changing the smooth start and smooth end options slows the start and finish of the animation effect for each data series marker.

   > **QUICK TIP**
   > Click the Play button at the bottom of the Custom Animation task pane to view the chart animation again.

8. **Click the Timing tab, click the Start list arrow, click After Previous, type 2.5 in the Delay text box, then click OK**
   Watch closely at how the changed settings affect the progression of the data series markers animation. Using the After Previous setting and a 2.5 second delay between animations ensures that each data series marker is emphasized. Compare your screen to Figure F-11.

9. **Close the Custom Animation task pane, then save the presentation**

FIGURE F-10: Screen showing added animation effect

- You may not see the Add-Ins tab on your computer
- Animation tag
- Custom Animation task pane
- Chart 5 list arrow

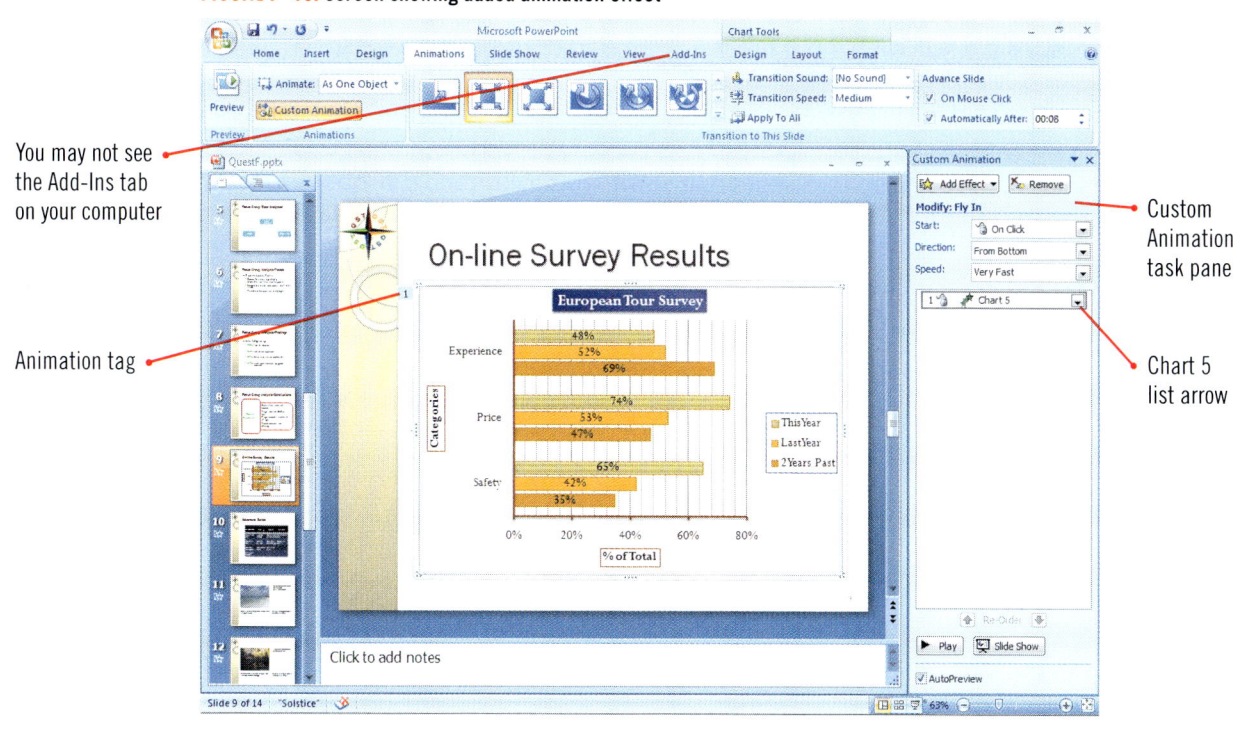

FIGURE F-11: Finished chart

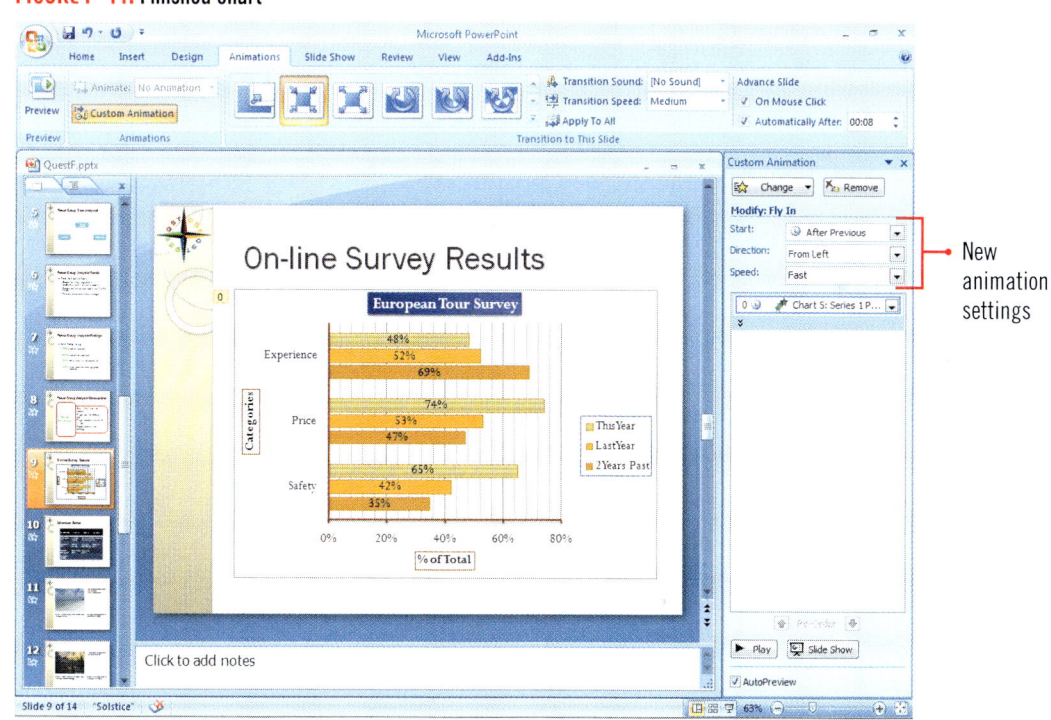

- New animation settings

Adding voice narrations

If your computer has speakers, a sound card, and a microphone, you can record a voice narration and then play it during your slide show. If you have a narration and other sounds that play automatically on the same slide, the voice narration takes precedence over the other sounds and will not play until you click them. To record a narration, click the Record Narration button in the Set Up group on the Slide Show tab. If you want the recording to be linked to the presentation, click the Link narrations in check box. If you do not select this option, the recording will be embedded in the presentation. If the Record Narration command is not available, then you do not have the necessary hardware.

Enhancing Charts   **PowerPoint 131**

Embedding an Excel Chart

UNIT F — PowerPoint 2007

When a chart is the best way to present information on a slide, you can create one within PowerPoint or you can embed an existing Excel chart directly to the slide. When you use another program to create an object, the program, Excel in this case, is known as the **source program**. The object you create with the source program is saved to a file called the **source file**. When you insert a chart into a presentation, the presentation file in which the chart is inserted becomes the **destination file**. Ellen wants to include supporting data from last year's sales numbers, so you insert an Excel chart on a new slide.

STEPS

> **QUICK TIP**
> You can also press [Ctrl][D] to duplicate a slide.

1. **With Slide 9 still selected, click the Home tab on the Ribbon, click the New Slide button list arrow in the Slides group, then click Duplicate Selected Slides**
   A new slide with a duplicate chart appears in the Slide pane and in the Slides tab.

2. **Select the slide title On-line Survey Results, type Quarterly Sales Figures, click the chart, then press [Backspace]**
   The slide has a new title and the duplicate chart is deleted.

3. **Click the Insert tab on the Ribbon, then click the Object button in the Text group**
   The Insert Object dialog box opens. Using this dialog box, you can create a new chart or locate an existing one to insert on a slide.

> **QUICK TIP**
> You can also open the chart in Excel, copy it, and then paste it into your slide.

4. **Click the Create from file option button, click Browse, locate the file PPT F-2.xlsx in the drive and folder where you store your Data Files, click OK, then click OK in the Insert Object dialog box**
   The chart containing the quarterly sales data appears and is embedded on the slide. Notice that the chart is not completely visible. You can open the chart and use Excel's commands to alter it.

5. **Double-click the chart to open Microsoft Office Excel**
   The chart appears inside an Excel worksheet on the slide. Excel commands and tabs appear on the Ribbon under the PowerPoint title bar as shown in Figure F-12.

> **QUICK TIP**
> If the chart you want to insert is in another presentation, you can open both presentations and then copy and paste the chart from one presentation to the other.

6. **Drag the Excel worksheet window lower-middle sizing handle until the axis labels at the bottom of the chart are visible, then drag the window right-middle sizing handle until the legend is visible**
   The entire chart is in the visible viewing area.

7. **Click the Chart Tools Design tab on the Ribbon, click the Chart Styles More button, then click Style 40 (row 5 last column)**
   The chart style changes with new data marker colors and a new plot area color.

8. **Right-click the Vertical (Value) Axis, click the Bold button B on the Mini toolbar, click the category axis, then press [F4]**
   Both the value and category axes labels are bold and now easier to read.

9. **Click outside the chart to exit Excel, drag the chart so its upper-left corner is under the word Quarterly, then drag the lower-right sizing handle down and to the right**
   Compare your screen to Figure F-13.

10. **Click a blank area of the slide, then save the presentation**

FIGURE F-12: Inserted Excel chart

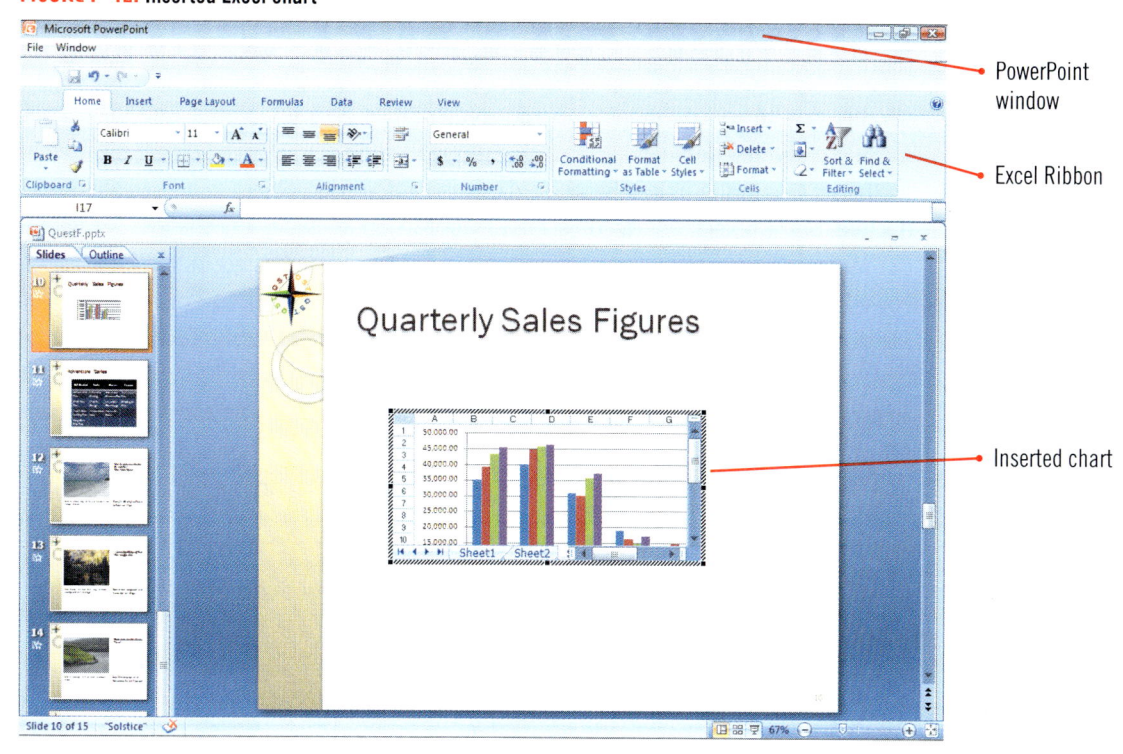

- PowerPoint window
- Excel Ribbon
- Inserted chart

FIGURE F-13: Formatted Excel chart

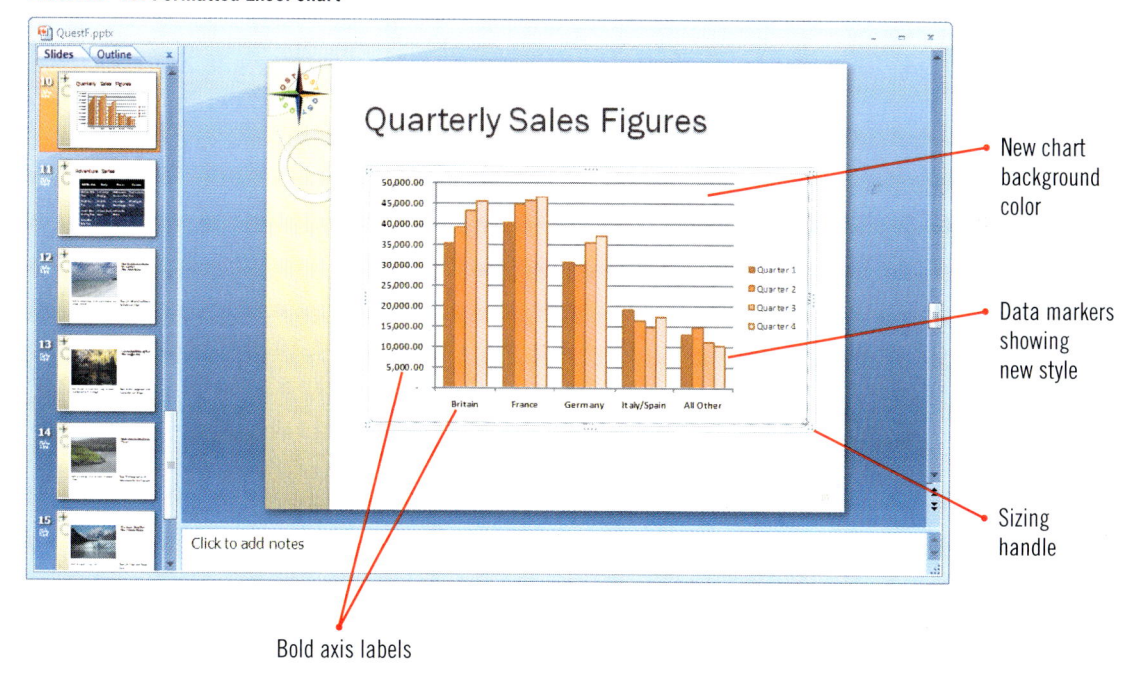

- New chart background color
- Data markers showing new style
- Sizing handle
- Bold axis labels

Embedding a worksheet

You can embed all or part of an Excel worksheet in a PowerPoint slide. To embed an entire worksheet, go to the slide where you want to place the worksheet. Click the Insert tab on the Ribbon, then click the Object button in the Text group. The Insert Object dialog box opens. Click the Create from file option button, click Browse, locate and double-click the worksheet filename, then click OK. The worksheet is embedded in the slide. Double-click it to edit it using Excel commands as needed to work with the worksheet. To insert only a portion of a worksheet, open the Excel workbook and copy the cells you want to include in your presentation.

Enhancing Charts

Linking an Excel Worksheet

UNIT F — PowerPoint 2007

Another way to connect objects to your presentation is to establish a **link**, or connection, between the source file and the destination file. Unlike embedded objects, a linked object is stored in its source file, not on the slide or in the presentation file. So when you link an object to a PowerPoint slide, a representation (picture) of the object, not the object itself, appears on the slide. Any changes made to the source file using the source program of a linked object are automatically reflected in the linked representation in your PowerPoint presentation. Some of the objects that you can link to PowerPoint include bitmap images, Microsoft Excel worksheets, and PowerPoint slides from other presentations. Use linking when you want to be sure your presentation contains the latest information and when you want to include an object, such as an accounting spreadsheet, that may change over time. See Table F-1 for suggestions on when to embed an object and when to link an object. You need to link and format an Excel worksheet to the presentation. The worksheet was created by the Quest Specialty Travel Accounting Department earlier in the year.

STEPS

> **QUICK TIP**
> If you plan to do the steps in this lesson again, make a copy of the Excel file PPT F-3.xlsx to keep the original data intact.

1. **Click the Home tab on the Ribbon, click the New Slide button, then type Quest Specialty Travel**
   The new Slide 11 is created and appears in the Slide pane with the title Quest Specialty Travel.

2. **Click the Insert tab on the Ribbon, then click the Object button in the Text group**
   The Insert Object dialog box opens.

3. **Click the Create from file option button, click Browse, locate the file PPT F-3.xlsx in the drive and folder where you store your Data Files, click OK, click the Link check box, then click OK**
   The Excel worksheet appears on the slide. The worksheet would be easier to see if it were larger.

4. **Drag the lower-right sizing handle down and to the right, drag the lower-left sizing handle down and to the left, then position the worksheet in the middle of the slide**
   The worksheet should be about as wide on the slide as shown in Figure F-14. If the worksheet has a background fill color, it would be set off from the slide and help to focus audience's attention.

> **QUICK TIP**
> Another way to link objects like a worksheet is to create a hyperlink. Copy the object in its source program, click the Paste button list arrow in PowerPoint, then click Paste as Hyperlink.

5. **Right-click the worksheet, then click Format Object on the shortcut menu**
   The Format Object dialog box opens.

6. **Drag the dialog box to the left out of the way if it is blocking the worksheet, in the Fill section click the Color list arrow, click Automatic, then click Preview**
   A dark teal color is applied behind the worksheet. The color is too dark for the presentation.

7. **In the Fill section, type 50 in the Transparency text box, then click Preview**
   The intensity of the background color is at 50 % and looks better.

8. **In the Line section click the Color list arrow, click Automatic, click the Weight up arrow once, click OK, then click a blank area of the slide**
   The worksheet appears with the new background color and border. Compare your screen to figure F-15.

9. **Save the presentation, then close the presentation**
   The PowerPoint file closes but PowerPoint remains open.

FIGURE F-14: Slide with linked Excel worksheet

Linked Excel chart

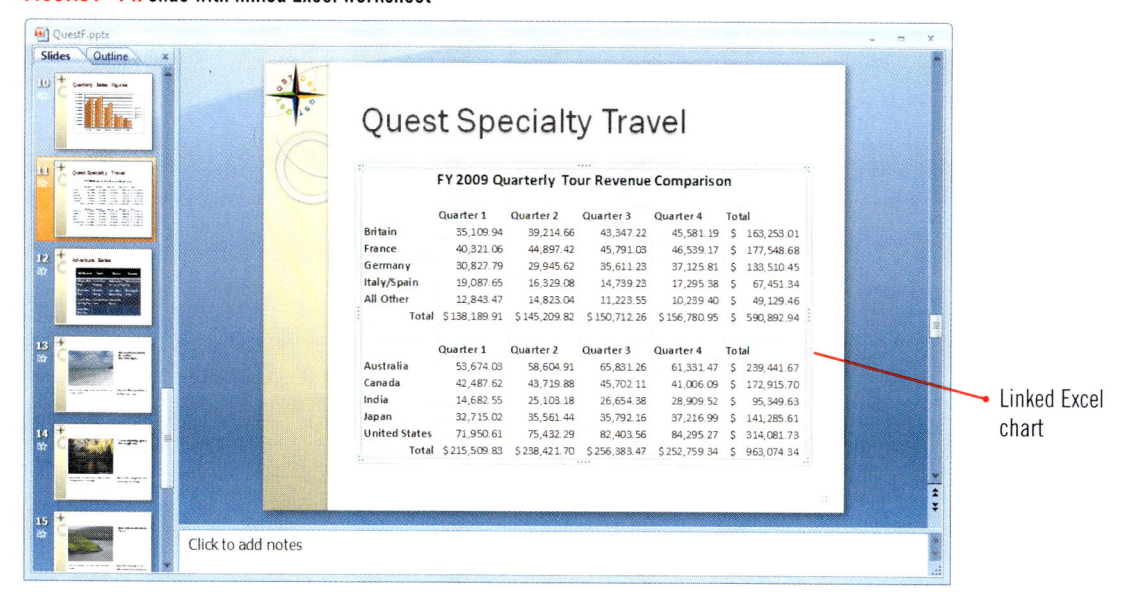

FIGURE F-15: Formatted linked worksheet

Formatted chart

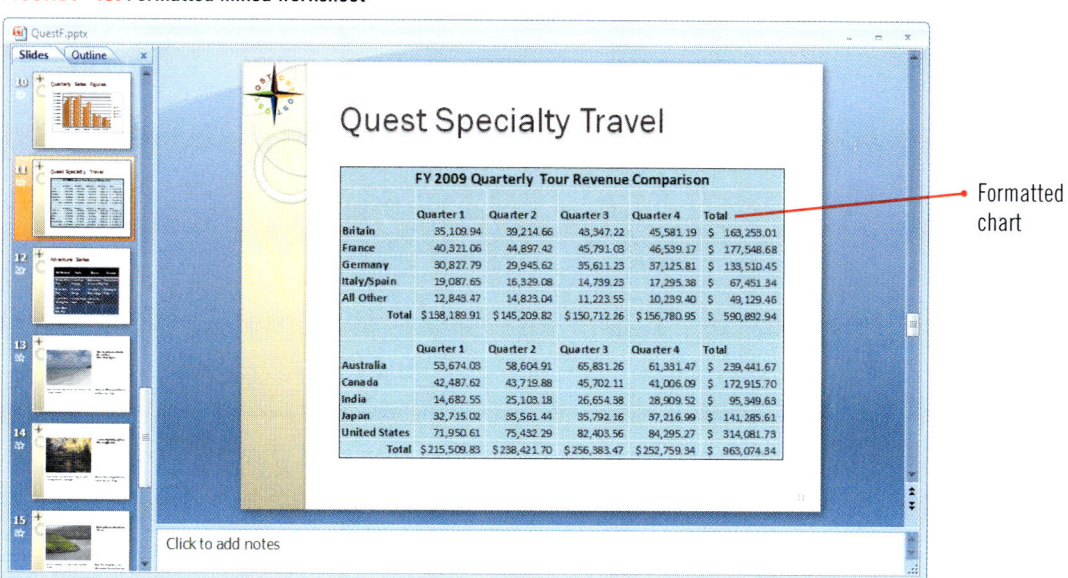

TABLE F-1: Embedding Versus Linking

situation	action
When you are the only user of an object and you want the object to be a part of your presentation	Embed
When you want to access the object in its source program, even if the original file is not available	Embed
When you want to update the object manually while working in PowerPoint	Embed
When you always want the latest information in your object	Link
When the object's source file is shared on a network or when other users have access to the file and can change it	Link
When you want to keep your presentation file size small	Link

Enhancing Charts

Updating a Linked Excel Worksheet

To edit or change the information in a linked object, you must open the object's source file in its source program. For example, you must open Microsoft Word to edit a linked Word table, or you must open Microsoft Excel to edit a linked Excel worksheet. You can open the source program by double-clicking the linked object in the PowerPoint slide, as you did with embedded objects, or by starting the source program directly using any method you prefer. When you work on a linked object in its source program, your PowerPoint presentation can be either open or closed. You have just received an e-mail that some of the data in the Excel worksheet is incorrect. You decide to start Excel and change the data in the source file and then update the linked object in the presentation.

STEPS

QUICK TIP
To edit or open a linked object in your presentation, the object's source program and source file must be available on your computer or network.

1. **Click the Start button on the Taskbar, point to All Programs, click Microsoft Office, click Microsoft Office Excel 2007, click the Office button, click Open, locate the file PPT F-3.xlsx in the drive and folder where you store your Data Files, then click Open**
   The worksheet PPT F-3.xlsx opens up in the Microsoft Excel window.

2. **Click cell B4, press [Shift], click cell E8, release [Shift], right-click cell E8, then click the Accounting Number Format button $ on the Mini toolbar**
   All of the selected cells now have the accounting format and display the dollar symbol.

3. **Click cell B12, drag to cell E16, press [F4], then click cell B14**
   The same accounting number format is applied to these cells.

4. **Type 18630.51, click cell E8, type 13427.34, then press [Enter]**
   The Quarter 1 value for India and the Quarter 4 value for All Other in the worksheet change. All totals that include these values in the Total cells are updated accordingly. Compare your screen to Figure F-16.

5. **Click cell F9, press [Ctrl], click cell F17, click the Bold button B in the Font group, click the Excel window Close button, then click Yes to save your changes**
   The bold attribute is added to these cells to highlight the overall totals, and the Excel window closes.

QUICK TIP
The destination file can remain open when you update links. After you change the source file and switch back to the destination file, the linked object is updated.

6. **In the PowerPoint program window click the Office button, then click 1 QuestF.pptx in the Recent documents list**
   A Microsoft Office PowerPoint Security Notice dialog box opens, telling you that the presentation contains links and asking if you want to update them. This message appears whenever you open a presentation that contains linked objects that have been changed.

7. **Click Update Links**
   The Excel worksheet in the QuestF.pptx presentation file is now updated with the new data.

8. **Click the View tab on the Ribbon, click Arrange All in the Window group, click Slide 11 in the Slides tab, then click the linked worksheet**
   Compare your screen to Figure F-17. The linked Excel worksheet shows the new numbers and the formatting changes you made. PowerPoint automatically makes all of the changes when you update the links.

9. **Save the presentation, add your name as the footer to the handouts, print handouts 4 per page, then exit PowerPoint**

FIGURE F-16: Modified Excel worksheet

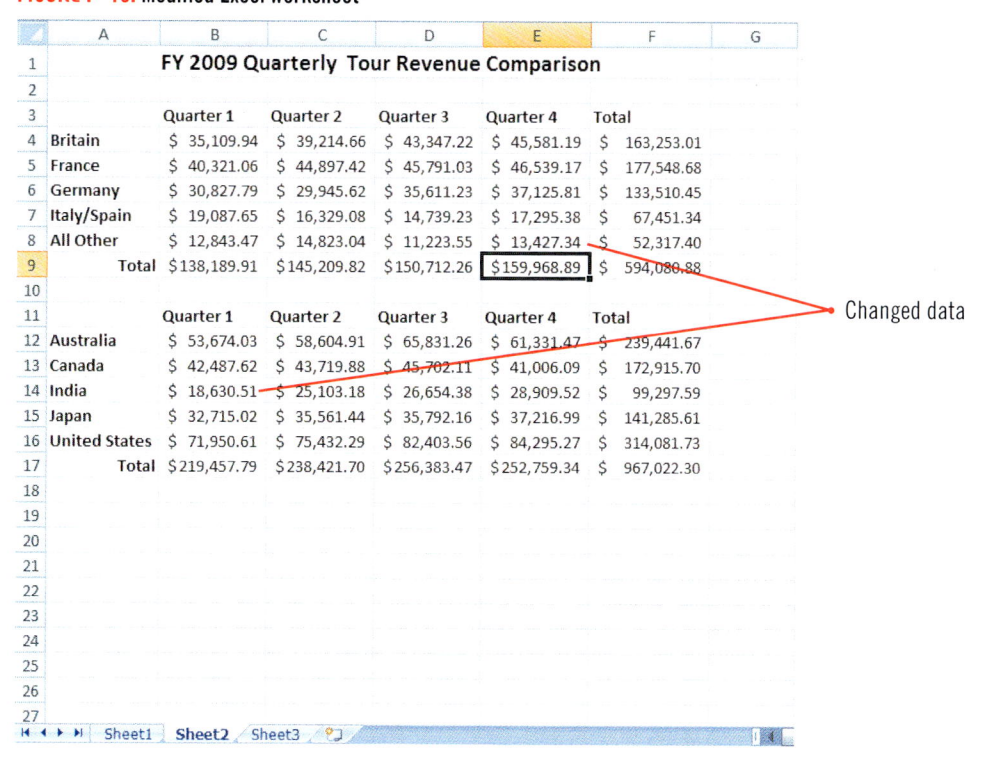

	A	B	C	D	E	F	G
1		FY 2009 Quarterly Tour Revenue Comparison					
2							
3		Quarter 1	Quarter 2	Quarter 3	Quarter 4	Total	
4	Britain	$ 35,109.94	$ 39,214.66	$ 43,347.22	$ 45,581.19	$ 163,253.01	
5	France	$ 40,321.06	$ 44,897.42	$ 45,791.03	$ 46,539.17	$ 177,548.68	
6	Germany	$ 30,827.79	$ 29,945.62	$ 35,611.23	$ 37,125.81	$ 133,510.45	
7	Italy/Spain	$ 19,087.65	$ 16,329.08	$ 14,739.23	$ 17,295.38	$ 67,451.34	
8	All Other	$ 12,843.47	$ 14,823.04	$ 11,223.55	$ 13,427.34	$ 52,317.40	
9	Total	$138,189.91	$145,209.82	$150,712.26	$159,968.89	$ 594,080.88	
10							
11		Quarter 1	Quarter 2	Quarter 3	Quarter 4	Total	
12	Australia	$ 53,674.03	$ 58,604.91	$ 65,831.26	$ 61,331.47	$ 239,441.67	
13	Canada	$ 42,487.62	$ 43,719.88	$ 45,702.11	$ 41,006.09	$ 172,915.70	
14	India	$ 18,630.51	$ 25,103.18	$ 26,654.38	$ 28,909.52	$ 99,297.59	
15	Japan	$ 32,715.02	$ 35,561.44	$ 35,792.16	$ 37,216.99	$ 141,285.61	
16	United States	$ 71,950.61	$ 75,432.29	$ 82,403.56	$ 84,295.27	$ 314,081.73	
17	Total	$219,457.79	$238,421.70	$256,383.47	$252,759.34	$ 967,022.30	

Changed data

FIGURE F-17: Slide showing updated linked worksheet

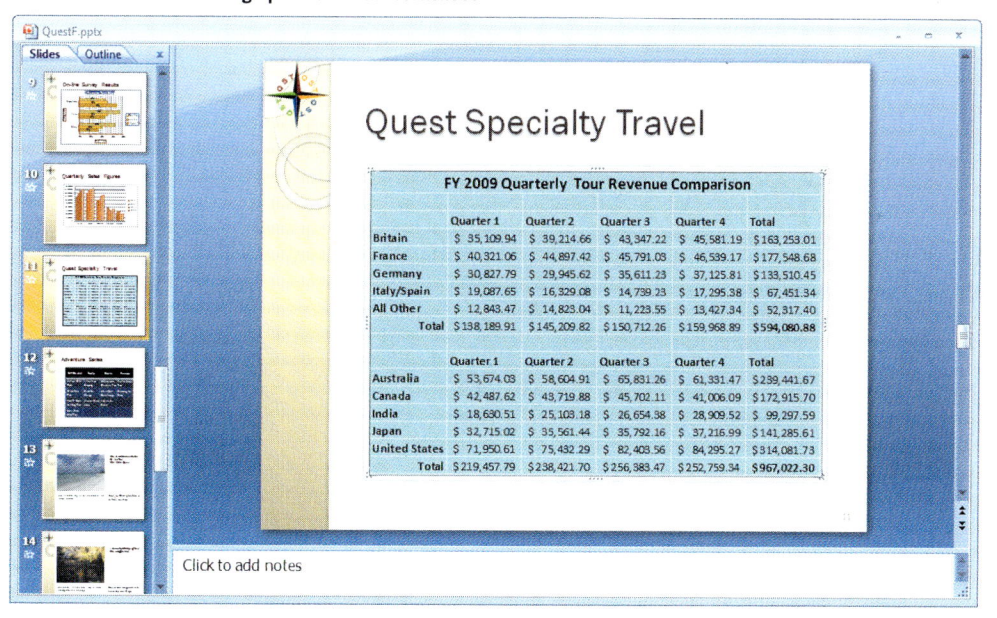

Using Paste Special

Paste Special is used to paste text or objects into PowerPoint using a specific file format. For example, you may want to paste some text as a picture or as plain text without formatting. Copy the text, then in PowerPoint click the Paste button list arrow, click Paste Special, then select the appropriate file format option. You can also link an object or selected information from another program to PowerPoint using the Paste Special command. This technique is useful when you want to link part of an Excel worksheet or a chart from a workbook that contains both a worksheet and a chart. To link just the chart, open the Microsoft Excel worksheet, then copy the chart. Leaving Excel and the source file open, click the Paste button list arrow, click Paste Special, click the Paste link option button, then click OK.

Enhancing Charts

Practice

▼ CONCEPTS REVIEW

Label each of the elements of the PowerPoint window shown in Figure F-18.

FIGURE F-18

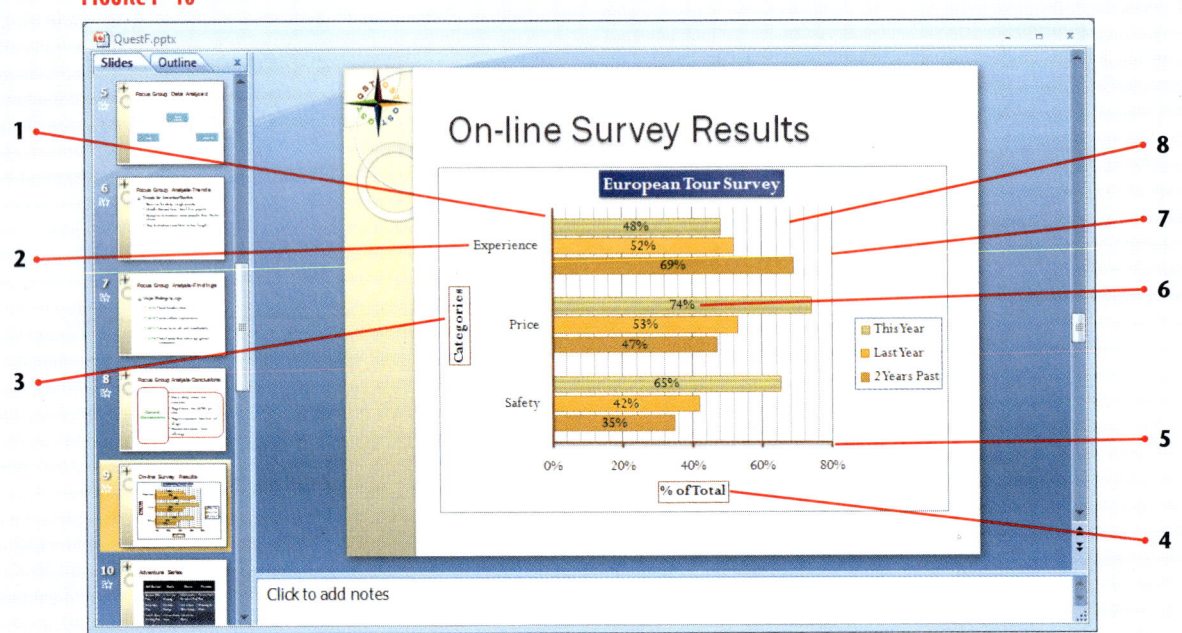

Match each of the terms with the statement that describes its function.

9. Create and then reuse to make a customized chart type
10. The file that contains the Excel chart that you embed into a PowerPoint file
11. The PowerPoint file where you embed an Excel chart
12. The connection between a source file and a destination file
13. The specific file format that locks the file from future change

a. Fixed layout format
b. Destination file
c. Template
d. Link
e. Source file

PowerPoint 138   Enhancing Charts

Select the best answer from the list of choices.

14. Which of the statements below is not true about working with charts in PowerPoint?
    a. Microsoft Graph is used to create a chart if Excel is not available.
    b. A linked chart is saved in the presentation.
    c. Document themes and effects are consistent between PowerPoint and Excel.
    d. An embedded chart's data is stored in an Excel worksheet.
15. Which of the following is not true about charts?
    a. A column chart displays a data series in proportion to the sum of all the data series.
    b. Cones and bubbles are examples of different chart types.
    c. Both Excel and PowerPoint use the same chart types.
    d. You can update a linked chart in its source program.
16. What is a data series?
    a. A graphical representation of a data series marker
    b. A range of data
    c. All of the data elements in a chart
    d. A column or row of data
17. Which animation method would you use to display each data series marker independently with the same color?
    a. By series
    b. Individually by category
    c. Individually by series
    d. By category
18. You use a(n) _____ program to create an object that you insert into PowerPoint.
    a. Support
    b. Linked
    c. Destination
    d. Source
19. Small lines that intersect an axis and identify categories are called:
    a. category markers.
    b. tick marks.
    c. plot layout lines.
    d. chart wedges.
20. Changes made to a _____ object's source file are automatically reflected in the destination file.
    a. embedded
    b. inserted
    c. linked
    d. Microsoft Graph

▼ SKILLS REVIEW

1. **Change chart design and style.**
   a. Start PowerPoint, open the presentation PPT F-4.pptx, then save it as **Italia Publishing** to the drive and folder where you store your Data Files.
   b. Select Slide 3, then select the chart.
   c. Open the Chart Tools Design tab, then apply Layout 7 from the Chart Layouts group.
   d. Change the axis label on the value axis to **Millions** and then change the category axis label to **Divisions**.
   e. Apply Style 37 from the Chart Styles group.
   f. Change the chart type to Clustered Cylinder. (*Hint*: A cylinder is a type of column chart.)

▼ SKILLS REVIEW (CONTINUED)

2. **Customize a chart layout.**
   a. Open the Chart Tools Layout tab, then change the horizontal gridlines to major gridlines and the vertical gridlines to major gridlines.
   b. Click the Chart Floor button in the Background group, click More Floor Options, click the Solid fill option button, type **35** in the Transparency text box, then click Close.
   c. Click the Chart Wall button in the Background group, then click None.
   d. Right-click the value axis label, click the Shape Outline button list arrow on the Mini toolbar, then click Blue-Gray, Accent 1.
   e. Select the category axis title, then press [F4].
   f. Click a blank area of the chart, then save your changes.

3. **Format chart elements.**
   a. Click the Chart Area list arrow in the Current Selection group, then click Series "2nd Qtr."
   b. Click the Format Selection button in the Current Selection group, then drag the Gap Width slider to the left to about 150%.
   c. Click Fill in the left pane, then change the fill to a Gradient fill, click the Direction list arrow, then click Linear Down.
   d. Click 3-D Format in the left pane, click the Material list arrow, click Dark Edge, then click Close.
   e. Right-click the value axis, then click Format Axis.
   f. Under Axis Options click the Major unit Fixed option button, then type **15** in the text box.
   g. Click the Major tick mark type list arrow, click Cross, click Close, then save your changes.

4. **Animate a chart.**
   a. Open the Animations tab, then click the Custom Animation button in the Animations group.
   b. Apply the Descend Entrance animation effect that is in the Moderate group to the chart.
   c. Click the animation list arrow (Object 4), click Effect Options, then click the Chart Animation tab.
   d. Change the animation to By Element in Series, click the check box to not draw the chart background, then click OK.
   e. Close the Custom Animation task pane, then save your changes.

5. **Embed an Excel chart.**
   a. Select Slide 4, then click the Insert tab.
   b. Click the Object button in the Text group, click the Create from file option button, click Browse, locate and open the file PPT F-5.xlsx from the drive and folder where you store your Data Files, then click OK.
   c. Double-click the chart, then drag the sizing handles so the entire chart is visible. You should see the value axis title and the category axis title as well as the legend.
   d. Click the chart, click the Chart Tools Design tab, then change the chart style to Style 36.
   e. Change the horizontal gridlines to display only major gridlines.
   f. Right-click the legend, click the Shape Outline button list arrow on the Mini toolbar, click Black, Text 1, then click outside the chart.
   g. Resize the chart so it fills most of the slide.
   h. Click a blank area of the slide, then save your changes.

6. **Link an Excel worksheet.**
   a. Add a new slide after the current slide with the Title Only layout.
   b. Type **Italia Publishing**, click the Insert tab, then click the Object button in the Text group.
   c. Click the Create from file option button, locate the file PPT F-6.xlsx in the drive and folder where you store your Data Files, then link it to the slide.
   d. Resize the worksheet object by dragging its sizing handles.
   e. Right-click the worksheet, click Format Object, click the Color list arrow, then click Automatic.
   f. Change the transparency to 40%, click OK, then save your changes.

▼ SKILLS REVIEW (CONTINUED)

7. **Update a linked Excel worksheet.**
   a. Right-click the worksheet, point to Linked Worksheet Object, then click Edit.
   b. Select cells B5 to F9, click the Accounting Number Format button list arrow in the Number group, then click Euro.
   c. Click cell F9, then click the Bold button in the Font group.
   d. Click cell D5, type **72492.38**, click cell E7, then type **87253.11**.
   e. Click the Excel window Close button, then click Yes to save your changes. The changes appear in the linked worksheet. Figure F-19 shows the completed presentation.
   f. Add your name to the handout footer, save your work, print the handouts 4 per page, close the presentation, and exit PowerPoint.

FIGURE F-19

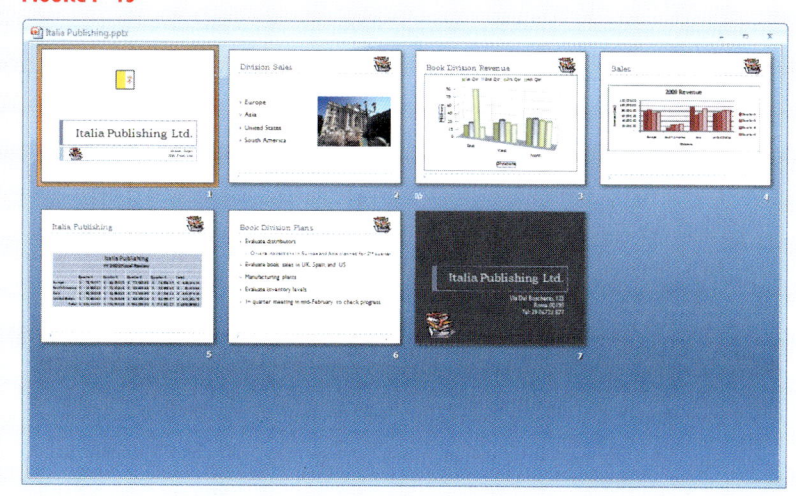

▼ INDEPENDENT CHALLENGE 1

You work for Business Builders Inc., a business consulting company that helps small and medium businesses organize or restructure themselves to be more efficient and profitable. You are one of four senior consultants who work directly with clients. To prepare for an upcoming meeting with executives at ComSystems, a mobile phone communications company, you create a brief presentation outlining typical investigative and reporting techniques, past results versus the competition, and the company's business philosophy. Use PowerPoint to customize a chart on Slide 5 of the presentation.

a. Start PowerPoint, open the presentation PPT F-7.pptx from the drive and folder where you store your Data Files, then save it as **Bz Builders**.
b. Select the chart on Slide 5, then apply Layout 3 from the Chart Layouts gallery.
c. Apply Style 26 from the chart Styles gallery, then type **AMPI Rating Comparison** in the chart title text box.
d. Change the chart type to Clustered Bar, then add minor vertical gridlines to the chart.
e. Open the Format Axis dialog box for the value axis, click Number in the left pane, click Number in the Category list, then type **1** in the Decimal Places text box.
f. Show data labels using the Inside End option.

Advanced Challenge Exercise

- Select the Value axis, open the Format Axis dialog box for the Value axis, in the Axis Options section click the Major unit Fixed option button, then type **0.5**.
- In the Axis Options section click the Minor unit Fixed option button, then type **0.1**.
- Select the category axis, open the Format Axis dialog box, click Alignment in the left pane, then type **–25** in the Custom angle text box.

g. Change the data labels to the Inside End option, then spell check and save your presentation.
h. Add your name as a footer to the slides and handouts, print the slides of the presentation, then submit your presentation plan and printouts.
i. View the presentation in Slide Show view, save the presentation, close the presentation, then exit PowerPoint.

Enhancing Charts

▼ INDEPENDENT CHALLENGE 2

One of your responsibilities working in the Delaware State Schools system is to provide program performance data for educational programs designed for disabled children in the state. You need to develop and give a presentation describing the program's results at a national education forum held this year in Cincinnati, Ohio. You have been working on the presentation and now you need to use PowerPoint to put the finishing touches on a chart.

a. Start PowerPoint, open the presentation PPT F-8.pptx from the drive and folder where you store your Data Files, then save it as **Delaware Schools**.
b. Select Slide 7, select the chart, then change the chart style to Style 27.
c. Open the Chart Tools Layout tab click the 3-D Rotation button, then in the Rotation section click the X down arrow once.
d. Open the Chart Tools Format tab, select the Reading data series, then change the shape fill to the gradient Linear Down (Dark Variation).
e. Change the Writing data series to the Woven mat texture shape fill, then change the Math data series to Linear Up (Light Variation).
f. Open the Custom Animation task pane, apply the Wipe Entrance effect to the chart, then slow the speed down to Fast.
g. Open the Effect Options dialog box for animation effect, change the animation so the data markers appear by category, then click the check box so the chart background does not animate.
h. Spell check and save the presentation.
i. Add your name as a footer to the slides and handouts, then print the final slide presentation.
j. View the presentation in Slide Show view, save and close the presentation, then exit PowerPoint.

▼ INDEPENDENT CHALLENGE 3

RNM Industries is a large company that develops and produces technical medical equipment and machines for operating and emergency rooms throughout the United States. You are one of the business managers in the company, and one of your assignments is to prepare a presentation for the stockholders on the profitability and efficiency of each division in the company. Use PowerPoint to develop the presentation.

a. Open the file PPT F-9.pptx from the drive and folder where you store your Data Files, then save it as **RNM Industries**.
b. Apply the Flow theme, then add at least two graphics to the presentation.
c. Add a new slide titled Company Divisions, then create a SmartArt graphic that identifies the company's seven divisions: Administration; Accounting; Sales and Marketing; Research and Development; Product Testing; Product Development; and Manufacturing.
d. Format the new SmartArt graphic using SmartArt Styles and colors.
e. Select the Division Performance slide, then insert the Excel file PPT F-10.xlsx from the drive and folder where you store your Data Files.
f. Double-click the chart, then drag the corner sizing handles so all of the chart is visible.

Advanced Challenge Exercise

- Right-click the value axis, then click Format Axis.
- Click the Axis labels list arrow, then click Low.
- Click the Minor tick mark type list arrow, click None, then click Close.

g. Apply the Style 42 chart style to the chart, deselect the chart, then increase the size of the chart and center it in the slide.
h. Select the Division Budgets slide, then link the Excel file PPT F-11.xlsx from the drive and folder where you store your Data Files.

▼ INDEPENDENT CHALLENGE 3 (CONTINUED)

i. Open the linked worksheet in Excel, select cells B5 through F12, click the Accounting Number Format button in the Number group, then close Excel.

j. Right-click the linked chart, click Format Object, then change the fill color to Automatic at 60% transparency.

k. Resize the worksheet to fill the slide, add your name as a footer to the slides and handouts, then print the final slide presentation.

l. View the presentation in Slide Show view, close the presentation and exit PowerPoint.

▼ REAL LIFE INDEPENDENT CHALLENGE

You are on staff at your college newspaper. One of your jobs is to review computer games and post a presentation on the paper's Web site. The presentation identifies the top computer games based on student testing and other reviews. Use PowerPoint to create a presentation that includes research and your own information. Use the basic presentation provided as a basis to develop this presentation.

As you create this presentation, follow these guidelines:
- Include three computer games in your presentation.
- Each game has at least one defined mission or task.
- Consumer satisfaction of each game is identified on a scale of 1.0 to 10.0.
- There are three categories of games: Adventure, Action, and Strategy.

If you have access to the Web, you can research the following topics to help you develop information for your presentation
- Consumer or industry reviews of computer games
- Computer game descriptions and pricing

a. Connect to the Internet, then use a search engine to locate Web sites that have information on PC computer games. Review at least two Web sites that contain information about computer games. Print the home pages of the Web sites you use to gather data for your presentation.

b. Open the presentation PPT F-12.pptx from the drive and folder where you store your Data Files, then save it as **PC Game Review**.

c. Add your name as the footer on all slides and handouts.

d. Your presentation should contain at least eight slides, including a title slide.

e. (Before you complete this step make a copy of the Data File PPT F-13.xlsx.) Link the Excel chart PPT F-13.xlsx from the drive and folder where you store your Data Files on the Game Reviews slide.

f. Resize the chart on the slide, then open the linked chart in Excel.

g. Click the Sheet 1 tab at the bottom of the Excel window, provide a name for each game, click the Sheet 2 tab, then save your changes.

h. Right-click the chart legend click Delete in the Shortcut menu, click the Page Layout tab, click the Colors button in the Themes group, then click Aspect.

i. Save your changes, then exit Excel.

j. Create at least one SmartArt diagram that briefly explains the story line of one of the games.

k. Create a table that lists the price of each game.

l. Enhance the presentation with clip art or other graphics, an appropriate design theme, and other items that improve the look of the presentation.

m. Modify the Slide Master as necessary and create a new slide layout, if necessary, to use in the presentation.

n. Spell check, save the presentation, then view the presentation in Slide Show view.

o. Add your name as a footer to the slides and handouts, print the slides of the presentation as handouts (4 slides per page).

p. Close the presentation and exit PowerPoint.

▼ VISUAL WORKSHOP

Create a slide that looks like the example in Figure F-20. Start a new presentation, then insert the Excel worksheet PPT F-14.xlsx from the drive and folder where you store your Data Files. Format the worksheet using PowerPoint's formatting features. Save the presentation as **Chase Products Inc.** Add your name as a footer on the slides, then save and print the presentation slides.

FIGURE F-20

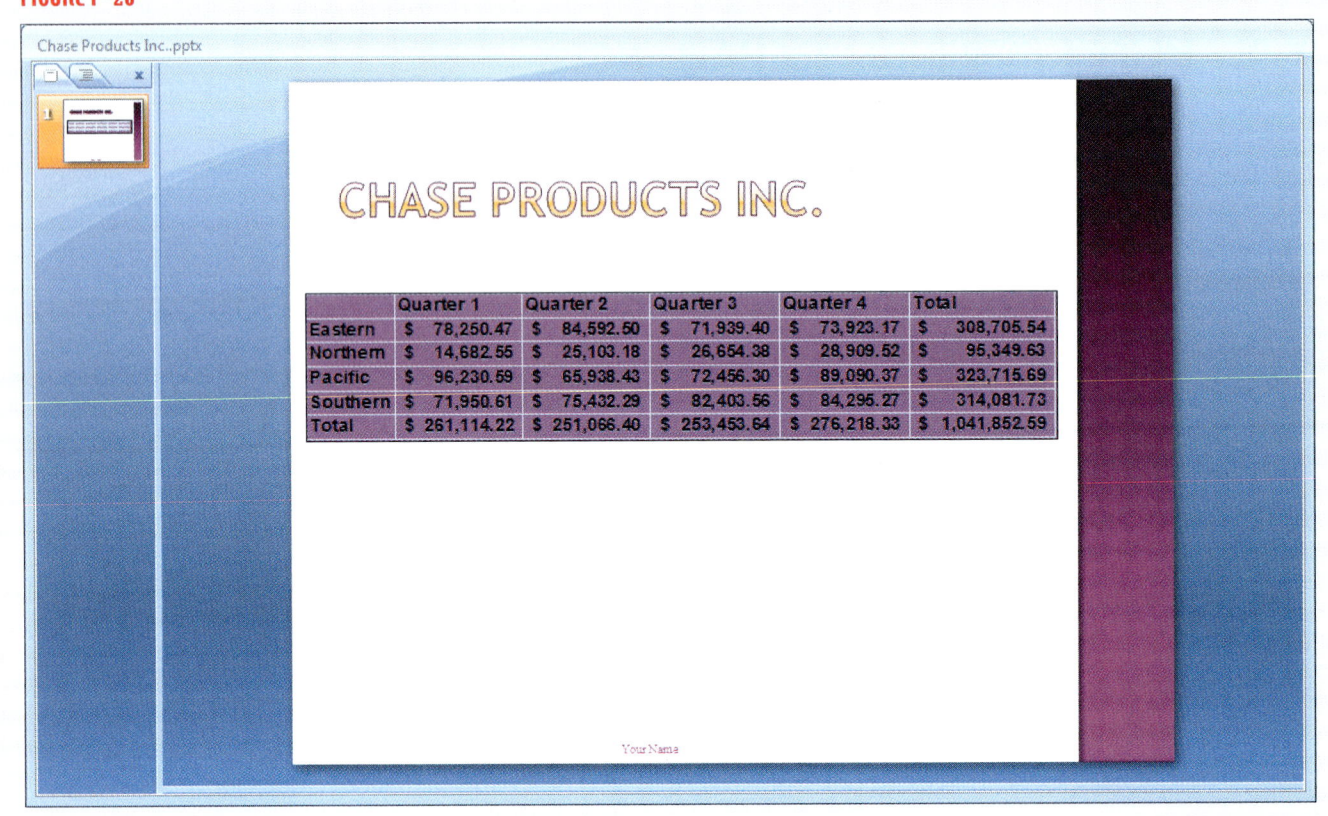

CHASE PRODUCTS INC.

	Quarter 1	Quarter 2	Quarter 3	Quarter 4	Total
Eastern	$ 78,250.47	$ 84,592.50	$ 71,939.40	$ 73,923.17	$ 308,705.54
Northern	$ 14,682.55	$ 25,103.18	$ 26,654.38	$ 28,909.52	$ 95,349.63
Pacific	$ 96,230.59	$ 65,938.43	$ 72,456.30	$ 89,090.37	$ 323,715.69
Southern	$ 71,950.61	$ 75,432.29	$ 82,403.56	$ 84,295.27	$ 314,081.73
Total	$ 261,114.22	$ 251,066.40	$ 253,453.64	$ 276,218.33	$ 1,041,852.59

Your Name

UNIT G
PowerPoint 2007

Inserting Illustrations, Objects, and Media Clips

Files You Will Need:
PPT G-1.pptm
PPT G-2.jpg
PPT G-3.jpg
PPT G-4.jpg
PPT G-5.jpg
PPT G-6.jpg
PPT G-7.jpg
PPT G-8.jpg
PPT G-9.jpg
PPT G-10.pptx
PPT G-11.docx
PPT G-12.pptx
PPT G-13.pptm
PPT G-14.jpg
PPT G-15.wav
PPT G-16.jpg
PPT G-17.docx
PPT G-18.pptx
PPT G-19.pptx
PPT G-20.pptx
PPT G-21.pptx
PPT G-22.pptm

PowerPoint provides you with many different types of graphics to improve your presentation. From customized tables and professional-looking diagrams to movies and sounds, you have a wide range of options when it comes to developing your presentation. You also have other advanced tools, such as hyperlinks, macros, and action buttons that help correlate, simplify, and assimilate information. In this unit, you will work on a short presentation for a specific tour that will be linked to the primary European Tours presentation that you have been working on for Ellen Latsky at Quest Specialty Travel. You will use PowerPoint's advanced features to customize a table and a SmartArt graphic, then you will insert a movie and sound that complements the information. Finally, you will use a macro to insert some pictures, create action buttons, and link one presentation to another one.

OBJECTIVES

Create custom tables
Design a SmartArt graphic
Format a SmartArt graphic
Insert an animation
Insert a sound
Use macros
Add action buttons
Insert a hyperlink

Creating Custom Tables

UNIT G
PowerPoint 2007

A table is a great way to display and organize related information. In PowerPoint 2007, you have the ability to create dynamic-looking tables. Tables you create in PowerPoint automatically display the style as determined by the theme assigned to the slide, including color combinations and shading, line styles and colors, and other attributes. It is easy to customize the layout of a table or change how data is organized. You can delete and insert rows or columns, merge two or more cells together, or split one cell into more cells. 🎨 You open a short presentation on Black Forest tours in Germany that you have been working on and finish customizing a table.

STEPS

1. **Start PowerPoint, open the presentation PPT G-1.pptm from the drive and folder where you store your Data Files, save the presentation as QuestG, then click OK in the privacy warning alert dialog box**

   The presentation opens. Notice that this presentation has the file extension .pptm instead of .pptx. The .pptm file extension identifies the PowerPoint file as having macros attached to it. A **macro** is an action or a set of actions that you use to automate tasks.

2. **Click the Options button in the Security Warning message bar, read the Microsoft Office Security Options dialog box, click the Enable this content option button, click OK, click the View tab on the Ribbon, then click the Arrange All button in the Window group**

   You have just enabled the macros attached to this presentation. As a rule, you should not enable macros from unfamiliar sources or those you do not trust because they could contain viruses.

3. **Click the table on Slide 1, click the Table Tools Design tab on the Ribbon, click the Pen Style button ─ in the Draw Borders group, then click the dash-dot style (4th line style from the top)**

   The pointer changes to ✏, which indicates that you are in drawing mode.

4. **Click the white vertical column line that divides the Pricing and Extras columns in the table, then click the vertical column line for each row in that column to the bottom of the table**

   See Figure G-1.

   QUICK TIP
   You can also press [Esc] to end drawing mode.

5. **Click the Draw Table button in the Draw Borders group, click the Table Tools Layout tab on the Ribbon, click the Hostel/Barn cell, then click the Split Cells button in the Merge group**

   Clicking the Draw Table button ends drawing mode and the pointer changes back to ⌕. The Split Cells dialog box opens. The default table is 2 columns and 1 row, and the Number of columns text box is selected.

   QUICK TIP
   To change the text direction in a text box or a table, select the text, click the Text Direction button in the Paragraph group, then click the appropriate option.

6. **Type 1, click the Number of rows up arrow once, then click OK**

   You split the cell so a new row is created.

7. **Drag to select the word Barn, press [Ctrl][X] to cut the word, click the new row, press [Ctrl][V] to paste the word, then delete the slash next to Hostel**

   The words Hostel and Barn are now in two separate rows within the Accommodations column.

8. **Repeat Steps 5–7 for the House/Farm cell and the Hotel/Inn cell**

   Compare your screen with Figure G-2.

9. **Click outside the table, click the Save button 💾 on the Quick Access toolbar, then click OK in the privacy warning alert dialog box**

FIGURE G-1: Table with new column line style

New column style

Pen pointer

FIGURE G-2: Formatted table

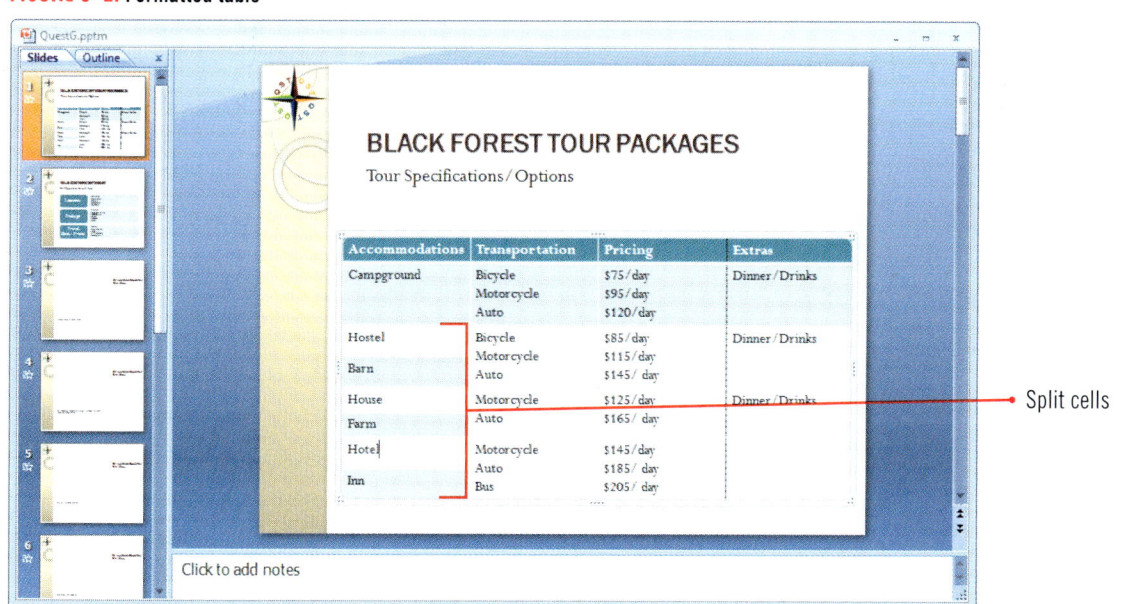

Split cells

Drawing tables

If you have limited space or a certain size table you want on a slide, you can draw it. Choose the slide where you want the table, click the Insert tab on the Ribbon, click the Table button in the Table group, then click Draw Table. The pointer changes to a pencil. Using the pencil to define the boundaries of the table, drag in the area of the slide where you want the table. A dotted outline appears as you draw. Next, you can create rows and columns. Click the Table Tools Design tab on the Ribbon, click the Draw Table button in the Draw Borders group, then using the pencil pointer draw lines for columns and rows. Be sure to draw within the boundary line of the table.

Inserting Illustrations, Objects, and Media Clips PowerPoint 147

Designing a SmartArt Graphic

The introduction of the SmartArt graphic in PowerPoint 2007 has dramatically improved your ability to create vibrant content on slides. You no longer have to struggle to combine your content with graphic illustrations. SmartArt allows you to easily combine your content with an illustrative diagram, improving the overall quality of your presentation and therefore, content understanding and retention by your audience. Now, in a matter of minutes you can create a SmartArt graphic using slide content that would otherwise have been placed in a simple bulleted list. You continue working on the Black Forest tours presentation by changing the graphic layout, adding a shape and text to the SmartArt graphic, and then changing its color and style.

STEPS

TROUBLE
If the Text Pane does not open automatically, click the Text Pane button in the Create Graphic group.

1. **Click Slide 2 on the Slides tab, click the Locations shape in the SmartArt graphic, then click the SmartArt Tools Design tab on the Ribbon**
   The Locations shape is selected and displays sizing handles and a rotate handle. Each shape in the SmartArt graphic is separate and distinct from the other shapes and can be individually edited, formatted, or moved within the boundaries of the SmartArt graphic. The SmartArt Text Pane is also open.

2. **Click the Add Bullet button in the Create Graphic group, then type Kehl-Kork in the Text Pane**
   A new bullet appears in the Text Pane and in the upper-right shape of the graphic. Compare your screen with Figure G-3.

3. **Click the More button in the Layouts group, then click Picture Accent List (1st column)**
   The SmartArt graphic layout changes.

4. **Click the Add Shape button list arrow in the Create Graphic group, click Add Shape After, then click next to the new bullet in the Text pane to place the insertion point**
   A new shape in the same style appears and a new bullet appears in the Text Pane.

5. **Type Other Offers, press [Enter], press [Tab], type Walking France, press [Enter], type Biking Austria, press [Enter], type Biking England, press [Enter], then type Walking Germany**

6. **Click the More button in the SmartArt Styles group, click Polished in the 3-D section, then click the Change Colors button in the SmartArt Styles group**
   A gallery of color themes appears showing the current theme applied to the graphic under Accent 1.

7. **In the Colorful section, click Colorful Range - Accent Colors 5 to 6**
   Each shape now has its own color.

8. **Click the Text Pane Close button, then click the Right to Left button in the Create Graphic group**
   The graphic flips and appears as a mirror image. You prefer the original view of the graphic.

9. **Click the Right to Left button in the Create Graphic group, click a blank area of the slide, then save your changes**
   Compare your screen to Figure G-4.

FIGURE G-3: SmartArt graphic with added text

— Text Pane
— Added text

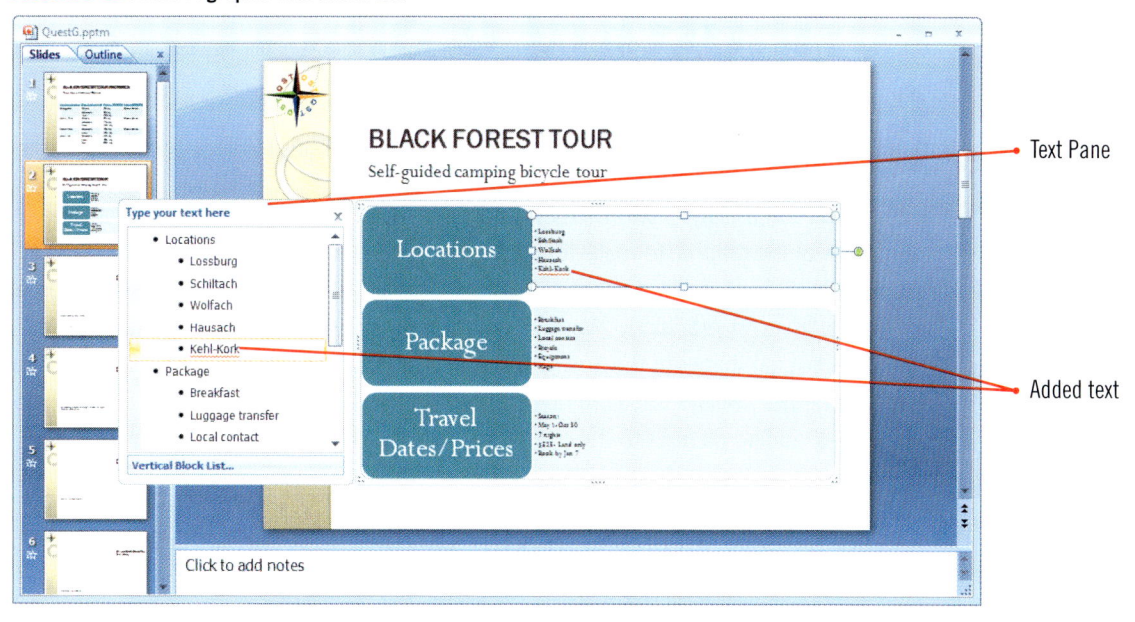

FIGURE G-4: SmartArt graphic with new design

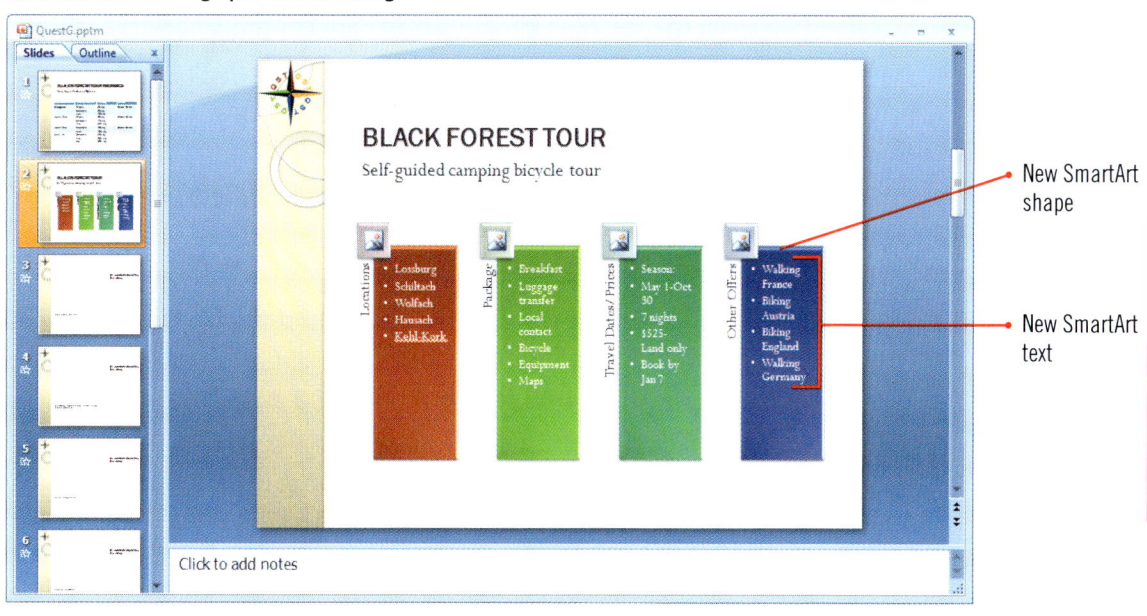

— New SmartArt shape
— New SmartArt text

Creating organizational charts

An organizational chart graphically illustrates the management structure of a business or organization. Organizational chart layouts are now incorporated within the SmartArt feature under the Hierarchy group. You can create organizational charts using SmartArt when your organizational chart has fewer than 30 shapes and you want to add effects or animate the chart. The Layout button in the Create Graphic group on the SmartArt Tools Design tab allows you to change the branch layout for the selected shape.

Inserting Illustrations, Objects, and Media Clips

Formatting a SmartArt Graphic

UNIT G
PowerPoint 2007

Though you can use styles and themes to format a SmartArt graphic, you still may need to refine individual aspects of the graphic to make it look the way you want it to look. You can use the commands on the SmartArt Tools Format tab to change shape styles, fills, outlines, and effects. You can also convert text within the SmartArt graphic to WordArt and format the text using any of the WordArt formatting commands. Individual shapes in the SmartArt graphic can be made larger or smaller, or altered into a different shape altogether. You continue working on the SmartArt graphic on Slide 2 by modifying four picture shapes, adding pictures to the picture shapes, and adjusting the text in the graphic.

STEPS

1. **Click the SmartArt graphic, click the SmartArt Tools Format tab on the Ribbon, move the pointer over the small shape behind the picture icon above the word Locations until it changes to ⁺⥊, then click the shape**
   The small shape behind the picture icon is selected.

2. **Click the Change Shape button in the Shapes group, then click Round Diagonal Corner Rectangle (the last shape in the Rectangles section)**
   The form of the small shape changes.

3. **Click the small shape above the word Package, press [F4], repeat this action for the other two small shapes, then click in a blank area of the SmartArt graphic**
   All four small shapes now have a new shape as shown in Figure G-5.

4. **Click the left-most picture icon above the word Locations**
   The Insert Picture dialog box opens.

5. **Locate the file PPT G-2.jpg from the drive and folder where you store your Data Files, then click Insert**
   A small thumbnail picture is placed in the picture shape.

6. **Click the picture icon above the word Package, insert the file PPT G-3.jpg, click the picture icon above the word Prices, insert the file PPT G-4.jpg, click the picture icon above the words Other Offers, then insert the file PPT G-5.jpg**
   All four shapes have pictures in them.

7. **Click a blank area inside the SmartArt graphic, drag the left sizing handle to the left to the edge of the white space on the slide, then drag the right sizing handle to the right edge of the slide**
   The SmartArt graphic fills the white area on the slide.

8. **Click a blank area of the slide, then save your work**
   Compare your screen with Figure G-6.

Inserting Illustrations, Objects, and Media Clips

FIGURE G-5: New shapes in SmartArt graphic

New Round Diagonal Corner Rectangle shapes

FIGURE G-6: Completed SmartArt graphic

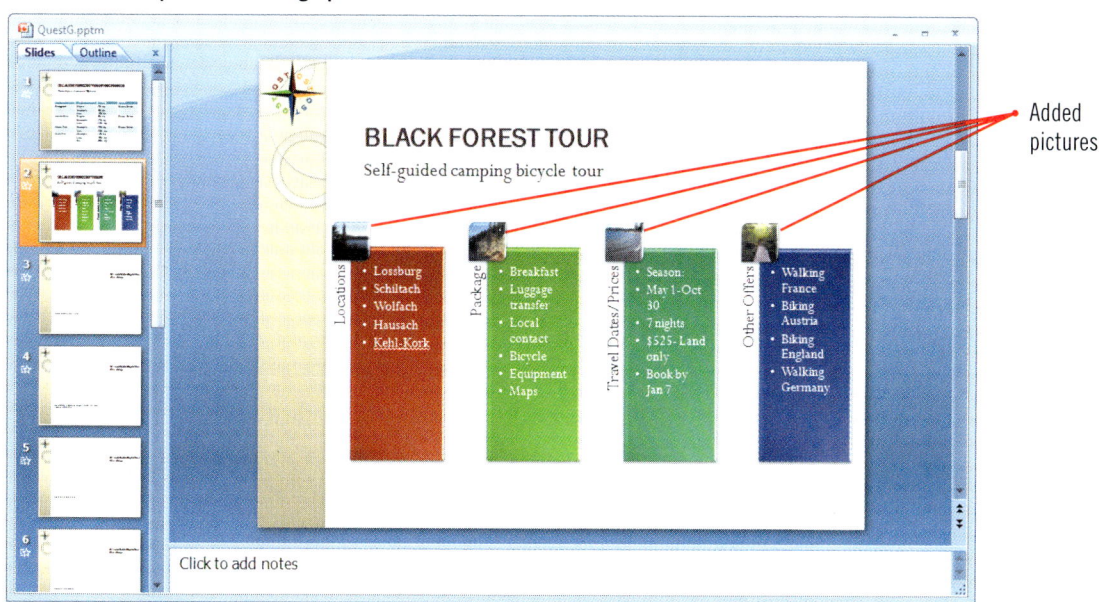

Added pictures

Changing page setup and slide orientation

When you need to customize the size and orientation of your presentation you can do so using the commands in the Page Setup group on the Design tab on the Ribbon. Click the Page Setup button to open the Page Setup dialog box. In the Page Setup dialog box, you can change the width and height of the slides to twelve different settings, including On-screen Show, Letter Paper, 35mm Slides, and Banner. You can also set a custom slide size by determining the height and width of the slides. If the presentation would work better in Portrait rather than Landscape mode, you can click the Slide Orientation button in the Page Setup group on the Design tab to change the orientation of the presentation. The orientation setting for the slides is separate from the orientation setting for the notes, handouts, and outline. You can set the slide orientation in the Page Setup dialog box or by clicking the Slide Orientation button in the Page Setup group.

Inserting Illustrations, Objects, and Media Clips   PowerPoint 151

Inserting an Animation

UNIT G
PowerPoint 2007

In your presentations, you may want to use special effects to illustrate a point or capture the attention of your audience. You can do this by inserting an animation or a movie. An **animation** contains multiple images that stream together or move when you run a slide show to give the illusion of motion. Animations are stored as Graphics Interchange Format (GIF) files. PowerPoint comes with a number of animated GIFs, which are stored in the Microsoft Clip Organizer. The **Clip Organizer** contains various drawings, photographs, clip art, sounds, animated GIFs, and movies that you can insert into your presentation. A **movie** is live action captured in digital format by a movie camera. You continue to develop your presentation by inserting an animation of a bicyclist in the forest.

STEPS

1. Click Slide 1 in the Slides tab

2. Click the Insert tab on the Ribbon, click the Movie button list arrow in the Media Clips group, then click Movie from Clip Organizer
   The Clip Art task pane opens and displays animations.

3. Type bicycle in the Search for text box, then click Go
   PowerPoint searches for bicycle animations.

   TROUBLE
   If you do not see the GIF file in Figure G-7, choose a different GIF or ask your instructor or technical support person for help.

4. Click the down scroll arrow until you see the thumbnail of the bicyclist shown in Figure G-7, then click the thumbnail
   The animation appears in the center of the slide.

5. Click the Clip Art task pane Close button ✖
   The Clip Art task pane closes and the Picture Tools Format tab is open on the Ribbon.

6. Right-click the animation, then click Size and Position on the shortcut menu
   The Size and Position dialog box opens.

7. In the Scale section double-click the number 100 in the Height text box, type 150, click the Position tab in the dialog box, select the number in the Horizontal text box, type 8.12, press [Tab] twice, type 6 in the Vertical text box, then click Close
   The animation moves to a new location on the slide and increases in size.

8. Click the Brightness button in the Adjust group, click +20 %, then click a blank area of the slide
   The animation is a little brighter and fits better with the other slide elements. Compare your screen with Figure G-8. The animation won't begin unless you view it in Slide Show view.

   QUICK TIP
   An animated GIF file will also play if you publish the presentation as a Web page and view it in a browser such as Internet Explorer.

9. Click the Slide Show button on the status bar, watch the animation for a few seconds, press [Esc], then save your work

Inserting Illustrations, Objects, and Media Clips

FIGURE G-7: Clip Organizer showing animation files

Click this animation

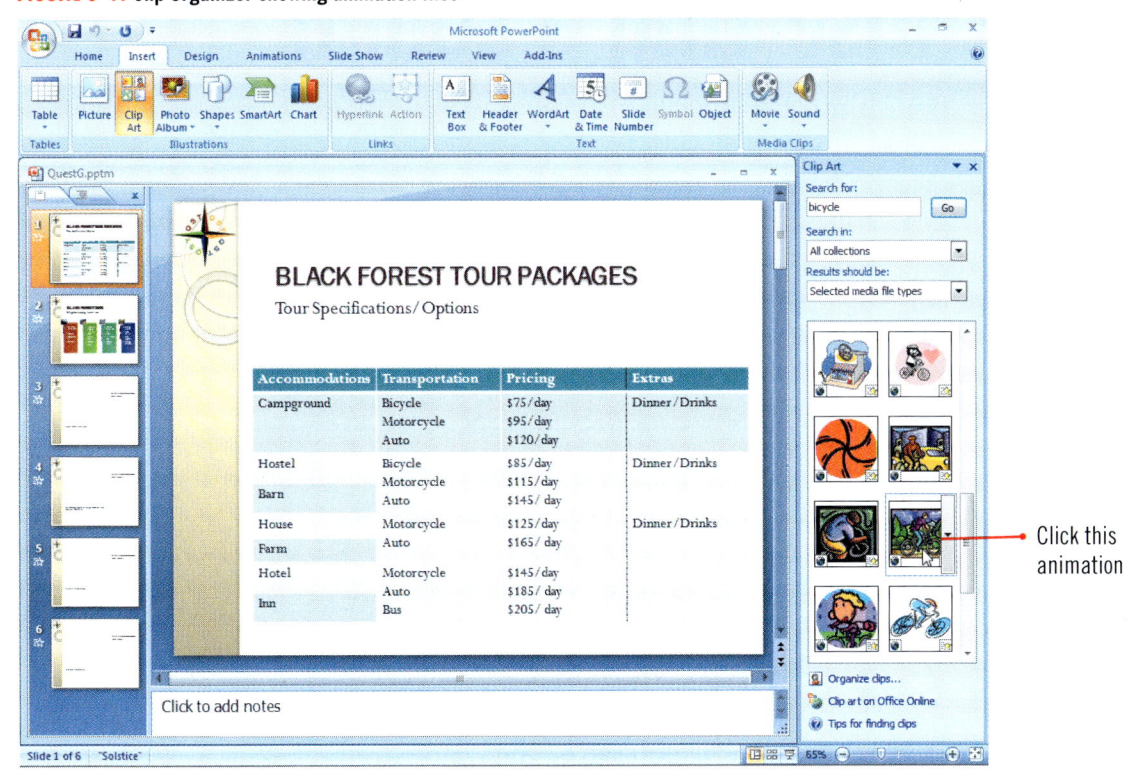

FIGURE G-8: Slide showing formatted animation

Animation

Inserting movies

You can insert movies from the Microsoft Clip Organizer, the Microsoft Web site, or from other sources. To insert a movie from your computer hard drive or a removable disk, click the Insert tab on the Ribbon, click the Movie button list arrow in the Media Clips group, then click Movie from File. Navigate to the location of the movie you want, then insert it. If you're using the Clip Art task pane, search for the file you want, then insert it. After you insert a movie, you can edit it using the Picture Tools Format tab. You can also open the Custom Animation task pane and apply an effect to the movie. From the Custom Animation task pane, you can indicate whether to continue the slide show or to stop playing the movie.

Inserting Illustrations, Objects, and Media Clips

Inserting a Sound

PowerPoint allows you to insert sounds in your presentation in the same way you insert animations or movies. You can add sounds to your presentation from files on a disk, the Microsoft Clip Organizer, the Internet, or a drive on a network. The primary use of sound in a presentation is to provide emphasis to a slide or an element on the slide. For example, if you are creating a presentation about a raft tour of the Colorado River, you might insert a rushing water sound on a slide showing a photograph of people rafting. If you try to insert a sound that is larger than 100 KB, PowerPoint will automatically link the sound file to your presentation. You can change this setting in the Advanced section of the PowerPoint Options dialog box. You insert a wind sound on Slide 1 of the presentation to enhance the animation on the slide.

STEPS

1. **Click the Insert tab on the Ribbon, click the Sound button list arrow in the Media Clips group, then click Sound from Clip Organizer**

   The Clip Art task pane opens and displays all the sound files installed with PowerPoint. PowerPoint sounds are Windows Audio (.wav) files, but you can also install other types of sound files, such as (.aiff), (.au), (.mid), (.mp3), and (.wma).

2. **Type wind in the Search for text box, then click Go**

   PowerPoint searches for wind sounds.

3. **Click the sound file labeled Strong Wind**

   A dialog box opens asking if you want the sound to play automatically or if you want it to play only when you click the icon during the slide show.

   > **QUICK TIP**
   > The sound icon you see may be different from the one illustrated in Figure G-9 depending on your sound card software.

4. **Click Automatically**

   A small sound icon appears in the center of the slide, as shown in Figure G-9. The sound will play automatically during a slide show.

   > **TROUBLE**
   > If you do not hear a sound, your computer may not have a sound card installed. See your instructor or technical support person for help.

5. **Drag the sound icon to the lower-right corner of the slide, click the Sound Tools Options tab, click the Loop Until Stopped check box in the Sound Options group, click the Preview button in the Play group, listen to the sound a few seconds until you hear a pause at the loop, then click the Preview button**

   You know the sound has looped when you hear a brief pause and then the sound begins again.

6. **Click the Slide Show Volume button in the Sound Options group, click Low, click the Preview button in the Play group, listen to the sound for a few seconds, then click the Preview button**

   The sound volume is slightly softer.

7. **Click the Slide Show button on the status bar, watch the slide for a few seconds, then press [Esc]**

   Notice that the sound icon appears during the slide show.

8. **Click the Results should be list arrow, click the All media types check box, click Go, then click Clip Art task pane Close button**

   The default settings are now restored to the Clip Art task pane.

9. **Click a blank area of the slide, then save your changes**

   Compare your screen to Figure G-10.

FIGURE G-9: Slide showing small sound icon

Sound icon

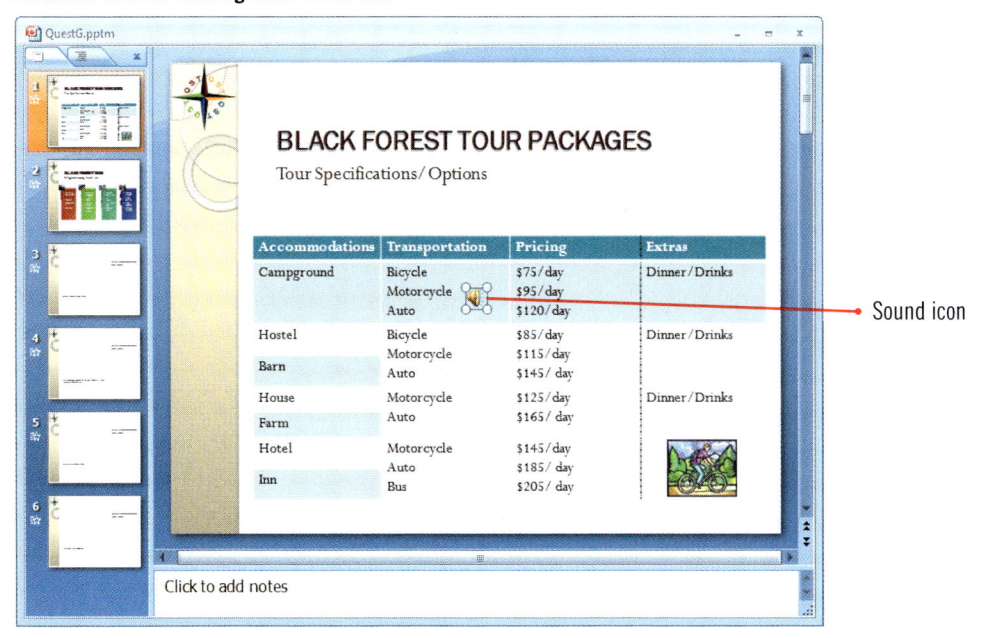

FIGURE G-10: Slide showing repositioned and formatted sound icon

Repositioned sound icon

Playing music from a CD

You can play a CD audio track during your slide show. Insert the CD into the CD drive, click the Insert tab on the Ribbon, click the Sound button list arrow, then click Play CD Audio Track. The Insert CD Audio dialog box opens. Select the beginning and ending track number and the timing options you want. See Figure G-11. When you are finished in the Insert CD Audio dialog box, click OK. A CD icon appears on the slide. You can indicate if you want the CD to play automatically when you move to the slide or only when you click the CD icon during a slide show. The CD must be in the CD-ROM drive before you can play an audio track.

FIGURE G-11: Insert CD Audio dialog box

Inserting Illustrations, Objects, and Media Clips

Using Macros

UNIT G — PowerPoint 2007

As you learned in the first lesson of this unit, a macro is a recording of an action or a set of actions that you use to automate tasks. The contents of a macro consist of a series of command codes that you create in the Visual Basic for Applications programming language using Microsoft Visual Basic, which you can access through the Developer tab in PowerPoint. You can use macros to automate almost any action that you perform repeatedly when creating presentations, which saves you time and effort. Any presentation with the .pptm file extension is saved with a macro. You use macros that you already created to format and place four pictures.

STEPS

1. **Click Slide 3 in the Slides tab, click the Office button, click PowerPoint Options at the bottom of the menu, click the Show Developer tab in the Ribbon check box, then click OK**
   The Developer tab appears on the Ribbon.

2. **Click the Developer tab on the Ribbon, then click the Visual Basic button in the Code group**
   The Visual Basic window opens displaying two small windows as shown in Figure G-12. Each window represents a separate macro. Each macro is designed to reduce the size of a picture and place it in a specific place on the slide. The difference between the two macros is that the Module2 macro unlocks the aspect ratio of a picture so that any size picture can be reduced within the designated parameters.

   > **QUICK TIP**
   > To learn more about macros and the Visual Basic for Applications programming language, click the Visual Basic button on the Developer tab to open the Visual Basic window, then click the Help button.

3. **Click the Close button on the Microsoft Visual Basic title bar, click the Insert tab on the Ribbon, click the Picture button in the Illustrations group, locate the file PPT G-6.jpg from the drive and folder where you store your Data Files, then click Insert**
   An oversized picture covers most of the slide.

4. **Click the Developer tab on the Ribbon, then click the Macros button in the Code group**
   The Macro dialog box opens displaying the two macros attached to this presentation file.

5. **Make sure the Module1.PictureReduction macro is selected, then click Run**
   The macro runs and the picture's size is reduced to fit within a certain area on the slide. The macro also positions the picture to precise coordinates on the slide.

6. **Click Slide 4 in the Slides tab, insert the picture file PPT G-7.jpg from the drive and folder where you store your Data Files, click the Developer tab on the Ribbon, click the Macros button in the Code group, click Module2.PictureReduction in the list, then click Run**
   This macro resizes and positions a picture with a portrait orientation.

7. **Insert the picture file PPT G-8.jpg on Slide 5, apply the Module1.PictureReduction macro to the picture, insert the picture file PPT G-9.jpg on Slide 6, then apply the Module1.PictureReduction macro to the picture**
   Compare your screen to Figure G-13.

8. **Click the Picture Tools Format tab on the Ribbon, click the Drop Shadow Rectangle style in the Picture Styles group, then apply this same picture style to the pictures on Slides 3, 4, and 5**
   Each of the pictures you inserted into the presentation is now formatted with the same drop shadow.

9. **Click, click PowerPoint Options, click the Show Developer tab in the Ribbon check box, click OK, then save your work**

Inserting Illustrations, Objects, and Media Clips

FIGURE G-12: Visual Basic window

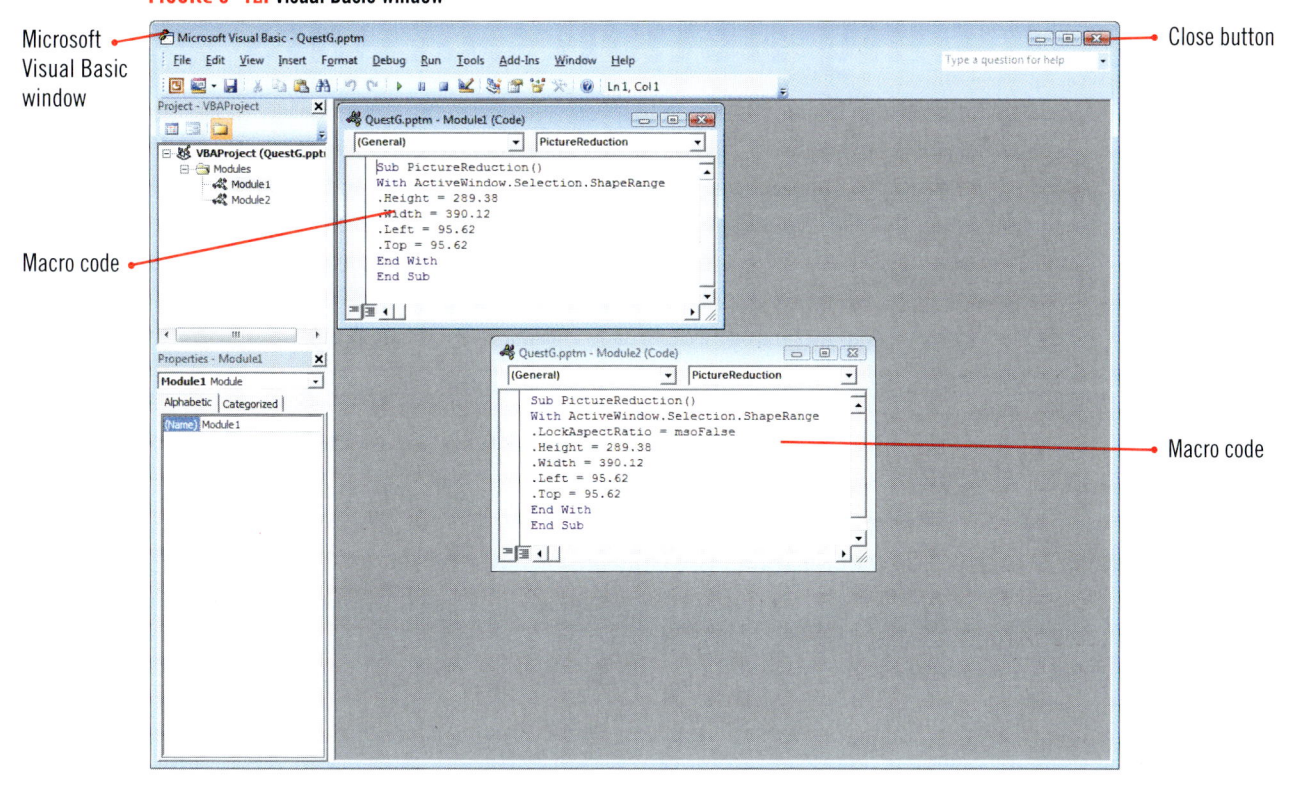

- Microsoft Visual Basic window
- Macro code
- Close button
- Macro code

FIGURE G-13: Screen showing inserted pictures

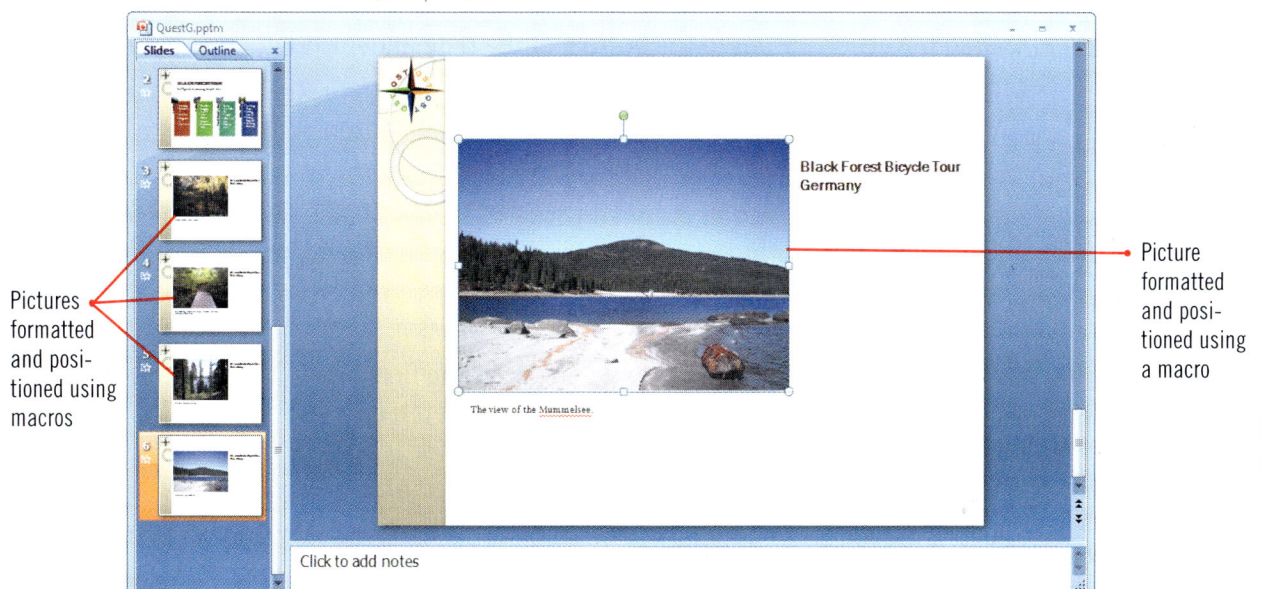

- Pictures formatted and positioned using macros
- Picture formatted and positioned using a macro

Macro security

There are certain risks involved when you enable macros on your computer. The macros used in this lesson are simple commands that automate the size reduction and relative position of picture on a slide; however, hackers can introduce harmful viruses or other malicious programs into your computer using macros. By default, PowerPoint disables macros when you open a presentation file that includes macros to prevent possible damage to your computer. To understand PowerPoint's security settings and how PowerPoint checks for harmful macros, click the Macro Security button on the Developer tab or click the Office button, click PowerPoint Options, then click Trust Center. The bottom line with macros is if you can't trust the source of the macro, do not enable it.

Inserting Illustrations, Objects, and Media Clips

Adding Action Buttons

An action button is an interactive button that you create from the Shapes gallery to perform a specific task. For example, you can create an action button to play a movie or a sound, or to hyperlink to another slide in your presentation. Action buttons can also hyperlink to an Internet address on the Web, a different presentation, or another file created in another program. You can also run a macro or another program using an action button. Action buttons are commonly used in self-running presentations and presentations published on the Web. You finish working on this presentation by adding action buttons to each slide, which will allow you to move from slide to slide and back to the first slide.

STEPS

1. Click Slide 1 in the Slides tab, then click the Home tab on the Ribbon, if it is not already selected

   Slide 1 appears in the Slide pane.

> **QUICK TIP**
> All of the shapes in the Shapes gallery as well as most other objects, including text, can be set as an action button.

2. Click the Shapes button in the Drawing group, click Action Button: Forward or Next in the Action Buttons section, press and hold [Shift], refer to Figure G-14 as you drag to create a button, then release [Shift]

   A small action button appears on the slide and the Action Settings dialog box opens.

3. Make sure Next Slide is selected in the Hyperlink to list, then click OK

   The dialog box closes.

4. Click the Drawing Tools Format tab on the Ribbon, click the More button in the Shape Styles group, then click Subtle Effect – Dark 1 in the first column

   The action button is easier to see.

> **QUICK TIP**
> You can soften the action button shape by removing its outline. Click the shape, click the Shape Outline button in the Shape Styles group, then click No Outline.

5. Drag the action button to the bottom of the slide under the left edge of the table

6. Click the Home tab on the Ribbon, click the Copy button in the Clipboard group, click Slide 2 in the Slides pane, then click the Paste button in the Clipboard group

   An exact copy of the action button is placed on the slide.

7. Paste a copy of the action button on Slides 3, 4, and 5, click Slide 6 in the Slides tab, click the Shapes button in the Drawing group, then click Action Button: Home in the Action Buttons section

   The action button is copied onto slides 1–5 of the presentation. You selected the Home Action button.

> **QUICK TIP**
> Use the arrow keys on your keyboard to nudge the action button into place.

8. Drag an action button about the same size as the first action button below the image on Slide 6, click OK, click the Drawing Tools Format tab on the Ribbon, click in the Shape Styles group, then click Subtle Effect – Dark 1

   This new action button is formatted the same as the other action buttons. Compare your screen to Figure G-15.

9. Click the Slide Show button on the status bar, click the Home action button, then click the action buttons to move from slide to slide, then press [Esc] to end the slide show

   The pointer changes to when you click each action button.

10. Save your changes, click , then click Close

FIGURE G-14: New action button

Action button

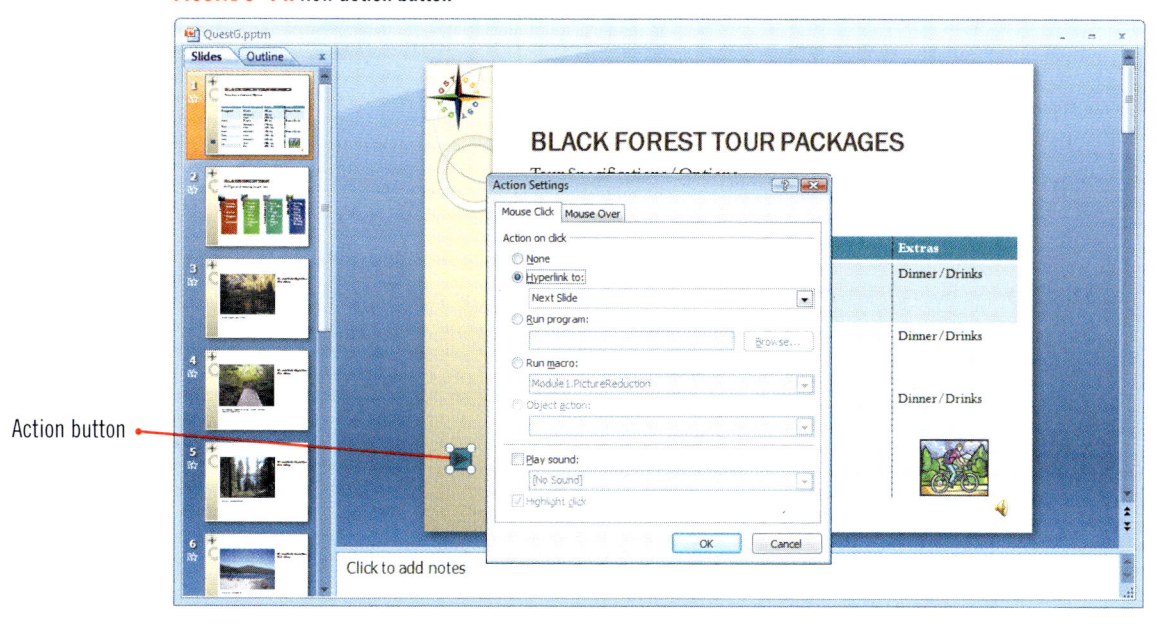

FIGURE G-15: Last slide showing Home action button

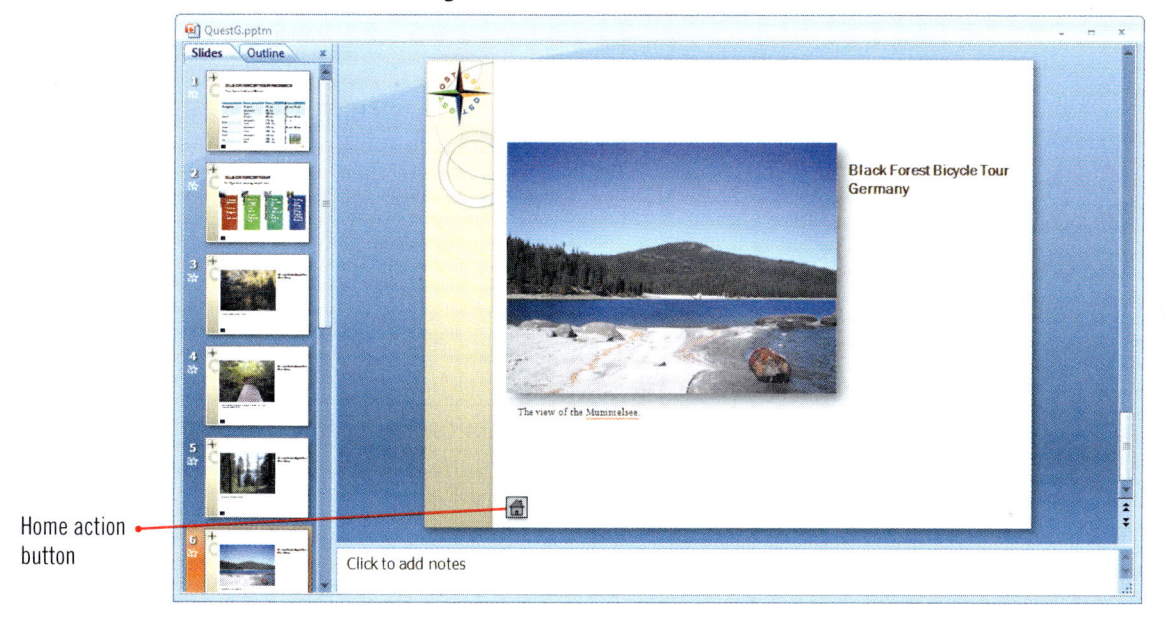

Home action button

The compatibility checker

In order to make certain that your PowerPoint 2007 presentation will open and function properly in an earlier version of PowerPoint, you need to run the Compatibility Checker. The Compatibility Checker analyzes your presentation and finds potential problems between your PowerPoint 2007 presentation and earlier versions of PowerPoint. After you run the Compatibility Checker, a report is created that identifies features you have used in your presentation that will be lost or degraded by saving your presentation in an earlier file format. For example, SmartArt graphics can't be edited in previous versions of PowerPoint. To run the Compatibility Checker, click the Office button, point to Prepare, then click Run Compatibility Checker.

Inserting Illustrations, Objects, and Media Clips   PowerPoint 159

UNIT G
PowerPoint 2007

Inserting a Hyperlink

Often you will want to view a document that either won't fit on the slide or is too detailed for your presentation. In these cases, you can insert a hyperlink, a specially formatted word, phrase, graphic, or drawn object that you click during your slide show to "jump to," or display, another slide in your current presentation; another PowerPoint presentation; a Word, Excel, or Access file; or a Web page on the Internet. Inserting a hyperlink is similar to linking because you can change the object in the source program after you click the hyperlink. You add two hyperlinks to the primary presentation you have been working on for Ellen that will provide access to more detail on the Black Forest bicycle tour.

STEPS

1. **Open the presentation PPT G-10.pptx from the drive and folder where you store your Data Files, save the presentation as QuestGFinal, click the View tab on the Ribbon, then click the Arrange All button in the Window group**

2. **Click Slide 12 in the Slides tab, select Biking Austria in the table, click the Insert tab on the Ribbon, then click the Hyperlink button in the Links group**

   The Insert Hyperlink dialog box opens. The Existing File or Web Page button is selected in the Link to: pane, and the Current Folder button is selected in the Look in page.

3. **Locate the file PPT G-11.docx from the drive and folder where you store your Data Files, click OK, then click in a blank area of the slide**

   Now that you have made "Biking Austria" a hyperlink to the file PPT G-11.docx, the text formatting changes to a green color, the hyperlink color for this presentation's theme, and is underlined. It's important to test any hyperlink you create.

4. **Click the Slide Show button on the status bar, point to Biking Austria to see the pointer change to 👆, then click Biking Austria**

   Microsoft Word opens, and the Word document containing a detailed description of the Biking Austria tour appears, as shown in Figure G-16.

5. **Click the down scroll arrow and read the document, then click the Word window Close button**

   The PowerPoint slide reappears in Slide Show view. The hyperlink is now an olive green, the color for followed hyperlinks in this theme, indicating that the hyperlink has been used or viewed.

6. **Press [Esc] to end the slide show, right-click the Information action button in the Black Forest Tour cell of the table, click Hyperlink, click the Hyperlink to option button, click the Hyperlink to list arrow, click the down scroll arrow, then click Other PowerPoint Presentation**

   The Hyperlink to Other PowerPoint Presentation dialog box opens.

7. **Locate the file PPT G-12.pptx from the drive and folder where you store your Data Files, then click OK**

   The Hyperlink to Slide dialog box opens. You can choose which slide of the presentation you want to link to.

8. **Click OK to link to Slide 1, click OK to close the Action Settings dialog box, click , click the Information action button, click through the presentation using the action buttons, press [Esc] to end the slide show, then press [Esc] again**

   The slide show ends. Both hyperlinks work correctly.

9. **Add your name to the Slide footer, save your changes, then click the Slide Sorter button**

   Compare your screen to Figure G-17.

10. **Print the outline and the slides, close the presentation, then exit PowerPoint**

PowerPoint 160   Inserting Illustrations, Objects, and Media Clips

FIGURE G-16: Linked Word document

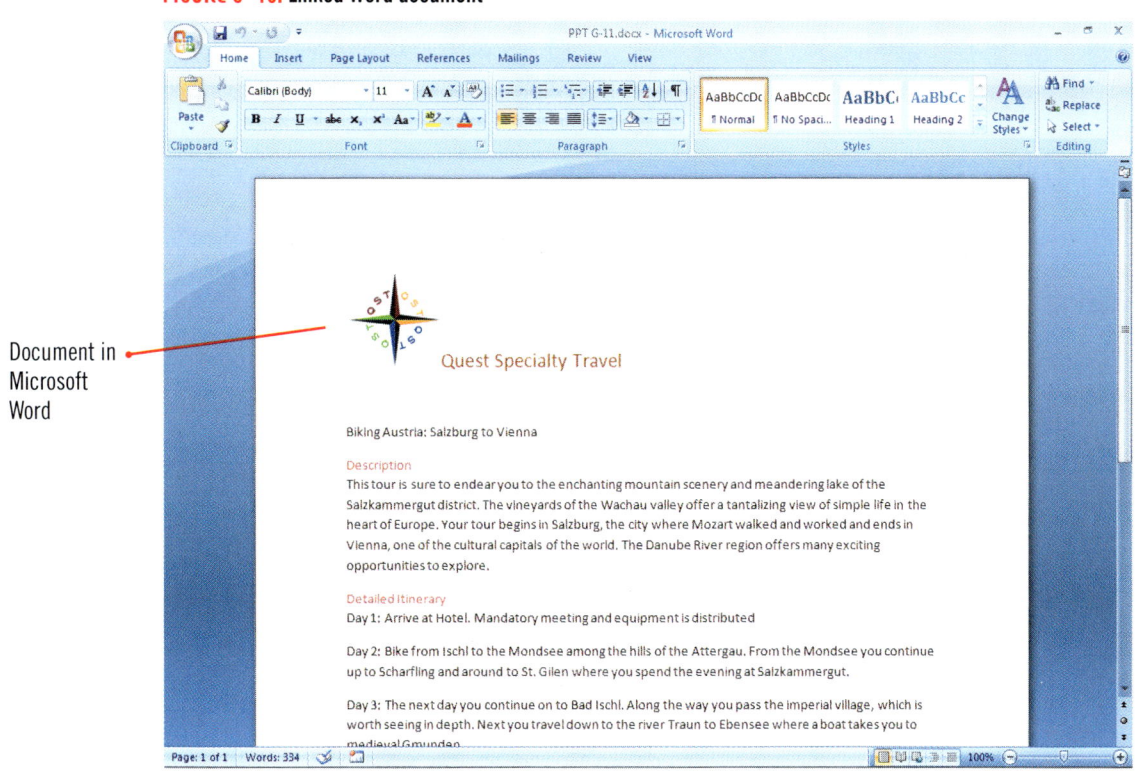

Document in Microsoft Word

FIGURE G-17: Final presentation in Slide Sorter view

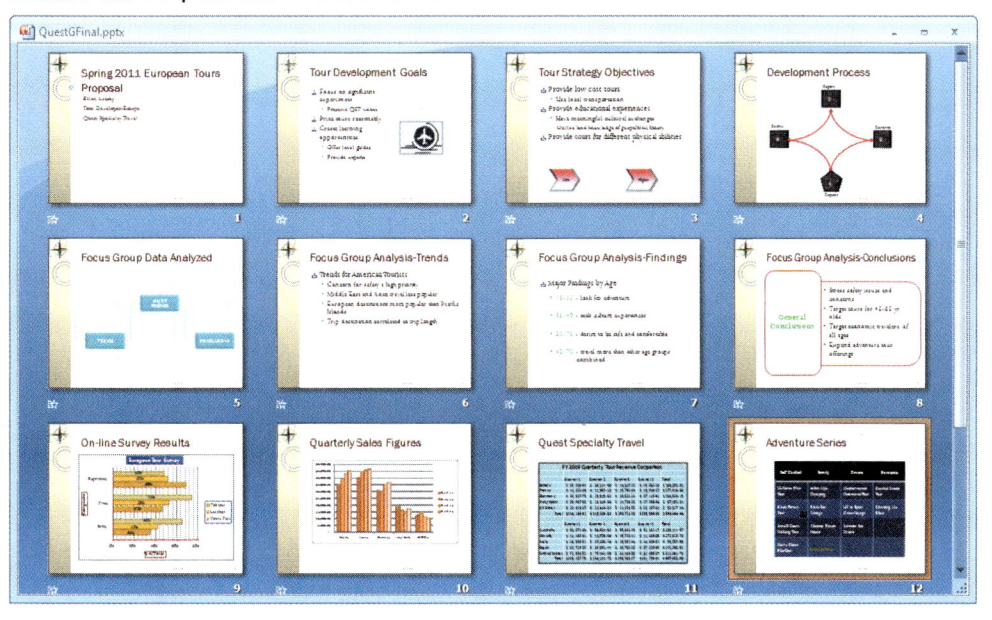

Changing PowerPoint options

You can customize your installation of PowerPoint by changing various settings and preferences. To change PowerPoint settings, click the Office button, then click PowerPoint Options to open the PowerPoint Options dialog box. In the dialog box there are eight sections identified by a word in the left pane, which offer you ways to customize PowerPoint. For example, the Popular area includes options for viewing the Mini toolbar, enabling Live Preview, and showing the Developer tab on the Ribbon.

Inserting Illustrations, Objects, and Media Clips

Practice

SAM — If you have a SAM user profile, you may have access to hands-on instruction, practice, and assessment of the skills covered in this unit. Log in to your SAM account (http://sam2007.course.com/) to launch any assigned training activities or exams that relate to the skills covered in this unit.

▼ CONCEPTS REVIEW

Label each element of the PowerPoint window shown in Figure G-18.

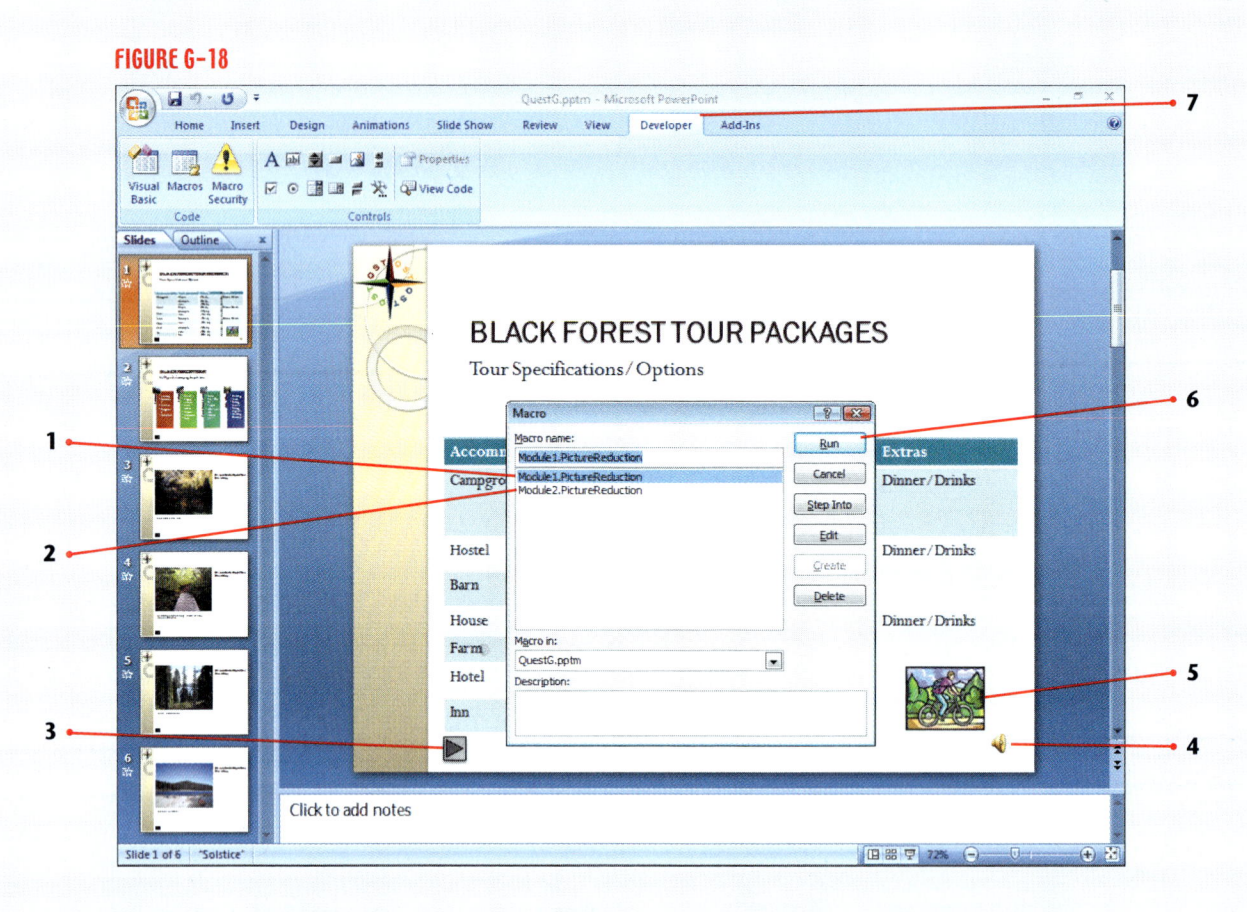

FIGURE G-18

Match each of the terms with the statement that best describes its function.

8. Clip Organizer
9. Macro-enabled presentation
10. Animation
11. Movie
12. Action button
13. Hyperlink

a. Multiple images that move when you run a slide show
b. A file with the .pptm file extension
c. A specially formatted word or graphic that you can click to jump to another document
d. An interactive shape that performs a specific task when clicked
e. A folder that stores media clips on the computer
f. Live action captured in digital format by a camera

Select the best answer from the list of choices.

14. A recording of an action that automates a task best describes which of the following:
    a. Hyperlink
    b. Action button
    c. Macro
    d. Movie
15. Which of the following combines content with an illustrative diagram?
    a. SmartArt
    b. Action button
    c. Hyperlink
    d. Table
16. Which statement best describes a hyperlink?
    a. A type of animation
    b. Another name for a macro
    c. A button used in a table to start a slide show
    d. A specially formatted shape that is clicked to display an Excel file
17. What is a GIF file?
    a. A movie
    b. An animation
    c. A sound
    d. A hyperlink

▼ SKILLS REVIEW

1. **Create custom tables.**
    a. Start PowerPoint, open the presentation PPT G-13.pptm from the drive and folder where you store your Data Files, then save it as **Cheese Cooperative**.
    b. Go to Slide 5, select the table, click the Table Tools Design tab, click the More button in the Table Styles group, then click the Light Style 2 – Accent 1 in the Light section in the second row.
    c. Click the Pen Weight button in the Draw Borders group, select a solid line style, select 2¼ pt, then apply the new line style to the bottom horizontal cell border in the first row.
    d. Apply the 2¼-pt line style to the vertical border lines between the cells in the first row, then click the Draw Table button.
    e. Open the Table Tools Layout tab, select the table, click the Cell Margins button in the Alignment group, then click Wide.
    f. Click anywhere in the upper-left cell, click the Select button in the Table group, click Select Row, then click the Center button in the Alignment group.
    g. Click anywhere in the bottom row, click the Insert Below button in the Rows & Columns group, click the left cell, type **Bleu de Gex**, press [Tab], type **Bethmale**, press [Tab], type **Agour Ossau-Iraty**.
    h. Save your changes.

2. **Design a SmartArt graphic.**
    a. Go to Slide 4, click the SmartArt graphic, then click the SmartArt Tools Design tab.
    b. Click the More button in the Layouts group, then click Vertical Picture Accent List in the third row.
    c. Open the Text Pane if necessary, click the Add Shape button list arrow in the Create Graphic group, then click Add Shape After.
    d. Type **Production**, press [Enter], click the Demote button in the Create Graphic group, type **Cow cheese 1.66 million tons**, press [Enter], type **Goat cheese 0.68 million tons**, press [Enter], type **Ewe cheese 0.52 million tons**.
    e. Close the Text Pane, click the Change Colors button in the SmartArt Styles group, then click Gradient Range – Accent 2 in the Accent 2 section.
    f. Resize and reposition the SmartArt graphic so it is centered on the slide, then save your changes.

3. **Format a SmartArt graphic.**
    a. Click the SmartArt Tools Format tab, click the top circle shape in the graphic, then click the Smaller button in the Shapes group twice.
    b. Following the instructions in the step above, decrease the size of the other two circle shapes.

▼ SKILLS REVIEW (CONTINUED)

    c. Click the picture icon in the bottom circle shape, then locate and insert the file PPT G-14.jpg from the drive and folder where you store your Data Files.

    d. Follow the above instructions and insert the file PPT G-14.jpg to the other two circle shapes.

    e. Save your changes.

4. **Insert an animation.**

    a. Go to Slide 7, then open the Clip Art task pane.

    b. Insert an animated GIF file of your choosing on the slide. Type the word **email** to search for an appropriate animated GIF.

    c. Resize and reposition the GIF file as necessary.

    d. Click the Contrast button in the Adjust group, then click +30%.

    e. Preview the animation in Slide Show view, then save your presentation.

5. **Insert a sound.**

    a. Go to Slide 2.

    b. Click the Insert tab, click the Sound button list arrow in the Media Clips group, then click Sound from File.

    c. Locate and insert the sound file PPT G-15.wav from the drive and folder where you store your Data Files. Set the sound to play when clicked.

    d. Drag the sound icon to the right side of the graphic of France.

    e. Click the Sound Tools Options tab on the Ribbon, click the Slide Show Volume button in the Sound Options group, then click Low.

    f. Click the Loop Until Stopped check box in the Sound Options group, click the Preview button in the Play group, then save your presentation.

6. **Use macros.**

    a. Go to Slide 6, click the Office button, click PowerPoint Options, then add the Developer tab to the Ribbon.

    b. Click the Insert tab on the Ribbon, click the Picture button in the Illustrations group, then locate and insert the file PPT G-16.jpg from the drive and folder where you store your Data Files.

    c. Click the Developer tab, click the Macros button in the Code group, then click Run in the Macro dialog box. Click OK to run the macro, if necessary.

    d. Click the Picture Tools Format tab on the Ribbon, click the More button in the Picture Styles group, then click Soft Edge Rectangle in the top row.

    e. Remove the Developer tab from the Ribbon.

7. **Add action buttons.**

    a. Go to Slide 1, click the Shapes button in the Drawing group, then click Action Button: Forward or Next.

    b. Draw a small button, click OK in the Action Settings dialog box, then position the button in the lower-left corner of the slide.

    c. Click the Drawing Tools Format tab on the Ribbon, click the More button in the Shape Styles group, then click Intense Effect – Accent 5 in the bottom row.

    d. Copy the action button to Slides 2–7.

    e. Go to Slide 8, click the Shapes button, click Action Button: Beginning, draw a small button, then click OK.

    f. Click Slide 7, click the action button, click the Format Painter button in the Clipboard group, click Slide 8, then click the action button.

    g. Position the button in the lower-left corner of the slide.

    h. Run the slide show from Slide 1 and test the action buttons, then save your work.

▼ SKILLS REVIEW (CONTINUED)

8. **Insert a hyperlink.**
   a. Go to Slide 6, then select the words Maria McNibs in the text object.
   b. Click the Insert tab on the Ribbon, click the Hyperlink button in the Links group, locate the file PPT G-17.docx from the drive and folder where you store your Data Files, then click OK.
   c. Click in the notes pane, then type **The hyperlink links to Maria's cheese review of the 2010 Camembert**.
   d. Open Slide Show view, click the hyperlink, read the review, then click the Word window Close button.
   e. Press [Esc], then add your name as a footer to notes and handouts.
   f. Run the spell checker, view the presentation in Slide Show view. Make any necessary changes. The completed presentation is shown in Figure G-19.
   g. Print the slides as Notes Pages, then save and close the presentation.

FIGURE G-19

▼ INDEPENDENT CHALLENGE 1

Tounger Engineering is a mechanical and industrial design company that specializes in designing manufacturing plants around the world. As a company financial analyst, you need to investigate and report on a possible contract to design and build a large manufacturing plant in China.

a. Open the file PPT G-18.pptx, then save it as **Chinese Plant**.
b. On Slide 3, apply the table style Medium Style 3 – Accent 3, then draw a dotted line down the center of the table using the Pen Style button.
c. Click in the top row of the table, insert a row above the top row, type **Line Item** in the left cell, then type **Budget** in the right cell.
d. Click the Overhead/Benefits cell, split the cell into two columns and one row, then move the word Benefits to the new cell and delete the slash.
e. Create a new SmartArt graphic on Slide 4 using the following process information: **Planning and Design**; **Site Acquisition and Preparation**; **Underground Construction**; **Above-ground Construction**; and **Final Building**.
f. Change the colors of the graphic to a colorful theme, then apply an intense SmartArt Style effect.
g. Change the shape of at least one shape in the SmartArt graphic using the Change Shape button, then click the Right to Left button in the Create Graphic group on the SmartArt Tools Design tab.
h. Add your name as a footer to the notes and handouts, then save your changes.

Advanced Challenge Exercise

- Create a new slide using the Title and Content slide layout, type **Project Organization** in the title placeholder, then create an organizational chart SmartArt graphic.
- Fill the text boxes with the following job titles: **Project Manager**; **Administrator**; **Project Foreman**; **Design Manager**; and **Project Coordinator**.
- Click the top shape, click the Layout button in the Create Graphic group, then click Right Hanging.
- Format the graphic by adding a new style and color theme, make any other necessary changes, then save the presentation as **Chinese Plant ACE**.

i. View the presentation in Slide Show view, print the presentation as handouts (two slides per page), then close the presentation and exit PowerPoint.

Inserting Illustrations, Objects, and Media Clips

▼ INDEPENDENT CHALLENGE 2

You are the director of operations at The Fisher Group, a large investment banking firm in New York. Fisher is considering merging with DuPont Financial Services, a smaller investment company in Miami, to form the 8th largest financial institution in the United States. As the director of operations, you need to present some financial projections regarding the merger to a special committee formed by The Fisher Group to study the proposed merger.

a. Open the file PPT G-19.pptx from the drive and folder where you store your Data Files, then save it as **Merger**.
b. Format the table on Slide 3 as directed in the following steps: (1) apply a table style from the Light Style 2 styles section of the Table Styles gallery; (2) draw three 1½-pt dotted vertical cell separator lines in the table; and (3) click the Total Row check box and the Last Column check box in the Table Style Options group.
c. Convert the text on Slide 5 to a SmartArt graphic using one of the List layouts.
d. Format the SmartArt graphic by: (1) applying an Accent 2 color theme, (2) changing the SmartArt style to Subtle Effect, (3) deleting the empty shape, and (4) applying a fill using the Shape Fill button in the Shape Styles group.
e. Insert an animation on Slide 3. Use the word **profits** to search for an appropriate animated GIF.
f. Select the word DuPont on Slide 2, click the Insert tab on the Ribbon, click the Hyperlink button in the Links group, locate the file PPT G-20.pptx from the drive and folder where you store your Data Files, then click OK.
g. Add your name as a footer to the notes and the handouts, save your changes, then view the presentation in Slide Show view. Be sure to click the hyperlink on Slide 2.
h. Print the final slide presentation as handouts (four per page), then close the presentation and exit PowerPoint.

▼ INDEPENDENT CHALLENGE 3

You have been recently hired at AsiaWorld Inc., a U.S. company that exports goods and services to companies in all parts of Asia, including Japan, Hong Kong, China, and the Philippines. One of your new responsibilities is to prepare short presentations on different subjects for use on the company Web site using data provided to you by others in the company.

a. Open the file PPT G-21.pptx from the drive and folder where you store your Data Files, then save it as **AsiaWorld**.
b. Add a design theme, background shading, or other objects to make your presentation look professional.
c. Convert the text on Slide 3 to a SmartArt graphic, then format the graphic using any of the formatting commands available.
d. Insert an appropriate animation on the last slide of the presentation.
e. Insert a sound on Slide 2. Use the word **harbor** to search for an appropriate sound.
f. Create, format, and position Forward action buttons on Slides 1–5.
g. Create, format, and position a Home action button on Slide 6.
h. Create, format, and position Back action buttons on Slides 2–6.

Advanced Challenge Exercise

- Go to Slide 1.
- Insert a CD of your choice into the CD drive of your computer, click the Insert tab on the Ribbon, then click the Sound button list arrow.
- Click Play CD Audio Track, select the start track, select the end track, set any other options you feel are necessary, then click OK.
- Click Automatically, click the sound icon if necessary, click the Play Track list arrow in the Set Up group, click Play across slides, then click the Slide Show button on the status bar.
- Press [Esc] when finished.

i. Add your name as a footer to the slides and notes and handouts, save your changes, then print the final slide presentation.
j. View the presentation in Slide Show view, then exit PowerPoint.

▼ REAL LIFE INDEPENDENT CHALLENGE

One of the assignments in your business course at the university is to give a 15 minute presentation on any subject to the class. The goal of the assignment is for you to persuade the class (and your instructor) to make an informed decision about the subject you are presenting based on your ability to communicate the facts. You decide to create a presentation using pictures and other media to play in the background while you give your presentation.

To develop the content of this presentation:

- Choose your own subject matter, for example, a favorite hobby or sport.
- Use your own media clips (pictures, sounds, or movies) on your computer. If you don't have your own media clips, you can search the Clip Organizer for appropriate clips.

a. Open the file PPT G-22.pptm from the drive and folder where you store your Data Files, then save it as **Business 410**. The file PPT G-22.pptm has no content, but is macro-enabled.
b. Add your name, the date, and the slide number as the footer on all slides, except the title slide.
c. Decide on a presentation subject, then think about what results you want to see and what information you will need to create the slide presentation.
d. Insert one picture (your own or one from the Clip Organizer) on each slide, then run the available macro for each picture.
e. Insert one or more appropriate sounds from your computer or the Clip Organizer.
f. Insert one or more appropriate animations or movies from your computer or the Clip Organizer.
g. Give each slide a title and add main text where appropriate. Create additional slides as necessary.
h. Apply an appropriate design theme.
i. Spell check the presentation, view the final presentation in Slide Show view, save the final version, then print the slides as handouts. See Figure G-20.
j. Close the presentation, then exit PowerPoint.

FIGURE G-20

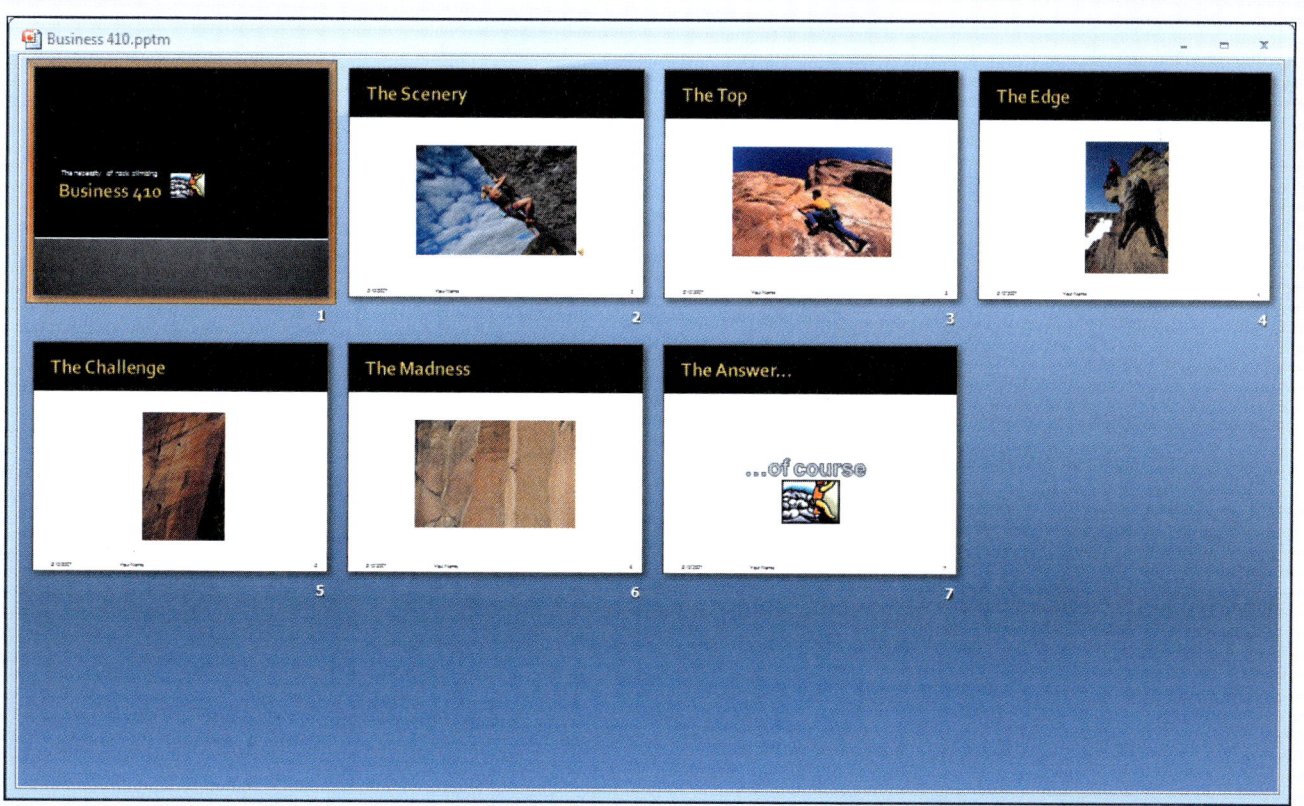

▼ **VISUAL WORKSHOP**

Create a slide that looks like the example in Figure G-21. The SmartArt is created using the Horizontal Bullet List layout with the Polished style and the colored Fill – Accent 1 color. Save the presentation as **California**. Add your name as a footer on the slide, then save and print the slide.

FIGURE G-21

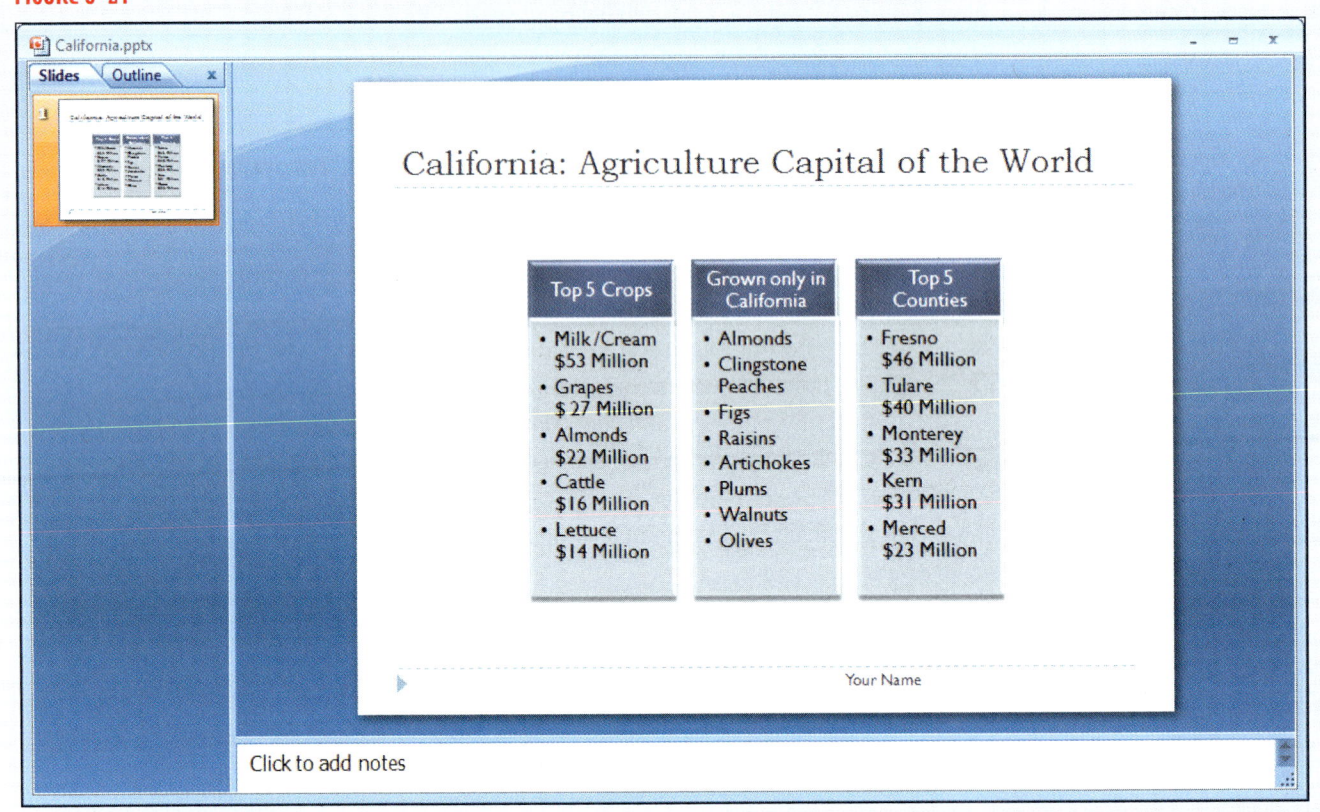

UNIT H
PowerPoint 2007

Using Advanced Features

Files You Will Need

PPT H-1.pptx
PPT H-2.pptx
PPT H-3.pptx
PPT H-4.jpg
PPT H-5.jpg
PPT H-6.jpg
PPT H-7.jpg
PPT H-8.jpg
PPT H-9.pptx
PPT H-10.pptx
PPT H-11.jpg
PPT H-12.jpg
PPT H-13.jpg
PPT H-14.jpg
PPT H-15.jpg
PPT H-16.jpg
PPT H-17.pptx
PPT H-18.pptx
PPT H-19.jpg
Pacific Theme.thmx

After your work on a presentation is complete, PowerPoint provides you with several options for preparing and distributing your final presentation. For example, you can send the presentation out for review and receive comments, package it to be used on another computer, or save it for viewing on the Web. At this stage in the process you can also create customized slide shows and use advanced options to set up a slide show. You have finished working on the content for the Quest Specialty Travel (QST) presentation that Ellen Latsky will use in an upcoming meeting. Now you need to send the presentation to Ellen so she can review it before you leave work for the weekend. You create a custom slide show, change slide show options, prepare the presentation for distribution, save it for viewing on the Web, then package the presentation. You end your day by having a little fun and creating a photo album of your trip to Ireland.

OBJECTIVES

Use templates and add comments
Send and review a presentation
Use advanced slide show options
Create a custom show
Prepare a presentation for distribution
Save a presentation for the Web
Package a presentation
Create a photo album

Using Templates and Adding Comments

UNIT H
PowerPoint 2007

PowerPoint 2007 offers you a variety of ways to create a presentation including beginning with a blank presentation, a theme, a template, or an existing presentation. Occasionally you may need a little help starting a new presentation. Looking through the templates in the New Presentation dialog box may provide just the inspiration you need to begin. PowerPoint divides the templates into two sections: Templates and Microsoft Office Online. The templates in the Templates section are installed on your computer and include the blank presentation, installed themes, and installed templates. The templates in the Microsoft Office Online section are designed for many different purposes and have professional layouts; you can download them from Microsoft Office Web site. You need to review available PowerPoint templates that could be used to display pictures of upcoming tour specials for the company Web site.

STEPS

1. **Start PowerPoint, click the Office button, then click New**
   The New Presentation dialog box opens. The Blank Presentation icon is selected in the center pane at the top of the dialog box by default.

2. **Click Installed Themes in the left pane, scroll through the themes, then click Installed Templates in the left pane**
   All of these themes and templates are installed on your computer and are available for you to use. The themes you see are the same themes you can access from the Design tab on the PowerPoint Ribbon. Each template comes with sample content including graphics and text. Themes do not have sample content.

3. **Make sure that Classic Photo Album is selected, click Create, click the Save button on the Quick Access toolbar, then save the file as Sample Album to the drive and folder where you store your Data Files**
   A new presentation with seven slides appears in the program window.

4. **Click the View tab on the Ribbon, click the Arrange All button in the Window group, click the Review tab on the Ribbon, then click the New Comment button in the Comments group**
   A new comment box appears next to the review comment thumbnail on the slide, as shown in Figure H-1.

5. **Type Ellen, is this sample photo album what you had in mind?, click Slide 5 in the Slides tab, click the New Comment button in the Comments group, then type This layout would work well for us., then click in a blank area of the slide**
   A new comment appears on Slide 5.

   > **QUICK TIP**
   > You can copy the text of a comment to the slide by clicking the review comment thumbnail, then dragging the comment text to the slide.

6. **Drag the review comment thumbnail so it is positioned over the left photograph, then click the Edit Comment button in the Comments group**
   The comment box opens and is ready to be modified.

7. **Type I like this picture style., then click the Previous button in the Comments group**
   The first comment on Slide 1 appears.

8. **Click the Show Markup button in the Comments group, then click the Show Markup button again**
   The Show Markup button is a toggle button, which alternates between showing and hiding comments.

9. **Click the Save button on the Quick Access toolbar**
   After you save the presentation, the review comment thumbnail changes to A1, as shown in Figure H-2, identifying the comment as being made by the author of the presentation.

Using Advanced Features

FIGURE H-1: Slide with new comment

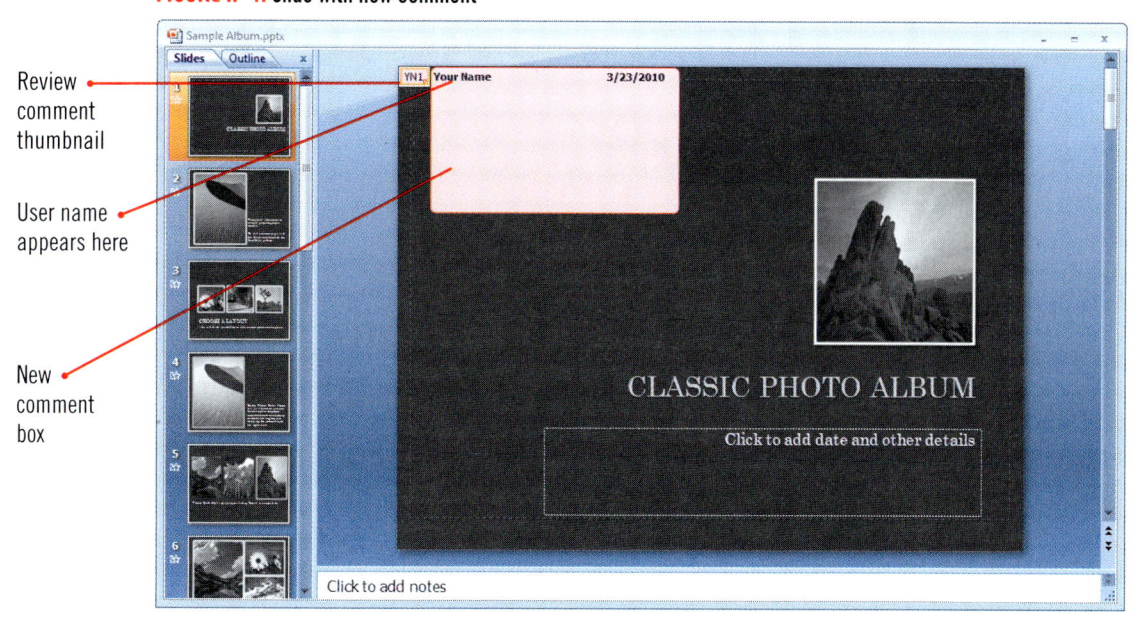

- Review comment thumbnail
- User name appears here
- New comment box

FIGURE H-2: Slide with completed comment

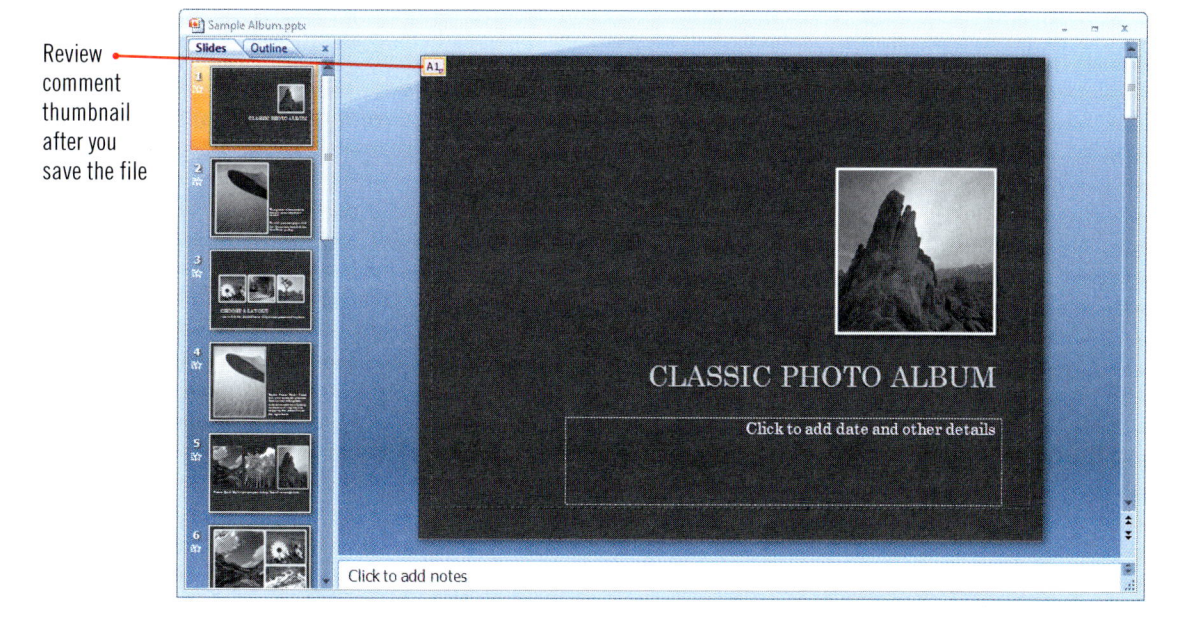

- Review comment thumbnail after you save the file

Creating a document workspace

You may be in a work environment where you work with several people who all collaborate on the same presentation. Instead of trying to manage different versions of the presentation as it passes from person to person, you can set up a document library on a Document Workspace Web site, where everyone involved with the presentation has access to the same file. A Document Workspace Web site is created on the Microsoft Windows SharePoint Services Web site, where you need permission to create a shared document library. Files located in this shared document library can be created, managed, and updated by anyone who has access to the site. One way to create a Document Workspace Web site is to click the Office button, click Publish, then click Create Document Workspace. Follow the directions in the Document Management task pane.

Using Advanced Features   PowerPoint 171

Sending and Reviewing a Presentation

UNIT H
PowerPoint 2007

When you finish creating a presentation, it is often helpful to have others look over the content for accuracy and clarity. When you are not in the same location as the reviewers, you can e-mail the presentation file. If you have Microsoft Outlook on your computer, you can open Outlook directly from PowerPoint and send a presentation file as an attachment in an e-mail. A reviewer can open the presentation on their computer, make changes and comments, and then e-mail it back to you. Use Outlook to send your presentation to Ellen to get her comments and then open the reviewed presentation.

STEPS

TROUBLE
If Outlook is not configured to send and receive e-mail on your computer, you will get a warning dialog box that the action cannot be completed. Click OK, then skip Steps 2–3.

1. **Click the Office button, point to Send, then click E-mail**
   Microsoft Outlook opens in a new window. The subject line is filled in for you and the Sample Album presentation is automatically attached to the e-mail. If you don't have Outlook installed on your computer, you will not be able to e-mail your presentation.

2. **Click the To text box, type your e-mail address, click in the message body window, then type Please review and get back to me. Thanks.**
   The e-mail is ready to send. Compare your screen to Figure H-3.

3. **Click the Send button, click, then click Close**
   Outlook sends the e-mail message with the attached presentation file, and the Outlook window closes. By clicking Close, the presentation closes, but PowerPoint remains open.

QUICK TIP
If the presentation you are sending for review includes linked files, you need to attach the linked files to your e-mail message or change the linked files to embedded objects.

4. **Open the presentation PPT H-1.pptx from the drive and folder where you store your Data Files, save the presentation as Sample Album Reviewed, click the View tab on the Ribbon, then click the Arrange All button in the Window group**

5. **Click the Review tab on the Ribbon, then click the review comment thumbnail in the upper-left corner of Slide 1**
   A small comment box opens.

6. **Click the Next button in the Comments group, read the comment, continue to click the Next button until you reach the comment on Slide 7, then click the Previous button in the Comments group**
   The previous comment on Slide 5 opens again.

7. **Click the Delete button list arrow in the Comments group, then click the Delete All Markup on the Current Slide button in the Comments group**
   The comments on Slide 5 are deleted. Compare your screen to Figure H-4.

8. **Click the Slide Sorter button on the status bar, click the Home tab on the Ribbon, click the Select button in the Editing group, then click Select All**
   All of the slides are selected in Slide Sorter view.

9. **Click the Animations tab on the Ribbon, click the No Transition option in the Transition to This Slide group, double-click Slide 1, then save your work**
   All of the transitions are removed from the presentation.

10. **Click the Office button, then click Close**

Using Advanced Features

FIGURE H-3: Outlook window

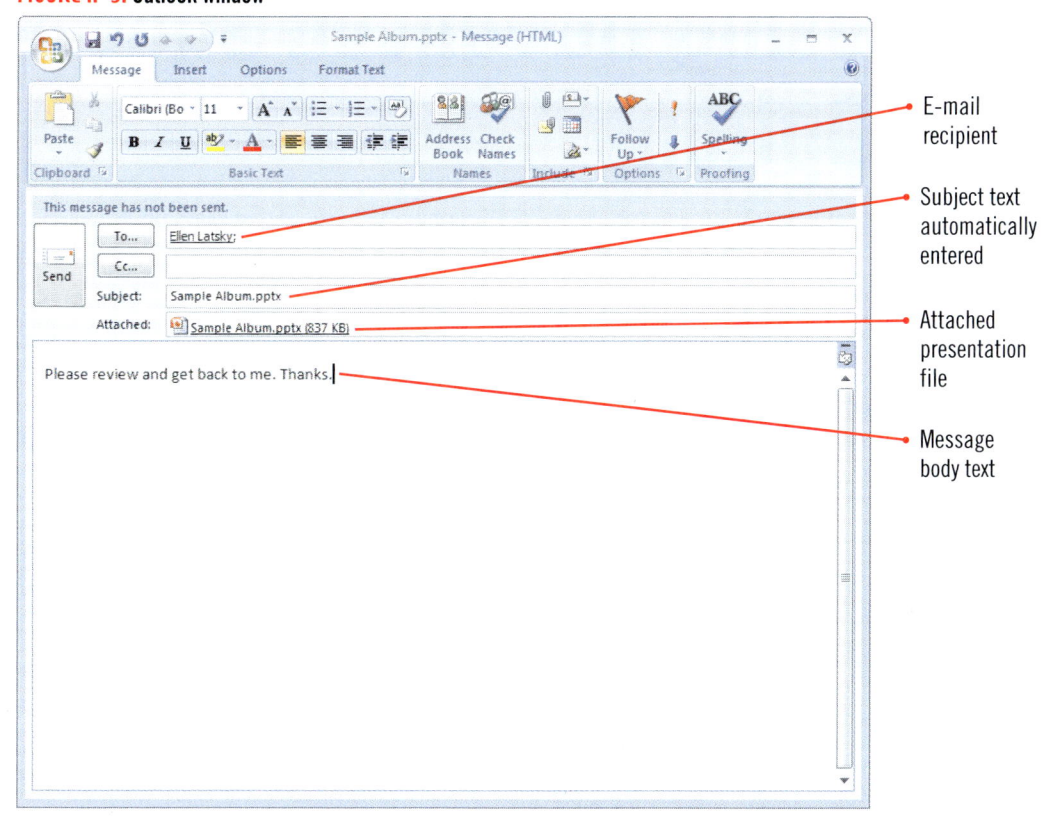

- E-mail recipient
- Subject text automatically entered
- Attached presentation file
- Message body text

FIGURE H-4: Slide with removed comments

Using PowerPoint's proofing tools

Along with the spell checker, PowerPoint has a research feature and a language feature that can help you in the development of your presentation. The research feature contains several tools which can help you research topics through encyclopedias and Internet sites, look up words using one of three different thesauruses, and translate words using 14 different languages. If you are working with text that is a different language than the default PowerPoint language (English), the language feature allows you to identify selected text in a presentation with its correct language. To access PowerPoint's proofing tools, click the Review tab on the Ribbon, then click a button in the Proofing group.

Using Advanced Features   PowerPoint 173

Using Advanced Slide Show Options

With PowerPoint, you can create a self-running slide show that plays on its own. For example, you can set up a presentation so viewers can watch a slide show on a stand-alone computer, called a **kiosk**, at a convention, mall, or some other public place. You can also create a self-running presentation on a CD or DVD for others to watch. You have a number of options when designing a self-running presentation; for example, you can include hyperlinks or action buttons to assist your audience as they move through the presentation. You can also add a synchronized voice that narrates the presentation and set either manual or automatic slide timings. You prepare the presentation so it can be self-running.

STEPS

1. **Open the presentation PPT H-2.pptx from the drive and folder where you store your Data Files, save the presentation as QuestH, click the View tab on the Ribbon, then click the Arrange All button in the Window group**

2. **Click the Slide Show tab on the Ribbon, click the Set Up Slide Show button in the Set Up group, then click the Browsed at a kiosk (full screen) option button in the Show type section of the Set Up Show dialog box**
   The Set Up Show dialog box has options you can set to specify how the show will run.

   > **QUICK TIP**
   > You must use automatic timings, navigation hyperlinks, or action buttons when you use the kiosk option, otherwise you will not be able to progress through the slides.

3. **Make sure the All option button is selected in the Show slides section, then make sure the Using timings, if present option button is selected in the Advance slides section**
   These settings include all the slides in the presentation and enable PowerPoint to advance the slides at time intervals you set. See Figure H-5.

4. **Click OK, click the Animations tab on the Ribbon, click the Automatically After check box in the Transition to This Slide group to select it, click the Automatically After up arrow until 00:05 appears, then click the Apply To All button in the Transition to This Slide group**
   Each slide in the presentation now has a slide timing of 5 seconds.

5. **Click the Slide Show button on the status bar, view the show, let it start again, press [Esc], then click the Slide Show tab on the Ribbon**
   PowerPoint advances the slides automatically at five-second intervals, or faster if someone advances the slide manually. After the last slide, the slide show starts over because the kiosk slide show option loops the presentation until someone presses [Esc].

6. **Click the Set Up Slide Show button, click the Presented by a speaker (full screen) option button, then click OK**
   The slide show options are back to their default settings.

   > **QUICK TIP**
   > To view a hidden slide while in Slide Show view, right-click the current slide, click Go to Slide, then click the hidden slide.

7. **Click Slide 1 in the Slides tab, click the Hide Slide button in the Set Up group, click the From Beginning button in the Start Slide Show group, then press [Esc]**
   The slide show begins with Slide 2. Notice that Slide 1 in the Slides tab is dimmed and has a hidden slide icon on its number indicating it is hidden, as shown in Figure H-6.

8. **Right-click Slide 1 in the Slides tab, then click Hide Slide in the shortcut menu**
   The hidden slide icon is removed.

9. **Save your changes**

FIGURE H-5: Set Up Show dialog box

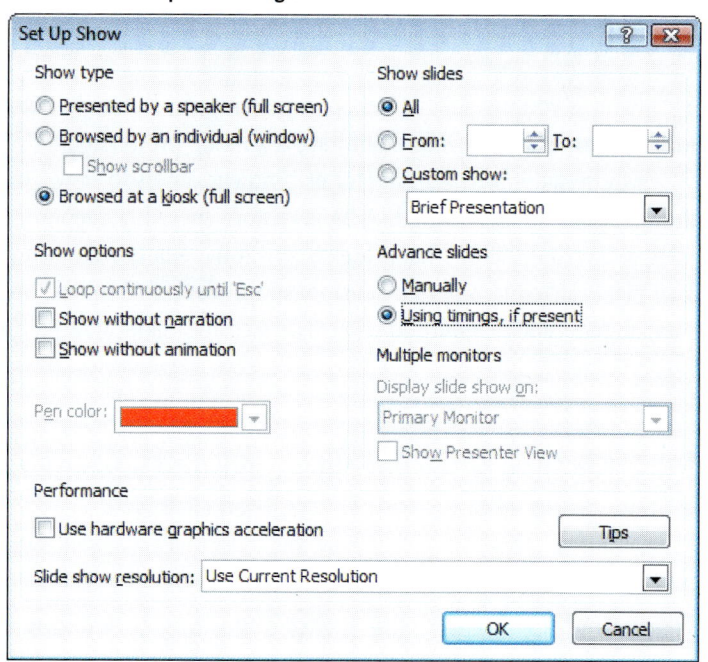

FIGURE H-6: Figure showing hidden slide

Hidden slide icon

Hidden slide

Using Presenter view

Presenter view is a special view that permits you to run a presentation through two monitors; one monitor that you see on your computer and a second monitor that your audience views. Running a presentation through two monitors provides you more control over your presentation, allowing you to click thumbnails of slides to jump to specific slides and run other programs, if necessary. Presenter view is designed with large icons, buttons, and other tools, which help you easily navigate through a presentation. Speaker notes are large and easy to read for the presenter. To use this feature, your computer must have multiple monitor capacity and you need to turn on multiple monitor support and Presenter view. To turn on multiple monitor support, click the Use Presenter View check box in the Monitors group on the Slide Show tab and follow the instructions.

Using Advanced Features

Creating a Custom Show

A custom show gives you the ability to adapt a presentation for use in different circumstances or with different audiences. For example, you might have a 25-slide presentation that you show to new customers, but only 12 of those slides are necessary for existing customers to view. PowerPoint provides two types of custom shows: basic and hyperlinked. A basic custom show is a separate presentation or a presentation that includes slides from the original presentation. A hyperlinked custom show is a separate (secondary) presentation that is linked to a primary custom show. You have been asked to create a version of the presentation for a staff meeting, so you create a custom slide show containing only the slides appropriate for that audience.

STEPS

1. **Click the Slide Show tab on the Ribbon, click the Custom Slide Show button in the Start Slide Show group, click Custom Shows, then click New**

   The Define Custom Show dialog box opens. The slides that are in your current presentation are listed in the Slides in presentation list box.

2. **Press and hold [Ctrl], click Slide 1, click Slides 6-8, click Slides 12-16, release [Ctrl], then click Add**

   The nine slides you selected move to the Slides in custom show list box, indicating that they will be included in the new presentation. See Figure H-7.

3. **Click 5. Adventure Series in the Slides in custom show list, then click the Slide Order up arrow button until the Adventure Series slide is at the top of the Slides in custom show list**

   The slide moves to the top of the list. You can arrange the slides in any order in your custom show using the Slide order up and down arrows.

4. **Click 2. Spring 2011 European Tours Proposal, click Remove, drag to select the existing text in the Slide show name text box, type Brief Presentation, then click OK**

   The Custom Shows dialog box lists your custom presentation. The custom show is not saved as a separate slide show on your computer even though you assigned it a new name. To view a custom slide show, you must first open the presentation you used to create the custom show in Slide Show view. You then can open the custom show from the Custom Shows dialog box.

   > **QUICK TIP**
   > To print a custom show, click the Office button, click Print, click the Custom Show option button in the Print range section, select the custom show you want in the Custom Show list box, set any other printing preferences, then click OK.

5. **Click Show, view the Brief Presentation slide show, then press [Esc] to end the slide show**

   The slides in the custom show appear in the order you set in the Define Custom Show dialog box. At the end of the slide show, you return to the presentation in Normal view.

6. **Click the Slide Show button on the status bar, right-click the screen, point to Custom Show, then click Brief Presentation, as shown in Figure H-8**

   The Brief Presentation custom show appears in Slide Show view.

7. **Press [Esc] at the end of the slide show, then save your changes**

FIGURE H-7: Define Custom Show dialog box

Selected slides

Slide Order up arrow button

Click to add slides to custom show

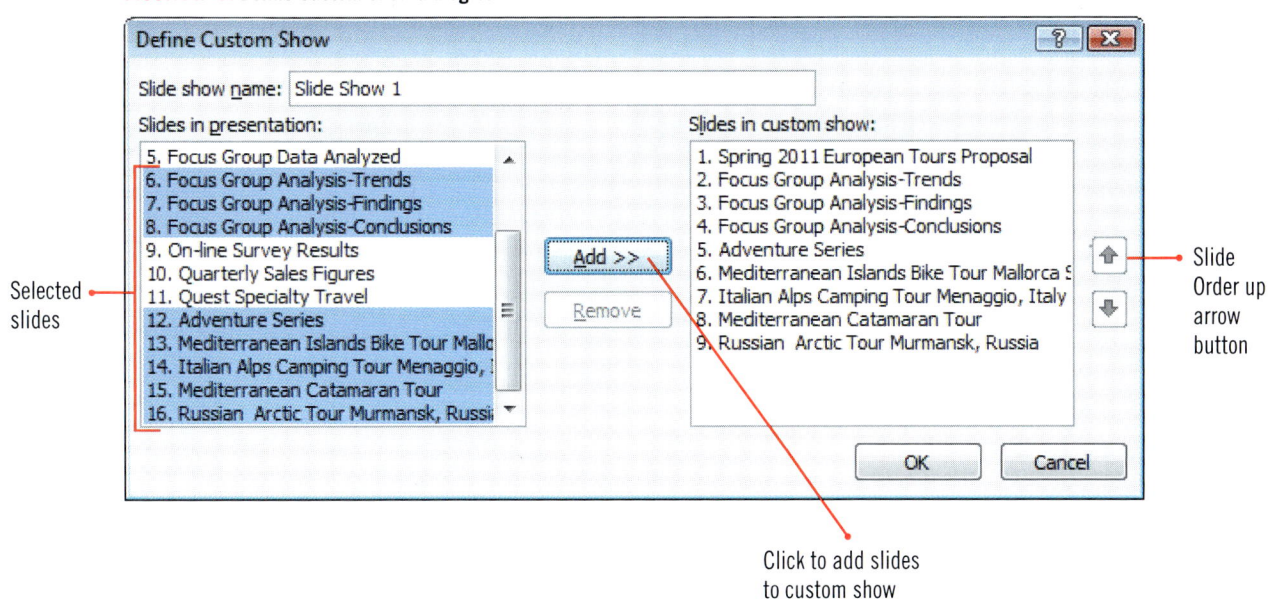

FIGURE H-8: Switching to the custom slide show

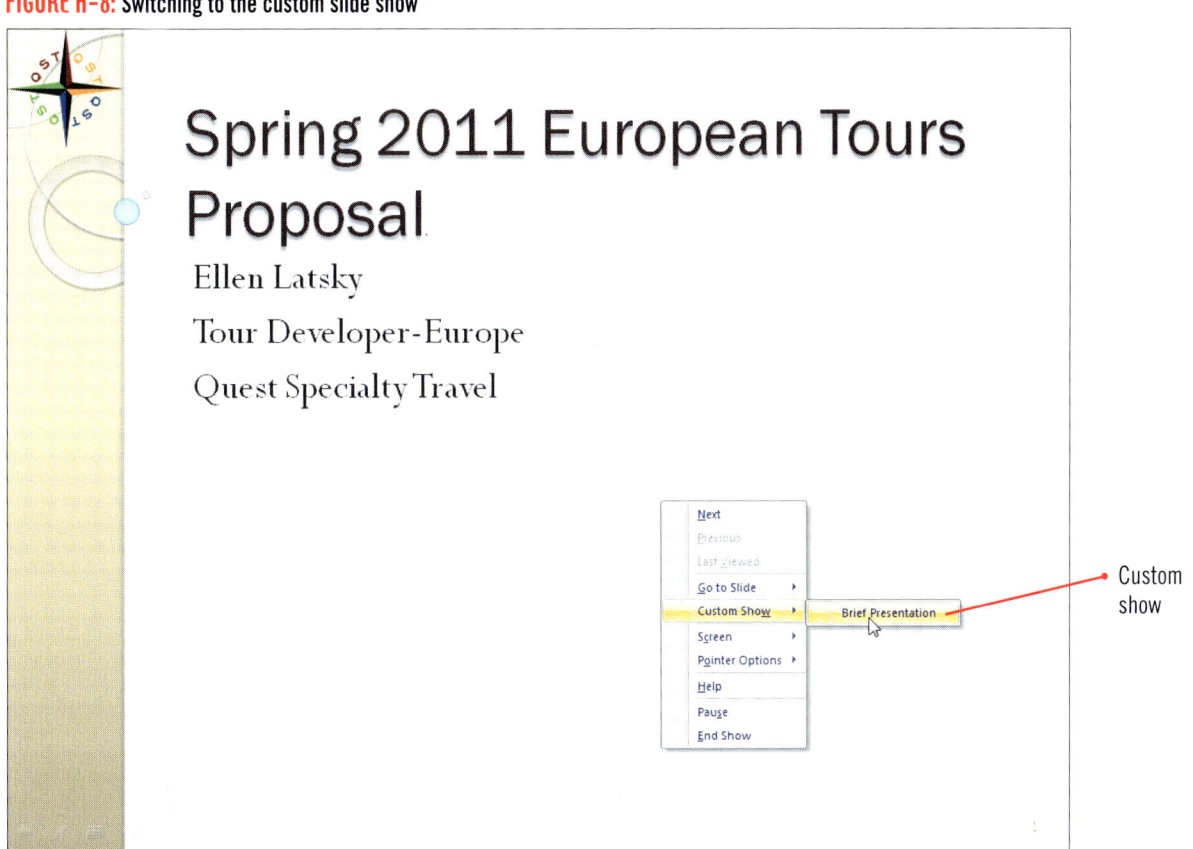

Custom show

Link to a custom slide show

You can use action buttons to switch from the "parent" show to the custom show. Click the Shapes button in the Drawing group on the Home tab, then click an action button. Draw an action button on the slide. Click the Hyperlink to list arrow, click Custom Show, click the custom show you want to link, then click OK. Now when you run a slide show you can click the action button you created to run the custom show. You can also create an interactive table of contents using custom shows. Create your table of contents entries on a slide, then hyperlink each entry to the section it refers to using a custom show for each section.

Using Advanced Features

UNIT H
PowerPoint 2007

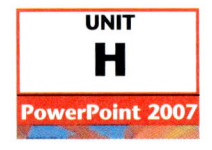

Preparing a Presentation for Distribution

Reviewing and preparing your presentation before you share it with others can be an essential step, especially with so many security issues on the Internet today. One way to help secure your PowerPoint presentation is to set a security password, so only authorized people can view or modify its content. If you plan to open a presentation in an earlier version of PowerPoint, it is a good idea to determine if the presentation is compatible. Some features in PowerPoint 2007, such as SmartArt graphics, are not compatible in earlier versions of PowerPoint. Ellen wants you to learn about PowerPoint's security and compatibility features so you can use them on presentations and other documents.

STEPS

1. **Click Slide 1 in the Slides tab, click the Office button, point to Prepare, then click Encrypt Document**

    The Encrypt Document dialog box opens.

2. **Type 123abc**

    As you type the password, solid black symbols appear in the text box and make the password unreadable. If anyone is looking while you type, this helps protect your privacy. Protecting a file is part of the **encryption**. See Figure H-9.

    > **TROUBLE**
    > If you mistype the password in the Confirm Password dialog box, an alert dialog box opens.

3. **Click OK to open the Confirm Password dialog box, type 123abc as shown in Figure H-10, then click OK**

    The presentation is now set with a password. Once the presentation is closed, this password must be entered in a Password dialog box to open the presentation.

4. **Click, click Close, click Yes to save changes, then open QuestH from the drive and folder where you store you Data Files.**

    The Password dialog box opens.

    > **QUICK TIP**
    > To set other password options, open the Save As dialog box, click Tools, then click General Options.

5. **Type 123abc, then click OK**

    The presentation opens. Be aware that if you don't remember your password, there is no way to retrieve it from the presentation or from Microsoft.

6. **Click, point to Prepare, click Encrypt Document, select the password, press [Delete], then click OK**

    The password is removed and is no longer needed to open the presentation.

7. **Click, point to Prepare, click Run Compatibility Checker**

    The Compatibility Checker analyzes the presentation, then the Microsoft Office PowerPoint Compatibility Checker dialog box opens, as shown in Figure H-11. Each item in the dialog box represents a feature that is not supported in earlier versions of PowerPoint. This means that if you try to run this presentation using an earlier version of PowerPoint, the items listed will function in a limited capacity or not at all.

8. **Click the down scroll arrow, read all of the items in the dialog box, click OK, add your name to the Notes and Handouts footer, then click the Slide Sorter button on the status bar**

    The dialog box closes. Compare your screen to Figure H-12.

9. **Save your work, then print the Handouts (4 slides per page)**

FIGURE H-9: Encrypt Document dialog box

FIGURE H-10: Confirm Password dialog box

FIGURE H-11: Compatibility Checker dialog box

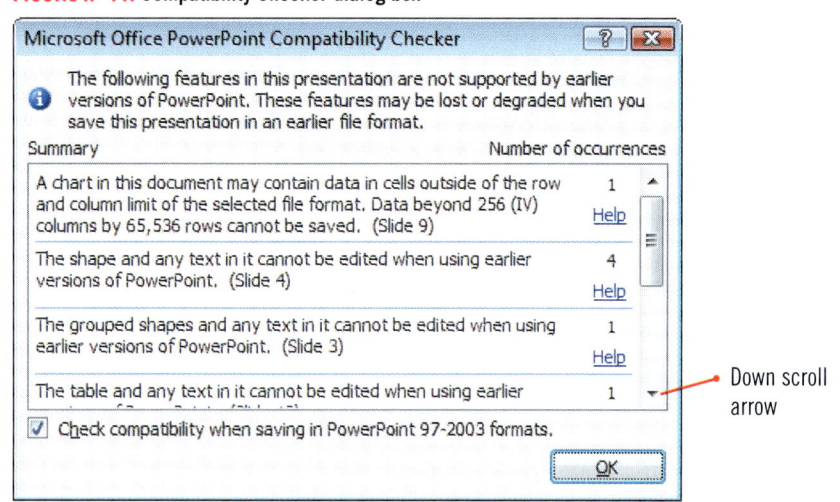

FIGURE H-12: Final presentation in Slide Sorter view

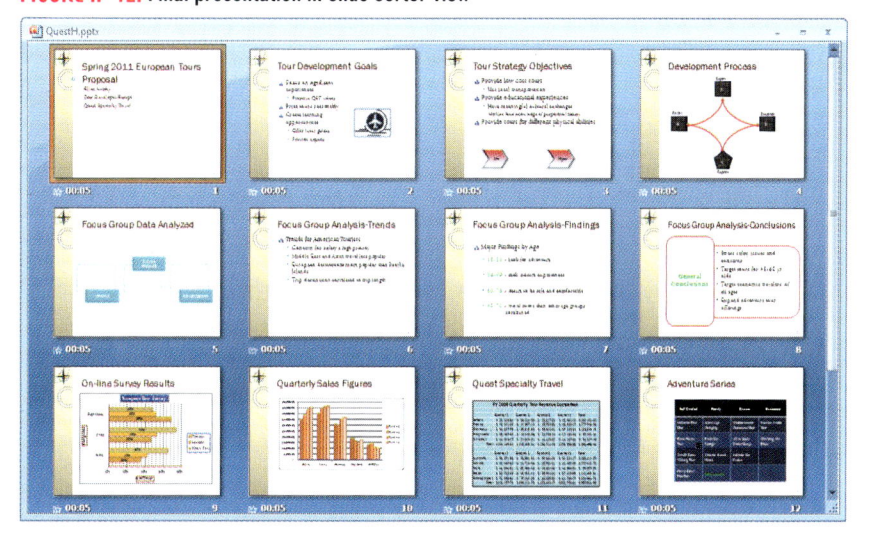

Creating a strong password

Creating a strong password is a vital part of securing your presentations, other sensitive documents, Internet accounts, and personal information. The strongest password is a random complex string of lowercase and uppercase characters and numbers. For example, the password used in this lesson, 123abc, is a weak password. Though it has both numbers and lowercase letters, it is an easy sequential password that someone could guess. Here are some simple guidelines to making a good password: (1) make the password long, 8 or more characters, (2) use a wide variety of uppercase and lowercase letters, symbols, and numbers, (3) if possible use words or phrases that you can remember that are difficult for others to guess, (4) keep your password secret and never reveal it in an e-mail, and (5) regularly change your password.

Using Advanced Features

Saving a Presentation for the Web

You can use PowerPoint to create presentations for viewing on the Web by saving the file in Hypertext Markup Language (HTML) format. You have two save options to choose from when saving a presentation for the Web. You can publish your entire presentation, including all of the information within the presentation and supporting documents, such as linked files, which creates a single file Web page. The other publishing option is to create a presentation as a Web page, which creates a separate folder that contains all supporting files, such as bullets, pictures, background objects, and linked files. Once your presentation is published to a computer that hosts Web pages called a **Web server**, others can view (but not change) the presentation on the Web. You want to publish the custom show version of the Spring 2011 European Tours Proposal presentation to be viewed on the company Web site.

STEPS

> **QUICK TIP**
> To save the presentation as a single file Web page, select the Single File Web Page file type in the Save as type list box.

1. **Click the Office button, click Save As, click the Save as type list arrow, then click Web Page (*.htm;*.html)**
   The Save As dialog box opens. As soon as you select the Web page file type, the Publish button appears in the Save As dialog box.

2. **Select the filename in the File name text box, type Webpres, then click Publish**
   The Publish as Web Page dialog box opens.

3. **Click the Custom show option button in the Publish what? section, then click the Display speaker notes check box to deselect it**

4. **In the Browser support section, click the All browsers listed above (creates larger files) option button**
   You want to make sure most browsers can view the HTML file you publish. At the bottom of the dialog box, notice that the default filename for the HTML file you are creating is the same as the presentation filename and that it will be saved to the same folder in which the presentation is stored.

5. **Click the Change button in the Publish a copy as section**
   The Set Page Title dialog box opens. The title displayed in this dialog box appears in the title bar of your Internet browser window.

6. **Type QST 2011 European Tours, click OK, then click the Open published Web page in browser check box to select it, if it is not already selected**
   The page title changes to the new title. See Figure H-13.

> **QUICK TIP**
> Once you publish a presentation and create the HTML files, you'll need to copy it to a Web server so others can open it from the Web.

7. **Click Publish, click the security bar in the Internet Explorer window if it appears, click Allow Blocked Content, then click Yes in the Security Warning dialog box**
   PowerPoint creates a copy of your presentation in HTML format and opens the published presentation in your default Internet browser. Your screen should look similar to Figure H-14, which shows the presentation in Internet Explorer 7. The slide titles on the left are hyperlinks to each slide.

8. **Click each slide title hyperlink in the left pane of the screen to see each presentation slide in the browser**
   You can also click the Slide Show button or the Next Slide and Previous Slide buttons at the bottom of the browser screen to view the presentation slides.

9. **Close your browser window, save your work, then close the presentation**
   Your original presentation closes but PowerPoint remains open.

FIGURE H-13: Publish as Web Page dialog box

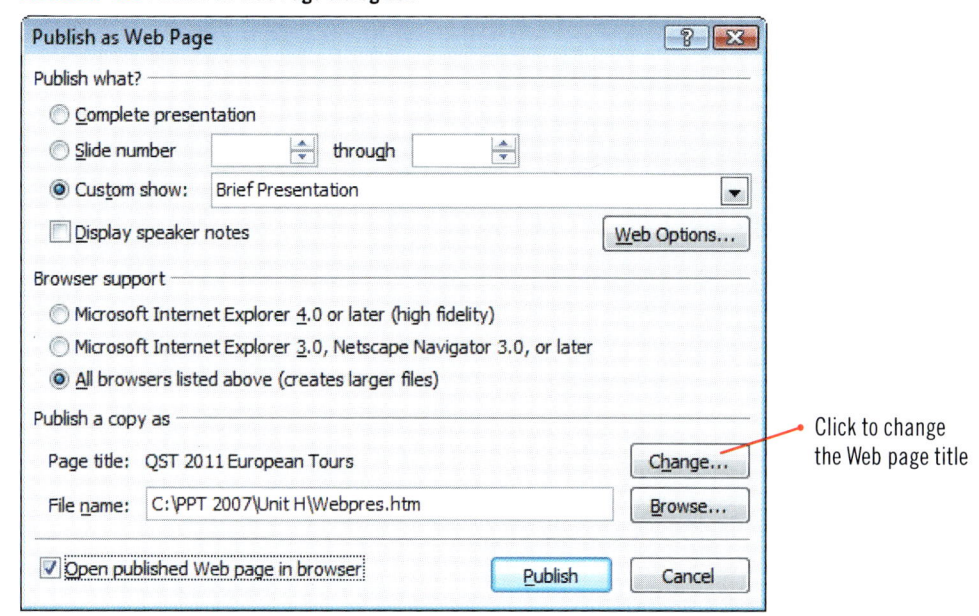

Click to change the Web page title

FIGURE H-14: Internet Explorer window displaying Web presentation

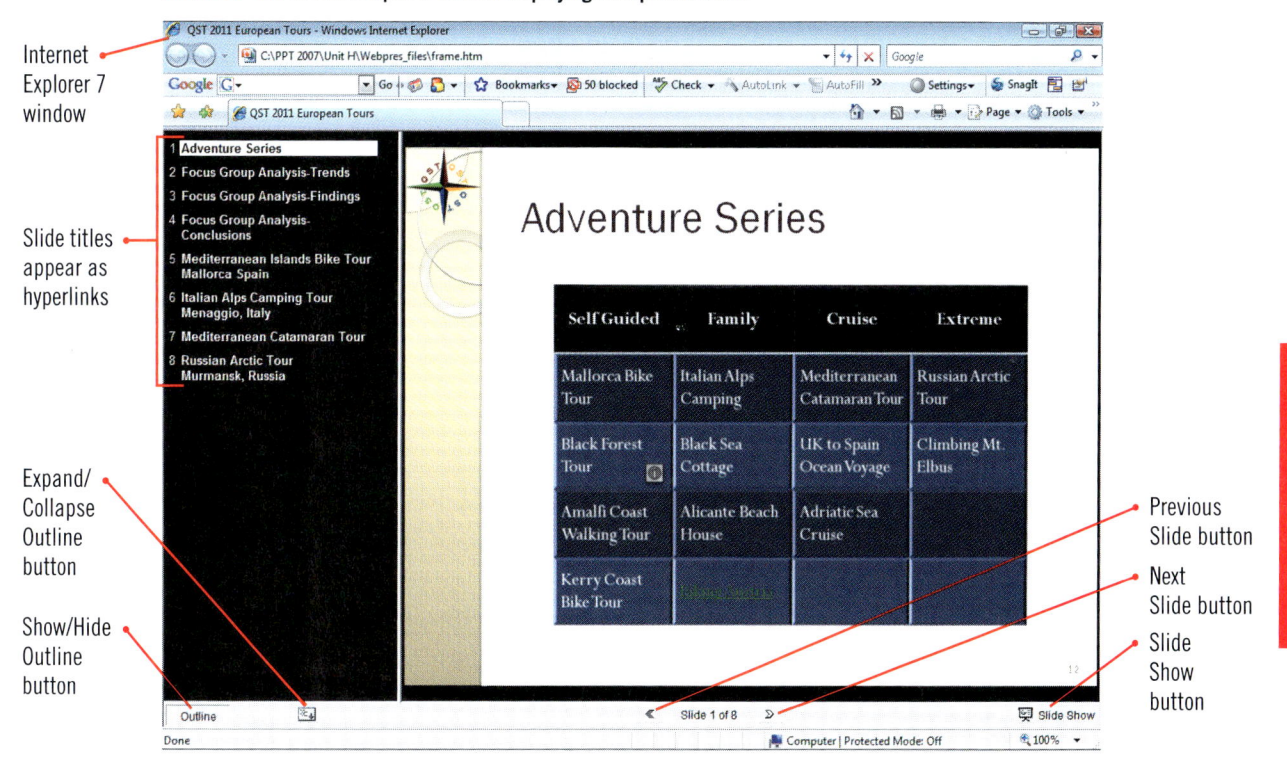

Internet Explorer 7 window

Slide titles appear as hyperlinks

Expand/Collapse Outline button

Show/Hide Outline button

Previous Slide button

Next Slide button

Slide Show button

Publish slides to a Slide Library

If your computer is connected to a network server running Office SharePoint Server 2007 software, you can store slides in a folder called a **Slide Library** for others to access, modify, and use. Using a Slide Library, others can make changes to your slides and you in turn can track and review all changes and have access to the latest version of your slides. To publish slides from PowerPoint 2007 to a Slide Library (after a Slide Library is created on a server), click the Office button, point to Publish, then click Publish Slides. The Publish Slides command only appears if you are connected to an Office SharePoint Server 2007 server. To add slides to your presentation from a Slide Library, click the Home tab, click the New Slide button arrow, then click Reuse Slides. Select the slides you want to insert into your presentation using the Reuse Slides task pane.

Using Advanced Features — **PowerPoint 181**

Packaging a Presentation

UNIT H
PowerPoint 2007

When you need to distribute one or more presentations or present a slide show using another Windows computer, you can package (or copy) your presentation to a CD, DVD, a network folder, or a local computer hard drive. To package the files you'll need to run a slide show on another computer (including your presentation, embedded and linked objects, and fonts), you'll use the Package for CD feature. Before you package a presentation, it is a good idea to inspect the presentation for hidden or personal data that may be inappropriate for others to view. The PowerPoint Viewer is included by default with a packaged presentation. The PowerPoint Viewer is a program that allows you to view a presentation in Slide Show view on a computer that does not have PowerPoint installed. You package a version of the European Tours Presentation using the Package to CD feature so Ellen can present it at an off-site meeting. You package the presentation to a new folder that you create on your computer's hard drive.

STEPS

1. Open the presentation PPT H-3.pptx from the drive and folder where you store your Data Files, then save the presentation as Packaged Presentation

2. Click the Office button, point to Publish, click Package for CD, then click OK to ensure the files are compatible with the PowerPoint Viewer if necessary
   The Package for CD dialog box opens.

    > **QUICK TIP**
    > If you want to package more than one presentation, click the Add Files button in the Package for CD dialog box, select the files, then click Add.

3. Click the Options button in the dialog box
   The Options dialog box opens.

4. Click the Embedded TrueType fonts check box, then click the Inspect presentations for inappropriate or private information check box
   Embedding TrueType fonts with the packaged presentation ensures that all of your fonts display properly on another computer. See Figure H-15.

5. Click OK, click the Copy to Folder button, then type Spring 2011 Packaged Pres
   The Copy to Folder dialog box opens and you create a new folder for the packaged presentation.

6. Click the Browse button to open the Choose Location dialog box, locate the drive and folder where you store your Data Files, then click Select
   Compare the Copy to Folder dialog box on your screen to Figure H-16.

7. Click OK, click Yes to include linked files in the package, click the Off-Slide Content check box in the Document Inspector dialog box, click Inspect, then click Close
   PowerPoint packages the presentation to the folder you created and displays the Package for CD dialog box.

8. Click Close to close the Package for CD dialog box, open Windows Explorer, navigate to the Spring 2011 Packaged Pres folder, then view the folder contents
   Compare your screen to Figure H-17. All the files you need to run the presentation are in this folder, including the linked files.

9. Close the Windows Explorer window, then close the presentation

FIGURE H-15: Options dialog box

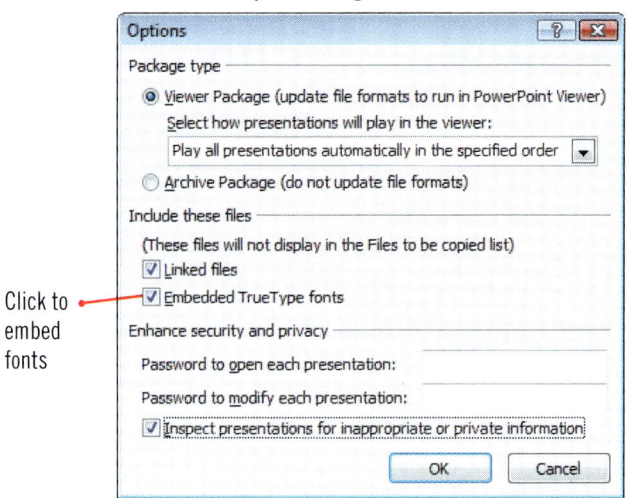

Click to embed fonts

FIGURE H-16: Package for CD dialog box

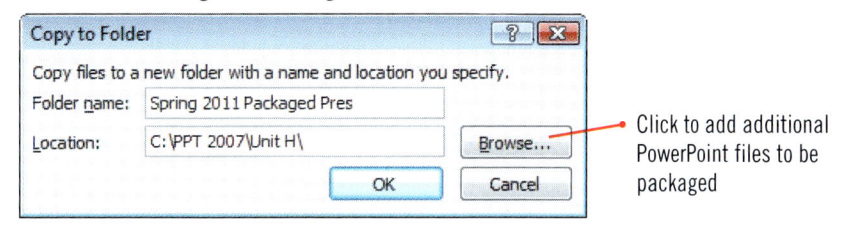

Click to add additional PowerPoint files to be packaged

FIGURE H-17: Windows Explorer window showing the packaged files

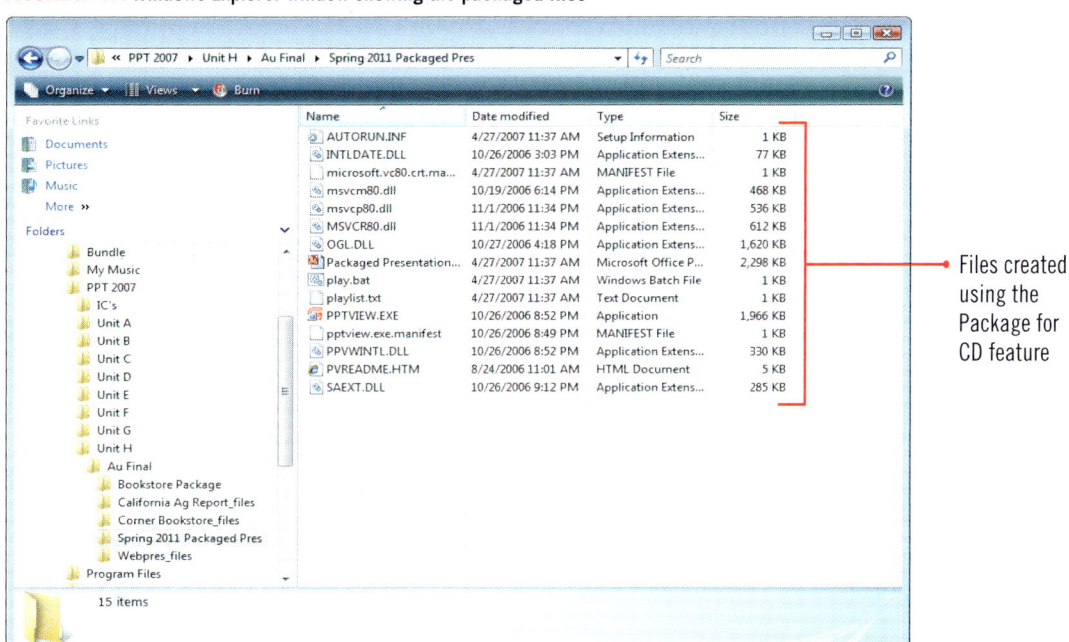

Files created using the Package for CD feature

Using the Microsoft PowerPoint Viewer

The Microsoft PowerPoint Viewer is a program used to show a presentation on a computer that doesn't have PowerPoint installed. The PowerPoint Viewer is a free program distributed by Microsoft from the Office Web site. The PowerPoint Viewer is included by default when you package a presentation. To view a presentation slide show using the PowerPoint Viewer, open the Microsoft Office PowerPoint Viewer dialog box by double-clicking the PPTVIEW.EXE file, then select the presentation you want to view. If you have a presentation that is only going to be shown as a slide show, you can save it with a special PowerPoint show file format (.ppsx), which opens the presentation up in Slide Show view instead of Normal view.

Using Advanced Features

Creating a Photo Album

A **PowerPoint photo album** is a special presentation designed specifically to display photographs. You can add pictures to a photo album from your hard drive, digital camera, scanner, or Web camera. As with any presentation, you can customize the layout of a photo album presentation by adding title text to slides, applying frames around the pictures, and applying a design template. You can also format the pictures of the photo album by adding a caption, converting the pictures to black and white, rotating them, and changing their brightness and contrast. You have a little extra time at the end of your day, so you decide to use PowerPoint to create a photo album of a recent trip to Ireland.

STEPS

1. Click the Insert tab on the Ribbon, then click the Photo Album button in the Illustrations group

   The Photo Album dialog box opens.

2. Click File/Disk, select the file PPT H-4.jpg from the drive and folder where you store your Data Files, then click Insert

   The photograph appears in the Preview box and is listed in the Pictures in album list, as shown in Figure H-18. The buttons below the Preview box allow you to rotate the photo or change its contrast or brightness.

3. Click File/Disk, click the file PPT H-5.jpg, press and hold [Shift], click the file PPT H-8.jpg, release [Shift], then click Insert

   Four more photographs appear in the dialog box. One photo is out of order.

4. Make sure PPT H-8.jpg is selected in the Pictures in album list, click the up arrow button below the list once, then click Create

   A new presentation opens. PowerPoint creates a title slide along with a slide for each photograph that you inserted. The computer user name appears in the subtitle text box by default.

5. Save the presentation as Ireland Trip to the drive and folder where you store your Data Files, change the slide title to Ireland Trip, click the Photo Album button list arrow in the Illustrations group, then click Edit Photo Album

   The Edit Photo Album dialog box opens. You can use this dialog box to format the photographs and slide layout of your photo album presentation.

6. Click PPT H-4.jpg in the Pictures in album list, press and hold [Shift], click PPT H-7.jpg, release [Shift], click the Picture layout list arrow in the Album Layout section, click 1 picture with title, click the Frame shape list arrow, click Center Shadow Rectangle, then click Update

   All of the slides now have a title text placeholder, and the photographs are formatted with a shadow.

7. Click Slide 5 in the Slides tab, click the title placeholder, type Why did I get shaved first?, enter your own title text on the other four slides, then click the Slide Sorter button on the status bar

   Compare your screen to Figure H-19.

8. Click Slide 1, click the Slide Show button on the status bar, advance through the slides, then double-click Slide 1

   All of the slides now have a title.

9. Add your name to the notes and handouts header, then print Handouts (1 per page)

10. Save your changes, close the presentation, then exit PowerPoint

> **QUICK TIP**
> If you want others to have access to your photo album on the Web, you can save the photo album presentation as a Web page.

> **QUICK TIP**
> To show a slide show in a different screen resolution, click the Slide Show tab, click the Resolution list arrow, then choose a resolution setting.

FIGURE H-18: Photo Album dialog box

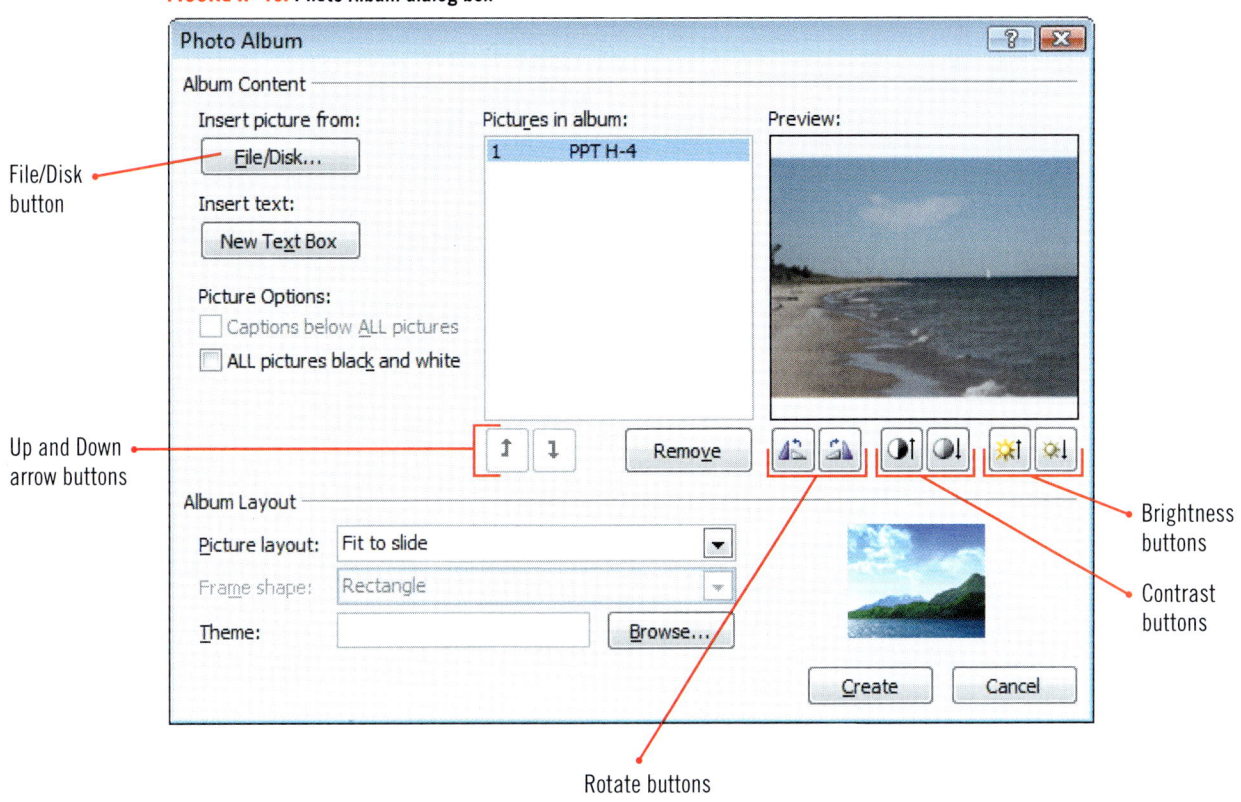

- File/Disk button
- Up and Down arrow buttons
- Brightness buttons
- Contrast buttons
- Rotate buttons

FIGURE H-19: Completed photo album presentation

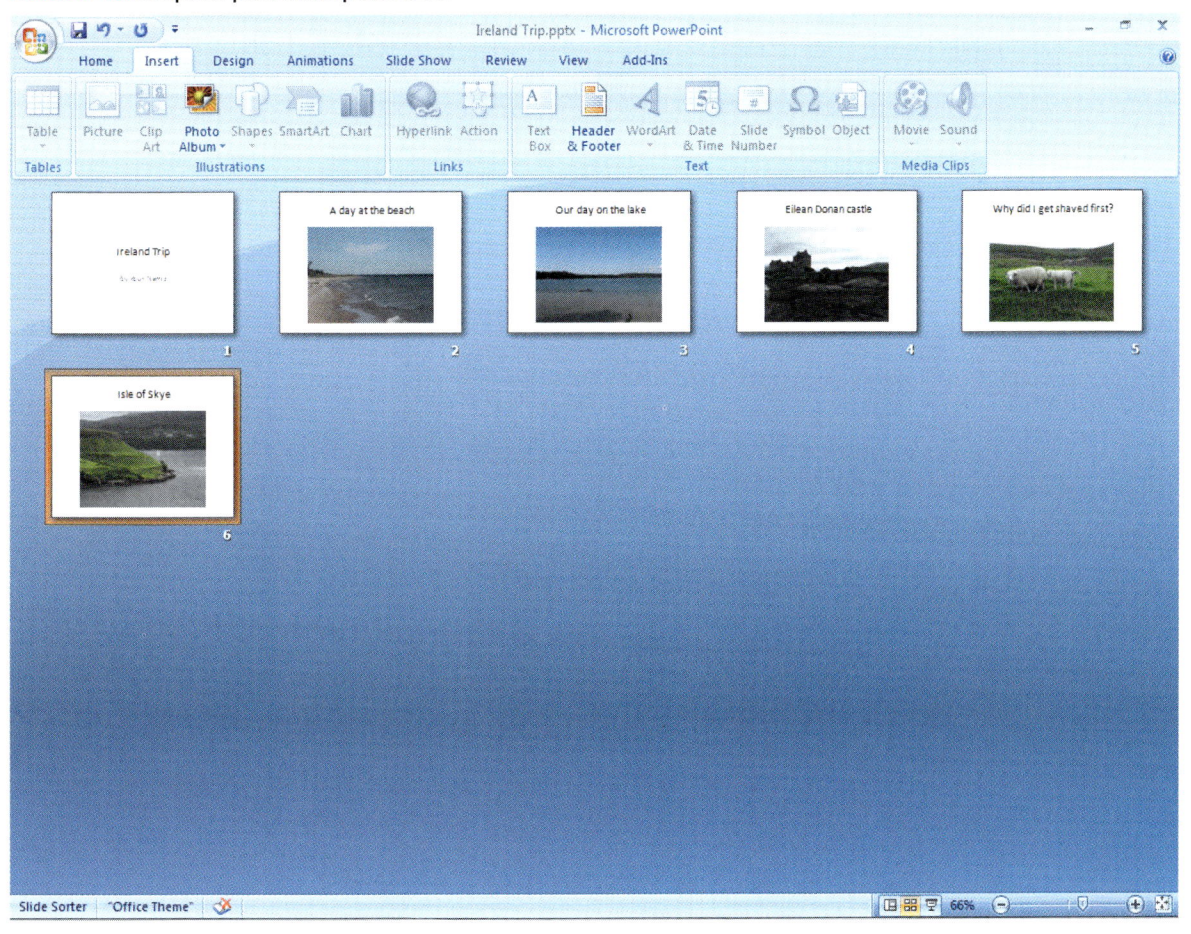

Using Advanced Features — **PowerPoint 185**

Practice

SAM — If you have a SAM user profile, you may have access to hands-on instruction, practice, and assessment of the skills covered in this unit. Log in to your SAM account (http://sam2007.course.com/) to launch any assigned training activities or exams that relate to the skills covered in this unit.

▼ CONCEPTS REVIEW

Label each element of the PowerPoint window shown in Figure H-20.

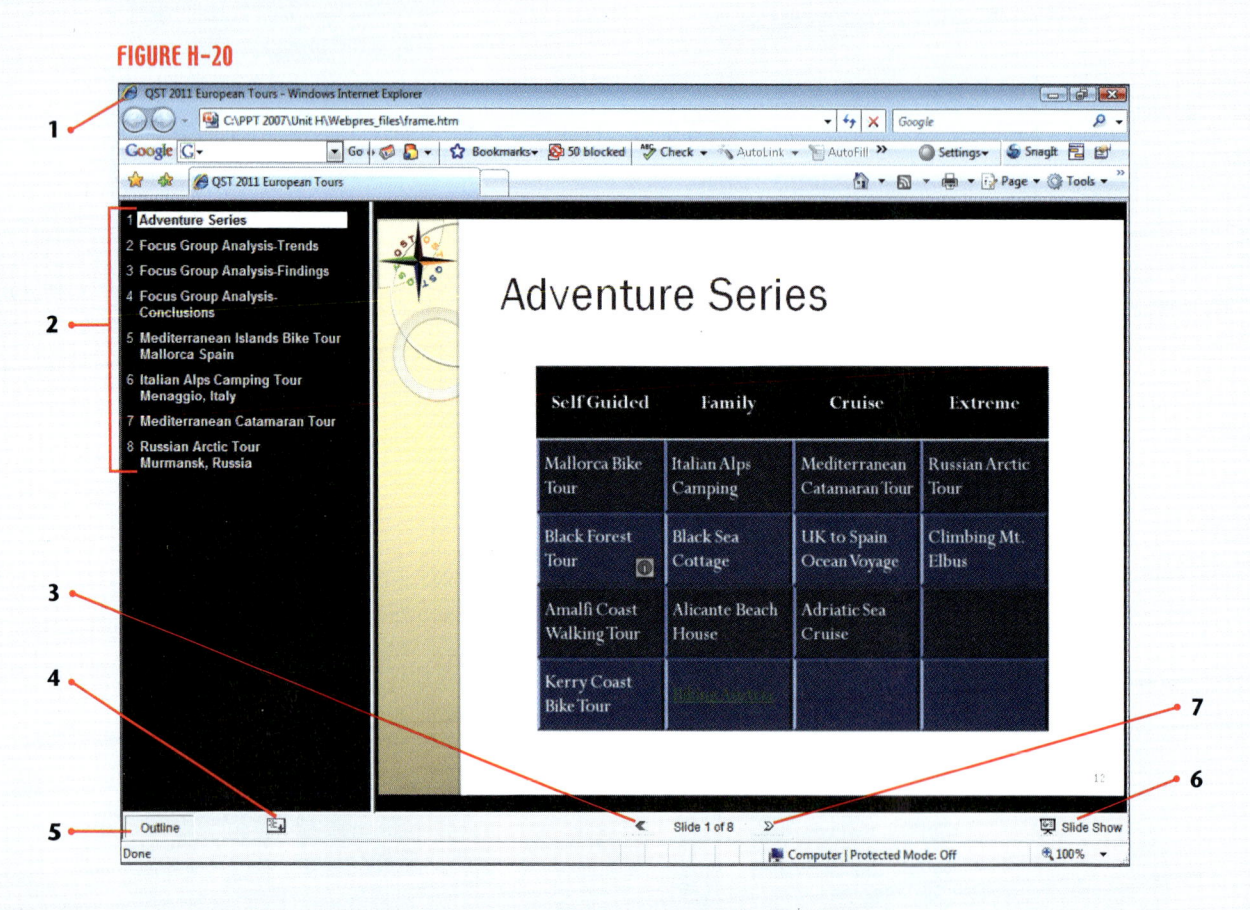

FIGURE H-20

Match each term with the statement that best describes its function.

8. Kiosk
9. Packaged presentation
10. Web server
11. Slide Library
12. Custom show

a. A stand-alone computer that can run a slide show without user intervention
b. A host computer where you can only view a presentation
c. A presentation you can open on a computer that does not have PowerPoint installed
d. A special slide show created from selected slides in a presentation
e. A folder that stores slides for others to access and modify

Select the best answer from the list of choices.

13. Which of the following statements is *not* true about a presentation set to run at a kiosk?
   a. The presentation loops continuously.
   b. The presentation works best with manual slide timings.
   c. You can use action buttons to progress through the slides.
   d. You don't have to be present to run the slide show.

14. Which view allows you to view a presentation using two monitors?
    a. Theater View
    b. Multiple Monitor View
    c. Slide Show View
    d. Presenter View
15. What is a basic custom show?
    a. A separate presentation that is linked to a primary custom show
    b. A presentation copied to a CD to be used on another computer
    c. A presentation that includes slides from the original presentation
    d. A photo album presentation
16. What does the PowerPoint Viewer allow you to do?
    a. View a presentation on the Web
    b. View and participate in an online meeting
    c. View a presentation in Slide Show view on any compatible computer
    d. View a presentation in all four views at the same time
17. The _____ identifies features that will not work in earlier versions of PowerPoint.
    a. PowerPoint Viewer
    b. Web server
    c. Document Inspector
    d. Compatibility Checker
18. When you save a presentation in Hypertext Markup Language, you are saving it to be used on _____.
    a. a Slide Library
    b. a custom show
    c. the Web
    d. a kiosk
19. When you type a password in the password text box, the text _____.
    a. Changes to small black symbols.
    b. Is transparent.
    c. Moves to a special folder.
    d. Converts to random symbols.
20. What is the primary purpose of packaging a presentation?
    a. To distribute it
    b. To create a backup copy of it
    c. To be able to post it to a Web server
    d. To see it in a Slide Library

▼ SKILLS REVIEW

1. **Use templates and add comments.**
    a. Start PowerPoint, click the Office button, click New, click Installed Templates, click Contemporary Photo Album, then click Create.
    b. Save the presentation as **Contemporary Album** to the drive and folder where you store your Data Files.
    c. Click the Review tab on the Ribbon, click the New Comment button, type **What do you think of this slide layout?**, then go to Slide 3.
    d. Add a new comment, type **This is an interesting photo layout.**, click the Previous button, then click the Edit Comment button.
    e. Type **I like it.**, then save your work.

▼ SKILLS REVIEW (CONTINUED)

2. **Send and review a presentation.**
   a. Click the Office button, point to Send, then click E-mail.
   b. Get approval and direction from your instructor before you send this e-mail to a colleague or friend, then close the presentation.
   c. Open the file PPT H-9.pptx from the drive and folder where you store your Data Files, then save it as **Reviewed Contemporary Album**.
   d. Click the Review tab, click the top-left review comment thumbnail, click the Next button, read the comment, then click the Next button until you read all the comments.
   e. Click the Previous button, click the Delete button arrow, then click Delete All Markup on the Current Slide.
   f. Save your changes, then close the presentation.

3. **Use advanced slide show options.**
   a. Open the file PPT H-10.pptx from the drive and folder where you store your Data Files, then save it as **Corner Bookstore**.
   b. Click the Slide Show tab, click the Set Up Slide Show button, then set up a slide show that will be browsed at a kiosk, using automatic slide timings.
   c. Set a slide timing of 4 seconds to each slide, run the slide show all the way through once, then press [Esc] to end the slide show.
   d. Set the slide show to run using manual slide timings and presented by a speaker.
   e. Run through the slide show from Slide 1 using the action buttons at the bottom of the slides. Move forward and backward through the presentation, watching the animation effects as they appear.
   f. Hide Slide 5, run through the slide show, then unhide Slide 5.
   g. When you have finished viewing the slide show, reset the slide timings to automatic, then save your changes.

4. **Create a custom show.**
   a. Create a custom show called **Goals** which includes Slides 2, 3, 4, and 5.
   b. Move Slide 3 Performance Series above Slide 2 Lecture Series.
   c. View the show from within the Custom Shows dialog box, then press [Esc] to end the slide show.
   d. Go to Slide 1, begin the slide show, then, when Slide 1 appears, go to the Goals custom show.
   e. View the custom slide show, return to Normal view, then save your changes.

5. **Prepare a presentation for distribution.**
   a. Click the Office button, point to Prepare, then open the Encrypt Document dialog box.
   b. Type **12345**, then type the same password in the Confirm Password dialog box.
   c. Close the presentation, save your changes, open the presentation, then type **12345** as the password in the Password dialog box.
   d. Open the Encrypt Document dialog box again, then delete the password.
   e. Click the Office button, point to Prepare, open the Compatibility Checker, read the information, then close the dialog box.
   f. Save your work, then add your name to the notes and handouts footer. The completed presentation is shown in Figure H-21.
   g. Print the slides in the presentation as Handouts (2 slides per page.)

   FIGURE H-21

6. **Save a presentation for the Web.**
   a. Click the Office button, click Save As, click the Save as type list arrow, then select Web Page.
   b. Click the Publish button, and make sure that speaker notes do not display and all browsers are supported.
   c. Change the page title to **Corner Bookstore Presentation**, then click Publish.

▼ SKILLS REVIEW (CONTINUED)

   d. View the presentation in your browser using the hyperlinks in the left pane, the Next Slide and Previous Slide buttons, and the action buttons on the slides.
   e. Close your browser, then save your work.
7. **Package a presentation.**
   a. Click the Office button, point to Publish, then open the Package for CD dialog box.
   b. Open the Options dialog box, embed TrueType fonts and inspect the presentation for appropriate content. Click OK.
   c. Click the Copy to Folder button, create a folder where you store your Data Files with the name **Bookstore Package**, then package the presentation.
   d. Run the Document Inspector, close the Document Inspector dialog box, then close the Package for CD dialog box.
   e. Open Windows Explorer, view the contents of the Bookstore Package folder, then close the Windows Explorer window.
   f. Save and close the presentation.
8. **Create a photo album.**
   a. Create a photo album presentation, then from the drive and folder where you store your Data Files, insert the files PPT H-11.jpg, PPT H-12.jpg, PPT H-13.jpg, PPT H-14.jpg, PPT H-15.jpg, and PPT H-16.jpg.
   b. Move picture PPT H-16.jpg so it is second in the list, move PPT H-14.jpg so it is last in the list, create the photo album, then save it as **Africa 2011** to the drive and folder where you store your Data Files.
   c. Change the title on the title slide to **Africa 2011**, then type your name in the subtitle text box.
   d. Open the Edit Photo Album dialog box, change the picture layout to 2 pictures with title, change the frame shape to a simple black frame, then update the presentation.
   e. Provide a title for rest of the slides, add your name as a footer to the slides, then save your changes.
   f. Print the slides of the presentation, then exit PowerPoint.

▼ INDEPENDENT CHALLENGE 1

You work for Pacific Island Tours, an international tour company that provides specialty tours to destinations throughout Asia and the Pacific. You have to develop presentations that the sales force can use to highlight different tours at conferences and meetings.

To complete the presentation, you need to create at least two of your own slides. Assume that Pacific Island Tours has a special (20% off regular price) on tours to Fiji and the Cook Islands during the spring of 2011. Also assume that Pacific Island Tours offers tour packages to the Philippines, Japan, Australia, and New Zealand.

   a. Start PowerPoint, open the presentation PPT H-17.pptx, then save it as **Pacific Tours** to the drive and folder where you store your Data Files.
   b. Open the Review tab on the Ribbon, use the Next button to view each comment, read the comment, then delete the last comment on the Departing Cities slide.
   c. Use the Previous button to move back to slides that have comments and write a response comment to each of the original comments.
   d. Use the Compatibility Checker on the presentation.
   e. Use the information provided above to help you develop additional content for two new slides.
   f. Insert at least three different media clips (pictures, animations, movies, clip art, or sounds). Use clips from PowerPoint or from other approved legal media sources.
   g. Apply slide transitions, timings, and animations to all the slides in the presentation.
   h. Apply a saved design theme. On the Design tab, click the More button in the Themes group, click Browse for Themes, then apply the Pacific Theme.thmx theme from the drive and folder where you store your Data Files.
   i. Convert the text on Slide 2 to a SmartArt diagram, then format the diagram using the techniques you learned in this book.
   j. Use the Compatibility Checker again on the presentation. Note any differences.
   k. View the presentation in Slide Show view.
   l. Add your name as a footer on all notes and handouts. Print the presentation as handouts (2 per page), close the presentation, then exit PowerPoint.

Using Advanced Features

▼ INDEPENDENT CHALLENGE 2

You work in Sacramento, California at the State Agricultural Statistics Agency. Part of your job is to compile agricultural information gathered from the counties of California and create presentations that display the data for public viewing. You are currently working on a summary presentation that will be made public on the agency Web site.

a. Start PowerPoint, open the presentation PPT H-18.pptx, then save it as **Ag Report** to the drive and folder where you store your Data Files.

b. Convert the information on Slide 5 to a SmartArt diagram using one of the List layouts. Use a layout that includes pictures and insert the file PPT H-19.jpg from the drive and folder where you store your Data Files to the SmartArt graphic.

c. Format the SmartArt diagram using the commands on the SmartArt Tools Design and Format tabs.

d. Format the table on Slide 4. Change the table layout so the table displays the information properly, split the Cattle and Calves cell into two cells, then format the table.

e. Create a custom slide show that displays four slides.

f. Insert appropriate media clips on at least two slides.

g. Save the presentation in HTML format for the Web, save it as **California Ag Report**, preview the presentation as a Web page in your browser, then close your browser.

Advanced Challenge Exercise (Internet connection and instructor approval required)

- Write at least two comments in the presentation, then send the presentation as an e-mail attachment to another student in your class.
- The reviewing student should create and insert their own comments, then send it back to you.
- Once you get the presentation back, review the comments.

h. Save the presentation, then view the presentation in Slide Show view.

i. Add your name as a footer on all notes and handouts. Print the presentation as handouts (2 per page), close the presentation, then exit PowerPoint.

▼ INDEPENDENT CHALLENGE 3

You are the assistant director of operations at NorthWest Cargo Inc., an international marine shipping company based in Seattle, Washington. NorthWest Cargo handles 65 percent of all the trade between Asia, the Middle East, and the West Coast of the United States. You need to give a quarterly presentation to the company's operations committee outlining the type and amount of trade NorthWest Cargo handled during the previous quarter.

Plan a presentation with at least six slides that details the type of goods NorthWest Cargo carries. Create your own content, but assume the following:

- NorthWest Cargo hauls automobiles from Tokyo to San Francisco. Northwest can usually haul between 2800 and 3500 automobiles in a quarter.
- NorthWest Cargo hauls large tractor equipment and parts made by Caterpillar Tractor and John Deere Tractor from the United States.
- NorthWest Cargo hauls common household goods that include electronic equipment, appliances, toys, and furniture.
- NorthWest Cargo owns five cargo ships that can operate simultaneously. All five ships were in operation during the last quarter.
- NorthWest Cargo hauled a total of 1.8 million tons during the last quarter.

a. Start PowerPoint, create a new presentation based on a template or theme in the New Presentation dialog box, then save it as **Cargo Report**.

b. Use the assumptions provided to help develop the content for your presentation. If you have Internet access, use the Internet to research the shipping business.

▼ INDEPENDENT CHALLENGE 3 (CONTINUED)

c. Use at least two different media clips to enhance your presentation.
d. Set transitions and animations, and rehearse slide timings.
e. View the presentation in Slide Show view.

Advanced Challenge Exercise

- Select one word and translate it to French using the Translate button in the Proofing group on the Review tab.
- Select one word, use the Thesaurus button in the Proofing group to find a different word, then apply the word.

f. Save your work, then add your name as a footer on all notes and handouts.
g. Print the final slide presentation as handouts (2 per page), close the presentation, then exit PowerPoint.

▼ REAL LIFE INDEPENDENT CHALLENGE

Your assignment for your cultural history class is to create a photo album based on your personal life and family history. You must use your own pictures of past and present family members, pets, a family home, a family business, or any other type of family activity that help tell the story of your personal family life and history.

a. Start PowerPoint, create a photo album presentation, insert your pictures to the presentation, then save it as **My Photo Album** to the drive and folder where you store your Data Files.
b. Add your name to the title slide and as the footer on the handouts.
c. Use the Edit Photo Album dialog box to format the pictures.
d. Spell check the presentation, then view the final presentation in Slide Show view.
e. Save the final version, print the slides, close the presentation, then exit PowerPoint. See Figure H-22.

FIGURE H-22

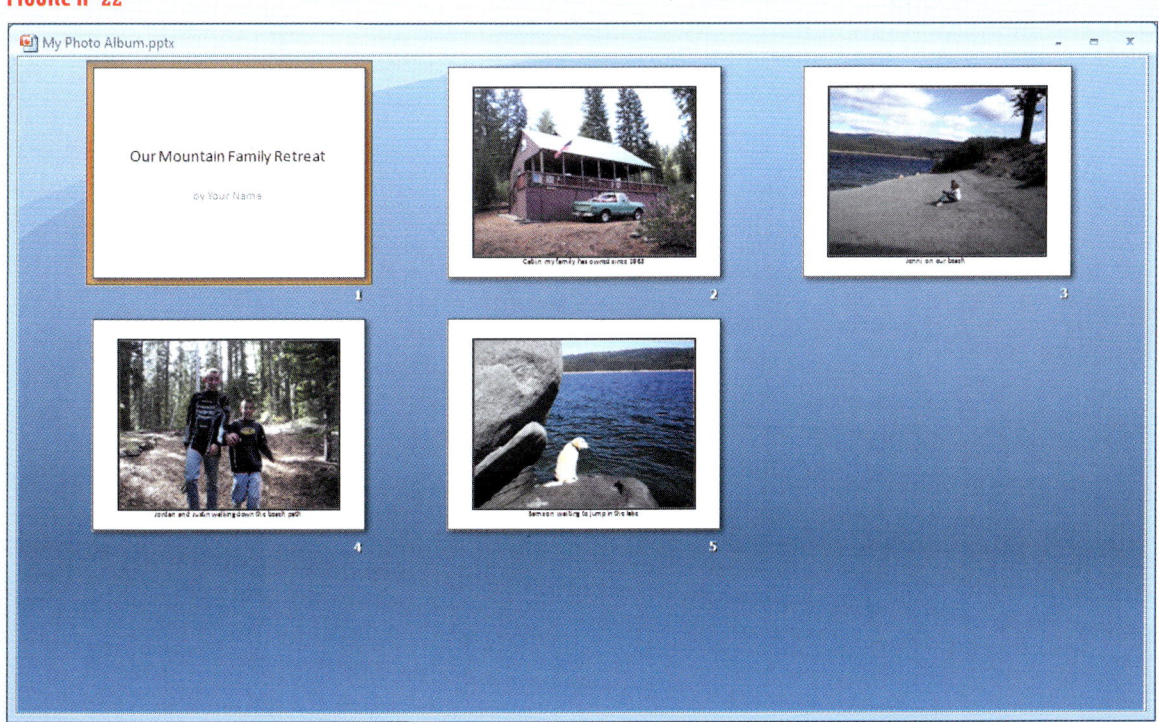

▼ VISUAL WORKSHOP

Create the slide shown in Figure H-23. Save the presentation as **Western Forests**. The SmartArt is a Vertical Box List layout. Convert the shapes in the SmartArt graphic to the Snip Diagonal Corner Rectangle shape, then apply the Cartoon SmartArt Style. Add your name to the slide footer, then print the slide of the presentation.

FIGURE H-23

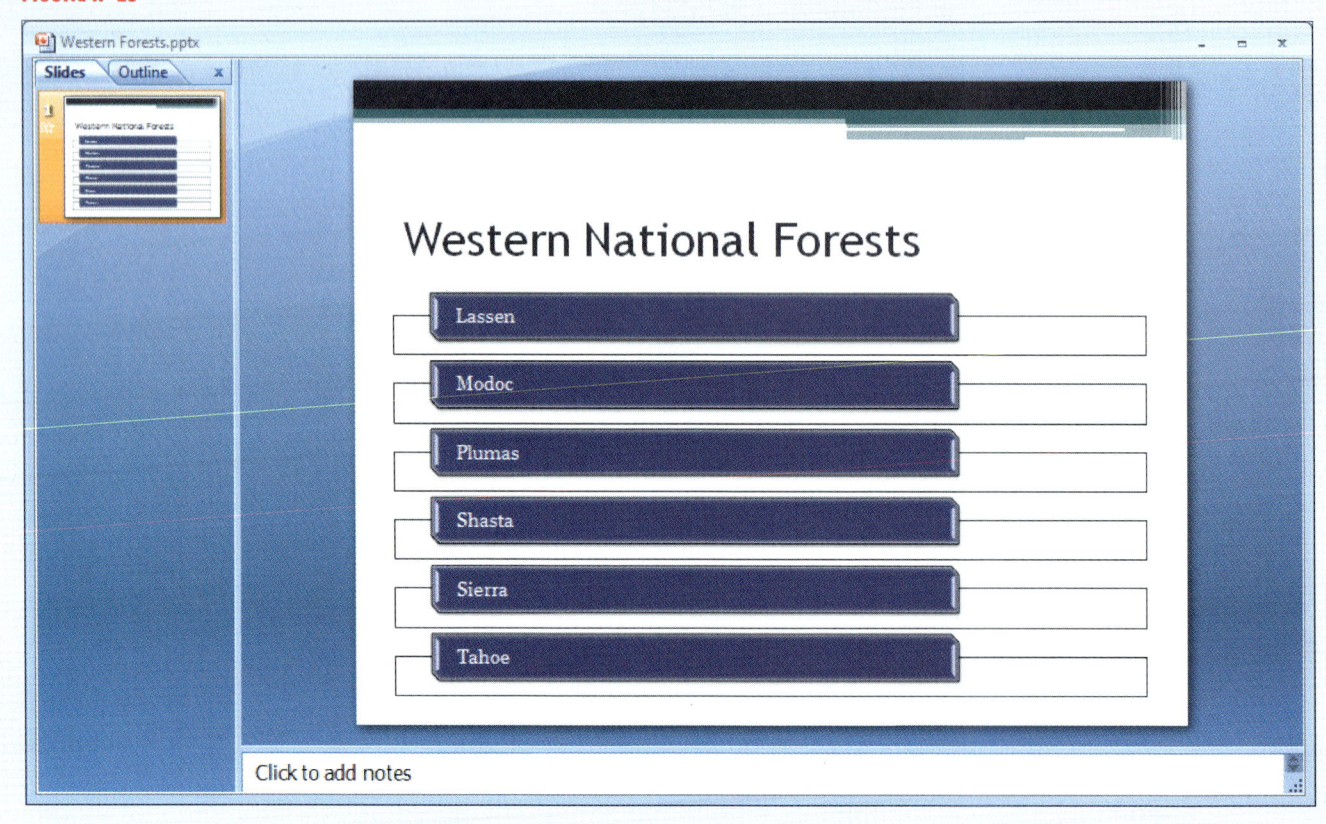

UNIT F
Integration

Integrating Word, Excel, Access, and PowerPoint

Files You Will Need:
INT F-1.pptx
INT F-2.accdb
INT F-3.docx
INT F-4.xlsx
INT F-5.docx
INT F-6.pptx
INT F-7.accdb
INT F-8.docx
INT F-9.xlsx
INT F-10.docx
INT F-11.docx
INT F-12.xlsx
INT F-13.pptx
INT F-14.accdb
INT F-15.accdb
INT F-16.xlsx

As you have learned in previous integration units, you can include objects from most Microsoft Office applications in most other Microsoft Office applications. For example, you can publish an Access report in Word, transfer an Excel chart to PowerPoint, or insert a PowerPoint slide in a Word document. Although you can exchange information between any Office programs, you are most likely to use Word or PowerPoint as the "host" programs because reports and presentations are most likely to contain objects from other applications. As the assistant to Bertram Lamont, the manager of the corporate division of QST London, you are in charge of compiling materials for a PowerPoint presentation and a Word report about the corporate tours offered in 2010. Bertram will deliver the presentation and report at an upcoming meeting of all the Quest Specialty Travel branch managers.

OBJECTIVES

Insert an Access table in PowerPoint
Insert Word objects in PowerPoint
Link an Excel file in PowerPoint
Publish PowerPoint slides in Word
Embed a PowerPoint slide in Word

UNIT F
Integration

Inserting an Access Table in PowerPoint

You can copy a table from Access and paste it into PowerPoint so that you can use PowerPoint tools to modify the table attractively for use in a presentation. However, you cannot create a link between Access and PowerPoint directly. As you learned in Unit C, you create a link from Access to PowerPoint by first copying a table to Excel then copying and pasting the Excel data into PowerPoint as a link. You already have an Access database containing information about the corporate tours offered by QST London in 2010. Because you don't need to link the database information to the presentation, you copy a query from the Access database, paste it directly into a PowerPoint slide, then format the query information attractively.

STEPS

1. **Start PowerPoint, open the file INT F-1.pptx from the drive and folder where you store your Data Files, save it as QST London Corporate Tours, then scroll through the presentation**
   The slides describe the corporate tours. The blank slides will contain objects that you import from other programs.

   TROUBLE
   To save the database with a new name, click the Office button, point to Save As, then click Access 2007 Database.

2. **Start Access, open the Data File INT F-2.accdb from the location where you store your Data Files, then save it as QST London Corporate Tours**
   The Access database contains two tables. The QST London Tours table lists all the tours offered by QST London in 2010, and the QST London Company table lists the companies that purchased tours in 2010. The QST London Tours query includes the list of companies and the tours they purchased.

3. **Click either instance of QST London Tours Query in the list of database objects, then click the Copy button in the Clipboard group**

4. **Switch to PowerPoint, go to Slide 4 (Top Corporate Customers), click Layout in the Slides group, select the Title Only slide layout, then click the Paste button in the Clipboard group**
   You change the default Title and Text slide layout to the Title Only layout before pasting so that the text placeholder does not overlap the pasted query datasheet.

5. **Click the Table Tools Design tab, click the More button in the Table Styles group, then select the Themed Style 1 – Accent 1 design, as shown in Figure F-1**
   You can use PowerPoint tools to format the pasted table.

6. **Click the Home tab, click any text in the pasted table, click Select in the Editing group, click Select All, then click the Increase Font Size button in the Font group four times**
   The font size is increased to 18 pt.

7. **Click anywhere in row 1, click the right mouse button, click Delete Rows, select all the text in the new row 1, increase the font size to 24 point, apply Bold formatting, then center the text**

8. **Double-click the column divider between Company Name and Tour Name, double-click the column divider between Tour Name and Location, verify that each tour name appears on one row, then save the presentation**
   The formatted table appears as shown in Figure F-2.

9. **Switch to Access, then exit the program, answering Yes to empty the clipboard**

FIGURE F-1: Selecting a table design in PowerPoint

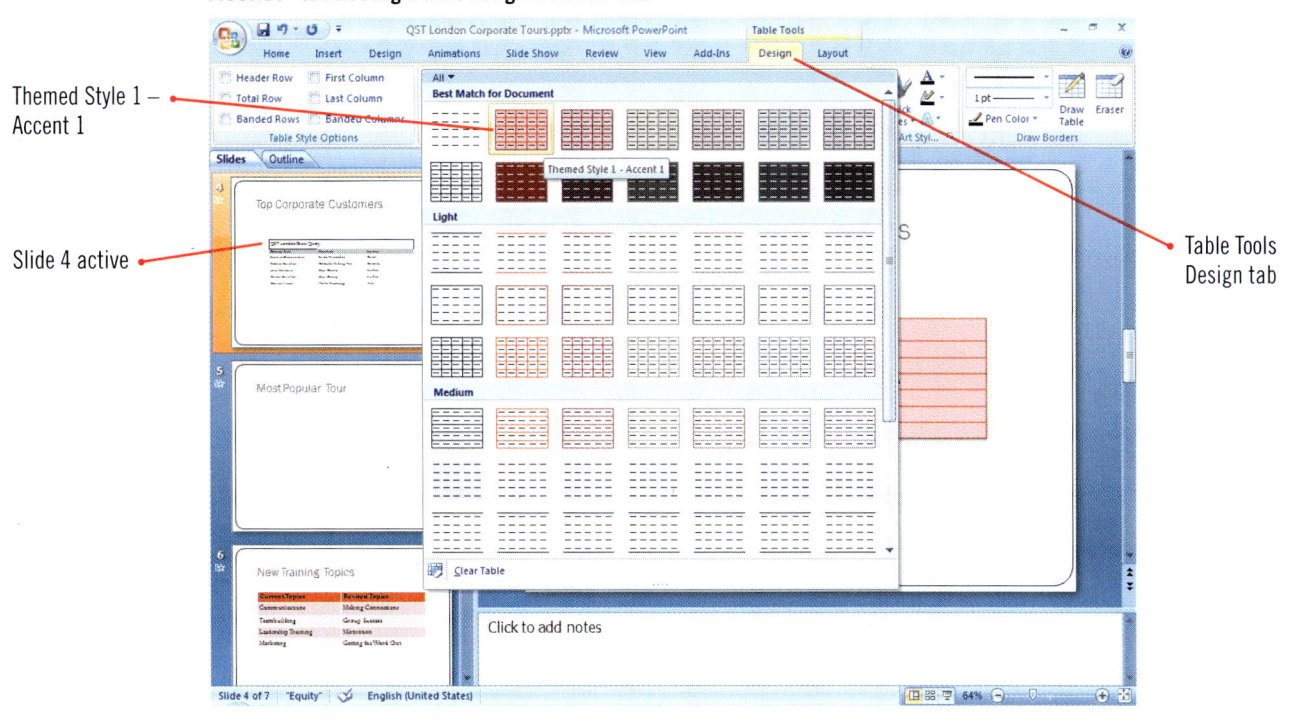

FIGURE F-2: Copied Access query formatted in PowerPoint

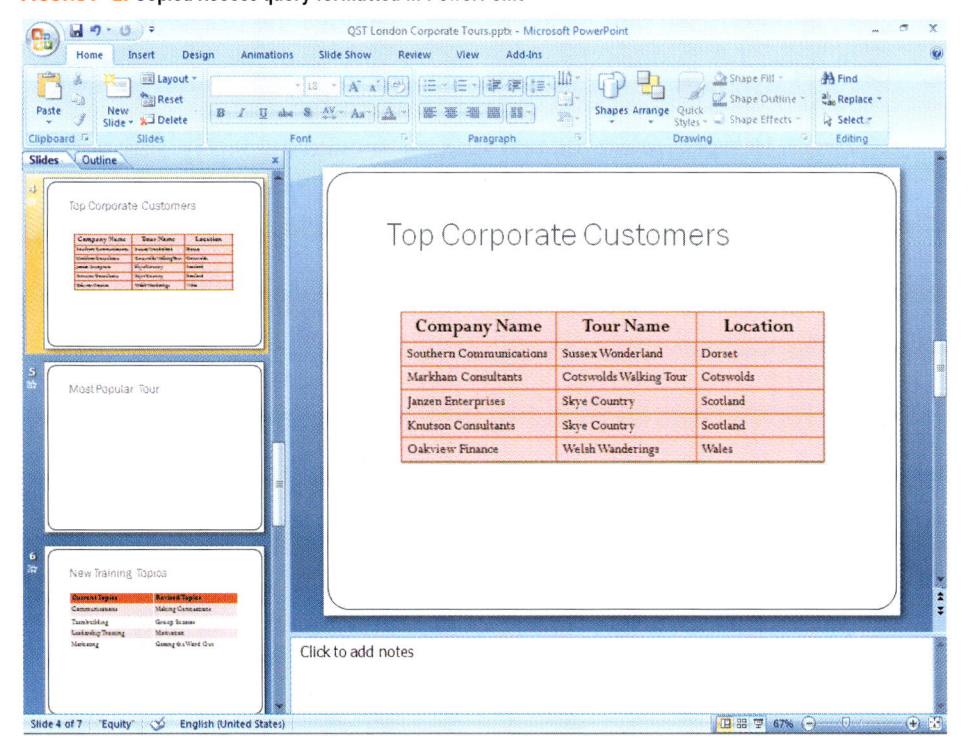

UNIT F
Integration

Inserting Word Objects in PowerPoint

Often you may need a PowerPoint presentation to include text that you have already entered in a Word document, such as a letter or a report. Instead of retyping the text in PowerPoint, you can copy it from Word and paste it into PowerPoint. The pasted text becomes a text box that you can then format and position using PowerPoint tools. You can choose to paste the object with or without linking it to the source document. You want information about QST's most popular tour to appear on Slide 5 of the presentation. The text that describes this tour is contained in a Word document.

STEPS

1. Start Word, open the file INT F-3.docx from the drive and folder where you store your Data Files, save it as QST London Tours, then select the Skye Country heading and paragraph

2. Click the Copy button in the Clipboard group, switch to PowerPoint, go to Slide 5, change the layout to Title Only, then click the Paste button

   The text is pasted into a text box that you can format in PowerPoint.

3. Click the Quick Styles button in the Drawing group, then click the Subtle Effect – Accent 2 quick style (fourth row, light rose colored)

4. Select all the text in the text box, then click the Increase Font Size button in the Font group twice

   The font size increases to 24 pt.

5. Drag the left and right sizing handles to modify the size of the pasted object as shown In Figure F-3, position the object on the slide as shown, then click away from the object to deselect it

6. Switch to Word, select the text rock climbing in the second line of the Skye Country tour description, copy it, switch to the PowerPoint presentation, click the Paste button, drag the pasted object below the text so its left edge is aligned with the left edge of the text box, then deselect it

7. Return to Word, select the text pony trekking in the third line of the Skye Country paragraph, copy it, switch to PowerPoint, click the Paste button, drag the pasted object below the text so its right edge is aligned with the right edge of the text box, then drag its green rotation handle to rotate the object as shown in Figure F-4

8. Select and rotate the rock climbing object slightly left, press and hold [Shift], click the pony trekking object, click the Drawing Tools Format tab, click the Shape Fill button in the Shape Styles group, then select the Dark Red, Accent 2, Lighter 80% color

9. Click the Shape Effects button in the Shape Styles group, point to Bevel, select the Angle bevel style as shown in Figure F-5, save the presentation, switch to Word, then close the document

   You formatted both rotated text objects with the same style.

FIGURE F-3: Sizing and positioning the copied text object

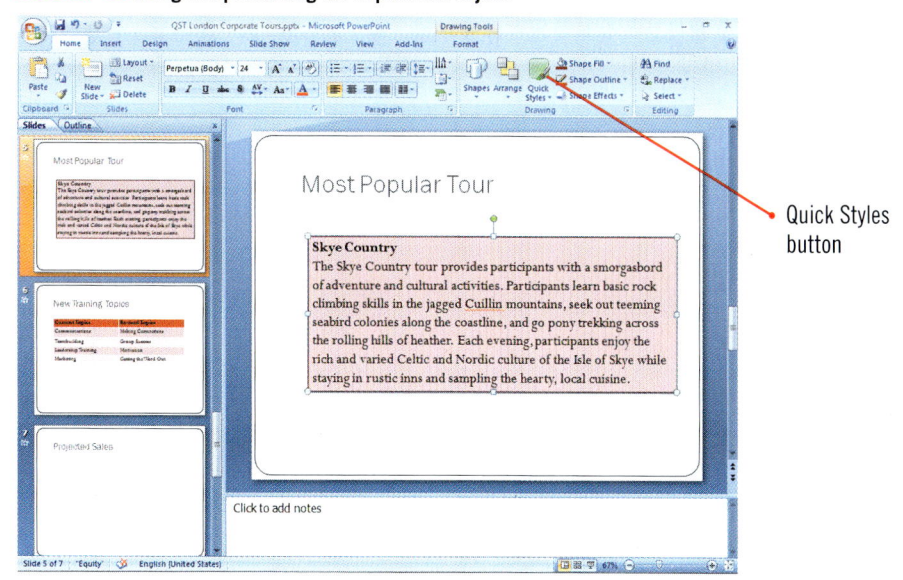

Quick Styles button

FIGURE F-4: Rotating a copied text object

Rotation handle

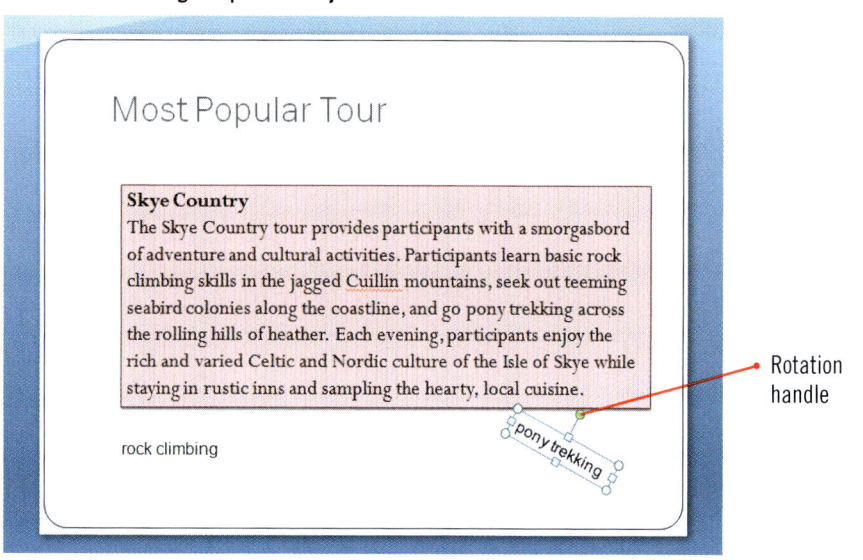

FIGURE F-5: Word text objects formatted and positioned

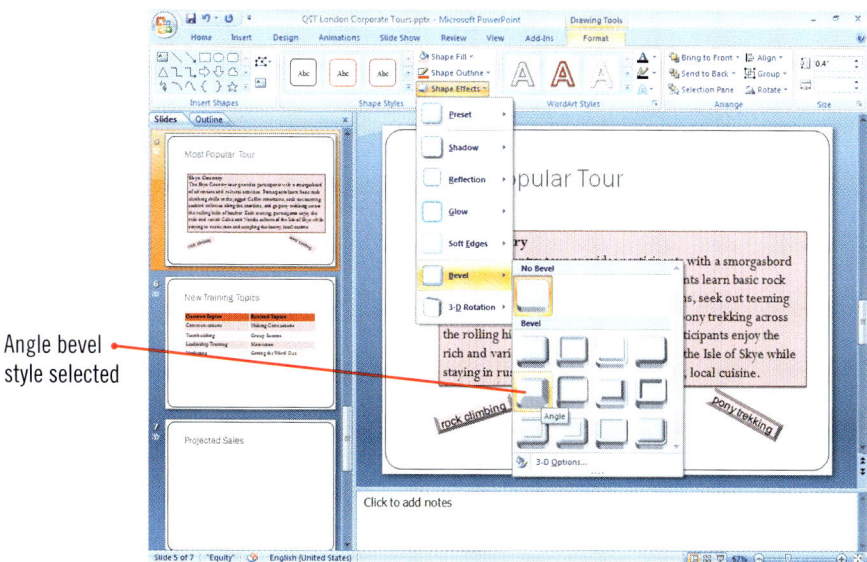

Angle bevel style selected

Integrating Word, Excel, Access, and PowerPoint

UNIT F
Integration

Linking an Excel File in PowerPoint

You can use the Object command to insert a linked Excel file into a PowerPoint presentation. To edit the content of the Excel file, you double-click it to open it in Excel, the source program. Changes you make to the file in Excel appear in PowerPoint and in the original Excel file. Slide 7 should contain information about projected sales for 2011. You already have this information stored in an Excel spreadsheet. You insert the Excel file in PowerPoint, then update selected content.

STEPS

1. Start Excel, open the file **INT F-4.xlsx** from the drive and folder where you store your Data Files, save it as **QST London Projected Revenue**, then close the file

QUICK TIP
Instead of applying the Title Only slide layout, you can just delete the 2nd placeholder.

2. Switch to PowerPoint, go to Slide 7, change the layout to **Title Only**, click the **Insert tab**, then click the **Object button** in the Text group

3. Click the **Create from file option button**, click **Browse**, navigate to the location where you stored the QST London Projected Revenue.xlsx file, then double-click **QST London Projected Revenue.xlsx**

4. Click the **Link check box** to select it, then click **OK**

   The Excel file appears on the PowerPoint slide as a worksheet object that you can resize as you would any object.

5. Drag the lower-left corner handle down to enlarge the worksheet object, then position the object on the slide as shown in Figure F-6

   You modify the linked object by double-clicking it so that you can use the tools of the source program (Excel) to make the changes.

QUICK TIP
You can edit the linked object by opening the file in Excel or by double-clicking it in Word.

6. Double-click the worksheet object, change the tour price for Wessex Wonderland to **£550** and the tour price for Cotswolds Walking Tour to **£300**, then save and close the workbook

7. In PowerPoint, verify that the prices have updated and that the total projected revenue is now **£491,250.00** in the worksheet object

8. Click the worksheet object to select it, click the **Drawing Tools Format tab**, click the **Shape Outline button** in the Shape Styles group, point to **Weight**, then select the 4½ point border weight as shown in Figure F-7

   The object is a linked file, which means that you cannot use all of the PowerPoint formatting tools to modify it. For example, you cannot apply a preset shape style or change the fill color.

9. Open **QST London Projected Revenue.xlsx** in Excel, verify that the total revenue is £491,250.00, close the workbook, then save the presentation

FIGURE F-6: Excel file inserted in PowerPoint

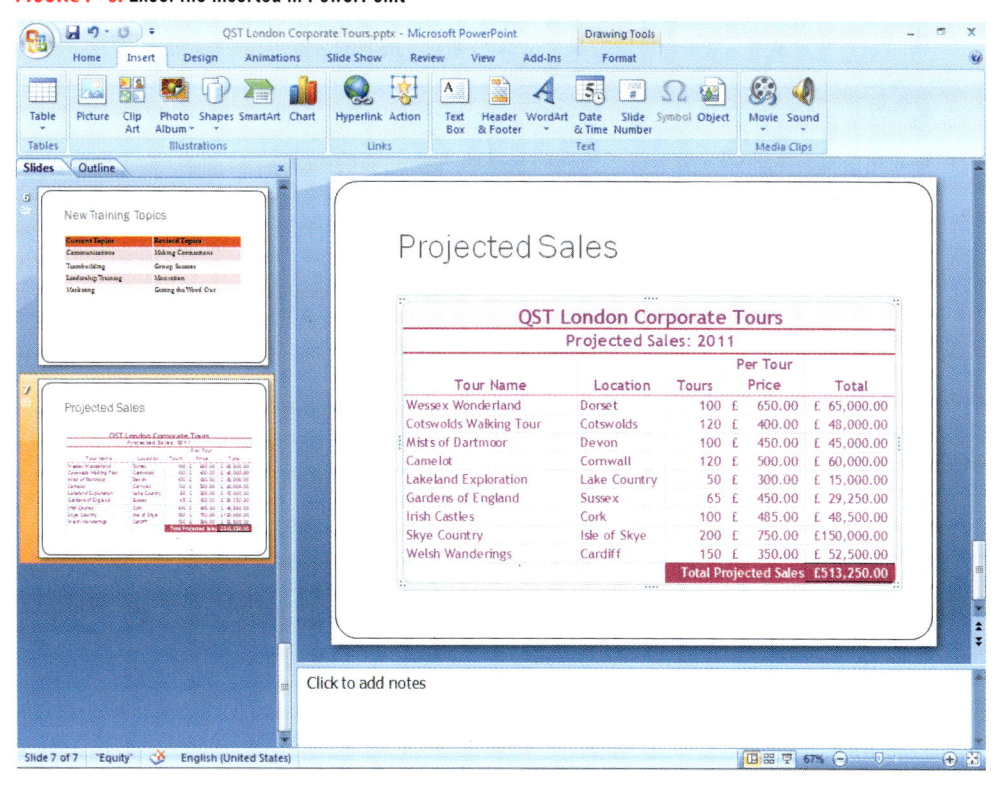

FIGURE F-7: Changing the border weight

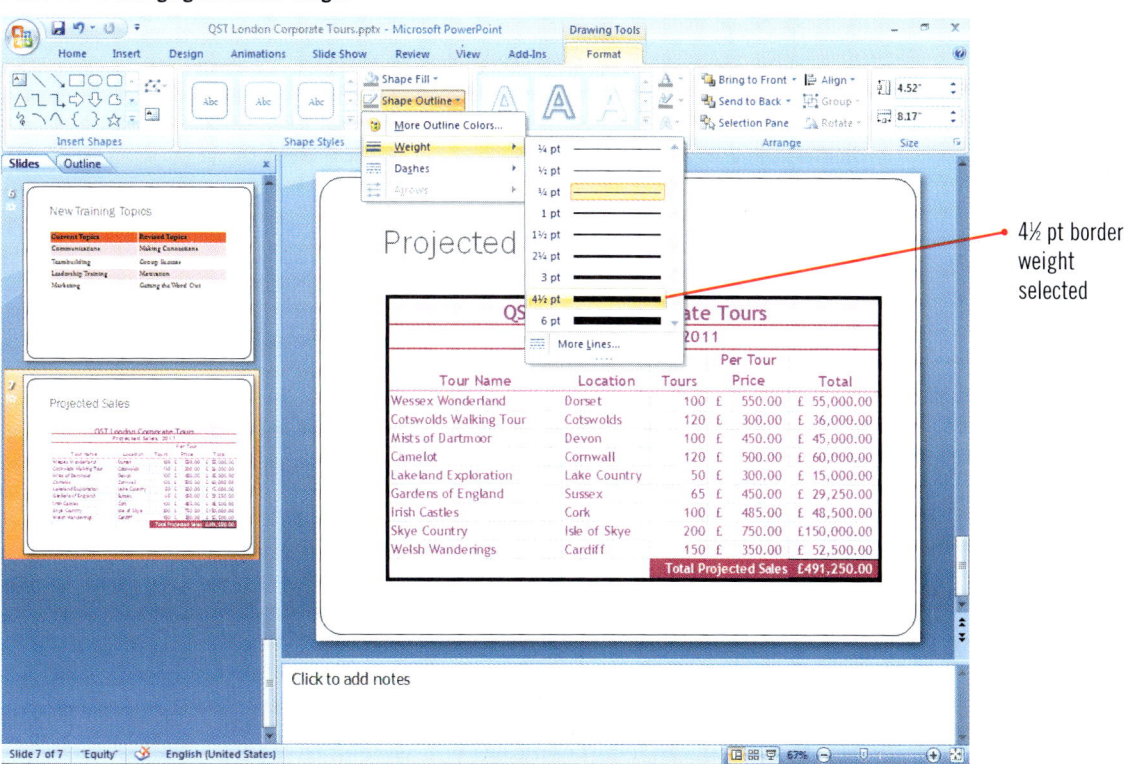

4½ pt border weight selected

Integrating Word, Excel, Access, and PowerPoint

UNIT F
Publishing PowerPoint Slides in Word

You can print slides as handouts directly from PowerPoint, or you can publish the slides in a Word document and use Word tools to modify the document further. Bertram asks you to publish the PowerPoint slides from his presentation to a Word document and then add the report text to it.

STEPS

1. In PowerPoint, click the Office button, point to Publish, click Create Handouts in Microsoft Office Word, verify that the Notes next to slides option button is selected, click the Paste link option button as shown in Figure F-8, then click OK

   In a few moments, the presentation appears in a three-column table in a new Word document.

2. Wait a few moments for the publishing process to finish, save the Word document as QST London Corporate Report, click to the left of Slide 6 at the bottom of page 2 to select the entire row, then click the Cut button in the Clipboard group

   When you delete slide content from the Word document, that slide is not deleted from the PowerPoint presentation, even though the presentation and the document are linked. You must delete it manually from the PowerPoint presentation. Similarly, if you delete a slide from PowerPoint, you need to delete it manually from the linked Word document.

3. Switch to PowerPoint, go to Slide 6, press [Delete], go to Slide 2, select New Training Topics, press [Delete], go to Slide 3, then insert Tours following Corporate in the slide title so it reads Corporate Tours Sales Focus

4. Switch to Word, click the Office button, point to Prepare, then scroll to and click Edit Links to Files

   In the Links dialog box, six entries appear. Each slide is linked separately to the PowerPoint presentation.

5. Press and hold [Shift], click the bottom link to select all six links as shown in Figure F-9, click Update Now, click OK, press [Ctrl][Home], then press [Enter] to insert a blank line above the table

   The text on Slides 2 and 3 in the Word document is updated. You insert a blank line before you paste new text into the document so that the copied text appears above the table.

6. Open the file INT F-5.docx from the drive and folder where you store your Data Files, click the Select button in the Editing group, click Select All, copy the text, then close the document

7. In Word, click the Paste button in the Clipboard group, click the table select icon, click the Cut button in the Clipboard group, click in the blank area above Conclusion on page 1, click the Paste button, then click after December 2010 in the paragraph above and press [Enter]

8. Select the table again, click the Table Tools Layout tab, click Properties in the Table group, click the Row tab, select the contents of the Specify height text box, type 2.2, then click OK

TROUBLE
Your table might paginate differently, depending on your printer setup.

9. Deselect the table, click the View tab, click the Two Pages button in the Zoom group, save the document, then compare your screen to Figure F-10

FIGURE F-8: Options in the Send To Microsoft Office Word dialog box

Paste link option button

FIGURE F-9: Selecting links in the Links dialog box

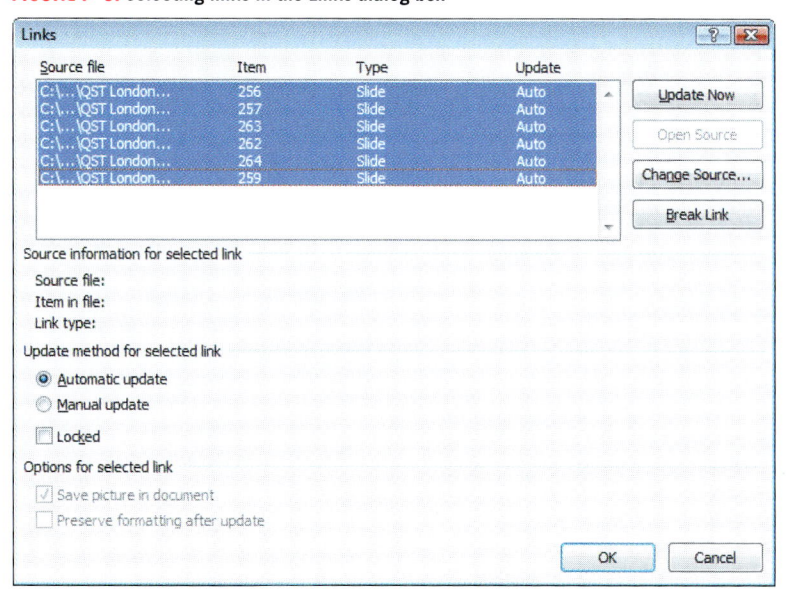

FIGURE F-10: Word document containing slides published from PowerPoint

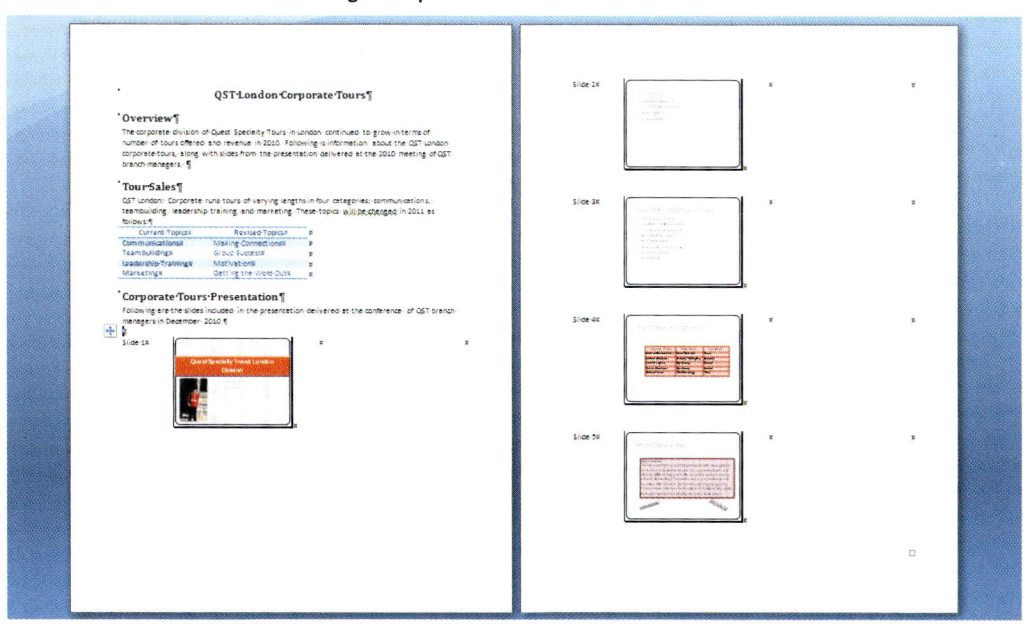

UNIT F Integration

Embedding a PowerPoint Slide in Word

You can embed a PowerPoint slide in a Word document and then, because it is embedded, use PowerPoint tools within Word to add text to the slide and apply formatting. The PowerPoint slide is not linked to a PowerPoint presentation. It exists only in the Word document. You can also copy a slide from PowerPoint, paste it into Word, then double-click it to make changes using PowerPoint tools. You want to replace the title of the Word report with an attractively formatted PowerPoint slide that includes the report title and your name. You also want to apply a consistent format to all the documents you have created in this unit. Finally, you decide to break all the links to the presentation and report so that you can send the document to other QST managers without sending the supporting PowerPoint file.

STEPS

1. **Return to 100% view, select the document title QST London Corporate Tours, press [Delete], click the Insert tab, click the Object button in the Text group, scroll to and click Microsoft Office PowerPoint Slide, then click OK**

   A blank PowerPoint slide appears in the Word document, along with the PowerPoint ribbon and tabs.

2. **Enter text on the embedded slide as shown in Figure F-11, click the Design tab, then click the Flow theme in the Themes group**

3. **Click to the left of Overview in the Word document, press [Enter], click to the left of the embedded slide to select it, click the Home tab, then click the Center button in the Paragraph group**

   You decide to make the theme consistent across all the linked files in PowerPoint, Word, and Excel.

4. **In Word, click the Page Layout tab, click Themes in the Themes group, click the Flow theme, switch to PowerPoint, click the Design tab, then select the Flow theme**

5. **Go to Slide 4, adjust the column widths of the table so the text does not wrap, center the table on the slide, go to Slide 5, select all the text in the Skye Country text box, click the Decrease Font Size button in the Font group once, then reposition the object as needed so that it appears centered on the slide**

   When you apply a new theme to a presentation, you often need to adjust the size and positioning of objects on the slides.

6. **Go to Slide 6, double-click the Excel worksheet object, click the Page Layout tab, click Themes, click the Flow theme, save and close the workbook, then return to PowerPoint and adjust the position of the Excel file on the slide**

   The Flow theme formats the Excel worksheet object in the PowerPoint presentation.

7. **In PowerPoint, open the Links dialog box, click the link, click Break Link, then click Close**

8. **View the slide show, print a copy of the presentation as handouts, six slides to a page, then save and close the presentation**

9. **Switch to Word, open the Links dialog box, select, update, and then break all the links, change Slide 7 to Slide 6 on page 3, preview the report, print a copy, save and close the document, then close all open programs**

   The three pages of the completed report appear as shown in Figure F-12. Table F-1 summarizes the integration activities you performed in this unit.

FIGURE F-11: Text entered on an embedded PowerPoint slide

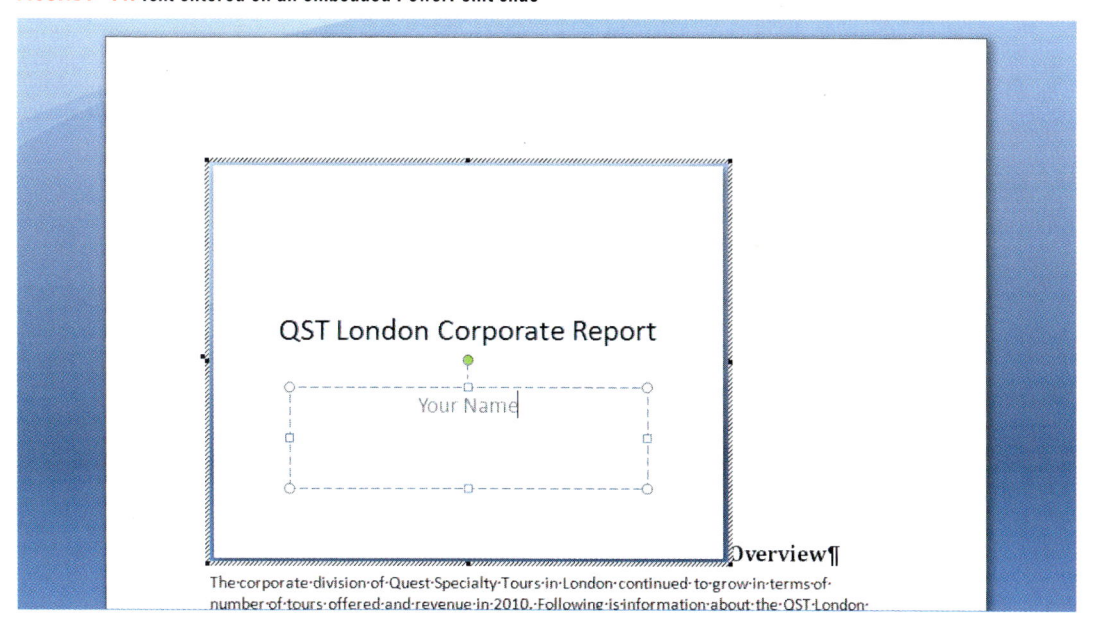

FIGURE F-12: Completed report

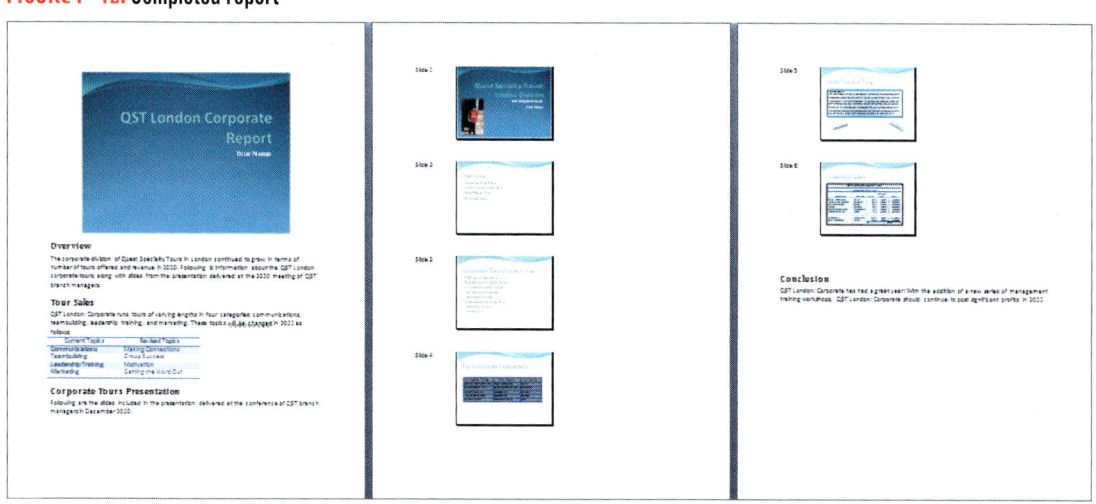

TABLE F-1: Unit F Integration activities

object	command(s)	source program	destination program	result	connection	page no.
Access table	Copy/Paste	Access	PowerPoint	Access table is pasted into the PowerPoint slide, then formatted with PowerPoint tools	None	82
Word text	Copy/Paste	Word	PowerPoint	Word text is pasted into the PowerPoint slide, then formatted with PowerPoint tools	None	84
Excel file	Copy/Paste Link	Excel	PowerPoint	Excel file is inserted into PowerPoint, then modified in Excel	Linked	86
PowerPoint slides	Publish	PowerPoint	Word	PowerPoint slides are published in a 3-column table in Word	Linked	88
PowerPoint slide	Object button in the Insert tab	PowerPoint	Word	PowerPoint slide is embedded in a Word document and updated with PowerPoint tools	Embedded	90

Integrating Word, Excel, Access, and PowerPoint

Practice

▼ CONCEPTS REVIEW

Match each term with the statement that best describes it.

1. Title Only
2. Paste Special
3. Object
4. Publish
5. PowerPoint slide

a. Click to insert an Excel file in PowerPoint
b. Slide layout that should be selected before a copied object is pasted on a PowerPoint slide
c. Select to send PowerPoint slides to Word
d. Select in PowerPoint to paste an object as a link
e. Insert in Word as an embedded object

Select the best answer from the list of choices.

6. Which of the following actions is not available when you copy a table from Access to PowerPoint?
   a. Paste the table
   b. Link the table
   c. Change the table fill color
   d. Delete a table row

7. How is a block of Word text pasted into PowerPoint?
   a. As a picture
   b. As a graphic object
   c. In a text box
   d. As a bulleted item

8. Which of the following formatting options can you apply to a linked Excel file in PowerPoint?
   a. Picture style
   b. Object style
   c. Border weight
   d. Theme

9. After clicking the Office button in PowerPoint, which option do you select if you want to send a PowerPoint presentation to Word?
   a. Prepare
   b. Send
   c. Publish
   d. Convert

10. After clicking the Office button in PowerPoint, which option do you select to access the Links dialog box?
    a. Prepare
    b. Send
    c. Publish
    d. Convert

▼ SKILLS REVIEW

1. **Insert an Access table in PowerPoint.**
   a. Start PowerPoint, open the file INT F-6.pptx from the drive and folder where you store your Data Files, save it as **Monroe Garden Club Presentation**, add your name where indicated on the title slide, then scroll through the presentation to identify what information is required.
   b. Start Access, open the file INT F-7.accdb from the drive and folder where you store your Data Files, then save it as **Monroe Garden Club Data**.
   c. Select either instance of the Garden Club Events Query in the list of database objects, copy it, switch to PowerPoint, go to Slide 4, then apply the Title Only slide layout.
   d. Paste the Access query information on the slide (don't worry if the background is white; it will change when you apply a table style), then apply the Themed Style 1 – Accent 4 table style. Select all the text in the table, then change the font size to 18 point.

▼ SKILLS REVIEW (CONTINUED)

e. Delete row 1, increase the font size of the text in the new row 1 to 20 point, then apply bold and center headings.

f. Adjust the column widths so none of the lines wrap, center the table on the slide, save the presentation, switch to Access, then close the database, answering yes to empty the clipboard and exit Access.

2. **Insert Word objects into PowerPoint.**

   a. Start Word, open the file INT F-8.docx from the drive and folder where you store your Data Files, save it as **Monroe Garden Club Events**, then select the Planting Fall Bulbs heading and the following paragraph.

   b. Copy the text, switch to PowerPoint, go to Slide 5, apply the Title Only slide layout, then paste the text.

   c. Apply the Moderate Effect - Accent 4 shape style to the text box, then increase the font size of all the text three time (28 pt).

   d. Size and position the object so that it fills the area attractively, then deselect it.

   e. In Word, select and copy the text "stunning tulips," paste the text object on the PowerPoint slide, drag the pasted object below the lower-left corner of the text box, then deselect it.

   f. Copy the text "dancing daffodils" from the Word document and paste it to the right of "stunning tulips" so its right edge aligns with the right edge of the text box. Rotate the two text objects, fill them with Lavender - Accent 4 - Darker 25%, then apply the Cool Slant Bevel shape effect.

   g. Save the presentation, switch to Word, then save and close the document.

3. **Link an Excel file in PowerPoint.**

   a. Start Excel, open the file INT F-9.xlsx from the drive and folder where you store your Data Files, save it as **Monroe Garden Club Budget**, then close the file.

   b. In PowerPoint, go to Slide 7, change the layout to Title Only, then insert the Monroe Garden Club Budget file as a linked object.

   c. Enlarge the linked worksheet object and position it so that it fills the slide attractively. The numbers will be easier to read when you change the presentation design in a later step.

   d. Edit the worksheet object in Excel by changing the Catering expense for Qtr 1 to $1,500 and the Speakers expense for Qtr 2 to $4,000, then save and close the Excel worksheet.

   e. In PowerPoint, verify that the two expense items were changed and that the total Profit/Loss is now $2,549.

   f. Format the worksheet object with a 6 pt outline, then save the presentation.

4. **Publish PowerPoint slides in Word.**

   a. In PowerPoint, publish the presentation in Word as a handout with a pasted link, using the Notes next to slides layout. (*Hint*: You need to wait for several moments to allow the publishing process to be completed. If you receive an error message, close the Word document, then try publishing the slides again.)

   b. Save the new Word document as **Monroe Garden Club Report**, then use the Cut command to delete the row containing Slide 6.

   c. Delete Slide 6 in PowerPoint (New Gardening Workshops), delete New Gardening Workshops on Slide 2, then change the title of Slide 3 to **Garden Club Focus**.

   d. In Word, update all the links.

   e. Move to the top of the Word document, then insert a blank line above the table containing the linked slides.

   f. Open the file INT F-10.docx from the drive and folder where you store your Data Files, select all the text, then copy it.

   g. Paste it above the slides in the Monroe Garden Club Report document, then close the INT F-10.docx document.

   h. Select the table containing the PowerPoint slides, cut the table, then paste it in the blank area above Conclusion on page 1.

   i. Change the row height of all the rows in the table containing the linked PowerPoint slides to 2.3", then change Slide 7 to Slide 6 at the end of the document.

5. **Embed a PowerPoint slide in Word.**

   a. Delete the document title Monroe Garden Club, then insert a PowerPoint slide.

   b. On the embedded slide, enter **Monroe Garden Club Annual Report** as the slide title and your name as the subtitle.

   c. Apply the Module design.

   d. Move Introduction down one line, then center the embedded slide.

   e. In Word, apply the Module theme, then in PowerPoint, apply the Module theme.

▼ SKILLS REVIEW (CONTINUED)

f. Go to Slide 6, double-click the Excel worksheet object, apply the Module theme, then save and close the workbook.

g. In PowerPoint, go to Slide Sorter view, compare the completed presentation to Figure F-13, then print a copy of the presentation as handouts, six slides to the page.

h. Switch to Word, update all the links, break all the links, print a copy of the report, compare it to Figure F-14, then save and close the document.

i. In PowerPoint, break the link, then save and close the presentation.

FIGURE F-13: Completed presentation in Slide Sorter view

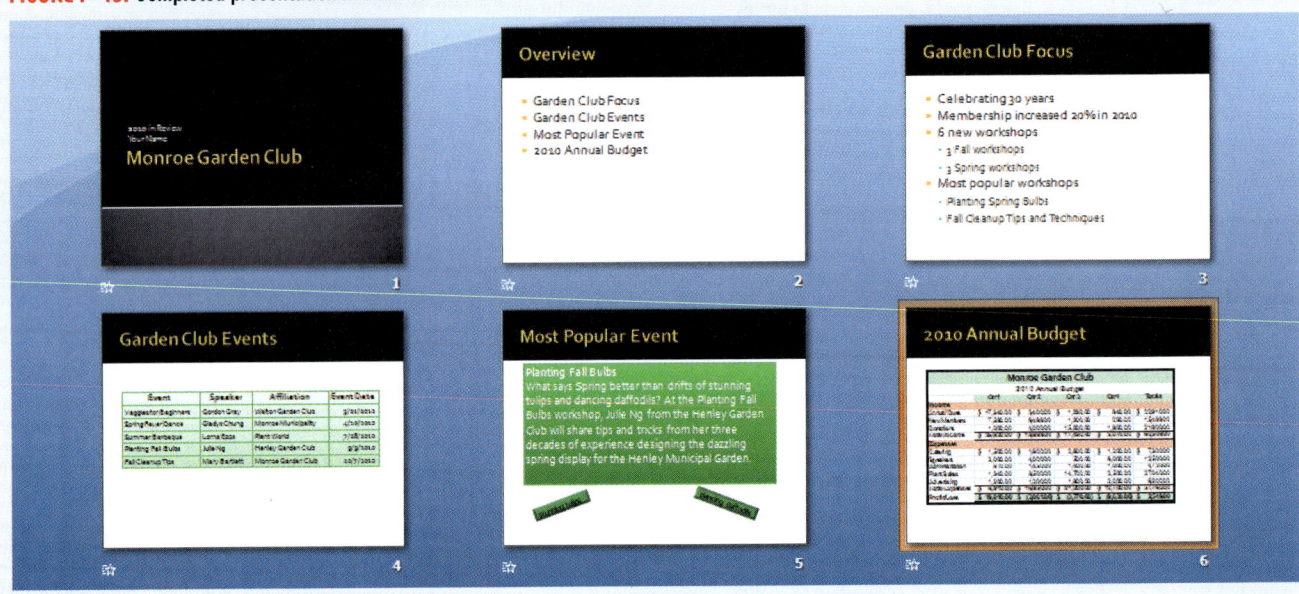

FIGURE F-14: Completed report

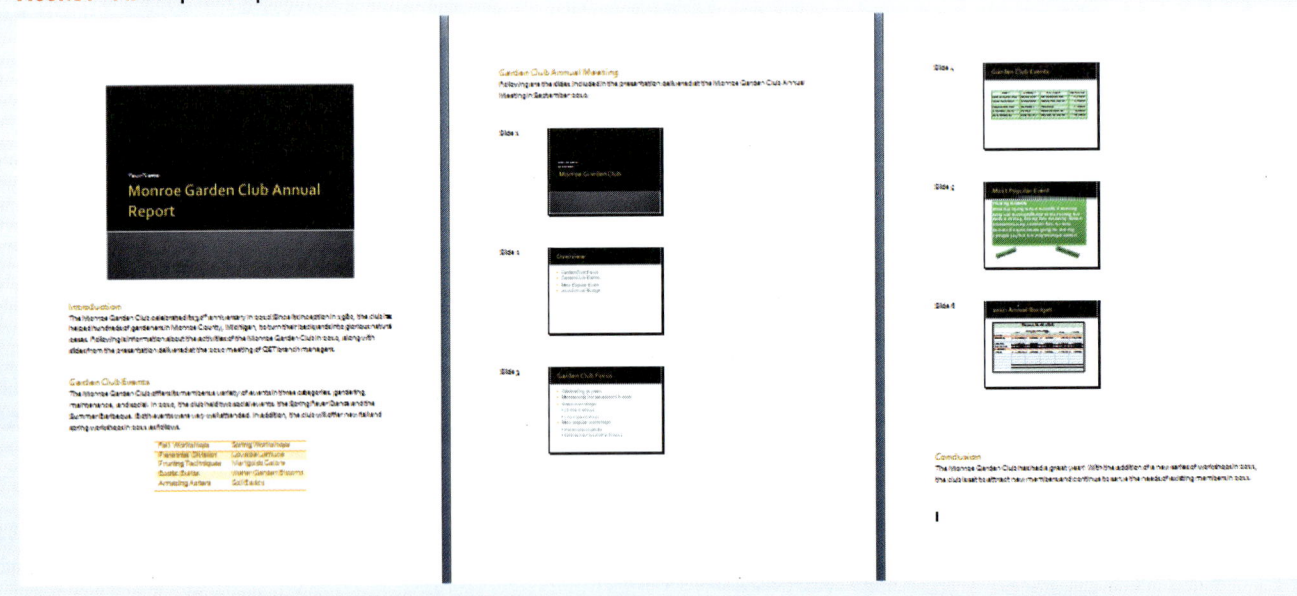

▼ INDEPENDENT CHALLENGE 1

You are the owner of a bed and breakfast establishment in downtown Chicago and a member of the Chicago Bed and Breakfast Association (CBBA), a small organization that meets monthly to discuss issues and sponsor events related to the hospitality industry. At the last meeting, you were asked to assemble the minutes shown in Figure F-15. You create the minutes in Word from a selection of materials contained in PowerPoint, Excel, and Access files.

a. Open the file INT F-11.docx from the drive and folder where your Data Files are located, then save it as **CBBA May 2010 Minutes**.

b. As shown in Figure F-15, insert a PowerPoint slide as an embedded object and enter the title text indicated followed by your name in the subtitle box. Apply the Metro theme, center the slide, then move the text after the slide down one line.

c. In Excel, open the file INT F-12.xlsx from the drive and folder where your Data Files are located, save it as **CBBA Data**, then close it.

d. In the Word document, replace the text EXCEL WORKSHEET with the CBBA Data inserted worksheet object. (Do not link the object.) Center the worksheet object.

e. In PowerPoint, open the file INT F-13.pptx, then save it as **CBBA Presentation**.

f. In Access, open the file INT F-14.accdb, copy the Events Query from Access, paste it on the appropriate slide in the PowerPoint presentation (the text will not be visible), apply the Themed Style 1 – Accent 5 table design, remove the first row, then increase the font size, bold the top row, and modify column widths so the table fills the space attractively. Close the Access database.

g. Save the presentation, then publish the PowerPoint slides in Word as linked slides using the default style. In PowerPoint, change the theme to Metro, then update the published slides. Copy the slides, paste them in the appropriate area of the minutes, answer No to update links, then reduce the height of the table rows to 2".

h. Break all links to the minutes, save the document, then print a copy.

i. Close the published slides without saving them, save and close the presentation, then close all open files and programs.

FIGURE F-15: Completed minutes

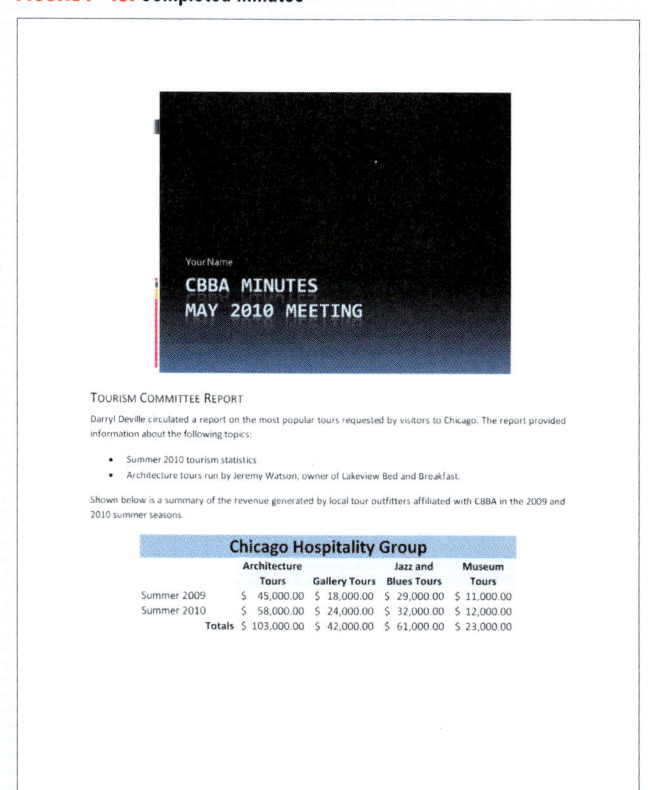

▼ VISUAL WORKSHOP

As the resident naturalist at the Maplewood Nature Preserve in North Vancouver, British Columbia, you are responsible for putting together presentations about the local wildlife for school and community groups. You need to create two slides that you can later use to integrate into other presentations. One slide contains query data from Access, and another slide contains data from an Excel worksheet. Open the Access database called INT F-15.accdb from the location where your Data Files are stored, copy the Bird Sightings query into a blank PowerPoint slide, close the Access database, then edit the slide and table text and format the slide and table as shown in Figure F-16. (*Hint*: The slide uses the Trek design, and the table uses the Themed Style 1 – Accent 1 table design.) Open the Excel workbook called INT F-16.xlsx from the location where your Data Files are stored, then save it as **Nature Preserve Data**. Insert a new slide in the presentation, insert the Nature Preserve Data file as an embedded object (only the table will be inserted), apply the Trek theme, then modify the font size and position the worksheet object as shown in Figure F-17. Copy the chart, then paste and position it as shown. Type your name in the slide footer (which appears in the upper-right corner of the slide in the Trek theme), save the presentation as **Nature Preserve**, print a copy of the slides, break the link, then close the files and exit all programs.

FIGURE F-16

MAPLEWOOD NATURE PRESERVE

Bird Sightings

Species	Date Sighted	Time
Canada Goose	06/06/2010	11:00:00 AM
Yellow-rumped Warbler	06/06/2010	12:00:00 PM
Palm Warbler	06/06/2010	4:00:00 PM
Northern Goshawk	06/06/2010	3:00:00 PM
American Kestrel	06/06/2010	5:00:00 PM

FIGURE F-17

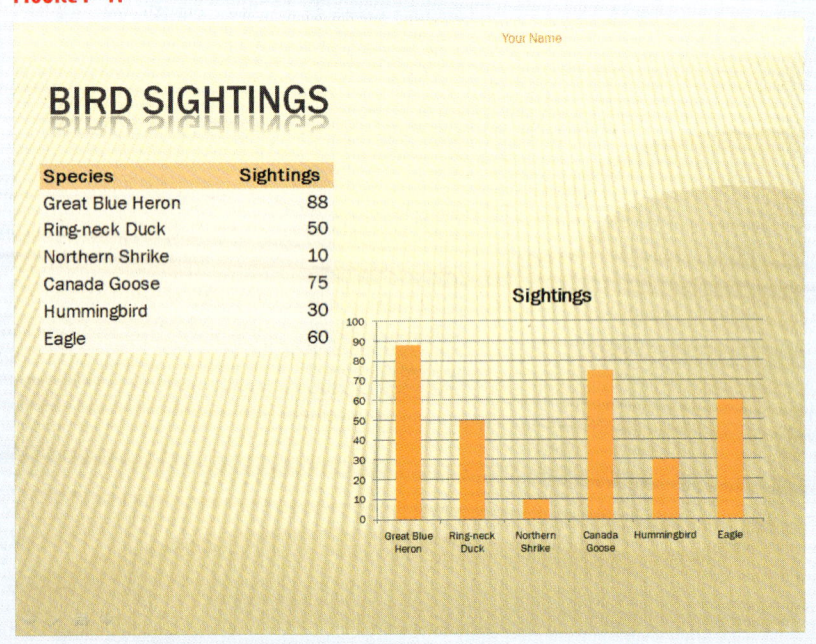

BIRD SIGHTINGS

Species	Sightings
Great Blue Heron	88
Ring-neck Duck	50
Northern Shrike	10
Canada Goose	75
Hummingbird	30
Eagle	60

UNIT A
Publisher 2007

Getting Started with Publisher 2007

Files You Will Need:
PB A-1.docx
PB A-2.jpg
PB A-3.docx
PB A-4.jpg
PB A-5.docx
PB A-6.docx

Microsoft Publisher 2007 is a desktop publishing program that helps you transform your ideas into visually appealing publications and Web sites for your business, organization, or home. In this unit, you will learn how to use one of Publisher's existing designs to create a publication that includes text and graphics. Then, you will save and print your publication before closing it and exiting Publisher. You have just been hired to work for Quest Specialty Travel. Juan Ramirez, the personnel director for QST, asks you to use Publisher to create a flyer announcing the QST employee summer barbecue.

OBJECTIVES

Define desktop publishing software
Start Publisher and view the Publisher window
Create a publication using an existing design
Replace text in text boxes
Format text
Resize and move objects
Insert a picture
Save, preview, and print a publication
Close a publication and exit Publisher

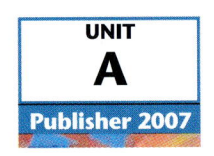

Defining Desktop Publishing Software

Desktop publishing programs let you integrate text, pictures, drawings, tables, and charts in one document, called a **publication**. You can design a publication from scratch, or you can customize an existing design. Figure A-1 shows three publications created using Publisher's premade designs. Juan wants the flyer for the barbecue to be informative and eye-catching. Figure A-2 shows the original flyer design and the notes you will use to customize the flyer. First, you review Publisher's features.

DETAILS

- **Create professionally designed publications**
  Publisher includes hundreds of **templates**—as well as many more available from the Microsoft Office Online Template Gallery—for creating newsletters, greeting cards, flyers, and many other types of publications. The templates include sample text and graphics, a sample layout, and sample color palettes. You plan to use the BBQ flyer design to create the flyer.

- **Create a set of publications with a common design**
  Publisher has several design themes that you can use to ensure consistency among related publications. For example, if you apply the same template design, such as Bubbles, to all the printed materials for QST, then all printed material, including postcards, business cards, catalogs, and e-mails, will have the same look and feel.

- **Change your publication's color scheme**
  Publisher includes more than 70 preset **color schemes** that you can apply to the publications. Each color scheme contains five colors that work well together. You will use the Sunset color scheme in the flyer.

- **Insert text and graphics created in other applications and insert clip art**
  You can insert files created in other programs into your publications, such as text from a Word file. You can insert photos, scanned images, or images drawn using Publisher or a drawing program. The Clip Art task pane provides access to thousands of downloadable images, sounds, and motion clips from the Web and is included with all Microsoft Office applications. You can also use the **Catalog Merge** feature to insert records from a data source, such as a database, to create publications with multiple records. Storing frequently used text and graphics to the **Content Library** allows you to insert them into your publications.

- **Arrange text and graphics easily**
  All elements of a publication are **objects**—boxes that contain text or frames that contain graphics that you can easily move, flip, resize, overlap, or color to control the overall appearance of a publication. Text in a text box is referred to as a **story**. Stories can be independent of one another, or you can link stories if you are continuing text onto additional pages in the publication. You can check the spelling and design of one story or all stories in a publication.

- **Choose from preset font schemes and format text easily**
  Fonts play a very important role in setting the mood and conveying the message of a publication. A **font** is the typeface or design of a set of characters, such as letters and numbers. Publisher includes more than 40 **font schemes**, or sets of fonts that look good together. You can also use Publisher's text-formatting features to enhance fonts by adding characteristics such as bold and italic. You use the Impact font scheme.

- **Print publications on a printer or prepare a publication for commercial printing**
  Publisher's commercial printing technology supports process color, spot color, black-and-white printing, the four major color models (RGB, HSL, CMYK, and PANTONE), as well as automatic and manual color trapping. You can also save publications as PDF files to export them without changing formatting.

- **Publish to the Web**
  You can create Web sites using Publisher's Web site premade designs or using the Easy Web Site Builder Wizard. You can also convert an existing publication to a Web page or e-mail.

FIGURE A-1: Sample Publisher publications

DAILY SPECIALS
June 14, 2010

Butternut Squash Soup — 5.00
Flavored with nutmeg and topped with sour cream

Fried Potato Strings — 3.95
Russet potatoes, fried with onions and garlic

Root Vegetable Casserole — 19.50
Buffalo mozzarella baked with root vegetables

Spinach Pie — 16.95
Feta cheese, spinach, & garlic... need we say more?

Good Eats Cafe
4 West Side Terrace
Seattle, Washington

We've Moved...

At new location:
February 13, 2010

Quill & Press Stationers

Come to our grand opening celebration on February 13th to enter to win one of three $100 gift certificates, see our new products, and get free demonstrations.

Quill & Press Stationers
14 John Paul Jones Avenue
Portsmouth, NH 03801-3298

Phone: 603-555-PENS
E-mail: info@quill&press.com
Web: www.quill&press.com

Placeholder graphic replaced with clip art

GIFT CERTIFICATE
The Major Chord

This certificate entitles

to

The Major Chord Music Store
1409 Great Road
Acton, MA 01720
(978) 555-2389

Authorized by
Expires
Number

Placeholder text replaced with your text

FIGURE A-2: Notes on how to modify the flyer

BBQ Title

- Rotate background image
- Change font scheme to Impact
- Change color scheme to Sunset
- Replace with time and date
- Time: 00:00
- Date: 00/00/00
- Replace this graphic with clip art
- Insert Word document with list of items to bring
- Describe your BBQ. Be sure to mention if attendees should bring anything. You may also want to include a description of planned activities or highlights.
- Replace this text with a proper name and contact information
- Contact person: 555 555 5555
- Add directions here
- Describe your location by landmark or area of town.
- Add QST logo to this area

Publisher 2007

Getting Started with Publisher 2007

Starting Publisher and Viewing the Publisher Window

You start Publisher in the same way you start other Windows applications—by using the Start menu. If you are familiar with other Windows applications, then many parts of the Publisher window will be familiar to you as well, such as tools you can use for formatting text and reviewing your publication. You start Publisher and look at important elements of the Publisher window.

STEPS

TROUBLE
If Microsoft Office is not on your All Programs menu or if the Privacy Options dialog box opens, ask your technical support person for assistance.

1. **Click the Start button on the taskbar, click All Programs, click Microsoft Office, then click Microsoft Office Publisher 2007**

   Publisher opens. The screen is divided into three panes, as shown in Figure A-3. The Microsoft Publisher pane on the left shows Getting Started selected, provides access to My Templates, and lists publication types available in Publisher. The **Publication Gallery** in the middle pane provides access to popular publication types. When you open a publication type folder, such as Flyers, you see **thumbnails**, or small representations, of the premade designs. You can select the publication type either in the left pane or in the Publication Gallery. The Recent Publications pane on the right is a list of recently opened or edited files.

TROUBLE
When the mouse rolls over a thumbnail it is highlighted, but it is not selected until you click it.

2. **Click Blank Page Sizes in the Publication Types section of the left pane, click A4 (Portrait), then click Create in the lower-right corner**

   A blank one-page publication appears in the publication window, as shown in Figure A-4. Until you save a publication and give it a name, the temporary name is Publication1.

The Publisher window displays the following elements:

- The **title bar** contains the name of your publication and the program name.
- The **menu bar** lists the names of menus that contain Publisher commands. Clicking a menu name displays a list of related commands.
- When you start Publisher, five **toolbars** appear by default, although your screen may differ.
- The **Standard toolbar** includes buttons for the most commonly used commands, such as opening, saving, or printing a publication.
- The **Publication Tasks toolbar** opens the Publisher Tasks task pane when clicked.
- The **Formatting toolbar** contains buttons for the most frequently used formatting commands, such as changing the font, and formatting and aligning text.
- The **Objects toolbar** includes buttons for selecting and creating text boxes, shapes, and picture frames, as well as buttons for working with other types of objects.
- The **Connect Text Boxes toolbar** gives you options for connecting overflow text from one part of your publication to another.
- The **publication window** includes the **publication page** or pages and a **desktop workspace** for storing text and graphics prior to placing them in your publication.
- The **vertical and horizontal rulers** help you to position, size, and align text and graphics precisely.
- The **vertical and horizontal scroll bars** work like scroll bars in any Windows program—you use them to display different parts of your publication in the publication window.
- The **status bar**, located below the publication window, displays the position and size of the selected object in a publication and shows the current page. You can use the **Page Navigation buttons** to jump to a specific page in your publication. You can use the **Object Position indicator** to position the pointer or an object containing text or graphics precisely, and the **Object Size indicator** to gauge the size of an object accurately.

FIGURE A-3: Opening window in Publisher

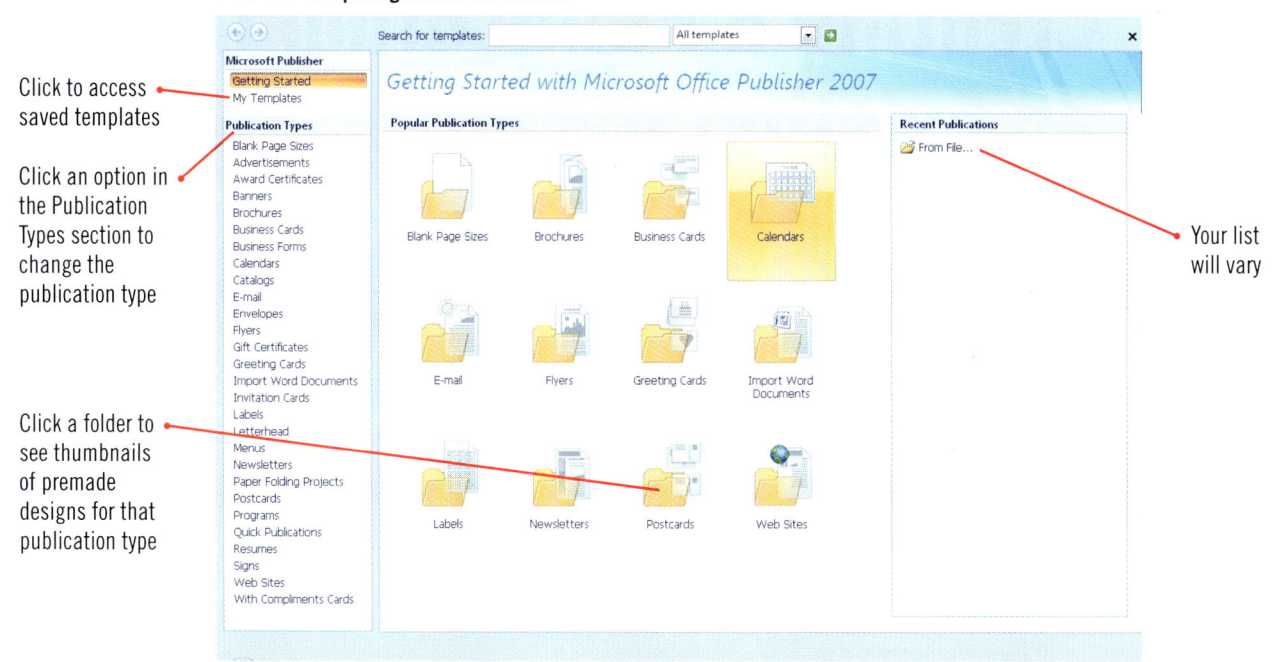

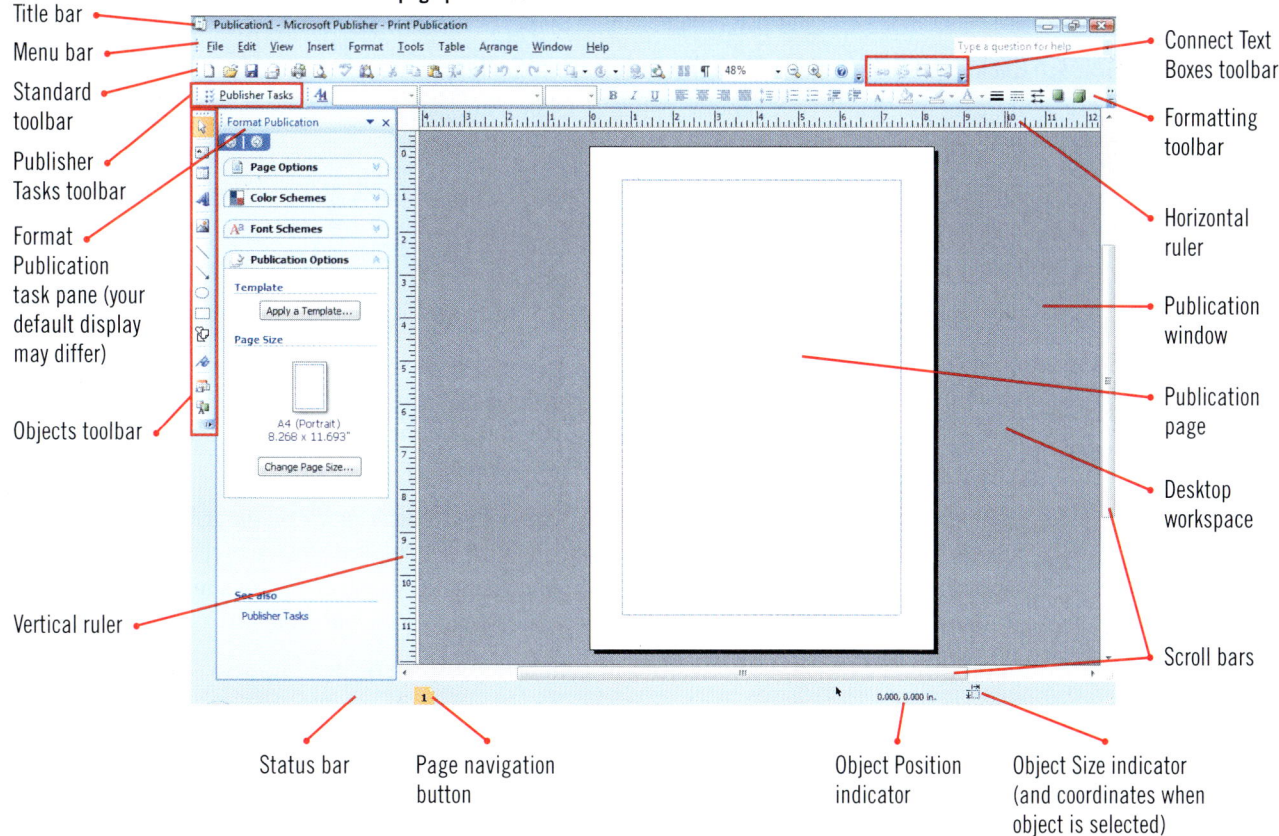

- Click to access saved templates
- Click an option in the Publication Types section to change the publication type
- Click a folder to see thumbnails of premade designs for that publication type
- Your list will vary

FIGURE A-4: Blank one-page publication

- Title bar
- Menu bar
- Standard toolbar
- Publisher Tasks toolbar
- Format Publication task pane (your default display may differ)
- Objects toolbar
- Vertical ruler
- Connect Text Boxes toolbar
- Formatting toolbar
- Horizontal ruler
- Publication window
- Publication page
- Desktop workspace
- Scroll bars
- Status bar
- Page navigation button
- Object Position indicator
- Object Size indicator (and coordinates when object is selected)

Publisher Tasks

The **Publisher Tasks task pane** has options for common Publisher features associated with creating, distributing, and following up. A task pane is a window that opens and provides contextual help with a task, such as inserting clip art or using Help. The **Creating your publication** section includes suggestions for adding appropriate text and images and for changing the design. The **Distributing your publication** section includes options for mailing, publishing, and distributing your publications. The **Following up** section can help you track the effectiveness of your marketing mailing as well as connect you to the Microsoft Small Business Center. Like any task pane, the Publisher Tasks task pane can be opened and closed as you wish.

Getting Started with Publisher 2007 — Publisher 5

Creating a Publication Using an Existing Design

Although you can always start from scratch, the easiest way to create a publication is to start from an existing design and then modify it to meet your needs and preferences. Publisher provides hundreds of pre-made designs, all containing sample layouts, font schemes, graphics, and color schemes. You can store modified or newly created templates in My Templates. You can search for templates and access templates that are stored online. You can also create information set profiles that store frequently used information, such as your contact information and company logo, for ease and consistency of use. You start a new publication and create the flyer for the company barbeque by beginning with an existing design.

STEPS

1. **Click Apply a Template in the Publication Options section of the Format Publication task pane**
   The Change Template window opens, displaying a list of templates on the left and thumbnails of Flyer publication types on the right.

2. **Click Flyers, then scroll down until Event is at the top of the Publication Gallery**
   The Publication Gallery displays thumbnails of Event Flyers.

3. **Click the BBQ thumbnail in the Publication Gallery**
   The right pane shows customization options, as shown in Figure A-5.

4. **Click OK**
   The BBQ flyer appears in the publication window. The Format Publication task pane displays options for modifying the layout of the flyer.

5. **Click Color Schemes in the task pane**
   The Apply a color scheme list appears in the task pane. Each color scheme includes five colors, including white, that work well together.

6. **Scroll through the alphabetical list of color schemes, then click Sunset**
   The Sunset color scheme is applied to the flyer in the publication window.

7. **Click Font Schemes in the task pane**
   The Apply a color scheme list closes and a list of named font schemes appears in the task pane, showing over 40 predefined sets of fonts that work well together. Font schemes make it possible to change the look of your publication quickly, assigning all text in major fonts to one style, and all text in a minor font to another style, ensuring that fonts are applied consistently throughout your publication.

   QUICK TIP
   If you don't like a color scheme or font scheme choice, click the Undo button on the Standard toolbar, click Color Schemes or Font Schemes, and then make a new choice.

8. **Scroll through the alphabetical list of font schemes, then click Impact**
   The new font scheme that includes the Impact font is applied to the BBQ flyer. Compare your screen to Figure A-6.

9. **Click the Close button in the task pane**
   The task pane closes, and the publication window expands to give you more room to work.

FIGURE A-5: Event flyers displayed in Publication Gallery

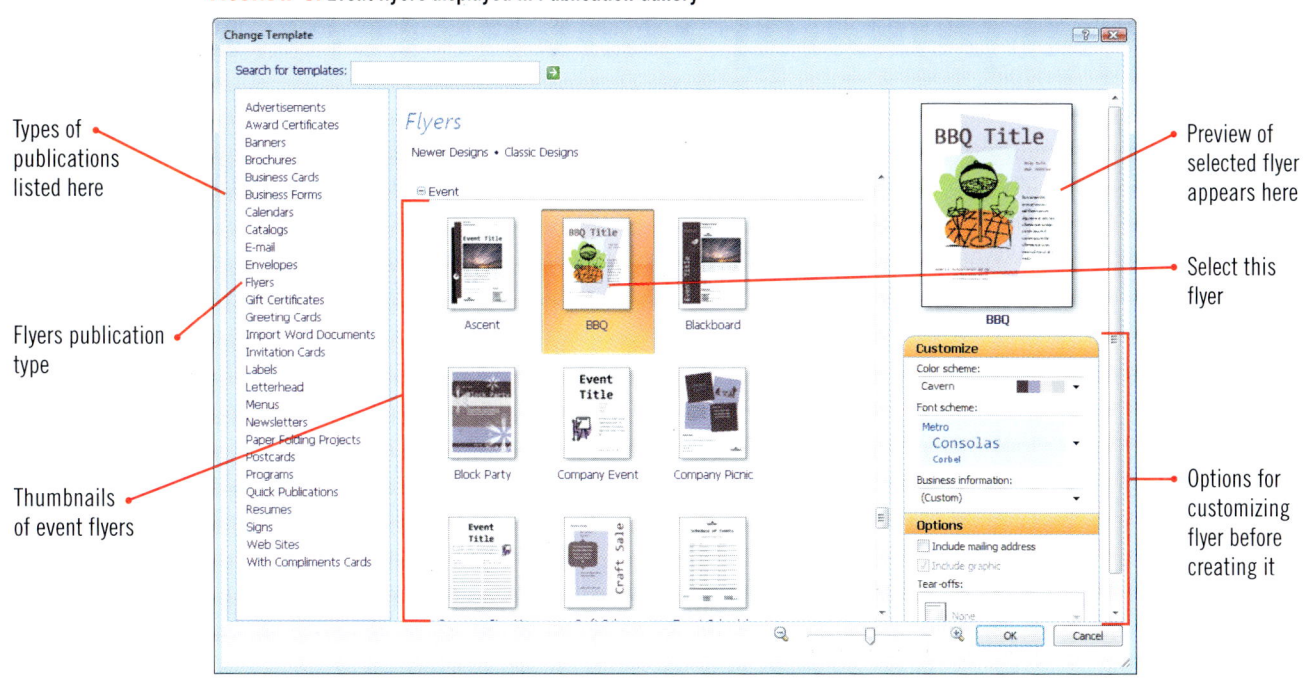

- Types of publications listed here
- Flyers publication type
- Thumbnails of event flyers
- Preview of selected flyer appears here
- Select this flyer
- Options for customizing flyer before creating it

FIGURE A-6: BBQ flyer with Sunset color scheme and Impact font scheme

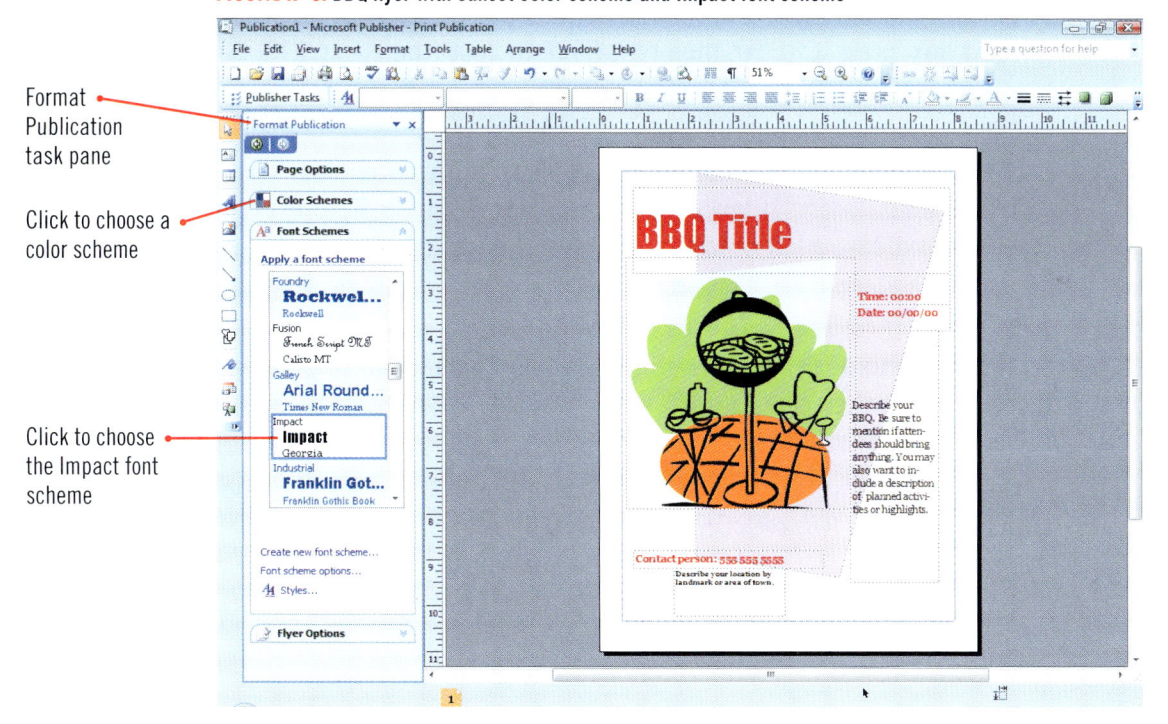

- Format Publication task pane
- Click to choose a color scheme
- Click to choose the Impact font scheme

Customizing Publisher

Publisher allows you to create and save templates for letterheads, address labels, and more using My Templates. Templates you save in My Templates are available from the Publication Gallery.

In addition to templates, you can create Business Information Set profiles that contain information you use frequently, such as contact information or a company logo. To create or update the Business Information Set, click Edit on the menu bar, click Business Information, then create or update your profile in the Create New Business Information Set dialog box. If you have created or updated the Business Information Set, your address and business information is automatically filled in for you, creating an instant, professional set of stationery items.

The Content Library allows you to store frequently used text and graphics, which can be easily inserted into your publications by clicking Insert on the menu bar, clicking Item from Content Library, selecting an item from the Content Library task pane, and then clicking OK.

Replacing Text in Text Boxes

UNIT A — Publisher 2007

In Publisher, every element in a publication is contained in a frame. A **frame** is an object that contains text or graphics. A **text box** is a frame that holds text. Before you can add text to a Publisher publication, you must first create a text box to hold the text. Once you create a text box, you can type text directly into the text box or insert text from a Word document file into it. To enter or insert text in a text box, you must select it. When you click a text box to select it, **sizing handles** appear around its edges. If you type or insert more text than fits in the text box, you can resize the text, resize the text box, or continue the text in another text box. You are ready to replace the placeholder text in the flyer. You type some of the text directly into the text boxes and insert other text describing the company barbecue from a Word file.

STEPS

QUICK TIP
The green circular handle at the top of the box is called a **rotation handle**. By dragging this handle, you can rotate the object freely or flip the object upside-down.

1. **Click in the center of the BBQ Title text box to select the placeholder text**
   The title placeholder text is selected and sizing handles appear around the text box, indicating that the box itself is also selected.

2. **Type Company BBQ, click 00:00 in the Time text box, then press [F9]**
   Pressing [F9] zooms in on the selected section of your publication, making it easier to see your work in detail. The [F9] key is a **toggle key**—press it once to zoom in, then press it again to zoom back out.

3. **Type Noon 'til ?, click 00/00/00 in the Date text box, then type Friday, 7/16**

4. **Scroll down and to the left to see the Contact person text box, click in the Contact person text box, press [Ctrl][A], then type RSVP to Your Name, ext. 213, by 7/6**
   Pressing [Ctrl][A] selects all the text in the text box. The text you type replaces the placeholder text and takes on the default formatting for the text box.

5. **Click the Describe your location text box to select the placeholder text in the frame, type Directions:, press [Enter], type Take I-5 N to Pershing St., press [Enter], then type Take Pershing, take a left onto Florida Drive, then follow signs to Zoo Place**
   If you are writing long stories, it's sometimes easier to create the document in Word and then insert the file into a text frame in Publisher.

6. **Scroll up and right-click the Describe your BBQ frame, point to Change Text on the shortcut menu, then click Text File**
   The Insert Text dialog box opens.

7. **Navigate to the drive and folder where you store your Data Files, click the file PB A-1.docx as shown in Figure A-7, click OK, then press [F9]**
   The text appears in the document. Compare your flyer with Figure A-8.

FIGURE A-7: Insert Text dialog box

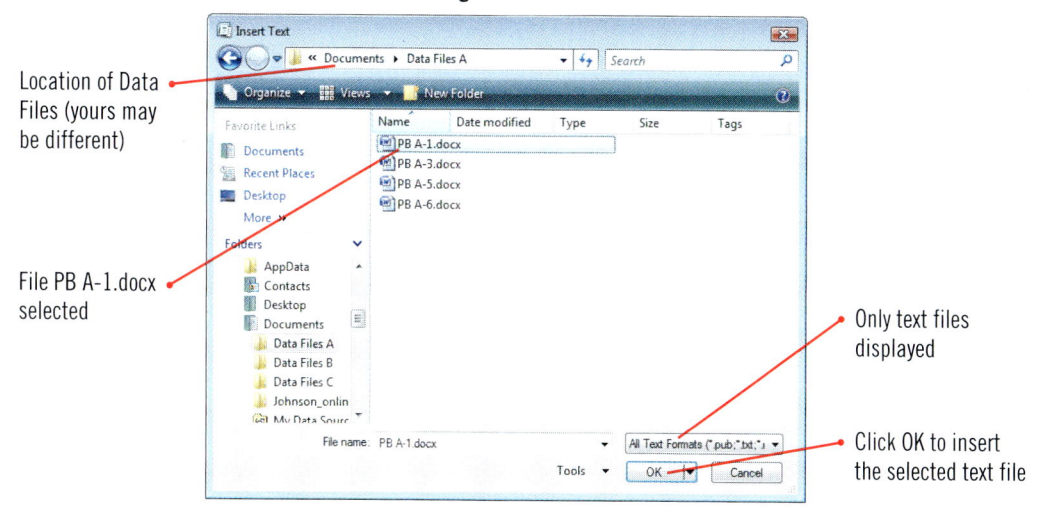

- Location of Data Files (yours may be different)
- File PB A-1.docx selected
- Only text files displayed
- Click OK to insert the selected text file

FIGURE A-8: BBQ flyer with placeholder text replaced

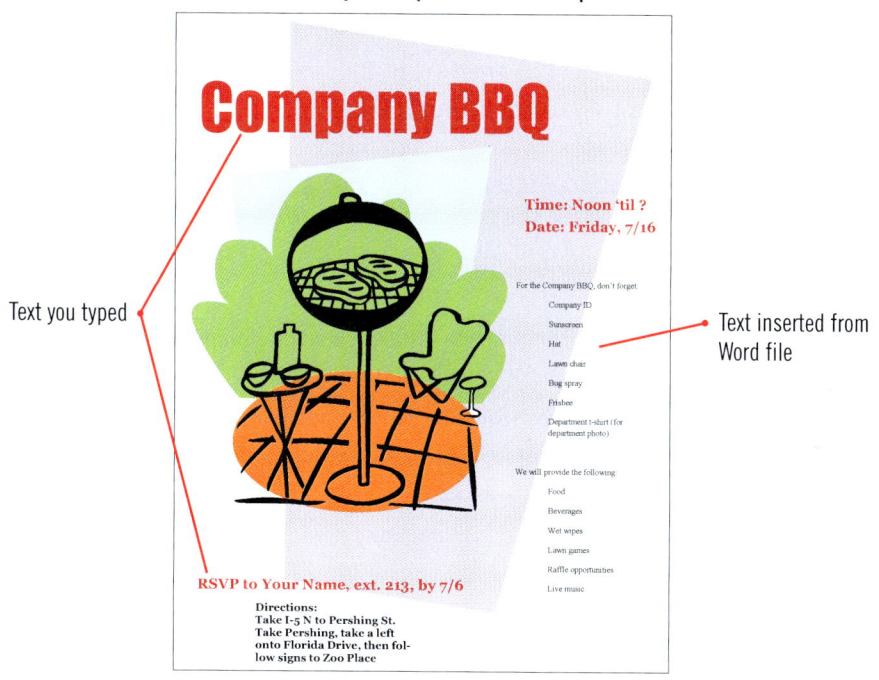

- Text you typed
- Text inserted from Word file

Creating text boxes

If you need additional text boxes in your publication or if you are creating a publication from scratch, you can easily create a new text box. To create a text box, click the Text Box button on the Objects toolbar. The pointer changes to a crosshair pointer. Position the pointer where you want one corner of the text frame to appear, press and hold the mouse button, then drag diagonally to create a rectangular frame, as shown in Figure A-9. Release the mouse button when the text box is the size and shape that you want. Then, you can enter text in the text box by clicking in the frame and typing or by inserting a Word file.

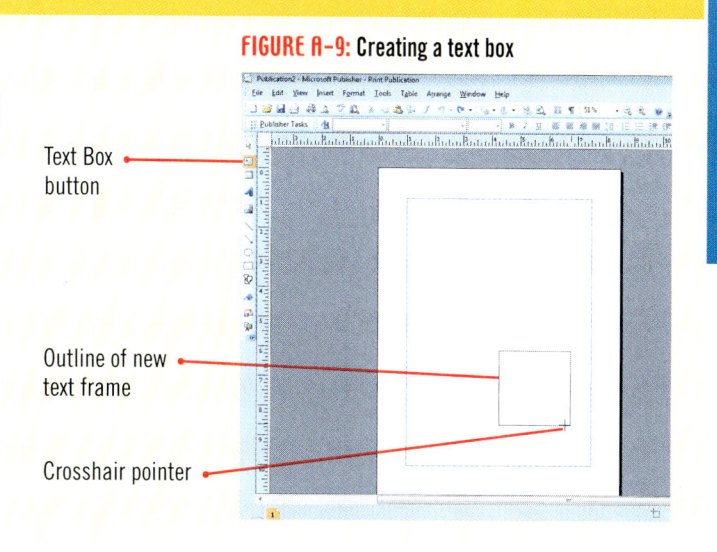

FIGURE A-9: Creating a text box

- Text Box button
- Outline of new text frame
- Crosshair pointer

Publisher 2007

Getting Started with Publisher 2007

UNIT A
Publisher 2007

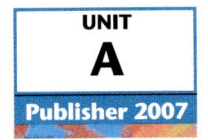

Formatting Text

Once you enter text in your publication, you can select it and then apply formatting to enhance its appearance. You can format text using the Formatting toolbar, which includes buttons for applying bold, italic, and underline to text, and for changing text alignment and text color. You can easily change the **font style**, which is the physical characteristics of a font, and the **font size**, which is the physical size of the characters measured in points. To change the font or font size, you use the Font list arrow or the Font Size list arrow on the Formatting toolbar. Another formatting feature is AutoFit. **AutoFit** automatically sizes text to fit it in a text box. You format the text to make the flyer more attractive and readable.

STEPS

1. **Click in the Company BBQ text box, press [F9] to zoom in, select the text, click Format on the menu bar, point to AutoFit Text, then click Best Fit**

   All the text in the Company BBQ text box is now bigger, as shown in Figure A-10. The font Impact and font size 89.9 of the selected text are displayed on the Formatting toolbar.

2. **Press [F9], then click in the For the Company BBQ text box**

3. **Press [Ctrl][A] to select all the text in the text box, press [F9] to zoom in, then click the Font list arrow on the Formatting toolbar**

   The names of the fonts in the Font list are formatted in the font they represent, making it easier for you to select the one that best suits your needs. Recently used fonts appear at the top of the font list as well as within the alphabetical list. You can select a font from either location.

4. **Scroll through the alphabetical list of fonts, then click Garamond on the Font list as shown in Figure A-11**

   The selected text changes to Garamond. It is a good idea to limit the number of fonts you use in a publication. Too many fonts can make a publication look cluttered.

> **QUICK TIP**
> Press [Ctrl][B] to quickly bold or unbold text after you select it.

5. **Scroll as needed, click in the Directions text box, press [Ctrl][A], click the Font list arrow, click Garamond, click the Bold button B on the Formatting toolbar to unbold the text, click the Font Color list arrow A·, then click the bright blue square**

   The text now is now formatted in Garamond bright blue. The Font Color button shows the color bright blue. You can click the Font Color button, instead of the Font Color list arrow, to apply the bright blue formatting to selected text.

> **TROUBLE**
> Throughout this unit, scroll as needed.

6. **Press [F9], click the text in the Time text box, press [Ctrl][A], then click B**

   The selected text is no longer boldface.

7. **Click the text in the Date text box, press [Ctrl][A], click B, click the text in the RSVP text box, press [Ctrl][A], then click B**

   The fonts are consistent, and the flyer looks professional.

FIGURE A-10: AutoFitting text in a frame

- Font of selected text
- Font size of selected text in text box
- AutoFit command creates larger text in text box
- Bold button

FIGURE A-11: Choosing a font

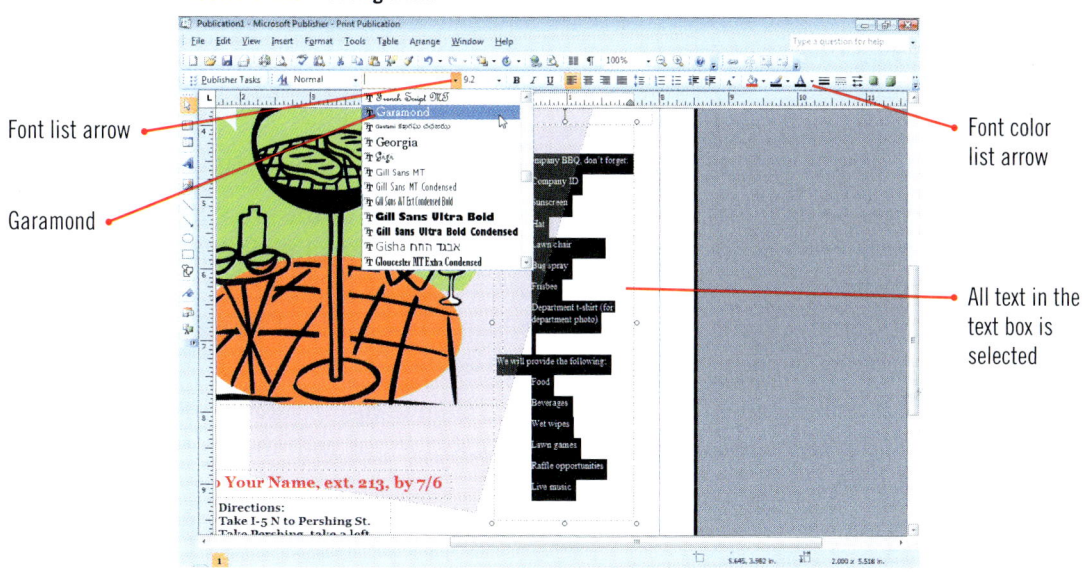

- Font list arrow
- Garamond
- Font color list arrow
- All text in the text box is selected

Checking your publication

Before you finalize a publication, you should check it for spelling and design errors. To have Publisher check for spelling errors in your publication, click Tools on the menu bar, point to Spelling, then click Spelling or click the Spelling button on the Standard toolbar. If there are words that Publisher does not recognize, the Check Spelling dialog box will open. In the Check Spelling dialog box, shown in Figure A-12, you can choose to ignore or change the words Publisher identifies as misspelled. You can also add a word to the dictionary. To check the spelling in every text box in your publication, make sure the Check all stories check box is selected in the Check Spelling dialog box.

In addition to spelling errors, Publisher can check for design errors. Design errors include text that runs off the page, overflow text, or graphics that are not scaled proportionally. To check for design errors, click Tools on the menu bar, then click **Design** Checker. In the Design Checker task pane, click an item in the Select an item to fix list to go to that item.

FIGURE A-12: Check the spelling of your publication

Click to check spelling in every text box

Publisher 2007

Getting Started with Publisher 2007

UNIT A
Publisher 2007

Resizing and Moving Objects

In the course of creating a publication, you might find it necessary to resize or move objects. For example, you might want to make a text box smaller because it contains too much white space, or you might want to move a picture closer to its caption. To move or resize an object, you must first select it. To resize an object, you drag a handle. To move an object, you click anywhere on the object (except on a handle) and drag it to a new location. 🎨 You resize and align text boxes. You also move the picture frame.

STEPS

1. **Click the Directions text box to select it**
   Handles appear around the edges of the text box.

   TROUBLE
   If the rulers do not appear, click View on the menu bar, then click Rulers.

2. **Position the pointer over the middle-right handle**
   When you position the pointer over a handle, a Resize pointer appears. Depending on the handle, the pointer is either a horizontal, vertical, or diagonal Resize pointer. See Table A-1 for a list of common pointer shapes. The rulers can be used as guides to align objects precisely as you resize and move them. A line moves along the ruler as you move the object to guide the placement.

3. **Drag the middle-right handle right to the 5" mark on the horizontal ruler as shown in Figure A-13**
   The text automatically expands to fill the resized text box area.

   TROUBLE
   If the Picture toolbar opens, click the toolbar Close button.

4. **Click the BBQ graphic, then press [F9]**
   The pointer changes to the Move pointer ✥. You use this pointer to move any Publisher object.

   QUICK TIP
   To change the length and width of a frame at the same time, drag a corner handle. To keep the center of the frame in the same location, press and hold [Ctrl] as you drag any corner handle.

5. **Click and drag the BBQ graphic down so the top of the graphic frame aligns with the bottom of the title frame and left so the left of the graphic frame aligns with the left margin, then release the mouse button**
   The handles still surround the graphic, with a green rotation handle at the top. You can **rotate**, or adjust, the angle of any object by dragging the **rotation handle**.

6. **Click the lavender background object, then drag the rotation handle to the left so that the top of the lavender background object aligns with the top of the Company BBQ text box**
   The lavender object is now less sharply angled. Compare your screen to Figure A-14.

TABLE A-1: Common pointer shapes

pointer shape	use to	pointer shape	use to
⤡⇐⤢	Resize an object in the direction of the arrows	▸	Drag selected text to a new location
+	Draw a frame	🗑	Indicates overflow text
✥	Move an object to a new location	🌀	Insert overflow text
T	Crop an object	↻	Rotate an object

Publisher 12

Getting Started with Publisher 2007

FIGURE A-13: Resizing an object

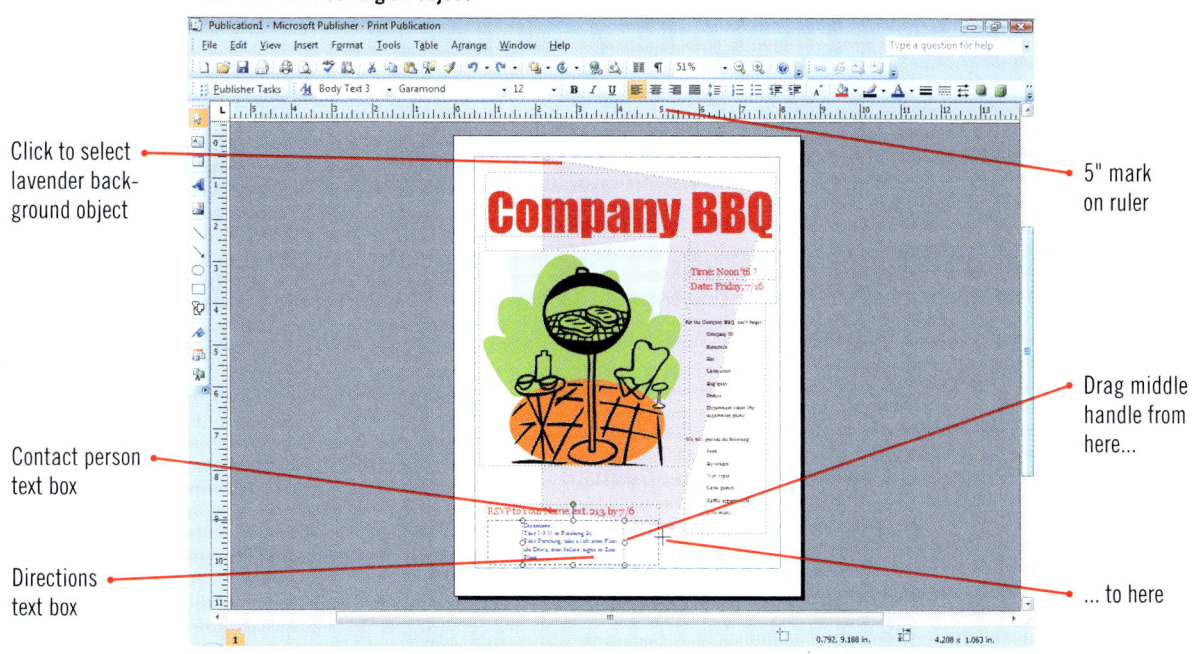

- Click to select lavender background object
- 5" mark on ruler
- Drag middle handle from here...
- Contact person text box
- Directions text box
- ... to here

FIGURE A-14: Moving and rotating an object

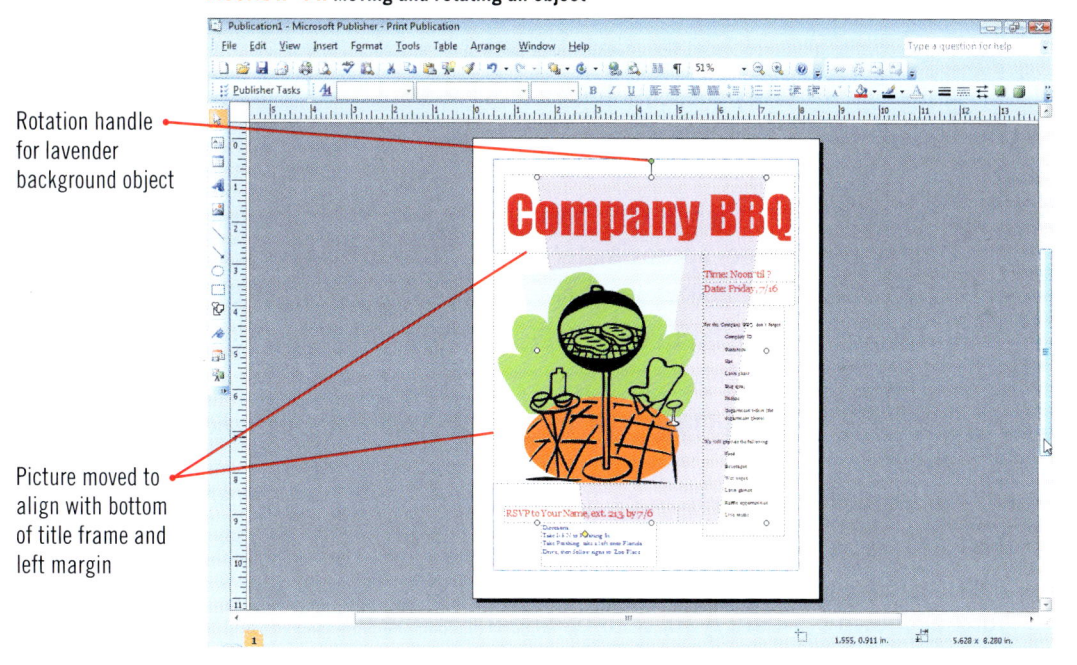

- Rotation handle for lavender background object
- Picture moved to align with bottom of title frame and left margin

Aligning objects

You can align objects to guides manually or you can have Publisher align them for you. A **guide** is a non-printing line that helps you place objects such as text boxes and graphics. To align an object manually, simply drag or resize the object using the mouse. You can use the Object Position and Object Size indicators in the status bar to place objects exactly. You can also use Publisher's Snap to and Nudge features to help you align objects precisely to guides. To turn on the Snap to feature, you must enable one or more of the following Snap commands on the Arrange menu: Snap To Ruler Marks, which snaps an object to the closest ruler mark; Snap To Guides, which automatically snaps an object to the closest layout guide; and Snap To Objects, which snaps an object to the closest object.

Publisher's Nudge feature allows you to move or **nudge** an object one small increment at a time. To nudge an object, select the object, click Arrange on the menu bar, point to Nudge, and then click Up, Down, Left, or Right. You can also nudge an object by pressing and holding [Alt] while pressing one of the arrow keys. To change the distance objects are nudged using the keyboard, click Tools on the menu bar, click Options, and then click the Edit tab in the Options dialog box. Select the Arrow keys nudge objects by check box, then type the nudging distance.

Getting Started with Publisher 2007

UNIT A
Publisher 2007

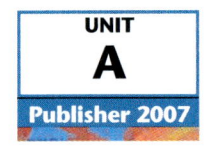

Inserting a Picture

Publications usually include both text and graphics. With Publisher, you can insert many types of graphic images into your publications, including clip art, images created in other applications (such as a logo or a chart), scanned images, or photographs taken with a digital camera. Before selecting an image to insert in a publication, you insert a blank picture frame, which you position where your image will go and then resize it. The Microsoft **Clip Organizer** is a library of art, pictures, sounds, video clips, and animations that all Office applications share. You can easily preview images from the Clip Organizer and insert them into your publications. You replace the placeholder clip art in the flyer with a different barbecue image from the Clip Organizer and insert the QST logo into a new blank picture frame.

STEPS

> **TROUBLE**
> Throughout this lesson, close any toolbars that open.

1. **Right-click the BBQ graphic, point to Change Picture, then click Clip Art**
   The Clip Art task pane opens.

2. **Click in the Search for text box, select any existing text, type barbecue, click Go, then if prompted to add clips from Microsoft Office Online, click No**
   The Results window opens in the task pane and displays images relating to the search term barbecue. It may take a minute or two to display all the images.

> **TROUBLE**
> If you don't see the image shown in Figure A-15, click another image.

3. **Scroll to and click the barbecue image in the Results window as shown in Figure A-15**
   The new barbecue image replaces the placeholder barbecue image on the flyer, as shown in Figure A-15.

4. **Close the Clip Art task pane, click the Picture Frame button on the Objects toolbar, then click Empty Picture Frame**
   The pointer changes to the Drawing pointer +.

> **QUICK TIP**
> Use the Object Size indicator on the status bar to view the size of the frame as you draw it.

5. **Press and hold [Shift], then use the pointer to draw a blank picture frame in the lower-right corner of the page, approximately 1.250 × 1.250**
   Pressing and holding [Shift] while creating a picture frame keeps the proportions the same.

6. **Right-click the frame, point to Change Picture, then click From File**
   The Insert Picture dialog box opens.

7. **Navigate to the drive and folder where you store your Data Files, click PB A-2.jpg, then click Insert**
   The QST logo is inserted in the frame and the frame size adjusts to 1.250 × 1.240 to fit the image.

8. **Press [F9] to zoom in on the logo if necessary, use the pointer to position the logo picture frame at approximately 6.750" on the horizontal ruler and 9.125" on the vertical ruler as shown in Figure A-16, then release the mouse button**
   Congratulations, you have successfully completed the flyer!

Considering image file size

To see the size of an image you are inserting, position the pointer over the image in the Clip Art task pane or in the Insert Picture dialog box and view the size in the ScreenTip that appears. Smaller file sizes make it easier to send files over e-mail or the Web.

FIGURE A-15: Clip Art search results

Results of search for barbecue images (your results may be different)

New image placed in frame

Click to insert this image in flyer (the image may appear in a different location in your task pane)

FIGURE A-16: Moving QST's logo

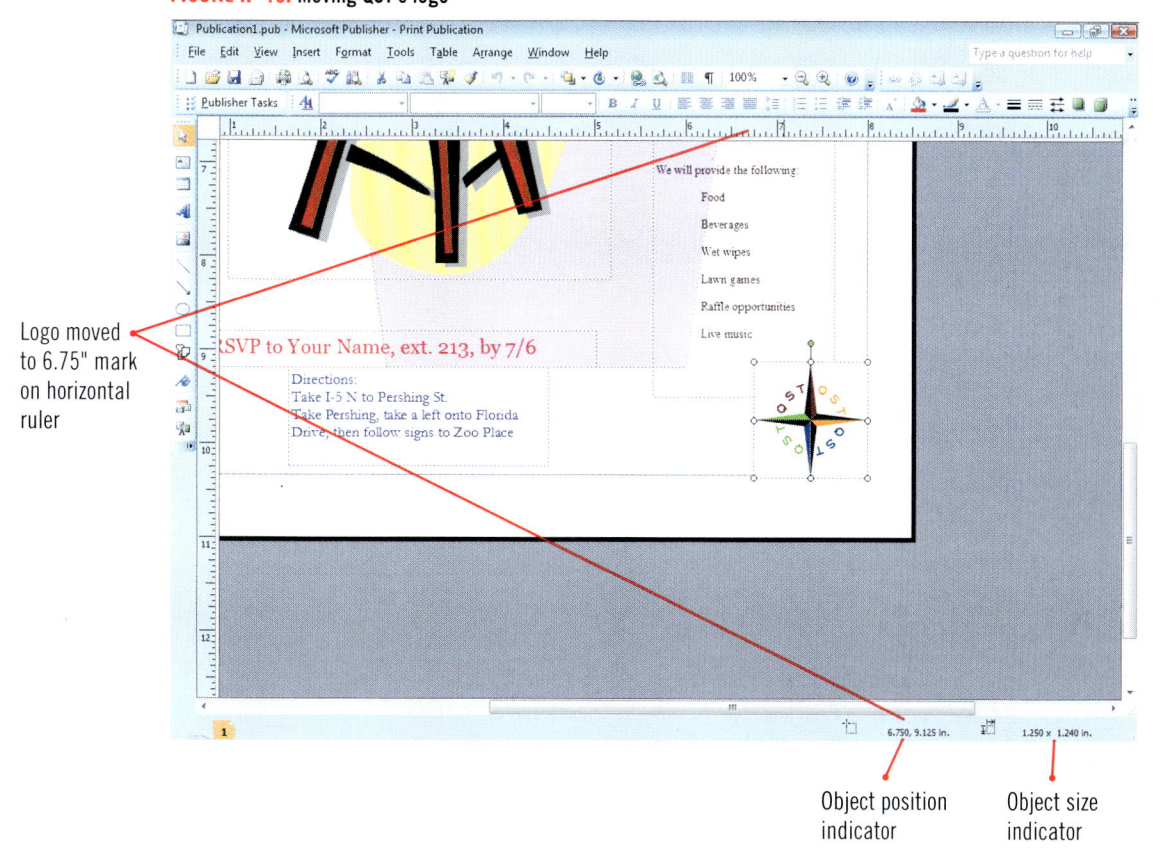

Logo moved to 6.75" mark on horizontal ruler

Object position indicator

Object size indicator

Getting Started with Publisher 2007

Publisher 2007

Saving, Previewing, and Printing a Publication

UNIT A — Publisher 2007

You need to save your work in order to store it permanently on a disk. You should save your work every 10 to 15 minutes, after any significant changes that you don't want to lose, and before you print your publication. By default, Publisher automatically saves your work every 10 minutes, so you can take advantage of the AutoRecover feature if you lose power or if you have a system problem. It is important to manually save your files often, since work you have done since the last automatic save will be lost otherwise. To save a file for the first time, you can use the Save or Save As command, or click the Save button on the Standard toolbar. After you've named and saved the file, you must continue to save any changes you make to the publication. It's a good idea to preview your publication as well as proofread it before you print it so that you can catch and fix any mistakes. You save the flyer, check it for mistakes, and then print it.

STEPS

> **QUICK TIP**
> After you've saved your publication for the first time, click the Save button on the Standard toolbar or press [Ctrl][S] to save changes quickly to your publication.

1. **Click File on the menu bar, then click Save**
   The Save As dialog box opens.

2. **Navigate to the drive and folder where you store your Data Files, type Barbecue in the File name text box, compare your dialog box with Figure A-17, then click Save**

3. **Click View on the menu bar, point to Zoom, then click Whole Page**
   The zoom level adjusts so that the whole page fits in the publication window. When you change the zoom level, you can select a specific zoom percentage, or a specific area to view. You can also click the Zoom list arrow on the Standard toolbar to change the zoom level.

4. **Click File on the menu bar, then click Print Preview**
   The publication opens in the Preview window and appears without nonprinting lines or paragraph marks. You use Print Preview view to view your publication exactly as it will print before you print it. If you need to make corrections, you can close Print Preview view and continue to work on your publication.

5. **Click Close on the Print Preview toolbar, click File on the menu bar, then click Print**
   The Print dialog box opens, as shown in Figure A-18.

> **QUICK TIP**
> Press [Ctrl][P] to access the Print dialog box quickly. Click the Print button on the Standard toolbar to print the publication with the default settings.

6. **Make sure the Number of copies is 1, then click Print**
   Your publication prints in color or in black and white, depending on your printer. Figure A-19 shows a copy of the completed flyer.

Using the Pack and Go Wizard

When you want to transfer your publication to another computer or to a commercial printing service, you can use the Pack and Go Wizard to assemble and compress all the files necessary for viewing and printing your publication in a different location. Packing your publication (that is, including the fonts and graphics that you used in your publication) ensures that it will look the same on another computer as it does on your computer. To use the Pack and Go feature, click File on the menu bar, point to Pack and Go, then click Take to Another Computer or Take to a Commercial Printing Service. After you make a selection, click Next, then click Finish when you have answered all of the wizard's questions.

FIGURE A-17: Save As dialog box

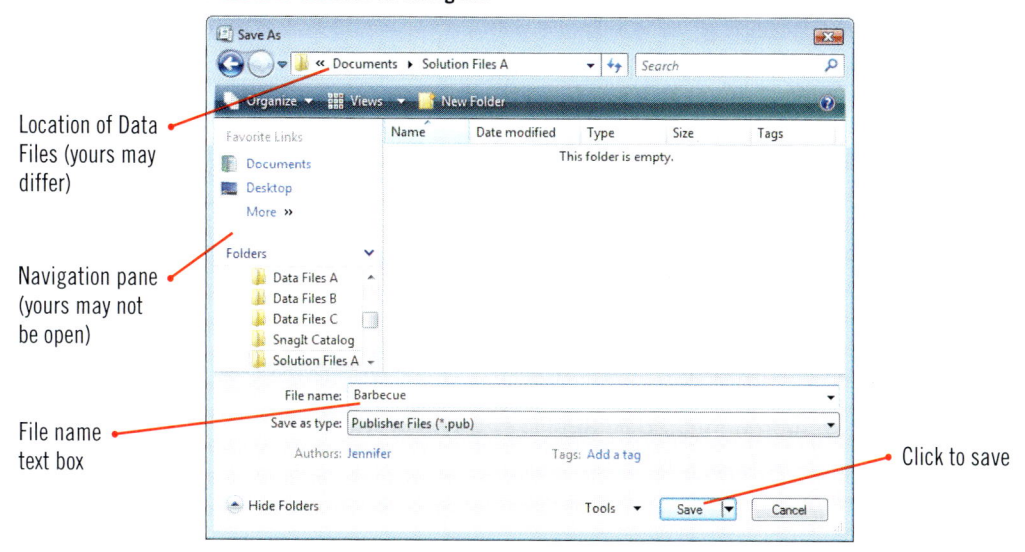

- Location of Data Files (yours may differ)
- Navigation pane (yours may not be open)
- File name text box
- Click to save

FIGURE A-18: Print dialog box

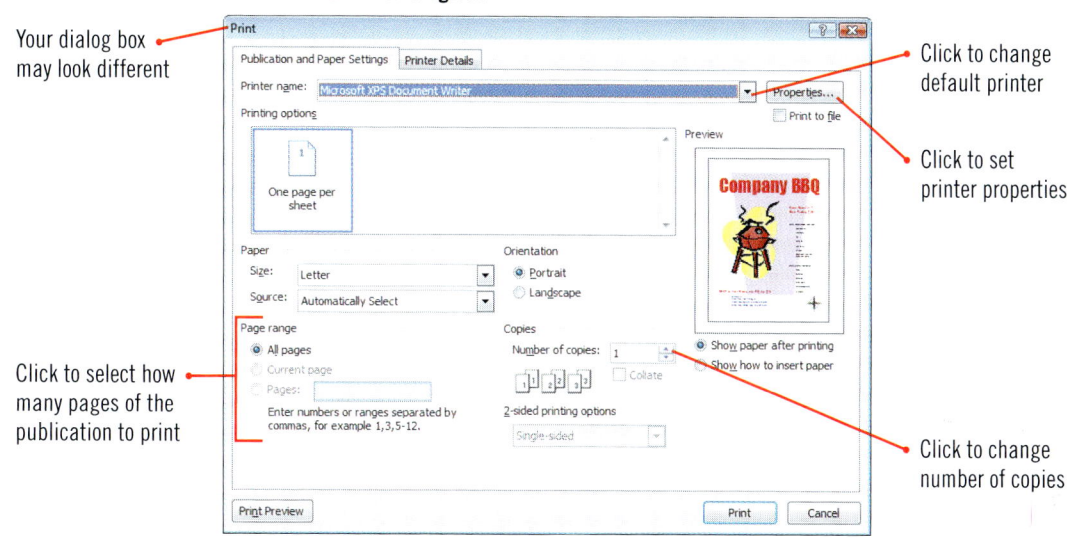

- Your dialog box may look different
- Click to select how many pages of the publication to print
- Click to change default printer
- Click to set printer properties
- Click to change number of copies

FIGURE A-19: Completed publication

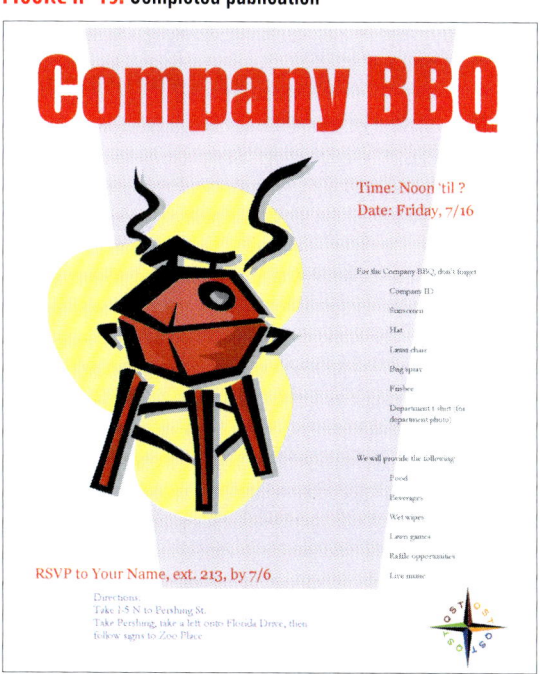

Getting Started with Publisher 2007 | Publisher 17

Publisher 2007

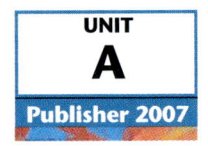

Closing a Publication and Exiting Publisher

UNIT A
Publisher 2007

When you are finished working on a publication and have saved your changes, you need to close it. You close a publication by using the Close command on the File menu. When you are finished working with Publisher, you can exit the program by using the Exit command on the File menu. You close the flyer and exit Publisher.

STEPS

1. **Click File on the menu bar, then click Close as shown in Figure A-21**
2. **If an alert box appears asking if you want to save changes before closing, click Yes to save your changes**
   The flyer closes and the Getting Started dialog box appears in the Publisher window. You can create a new publication or open an existing publication. If you are finished working with Publisher, you can exit the program.
3. **Click File on the menu bar, then click Exit, as shown in Figure A-22**
   The program closes; Publisher is no longer running.

Using Help

Publisher includes an extensive Help system that you can use to learn about features and commands. You can get help while working with Publisher by using the Help menu, by using the Research task pane, or by typing a question in the Type a question for help text box. To access Help online, click Help on the menu bar, then click Microsoft Office Online. The Help system allows you to search for topics or use an index to find what you want. You must be able to connect to the Internet to access the Web site.

The Research task pane, shown in Figure A-20, is another tool that can be used to get help. It provides access to resources such as dictionaries, encyclopedias, business and financial sites, and news sources.

FIGURE A-20: Research task pane

FIGURE A-21: Closing a publication

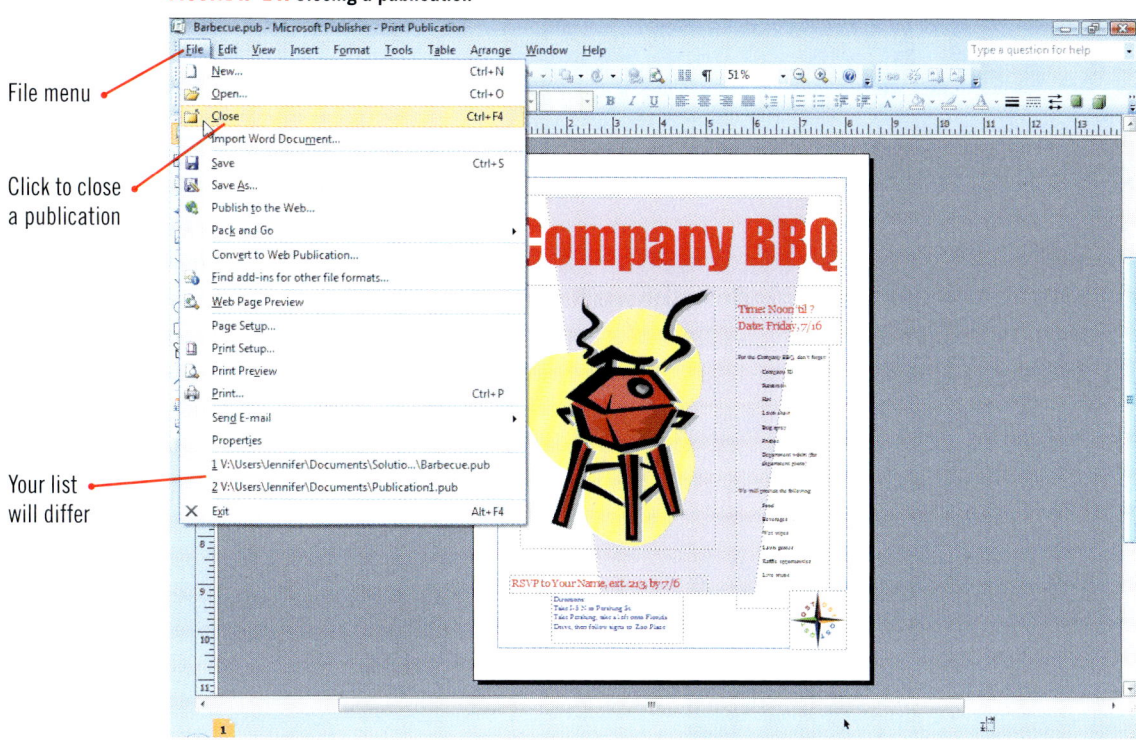

File menu

Click to close a publication

Your list will differ

FIGURE A-22: Exiting Publisher

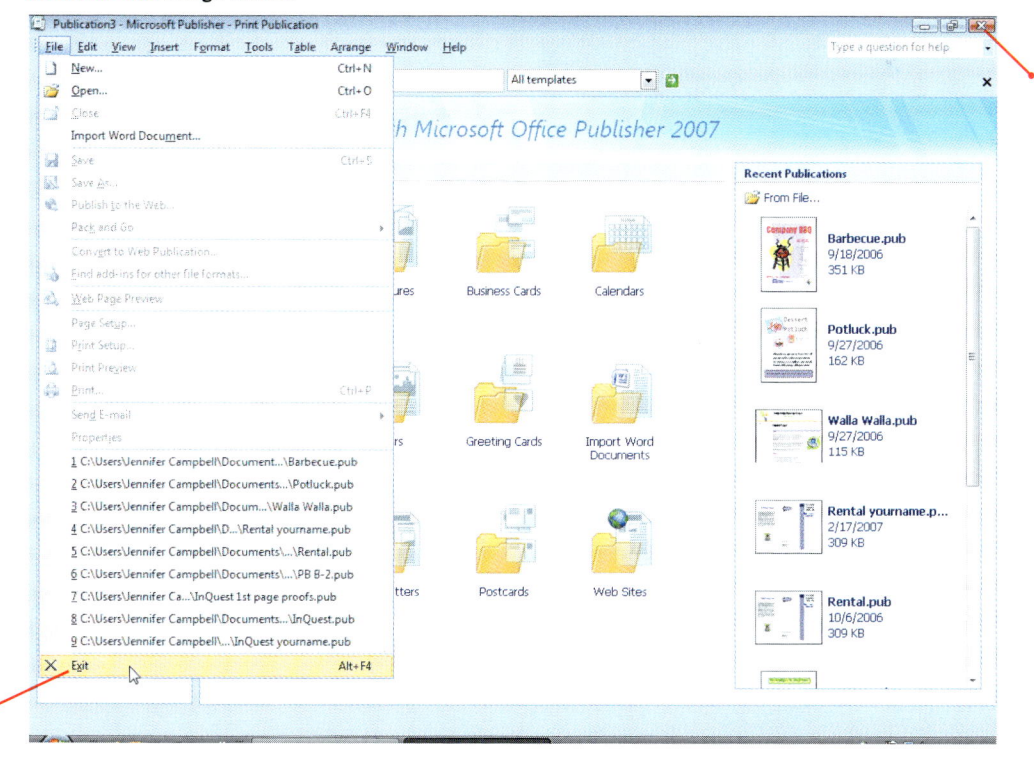

Click to close publication and exit Publisher at the same time

Click to exit Publisher

Getting Started with Publisher 2007   **Publisher 19**

Practice

SAM — If you have a SAM user profile, you may have access to hands-on instruction, practice, and assessment of the skills covered in this unit. Log in to your SAM account (http://sam2007.course.com/) to launch any assigned training activities or exams that relate to the skills covered in this unit.

▼ CONCEPTS REVIEW

Label each element of the Publisher window shown in Figure A-23.

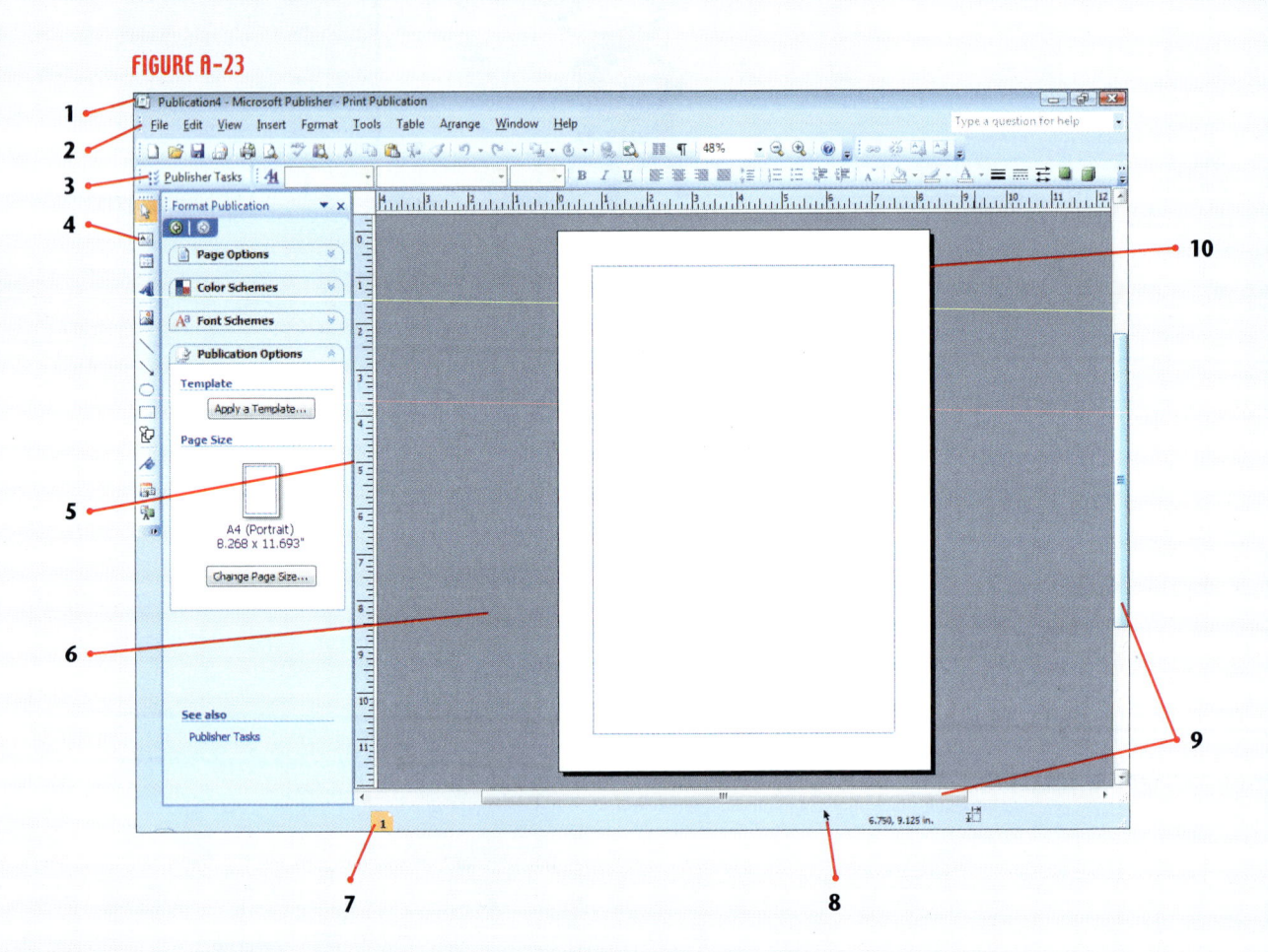

FIGURE A-23

Match each term with the statement that best describes it.

11. AutoFit
12. Frame
13. Research task pane
14. Color scheme
15. Font scheme

a. Preset colors used consistently throughout a publication
b. An object that can contain text or graphics
c. Help resource that connects you to online dictionaries, business sites, and other reference material
d. Preset fonts used consistently throughout a publication
e. Feature that resizes text to fit in a text box

▼ SKILLS REVIEW

1. **Start Publisher and view the Publisher window.**
   a. Start Publisher and open a blank publication of any size.
   b. Identify as many parts of the publication window as you can without referring to the unit material.
2. **Create a publication using an existing design.**
   a. Click Apply a Template in the task pane.
   b. In the Change Template dialog box, select Flyers, scroll to the Sale category and select the Borders House for Sale thumbnail, then click OK.
   c. Change the color scheme to Marine.
   d. Change the font scheme to Capital.
3. **Replace text in text boxes.**
   a. Close the task pane, zoom as needed (using [F9] or the Zoom list arrow), then type **$250,000** for the price.
   b. Select the Age of home text box, then type the following information, pressing [Enter] after each bullet except the last:
      - **Built in 1992**
      - **3 bedrooms**
      - **2 baths**
      - **Hardwood floors**
      - **Eat-in kitchen**
      - **2 acres**
   c. Select the Describe the special features text box, then insert the text file PB A-3.docx from the drive and folder where you store your Data Files into the text box.
   d. Select the text in the Contact person frame, and replace the text with **Call Your Name for more information**.
   e. Refer to Figure A-24 to fill in information in the remaining text boxes.

FIGURE A-24

▼ SKILLS REVIEW (CONTINUED)

4. **Format text.**
   a. Select the text box below the Call Your Name text box, then press [Ctrl][A] to select all of the text in the frame.
   b. Bold the text in that text box, then bold the text in the remaining contact text boxes.
   c. Select the text box with the directions, press [Ctrl][A], then format the text to AutoFit, Best Fit.
   d. Reduce the font size of the price text to 24 points.
   e. Change the color of the text in the Call your name text box to teal. (*Hint*: Use the Font Color button on the Formatting toolbar to choose another color in the scheme.)
   f. Change the Directions text to Perpetua and italic. Notice that the font size changes to fill the text box because you formatted the text earlier with AutoFit.

5. **Resize and move objects.**
   a. Drag the middle-left sizing handle of the House for Sale frame to the 1" mark on the horizontal ruler.
   b. Drag the middle-right sizing handle of the House for Sale frame to the 7½" mark on the horizontal ruler.
   c. Select the Directions text box and drag the upper-middle sizing handle up to the 5¾" mark on the vertical ruler. The text automatically resizes because you set it to AutoFit.
   d. Zoom as needed to see more of your publication.

6. **Insert a picture.**
   a. Right-click the sky picture frame at the top of the flyer, then click Delete Object.
   b. Click Insert on the menu bar, point to Picture, then click From File.
   c. Insert the file PB A-4.jpg from the drive and folder where you store your Data Files, then resize and reposition the image, if necessary.
   d. Delete the logo placeholder at the top of the flyer.

7. **Save, preview, and print a publication.**
   a. Save the publication as **House** to the drive and folder where you store your Data Files.
   b. Switch to Whole Page view to proof your publication and make any last-minute changes.
   c. Save your changes, then print your publication.

8. **Close a publication and exit Publisher.**
   a. Close the publication, then exit Publisher.

▼ INDEPENDENT CHALLENGE 1

Publisher provides templates for creating Web pages. You have volunteered to create a home page for your son's elementary school's Web site. You use Publisher to create the Web page.

   a. Start Publisher, in the Web Sites publication type and the Classic Designs category, choose the Kid Stuff Web Site design, then create the document. (*Note*: If a dialog box opens asking what you want the Web site to do, click Cancel.)
   b. Choose Iris as the color scheme and Casual as the font scheme.
   c. Enter information in text boxes using Table A-2 as a guide.
   d. AutoFit the text in the text frame into which you inserted the text file.
   e. Enter information into the Phone/Fax/E-mail text box at the bottom of the page.
   f. Apply bold formatting to the subheadings Vision and Mission, and change the text color to Violet. (*Hint*: Use the Font Color button.)

TABLE A-2

placeholder text frame	replace with
Business Name	Walla Walla Elementary School
Your business tag line here	Making Education Count!
This is the first page....	Text File PB A-6.docx
Frame below "To contact us"	Your Name Walla Walla Elementary School 23 School Street Walla Walla, Washington 99362-1950
Contact information frame	(713) 555-8912

▼ INDEPENDENT CHALLENGE 1 (CONTINUED)

g. Delete the placeholder logo at the top of the page and the picture caption placeholder text box.
h. Replace the placeholder graphic with one of your choosing.
i. Type **Home Page** as the page title.
j. Save the publication as **Walla Walla**.

Advanced Challenge Exercise

- Click Insert on the menu bar, point to Picture, then click WordArt.
- Choose a vertical style from the far-right column, then click OK.
- Type **Walla Walla**, then click OK.
- Right-click the WordArt, then click Format WordArt.
- Change the line color to light orange using the Format WordArt dialog box, then click OK.
- Position the WordArt to the left of the description and contact information text boxes.

k. Proof your publication, print and close the publication, then exit Publisher.

▼ INDEPENDENT CHALLENGE 2

Your cat had kittens and you would like to place them in good homes. You decide to post a flyer at the local veterinary clinic. You want the flyer to include tear-off tabs with your contact information. You use a Publisher template to create the flyer.

a. Start Publisher, then in the Flyers publication type, in the Sale category, select the Pets Available thumbnail, and create the publication.
b. Use Figure A-25 as a guide; replace the title and bullet placeholder text. Apply the Burgundy color scheme and the Archival font scheme.
c. Replace the text in the text frame with the description of the kittens by inserting the text file PB A-5.docx from the drive and folder where you store your Data Files. Change the font of the inserted text to Georgia.
d. Replace the placeholder graphic with a cat of your choosing from the Clip Art Gallery, then place and size the image appropriately.
e. Replace the contact information with the following: Please call Your Name for more information: 555-2307.
f. Replace the text in each tear-off frame with the following: Kittens Call Your Name: 555-2307 on two lines as shown in Figure A-25. (*Hint*: Type the information in one tear-off frame, then click in any other tear-off frame and all tear-off frames fill automatically with the same information.)
g. Save the publication as **Kittens**.

FIGURE A-25

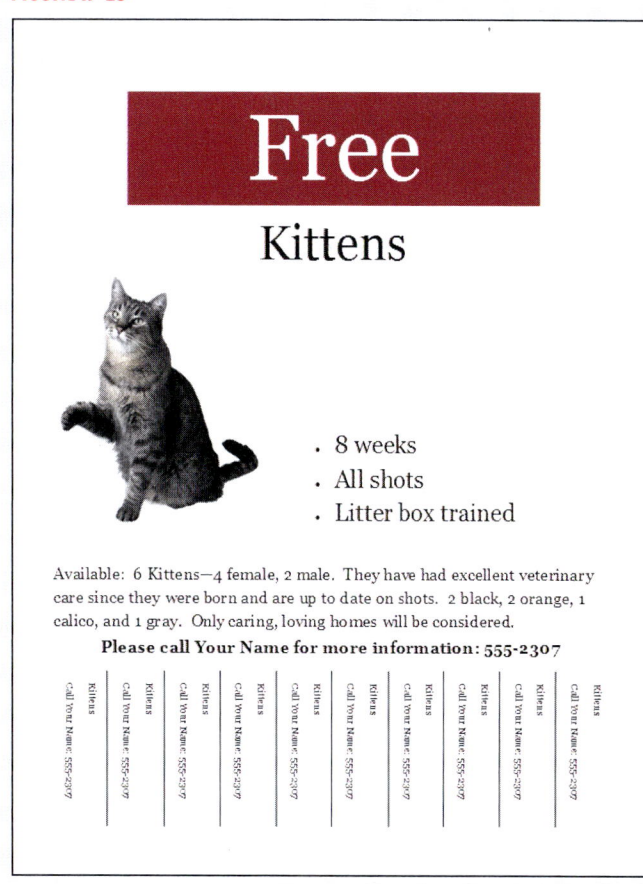

Advanced Challenge Exercise

- Select the subtext Kittens.
- Click the Font Color list arrow on the Formatting toolbar, then click More Colors.
- Select a color from the Standard or Custom tab in the Colors dialog box, then click OK.

h. Proof the flyer for mistakes, print and close the publication, then exit Publisher.

Getting Started with Publisher 2007

▼ INDEPENDENT CHALLENGE 3

Publisher provides a wide variety of templates for creating customized calendars. These calendars can include a company name, logo, and contact information. They can also include a list of events. You create a calendar for next month using a Publisher template.

a. Start Publisher, then in the Calendars publication type and Full Page category, click any one-page calendar thumbnail.
b. In the Options section of the pane on the right, be sure the one month per page option is selected, and set the date range from the beginning of next month to the end of next month. Do not include a schedule of events.
c. Choose a color and font scheme of your choice, then click Create.
d. Replace the placeholder text with text of your own, making sure to include your name somewhere on the calendar. Be sure to include text in the calendar grid, such as birthdays or meetings to remember. Format the text appropriately.
e. Customize the logo if a logo placeholder is part of the template. Replace any clip art with appropriate images.
f. Save the publication as **Calendar**, and compare your publication to Figure A-26.
g. Proofread and spell check your publication, print and close the publication, then exit Publisher.

FIGURE A-26

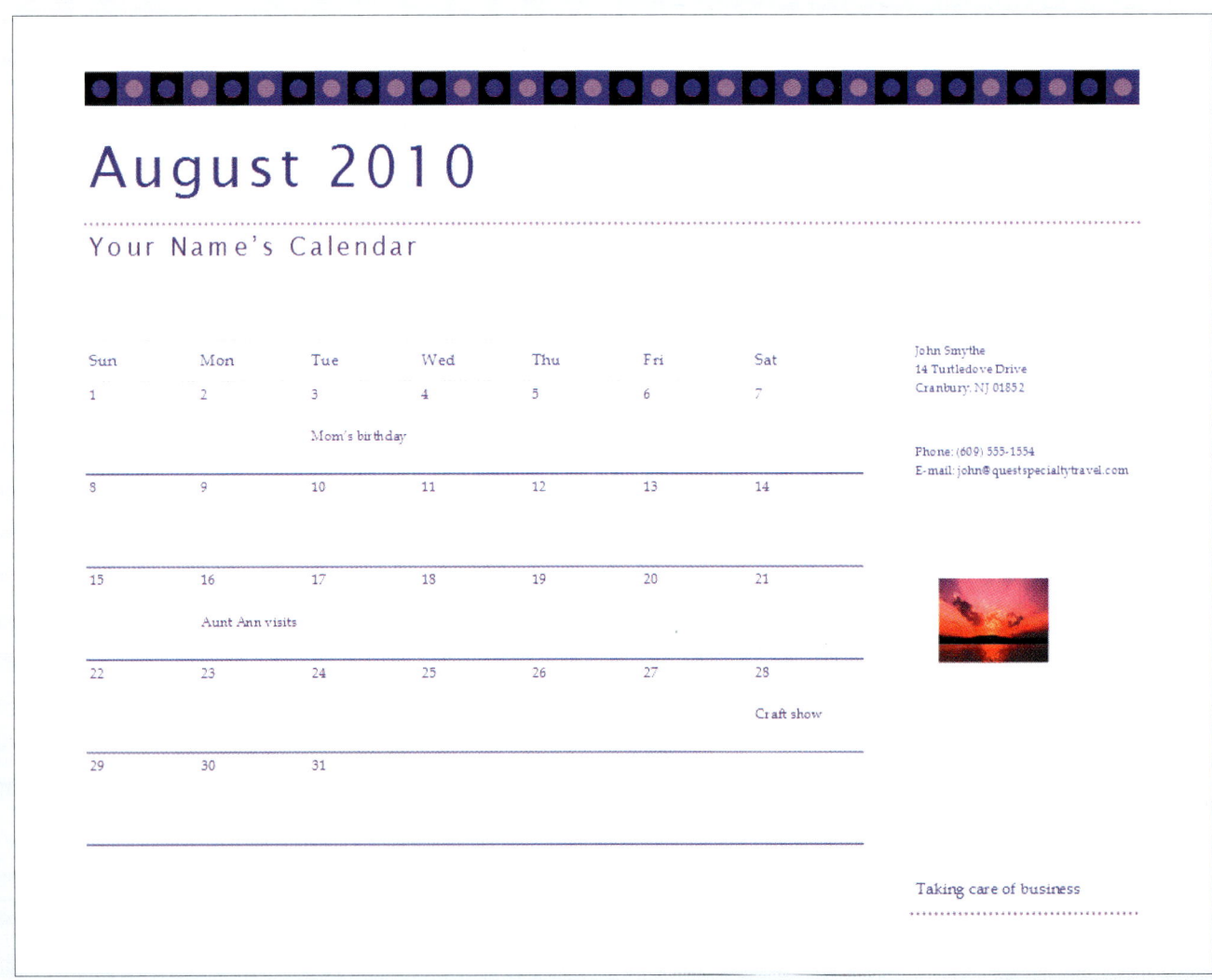

August 2010

Your Name's Calendar

Sun	Mon	Tue	Wed	Thu	Fri	Sat
1	2	3	4	5	6	7
		Mom's birthday				
8	9	10	11	12	13	14
15	16	17	18	19	20	21
	Aunt Ann visits					
22	23	24	25	26	27	28
						Craft show
29	30	31				

John Smythe
14 Turtledove Drive
Cranbury, NJ 01852

Phone: (609) 555-1554
E-mail: john@questspecialtytravel.com

Taking care of business

▼ VISUAL WORKSHOP

Create the flyer shown in Figure A-28. In the Flyers publication type and the Event category, select the Potluck thumbnail. Use the Cavern color scheme and the Metro font scheme, and include a mailing address. Replace the sandwich and cooking pot graphics with the clip art shown. (*Hint*: Open the Clip Art task pane, then search for dessert and coffee. If the images shown are not available, choose others.) Drag the green rotation handle to rotate the potholder graphic to the left. Replace all placeholder text using Figure A-28 as a guide. Resize the Hosted by text box so that the text aligns as shown in Figure A-28. Use AutoFit to adjust the text in the Please bring a dessert to share text box. Replace Janey Hoff's name with your name. Save the publication as **Potluck** to the drive and folder where you store your Data Files, then print a copy.

FIGURE A-28

Dessert Potluck

Date: October 9, 2010
Time: 7:00 PM

Hosted by: Mary Halvey, 144 Green St.

Please bring a dessert to share. We will provide coffee and beverages. Come to meet our new neighbors and see old friends. Babysitting will be provided.

RSVP to Mary Halvey (978) 555-3897 or Janey Hoff (978) 555-7800 by October 6

▼ REAL LIFE INDEPENDENT CHALLENGE

Publisher provides a wide variety of greeting card templates. You create a birthday greeting card using a Publisher template, and then you customize the greeting card to meet your needs. You know that once you learn how to create and customize a greeting card in Publisher, you can create additional cards when you need them.

a. Start Publisher, then in the Greeting Cards publication type and in the Birthday category, click any Birthday card thumbnail. An example of a greeting card made in Publisher is shown in Figure A-27.

b. Customize your birthday card by choosing a color scheme and a font scheme, then click Create.

c. Edit any placeholder text (be sure to use the page navigation buttons to see and edit the text on all pages), and replace any placeholder graphics. Add text boxes and graphics if necessary.

d. Include your name on the card.

e. Check the spelling, save the card with the filename **Birthday**, print and close the publication, then exit Publisher.

FIGURE A-27

UNIT B
Publisher 2007

Working with Text and Graphics

Files You Will Need
PB B-1.docx
PB B-2.pub
PB B-3.xls
PB B-4.docx
PB B-5.xls
PB B-6.docx
PB B-7.docx
PB B-8.xls
PB B-9.docx
book.bmp
box.bmp
cd.bmp
Ellen.jpg
frisbee.bmp
Fundraiser.pub
hippo.bmp
InQuest.pub
Juan.jpg
Keisha.jpg
makeup.bmp
maze.bmp
Nova Scotia.pub
Rental.pub
Ron.jpg

Publisher provides you with a wide array of tools to help you work with text and graphics. In this unit, you will learn how to create a newsletter. You will place text in columns and learn how to manage text that doesn't all fit in one text box. Then, you will insert a caption for a picture and learn how to wrap text around that and other objects. You will learn how to insert headers and footers that appear on every page of your publication. You will also learn about layering and grouping objects and inserting information from a data source. Juan Ramirez, marketing director for Quest Specialty Travel, has asked you to take over responsibility for the quarterly newsletter for QST employees. You start by planning the content of the *InQuest* newsletter. Then, you use the skills covered in this unit to create it.

OBJECTIVES

Plan a publication
Create columns of text
Work with overflow text
Use guides
Create picture captions
Create headers and footers
Wrap text around objects
Layer and group objects
Merge information from a data source

Planning a Publication

Before creating a publication, you must first plan its design and content. Careful planning helps to ensure that your publication is both informative and eye-catching. Before you start working on the newsletter, you plan the next edition of the *InQuest* newsletter. Figure B-1 shows your plan for the content, layout, and graphics. As you plan the newsletter, you review the factors that can be used to improve a publication.

DETAILS

Some factors you need to consider when planning a publication:

- **What layout to use**

  Choosing the layout is the first decision you need to make in planning a multipage publication. You can use one of the many sample designs that Publisher provides and customize it to meet your needs, or you can start from scratch. No matter which option you choose, you need to decide up front how many columns of text the publication will have, and how many pages it will be. You also need to decide how you want it to look when printed. For example, will the pages be folded or printed back to back? You plan to continue to use the same newsletter design for each issue of *InQuest* so that all issues have the same look and feel. For this issue, you decide to change the layout of the inside pages of the newsletter. As in the last issue, the pages will be printed back to back.

- **What text to include and how to present it**

  Once you've chosen your layout, you need to decide on your content. Write a list of all the articles you plan on including, similar to the list you created in the first column of Figure B-1. Next, decide how you want to present your content. In a publication you can present text in two ways—either as a story or as a table. A **story**, also called an article, is composed of text that is meant to be read from beginning to end. A **table** contains text or numbers in columns and rows. You use tables to organize information, such as the table of contents, so that it is easy to read at a glance. You will also use a catalog merge to create a publication introducing new employees at QST. As part of your plan, you make a list of all the stories the InQuest Editorial Board picked for this issue.

- **Where to place your text**

  Next, you have to plan where to place each story and table in the publication. Sometimes, all the text for a particular story won't fit in one text box and needs to continue into another text box in a different part of the publication. This type of text is called **overflow text**. In the plan in Figure B-1, you note that you need to use overflow text for The Common Review Date story on page 1, which you decide to continue on page 4.

- **What pictures and captions to include**

  Once you've settled on your stories, it's time to plan for graphics. A **picture caption** is a description that appears adjacent to a picture. When you add a picture or any object to your publication, you can choose to have Publisher wrap the text around that object or around the object's **frame**, which is its outside border. **Wrapping** means that the text flows around the object rather than over it. You plan to wrap text around graphics for three stories in the newsletter.

- **What content should appear on every page**

  A **header** is information that appears at the top of every page in your publication. A **footer** is information that appears at the bottom of every page in your publication. You will put the Volume and Issue number in the header of the newsletter, and will add a footer containing page numbers. You will specify not to show the header and footer on page 1.

- **What special effects to include**

  Publisher gives you many tools to create special effects. For example, you can add a **pull quote** or sidebar. A pull quote is a quotation from an article that is pulled out and treated like a graphic. A **sidebar** is text that is set apart from the major text but in some way relates to that text. You can also create unique effects by layering objects on top of each other to add depth and dimension to your publication. Figure B-2 shows the first page of the completed newsletter.

FIGURE B-1: Notes regarding content, layout, and graphics plan for the August issue of *InQuest*

Stories	Page	Contributor	Graphics
A Word from Our President	1	Jessica Long	Insert pull quote and wrap text around it; add success graphic at end
Common Review Date	1, 4	Me	
InQuest Needs You (sidebar)	1	Me	
Vision Service Plan	2	Jim Fernandez	Wrap text around eyeglasses graphic
401K Notes	2	John-Kyle Jones	
Employee Advisory Resource	2	Me	
True Fashion Confessions – You Wore What?!?	3	Namita Persand	Wrap text around pull quote between columns
What I Learned on My Vacation	4	Namita Persand	

- Stories for August issue
- Story requires overflow text

FIGURE B-2: Printout of page 1 of the completed newsletter

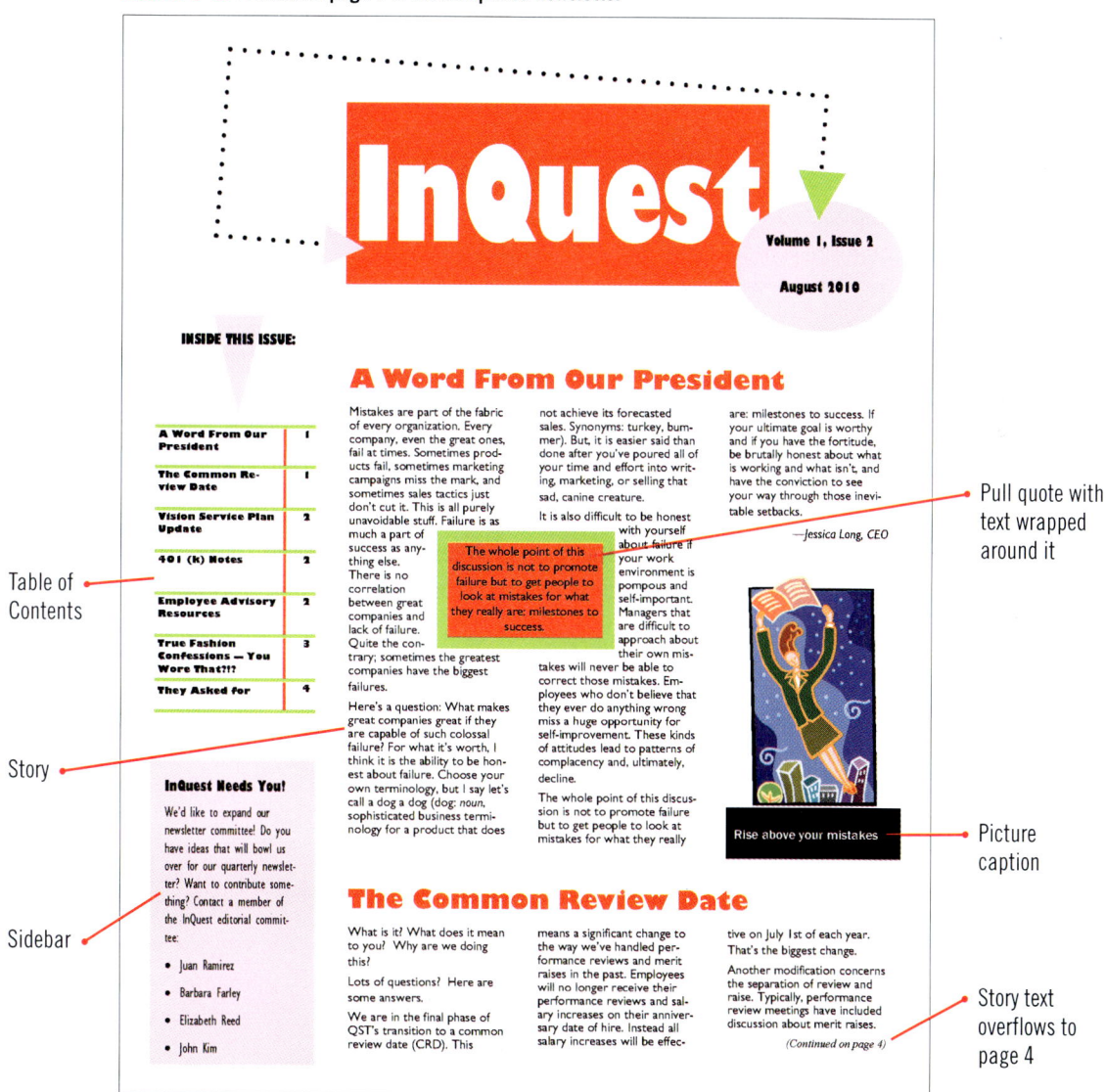

- Table of Contents
- Story
- Sidebar
- Pull quote with text wrapped around it
- Picture caption
- Story text overflows to page 4

UNIT B
Publisher 2007

Creating Columns of Text

Formatting text in columns can make text easier to read and more visually appealing. To create columns, you can either choose a Publisher design that includes columns, or you can format text into columns using options on the Newsletter Options task pane. You have been working on the newsletter for a few days. You used a Publisher sample design to create the newsletter, and then you replaced the placeholder text and graphics with the content for *InQuest*. Today, you plan to finish the newsletter. You begin by opening the partially completed publication and changing the column format on the inside pages.

STEPS

1. **Start Publisher, then click From File in the Recent Publications pane**
   The Open Publication dialog box opens.

2. **Navigate to the drive and folder where you store your Data Files, click InQuest.pub, then click Open**
   The newsletter opens with the first page displayed at 51%. Some graphic images, which you will use later in the unit, are in the workspace. The Mobile newsletter sample design with a three-column format was used to create the publication. The Page Navigation buttons on the status bar indicate that the publication has four pages.

3. **Save the file as InQuest your name to the drive and folder where you store your Data Files**

4. **Click the Page 2 Page Navigation button on the status bar, click the Zoom list arrow 51% on the Standard toolbar, then click Whole Page**
   Pages 2 and 3 appear in the Publication window, as shown in Figure B-3. Pages 2 and 3 are a **two-page spread**. In a bound, printed publication, such as a book, pages on a two-page spread face each other.

5. **Click Page Options in the Format Publication task pane, then make sure Left inside page appears in the Select a page to modify text box**
   Compare your Format Publication task pane to Figure B-4. The options on the task pane apply to the left page because you have selected the Left inside page as the page to modify.

   > **QUICK TIP**
   > You can quickly apply column-formatting changes to the selected page by clicking the appropriate column icon in the Columns on left page section in the task pane.

6. **Position the pointer over the 2 column icon in the Columns on left page section in the task pane, click the down arrow that appears, then click Apply to the Page**
   Publisher reformats the left inside page with two columns and automatically inserts four graphics on the left page. At this point, you could change the way the content is formatted by opening the Content for Left Page menu in the task pane and selecting a different formatting option, but you are happy with the selected formatting option of three stories.

   > **TROUBLE**
   > Be sure the entire graphic is deleted. If it is not, click the graphic frame and press [Delete].

7. **Click the footprints graphic, press [Delete], then repeat to delete the pull quote, the phone graphic, and the pink circle containing the page number**
   You decide that you like the contrast between two columns on the left page and three columns on the right page.

8. **Close the task pane to view more of your workspace**
   With the task pane closed, you can now see more of the newsletter.

9. **Save your changes to the newsletter**

FIGURE B-3: Pages 2 and 3 of the newsletter

- Format Publication task pane
- Design template used to create InQuest publication
- Clip art in workspace
- Page Navigation buttons
- Zoom list arrow
- Pages 2 and 3 appear as facing pages

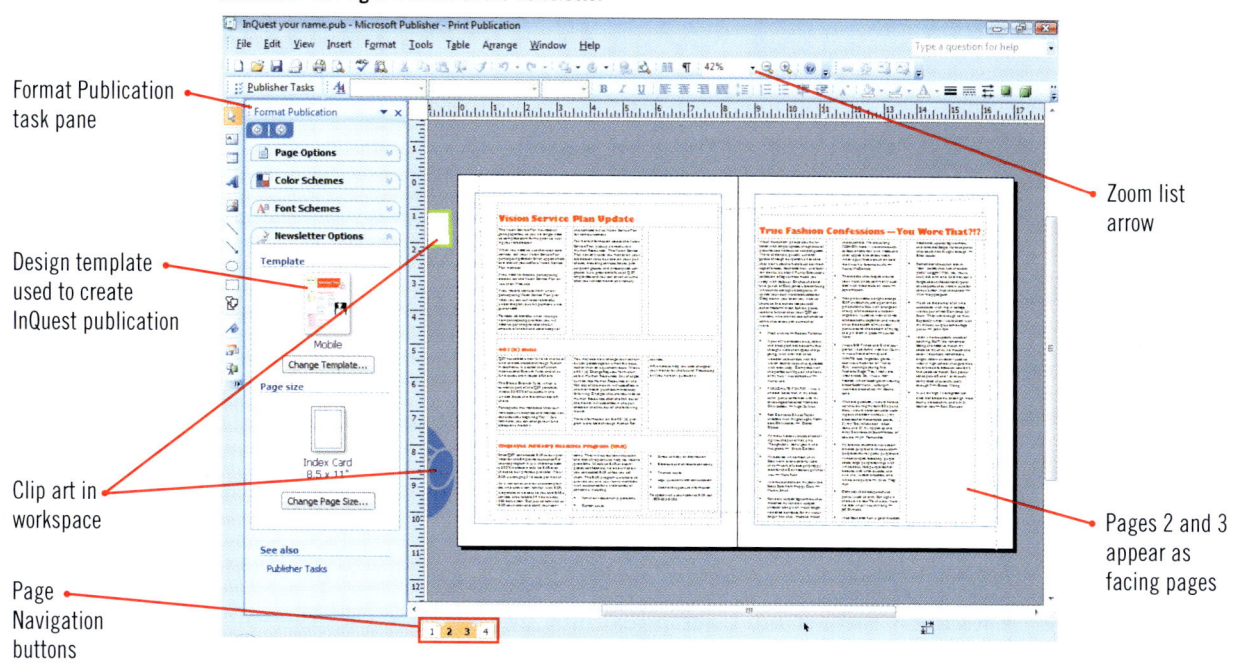

FIGURE B-4: Changing the number of columns with the Format Publication task pane

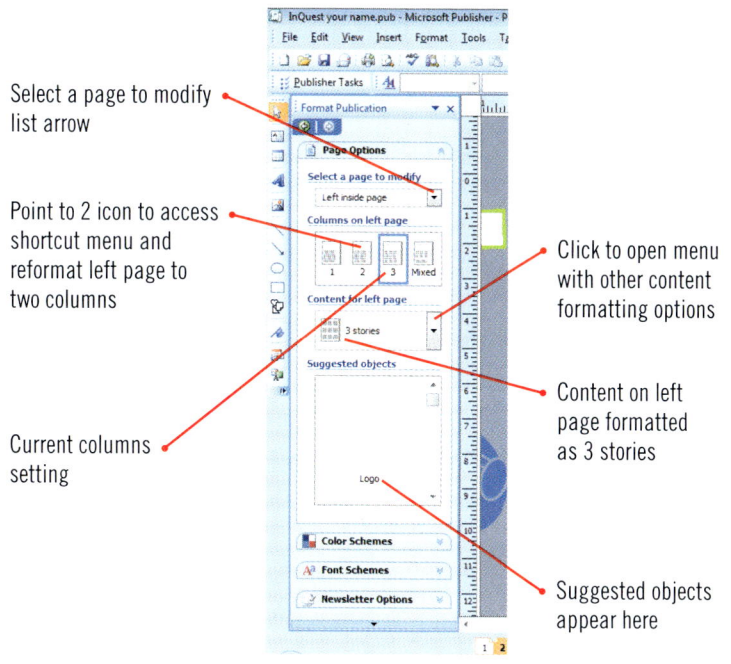

- Select a page to modify list arrow
- Point to 2 icon to access shortcut menu and reformat left page to two columns
- Current columns setting
- Click to open menu with other content formatting options
- Content on left page formatted as 3 stories
- Suggested objects appear here

Creating columns in existing text boxes

You can also change the number of columns of text in existing text boxes. Sometimes it is easier to read narrower columns. For example, you could turn one wide column of text into two or three more-readable columns. To create columns in an existing text box, right-click the text box, then click Format Text Box on the shortcut menu. Click the Text Box tab, click Columns to open the Columns dialog box, then specify the number of columns and the amount of spacing between the columns, as shown in Figure B-5.

FIGURE B-5: Columns dialog box

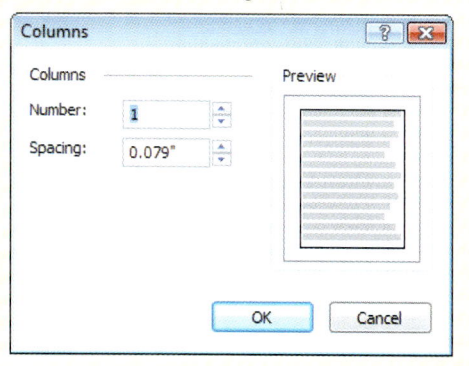

Working with Text and Graphics — Publisher 31

Working with Overflow Text

UNIT B — Publisher 2007

When there isn't enough room in a text box to hold all of the text for a particular story, a Text in Overflow icon appears at the bottom of the text box. To display all the text, you either must enlarge the text box or continue the story in another text box, either on the same page or on a different page of the publication. To continue a story in another text box, you connect the text box that contains overflow text to the text box you want to "pour" the overflow text into. 🎨 You asked one of your colleagues to write a 500-word article in Microsoft Word for the newsletter on QST's new annual review policy. You plan to begin this story on page 1 and continue it on page 4.

STEPS

1. **Click the Page 1 Page Navigation button, click the first column text box beneath the headline "The Common Review Date" to select it, press [F9], click the Create Text Box Link button 🔗 on the Connect Text Boxes toolbar, then move the pointer to the first column text box**

   The pointer changes to a pitcher 🫗. See Table B-1 for a description of the different text flow icons.

2. **Click the empty second column text box, click 🔗, then click the empty third column text box**

   When the pointer is over a text box you want to connect to, the pitcher changes to 🫗. When you click, the text boxes are **connected**. You know text boxes are connected when you see the Go to Next Text Box icon ➡️, which indicates that the selected text box is linked to another text box, or the Go to Previous Text Box ⬅️, as shown in Figure B-6, which indicates the selected text box is linked to a previous text box.

   > **QUICK TIP**
   > When you use **autoflow**, Publisher automatically flows text to the next empty text box, asking for confirmation before it flows into each text box.

3. **Click the empty first column text boxes, click Insert on the menu bar, click Text File to open the Insert Text dialog box, navigate to the drive and folder where you store your Data Files, click PB B-1.docx, then click OK**

   Text from the Word document automatically pours into the three connected text boxes on page 1, but because there is too much text to fit in the three boxes, Publisher prompts you to use autoflow.

4. **Click No in the Microsoft Office Publisher dialog box**

   The Text in Overflow icon 🅰… appears at the bottom of the third text box.

   > **QUICK TIP**
   > You can press [Ctrl][G], enter a page number, then click OK to move to another page in your publication.

5. **Click 🔗 on the Connect Text Boxes toolbar, click the Page 4 Page Navigation button, scroll until the headline "The Common Review Date (continued)" is at the top of the window, position the 🫗 pointer in the first column text box under the headline, then click**

   Again, the text does not entirely fit in the text box, as shown in Figure B-7.

6. **Click 🔗, click the second column text box, click 🔗, then click the third column text box**

   > **QUICK TIP**
   > If you add pages to a publication, Publisher automatically updates the Continued on page numbers.

7. **Go to page 1, right-click the third column text box of the story, click Format Text Box on the shortcut menu, then click the Text Box tab**

   Figure B-8 shows options for continuing text. When a story continues on another page, continued notices provide cues that help the reader find the rest of the story.

8. **Click the Include "Continued on page…" check box to select it, then click OK**

   Publisher adds the text "(Continued on page 4)" to the bottom of the text box.

9. **Go to page 4, right-click the first column text box of the story, click Format Text Box, click the Text Box tab, click the Include "Continued from page…" check box to select it, click OK, then save your work**

   Publisher adds the text "(Continued from page 1)" to the top of the text box.

Working with Text and Graphics

FIGURE B-6: Three connected text boxes

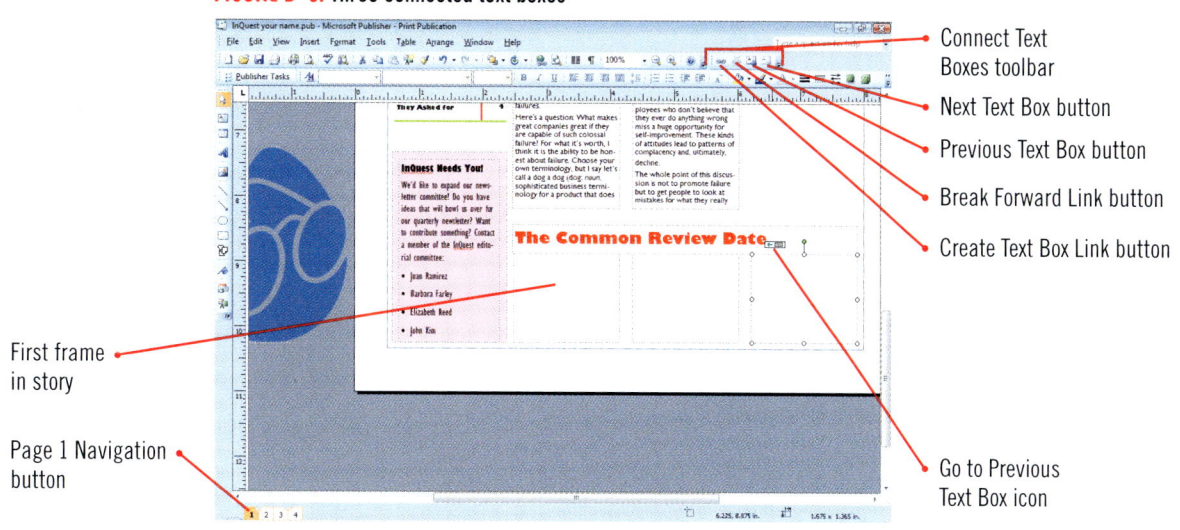

- Connect Text Boxes toolbar
- Next Text Box button
- Previous Text Box button
- Break Forward Link button
- Create Text Box Link button
- First frame in story
- Page 1 Navigation button
- Go to Previous Text Box icon

FIGURE B-7: Connecting text from one frame to another

- Go to Previous Text Box icon
- Page 4
- Text in Overflow icon

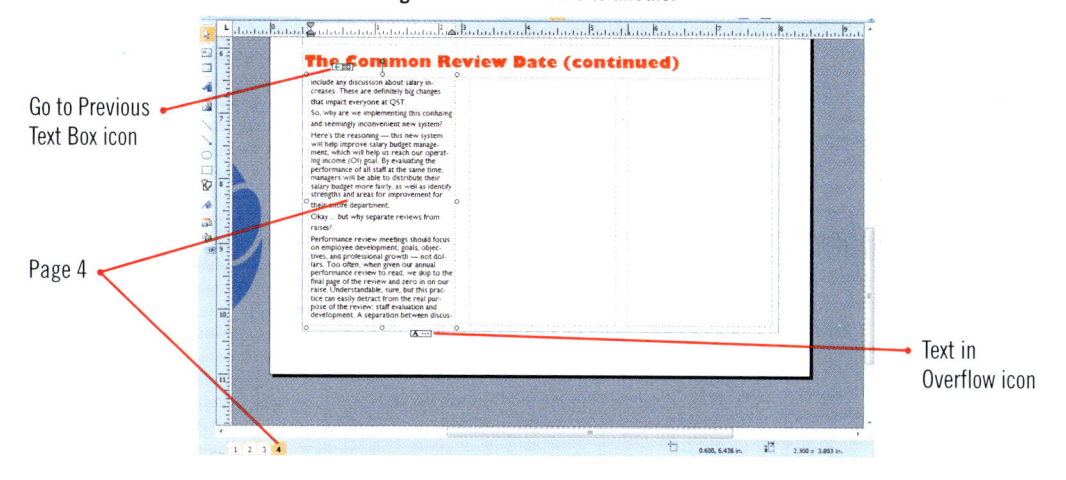

FIGURE B-8: Format Text Box dialog box with Text Box tab displayed

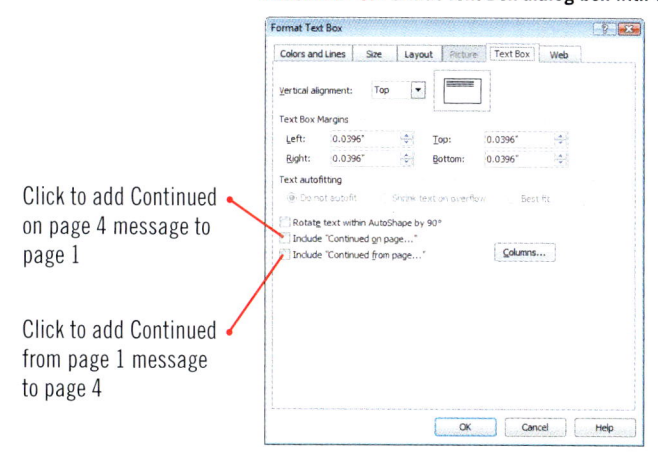

- Click to add Continued on page 4 message to page 1
- Click to add Continued from page 1 message to page 4

TABLE B-1: Text Flow icons

text flow icon	description
→	Indicates that text box is connected to another text box and that text flows from this text box to the next one. Click to move quickly to the next text box.
←	Indicates that text box is connected to another text box and that text flows from that text box to this text box. Click to move quickly to the previous text box.
A...	Indicates that text box is not connected to another text box and that there is more text that does not fit in the text box.

Working with Text and Graphics

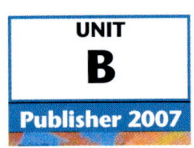

Using Guides

When you are working with columns, it can be helpful to use layout and ruler guides. **Layout guides** are nonprinting lines that help you align text, pictures, and other objects into columns and rows so that your publication has a consistent look across all pages. Layout guides appear on every page of your publication and are represented by blue dotted lines on the screen. **Ruler guides** are similar to layout guides but appear only on a single page. Use ruler guides whenever you need a little extra help aligning an object on a page. Ruler guides are represented by green dotted lines on the screen. You notice that the objects in the column containing the Table of Contents and sidebar on page 1 are not the same width as the other columns on the page. Setting vertical layout guides can help you fix this. Setting a ruler guide can help you position a picture more precisely.

STEPS

1. Go to page 1, click the Zoom list arrow, click Whole Page, click Arrange on the menu bar, then click Layout Guides

   The Layout Guides dialog box opens with the Margin Guides tab selected, as shown in Figure B-9. Use this dialog box to adjust the margin guides, grid guides, and baseline guides. The **margin guides** appear in blue on the screen and outline the **margin**, or perimeter, of the page. The **grid guides** appear in blue on the screen and provide a perimeter for each column on the page. **Baseline guides** are horizontal, brown, dotted lines and help to align text among columns in text boxes.

2. Click the Grid Guides tab, then click the Columns up arrow until 4 displays in the Columns text box

   The Preview shows blue grid guides dividing the page into four columns.

3. Click OK

   Four grid layout guides appear on the newsletter.

4. Click the Table of Contents, then press [F9] to zoom in as shown in Figure B-10

   Because the Table of Contents and design element above it are grouped, as indicated by the group icon at the bottom of the selected object, both objects will be resized together.

   > **QUICK TIP**
   > Click the Undo button on the Standard toolbar if you are not satisfied with the result, then try again.

5. Point to the middle sizing handle on the right border of the table until the pointer changes to ↔, drag left using the ↔ pointer to align the right edge of the selected object with the blue grid guide, then click outside to check your work

   The grouped object, the Table of Contents and the design element, is now the same width as the grid guide.

6. Scroll down and click the light pink sidebar *InQuest* Needs You! text box, drag the middle-right sizing handle left using the ↔ pointer to align with the blue grid guide, then click outside the text box to check your work

   The elements in the first column have been resized to fit the column width.

   > **QUICK TIP**
   > To clear all ruler guides, click Arrange on the menu bar, point to Ruler Guides, then click Clear All Ruler Guides.

7. Scroll up and to the right until the top of the red banner is at the top of the window, click Arrange on the menu bar, point to Ruler Guides, then click Add Horizontal Ruler Guide

   A greenish-blue horizontal line appears on the page near the top of the story, A Word From Our President.

8. Place the pointer over the green line in the left margin so the pointer changes to the Adjust pointer ⇅, then click and drag to align with the 5½" mark on the vertical ruler

   The ruler guide is now set as shown in Figure B-11. You will use this newly created ruler guide in the next lesson.

9. Save your changes

FIGURE B-9: Layout Guides dialog box with Margin Guides tab displayed

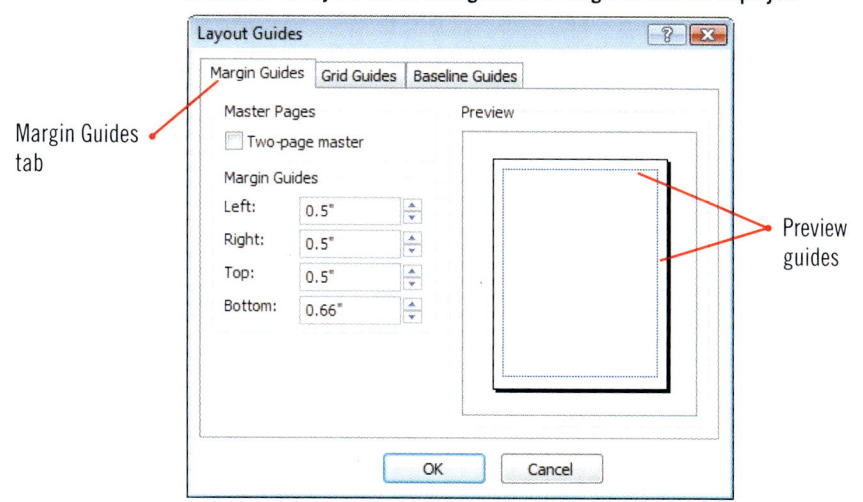

FIGURE B-10: Table of Contents table frame

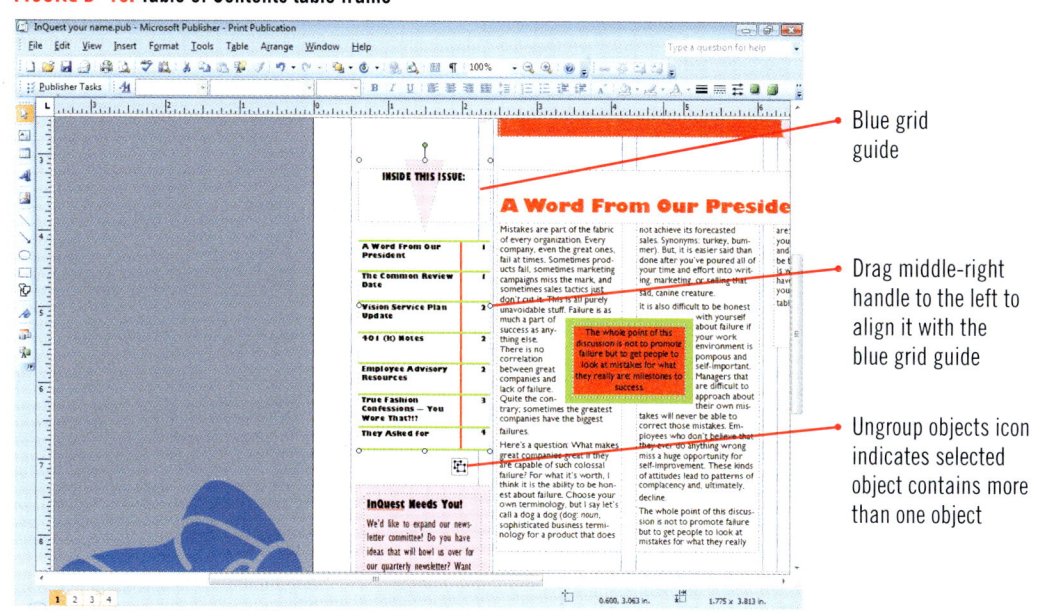

FIGURE B-11: Setting a ruler guide

Using baseline guides

Baseline guides are used to align text across multiple columns. They are brown, dotted horizontal lines that are spaced evenly throughout the publication and indicate where text lines start. In order to make the last row of text align with the bottom margin, you need to set the baseline guides at a multiple of the space between the top and bottom margins. Since text is measured in points, it is helpful to use point sizes when setting the margin guides and baseline guides so that it is easy to adjust both to coordinate the text properly. To add baseline guides to your publication, click Arrange on the menu bar, click Layout Guides, click the Baseline Guides tab in the Layout Guides dialog box, then adjust the settings as needed.

UNIT B
Publisher 2007

Creating Picture Captions

A **picture caption** is text that describes or provides additional information about a picture. Captions can be located above, below, or next to a picture. You can create a picture caption by typing text in a text box that you create, or you can use Publisher's Design Gallery to choose one of the picture caption designs. The design collection includes objects such as picture captions, logos, and calendars. You can also create and save your own objects in the Design Gallery. You would like to add a piece of motivational clip art at the bottom of the president's article on page 1. You do this by using one of Publisher's preset picture captions in the Design Gallery and choosing an appropriate piece of clip art.

STEPS

1. On page 1, select the **first column text box** below the "A Word From ..." text box

2. Click the **Design Gallery Object button** on the Objects toolbar
   The Microsoft Office Publisher Design Gallery opens, as shown in Figure B-12. The categories list in the left pane shows the large variety of predesigned objects you can use to enhance your publication. The right pane shows thumbnails of predesigned objects for the selected category.

   QUICK TIP
   Designs are organized by category and design type.

3. Click **Picture Captions** in the left pane, click the **Solid Bar thumbnail**, then click **Insert Object**
   The object, an image with "Caption describing picture or graphic" text, appears on top of the article.

4. Scroll to view the bottom of the third column of that story, then drag the **object** using the Move pointer ✥ so that the upper-left handle of the object is positioned at the intersection of the ruler guide and the layout guide, as shown in Figure B-13

   TROUBLE
   If the Picture toolbar opens at any time, click the Close button.

5. Drag the **lower-right corner handle** up and to the left using the Resize pointer ✥ to resize the frame so that it is aligned with the bottom of the column at the 8 3/16" mark on the vertical ruler and the 8" mark on the horizontal ruler
   As you drag, one guide moves along the vertical ruler and another guide moves along the horizontal ruler. The elements in a design gallery object are grouped, but can be individually modified.

   QUICK TIP
   Small, gray handles appear around the picture when it is selected.

6. Click the **picture of the deer**, right-click, point to **Change Picture**, then click **Clip Art**
   The Clip Art task pane opens.

   TROUBLE
   You need an active Internet connection to access this picture. If you don't see this picture, click another image.

7. Type **success** in the Search for text box, click **Go**, then scroll down the results to display the picture of a woman flying over buildings
   The Clip Art task pane displays the results of your search.

8. Click the **picture of a woman flying over buildings** to insert it, click the **placeholder caption text** to select it, type **Rise above your mistakes**, click outside the object, compare your screen to Figure B-14, then save your changes
   The placeholder picture and caption are replaced with a relevant image and text.

Adding your own objects to the Content Library

If you design or modify an object, such as a pull quote or a logo, that you intend to use in every edition of a publication, you can save it to the Content Library for use in future publications. To add an item to the Content Library, select the object you want to save, click Insert on the menu bar, and then click Add to Content Library. In the Add Item to the Content Library dialog box, type a title for the object, add or choose a category, then click OK. This object is saved to the Content Library. To open the Content Library task pane, click Insert on the menu bar, and then click "Item from Content Library." The Content Library task pane opens, and items you have saved to the Content Library appear in the task pane. To delete an object from the Content Library, position the pointer over the object, right-click the object, click Delete on the shortcut menu, then click OK to confirm the deletion.

FIGURE B-12: Microsoft Office Publisher Design Gallery

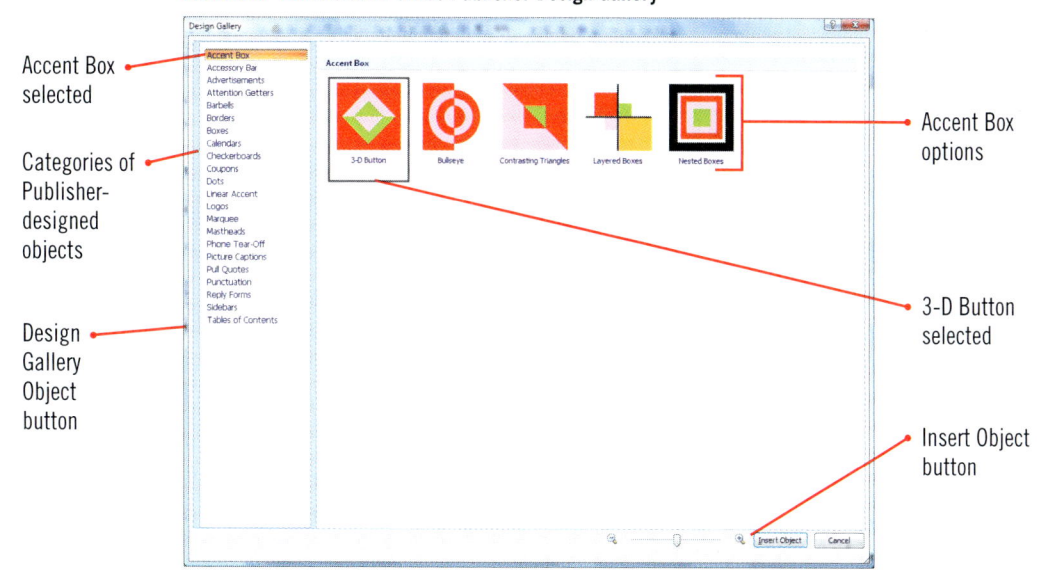

- Accent Box selected
- Categories of Publisher-designed objects
- Design Gallery Object button
- Accent Box options
- 3-D Button selected
- Insert Object button

FIGURE B-13: Positioning the object using guides

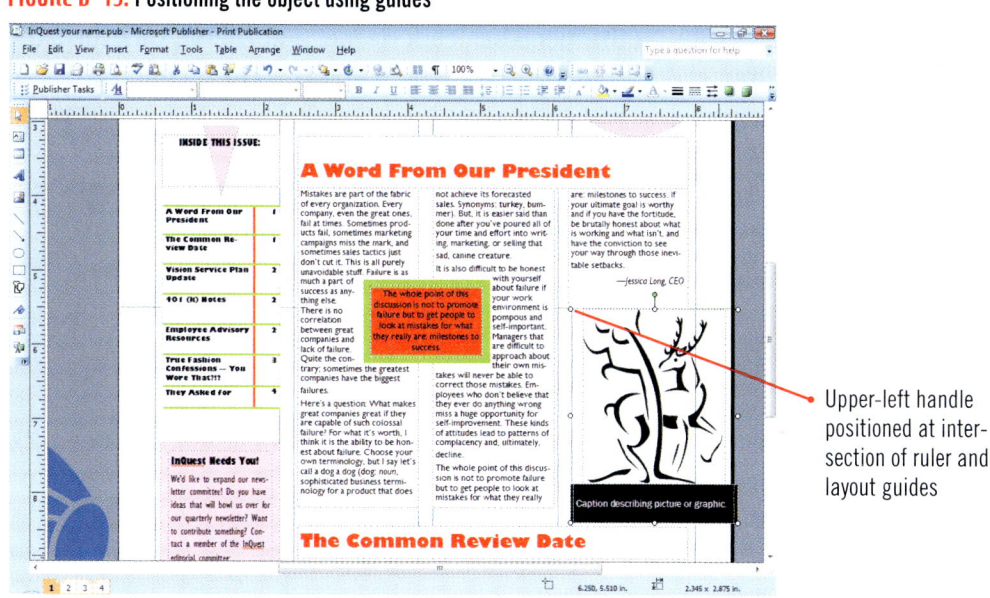

- Upper-left handle positioned at intersection of ruler and layout guides

FIGURE B-14: Inserting clip art using the task pane

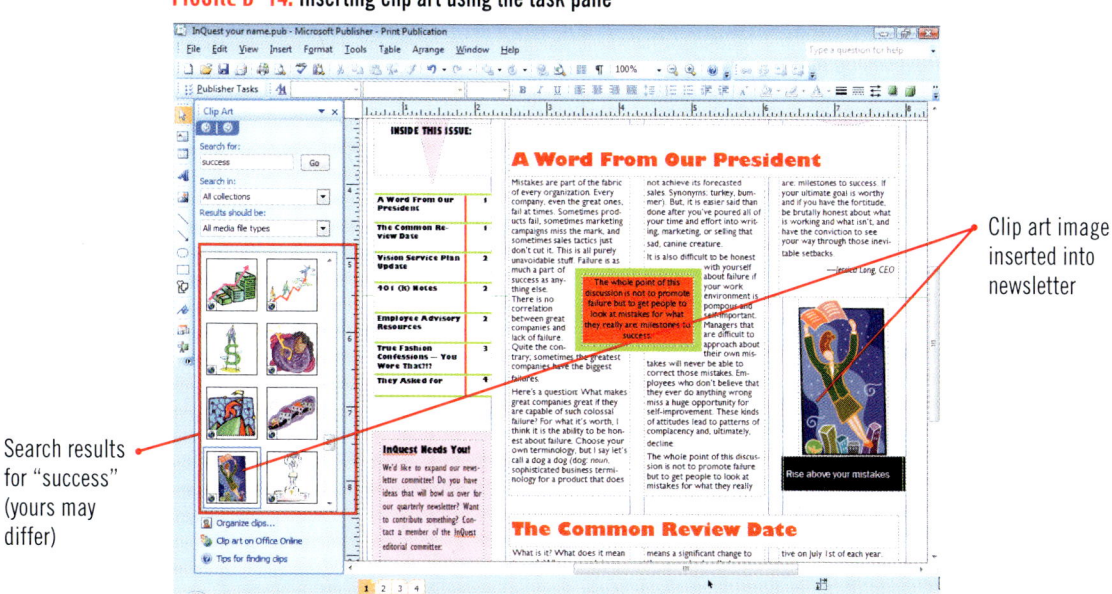

- Search results for "success" (yours may differ)
- Clip art image inserted into newsletter

Working with Text and Graphics

Publisher 2007

Publisher 37

Creating Headers and Footers

A **header** is information that appears on the top of every page of a publication, such as the name of the publication. A **footer** is information that appears on the bottom of every page of a publication, such as a page number. When you create a header or footer in Publisher, you use the **master page**, also known as the **background**, which is a layer that appears behind every page in a publication. If you want certain objects or information to appear in the same place on every page of a publication, you must place them on the master page. The **foreground** sits on top of the background and consists of the objects that appear on a specific page of a publication. In a multipage publication you can create separate master pages to apply to two facing pages, and choose not to have master page elements such as header, footer, or page numbers appear on the first page of the publication. You add a header and a footer to the master pages, and you make sure the header and footer do not appear on page 1.

STEPS

1. Click **View** on the menu bar, click **Header and Footer**, click the **Other Task Panes list arrow**, click **Edit Master Pages**, then press **[F9]** to zoom out

   The background right master page appears, and the Edit Master Pages task pane opens. The page navigation button is an "R," indicating there is one master page and it is a right-hand one.

2. Be sure the insertion point is in the **header text box**, type **VOLUME 1 ISSUE 2**, then click the **Align Text Right button** on the Formatting toolbar

3. Scroll down if necessary, click in the **footer text box**, press **[F9]**, type **Page**, press **[Spacebar]**, click the **Insert Page Number button** on the Header and Footer toolbar, click, then press **[F9]**

   The page number appears as shown in Figure B-15.

   > **QUICK TIP**
   > The master page on the left is a duplicate of the master page on the right, so it is labeled "R."

4. Point to the **Master R** icon in the Edit Master Pages task pane, click the **list arrow that appears on the Master R icon**, click **Change to Two-page**, zoom to whole page, then drag and resize the header text box and the footer text box on the left page to the position shown in Figure B-16 if necessary and left-align the text in both text boxes

   The Page Navigation buttons now indicate there are two master pages, both labeled "R." The information you added to the header and footer on the first master page appears on both master pages.

   > **QUICK TIP**
   > Press [Ctrl][M] to toggle quickly between the publication page and the background.

5. Press **[Ctrl][M]**, use the Page Navigation buttons to view all pages of your publication, then close the task pane

   You can see a header and a footer on each page.

6. Go to page 1, click **View** on the menu bar, click **Ignore Master Page**, then save the document

   The header and footer no longer appear on page 1 but still appear on pages 2–4 with pagination continuing from page 1.

Creating a drop cap

A **drop cap** is a specially formatted first letter of the first word of a paragraph. Usually, a drop cap is in a much larger font size than the paragraph text itself, and sometimes the drop cap is formatted in a different font. To create a drop cap, click anywhere in the paragraph where you want the drop cap to appear, click Format on the menu bar, click Drop Cap, click one of the available drop cap styles in the Drop Cap dialog box, then click OK. You can also use the options on the Custom Drop Cap tab to create your own drop cap style.

FIGURE B-15: Completed footer

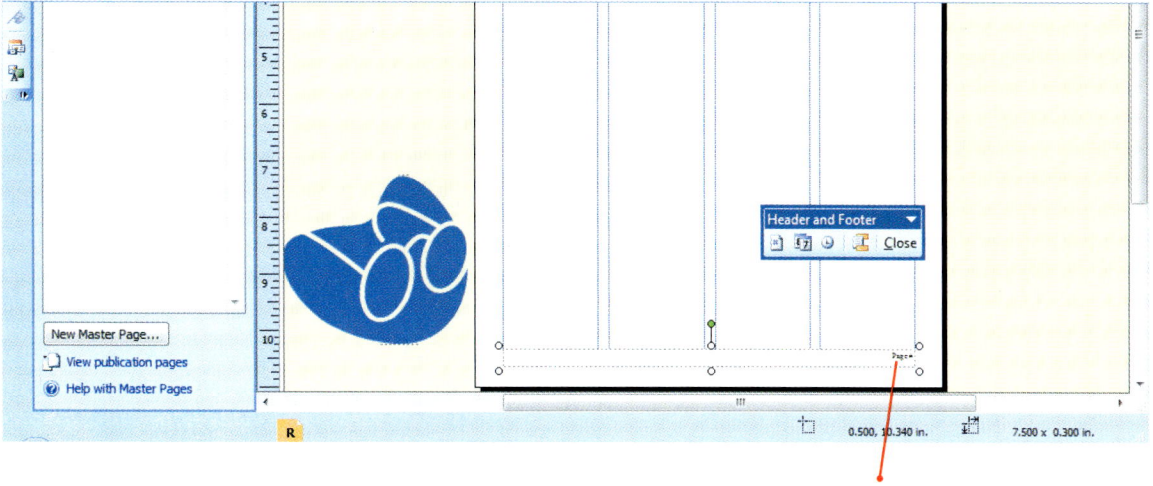

Pound sign indicates page number placeholder

FIGURE B-16: Completed master pages

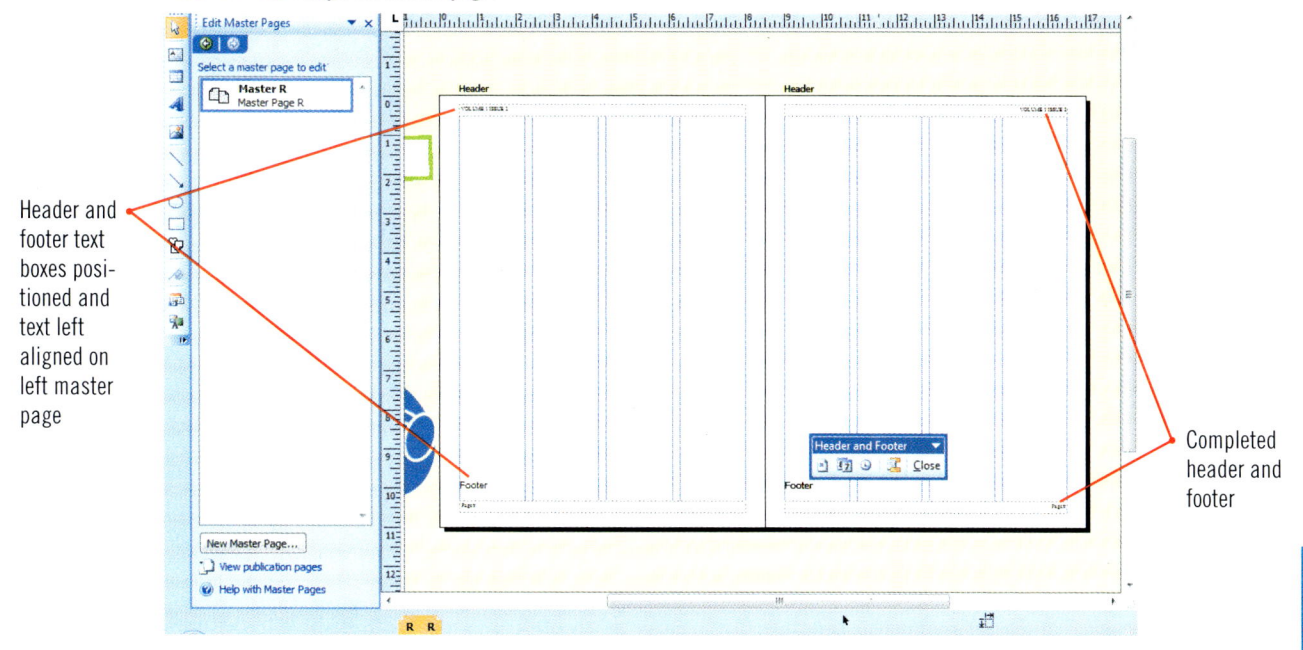

Header and footer text boxes positioned and text left aligned on left master page

Completed header and footer

Working with text styles

A text style is a set of formatting characteristics that you can quickly apply to text in selected paragraphs. A style contains all text formatting information: font and font size, font color, alignment, indents, character and line spacing, tabs, and special formatting, such as numbered lists. You can apply preset styles included with Publisher, you can import text styles from other publications, or you can define your own styles. To apply a text style, select the text you want to format, click the Style list arrow on the Formatting toolbar, then choose from the list of styles. To modify a style or create a new style, use the Styles command on the Format menu to open the Styles task pane.

UNIT B
Publisher 2007

Wrapping Text Around Objects

To help make your stories more visually interesting, Publisher gives you the ability to wrap text around any object. **Wrapping** means that the text flows around the object rather than on top of or behind it. You can wrap text around pictures or around other text, such as pull quotes. A **pull quote** is a quotation from a story that is pulled out into its own frame and treated like a graphic. You can choose to wrap text around an object's frame or around the object itself. You can store clip art on the desktop workspace for use in the publication. However, when you are finished with your publication, you should delete any unused clip art because it increases the file size of your publication. You are ready to add the graphics you placed on the workspace to the stories on pages 2 and 3.

STEPS

> **QUICK TIP**
> If the Picture toolbar opens at any time, click the Close button.

1. Go to page 2, then zoom out to view the whole page, if necessary

2. Drag the eyeglass clip art located on the left of your desktop workspace so that it is centered between the two columns of text in the "Vision Service Plan Update" story, click Arrange on the menu bar, point to Order, then click Bring to Front

   Once you perform an Order command, an Order button, in this case the Bring to Front button, appears on the Standard toolbar. The text in the article automatically wraps around the square-shaped frame containing the eyeglasses.

> **QUICK TIP**
> To manually adjust how close the text is to certain areas of the object, click Arrange on the menu bar, point to Text Wrapping, then click Edit Wrap Points. When you click this option, handles appear that you can use to resize the wrap around the object.

3. Click Arrange on the menu bar, point to Text Wrapping, click Tight, click Yes in the message box, then deselect the object

   The text now wraps tightly around the contours of the eyeglasses.

4. Click Insert on the menu bar, click Design Gallery Object, then click Pull Quotes in the Categories list

   The Design Gallery displays an alphabetical list of thumbnails of the preset Pull Quote designs, as shown in Figure B-17.

5. Scroll down, click the Tilt thumbnail, then click Insert Object

   The pull quote placeholder appears on top of the publication text, between pages 2 and 3.

> **QUICK TIP**
> Don't place an object in the middle of a single column so that the object divides lines of text. It is difficult to read lines of text separated by a graphic.

6. Drag the Pull Quote frame to the "True Fashion Confessions" story on page 3 so that its right edge is on the left edge of the third column and the top edge is approximately at the 4" mark on the vertical ruler

   Notice that the text automatically wraps around the pull quote frame.

7. Zoom in on the lower-right corner of page 3, drag to select the last bulleted item in the third column, beginning with In junior high..., including Ron Dawson, then click the Copy button on the Standard toolbar

   Text can be copied from one text box to another.

8. Click to select the placeholder text in the Pull Quote frame, click the Paste button on the Standard toolbar, then delete the bullet in the pull quote object if necessary

   The quote from Ron Dawson is pulled out and highlighted in the pull quote on the page.

9. Select all the text in the pull quote, click the Font list arrow on the Formatting toolbar, click Times New Roman, click the Font Size list arrow, click 10, click the Italic button, click the Center button, zoom out to see the whole page, click the desktop workspace, then save your changes

   Compare your publication with Figure B-18.

Publisher 40 Working with Text and Graphics

FIGURE B-17: Design Gallery with Pull Quotes category selected

Pull Quotes category selected

Design currently used in the publication

Scroll to see more options

Thumbnails of pull quote designs

FIGURE B-18: Wrapping text around clip art and pull quotes

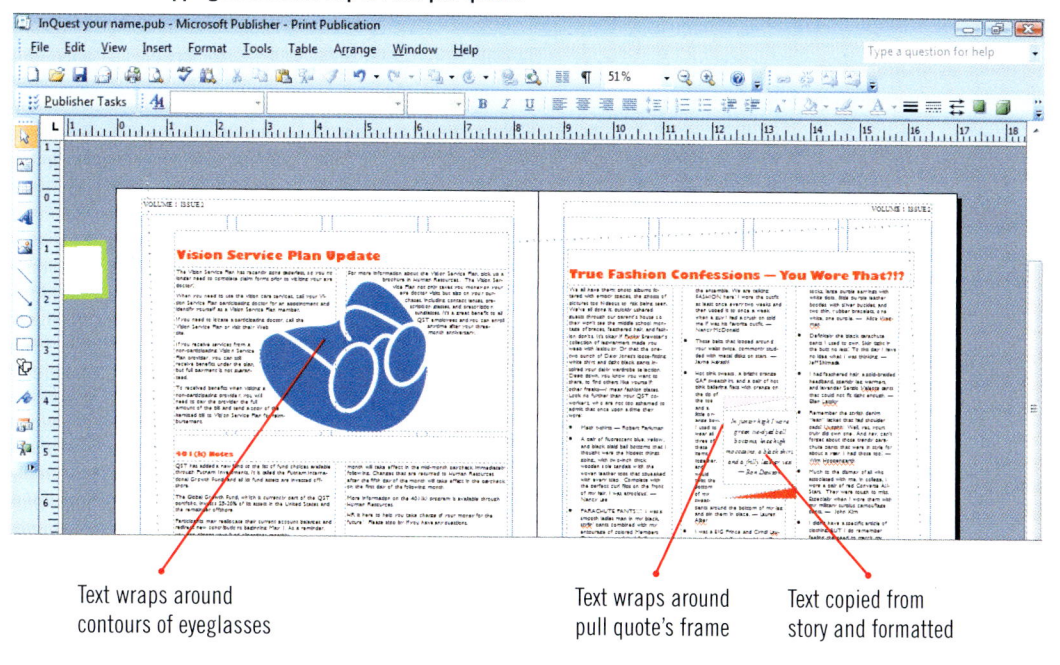

Text wraps around contours of eyeglasses

Text wraps around pull quote's frame

Text copied from story and formatted

Rotating and flipping objects

You can create interesting effects in a publication by rotating or flipping text and objects. When you **rotate** an object, you change its angle in degrees relative to a baseline. For example, text that is rotated 90 degrees appears vertically rather than horizontally. To rotate an object in 90-degree increments, select the object, click Arrange on the menu bar, point to Rotate or Flip, then click the option you want. To rotate an object by dragging it, select the object, then point to the green rotation handle at the top of the frame. Drag the mouse in the direction you want to rotate the object. To rotate the object in 15-degree increments using the dragging method, press and hold [Shift] while dragging the rotation handle.

Working with Text and Graphics

Publisher 2007

Publisher 41

UNIT B
Publisher 2007

Layering and Grouping Objects

You can layer two or more objects on top of each other in a publication to create an interesting visual effect. When you **layer** objects, they appear on the page in the order you placed them, as if you had placed different pieces of paper on top of one another. You can change the layer order by using the Bring to Front, Send to Back, Bring Forward, or Send Backward commands. When you are happy with the arrangement of your layered objects, you can group them so you can work with the objects as a single object. Grouping objects allows you to move and resize the group rather than each object individually, saving time. You want to improve the look of the QST logo on page 4 of *InQuest*. You decide to layer the logo on top of several different rectangle shapes to make it more attractive. You also add the correct contact information.

STEPS

> **QUICK TIP**
> AutoShapes provide you with a wide variety of shapes, connectors, callouts, and arrows. To access them, click the AutoShapes button on the Objects toolbar.

1. **Go to page 4, then zoom in on the upper-left corner of the page and the desktop workspace to the left of the page**

    The QST logo is positioned above the gold box, and an AutoShape graphic with a green border is seen in the top left of the desktop workspace. An **AutoShape** is a predesigned shape provided with Publisher that you can use in your publications.

2. **Select the green-bordered rectangle in the desktop workspace, then drag it to the publication page so that the upper-left corner is positioned at the .5" mark on the horizontal ruler and .5" on the vertical rulers**

    Compare your screen to Figure B-19.

> **TROUBLE**
> If you send the wrong frame to the back, click the Undo button on the Standard toolbar and repeat the step.

3. **Click the yellow rectangle to select it, click Arrange on the menu bar, point to Order, then click Send to Back**

    The yellow rectangle is now positioned behind the green-bordered rectangle.

4. **Click the logo, close the Picture toolbar if it opens, double-click the Object Position on the status bar, verify .75 is in the x text box in the Measurement toolbar, type .75 in the y text box, then close the Measurement toolbar**

5. **Verify that the logo is still selected, press and hold [Shift], click the green-bordered rectangle, then click the yellow rectangle**

    Notice that all three objects are selected and the Group Objects button appears under the objects.

6. **Click the Group Objects button beneath the objects**

    The objects are now grouped as shown in Figure B-20. You can move, resize, or format them as a whole. The Group Objects button has changed to an Ungroup Objects button now that the selected object is a group. You can click this button to ungroup the objects and work with the objects individually.

7. **Replace the contact information with your information, replace Business Name with Quest Specialty Travel, and delete the tag line on page 4, then save your changes to the newsletter**

> **QUICK TIP**
> Be sure that all names are spelled correctly.

8. **Click the Spelling button on the Standard toolbar, check all the stories in the publication, correct any misspelled words, compare your newsletter to Figure B-21, save any changes, then print and close the file**

FIGURE B-19: Working with three layers

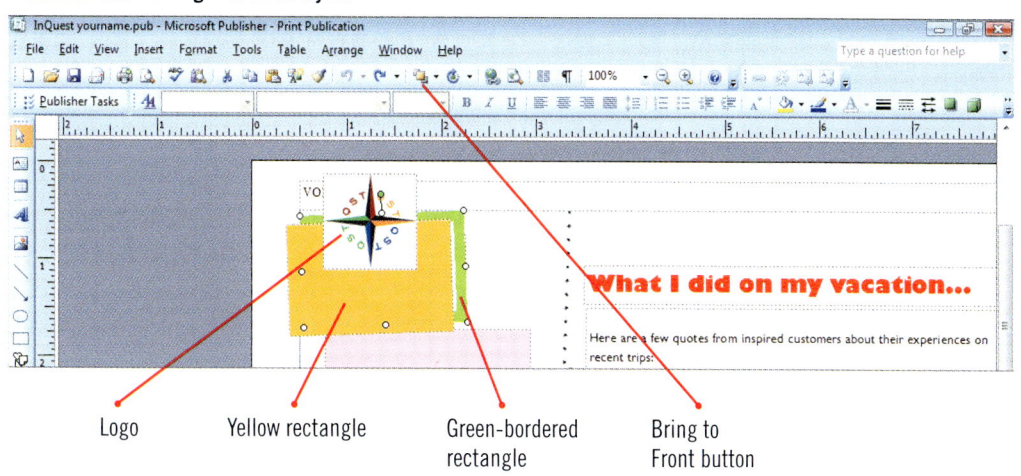

- Logo
- Yellow rectangle
- Green-bordered rectangle
- Bring to Front button

FIGURE B-20: Grouping objects

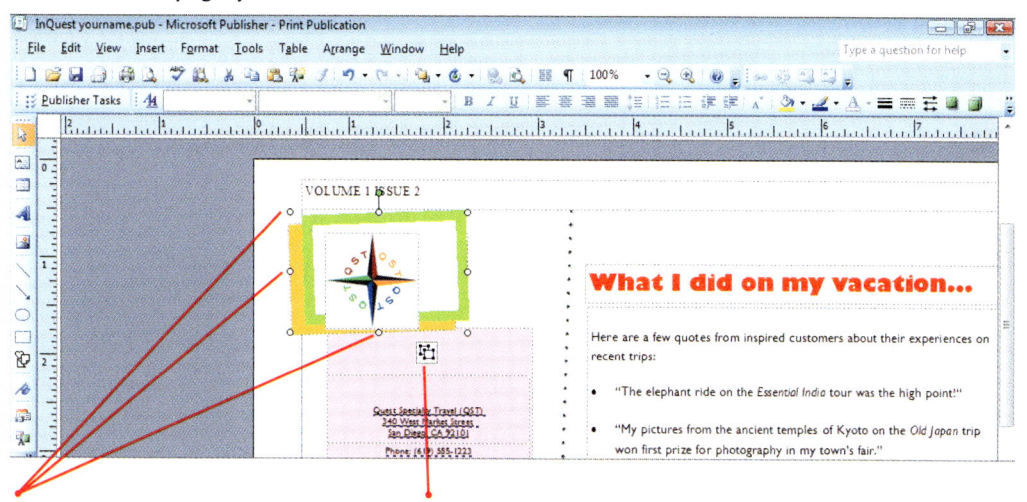

- Sizing handles around all objects indicate objects are selected as a group
- Ungroup Objects button

FIGURE B-21: Completed newsletter

Working with Text and Graphics

Publisher 2007

Publisher 43

Merging Information from a Data Source

UNIT B
Publisher 2007

With the Catalog Merge feature, you can use information from a data source to create a brochure or add an additional page or pages to an existing publication. Using the Catalog Merge task pane, you can choose to create an address list or catalog file, then choose a source, such as a database or spreadsheet, or create a new product list. Once your data source is selected, you can add fields from your data source in any order and position them to create the look you want. You can define your data source fields as text or picture fields. Adding a picture field is useful when you have graphics or images you want to display in your publication. When positioning and formatting fields, Publisher displays each change you make immediately. You need to create a one-page listing of the QST employees that everyone should know so it can be posted around the offices. You use the Catalog Merge feature to create the new publication.

STEPS

1. Open the file PB B-2.pub from the drive and folder where you store your Data Files

TROUBLE
Close any toolbars that open during this lesson.

2. Click Tools on the menu bar, point to Mailings and Catalogs, then click Catalog Merge
   The Catalog Merge task pane opens, as shown in Figure B-22.

3. Verify that the Use an existing list option button is selected, click Next: Create or connect to a product list at the bottom of the Catalog Merge task pane, navigate to the drive and folder where you store your Data Files, click PB B-3.xls, then click Open
   The Select Table dialog box opens, displaying the Excel data sheets.

4. Verify that Sheet1$ is selected, click OK, then click OK in the Catalog Merge Product List dialog box
   The fields from the data source are listed in the Prepare your publication section.

5. Click FirstName in the Catalog Merge task pane, click LastName, then click Title
   The fields you selected appear in text boxes in the **work area canvas**. The work area canvas holds all fields for one record. All positioning and formatting changes made to fields in the work area canvas are applied to those same fields throughout the publication.

6. Click Product Picture under More items, select the Photo field in the Insert Picture Field dialog box if necessary, then click OK
   A placeholder text box for the photo field is added to the work area canvas.

TROUBLE
If the work area closes, click the first picture to display the work area again.

7. Move the work area canvas to position it under the header, use the bottom-middle sizing handle to resize the work area canvas so that the bottom of it aligns with 3¾" on the vertical ruler, use the rulers and Figure B-23 as your guide to position and size the fields in the work area canvas, format the two name fields using 20-point Perpetua bold and the Title field using 16-point Perpetua bold, then click outside the work area
   The positioning, size, and formatting changes are applied to the fields in the work area canvas and to all fields in the publication.

8. Click Next: Create merged publications, click Merge to a new publication, click File on the menu bar, click Save As, navigate to where you store your Data Files, name the merged publication as Employees.pub, then click Save

TROUBLE
Click View on the menu bar, then click Boundaries and Guides to turn off the display of guides.

9. Compare your finished publication to Figure B-24, add your name somewhere in the document, close Employees.pub, close PB B-2.pub without saving changes, then exit Publisher

Working with Text and Graphics

FIGURE B-22: Catalog Merge task page

Data source options

Click link to select data source

Use the work area canvas to set up one record; fields in all records in the publication will use the same positioning, size, and formatting

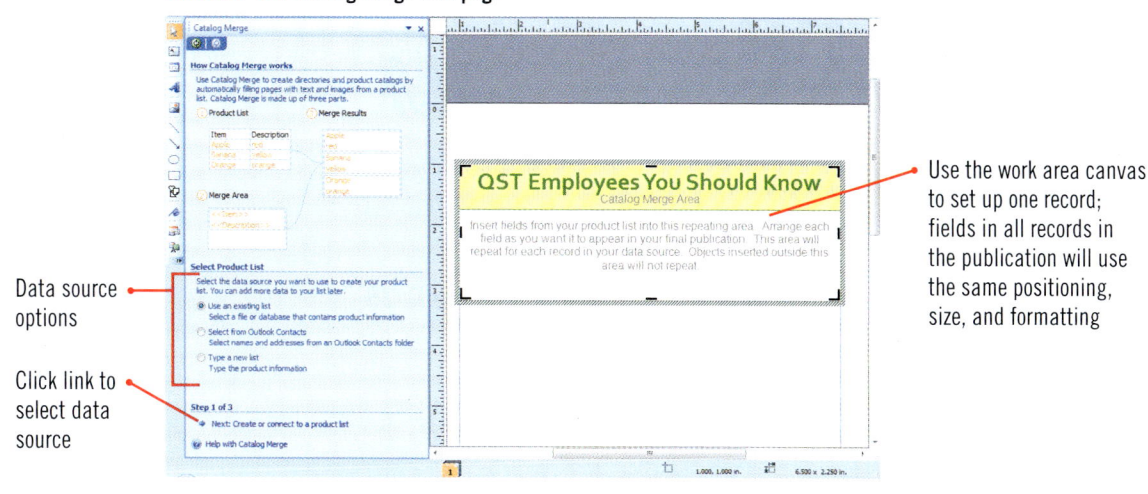

FIGURE B-23: Fields inserted and formatted in merge template

Fields from data source; moved to work area canvas

First name field positioned, sized, and formatted

Last name field positioned, sized, and formatted

Title field positioned, sized, and formatted

Photo field positioned, sized, and formatted

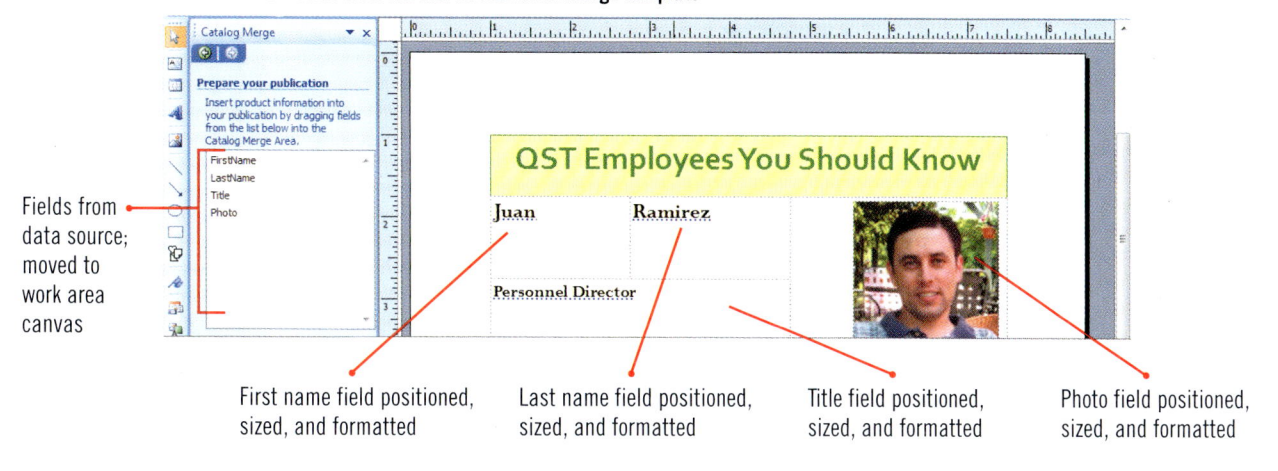

FIGURE B-24: Employee page with formatting complete

Using marketing tools

Microsoft Publisher 2007 can be used not only to create business publications such as print mailings, e-mails, and catalogs, it also comes with tools that can help you customize and track your mailings to customers. If you have purchased Publisher 2007 as a part of either the Office Small Business 2007 suite or the Office Professional 2007 suite, Publisher can be integrated with Business Contact Manager, a tool that comes with Office Outlook 2007. **Business Contact Manager** can be used to organize and centralize your customer information, manage sales leads, track your marketing activities, and coordinate project information. Using the Mail Merge feature in Publisher, you can combine and edit customer lists from multiple sources into a single list.

Working with Text and Graphics

Practice

If you have a SAM user profile, you may have access to hands-on instruction, practice, and assessment of the skills covered in this unit. Log in to your SAM account (http://sam2007.course.com/) to launch any assigned training activities or exams that relate to the skills covered in this unit.

▼ CONCEPTS REVIEW

Label each element of the publication shown in Figure B-25.

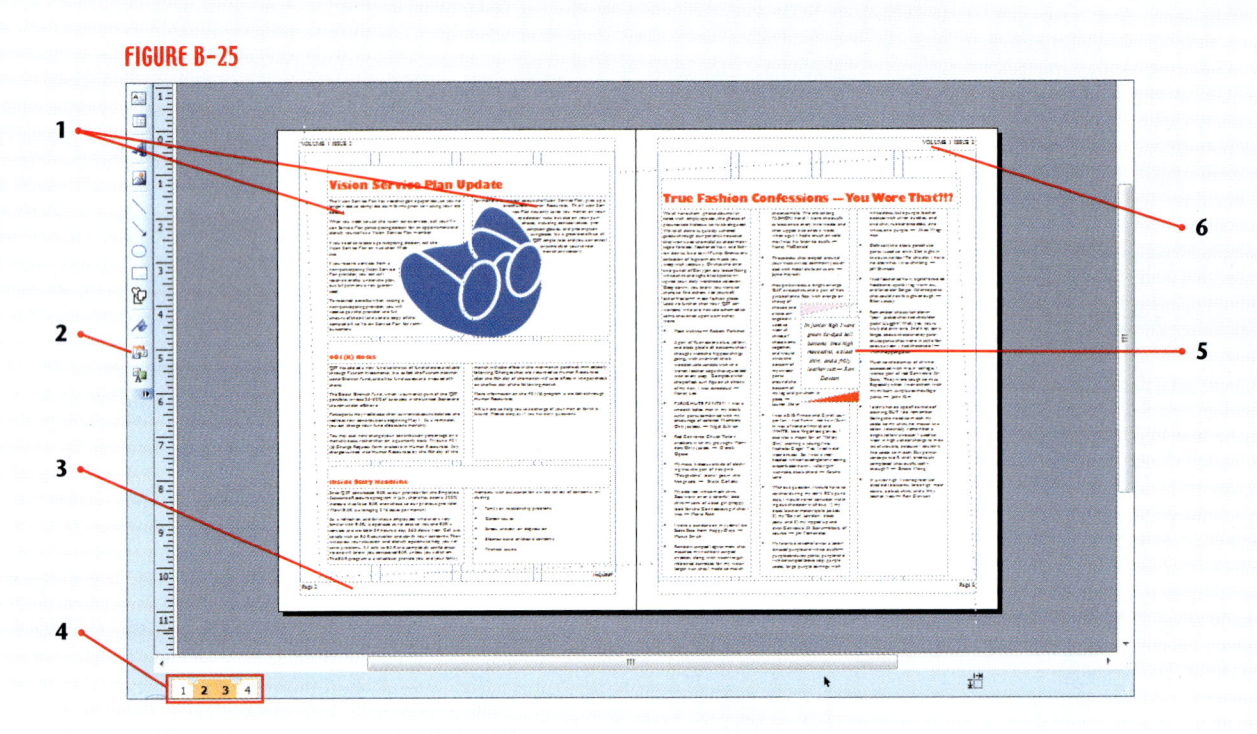

FIGURE B-25

Match each term with the statement that best describes it.

7. Master page
8. Data source
9. Baseline guides
10. Send to Back
11. Sidebar
12. Wrapping
13. Autoflow
14. Header

a. The layer where you place objects that you want to appear on every page
b. Text that relates to a story and is used to capture the reader's eye
c. Feature that flows text from one text box to another
d. The flow of text around an object, such as a clip art image or pull quote
e. A file, such as a database or spreadsheet, that provides merged information
f. Information that appears at the top of every page of a publication
g. Nonprinting lines that indicate where text lines start
h. Command used to send an object behind a stack of objects

▼ CONCEPTS REVIEW (CONTINUED)

Multiple Choice

15. In Publisher, a story is _____.
    a. Text aligned in rows and columns
    b. An article
    c. A box with text that relates to an article
    d. A box containing text
16. A _____ is a nonprinting line used to align text and graphics.
    a. Margin
    b. Scroll bar
    c. Ruler guide
    d. Layer

▼ SKILLS REVIEW

1. **Create columns of text.**
    a. Start Publisher, open the file Rental.pub from the drive and folder where you store your Data Files, then save the file as **Rental yourname.**
    b. Select the text box beneath the heading About Us, open the Format Text Box dialog box, click Columns on the Text Box tab to change the number of columns in this text box to 2, with .14" of space in between, then click OK in all open dialog boxes.
2. **Work with overflow text.**
    a. Select the empty text box below the Why Rent a Computer text box, insert the file PB B-4.docx, then click No when asked if you want to use autoflow.
    b. Connect the text box containing PB B-4.docx text to the empty text box in column 2 on page 2, then connect the text box in column 2 on page 2 to the empty text box in column 3 on page 2.
    c. Go to page 1. Insert a Continued on notice at the end of the text box in column 3, then insert a Continued from notice at the beginning of the text box in column 2 on page 2.
3. **Use guides.**
    a. Go to page 1. Create grid guides for three columns.
    b. In column 1 on page 1, increase the width of the text box containing the two-column text so that the right side of the text box is aligned with the blue layout guide and the left side is ⅛" from the edge of the page.
    c. Drag the lower-middle handle of the text box up to the 4" mark on the vertical ruler.
4. **Create picture captions.**
    a. In column 2 on page 1, insert a picture caption in the white space below the graphic element at the top of the page. Choose the Thin Frame design.
    b. Resize and move the picture so that its top edge is at the 2" mark on the vertical ruler, and its bottom edge is at the 5½" mark on the vertical ruler.
    c. Replace the placeholder graphic with a picture of a computer from the Clip Art task pane, then replace the placeholder caption text with **Don't buy — rent!**
    d. Change the font of the picture caption to 14-point Book Antiqua, bold, and center-aligned.
5. **Create headers and footers.**
    a. Insert a header at the top of the second column that contains this text: **Visit us at www.coronadocomputerrentals.com!** (*Hint*: Click View on the menu bar, then click Header and Footer.)
    b. Insert a footer at the bottom of the second column that contains this text: **Call Coronado Computer Rentals today at (713) 555-9988!**
    c. Verify that the footer and header text is center-aligned, format the footer and header text in 10-point Book Antiqua and italic, then close Master Page view.

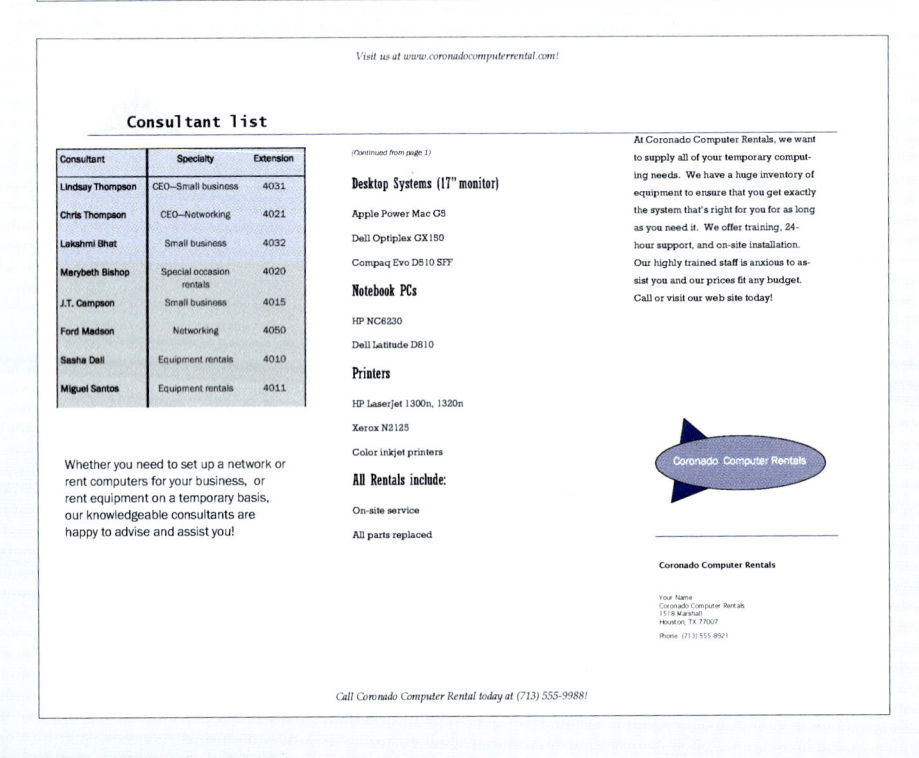

▼ SKILLS REVIEW (CONTINUED)

6. **Wrap text around objects.**

   a. Go to page 1, select the photo in column 1 and move it up into the paragraph of text, so it is centered between the two columns of text and its top edge is at the 2¼" mark on the vertical ruler. Choose the square text wrapping option.

   b. Go to the story in column 3 of page 1, then insert a pull quote using the Design Box design.

   c. Resize the pull quote to 1.00 × 1.500.

   d. Replace the placeholder text with **Always have a state-of-the-art system at your fingertips**, then format the text in 9-point Book Antiqua. Refer to Figure B-26, position and resize the pull quote frame as needed so that the text wraps as seen in the figure and so the story ends with the same line of text.

FIGURE B-26

▼ SKILLS REVIEW (CONTINUED)

7. **Layer and group objects.**
   a. In the workspace to the right of the brochure, create the Coronado Computer Rentals logo by assembling the Coronado Computer Rentals text with the purple oval and the blue triangle. Use the logo at the top of page 1 as a model.
   b. Use the Order buttons as necessary to complete this task. When the logo is assembled correctly, group the items and move the logo to just above the address on page 2.
   c. Go to page 2, then type your name in column 2 above the address.
   d. Proofread and spell check all stories, adjust text boxes as needed to accommodate stories, save your changes, then print and close the publication.

8. **Merge information from a data source.**
   a. In order to create a cover sheet that can be tri-folded with the mailing addresses on it, start a new blank publication using the Letter 8.5 × 11" template.
   b. Change the task pane to the Mail Merge task pane, use Sheet1$ from PB B-5.xls from your Data Files as the data source and choose to add all of the recipients.
   c. Click Address block in the task pane, then accept the default settings in the Insert Address Block dialog box.
   d. Use the Measurement toolbar to position and size the address block so that x = 3, y = 3, width = 2, height = 1.
   e. Preview each record in the publication to make sure the text fits in the address block, then complete the merge to a new publication. (*Hint*: Your publication should have four pages.) Save it as **Addresses**, then close the publication. Close the template without saving changes, then exit Publisher.

▼ INDEPENDENT CHALLENGE 1

You are a travel agent with Escape Travel. You are in charge of creating a brochure on vacations to Nova Scotia. You started the brochure a few days ago. You have received additional marketing text and you are ready to add the finishing touches.

a. Start Publisher, open the file Nova Scotia.pub from the drive and folder where you store your Data Files, save the file as **Nova Scotia yourname**, then add layout grid guides for three columns.
b. On page 2, insert the Data File PB B-6.docx from the drive and folder where you store your Data Files into the two empty columns. Do not use autoflow. (*Hint*: Connect the text boxes.)
c. Insert a picture caption in column 2 of page 1. Choose a picture frame that you like and change the placeholder text to **Don't wait to get away!** Format the caption text in 11-point Arial Black. Replace the picture with a map of Nova Scotia from the Clip Art task pane. (*Hint*: Search for Nova Scotia.)
d. Insert a right-aligned footer with the text **Call Escape Travel at (207) 555-0761 for more information**, then create a left-aligned header that contains your name. Adjust the header and footer so they appear only in column 3.

Advanced Challenge Exercise
- Create a logo using a text box, AutoShape, and Clip Art image.
- Experiment with layering orders and grouping to position the logo to your liking.
- Place the logo in column 2 on page 1.

e. Proofread, spell check, save, and print the publication.

▼ INDEPENDENT CHALLENGE 2

You are the development director for the Walden Pond Arts Academy. You have partially completed a brochure announcing the annual fundraiser. You need to finish formatting and placing objects in the publication.

a. Start Publisher, and open the file Fundraiser.pub from the drive and folder where you store your Data Files, then save the file as **Fundraiser yourname**.

b. Replace the text <name> in the text boxes in columns 2 and 3 on page 1 with **Walden Pond Arts Academy**.

c. In column 1 on page 1, replace the text Back Panel Heading with **Live Onstage**. In the text box below this heading, insert two pieces of clip art that illustrate the paragraph text. Resize the graphics to appropriate sizes and specify the text wrapping of your choice.

d. In column 1 on page 2, insert PB B-7.docx in the text box below Our annual fundraising gala!, increase the size of the text box by aligning the right edge with the grid guide, then format the text into two columns.

e. Insert any pull quote frame centered between the two columns of text. Use the Carla Davis quote from the paragraph, and format the text in 9-point Century, italic, and center-aligned. Reduce the size of the pull quote box to 1" tall by 1" wide. Adjust the text box so that the two-column text is balanced across columns. (*Hint*: Drag the bottom of the text box up until the text is evenly distributed.)

Advanced Challenge Exercise

- Rotate one of the inserted clip art images using the green rotation handle.
- Edit the wrap points on one of the inserted clip art images.
- Insert a custom drop cap in both the Gala and Live Onstage stories. Readjust the text boxes as needed.

f. In the top text box in column 2 on page 1, replace the text "<designer> for" with your name, proofread, spell check, make any other adjustments, save, print, and close the publication.

▼ INDEPENDENT CHALLENGE 3

You own a small novelty store and you need to create a two-page brochure to promote your new summer items. You use the Mail and Catalog Merge features to create a catalog that uses an Excel spreadsheet as a data source. You format the fields so that the fonts and positions are attractive and legible.

a. Start Publisher, open a new blank publication using the first size A4 template, then choose Catalog Merge from the Mailings and Catalogs option on the Tools menu.

b. Select PB B-8.xls from the drive and folder where you store your Data Files as the data source, select Sheet1$, then click OK.

c. In the Catalog Merge Product List table, sort the items in ascending order by price, then click OK. (*Hint*: Click the Price column head, and select the sort order.)

d. Insert all fields, making sure that the Photo field is inserted as a photo field.

e. Position and resize the text boxes and photo field in any order you wish.

f. Format the fonts and insert at least one filled AutoShape behind a text box.

g. Preview the catalog, merge it to a new publication, then save the publication as **Toy Catalog** to the drive and folder where you store your Data Files.

h. Add a footer that includes your name, and then add a WordArt title above the work area canvas.

i. Proofread and spell check, save the publication, print, close it, then close the template without saving changes.

▼ REAL LIFE INDEPENDENT CHALLENGE

You want to create a two-page flyer that announces a service you can offer to friends, colleagues, fellow students, or neighbors. Include a story that flows to several text boxes, a graphic that you can add a caption to, and a pull quote from your story. Create a logo for your service.

a. Start a new publication, select brochure as the publication type, choosing a two-page design template and your choice of color schemes and font schemes.

b. Using a word processing program, type a 200-word story that describes your service. Include quotes from satisfied customers.

c. Insert the article into a first text box, then connect that text box to the next text box, and continue to do so until all of the text from the article is placed in the brochure.

d. Insert a pull quote design in the story. Size and place the pull quote placeholder as you wish, wrap the story text around it, and then add a quote from a satisfied customer.

e. Add a graphic to the brochure. Size and place it as you wish, wrap the text around it if necessary, then add a caption.

f. Create a logo by using AutoShapes and Clip Art, and by layering and rotating the objects. When your logo is done, group all of the pieces together. Place the logo somewhere on the front page of the brochure.

g. Make any other formatting changes you wish, replace remaining placeholder text, and delete extra placeholder graphics and text boxes until you are satisfied with your publication. Be sure your name is somewhere on the brochure.

h. Save your publication as **My Service Flyer** to the drive and folder where you store your Data Files, then spell check, print, and close the publication. A sample service flyer is shown in Figure B-27.

FIGURE B-27

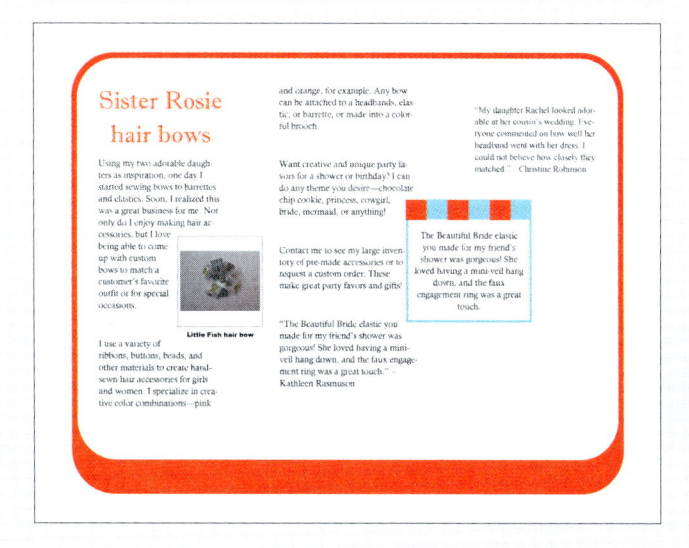

▼ VISUAL WORKSHOP

Create the advertisement for the play shown in Figure B-28. Use the Floating Oval Event Flyer, the Peach color scheme, and the Perspective font scheme. Delete the photograph placeholder. Group the text boxes containing date, time, location, and contact information, and then move them into the position shown in Figure B-28. Replace the placeholder clip art with the clip art image of Romeo and Juliet. (*Hint*: Search for Romeo.) Delete the remaining placeholders and add text as shown in the top of Figure B-28. Add your name to the contact information. Delete the placeholders in the black box at the bottom of the flyer. Create a new text box over the black box, then insert the text file PB B-9.docx from the drive and folder where you store your Data Files in the new text box. Be sure the inserted text is formatted using white, and make the text box two columns. (*Hint*: Click inside the text box, press [Ctrl][A] to select all the text, then change the font color to white.) Format the text in the text box as Franklin Gothic Heavy 12 pt. Insert a pull quote, choosing the Linear Accent pull quote design from the Design Gallery and using the Fill Color button on the Formatting toolbar to add color to the frame. Move, format, and resize objects as necessary to make your flyer look like Figure B-28. Save your publication with the name **Play flyer.pub** to the drive and folder where you store your Data Files.

FIGURE B-28

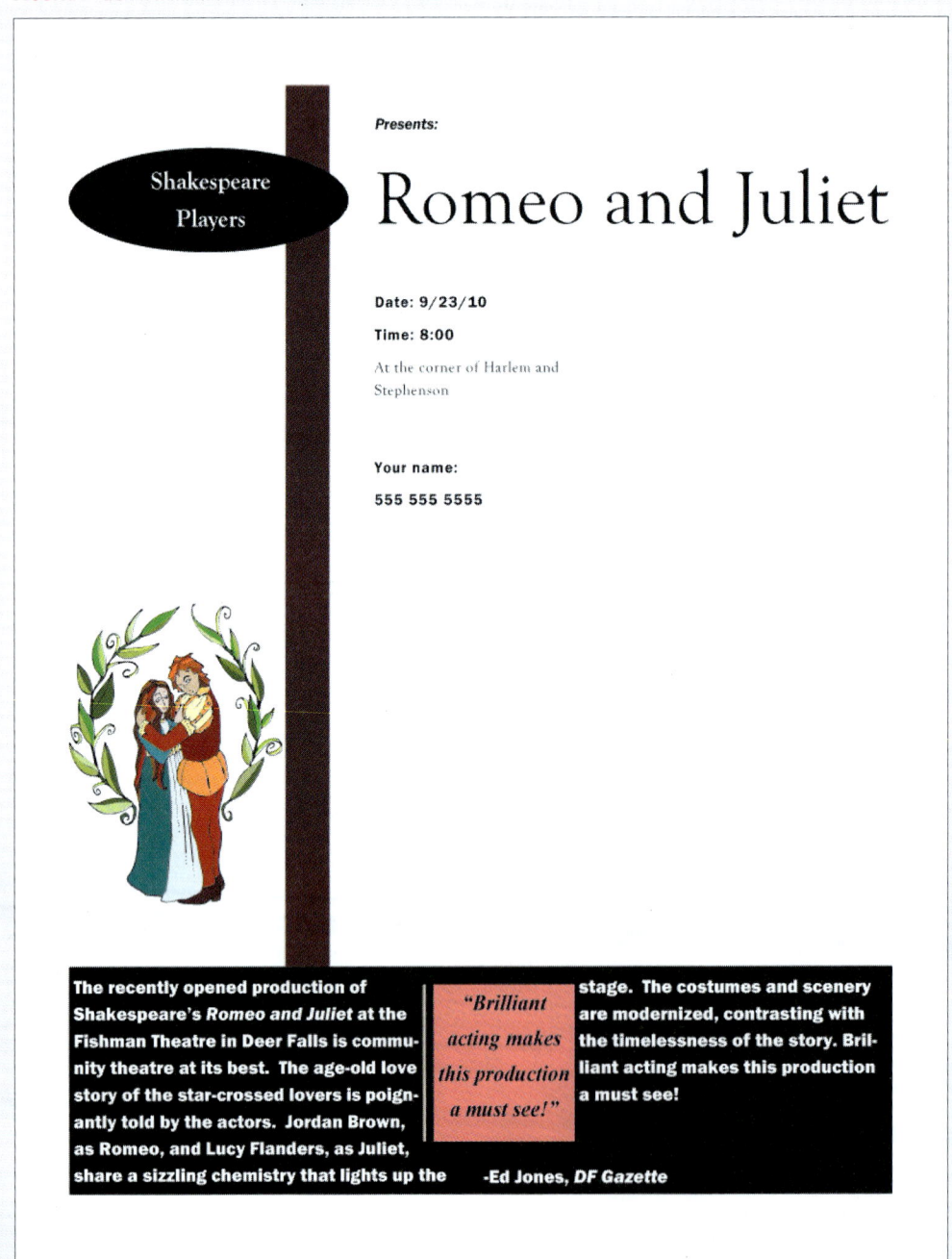

UNIT C
Publisher 2007

Creating a Web Publication

Files You Will Need:
PB C-1.jpg
PB C-2.docx
PB C-3.pub
PB C-4.jpg
PB C-5.docx
PB C-6.pub
PB C-7.docx
PB C-8.docx
PB C-9.docx

Publisher lets you create Web pages quickly and easily. Publisher provides many tools that facilitate the development of Web pages. You can start with a premade design and customize it to meet your needs. You can also convert an existing publication to a layout suitable for the Web. Juan Ramirez, the personnel director for QST, asks you to use Publisher to create a two-page Web site, *InQuest Online*. You will use one of the Web site designs available from the Publication Gallery to create the Web site. You will also convert the most recent issue of *InQuest* to a Web layout.

OBJECTIVES

Understand and plan Web publications

Create a new Web publication

Format a Web publication

Modify a Web form

Add form controls

Preview a Web publication

Convert a Web publication to a Web site

Send a publication as an e-mail

Understanding and Planning Web Publications

The **World Wide Web**, or simply the **Web**, is a collection of electronic documents available to people around the world through the **Internet**, a global computer network. **Web pages** are the documents that make up the Web. A group of associated Web pages is known as a **Web site**. Anyone with Internet access can create Web pages and Web sites and then post them to a network, such as the Internet or a company intranet. **Web browser** software allows anyone to view Web sites. All Web pages are written in a common programming language called **Hypertext Markup Language (HTML)**. With Publisher, you can create a **Web publication**—a publication that you later convert to either a Web page or a Web site—without needing to know HTML. You use your Publisher skills to design and create the content for the Web site, and then let Publisher create the HTML code. Figure C-1 shows how one Web page created using a Publisher Web site template looks when previewed in a Web browser.

DETAILS

An overview of Web components you need to consider when creating a Web site follows:

- Planning is an important first step when designing a Web site. A detailed outline of the entire site, also known as a **storyboard**, should include a description of each Web page, which elements should appear on each Web page as well as the placement of the elements, and any special graphics you might need. You plan which features you will add to your Web site. Figure C-2 shows a sketch of your plan.

- A **home page** is the introductory page of a Web site, which usually gives an overview of the site's contents and provides easy access to other pages in the Web site.

- A **hyperlink**, or simply a **link**, is specially formatted text or a graphic that a user can click to open an associated Web page. Links serve as the foundation of the Web. Almost all Web pages are connected to other Web pages through links. Each Web page can contain many links to many different Web sites. Your storyboard should indicate all links on a Web page. You will place a welcome paragraph on the home page that describes the features of *InQuest Online*, and then you will create the phrase *feedback form* as a link to the Web page with the feedback form.

- When your Web site has multiple pages, it's important to provide users with an easy and consistent method of navigating between them. A **navigation bar** provides a set of links to the most important pages in a Web site, displayed in the same location on each page. When you create a Web publication using one of the Web site designs in the Publication Gallery, Publisher can automatically create one or more navigation bars on the main pages and update them as you add or delete pages. You will insert navigation bars at the top and bottom of both pages, making it easier for viewers to jump quickly to where they want to go.

- In addition to elements such as links, navigations bars, and graphics, a Web page can contain a form. **Forms** are Web page elements that allow users to input information, such as their name, address, and credit card number. Much like its paper counterpart, a **Web form** can include areas for text input, such as name and address, and provide an easy way for a user to submit information. Unlike its paper counterpart, a Web form can include text boxes, lists, and buttons that users click to submit information via the Web. Many organizations that do business online allow users to select products or services using a Web form. You will add a feedback form to the *InQuest Online* Web site, so users can provide comments to a specific question.

FIGURE C-1: Preview of Web page created using Publisher in a Web browser

Navigation bar provides links to other Web pages

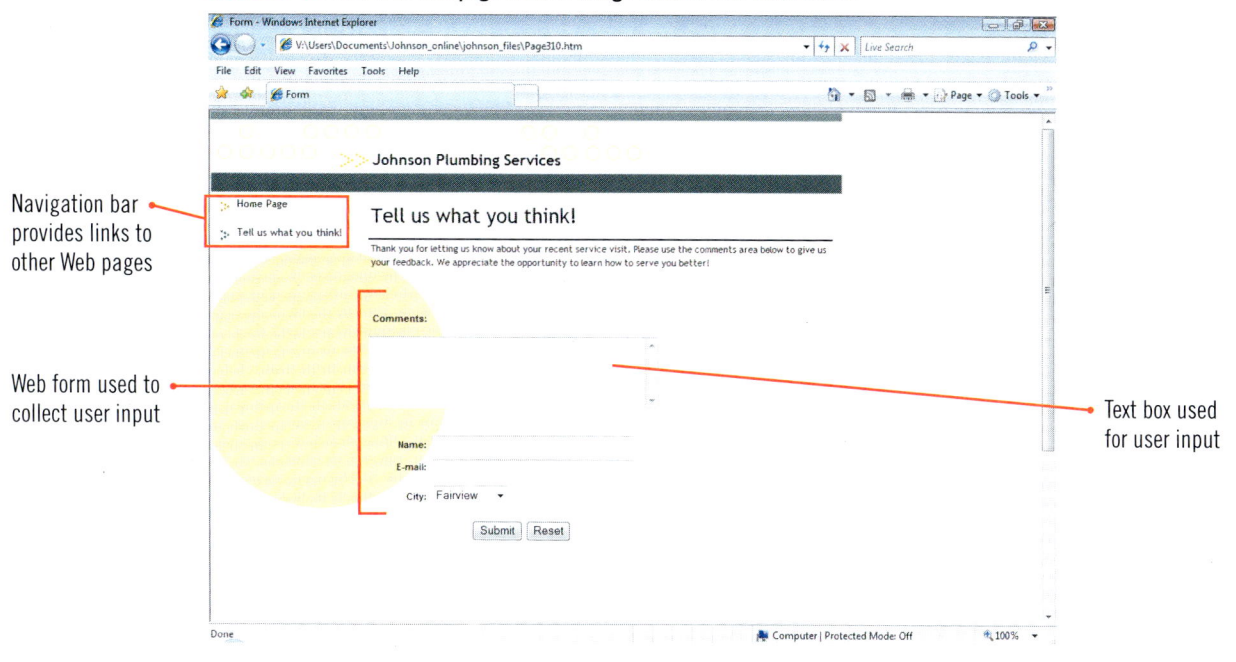

Web form used to collect user input

Text box used for user input

FIGURE C-2: Your content, layout, and graphics plan for *InQuest Online*

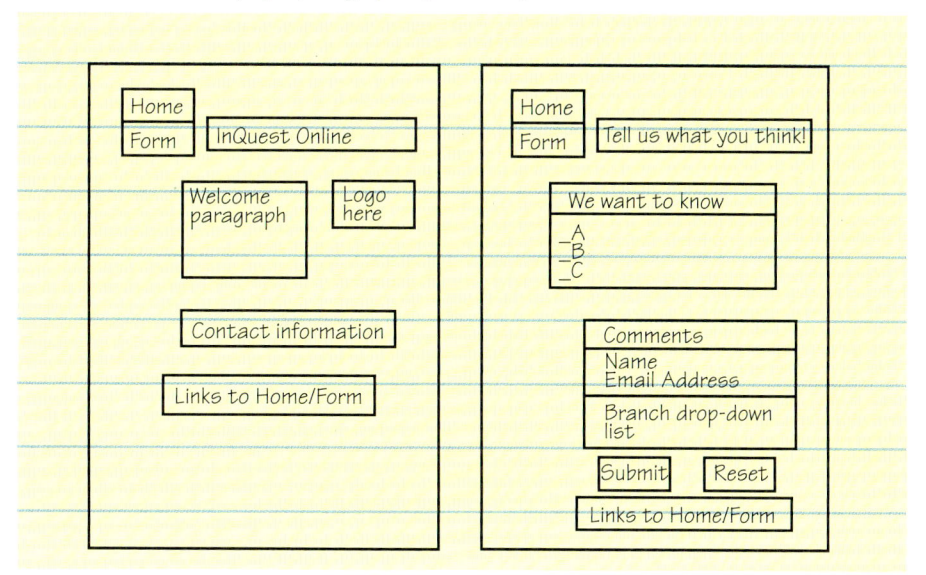

Publishing a Web site

If you want to make your Web site available to all users of the Internet, you need to publish it. When you publish your Web site, you post your Web site files on a Web server, known as a **host**. Your Web site files are stored on the Web server, and since a Web server is always connected to the Web, your pages are available to anyone with Web access. Some commercial Internet service providers (ISPs) and schools provide space for their subscribers or students to post a Web site as part of their account agreement. Additionally, several Internet companies offer free space for Web pages on their servers; in exchange, they place an advertisement on each page in your Web site. All Web servers impose limits on the amount of data you can store; be sure to check these limits before publishing your Web site. Remember though, a graphics-heavy site can quickly mushroom in size, so it is important to use graphics sparingly in your Web pages if your allotted space is small.

Creating a Web Publication   Publisher 55

Creating a New Web Publication

You can use one of the Web site designs in the Publication Gallery to create a single Web page, or a Web site containing several pages. If you want to create a Web presence but have little information to publicize, you may be able to fit all the information on a single Web page. However, if you need more than one page, then you want to be sure all design elements, such as the font scheme, the color scheme, and the design, are applied consistently to all Web pages in the Web site. If you use a Publisher Web site template, the design elements are automatically applied consistently to all Web pages in the Web site. The QST Web site will eventually have many pages that link to past issues of *InQuest*. For now, though, you use a Web site design in the Publication Gallery to create a home page and a feedback form.

STEPS

QUICK TIP
If the Web Tools toolbar opens during this lesson, close it.

1. **Start Publisher, then click Web Sites in the Publication Types list**

2. **Scroll down the Publication Gallery, click the Mobile thumbnail in the Classic Designs section, then verify that the Vertical and Bottom icon is selected as the Navigation bar type in the Options section of the right pane**
   A navigation bar will be placed at the top left (Vertical navigation bar) and the bottom (Horizontal navigation bar) of every page of your site, providing a consistent look and feel to the site. The Publication Gallery shows the choices you've made, as shown in Figure C-3.

3. **Deselect the Use Easy Web Wizard check box if necessary, then click Create**
   A new publication opens based on the Mobile template. The Format Publication task pane provides access to page options, color schemes, font schemes, and other Web site options.

4. **Under the Web Site Options section of the task pane, click Insert a page, click Forms in the Insert Web Page dialog box, click Response Form, then click OK**
   A second page, which includes a response form, is added to the Web site. In addition to forms, Publisher includes templates for other types of specialized Web pages as listed in the Insert Web Page dialog box. Table C-1 provides a list of some of the different kinds of specialized Web pages you can add using a Publisher template.

5. **Click Color Schemes in the task pane, then scroll to and click Plum from the Apply a color scheme list**
   The colors change throughout the Web site; for example, the bar at the top of the page is now plum.

6. **Click Font Schemes in the task pane, scroll up if necessary, click Archival in the Apply a font scheme list, close the task pane, zoom to 50%, then click the Page 1 Navigation button and scroll to see all content on the page**
   The Archival font scheme uses the Georgia font. Publisher reformats the Web page so that the placeholder text font is Georgia, sometimes with bold or italic applied. Compare your page 1 to Figure C-4.

7. **Save the file as qstweb to the drive and folder where you store your Data Files**
   The file is saved in Publisher publication format with a .pub file extension.

FIGURE C-3: Web site designs in Publication Gallery

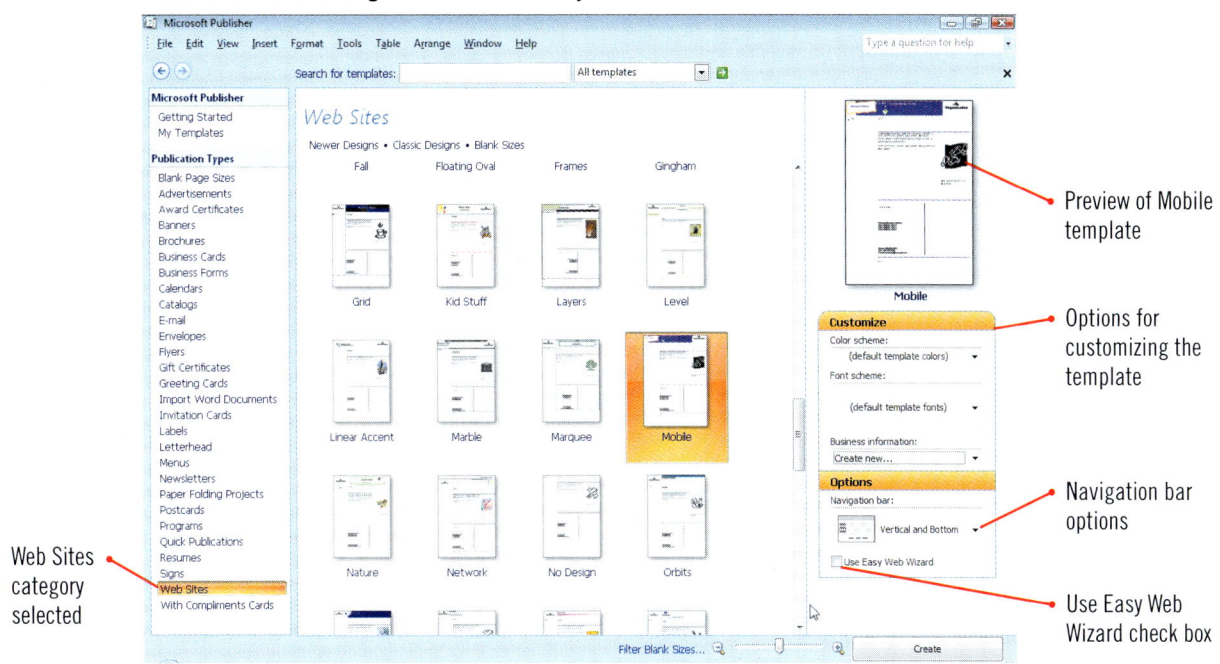

- Web Sites category selected
- Preview of Mobile template
- Options for customizing the template
- Navigation bar options
- Use Easy Web Wizard check box

FIGURE C-4: Customized home page

- Archival font scheme—Georgia font applied to text
- Vertical navigation bar
- Page 2 contains form template
- Plum color scheme applied to elements
- Bottom navigation bar

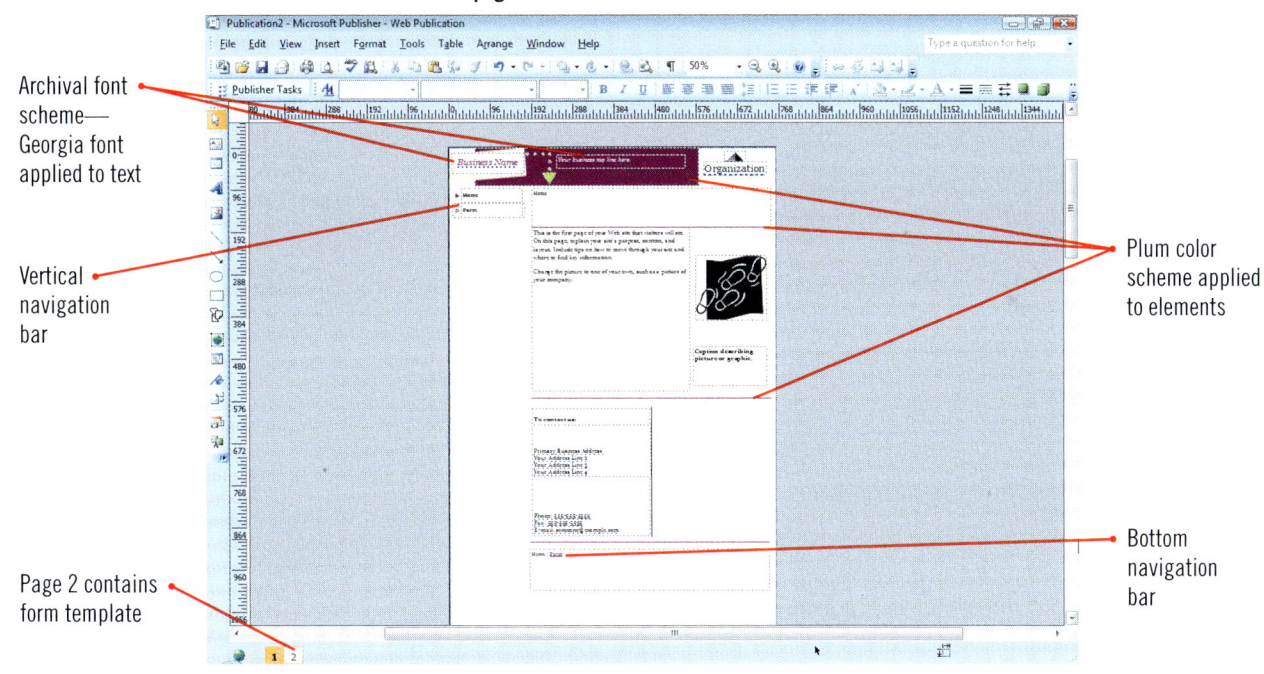

TABLE C-1: Some types of Web pages you can create using the Insert a page command

Web page type	useful for
FAQ	A list of frequently asked questions about your organization
Calendar	A list of upcoming important dates/events with or without links to more information
Event	Information about an upcoming event
Special Offer	Details of a sale or discount
Photos	Presenting photos with captions, links, or in a gallery
Related Links	Descriptions and links for other relevant Web sites or pages within the site

Creating a Web Publication

UNIT C
Publisher 2007

Formatting a Web Publication

After you create a Web publication using a design from the Publication Gallery, you need to personalize the contents and adjust the formatting to meet your needs. In addition to the standard formatting options available for all publications, Publisher offers several tools specifically for use in Web publications. Table C-2 shows some of the special toolbar buttons and explains how to use them. You start customizing your Web publication by changing the default home page text and graphics.

STEPS

> **TROUBLE**
> The placeholder text may differ if the Business Information dialog box has been completed for your installation of Publisher.

1. Zoom in and scroll as necessary, triple-click the Business Name placeholder text in the rectangular frame in the upper-left corner of the page, type Quest Specialty Travel, then click outside the frame

2. Select the text Your business tag line here. in the plum banner at the top of the page, then type What's up at QST?

3. Select the Home placeholder text in the large frame under the text you just typed, type InQuest Online, select the text, then resize the text to 36 pt

> **TROUBLE**
> Make sure you delete the picture caption text box and not just the text inside of it.

4. Select the picture caption text box beneath the footprints, press [Delete], right-click the clip art of the footprints, point to Change Picture, click From File, select the file PB C-1.jpg from the drive and folder where you store your Data Files, then click Insert

   The QST logo appears in the picture frame.

5. Select both paragraphs of body text, right-click, point to Change Text, click Text File, select the file PB C-2.docx from the drive and folder where you store your Data Files, then click OK

   The new text now appears in the text box. Compare your screen with Figure C-5.

6. Select the text Feedback Form in the second paragraph, then click the Insert Hyperlink button on the Standard toolbar

   The Insert Hyperlink dialog box opens.

7. Click the Place in This Document icon, click Page 2. Form in the Select a place in this document list, then click OK

   The text "Feedback Form" appears underlined and in color, indicating that it is a link. Web site visitors can click the Feedback Form link to open the Web page that contains the feedback form.

> **TROUBLE**
> If the text boxes differ, it's because your business information has been set up. Use Figure C-6 as a guide to delete one text box, then add and format text.

8. Click the pyramid image to select the Organization logo, press [Delete], scroll down to view the To contact us information, select the text box with phone numbers, press [Delete], delete the text in the Primary Business Address text box, type the contact information and format the text for QST as shown in Figure C-6, then expand the text box if necessary

9. Save the publication

Publisher 58   Creating a Web Publication

FIGURE C-5: Top section of home page

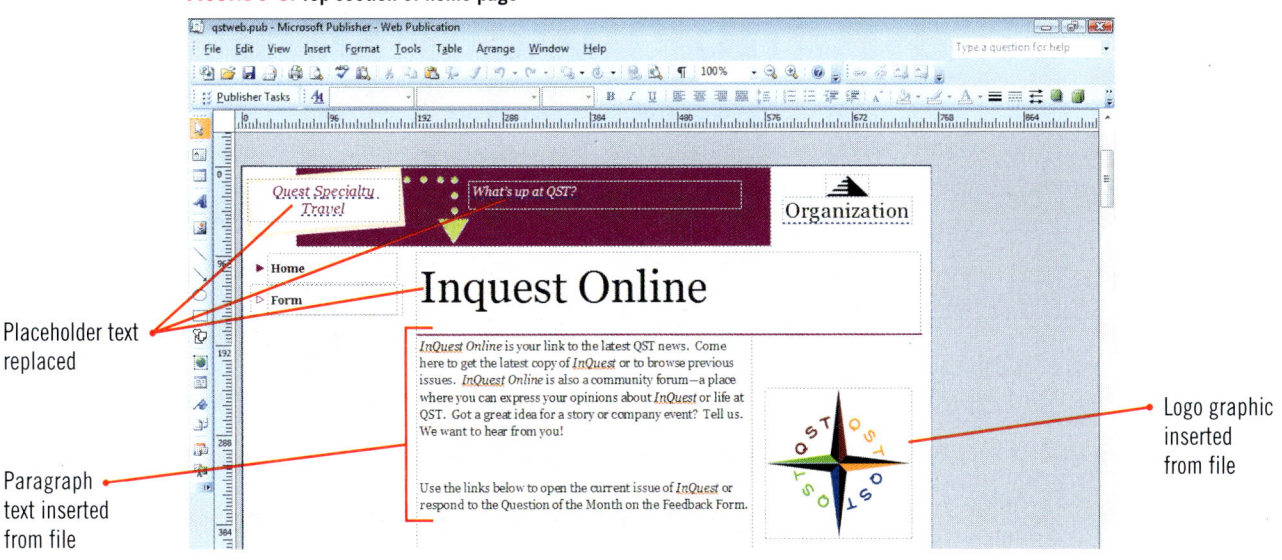

- Placeholder text replaced
- Paragraph text inserted from file
- Logo graphic inserted from file

FIGURE C-6: *InQuest* contact information

- *InQuest* contact information

TABLE C-2: Some Web page formatting options*

option	button	description
Web Page Preview		Opens the current Web page using your system's default Web browser
Insert Hyperlink		Adds a hyperlink to the selected object
Hot Spot		Formats a single graphic with links to multiple Web pages
Form Control		Inserts a form field for user input, such as a text box or check box
HTML Code Fragment		Allows advanced users to add additional HTML code to a specific part of a publication

*These buttons are available on the Web Tools toolbar, and some are available on the Objects toolbar. If a toolbar is not open, you can open it using the Toolbars submenu on the View menu.

Creating a Web Publication   Publisher 59

Publisher 2007

Modifying a Web Form

UNIT C — Publisher 2007

Including a form in a Web page is a great way to encourage users to interact with your Web site. Using forms, you can collect valuable information, such as customer names and addresses, or feedback on a product. The publication's second page contains the feedback form you selected in the Insert Web Page Options dialog box. The response form contains four placeholder questions, a comments text area, and user contact information text boxes. You customize the response form to suit your needs.

STEPS

TROUBLE
Change the banner text to match Figure C-7 if it does not update automatically.

1. **Click the Page 2 Navigation button, then zoom in on the top of the page**
   Text fields at the top reflect the change you made to the corresponding fields on the home page.

2. **Select the pyramid logo, then press [Delete]**

3. **Select the text Response Form, type Tell us what you think!, resize the text to 28 pt, select the Ask readers text box, press [Delete], click Response form title, type We want to know, click Type a description, then type Answer the question below and use the comments area to tell us your opinions about** *Quest Specialty Travel.*
   Compare your screen with Figure C-7.

4. **Click Question 1, type Which job perk is most important to you?, click Answer A, type Summer hours, click Answer B, type On-site childcare, click Answer C, then type Telecommuting policy**
   The question and three choices are complete. To select multiple objects, drag the selection pointer diagonally to create a rectangular shape around the objects. This is called dragging a selection rectangle.

TROUBLE
Be sure to include all parts of each object when dragging a selection rectangle. If your selection box doesn't include all the desired objects or you select too many objects, press [Shift], then click the additional or extraneous objects.

5. **Scroll so the text We want to know is at the top of the window, use the ▷ pointer to drag a selection rectangle around Question 3 and its three answers and Question 4 and its three answers so all eight objects are selected, then press [Delete]**
   You deleted two of the placeholder questions and answer options.

6. **Use the ▷ pointer to drag a selection rectangle around Question 2 and its three answers, then press [Delete]**

7. **Use the ▷ pointer to drag a selection rectangle around the Comments label and the Comments multiline text box to select both objects, drag them up until they are just below Telecommuting policy, click the workspace area, then save your changes**
   Compare your screen with Figure C-8.

Adding multimedia components to a Web publication

Publisher allows you to add multimedia elements to make the site more eye-catching and to make more information available to your viewers. In the Page Options section on the Format Publication task pane, you can select a background fill as well as sound, which plays on the user's browser when the page opens. To insert and format a sound, click the Page Options link on the Format Publication task pane, click Background fill and sound, click Background sound to open the Web Page Options dialog box, then type the location of the sound file you want to use in the Background sound File name text box. You can choose to have the sound loop continuously or play as many times as you specify.

You can add simple animation to a site by inserting an **animated GIF**. GIF stand for graphics interchange file, and is a standard format for displaying images on Web pages. An animated GIF is a short animation that plays repeatedly when opened in a browser. To add GIFs to your Web publication, click Insert on the menu bar, point to Picture, click From File, then type the name and location of the .gif file you want to add. Some .gif files are available in the Clip Organizer.

You can also add video and other objects by selecting Object on the Insert menu, clicking the Create from File option button, then specifying the object's location in the dialog box. Remember, all of these elements increase the size of your Web site and can lengthen the time these files take to open in a Web browser. Be sure to add only those elements that support the Web site message.

FIGURE C-7: Form Page with new heading text

Reflects changes made to home page

Heading text replaces placeholder text

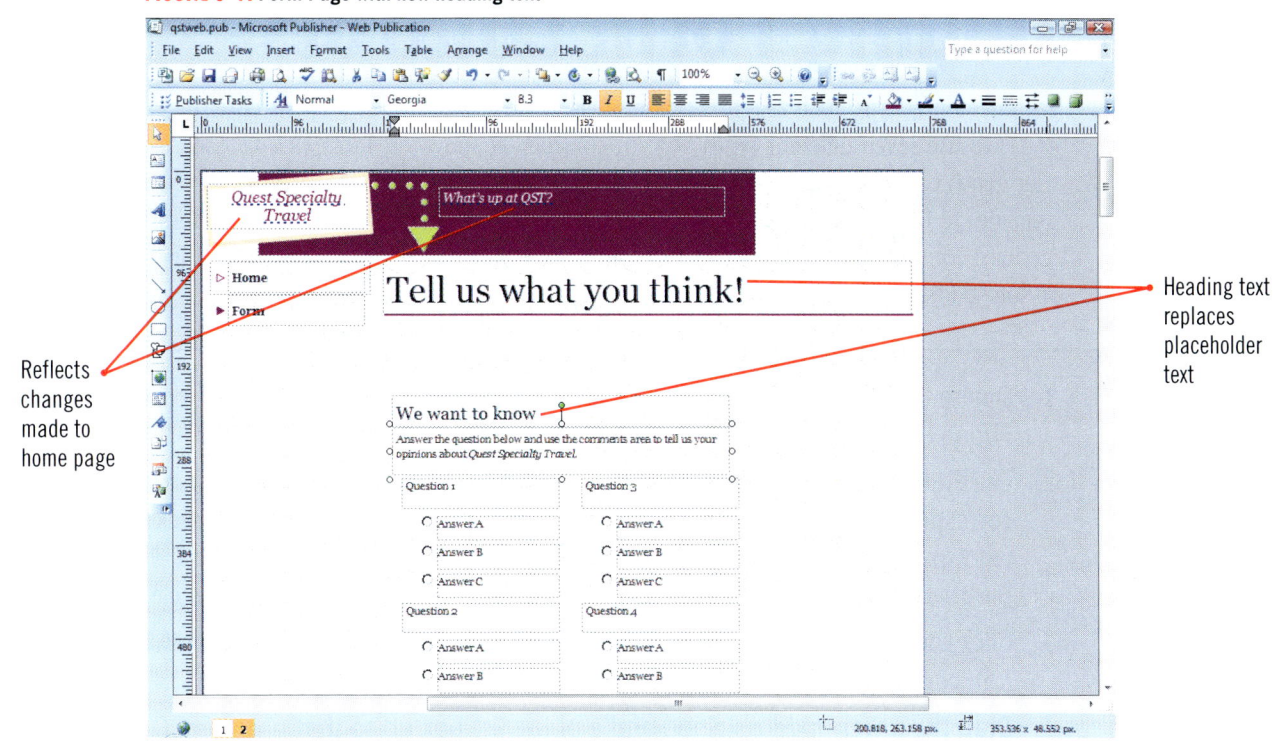

FIGURE C-8: Form page with modified question and comments fields moved

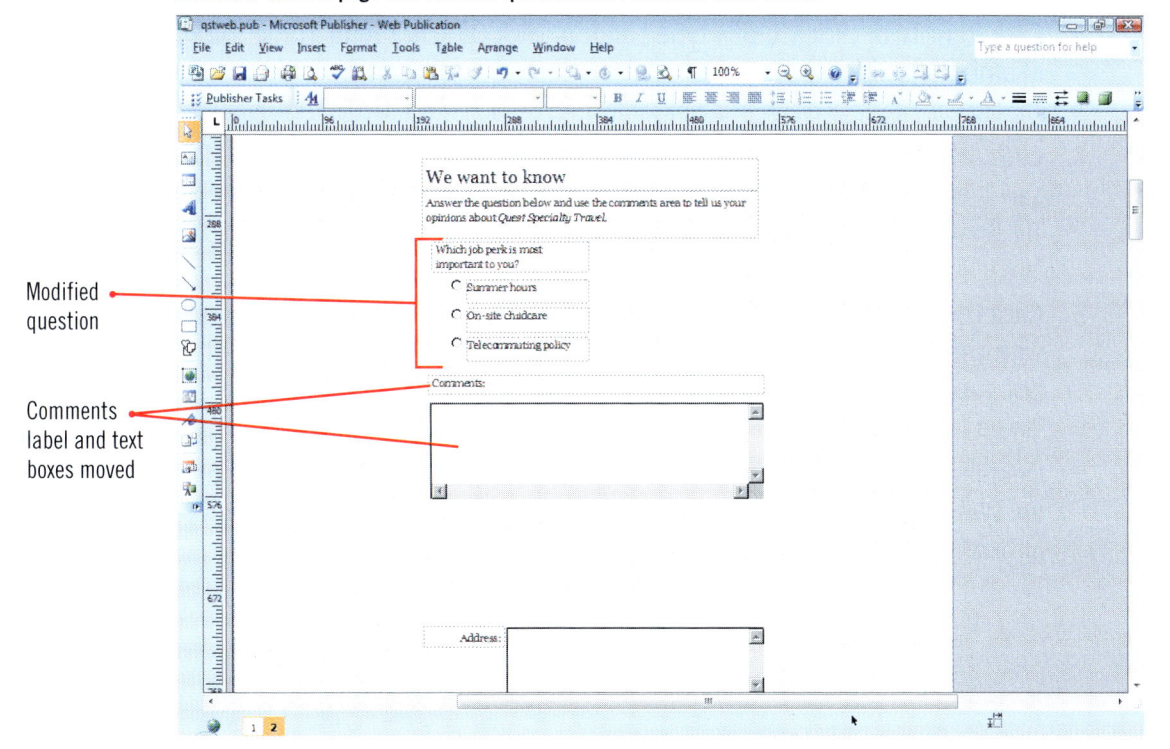

Modified question

Comments label and text boxes moved

Creating a Web Publication

Publisher 61

Adding Form Controls

Each item in a form, such as a text box or a check box, is known as a **form control**. HTML allows Web pages to use seven different types of form controls, as shown in Table C-3, to collect information from users. Each control is usually associated with a text box, which can display a label or question, or provide guidance to the user about the type of information to be collected. You continue to customize the feedback form by modifying and moving form controls and labels. You also add a drop-down list for Web visitors to identify their branch location.

STEPS

1. Delete the text box control and corresponding text label for Address, scroll down, click Phone in the Phone text box, then type Name:

2. Use Figure C-9 as your guide to position the Name and E-mail controls and their corresponding labels, the Submit button, and the Reset button, then click the workspace area

   You deleted and rearranged controls, their corresponding labels, and buttons to better meet your needs.

3. Click the Form Control button on the Objects toolbar, then click List Box

   A list box appears showing placeholders for three items.

4. Drag the lower-middle sizing handle of the list box up so that only Item One appears, then drag the list box to just below the E-mail: text box control

   You modified the list box to show only one item at a time.

5. Double-click the list box, select Item One in the Appearance section of the List Box Properties dialog box, click Modify, type Chicago in the Item text box, click the Not selected option button, then click OK

6. Click Item Two, click Modify, type London, click OK, click Item Three, click Modify, type Miami, then click OK

   The List Box Properties dialog box shows three items: Chicago, London, and Miami.

7. Click Add, type New York in the Item text box, click OK, continue to add the following: San Diego, Sydney, Toronto, and Vancouver, then click OK

   The list box displays the text "Chicago." QST employees who use this form will be able to click the arrow next to the text and select the city where they work.

8. Click the E-mail text box, press and hold [Ctrl], drag to create a copy of the text box with the E-mail label to the left of the list box, select the text E-mail in the text box you just copied, type Branch:, then click the workspace area

   The list box now has the label Branch next to it. Compare your screen with Figure C-10.

TROUBLE
This button will not work unless your Web server is set up to save Web data.

9. Double-click the Submit button, click Form Properties, click the Save the data in a file on my Web server option button, click OK twice, then save your publication

   All data entered by users will be stored in a file on the QST Web server.

FIGURE C-9: Modified form page

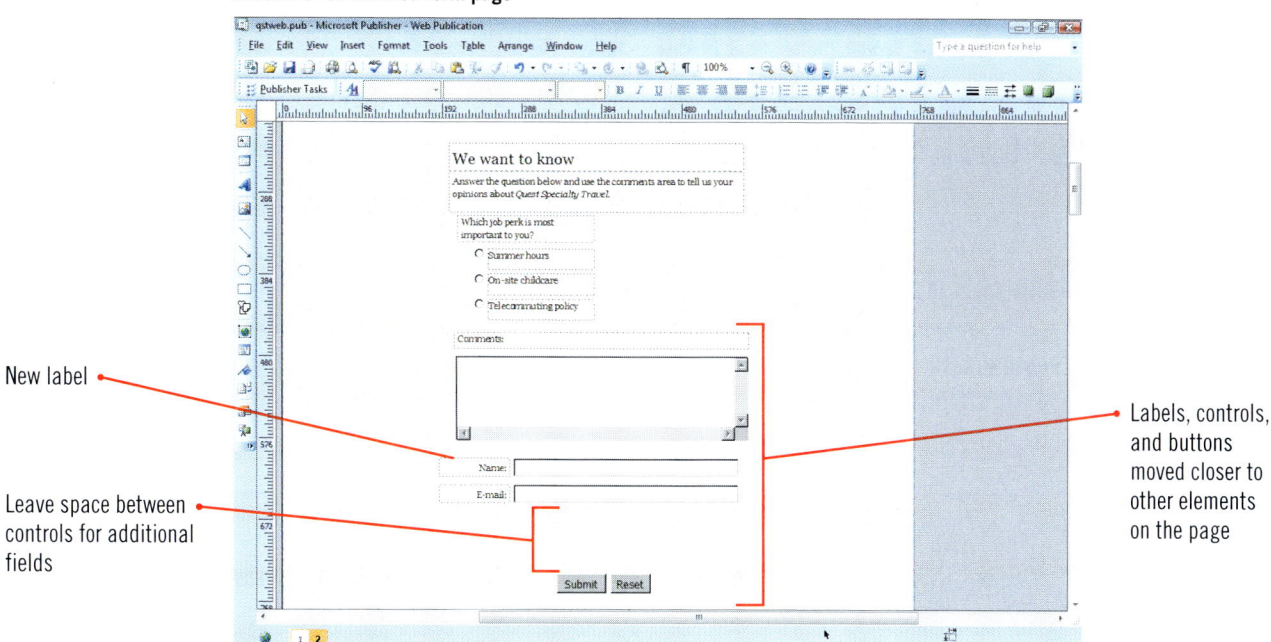

- New label
- Leave space between controls for additional fields
- Labels, controls, and buttons moved closer to other elements on the page

FIGURE C-10: Completed form

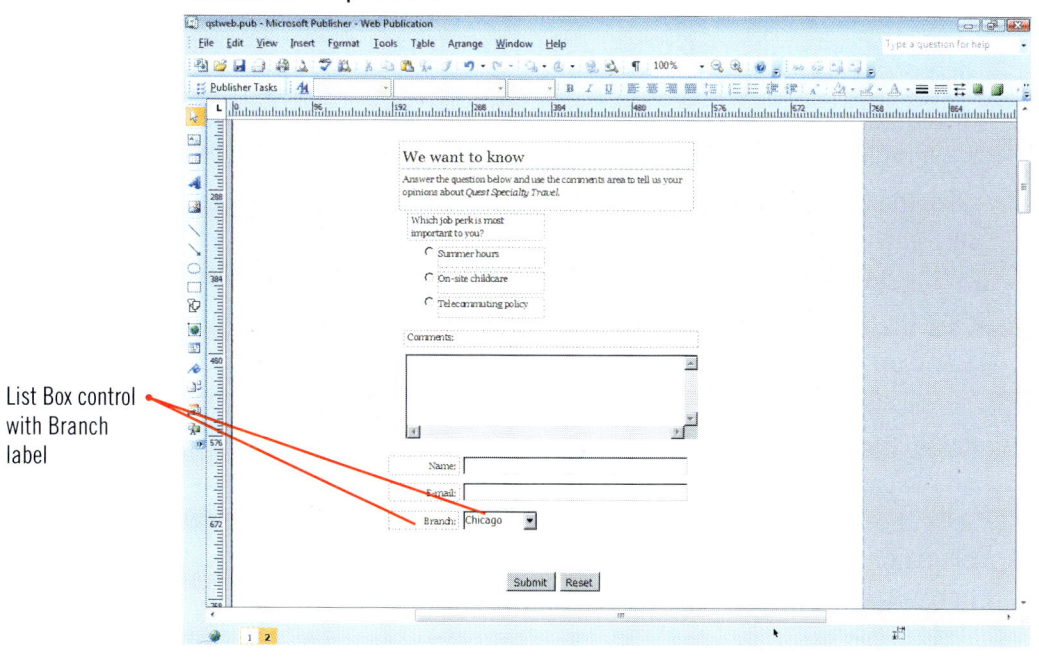

- List Box control with Branch label

TABLE C-3: Web page form controls

control name	uses
Textbox	Short input, such as a name or e-mail address
Text Area	Longer input, such as comments
Checkbox	A question or option that the user can select, such as not being added to a mailing list
Option Button	A list of choices, of which the user should pick a limited number
List Box	A drop-down menu providing a list of choices
Submit Button	A command button, used to submit information entered in the form
Reset Button	A command button, used to clear information from a form

Creating a Web Publication

Previewing a Web Publication

Creating and editing your Web publication in Publisher gives you an idea of the appearance of your final Web site. However, whenever you develop a Web site, it's best to look at the publication in a Web browser before saving it in HTML and making it available on a network, such as the Internet or a company intranet. Because some aspects of the publication can appear differently in a browser, Publisher provides **Web Page Preview**, a tool that lets you preview the publication in a Web browser to ensure that it appears the way you want. Upon review, you can make changes to the publication, if necessary, before publishing it on a network. You preview *InQuest Online* in your browser and make final adjustments.

STEPS

1. **Click the Web Page Preview button on the Standard toolbar, then, when the page opens in your Web browser, click Home on the navigation bar to view the home page, if necessary**

   Publisher creates a temporary version of your Web site in HTML and opens the file in your Web browser, as shown in Figure C-11.

2. **Scroll down the home page to view the entire contents, click Form on the navigation bar at the bottom of the Web page to open the Web page with the form, then scroll to view all the contents of the Web page**

   On each Web page, notice the large gaps between the elements at the top and the bottom. You make adjustments to minimize the amount of white space between elements.

3. **Click the Microsoft Publisher program button on the taskbar to return to Publisher, be sure you are on the Web page with the form, then drag the center-right sizing handle on the question text box to the right so that the question fits on one line**

4. **Click the Page 1 Navigation button of the publication, click the Zoom list arrow on the Standard toolbar, click 50%, then scroll as needed to view the entire Web page**

   You can now view all of the page contents.

> **QUICK TIP**
> Use the Object Position coordinates on the status bar to help you position elements as closely to the given coordinates as possible.

5. **Resize the text box with the text file you imported so that its bottom line is at about 384 on the vertical ruler, delete the vertical black line to the right of the contact information, select the top plum line and two contact information text boxes, drag them so that the plum horizontal line is at about 440 on the vertical ruler, then drag the bottom plum horizontal line and the bottom navigation bar so that the line is at about 664 on the vertical ruler**

   The entire contents of the home page are now closer to the top of the page.

6. **Click the Page 2 Navigation button, use the pointer to drag a selection rectangle around all the objects from the We want to know text box to the Submit and Reset buttons, drag the selected items so that the top of the We want to know text box is at about 192 on the vertical ruler, then drag the bottom plum line and the navigation bar so that the plum line is at about 744 on the vertical ruler**

7. **Save your publication, click , then scroll to view the page**

   The form page appears with all the elements consolidated, as shown in Figure C-12.

8. **Test the links on the navigation bars to view the Web pages, then close the browser**

FIGURE C-11: Preview of home page in Web browser

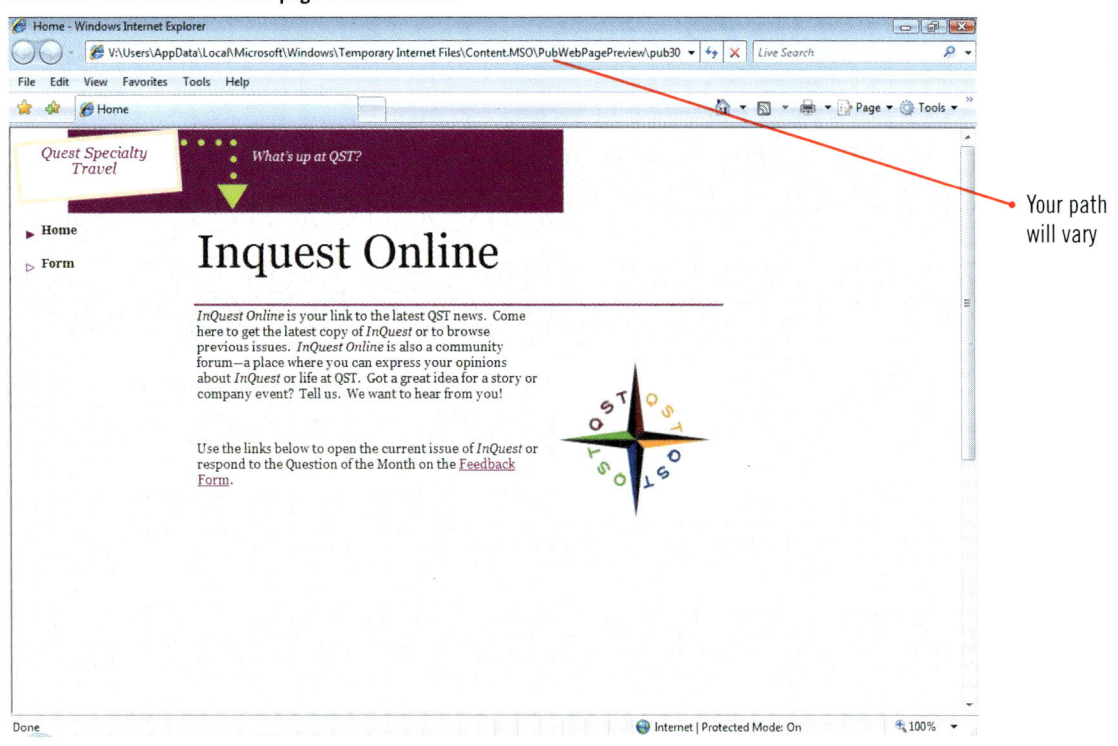

Your path will vary

FIGURE C-12: Preview of form page in Web browser

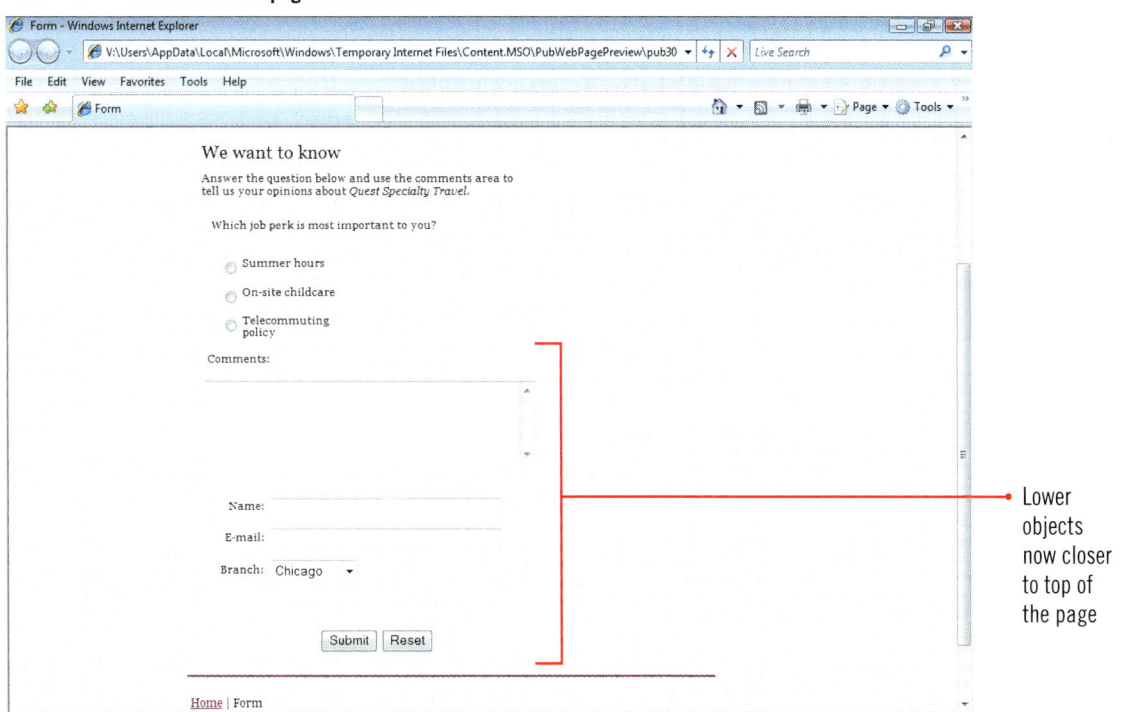

Lower objects now closer to top of the page

Creating a Web Publication

Publisher 65

UNIT C
Publisher 2007

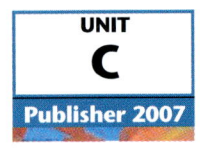

Converting a Web Publication to a Web Site

In your work on the Web site so far, you have edited and saved the publication in the Publisher file format (which has the file extension .pub). When you are satisfied with the publication's appearance and layout, you need to convert the publication to HTML format (which has the file extension .htm). The HTML document you produce can then be published on a network (either the Internet or an intranet) and displayed by Web browsers. You are satisfied with the preview of your Web site in the Web browser and are ready to convert the publication to an HTML document.

STEPS

1. **If necessary, click the Microsoft Publisher program button on the taskbar to return to Publisher**

2. **Click File on the menu bar, then click Publish to the Web**

   The Publish to the Web dialog box opens, as shown in Figure C-13.

   > **TROUBLE**
   > Click OK or close in any alert boxes that open during this lesson.

3. **Navigate to the drive and folder where you store your Data Files, click the Organize list arrow, click New Folder, type qst_on, press [Enter], select index.htm in the File name text box, type qstweb, then click Save**

   A separate folder is created just for this Web site so that all the files, including the graphics for the top and bottom page borders, are grouped together.

4. **Click File on the menu bar, click Close, start Internet Explorer (or your default browser), click File on the Internet Explorer menu bar, click Open, click Browse, open the qst_on folder, click qstweb.htm, click Open, then click OK**

   > **TROUBLE**
   > Right-click a toolbar, then click Menu Bar if necessary.

   The *InQuest Online* Web page, now saved as an HTML file, appears in your default Web browser.

5. **Click the Form link on the navigation bar**

   The second page of the Web site opens, as shown in Figure C-14.

6. **Type your name in the Name text box, click File on the menu bar, click Print, then click Print**

   You printed the form page with your name on it.

7. **Close the browser window**

   You exited the browser, but Publisher is still open.

Formatting Web publications for different audiences

When you create a Web page, you want to make it available to the largest possible audience. Web pages created in Publisher can be viewed in Internet Explorer or Netscape Navigator, Mozilla Firefox, or other browsers. Some features, such as tables and cascading style sheets, may not appear properly if viewed in early versions of these popular browsers. If your site is going to be viewed only on an intranet where all users have Internet Explorer 7.0, you might want to optimize your site and include features that can only be viewed with this version of the browser. However, if your site is being viewed on the Internet by a wide range of users, you will want to make sure that you optimize the site for an earlier browser version. It is important to test your site using a variety of browser versions before making it available to a wide audience to ensure that it can be read by all.

FIGURE C-13: Publish to the Web dialog box

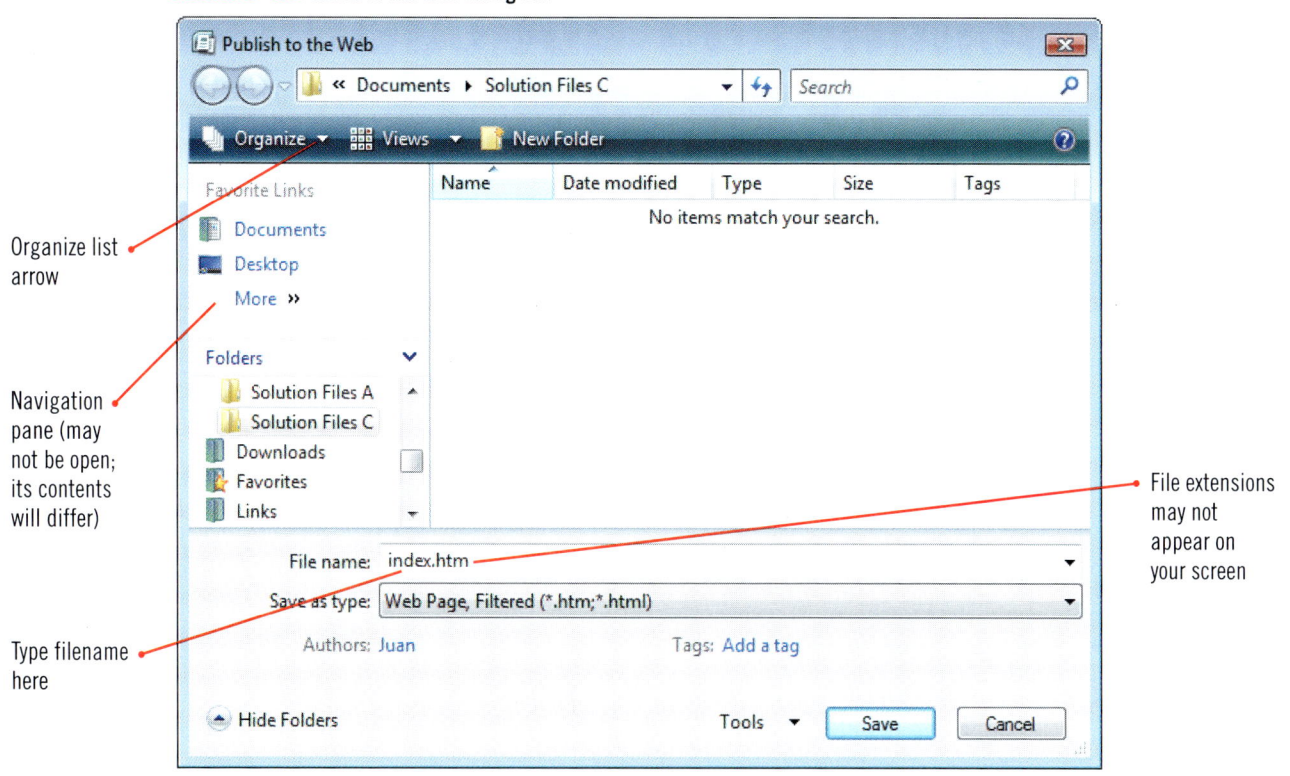

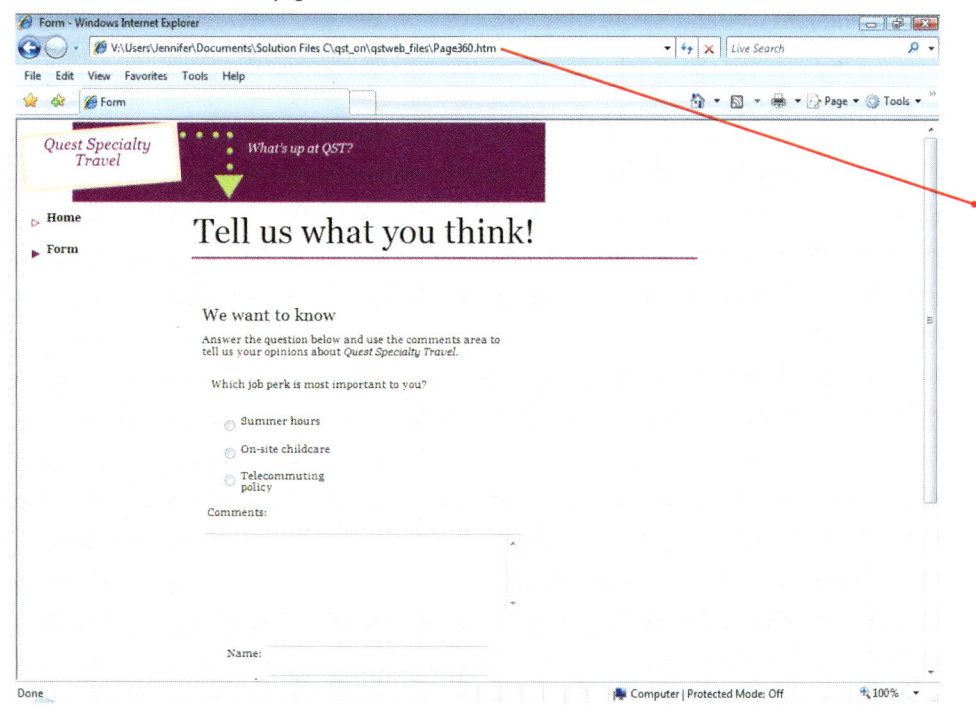

- Organize list arrow
- Navigation pane (may not be open; its contents will differ)
- Type filename here
- File extensions may not appear on your screen

FIGURE C-14: Feedback form page in Web browser

- Your path will differ

Publisher 2007

Creating a Web Publication — Publisher 67

Sending a Publication as an E-mail

UNIT C
Publisher 2007

Using Publisher, you can send a page of a document as an e-mail message or an entire document as an attachment if you have Microsoft Outlook 2007 or Microsoft Outlook Express (version 6.0 or later) as your default e-mail program. This can be an effective way to distribute an electronic newsletter. When converting a publication for e-mail, you should always use the preview feature, and also send a test copy to yourself to check for any formatting issues before sending it to your audience. **Design Checker** can help you identify areas that need to be fixed. Many e-mail programs (although not all) can read e-mails that have formatting, graphics, and links to Web sites. Your recipients can have other e-mail programs, but may not be able to see all features. If you know that the publication you are creating is going to be distributed via e-mail, consider using one of the Publisher e-mail templates that are formatted specifically for e-mail. You want to explore making the *InQuest* newsletter available as an e-mail to QST employees. You start by converting page 1.

STEPS

TROUBLE
If you do not have Microsoft Outlook 2007 or Microsoft Outlook Express 6.0 or later, you will not be able to complete this lesson.

1. **Be sure Publisher is the active program, click File on the menu bar, click Open, then open the file PB C-3.pub from the drive and folder where you store your Data Files**
   The first page of *InQuest* appears in the workspace.

2. **Click File on the menu bar, point to Send E-mail, then click E-mail Preview**
   The first page of the newsletter appears in your browser, as shown in Figure C-15. Although the margins look good, you know that you will have to create links to other articles and do more work on the newsletter before you can send it as an e-mail. You decide to send it to yourself as an e-mail to see what it looks like and to see if any other changes are needed.

3. **Return to the Publisher file, click File on the menu bar, point to Send E-mail, click Send as Message, click the Send current page only option button in the Send as Message dialog box, then click OK**
   An e-mail message header opens with text boxes for e-mail addresses and a subject.

4. **Click Design Checker on the E-mail toolbar**
   The Design Checker task pane opens, as shown in Figure C-16. You do not fix problems identified by the Design Checker at this time because you want to see what the page looks like when it is sent as is in an e-mail.

5. **Type your e-mail address in the To text box, type Test in the Subject text box, then click the Send button**
   An Outlook status dialog box opens while the e-mail is sent. After a few minutes, check your e-mail to see if it appears in your inbox. Open the e-mail, review its contents, then delete the e-mail.

6. **Close the PB C-3.pub file without saving changes, then exit Publisher**

Converting a print publication to a Web site

When you create a Web site from scratch, you format the text, preview it using the Web Page Preview button, make adjustments as necessary, and then save it as a Web page. You can use this same process to convert print publications such as flyers and newsletters into Web pages. Each page in your publication becomes a separate page in the Web site, and you can add a navigation bar and other links easily. To convert a print publication to a Web site, open the Publisher Tasks task pane, click Post to a Web site in the Distributing your publication section, then click Publish to the Web. Click Convert to Web Publication in the Publish to the Web dialog box. A Wizard opens, asking if you want to save your print publication first and save your Web publication as a new document. Click Next, choose the appropriate navigation bar option, then click Finish in the Wizard. You will need to reposition some objects, and create links to the navigation bar, but creating a Web site from an existing publication is easy.

Creating a Web Publication

FIGURE C-15: First page of *InQuest* issue viewed as an e-mail preview

Your path will differ

FIGURE C-16: Sending a publication as an e-mail

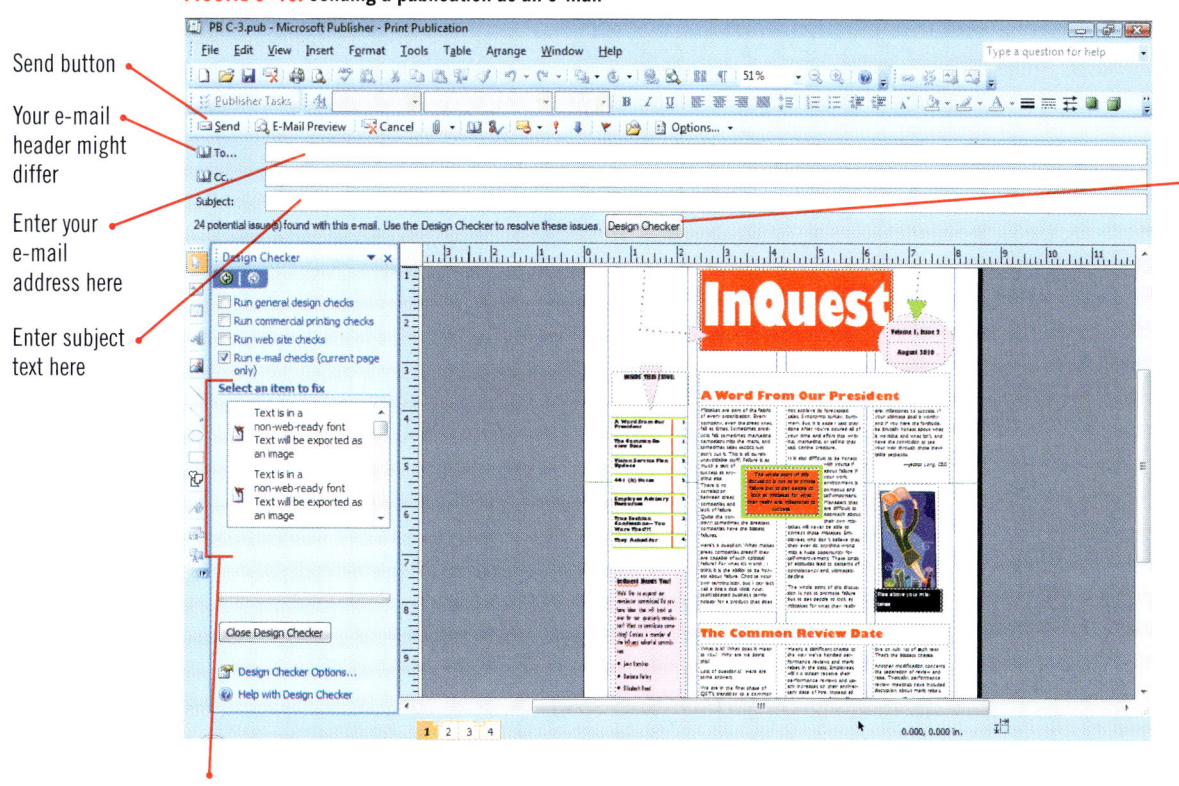

Send button

Your e-mail header might differ

Enter your e-mail address here

Enter subject text here

Design Checker button

List of problems identified by the Design Checker, scroll to see more items

Creating a Web Publication

Publisher 69

Practice

▼ CONCEPTS REVIEW

If you have a SAM user profile, you may have access to hands-on instruction, practice, and assessment of the skills covered in this unit. Log in to your SAM account (http://sam2007.course.com/) to launch any assigned training activities or exams that relate to the skills covered in this unit.

Label each item marked in Figure C-17.

FIGURE C-17

Match each item with its definition.

6. HTML
7. Web form
8. Reset
9. Check box
10. navigation bar
11. browser

a. Can be used to select or deselect options, such as the option to have your name added to a mailing list
b. A means for users of a Web page to enter and submit information
c. Special software for viewing Web pages and Web sites
d. Area on a Web page that provides links to the most important pages in a Web site, in the same location on each page
e. A command button that clears information entered into a form
f. The programming language in which all Web pages are created

Select the best answer from the list of choices.

12. Which Web page control would most commonly be found in a form?
    a. Image box
    b. List box
    c. Navigation bar
    d. Link

13. Which is *not* true about Web pages and Web sites?
    a. They can be created and added to the network by anyone with Internet access.
    b. They are written in a common programming language called Hypertext Markup Language (HTML).
    c. They can be viewed with special software called Web browsers.
    d. They can be created only by using software designed exclusively for that purpose.

14. If you want a user to open a Web page by clicking on text or graphics, you insert a(n)
    a. Form control
    b. User input field
    c. Hyperlink
    d. HTML code fragment

15. Which Web Page formatting button inserts a form field?
    a.
    b.
    c.
    d.

▼ SKILLS REVIEW

1. **Create a new Web publication.**
   a. Refer to Figure C-18, which shows the completed Web pages, as needed while completing this Skills Review.
   b. Start Publisher, in the Publication Types list, click Web Sites, then scroll down and, in the Classic Design section in the Publication Gallery, click the Spotlight thumbnail.
   c. In the right pane, verify that Vertical and Bottom is selected in the Navigation bar area and that the Use Easy Web Wizard check box is deselected, then click Create.
   d. Insert a new page with a sign-up form.
   e. Choose the Prairie color scheme.
   f. Choose the Casual font scheme, then close the task pane.

2. **Format a Web publication.**
   a. Switch to and zoom in on the top of page 1, click the image of the pagoda at the top of the page twice to select the pagoda. (*Hint*: If the Format Object dialog box opens, click Cancel, then click the pagoda two times slowly). Right-click the pagoda, point to Change Picture, click From File, select the file PB C-4.jpg from the drive and folder where you store your Data Files, then click Insert. (*Hint*: When the pagoda is selected it will have grey, filled handles around it.)
   b. Replace the graphic of the dragon with a clip art image of your choice relating to sports, size it appropriately, then delete the caption placeholder and its related text box.
   c. Select the text Home, then type **Barlee Recreation**.
   d. Select the text Your business tag line here above Barlee Recreation, then type **And you thought your job was fun!**
   e. Delete the Business Name text box at the top of the page and the pyramid placeholder logo and graphic, but leave the white box.
   f. Right-click the paragraph placeholder text, point to Change Text, click Text File, then insert the file PB C-5.docx from the drive and folder where you store your Data Files.
   g. Select the text sign-up form in the last line of the paragraph before the list of events, then click the Insert Hyperlink button on the Standard toolbar.
   h. Click the Place in This Document option, click Page 2. Form, then click OK.
   i. Scroll to the bottom of the page, type the following information in the two text boxes below To contact us:, then position them side by side and delete the black line. Change the font to Verdana 8 point.

   Barlee Consulting   **Phone: (815) 555-7998**
   Your Name   **Fax: (815) 555-8779**
   282 West Wayne Street   **E-mail: Recreation@barleeconsulting.com**
   Freeport, IL 61032

   j. Resize the text boxes as necessary to make the text fit, reposition the navigation bar and contact information as necessary to avoid gaps, then save your publication as **recsite** to the drive and folder where you store your Data Files.

▼ SKILLS REVIEW (CONTINUED)

3. **Modify a Web form.**
   a. Navigate to page 2 of the publication and zoom in on the top of the page.
   b. Delete the Business name text box and replace the picture on the right with the Barlee logo (PB C-4.jpg). Delete the pyramid placeholder logo, but not the white box behind it.
   c. Select the text Sign Up Form, type **Event Registration**, delete the text box below Event Registration, replace the Sign-up form title with **Sign up today to attend an event!**, then drag the text box up so it is just under the blue line.
   d. Use the pointer to drag a selection rectangle around all the controls and text labels from the Sign up for: label through the Total: control, then press [Delete].
   e. Select and delete the text labels and controls from Method of Payment through Exp. Date. (Hint: Make sure you delete the text box containing security information.)
   f. Replace the Address label text with **Event**, then add a label and textbox form control for **Number of guests:** below the E-mail text box and label. Resize the label to the left so that the text fits on one line. Resize the text box as shown in Figure C-18.
   g. Drag the Submit and Reset buttons up so they are positioned just below the Number of guests control, then select from Name through Reset and drag all elements up so they are just under the text box with the phrase Sign up today.

FIGURE C-18

▼ SKILLS REVIEW (CONTINUED)

4. **Add form controls.**
   a. Click the Event: text area, then press [Delete]. (*Hint*: Do not delete the Event label.)
   b. Click the Form Control button, click List Box, drag to create a one-line list box in the space formerly occupied by the Event text box, then double-click the list box you inserted.
   c. Select Item One in the Appearance section, click Modify, replace the text in the Item text box with Miniature golf, click the Not selected option button, then click OK.
   d. Replace the Item Two text with **Comedy Club night**, and the Item Three text with **Barbeque and softball game**.
   e. Click Add, type **Riverboat dinner cruise** in the Item text box, click OK, create three new items with the text **Art museum tour**, **Picnic in the park**, and **Walking tour of historic downtown**, then click OK to close the List Box Properties dialog box.
   f. Double-click the Submit button, click Form Properties, click the Save the data in a file on my Web server option button, click OK, click OK, then save your changes.

5. **Preview a Web publication.**
   a. Click the Web Page Preview button.
   b. Scroll down your form page to view the entire contents, click Home on the navigation bar to open the first page, then scroll to view all the page's content.
   c. Click the Publisher program button on the taskbar.
   d. Click the Page 1 Navigation button, drag to select the three text boxes containing Barlee contact information at the bottom of the page, click the Copy button on the Standard toolbar, click the Page 2 Navigation button, click the Paste button on the Standard toolbar, then position the contact information below the Submit and Reset buttons.
   e. Select the bottom navigation bar, then drag it up to just below the contact information. Make any other adjustments using Figure C-18 as a guide.
   f. Save your changes, click the Web Page Preview button, then review your changes.
   g. Close the browser window.

6. **Convert a Web publication to a Web site.**
   a. Click the Publisher program button on the taskbar to view the recsite publication.
   b. Click File on the menu bar, click Publish to the Web, then click OK in the alert box if necessary.
   c. Locate the drive and folder where you store your Data Files, create a new folder called **barleerec**, name the .htm file **recsite**, press [Enter], then click OK in the alert box if necessary.
   d. Open your default Web browser. Click File on the menu bar, click Open, browse to and open the barleerec folder, double-click the file recsite.htm, then click OK. (*Note*: If a warning message opens, click OK.)
   e. Click the Form link on the navigation bar.
   f. Type your name in the Name field, then click the Print button on the browser toolbar.
   g. Close the browser window, then close the recsite file, but keep Publisher open.

7. **Send a publication as an e-mail.**
   a. Open the file PB C-6.pub from the drive and folder where you store your Data Files. (*Note*: If you do not have Microsoft Outlook 2007 or Microsoft Outlook Express 6.0 or later, you will not be able to complete this lesson.)
   b. Click File on the menu bar, point to Send E-mail, click E-mail Preview, then review the page that opens.
   c. Close the e-mail preview, click File on the menu bar, point to Send E-mail, click Send as Message, then click the Send current page only option button. Use the Design Checker to review suggested changes.
   d. Type your e-mail address in the To text box, type **Wallaby Inn test** in the subject line, then click the Send button.
   e. Check your e-mail to see if it appears in your inbox. Open the e-mail, delete it, then close your e-mail program.
   f. Click the Publisher program button on the status bar, close PB C-6.pub without saving changes, then exit Publisher.

▼ INDEPENDENT CHALLENGE 1

You have been hired by a local café to advertise its Saturday Karaoke Night series. You have decided to create a Web page describing the series that the café can publish on its ISP's Web server. You start by creating a Web publication.

a. Start Publisher, select the Accent Box Web page site template, choose Horizontal and Bottom navigation bars, choose a color scheme and font scheme that appeal to you, then click Create.

b. Insert a sign-up form as the second page.

c. Replace the text Home on page one with **Sing at Java Jerry's Café!**, delete the business tag line, business name, and logo placeholders, then replace the main paragraph text with the contents of the file PB C-7.docx (located on the drive and in the folder where you store your Data Files). Format the text as Impact 10 pt.

d. Replace the calculator graphic with an appropriate piece of clip art, then delete the picture caption.

e. Scroll to the bottom of the page, insert the following text in the text box below To contact us:, then delete the phone number text box.
Your Name, Karaoke Coordinator
Phone: (415) 555-5232
E-mail: javajerryscafe@isp-services.com
98 Danvers Street
San Francisco, CA 94114

f. Create a hyperlink from the text "sign-up form" in the second paragraph on the first page to the form page, then save the publication with the name **karaoke**.

g. Open page 2 of the publication, delete the business tag line, business name, and logo placeholders, delete the text box below Sign Up Form, replace the text Sign Up Form with **Karaoke Night Registration**, replace the Sign-up form title text with **Sing at Java Jerry's!**, delete all the labels and controls from Sign up for through Total, then delete all the labels and controls from Method of Payment through Exp. date:. (*Hint*: Make sure you delete the text box containing security information.)

h. Just below the E-mail label, insert a text box for a label, then type **Song Style** in the text box as the new label.

i. Insert a list box to the right of the Song Style label that contains the following items (none of which is selected by default): **Country**, **Hip Hop**, **Pop**, **R&B**, **Show tunes**, and **Other**, and resize the list box so that only the first item is showing.

j. Select and drag the controls and labels to fill in the empty space on the page, double-click the Submit button, click Form Properties, click the Save the data in a file on my Web server option button, click OK twice, then save your publication.

k. Preview your pages in a Web browser, then make any necessary formatting adjustments in Publisher, and save your publication as a Web page named **karaoke.htm** in a folder called **karaoke** in the drive and folder where you store your Data Files.

l. Open the file in your browser, type your name in the Name text box on the form, print the form page, close your browser, close the publication, then exit Publisher.

▼ INDEPENDENT CHALLENGE 2

You are the human resources director for Jasmine Herbal Harvest, a producer of herbal products. You are conducting a contest for your sales force, offering prizes for the best success story relating to your line of herbal products. You will post the information about the contest on your company intranet using Figure C-19 as an example.

a. Start Publisher. Create a Web site with a horizontal navigation bar, using the Brocade Web site design.
b. Add a second page with a response form, then save the file as **jasmine.pub**.
c. Choose a color and font scheme that you like, and replace any graphics with appropriate ones and delete the caption placeholder.
d. Delete the Business tag line, Business name, and logo placeholders on both pages. On the home page, delete the phone text box and the vertical line next to it.
e. On the home page, scroll down and insert the following contact information, replacing the placeholder text as appropriate:
   Jasmine Herbal Harvest, Your Name, Customer Relations, 2230 Red Rock Way, Sedona, Arizona 86336, (520) 555-9010
f. On the home page, scroll up as needed and replace Home with **Jasmine Herbal Harvest** in the text box above the body text.
g. Replace the paragraph text with the file PB C-8.docx. Don't use Autoflow and be sure you can view all the text in the text box, and format the text as necessary. Autofit the text to fit into the text box. Then create a link from Contest Form at the end of the body text to the contest form on page 2.
h. On page 2, replace the placeholder Form headings with the following:

Form heading placeholder	Replace with:
Response Form	**Success Story Contest**
Ask readers to…	Delete the text box and text
Response Form Title	**Win a trip to Bermuda for two!**
Type a description…	**Describe the best success story you've heard from a customer about Jasmine Herbal Harvest products.**

i. Delete all the placeholder questions and the comments label, then drag the Comment text box control up to close up the empty space.
j. Modify the remaining placeholder controls and labels so that the form contains only an E-mail label and text box and Submit and Reset buttons. Create a list box below the E-mail text box with four items (show one, with none selected) as follows: **North**, **South**, **East**, and **West**, then add a label with the text **Sales Territory**.
k. Drag all the remaining elements up to close the empty space.
l. Double-click the Submit button, click Form Properties, click the Save the data in a file on my Web server option button, then click OK twice.

Advanced Challenge Exercise

- Right-click the navigation bar, then click Delete Object. (*Hint*: Do this for all pages.)
- Click Insert on the menu bar, point to Navigation Bar, then click New.
- Choose a horizontal navigation bar from the Design Gallery, click Insert Object, then position it as necessary.
- Copy and paste this new navigation bar onto every page of your Web site and reposition as necessary.

m. Preview your Publication in a browser using the Web Page Preview button, then make necessary changes. Save the publication as a Web page called **jasmine.htm**, in a new folder called **jasmine** in the drive and folder where you store your Data Files.
n. View the pages in your browser, type your name in the Comments text box, print the forms page, close the browser, then exit Publisher.

▼ INDEPENDENT CHALLENGE 2 (CONTINUED)

FIGURE C-19

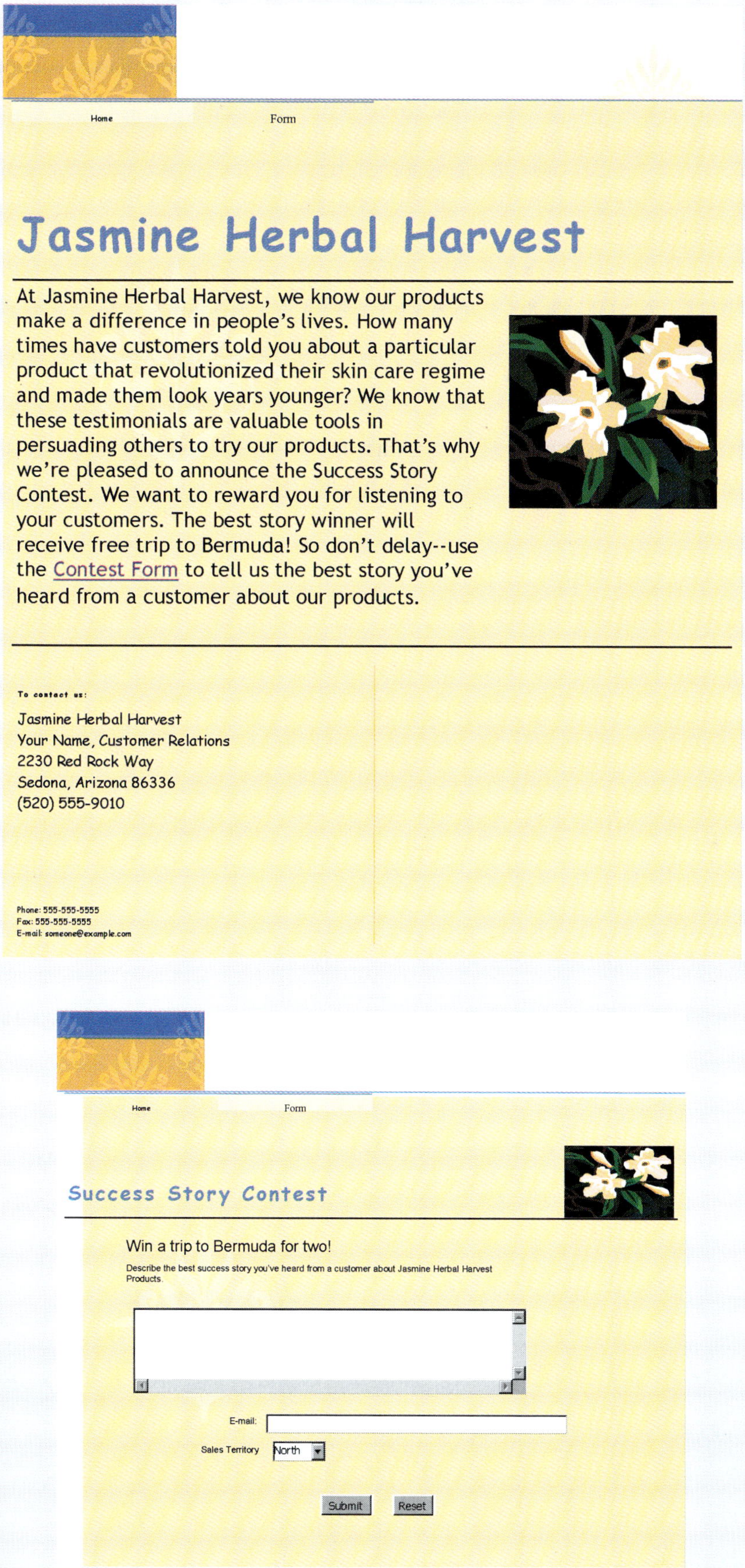

▼ INDEPENDENT CHALLENGE 3

There are many organizations that help people worldwide. Pick a cause that is important to you that affects the global community. It could be a health issue, a political cause, or a charitable organization. Research the cause using the Internet, your library, or periodicals you subscribe to and create a Web site about this topic. See Figure C-20 for an example.

a. To create the Web site, choose a Web site design, color scheme, and font scheme that appeal to you, and appropriate graphics. Your site should have at least three pages, including a home page, a response form page, and a related links page. On the home page, include a paragraph written by you that provides an overview of the topic. Insert links from the paragraph to the related links page and the response form page. Save the Publisher file as **mycause.pub**.

b. On the response form page, include at least one survey question for your viewers to answer relating to your cause. Make sure that the Submit form will save the data to your Web server.

c. On the related links page, insert at least three links to other Web sites that relate to your topic.

d. Type your name somewhere on the home page, use the Web Page Preview button to preview your work, then make any necessary adjustments in Publisher. Save your changes, then save the publication as a Web page named **mycause.htm** in a folder called **my_cause**.

Advanced Challenge Exercise

- Click Format on the menu bar, click Background, then click the More backgrounds link on the task pane.
- In the Fill Effects dialog box, choose a textured or patterned background, then click OK.
- Apply the same background or choose a different background for every page in your Web site.

e. View the page in Publisher, and then view the page in your default browser. Print page 1.

f. Close your browser, and then exit Publisher.

FIGURE C-20

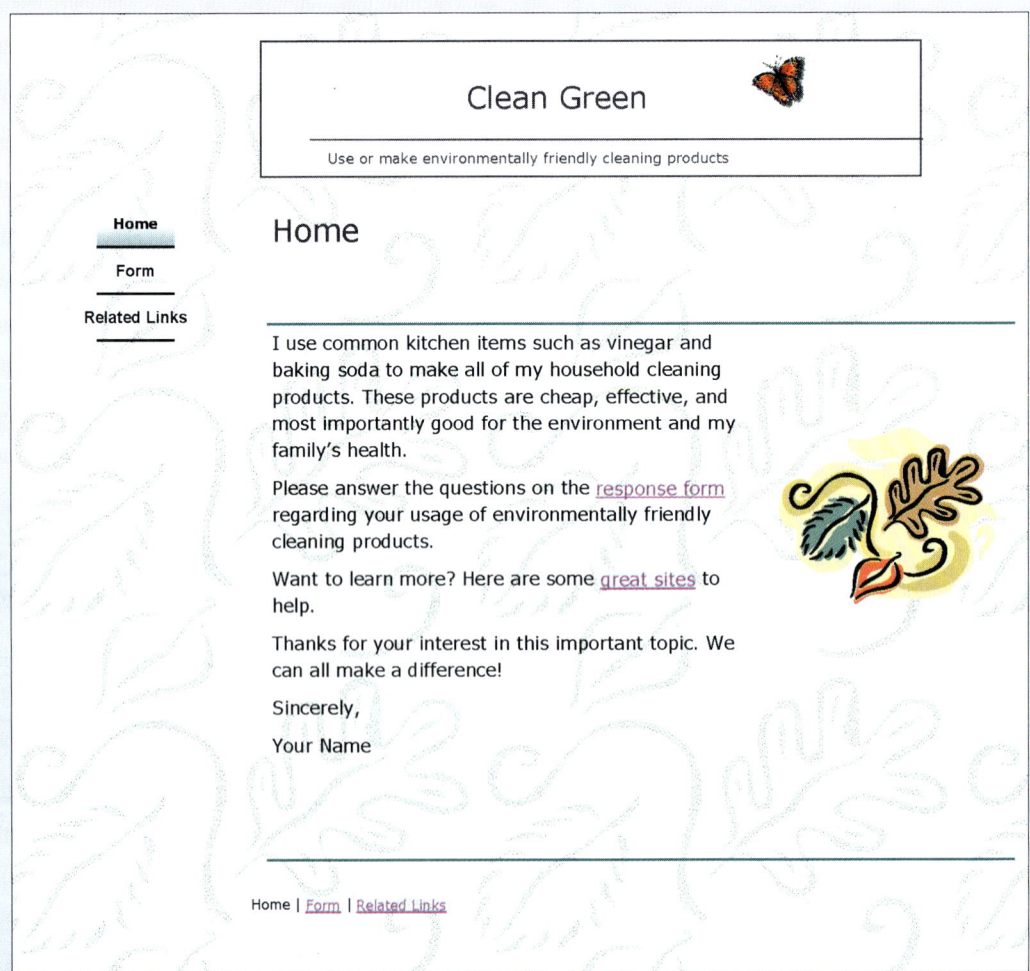

Clean Green
Use or make environmentally friendly cleaning products

Home

Form

Related Links

Home

I use common kitchen items such as vinegar and baking soda to make all of my household cleaning products. These products are cheap, effective, and most importantly good for the environment and my family's health.

Please answer the questions on the response form regarding your usage of environmentally friendly cleaning products.

Want to learn more? Here are some great sites to help.

Thanks for your interest in this important topic. We can all make a difference!

Sincerely,

Your Name

Home | Form | Related Links

▼ REAL LIFE INDEPENDENT CHALLENGE

Create a Web site called **myweb** about yourself using your Publisher Web site creation skills.

a. Start by planning the information you want to include in your site. Remember that you can include several pages in your site, so you should plan on breaking the information up logically into separate Web pages. Make a list of information you want your site to contain, and create an outline of the site showing what information will appear on each page. Figure C-21 provides an example of a home page.

b. Start Publisher, choose a Web site design from the Publication Gallery, then select the options you want to use for your Web site. In addition to your home page, include at least one form page and one other page. You may include additional pages if you want.

c. Replace the placeholder text and graphics on your Web site with graphics that are appropriate for you. If you need to add additional pages, click Insert a page on the Format Publication task pane.

d. Save your publication with the name **myweb.pub**.

e. Preview your publication in a browser using the Web Page Preview button, make necessary changes, then use the Publish to the Web command to save the file as myweb.htm to a new folder called **myweb**.

f. View the pages in a browser, print the pages, close the browser, close the file, then exit Publisher.

FIGURE C-21

▼ VISUAL WORKSHOP

Use Publisher to create the Web page shown in Figure C-22. Use the Orbits design, a Vertical navigation bar, the Tidepool color scheme, and the Opulent font scheme. Insert or replace any existing graphics with the teacup graphic and delete the caption. Resize, rotate, and move the graphic to the position shown in the figure, then import the paragraph text from the file PB C-9.docx. Format the paragraph text in 11-point Arial. Resize the text box so that the paragraph fits as shown. Create the controls shown using the Form Control button. Add the E-mail address label. Make any other changes based on Figure C-22. Save the publication as **inn_site.pub**, then save it as a Web page called **inn_site.htm** in a new folder titled **inn**. View the publication in your default browser, type your name in the E-mail address text box on the page, then print it. Close the browser, then exit Publisher.

FIGURE C-22

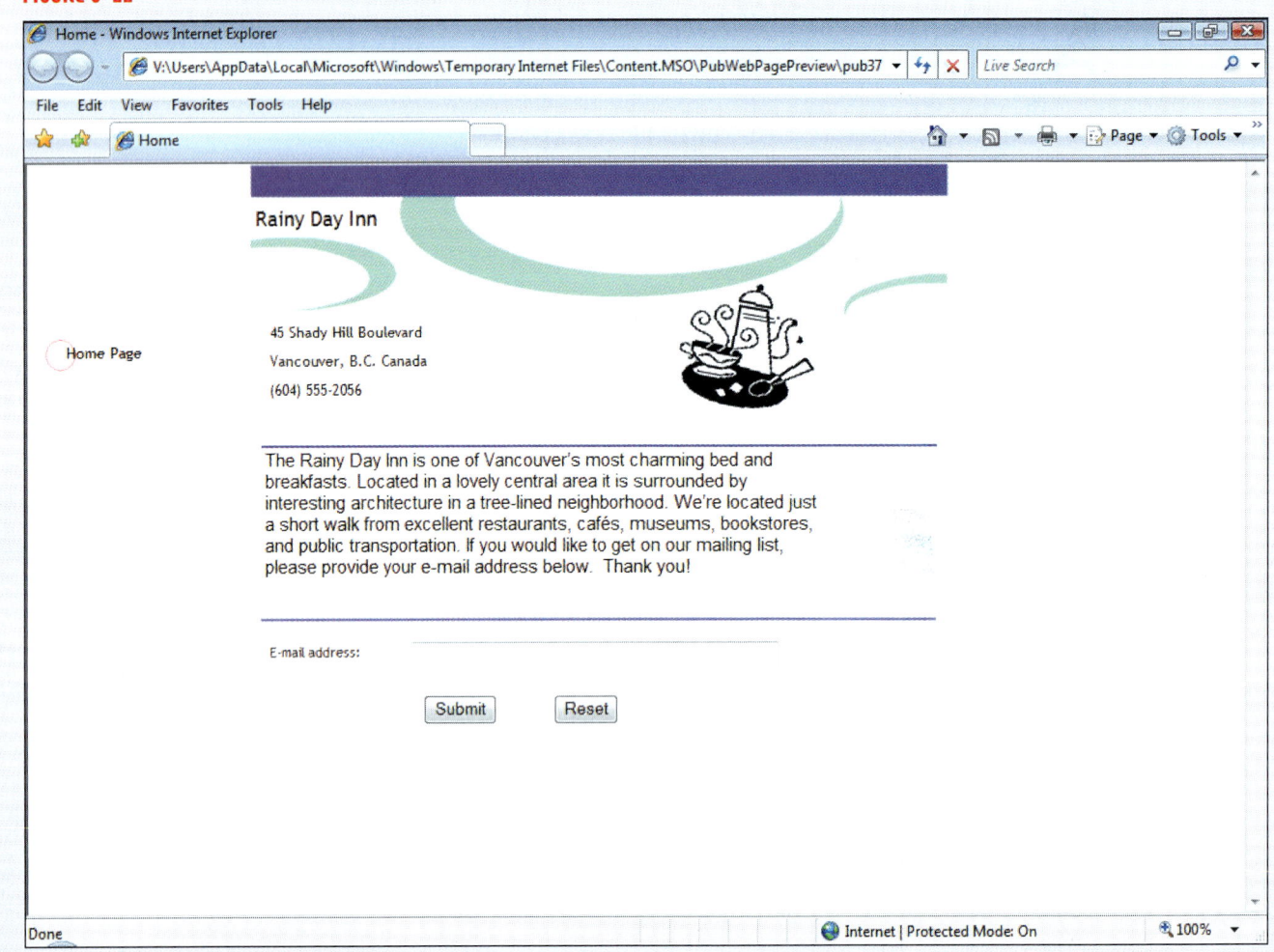

Appendix A

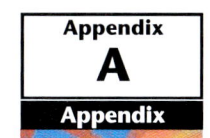

Restoring Defaults in Windows Vista and Disabling and Enabling Windows Aero

Files You Will Need:
No files needed.

Windows Vista is the most recent version of the Windows operating system. An operating system controls the way you work with your computer, supervises running programs, and provides tools for completing your computing tasks. After surveying millions of computer users, Microsoft incorporated their suggestions to make Windows Vista secure, reliable, and easy to use. In fact, Windows Vista is considered the most secure version of Windows yet. Other improvements include a powerful new search feature that lets you quickly search for files and programs from the Start menu and most windows, tools that simplify accessing the Internet, especially with a wireless connection, and multimedia programs that let you enjoy, share, and organize music, photos, and recorded TV. Finally, Windows Vista offers lots of visual appeal with its transparent, three-dimensional design in the Aero experience. This appendix explains how to make sure you are using the Windows Vista default settings for appearance, personalization, security, hardware, and sound and to enable and disable Windows Aero. For more information on Windows Aero, go to *www.microsoft.com/windowsvista/experiences/aero.mspx*.

OBJECTIVES

Restore the defaults in the Appearance and Personalization section

Restore the defaults in the Security section

Restore the defaults in the Hardware and Sound section

Disable Windows Aero

Enable Windows Aero

Appendix A

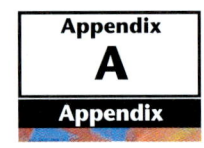

Restoring the Defaults in the Appearance and Personalization Section

The following instructions require a default Windows Vista Ultimate installation and the student logged in with an Administrator account. All of the following settings can be changed by accessing the Control Panel.

STEPS

- **To restore the defaults in the Personalization section**
    1. Click Start, and then click Control Panel. Click Appearance and Personalization, click Personalization, and then compare your screen to Figure A-1
    2. In the Personalization window, click Windows Color and Appearance, select the Default color, and then click OK
    3. In the Personalization window, click Mouse Pointers. In the Mouse Properties dialog box, on the Pointers tab, select Windows Aero (system scheme) in the Scheme drop-down list, and then click OK
    4. In the Personalization window, click Theme. Select Windows Vista from the Theme drop-down list, and then click OK
    5. In the Personalization window, click Display Settings. In the Display Settings dialog box, drag the Resolution bar to 1024 by 768 pixels, and then click OK

FIGURE A-1

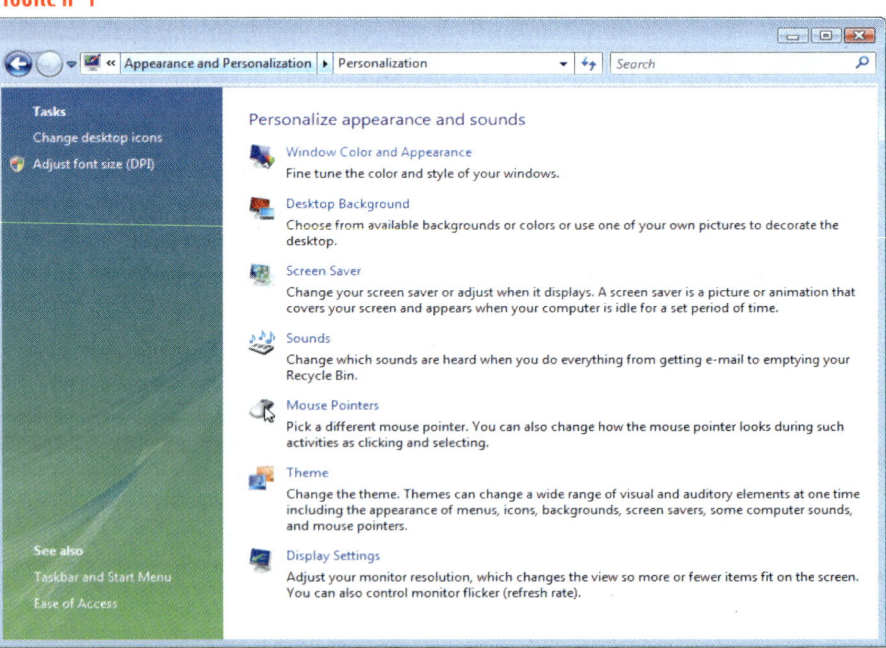

- To restore the defaults in the Taskbar and Start Menu section
    1. Click Start, and then click Control Panel. Click Appearance and Personalization, click Taskbar and Start Menu, and then compare your screen to Figure A-2
    2. In the Taskbar and Start Menu Properties dialog box, on the Taskbar tab, click to select all checkboxes except for "Auto-hide the taskbar"
    3. On the Start Menu tab, click to select the Start menu radio button and check all items in the Privacy section
    4. In the System icons section on the Notification Area tab, click to select all of the checkboxes except for "Power"
    5. On the Toolbars tab, click to select Quick Launch, none of the other items should be checked
    6. Click OK to close the Taskbar and Start Menu Properties dialog box

- To restore the defaults in the Folder Options section
    1. Click Start, and then click Control Panel. Click Appearance and Personalization, click Folder Options, and then compare your screen to Figure A-3
    2. In the Folder Options dialog box, on the General tab, click to select Show preview and filters in the Tasks section, click to select Open each folder in the same window in the Browse folders section, and click to select Double-click to open an item (single-click to select) in the Click items as follows section
    3. On the View tab, click the Reset Folders button, and then click Yes in the Folder views dialog box. Then click the Restore Defaults button
    4. On the Search tab, click the Restore Defaults button
    5. Click OK to close the Folder Options dialog box

- To restore the defaults in the Windows Sidebar Properties section
    1. Click Start, and then click Control Panel. Click Appearance and Personalization, click Windows Sidebar Properties, and then compare your screen to Figure A-4
    2. In the Windows Sidebar Properties dialog box, on the Sidebar tab, click to select Start Sidebar when Windows starts. In the Arrangement section, click to select Right, and then click to select 1 in the Display Sidebar on monitor drop-down list
    3. Click OK to close the Windows Sidebar Properties dialog box

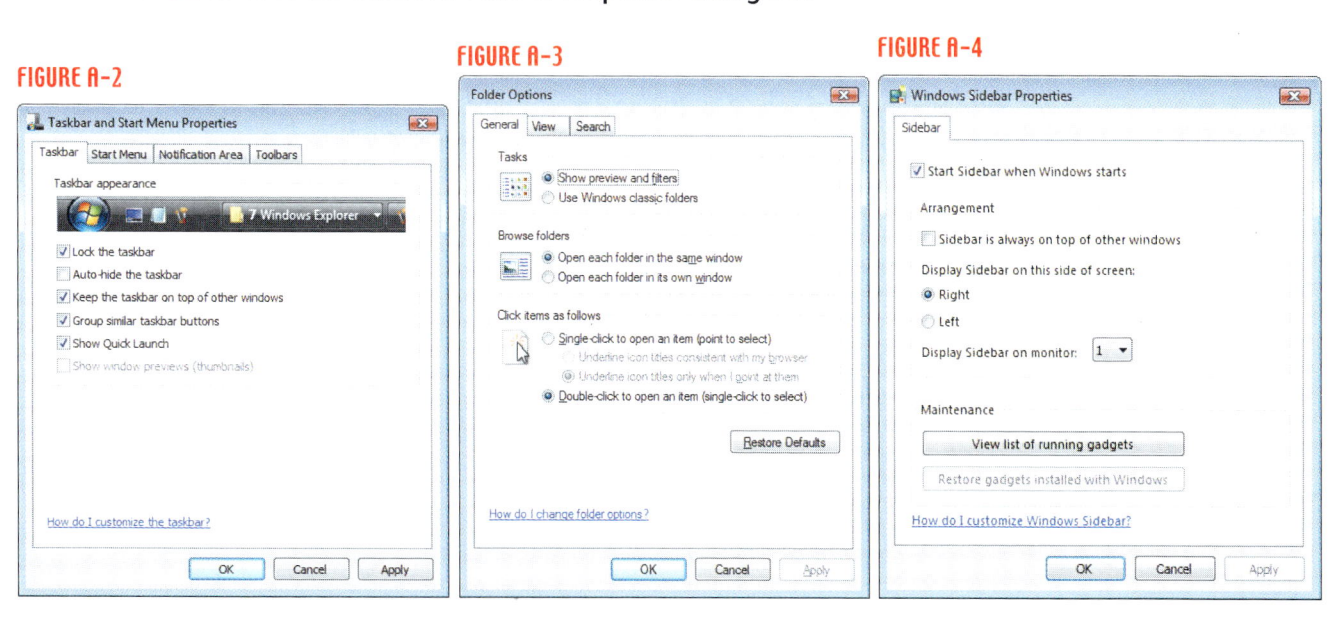

FIGURE A-2

FIGURE A-3

FIGURE A-4

Appendix 3

Appendix A

Restoring the Defaults in the Security Section

The following instructions require a default Windows Vista Ultimate installation and the student logged in with an Administrator account. All of the following settings can be changed by accessing the Control Panel.

STEPS

- **To restore the defaults in the Windows Firewall section**
    1. Click Start, and then click Control Panel. Click Security, click Windows Firewall, and then compare your screen to Figure A-5
    2. In the Windows Firewall dialog box, click Change settings. If the User Account Control dialog box appears, click Continue
    3. In the Windows Firewall Settings dialog box, click the Advanced tab. Click Restore Defaults, then click Yes in the Restore Defaults Confirmation dialog box
    4. Click OK to close the Windows Firewall Settings dialog box, and then close the Windows Firewall window

- **To restore the defaults in the Internet Options section**
    1. Click Start, and then click Control Panel. Click Security, click Internet Options, and then compare your screen to Figure A-6
    2. In the Internet Properties dialog box, on the General tab, click the Use default button. Click the Settings button in the Tabs section, and then click the Restore defaults button in the Tabbed Browsing Settings dialog box. Click OK to close the Tabbed Browsing Settings dialog box
    3. On the Security tab of the Internet Properties dialog box, click to uncheck the Enable Protected Mode checkbox, if necessary. Click the Default level button in the Security level for this zone section. If possible, click the Reset all zones to default level button
    4. On the Programs tab, click the Make default button in the Default web browser button for Internet Explorer, if possible. If Office is installed, Microsoft Office Word should be selected in the HTML editor drop-down list
    5. On the Advanced tab, click the Restore advanced settings button in the Settings section. Click the Reset button in the Reset Internet Explorer settings section, and then click Reset in the Reset Internet Explorer Settings dialog box
    6. Click Close to close the Reset Internet Explorer Settings dialog box, and then click OK to close the Internet Properties dialog box

FIGURE A-5

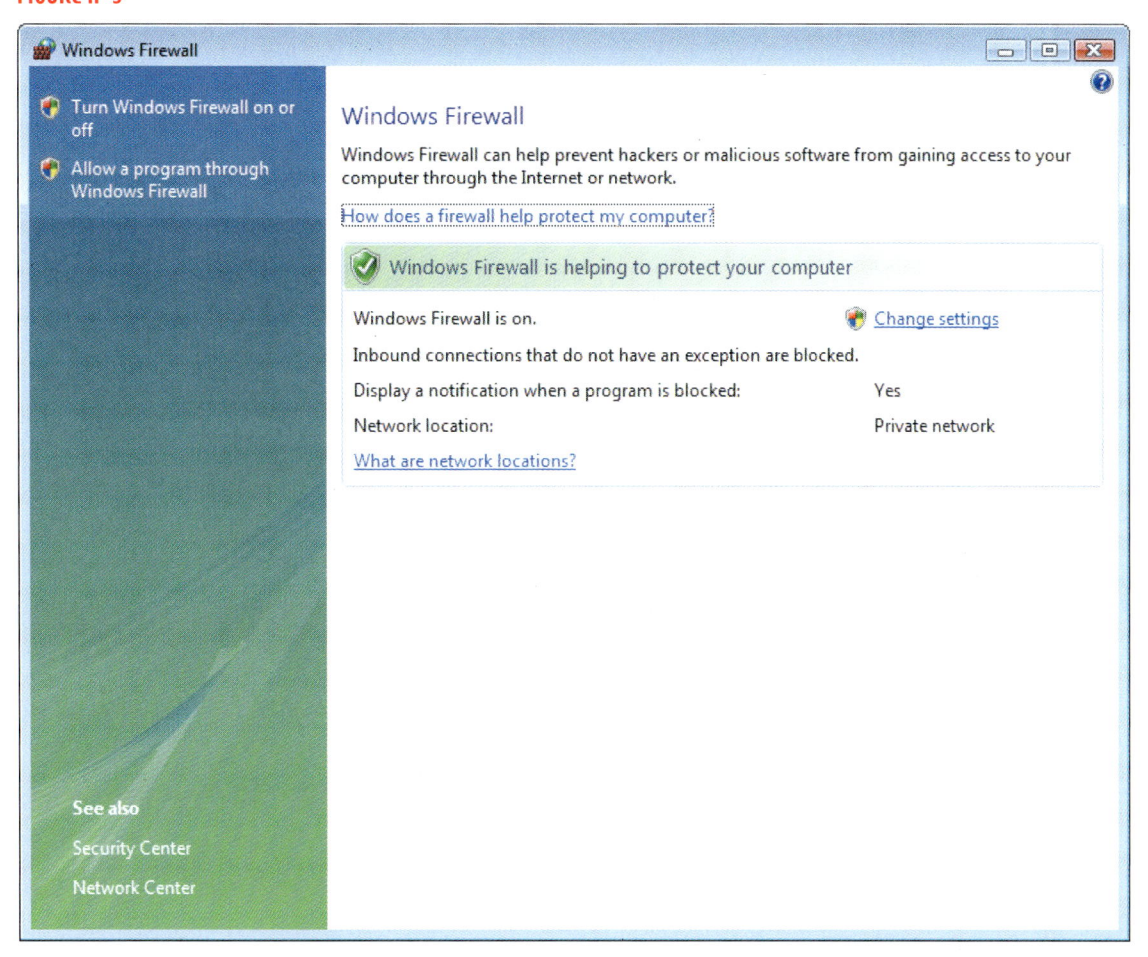

FIGURE A-6

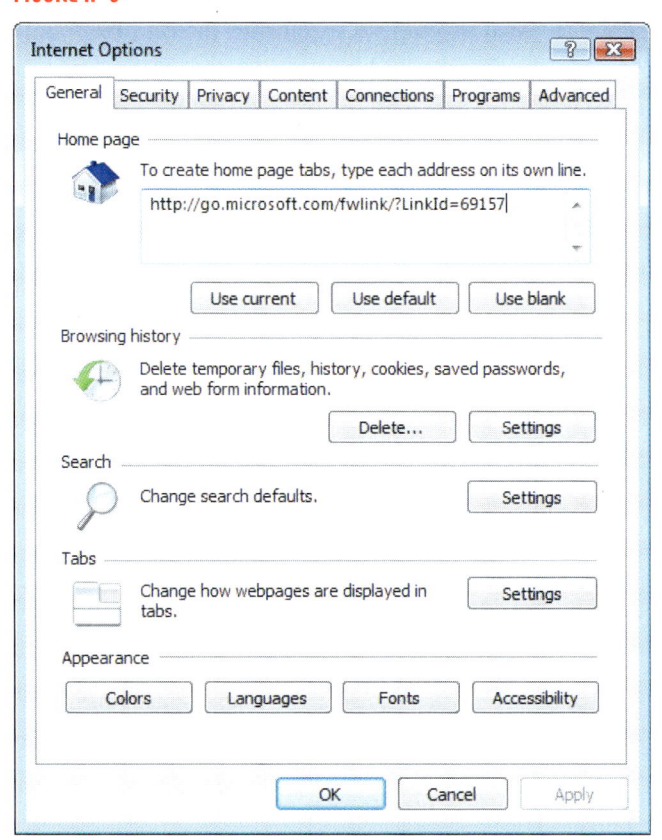

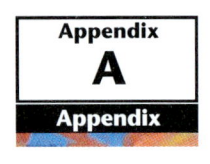

Restoring the Defaults in the Hardware and Sound Section

The following instructions require a default Windows Vista Ultimate installation and the student logged in with an Administrator account. All of the following settings can be changed by accessing the Control Panel.

STEPS

- To restore the defaults in the Autoplay section
    1. Click Start, and then click Control Panel. Click Hardware and Sound, click Autoplay, and then compare your screen to Figure A-7. Scroll down and click the Reset all defaults button in the Devices section at the bottom of the window, and then click Save

- To restore the defaults in the Sound section
    1. Click Start, and then click Control Panel. Click Hardware and Sound, click Sound, and then compare your screen to Figure A-8
    2. In the Sound dialog box, on the Sounds tab, select Windows Default from the Sound Scheme drop-down list, and then click OK

- To restore the defaults in the Mouse section
    1. Click Start, and then click Control Panel. Click Hardware and Sound, click Mouse, and then compare your screen to Figure A-9
    2. In the Mouse Properties dialog box, on the Pointers tab, select Windows Aero (system scheme) from the Scheme drop-down list
    3. Click OK to close the Mouse Properties dialog box

FIGURE A-7

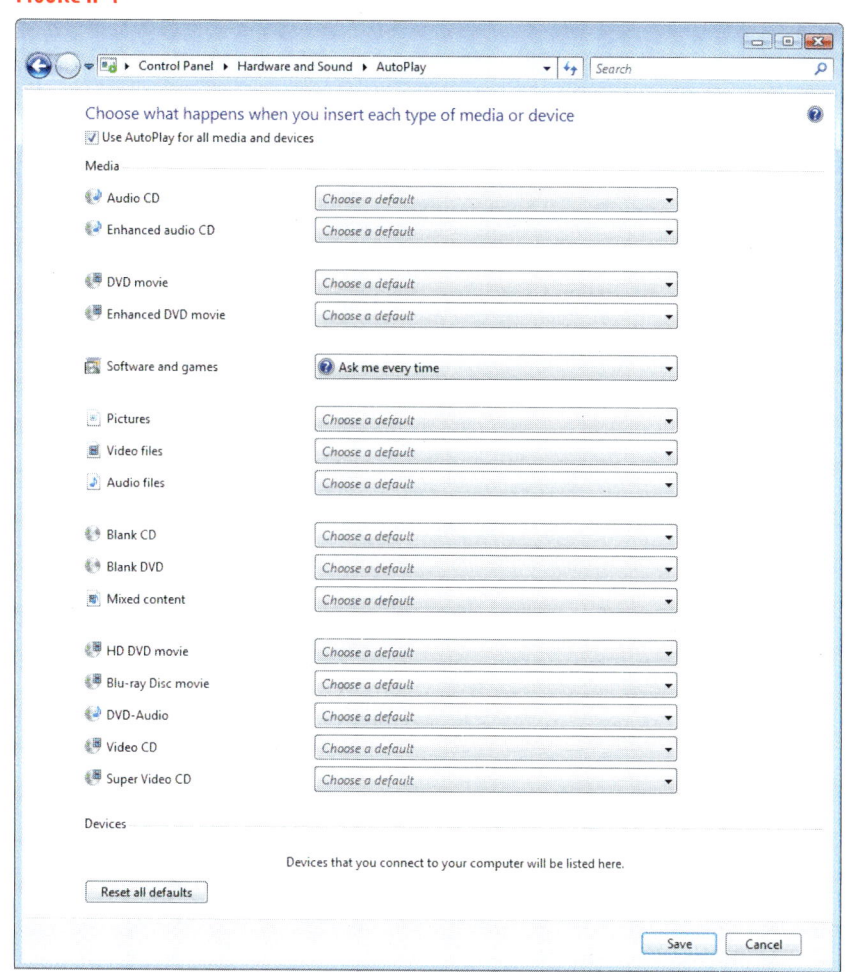

FIGURE A-8

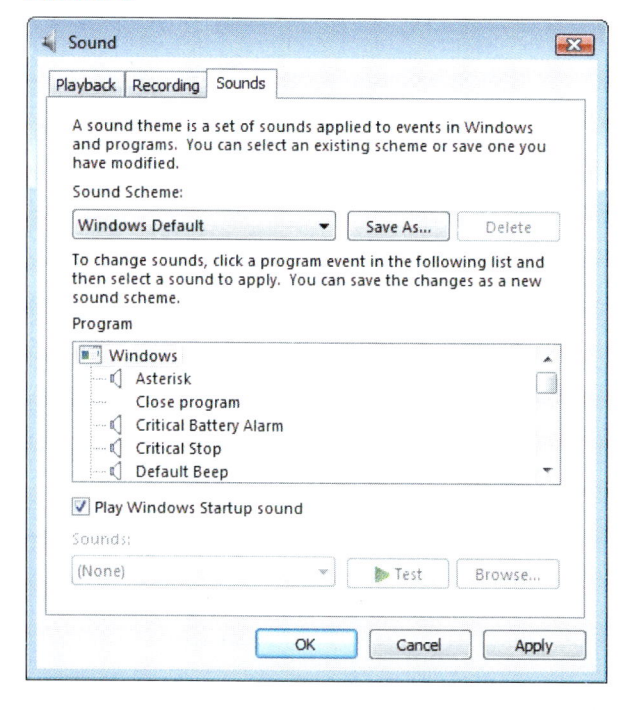

FIGURE A-9

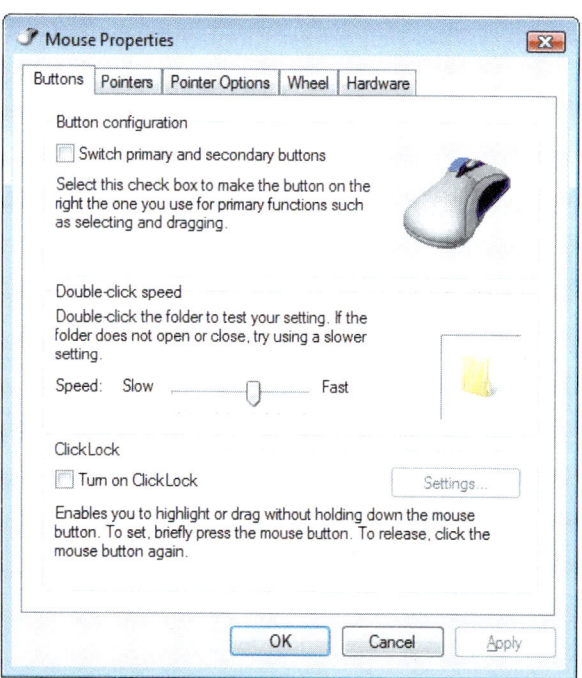

Appendix A

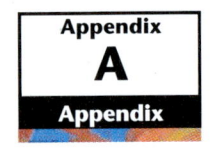

Disabling and Enabling Windows Aero

Unlike prior versions of Windows, Windows Vista provides two distinct user interface experiences: a "basic" experience for entry-level systems and more visually dynamic experience called Windows Aero. Both offer a new and intuitive navigation experience that helps you more easily find and organize your applications and files, but Aero goes further by delivering a truly next-generation desktop experience.

Windows Aero builds on the basic Windows Vista user experience and offers Microsoft's best-designed, highest-performing desktop experience. Using Aero requires a PC with compatible graphics adapter and running a Premium or Business edition of Windows Vista.

The following instructions require a computer capable of running Windows Aero, with a default Windows Vista Ultimate installation and student logged in with an Administrator account.

STEPS

- **To Disable Windows Aero**

We recommend that students using this book disable Windows Aero and restore their operating systems default settings (instructions to follow).

1. Right-click the desktop, select **Personalize**, and then compare your screen in Figure A-10. Select **Window Color and Appearance**, and then select **Open classic appeareance properties for more color options**. In Appearance Settings dialog box, on the Appearance tab, select any non-Aero scheme (such as **Windows Vista Basic** or **Windows Vista Standard**) in the Color Scheme list, and then click OK. Figure A-11 compares Windows Aero to other color schemes. Note that this book uses Windows Vista Basic as the color scheme

- **To Enable Windows Aero**

1. Right-click the desktop, and then select **Personalize**. Select **Window Color and Appearance**, then select **Windows Aero** in the Color scheme list, and then click OK in the Appearance Settings dialog box

FIGURE A-10

FIGURE A-11

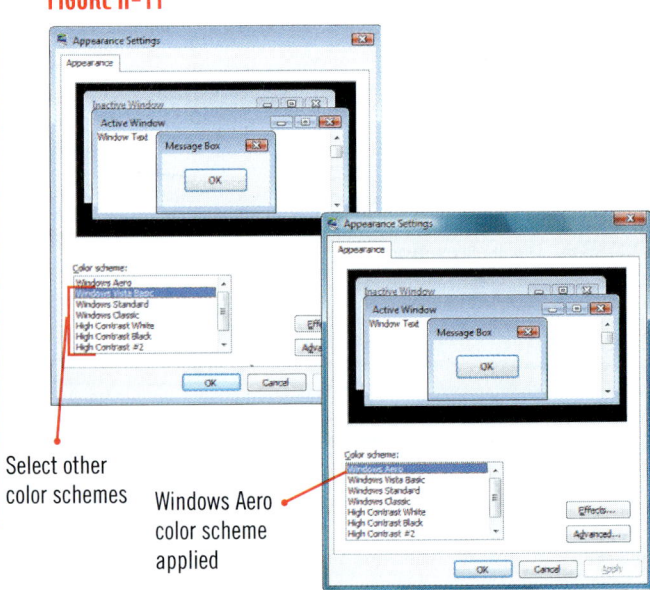

Select other color schemes

Windows Aero color scheme applied

Glossary

.accdb The file extension that usually means the database is an Access 2007 format database.

.bmp The file extension for the bitmap graphics file format.

.gif The file extension for the graphics interchange format.

.jpg The file extension for the JPEG (Joint Photographic Experts Group) File Interchange Format.

.mdb The file extension for Access 2000 and 2002-2003 databases.

3-D reference A reference that uses values on other sheets or workbooks, effectively creating another dimension to a workbook.

Action button An interactive button that you click in Slide Show view to perform an activity, such as advancing to the next slide.

Add-in An extra program, such as Solver and the Analysis ToolPak, that provides optional Excel features. To activate an add-in, click the Office button, click Excel options, click Add-Ins, then click Go. Select or deselect add-ins from the list.

Adjustment handle The yellow diamond that appears when certain shapes are selected; used to change the shape, but not the size, of a shape.

Aggregate function A function such as Sum, Avg, and Count used in a summary query to calculate information about a group of records.

Allow Value List Edits A property you specify to determine whether the Edit List Items button is active in a combo box list.

Alternate Back Color A property that determines the color that alternates with white in the background of a report section.

Anchored The state of a floating graphic that moves with a paragraph or other item if the item is moved; an anchor symbol appears next to the paragraph or item when the floating graphic is selected and formatting marks are displayed.

AND condition A filtering feature that searches for records by specifying that all entered criteria must be matched.

Animated GIF A file format used to display animations in Web pages.

Animation The illusion of making a static object appear to move. Some graphics, such as an animated .gif (Graphics Interchange Format) file, have motion when you run the slide show.

Ascending order In sorting data, the lowest value (the beginning of the alphabet, or the earliest date) appears at the beginning of the sorted data.

Attachment field A field that allows you to attach an external file such as a Word document, PowerPoint presentation, Excel workbook, or image file to a record.

AutoFilter A table feature that lets you click a list arrow and select criteria by which to display certain types of records; *also called* filter.

AutoFilter list arrows List arrows that appear next to field names in an Excel table; used to display portions of your data; *also called* filter list arrows.

AutoFit A feature that automatically sizes text to fit in a frame.

Autoflow A feature that flows text automatically from one existing empty text frame to the next, asking for confirmation before it flows to the next text frame.

AutoFormat A predefined format that you can apply to a form or report to set the background picture, font, color and alignment formatting choices.

AutoShape A drawing object, such as a rectangle, oval, triangle, line, block arrow, or other shape, that you create using the tools on the Drawing toolbar.

Back Color A property that determines the background color of a report section.

Background A layer that appears behind every page in a publication and the layer on which you put objects, such as headers, that you want repeated on each page.

Banding Worksheet formatting in which adjacent rows and columns are formatted differently.

Baseline guide A horizontal, brown, dotted line that helps to align text among columns in text boxes.

Bitmap graphic A graphic that is composed of a series of small dots called "pixels" and often saved with a .bmp, .png, .jpg, .tif, or .gif file extension.

Boilerplate text Text that appears in every version of a merged document.

Border A line that can be added above, below, or to the sides of a paragraph, text, or a table cell; a line that divides the columns and rows of a table.

Brightness The relative lightness of a photograph.

Building block A reusable piece of formatted content or a document part that is stored in a gallery.

Bullet A small graphic symbol, usually a round or square dot, often used to identify items in a list.

Business Contact Manager A feature that allows you to organize and centralize customer information, track marketing activities, and coordinate project information.

Calculated columns In a table, a column that uses one formula that automatically adjusts to accommodate additional rows.

Calculated field A field created in Query Design View that results from an expression of existing fields, Access functions, and arithmetic operators. For example, the entry Profit: [RetailPrice]-[WholesalePrice] in the field cell of the query design grid creates a calculated field called Profit that is the difference between the values in the RetailPrice and WholesalePrice fields.

Catalog Merge A feature that lets you insert text and pictures from a data source, such as a spreadsheet or database, in order to create catalogs, address books, or other publications that include multiple records.

Category axis The horizontal axis in a chart or PivotChart; *also called* the x-axis.

Cell reference A code that identifies a cell's position in a table. Each cell reference contains a letter (A, B, C, and so on) to identify its column and a number (1, 2, 3, and so on) to identify its row. The cell reference A4 refers to the cell in column A, row 4.

Cell The box formed by the intersection of a table row and table column.

Chart A graphical representation of numerical data from an Excel worksheet. Chart types include 2-D and 3-D column, bar, pie, area, and line charts.

Chart Field List A list of fields in the underlying record source for a PivotChart.

Clip art Predesigned graphic images you can insert in any document or presentation to enhance its appearance.

Clip Organizer A library of art, pictures, sounds, video clips, and animations that all Office applications share.

Color scale In conditional formatting, a formatting scheme that uses a set of two, three, or four fill colors to convey relative values of data.

Color scheme A named set of five colors, including white, which can be applied consistently throughout a publication.

Combo box A bound control used to display a list of possible entries for a field in which you can also type an entry from the keyboard. It is a "combination" of the list box and text box controls.

Combo Box Wizard A bound control used to display a list of possible entries for a field in which you can also type an entry from the keyboard.

Command button An unbound control used to provide an easy way to initiate an action.

Comment A note you attach to a slide.

Compatibility Checker Finds potential compatibility issues between a PowerPoint 2007 presentation and earlier versions of PowerPoint.

Conditional formatting Formatting that is based on specified criteria. For example, a text box may be conditionally formatted to display its value in red if the value is a negative number.

Connect Text Boxes toolbar A toolbar that gives you options for connecting overflow text from one text box in your publication to another text box.

Connected text box A text box whose text flows either from or to another text box.

Consolidate To combine data on multiple worksheets and display the result on another worksheet.

Content control An interactive object that is embedded in a document and which expedites your ability to customize the document with your own information.

Content Library A feature that allows you to store frequently used text and graphics, which can be easily inserted into your publications.

Contrast The difference in brightness between the darkest and the lightest areas of a photograph.

Criteria range In advanced filtering, a cell range containing one row of labels (usually a copy of column labels) and at least one additional row underneath it that contains the criteria you want to match.

Crop To trim away part of a graphic.

Crosstab query A query that presents data in a cross-tabular layout (fields are used for both column and row headings), similar to PivotTables in other database and spreadsheet products.

Crosstab Query Wizard A wizard used to create crosstab queries and which helps identify fields that will be used for row and column headings, and fields that will be summarized within the datasheet.

Crosstab row A row in the query design grid used to specify the column and row headings and values for the crosstab query.

Data entry area The unlocked portion of a worksheet where users are able to enter and change data.

Data field A category of information, such as last name, first name, street address, city, or postal code.

Data record A complete set of related information for a person or an item, such as a person's contact information, including name, address, phone number, e-mail address, and so on.

Data series A column or row in a datasheet.

Data series marker A graphical representation of a data series, such as a bar or column.

Data source In a mail merge, the file with the unique data for individual people or items.

Default View property A form property that determines whether a subform automatically opens in Datasheet or Continuous Forms view.

Delimiter A separator such as a space, comma, or semicolon between elements in imported data.

Descending order The order of data that is in reverse alphabetical or sequential order (from Z to A, 9 to 0, or latest to earliest).

Design Checker A feature that searches for errors in your publication, such as text outside margins, and provides suggestions for fixing the errors.

Desktop publishing program A program for creating publications containing text and graphics.

Desktop workspace The area around the publication page that you can use to store text and graphics prior to placing them in a publication.

Destination file The file an object is embedded into, such as a presentation.

Dialog box A window that opens when a program needs more information to carry out a command.

Display When property A control property that determines whether the control appears only on the screen, only when printed, or at all times.

Document properties Details about a file, such as author name or the date the file was created, that are used to describe, organize, and search for files.

Domain The recordset (table or query) that contains the field used in a domain function calculation.

Domain function A function used to display a calculation on a form or report using a field that is not included in the Record Source property for the form or report; *also called* domain aggregate function.

Drawing canvas A workspace for creating graphics.

Drawing gridlines A grid of nonprinting lines that appear within the margins in Print Layout view to help you size, align, and position graphics.

Drop area A position on a PivotChart or PivotTable where you can drag and place a field. Drop areas on a PivotTable include the Filter field, Row field, Column field, and Totals or Detail field. Drop areas on a PivotChart include the Filter field, Category field, Series field, and Data field.

Drop cap A large dropped initial capital letter that is often used to set off the first paragraph of an article.

Dynamic page breaks In a larger workbook, horizontal or vertical dashed lines that represent the place where pages print separately. They also adjust automatically when you insert or delete rows or columns, or change column widths or row heights.

Edit List Items button A button you click to add items to the combo box list in Form View.

Embedded object An object that is created in one application and copied to another. Embedded objects remain connected to the original program file in which they were created for easy editing.

Enabled property A control property that determines whether the control can have the focus in Form View.

Error bars Bars that identify potential error amounts relative to each data marker in a data series.

Error Indicator button A smart tag that helps identify potential design errors in Report or Form Design View.

Exception A Formatting change that differs from the slide master.

External reference indicator The exclamation point (!) used in a formula to indicate that a referenced cell is outside the active sheet.

Extract To place a copy of a filtered table in a range you specify in the Advanced Filter dialog box.

Field (Excel) In a table (an Excel database), a column that describes a characteristic about records, such as first name or city. (Word) A code that serves as a placeholder for data that changes in a document, such as a page number.

Field name A column label that describes a field.

Field properties Characteristics that further define a field.

File format A file type, such as .pptx, .bmp, .jpg, or .gif.

Filter arrows *See* AutoFilter list arrows.

Filter (Excel) To display data in an Excel table that meet specified criteria. *See also* AutoFilter. (Word) In a mail merge, to pull out records that meet specific criteria and include only those records in the merge.

Find Duplicates Query Wizard A wizard used to create a query that determines whether a table contains duplicate values in one or more fields.

Find Unmatched Query Wizard A wizard used to create a query that finds records in one table that doesn't have related records in another table.

Fixed layout format A specific file format that locks the file from future change.

Floating graphic A graphic to which a text wrapping style has been applied, making the graphic independent of text and able to be moved anywhere on a page.

Folder A subdivision of a disk that works like a filing system to help you organize files.

Font scheme A named set of two fonts or font styles that are applied consistently throughout a publication.

Font size The size of characters, measured in units called points (pts).

Font style The physical characteristics of a font.

Font The typeface or design of a set of characters (letters, numbers, symbols, and punctuation marks).

Footer Information that prints at the bottom of each printed page.

Foreground The layer that sits on top of the background layer and consists of the objects that appear on a specific page of a publication.

Form A type of Web page that provides an easy way for a user to submit information.

Form control An item in a form that is used for gathering information from a user, such as a text box, list box, command button, or check box.

Format Painter A tool you can use when designing and laying out forms and reports to copy formatting characteristics from one text object or control to another.

Format property A field property that controls how information is displayed and printed.

Formatting toolbar A toolbar that contains buttons for frequently used formatting commands.

Frame A container that holds an object, such as a text box or graphic.

Freeze To hold in place selected columns or rows when scrolling in a worksheet that is divided in panes. *See also* Panes.

Gallery A location where styles, themes, or building blocks, such a headers, footers, and text boxes, are stored.

Grid guide A nonprinting line that is used to position text and objects.

Gridlines Nonprinting blue dotted lines that show the boundaries of table cells.

Group controls To allow you to identify several controls as a group to quickly and easily apply the same formatting properties to them.

Group selection handles Selection handles that surround grouped controls.

Guide A nonprinting line that helps you place objects, such as text boxes and graphics.

Handout master The master view for printing handouts.

Hanging indent A format in which the first line of a paragraph begins to the left of all subsequent lines of text.

Header Information, such as text, a page number, or a graphic, that appears at the top of every page.

Header row In an Excel or Word table, the first row that contains the field names.

Hexadecimal Numbers that consist of numbers 0-9 as well as letters A-H.

Home page The main page of a Web site and the first page viewers see when they visit a site.

Horizontal ruler A ruler that appears at the top of the publication window.

Horizontal scroll bar The bar on the bottom edge of the document window that is used to display different parts of the document in the document window.

Host A computer with an always on connection to a network, such as the Internet or an intranet, on which you can store the files for a Web site.

HTML (Hypertext Markup Language) A programming language, which is a set of codes inserted into a text file that browser software, such as Internet Explorer, can use to determine the way text, hyperlinks, images, and other elements appear on a Web page.

Hyperlink An object or link (a filename, word, phrase, or graphic) that, when clicked, "jumps to" another location in the current file or opens another PowerPoint presentation, a Word, Excel, or Access file, or an address on the World Wide Web; *also called* a link. *See also* Target.

Icon sets In conditional formatting, groups of images that are used to visually communicate relative cell values based on the values they contain.

Indent levels Text levels in the master text placeholder. Each level is indented a certain amount from the left margin, and you control their placement by dragging indent markers on the ruler.

Indent markers Small markers (two triangles and one square) on the horizontal ruler that indicate the indent settings for the selected text.

Inline graphic A graphic that is part of a line of text in which it was inserted.

Input Mask property A field property that provides a visual guide for users as they enter data.

Instance A worksheet in its own workbook window.

Internet A system of connected computers and computer networks located around the world by telephone lines, cables, satellites, and other telecommunications media.

Intranet An internal network site used by a group of people who work together.

JPEG Acronym for Joint Photographic Experts Group, which defines the standards for the compression algorithms that allow image files to be stored in an efficient compressed format.

Junction table A table created to establish separate one-to-many relationships to two tables that have a many-to-many relationship.

Key field combination Two or more fields that, as a group, contain unique information for each record.

Keywords Terms added to a workbook's Document Properties that help locate the file in a search.

Kiosk A freestanding computer used to display information, usually in a public area.

Layer To stack objects, such as text boxes or graphics, on top of one another.

Layout The general arrangement in which a form displays the fields in the underlying recordset. Layout types include Columnar, Tabular, Datasheet, Chart, and PivotTable. Columnar is most popular for a form, and Datasheet is most popular for a subform.

Layout guide A nonprinting line that appears in every page of a publication to help you align text, pictures, and other objects into columns and rows so that your publication will have a consistent look across all pages.

Leading The spacing between lines of text in a text object within the same paragraph.

Like operator An Access comparison operator that allows queries to find records that match criteria that include a wildcard character.

Limit to List A combo box control property that allows you to limit the entries made by that control to those provided by the combo box list.

Link A connection between a source file and a destination file, which when the source file is updated, the destination file can also be updated. Can also refer to a hyperlink. *See also* Hyperlink. (Word) A connection between two or more text boxes so that the text flows automatically from one text box to another.

Link Child Fields A subform property that determines which field serves as the "many" link between the subform and main form.

Link Master Fields A subform property that determines which field serves as the "one" link between the main form and the subform.

Linking The dynamic referencing of data in other workbooks, so that when data in the other workbooks is changed, the references in the current workbook are automatically updated.

List arrows *See* AutoFilter list arrows.

List box A bound control that displays a list of possible choices for the user. Used mainly on forms.

Lock To secure a row, column, or sheet so that data in that location cannot be changed.

Locked property A control property that specifies whether you can edit data in a control on Form View.

Logical conditions Using the operators And and Or to narrow a custom filter criteria.

Logical formula A formula with calculations that are based on stated conditions.

Logical test The first part of an IF function; if the logical test is true, then the second part of the function is applied, and if it is false, then the third part of the function is applied.

Lookup field A field that has lookup properties. Lookup properties are used to create a drop-down list of values to populate the field.

Lookup properties Field properties that allow you to supply a drop-down list of values for a field.

Lookup Wizard A wizard used in Table Design View that allows one field to "look up" values from another table or entered list. For example, you might use the Lookup Wizard to specify that the Customer Number field in the Sales table display the Customer Name field entry from the Customers table.

Macro An action or a set of actions that you use to automate tasks.

Mail merge To merge a main document that contains standard text with a file that contains customized information for many individual items to create customized versions of the main document.

Main document In a mail merge, the document with the standard text.

Main form A form that contains a subform control.

Main report A report that contains a subreport control.

Major gridlines Identify major units on a chart axis and are identifies by tick marks.

Many-to-many relationship The relationship between two tables in an Access database in which one record of one table relates to many records in the other table and vice versa. You cannot directly create a many-to-many relationship between two tables in Access. To relate two tables with such a relationship, you must establish a third table called junction table that creates separate one-to-many relationships with the two original tables.

Margin (Publisher, Word) Perimeter of the page outside of which nothing will print; the blank area between the edge of the text and the edge of a page. (PowerPoint) The distance between the edge of the text and the edge of the text box.

Margin guide A nonprinting line that appears in blue on the screen and outlines the margin, or perimeter, of the page.

Master page The page where you place any object that you want to repeat on every page of a publication.

Master view A specific view in a presentation that stores information about font styles, text placeholders, and color scheme. There are three master views: Slide Master view, Handout Master view, and Notes Master view.

Menu bar The bar beneath the title bar that contains the names of menus; clicking a menu name opens a menu of program commands.

Merge To combine adjacent cells into a single larger cell. *See also* Mail merge.

Merge field A placeholder that you insert in the main document to indicate where the data from each record should be inserted when you perform a mail merge.

Metadata Information that describes data and is used in Microsoft Windows document searches.

Minor gridlines Identify minor units on a chart axis.

Movie Live action captured in digital format by a movie camera.

Multilevel sort A reordering of table data using more than one column at a time.

Multivalued field A field that allows you to make more than one choice from a drop-down list.

Named range A contiguous group of cells given a meaningful name; it retains its name when moved and can be referenced in a formula.

Navigation bar The bar that provides a set of links to pages in a Web site.

Nested table A table inserted in a cell of another table.

Normal view A presentation view that divides the presentation window into three sections: Slides or Outline tab, Slide pane, and Notes pane.

Notes master The master view for Notes Page view.

Notes Page view A presentation view that displays a reduced image of the current slide above a large text box where you can type notes.

Notes pane The area in Normal view that shows speaker notes for the current slide; also in Notes Page view, the area below the slide image that contains speaker notes.

Nudge (Word, Publisher) To move a graphic or object a small amount in one direction using the arrow keys.

Null entry The state of "nothingness" in a field. Any entry such as 0 in a numeric field or a space in a text field is not null. It is common to search for empty fields by using the Null criterion in a filter or query. The Is Not Null criterion finds all records where there is an entry of any kind.

Object (PowerPoint) An item you place or draw on a slide that can be modified. Objects are drawn lines and shapes, text, clip art, imported pictures, and other objects. (Publisher) Any element in a publication that contains text or graphics and that can be moved or resized.

Object Position indicator An indicator on the status bar used to precisely position an object.

Object Size indicator An indicator on the status bar used to accurately gauge the size of an object.

Objects toolbar A toolbar that contains buttons for selecting and creating text boxes, shapes, and picture frames, as well as buttons for working with other types of objects.

Option button A bound control used to display a limited list of mutually exclusive choices for a field, such as "female" or "male" for a gender field in form or report.

Option group A bound control placed on a form that is used to group together several option buttons that provide a limited number of values for a field.

Or condition The records in a search must match only one of the criterion.

Organization chart A diagram of connected boxes that shows reporting structure in a company or organization.

Outline tab The area in Normal view that displays a presentation text in the form of an outline, without graphics.

Overflow text Text that won't fit in a text frame.

Page Navigation buttons The buttons at the bottom of the publication window that are used to jump to a specific page in your publication.

Pane A section of the PowerPoint window, such as the Slide or Notes pane.

Panes Sections into which you can divide a worksheet when you want to work on separate parts of the worksheet at the same time; one pane freezes, or remains in place, while you scroll in another pane until you see the desired information.

Paragraph spacing The space before and after paragraph text.

Parameter report A report that prompts you for criteria to determine the records to use for the report.

Photo album A type of presentation that displays photographs.

Picture caption Text that appears next to, above, or below a picture to describe or elaborate on the picture.

PivotChart A graphical presentation of the data in a PivotTable.

PivotChart View The view in which you build a PivotChart.

PivotTable An arrangement of data that uses one field as a column heading, another as a row heading, and summarizes a third field, typically a Number field, in the body.

PivotTable View The view in which you build a PivotTable.

Placeholder A dashed line box where you place text or objects.

PowerPoint Viewer A special application designed to run a PowerPoint slide show on any compatible computer that does not have PowerPoint installed.

PowerPoint window A window that contains the running PowerPoint application. The PowerPoint window includes the Ribbon, the panes, and Presentation window.

Presentation software A software program used to organize and present information.

Presenter view A special view that permits you to run a presentation through two monitors.

Print area A portion of a worksheet that you can define using the Print Area button on the Page Layout tab; after you select and define a print area, the Quick Print feature prints only that worksheet area.

Print title In a table that spans more than one page, the field names that print at the top of every printed page.

Properties File characteristics, such as the author's name, keywords, or the title, that help others understand, identify, and locate the file.

Property control A control that contains document property information or a placeholder for document property information, and which can be used to assign or update the document property directly from the document.

Publication A file created in Publisher.

Publication Gallery A pane that displays thumbnails of ready-made Publisher designs for the selected category.

Publication page A visual representation of your publication that appears in the publication window.

Publication Tasks task pane Task pane with options for common Publisher features associated with creating, distributing, and tracking the success of your publication.

Publication Tasks toolbar A toggle button located with the other toolbars at the top of the Publisher window that opens or closes the Publication Tasks task pane.

Publication window The area that includes the workspace for the publication page or pages and a desktop workspace for storing text and graphics prior to placing them in your publication.

Publish To save a version of an Office document in HTML format so that others can access it using their Web browsers. You can save the HTML files to a disk or save them directly to an intranet or Web server.

Pull quote A text box that contains a quotation or excerpt from an article, "pulled out" and formatted in a larger font size and placed on the same page, like a graphic.

Q

Query Datasheet View The view of a query that shows the selected fields and records as a datasheet.

Quick Part A reusable piece of content that can be inserted into a document, including a field, document property, or a preformatted building block.

Quick Style set A group of related styles that share common fonts, colors, and formats, and that can be used together in a document to give it a polished look.

R

Read-only format Data that users can view but not change.

Record In a table (an Excel database), data about an object or a person.

Report In Access, a flexible way to display and print data. *See also* Parameter report, Summary report, and Subreport.

Resize bar A thin gray bar that separates the field lists from the query design grid in Query Design View.

Return In a function, to display the result in a cell.

Ribbon A wide (toolbar-like) band that runs across the Office program windows that organizes primary commands into tabs; a new feature in Office 2007 that replaces Office 2003 menus and toolbars.

Rotate To change the angle of a selected object.

Rotation handle A green circular handle at the top of a selected object that you can drag to rotate the selected object to any angle between 0 to 360 degrees.

Row Source The Lookup property that defines the list of values for the Lookup field.

Ruler guide A nonprinting line that appears on a single page of your publication and that helps you align text, pictures, and other objects into columns and rows.

Run a query To open a query and view the fields and records that you have selected for the query presented as a datasheet.

S

Scale To resize a graphic so that its height-width ratio remains the same.

Scope In a named cell or range, the worksheets where the name can be used.

Scroll To use the scroll bars or arrow keys to display different parts of a window.

Search criterion In a workbook or table search, the text you are searching for.

Section A location on a form or report that contains controls. The section in which a control is placed determines where and how often the control prints.

Section properties Characteristics that define each section in a report.

Select query The most common type of query that retrieves data from one or more linked tables and displays the results in a datasheet.

Shape A drawing object, such as a rectangle, oval, triangle, line, block arrow, or other shape that you create using the Shapes command.

Shared workbook An Excel workbook that several users can open and modify.

Sidebar A text box that is positioned adjacent to the body of a document and contains auxiliary information.

Simple Query Wizard A wizard used to create a select query.

Single-file Web page A Web page that integrates all of the worksheets and graphical elements from a workbook into a single file in the MHTML file format, making it easier to publish to the Web.

Sizing handles Small boxes or circles appearing along the corners and sides of an object when that object is selected and that are used for moving and resizing.

Slide layout The arrangement that determines where all of the elements on a slide are located, including text and content placeholders.

Slide Library A folder where you store presentation slides for others to access, modify, or use.

Slide pane The section of Normal view that contains the current slide.

Slide Show view A view that shows a presentation as an electronic slide show; each slide fills the screen.

Slide Sorter view A view that displays a thumbnail of all slides in the order in which they appear in a presentation; used to rearrange slides and add special effects.

Slide timing The amount of time a slide is visible on the screen during a slide show. You can assign specific slide timings to each slide, or use the PowerPoint Rehearse Timings feature to simulate the amount of time you will need to display each slide in a slide show.

Slide transition The special effect that moves one slide off the screen and the next slide on the screen during a slide show. Each slide can have its own transition effect.

Slides tab The section in Normal View that displays the slides of a presentation as small thumbnails.

Smart tag A button that provides a small menu of options and automatically appears under certain conditions to help you work with a task, such as correcting errors. For example, the AutoCorrect Options button, which helps you correct typos and update properties, and the Error Indicator button, which helps identify potential design errors in Form and Report Design View, are smart tags.

SmartArt A professional quality graphic diagram, such as a diagram, list, organizational chart, or other graphic, that visually illustrates text; created using the SmartArt Command.

SmartArt text pane A small text pane attached to a SmartArt graphic where you can enter and edit text.

Sort To change the order of Access or Excel records, or Word table rows or mail merge records, according to one or more fields; sort order can be ascending or descending. *See also* Ascending order and Descending order.

Sort keys Criteria on which a sort, or a reordering of data, is based.

Source file Where an object you create with the source program is saved.

Source program The program in which a file was created.

Split To divide a cell into two or more cells.

Split form A form that shows you two views of the same data at one time: a traditional form and a datasheet view.

Standard toolbar The toolbar containing the buttons that perform some of the most commonly used commands, such as Cut, Copy, Paste, Save, Open, and Print.

Stated conditions In a logical formula, criteria you create.

Status bar The bar at the bottom of an Office program window that indicates the current page, the position and size of the selected object in the publication, and other program-specific information.

Story A single article that is contained in either one text box or a series of connected text boxes.

Storyboard A detailed outline of a Web site, including position of elements, necessary links, and graphics placement.

Structured reference Allows table formulas to refer to table columns by names that are automatically generated when the table is created.

Style A named collection of character and/or paragraph formats that are stored together and can be applied to text to format it quickly.

Subform A form placed within a form that shows related records from another table or query. A subform generally displays many records at a time in a datasheet arrangement.

Subform/Subreport control A control you use to start the Subform Wizard, which guides you through adding the subform to the main form in Form Design View.

Subreport A report placed as a control in another report.

Summary query A query used to calculate and display information about records grouped together.

Summary report A report that calculates and displays information about records grouped together.

Tab control An unbound control used to create a three-dimensional aspect to a form so that other controls can be organized and shown in Form View by clicking the "tabs."

Tab selector Cycles through the tab alignment options.

Table (Publisher, Word, and PowerPoint) A grid made up of rows and columns of cells that you can fill with text and graphics. (Excel) An organized collection of rows and columns of similarly structured data on a worksheet; formerly called a list in Excel 2003.

Table Design View The view in which you can add, delete, or modify fields and their associated properties.

Table style A named set of table format settings that can be applied to a table to format it all at once.

Table total row The area at the bottom of a table used for calculations with the data in the table columns.

Target The location that a hyperlink displays after you click it.

Task pane A window that provides quick access to common tasks organized by categories, such as Format Publication and Clip Art task panes (Publisher) or the Custom Animation task pane (PowerPoint).

Template A premade publication that contains formatting specifications for text, fonts, and colors, as well as placeholders for text and graphics, which can be used as a basis for a new publication.

Text box A frame that you can fill with text and graphics, which can be moved or resized.

Text placeholder A box with a dashed-line border and text that you replace with your own text.

Theme A set of unified design elements, including theme colors, theme fonts for body text and headings, and theme effects for graphics that can be applied to a document all at once.

Thumbnail A small image of a Publisher template.

Tick mark A small line of measurement that intersects an axis and identifies the categories, values or series of a chart.

Tiled Repeated, like a graphic in a worksheet background.

Timing *See* Slide timing.

Title bar The bar at the top of the program window that indicates the program name and the name of the current file.

Toggle key A key that switches between two options – press once to turn the option on, press again to turn it off.

Toolbar A bar that contains buttons that you can click to perform commands.

Total row Row in the query design grid used to specify how records should be grouped and summarized with aggregate functions.

Track To identify and keep a record of who makes which changes to a workbook.

Trendline A graphical representation of an upward or downward trend.

Two-page spread Pages that will face each other when a publication is printed.

Validation Rule
A field property that helps eliminate unreasonable entries by establishing criteria for an entry before it is accepted into the database.

Validation Text A field property that determines what message appears if a user attempts to make a field entry that does not pass the validation rule for that field.

Value axis On a chart or PivotChart, the vertical axis; *also called* the y-axis.

Value field A numeric field, such as Cost, that can be summed or averaged.

Vertical ruler A ruler that appears on the left side of the publication window.

Vertical scroll bars The bars on the right edge of the document window that is used to display different parts of the document in the document window.

View (Excel) A set of display or print settings that you can name and save for access at another time. You can save multiple views of a worksheet. (PowerPoint) A way of displaying a presentation, such as Normal view, Notes Page view, Slide Sorter view, and Slide Show view.

View Shortcuts The buttons on the status bar of the PowerPoint window that you click to switch among views.

Watermark
A translucent background design on a worksheet that is displayed when the worksheet is printed. Watermarks are graphic files that are inserted into the document header. Worksheet backgrounds created with the Background button on the Page Layout tab do not print.

Web *See* World Wide Web.

Web browser Software used to view Web pages and Web sites.

Web form A form that provides an easy way for a user to submit information via the Web.

Web Page Preview The view that shows how a Web page will appear in a browser when it is published.

Web page A document that can be stored on a computer called a Web server and viewed on the World Wide Web or on an intranet using a browser.

Web publication A publication that you can convert to either a Web page or a Web site.

Web server A computer that hosts Web pages.

Web site A group of associated Web pages that are linked together with hyperlinks.

Wildcard A special symbol that substitutes for unknown characters in defining search criteria in the Find and Replace dialog box. The most common types of wildcards are the question mark (?), which stands for any single character, and the asterisk (*), which represents any group of characters.

Window A rectangular area of the screen where you view and work on the open file.

WordArt A drawing object that contains text formatted with special shapes, patterns, and orientations.

Work area canvas Holds all fields for one record during a catalog merge.

Worksheet The component in Excel that contains the numerical data displayed in a chart.

Workspace An Excel file with an .xlw extension containing information about the identity, view, and placement of a set of open workbooks. Instead of opening each workbook individually, you can open the workspace file instead.

World Wide Web (WWW) A collection of electronic documents available to people around the world via the Internet; commonly referred to as the Web.

Wrapping The flow of text around an object rather than over it or behind it.

Index

KEY TO PAGE NUMBER ABBREVIATIONS

Access	AC
Excel	EX
Integration	INT
PowerPoint	PPT
Publisher	PB
Word	WD

SPECIAL CHARACTERS

\> (greater than operator), AC 143, EX 117
< (less than operator), AC 143, EX 117
<> (not equal to operator), AC 143, EX 117
* (asterisk), AC 142, AC 145, AC 146, AC 147, EX 160
\+ (plus sign), AC 146, AC 147
– (minus sign), AC 146, AC 147
/ (slash), AC 146, AC 147
= (equal sign), EX 117
\>= (greater than or equal to operator), AC 143, EX 117
<= (less than operator), AC 143
<= (less than or equal to operator), AC 143, EX 117
? (question mark), AC 145, EX 160
^ (caret), AC 146, AC 147

A

.accdb file extension, AC 123
Access, integrating with Word and Excel. *See* integrating Word, Excel, and Access
Access tables
 exporting to Excel, INT 72–73
 exporting to Word, INT 70–71
 inserting in PowerPoint, INT 82–83
 merging to Word, INT 66–67
action buttons, PPT 158–159
Add View dialog box, EX 134, EX 135
addition operator (+), AC 146, AC 147
Address Block command, WD 189
Advanced Filter command, EX 182–183
advanced formatting, PPT 122
 tools, PPT 100–101
aggregate functions, AC 148, AC 149
alignment, objects, PB 13, WD 143
Allow Value Lists Edits property, combo boxes, AC 170
And condition, EX 182
AND criteria, AC 142–143
AND function, building logical formulas with, EX 118–119
animation
 animated GIFs, PB 60
 charts, PPT 130–131
 customizing effects, PPT 102–103
 inserting in presentations, PPT 152–153
 timings, PPT 103
arithmetic operators, AC 146, AC 147
Arrange Windows dialog box, EX 130, EX 131
articles. *See* stories
ascending order, EX 164, WD 112

asterisk (*)
 multiplication operator, AC 147
 wildcard, AC 142, AC 145, EX 160
Attachment fields, AC 122–123
Auto Check for Errors command, WD 189
AutoFit, PB 10, PB 11
autoflow, PB 32
AutoFormats, AC 194, AC 195
AutoShapes, PB 42
AVERAGE function, EX 192
AVERAGEIF function, EX 108
Avg function, AC 148, AC 149

B

Back button, Quick Access toolbar, EX 140
backgrounds, PB 38
 worksheets, EX 136–137
banding, EX 157
baseline guides, PB 34, PB 35
Between...And operator, AC 143
bitmap graphics, WD 130
blank table cells, WD 116
boilerplate text, WD 178
borders, tables, WD 106
bound controls, option groups, AC 174–175
brightness of graphics, WD 131
building blocks, WD 160
 creating, WD 166–167
 editing, WD 167
 editing content, WD 168
 inserting, WD 168–169
 renaming, WD 167
Building Blocks Organizer, WD 168, WD 169
bullets
 default, resetting to, PPT 106
 picture, inserting, PPT 106, PPT 107
Business Contact Manager, PB 45
Business Information Set profiles, PB 7
buttons
 action, PPT 158–159
 command, forms, AC 176–177
Byte property, Number fields, AC 117

C

calculated columns, EX 166
calculated fields, AC 146–147
calculations, tables, WD 116–117
calendar pages, PB 57
caption(s), pictures, PB 28, PB 29, PB 36–37
Caption property, Text fields, AC 115
caret (^), exponentiation operator, AC 147
case sensitivity, sorting, EX 164
Catalog Merge feature, PB 2
Catalog Merge task page, PB 44, PB 45
Category Field drop area, PivotChart View, AC 153
CDs, playing music from, PPT 155

cell(s)
 locking and unlocking, EX 132, EX 133
 Word tables. *See* table cells
cell references, WD 116, WD 117
Center-aligned tab marker, PPT 109
Change Picture button, WD 134
chart(s), PPT 121–137, WD 142–143
 animation, PPT 130–131
 changing type, WD 142
 creating using Excel from PowerPoint, PPT 122, PPT 123
 editing data, WD 142
 embedding, PPT 122, PPT 132–133
 formatting elements, PPT 128–129
 layout, PPT 122, PPT 124, PPT 125, PPT 126–127
 linking, PPT 122
 organizational, PPT 149
 saving as templates, PPT 125
 styles, PPT 122, PPT 124, PPT 125
chart elements, formatting, WD 142
Chart Field List, PivotChart View, AC 152, AC 153
Check Spelling dialog box, PB 11
checkboxes, Web page forms, PB 63
circles, drawing, WD 140
circular references, correcting, EX 112
clearing ruler guides, PB 34
Clip Organizer, PB 14, PPT 152
closing publications, PB 18, PB 19
color
 graphics, WD 131
 Quick Style sets, WD 154
 sections in reports, AC 198
color scale, EX 183
color schemes
 publications, PB 2
column(s), PB 30–31
 datasheets, resizing, AC 140
 existing text boxes, PB 31
 tables. *See* table columns
 text boxes, PPT 101
 worksheets. *See* worksheet columns
Column Field drop area, PivotTable View, AC 153
Columnar layout, forms, AC 163
combo box(es), AC 170–173
 data entry, AC 170–171
 finding records, AC 172–173
Combo Box Wizard, AC 170, AC 172, AC 173
command(s). *See also specific commands*
 Mailings tab, WD 189
 Table menu, WD 106
command buttons, forms, AC 176–177
comments, PPT 170, PPT 171
comparison operators, AC 142, AC 143, EX 117
Compatibility Checker, PPT 159
Compatibility Checker dialog box, PPT 178, PPT 179
compatibility mode, EX 142, EX 143
CONCATENATE function, EX 106

condition(s)
  stated, EX 116
  summing data ranges based on, EX 108–109
conditional formatting, AC 190–191
  advanced options, EX 183
  multiple rules, EX 181
  sorting tables, EX 164
Conditional Formatting dialog box, AC 190, AC 191
Confirm Password dialog box, PPT 178, PPT 179
Connect Text Boxes toolbar, PB 4, PB 5
connecting text boxes, PB 32, PB 33
connector tools, PPT 98–99
consolidating data, using formulas, EX 110–111
Content Library, PB 2, PB 7
  adding objects, PB 36
contrast, graphics, WD 131
controls in forms, AC 161
  bound, AC 174–175
  combo boxes. *See* combo box(es)
  list boxes, AC 170, AC 171
  option groups, AC 174–175
  Subform/Subreport control, AC 162
  tab controls, AC 168–169
controls in reports
  adding lines to reports, AC 192–193
  group controls, AC 190
controls in Web pages, PB 62–63
Convert Text to Columns dialog box, EX 106, EX 107
Convert Text to Table command, WD 106
converting
  print publications to Web sites, PB 68
  shapes to text boxes, WD 140
  between tables and text, WD 107
  Web publications to Web sites, PB 66–67
copying
  table columns, WD 109
  table rows, WD 109
copy-to location, EX 185
correcting errors, circular references, EX 112
COUNT function, EX 192
Count function, AC 148, AC 149
COUNTIF function, EX 108, EX 109
cover pages, WD 164–165
Create New Building Block dialog box, WD 166, WD 167
Create New Theme Colors dialog box, WD 158, WD 159
Create New Theme Fonts dialog box, WD 158, WD 159
Creating your publication section, Publisher Tasks task pane, PB 5
criteria, AC 142
  AND, AC 142–143
  OR, AC 144–145
criteria ranges, EX 182, EX 183, EX 185
cropping graphics, WD 132
crosstab queries, AC 150–151
Crosstab Query Wizard, AC 150
Currency fields, AC 116, AC 117
Custom AutoFilter dialog box, EX 181
custom filters, EX 180–181
custom formats, tables, WD 120–121
custom shows, PPT 176–177
  links to, PPT 177
  printing, PPT 175
custom tables, creating, PPT 146–147
custom views, saving, EX 134–135

customizing
  animation effects, PPT 102–103
  PowerPoint installation, PPT 161
  Publisher, PB 7
  slide layouts, PPT 104–105
  themes, WD 158–159

D

data
  consolidating using formulas, EX 110–111
  protecting in forms, AC 174
  redundant, AC 106
  tables. *See* table(s); table data
data entry, combo boxes, AC 170–171
data entry area, EX 132
Data Field drop area, PivotChart View, AC 153
data fields, data sources, WD 178
data records, data sources, WD 178
data series, worksheets, PPT 123
data series mark, PPT 123
data sources, WD 178
  Access, filtering, INT 68–69
  data fields, WD 178
  data records, WD 178
  designing, WD 182–183
  editing records, WD 184–185
  file names, WD 178
  filtering records, WD 192, WD 193
  merging data into main document, WD 178
  merging information from, PB 44–45
  Outlook, WD 183
  sorting records, WD 192, WD 193
Data Validation dialog box, EX 190, EX 191
database(s)
  formats, AC 123
  merging to Word, INT 66–67
datasheet(s), resizing columns, AC 140
Datasheet layout, forms, AC 163
DATE function, AC 146, AC 147
Date/Time fields, AC 118–119
DAVERAGE function, EX 189
DCOUNT function, EX 189
DCOUNTA function, EX 189
Decimal Places property, Number fields, AC 117
Decimal-aligned tab marker, PPT 109
default theme, changing, WD 157
Default Value property, Text fields, AC 115
Default View property, AC 162
deleting
  data in tables, EX 162–163
  hyperlinks, INT 53
  table columns, WD 108, WD 109
  table rows, WD 108, WD 109
delimiters, EX 106
descending order, EX 164, WD 112
Design Checker, PB 11, PB 68
desktop publishing programs, PB 2–3. *See also* Publisher
desktop workspace, PB 4, PB 5
destination file, PPT 132
Detail Field drop area, PivotTable View, AC 153
Detail section, AC 187
  forms, AC 176
DGET function, EX 186, EX 189
dialog box(es). *See also specific dialog boxes*
digital signatures, EX 139
displaying rulers, WD 132

Distributing your publication section, Publisher Tasks task pane, PB 5
distribution
  preparing presentations for, PPT 178
  saving workbooks for, EX 142–143
division operator, AC 146, AC 147
document(s)
  merging. *See* mail merge
  saving as Web pages, WD 155
Document Inspector dialog box, EX 138, EX 139
document properties, updating, WD 162
Document Properties panel, EX 138, EX 139
Document Workspace Web site, PPT 171
domain(s), AC 200
domain (aggregate) functions, AC 200–201
Double property, Number fields, AC 117
dragging
  moving graphics, WD 134, WD 135
  resizing graphics, WD 132, WD 133
Draw Table command, WD 106
drawing
  freeform shapes, PPT 99
  shapes, WD 140–141
  SmartArt graphics, PPT 148–149
  tables, PPT 147, WD 121
  text boxes, WD 136
drawing canvas, WD 141
drop area, PivotTable and PivotChart Views, AC 152, AC 153
drop caps, PB 38
DSUM function, EX 188, EX 189
dynamic page breaks, EX 135

E

Edit Data Source dialog box, WD 184, WD 185
Edit List Items button, AC 170, AC 171
Edit Recipients List command, WD 189
Edit relationships dialog box, AC 110, AC 111
  one-to-many line, AC 110
editing
  building block content, WD 168
  building blocks, WD 167
  chart data, WD 142
  data source records, WD 184–185
  hyperlinks, INT 53
e-mail, sending publications as, PB 68–69
embedded objects, formatting, INT 56
embedding
  charts, PPT 122
  Excel charts in slides, PPT 132–133
  Excel files in Word, INT 56–57
  linking versus, PPT 135
  PowerPoint slides in Word, INT 90–91
  worksheets in slides, PPT 133
Enabled property, forms, AC 174
Encrypt Document dialog box, PPT 178, PPT 179
envelope(s), printing, WD 191
envelope mail merges, WD 190
Envelopes and labels dialog box, WD 191
Envelopes command, WD 189
equal sign (=), equal to operator, EX 117
error(s)
  checking formulas for, EX 112–113
  correcting. *See* correcting errors
  error values, EX 113
  validating table data, EX 190–191
Error Alert tab, Data Validation dialog box, EX 191

error bars, PPT 122, PPT 123
error correction, PB 11
error indicator(s), forms, AC 164
Error Indicator button, AC 119
event pages, PB 57
Excel
   creating charts using, from PowerPoint, PPT 122
   integrating with Word. *See* integrating Word and Excel
   integrating with Word, Access, and PowerPoint. *See* integrating Word, Excel, Access, and PowerPoint
   integrating with Word and Access. *See* integrating Word, Excel, and Access
Excel Spreadsheet command, WD 106
exceptions, Slide Master, PPT 107
exiting Publisher, PB 18, PB 19
exponentiation operator (^), AC 146, AC 147
exporting
   Access reports to Word, INT 74–75
   Access tables to Excel, INT 72–73
   Access tables to Word, INT 70–71
expressions, calculated fields, AC 146
extracting table data, EX 184–185

▶ F

FAQs, PB 57
field(s)
   calculated, AC 146–147
   data, data sources, WD 178
   foreign key, AC 109
   Lookup, AC 112–113
   matching in mail merge, WD 186
   merge. *See* merge fields
   multivalued, AC 112
   tables, EX 154
field lists, AC 138
field names, EX 154
field properties, AC 114–115
field selector button, AC 114
Field Size property
   Number fields, AC 117
   Text fields, AC 115
file extensions
   databases, AC 123
   workbook formats, EX 143
filenames, data sources, WD 178
Filter Field drop area, PivotTable and PivotChart Views, AC 153
filter list arrows, EX 178
filtering records in data source, WD 192, WD 193
filtering tables, EX 178–183
   Advanced Filter command, EX 182–183
   clearing filters, EX 178
   custom filters, EX 180–181
Final Relationships window, AC 110, AC 111
Find & Select button, EX 160, EX 161
Find and Replace dialog box, EX 160, EX 161
Find Duplicates Query Wizard, AC 151
Find recipient command, WD 189
Find Unmatched Query Wizard, AC 151
finding
   data in tables, EX 160–161
   records, using combo boxes, AC 172–173
Finish & Merge command, WD 189
First function, AC 149
First line indent marker, PPT 109
fixed layout format, PPT 129
flipping objects, PB 41

floating graphics, WD 130, WD 131, WD 134
Following up section, Publisher Tasks task pane, PB 5
font(s)
   publications, PB 2
   Quick Style sets, WD 154
font schemes, PB 2
font sizes, PB 10
font styles, PB 10
footers, PB 28, PB 38, PB 39
foreground, PB 38
foreign key field, AC 106
   data type, AC 109
   null entries, AC 111
form(s), AC 161–177, PB 54
   command buttons, AC 176–177
   controls. *See* controls in forms
   layout, AC 162, AC 163
   linking with subforms, AC 165
   main, AC 162, AC 163
   option groups, AC 174–175
   protecting data, AC 174
   sections, AC 176
   split, AC 166–167
   subforms. *See* subforms
form control(s), Web pages, PB 62–63
Form Control button, PB 59
Form design View, tab controls, AC 168–169
Form Footer section, AC 176
Form Header section, AC 176
Form Wizard, AC 162, AC 163
format(s), workbooks, EX 143
Format Cells dialog box, Protection tab, EX 132, EX 133
Format Picture dialog box, WD 131
Format property
   Date/Time fields, AC 118
   Text fields, AC 115
FormatPainter, AC 194, AC 195
formatting
   advanced, PPT 100–101, PPT 122
   chart elements, PPT 128–129, WD 142
   charts, PPT 122
   conditional, AC 190–191. *See* conditional formatting
   custom formats for tables, WD 120–121
   data using text functions, EX 106–107
   master text, PPT 106–107
   modifying using Paste Special, INT 50–51
   pasted, embedded, and linked objects, INT 56
   reports, AC 190–191
   SmartArt graphics, PPT 150–151
   text, PB 10–11
   Web publications, PB 58–59
   Web publications for different audiences, PB 66
formatting tools, advanced, PPT 100–101
formulas, EX 105–121
   calculating payments with PMT function, EX 120–121
   checking for errors, EX 112–113
   consolidating data, EX 110–111
   constructing using names ranges, EX 114–115
   hiding, EX 132
   logical, building, EX 116–119
   summing data ranges based on conditions, EX 108–109
   tables, EX 166–167, WD 116, WD 117
   text, formatting data using, EX 106–107
frames, PB 8, PB 28
   resizing, PB 12
freeform shapes, drawing, PPT 99
freezing rows and columns, EX 132

function(s), AC 146, AC 147
   aggregate, AC 148, AC 149
   domain (aggregate), AC 200–201
Function Arguments dialog box, EX 188, EX 189
future value, calculating with FV function, EX 121
FV function, EX 121

▶ G

GIF files, PPT 152
graphics, WD 129–145
   bitmap, WD 130
   brightness, WD 131
   changing proportions, WD 132
   changing shape, WD 135
   charts, WD 142–143
   color, WD 131
   contrast, WD 131
   cropping, WD 132
   drawing shapes, WD 140–141
   file size, PB 14
   floating, WD 130, WD 131, WD 134
   inline, WD 130, WD 131
   inserting in documents, WD 130–131
   inserting in publications, PB 14–15
   page layout, WD 144–145
   positioning, WD 130, WD 134–135
   publications, PB 28, PB 29
   rotating, WD 140, WD 141
   scaling, WD 132, WD 133
   shadows, WD 139
   shifting order of layers in stack, WD 140
   sizing, WD 132, WD 133
   SmartArt. *See* SmartArt graphics
   text boxes, WD 136–137
   3-D effects, WD 139
   visual effects, WD 135
   WordArt, WD 138–139
Graphics Interchange Format files, PPT 152
greater than operator (>), AC 143, EX 117
greater than or equal to operator (>=), AC 143, EX 117
Greeting Line command, WD 189
grid guides, PB 34
gridlines
   major, PPT 126
   minor, PPT 126, PPT 127
   tables, WD 119, WD 162
group controls, AC 190
Group Footer section, AC 187
Group Header section, AC 187
group selection handles, AC 190
grouping
   objects, PB 42–43
   worksheets, EX 144–145
guides, PB 13, PB 34–35

▶ H

handouts, PPT 112, PPT 113
   creating in Word, PPT 113
Hanging indent marker, PPT 109
header(s), PB 28, PB 38, PB 39
header rows, EX 154
   repeating on every page of table, WD 112
Help system, PB 18
hiding
   formulas, EX 132
   worksheets, EX 130
Highlight Merge Fields command, WD 189

HLOOKUP function, EX 187
home pages, PB 54
horizontal ruler, PB 4, PB 5
hosts, PB 55
Hot Spot button, PB 59
HTML Code Fragment button, PB 59
hyperlinks, PB 54. *See also* linking
   changing link sources, INT 58–59
   editing, INT 53
   inserting, PPT 160–161
   re-establishing, INT 59
   removing, INT 53
   between Word and Excel, INT 52–53, INT 57
   workbooks, EX 140–141
Hypertext Markup Language (HTML), EX 142, PB 54

I

icon sets, EX 183
IF function, building logical formulas, EX 116–117
IFERROR function, EX 112
images. *See* graphics
In operator, AC 143
indent(s), master text, PPT 108–109
indent levels, PPT 108, PPT 109
indent markers, PPT 108, PPT 109
Information Rights Management (IRM), EX 138
inline graphics, WD 130, WD 131
Input Mask property, Text fields, AC 115
Input Message tab, Data Validation dialog box, EX 191
Insert Address Block dialog box, WD 186, WD 187
Insert Hyperlink button, PB 59
Insert Hyperlink dialog box, EX 140, EX 141, INT 52, INT 53
Insert Merge Field command, WD 189
Insert Table command, WD 106
Insert Text dialog box, PB 8, PB 9
inserting files into publications, PB 2
Integer property, Number fields, AC 117
integrating Word, Excel, Access, and PowerPoint, INT 81–91
   embedding PowerPoint slides in Word, INT 90–91
   inserting Access tables in PowerPoint, INT 82–83, INT 91
   inserting Word objects in PowerPoint, INT 84–85, INT 91
   linking Excel files in PowerPoint, INT 86–87, INT 91
   publishing PowerPoint slides in Word, INT 88–89, INT 91
   summary, INT 91
integrating Word, Excel, and Access, INT 65–75
   exporting Access reports to Word, INT 74–75
   exporting Access tables to Excel, INT 72–73, INT 75
   exporting Access tables to Word, INT 70–71, INT 75
   filtering Access data sources, INT 68–69, INT 75
   merging from Access to Word, INT 66–67, INT 75
   summary, INT 75
integrating Word and Excel, INT 49–59
   changing link sources, INT 58–59
   creating Excel spreadsheets in Word, INT 54–55, INT 57
   creating hyperlinks, INT 52–53, INT 57
   embedding Excel files in Word, INT 56–57
   modifying formatting using Paste Special, INT 50–51, INT 57
   summary, INT 57
intranets, EX 142
Invalid Data warning, EX 190, EX 191
Is Not Null operator, AC 143

J

JPEG images, AC 122, AC 123
junction tables, AC 106

K

key field combinations, AC 106
keywords, EX 138
kiosks, PPT 174

L

label(s)
   creating, WD 190–191
   printing, WD 191
Label Options dialog box, WD 190, WD 191
Labels command, WD 189
Last function, AC 149
layering objects, PB 42–43
layout. *See also* page layout
   charts, PPT 122, PPT 124, PPT 125, PPT 126–127
   forms, AC 162, AC 163
   publications, PB 28, PB 29
   Slide Master, restoring, PPT 105
   slides, custom, PPT 104–105
layout, pages. *See* page layout
layout guides, PB 34, PB 35
leading, PPT 110
LEFT function, AC 146, AC 147
Left indent marker, PPT 109
Left-aligned tab marker, PPT 109
LEN function, AC 146, AC 147
less than operator (<), AC 143, EX 117
less than or equal to operator (<=), AC 143, EX 117
Like operator, AC 142, AC 143
Limit to List Lookup property, AC 112
Limit to List property, combo boxes, AC 170
line(s)
   adding to reports, AC 192–193
   problems, AC 195
line spacing, PPT 110, PPT 111
link(s). *See* hyperlinks; linking
Link Child Fields, AC 165
Link Master Fields, AC 165
linked objects, formatting, INT 56
linking. *See also* hyperlinks
   charts, PPT 122
   to custom shows, PPT 177
   data between workbooks, EX 110, EX 111
   embedding versus, PPT 135
   text boxes, WD 136
   updating linked Excel worksheets, PPT 136–137
   worksheets to slides, PPT 134–135
Links dialog box, INT 88, INT 89
list(s), sorting, WD 113
list arrows, EX 178
list boxes, AC 170, AC 171
   Web page forms, PB 63
Lock aspect ratio check box, WD 132
Locked property, forms, AC 174
locking cells, EX 132, EX 133
logical conditions, EX 180
logical formulas
   building with AND function, EX 118–119
   building with IF function, EX 116–117
logical tests, EX 116
logical view, AC 138
Long Integer property, Number fields, AC 117

looking up table values, EX 186–187
Lookup fields, AC 112–113
Lookup Wizard, AC 112
LOWER function, EX 107

M

macros, PPT 156–157
   security, PPT 157
mail merge, WD 177–193
   data source. *See* data sources
   envelopes, WD 190
   labels, WD 190–191
   main document. *See* main document
   performing merges, WD 188–189
   process, WD 178, WD 179
   templates, WD 181
Mail Merge Recipients dialog box, WD 184, WD 185
Mailings tab, commands, WD 189
main document, WD 178
   creating, WD 180–181
   inserting individual merge fields, WD 193
   merge fields, WD 178, WD 186–187
   merging data from data source into, WD 178
main form, AC 162, AC 163
main report, AC 196
major gridlines, PPT 126
many-to-many relationships, AC 106
margin(s), PB 34, PPT 110, PPT 111
   cells in tables, WD 115
margin guides, PB 34, PB 35
marketing tools, PB 45
Master Layout dialog box, PPT 105
master pages, PB 38, PB 39
master text
   formatting, PPT 106–107
   indents, PPT 108–109
Match Fields command, WD 189
MATCH function, EX 187
matching fields, mail merge, WD 186
MAX function, EX 192
Max function, AC 148, AC 149
.mdb file extension, AC 123
menu bar, PB 4, PB 5
merge fields, WD 178
   inserting, WD 193
   main document, WD 186–187
merging
   from Access to Word, INT 66–67
   cells, WD 114, WD 115
   documents. *See* mail merge
   information from data sources, PB 44–45
metadata, EX 138
Microsoft Office Publisher Design Gallery, PB 36, PB 37
Microsoft PowerPoint Viewer, PPT 183
MIN function, EX 192
Min function, AC 148, AC 149
minor gridlines, PPT 126, PPT 127
minus sign (–), subtraction operator, AC 147
mouse, resizing graphics,, WD 132, WD 133
movies, inserting in presentations, PPT 153
moving
   objects, PB 12, PB 13
   table columns, WD 109
   table rows, WD 109
multilevel sorts, EX 164
multiple rules, conditional formatting, EX 181
multiplication operator (*), AC 146, AC 147

multivalued fields, AC 112
music, playing from CDs, PPT 155
My Templates, PB 7

▶ N

name(s)
　data sources, WD 178
　field, EX 154
　workbooks, EX 115
named ranges, constructing formulas, EX 114–115
navigation bars, PB 54
Navigation Pane, AC 108, AC 109
　renaming objects, AC 144
nested tables, WD 119
New Address List dialog box, WD 182, WD 183, WD 184, WD 185
New Name dialog box, EX 114, EX 115
not equal to operator (<>), AC 143, EX 117
NOT function, EX 118
Not operator, AC 143
notes masters, PPT 112, PPT 113
nudging objects, PB 13
null entries, AC 111
Null operator, AC 143
Number fields, AC 116, AC 117

▶ O

object(s). *See also* form(s); queries; report(s); table(s)
　adding to Content Library, PB 36
　aligning, PB 13
　embedded, formatting, INT 56
　flipping, PB 41
　grouping, PB 42–43
　layering, PB 42–43
　linked, formatting, INT 56
　moving, PB 12, PB 13
　nudging, PB 13
　pasted, formatting, INT 56
　publications, PB 2
　resizing, PB 12, PB 13
　rotating, PB 41
　selecting, PB 12
　wrapping text around, PB 28, PB 29, PB 40–41
Object Position indicator, PB 4, PB 5, PB 13
Object Size indicator, PB 4, PB 5, PB 13, PB 14, PB 15
Objects toolbar, PB 4, PB 5
OLE data type, AC 122
one-to-many join lines, AC 138, AC 139
one-to-many line, Edit relationships dialog box, AC 110
one-to-many relationships, AC 107, AC 110–111
option buttons, Web page forms, PB 63
Option Group Wizard, AC 174, AC 175
option groups, forms, AC 174–175
Options dialog box, PPT 182, PPT 183
Or condition, EX 182
OR criteria, AC 144–145
OR function, EX 118
organizational charts, PPT 149
Outlook, data sources, WD 183
Outlook window, PPT 172, PPT 173
overflow text, PB 28, PB 29, PB 32–33

▶ P

Pack and Go wizard, PB 16
Package for CD dialog box, PPT 182, PPT 183
packaging presentations, PPT 182–183

page(s). *See also* Web pages
　margin, PB 34
　master, PB 38, PB 39
page break(s), dynamic, EX 135
Page Break Preview button, EX 135
Page Footer section, AC 187
　forms, AC 176
Page Header section, AC 187
　forms, AC 176
page layout
　graphics, WD 144–145
　tables, WD 119
Page Navigation buttons, PB 4, PB 5
page setup, changing, PPT 151
panes, EX 132
paragraph(s), sorting, WD 113
paragraph spacing, PPT 110, PPT 111
parameter queries, AC 188, AC 189
parameter reports, AC 188–189
passwords, PPT 178, PPT 179
　strong, PPT 179
Paste Special command, PPT 137
　modifying formatting, INT 50–51
pasted objects, formatting, INT 56
payments, calculating with PMT function, EX 120–121
PDF format, EX 142
　saving files, PPT 129
photo album(s), PPT 184–185
Photo Album dialog box, PPT 184, PPT 185
photo pages, PB 57
picture captions, PB 28, PB 29, PB 36–37
PivotChart(s), AC 152, AC 153
PivotChart layout, forms, AC 163
PivotChart View, AC 152, AC 153
PivotTable(s), AC 152, AC 153
PivotTable layout, forms, AC 163
PivotTable View, AC 152, AC 153
planning
　publications, PB 28–29
　tables, EX 154–155
plus sign (+), addition operator, AC 147
PMT function, AC 146, AC 147, EX 120–121
pointer shapes, PB 12
positioning graphics, WD 130, WD 134–135
PowerPoint photo albums, PPT 184–185
PowerPoint versions, checking, PPT 159
presentations
　animation, PPT 152–153
　custom shows, PPT 176–177
　inserting movies, PPT 153
　packaging, PPT 182–183
　preparing for distribution, PPT 178
　reviewing, PPT 172, PPT 173
　saving for Web, PPT 180–181
　self-running, PPT 174, PPT 175
　sending, PPT 172, PPT 173
　sound, PPT 154–155
Presenter view, PPT 175
Preview Results command, WD 189
previewing
　publications, PB 16, PB 17
　Web publications, PB 64–65
primary key field, AC 106
print area, setting, EX 169
Print dialog box, PB 16, PB 17
printing
　custom shows, PPT 175
　envelopes, WD 191

labels, WD 191
　publications, PB 2, PB 16, PB 17
　tables, EX 168–169
programs. *See also specific programs*
　source, PPT 132
proofing tools, PPT 173
PROPER function, EX 106
properties. *See also specific properties*
　fields, AC 114–115
　toggling through choices, AC 192
properties, workbooks, EX 138
Property Update Options button, AC 116, AC 117
proportions, graphics, changing, WD 132
Protect Sheet dialog box, EX 132, EX 133
Protection tab, Format Cells dialog box, EX 132, EX 133
publication(s), PB 2, PB 3. *See also* Publisher
　checking for spelling and design errors, PB 11
　closing, PB 18, PB 19
　creating using an existing design, PB 6–7
　graphics, PB 28, PB 29
　inserting files created in other programs, PB 2
　inserting graphics, PB 14–15
　layout, PB 28, PB 29
　planning, PB 28–29
　previewing, PB 16, PB 17
　printing, PB 2, PB 16, PB 17
　publishing to Web, PB 2
　saving, PB 16, PB 17
　text, PB 28, PB 29
Publication Gallery, PB 4, PB 6, PB 7, PB 56, PB 57
publication page, PB 4, PB 5
Publication Tasks toolbar, PB 4, PB 5
publication window, PB 4, PB 5
Publish as Web Page dialog box, PPT 180, PPT 181
Publish to the Web dialog box, PB 66, PB 67
Publisher
　customizing, PB 7
　exiting, PB 18, PB 19
　starting, PB 4, PB 5
Publisher Tasks task pane, PB 5
Publisher window, PB 4, PB 5
publishing
　PowerPoint slides in Word, INT 88–89
　saving workbooks for, EX 142–143
　slides to Slide Libraries, PPT 181
　Web sites, PB 55
pull quotes, PB 28, PB 29, PB 40, PB 41, WD 160

▶ Q

queries, AC 137–153
　calculated fields, AC 146–147
　AND criteria, AC 142–143
　criteria. *See* criteria
　crosstab, AC 150–151
　datasheets. *See* datasheet(s)
　multiple sort orders, AC 140–141
　OR criteria, AC 144–145
　parameter, AC 188, AC 189
　PivotTables and PivotCharts, AC 152–153
　running, AC 138
　select, AC 137, AC 138–139
　summary, AC 148–149
Query Datasheet View, AC 138
query design grid, AC 138, AC 139
Query Design View, AC 138, AC 139
　multiple sort orders, AC 140–141
　resizing, AC 139

question mark (?), wildcard, AC 145, EX 160
Quick Access toolbar, Back button, EX 140
Quick Parts feature, WD 162–163
Quick Style sets, WD 154–155
Quick Tables command, WD 106

R

record(s)
    data sources. *See* data sources
    finding using combo boxes, AC 172–173
    tables, EX 154
Record Source property, forms, AC 164
redundant data, AC 106
re-establishing hyperlinks, INT 59
referential integrity, AC 111
related links pages, PB 57
relational database(s)
    Attachment fields, AC 122–123
    date/time fields, AC 118–119
    lookup fields, AC 112–113
    many-to-many relationships, AC 106
    number and currency fields, AC 116–117
    one-to-many relationships, AC 107, AC 110–111
    overview, AC 106–107
    related table design, AC 106, AC 108–109
    text fields, AC 114–115
    validation properties, AC 120–121
Remove Duplicates dialog box, EX 162, EX 163
removing hyperlinks, INT 53
renaming building blocks, WD 167
replacing
    data in tables, EX 160–161
    text in text boxes, PB 8–9
report(s), AC 185–201
    Access, exporting to Word, INT 74–75
    adding lines, AC 192–193
    AutoFormats, AC 194, AC 195
    conditional formatting, AC 190–191
    domain (aggregate) functions, AC 200–201
    FormatPainter, AC 194, AC 195
    formatting, AC 190–191
    main, AC 196
    parameter reports, AC 188–189
    section properties, AC 198–199
    sections, AC 187
    subreports, AC 196–197
    summary reports, AC 186–187
Report Header section, AC 187
Required property, Text fields, AC 115
Research task pane, EX 141, PPT 127
reset buttons, Web page forms, PB 63
resize bar, AC 139
resizing
    datasheet columns, AC 140
    frames, PB 12
    objects, PB 12, PB 13
    Query Design View, AC 139
    tables, WD 110, WD 111
reviewing presentations, PPT 172, PPT 173
RIGHT function, AC 146, AC 147
Right-aligned tab marker, PPT 109
rotate handle, WD 130
rotating
    graphics, WD 140, WD 141
    objects, PB 41
rotation handles, PB 8
row(s)
    tables, planning, EX 154
    worksheets. *See* worksheet rows

Row Field drop area, PivotTable View, AC 153
Row Source lookup property, AC 112
Row Source Type property, combo boxes, AC 170, AC 171
rows, tables. *See* table rows
RTF File dialog box, INT 70, INT 71
.rtf format, exporting Access tables to Word, INT 70
ruler(s), PB 4, PB 5, PB 12
    displaying, WD 132
ruler guides, PB 34, PB 35
    clearing, PB 34
Rules command, WD 189
running queries, AC 138

S

Save As dialog box, PB 16, PB 17
saving
    custom views, EX 134–135
    documents as Web pages, WD 155
    files in PDF and XPS file formats, PPT 129
    presentations for Web, PPT 180–181
    publications, PB 16, PB 17
    workbooks for distribution, EX 142–143
scaling graphics, WD 132, WD 133
scope, EX 114
search criteria, EX 178
section(s)
    colors, AC 198
    forms, AC 176
section properties, AC 198–199
security
    macros, PPT 157
    passwords, PPT 178, PPT 179
select queries, AC 137, AC 138–139
Select Recipients command, WD 189
selecting
    objects, PB 12
    table cells, WD 108
selection handles, group, AC 190
Send to Microsoft Office Word dialog box, INT 88, INT 89
sending presentations, PPT 172, PPT 173
Series Field drop area, PivotChart View, AC 153
Set Up Show dialog box, PPT 174, PPT 175
shadows, graphics, WD 139
shapes
    connecting, PPT 98–99
    converting to text boxes, WD 140
    drawing, WD 140–141
    freeform, drawing, PPT 99
    graphics, changing, WD 135
shared workbooks, EX 139
sheet(s), linking data between, EX 110
Show Table dialog box, AC 138
sidebars, PB 28, PB 29, WD 160–161
signatures, digital, EX 139
Simple Query Wizard, AC 138
single file Web pages, EX 142, EX 143
Single property, Number fields, AC 117
Size dialog box, WD 132, WD 133
sizing graphics, WD 132, WD 133
sizing handles, PB 8, WD 130
slash (/), division operator, AC 147
slide(s)
    embedding Excel charts, PPT 132–133
    embedding in Word, INT 90–91
    embedding worksheets, PPT 133
    linking worksheets, PPT 134–135

    publishing in Word, INT 88–89
    publishing to Slide Libraries, PPT 181
Slide Libraries, publishing slides to, PPT 181
Slide Master
    exceptions, PPT 107
    restoring layout, PPT 105
slide orientation, changing, PPT 151
slide shows, voice narrations, PPT 131
Smart Tags, AC 119
SmartArt graphics, WD 143
    drawing, PPT 148–149
    formatting, PPT 150–151
Snap to feature, PB 13
Sort dialog box, EX 164, EX 165
sorting
    custom sort order, EX 165
    data tables, EX 164–165
    lists, WD 113
    multiple sort orders, AC 140–141
    paragraphs, WD 113
    records in data source, WD 192, WD 193
    secondary sort order, AC 141
    table data, WD 112–113
    tables with conditional formatting, EX 164
sound, inserting in presentations, PPT 154–155
source file, PPT 132
source program, PPT 132
spacing, text, PPT 110, PPT 111
special offer pages, PB 57
spell checking, PB 11
Split Cells dialog box, WD 114, WD 115
split forms, AC 166–167
splitting cells, WD 114, WD 115
spreadsheets. *See also* worksheet(s)
    Excel, creating in Word, INT 54–55
SQL (structured query language), AC 140
St Dev function, AC 149
Standard toolbar, PB 4, PB 5
Start Mail Merge command, WD 189
starting Publisher, PB 4, PB 5
stated conditions, EX 116
status bar, PB 4, PB 5
stories, PB 28, PB 29
    publications, PB 2
storyboards, PB 54
strong passwords, PPT 179
Structured Query Language (SQL), AC 140
structured references, EX 166, EX 167
styles
    charts, PPT 122, PPT 124, PPT 125
    definition, WD 154
    Quick Style sets, WD 154–155
    tables, WD 118–119
subforms, AC 161, AC 162–165
    creating, AC 162–163
    linking with forms, AC 165
    modifying, AC 164–165
Subform/Subreport control, AC 162
submit buttons Web page forms, PB 63
subreports, AC 196–197
SUBSTITUTE function, EX 107
subtotal(s), EX 192–193
Subtotal dialog box, EX 192, EX 193
subtraction operator (–), AC 146, AC 147
Sum function, AC 148, AC 149
SUMIF function, EX 108, EX 109
summarizing table data, EX 188–189
summary information, viewing, EX 138
summary queries, AC 148–149

Index 23

summary reports, AC 186–187
summing data ranges based on conditions, EX 108–109
Symbol dialog box, PPT 106, PPT 107
Synchronous Scrolling button, EX 130

T

tab controls, forms, AC 168–169
tab markers, PPT 108, PPT 109
tab selector, PPT 108
table(s), EX 153–169, PB 28, PB 29, WD 105–121
   Access. *See* Access tables
   advanced properties, WD 111
   borders, WD 106
   calculations, WD 116–117
   cells. *See* table cells
   columns. *See* table columns
   converting between text and, WD 107
   creating, EX 156–157
   custom, creating, PPT 146–147
   custom formats, WD 120–121
   data. *See* filtering tables; table data
   definition, WD 106
   drawing, PPT 147, WD 121
   fields, EX 154
   formulas, EX 166–167, WD 116, WD 117
   gridlines, WD 119, WD 162
   junction, AC 106
   nested, WD 119
   page layout, WD 119
   planning, EX 154–155
   printing, EX 168–169
   records, EX 154
   related, design, AC 106, AC 108–109
   repeating header row on every page, WD 112
   resizing, WD 110, WD 111
   rows. *See* table rows
   sorting data, WD 112–113
   splitting and merging cells, WD 114–115
   styles, WD 118–119
table cells, WD 106
   blank, WD 116
   changing margins, WD 115
   merging, WD 114, WD 115
   selecting, WD 108
   splitting, WD 114, WD 115
table columns
   copying, WD 109
   deleting, WD 108, WD 109
   inserting, WD 108, WD 109
   modifying, WD 110–111
   moving, WD 109
   planning, EX 154
table data, EX 177–193
   adding, EX 158–159
   deleting, EX 162–163
   extracting, EX 184–185
   filtering. *See* filtering tables
   finding and replacing, EX 160–161
   looking up values, EX 186–187
   sorting, EX 164–165
   subtotals, EX 192–193
   summarizing, EX 188–190
   validating, EX 190–191
Table Design view, AC 108, AC 109
   related table design, AC 108–109
Table menu, commands, WD 106

Table Properties dialog box, WD 111
table rows
   copying, WD 109
   deleting, WD 108, WD 109
   inserting, WD 108, WD 109
   modifying, WD 110–111
   moving, WD 109
table styles, EX 156, WD 118–119
   changing options, EX 156
   coordinating with document, EX 156
table total row, EX 166
Tabular layout, forms, AC 163
targets, EX 140, EX 141
templates, PB 7, PPT 170
   mail merge, WD 181
   publications, PB 2
   saving charts as, PPT 125
text
   boilerplate, WD 178
   columns, PB 30–31
   converting between tables and, WD 107
   formatting, PB 10–11
   overflow, PB 28, PB 29, PB 32–33
   publications, PB 28, PB 29. *See* stories
   Quick Style sets, WD 154–155
   replacing in text boxes, PB 8–9
   Word, inserting in PowerPoint, INT 84–85
   wrapping, PB 28, PB 29, PB 40–41
text area, Web page forms, PB 63
text boxes, WD 136–137
   columns, PB 31, PPT 101
   connecting, PB 32, PB 33
   converting shapes to, WD 140
   creating, PB 9
   drawing, WD 136
   linking, WD 136
   replacing text, PB 8–9
   Web page forms, PB 63
text flow icons, PB 33
text functions, formatting data using, EX 106–107
text objects, adjusting, PPT 110–111
text spacing, PPT 110, PPT 111
text styles, PB 39
themes
   applying, WD 156–157
   customizing, WD 158–159
   default, changing, WD 157
3-D effects, graphics, WD 139
3-D references, EX 110
thumbnails, PB 4, PB 5
tick marks, PPT 122, PPT 123
timings, animation, PPT 103
title bar, PB 4, PB 5
toolbar(s), PB 4, PB 5
toolbar buttons, Web page formatting, PB 58, PB 59
Total row, AC 148
Totals Field drop area, PivotTable View, AC 153
tracking modifications, EX 139
trendlines, PPT 122

U

unlocking cells, EX 132, EX 133
Update Labels command, WD 189
updating
   document properties, WD 162
   linked Excel worksheets, PPT 136–137
UPPER function, EX 107

V

validating table data, EX 190–191
Validation Rule field property, AC 120, AC 121
Validation Text field property, AC 120, AC 121
value(s)
   error, EX 113
   future, calculating with FV function, EX 121
   looking up table values, EX 186–187
Var function, AC 149
vertical ruler, PB 4, PB 5
view(s), logical, AC 138
View Side by Side button, EX 130
viewing summary information, EX 138
Visual Basic window, PPT 156, PPT 157
visual effects, graphics, WD 135
VLOOKUP function, EX 186–187

W

watermarks, EX 136
Web. *See* World Wide Web
Web browsers, PB 54
Web forms, PB 54
Web page(s), PB 54, PB 55
   form controls, PB 62–63
   forms, PB 60–61
   single file, EX 142, EX 143
   types, PB 57
Web Page Preview, PB 64–65
Web Page Preview button, PB 59
Web publications, PB 53–69
   converting to Web sites, PB 66–67
   form controls, PB 62–63
   formatting, PB 58–59
   formatting for different audiences, PB 66
   modifying Web forms, PB 60–61
   multimedia components, PB 60
   new, creating, PB 56–57
   planning, PB 54–55
   previewing, PB 64–65
   sending as e-mail, PB 68–69
Web servers, PPT 180
Web sites, PB 54
   components, PB 54
   converting print publications to, PB 68
   converting Web publications to, PB 66–67
   publishing, PB 55
wildcards, AC 142, AC 145, EX 160
Word, integrating with other programs. *See* integrating Word, Excel, Access, and PowerPoint; integrating Word, Excel, and Access; integrating Word and Excel
WordArt, WD 138–139
workbooks
   formats, EX 143
   hyperlinks, EX 140–141
   linking data between, EX 110, EX 111
   names, EX 115
   preparing for distribution, EX 138–139
   properties, EX 138
   protecting, EX 132–133
   saving for distribution, EX 142–143
   shared, EX 139
   tracking modifications, EX 139
worksheet(s)
   arranging, EX 130, EX 131
   backgrounds, EX 136–137
   columns. *See* worksheet columns

data series, PPT 123
embedding in slides, PPT 133
formulas. *See* formula(s)
grouping, EX 144–145
hiding, EX 130
linked, updating, PPT 136–137
linking to slides, PPT 134–135
protecting, EX 132–133
rows. *See* worksheet rows

saving custom views, EX 134–135
splitting into multiple panes, EX 131
viewing, EX 130, EX 131
worksheet columns
   calculated, EX 166
   freezing, EX 132
worksheet rows, freezing, EX 132
workspaces, EX 144
World Wide Web. *See also* Web *entries*

   publishing to, PB 2
   saving presentations for, PPT 180–181
World Wide Web (Web), PB 54
wrapping text around objects, PB 28, PB 29, PB 40–41

▶ X

XPS format
   saving files, PPT 129